Handbook of Environmental and Resource Economics

Handbook of Environmental and Resource Economics

Edited by
Jeroen C.J.M. van den Bergh

Professor of Environmental Economics
Free University, Amsterdam, The Netherlands

Edward Elgar
Cheltenham, UK • Northampton, MA, USA

Published by
Edward Elgar Publishing Limited
Glensanda House
Montpellier Parade
Cheltenham
Glos GL50 1UA
UK

Edward Elgar Publishing, Inc.
136 West Street
Suite 202
Northampton
Massachusetts 01060
USA

A catalogue record for this book
is available from the British Library

Library of Congress Cataloguing in Publication Data

Handbook of environmental and resource economics / edited by Jeroen C.J.M. van den Bergh.
   Includes index.
   1. Environmental policy.   2. Natural resources.   3. Economics.
I. Bergh, Jeroen C.J.M. van den, 1965–
HC79.E5H3284   1999
333.7—dc21
                                                            98–42887
                                                            CIP

ISBN 1 85898 375 4 (cased)

Printed and bound in Great Britain by MPG Books Ltd, Bodmin, Cornwall

Contents

PART I   INTRODUCTION

PART II   ECONOMICS OF NATURAL RESOURCES

PART III   ECONOMICS OF ENVIRONMENTAL POLICY

PART IV   INTERNATIONAL ASPECTS OF ENVIRONMENTAL
ECONOMICS AND POLICY

PART V   SPACE IN ENVIRONMENTAL ECONOMICS

PART VI   ENVIRONMENTAL MACROECONOMICS

PART VII   ECONOMIC VALUATION AND EVALUATION

PART VIII   INTERDISCIPLINARY ISSUES

PART IX   METHODS AND MODELS IN ENVIRONMENTAL
          AND RESOURCE ECONOMICS

PART X   PROSPECTS

Figures

Tables

Contributors

D.G. Abler, Department of Agricultural Economics and Rural Sociology, Pennsylvania State University, University Park, USA.

B.W. Ang, Department of Industrial and Systems Engineering, National University of Singapore, Singapore.

T. Aronsson, Department of Economics, University of Umeå, Sweden.

R.U. Ayres, INSEAD, Fontainebleau, France.

D. Banister, University College London, UK.

E.B. Barbier, Environmental Department, University of York, UK.

W. Beckerman, Oxford, UK.

J.C.J.M. van den Bergh, Department of Spatial Economics, Vrije Universiteit, Amsterdam, The Netherlands.

R.K. Blamey, Urban Research Program Research School of Social Sciences, Australian National University, Canberra, Australia.

S.M. de Bruyn, Department of Spatial Economics, Vrije Universiteit, Amsterdam, The Netherlands.

K.J. Button, Institute of Public Policy, George Mason University, Fairfax, USA.

C. Carraro, Department of Economics, University of Venice, Italy.

H. Cesar, Institute for Environmental Studies, Vrije Universiteit, Amsterdam, The Netherlands.

C.W. Clark, Institute of Applied Mathematics, The University of British Columbia, Vancouver, Canada.

C.J. Cleveland, Center for Energy & Environmental Studies, Boston University, USA.

M.S. Common, Graduate School of Environmental Studies, University of Strathclyde, UK.

K. Conrad, Department of Economics, Mannheim University, Germany.

T.D. Crocker, Department of Economics and Finance, University of Wyoming, Laramie, USA.

J.R. Crooker, Department of Economics, Iowa State University, Ames, USA.

H.E. Daly, School of Public Affairs, University of Maryland, College Park, USA.

F.J. Dietz, Department of Public Administration, Erasmus University, Rotterdam, The Netherlands.

F. Duchin, School of Humanities and Social Sciences, Rensselaer Polytechnic Institute, Troy, USA.

S. El Serafy, International Consultant (formerly Senior Economic Adviser, The World Bank), Arlington, USA.

S. Faucheux, Centre d'Economie et d'Ethique pour l'Environnment, Université de Versailles Saint-Quentin-en-Yvelines, France.

T. Feenstra, IMTA, Erasmus University, Rotterdam and RIVM, Bilthoven, The Netherlands.

C. Folke, The Beijer International Institute for Ecological Economics and Natural Resources Management, Department of Systems Ecology, Stockholm University, Sweden.

H. Folmer, Department of Economics, Agricultural University Wageningen and CentER, Tilburg University, The Netherlands.

A.J. Gilbert, Institute for Environmental Studies, Vrije Universiteit, Amsterdam, The Netherlands.

H. Glasser, Environmental Studies Program, Western Michigan University, Kalamazoo, Michigan, USA.

R. Goodland, Environmental Department, World Bank, Washington DC, USA.

J.M. Gowdy, School of Humanities and Social Sciences, Rensselaer Polytechnic Institute, Troy, USA.

N. Hanley, Institute of Ecology and Resource Management, University of Edinburgh, UK.

B. Hannon, Geography Department, University of Illinois, Urbana, USA.

R.J. Heintz, World Bank, Washington DC, USA.

G.E. Helfand, School of Natural Resources and Environment, The University of Michigan, Ann Arbor, USA.

R.A. Herendeen, Illinois Natural History Survey, University of Illinois, Champagne, USA.

M. Hoel, Department of Economics, University of Oslo, Norway.

M.W. Hofkes, Institute for Environmental Studies, Vrije Universiteit, Amsterdam, The Netherlands.

T.M. Hurley, Department of Environmental and Natural Resource Economics, University of Rhode Island, Kingston, USA.

E.C. van Ierland, Department of Economics, Agricultural University Wageningen, The Netherlands.

R. Janssen, Institute for Environmental Studies, Vrije Universiteit, Amsterdam, The Netherlands.

P.-O. Johansson, Stockholm School of Economics, Sweden.

C.L. Kling, Department of Economics, Iowa State University, Ames, USA.

P. Kort, Department of Econometrics, University of Tilburg, The Netherlands.

P. Koutstaal, IRF – Bureau for Policy Research, Ministry of Finance, The Hague, The Netherlands.

B. Kriström, Department of Forest Economics, Swedish University of Agricultural Sciences, Umeå, Sweden.

K. Krutilla, School of Public and Environmental Affairs, Indiana University, Bloomington, USA.

O.J. Kuik, Institute for Environmental Studies, Vrije Universiteit, Amsterdam, The Netherlands.

S. Kverndokk, Foundation for Research in Economics and Business Administration, Oslo, Norway.

F. Levarlet, Institut Français de l'Environnement, Orléans, France.

L. Lipper, Department of Agricultural and Resource Economics, University of California, Berkeley, USA.

K.-G. Löfgren, Department of Economics, University of Umeå, Sweden.

N.V. Long, Department of Economics, McGill University, Montréal, Canada.

J.R. Markusen, Department of Economics, University of Colorado, Boulder, USA.

J. Martínez-Alier, Department of Economics and Economic History, Universitat Autonòma de Barcelona, Bellaterra, Spain.

W.B. Meyer, George Perkins Marsh Institute, Clark University, Worcester, USA.

R.A. de Mooij, Research Centre for Economic Policy, Erasmus University Rotterdam and Netherlands Bureau for Economic Policy Analysis, The Hague, The Netherlands.

M. Munasinghe, Environmental Policy and Research, World Bank, Washington DC, USA.

G. Munda, Department of Economics and Economic History, Universitat Autònoma de Barcelona, Bellaterra, Spain.

P.A. Neher, Department of Resource Economics, University of British Columbia, Vancouver, Canada.

P. Nijkamp, Department of Spatial Economics, Vrije Universiteit, Amsterdam, The Netherlands.

M. O'Connor, Centre d'Economie et d'Ethique pour l'Environnement, Université de Versailles Saint-Quentin-en-Yvelines, France.

R.B. Palmquist, Department of Economics, North Carolina State University, Raleigh, USA.

D.W. Pearce, Centre for Social and Economic Research on the Global Environment, University College London, UK.

P.T. Powell, University of Indiana School of Business, Bloomington, USA.

J.L.R. Proops, Department of Economics and Management Science, University of Keele, UK.

S. Proost, Center for Economic Studies, Catholic University of Leuven, Belgium.

M. Rauscher, Faculty of Economics, Universtät Rostock, Germany.

P. Rietveld, Department of Spatial Economics, Vrije Universiteit, Amsterdam, The Netherlands.

A. Rose, Department of Energy, Environmental and Mineral Economics, The Pennsylvania State University, University Park, USA.

C.S. Russell, Institute for Public Policy Studies, Vanderbilt University, Nashville, USA.

M. Ruth, Center for Energy and Environmental Studies, Boston University, USA.

J.F. Shogren, Department of Economics and Finance, University of Wyoming, Laramie, USA.

J.S. Shortle, Department of Agricultural Economics and Rural Sociology, The Pennsylvania State University, University Park, USA.

D. Siniscalco, Fondazione Eni Enrico Mattei, Milan, Italy.

S. Smith, Department of Economics, University College London, UK.

S. Smulders, Department of Economics and CentER, Tilburg University, The Netherlands.

A.E. Steenge, Faculty of Public Administration and Public Policy, University of Twente, Enschede, The Netherlands.

K.W. Steininger, Department of Economics, University of Graz, Austria.

D.I. Stern, Centre for Resource and Environmental Studies, Australian National University, Canberra, Australia.

T. Tietenberg, Department of Economics, Colby College, Waterville, USA.

R.K. Turner, Centre for Social and Economic Research on the Global Environment, University of East Anglia, Norwich, UK.

A.M. Ulph, Department of Economics, University of Southampton, UK.

J.W. Velthuijsen, Foundation for Economic Research, University of Amsterdam, The Netherlands.

H. Verbruggen, Institute for Environmental Studies, Vrije Universiteit, Amsterdam, The Netherlands.

E.T. Verhoef, Department of Spatial Economics, Vrije Universiteit, Amsterdam, The Netherlands.

H.R.J. Vollebergh, Research Centre for Economic Policy, Erasmus University, Rotterdam, The Netherlands.

C.A.A.M. Withagen, Department of Spatial Economics, Vrije Universiteit, Amsterdam and Department of Economics, Tilburg University, The Netherlands.

E. Worrell, Lawrence Berkeley National Laboratory, University of California, Berkeley, USA.

A. Xepapadeas, Department of Economics, University of Crete, Iraklion, Greece.

A. de Zeeuw, Department of Economics and CentER, Tilburg University, The Netherlands.

D. Zilberman, Agricultural and Resource Economics, University of California, Berkeley, USA.

Preface

The aim of this handbook is to bring together in a systematic structure advanced but accessible surveys of a wide range of topics in 'environmental and resource economics' (E&RE). These are aimed principally at informing environmental economists about recent progress. E&RE has developed into various specialized sub-areas, indicated by the main structure of the book. Many new tools, theories and empirical studies have appeared over the last decade, which are only partly covered by other handbooks, monographs and advanced textbooks. Environmental economists – whether involved in teaching, research or management – will want to maintain a grand overview of developments in E&RE, otherwise it is virtually impossible to assess the partiality of particular insights. This has been my main motivation for organizing this handbook.

The contributions to the book are generally at an advanced level, beyond the undergraduate textbook level, and require in some cases a certain minimum knowledge of economics or environmental economics. In this sense, the book could act as a useful complement to an advanced textbook in graduate courses. In addition, many chapters can certainly be useful as concise introductions to specific topics in E&RE for a wider group of readers than economists, notably researchers in the natural and social sciences involved in environmental research. Most contributions keep technical discussion to a minimum, focusing instead on a verbal presentation of the main ideas and arguments, and complementing these with technical statements only where these are regarded as being essential to the exposition.

Without doubt, most readers will judge Parts IV, V, VI, VIII and IX as the main distinguishing feature of this handbook relative to other handbooks on E&RE. International and spatial aspects of environmental policy have received a great deal of attention in the last decade, and the same holds for empirical and theoretical macroeconomic research into growth and sustainability. Parts IV, V and VI deal with these issues from many angles. Part VIII contains various contributions that provide basic information on relevant insights from natural sciences, as well as on broader perspectives such as ethics and economic evolution in relation to environmental economics and policy. These contributions have been specifically oriented towards the needs and basic knowledge of environmental economists, but may also be of interest to a wider group of readers. They link clearly to discussions in the younger 'sister field' of ecological economics, which can be regarded as being more pluralistic in approach than conventional environmental and resource economics. These two fields are, however, closely related, and study similar problems. I think that mutual understanding, interaction and debate between them will be important for development of each. Lastly, Part IX contains accessible introductions to methods that are often used in E&RE, along with short surveys of main applications. Apart from serving as general introductions and surveys, these chapters may provide background information for discussions in other parts of the book where reference is made to specific methods. It should be noted that the other three larger Parts, II, III and VII – although more in line with E&RE as it is traditionally structured, that is, resource economics, environmental policy theory and economic valuation – also contain various chapters that offer innovative perspectives on important topics. Finally, the opening and closing Parts, I and X, offer an overview of the book, a short history of E&RE, and monodisciplinary and multidisciplinary perspectives on the future of E&RE.

All contributions have been personally commissioned, and I have tried to coordinate the outlines and contents of the various contributions so as to avoid overlap between them, unless it involved alternative (conflicting or complementary) perspectives. Draft chapters were revised in a first round on the basis of my suggestions. Each chapter was then reviewed by two or three referees and revised at least once more on the basis of their comments and criticism. In spite of the suggested completeness, it is inevitable that some readers will feel that certain topics are missing from this collection. I have tried to indicate a few of these in Chapter 1, along with suggestions for further reading. This chapter also provides a short overview of the contents and particularities of each chapter in the book, and gives a systematic account of topics that receive attention in multiple chapters.

I hope that this handbook will serve as a useful source of information on past and ongoing research in E&RE and that it will allow readers from both inside and outside E&RE to appreciate the subtlety and diversity of analyses, methods and insights in E&RE. Moreover, it is my wish that the book will contribute to a mutual understanding of supporters of different perspectives on problems and research methods in environmental and resource economics.

JvdB
Amsterdam

Acknowledgements

I would like to thank all participants in this project – authors, reviewers and advisers – for bearing with my e-mails, and a few letters, that were aimed to provide suggestions, constructive criticism and – in most cases – deadline reminders. Of course, my greatest gratitude is to the authors, who gave so much of their time to writing and revising their chapters, as well as reviewing other chapters. I am also indebted to various colleagues and friends for specific support in a number of ways. Robert Ayres, Cees van Beers, Carlo Carraro, Kerry Krutilla, Peter Nijkamp, Hans Opschoor, Adam Rose, Jason Shogren and Jan van der Straaten provided comments on the initial outline. I am very grateful to Ada Ferrer Carbonell, Piet Rietveld and Cees Withagen for suggestions on rearranging the pre-final outline, as well as comments on a draft of the introductory chapter. While most chapters were reviewed by authors of other chapters, Glen Harrison, Paul Ekins and Cees van Beers were so kind as to evaluate chapters for which I could not find a suitable reviewer inside the project. Furthermore, several participants reviewed three instead of the standard two other chapters. Sander de Bruyn and Erik Verhoef generously reviewed a chapter within a few days when time was pressing me. I would also like to acknowledge Klaus Conrad for quick production and revisions of his chapter, which was suddenly required when the initial author dropped out at a late stage of the project. I would like to thank Island Press for permission to include a shortened and slightly revised version of a chapter by Bruce Hannon, which was originally published as: B. Hannon, 1992, 'Measures of economic and ecological health', in R. Costanza, B.G. Norton and B.D. Haskell (eds), *Ecosystem Health*, Island Press, Washington, DC. Lastly, I would like to express my gratitude to Edward Elgar Publishing for arranging a marvellous typesetting job, to my managing editor, Julie Leppard, for very reliable support and useful advice, and to Edward Elgar for his confidence in this ambitious project from the outset.

PART I

INTRODUCTION

1 An overview of environmental and resource economics

Jeroen C.J.M. van den Bergh

1. Introduction

The field of environmental and resource economics (E&RE) is developing rapidly, as is reflected by a large number of conferences, workshops, journals, monographs, edited books, and textbooks.[1] The variety of contributions is also increasing. To some extent this is due to economists from various sub-disciplines of economics showing an interest in environmental and resource economics and contributing to its progress. In addition, the multidisciplinary nature of some of the questions raised in environmental economics research has caused an increase in the interaction between economists and scientists from various other disciplines, for the purposes of either communication or integration of insights and tools. All these developments are reflected in the appearance of various new journals in the last decade, the main ones of interest for economists being *Environmental and Resource Economics, Ecological Economics,* and *Environment and Development Economics*. A consequence of these developments is that it is becoming increasingly difficult to stay well informed about the range of issues dealt with in E&RE. Established textbooks do not cover all of these, since many issues concern too recent or too advanced material. Moreover, the number of monographs comprising a thorough and complete discussion of specific topics within E&RE remains relatively small, as opposed to the number of edited books with less internal cohesion. Survey articles on environmental or resource economics are rare, the main ones being Fisher and Peterson (1976), Peterson and Fisher (1977), Cropper and Oates (1992) and Krautkramer (1998). There now exist various collections of reprints of 'classic articles' in E&RE that, although individually necessarily biased and incomplete, together provide a most diverse and comprehensive picture of important insights in E&RE (Costanza et al., 1997a; Dorfman and Dorfman, 1993; Heal, 1993; Krishnan et al., 1995; Daly and Townsend, 1993; Markandya and Richardson, 1992; and Oates, 1992). More such collections are being prepared. Other recent initiatives worth mentioning are a yearly series of advanced surveys of selected topics in E&RE (Folmer and Tietenberg, 1997, 1999; Tietenberg and Folmer, 1998), and a special issue of *Environmental and Resource Economics* on 'Frontiers in

Environmental and Resource Economics' (Sterner and van den Bergh, 1998). Last, but not least, there are two other handbooks on E&RE, namely Kneese and Sweeney (1985/1993) and Bromley (1995). Both contain excellent surveys at an advanced level. However, most contributions to the first collection are already more than 13 years old, while the second collection is rather a mix of surveys and in-depth articles. Most importantly, these handbooks omit a number of exciting and modern research areas in E&RE. The present collection aims to offer a more comprehensive as well as up-to-date advanced survey of E&RE – complementary to rather than a substitute for these earlier handbooks.

The purpose of this chapter is threefold. First, it offers a short overview of research topics in E&RE, based on a discussion of the main contents of each chapter in the handbook. Along the way, where relevant, classic contributions and more extensive surveys will be mentioned. It should be noted that, given the large number of chapters, it is inevitable that the presentation omits backgrounds and explanations, and instead focuses on broad aspects and key issues. A second objective of this chapter is to indicate which particular topics are discussed in multiple chapters. This is done because chapter titles cannot possibly reflect all the issues discussed. Furthermore, several issues are approached from alternative perspectives, leading to complementary and sometimes opposite approaches. For a number of selected topics I have tried to indicate where in the book such alternative perspectives can be found. One may argue that a 'subject index' is intended to serve this purpose, but I doubt whether readers would prefer to sift through an index. The overview given in this chapter will allow readers to glance through the list of topics and see if there are any corresponding with their interest. Finally, the book is certainly not complete in terms of its coverage of topics in the realm of E&RE. I have therefore tried to indicate, for a few significant omissions, which literature sources can be consulted in case readers are interested in learning more about the respective topics.

The organization of this chapter is as follows. Section 2 provides an overview of the contents of the book. Section 3 indicates the topics that receive discussion in multiple chapters. Lastly, Section 4 presents a list of omitted topics and suggests some entrances to the literature on these.

2.   An overview of the handbook

The present Part I of the book contains one other chapter (2), which offers a short and elegant history of environmental economics. I recommend this without hesitation as essential reading. The remainder of this section is devoted to a short account of the main issues addressed in Parts II to X of the book. In places this is complemented by information on classic publications, more elaborated surveys or introductions to the respective topics. As a result, this summary of the handbook can also be regarded as a broad survey of E&RE.

Part II   Economics of natural resources (Chapters 3-12)
The second part of the book considers selected topics in natural resource economics. These relate to particular problems, resources or sectors. First, the conventional non-renewable resource economics theory is presented at an advanced level, in four chapters (3-6). Chapter 3 addresses optimal extraction under competitive conditions without capital (the Hotelling cake-eating problem) and with capital (the Ramsey growth problem and the Hartwick rule). Attention is also given to extraction under uncertainty and to research and development. Chapter 4 reviews resource markets under imperfect competition. Two general cases are considered, namely monopoly and oligopolistic markets. The latter involve cartel-versus-fringe models in which Stackelberg-type of strategic behaviour equilibria are examined. Chapter 5 contains a concise discussion of optimal revenue and Pigouvian taxation analysed in resource models. Chapter 6 is devoted to the international trade aspects of resource markets under various market configurations. Attention is also given here to the well-known Hartwick rule on sustainable consumption, which has received much attention due to its relation to sustainable development and growth. Topics in resource economics have been best covered in the classic text by Dasgupta and Heal (1979), and in the third volume of Kneese and Sweeney (1993), which is entirely devoted to advanced resource economics. Accessible introductions to the theory are Hartwick and Olewiler (1998) and Neher (1990), while Howe (1979) pays more attention to broader and practical economic issues of resource use.

Following the first set of chapters, which address mainly theoretical issues, Chapter 7 is devoted to indicators of resource scarcity. It offers a combination of theory, empirical results and weaknesses for three classes of approaches. These are based on classical, neoclassical and biophysical models of scarcity.

Subsequently, recent developments are surveyed in two areas of renewable resources: fisheries and forestry. Chapter 8 on fisheries addresses a range of issues, from basic textbook issues to topics such as alternative management techniques, uncertainty, investment, and marine reserves. Chapter 9 on forestry deals with theoretical, empirical and multiple-use issues. The classic introduction to renewable resource economics (sometimes referred to as 'bio-economics') is Clark (1990). For a more detailed account of fisheries economics, see Clark (1985) and Hannesson (1993), and for a perspective focusing on uncertainty, see Walters (1986). Forestry is discussed thoroughly in Johansson and Löfgren (1985).

Finally, environmental economics aspects of three specific resources or sectors receive detailed attention, namely water resources, agriculture and energy resources. These include general issues that link to some of the previous chapters, as well as specific issues related to the features of the resources or the institutional setting of the problems examined. Chapter 10 on water resources deals with farm-level decisions on irrigation, surface and groundwater allocation mechanisms, the spatial management of water, and the economic analysis of water projects. The latter includes discussions on irreversibility, externalities, institutions, restoration and equity. Chapter 11 on agriculture and the environment adopts a broad economic approach, and surveys different categories of pollution originating from agricultural practices, technical progress and policy trends, land conversion and degradation issues, rural amenities, and the impact of environmental pollution on agricultural production. Chapter 12 on energy and the environment also adopts a broad approach, and considers environmental impacts of energy use, energy demand, energy conservation and efficiency, the liberalization of energy markets, renewable energy and energy policy. For various collections of articles on agriculture and environment see Hoggart (1992), OECD (1994) and Ruttan (1994). Bredahl et al. (1996), Merrett (1997), and Spulber and Sabbaghi (1997) discuss economic aspects of using water resources. A variety of perspectives on energy, environment and policy is offered by Kneese and Sweeney (1993), Martínez-Alier (1991) and Peet (1992).

Part III   Economics of environmental policy (Chapters 13–25)
This part of the book on pure environmental economics and policy covers the standard theory and insights, as discussed most thoroughly in the classic text by Baumol and Oates (1988). In addition, surveys of topics were sought that are usually only marginally addressed or even ignored in (advanced) textbooks. The part opens with two chapters on fundamental concepts, namely externalities and environmental risk. Chapter 13 includes a general discussion of market failures, a careful consideration of a definition of externalities, and various insights into the relationship between allocative efficiency and equity. Chapter 14 focuses on risk situations where individuals can alter risk by choice. Attention is devoted to the theory, assessment, valuation and management of endogenous risk.

Many of the remaining chapters in this part of the book are concerned with the choice of policy instruments in relation to efficiency, equity and other criteria. First, the archetypal opposition of standards and taxes is considered in Chapter 15, which discusses the efficiency advantages of taxes over standards, as well as qualifications to these. The literature on uncertainty, and on other criteria such as equity, political and ethical perspectives, is also surveyed.

The next few chapters cover modern topics such as imperfect markets, technological innovation, transaction costs, tradable permits and environmental tax reform. The cases of environmental policy under monopoly and oligopoly are surveyed in Chapter 16, which reviews the literature on market entry, the use of policy instruments, and impacts of environmental degradation on market demand or supply. The last section of this chapter deals with the impact of environmental policy on R&D related to environmental characteristics of production. Next, Chapter 17 considers the implications of transactions costs on the design of environmental regulation. Transactions costs arise from exchange and maintenance of ownership and use rights, are related to informational imperfections and asymmetries, and may apply to both market parties and regulating institutions. The chapter presents a broad overview, giving attention to policy choice, policy implementation, the operational phase of policy, and interactions between these three policy stages. Subsequently, two chapters discuss advanced theory and practical lessons of experience with tradable permits. Chapter 18 treats tradable permits under imperfect competition and barriers to entry, the lack of trade in permit markets, and the auctioning of permits. Chapter 19 draws lessons from the experience with permit-trading programmes in the US, considering different local and global environmental problems related to lead in petrol, ozone depletion, acid rain, and so on. The evolution of the regulation programmes is carefully traced, by examining programme design goals such as cost-effectiveness, reduction of transactions costs and improved air quality. Spatial issues and the context of developing countries are also considered. Chapter 20 reviews the debate on the double dividend of environmental tax reforms. It opens with the theory of second-best environmental taxation, distinguishing between three versions of double dividend, namely 'weak double', 'strong double' and 'employment double'. Subsequently, a survey of empirical studies is presented. The chapter ends with a consideration of political implications, and concludes that a double dividend cannot occur without shifts in income distribution. For more discussion of this topic, see Bovenberg and Cnossen (1995), Carraro and Siniscalco (1996) and O'Riordan (1997).

The policy perspective is widened by the last five chapters in this part of the book, which address a broader range of criteria for instrument choice and in particular deal with distribution issues in environmental policy. In Chapter 21 on comparison of instruments, 10 categories of instruments are evaluated on the basis of 12 criteria. These criteria cover, among others, static and dynamic efficiency, informational demands, ease of monitoring and enforcement, flexibility, the institutional demands of agencies and regulated parties, political dimensions and perceived *a priori* risks. For other surveys of instruments in practice, with a particular focus on market-based instruments, see, for instance, Sterner (1994) and Opschoor et al. (1994).

Chapter 22 is devoted to public economics and environmental policy. Cooperative and non-cooperative mechanisms in the provision of environmental goods and services as public goods are discussed, while attention is also given to the use of public funds and environmental policy design. Chapter 23 considers political aspects of the evolution of environmental regulation. Attention is devoted to political pressure from various interest groups, such as polluters and environmentalists, and to the role of actors in the public sector, such as politicians and bureaucrats. The final two chapters on distribution or equity may be of special interest to many readers, as together they provide a balanced account of the economic analysis of distribution issues in environmental economics. Chapter 24 presents a historical background and discusses efficiency–equity trade-offs in the context of standard welfare theory. It then goes on to consider extensions and alternatives, such as utilitarianism, Rawlsian theories of justice, and libertarian thought. Subsequently, principles of equity and efficiency are discussed, and the use of cost–benefit analysis is examined from the equity perspective. All these elements are examined further in an application to global warming. Chapter 25 takes a more critical approach to welfare-based evaluations of the distribution impacts on environmental regulation, and offers a broad literature review of critiques and alternative suggestions for conceptualizing equity issues. It is argued that efficiency and distribution in general equilibrium models are non-separable, and that a unique determination of 'correct' prices is impossible. As an alternative approach, neo-Ricardian and Sraffian reproductive modelling instead of allocative modelling of economic and ecological distribution is discussed. The chapter ends with a consideration of the intergenerational distribution issues related to sustainability and time discounting.

Part IV International aspects of environmental economics and policy (Chapters 26–34)
Since the mid-1980s E&RE has included much research on the international dimension of environmental economics and policy. Until then, most policy theory was dominated by insights based on models of closed economies. One can consider three main topics in E&RE that have an international dimension: cross-boundary and global environmental problems; the interface between foreign trade and environmental externalities; and international policy coordination and trade agreements. Some of this material has reached a few recent advanced textbooks, but these are unsuitable to convey the diversity of approaches, models and insights as presented

here. Moreover, good monographs surveying the approaches and applications are lacking.

Trade issues are covered here by five chapters that address theoretical and empirical issues, a range of equilibrium approaches, and the context of developing countries. Chapter 26 provides a broad introduction to the environmental policy dimension of foreign trade, focusing on environmental policy as trade policy, the restriction of trade for environmental reasons, 'environmental protectionism', and the GATT/WTO. The other chapters consider in detail particular formal approaches to analyse the trade–environment interface. Chapter 27 evaluates partial equilibrium analysis of the trade–environment interface. This is a sensible approach when economy-wide effects of environmental policy can be assumed negligible, and the 'rest of the world' does not act strategically. The environmental impacts of trade liberalization and environmental policy are examined for a number of cases: production and consumption externalities; small and large countries (that is, fixed or variable terms of trade); and local and transboundary pollution. The use of 'general models' is surveyed in Chapter 28. These models can address questions related to specialization patterns, interlinkages of economic production sectors and markets, the feedback effects of policies, distribution issues, and leakage effects. A detailed consideration of Heckscher–Ohlin models extended with environmental variables is followed by discussions of statistical–econometric and applied general equilibrium models. These three 'general model' categories are regarded as being largely complementary to each other. Some important conclusions are that research on trade–environment interactions needs to address spatial distances, technological innovation and particular features of developing countries. Next, Chapter 29 addresses strategic environmental policy in the context of transboundary pollution or international trade characterized by imperfect competition. Among other things, ecological dumping and the Porter hypothesis related to the impacts of environmental regulation on R&D efforts are discussed in this context. The last survey on trade issues, in Chapter 30, focuses on the environment–trade interface in relation to developing countries. It opens with a discussion of alternative conceptual models of this relationship, based on concepts such as environmental capital, equity, harmonization and diversity. Subsequently, a number of issues are considered, including political dimensions and the Rio Declaration on Environment and Development, foreseeable and potential changes in North–South comparative advantages, and policy issues focusing on multilateral agreements and eco-labelling.

The rest of this part of the book is devoted to other topics in 'international environmental economics'. In Chapter 31 a survey is offered of formal modelling of environmental conflict, bargaining and cooperation.

Attention focuses here on self-enforcement and the stability of international environmental agreements, using models derived from game theory. Two specific issues are addressed: transfers to compensate countries that lose by signing an agreement, and issue linkage aimed at improving the profitability and stability of agreements.

The final three chapters address specific categories of environmental problems. Transboundary environmental problems are considered in Chapter 32. A general formalization of these problems is presented, followed by focused discussions on 'acid rain' and 'global warming'. Various models are surveyed, of non-cooperative and cooperative solutions, the design of international agreements, and the relations between trade and transboundary pollution. Global environmental issues are treated further in the last two chapters. Chapter 33 discusses 'global warming', stratospheric ozone and biodiversity, and tries to consider these problems within a single economic framework. Attention is devoted to economic value, uncertainty aspects and policy instruments. Chapter 34 presents a mixed theoretical–empirical discussion of a specific category of policy instruments that has received much attention in the context of curbing CO_2 emissions, namely 'carbon taxes'. This includes, among other things, considerations of efficient specification, dynamic issues, interactions with other taxes, international bargaining and coordination, and barriers and problems.

Publications that offer a good introduction to international and global dimensions of environmental economics and policy are Anderson and Blackhurst (1992), Low (1992), Mabey et al. (1997), Siebert (1995), and Pearce and Warford (1993). On economics and climate change see the relevant IPCC report (Bruce et al., 1996). An accessible summary of the IPCC approach and methods is given by Parry and Carter (1998). For different views on modelling and the analysis of climate change see, for instance, the economic approach by Nordhaus (1994), and the 'integrated assessment' approach by Rotmans and de Vries (1997). Critical evaluations of many related issues have been provided by Daly and Cobb (1989) and Rugman and Kirton (1998). An interesting and accessible discussion of the relationship between ecology and biodiversity, oriented towards economists, is Holling et al. (1995). See further Chapter 61.

Part V   Space in environmental economics (Chapters 35–40)
Economists seem to have paid little attention to the spatial dimensions of environmental problems, environmental policy, and environment–economy interactions, including issues of growth and environmental sustainability. There is still much to do in this area, especially in a multidisciplinary setting where information from natural sciences is used. For

instance, in hydrology, geography and ecology, spatial disaggregate frameworks and models are very common (see Part VIII). Spatial mismatches between environmental, economic and policy systems and processes may offer important and interesting research themes.

This part of the book addresses the conventional issues that have received some attention, such as non-point source pollution, land use, urban environmental problems, location choice and transport. Chapter 35 offers a broad introduction, relating historical developments in environmental and spatial economics. To motivate the interconnection it is argued that 'space' is the geographical medium for environmental externalities, which is both heterogeneous and scarce. Next, a survey is offered of how the interconnection of spatial and environmental economics has occurred in theory, in modelling and in applied policy studies. Chapter 36 considers the problem of non-point source pollution, which has so far received little attention in advanced textbooks. This is a relevant problem in the context of diffuse sources such as farmers, households and mobile sources (transport vehicles). It can be regarded as both a spatial and an information asymmetry problem, where the latter results from the imperfect observability of the polluters by the regulator. Different incentive schemes, such as input and ambient taxes, are examined on a theoretical level, while applied issues are also briefly discussed. Next, Chapter 37 is devoted to land use and environmental quality, adopting a broad perspective. This includes a short introduction to non-residential land use and environmental issues at the global level, followed by a discussion of the mutual dependence between environmental quality and residential land use. The conceptual model used to structure the survey is based on the impact of the environment on land use via amenities and disamenities. Attention is devoted to issues surrounding the interpretation of hedonic price studies and urban development and land price theories. Chapter 38 provides a short but broad account of studies on urban sustainability issues. This is done by considering three dimensions, namely land, energy and transport, and by referring to a range of applied studies. Subsequently, in Chapter 39, the issue of endogenous location of plants induced by relative strictness of environmental regulation is surveyed, a phenomenon that is sometimes referred to as 'relocation' or 'capital flight'. First, a general model with graphical illustrations of the location problem is presented, which gives rise to considerations of economies of scale, market structure, multinationals, and transport costs. Next, policy competition between regions or countries in the presence of footloose industries is surveyed in more detail. A final section examines the empirical support for some of the hypotheses generated by the theoretical literature. Chapter 40 offers a concise survey of research on transport and the environment. It opens with some illustrations of social costs and the energy efficiency of transport, followed by an account of demand-side developments in the areas of passenger and freight transport. It closes with a discussion of the economic and social feasibility characteristics of transport–environment policies.

Some of the topics in this part of the book can also be regarded as relevant at an international level, in which case the distinction from Part IV becomes rather vague. The purpose of both Parts IV and V is to broaden the horizon of the non-spatial and closed-economy environmental policy discussions that have long been common in many E&RE textbooks and policy discussions. A very accessible introduction to both spatial and international dimensions in environmental economics is provided by Siebert (1985, 1995).

Part VI   Environmental macroeconomics (Chapters 41–50)

'Environmental macroeconomics' is a term coined by Daly (1991b), who argues that environmental issues have barely been discussed or even noted in standard macroeconomic textbooks. Environmental macroeconomics may be regarded as covering theoretical and empirical issues related to growth, sustainable development, and the physical scale of the economy. These have given rise to much debate among economists, and between economics and other sciences. This part of the book aims to survey the various approaches and stances. It includes a somewhat diverse collection of contributions, many of which relate to research on growth and sustainable development.

The opening Chapter 41 offers a general account of macroeconomics and modelling in environmental economics, while also devoting attention to economics in global modelling and integrated assessment. Macroeconomics is discussed in relation to regionalized world models, environmental input–output models and qualitative scenario studies. The topic of endogenous growth and the environment receives separate treatment in Chapter 42, as it has been the subject of numerous articles in recent years. This chapter discusses the general structure of such models, presents an archetype model, and examines the role of behaviour and policy. It ends by considering the question of whether sustainable growth is possible from the perspective of modern growth theory. In this context, some empirical findings are also referred to.

Next, several chapters offer elements of the growth debate. This debate is most clearly presented by two opposing views, a 'growth-optimistic view' by W. Beckerman in Chapter 43, and a 'growth-pessimistic view' by H.E. Daly in Chapter 44. Following these, Chapter 45 suggests a typology of perspectives in the broader growth debate. This includes main perspectives, that of the moralist, the pessimist, the technocrat, the opportunist and the optimist. This categorization essentially follows three questions: Is growth desirable? Is growth feasible? Can growth be controlled or directed? The various stances in this debate are considered in more detail in the following publications: Lecomber (1975), Mishan (1977), Daly and Townsend (1993), and Myers and Simon (1994).

Next, Chapter 46 presents a survey of empirical research with a macro-economic orientation towards growth and environment, dominated by a search for 'environmental or green Kuznets curves'. Here attention is devoted to the choice of indicators, data, statistical methods, the interpretation of empirical results, and policy implications. The final survey related to growth, in Chapter 47, reviews studies on national or economy-wide policies in the context of growth and environment. This contribution looks, among other things, at the environmental impacts of such policies and their timing and sequencing. An action impact matrix is discussed as a general tool for policy analysis, formulation and coordination. A large number of studies is reviewed, covering macroeconomic and sectoral reforms, stabilization policies, and so on.

Four chapters deal explicitly with 'sustainable development', namely Chapters 38, 48, 49 and 72. Chapter 48 provides a definition and a short history of sustainability as a general concept. It distinguishes environmental from economic and social sustainability, and relates intergenerational to intragenerational equity. Subsequently, it tries to answer the question of what should be sustained, such as environmental source or sink capacities, life support functions, or biodiversity. It concludes by considering the relationship between sustainability and substitutability, arguing that the latter is the exception, rather than the rule. Chapter 49 surveys the literature on indicators of sustainable development. This covers a conceptual framework for indicator development, and discussions of aggregation and spatial and analytical demarcation. Three types of approaches are recognized: (i) a single aggregate indicator such as 'green GDP', genuine savings measures, and so on; (ii) multiple economic and environmental indicators, each closely linked to the economic system, for example, based on the system of national accounts; and (iii) 'free form' indicators which can address all elements of economic–environmental cause–effect chains.

A final survey in this part of the book, Chapter 50, addresses the relation between poverty and environment in developing countries, taking the sustainability perspective to a different level. It starts by framing the UNCED/Rio 1992 benchmark, in which development and environment were firmly linked at a political level. Subsequently, resource dependence in developing countries is examined, and it is concluded that the natural asset base of the poorest economies is being quickly eroded, while economic growth is largely absent. Next, the concentration of poor people in

marginal areas is considered, and it is argued that environmental degradation creates the greatest threat for the poorest people in developing countries. Lastly, the poverty–environment trap is examined, that is, the question
whether poverty causes environmental degradation; it is emphasized that
the determinants of behaviour need more study, and that the poor should
not be treated as a homogenous group.

Readers interested in good surveys of theoretical economic views on
growth, environment and sustainability may want to consult the excellent
article by Toman et al. (1995), the older but very readable Pezzey (1989)
(which includes a long list of definitions of sustainable development), or
recent contributions by Hartwick (1997) and by Aronsson et al. (1997). A
wide range of indicators of sustainable development is presented in
Atkinson et al. (1997). An interesting systems perspective on sustainability
has been put forward by Clayton and Radcliffe (1996). A broad view on
development, poverty and environment is provided by Pearce and Warford
(1993). For less orthodox discussions of environmental problems in developing countries see Martínez-Alier (1995) and Guha and Martínez-Alier
(1997).

Part VII   Economic valuation and evaluation (Chapters 51–58)
Valuation has received ample attention in E&RE textbooks, and has also
been well covered at the theoretical and methodological level in monographs (Freeman, 1993; Johansson, 1987) and edited volumes (Braden and
Kolstad, 1991; Bromley, 1995). An accessible introduction to this theme is
Hanley and Spash (1993). Although some repetition of these excellent
surveys seems inevitable, both the theory and the main methods have been
included in a number of separate chapters here, covering recreation demand
models, hedonic pricing models, and contingent valuation (CV) approaches.

Chapter 51 reviews recent progress on environmental valuation theory. It
provides a short introduction to compensated money measure concepts,
and a survey of, among other things, important conditions for market
valuation, the logical properties of money measures, altruism and other
non-use values. Chapter 52 on recreation models reviews progress on valuation methods that includes indirect methods, recreation demand models
and traditional travel costs models, all using travel costs as core information. The differences between these relate to continuity versus discreteness
of demand, that is, they focus on the number of visits to a particular site
versus the choice between alternative sites, respectively. Chapter 53 surveys
the development and application of hedonic pricing methods, with detailed
attention being devoted to various sophisticated theoretical and statistical
refinements, such as the timing of adverse impacts of environmental pollution on property values, functional forms and two-stage models. Some of

this refers to the results of meta-analysis of hedonic studies. Next, Chapter 54 on contingent valuation (CV) offers a very thorough overview of the huge amount of research that has developed and applied this method in the last decade. This pays attention to the construction of CV experiments, and a number of strongly debated issues, such as altruism, the comparison of elicitation formats, embedding and sequencing, the willingness to accept/willingness to pay (WTA/WTP) disparity and the focus on mean versus median. Two early books on CV are Mitchell and Carson (1989) and Cummings et al. (1990). After the Exxon Valdez oil spill in Alaska in 1989, the method was heavily debated (see Carson et al., 1992; Hausman, 1993; Arrow et al., 1993). Since then, many publications on the subject have appeared (for example, Bjornstad and Kahn, 1996; Kopp et al., 1997). Some aspects of CV research relate to experimental economics, which is covered separately in Part IX of the book.

Next, two less common topics are addressed. The first of these, meta-analysis, treated in Chapter 55, has recently received some attention, also in relation to benefit or value transfer. This is approached from a broad perspective, covering conceptual issues, statistical issues, alternative methods, the relation with benefits transfer, and the fundamental and practical limits to meta-analysis (see van den Bergh et al., 1997). The second less common topic, surveyed in Chapter 56, is concerned with the ethical dimensions of economic valuation, an issue which is conspicuously absent in many environmental economics textbooks (note that a broader perspective on ethics in relation to environmental policy is discussed in Chapter 66 in Part VIII). This chapter discusses subtle criticisms of the standard assumptions of economic valuation methods. This concerns issues of altruism, ethical attitudes and CV responses, 'citizen responses' (Sagoff, 1988) and the non-existence of ordinary utility functions, due to lexicographic preferences, responsibility considerations, moral satisfaction, and the like. In addition, the use of estimated economic values in cost–benefit analysis is considered from an ethical perspective.

This part of the book ends with two chapters on methods for project or policy evaluation. Chapter 57 discusses the conventional cost–benefit analysis (CBA) approach. It gives a short introduction and includes discussions, among other topics, of irreversibility, complexity, discounting and discount rates, and sustainable development and CBA. Chapter 58 presents multi-criteria evaluation methods. A conceptual and methodological discussion is offered, which includes a typology of methods, a treatment of uncertainty and 'fuzzy evaluation' problems, and an example illustrating many of the elements and methods discussed. An accessible introduction to multi-criteria evaluation in the context of environmental economics is Janssen (1992).

Part VIII   Interdisciplinary issues (Chapters 59–67)
The purpose of this part is to offer a more detailed background on insights from the natural sciences relevant to studies of environmental problems than is usual in (advanced) environmental economics textbooks. The contributions have been specifically oriented towards the demands and knowledge of environmental and resource economists. The first set of chapters addresses issues related to physics and biology, offering information about material flows, energy transformation and ecological processes that may be regarded as required basic knowledge for economists involved in environmental research.

Chapter 59 on 'physical principles' provides a short introduction to the material balance principle and the 'entropy law', and then considers how these have been incorporated into environmental economics studies. This survey is categorized according to production processes, economy–environment interactions, and long-run growth. Chapter 60 presents a detailed discussion on materials in relation to environmental problems. It offers short informative introductions to four main groups of materials, namely fuels, metals, non-fuel minerals, and packaging materials and synthetics. Subsequently, it discusses product cycles, 'dematerialization' and recycling, and related policy issues. The topics of these two chapters – materials, energy and thermodynamics in relation to economics and the environment – are more extensively discussed in a variety of ways in Ayres (1978 and 1988), Ayres and Ayres (1996), Daly and Umaña (1981), Faber et al. (1987), Georgescu-Roegen (1971, 1976), Kandelaars (1999), Kneese et al. (1970), Martínez-Alier (1991), Noorman and Uiterkamp (1998), Peet (1992), Perrings (1987) and Ruth (1993).

Chapter 61 considers another set of basic insights to E&RE, namely 'ecological principles'. This chapter devotes attention to the structure, classification, succession, development and management of ecosystems. Subsequently, the importance of biological diversity for ecosystem functioning is examined. Next, economic issues are introduced, focusing on ecosystems as factors of production, and improvement of the interaction between humans and ecosystems. More descriptive details of global nutrient cycles and human interference in these is covered in Chapter 62. Here, information from ecology, physics, chemistry and economics is combined, which is referred to as 'industrial metabolism'. A four-box scheme is put forward to describe biogeochemical reservoirs and cycles of the nutrients carbon, nitrogen, sulphur and phosphorus, which are important as they can be considered 'scarce' in the biosphere. In addition to a detailed discussion of each of these cycles, two fundamental issues are raised, namely the thermodynamic disequilibrium of these cycles, and the slow acidification of the environment at the global level, that is, beyond the usually emphasized local effects. For a set of more pragmatically oriented perspectives on several of these issues see Klijn (1994).

Two additional chapters provide creative views on macro or system indicators and energy systems analysis that have received some attention in ecology and ecological economics. Chapter 63 is devoted to indicators of economic and ecological health (see also Costanza et al., 1992). Here it is argued that ecologists can come up with measures of ecological health at a national level by combining elements of ecology and economics. The discussion pays attention to characteristics of GNP and accounting, ecosystem goals and outputs, aggregation, discounting, and so on. The chapter ends by discussing the integration of economic and ecosystem output measures in a single system 'health' indicator. Chapter 64 deals with 'EMERGY analysis' (note the 'm' instead of the 'n'), developed by H.T. Odum, which is aimed at quantifying the role of the environment in supporting economic activity. This involves a comprehensive method that traces all environmental services back to the 'captured energy' of sunlight. The basis of this method is the principle of maximum power, which is regarded as relevant for both ecosystems and economic processes. Differences from conventional energy analysis are briefly indicated (see also Brown and Herendeen, 1996). The chapter ends by outlining applications to various problems.

Following these natural science backgrounds to research in environmental economics, Chapter 65 is devoted to evolutionary perspectives in economics as applied to the context and problems of environmental economics. Attention is devoted to traditional and modern insights of evolutionary biology and how these have influenced evolutionary economics. Other influences are also discussed, notably Schumpeterian theories and thermodynamics. This is followed by an account of modelling of evolutionary systems. Special attention is given to a number of topics, including mechanisms for the selection of economic agents, hierarchical organization, structural economics, and the management of evolutionary natural systems. It seems that there are almost as many evolutionary perspectives in environmental economics as there are authors addressing this issue, which is partly due to the fact that such perspectives are still exceptional. Some relevant publications are Boulding (1978), Clark et al. (1995), Faber and Proops (1990), Gowdy (1994), Munro (1997) and Norgaard (1994).

Next, Chapter 66 discusses alternative ethical stances and their relationship with environmental policy. It is argued that clarifying the role of ethics in the preparation of, and the choices made in, environmental policy can sharpen the debate on issues which increasingly involve complexity, uncertainty, conflict and irreversibility. For this purpose, a number of steps are taken. The discussion opens with the link between normative collective decisions and ethics. Next, a number of deficiencies of standard environmental economics practice, according to various authors, are briefly mentioned. The main body of the chapter is devoted to a review of the ethical bases for environmental concern. These are classified into humanism, ethical extensionism, and strong non-anthropocentrism. Attention is also given to environmental values of the public (or lay people). A final section examines the relationship between consequentialism, deontology and the use of evaluation frameworks and methods in environmental economics. Introductions to ethical issues are provided by Maclean and Brown (1983), Devall and Sessions (1984) and Pierce and Vandeveer (1995). The latter offers a very rich collection of views from economists, natural scientists and philosophers.

Many of the foregoing issues in this part of the handbook receive more explicit attention in ecological economics than they do in conventional environmental economics. Chapter 67 goes into more detail about what the essential differences are between these two areas. It examines whether ecological economics offers an alternative and competing paradigm to that represented by conventional environmental economics. It is argued that the mild acceptance of ecological-economics-oriented research in various mainstream journals implies that ecological economics is a fruitful field of interdisciplinary cooperation rather than an alternative paradigm. Some focal points and core concepts of ecological economics are briefly examined, covering sustainability, technical change, optimal scale, thresholds, resilience, valuation, ethics and sociology. An earlier attempt to indicate differences between ecological economics and standard environmental economics is Turner et al. (1997).

Introductions to ecological economics are provided by Costanza et al. (1997a,b). Collections of articles from ecological economics conferences offer a good impression of the variety of views and approaches in this field: Costanza (1991), Costanza et al. (1996), Jansson et al. (1994), and van den Bergh and van der Straaten (1994, 1997). Ecological economics critiques, based on considerations of an institutional, ecological or physical nature, have been largely neglected by mainstream environmental economists. Several publications have offered criticism and alternative views on how environmental economics should proceed, for instance: Boulding (1978), Costanza (1991), Daly (1991a), Daly and Cobb (1989), Ekins and Max-Neef (1992), Faber and Proops (1990), Georgescu-Roegen (1971), Norgaard (1994), and Sagoff (1988). A pluralistic introduction to economics oriented towards non-economists interested in environmental issues is offered by Gowdy and O'Hara (1996). Many of these authors argue that standard environmental economics focuses too strongly on static equilibrium processes and isolated rational individuals, and should take more account of physical, historical and cultural processes in economics, extreme uncertainty and surprises, social contexts and other models of behaviour, and institutions in a broader sense than merely markets and policy instruments.

I have explicitly chosen to mention a relatively large number of references here, so as to provide an easy entry into ecological economics, particularly for economists and other social scientists. Some readers may wonder why I spend so much time on this in a survey of environmental economics. In my view, the divide that presently exists between ecological and 'standard' (or 'mainstream', 'orthodox', 'neoclassical') E&RE is undesirable, and the two areas should communicate and reinforce each other in the long run. This may require more open-mindedness from neoclassical economists, especially those who think that a single method of scientific research is sufficient to understand our complex reality and to suggest solutions to pressing problems. To me it is evident that science and pluralism go hand in hand, which is perfectly consistent with individuals specializing in one specific method of research. Some regard scientific pluralism as essential for the survival of science and the planet in the long run, regarding both of these as subject to evolutionary processes that require a minimal amount of internal diversity, as has been most clearly expressed by Richard Norgaard (1985, 1989, 1994). Any scientific approach misses out on some aspects of reality and is partial in some sense, and from a multidisciplinary perspective the same is true for any monodisciplinary research approach. Environmental economics certainly seems one of those areas inside economics where a mind open to multidisciplinary aspects and problems is essential in order to come up with relevant and socially acceptable suggestions for solutions. 'Multidisciplinary' refers not only to natural science, but certainly also to social science in a broad sense, including history, sociology, political science, institutional economics and evolutionary thought.

On the other hand, many 'ecological economists' (ecologists, economists and others) may realize that 'neoclassical' economics is the only approach that has been able to come up with an impressive and coherent structure of rigorous, clearly founded and subtle insights, in particular related to environmental policy analysis and economic valuation of environmental change. Given the long tradition and large body of work in 'mainstream' E&RE, the approach associated with this dominates in the present book. Summarising this intermezzo, the collection of authors and contributions in this book is aimed to offer a greater diversity of perspectives on E&RE than is usual in most other surveys.

Part IX   Methods and models in environmental and resource economics
(Chapters 68–77)
This part of the book presents a range of methods that are frequently applied in E&RE research, and in fact have been mentioned, or underlie most insights discussed, elsewhere in the book. The chapters here cover general features of the methods, specific issues relevant to their application to E&RE, and a survey of such applications. The main method used in environmental economics is (partial or general) equilibrium analysis. A specific treatment of this is not included here, as it is well covered in standard economic and environmental economics textbooks (notably in Baumol and Oates, 1988). Elements of it appear in various places in the book, notably in the opening chapter of Part III and in Chapter 69.

Chapter 68 presents a survey of the use of input–output (I–O) analysis in environmental economics. It includes an introduction to standard I–O analysis, various extensions in environmental economics applications, materials balance and physical models, dynamic models, and social accounting matrices extended with economy–environmental flows. This chapter concludes by proposing a 'structural economics' on the basis of I–O analysis and the previous extensions, focused on issues, scenarios and a minimum of assumptions. Chapter 69 surveys the use of applied or computable general equilibrium (CGE) models to answer questions in environmental economics. This chapter covers methodological principles and the standard elements related to producer and consumer behaviour, foreign trade, multiregional models, dynamics, and closure rules. In addition, specific environment-related elements are discussed, such as abatement technologies, environmental policy instruments, and measures of welfare change. Lastly, a survey is presented of important applications of CGE models to environmental policy questions.

The following two chapters shift attention to more theoretical methods. Chapter 70 is devoted to game theory in environmental policy analysis. It opens with a short introduction to core concepts and approaches in modern game theory. Next, it examines three areas of application in environmental economics, namely international environmental problems, interaction between a regulator and regulated agents, and strategic competition between governments or between economic agents. Chapter 71 considers optimal control techniques, which are used to solve environmental economic problems formulated as continuous dynamic optimization models. After a discussion of a basic resource–environment model and aspects of the technique as applied in economics, specific models are surveyed.

In the next two chapters, broader categories of models are discussed. Chapter 72 addresses alternative concepts and models of sustainable development. It distinguishes between discounted utilitarianism, intergenerational equity, weak and strong sustainability, stationary state and optimal scale, and ecological stability and resilience. Subsequently, four ways of modelling sustainable development are given more detailed attention, as follows: economic growth theory; sectorally disaggregate models; disequilibrium, evolutionary and integrated models; and empirical studies. Books by Faucheux et al. (1996), van den Bergh (1996), and van den Bergh and Hofkes (1998) provide a range of economic modelling perspectives on sustainable development. Chapter 73 surveys models that consider the relationship between economic structure, energy and the environment. This contains discussions of energy resource modelling based on economic and physical inputs, and output-oriented models including integrated assessment models (see Rotmans and de Vries, 1997). Furthermore, a number of issues are examined, such as aggregation, top–down versus bottom–up structure, neo-Keynesian versus CGE models, and time dimensions.

The subsequent two chapters introduce decomposition methods for analysing changes in economic structure as related to energy, material and environmental indicators. These have been mostly applied to energy demand analysis, but may be applied to a range of issues in environmental economics, using environmental indicators, so that it seems useful that environmental economists take note of these methods. Chapter 74 addresses methods related to the solutions to index number problems in economics. It starts with a basic form model founded on aggregate energy intensity, discusses different index methods, and reviews past applications. Next, methods for energy consumption level and energy elasticity approaches are considered. Subsequently, alternative formulations of these models are presented. This is followed by a discussion and survey of the decomposition of environment-related indicators. The chapter concludes by discussing a number of application issues, such as method selection, residual treatment, data, period-wise versus time-series analysis, and sector disaggregation. The presentation is supported by showing what information each method generates based on a single numerical example for 2 sectors and 2 years. Chapter 75 explains decomposition analysis of economic change by way of comparative static changes in input–output tables. After a discussion of basic elements and extended decomposition analysis comes a survey of theoretical underpinnings and applications.

Next, Chapter 76 is devoted to the use of experimental methods in environmental economics. Some historical notes, interpretations of 'experiment' and discussion of methods are followed by two main categories of applications in environmental economics: institutional experiments aimed at examining the impact of environmental control on the allocation of scarce resources, via market and other mechanisms; and valuation experiments aimed at discovering private preferences for market or non-market goods by controlling behaviour. Finally, Chapter 77 considers a method specifically developed for environmental policy and management, namely natural resource accounting. It discusses resource and pollution accounting, different systems of national accounts, stock accounting, and a range of accounting approaches to valuation. In the latter context, the net-price method, the user-cost approach, renewable resources and shadow pricing receive detailed attention. Finally, some attention is given to mixed systems of measurement such as NAMEA – 'national accounting matrix including environmental and economic accounts' (see also the chapter on I–O analysis – Chapter 75).

Part X   Prospects (Chapters 78 and 79)
The final part of the book contains two short chapters that look towards the future of E&RE along monodisciplinary and multidisciplinary dimensions, respectively. Chapter 78 considers recent developments in economic theory that may be relevant to environmental economics research. This chapter opens with a broad policy context, concluding that the general framework of environmental economics has changed from one characterized by partial externalities studies to one which regards environmental issues as a particular dimension of human development. A number of major research areas are indicated, namely sustainable development (or environment and development), transboundary and transnational environmental issues and policy, uncertainty and the role of information, environmental management, and urban issues. This chapter also presents a very interesting and informative evaluation of trends in the environmental economics literature, based on a survey of over 1400 papers from two main journals (*Environmental and Resource Economics* and the *Journal of Environmental Economics and Management* (*JEEM*)) and annual European conferences, between 1990 and 1997 (a similar survey was done for *JEEM* by Deacon et al., 1998).

Chapter 79 presents a broad perspective on the integration of views from economics, ecology and the social sciences. It describes the prospects of communication between environmental economics and other disciplines. This will involve a preparedness to shift from a multidisciplinary to a transdisciplinary approach. Subsequently, it is discussed how to address the biophysical foundations of, and natural constraints to, economic activities, based on physics and ecology. More detailed discussions are provided of thermodynamics, resilience and evolutionary modelling. Finally, environmental philosophy is considered, where a distinction is made between ethical and epistemological issues. In both multidisciplinary and economic directions much further work remains to be done, and readers may find some useful ideas in these final chapters.

3. An overview of multiple treatments of particular topics

The handbook contains various sets of chapters that offer multiple views on specific topics. These are either complementary or opposing. This section is intended to offer a systematic account of them.

Several views on criteria for choosing environmental policy instruments are put forward in Part III, notably in Chapters 15 and 21. Contributions offering complementary views to the standard externality-based theory of optimal environmental policy relate to risk (Chapter 14), to transaction costs (Chapter 17), to distribution issues (Chapters 24 and 25), to steady state and optimal scale (Chapter 44), to sustainability (Chapter 48), to ethics (Chapter 66), to incommensurability (Chapter 58), to evolution (Chapters 65 and 79), and to various issues considered in ecological economics (Chapter 67).

On the topic of distribution and equity there are two main chapters (24 and 25). In addition, Chapters 13, 15, 20, 21, 22, 23, 66 and 67 devote brief attention to issues related to equity and fairness. Together, these various chapters provide a complete and diverse survey of distribution issues in environmental policy.

A number of chapters in Part IV (26–30) address the relation between trade and environment, adopting various theoretical and empirical perspectives, as well as considering the context of developing countries. In addition to these, Chapter 6 considers natural resources from an international trade perspective, and Chapter 39 surveys models of international relocation or 'capital flight'.

Global environmental issues are explicitly discussed in Chapters 24, 32, 33, 34, 41, 62 and 73. Biodiversity is discussed from an economic perspective in Chapter 33, and from an ecological perspective in Chapter 61. Chapter 79 also contains a short discussion on biodiversity.

Spatial issues are mainly discussed in Part V. However, land use and non-point source pollution issues not only receive attention in Chapters 36 and 37, but also in Chapters 10 and 11 on water resources and agriculture.

Environmental sustainability and sustainable development are the subject of a number of chapters, namely Chapter 8 on fisheries, Chapter 33 on global environmental issues, Chapter 38 on urban sustainability, Chapter 48 on the biophysical foundation of sustainability, Chapter 49 on indicators, Chapter 60 on global nutrient cycles, and Chapter 72 on perspectives and models. The link between sustainability, discount rates and future generations is discussed in Chapter 25. Discounting is also discussed in Chapters 57, 63 and 72.

Multiple chapters in Part VI discuss economic growth and environment (Chapters 41–47). A survey of neoclassical exogenous growth models has not been separately included, but is treated briefly in Chapters 3, 41 and 72.

Endogenous growth is dealt with in Chapter 42. Evolutionary perspectives and long-run modelling in environmental economics are discussed in Chapters 65, 72 and 79.

Several chapters, spread throughout the book, address energy-related issues: see Chapters 12, 59, 62, 63, 64, 73, 74 and 75. Chapters 74 and 75 survey decomposition methods, applications of which have been mostly related to industrial energy demand. Similarly, various chapters address the physical–material dimension of the economy, notably Chapters 59 and 60 and, on a more abstract level, Chapters 3–7.

Indicators of various types are discussed in Chapters 7, 46, 48, 49, 58, 63, 64 and 77. Valuation approaches are discussed in a number of chapters in Part VII (51–55), and from an accounting perspective in Chapter 77. Meta-analysis in relation to valuation is discussed from a broad perspective in Chapter 55, and in relation to hedonic pricing models in Chapter 53. Evaluation methods are discussed from the perspective of methods in Chapter 57 (cost–benefit analysis) and 58 (multi-criteria analysis), and from an ethical perspective in Chapters 24, 56 and 57. Ethical issues are extensively discussed in Chapters 56 and 66, and briefly in Chapters 15, 21, 24, 67 and 79.

4.   Missing topics and recommended reading

It is fair to say that even if the book gives an impression of completeness at first sight, there are a few topics that have not been included, as no suitable authors could be found, or the respective authors dropped out at a late stage of the project, or the subject was simply forgotten. The most important area omitted is perhaps environmental management or 'business and the environment' (see Chapter 78). This covers topics such as environmental care systems, environmental strategies, internal organization, environmental accountancy, environmental reporting, environmental cost accounting and green marketing.[2] Most textbooks do not integrate environmental economics and environmental management. The reason is perhaps that the group of readers interested in 'general' environmental economics seems quite disconnected from those interested in environmental business management. Evidently, this handbook has been limited to cover only the first area. Adequate treatment of the second area would very likely need a separate volume in itself. Fischer and Schot (1993), Welford and Starkey (1996) and Folmer et al. (1995, part 3) have presented various interpretations of the contents of environmental management.

Other topics have been omitted. I will mention some of them, and make a few reading suggestions. First, institutions and property rights are not discussed in a separate chapter here (see Bromley, 1991 and 1997). Green GDP has not received much attention either (see Chapter 49), although a related topic on natural resource accounting is discussed in Chapter 77 (see Aronsson et al., 1997; Daly and Cobb, 1989; and Hueting et al. 1992). The question whether discounting is (ethically) indefensible, or whether discount rates should be adapted for projects or investments with (irreversible) environmental consequences, is not discussed in a separate chapter, although short discussions on discounting have been included in various chapters (see the previous section). A classic text is Lind (1982), a concise account of the main issues Markandya and Pearce (1988), and a recent discussion Azar and Sterner (1996). Regrettably, population and environment were not given separate attention. Informative short introductions are provided by Perman et al. (1999, ch. 11), Tietenberg (1994, ch. 5), and Dasgupta (1995). The relation between development, poverty and population issues is surveyed in Demeny and McNicoll (1998), and a very thorough account of population issues is Cohen (1995). Although climate issues are dealt with in several places in this book (see the previous section), more could have been said about the subject. A collection of 'classic articles' is contained in Tietenberg (1997). Joint implementation is a related topic that is also missing; it has recently received much attention, notably in the context of the Kyoto negotiations to reduce greenhouse gas emmissions (see Kuik et al., 1994; Jepma, 1995; see also the newsletter *Joint Implementation Quarterly*). More information on the neoclassical exogenous growth theory with natural resources and environment, mainly developed in the 1970s, can be found in Dasgupta and Heal (1979), Beltratti (1996), Chichilnisky et al. (1997) and Toman et al. (1995). In the context of valuation some topics are missing here, notably related to uncertainty, ecosystems and biodiversity. Excellent discussions and surveys of valuation under uncertainty, option value and quasi-option value can be found in Freeman (1993) and Bromley (1995). The valuation of ecosystem changes is discussed in Barbier et al. (1994) and Gren et al. (1994). Biodiversity can be approached from the perspectives of economic valuation, systems stability or sustainability (see Perrings et al., 1995a and b). For broader and critical views by natural and social scientists, see Gowdy (1997) and various papers in Wilson (1988). I hope the most important omitted topics are covered in this short list.

Notes
1. Many introductory and advanced textbooks have recently appeared or been revised, for instance: Bowers (1997); Callan and Thomas (1996); Common (1996); Costanza et al. (1997b); Dodds et al. (1997); Field (1996); Folmer et al. (1995); Goodstein (1995); Hanley et al. (1997); Hartwick and Olewiler (1998); Kahn (1998); Lesser et al. (1997); Perman et al. (1996); Siebert (1995); Tietenberg (1996); and Turner et al. (1994).
2. A survey chapter on this young field was originally planned.

References

Anderson, K. and R. Blackhurst (eds) (1992), *The Greening of World Trade Issues*, New York: Harvester Wheatsheaf.

Aronsson, T., P.-O. Johansson and K.-G. Löfgren (1997), *Welfare Measurement, Sustainability and Green National Accounting: A Growth Theoretical Approach*, Cheltenham, UK and Lyme, US: Edward Elgar.

Arrow, K.J., R. Solow, P. Portney, E. Leamer, R. Radner and H. Schuman (1993), *Report of NOAA Panel on Contingent Valuation*, 58 Fed. Reg. 46.

Atkinson, G., R. Dubourg, K. Hamilton, M. Munasinghe, D. Pearce and C. Young (1997), *Measuring Sustainable Development: Macroeconomics and the Environment*, Cheltenham, UK and Lyme, US: Edward Elgar.

Ayres, R.U. (1978), *Resources, Environment and Economics: Applications of the Materials/Energy Balance Principle*, New York: Wiley-Interscience.

Ayres, R.U. (1998), *Accounting for Resources. Applications of Mass Balance and Energy Balance Principles*, Cheltenham: Edward Elgar.

Ayres, R.U. and L.W. Ayres (1996). *Industrial Ecology: Towards Closing the Materials Cycle*, Cheltenham, UK and Brookfield, US: Edward Elgar.

Azar, C. and T. Sterner (1996), 'Discounting and distributional considerations in the context of global warming', *Ecological Economics*, **19**, 169–84.

Barbier, E.B., J.C. Burgess and C. Folke (1994), *Paradise Lost? The Ecological Economics of Biodiversity*, London: Earthscan.

Baumol, W.J. and W.E. Oates (1988), *The Theory of Environmental Policy*, 2nd edn, Cambridge, UK: Cambridge University Press.

Beltratti, A. (1996), *Models of Economic Growth with Environmental Assets*, Dordrecht: Kluwer Academic Publishers.

Bergh, J.C.J.M. van den (1996), *Ecological Economics and Sustainable Development: Theory, Methods and Applications*, Cheltenham, UK and Brookfield, US: Edward Elgar.

Bergh, J.C.J.M. van den and M.W. Hofkes (eds) (1998), *Theory and Implementation of Economic Models for Sustainable Development*, Dordrecht: Kluwer Academic Publishers.

Bergh, J.C.J.M. van den and J. van der Straaten (eds) (1994), *Toward Sustainable Development: Concepts, Methods and Policy*, Washington, DC: Island Press.

Bergh, J.C.J.M. van den and J. van der Straaten (eds) (1997), *Economy and Ecosystems in Change: Analytical and Historical Approaches*, Cheltenham, UK and Lyme, US: Edward Elgar.

Bergh, J.C.J.M. van den, K.J. Button, P. Nijkamp and G.J. Pepping (1997), *Meta-analysis in Environmental Economics*, Dordrecht: Kluwer Academic Publishers.

Bjornstad, D.J. and J.R. Kahn (eds) (1996), *The Contingent Valuation of Environmental Resources: Methodological Issues and Research Needs*, Cheltenham, UK and Brookfield, US: Edward Elgar.

Boulding, K.E. (1978), *Ecodynamics: A New Theory of Societal Evolution*, Beverly Hills: Sage Publications.

Bovenberg, L. and S. Cnossen (eds) (1995), *Public Economics and the Environment in an Imperfect World*, Dordrecht: Kluwer Academic Publishers.

Bowers, J. (1997), *Environmental Economics: An Alternative Text*, London: Addison-Wesley Longman.

Braden, J.B. and C.D. Kolstad (eds) (1991), *Measuring the Demand for Environmental Quality*, Amsterdam: North-Holland.

Bredahl, M.E., N. Ballenger and J.C. Dunmore (eds) (1996), *Agriculture, Trade, and the Environment: Discovering and Measuring the Critical Linkages*, Boulder, CO: Westview Press.

Bromley, D.W. (1991), *Environment and Economy: Property Rights and Public Policy*, Oxford: Basil Blackwell.

Bromley, D.W. (ed.) (1995), *Handbook of Environmental Economics*, Oxford: Blackwell.

Bromley, D.W. (1997), 'Property regimes in environmental economics', in H. Folmer and T. Tietenberg (eds), *The International Yearbook of Environmental and Resource Economics 1997/1998: A Survey of Current Issues*, Cheltenham, UK and Lyme, US: Edward Elgar.

Brown, M.T. and R.A. Herendeen (1996), 'Embodied energy analysis and EMERGY analysis: a comparative view', *Ecological Economics*, **19**, 219–35.

Bruce, J.P., H. Lee and E.F. Haites (eds) (1996), *Climate Change 1995: Economic and Social Dimensions of Climate Change*, Cambridge, UK: Cambridge University Press.

Callan, S. and J. Thomas (1996), *Environmental Economics and Management: Theory, Policy, and Applications*, New York: McGraw-Hill.

Carraro, C. and D. Siniscalco (eds) (1996), *Environmental Fiscal Reform and Unemployment*, Dordrecht: Kluwer Academic Publishers.

Carson, R.T., W.M. Hanemann, R.J. Kopp, S. Presser and P. Ruud (1992), 'A contingent valuation study of lost passive use values resulting from the Exxon Valdez oil spill', Attorney General of the State of Alaska, Anchorage.

Chichilnisky, G., G. Heal and A. Vercelli (eds) (1997), *Sustainability: Dynamics and Uncertainty*, Dordrecht: Kluwer Academic Publishers.

Clark, C.W. (1985), *Bioeconomic Modelling and Fisheries Management*, New York: Wiley-Interscience.

Clark, C.W. (1990), *Mathematical Bioeconomics: The Optimal Management of Renewable Resources*, 2nd edn, New York: Wiley.

Clark, N., F. Perez-Trejo and P. Allen (1995), *Evolutionary Dynamics and Sustainable Development: A Systems Approach*, Aldershot, UK and Brookfield, US: Edward Elgar.

Clayton, A.M.H. and N.J. Radcliffe (1996), *Sustainability: A Systems Approach*, London: Earthscan.

Cohen, J.E. (1995), *How Many People can the Earth Support?* New York: Norton.

Common, M. (1996), *Environmental and Resource Economics*, 2nd edn, London: Addison-Wesley Longman.

Costanza, R. (ed.) (1991), *Ecological Economics: The Science and Management of Sustainability*, New York: Columbia University Press.

Costanza, R., B.G. Norton and B.D. Haskell (eds) (1992), *Ecosystem Health*, Washington, DC: Island Press.

Costanza, R., C. Perrings and C.J. Cleveland (eds) (1997a), *The Development of Ecological Economics*, Cheltenham, UK and Lyme, US: Edward Elgar.

Costanza, R., J. Cumberland, H. Daly, R. Goodland and R. Norgaard (1997b), *An Introduction to Ecological Economics*, Washington, DC: Island Press.

Costanza, R., O. Segura and J. Martínez-Alier (eds) (1996), *Getting Down to Earth: Practical Applications of Ecological Economics*, Washington, DC: Island Press.

Cropper, M.L. and W.E. Oates (1992), 'Environmental economics: A survey', *Journal of Economic Literature*, **30**, 675–740.

Cummings, R.G., D. Brookshire and W. Schulze (eds) (1990), *Valuing Environmental Goods: An Assessment of the Contingent Valuation Method*, Totawa, NJ: Rowman & Littlefield.

Daly, H.E. (1991a), *Steady-State Economics*, 2nd edn, Washington, DC: Island Press.

Daly, H.E. (1991b), 'Elements of environmental macroeconomics', in R. Costanza (ed.), *Ecological Economics: the Science and Management of Sustainability*, New York: Columbia University Press.

Daly, H.E. and W. Cobb (1989), *For the Common Good: Redirecting the Economy Toward Community, the Environment and a Sustainable Future*, Boston: Beacon Press.

Daly, H.E. and K.N. Townsend (eds) (1993), *Valuing the Earth: Economics, Ecology and Ethics*, Boston: MIT Press.

Daly, H.E. and A.F. Umaña (eds) (1981), *Energy, Economics and the Environment*, AAAS Selected Symposia Series, Boulder, COL: Westview Press.

Dasgupta, P. (1995), 'The population problem: theory and evidence', *Journal of Economic Literature*, **33**, 1879–902.

Dasgupta, P.S. and G.M. Heal (1979), *Economic Theory and Exhaustible Resources*, Cambridge, UK: Cambridge University Press.

Deacon, R.T., D.S. Brookshire, A.C. Fisher, A.V. Kneese, C.D. Kolstad, D. Scrogin, V.K. Smith, M. Ward and J. Wilen (1998), 'Research trends and opportunities in environmental and natural resource economics', *Environmental and Resource Economics*, **12** (1–3), special issue 'Frontiers of Environmental and Resource Economics'.

Demeny, P. and G. McNicoll (eds) (1998), *The Earthscan Reader in Population and Development*, London: Earthscan.

Devall, B. and G. Sessions (1984), *Deep Ecology*, Layton, UT: Peregrine Smith.

Dodds, D.E., J.A. Lesser and R.O. Zerbe (1997), *Environmental Economics and Policy*, London: HarperCollins.

Dorfman, R. and N.S. Dorfman (eds) (1993), *Economics of the Environment: Selected Readings*, 3rd edn, New York: W.W. Norton & Co.

Ekins, P. and M. Max-Neef (eds) (1992), *Real-life Economics: Understanding Wealth Creation*, London: Routledge.

Faber, M. and J.L.R. Proops (1990), *Evolution, Time, Production and the Environment*, Heidelberg: Springer-Verlag.

Faber, M., H. Niemes and G. Stephan (1987), *Entropy, Environment and Resources: An Essay in Physico-Economics*, Heidelberg: Springer-Verlag.

Faucheux, S., D. Pearce and J. Proops (eds) (1996), *Models of Sustainable Development*, Cheltenham, UK and Brookfield, US: Edward Elgar.

Field, B.C. (1996), *Environmental Economics: An Introduction*, 2nd edn, New York: McGraw-Hill.

Fischer, K. and J. Schot (eds) (1993), *Environmental Strategies for Industry: International Perspectives on Research Needs and Policy Implications*, Washington, DC: Island Press.

Fisher, A.C. and F.M. Peterson (1976), 'Economics of the Environment', *Journal of Economic Literature*, **14**, 1–33.

Folmer, H., H. Landis Gabel, J.B. Opschoor (eds) (1995), *Principles of Environmental and Resources Economics: A Guide for Students and Decision Makers*, Aldershot, UK and Brookfield, US: Edward Elgar.

Folmer, H. and T. Tietenberg (eds) (1997), *The International Yearbook of Environmental and Resource Economics 1997/1998*, Cheltenham, UK and Lyme, US: Edward Elgar.

Folmer, H. and T. Tietenberg (eds) (1999), *The International Yearbook of Environmental and Resource Economics 1999/2000*, Cheltenham, UK and Northampton, MA, USA: Edward Elgar.

Freeman III, A.M. (1993), *The Measurement of Environmental and Resource Values: Theory and Methods*, Baltimore, MD: Resources for the Future.

Georgescu-Roegen, N. (1971), *The Entropy Law and the Economic Process*, Cambridge, MA: Harvard University Press.

Georgescu-Roegen, N. (1976), *Energy and Economic Myths*, New York: Pergamon.

Goodstein, E.S. (1995), *Economics and the Environment*, Englewood Cliffs, NJ: Prentice Hall.

Gowdy, J.M. (1994), *Coevolutionary Economics: The Economy, Society and the Environment*, Dordrecht: Kluwer Academic Publishers.

Gowdy, J.M. (1997), 'The value of biodiversity: markets, society and ecosystems', *Land Economics*, **73**, 25–41.

Gowdy, J.M. and S. O'Hara (1996), *Economic Theory for Environmentalists*, Delray Beach, Florida: Saint Lucie Press.

Gren, I.-G., C. Folke, K. Turner and I. Bateman (1994), 'Primary and secondary values of wetland ecosystems', *Environmental and Resource Economics*, **4**, 55–74.

Guha, R. and J. Martínez-Alier (1997), *Varieties of Environmentalism: Essays from North and South*, London: Earthscan.

Hanley, N. and C.L. Spash (1993), *Cost–Benefit Analysis and the Environment*, Aldershot, UK and Brookfield, US: Edward Elgar.

Hanley, N., J.F. Shogren and B. White (1997), *Environmental Economics – In Theory and Practice*, London: Macmillan.

Hannesson, R. (1993), *Bioeconomic Analysis of Fisheries*, Oxford: Fishing News Book.

Hartwick, J.M. (1997), 'National wealth, constant consumption and sustainable development', in H. Folmer and T. Tietenberg (eds), *The International Yearbook of Environmental and Resource Economics 1997/1998: A Survey of Current Issues*, Cheltenham, UK and Lyme, US: Edward Elgar.

Hartwick, J.M. and N.D. Olewiler (1998), *The Economics of Natural Resource Use*, 2nd edn, New York: Addison-Wesley.

Hausman, J.A. (ed.) (1993), *Contingent Valuation: A Critical Assessment*, Amsterdam: North-Holland.

Heal, G. (ed.) (1993), *The Economics of Exhaustible Resources*, The International Library of Critical Writings in Economics Series, Aldershot, UK and Brookfield, US: Edward Elgar.

Hoggart, K. (ed.) (1992), *Agricultural Change, Environment and Economy*, San Francisco: Mansell.

Holling, C.S., D.W. Schindler, B.W. Walker and J. Roughgarden (1995), 'Biodiversity in the functioning of ecosystems: an ecological synthesis', in C. Perrings, K.-G. Mäler, C. Folke, C.S. Holling and B.-O. Jansson (eds) (1995b).

Howe, C.W. (1979), *Natural Resource Economics: Issues, Analysis and Policy*, New York: Wiley.

Hueting, R., P. Bosch and B. de Boer (1992), 'Methodology for the calculation of sustainable national income', Publication M44, Central Bureau for Statistics, Voorburg.

Janssen, R. (1992), *Multiobjective Decision Support for Environmental Management*, Dordrecht: Kluwer Academic Publishers.

Jansson, A.M., M. Hammer, C. Folke and R. Costanza (eds) (1994), *Investing in Natural Capital: The Ecological Economics Approach to Sustainability*, Washington, DC: Island Press.

Jepma, C.J. (ed.) (1995), *The Feasibility of Joint Implementation*, Dordrecht: Kluwer Academic Publishers.

Johansson, P.-O. (1987), *The Economic Theory and Measurement of Environmental Benefits*, Cambridge, UK: Cambridge University Press.

Johansson, P.O. and K.G. Löfgren (1985), *The Economics of Forestry and Natural Resources*, Oxford: Basil Blackwell.

Kahn, J.R. (1998), *The Economic Approach to Environmental and Natural Resources*, 2nd edn, Orlando, FL: The Dryden Press/Harcourt Brace College Publishers.

Kandelaars, P.P.A.A.H. (1999), *Economic Models of Material–Product Chains for Environmental Policy Analysis*, Dordrecht: Kluwer Academic Publishers.

Klijn, F. (ed.) (1994), *Ecosystem Classification for Environmental Management*, Dordrecht: Kluwer Academic Publishers.

Kneese, A.V. and J.L. Sweeney (eds) (1985–93), *Handbook of Natural Resource and Energy Economics*, vols 1–3, Amsterdam: North-Holland.

Kneese, A.V., R.U. Ayres and R.C. D'Arge (1970), *Economics and the Environment: A Materials Balance Approach*, Baltimore, MD: Johns Hopkins University Press.

Kopp, R.J., W.W. Pommerehne and N. Schwarz (eds) (1997), *Determining the Value of Non-Marketed Goods: Economic, Psychological, and Policy Relevant Aspects of Contingent Valuation Methods*, Dordrecht: Kluwer Academic Publishers.

Krautkramer, J.A. (1998), 'Nonrenewable resource scarcity', *Journal of Economic Literature*, **36**, 2065–2107.

Krishnan, R., J. Harris and N. Goodwin (eds) (1995), *A Survey of Ecological Economics*, Washington, DC: Island Press.

Kuik, O., P. Peters and N. Schrijver (eds) (1994), *Joint Implementation to Curb Climate Change: Legal and Economic Aspects*, Dordrecht: Kluwer Academic Publishers.

Lecomber, R. (1975), *Economic Growth versus the Environment*, London: Macmillan.

Lesser, J.A., D.E. Dodds and R.O. Zerbe Jr (1997), *Environmental Economics and Policy*, London: Addison-Wesley.

Lind, R. (ed.) (1982), *Discounting for Time and Risk in Energy Policy*, Baltimore, MD: Johns Hopkins University Press.

Low, P. (1992), *International Trade and Environment*, World Bank Discussion Papers, 159, Washington, DC: World Bank.

Mabey, N., S. Hall, C. Smith and S. Gupta (eds) (1997), *Argument in the Greenhouse: The International Economics of Controlling Global Warming* (Global Environment Change Series), London: Routledge.

Maclean, D. and P.G. Brown (eds) (1983), *Energy and the Future*, Totowa, NJ: Rowman and Littlefield.

Markandya, A. and D.W. Pearce (1988), 'Natural environments and the social rate of discount', *Project Appraisal*, **3**, 2–12.
Markandya, A. and J. Richardson (eds) (1992), *The Earthscan Reader in Environmental Economics*, London: Earthscan.
Martínez-Alier, J. (1995), 'The environment as a luxury good or "too poor to be green"?', *Ecological Economics*, **13**, 1–10.
Martínez-Alier, J. with K. Schluepmann (1991), *Ecological Economics: Environment, Energy and Society*, 2nd edn, Oxford: Basil Blackwell.
Merrett, S. (1997), *Introduction to the Economics of Water Resources: An International Perspective*, Totowa, NJ: Rowman & Littlefield.
Mishan, E.J. (1977), *The Economic Growth Debate: An Assessment*, London: George Allen & Unwin.
Mitchell, R. and R. Carson (1989), *Using Surveys to Value Public Goods: The Contingent Valuation Method*, Washington, DC: Resources for the Future.
Munro, A. (1997), 'Economics and biological evolution', *Environmental and Resource Economics*, **9**, 429–49.
Myers, N. and J.L. Simon (1994), *Scarcity or Abundance? A Debate on the Environment*, New York: W.W. Norton.
Neher, P.A. (1990), *Natural Resource Economics: Conservation and Exploitation*, New York: Cambridge University Press.
Noorman, K.J. and T.S. Uiterkamp (eds) (1998), *Green Households? Domestic Consumers, Environment and Sustainability*, London: Earthscan.
Nordhaus, W.D. (1994), *Managing the Global Commons: The Economics of Climate Change*, Cambridge, MA: MIT Press.
Norgaard, R.B. (1985), 'Environmental economics: an evolutionary critique and a plea for pluralism', *Journal of Environmental Economics and Management*, **12**, 382–94.
Norgaard, R.B. (1989), 'The case for methodological pluralism', *Ecological Economics*, **1**, 37–57.
Norgaard, R.B. (1994), *Development Betrayed: The End of Progress and a Coevolutionary Revisioning of the Future*, London and New York: Routledge.
Oates, W.E. (ed.) (1992), *The Economics of the Environment*, The International Library of Critical Writings in Economics Series, Aldershot, UK and Brookfield, US: Edward Elgar.
OECD (1994), *Agriculture and the Environment in the Transition to a Market Economy*, Paris: OECD.
Opschoor, J.B., A.F. de Savornin Lohman and J.B. Vos (1994), *Managing the Environment: The Role of Economic Instruments*, Paris: OECD.
O'Riordan, T. (ed.) (1997), *Ecotaxation*, London: Earthscan.
Parry, M. and T. Carter (1998), *Climate Impact and Adaptation Assessment*, London: Earthscan.
Pearce, D.W. and J.J. Warford (1993), *World Without End: Economics, Environment and Sustainable Development*, Oxford: Oxford University Press.
Peet, J. (1992), *Energy and the Ecological Economics of Sustainability*, Washington, DC: Island Press.
Perman, R., Y. Ma, J. McGilvray and M. Common (1999), *Natural Resource and Environmental Economics*, 2nd edn, London: Longman.
Perrings, C. (1987), *Economy and Environment*, New York: Cambridge University Press.
Perrings, C., K.-G. Mäler, C. Folke, C.S. Holling and B.-O. Jansson (eds) (1995a), *Biodiversity Conservation*, Dordrecht: Kluwer Academic Publishers.
Perrings, C., K.-G. Mäler, C. Folke, C.S. Holling and B.-O. Jansson (eds) (1995b), *Biodiversity Loss*, Cambridge, UK: Cambridge University Press.
Peterson, F.M. and A.C. Fisher (1977), 'The optimal exploitation of extractive resources: a survey', *The Economic Journal*, **87**, 681–721.
Pezzey, J. (1989), *Economic Analysis of Sustainable Growth and Sustainable Development*, Environmental Department Working paper no. 15, Environmental Department, World Bank.
Pierce, C. and D. Vandeveer (1995), *People, Penguins, and Plastic Trees: Basic Issues in Environmental Ethics*, 2nd edn, Belmont, CA: Wadsworth.

Rotmans, J. and B. de Vries (1997), *Perspectives on Global Change: The Targets Approach*, Cambridge, UK: Cambridge University Press.

Rugman, A.M. and J.J. Kirton (eds) (1998), *Trade and the Environment. Economic, Legal and Policy Perspectives*, The International Library of Critical Writings in Economics Series, Cheltenham, UK and Lyme, US: Edward Elgar.

Ruth, M. (1993), *Integrating Economics, Ecology and Thermodynamics*, Dordrecht: Kluwer Academic Publishers.

Ruttan, V.W. (ed.) (1994), *Agriculture, Environment, and Health: Sustainable Development in the 21st Century*, Minneapolis: University of Minnesota Press.

Sagoff, M. (1988), *The Economy of the Earth*, Cambridge, UK: Cambridge University Press.

Siebert, H. (1985), 'Spatial aspects of environmental economics', in A.V. Kneese and J.L. Sweeney (eds), *Handbook of Natural Resource and Energy Economics*, vol. 1, Amsterdam: North-Holland.

Siebert, H. (1995), *Economics of the Environment: Theory and Policy*, 4th edn, Berlin: Springer-Verlag.

Spulber, N. and A. Sabbaghi (1997), *Economics of Water Resources: From Regulation to Privatization*, Boston: Kluwer Academic Publishers.

Sterner, T. (ed.) (1994), *Economic Policies for Sustainable Development*, Dordrecht: Kluwer Academic Publishers.

Sterner, T. and J.C.J.M. van den Bergh (eds) (1998), 'Frontiers of environmental and resource economics', *Environmental and Resource Economics*, **12** (1–3), special issue.

Tietenberg, T. (1994), *Environmental Economics and Policy*, New York: HarperCollins.

Tietenberg, T. (1996), *Environmental and Natural Resource Economics*, 4th edn, New York: HarperCollins.

Tietenberg, T. (ed.) (1997), *The Economics of Global Warming*, The International Library of Critical Writings in Economics Series, Cheltenham, UK and Lyme, US: Edward Elgar.

Tietenberg, T. and H. Folmer (eds) (1998), *The International Yearbook of Environmental and Resource Economics 1998/1999*, Cheltenham, UK and Lyme, US: Edward Elgar.

Toman, M.A., J. Pezzey and J. Krautkraemer (1995), 'Neoclassical economic growth theory and "sustainability",' in D.W. Bromley (ed.), *Handbook of Environmental Economics*, Oxford: Blackwell.

Turner, R.K., D.W. Pearce and I. Bateman (1994), *Environmental Economics, An Elementary Introduction*, Hemel Hempstead: Harvester Wheatsheaf.

Turner, R.K., C. Perrings and C. Folke (1997), 'Ecological economics: paradigm or perspective', in J.C.J.M. van den Bergh and J. van der Straaten (eds), *Economy and Ecosystems in Change: Analytical and Historical Approaches*, Cheltenham, UK and Lyme, US: Edward Elgar.

Walters, C. (1986), *Adaptive Management of Renewable Resources*, New York: Macmillan.

Welford, R. and R. Starkey (eds) (1996), *The Earthscan Reader in Business and the Environment*, London: Earthscan.

Wilson, E. O. (ed.) (1988), *Biodiversity*, Washington, DC: National Academy of Science Press.

2 A short history of environmental and resource economics

Thomas D. Crocker

1 Introduction

As late as 300 years ago, nearly everyone was fatalistic about nature. Whatever transactions people undertook left all but their immediate environment and the social order in which they nested pretty much undisturbed (Chayanov, 1966; Sahlins, 1974). People lived in self-contained groups which left them few options but to adapt to the idiosyncrasies of their natural surroundings. Many were unlucky and suffered famine, flood and pestilence. The intellectual ferment of the eighteenth-century Enlightenment changed this. Over about two centuries the idea that the social order may influence nature – for good – spread over the world. A broad consensus that this same order may also influence nature for ill was reached only in the last half of the twentieth century. Though economists have studied the original endowment of the earth since the beginnings of their discipline, it took an awakening realization in 1950s North America that all was not well with the management of the region's natural resource asset base to make environmental and resource economics (resource economics, for brevity) a distinct field.

As in general economics the history of resource economics can be viewed as a sequence of thought experiments or models and organized empirical observations directed at a common set of questions about economic scarcity and thus choice. For resource economics the models and the findings are meant to explain the roles that the natural environment plays in decisions under the curse of Adam and Eve, decisions that are a universal problem of the human condition and which therefore should be of keen interest to all, economists and non-economists alike. This brief essay traces the contributions of economics to the evolution of approaches to this problem and the forms these approaches currently take in the specialized field of resource economics.

2. Predecessors

In order to hear their modern echoes, this section portrays the thinking of the pre-World War II predecessors to the modern field of resource economics. According to Smith (1776), Ricardo (1817) and Marx (1865), natural resources are worthy of distinctive analytical treatment because the services they offer are gratis. Payments to the owners of the resources are therefore rents or unearned increments. Marshall (1920) concluded that such payments combine rents and royalties because extraction of the potential services that nature freely provides requires effort. Exhaustibility was not an issue, but, because resources differ in their service potentials, depletion may be realized by different declines in the quality of supply sources. Such declines were shown to be the source of dissimilar land rents across space.

Exceptions to this early, rather sterile debate about labels were few and melancholy. Malthus (1798) told a grim tale of immiseration caused by limited agricultural land and exponential population growth. Darwin (1876, p. 388) granted that this tale inspired his theory of evolution. The rising land rents induced by diminishing returns were the ultimate check upon growth in population and in wealth (Ricardo, 1817). George (1879) worried about the wealth and power consequences of landowners' unearned rents. Jevons (1865) gloomily spoke of industrial decay due to the depletion of the quantity and quality of coal stocks. Other than Mill's (1865, p. 750) brief remarks, no economist of stature deliberated upon the life support and amenity services that natural environments offer. Exept for Faustmann's (1849) prescient treatment of the optimal time to harvest a forest when current harvesting affects the growth and thus the time distribution of future returns, and Pressler's (1860) use of the same problem to anticipate marginal analysis, questions that would later become prominent about optimal rates of resource depletion and levels of environmental quality were simply not asked. Natural resources were regarded as another factor of production similar, aside from their free provision by nature, to heterogeneous capital which never gets out of the market process. In modern terms the economics of the time offered up a simple present-value maximization criterion in an assumed setting of complete markets. The criterion was thereby blind to the life support and amenity services of the environment and presumed that present consumption of resource stocks did not impact on future consumption and production opportunities.

Not until the early twentieth century did economists begin to explore systematically the tension between present-value maximization as if the entire economy were a single, fully informed, incentive-compatible firm indifferent to the foreclosure of its future options and to the depletion and non-market features which pervade natural resource issues. Gray (1914) initiated this thrust by showing that in a world of complete markets and rational expectations a firm employing the present-value maximization criterion would distribute its depletable resource extraction activities over time such that its rents would increase at the market rate of interest. A heretofore unrecognized cost over and above the costs of extraction and processing, the opportunity cost of depletion, or 'user cost', drove this result. Ise (1925) showed how the rent path of the resource was sensitive to the prices of substitutes and other exogenous economic factors. For regenerative biological resources, an opportunity cost of *not* harvesting, the foregone growth of the stock remaining after the harvest, must also be taken into account. Hotelling (1931) extended Gray (1914) to the entire economy by demonstrating, again in a world of complete markets and rational expectations, that the price for a depletable resource would increase at the rate of interest. Private and socially optimal price paths would coincide. However, Gray (1913) has earlier set aside the complete markets condition to express concern that user costs accruing to future generations would then be inadequately reflected in current extraction decisions. Ely (1918), expressing the same concern about the erosion of society's resource base, proposed to reduce the biases that incomplete markets have for the present by joining economic analysis with the understanding that natural scientists and the like have about the future productive powers of natural resources. Pigou (1920) took the incomplete markets theme further to demonstrate how the price system is likely to understate the collective scarcity value of the life support and amenity services of the natural environment.

During the 1930s, economists' interest in resource questions languished except for the institutionalist school associated with the work of Commons (1934). This enclave, which was virtually a subset of the agricultural economics of the time, insisted that market prices are only a part of the information that economic agents employ to make decisions. The social commitments and norms that property and other collective institutions induce, and the coordination of expectations among agents that they thereby offer, are forms of value expression and social interaction just as valid as those of the market, especially when issues of equity are granted intellectual stature equal to that of allocative efficiency and economic growth. Natural resource institutions were frequently the vehicle employed to carry forward these arguments.

Though natural resources played little if any role in their development, two strands of thought emerged in these interwar years that were to be influential for the evolution of resource economics after World War II. The Austrian school, whose exemplar is Hayek (1937), stressed the subjective nature of human preferences and the dominant roles that information and incentives play in individuals' decisions. Simultaneously, Hicks (1936) and others laid the foundations for inferring individuals' changes in preference satisfaction or welfare from observations of the choices that they make. With these two strands the intellectual tools needed for a resurgence of interest in natural resource economics lay ready at the end of World War II. However, if in the 1930s the United States federal government, drawing upon a tradition in water resources planning going back to Dupuit (1844), had not insisted that proposed federal water developments undergo a rigorous assessment of their benefits and the alternatives that the projects denied, applications of these new tools might well have stalled (Eckstein, 1958). The potential applications of resource economics to water resources planning induced strong demands to advance the state of the art, especially with respect to non-marketed environmental values.

3. Post-World War II

Economic activity consists of two types of transformations: the conversion of resources into goods and services through the creation of form, place, and time utility; and the exchange of the results of these conversions for other goods and money. By the early 1950s, general economics had a set of core behavioural assumptions or working hypotheses in place that allowed it to focus primarily on the second of these transformations. The six conventions are: (1) economic agents exist; (2) these agents have invariant, complete preferences over outcomes; (3) they optimize independently of each other over natural and man-made constraints; (4) their choices are all made in fully integrated markets; (5) they have full, relevant knowledge of their decision problems; and (6) observable outcomes are fully coordinated and must therefore be discussed with respect to equilibrium states (Weintraub, 1985). This core set the stage for tensions which still persist between general economics and resource economics and within resource economics. Because its core conventions did not require recognition that resource conversions were antecedent to the exchange process, general economics has been able to progress by elaborating stylized consistencies between the conventions and equilibrium prices. All economic issues about the environmental and natural resource base are implicitly assumed to have already been solved. Too infrequently, say some observers (McCloskey, 1983), are the consistencies used to design empirical tests of specific hypotheses and to interpret the sources and the consequences of observed events related to exchange. Too frequently are abstraction and mathematical formalism raised above all else and too often is empirical work restricted to a slim set of econometric practices that approved method elevates above systematic observation. In contrast to the well-ordered, narrow path conferred by the universal paradigm of its parent discipline, the frequent demands starting in the 1930s for public policy applications in resource economics have given life to an eclectic interplay between real problems and abstract theory. Though there can be considerable differences among resource economists about the appropriate degree of adherence to the general paradigm (Randall, 1985), there is near-universal agreement that progress in the field demands violations of one or more of the core conventions, attention to the historical antecedents of problems, and flexibility in empirical method.

Contemporary resource economics departs from the core assumption that all choices are made in fully integrated markets (Kapp, 1950; Coase, 1960). Thinness in markets and in other exchange processes for natural resources, rather than increasing marginal costs caused by diminishing returns in supply, motivate the field to look in depth at the manners in which resource transformations create form, time and place utilities. Questions of internal consistency between the standard behavioural conventions and the formal definition of a general equilibrium set of prices for natural resources as well as for other commodities have, as in Mäler (1974) and in Baumol and Oates (1975), attracted occasional interest. Applications of these general equilibrium concepts to the detailed behavioural as opposed to the gross mechanistic properties of economy–ecosystem interactions have only recently appeared (van den Bergh and Nijkamp, 1991; Crocker and Tschirhart, 1993; Swallow, 1996). The field has instead concentrated on the development of auxiliary conditions in partial equilibrium settings which allow at least some features (for example, invariant preferences) of the standard paradigm to fit observed phenomena. Considerable effort has thus been devoted to the task of identifying the exact conditions in a resources context which cause allocation system failures, where 'failure' means that the system fails to exhaust all potential economic surpluses. These sources of failure include rivalrous open access (Gordon, 1954), non-rivalrous indivisibilities in consumption (Samuelson, 1954), informational asymmetries (Weitzman, 1974), non-separabilities (Montgomery, 1976) and non-convexities (Starret, 1972) in production, and transferable externalities (Bird, 1987). The perceived pervasiveness of these sources of failure has in turn led many in the field to reconsider the appropriateness of the invariance and the completeness of preferences (Shogren et al., 1994; Spash and Hanley, 1995), the independence of optimization (Marglin, 1963; Kahneman and Knetsch, 1992), and the fullness and relevance of knowledge conventions (Pigou, 1920; Norgaard, 1990) for the analysis of environmental and resource issues. Arguably the field has therefore displayed a lesser willingness than its parent discipline to protect theory from data.

Given that allocation system failures exist, the field perceives the second of its tasks to be measurement of the surpluses foregone due to these failures. A variety of clever observed behaviour techiques, for example, travel cost (Clawson, 1959), dual profit functions (Garcia et al., 1986), hedonics (Ridker and Henning, 1967; Freeman, 1971), household production (Becker, 1965), mathematical programming (Adams et al., 1982), have been developed. All rely upon specification of a complementary or substitution relation between a market good and the non-marketed, environmental good of interest. A stated behaviour method commonly called contingent valuation (Knetsch and Davis, 1966) has recently attracted wide interest among policy makers responsible for providing and protecting non-marketed environmental goods, though the meaning of the results of the technique in terms of the core behavioural assumptions of general economics remains open to considerable doubt (Diamond and Hausman, 1994; Hanemann, 1994). Insights from psychology have, however, proved fruitful in structuring and interpreting contingent valuation studies (for example, Kahneman and Knetsch, 1992).

Resource economists have also identified new types of surplus to measure. The most defensible in terms of economic theory are option value or the value of avoiding commitments that are costly to reverse (Weisbrod, 1964), quasi-option value or the value of maintaining opportunities to learn about the benefits and costs of avoiding possibly irreversible future states (Arrow and Fisher, 1974; Henry, 1974), bequest value or the value of contributing to the welfare of future generations (Cropper and Sussman, 1988), and existence or pure non-use value (Krutilla, 1967). Limited empirical work (for example, Schulze et al., 1983) indicates that these types of value can be a greater portion of the total value of environmental goods than is traditional use value. Dixit and Pindyck (1994), while drawing upon results in financial economics, have recently expanded understanding of the set of observed behaviour techniques available to assess option and quasi-option values, including land development (Capozza and Li, 1994). Controlled experiments designed to be incentive-compatible are increasingly used to inform and to assess the reliability of valuation work in the field (Cummings et al., 1995).

A third task for the resource economics research programme has been the design of allocation systems capable of realizing the foregone surpluses. The efficiency or incentive-compatibility properties of mandated effluent or ambient standards versus effluent charges (Kneese and Schulze, 1975), tradable rights (Crocker, 1966) or permits (Dales, 1968), and environmental bonds (Shogren et al., 1993) or liability (Kolstad et al., 1990) in the presence of asymmetric information between non-cooperating regulators and polluters (Segerson, 1988; Xepapadeas, 1991) now dominate the discussion. Much of the related empirical work is sophisticated in natural science as well as in economic terms (Russell and Spofford, 1977; Atkinson and Tietenberg, 1982). Game-theoretic approaches to understanding sufficient conditions for cooperative agreements about pollution problems also now frequently appear (Hoel, 1991; Barrett, 1992). Again, controlled experiments are increasingly used to gain empirical insights about the efficiency and distributional properties of alternative designs (Cason, 1995). A major finding of all this design work is that single-price market devices are not the only or always the best ways to allocate environmental and natural resources. Both economic theory and empirical observation demonstrate that voluntary, cooperative non-market institutions built upon rules of access to and use of a resource held in common can be very effective at capturing surplus and pooling risks (Bromley, 1991).

Elucidation of the sources of and corrections for market, regulatory, and household failures, and the measurement of the associated foregone and potential surpluses, have been approached using the perspective of microeconomics. The fourth task that post-World War II resource economics has undertaken focuses on depletion, large macroeconomic-like questions about trends in the availability of environmental, biological and mineral resources and their effects upon economic growth. Starting with Barnett and Morse (1963), numerous studies assess the ability of the price system and of human inventiveness to overcome the diminishing returns principle of Malthus (1798) and Ricardo (1817). Because adaptive expectations rather than rational expectations appear to dominate the behaviours of extractive industries (Farzin, 1992; Pesaran, 1990), the validity of applying Hotelling (1931) principles to test the increasing scarcity hypothesis has been questioned (Eagan, 1987). Treatments of the life support, amenity and waste disposal services of the natural environment as free in general economics studies of man-made capital formation are nevertheless shown to have led to exaggerated estimates of rates of growth in economies (Nordhaus and Tobin, 1972). In addition, the axis of the depletion discussion has shifted from the stand-alone service flows of individual environmental goods to a view of these goods as bundles of assets (Mohring and Boyd, 1971) that demand attention to the sequential and spatial patterns of their uses and abuses (Keeler et al., 1972; Forster, 1973). The result has been greatly increased attention to the joint products that the assets offer and to the impact of the often subtle connected global and ubiquitous local cumulative impacts of environmental change upon the ability of competitive but incomplete markets to sustain these offerings (Plourde, 1972; Dasgupta and Heal, 1979). These subtleties inspire increasing use of simulation techniques to test analytical results and to gain insight about detailed structural responses to system perturbations (Deacon, 1993). There is controversy as to whether the economic scarcity of mineral and immobile biological resources has been increasing (Norgaard, 1990; Devarajan and Fisher, 1982). For other biological and environmental resources such as fisheries and water quality the consensus is that depletion governs (Smith and Krutilla, 1979), partly because of the stress that the extraction and consumption of mineral and immobile biological resources place upon them. However, limited empirical evidence shows an inverted U relation between pollution flows and economic growth whereby initial increases in pollution flows with growth are eventually offset by increased abatement effort at higher levels of development (Grossman and Krueger, 1995). The increasing scarcity discourse has generated a rapidly expanding analytical and empirical management literature dealing with intergenerational equity and efficiency (Solow, 1974; Hartwick, 1977) and thus conservation ethics (Page, 1977), accounting for resource depletion in macroeconomic indicators (Peskin, 1972), the double dividend fiscal implications of pollution and depletion taxes (Munasinghe and Cruz, 1994), the relationships between environmental life support and amenity depletion and economic growth (Vousden, 1973; Daly, 1977), environmental quality and poverty (Dasgupta, 1993), and environmental quality and international trade (d'Arge and Kneese, 1972).

Starting with Boulding's (1966) application of the conservation of mass principle and Georgescau-Roegen's (1971) advocacy of greater economic attention to the entropy principle, resource economists have commonly used prior information from the natural sciences to restrict the dimensionalities of their positive models of economy–environment interactions (Ayres, 1978; Clark, 1976), and to develop normative criteria other than consumer sovereignty for sustaining the potential of natural capital assets to contribute to well-being (Pezzey, 1986; Common and Perrings, 1992). Scholars who choose to make the reciprocities between ecological system functions and economic systems dominate their normative thinking now identify themselves as ecological economists. They propose that their view of ecological processes as a reciprocating part of economic activity (Norgaard, 1985), rather than as an independent background support upon which this activity feeds, distinguishes them from standard resource economics practice. Though the distinction has some validity for a general economics that centres upon exchange rather than resource transformations, it probably claims too much relative to the actual traditions of resource economics. After all, *sustainability* or risk aversion against environmental change, the badge of the ecological economics club, was a primary concern of Ciriacy-Wantrup (1952), Scott (1955), Solow (1974), Hartwick (1977), and even of Hicks (1936), the archetypical general economist. Though the ecological economists have demonstrated it under restricted conditions, these predecessors clearly suspected that the price system favoured by the current generation and its immediate progeny and the pace of human capital accumulation may be insufficient to sustain human well-being across generations.

Unfortunately the resource economics research programme has evolved in a setting of environmentalist scepticism, even outright hostility, toward its content and implications (for example, Anderson, 1993). At root, these feelings stem from the nearly two-centuries-old shallow-brained propensity of intellectuals to avoid reading economics and to complain, without reading, that its content and arguments correspond perfectly to commercial interests. With natural resources, the correspondence is reflected in the reluctance of environmentalists to grant that natural assets can be traded off against other entities that humans desire. The reluctance is encouraged by the inattention that ecological theory gives to the roles of human discretion in ecosystem behaviours. Environmental policy making has often manifested these feelings. Witness the neglect of economic analysis in environmental risk assessment practice in the United States, as if human choice plays no role in observed pollution exposures and damages. Policy has thus typically lagged far behind the findings and insights of the field until the pressure of events (rapidly escalating control costs, obvious rent dissipation, citizen resistance to bureaucratic rigidities) forces a reconsideration of the economic dimension. Recent political rhetoric about replacing command-and-control schemes of pollution control with economic incentives such as tradable rights is a prime example. Greater attention by the field to problems of providing operational guidelines for its findings would undoubtedly reduce the lag. Resource economics can no longer validly be viewed by practical people as a collection of 'empty boxes' (Clapham, 1922).

4.   Conclusions

It is easy to be impressed with the depth and the breadth of knowledge that the serious environmental and resource economist must now command. This necessary knowledge spans the domain from the extremely practical to the highly abstract and general – from doing a cost–benefit analysis of a particular project to modelling dynamic economies with increasing returns and incomplete markets. Environmental and resource economics has done more than any other field to bring natural science and psychology into economics. Because of the significant role that institutional and property rights design issues play in environmental questions, the same assertion might be made about the law. This drive toward a multidisciplinary focus is caused by the frequent absence in resource settings of prices that bring together the laws of nature and rules of man relevant to the burden of scarcity. The focus suggests that many of the great discoveries in resource economics have yet to be made. All the veins of environmental and natural resource questions to which economics can be applied and from which economics can learn have not yet been mined or even discovered.

Nevertheless, one might readily question whether the substantial intellectual talents the field attracts are now being allocated in the most productive manner across its four self-elected tasks.

Practical matters of legal suits and bureaucratic rule making have caused some of the best minds in the field to turn inward toward technical economic minutiae associated with the humdrum everyday business of valuing site- and time-specific non-marketed environmental goods. Bigger at the margin but less commercialized questions about the sources of environmental problems, the institutional means to resolve them, and their intergenerational consequences have partly become the province of some natural scientists, especially ecologists, and general economists who choose to face outward. This recruitment of fresh talent is what will keep the field dynamic and continue to enrich its explanatory power and its normative punch.

References

Adams, Richard M., Thomas D. Crocker and Narongsakdi Thanavibulchai (1982), 'An economic assessment of air pollution damages to selected annual crops in southern California', *Journal of Environmental Economics and Management*, 9 (1), 42–58.

Anderson, Ellen (1993), *Values in Ethics and Economics*, Cambridge, MA: Harvard University Press.

Arrow, Kenneth J. and Anthony C. Fisher (1974), 'Environmental preservation, uncertainty, and irreversibility', *The Quarterly Journal of Economics*, 88 (2), 313–19.

Atkinson, Scott E. and Thomas H. Tietenberg (1982), 'The empirical properties of two classes of designs for transferable discharge permit markets', *Journal of Environmental Economics and Management*, 9 (2), 101–21.

Ayres, Robert U. (1978), *Resources, Environment and Economics*, New York: John Wiley and Sons.

Barnett, Harold, J. and Chandler Morse (1963), *Scarcity and Growth: The Economics of Natural Resource Availability*, Baltimore, MD: Johns Hopkins University Press.

Barrett, Scott (1992), 'International environmental agreements as games', in Rudi Pethig (ed.), *Conflicts and Cooperation in Managing Environmental Resources*, Berlin: Springer-Verlag, pp. 11–36.

Baumol, William J. and Wallace E. Oates (1975), *The Theory of Environmental Policy*, Englewood Cliffs, NJ: Prentice-Hall.

Becker, Gary S. (1965), 'A theory of the allocation of time', *The Economic Journal*, 75 (Sept.), 495–517.

Bergh, Jeroen C.J.M. van den and Peter Nijkamp (1991), 'Operationalizing sustainable development: dynamic ecological economic models', *Ecological Economics*, 4 (1), 11–33.

Bird, Peter J.W.N. (1987), 'The transferability and depletability of externalities', *Journal of Environmental Economics and Management*, 14 (1), 54-7.

Boulding, Kenneth (1966), 'The economics of the coming Spaceship Earth', in Henry Jarret (ed.), *Environmental Quality in a Growing Economy*, Baltimore, MD: Johns Hopkins University Press, pp. 3–14.

Bromley, Daniel W. (1991), *Environment and Economy: Property Rights and Public Policy*, Oxford: Basil Blackwell.

Capozza, Dennis, and Uuming Li (1994), 'The intensity and timing of investment: the case of land', *The American Economic Review*, 84 (4), 889–904.

Cason, Timothy N. (1995), 'An experimental investigation of the seller incentives in the EPA's emission trading auction', *The American Economic Review*, 85 (4), 905–22.

Chayanov, A.V. (1966), 'On the theory of non-capitalist economic systems', in D. Thorner and B. Kerblay (eds), *The Theory of the Peasant Economy*, Homewood, IL: R.D. Irwin, pp. 1–51.

Ciriacy-Wantrup, S.V. (1952), *Resource Conservation: Economics And Politics*, 3rd edn, Berkeley, CA: University of California Press.

Clapham, J.H. (1922), 'Of empty economic boxes', *The Economic Journal*, **32** (Sept.), 305–14.

Clark, Colin W. (1976), *Mathematical Bioeconomics: The Optimal Management of Renewable Resources*, New York: John Wiley and Sons.

Clawson, Marion (1959), *Methods of Measuring the Demand for and Value of Outdoor Recreation*, RfF Reprint no. 10, Washington, DC: Resources for the Future.

Coase, Ronald H. (1960), 'The problem of social cost', *Journal of Law and Economics*, **3** (1), 1–44.

Common, Mick and Charles Perrings (1992), 'Towards an ecological economics of sustainability', *Ecological Economics*, **6** (1), 7–34.

Commons, John R. (1934), *Institutional Economics*, New York: Macmillan and Co.

Crocker, Thomas D. (1966), 'Structuring of atmospheric pollution control systems', in H. Wolozin (ed.), *The Economics of Air Pollution*, New York: W.W. Norton and Co, pp. 61–86.

Crocker, Thomas D. and John Tschirhart (1993), 'Ecosystems, externalities, and economies', *Environmental and Resource Economics*, **2** (4), 551–68.

Cropper, Maureen L. and Frances G. Sussman (1988), 'Families and the economics of risks to life', *The American Economic Review*, **78** (1), 225–60.

Cummings, Ronald G., Glenn W. Harrison and E. Elisabet Rutström (1995), 'Homegrown values and hypothetical surveys: is the dichotomous choice approach incentive-compatible?', *The American Economic Review*, **85** (1), 260–66.

Dales, John H. (1968), *Pollution, Property and Prices*, Toronto: University of Toronto Press.

Daly, Herman E. (1977), *Steady State Economics*, San Francisco, CA: W. B. Freeman & Co.

D'Arge, Ralph C. and Allen V. Kneese (1972), 'Environmental quality and international trade', *International Organization*, **26** (3), 419–65.

Darwin, Charles ([1876]1963), 'The autobiography', in Stanley E. Hyman (ed.), *Darwin for Today*, New York: Viking Press, pp. 325–404.

Dasgupta, Partha S. (1993), *An Inquiry into Well-Being and Destitution*, Oxford: Oxford University Press.

Dasgupta, Partha S. and Geoffrey M. Heal (1979), *Economic Theory and Exhaustible Resources*, Welwyn, UK: James Nisbet & Co.

Deacon, Robert T. (1993), 'Taxation, depletion, and welfare: a simulation study of the U.S. petroleum resource', *Journal of Environmental Economics and Management*, **24** (2), 159–87.

Devarajan, Shamtayanan and Anthony C. Fisher (1982), 'Exploration and scarcity', *Journal of Political Economy*, **90** (6), 1279–90.

Diamond, Peter A. and Jerry A. Hausman (1994), 'Contingent valuation: is some number better than no number?', *The Journal of Economic Perspectives*, **8** (1), 45–64.

Dixit, Avinash K. and Robert S. Pindyck (1994), *Investment under Uncertainty*, Princeton, NJ: Princeton University Press.

Dupuit, Jules ([1844]1952), 'On the measurement of the utility of public works', (English translation), *International Economic Papers*, **2**, London: Macmillan.

Eagan, Vince (1987), 'The optimal depletion of the theory of exhaustible resources', *Journal of Post Keynesian Economics*, **9** (4), 565–71.

Eckstein, Otto (1958), *Water Resource Development: The Economics of Project Evaluation*, Cambridge, MA: Harvard University Press.

Ely, Richard T. (1918), 'Conservation and economic theory', in R.T. Ely et al. (eds), *The Foundations of National Prosperity*, New York: Macmillan, pp. 1–77.

Farzin, Y. H. (1992), 'The time path of scarcity rent in the theory of exhaustible resources', *The Economic Journal*, **102** (413), 813–30.

Faustmann, Martin ([1849]1995), 'Calculation of the value which forest land and immature stands possess for forestry', *Journal of Forest Economics*, **1** (1), 7–44.

Forster, Bruce A. (1973), 'Optimal consumption planning in a polluted environment', *Economic Record*, **49** (Dec.), 534–45.

Freeman, A. Myrick III (1971), 'Air pollution and property values: a methodological comment', *Review of Economics and Statistics*, **53** (4), 415–16.

Garcia, Philip, Bruce L. Dixon, James W. Mjelde and Richard M. Adams (1986), 'Measuring the benefits of environmental change using a duality approach: The case of ozone and Illinois cash grain farms', *Journal of Environmental Economics and Management*, **13** (1), 69–80.

George, Henry (1879), *Progress and Poverty*, San Francisco, CA: W.M. Hinton.

Georgescu-Roegen, Nicholas (1971), *The Entropy Law and the Economic Process*, Cambridge, MA: Harvard University Press.

Gordon, H. Scott (1954), 'Economic theory of common property resources', *Journal of Political Economy*, **62** (1), 124–42.

Gray, Lewis C. (1913), 'Economic possibilities of conservation', *The Quarterly Journal of Economics*, **27** (May), 497–519.

Gray, Lewis C. (1914), 'Rent under the assumption of exhaustibility', *The Quarterly Journal of Economics*, **28** (May), 466–89.

Grossman, Gene M. and Allan B. Krueger (1995), 'Economic growth and the environment', *The Quarterly Journal of Economics*, **110** (2), 353–78.

Hanemann, W. Michael (1994), 'Valuing the environment through contingent valuation', *The Journal of Economic Perspectives*, **8** (4), 19–44.

Hartwick, John M. (1977), 'Intergenerational equity and the investing of rents from exhaustible resources', *The American Economic Review*, **67** (4), 972–4.

Hayek, F. A. (1937), 'Economics and knowledge', *Economica*, **4** (February), 33–54.

Henry, Claude (1974), 'Investment decisions under uncertainty', *The American Economic Review*, **64** (6), 1006–12.

Hicks, John R. (1936), *Value and Capital*, Oxford: Oxford University Press.

Hoel, Michael (1991), 'Efficient international agreements for reducing emissions of CO_2', *Energy Journal*, **12** (2), 93–108.

Hotelling, Harold (1931), 'The economics of exhaustible resources', *Journal of Political Economy*, **39** (2), 137–75.

Ise, John (1925), 'The theory of value as applied to natural resources', *The American Economic Review*, **15** (2), 284–9.

Jevons, W. Stanley (1865), *The Coal Question*, London: Macmillan.

Kahneman, Daniel and Jack L. Knetsch (1992), 'Valuing public goods: the purchase of moral satisfaction', *Journal of Environmental Economics and Management*, **22** (1), 57–70.

Kapp, K. William (1950), *The Social Costs of Private Enterprise*, Cambridge, MA: Harvard University Press.

Keeler, Theodore E., Michael Spence and Richard Zeckhauser (1972), 'The optmal control of pollution', *Journal of Economic Theory*, **4** (1), 19–34.

Kneese, Allen V. and Charles Schulze (1975), *Pollution, Prices, and Public Policy*, Washington, DC: The Brookings Institution.

Knetsch, Jack L. and Robert K. Davis (1966), 'Comparison of methods for recreation evaluation', in A.V. Kneese and S.C. Smith (eds), *Water Research*, Baltimore, MD: Johns Hopkins University Press, pp. 125–42.

Kolstad, Charles D., Thomas S. Ulen and Gary V. Johnson (1990), 'Expost liability for harm vs. expost safety regulation: substitutes or complements', *The American Economic Review*, **80** (4), 888–901.

Krutilla, John V. (1967), 'Conservation reconsidered', *The American Economic Review*, **57** (4), 777–86.

Mäler, Karl-Goren (1974), *Environmental Economics: A Theoretical Inquiry*, Baltimore, MD: Johns Hopkins University Press.

Malthus, Thomas ([1798]1960), *On Population*, Modern Library Edition, New York: Random House.

Marglin, Stephen A. (1963), 'The social rate of discount and the optimal rate of investment', *The Quarterly Journal of Economics*, **77** (1), 95–111.

Marshall, Alfred (1920), *Principles of Economics*, 8th edn, London: Macmillan.

Marx, Karl ([1865]1906), *Capital*, F. Engels, trans., Modern Library Edition, New York: Random House.

McClosky, Donald (1983), 'The rhetoric of economics', *Journal of Economic Literature*, **21** (2), 481–517.

Mill, John S. ([1865]1965), *Principles of Political Economy*, 6th edn, New York: Augustus M. Kelley.

Mohring, Herbert and J. Hayden Boyd (1971), 'Analyzing externalities: direct interaction vs. asset utilization frameworks', *Economica*, **38** (November), 347–61.

Montgomery, W. David (1976), 'Separability and vanishing externalities', *The American Economic Review*, **66** (1), 174–7.

Munasinghe, Mohan and W. Cruz (1994), *Economywide Policies and the Environment*, Washington, DC: The World Bank.

Nordhaus, William D. and James Tobin (1972), *Is Growth Obsolete?* 5th Anniversary Volume of the NBER, *Economic Growth*, New York: Columbia University Press.

Norgaard, Richard B. (1985), 'Environmental economics: an evolutionary critique and a plea for pluralism', *Journal of Environmental Economics and Management*, **12** (4), 382–94.

Norgaard, Richard B. (1990), 'Economic indicators of resource scarcity: A critical essay', *Journal of Environmental Economics and Management*, **19** (1), 19–25.

Page, Talbot (1977), *Conservation and Economic Efficiency: An Approach to Materials Policy*, Baltimore, MD: Johns Hopkins University Press.

Pesaran, M. Hasham (1990), 'An econometric analysis of exploration and extraction of oil in the U.K. continental shelf', *The Economic Journal*, **100** (1), 367–90.

Peskin, Henry M. (1972), *National Accounting and the Environment*, Oslo, Norway: Central Bureau of Statistics.

Pezzey, John (1986), 'Conservation of mass and instability in a dynamic economy–environment system', *Journal of Environmental Economics and Management*, **13** (3), 199–211.

Pigou, Arthur C. (1920), *The Economics of Welfare*, London: Macmillan.

Plourde, Charles G. (1972), 'A model of waste accumulation and disposal', *Canadian Journal of Economics*, **5** (1), 119–25.

Pressler, Max R. ([1860]1995), 'For the comparison of net revenue silviculture and the management objectives derived thereof', *Journal of Forest Economics*, **1** (1), 45–88.

Randall, Alan (1985), 'Methodology, ideology, and the economics of policy: why resource economists disagree', *American Journal of Agricultural Economics*, **67** (5), 1022–9.

Ricardo, David ([1817]1951), 'Principles of political economy and taxation', in P. Sraffa and Maurice H. Dobb (eds), *The Works of David Ricardo*, Cambridge: Cambridge University Press.

Ridker, Ronald G. and John A. Henning (1967), 'The determinants of residential property values with special reference to air pollution', *The Review of Economics and Statistics*, **49** (2), 246–57.

Russell, Clifford S. and Walter D. Spofford, Jr (1977), 'A regional environmental management model', *Journal of Environmental Economics and Management*, **4** (2), 89–110.

Sahlins, M. (1974), *Stone Age Economics*, London: Tavistock Press.

Samuelson, Paul A. (1954), 'The pure theory of public expenditure', *The Review of Economics and Statistics*, **36** (4), 387–90.

Schulze, William D., David S. Brookshire, Edward G. Walther, Kenneth K. McFarland, Mark A. Thayer, Richard L. Whitworth, Saul Ben-David, Walter Malm and John Malenar (1983), 'The economic benefits of preserving visibility in the national parklands of the southwest', *Natural Resources Journal*, **23** (1), 149–73.

Scott, Anthony D. (1955), 'The fishery: the objectives of sole ownership', *Journal of Political Economy*, **63** (2), 116–24.

Segerson, Kathleen (1988), 'Uncertainty and incentives for nonpoint pollution control', *Journal of Environmental Economics and Management*, **15** (1), 87–98.

Shogren, Jason F., Joseph A. Herriges and Ramu Govindasamy (1993), 'Limits to environmental bonds', *Ecological Economics*, **8** (2), 109–34.

Shogren, Jason F., Seung Y. Shin, Dermot J. Hayes and James B. Kliebenstein (1994), 'Resolving differences in willingness to pay and willingness to accept', *The American Economic Review*, **84** (1), 255–70.

Smith, Adam ([1776]1937), *The Wealth of Nations*, edited by E. Cannan, Modern Library Edition, New York: Random House.

Smith, V. Kerry and John V. Krutilla (1979), 'Resource and environmental constraints to growth', *American Journal of Agricultural Economics*, **61** (3), 395–408.

Solow, Robert M. (1974), 'Intergenerational equity and exhaustible resources', *Review of Economic Studies, Symposium on the Economics of Exhaustible Resources*, **41** (Supp.), 29–45.

Spash, Clive L. and Nick Hanley (1995), 'Preferences, information and biodiversity preservation', *Ecological Economics*, **12** (3), 191–208.

Starret, David A. (1972), 'Fundamental non-convexities in the theory of externalities', *Journal of Economic Theory*, **4** (2), 180–99.

Swallow, Stephen K. (1996), 'Resource capital theory and ecosystem economics: developing nonrenewable habitats with heterogeneous quality', *Southern Economic Journal*, **63** (1), 106–23.

Vousden, Nicholas (1973), 'Basic theoretical issues in resource depletion', *Journal of Economic Theory*, **6** (2), 126–43.

Weintraub, E. Roy (1985), *General Equilibrium Analysis*, New York: Cambridge University Press.

Weisbrod, Burton A. (1964), 'Collective consumption services of individual consumption goods', *The Quarterly Journal of Economics*, **77** (1), 71–7.

Weitzman, Martin (1974), 'Prices vs. quantities', *Review of Economic Studies*, **41** (4), 477–91.

Xepapadeas, A. P. (1991), 'Environmental policy under imperfect information: incentives and moral hazard', *Journal of Environmental Economics and Management*, **20** (2), 113–27.

PART II

ECONOMICS OF
NATURAL RESOURCES

3 Optimal extraction of non-renewable resources

Cees Withagen

1. Introduction

This chapter reviews the optimal exploitation of exhaustible resources. The literature on this subject is so huge that it is impossible to do justice to all the important contributions that have been made. We shall concentrate on theoretical issues of resource depletion under certainty, while some remarks about uncertainty will be made at the end of this chapter. We shall consider optimal depletion in a closed economy from the point of view of a social planner and compare the Rawlsian and the utilitarian outcomes. We shall not go into the question how the welfare optimum can be implemented in a decentralized economy, nor shall we deal with matters such as imperfect competition. For these issues the reader is referred to other chapters of this handbook (see also Withagen, 1990).

Since we are dealing with optimal exploitation over time, intergenerational welfare has to be given attention at the outset. An excellent introduction to the theory of intergenerational welfare is provided by Dasgupta and Heal (1979). Here we shall restrict ourselves to a very brief statement of the questions involved. The number of people living at date t is denoted by $L(t)$, where the the initial population, at $t = 0$, is normalized to unity. The growth rate of the population is given by π. As far as labour is an input in a production process, it is assumed throughout that this is a given constant fraction of the population. Without loss of generality it is assumed that this fraction equals unity. We shall assume that the individual preferences of all agents living at present and in the future depend only on their own consumption of a single composite commodity. The preference relations of all agents are the same and can be represented by an instantaneous utility function u. If u is concave, instantaneous total utility is then maximized by giving equal consumption shares. The technological constraints facing the economy restrict the set of feasible consumption patterns and it is the task of the planner to select from the set one element according to some criterion. The first criterion we shall deal with is the Rawlsian one. Here a feasible consumption pattern is optimal if per capita consumption is constant over time and there is no other feasible consumption pattern that is lying entirely above it. A consumption pattern is optimal in the utilitarian sense if it maximizes

$$\int_0^T e^{-\rho t} L(t) u\big(C(t)/L(t)\big) dt$$

where ρ denotes the rate of pure time preference, T is the final time, which is in some cases endogenous, and $C(t)$ is total available consumption at time t. We do not want to go into the ethical aspects of discounting (see Heal (1993) on this topic); we merely remark that we will consider the case where ρ is zero as well as the case where it is positive.

In Section 2 we shall deal with the so-called cake-eating problem, where the natural resource itself provides the consumer commodity. In Section 3 we introduce man-made capital and the raw material as an input into the production process of the composite commodity. In Section 4 we go briefly into the issue of uncertainty and R&D. Section 5 concludes.

2.   The cake-eating problem

The simplest setting in which the optimal depletion of an exhaustible resource can be studied is the so-called cake-eating problem, which concerns the optimal allocation over time of the raw material from an exhaustible resource stock, where the raw material is the only source of well-being. This problem was addressed as early as the 1930s, in Fisher's (1930) work on interest rates (the hardtrack example of stranded sailors) and of course in Hotelling's (1931) seminal work on exhaustible resources. In the utilitarian framework (with constant population) the model can be formulated as follows. Maximize

$$\int_0^T e^{-\rho t} u\big(C(t)\big) dt \qquad (3.1)$$

subject to

$$\dot{S}(t) = -C(t), \quad S(t) \geq 0, \quad S(0) = S_0, \text{ given} \qquad (3.2)$$

$$C(t) \geq \bar{C} \qquad (3.3)$$

Here u is the instantaneous utility function which is increasing, continuously differentiable on $(\bar{C}, \infty)$, and strictly concave. Moreover, $u'(\bar{C}) = \infty$ and u is positive for some $C \geq \bar{C}$. $\bar{C} (\geq 0)$ is the given constant subsistence level, S denotes the stock of the exhaustible resource, and ρ, C and T are as indicated in the previous section. Clearly, if $\bar{C} > 0$, a constant positive consumption stream cannot be maintained indefinitely.

The Hamiltonian for this problem is

$$\mathcal{H}(C,S,p,t):=e^{-\rho t}u(C)+p[-C]$$

(see Seierstad and Sydsaeter, 1987). Necessary conditions for optimality include the maximization of the Hamiltonian with respect to consumption subject to the constraint (3.3), the constancy of the shadow price p of the resource stock, due to the fact that the resource stock does not enter the Hamiltonian (this is the well-known Hotelling rule), and the requirement that, if there is an optimal final time, the Hamiltonian equals zero at that final time. Several cases can be distinguished. First assume that $\bar{C}=\rho=0$. It was pointed out by Gale (1967) that this does not produce a solution. If it did, the rate of consumption would be constant over time, which implies that consumption is zero for ever, which is clearly suboptimal. Note also that there exists a Rawlsian optimum (with zero consumption throughout), which is clearly inefficient in the Pareto sense. If $\bar{C}>0$ and $\rho=0$, then the optimal rate of consumption is constant over time and follows from the requirement that at the optimal final date the Hamiltonian should be zero and from the fact that the Hamiltonian is maximized with respect to C. The optimal C satisfies $u'(C)C=u(C)$; the optimal final time is $T=S_0/C$. If $\bar{C}=0$ and $\rho>0$, then we have $\dot{C}/C=\rho/\eta(C)$ where $\eta(C)$ denotes the elasticity of marginal utility $\left(\eta(C):=u''(C)C/u'(C)\right)$. Therefore, consumption will monotonically decrease toward zero as time goes to infinity. It is easily seen that if the elasticity of marginal utility is constant $\left(\eta(C)=\eta\right)$, then the optimum is given by $C(t)=-(\eta/\rho)S_0e^{\rho t/\eta}$. Let us finally see what happens if $\bar{C}>0$ and $\rho>0$. Clearly, as long as $C>\bar{C}$, we should have that $\dot{C}/C=\rho/\eta(C)$. Since T is free, we should also have $e^{-\rho T}u\left(C(T)\right)=e^{-\rho T}u'\left(C(T)\right)C(T)$. This determines the final rate of consumption. It now follows that 'discounting advances the doomsday' since a high rate of time preference induces higher consumption initially, until the resource is exhausted (see Koopmans, 1973, 1974; Vousden, 1973 also deals with this issue).

3. Man-made capital and exhaustible resources
A straightforward extension of the model of the previous section is to embed it into a Ramsey (1928) type growth model with man-made capital. The idea here is that the raw material from the resource enters the production of a commodity yielding welfare. The first contributions in this area were made by Anderson (1972) and Koopmans (1973). A prototype model would involve

$$\dot{K}=F(K,R,L,t)-\mu K-C, \quad K(0)=K_0 \text{ given}$$

$$\dot{S} = -R, \ S \geq 0, \ R \geq 0, \quad S(0) = S_0 \text{ given}$$

$$\dot{L} = \pi L, \quad L(0) = L_0 = 1$$

where K is man-made capital, R is the rate of use and of extraction of the exhaustible resource and L is labour input. The production function is F and allows for technical progress. The parameter μ refers to the depreciation of the capital stock. The first question addressed in this framework is whether this economy is capable of producing a positive constant per capita rate of consumption. Let us consider a CES production function:

$$Y = F(K,R,L,t) = \left[\delta_1^{-\psi} + \delta_2 R^{-\psi} + \delta_3 (e^{\lambda t} L)^{-\psi}\right]^{-1/\psi} \tag{3.4}$$

with $\delta_i \geq 0$ (all i) and with λ the rate of Harrod-neutral, labour-augmenting, technical progress. The elasticity of substitution is $\sigma = 1/(1 + \psi)$.

If $\sigma > 1$, none of the inputs is necessary for production and positive per capita consumption can be maintained: the resource is called inessential. On the other hand, if $\sigma < 1$, total production over time is bounded from above (because $Y/R < \delta_2^{-1/\psi}$) and hence consumption will necessarily go to zero. In a more general framework Dasgupta and Heal (1979) argue that in the absence of technical progress what matters is the behaviour of the elasticity of substitution as a function of R/K when R/K tends to zero. The intuition behind this result is that R/K must necessarily decline to zero, and that capital must be capable of substituting enough for the raw material.

So, an interesting border case turns out to the Cobb–Douglas production function

$$Y = F(K,R,L,t) = K^{\alpha_1} R^{\alpha_2} (e^{\lambda t} L)^{\alpha_3} \tag{3.5}$$

Before proceeding we have to elaborate on the notion of efficiency. A consumption pattern will be called efficient if it is feasible and if there is no feasible consumption trajectory that is lying entirely above it.

Clearly, we can restrict ourselves to efficient consumption patterns. It can be shown (see, for example, Withagen, 1990) that a necessary condition for efficiency is that $\dot{F}_R/F_R = F_K$. Here indices refer to partial derivatives. This rule is called the Hotelling rule. It can be obtained as follows. Consider two adjacent periods in discrete time. Consider two feasible trajectories of the economy, starting at the beginning of the first period and ending after the second period with the same stocks of capital and of the natural resource. It should not be possible to deviate from, say, the first path in the first period, maintaining the rate of consumption in that period and increasing the rate of consumption in the second period. This is what the rule boils down to. Using the Hotelling rule, the following results can be obtained for the Cobb–Douglas case (see Stiglitz, 1974 and Withagen, 1990). If the natural growth rate $(\pi + \lambda)$ equals zero, then a necessary and sufficient condition for the resource to be inessential is that $\mu = 0$ and $\alpha_1 > \alpha_2$. If the natural growth rate is positive, then a necessary and sufficient condition for the resource to be inessential is that $\alpha_3(\pi + \lambda) > \pi(1 - \alpha_1)$. The derivation of these conditions is rather tedious but their interpretation is straightforward. In the absence of technical progress and of population growth we need that capital can sufficiently substitute for the unavoidable decrease in the raw material input. Therefore, the production elasticity of capital should exceed the production elasticity of the raw material. But since capital must go to infinity it is also required that there is no depreciation. For the case of population growth and technical progress it is required that technical progress is high enough and that the production elasticity of capital is sufficiently large.

If the conditions established above are satisfied, one might ask what is the maximal constant per capita rate of consumption. It has been shown by Solow (1974) that for the case of no natural growth and a Cobb–Douglas production function it is equal to

$$C^* = (1 - \alpha_2)\left\{(\alpha_1 - \alpha_2)^{\alpha_2} S_0^{\alpha_2} K_0^{\alpha_1 - \alpha_2}\right\}^{\frac{1}{1 - \alpha_2}}$$

It can be shown that this rate of consumption results if the savings rate $(\dot{K}/Y)$ equals α_2. It can also be shown that $\dot{K} = F_R R$: the share of the natural resource in production should be invested in man-made capital. This is known as Hartwick's rule (after Hartwick, 1977). For the case of a positive natural growth rate the asymptotic savings rate is also a constant.

Turning now to the utilitarian optimum, it should be clear that no closed expressions for consumption and extraction can be obtained. In the literature attention is mostly restricted to isoelastic utility functions (meaning that the elasticity of marginal utility is constant). Stiglitz (1974) (for a logarithmic utility function) and Withagen (1990) (for the general constant elasticity case) consider the utilitarian optimum with a Cobb–Douglas production function, including technical progress and growth of the labour force and allowing for increasing returns to scale, whereas Dasgupta and Heal (1974) deal with a CES production function with constant returns to scale with respect to capital and raw material. In both cases one of the necessary conditions is, of course, the Hotelling rule discussed above. But, in addition, we now have the so-called Ramsey rule as a necessary condition. This rule reads

$$\eta(c)\dot{c}/c = -F_K + \rho$$

where $c := C/L$. For a derivation of this rule see, for example, Dasgupta and Heal (1979). The central idea can be sketched as follows. Consider two adjacent periods in discrete time. Increase investments in the first period. This yields less consumption now, but gives better opportunities next period. It should not be possible to gain more total utility over the two periods without ending up with a smaller final stock of capital.

In the Cobb–Douglas case the Hotelling rule and the Ramsey rule allow us to derive a system of differential equations in capital productivity (Y/K) and consumption per unit of capital (C/K). It is shown by the authors mentioned above that if the rate of time preference is large enough, there exists a utilitarian optimum, along which Y/K and C/K converge to constants. In the case of no technical progress, no population growth and constant returns to scale in capital and the raw material, the asymptotic growth rate of consumption and capital is ρ/η. Moreover, the rate of exploitation will have a constant rate of decline eventually. Per capita consumption need not be monotonic. For example, if an economy is initially very capital-rich, it is possible to construct an example where per capita consumption initially falls but increases eventually. This U-shaped consumption profile does, however, not occur when the natural growth rate is zero. This is shown by Pezzey and Withagen (1998) for the case of a general production function displaying constant returns to scale. Dasgupta and Heal (1974) pay attention to a CES specification of technology. It is assumed that only capital and the raw material are factor inputs and that there are constant returns to scale. So, we have (3.4) with $\alpha_3 = 0$ and $\alpha_1 + \alpha_2 = 1$. If the elasticity of substitution is smaller than unity ($\sigma < 1$), then the asymptotic growth rates of consumption, capital and resource extraction are all ρ/η. On the other hand, with an elasticity of substitution exceeding unity, it is required for the existence of an optimum that the rate of time preference is large enough $\left(\text{in particular } \rho > \alpha_1^{-1/\psi}(1 + \eta)\right)$. The asymptotic growth rates of consumption and capital are $(\rho - \alpha_1^{-1/\psi})/\eta$. For the asymptotic growth rate of exploitation we have $\left[(\rho - \alpha_1^{-1/\psi})/\eta\right] - \sigma\alpha_1^{-1/\psi}$. So, if the rate of time preference is not too large, optimal consumption might eventually increase in this case. Finally, Dasgupta and Heal (1979) consider the Cobb–Douglas production function in some detail for the case of a time preference equal to zero. They also find that consumption might increase indefinitely along an optimum. Figure 3.1 presents a set of possible outcomes of the utilitarian optimum in the case of no technical progress.

The large number of possibilities and their diversity brings to mind the words of Koopmans (1965): 'Ignoring realities in adopting "principles" may lead one to search for a nonexistent optimum, or to adopt an optimum

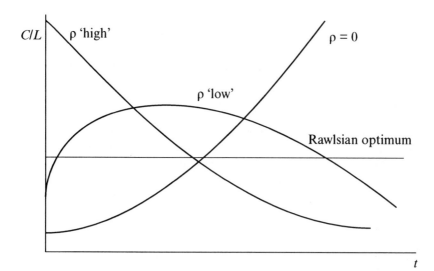

Figure 3.1   Optimal consumption trajectories

that is open to unanticipated objections.' In fact, it is not true in general that the utilitarian optimum severely harms future generations, e.g. if the rate of time preference equals zero.

4.   Uncertainty and research and development
It is unquestionable that uncertainty is pertinent to almost every aspect of the economics of exhaustible resources. It would go far beyond the scope of the present survey to give a full account of the abundant literature on this topic. We restrict ourselves here to some general observations. For a more detailed survey the reader is referred to Crabbe (1982) and Mangel (1985).

Uncertainty with respect to the *size of the exhaustible resource* is treated by Gilbert (1979), Kemp (1976), Loury (1978) and Pindyck (1980). A general outcome of these models is that the extraction rate under uncertainty is more conservative than under certainty. Uncertainty can also refer to the process of *exploration*, not dealt with above. The questions that are studied include how much effort should be invested in exploration, if there is an unknown number of deposits of known size (Arrow and Chang, 1980 and Pindyck, 1980). Kemp and Long (1980) study the case where the location of resources of known sizes is unknown. Another source of uncertainty can be the *horizon* of the economy. For example, at each instant of time there might be a positive probability that life ceases or, as is discussed in Long (1975), there is uncertainty about the *possible nationalization* of the resource. The transition from the use of exhaustible resources to a *substitute* is a topic which is given much attention in the literature. Here uncertainty can have to do with the (exogenous) date on which the substitute becomes available (Dasgupta and Heal, 1974; Dasgupta and Stiglitz, 1981 and Heal, 1979). The case of an endogenous date of invention, depending on the R&D efforts undertaken, is studied by Dasgupta et al. (1976), Dasgupta et al. (1980) and Davidson (1978). Hoel (1978) considers the situation where the substitute has an uncertain cost but becomes available at some fixed instant of time. He shows that a mean-preserving increase in uncertainty leads to an increase in the extraction rate of the conventional resource, if the instantaneous utility function displays risk-neutrality and the resource is not depleted at the time the substitute becomes available.

5.   Conclusion

In this chapter a brief account has been given of some analytical issues related to the optimal depletion of exhaustible resources. For reasons of space many interesting aspects have been neglected. We have paid no attention to extraction costs (see Heal, 1976; Levhari and Leviathan, 1977 and Solow and Wan, 1976 and Chapter 5 in this handbook), or the optimal exploitation in open economies (see Aarrestad, 1978 and Chapter 6 in this handbook). Another very interesting question refers to the current debate on net national product as an indicator for welfare in the utilitarian or the Rawlsian sense (see, for example, Solow, 1993 and Vellinga and Withagen, 1996), based on the literature discussed in the present chapter. Nevertheless it is hoped that this chapter demonstrates some analytical fundamentals and the crucial role technology and preferences play in the choice of the optimal exploitation rate.

References
Aarrestad, J. (1978), 'Optimal savings and exhaustible resources in an open economy', *Journal of Economic Theory*, **19**, 163–79.
Anderson, K. (1972), 'Optimal growth when the stock of resources is finite and depletable', *Journal of Economic Theory*, **4**, 256–67.
Arrow, K. and S. Chang (1980), 'Optimal pricing, use and exploration of uncertain natural resource stocks', in P. Liu (ed.), *Dynamic Optimization and Mathematical Economics*, New York: Plenum Press, pp. 105–16.
Crabbe, P. (1982), 'Sources and types of uncertainty, information and control in stochastic economic models of non-renewable resources', in G. Feichtinger (ed.), *Optimal Control Theory and Economic Applications*, Amsterdam: North-Holland.
Dasgupta, P. and G. Heal (1974), 'The optimal depletion of exhaustible resources', *Review of Economic Studies*, Symposium, pp. 3–28.
Dasgupta, P. and G. Heal (1979), *Economic Theory and Exhaustible Resources*, Cambridge, UK: Cambridge University Press.

Dasgupta, P. and Stiglitz, J. (1981), 'Resource depletion under technological uncertainty', *Econometrica*, **49**, 85–104.

Dasgupta, P., G. Heal and M. Majumdar (1976), 'Resource depletion and research and development', in M. Intriligator (ed.), *Frontiers of Quantitative Economics IIIb*, Amsterdam: North-Holland, pp. 483–506.

Dasgupta, P., G. Heal and A. Pand (1980), 'Funding research and development', *Applied Mathematical Modelling*, **4**, 87–94.

Davidson, R. (1978), 'Optimal depletion of an exhaustible resource with research and development towards an alternative technology', *Review of Economic Studies*, **45**, 355–68.

Fisher, I. (1930), *The Theory of Interest*, New York: Macmillan.

Gale, D. (1967), 'On optimal development in a multi-sector economy', *Review of Economic Studies*, **34**, 1–18.

Gilbert, R. (1979), 'Optimal depletion of an uncertain stock', *Review of Economic Studies*, **46**, 47–57.

Hartwick, J. (1977), 'Intergenerational equity and the investing of rents from exhaustible resources', *American Economic Review*, **66**, 972–4.

Heal, G. (1976), 'The relationship between price and extraction costs for a resource with a backstop technology', *Bell Journal of Economics*, **1**, 371–8.

Heal, G. (1979), 'Uncertainty and the optimal supply policy for an exhaustible resource', in R. Pindyck (ed.), *Advances in the Economics of Energy Resources*, Greenwich, CT: JAI Press, pp. 119–47.

Heal, G. (1993), 'The optimal use of exhaustible resources', in A. Kneese and J. Sweeney (eds), *Handbook of Natural Resource and Energy Economics*, Amsterdam: North-Holland, pp. 855–80.

Hoel, M. (1978), 'Resource extraction when a future substitute has an uncertain cost', *Review of Economic Studies*, **45**, 637–43.

Hotelling, H. (1931), 'The economics of exhaustible resources', *Journal of Political Economy*, **31**, 137–75.

Kemp, M. (1976), 'How to eat a cake of unknown size', in M. Kemp (ed.), *Three Topics in the Theory of International Trade*, Amsterdam: North-Holland, pp. 297–308.

Kemp, M. and N. Long (1980), 'Optimal search and extraction: a general equilibrium formulation', in M. Kemp and N. Long (eds), *Exhaustible Resources, Optimality, and Trade*, Amsterdam: North-Holland, pp. 155–63.

Koopmans, T. (1965), 'On the concept of optimal economic growth', *The Econometric Approach to Development Planning*, Pontificiae Academiae Scientiarium Scriptum Varia, Amsterdam: North-Holland, pp. 225–87.

Koopmans, T. (1973), 'Some observations on "optimal" economic growth and exhaustible resources', in H. Bos, H. Linneman and P. de Wolff (eds), *Economic Structure and Development*, Essays in Honour of Jan Tinbergen, Amsterdam: North-Holland, pp. 239–55.

Koopmans, T. (1974), 'Proof for a case where discounting advances doomsday', Review of Economic Studies, Symposium, pp. 117–20.

Levhari, D. and N. Leviathan (1977), 'Notes on Hotelling's economics of exhaustible resources', *Canadian Journal of Economics*, **10**, 177–92.

Long, N.V. (1975), 'Resource extraction under the uncertainty about possible nationalization', *Journal of Economic Theory*, **10**, 42–53.

Loury, G. (1978), 'The optimal exploitation of an unknown resource', *Review of Economic Studies*, **45**, 621–36.

Mangel, M. (1985), *Decision and Control in Uncertain Resource Systems*, Orlando, FL: Academic Press.

Pezzey, J. and C. Withagen (1998), 'The rise, fall and sustainability of capital-resource economies', *Scandinavian Journal of Economics*, **100** (2), 513–27.

Pindyck, R. (1980), 'Uncertainty and exhaustible resource markets', *Journal of Political Economy*, **88**, 1203–25.

Ramsey, F. (1928), 'A mathematical theory of saving', *Economic Journal*, **38**, 543–59.

Seierstad, A. and K. Sydsaeter (1987), *Optimal Control Theory with Economic Applications*, Amsterdam: North-Holland.

Solow, R. (1974), 'Intergenerational equity and exhaustible resources', *Review of Economic Studies*, Symposium, pp. 29–45.

Solow, R. (1993), 'An almost practical step toward sustainability', *Resources Policy*, **19**, 162–72.

Solow, R. and H. Wan (1976), 'Extraction costs in the theory of exhaustible resources', *Bell Journal of Economics*, **17**, 359–70.

Stiglitz, J. (1974), 'Growth with exhaustible natural resources: efficient and optimal growth paths', *Review of Economic Studies*, Symposium, pp. 123–37.

Vellinga, N. and C. Withagen (1996), 'On the concept of green national income', *Oxford Economic Papers*, **48**, 499–514.

Vousden, N. (1973), 'Basic theoretical issues of resource depletion', *Journal of Economic Theory*, **6**, 126–43.

Withagen, C. (1990), 'Topics in resource economics', in F. van der Ploeg (ed.), *Advanced Lectures in Quantitative Economics*, London: Academic Press, pp. 381–420.

4 Imperfect competition in natural resource markets

Cees Withagen and Aart de Zeeuw

1. Introduction

This chapter intends to survey the results of theoretical models on the extraction of an exhaustible natural resource in the tradition of Hotelling (1931). The main focus will be on the differences in extraction schedules resulting from different market structures for the suppliers of the resource. The approach is analytical and combines the dynamics of resource extraction with imperfect competition on the supply side. Special attention will be given to an oligopolistic structure with one big coherent cartel and a large number of small suppliers which was introduced in the literature in the 1970s due to the developments on the oil market.

In order to allow a complete analysis, the basic model is simple in all other aspects. The suppliers are profit maximizers, demand is linear, the market will clear, the resource stocks are given at the initial time and the marginal extraction costs are constant. We do not deal with exploration (see for example Devarajan and Fisher, 1980). Also the important issue of innovation and backstop technologies will not be covered (see for example Hoel, 1978, Heal, 1976 and Dasgupta et al., 1982). Finally, we do not address the question of internal stability of the cartel, although this is obviously important in the explanation of the events that have occurred on the oil market. This chapter is restricted to an exposition of the theory. No attempt is made to confront the results with observations on markets for exhaustible resources (see for example Griffin, 1985 or Teece et al., 1993). In Section 2 the main issue is the comparison between perfect competition and monopoly. In Section 3 the topic is the complex cartel-versus-fringe model. It can be viewed as an extension of the excellent survey of Karp and Newbery (1993) by adding the time-consistent equilibrium. Section 4 concludes the chapter.

2. Perfect competition and monopoly

We depart from $N+1$ ($N \geq 0$) suppliers (indexed by i) of the exhaustible resource. For each $i \in \{0,1, ..., N\}$ we denote by S_{0i}, $E_i(t)$, $S_i(t)$ and k_i the initial resource stock, the rate of extraction at time t, the resource stock at time t and the constant marginal extraction costs. The suppliers are ordered in such a way that $k_0 \leq k_1 \ldots \leq k_N$. For expositional purposes and for mathematical convenience it is assumed that the demand schedule for the raw material is linear and constant over time

$$p(t) = \bar{p} - X(t)$$

where $p(t)$ denotes the market price, $\bar{p}$ is the price of a backstop and $X(t)$ is demand. It is assumed that $\bar{p} > k_N$, in order to avoid the phenomenon of limit pricing (see for example Dasgupta and Stiglitz, 1982). The suppliers want to maximize their total discounted profits over time, where all use the same rate of interest $r(>0)$. We define for each supplier the set of feasible extraction trajectories:

$$\mathcal{F}_i := \left\{ E_i : [0,\infty) \to \mathbb{R}_+ \mid \int_0^\infty E_i(t)dt \leq S_{0i} \right\} \quad i = 0, 2, \ldots, N$$

We also define the set $\mathcal{F}$ of price-extraction trajectories that may occur as market equilibria:

$$\mathcal{F} := \left\{ (p, E_0, \ldots, E_N) : [0,\infty) \to \mathbb{R}_+^{N+2} \mid E_i \in \mathcal{F}_i \text{ (all } i) \text{ and} \right.$$

$$\left. p(t) = \bar{p} - \sum_{i=0}^N E_i(t) \text{ (all } t) \right\}$$

We are now in a position to define several equilibrium concepts that will be used in the sequel. First we introduce the notion of profit maximization. Fix some i and some $p : [0,\infty) \to \mathbb{R}_+$. We say that $E_i \in \mathcal{F}$ is profit-maximizing at p if E_i maximizes

$$\int_0^\infty e^{-rt} \left(p(t) - k_i \right) E_i(t)dt$$

over all elements of $\mathcal{F}_i$. $(p, E_0, \ldots, E_n) \in \mathcal{F}$ is a *competitive equilibrium* if E_i is profit-maximizing at p (all i). It follows from a simple arbitrage argument that marginal discounted profits from exploitation should be constant along intervals where exploitation takes place. This is called Hotelling's rule (Hotelling, 1931). Hence, a vector λ of positive constants $(\lambda_0, \ldots, \lambda_N)$ exists such that for $E_i(t) > 0$ we have

$$p(t) = k_i + \lambda_i e^{rt} \quad (i = 0, 1, \ldots, N) \tag{4.1}$$

The resources are exploited according to their cost of extraction: the cheapest resources are exploited first. This can be seen by noting that the price paths in (4.1) have the k_is as asymptotes.

Monopoly occurs when there is only one supplier, say agent 0. $(p, E_0) \in \mathcal{F}_0$ is a *monopoly* with agent 0 as monopolist if E_0 maximizes

$$\int_0^\infty e^{-rt}\left(\bar{p} - E_0(t) - k_0\right)E_0(t)dt$$

over $\mathcal{F}_0$. In the case at hand the firm has to be indifferent with respect to when extraction takes place in order to have an equilibrium. Hence a $\lambda_0 > 0$ exists (in general unequal to the λ_0 of (4.1)) such that as long as $E_0(t) > 0$,

$$p(t) = \tfrac{1}{2}(\bar{p} + k_0^c) + \tfrac{1}{2}\lambda_0 e^{rt} \qquad (4.2)$$

It is straightforward to compare the competitive and the monopoly outcomes. Suppose that $k_i = k_0$ for all i. The competitive price path is given by (4.1) and the monopoly price path is given by (4.2). The locus of these curves (and thereby the λs) is determined by the total amounts extracted. If, to make a fair comparison, it is assumed that these amounts are the same, it is straightforward to see that the competitive price path is steeper than the monopoly price path, as is illustrated in Figure 4.1. The curves have k_0 and $\tfrac{1}{2}(\bar{p} + k_0)$, respectively, as asymptotes with $k_0 < \tfrac{1}{2}(\bar{p} + k_0)$. If total amounts extracted are the same, the competitive price path must cross the monopoly price path and must therefore be steeper. This implies that it takes the monopolist longer to exhaust the resource.

This is by now textbook wisdom and can be seen as a direct application of Hotelling's rule. It explains the adage: 'the monopolist is the conservationist's best friend'. The monopolist can and will keep extraction lower and prices higher and is therefore more careful with extracting the material resource. However, Stiglitz (1976) shows that in the case of constant price elasticity of demand the two price curves coincide. If the price elasticity is decreasing then the monopoly price path is steeper, as was shown by, among others, Dasgupta and Heal (1979).

3. Oligopolistic markets
Next we consider the case of oligopolists, who act simultaneously without a leader–follower structure (Lewis and Schmalensee, 1980a and b).

$(p, E_0, ..., E_N) \in \mathcal{F}$ is called an *open-loop Nash equilibrium* if E_i maximizes

$$\int_0^\infty e^{-rt}\left(\bar{p} - \sum_j E_j(t) - k_i\right)E_i(t)dt$$

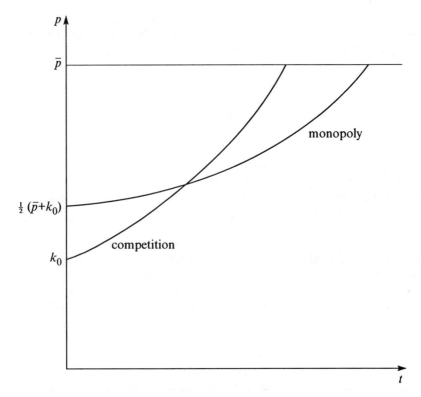

Figure 4.1   Competitive and monopoly price paths

over $\mathcal{F}_i$ (all i). Again, according to Hotelling's rule, a vector λ of positive constants $(\lambda_0, ..., \lambda_N)$ exists such that for $E_i(t) > 0$ we have

$$p(t) = k_i + \lambda_i e^{rt} + E_i(t) \tag{4.3}$$

Lewis and Schmalensee (1980a and b) prove for the case of equal costs that the larger the number of suppliers, the more competitive the price path will be.

The main case to be considered in this section is the so-called cartel-versus-fringe model, which, because of the developments on many resource markets, has attracted much attention. The idea is that the supply side of the market can be characterized by a cartel and a 'large' number of small suppliers, which prevent the cartel from acting as a pure monopolist. This idea was first introduced by Salant (1976). Ulph and Folie (1980) give a full characterization of the Cournot–Nash equilibrium for this model (see also Salant, 1982). In these papers the fringe members are modelled as price takers. Furthermore, the fringe members are aggregated, assuming identical marginal extraction costs. We have to modify the notation a little bit in this respect. The index c refers to the cartel and the index f refers to the (aggregate) fringe. The sets $\mathcal{F}_i$ and $\mathcal{F}$ are redefined accordingly.

$(p, E^c, E^f) \in \mathcal{F}$ is an *open-loop Nash equilibrium for the cartel-versus-fringe model* if E^f is profit-maximizing at p and E^c maximizes

$$\int_0^\infty e^{-rt}(\bar{p} - E^c(t) - E^f(t) - k^c)E^c(t)dt$$

over $\mathcal{F}_c$. This is exactly the model studied by Ulph and Folie (1980). In the definition presented above the term 'open-loop' refers to the assumption that the decisions are taken at the initial instant of time and are fixed. It is important to note that in a Nash equilibrium the cartel takes the output of the fringe as given. The results are summarized in Table 4.1, where we list the exploitation sequences. Here C^c, C^m, F and S denote intervals of time where the cartel is supplying alone at the competitive price $(p = k^f + \lambda^f e^{rt})$, where the cartel is supplying alone at the monopoly price $\left(p = \frac{1}{2}(\bar{p} + k^c) + \lambda^c e^{rt}\right)$, where the fringe is supplying alone and where there is simultaneous supply, respectively. Besides the cost parameters, the relative size of the initial stock of the cartel is an important determinant of the results. The effect is also presented in Table 4.1.

Table 4.1   Open-loop Nash equilibrium

Open-loop Nash equilibrium sequences		
Marginal costs	Endowment cartel	Exploitation sequence
$k^f > \frac{1}{2}(\bar{p} + k^c)$	large	$C^c \rightarrow S \rightarrow F$
$k^f > \frac{1}{2}(\bar{p} + k^c)$	small	$S \rightarrow F$
$k^f = \frac{1}{2}(\bar{p} + k^c)$		$S \rightarrow F$
$k^c < k^f < \frac{1}{2}(\bar{p} + k^c)$	small	$S \rightarrow F$
$k^c < k^f < \frac{1}{2}(\bar{p} + k^c)$	intermediate	S
$k^c < k^f < \frac{1}{2}(\bar{p} + k^c)$	large	$S \rightarrow C^m$
$k^c = k^f$		$S \rightarrow C^m$
$k^c > k^f$	large	$S \rightarrow C^m$
$k^c > k^f$	small	$F \rightarrow S \rightarrow C^m$

The basic schedule for large k^f is $S \rightarrow F$. If the cartel has a big initial stock, this can be preceded by a phase C^c. The basic schedule for small k^f

is $S \rightarrow C^m$. If the fringe has a big initial stock, this can be preceded by a phrase F. Salant (1976) and Ulph and Folie (1980) offer an interesting discussion on who benefits from cartelization. Salant shows that the formation of the cartel will raise the profits of the fringe relatively more than the profits of the cartel if the costs are equal ($k^f = k^c$). However, Ulph and Folie show that the formation of the cartel can lower the fringe's profitability if the cartel has a considerable cost advantage. The intuition behind this result is that in that case the cartel can act as a monopolist initially at prices that prevent the fringe from producing. The fringe is then forced to supply at the end of lower discounted prices.

Gilbert (1978) was the first to introduce the von Stackelberg equilibrium concept in order to characterize the market power of the cartel. Newbery (1981), Ulph and Folie (1981) and Ulph (1982) have elaborated on this. They all use the open-loop von Stackelberg equilibrium. The suppliers cannot react to observed changes in the resource stocks. In the von Stackelberg equilibrium the cartel takes account of the reactions of the fringe to its own decisions.

$(p, E^c, E^f) \in \mathcal{F}$ is an *open-loop von Stackelberg equilibrium for the cartel-versus-fringe model* if E^f is profit-maximizing at p and if there is no $(\hat{p}, \hat{E}^c, \hat{E}^f) \in \mathcal{F}$ such that $\hat{E}^f$ is profit-maximizing at $\hat{p}$ and

$$\int_0^\infty e^{-rt}\left(\hat{p}(t) - k^c\right)\hat{E}^c(t)dt > \int_0^\infty e^{-rt}\left(p(t) - k^c\right)E^c(t)dt$$

Initially this equilibrium was derived by means of calculus of variation, *assuming* that the equilibrium price trajectory is continuous over time. However, as is demonstrated by Groot et al. (1990 and 1992), that need not be the case. The equilibrium is given in Groot et al. (1995) and can be characterized as in Table 4.2.

From an economic point of view the case $k^c < k^f < \frac{1}{2}(\bar{p} + k^c)$ is the most interesting one. The price trajectory is discontinuous at points in time where there is a transition from F to C^m and where there is a transition from C^m to F. But, more importantly, the phenomenon of dynamic inconsistency might arise, as was already demonstrated by Newbery (1981) and Ulph and Folie (1981). To see this, note that it is always optimal to have an initial phase where the cartel supplies at the competitive price. If the initial resource stock of the cartel is large, its resource is not exhausted when this phase ends. If the cartel reconsiders its choice it would like to have an initial C^c phase again. In the absence of binding contracts, this will indeed happen, which implies dynamic inconsistency of the cartel's extraction path. Dynamic inconsistency also occurs when $k^c > k^f$. After the fringe has exhausted its resource, the cartel will always supply at the monopoly price

Table 4.2   Open-loop von Stackelberg equilibrium

Open-loop von Stackelberg equilibrium sequences		
Marginal costs	Endowment cartel	Exploitation sequence
$k^f > \frac{1}{2}(\bar{p} + k^c)$	large	$C^m \to C^c \to F$
$k^f > \frac{1}{2}(\bar{p} + k^c)$	small	$C^c \to F$
$k^f = \frac{1}{2}(\bar{p} + k^c)$		$C^c \to F$
$k^c < k^f < \frac{1}{2}(\bar{p} + k^c)$	small	$C^c \to F$
$k^c < k^f < \frac{1}{2}(\bar{p} + k^c)$	intermediate	$C^c \to F \to C^m$
$k^c < k^f < \frac{1}{2}(\bar{p} + k^c)$	large	$C^c \to C^m \to F \to C^m$
$k^c = k^f$		$S \to C^m$
$k^c > k^f$	large	$S \to C^m$
$k^c > k^f$	small	$F \to C^c \to C^m$

and not at the competitive price initially. These observations make it necessary to study an alternative equilibrium concept, namely the feedback or
rational expectations or Markov-perfect von Stackelberg equilibrium. We
shall not give a formal definition here but just note that the players now
condition their actions on the state variables, which are the current resource
stocks. An equilibrium is an element in the set of mappings from the state
space into the space of extraction rates. It was conjectured that in such an
equilibrium there are stages with simultaneous supply, which do not occur
in the open-loop equilibrium (except when $k^f = k^c$), but the derivation of
the individual extraction rates along such a phase proved to be rather
difficult (see Karp and Newbery, 1991 and 1992). Recently Groot et al.
(1996) were able to establish the equilibrium. The outcomes are summarized in Table 4.3.

Time inconsistency and price discontinuities have now been resolved. The
extraction shows again basic schedules for large $k^f (C^c \to F)$ and small
$k^f (S \to C^m)$, with possibly preceding stages in case the initial stock of the
cartel is relatively large and in case the initial stock of the fringe is relatively
large. The first-mover advantage of the cartel in the von Stackelberg equilibrium concept reflects itself mainly for large k^f. When compared with the
open-loop von Stackelberg equilibrium, simultaneous extraction returns as
an important case, which seems more in line with reality. Karp and
Tahvonen (1996) were able to calculate the feedback von Stackelberg equilibrium for the case of extraction costs which are linearly decreasing with the
remaining resource stock. They also find intervals with simultaneous supply.

Table 4.3   Feedback von Stackelberg equilibrium

Feedback von Stackelberg equilibrium sequences		
Marginal costs	Endowment cartel	Exploitation sequence
$k^f > \frac{1}{2}(\bar{p} + k^c)$	large	$C^m \to C^c \to F$
$k^f > \frac{1}{2}(\bar{p} + k^c)$	small	$C^c \to F$
$k^f = \frac{1}{2}(\bar{p} + k^c)$		$C^c \to F$
$k^c < k^f < \frac{1}{2}(\bar{p} + k^c)$	small	$C^c \to F$
$k^c < k^f < \frac{1}{2}(\bar{p} + k^c)$	large	$S \to C^m$
$k^c = k^f$		$S \to C^m$
$k^c > k^f$	large	$S \to C^m$
$k^c > k^f$	small	$F \to S \to C^m$

4. Conclusion

In the 1970s and 1980s the well-known Hotelling rule for the price path corresponding to the optimal extraction of an exhaustible natural resource was extended to situations with imperfect competition. Developments on the oil market, in particular, inspired the analysis of the so-called cartel-versus-fringe model. A difficulty in this model was the occurrence of dynamic inconsistency of the extraction path of the cartel, but this problem has recently been solved. This chapter surveys some theoretical results in oligopolistic market structures with a special emphasis on this cartel-versus-fringe model. Further research can be expected on relaxing some simplifying assumptions in the theoretical model and on confronting the theoretical results with empirical observation in the resource markets.

References

Dasgupta, P. and G. Heal (1979), *Economic Theory and Exhaustible Resources*, Welwyn, UK: James Nisbet and Co.
Dasgupta, P. and J. Stiglitz (1982), 'Market structure and resource depletion: a contribution to the theory of intertemporal monopolistic competition', *Journal of Economic Theory*, **28**, 128–64.
Dasgupta, P., R. Gilbert and J. Stiglitz (1982), 'Invention, innovation under alternative market structures: the case of natural resources', *Review of Economic Studies*, **49**, 567–82.
Devarajan, S. and A. Fisher (1980), 'Exploration and scarcity', *Journal of Political Economy*, **90**, 1279–90.
Gilbert, R. (1978), 'Dominant firm pricing policy in a market for an exhaustible resource', *Bell Journal of Economics*, **9**, 385–95.
Griffin, J. (1985), 'OPEC behavior: a test of alternative hypotheses', *American Economic Review*, **75**, 954–63.
Groot, F., C. Withagen and A. de Zeeuw (1990), 'Theory of natural exhaustible resources: the cartel-versus-fringe model reconsidered', *Center Discussion Paper* 8924, Tilburg University.

Groot, F., C. Withagen and A. de Zeeuw (1992), 'Note on the open-loop von Stackelberg equilibrium in the cartel-versus-fringe model', *The Economic Journal*, **102**, 1478–84.

Groot, F., C. Withagen and A. de Zeeuw (1995), 'Open-loop von Stackelberg equilibrium in the cartel-versus-fringe model', *Memorandum COSOR 95-29*, Eindhoven University of Technology.

Groot, F., C. Withagen and A. de Zeeuw (1996), 'Strong time-consistency in the cartel-versus-fringe model', *Tinbergen Institute Discussion Paper* 96-43/4, Erasmus University Rotterdam.

Heal, G. (1976), 'The relationship between price and extraction cost for a resource with a backstop technology', *The Bell Journal of Economics*, **7**, 371–8.

Hoel, M. (1978), 'Resource extraction, substitute production and monopoly', *Journal of Economic Theory*, **19**, 28–37.

Hotelling, H. (1931), 'The economics of exhaustible resources', *Journal of Political Economy*, **39**, 137–75.

Karp, L. and D. Newbery (1991), 'Optimal tariffs on exhaustible resources', *Journal of International Economics*, **30**, 285–99.

Karp, L. and D. Newbery (1992), 'Dynamically consistent oil import tariffs', *The Canadian Journal of Economics*, **25**, 1–21.

Karp, L. and D. Newbery (1993), 'Intertemporal consistency issues in depletable resources', in A. Kneese and J. Sweeney (eds), *Handbook of Natural Resource and Energy Economics*, Amsterdam: North-Holland, pp. 881–931.

Karp, L. and O. Tahvonen (1996), 'International trade in exhaustible resources: a cartel-competitive fringe model', *Working Paper* no. 754, University of California.

Lewis, T. and R. Schmalensee (1980a), 'On oligopolistic markets for non-renewable natural resources', *Quarterly Journal of Economics*, **95**, 475–91.

Lewis, T. and R. Schmalensee (1980b), 'Cartel and oligopoly pricing of non-replenishable natural resources', in P. Liu (ed.), *Dynamic Optimization and Application to Economics*, New York: Plenum Press, pp. 133–56.

Newbery, D. (1981), 'Oil prices, cartels, and the problem of dynamic consistency', *The Economic Journal*, **91**, 617–46.

Salant, S. (1976), 'Exhaustible resources and industrial structure: a Nash–Cournot approach to the world oil market', *Journal of Political Economy*, **84**, 1079–94.

Salant, S. (1982), 'Imperfect competition in the international energy market: a computerized Nash–Cournot model', *Operations Research*, **30**, 252–80.

Stiglitz, J. (1976), 'Monopoly and the rate of extraction of exhaustible resources', *American Economic Review*, **66**, 655–61.

Teece, D., D. Sunding and E. Mosakowski (1993), 'Natural resource cartels', in A. Kneese and J. Sweeney (eds), *Handbook of Natural Resource and Energy Economics*, part 3, Amsterdam: North-Holland.

Ulph, A. (1982), 'Modeling partially cartelized markets for exhaustible resources' in W. Eichhorn et al. (eds), *Economic Theory of Natural Resources*, Würzburg: Physica Verlag, pp. 269–91.

Ulph, A. and G. Folie (1980), 'Exhaustible resources and cartels: an intertemporal Nash–Cournot model', *The Canadian Journal of Economics*, **13**, 645–58.

Ulph, A. and G. Folie (1981), 'Dominant firm models of resource depletion', in D. Curry, D. Peel and W. Peters (eds), *Microeconomic Analysis*, London: Croom Helm, pp. 77–106.

5 Economics of mining taxation
Philip A. Neher

1. Introduction

The economics of mining has traditionally encompassed the taxation of mining enterprises for the purposes of raising revenue. The scope of economic inquiry now extends to taxes for the purpose of generating efficient prices for collateral damage of environmental assets from mining activity. These are described as Pigouvian taxes because they stem from the early work of Pigou (1952) on using taxes to correct for missing or incomplete markets for these assets and their services.

The plan is to review first the economics of revenue taxation, moving from traditional to more modern formulations. The next step shows how Pigouvian taxation can be applied to achieve efficient production of external environmental harm from mining. Then these two taxes are related with some reference to practical applications.

Dynamic efficiency criteria are used because mining activity necessarily extends over time. The natural resource is a durable and depletable asset, reflecting the fact that concentrations of it are strictly limited in quantity and grade. This ultimate scarcity restricts the appropriate use of static efficiency analysis.

2. Revenue taxation

Traditional economic analysis has focused on the efficiency of taxation regimes with the more or less explicit understanding that the mining activity is embedded in an otherwise efficient economy.[1] Then the objective is to devise a tax which does not distort the extraction profile which maximizes private wealth.

The normal case is a tax-free, competitive mining activity with no external effects.[2] The objective is to maximize the present value (V) of a profile of extractions (x) from a known body (pool) of underground resource (b). The product sells for a given market price (p). The cost of extraction is $C = C(\overset{+}{x}, \bar{b})$ such that average cost function, C/x, is 'U'-shaped in x for given b, indicating scale (dis)economies for small (large) x. Economies of scale stem from spreading out development (set-up) costs (sinking shafts, drilling tunnels, removing overburden) over more output. Diseconomies stem from declining marginal productivity of operational mining effort. Also, for given x, depletion of b increases C ($C_b < 0$) at an increasing rate ($C_{bb} > 0$) while increasing marginal operating costs ($C_{xb} < 0$).

In short, operating profit $\pi(x, b)$ is

$$p \cdot x - C(\overset{+}{x}, \overset{-}{b})$$

where x (a flow) and b (a stock) are functions of time (v) so that the objective (functional) is

$$V(x, b; t) = \int_{v=0}^{T} \pi(x, b) \cdot D(t) \, dv \tag{5.1}$$

where $D(t)$ is the discount factor equal to $\exp(-rt) \leq 1$, using the appropriate discount rate (r).

This is to be maximized by choosing the control function, $x(v)$, over the open time interval $(0, T)$. T is also to be chosen.

Maximizing (5.1) is subject to the extractions constraint that mine production during $(0, T)$ cannot exceed the initial stock (b_0).

$$\int_{v=0}^{T} x \, dv \leq b_0 \tag{5.2}$$

The performance indicator for this problem (H) is current operating profit minus physical depletion (disinvestment $= -\dot{b} = x$) valued at the current value shadow price. This will be called the 'resource price' (q).

$$H(x, q, b) = \pi(x, b) - qx \tag{5.3}$$

Necessary for optimality are:

first-order (all v) conditions (FOCs)

$$H_x = \pi_x - q = (p - q) - C_x = 0 \tag{5.4}$$

$$H_q = \dot{b} \tag{5.5}$$

$$H_b = rq - \dot{q} = -C_b \tag{5.6}$$

terminal (at $v = T$) conditions (TCs)

$$H(T) = 0 \tag{5.7}$$

$$q(T)b(T) = 0 \tag{5.8}$$

Together, (5.3)–(5.8) determine time paths for (q, x, b). Begin by using (5.4) written as

$$x = X(q, b)$$

Then

$$\dot{b}(q, b) = -X(q, b) \tag{5.9}$$

$$\dot{q}(q, b) = rq + C_b(b, X(q, b)) \tag{5.10}$$

are the differential equations of motion (*EM*) in (q, b). Alternatively, *EM* can be found in (x, b) by using (5.4) written as

$$q = Q(x, b)$$

Second, use the TCs. The operation has become terminally 'uneconomic' at T when these are satisfied. Use (5.4) along with (5.7) to find that

$$C_x = C/x$$

at T. This is a critical result. The operations end when average equals marginal cost of extraction at the low point of the average cost curve $C(x(T), b(T))/x(T)$ with $b(T)$ positive. During operations before T, x and b are falling. The resource price falls from $q(0)$ to $q(T)$. Then (5.8) indicates that the terminal resource price, the 'scrap value', is zero $(q(T) = 0)$.

It is evident that this normative case will not be replicated if a private mining activity is subject to a positive revenue tax (t^G) falling on *gross* revenue (a royalty). Then the activity will choose a profile of x to maximize

$$V(x, b; t) = \int_{v=0}^{T} ((1 - t^G)px - C(x, b)) \cdot D \, dv$$

Accordingly, for the activity,

$$H_x = (1 - t^G)p - C_x - q = 0 \tag{5.11}$$

The marginal cost of extraction, $C_x(x, b)$, is smaller for higher t^G throughout $(0, T)$. However, since $H = (1 - t^G) px - C - qx$ equals zero at T, it remains from (5.11) that $C_x = C/x$ at T. Hence, $x(T)$ is unaffected by t^G. So the lower marginal cost of extraction at T must be caused by $b(T)$ being larger. More remaining ore is abandoned when the mine is closed if t^G is higher. In this case, the royalty is not economic (not efficient).

But suppose a revenue tax (t^N) on *net* revenue (π). Then the private activity will choose a profile of x to maximize

$$V(x, b;\, t) = (1 - t^N) \int_{v=0}^{T} \big(px - C(x, b)\big) \cdot D\, dv$$

None of the necessary normative conditions of optimality are affected by the profit tax. It falls on pure resource rent and is therefore economic if the activity is otherwise economic. The achievable maximum private value (V) of the resource is lower if t^N is higher, however. But the corresponding social value of it is not diminished.

This observation begs the question of discovery rates of new resources. Exploration is, after all, motivated by the private expectation of private Vs in the extraction phase. This suggests revenue taxation of consolidated profit from exploration and extraction activities. A tax which does this is called a resource rent tax (RRT). The RRT promises a more 'neutral' tax regime which is theoretically based on the pure rent potential of activity having origins in 'green fields' and carried forward through discovery, development and extraction. By extension, the RRT should encompass a terminal clean-up phase as well.

3. Environmental taxes

Pigouvian taxation is intended to internalize the social cost of environmental harm which otherwise would be externalized by decision makers in uncontrolled mining activities.[3] Here, these costs will be related to the rate of extraction $\big(x\,(v)\big)$ and also to cumulative extraction $\big(b_0 - b(T)\big)$.

Flow-related environmental costs are here strictly transitory, as from unsightly unit trains, annoying noise, or a smoke plume besmirching an otherwise pristine sylvan scene. These costs are denoted by

$$F(x);\ F' > 0,\ F'' > 0 \tag{5.12}$$

Stock-related environmental costs are persistent, as from disinterred hydrocarbons which become CO_2 in the atmosphere or from mercuric compounds mixed in alluvium. These costs are computed at T as the present value of environmental costs which persist into the future.[4] Denote these as

$$S\big(b_0 - b(T)\big);\ S' > 0,\ S'' > 0$$

The objective (functional) for the social problem including flow- and stock-related damage is

$$V(x, b; t) = \int_{v=0}^{T} \left((\pi(x, b) - F(x))D(t)dv - S(b_0 - b(T))D(t) \, dv \right.$$

$$\pi(x, b) = px(v) - C(x(v), b(v))$$

The extraction constraint is as before. The performance indicator (*H*) now includes the flow-related (*x*) environmental cost.

$$H(x, q, b) = \pi(x, b) - qx - F(x)$$

The first-order conditions are found similarly, H_b and H_q are not changed. But

$$H_x = \pi_x - q - F' = (p - q) - C_x - F' = 0$$

and the marginal external cost of transient damage ranks as a social cost along with marginal extraction cost (C_x) and depletion (*q*).

The TCs are found similarly. The first one, $H(T) = 0$, is not changed. But the second one is now

$$q(T)b(T) = S'(T)b(T)$$

Apparently, the appropriate Pigouvian tax rates are

$$t^F(v) = F'(x(v))$$

$$t^S(T) = S'(b_0 - b(T))$$

4.   Comparisons

These Pigouvian taxes can be substituted into the first-order and transversality conditions to see how environmental taxes and revenue taxes are related.

The base case is for 'neutral' net revenue taxation. Rewrite (5.4) using t^N to indicate the rate of net profit taxation at t^N.

$$(1 - t^N)(p - C_x) - q = 0 \tag{5.4a}$$

A higher t^N reduces *q* but does not affect the extraction profile.

A gross profit tax at t^G encourages slower extraction by reducing after tax unit marginal revenue relative to unit extraction cost. With lower marginal revenue, marginal cost and the extraction rate are lower too.

$$(1 - t^G)p - C_X - q = 0 \tag{5.4b}$$

In a similar way, a flow-related environmental tax (t^F) also lowers the extraction rate:

$$p - t^F - C_X - q = 0 \tag{5.4c}$$

A gross revenue tax can mimic an efficient environmental tax $(t^G = t^F/p)$, even though it is differently motivated.

The first transversality condition (5.4) plus (5.7) is satisfied with $b(T)$ positive where $C_X(T) = C(T)/x(T) = p$. The second transversality condition (5.5) is also satisfied there with $q(T)$, the value of ore underground equal to minus its negative 'scrap value'.

For the base case, this scrap value is zero (see above):

$$q(T)B(T) = 0 \tag{5.8}$$

But if extracted material is causing environmental harm, its scrap value is the marginal environmental harm of having extracted, $S'\big(b_0 - b(T)\big)$ and so this is the (negative) tax rate on the marginal conservation at $t = T$.

$$- q(T)b(T) = t^S \cdot b(T) = (-) \tag{5.8a}$$

It is interpreted as a subsidy on unmined ore, $b(T)$. The value of this ore below the ground is greater to society than it is above the ground to the private activity. Alternatively, the negative of t^S is the (positive) tax rate on marginal extraction at $t = T$.

5. Applications

In practice, taxation is an art and a science. In science it is sometimes convenient to ignore complications of implementation so that, for example, a subsidy is simply a negative tax. Science also suggests that a tax system should first enlarge the revenue tax base by applying Pigouvian taxes to correct for externalities. This achieves Paretian efficiency and, as a by-product, diverts revenue to the tax authority as an administrative surplus. This can be used to reduce general revenue taxes and pay lump sum subsidies as required to maintain some desired balance of public and private goods.

Notes

1. A good survey is in Heaps and Helliwell (1987).
2. Early analysis of underground materials as economic assets is in Gray (1913). Hotelling's (1931) work was novel for applying the classical calculus of variations to the wealth-maximizing problem. The Dasgupta and Heal (1974) paper employs modern dynamic

optimization to extend and generalize the work begun by Hotelling. For technique, see Kamien and Schwartz (1991).
3.   A well-known application of Pigou's earlier work to environmental economics is by Baumol and Oates (1988).
4.   Stock- and flow-related environmental costs are unnaturally dichotomized here as polar cases. The first does not accumulate at all although it can persist for the active life of the mine. The second notably does accumulate, and the present value of the damage can, in principle, be charged to the programme when it is created. CO_2 release is an example. In practice, 'cleanup costs' are often assessed when operations are terminated. Geophysical harm, for example, is economically assessed when operations are terminated and are subsequently mitigated by recontouring the affected surface or by converting an ugly pit into a scenic lake or formal garden. In these cases, significant damages of accumulation during operations can be compounded forward and added to the discounted value of future damage. In a 'full information' setting, the present dichotomy disappears. As it is, the idea that remaining ore in the ground has value as an environmental asset seems a useful one.

References

Baumol, W. and W. Oates (1988), *The Theory of Environmental Policy*, 2nd edn, Cambridge UK: Cambridge University Press.
Dasgupta, P. and G. Heal (1974), 'The optimal depletion of exhaustible resources', *Review of Economic Studies*, Symposium, pp. 3–28.
Gray, L.C. (1913), 'The economic possibilities of conservation', *Quarterly Journal of Economics*, **27**, 497–519.
Heaps, T. and J. Helliwell (1987), 'The taxation of natural resources', ch. 8 in A.J. Auerbach and M. Feldstein, *Handbook of Public Economics*, vol. II, Amsterdam: North-Holland.
Hotelling, H. (1931), 'The economics of exhaustible resources', *Journal of Political Economy*, **31**, 137–75.
Kamien, M.I. and Nancy L. Schwartz (1991), *Dynamic Optimization*, 2nd edn, Amsterdam: North-Holland.
Pigou, A.C. (1952), *Economics of Welfare*, 4th edn, London: Macmillan.

6 International trade and natural resources
Ngo Van Long

1. Introduction

There are two streams of literature on the role of natural resources in international trade. The first stream deals with the short-run macroeconomic consequences of a resource boom. The second stream is in the tradition of the pure theory of international trade: it focuses on long-run issues and abstracts from macroeconomic adjustment problems such as changes in the exchange rates, inflation, unemployment and balance of payments disequilibrium.

Corden (1984) provides a useful survey of the first stream of literature. He shows how a country experiencing a resource boom (caused by increased international demand and/or price for its natural resources, or by new discoveries of deposits) can, as a consequence, suffer from an illness called 'de-industrialization', that is, the demise of the manufacturing sector. He explains this in terms of two effects, the spending effect and the resource movement effect. The former operates in the same manner as an income transfer. At given relative prices, the higher income brought about by the resource boom results in an excess demand for non-traded goods. This causes a rise in non-traded goods prices relative to traded goods prices; this is called a 'real appreciation'. The result is the contraction of the non-resources traded goods sector. This effect is reinforced by the resource movement effect if the booming natural resource sector requires significant inputs which must be bid away from the other sectors. If the wage rate is not flexible, and if labour mobility is limited, the spending effect may cause unemployment in the manufacturing traded goods sector. On the other hand, if labour mobility is high, the resource movement effect may make it more likely that labour shortage rather than unemployment will emerge; see van Wijnbergen (1984). If the nominal exchange rate is fixed, a resource boom tends to lead to domestic inflation. Corden points out that fixing the nominal exchange rate and sterilizing the inflow of foreign currencies would mitigate the extent of de-industrialization.

The literature surveyed by Corden abstracts from the intertemporal optimization behaviour of the resource-extracting firms. The purpose of this chapter is to survey the second stream of literature mentioned above which is firmly based on the intertemporal optimization foundation: the resource-extracting firm is viewed as a forward-looking entity that seeks to maximize the discounted stream of net cash flows subject to a stock constraint (in the case of non-renewable resources) or to the dynamics of stock growth (in the case of renewable resources such as timber and marine species).

In Section 2, we survey models of trade involving resource firms that have perfect foresight of future prices which they take as given. In Section 3, we review trade models that incorporate elements of game theory: optimal tariff, resource oligopoly, cartel behaviour, and so on. Section 4 addresses the issue of sustainability of resource-poor and resource-rich economies. Some empirical issues are reviewed in Section 5. Section 6 suggests some topics for future research.

2.   Perfect competition models

The standard theory of international trade abstracts from the exhaustibility of natural resources and from the dynamics of renewable resources. That theory has provided us with a number of important theorems that explain the pattern of trade, the effects of changes in relative price on real factor rewards, and the effects of changes in endowment on outputs. The fourfold theorems of Heckscher–Ohlin, Stolper–Samuelson, Rybczynski, and factor price equalization are at the heart of trade theory. (In their simplest versions, with two goods, two factors, and two countries, these four theorems say, respectively, that (i) a country tends to export the good that uses intensively the factor it has in relative abundance; (ii) an increase in the relative price of a good will lead to a rise in the real reward of the factor used intensively in the production of that good, and a fall in the real reward of the other factor; (iii) an increase in a country's endowment of a factor will result in an expansion of the sector which uses that factor intensively, and a contraction of the other sector; and (iv) free trade will promote the international equalization of factor prices.)

The oil price shocks of the 1970s and recent concerns about deforestation and the possible extinction of various marine species reveal that the traditional framework of trade theory must be expanded to take into account the exhaustibility of natural resources as inputs, and the importance of natural resources management. The first generation of models of trade with non-renewable natural resources in an intertemporal optimization context includes Vousden (1974), Long (1974), Kemp and Suzuki (1975), and Kemp and Long (1980b). For two reviews of this early literature, see Kemp and Long (1984) and Withagen (1985).

In the Kemp–Long review, the four standard trade theorems were shown to have their counterparts in a dynamic framework, where firms and individuals are intertemporal maximizers. Their survey displays three classes of models: the anti-Heckscher–Ohlin model, the hybrid model, and the generalized Heckscher–Ohlin model (or GHOM). In the anti-H–O model, two final goods are produced using two exhaustible natural resources. In the hybrid model, one input is an exhaustible natural resource and the other input is a primary non-exhaustible factor; these are called the Hotelling factor and the Ricardian factor respectively. In the GHOM formulation, there are two Ricardian factors and at least one Hotelling factor. Within the GHOM framework, Kemp and Long (1984) show that the four standard theorems can be readily generalized. Their formulation may be given the following interpretation: capital and labour produce two intermediate inputs, one for each sector, which are then combined with an exhaustible natural resource input to produce two final goods. They postulated that the production functions for the final goods are $Q_i = E_i^{\alpha_i} F_i(K_i, L_i)$, where F_i is homogenous of degree $1 - \alpha_i$, $i = 1,2$, and F_1 is relatively more capital-intensive than F_2.

Kemp and Long assume that the value share of the natural resource in the two final goods are identical (that is $\alpha_1 = \alpha_2$). It follows from this assumption and the homotheticity of preferences that the world economy will produce the same mix of final goods at all points in time. Osei and Lapan (1996) generalize the Kemp–Long model by allowing the value shares of the resource to differ: $\alpha_1 \neq \alpha_2$. They show that the production pattern may change over time. For the resource-rich country, a decline in the share of the resource-intensive industry in GDP may be expected as the resource base of the country decreases. Furthermore, a capital-rich country may not always export the capital-intensive good. These results may help explain the Leontief paradox (which is based on Leontief's finding that US exports were labour-intensive even though the USA seemed to be relatively well endowed with capital) and other empirical observations which may seem to contradict the standard H–O theorem.

The models mentioned above do not deal with capital accumulation. This issue was taken up by Chiarella (1980) who generalized an earlier general equilibrium model of Kemp and Long (1979) where there was resource dynamics but no capital formation. Chiarella assumed the Cobb–Douglas functional form with three inputs (the resource input, capital and labour) and specified that technological knowledge grows at an exogenous rate. He analysed, in continuous time, the stability properties of the general equilibrium time path of trade between a resource-poor economy (having capital but no natural resources) and a resource-rich economy (having natural resources but no capital). Each country's consumption share, and the growth rate of the resource price, were shown to converge to their long-run equilibrium values. A continuous-time model in which both countries own natural resource stocks (as well as accumulate capital) is studied by Elbers and Withagen (1984), but the focus is on existence and Pareto optimality rather than on convergence. (For existence results in discrete time, see van Geldrop et al., 1991.) In a recent paper, van Geldrop and Withagen (1993) consider the case of *n* countries, each owning a stock of natural resource and a stock of capital, and the production function need not be Cobb–Douglas. They prove the existence of a general equilibrium under constant returns to scale, and show that, in the absence of technical progress, (i) the interest rate must either fall over time or remain constant for ever, (ii) capital intensity is non-decreasing, and (iii) consumption will eventually fall.

A common feature of all the models mentioned above is the absence of a backstop technology. An interesting topic for future research is the accumulation of capital which is necessary for harnessing alternative sources of energy such as wind or solar energy. How would the pattern of trade and consumption evolve in this case?

We now turn to models of trade involving renewable resources such as timber and fish. Earlier works include the static model of Markusen (1976), and the dynamic models of McRae (1978) and Tawada (1982, 1984); see also the survey of Kemp and Long (1984). The authors of these early dynamic models assumed that property rights are well defined. Recent concerns about the sustainability of forests have given rise to a number of significant contributions to the economics of renewable resources in the absence of well-defined property rights. In this context, Barbier et al. (1995) developed a simulation model and showed that international trade in timber played an important factor in forest depletion in Indonesia. Bee (1987) made similar remarks concerning trade-induced deforestation in the Philippines. Chichilnisky (1994) uses a static model to show that North–South trade tends to enlarge the problems of the commons, and that taxing the use of common property resources in the South can aggravate overextraction. The assignment of property rights would ensure efficiency. Brander and Taylor (1995) develop a two-sector model of a small open economy with an open-access renewable resource. They compare the steady state under autarchy with that under free trade. Since the resource is not privately owned, common access implies overexploitation in both steady states, but in their model the damage is worse under free trade if the country exports the natural resource good. They show that under these conditions, the steady-state utility under free trade is lower than under autarchy, and increases in the world price of exports are welfare-reducing.

If the quality of the environment is considered as a renewable resource, then one should mention some recent (static) models of trade in goods whose production processes generate pollutants. Among these are Copeland and Taylor (1994, 1995). They argue that since environmental quality is a normal good, higher-income countries would choose stricter pollution regions. These countries would therefore endogenously develop a comparative advantage in the relatively clean goods. Because trade shifts the location of pollution-intensive industries to countries with the weakest pollution regulations, trade liberalization could increase world pollution.

3.   Game-theoretic models

In the models surveyed in Section 2, it is assumed that firms are price-takers and governments do not interfere with the trade flow. We now turn to models where these assumptions are relaxed.

The traditional static trade literature has taught us that a large country will gain by imposing a suitable level of tariff on its imports, because the resulting improvement in the terms of trade will outweigh the loss that arises from consumption and production distortions (see Vousden, 1990, for example, for an exposition of the concept of optimal tariff). For a big oil-importing country, what is the time path of the optimal tariff? This question was explored by Newbery (1976) and Kemp and Long (1980b, Essay 18), where the concept of dynamic inconsistency played a central role. These authors show that if a big oil-importing country can commit itself to a time path of tariff rate, then the optimal *ad valorem* tariff on oil is a constant over time. This is because, given any cumulative volume of oil import over time interval $[0, T]$, for optimal consumption in the importing country, consumers' price must rise at the rate of discount during this inter-val so that discounted marginal utilities are equalized. Oil producers' price also rises at the rate of discount, due to Hotelling's rule. The constant rate of growth of these two prices implies a constant *ad valorem* tariff.

It is clear, however, that such a constant tariff rate policy is dynamically inconsistent, in the sense that at some time in the future, the oil-importing country will want to lower the tariff rate if it can renege on its originally announced (constant) time path of tariff. This is most easily seen at the point of time when, according to the original plan, the consumers' price in the importing country reaches the level – called the 'choke price' – at which domestic demand for oil is zero (as these consumers switch to a substitute whose cost of production equals the choke price). At this point, oil is still being sold in the rest of the world at a price below the choke price. The tariff-imposing country therefore would gain by cutting the tariff to encour-age oil imports as oil is cheaper than the substitute energy source. This explains the dynamic inconsistency. In fact, if the importing country could choose only a time t_1 at which it reneges on its constant tariff commitment (assuming that this is unforeseen by oil producers, and that it can only renege once), then it might do so before T.

However, if oil producers are smart, this extra demand caused by a tariff cut at time T (or before T) will be anticipated, and the market price path over the entire interval [0, *T*] will be higher than the one implied by the pre-committed path of demand associated with the pre-committed constant tariff rate. Thus the possibility of reneging on the part of the tariff-imposing country reduces its monopsony power. (Technically, this illustrates the fact that in a dynamic game with a Stackelberg leader playing an open-loop strategy, the solution is dynamically inconsistent, in general.)

The study of tariff paths that are dynamically consistent was undertaken by Maskin and Newbery (1990) and Karp and Newbery (1991). To ensure dynamic consistency, they impose the 'subgame perfection' condition, which is stronger than time consistency. Time consistency requires only that the continuation of the proposed equilibrium is itself an equilibrium for the remaining part of the game, when no player has deviated. Subgame perfection insists that the proposed equilibrium strategy profile remain an equalibrium for any level of the stock.

Karp and Newbery (1991) assume that players use only stationary Markovian strategies. This means that agents base their decisions only on information that has direct economic relevance and is currently observable. They consider two models. In their 'exporters-move-first' model, at each point of time output decisions are made before knowing the tariff rate. The reverse assumption is made in the 'importers-move-first' model. They show that the equilibrium time paths of the tariff are quite different in the two models.

The above models are relatively simple because all the market power is concentrated in the hand of one player and the relevant state variable is the world's stock of resource. If oil exporters were oligopolists, there would be several state variables, and the analysis would become very complicated when subgame perfection is imposed. (Eswaran and Lewis, 1985, showed that only under exceptionally restrictive assumptions can one fully characterize Markov-perfect equilibria with many oil stocks.) Another important point is the possibility that one of the oil producers will eventually become a monopolist when the others have depleted their stocks. Gaudet and Long (1994) show that in the case of a duopoly with different initial stock levels, the anticipation of a final phase where one firm would become a monopolist will have important effects on the equilibrium extraction path.

The assumption that firms are restricted to stationary Markov strategies, together with the natural requirement of eventual exhaustion, ensures that the equilibrium in the Karp–Newbery model is unique, even though in general this assumption alone is not sufficient for uniqueness. In addition to the possible multiplicity of equilibria under stationary Markovian strategies (see for example Dockner et al., 1996), the number of equilibria increases when agents are allowed to use trigger, or punishment strategies;

see Olsen (1989). This result is similar to the multiplicity of equilibria in repeated games.

Other strategic aspects of trading between resource-poor and resource-rich economies are considered in Hillman and Long (1983, 1985), and Ulph (1982). The possibility of a trade embargo by the resource-rich country may cause the resource-poor country to be more conservative in its extraction of its small resource stock. A resource-rich country may also take into account the fact that its export revenue, when invested (as opposed to consumed), will depress the world rate of interest. Ulph (1982) considers the case where a resource cartel acts as a Stackelberg leader while other small resource producers, called the competitive fringe, are price-takers. He shows that there will be a competitive phase during which the fringe produces, and this is followed by a monopolistic phase. This model is based on the assumption that the cartel can pre-commit itself to a pre-announced time path. As one would expect, such an equilibrium is dynamically inconsistent, as is the open-loop Nash–Cournot model of Salant (1976). Dynamic inconsistency arises in Ulph's model because the player with market power (the cartel) plays an open-loop game against a competitive fringe. A similar result is reported in Newbery (1981). Under the alternative assumption that the cartel uses a Markovian strategy, dynamic consistency can be assured. The dynamically consistent equilibrium is characterized by Karp and Tahvonen (1995) for the case where extraction costs depend linearly on the remaining stock. The complete solution under the alternative assumption that marginal costs are independent of stocks is given by Groot et al. (1995).

Prominent among models of international games involving renewable resources are those of Levhari and Mirman (1980), Kaitala and Pohjola (1988), and Fischer and Mirman (1992). In a recent game-theoretic model of trade with renewable resources, Datta and Mirman (1994) consider two countries exploiting two separate and distinct stocks of fish. If there are biological interactions between the two fish species, the Cournot–Nash equilibrium is inefficient. However, they show that if there is international trade in fish, and the marginal rates of substitution are the same across countries, then such inefficiency disappears. This is a surprising result, and seems to hinge on the specific functional forms they assume.

If the quality of the environment is considered as a renewable resource, then models of transfrontier pollution games should be mentioned in this section. Intertemporal models of global pollution games include Dockner and Long (1993) and Dockner et al. (1996). The former paper is a continuous-time model, in which there are many Markov-perfect equilibria, some of which approximate the first-best cooperative outcome. The latter paper presents a discrete-time model, thereby allowing some degree of pre-commitment; this model possesses two types of Markov-perfect equilibria that coexist under the same initial conditions and parameter values. The first type exhibits monotone convergence of the pollution stock, while the second type displays a chaotic time path of pollution. Furthermore, depending on parameter values, a chaotic equilibrium may be Pareto-superior to a non-chaotic one.

4. Sustainability and trade in natural resources

If natural resources are essential inputs, is it possible to maintain positive consumption for ever? And for an open economy that exports or imports an exhaustible resource, is there a saving rule that ensures constant consumption? What are the adjustments that must be made to obtain a correct measure of national income for a resource-exporting (or -importing) country? These issues have spawned a stream of articles, and continue to be a topic of lively debate.

It is known that if the production function is Cobb–Douglas and the capital share exceeds the resource share, then it is possible to maintain a constant level of consumption for ever, provided that the capital stock does not depreciate (see Solow, 1974, Dasgupta and Heal, 1979, ch. 7, and for a transparent control-theoretic proof, Léonard and Long, 1992, pp. 300–304). Kemp et al. (1984) provide more general sufficient conditions. For a resource-importing country, Kemp and Long (1982a) show that if the resource price rises exponentially at a constant rate, positive consumption can be maintained provided that the rate of technical progress is sufficiently high. However, in a world where capital is being accumulated to substitute for the resource, one expects that the interest rate will fall steadily. It is therefore possible for a resource-importing country to maintain a constant flow of consumption without technical progress; see Asheim (1986).

There are no compelling reasons why a country ought to maintain a constant stream of consumption. However, a hypothetical constant stream of consumption may serve as a useful measure of sustainability. In fact, Weitzman (1995), generalizing the results of Weitzman (1976) and Kemp and Long (1982b), has shown that, under quite general conditions, net national product (NNP), if properly defined to take into account resource depletion and technical progress, is equivalent to a hypothetical level of consumption which, if maintained for ever, will yield the same present value as that of the non-constant stream of consumption that is the solution to the intertemporal optimization problem of the representative consumer.

While Weitzman assumes that the rate of discount is an exogenously given constant, Kemp and Long (1998) address the same issue using the endogenous discounting framework. They show that the correct NNP measure should also include anticipated changes in both atemporal and intertemporal terms of trade. Neither Weitzman nor Kemp and Long are concerned with saving rules that ensure constant consumption. This issue is taken up by Hartwick (1977), whose result inspires the work of Dixit et al. (1980) who investigate the necessity and sufficiency of the now celebrated Hartwick's rule: all resource rents must be invested to ensure constant consumption. Their results are further generalized by Hartwick and Long (1995) to allow for technical progress and terms of trade changes. They show that, in the case of a constant interest rate, if the economy invests an amount equal to the economic depreciation of a suitably defined aggregate of its productive assets (which include natural resources and their expected future prices), then constant consumption and constant wealth are ensured. In the case of a non-constant interest rate, the saving formula has to be modified to take into account future changes in the interest rate. By specializing in the case of constant returns to scale in the capital stocks, Asheim (1996) obtains the interesting result that the current value of the capital stocks equals the value of the discounted stream of consumption. In this case, the future changes in the terms of trade and the interest rate are fully reflected in a capital gain term, and a term involving the current change in the long-term interest rate.

Sefton and Weale (1996) model a world economy with a resource-importing and a resource-exporting country. They argue that since the resource price is expected to rise in the future, the conventional NNP measure for resource-importing countries such as Japan overstates its sustainable welfare. This conclusion is in the same spirit as that of Kemp and Long (1998) and Hartwick and Long (1995). For related discussions, see Hartwick (1995), Lozada (1995), and Vincent et al. (1995). These authors show how economic depreciation should be calculated under various specifications of technology and terms of trade changes. Vellinga and Withagen (1996) provide a useful survey on green national income. See also El Serafy's chapter in this volume (Chapter 77) for further discussion of this topic.

5.   Some remarks on related empirical work
While the theory of trade with natural resources is characterized by its richness in theoretical issues and approaches, the related empirical works have concentrated on testing the Heckscher–Ohlin theory, with natural resources being treated in much the same way as other capital stocks. There is a voluminous literature on testing the H–O theory. Deardorff (1984) and Leamer and Levinsohn (1995) provide useful surveys. Deardorff, noting that the H–O theorem is a relationship among three variables (factor abundance, factor intensity and trade), pointed out that 'most of the studies

reviewed so far have looked at only two of these – usually trade and factor intensities – and have therefore not even pretended to test the theorem' (p. 492).

Leamer and Levinsohn (1995) argue that after allowing for factors such as technological differences, home bias, and multiple cones of diversification, 'there appears to be a substantial effect of relative factor abundance on the commodity composition of trade' (p. 1375). In a recent empirical study of regional trade within the USA, Kim (1995) also finds that trade and industry localization are influenced by the geographic distribution of natural resources.

The empirical question of necessary savings to ensure constant consumption has been addressed in Proops and Atkinson (1994), and Stollery (1996). Empirical green accounting for a number of countries (Mexico, Papua New Guinea, Australia) was reported in the volume edited by Lutz (1993).

6. Topics for further research

Recent developments in the endogenous growth theory raise the following question: is it possible to have consumption per head rising at a constant rate if natural resources are essential in production? It seems that the answer is 'yes' for a variety of models. Take for instance the constant consumption model of Dasgupta and Heal (1979). Clearly it can be modified to generate a positive constant growth rate. For example, suppose the consumption good is produced under the Cobb–Douglas production function with constant returns to scale, where the two inputs are human capital and an intermediate input. If the latter is held constant, and human capital grows at a constant proportional rate, then consumption will grow at the same rate. Suppose the intermediate input itself is produced with two inputs, capital and oil, where the capital share exceeds the oil share, and that capital is produced under a similar production function. Then the capital stock can grow linearly, that is, $K(t) = K(0) + mt$, ensuring that a constant amount of intermediate good is produced at each t. It follows that a constant consumption growth rate is feasible if human capital can grow exponentially by means of education. It remains to see if less extreme assumptions would be sufficient for endogenous growth. Trade between resource-poor and resource-rich economies can be studied in this context.

It is important to bear in mind that what is technically feasible is not necessarily an equilibrium. For example, in an overlapping generations model without bequests, constant consumption (not constant consumption growth, as in the preceeding paragraph) in the case of an essential exhaustible resource is not an equilibrium outcome. A tax and transfer mechanism must be put in place to achieve constant consumption. See Long et al. (1995) for details. This consideration should be taken into account in formulating models of endogenous growth with exhaustible resources.

Other interesting topics for research include (i) differential games between resource-poor and resource-rich economies, where both countries use strategies that are dependent on the stocks of capital and resources, (ii) international trade and investment in natural resources under asymmetric information (see Gaudet et al., 1995 and Osmundsen, 1996, on extracting resource royalties under informational asymmetry), (iii) privatization of natural resources in the context of global capital flows, possibly under risk of policy reversal (see Long, 1975 and Konrad et al. 1994, for a starting point on risks of nationalization), (iv) efficient order of exploitation of deposits when trade liberalization is anticipated (see Kemp and Long, 1980d and Amigues et al., 1998 on some unexpected results on order of exploitation), and (v) the gains from trade in overlapping models where resources are essential inputs.

References

Amigues, J.-P., P. Favard, G. Gaudet and M. Moreaux (1998), 'On the optimal order of natural resource use when the capacity of the inexhaustible resource substitute is limited', *Journal of Economic Theory*, **80**, 153–70.

Asheim, G. (1986), 'Hartwick's rule in open economies', *Canadian Journal of Economics*, **19**, 395–402.

Asheim, G. (1996), 'The Weitzman Foundation of NNP with non constant interest rate', typescript, University of Oslo.

Barbier, E., N. Bockstael, J. Burgess and I. Strand (1995), 'The linkage between the timber trade and tropical deforestation', *The World Economy*, **18**, 411–43.

Bee, O.J. (1987), 'Depletion of the forest resources in the Philippines', *Field Report Series No. 18*, Institute of Southeast Asian Studies.

Brander, J. and M.S. Taylor (1995), 'International trade and open access renewable resources: the small country case', NBER working paper 5021.

Chiarella, C. (1980), 'Trading between resource-poor and resource-rich economies as a differential game', in M.C. Kemp and N.V. Long (eds), *Exhaustible Resources, Optimality, and Trade*, Amsterdam: North-Holland, pp. 219–46.

Chichilnisky, G. (1994), 'North–South trade and the global environment', *American Economic Review*, **84**, 851–74.

Copeland, B. and M.S. Taylor (1994), 'North–South trade and the environment', *Quarterly Journal of Economics*, **109**, 755–87.

Copeland, B. and M.S. Taylor (1995), 'Trade and transboundary pollution', *American Economic Review*, **85**, 716–37.

Corden, W.M. (1984), 'Booming sector and Dutch disease economics: survey and consolidation', *Oxford Economic Papers*, **36**, 359–80.

Dasgupta, P. and G. Heal (1979), *Economic Theory and Exhaustible Resources*, Cambridge, UK: James Nesbitt and Cambridge University Press.

Datta, M. and L. Mirman (1994), 'Dynamic capital market interactions, externalities, and trade', CORE discussion paper 9409, Université Catholique de Louvain.

Deardorff, A.V. (1984), 'Testing trade theory', in R.W. James and P. Kenen (eds), *Handbook of International Economics, vol. I*, Amsterdam: North-Holland.

Dixit, A., P. Hammond and M. Hoel (1980), 'On Hartwick's rule for regular maximin paths of capital accumulation', *Review of Economic Studies*, **47**, 551–6.

Dockner, E. and N.V. Long (1993), 'International pollution control: Cooperative versus non-cooperative strategies', *Journal of Environmental Economics and Management*, **24**, 13–29.

Dockner, E., N.V. Long and G. Sorger (1996), 'Analysis of Nash equilibria in a class of capital accumulation games', *Journal of Economic Dynamics and Control*, **20**, 1209–35.

Elbers, C. and C. Withagen (1984), 'Trading in exhaustible natural resources in the presence of conversion cost: a general equilibrium approach', *Journal of Economic Dynamics and Control*, **8**, 197–209.

Eswaran, M. and T. Lewis (1985), 'Exhaustible resources and alternative equilibrium concepts', *Canadian Journal of Economics*, **18**, 459–73.

Fischer, R.D. and L.J. Mirman (1992), 'Strategic dynamic interactions: fish wars', *Journal of Economic Dynamics and Control*, **16**, 276–87.

Gaudet, G. and N.V. Long (1994), 'On the effect of the distribution of initial endowments in a non-renewable resource duopoly', *Journal of Economic Dynamics and Control*, **18**, 1189–98.

Gaudet, G., P. Lasserre and N.V. Long (1995), 'Optimal resource royalties with unknown and temporally independent extraction cost structures, *International Economic Review*, **36**, 715–49.

Geldrop, J. van and C. Withagen (1993), 'General equilibrium and international trade with exhaustible resources', *Journal of International Economics*, **34**, 341–57.

Geldrop, J. van, J. Shou and C. Withagen (1991), 'Existence of general equilibria in economies with natural exhaustible resources and an infinite time horizon', *Journal of Mathematical Economics*, **20**, 225–48.

Groot, F., C. Withagen and A. de Zeeuw (1996), 'Strong time consistency in the cartel-versus-fringe model', typescript, Eindhoven University.

Hartwick, J.M. (1977), 'Intergenerational equity and the investing of rents from exhaustible resources', *American Economic Review*, **66**, 972–4.

Hartwick, J.M. (1995), 'Sustainability and constant consumption path in open economies with exhaustible resources', *Review of International Economics*, **3**, 275–83.

Hartwick, J.M. and N.V. Long (1995), 'Constant consumption and economic depreciation of natural capital', typescript, Queen's University, to appear in *International Economic Review*.

Hillman, A.L. and N.V. Long (1983), 'Pricing and depletion of an exhaustible resource when there is an anticipation of trade disruption', *Quarterly Journal of Economics*, **390**, 215–33.

Hillman, A.L. and N.V. Long (1985), 'Monopolistic recycling of oil revenue and intertemporal bias in oil depletion and trade', *Quarterly Journal of Economics*, **100**, 597–624.

Kaitala, V. and M. Pohjola (1988), 'Optimal recovery of a shared resources stock: a differential game with efficient memory equilibria', *Natural Resource Modelling*, **3**, 91–119.

Karp, L. and D. Newbery (1991), 'Optimal tariffs on exhaustible resources', *Journal of International Economics*, **30**, 285–300.

Karp, L. and O. Tahvonen (1995), 'International trade and exhaustible resources: a cartel-competitive fringe model', Working paper no. 754, Department of Agricultural and Resource Economics, University of California at Berkeley.

Kemp, M.C. and N.V. Long (1979), 'The interaction between resource poor and resource rich economies', *Australian Economics Papers*, **18**, 258–67.

Kemp, M.C. and N.V. Long (1980a), 'On two folk theorems concerning the extraction of exhaustible resources', *Econometrica*, **48**, 663–73.

Kemp, M.C. and N.V. Long (1980b), *Exhaustible Resources, Optimality, and Trade*, Amsterdam: North-Holland.

Kemp, M.C. and N.V. Long (1982a), 'Conditions for survival of a small resource-importing economy', *Journal of International Economics*, **13**, 135–42.

Kemp, M.C. and N.V. Long (1982b), 'On the evaluation of social income in a dynamic economy', in G.R. Feiwell (ed.), *Samuelson and Neoclassical Economics*, Boston: Kluwer-Nijhoff.

Kemp, M.C. and N.V. Long (1984), 'The role of natural resources in trade models', ch. 8 in R.W. Jones and P.B. Kenen (eds), *Handbook of International Economics, Vol. I*, Amsterdam: North-Holland.

Kemp, M.C. and N.V. Long (1998), 'On the evaluation of national income in a dynamic economy: generalisations', in K. Jager and K.-J. Koch (eds), *Trade, Growth, and Economic Policies in Open Economies*, Berlin: Springer Verlag, 101–10.

Kemp, M.C. and H. Suzuki (1975), 'International trade with a wasting but possibly replenishable resource', *International Economic Review*, 16, 712–32.

Kemp, M.C., N.V. Long and K. Shimomura (1984), 'The problem of survival: A closed economy', Essay 2 in M.C. Kemp and N.V. Long (eds), *Essays in the Economics of Exhaustible Resources*, Amsterdam: North-Holland.

Kim, S. (1995), 'Expansion of markets and the geographic distribution of economic activities: the trends in US regional manufacturing structure, 1890–1987', *Quarterly Journal of Economics*, 110, 881–908.

Konrad, K.A., T.E. Olsen and R. Schöb (1994), 'Resource extraction and threat of possible expropriation: the role of Swiss bank accounts', *Journal of Environmental Economics and Management*, 26, 149–62.

Leamer, E. and J. Levinsohn (1995), 'International trade theory: the evidence', ch. 26 in G. Grossman and K. Rogoff (eds), *Handbook of International Economics, Vol. III*, Amsterdam: Elsevier.

Léonard, D. and N.V. Long (1992), *Optimal Control Theory and Static Optimization in Economics*, New York: Cambridge University Press.

Levhari, D. and L.J. Mirman (1980), 'The Great Fish War: An example using a dynamic Nash–Cournot solution', *Bell Journal of Economics*, 11, 322–34.

Long, N.V. (1974), 'International borrowing for resource extraction', *International Economic Review*, 15, 168–83.

Long, N.V. (1975), 'Resource extraction under the uncertainty about possible nationalization', *Journal of Economic Theory*, 10, 42–53.

Long, N.V., T. Mitra and G. Sorger (1995), 'Equilibrium growth and sustained consumption with exhaustible resources', Center for Analytic Economics, *Working paper 95–02*, Cornell University.

Lozada, G. (1995), 'Resource depletion, national income accounting, and the value of optimal dynamic programs', *Resource and Energy Economics*, 17, 137–54.

Lutz, E. (1993), *Toward Improved Accounting for the Environment*, Washington, DC: The World Bank.

Markusen, J.R. (1976), 'Production and trade from international common property resources', *Canadian Journal of Economics*, 9, 309–19.

Maskin, E. and D. Newbery (1990), 'Disadvantageous oil tariffs and dynamic consistency', *American Economic Review*, 80, 143–56.

McRae, J. (1978), 'Optimal and competitive use of replenishable natural resources by open economies', *Journal of International Economics*, 8, 29–54.

Newbery, D. (1976), 'A paradox in tax theory: optimal tariffs on exhaustible resources', SEER Technical Paper, Stanford University.

Newbery, D. (1981), 'Oil prices, cartels and the problem of dynamic inconsistency', *The Economic Journal*, 91, 617–46.

Olsen, T. (1989), 'A folk theorem for rent extracting tariff on exhaustible resources', unpublished working paper, Norwegian Centre for Research in Organization and Management, Bergen, Norway.

Osei, E. and H. Lapan (1996), 'The generalized H–O Model with different natural resource intensities', Staff Paper no. 274, Department of Economics, Iowa State University.

Osmundsen, P. (1996), 'Dynamic taxation of non-renewable natural resources: Asymmetric information about reserves', typescript, Norwegian School of Economics and Business Administration.

Proops, J. and G. Atkinson (1994), 'A practical sustainability criterion when there is international trade', *Proceedings of the Conference on Models of Sustainable Development*, Université Panthéon-Sorbonne, March, pp. 819–45.

Salant, S. (1976), 'Exhaustible resources and industrial structure: a Nash–Cournot approach', *Journal of Political Economy*, 84, 1079–93.

Sefton, J.A. and M.R. Weale (1996), 'The net national product and exhaustible resources: the effects of foreign trade', *Journal of Public Economics*, 3, 21–47.

Solow, R. (1974), 'Intergenerational equity and exhaustible resources', *Review of Economic Studies* (Symposium), 29–45.

Stollery, K. (1996), 'Constant utility paths and irreversible global warming', typescript, University of Waterloo.

Tawada, M. (1982), 'A note on international trade with renewable resources', *International Economic Review*, **23**, 157–63.

Tawada, M. (1984), 'International trade with a replenishable resource: the steady state analysis', *Economic Studies Quarterly*, **35**, 33–45.

Ulph, A.M. (1982), 'Modelling partially cartelized markets for exhaustible resources', in W. Eichhorn (ed.), *Economic Theory and Natural Resources*, Würzburg: Physica Verlag, 269–91.

Vellinga, N. and C. Withagen (1996), 'On the concept of Green national income', *Oxford Economic Papers*, **48**, 499–514.

Vincent, J., T. Panayotou and J.M. Hartwick (1995), 'Resource depletion and sustainability in small open economies', typescript, Queen's University, Kingston, Canada.

Vousden, N. (1974), 'International trade and exhaustible resources: a theoretical model', *International Economic Review*, **15**, 149–67.

Vousden, N. (1990), *The Economics of Trade Protection*, New York: Cambridge University Press.

Weitzman, M. (1976), 'On the welfare significance of national product in a dynamic economy', *Quarterly Journal of Economics*, **90**, 156–62.

Weitzman, M. (1995), 'Sustainability and the welfare significance of national product revisited', Discussion Paper 1737, Harvard Institute of Economic Research.

Wijnbergen, S. van (1984), 'Inflation, employment and the Dutch disease in oil exporting economies: a short-run disequilibrium analysis', *Quarterly Journal of Economics*, **99**, 233–50.

Withagen, C. (1985), *Economic Theory and International Trade in Natural Exhaustible Resources*, Lecture Notes in Economics and Mathematical Systems, Berlin: Springer-Verlag.

7 Indicators of natural resource scarcity: a review and synthesis

Cutler J. Cleveland and David I. Stern

1. Introduction

There is considerable uncertainty about the extent to which human economic aspirations are limited by biophysical constraints. One aspect of this question is natural resource scarcity. In general terms, an increase in scarcity is defined by a reduction in economic well-being due to a decline in the quality, availability or productivity of natural resources and vice versa. A major issue in the literature on the measurement of natural resource scarcity is which of the alternative indicators of scarcity, such as unit costs, prices, rents, elasticities of substitution and energy costs, is superior (for example Brown and Field, 1979; Fisher, 1979; Hall and Hall, 1984; Cairns, 1990; Cleveland and Stern, 1993). Most neoclassical economists argue that, in theory, price is the ideal measure of scarcity (see Fisher, 1979), although some argue in favour of rents (Brown and Field, 1979; Farzin, 1995). Barnett and Morse (1963) developed the unit cost indicator from their reading of Ricardo as an alternative to the neoclassical indicators. Some ecological economists favour a biophysical model of scarcity and derive energy-based indicators (for example Cleveland et al., 1984; Hall et al., 1986; Gever et al., 1986; Cleveland, 1991a, 1992; Ruth, 1995). The central point of this debate has been under what economic, technological, institutional and environmental conditions each indicator provides clear or ambiguous signals of scarcity.

The purpose of this chapter is to review the different methods used to analyse resource scarcity, including their underlying theories, methodologies and principal empirical results. We attempt to put the issue in perspective by stepping back and asking the question, 'What do we actually mean by scarcity?', a question rarely addressed in the literature, and answer it in the context of the various approaches. We propose the terms *use scarcity* and *exchange scarcity* to distinguish between two broad approaches to measuring scarcity. These terms relate to the classical concepts of use and exchange value. Definitions of use and exchange value have varied among different economic paradigms, but broadly speaking use value is the value derived from consumption of a good, while exchange value is the value of goods or money that can be obtained in exchange for the good in an actual or potential market. Our usage of the term use value does not refer to that common among some environmental economists, where it is used to describe value derived from active use of the resource in consumption or production as opposed to 'non-use values' of environmental resources that contribute to utility through, for example, knowledge of their existence.

As proposed in this chapter, exchange scarcity is commonly measured by price or rent, depending on whether the scarcity of *in situ* natural resources or resource commodities is being measured. Use scarcity refers to the ability of natural resources to generate use value and is typically measured in terms of the balance between the productivity and availability of the resource base and the level of technology (Cleveland and Stern, 1993). The first three sections of the chapter review classical, neoclassical and biophysical indicators in terms of their theoretical background, empirical results and critiques of these methods. The fourth section presents our synthesis in terms of use and exchange scarcity. The fifth section and conclusion discuss some issues that emerge from the discussion and present some suggested directions for future research.

2. The classical model of scarcity

Ricardo and Marx argued that the labour cost of production is a common unit of measurement of the use value of commodities, and that use value, rather than exchange value, was the 'real' measurement of value. Ricardo viewed nature not as a factor of production, but as a force resisting the efforts of labour to produce use value (Commons, 1934). The poorer the quality of the resource base, the more it resists the efforts of labour. Thus, interpreters of the classical model such as Barnett and Morse (1963) define an increase in scarcity as an increase in the resistance of nature to the efforts of people to produce resource commodities. The classic example is Ricardo's case of the declining fertility of land at the extensive margin. From this perspective, the appropriate measure of scarcity is the labour required to produce a unit of the commodity. Rising resistance or rising scarcity means that more labour is required. This is the source of the unit cost measure which in its simplest form is the inverse of labour productivity. The term unit cost is somewhat unfortunate. Some analysts (for example Farzin, 1995; Uri and Boyd, 1995) erroneously assume that unit cost is the average cost of extraction. Barnett and Morse also combine the Ricardian model with a neoclassical production function to derive a more comprehensive measure of scarcity that accounts for capital inputs.[1] In this case unit cost is the inverse of multi-factor productivity defined with respect to labour and capital. Hall et al. (1988) expanded the definition to include energy.

Barnett and Morse (1963) defined unit cost as:

$$UC_t = \frac{\alpha_t(L_t/L_b) + \beta_t(K_t/K_b)}{Q_t/Q_b}$$
(7.1)

where:

UC_t = unit cost of extraction at time t

Q_t = net output (value added) in constant dollars

L_t = labour cost measured as number of persons employed

K_t = capital cost measured as net fixed capital stock in constant dollars

Q_b, L_b, K_b = output, labour and capital inputs in the base year b

$\alpha_t = I_t^L/I_t^T$ where I^L is total labour compensation and I^T is value added originating in the industry in question (other indexation procedures such as Divisia aggregation can be used).

The classical model from which Barnett and Morse derive the unit cost index assumes that resources are used in order of descending quality. With unchanging technology, cumulative extraction will be associated with an increase in the quality of labour and capital required to extract a unit of the resource. Technological innovations work in the opposite direction, reducing required labour and capital inputs per unit output. In real-world cases, where resources are not used in strict order of quality, new discoveries of higher-quality resources can also lower unit cost. Barnett and Morse argued that unit cost reflects the net effect of these opposing forces, and thus measures the long-run productivity of the resource base. As we show below, the overall quantity of resource stock under exploitation also affects unit cost – using more natural capital with given inputs of capital and labour will normally raise the productivity of the latter inputs.

Empirical results of the classical model

Barnett and Morse calculated the unit cost index for aggregate resource industries (agriculture, forestry, fisheries, mining) and individual resource commodities in the US from 1870 to 1957. They found an almost universal decline in unit cost, which they viewed as a rejection of the classical school's 'iron law of diminishing returns'. The sole exception was the forest products sector, which showed an overall increase in labour used per unit output.

Johnson et al. (1980) used regression analysis to update Barnett and Morse through 1966, and used a dummy variable to test for a significant change in the trend in scarcity after 1957. They found the cost of aggregate agricultural and mineral commodities fell at a *faster* rate from 1957 to 1966 compared to the period before 1957. Johnson et al. also found an overall increase in the cost of forestry products from 1870 to 1970, although costs generally declined after 1957. This trend was confirmed by Cleveland and Stern (1993) for the subsequent years to 1990 as well.

Hall and Hall (1984) updated the unit cost analysis for a number of resources, and used regression analysis to test for a significant change in scarcity between 1960 and 1980, and for the possible effects of the energy price shocks on unit cost. They found that the unit cost of petroleum and coal began to increase in the 1970s, but not for agriculture, electricity and metals. The authors emphasized that costs turned upward prior to the energy price increases, indicating that the actions of the OPEC cartel were not the principal cause of the increase in cost.

The cost of oil resources in the US has attracted considerable attention. Cleveland (1993) calculated the unit cost index for petroleum (oil and gas) extraction in the US from 1880 to 1990. He found a precipitous decline in cost through the 1960s, followed by a sharp increase in cost through 1990. Like the Hall and Hall results, costs turned upward prior to the energy price shocks. Cleveland (1991b) also calculates the average (not unit) cost of oil discovery and production in the US from 1936 to 1988. He finds that the time paths for both are consistent with Slade's (1982) U-shaped time path for scarcity. The cost of oil discovery has increased steadily since the 1930s, while the cost of production began to increase in the 1960s. Like Hall and Hall (1984), Cleveland's econometric analysis indicates that the actions of the OPEC cartel accelerated, but did cause, the cost increase.

Critique of the classical model
Barnett and Morse argued for the use of unit costs and against the use of rents as a scarcity indicator because changes in rent may be due to 'changes in interest rates, the relative demand, and expectations concerning future resource availability' (p. 225) – in other words, forces that obscure the issue of productivity. As Smith (1980) stated, 'Their objective would seem to call for measuring resource scarcity without judging the legitimacy of society's ends ... Thus [Barnett and Morse] implicitly accepted the notion that there was an objective measure of scarcity independent of consumer preferences' (p. 261). Neoclassical economists criticize Barnett and Morse's unit cost measure because, *inter alia*, 'Whether a resource is becoming scarce or not, for example, ought to depend in part on expectations about future supplies' (Brown and Field, 1979, p. 230). In other words, an indicator that excludes any factor that determines exchange value is inadmissible.

One significant shortcoming is that unit cost excludes all inputs other than capital and labour, and output is measured in value-added terms.

Fuel, water and other purchased inputs are excluded, though this problem is addressed by Hall et al. (1988) and is not a fundamental problem. The most serious computational issue is that unit cost is a constructed index, which requires assumptions about the best way to measure output, inputs and the weighting factors (Brown and Field, 1979; Howe, 1979). Particularly troublesome is the measurement of capital input and how the capital stock is depreciated over time. The weighting factors are also problematic because the return to capital is typically unobserved and combined with the compensation for land in a single measure of total profit.

Brown and Field (1979) showed that labour-only unit cost would rise in the face of an increase in the price of the resource stock relative to wages. But, they argued, the impact would be greater the greater the ease of substitution between resources and labour in producing resource commodities. This relationship stands to reason, as the optimal ratio of labour use to resource use will shift more, the easier substitution is. Innnovations that make it easier to substitute away from the resources base will accelerate the rate of increase in unit cost. This, they state, is perverse.

The more general point is that, contrary to Barnett and Morse's assertions, unit cost does depend on factor and output prices and all the variables that drive those prices. As discussed in the next section, similar problems affect the biophysical indicators. It is, however, possible to calculate a generalized unit cost (U) indicator that is more independent of price movements.

The starting point is a production function for a resource commodity Q:

$$Q = f(A_1, ..., A_n, A_R, X_1, ..., X_n, R, S) \qquad (7.2)$$

where Q is gross output, R is the resource base from which the resource is extracted, and S is a vector of additional uncontrolled natural resource inputs such as rainfall and temperature. The X_i are other factors of production controlled by the extractor, and the A_i are augmentation factors associated with the respective factors of production. A_R is the augmentation (or depletion) index of the resource base. In theory we could also allow the effective units per crude unit of S to vary, though in most applications it will be assumed that the augmentation index is constant. Equation (7.2) can obviously be generalized to multiple outputs and multiple resource inputs. A useful simplifying assumption is that the production function exhibits constant returns to scale in all inputs including the resource inputs. Again, generalizations can be made. Note that if S is measured in terms of rainfall, temperature and so on, rather than water, heat and so on, the relevant constant returns relates to the expansion of X and R but not S.

Taking the time derivative of $\ln Q$ yields:

$$\dot{Q} = \Sigma\, \sigma_i \dot{A}_i + \sigma_R \dot{A}_R + \Sigma\, \sigma_i \dot{X}_i + \Sigma\, \sigma_j \dot{S}_j + \sigma_R \dot{R} \tag{7.3}$$

where the σ_i are the output elasticities of the various inputs. A dot on a variable indicates the derivative of the logarithm with respect to time. Then the change in the logarithm of U, a generalized unit cost indicator, is defined as:

$$\dot{U} = \Sigma\, \sigma_i \dot{X}_i - \dot{Q} \tag{7.4}$$

Typically the change in $\ln U$ will be calculated using a Divisia index of input where σ_i is replaced with the relevant revenue share. In equilibrium $\Sigma\, \sigma_i = C/V$, where C is cost and R is revenue. The remaining profit is distributed as rent to the resource owners. The traditional definition of unit cost, (7.1), differs by the premultiplication of $\Sigma\, \sigma_i \dot{X}_i$ by V/C. From (7.3) and (7.4) we find that U can alternatively be defined as:

$$\dot{U} = \Sigma\, \sigma_i \dot{A}_i - \sigma_R \dot{A}_R - \Sigma\, \sigma_j \dot{S}_j - \sigma_R \dot{R} \tag{7.5}$$

Thus, changes in U are the sum of the four terms in (7.5), respectively:

1.   Technical change
2.   Resource depletion or augmentation
3.   Change in uncontrolled natural resource inputs such as rainfall and temperature in agriculture
4.   Change in the dimension of the resource base.

These components seem to cover the dynamics that unit cost proponents have tried to capture without distortions caused by shifts in input or output prices. Factor prices still affect U because, in general, the output elasticities will be functions of input quantities. For the special case of the Cobb–Douglas production function the indicator is completely independent of prices. Equation (7.5) demonstrates most clearly what U is intended to capture and equation (7.4) shows that such an indicator can be calculated.

3.   The neoclassical model of scarcity

The neoclassical view of scarcity begins with the theory of optimal depletion (Hotelling, 1931) in which resource owners are assumed to maximize the discounted profits from the extraction and sale of the resource. Solution of the model suggests two possible scarcity indicators: price and rent.

Fisher (1979) demonstrates this with a simple optimal control problem for non-renewable resource extraction in which the private profit-maximizing resource owner faces the following problem:

$$\text{Maximize} \int_{0}^{\infty} [PY - WE]e^{-rt}dt$$

subject to:

$$dX/dt = -Y$$

$$Y = f(E,X,t) \tag{7.6}$$

where P is market price, W is the price of hiring a unit of effort E, Y is the quantity of the resource commodity produced from the stock X, and $f()$ is the production function. In equilibrium the following condition is met:

$$P = W/(\partial Y/\partial E) + q \tag{7.7}$$

where q is the costate variable attached to the constraint in the Hamiltonian. Market price, therefore, has the attractive feature of capturing the sum of direct sacrifices such as the cost of hiring labour, and indirect sacrifices such as the change in the net present value of future profits caused by reducing the size of the remaining resource stock. The quantity q is known as the shadow price of the stock, user cost, or rent. If we are only interested in the direct and indirect sacrifices associated with depleting the stock, rather than producing the commodity, q is a better indicator. Therefore, market prices are the appropriate scarcity indicator for resource commodities and rents for resource stocks.

Several authors have developed theoretical time paths for rent and price as a resource is depleted for both renewable and non-renewable resources (for example Hotelling, 1931; Fisher, 1979; Lyon, 1981; Sedjo and Lyon, 1990; Slade, 1982; Farzin, 1992, 1995). In Hotelling's simple model both price and rent rise monotonically at the rate of interest. In Fisher's model price still rises monotonically but rent may follow a non-monotonic path. Slade (1982) developed a more complex model where the path of prices over time may follow a U shape, implying that declining prices may be a misleading signal for long-run scarcity. Farzin (1992, 1995) derives a variety of time paths under varying assumptions. The theoretical literature indicates that for sufficiently general models, any time path may be possible. Lyon (1981) and Sedjo and Lyon (1990) derived specific models for forest products. The resulting time path is an S-curve, a path which both rents and prices have followed remarkably closely in the US in the last couple of centuries (Cleveland and Stern, 1993).

Empirical results of the neoclassical model

The empirical analysis of price and rent is characterized by applying increasingly sophisticated econometric tools to time-series data. Barnett and Morse's (1963) visual inspection of prices from 1870 to 1957 led them to reject the hypothesis of increasing scarcity for agriculture and minerals (metals, non-metals and fuels), and accept it in forestry. The trend for fisheries was indeterminate.

Smith (1979) uses Brown–Durbin CUSUM (cumulative sum of squares) and Quandt log-likelihood tests to examine the stability of the coefficients from a simple linear regression of real prices as a function of time for four broad industry groups from 1900 to 1973. He finds significant instability, and concludes that any judgements as to a consistent pattern of change in the price series would be 'hazardous'.

Devarajan and Fisher (1982) develop a two-period model of optimal depletion which indicates that marginal discovery cost is a close proxy of rent. They found that the average cost of oil discovery in the US showed a statistically significant increase from 1946 to 1971, indicating a clear increase in scarcity.

Slade (1982, 1985) develops a model of optimal depletion in which the long-run path of price is U-shaped due to changes in the effects of depletion and technical change. She tested the U-shape model by estimating a quadratic time-trend model for 12 non-renewable resources in the US from 1870 to 1978. She found significant U shapes for 11 of the 12 resources, and noted that all had passed the minimum points on their fitted U-shaped curves, indicating growing scarcity.

Ozdemiroglu (1993) updated Slade's (1982) analysis by fitting a quadratic model to time-series price data for 39 resources in five categories from a number of developed and developing nations. Of the nine resources that have significant trend coefficients, five show an inverted U shape, contrary to Slade's finding of a pervasive U shape for the US extractive sector. Ozdemiroglu's series are much shorter (as short as 12 years in the case of coal) than those used by Slade. Given that Slade's hypothesis is about long-run trends, it is doubtful that his analysis really tests Slade's hypothesis.

Hall and Hall (1984) estimated a time-trend model for 14 resource commodities in the US from 1960 to 1980, and tested for the possible effects of the energy price shocks on price. They found that the real price of fuels and electricity increased in the 1970s, and the actions of the OPEC cartel accelerated – but did not cause – the observed increase in price.

Forest products in the US have received considerable attention. Brown and Field (1979) found that the rental value of Douglas fir (as measured by its stumpage price) relative to its lumber price increased significantly from 1930 to 1970. They noted that this increase occurred at the same time as the unit cost of forest products (L/Q) declined. Brown and Field also found that the stumpage price of Douglas fir relative to a quality-adjusted wage rate increased from 1920 to 1970. Their empirical results are consistent with the growing importance of forest plantations in the US, a form of backstop technology which produces forest products at a higher but relatively constant cost compared to virgin forests. Cleveland and Stern (1993) test econometrically for trends in lumber prices from 1800 to 1990 and for trends in stumpage prices from 1910 and 1989 in the US. They find that both series can be represented by a logistic function. Prices for lumber products and rental rates for timberland are much higher today than in the past, but have levelled off in recent decades.

An issue ignored in most studies of scarcity indicator trends, whether classical, neoclassical or biophysical, is the time-series properties of the series in question. Recently Uri and Boyd (1995) and Berck and Roberts (1996) have addressed this question. Berck and Roberts (1996) revisit Slade's (1982) results. They find that most of the series are difference-stationary rather than trend-stationary, that is, they can be represented by unit root processes. Forecasting 1991 prices using a model estimated on 1940 to 1976 data, an ARIMA model generates more accurate predictions than Slade's quadratic model for all commodities except copper. The prices forecast by the ARIMA model are also lower for all commodities except copper. Using the quadratic model to predict 2000 prices from a 1991 base, the quadratic model gives a probability of an increase in price of more than 75 per cent for every commodity and a mean probability of 87 per cent. The ARIMA model has a mean probability of increase of 57 per cent with only one commodity having a probability of less than 50 per cent. So while price rises are seen to be less likely when a more appropriate model is fitted, the odds are still above even for an increase in prices in the future.

Uri and Boyd (1995) also find that average cost of extraction and real resource price series for a group of metals are all unit root series. They attempt to find cointegration between each of these two indicators and US GDP. They find no cointegration and argue that this means that resource scarcity has not constrained economic growth. However, there are two problems with this approach. First, testing for cointegration between GDP and each price separately implies that either all the price series cointegrate themselves and share the same stochastic trends so that any one of them can represent the others in their effect on GDP, or only one of the series has an effect on GDP and none of the others do. Second, the test implies that GDP and the scarcity indicators do not contain any non-common trends –

any other non-stationary variables driving GDP are also assumed to drive prices and vice versa. Both sets of assumptions seem rather unlikely.

Critique of the neoclassical model

Price has a number of practical advantages relative to unit cost (Cleveland, 1993). First, the prices of most natural resources are readily observable, avoiding the pitfalls of having to construct an index from secondary data. Second, the joint effects of the physical, technological and market factors that influence scarcity are subsumed in a single index. Third, price is not hampered by the joint product problem in industries such as oil and gas extraction, which complicates measurement of unit cost. Natural gas and crude oil have separate and distinct market prices. Rent, however, does not have many of these advantages.

There also are numerous caveats to the theoretical properties of price and rent. Most importantly, market prices and rents only indicate *private* scarcity (Fisher, 1979). In the presence of market imperfections or market failure, social indicators of scarcity will diverge from the private indicators.

The arguments for price are based on highly simplified models of optimal resource depletion that rest on restrictive assumptions about market structure, technical change, uncertainty about future cost and market conditions, and other factors that determine price. In the real world there are many practical problems with price that negate some of its theoretical advantages. The price of natural resources is determined in markets that are far more complex than those described in many of the theoretical models. Furthermore, the trend in scarcity suggested by price is sensitive to the benchmark that nominal prices are compared to (Brown and Field, 1979).

Rent faces similar problems as a scarcity indicator. Mattey (1990) shows that stumpage prices, the resource rent in the forestry sector, are influenced more by government policy and economic forecasts than by changes in the difficulty of production. Fisher (1979) describes the possibility of rent falling to zero as a low-grade backstop resource was substituted for a depleted higher-quality resource, and thus sending perverse signals about the impact on social well-being.

Norgaard (1990) presented what he argued was a logical fallacy in the empirical scarcity literature. The argument boils down to two points: imperfect information means that price or rent is not an accurate scarcity indicator for a resource owner, and that in addition imperfect or non-existent markets mean that price or rent are not indicators of social scarcity. Neither of these points is new, and they are explicit in earlier studies (for example Barnett and Morse 1963; Fisher, 1979). Norgaard also argues that if resource owners actually did have perfect information about resource scarcity, then economists could ask them directly for this information. Yet economists generally prefer to use market data to investigate people's preferences rather than asking them directly. Stated preference methods such as contingent valuation are normally only used in the absence of markets for the resource or other indirect market information such as hedonic pricing or the travel cost method. So even if resource owners had perfect information, it might be useful to exploit market data where available.

4. The biophysical model of scarcity

The biophysical approach begins by redrawing the conventional boundaries of the economic system. The economic process is a work process and as such it is sustained by a flow of low-entropy energy and matter from the environment. As materials and energy are transformed in production and consumption, higher-entropy waste heat and matter are ultimately released to, and assimilated by, the environment. Analysis of exchange in markets, which grabs the spotlight in conventional economic analysis, is given less attention as an intermediate step in the process of fulfilling human needs and desires by the flow of energy and materials from resources to production, pollution and environmental assimilation.

The biophysical approach defines the resource transformation process as one that uses energy to upgrade the organization of matter to a more useful state (Ayres, 1978; Cook, 1976; Gever et al., 1986; Hall et al., 1986; Cleveland, 1991b; Ruth, 1993). In their natural state resources are not useful inputs to the production process. They must be located, extracted, refined, transported, and generally transformed into useful raw materials or products. By definition, lower-quality resources require more energy to upgrade to a given state. The same fundamental relationship exists for renewable and non-renewable natural resources (Hall et al., 1986). Just as more energy is required to isolate copper metal from a lower-grade ore, more energy is required to pump oil from deeper and smaller fields, harvest food from less fertile soil, and catch fish from smaller and more remote areas.

A second tenet of the biophysical model emphasizes the role that energy plays in implementing technical innovations in the extractive sector. Technical improvements have tended to be energy-using and labour-saving, achieved through the use of more powerful energy converters (Georgescu-Roegen, 1975). Empirical research demonstrates a significant relationship between labour productivity, the quantity of installed horsepower (Maddala, 1965) and fuel use (Hall et al., 1986) per worker in the US extractive sector. Energy converters have also evolved towards the use of higher-quality forms of energy. Animate energy converters such as human labour and draught animals were replaced by inanimate energy converters burning wood and coal, then oil and natural gas, and eventually electricity.

The energy used to extract a resource is mirrored by the additional use of renewable resources and ecosystem services, such as clean water and air, and the land used to support the extraction process. The increase in throughput of energy and materials also increases the generation of wastes which, in turn, increases the use of natural capital in various forms for waste assimilation. The increase in the overall scale of extraction that accompanies the cumulative depletion of a resource increases the demand for natural capital in various forms for waste assimilation. The increase in the overall scale of extraction that accompanies the cumulative depletion of a resource increases the demand for natural capital inputs because that expansion often diverts larger portions of the landscape to extraction activities. Changes in the quality of the resource base affect all of these costs, just as they affect the energy cost of extraction. For example, the decline in quality of the US oil resource base has increased the energy cost of oil extraction. In turn, this has increased the amount of CO_2 released by the fuel burned to extract the oil, and the amount of water used per barrel of oil (Kaufmann and Cleveland, 1991; Cleveland, 1993). In surface metal and coal mines, a decline in resource quality increases the stripping ratio and hence the amount of waste produced per unit of the product (Gelb, 1984).

Empirical results of the biophysical model
The energy cost of extracting a unit of resource in the US shows some important differences relative to the trends in unit cost and price. The most thoroughly examined resources are fossil fuels (Cleveland et al., 1984; Hall et al., 1986; Gever et al., 1986; Cleveland, 1991b; Cleveland, 1992; Cleveland, 1993). The energy cost of extracting oil and gas increased by 40 per cent from 1970 to the 1990s, indicating a significant increase in scarcity. The energy cost of coal extraction increased by a similar magnitude.

The energy cost of agricultural output increased steadily from 1910 through the late 1970s as the direct and indirect use of fossil fuels replaced labour and draught animals (Cleveland, 1991a; Cleveland, 1995a, 1995b). Since the second energy price shock energy costs have declined due to reduction in the rate of energy use per hectare, a reduction in the number of harvested hectares, and larger firms. Cleveland (1995a) finds no evidence that resource degradation has diminished the productivity of energy use in US agriculture.

The energy cost of metals such as silver, bauxite and iron shows their increasing scarcity in the US while copper, lead and zinc show stable or decreasing scarcity (Cleveland, 1991a). Most non-metals show no signs of increasing scarcity measured by their energy cost.

Cleveland and Stern (1993) develop an index of energy cost of forest products in the US that adjusts for energy quality by using a Divisia index to aggregate energy inputs. Unit energy costs of forest products showed a decrease in scarcity since 1947.

Critique of the biophysical model
Stern (1994) argues that a biophysical theory of production need not reduce to an energy theory of production. Low-entropy energy and matter are not the only non-reproducible inputs to production. According to Stern, information could be seen in an analogous way to energy as a primary input. This information is accumulated as knowledge. Technology consists of the designs for the products to be manufactured, the ideas for which come in part from human imagination, and the techniques used in producing those products. These techniques consist purely of the application of the knowledge of physical laws and the chemical and biological properties of resources to the production process, though of course the techniques used at any one time are contingent on the path of knowledge accumulation to that date. This latter knowledge is the result of the extraction of information from the environment. Capital, labour and energy are required to extract that knowledge from the environment and render it into a productive form. Capital, labour and other intermediate goods are produced within the economy by applying to matter the two primary factors of production: low-entropy energy and knowledge. From the perspective of Ricardo and Marx the use value of the products is not a function of energy alone, but also of the knowledge employed. For example, knowledge is embodied in the physical arrangement of capital, say, the shape and design of machines. From a more neoclassical perspective, knowledge can be used either in an embodied form in the capital and labour inputs or in the combination of the factors of production in the production process. The implication is that the economic value of capital and labour is not a linear function of the energy used in their production alone, even if we ignore the fact that two different products embodying the same energy and knowledge may have different values in their use by people.

Stern (1996) shows that unless we subscribe to an energy theory of value where the productivity of non-energy inputs is a linear function of the energy used in their manufacture, energy cost could be a misleading indicator of scarcity. In particular, for most reasonable estimates of the elasticity of substitution of energy for capital and labour, energy cost could rise as the relative price of energy falls, even though no change has occurred in the productivity of the resource base or in the state of technology. This is the same argument as that levelled against unit cost by Brown and Field (1979) discussed above. This finding is supported by empirical studies

(Cleveland, 1995a; Mitchell and Cleveland, 1992) that show rising energy cost as the relative price of energy to capital and labour declined.

That productivity is not a function of energy alone is clear from the issue of varying energy quality (Berndt, 1978; Kaufmann, 1994). Petroleum is considered to be a higher-quality fuel than coal because of the accompanying physical and chemical properties of the fuel vector and the technologies available for using the fuels. This difference cannot be explained purely in terms of the embodied environmental energy in the fuels, that is, petroleum has not undergone considerably more processing in the environment than has coal. This problem can be addressed by using quality-weighted indices of energy inputs (Cleveland, 1993; Cleveland and Stern, 1993; Stern, 1993), typically the relative prices of the fuels. This is only a partial solution which implies certain separability conditions on the production function.

5.   Towards a synthesis: use and exchange scarcity
Much of the debate about the strengths and weaknesses of various scarcity indicators ignores a fundamental point: different indicators measure different types of scarcity. We elaborate this point below using the concepts of *use scarcity* and *exchange scarcity*.

The two fundamental concepts of value in economics are use value and exchange value. The exchange value of a commodity is identical with its price. For an individual wishing to acquire a resource commodity, market price is a valid indicator of exchange value. A resource becomes more scarce if its exchange value increases or the sacrifices required to obtain it increase. It is this meaning of scarcity that we term exchange scarcity. Note that these sacrifices do not necessarily relate to changes in the difficulty of obtaining the resource from the environment itself, although the two obviously may be related.

Use value was always a problematic concept because either it was impossible to measure or the units of measurement were unclear. Ricardo and Marx's labour theories of value were intended to solve this problem but created as many difficulties as they cleared up. In the neoclassical view, use value is represented by some indicator of total utility such as consumer surplus, while exchange value represents marginal utility.

Commons (1934) paralleled the concepts of exchange and use value by his categories of 'scarcity' and 'efficiency'. Efficiency is a measure of productivity and is defined as the rate of production of use value by the factors of production, or output per unit input. The inverse of this output/input ratio is unit cost. When there are several factors of production, it is impossible to identify *a priori* the contribution of each to use value. But if the input/output ratio is calculated omitting one of the factors, that is, land, a rise in the ratio implies, *ceteris paribus*, a decline in the use value produced by the omitted factor and an increase in what we call use scarcity. The parallel exchange value concept is the revenue/cost ratio, the rate of revenue generation per unit of expenditure on inputs, or the profit mark-up rate. If only land is omitted from the calculation of expenditure on inputs, then the profit mark-up rate is $M = 1 + rR/C = pQ/C$ where r is the rental rate, R, is land, C is cost of all other inputs, p is the output price, and Q the output quantity. Thus unit cost is a use-value indicator of natural resource scarcity and rent, prices and average costs are related components of Commons's own scarcity measure, M.

Commons (1934) defined use value in terms of quantities of commodities, though he recognized that use value did change with what we would now call changes in preferences, in household production functions, or in capital stocks associated with household production (Stigler and Becker, 1977), so a 'commodity theory of value' was not really satisfactory. In the neoclassical view, unless functions are linear in commodities, use value is also a function of the quantities of other commodities consumed. Calculation of the consumers' utility derived from natural resources also needs to take into account the efficiency of production downstream from the resource sector. The unit cost indicator is an 'upstream indicator' of scarcity. The prices of resource commodities do not necessarily move in the same direction as rent (Fisher, 1979), and downstream use scarcity does not necessarily move in the same direction as unit cost. To our knowledge no one has attempted to construct a 'downstream indicator' of use scarcity.

Now we can explain Fisher's (1979) comments on the inadequacy of rent as a scarcity indicator noted above. Rent falls to zero as a stock of minerals of variable quality is depleted. The average use value of the remaining mineral deposits declines, but so does their exchange value. In the extreme case, nobody wants to buy useless rocks and therefore their rent declines to zero. The scarcity of use value embodied in the minerals has increased sharply and this will be correctly reflected in the rise in unit cost noted by Fisher. Society is indeed much worse off – its ability to produce use value is much diminished. In order to obtain a full picture of the scarcity of natural resources in both its dimensions, we must examine both exchange value and use value, exchange scarcity and use scarcity.

6.   Discussion

The problem with all natural resource scarcity indicators is that we can only look at the historic time path of the indicator and guess what the trend will be in the future. The recent literature on the time paths of prices and rent (Farzin, 1992) indicates that many time paths are possible, and assuming that the trend will continue is problematic. In order to develop more effective forecasts of future resource scarcity we need to look beyond the indicators to the production technologies, natural resource bases and market structures that determine the indicators. We propose here a generalized unit cost indicator. As we describe, one advantage is that it directly decomposes into a number of more fundamental trends, such as the effects of depletion, technical change and the size of the resource base. These underlying components can also be connected with price and rent movements. Barnett and Morse (1963) attempted a simple version of this decomposition with their index of relative unit cost – the ratio of unit cost in the extractive sector to unit cost in the non-extractive sector. The idea was to remove the overall technical change trend in the economy from the use scarcity indicator so that it more accurately reflected the results of depletion alone.

Future trends in use scarcity might be better understood if we could estimate each of these components separately. Most analyses of use scarcity assume that the net result of these opposing forces is reflected in the historical trend of the indicator, and they do not explicitly measure the effects of depletion and innovation. One exception is the analysis of the cost of oil extraction in the US, for which sufficient data are available to describe or proxy depletion and innovation (Norgaard, 1975; Cleveland, 1991b). We have carried out a number of studies that model resource availability and productivity providing estimates of underlying variables that can be used to develop scenarios about future trends. Cleveland and Kaufmann (1991) model long-run oil supply in the US in terms of physical and economic factors. Perrings and Stern (1995) model rangeland degradation in Botswana as the outcome of physical processes and a changing economic environment. Cleveland and Stern (1998) decompose output growth in US agriculture as in equation (7.3) by using an econometric model of the agricultural sector.

An interesting corollary of equation (7.3) is that all previous studies of biased technical change in the extractive sector of the economy aggregate technical change, resource depletion and resource availability. For example some studies (Abt, 1987; Constantino and Haley, 1988; Merrifield and Haynes, 1985) of the forest products industry indicate that technical change has tended to be wood-using. This has been taken to indicate that wood is relatively less scarce than the other factors of production (Stier and Bengston, 1992). However, the finding of a wood-using bias could indicate that the quality of the resource base has declined, and a wood-saving bias could indicate an improvement in the quality of the resource base. In general, the bias of 'technological change' in an extractive industry does not provide useful data on the scarcity of the natural resources in question unless further information is available which allows the researcher to separate the effects of depletion from the effects of technological change.

Finally, though Uri and Boyd (1995) and Berck and Roberts (1996) have both shown that scarcity indicator series are difference-stationary rather than trend-stationary, neither explicitly revisited the question of the presence of a trend in scarcity using recent time-series techniques. Berck and Roberts (1996) instead focused on the forecasting abilities of different models, while Uri and Boyd (1995) took a detour into cointegration analysis. This clearly is an issue that needs further investigation.

7.   Conclusions

There is no 'correct' way to measure resource scarcity. To a large extent arguments over the meaning and indicators of scarcity reflect fundamental disagreements among economists regarding the nature and purposes of economics (Cole et al., 1983). However, we have tried to show how these different views are complementary.

There are at least two meanings attached to the term 'scarcity' in the economic literature which we name exchange scarcity and use scarcity. They relate to the Hotelling or Ricardian scarcity models. Rents and prices measure the private exchange scarcity of stocks and commodities respectively for those wishing to purchase them. They are not necessarily good measures of scarcity for society as a whole or for resource owners. Generalized unit cost is a possible indicator of use scarcity, but it may not reflect downstream technical improvements in resource use, the possibility of non-linear utility functions, or, as in the case of price, the impact of environmental damage associated with resource extraction on welfare. Correctly calculated, unit cost is less affected by information and market imperfections than the exchange scarcity indicators. Each indicator measures the aspect of scarcity for which it is designed. In our opinion, the argument that a particular indicator does not reflect the true movement in scarcity in most cases reflects either a problem with the question being asked or with the method of calculating the indicator rather than with the type of indicator itself.

Despite this, a research programme aimed at modelling resource supply that takes into account both physical and economic factors would perhaps be more useful than the simple calculation of scarcity indicators. Rather than just observing the trend in unit costs or prices and assuming that this will continue into the future, this approach would seek to differentiate between the various causes of change in scarcity. This would give us a better picture of the limits to improvements in the future. Together with information on the possibilities for future technical change and natural processes, such models could be used to produce scenarios about possible future scarcity trends that could inform debate and policy making. We believe that this would be a more productive endeavour than the search for the perfect resource scarcity indicator.

Note
1. Capital refers to manufactured capital, although occasionally we use the term 'natural capital', which can be understood as referring to the resource stock or resource base. Natural capital emphasizes the active contribution resource stocks play in production – for example pressure in oil reservoirs forces oil to the surface.

References
Abt, R.C. (1987), 'An analysis of regional factor demand in the US lumber industry', *Forest Science*, **33**, 164–73.
Ayres, R.U. (1978), *Resources, Environment, and Economics: Applications of the Materials/ Energy Balance Principle*, New York: John Wiley and Sons.
Barnett, H. and C. Morse (1963), *Scarcity and Growth: The Economics of Natural Resource Availability*, Baltimore, MD: Johns Hopkins University Press.
Berck, P. and M. Roberts (1996), 'Natural resource prices: will they ever turn up?' *Journal of Environmental Economics and Management*, **31**, 65–78.
Berndt, E.R. (1978), 'Aggregate energy, efficiency, and productivity measurement', *Annual Review of Energy*, **3**, 225–73.
Brown, G.M. and B. Field (1979), 'The adequacy of scarcity measures for signaling the scarcity of natural resources', in V.K. Smith (ed.), *Scarcity and Growth Reconsidered*, Baltimore, MD: Johns Hopkins University Press, pp. 218–48.
Cairns, R.D. (1990), 'A contribution to the theory of depletable resource scarcity and its measures', *Economic Inquiry*, **28**, 744–55.
Cleveland, C.J. (1991a), 'Natural resource scarcity and economic growth revisited: Economic and biophysical perspectives', in R. Costanza (ed.), *Ecological Economics: The Science and Management of Sustainability*, New York: Columbia University Press.
Cleveland, C.J. (1991b), 'Physical and economic aspects of resource quality: the cost of oil supply in the lower 48 United States, 1936–1988', *Resources and Energy*, **13**, 163–88.
Cleveland, C.J. (1992), 'Energy quality and energy surplus in the extraction of fossil fuels in the US', *Ecological Economics*, **6**, 139–62.
Cleveland, C.J. (1993), 'An exploration of alternative measures of natural resource scarcity: the case of petroleum resources in the US', *Ecological Economics*, **7**, 123–57.
Cleveland, C.J. (1995a), 'Resource degradation, technical change, and the productivity of energy use in US agriculture', *Ecological Economics*, **13**, 185–201.
Cleveland, C.J. (1995b), 'The direct and indirect use of fossil fuels and electricity in USA agriculture, 1910–1990', *Agriculture, Ecosystems, and the Environment*, **55**, 111–21.
Cleveland, C.J. and R.K. Kaufmann (1991), 'Forecasting ultimate oil recovery and its rate of production: Incorporating economic forces into the models of M. King Hubbert', *The Energy Journal*, **12** (2), 17–46.
Cleveland, C.J. and D.I. Stern (1993), 'Productive and exchange scarcity: an empirical analysis of the US forest products industry', *Canadian Journal of Forest Research*, **23**, 1537–49.
Cleveland, C.J. and D.I. Stern (1998), 'Measuring natural resource scarcity: A review, synthesis, and application to US agriculture', in J.C.J.M. van den Bergh and M.W. Hofkes (eds), *Theory and Implementation of Economic Models for Sustainable Development*, Dordrecht: Kluwer Academic Publishers, 113–38.
Cleveland, C.J., R. Costanza, C.A.S. Hall and R. Kaufmann (1984), 'Energy and the US economy: a biophysical perspective', *Science*, **255**, 890–97.
Cole, K., J. Cameron and C. Edwards (1983), *Why Economists Disagree: The Political Economy of Economics*, New York: Longman.
Commons, J.R. (1934), *Institutional Economics*, New York: Macmillan.
Constantino, L.F. and D. Haley (1988), 'Wood quality and the input and output choices of

sawmilling producers for the British Columbia coast and United States Pacific Northwest, west side', *Canadian Journal of Forest Research*, **18**, 202–8.

Cook, E.F. (1976), 'Limits to the exploitation of nonrenewable resources', *Science*, **210**, 1219–24.

Devarajan, S. and A.C. Fisher (1982), 'Exploration and scarcity', *Journal of Political Economy*, **90**, 1279–90.

Farzin, Y.H. (1992), 'The time path of scarcity rent in the theory of exhaustible resources', *Economic Journal*, **102**, 813–31.

Farzin, Y.H. (1995), 'Technological change and the dynamics of resource scarcity measures', *Journal of Environmental Economics and Environmental Management*, **29**, 105–20.

Fisher, A.C. (1979), 'Measures of natural resource scarcity', in V.K. Smith (ed.), *Scarcity and Growth Reconsidered*, Baltimore, MD: Johns Hopkins University Press.

Gelb, B. (1984), 'A look at energy use in mining: it deserves it', International Association of Energy Economists, San Francisco, pp. 947–59.

Georgescu-Roegen, N. (1975), 'Energy and economic myths', *Southern Economic Journal*, **41**, 347–81.

Gever, J., R. Kaufmann, D. Skole and C. Vorosmarty (1986), *Beyond Oil: The Threat to Food and Fuel in the Coming Decades*, Cambridge: Ballinger.

Hall, C.A.S., C.J. Cleveland and R. Kaufmann (1986), *Energy and Resource Quality: The Ecology of the Economic Process*, New York: Wiley Interscience.

Hall, D.C. and J.V. Hall (1984), Concepts and measures of natural resource scarcity with a summary of recent trends', *Journal of Environmental Economics and Management*, **11**, 363–79.

Hall, D.C., J.V. Hall and D.X. Kolk (1988), 'Energy in the unit cost index to measure scarcity', *Energy*, **13**, 281–6.

Hotelling, H. (1931), 'The economics of exhaustible resources', *Journal of Political Economy*, **39**, 137–75.

Howe, C.W. (1979), *Natural Resource Economics*, New York: John Wiley and Sons.

Johnson, M.H., J.T. Bell and J.T. Bennett (1980), 'Natural resource scarcity: empirical evidence and public policy', *Journal of Environmental Economics and Management*, **7**, 256–71.

Kaufmann, R.K. (1994), 'The relation between marginal product and price in US energy markets', *Energy Economics*, **16**, 145–58.

Kaufmann, R.K. and C.J. Cleveland (1991), 'Policies to increase US oil production: Likely to fail, damage the economy, and damage the environment', *Annual Review of Energy and Environment*, **16**, 379–400.

Lyon, K.S. (1981), 'Mining of the forest and the time path of the price of timber', *Journal of Environmental Economics and Management*, **8**, 330–44.

Maddala, G.S. (1965), 'Productivity and technological change in the bituminous coal industry, 1919–1954', *Journal of Political Economy*, **73**, 352–65.

Mattey, J.P. (1990), *The Timber Bubble that Burst: government policy and the bailout of 1984*, New York: Oxford University Press.

Merrifield, D.E. and R.W. Haynes (1985), 'A cost analysis of the lumber and plywood industries in two Pacific Northwest sub-regions', *Annals of Regional Science*, **19** (3), 16–33.

Mitchell, C. and C.J. Cleveland (1992), 'Resource scarcity, energy use and environmental impact: A case study of the New Bedford, Massachusetts fisheries', *Environmental Management*, **17**, 305–18.

Norgaard, R.B. (1975), 'Resource scarcity and new technology in US petroleum development', *Natural Resources Journal*, **15**, 265–82.

Norgaard, R.B. (1990), 'Economic indicators of resource scarcity: A critical essay', *Journal of Environmental Economics and Management*, **19**, 19–25.

Ozdemiroglu, E. (1993), 'Measuring natural resource scarcity: the study of the price indicator', Centre for Social and Economic Research on the Global Environment, University of East Anglia, Norwich, England, *Working paper GEC 93-14*.

Perrings, C.A. and D.I. Stern (1995), 'Modelling the resilience of agroecosystems: theory and application to rangeland degradation in Botswana', paper presented at Ulvön Workshop of Beijer Institute for Ecological Economics Resilience Network, Ulvön, Sweden, June.

Ruth, M. (1993), *Integrating Economics, Ecology, and Thermodynamics*, Dordrecht: Kluwer Academic Publishers.

Ruth, M. (1995), 'Thermodynamic implications for natural resource extraction and technical change in US copper mining', *Environmental and Resource Economics*, **6**, 187–206.

Sedjo, R.A. and K.S. Lyon (1990), *The Long-Term Adequacy of World Timber Supply*, Washington, DC: Resources for the Future.

Slade, M.E. (1982), 'Trends in natural-resource commodity prices: An analysis of the time domain', *Journal of Environmental Economics and Management*, **9**, 122–37.

Slade, M.E. (1985), 'Trends in natural-resource commodity prices: U-shaped price paths explored', *Journal of Environmental Economics and Management*, **12**, 181–92.

Smith, V.K. (1979), 'Natural resource scarcity: a statistical analysis', *Review of Economics and Statistics*, **61**, 423–7.

Smith, V.K. (1980), 'The evaluation of natural resource adequacy: elusive quest or frontier of economic analysis?', *Land Economics*, **56**, 257–98.

Stern, D.I. (1993), 'Energy use and economic growth in the USA: a multivariate approach', *Energy Economics*, **15**, 137–50.

Stern, D.I. (1994), 'Natural resources as factors of production: three empirical studies', PhD dissertation, Department of Geography, Boston University, Boston, MA.

Stern, D.I. (1996), 'The theory of natural resource scarcity indicators: towards a synthesis', *CEES Working Papers* 9601, Center for Energy and Environmental Studies, Boston University (available on WWW at: http://cres.anu.edu.au/~dstern/CEES_WP/9604.ps).

Stier, J.C. and D.N. Bengston (1992), 'Technical change in the North American forestry sector: A review', *Forest Science*, **38**, 134–59.

Stigler, G.J. and G.S. Becker (1977), 'De gustibus non est disputandum', *American Economic Review*, **67**, 76–90.

Uri, N.D. and R. Boyd (1995), 'Scarcity and growth revisited', *Environment and Planning*, A 27, 1815–32.

8 Renewable resources: fisheries
Colin W. Clark

1. Introduction

Marine fisheries the world over are in trouble. Depletion of once-productive fish stocks, a sporadic occurrence earlier in the twentieth century, has progressively become a common event. The declaration of 200-mile fishing zones by most of the world's coastal nations in the late 1970s, which was a reaction to overfishing by foreign fleets, has had limited success in terms of conservation. To name one extreme example, the Northern cod fishery in the Western Atlantic collapsed in 1992, in spite of intense management activity by the Canadian government. The collapse, caused by extreme overfishing (by Canadian fishers) has destroyed the economy of the Province of Newfoundland, throwing some 30 000 fishers and plant workers on to the unemployment roster. Only limited signs of recovery of this historical fishery had appeared by 1999.

The economic causes of overfishing are well understood for the case of unregulated, open-access fisheries. As explained more fully later, an unregulated fishery will tend to reach a bionomic equilibrium, in which revenues from fishing are exactly balanced by opportunity costs, and potential economic rents are entirely dissipated. This theory, due to Gordon (1954), predicts that depletion (that is, suboptimal fish stocks) will become more prevalent as demand increases and as fishing technology improves; it also predicts that fishermen will become and remain impoverished. These properties are characteristic of many marine fisheries – but there have been some notable exceptions.

Understanding the depletion, not to mention collapse, of managed fisheries is more problematic. It will be argued later that this is usually the result of a combination of circumstances, including discounting the future, initial overcapitalization, and inadequate consideration of the high levels of uncertainty encountered in marine ecosystem dynamics and management.

2. Fisheries as natural capital

Modern economic theory treats renewable resource stocks as forms of natural capital (Jansson et al., 1994). To describe a generic model based on this idea (Clark, 1990), let $x(t)$ denote the biomass of a given fish population at time t. When the biomass is x, the net rate of population growth equals $F(x)$. Harvesting at the rate h reduces the net population growth rate accordingly:

$$\frac{dx}{dt} = F(x) - h \tag{8.1}$$

The economically literate reader will immediately recognize equation (8.1) as a form of the standard model of capital accumulation and consumption: x corresponds to the capital stock, while h corresponds to the rate of consumption. Here the production of natural capital, $F(x)$, is facilitated by the natural environment (driven ultimately by solar energy), rather than by labour as in the capital theory model. Positive investment in natural capital occurs if $h < F(x)$, whereas disinvestment occurs if $h > F(x)$. Equilibrium at stock level x is achieved if $h = F(x)$.

One important difference between the two models, however, concerns the properties of the natural production function $F(x)$. In capital theory it is usually assumed that F is increasing and concave down ($F' > 0$, $F'' < 0$), reflecting decreasing returns to scale. In the fishery model it is assumed that F peaks at some value $x = x_{MSY}$ and then decreases to zero (see Figure 8.1):

$$F(0) = 0, \quad F(K) = 0, \quad F''(x) < 0$$
$$\max F(x) = F(x_{MSY}) = h_{MSY} \tag{8.2}$$

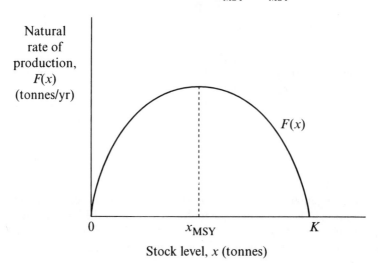

Notes: x is the size of the stock (tonnes), and $F(x)$ is the net annual rate of increase of the stock (tonnes/yr). The level $x = K$ is the natural equilibrium stock size, or carrying capacity. Maximum sustainable yield (MSY) occurs at an intermediate stock size $x = x_{MSY}$, when the sustainable harvest h achieves a maximum value. In spite of many shortcomings (Larkin, 1977; Holt and Talbot, 1978; Mangel et al., 1996), the concept of MSY has continued to dominate fisheries management.

Figure 8.1   A model of the natural production function for a fish stock

Here K is called the environmental carrying capacity of the population; $x = K$ is a stable equilibrium (when $h = 0$) of the natural population. The harvest rate h_{MSY} given by equation (8.2) is the maximum sustainable yield (MSY) that can be harvested from the population. MSY has been the traditional management objective for most fisheries, but achieving this objective in a stable, efficient and equitable way has proved to be more difficult than anticipated, for reasons discussed below.

Next we introduce the quantity E, fishing effort (for example, the number of standardized fishing vessels in operation at time t), and assume that

$$h = qEx \qquad (8.3)$$

Here q, the catchability coefficient, may in general depend on the current stock size x; for simplicity, however, we assume q constant. If c denotes the unit cost of effort, and p the landed price of fish, then the net flow of revenue (economic rent) equals

$$R = ph - cE = (pqx - c)E \qquad (8.4)$$

On the basis of this simple model we can discuss the concepts of bionomic equilibrium, depletion and optimal exploitation. Extensions and limitations of the model will be discussed later.

3.   Bionomic equilibrium

Imagine now an unregulated fishery exploited by numerous fishers. If $pqx - c > 0$, the net returns to effort E are positive. It will therefore pay a fisher to increase his effort; also additional fishers will be attracted to the fishery. Thus E will tend to increase, resulting in a decrease in x. Bionomic equilibrium is achieved when $pqx - c = 0$, that is, when

$$x = x_{BE} = \frac{c}{pq} \qquad (8.5)$$

This equation has several implications. Bionomic equilibrium depends on the cost/price ratio c/p; lower costs or higher prices lead to reduced biomass levels at equilibrium. Likewise, increased vessel efficiency, as reflected by increased catchability q, also reduces the bionomic equilibrium. If these changes take place slowly over time, fish stocks will slowly decline. Sustainable yield equals $F(x_{BE})$; this will increase in the early development of the fishery, but will subsequently decline once x_{BE} falls below x_{MSY}. This latter situation, involving low fish stocks and low catches, characterizes overfishing in the usual sense of this term. The model thus predicts that overfishing is inevitable in an unregulated, open-access fishery, provided that demand is high relative to fishing costs. The histories of countless fisheries support this prediction.

4.   Externalities

Overfishing is sometimes attributed to externalities in the operation of individual firms (fishers) competing in the fishery. In the above model externalities arise because each fisher bases his decisions solely on current returns to effort ($pqx - c$), and does not consider the effects of his catches on future stock levels x. Such dynamic externalities are central throughout resource and environmental economics. They are the essence of the 'tragedy of the commons' (Hardin, 1968).

Additional, short-term externalities may arise if fishing vessels interfere with one another during search or capture activities. While such 'crowding' externalities may influence the economic efficiency of fishing in important ways, they are probably less significant in terms of overfishing than the dynamic stock externality described above. A third form, 'by-catch' externalities, occurs when fishermen seeking a particular species (for example, shrimp) catch or otherwise destroy other species (such as juvenile fish) that may also have value, either directly or as food for other targeted species.

5.   Traditional management

Excessive harvesting having been recognized as the cause of overfishing, traditional management approaches have concentrated on controlling annual catches. Typically the management agency determines a total allowable annual catch (TAC). The cumulative year's catch is tracked, and the fishery closed once the TAC has been reached. Alternatively, the length of the fishing season may be determined in advance, based on an estimate of the fleet's capture efficiency. Assuming that the TAC has been correctly calculated, and that actual catches are quickly and accurately reported, this method has the potential for protecting vulnerable fish populations. However, there are usually unfortunate economic side-effects. The restricted seasonal opening forces fishers to compete vigorously for their share of the TAC, and also motivates them to increase vessel capacity so as to maximize their catches. In order to balance this effect, the length of the fishing season must be progressively reduced. For example, in the Pacific halibut fishery, the TAC approach had resulted, by the early 1990s, in a fishing season lasting only three days out of each year. A new 'regulated bionomic equilibrium' became established, with economic rents being dissipated through the costs of overcapacity. Other side-effects included reduced market prices for halibut, and potentially dangerous fishing conditions as fishers were forced to go to sea during the brief openings, regardless of weather conditions.

This scenario – overcapacity, brief fishing seasons, and regulated bionomic equilibrium – is characteristic of TAC-based fishery management. Eventually the pressure on the management agency to increase the TAC (or to retain the current TAC even though it may be excessive) may destabilize the fishery and precipitate a collapse. Most fish populations undergo environmentally induced fluctuations, from which they usually recover under natural conditions. When an overcapitalized fishery is dependent on the stock, such a fluctuation may result in a population collapse unless the management agency responds quickly by reducing the TAC.

6. Alternative management techniques

To prevent overcapacity, management agencies may be forced to regulate vessel size, horsepower and fishing gear. They may also limit the number of vessels licensed to participate in the fishery. Such regulations tend to interfere with market-based individual decisions, and lead to an increasingly unwieldy management system.

An alternative approach, now being used with increasing frequency, employs individual transferable quotas (ITQs). Each fisher has a specified annual quota, which may be caught whenever and however the fisher desires. Quota units may be bought from or sold to other fishers. Total quotas are determined by the management authority, as usual. (Individual quotas may consist of shares of this total quota.) Provided that illegal catches can be prevented, the ITQ approach has many advantages arising from decentralized decision making and the elimination of competition among fishers. Economic rents are preserved, and distributed among quota owners. ITQs were adopted in the Pacific halibut fishery in 1993 for the Canadian sector, and were under consideration for US fishers by 1996. The results in the Canadian sector have been increased incomes to fishers, availability of fresh halibut throughout most of the year, and a system of reporting and verification of catches devised and controlled by the fishers themselves.

ITQs may be criticized on the grounds that quota owners receive a valuable endowment denied other citizens. In practice ITQs are usually awarded to those with a history of participation in the fishery; if distributional fairness is deemed important, ITQs can be taxed or sold at auction.

An alternative approach to ITQs is the use of taxes, or royalties, imposed on the landed catch. By reducing the net price (p) paid to fishermen, a landing tax reduces the incentive for overfishing; a properly determined tax could – in principle, at least – achieve any desired target equilibrium stock level x. All resource rents are then retained by government, in the form of tax revenues.

That this solution to the problem of overfishing has seldom been tried comes as no surprise. Fishers would be no better off than before the tax programme; indeed they would initially be worse off. In terms of preserving resource rents, taxes and ITQs are theoretically equivalent in a deterministic world. In reality, the world of fisheries management is far from deterministic. The quantitative impact of a given landings tax could probably not be forecast with any degree of certainty. In contrast, ITQs can be effective provided only that the management authority has a reasonably accurate model of the biological resource. How to manage a fishery when even this knowledge is lacking is a difficult but important issue, which is discussed further below.

7.   An optimization model

How can an optimal harvesting strategy be identified for our generic fishery model? Let r denote the annual discount rate, and consider the present value of future economic rents.

$$PV = \int_0^\infty e^{-rt}(pqx - c)E \, dt \tag{8.6}$$

subject to

$$\frac{dx}{dt} = F(x) - qxE, \quad x \geq 0, \, E \geq 0 \tag{8.7}$$

The optimal effort/harvesting strategy can be determined by an elementary calculation (Clark, 1990, p. 50). First, there is an optimal equilibrium biomass $x = x^*$, determined by the equation.

$$F'(x^*) - \frac{c'(x^*)F(x^*)}{p - c(x^*)} = r \quad \text{where } c(x) = \frac{c}{qx} \tag{8.8}$$

The optimal strategy is then given by

$$E = E^*(x) = \begin{cases} E_{\max} & \text{if } x > x^* \\ F(x^*)/qx^* & \text{if } x = x^* \\ 0 & \text{if } x < x^* \end{cases} \tag{8.9}$$

(where $E_{\max}$ denotes maximum feasible effort). This effort strategy adjusts the biomass x to the optimal level x^* as rapidly as possible.

Equation (8.8) is a modified form of the well-known 'golden rule' of capital accumulation, $F'(x) = r$. (The modification consists of an additional term that accounts for the fact that the cost of consumption $h = qEx$

is a function of the current stock size x.) The optimal biomass x^* depends on the biological production function $F(x)$, as well as on the economic factors of price p, cost c, and discount rate r. Higher price/cost ratios p/c result in lower optimal stocks x^*. Higher discount rates also result in lower x^*; bionomic equilibrium x_{BE} occurs as the limiting case as $r \rightarrow +\infty$. If the resource owner discounts the future utterly, he will prefer to maximize short-term benefits at the expense of long-term sustainable returns, leading to the same result as uncontrolled exploitation (Scott, 1955).

How high do discount rates have to be for this effect to be important? Table 8.1 shows optimal equilibrium stock levels x^* calculated for Antarctic baleen whales, based on economic data from the 1950s, the heyday of Antarctic pelagic whaling (Clark and Lamberson, 1982). In this example, the low biological productivity of whale populations ($F'(x) < 0.05$ per annum) implies that discounting at normal rates has a strong influence on whale stocks. In short, whaling companies almost certainly preferred to deplete the resource and abandon whaling, rather than to maintain a sustainable whale fishery. While it lasted, whaling was one of the most lucrative fisheries ever. (Additional aspects of the whaling industry are described later.)

Table 8.1   *Optimal stock levels and optimal sustained yields for Antarctic baleen whales*

Discount rate (per cent per annum)	Optimal stock level (BWU)	Optimal sustainable yield (BWU per annum)
0	227 500	4905
3	141 200	4700
5	119 500	4190
10	85 300	3355
20	68 600	2845
$+\infty$	55 000	2370

Notes: Parameter values: r (intrinsic growth rate) = 0.05 yr^{-1};
K (carrying capacity) = 400 000 blue whale units (BWU); p (price) = \$7000 BWU^{-1};
c (cost of effort) = \$5000 (catcher day)$^{-1}$; q (catchability) = 1.3×10^{-5} (catcher day)$^{-1}$

Source: Clark and Lamberson (1982).

The above dynamic optimization model has never actually been used to manage a fishery – that is not its purpose. The model does suggest, however, that financial considerations may motivate the fishing industry to deplete their resource base because of dominant short-term interests. In the case of

Newfoundland cod, it appears that the 1992 collapse resulted from a combination of causes, including overcapacity, large-scale subsidization, industry insistence on maintaining large quotas, and ultimately a failure in recruitment (Myers et al., 1997). Undue optimism that the resource was highly stable may also have contributed to the disaster. As in most fisheries, the role of discounting was never considered explicitly in cod management models, but this by no means implies that the discounting of future revenues is irrelevant to the motivations of fishers. The fact that the future course of the fish stocks is uncertain (and increasingly so as the capacity of the fleets continues to expand) only exaggerates the fishers' desire to catch the available stock immediately. Management programmes that fail to take account of these universal economic motives will continue to fail, as they have failed in the past.

8.   Some bionomic complexities

The generic model discussed above is highly oversimplified in both biological and economic terms. Neglected biological aspects include age structure of fish populations, spatial distribution, multi-species and ecosystem dynamics, population genetics, and environmental factors and fluctuations. On the economic side, industry structure and dynamics, capital investment, markets and demand, technological change, pollution and habitat degradation all play important economic roles. Finally, the generic model presumes completely unrealistic levels of knowledge, certainty and determinism. Space limitations preclude a full discussion of all these topics, and the ensuing discussion is selective. Most of these complexities are poorly understood in general, and their effects on particular fisheries and management strategies are largely unknown. How to effectively manage fishery resources in the face of such lack of knowledge is perhaps the most important and difficult problem facing the fishing industry today.

Age structure

Let $N(t)$ denote the number (a continuous variable, for simplicity) of fish in a certain cohort. We have

$$\frac{dN}{dt} = -(M+F)N, \quad N(t_0) = R \tag{8.10}$$

where M and F denote natural and fishing mortality, respectively, and R denotes recruitment of the cohort to the fishery, at time t_0. Time $t = 0$ is taken as the birth of the cohort (so cohort age also equals t in this model). Total cohort biomass is

$$B(t) = N(t)w(t) \tag{8.11}$$

where $w(t)$ is the weight of a fish of age t. Yield per recruit from the cohort can be expressed as

$$Y(F) = \frac{1}{R} \int_{t_0}^{\infty} FB_F(t)dt \tag{8.12}$$

where the subscript F is used to emphasize that $B(t)$ in equation (8.11) depends on F.

A widely accepted criterion of optimal fishery exploitation is the so-called $F_{0.1}$ level of fishing mortality, defined as the value of F such that

$$Y'(F) = 0.1 Y'(0) \tag{8.13}$$

(where prime signifies the derivative). Originally proposed by J. Gulland (1968), the $F_{0.1}$ criterion was viewed as a method of keeping fishing mortality below the estimated MSY level, at which $Y'(F) = 0$. This would lower the unit costs of harvesting, and also provide positive protection for the fish populations, allowing a safety factor in the event of measurement errors in stock levels or actual catches.

In spite of its popularity, the $F_{0.1}$ management criterion has several important disadvantages. First, calculation of $F_{0.1}$ depends on an accurate knowledge of M (natural mortality), besides assuming that this parameter is independent of age t. But measuring M for a wild fish stock is notoriously difficult. Second, the yield-per-recruit characterization ignores any density-dependent stock–recruitment relationship. While the estimation of such relationships is also extremely difficult, the grounds for ignoring this aspect are shaky indeed. Finally, implementation of the estimated $F_{0.1}$ level of fishing mortality requires accurate current estimates of the stock size $N(t)$, another exceedingly difficult (and expensive) task for most marine fish stocks. Yet the above model has remained the principal scientific component of management advice for many important commercial fisheries, including Northern cod.

This discussion of the $F_{0.1}$ concept serves to indicate the wide gap that exists between what fisheries scientists need to know, and what they do know, or can know. The underlying level of uncertainty, though widely, if quietly, admitted by most fishery scientists, is seldom taken fully into account in designing management strategies. Dealing rationally with this uncertainty is rendered all the more difficult by the ever-persistent demands of the fishing industry for maximum quotas. Placed in a position of having to justify the need for reduced quotas, the scientist is at a great disadvantage relative to the economic and political power of the fishing industry. Severe overcapitalization often further exacerbates the problem, leading to greater demands for increased catch quotas. We turn next to this issue (bypassing for the moment many other biological complexities).

Capital investment
Fish stocks are harvested by fishing fleets, whose catches are processed by factories ashore or at sea. The costs of acquiring these capital assets can be large, and the losses from overexpansion can be considerable. Yet typically today's high-technology fishing fleets tend to be several times larger than needed for any sustainable harvest. The whaling nations, for example, constructed 26 pelagic factory fleets (processing factories with associated catchers) following the postwar resumption of Antarctic whaling. The estimated maximum sustained yield of Antarctic whales could have been captured by one, or at most two, such fleets. At several million US dollars per fleet, the cost of overcapacity was non-trivial in a capital-starved postwar world.

Although prewar whaling had reduced the Antarctic populations considerably, the whales in the Southern Ocean were still a valuable resource. Early entrants could recoup the cost of an entire fleet in one or two seasons of whaling. The temptations to enter the industry were great, and few companies worried about long-term conservation problems. The following model of optimal capital investment (Clark et al., 1979) can be used to estimate the optimal capitalization in postwar whaling fleets (Clark and Lamberson, 1982).

Maximize

$$PV = \int_0^\infty e^{-rt}(pqxE - cE - c_1 I)dt \qquad (8.14)$$

subject to

$$\frac{dx}{dt} = F(x) - qEx \qquad (8.15)$$

$$0 \leq E(t) \leq K_f(t) \qquad (8.16)$$

$$\frac{dK_f}{dt} = I - \gamma K_f \qquad (8.17)$$

$$I \geq 0 \qquad (8.18)$$

Here $K_f(t)$ denotes total fleet capacity, I is the rate of investment in fleet construction, $\gamma > 0$ is the depreciation rate, and c_1 is the cost of unit construction. Other symbols are as before. In this model, effort is limited by the existing fleet capacity $K_f(t)$; also, investment in K_f is assumed to be irreversible (see equation 8.18), on the grounds that whaling fleets are highly specialized and cannot be readily converted to other uses. (The case of completely reversible investment is trivial; for the possibility of disinvestment at a reduced scrap value see Clark et al., 1979.) Solution of the above model via optimal control theory is distinctly non-trivial, but a rigorous solution with fully synthesized feedback control is presented in the reference.

When applied to postwar Antarctic whaling, the above model predicts an optimal capacity in 1948 of approximately 13 fleets (Clark and Lamberson, 1982). This is about half of the actual capacity that entered the whale fishery in the postwar era. More interesting is the fact that the optimal capacity greatly exceeds the capacity (one fleet) required to harvest the optimal sustained yield. This large initial fleet is used to rapidly reduce the initial stock to the ultimate equilibrium, providing transitional revenues that more than repay the costs of the 12 surplus vessels (which are then simply tied up or scrapped).

As indicated by this model, the initial revenues obtainable from developing a previously unexploited (or lightly exploited) fish stock can attract large-scale investment in harvesting capacity. This initial capacity will be greater under competitive, open-access conditions than under present value maximization. But in any event, the built-up initial capacity may far exceed what is needed for the ultimate sustainable yield. Unless this excess capacity is removed once the initial stock reduction is completed, severe overfishing is likely to occur.

These capital dynamics – a sort of boom-and-bust cycle – are unusual for an economic system, but are a logical consequence of the biology of a renewable resource. In many fisheries the profits generated from the initial stock reduction greatly exceed those generated later during the sustainable-yield phase. (In the case of Antarctic whaling *all* the profits came from stock reduction. Economically speaking, whale stocks were treated as an exhaustible resource.) In fact the optimal dynamics are somewhat more complex than described above, in the sense that the optimal stock level is temporarily fished down below the long-term optimal equilibrium $\bar{X}$ (see Clark et al., 1979). This temporary, optimal overfishing is explained by the temporary, optimal surplus capacity, for which the opportunity costs of capital are irrelevant. (This would not be the case if the fishers had to rent the vessels from some U-fish company.)

Obviously the phase of overcapacity is a dangerous time for the fish population. Given that population and ecosystem dynamics are inevitably poorly understood, the likelihood of a disastrous, unexpected collapse of the fishery cannot be ignored. Various political, economic and psychological factors may further increase the likelihood of a collapse. The fact that annual catches experienced during the initial stage of exploitation cannot be continued indefinitely is difficult for the industry to comprehend. Steady increases in the efficiency of search and capture can mask the decline of the resource. In the Northern cod fishery, for example, catch-per-unit-effort statistics in the late 1980s failed to indicate any significant decrease in cod stocks, although subsequent analysis proved that these stocks were in extreme decline during this period (Myers et al., 1997).

Clearly many factors combine to bias fisheries towards overexpansion and overfishing. Most experienced fishers probably know that ultimate overfishing is highly likely. Consequently any sacrifice of current income in the hope of maintaining a sustainable fishery in the future is not likely to pay off. Because they know that fish are still available, it is only natural that fishers will want to catch them. Lack of well-defined access rights, excess industry capacity, together with major scientific uncertainty and inability to forecast future stock levels, all combine to make large current catches more attractive than the hope for a sustainable future.

9.   Countering uncertainty and bias: marine reserves

A new approach is desperately needed to reverse the trend of destruction of marine populations. The first step, recognizing that a fixed annual quota (based on estimated MSY) is not likely to be sustainable on a long-term basis because of natural fluctuations in recruitment, has now generally been taken. Responses include regular stock assessment and corresponding changes in TACs, as well as a safety margin in the TAC specification. Unless combined with some strategy (such as ITQs) for controlling competition and capacity, these methods are unlikely to succeed over the long term.

A new approach that has recently been recommended is the use of extensive marine reserves, or marine protected areas (Shackell and Willison, 1995; Lauck et al., 1998). Such reserves, in which fishing is completely prohibited, could serve as a source for replenishment of stocks that may be overfished elsewhere. The potential advantages of MPAs include:

- increased stability of fish stocks
- protection of spawning populations
- a hedge against uncertainty and management error
- an increase in the average age and size of fish caught
- reduced management costs
- protection of ocean biodiversity
- a venue for controlled marine research.

Fisheries management in the twentieth century has been based on a paradigm of the perfectibility of scientific knowledge and technique. The observed results of this philosophy are sufficient proof of its invalidity. Thousands of millennia of evolution by natural selection have produced – we don't fully understand how – highly resilient ecosystems. The use of marine reserves as a major component of fisheries management could transfer some of nature's good sense for our own long-term benefit. Designing and implementing truly sustainable management strategies for commercial fisheries is a challenge facing today's scientists, fishers and managers.

Many other aspects which have been excluded from this chapter because of space limitations also need to be addressed. Examples include multispecies interactions, economic intervention through taxation or subsidies and long-term evolutionary implications of exploitation and management. Protected marine reserves might help to defuse the current climate of perpetual crisis, allowing time to address some of these basic issues.

References

Clark, C.W. (1990), *Mathematical Bioeconomics: the Optimal Management of Renewable Resources*, New York: Wiley.

Clark, C.W. and R H. Lamberson (1982), 'An economic history and analysis of pelagic whaling', *Marine Policy*, **6**, 103–20.

Clark, C.W., F.H. Clarke and G.R. Munro (1979), 'The optimal exploitation of renewable resource stocks: problems of irreversible investment', *Econometrica*, **47**, 25–49.

Gordon, H.S. (1954), 'The economic theory of a common-property resource: the fishery', *Journal of Political Economy*, **62**, 124–42.

Gulland, J.A. (1968), 'The concept of marginal yield from exploited fish stocks', *Journal du Conseil International pour L'Exploration de la Mer*, **32**, 256–61.

Hardin, G. (1968), 'The tragedy of the commons', *Science*, **162**, 1243–7.

Holt, S.J. and L.M. Talbot (1978), 'New principles for the conservation of wild living resources', *Wildlife Monographs* no. 59.

Jansson, A.M., M. Hammer, C. Folke and R. Costanza (1994), *Investing in Natural Capital*, Washington, DC: Island Press.

Larkin, P.A. (1977), 'An epitaph for the concept of Maximum Sustainable Yield', *Transactions of the American Fisheries Society*, **106**, 1–11.

Lauck, T., C.W. Clark, M. Mangel and G.R. Munro (1997), 'Implementing the precautionary principle in fisheries management through marine reserves', *Ecological Applications*, **8** (1), Supplement, S72–S78.

Mangel, M. et al. (1996), 'Principles for the conservation of wild living resources', *Ecological Applications*, **6**, 338–62.

Myers, R.A., J.A. Hutchings and N.J. Burrowman (1997), 'Why do fish stocks collapse? The example of cod in Atlantic Canada', *Ecological Applications*, **7**, 91–106.

Scott, A.D. (1955), 'The fishery: the objectives of sole ownership', *Journal of Political Economy*, **63**, 116–24.

Shackell, N.L. and J.H.M. Willison (eds) (1995), *Marine Protected Areas and Sustainable Fisheries*, Acadia University, Wolfville, Nova Scotia, Canada: Centre for Wildlife and Conservation Biology.

9 Renewable resources: forestry
Thomas Aronsson and Karl-Gustaf Löfgren

1. Introduction

The proper economic management of forests is one of the classic problems in renewable resource economics. Already at the beginning of the nineteenth century there was a public discussion in Germany about the best time to cut down a forest stand and start a regeneration. The famous German location theorist, Johan von Thünen, attacked the problem in the third volume of *Der Isolierte Staat* (1826), which was published posthumously in 1863 by H. Schumacher. As it turned out, von Thünen's solution was not quite correct. In the middle of the century, however, the German forester, Martin Faustmann, in an attempt to rectify an error in a previous paper by von Gehren, posed the problem in a correct manner. He formulated it as a rotation problem, where a new generation follows upon each harvest. The land value, in this context, is found by calculating the present value of all future net revenues from the harvests. Von Gehren had only considered the case when the forest land is bare of trees, and in the calculations in his main text he used the geometric mean interest, whereas Faustmann used compound interest rates. Faustmann also studied the case in which the valuation problem starts with trees standing on the forest land.

To maximize land value, one has to choose the harvest time optimally. It is intuitively obvious that, if prices, the interest rate, and the biotechnology remain unchanged, then each rotation will, under an infinite time horizon, be of the same length. To see this, suppose that the first rotation has been optimally chosen conditional on all future rotations also being optimally chosen. Since no conditions relevant for forestry have changed, incentives remain unchanged, which means that the second rotation period will have the same length as the first. This result can be proved formally by mathematical induction. Both Faustmann and von Gehren realized this, but neither of them was able to state the correct conditions for an optimal rotation. It was Max Robert Pressler who, in 1860, introduced the concept of 'das Weizerprozent', (defined on page 125) as an important building block in a rule to decide whether trees are mature to harvest or not.

For a long time it was believed that either Faustmann or Pressler was the first to solve the optimal rotation problem in a correct manner. Very recently, however, new material has surfaced. It turns out that a Bishop of

Llandaff by the name of Watson, who was also a plantation owner, had already invented 'Jevons's wine ageing formula' in 1794. However, as explained below, this formula is not a suitable basis for forestry, because it misses the important fact that a forest must be cut down before a new rotation is started. William Marshall, an agriculturalist and honorary member of the newly formed 'Board of Agriculture and Internal Improvement', commented on Watson's writings and added the crucial missing component to his cutting rule. Marshall's paper was published in 1808, but there are indications that he already had the right idea in 1790. The reader is referred to Scorgie and Kennedy (1996) for further details.

This chapter is structured as follows. Section 2 concerns the classic problem of finding the optimal rotation period. In Section 3, we turn to the issue of so-called normal forests, that is, stands of equal area and one age class in each such area up to the optimal rotation period. We shall, in particular, examine the conditions for convergence to a unique optimal normal forest. Supply and demand curves for timber, as well as the timber market, are discussed in Section 4. We also review some of the empirical attempts to estimate supply and demand curves. Section 5 examines the forest management problem from another angle, by asking the question of when the (frequently made) assumption that forest owners maximize the present value of profits from forestry is a suitable starting point for empirical analysis. Finally, Section 6 discusses multiple-use considerations and, in particular, to what extent the socially optimal rotation period will diverge from a 'commercial' rotation, when the forest stand produces amenity values.

2. The optimal cutting rule

Trees are biological resources in the same way as fish and crops, and the principles of forest management should, under well-defined property rights, be analogous to what we have learnt from previous chapters on renewable resources. As we have just seen (in Chapter 8), a fish stock should, in a steady state, be kept at a level where the yield from an extra unit added to the stock coincides with the real interest rate from an extra unit harvested and invested in a bank account. This is a rule which is completely analogous to the fundamental principle of profit maximization in microeconomic theory: marginal revenue is equal to marginal cost. The marginal cost (yearly) of keeping the fish in the fishing bank is the opportunity cost of not putting the market value of the fish in a bank, that is, the ruling interest rate. The marginal benefit (yearly) of an extra unit of the biomass is what it contributes to the stock over the period, and, at the optimal steady state, it coincides with the interest rate. This is a steady-state criterion for the economically optimal stock. To preserve the stock at the steady-state level, we have to harvest the yearly yield generated at the steady-state level of the stock.

What distinguishes trees from fish is that, for the latter population, it is neither practically feasible nor theoretically necessary to distinguish between fish in different age classes. Instead we adapt the fishing-tackle to catch the more mature 'individuals'. On the other hand, it is both practically and theoretically crucial to keep track of the age distribution in forestry. In this case, it turns out to be more practical to focus on non-stationary conditions and decide the conditions for the optimal time to harvest an even-aged stand. We shall return later to steady-state considerations.

An approach which can be used to find the optimal economic decision is to consider marginal revenue and marginal costs. The marginal revenue from preserving the stand intact until the next period is the growth of the biomass over the period times the market price of timber. The opportunity cost of preserving the stand one more period is the interest on the revenue from selling the harvest, but also the interest on the value of the bare land. As we indicated above, the latter component of the marginal cost of not harvesting the trees now surfaces, since you cannot start a new rotation without cutting down the standing trees. The marginal cost of keeping the tree capital over the period is the interest on the capital. Hence, this cost of keeping the stand intact can be decomposed into two components: the interest on the value of the standing trees, and the interest on the value of the bare land.

We can sum up the discussion on the optimal rotation period under stationary external conditions (constant prices, constant technology, and a constant interest rate) in the following manner:

Theorem 1: (Faustmann–Marshall–Pressler) A forest stand should be harvested when the change in its value with respect to time is equal to the interest on the value of the stand plus the interest on the value of the bare forest land.

The proof of the theorem is straightforward. Let P be the (constant) timber price, r the (constant) interest rate and $f(T)$ the forest biomass as a function of time. If we, for notational convenience, neglect harvesting and regeneration costs, the land value (Faustmann formula) is written

$$V(T) = Pf(T)e^{-rT}\left[1 + e^{-rT} + (e^{-rT})^2 + \ldots\right] = \frac{Pf(T)e^{-rT}}{1 - e^{-rT}} \qquad (9.1)$$

The right-hand-side expression is explained by the fact that the present value of profits from *all* future rotations is an infinite series with a finite sum (due to discounting). The first-order condition for a maximum of the forest land value is obtained by differentiating equation (9.1) with respect to T and setting the derivative equal to zero. By rearranging the first-order condition, we obtain

$$Pf'(T^*) = rPf(T^*) + rV(T^*) \qquad (9.2)$$

where T^* is the length of the optimal rotation period. The left-hand side measures the change in the value of the stand, and the right-hand side is the sum of the interest on the value of the stand and the interest on the value of the bare land. Clearly, if the rate of change in the value of the stand (the marginal revenue from keeping the stand another year) exceeds the opportunity cost of the forest (the marginal cost of keeping the trees another period), the forest will be maintained for yet another period. Note that the value of the forest at harvesting is the value of the standing trees plus the value of the bare land. Hence the decomposition of the opportunity cost is artificial in the sense that this cost is simply the interest on the value of the forest land (including the standing trees).

According to the above interpretation of equation (9.2), it is clear that an alternative basis for choosing whether or not to cut the forest is to compare, on the one hand, the growth rate of the forest and, on the other, the interest on the value of the forest land (including the value of the standing trees) divided by the value of the stand. This gives Pressler's (1860) concept of 'das Weizerprozent', $i(T)$, which is defined as

$$i(T) = \frac{f'(T)}{f(T)} - \frac{re^{-rT}}{1 - e^{-rT}} \qquad (9.3)$$

meaning that the sign of $i(T)$ provides a qualitative indicator of whether or not to cut the stand. A comparison with equation (9.2) reveals that the cutting rule will be to harvest if $i(T) \leq 0$, while maintaining the forest if $i(T) > 0$.

What von Thünen missed in his analysis of the rotation problem, and what many prominent economists have overlooked after him, was the interest on the value of the land. His harvesting criterion, the equality between the rate of change in value, and the interest rate is more appropriate for wine ageing, which was treated by Jevons around 1870. You can, as a rule, start a new vintage of wine without getting rid of an already maturing one.

Since conditions are assumed to be stationary, it also follows that the value of the bare land is independent of whether it carries trees or not. Regardless of whether it is fully stocked or not, the difference in the value of the forest is attributable solely to differences in the stand value. This observation had already been made by Faustmann.

3.   Convergence towards the normal forest

A synchronized normal forest is a forest with stands of equal area, and exactly one stand in each age class up to the optimal rotation period. Foresters have long had a feeling that once the forest has been transformed into a normal forest, it is optimal to preserve the steady state, but formal proofs have not been available until fairly recently. Whether the forest, along an optimal programme from any initial composition, converges to a steady state has been even more unclear. Both problems are solved in two papers by Mitra and Wan (1985, 1986).[1]

The purpose of this section is to try to give the reader an intuitive feeling for the logic behind the Mitra and Wan convergence results. To this end, we start by noting that a necessary condition for a steady state or normal forest is that the same amount is harvested in each year. A convergence towards a normal forest, however, also means that the land areas containing trees of a given age class converge towards a common size. This is very difficult to handle in an intuitive manner, although it would be strange to end up in a situation in which the same amount is cut each year, at the same time as the area of the stand(s) that is (are) cut each year varies. If the technology is kept constant, such a situation means that different age classes are cut the same year. This sounds wrong if the net price is an increasing function of age.

We shall, however, disregard the age distribution here and treat the forest as a homogeneous biomass. It is, under these conditions, obvious that we can write the profit from forestry as a function of the cut. If this function is linear, it holds that a marginally increased cut in a period yields the same return independently of how much was cut initially, that is, there are constant returns to scale. Under constant returns to scale, there are neither gains from merging cuttings, nor from trying to even out the initial age distribution. It means that each forest stand should be cut down in the period when the present value of the stand is at its maximum. It also means that the harvesting point of time will be independent of the composition of the initial endowment, and the optimal rotation period of each stand will be determined by the rule in Theorem 1. Therefore, the following statement is true:

Theorem 2:   If the profit in each period is linear in the cut, it is optimal to treat the forest stand by stand. The optimal rotation period of each stand is equal to the Faustmann–Marshall–Pressler rotation period, and the forest will not converge towards the normal forest.

Theorem 2 is a theoretical justification for the old practice – initiated by, among others, Faustmann – of treating the forest management problem at the stand level. It means, for example, that if one starts with a bare tract of land and plants trees, the harvest will take place at the Faustmann–Marshall–Pressler age. If the tract is not bare, all trees older than or equal to this age will be cut down immediately, and, from the second period and onwards, only trees which reach the Faustmann–Marshall–Pressler age will be harvested.

The intuition behind Theorem 2 is also conveyed by Figure 9.1. Let c_1 and c_2 be the harvest 'today' and 'tomorrow' under an uneven cutting pattern generated by a non-uniform age distribution and a Faustmann–Marshall–Pressler solution. If we move to an even cutting pattern, we must diverge from the optimal rotation period and this involves an 'inoptimality loss'. However, since $\pi(\bar{c}) = \left[\pi(c_1) + \pi(c_2)\right]/2$, there is no additional revenue from an even cutting pattern, and it is not optimal to move towards the normal forest.

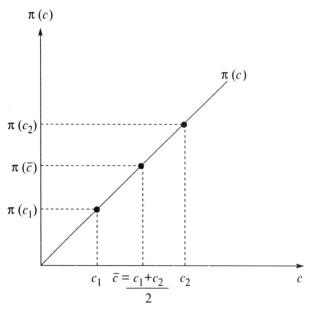

Figure 9.1   The periodic solution under a linear objective function

What about the realism of a profit which is linear in the cut? Given that prices are set in competitive markets, it is reasonable to assume that the revenue side is linear in the cut, but this is not necessarily true for the cost function. Up to a certain point it may be profitable to merge nearby cuttings, even if the stands consist of different age classes, as there are increasing returns to scale. After this point, marginal cutting costs increase with the volume cut, as there are decreasing returns to scale.

Decreasing returns to scale throughout implies that the profit in each period is strictly concave as a function of the cut, and the forest management problem can no longer be treated stand by stand. Similarly, if there are increasing returns to scale throughout, the profit is strictly convex in the cut. Since it is now worthwhile to merge cuttings in different age classes, one would not expect a convergence towards a normal forest. The remaining case is then the possible convergence towards the normal forest under a strictly concave profit expression. It turns out that the following claim is true:[2]

Theorem 3: (Mitra and Wan, 1986) When future profits are not discounted, and the profit in each period is strictly concave in the cut, an optimal programme will, from any initial situation, converge to a unique optimal normal forest. The yearly cut along the steady-state programme will be equal to the maximum sustainable yield, and the Faustmann–Marshall–Pressler rotation period is optimal.

In other words, if the interest rate is zero and the marginal profit from the last cubic metre of the harvest is decreasing, the composition of the forest land will asymptotically reach the normal forest. The intuition behind this result is, to some extent, clarified by Figure 9.2.

To interpret Figure 9.2, let $(c_1 + c_2)/2 = \bar{c}$ represent the yearly cut under an even cutting pattern resulting from a uniform age distribution. Obviously, the uniform cutting pattern is preferred $\pi(\bar{c}) > \big(\pi(c_1) + \pi(c_2)\big)/2$ to the non-uniform, indicating that it pays gradually to smooth out the age distribution of the forest. If the objective function is strictly concave and profits are not discounted, it is, loosely speaking, true that the total gain from a transformation to a more smooth cutting pattern is unbounded, while the opportunity cost along a path towards the normal forest is bounded. No wonder that the solution converges towards the normal forest. It can, however, be shown by a counter-example (see Mitra and Wan, 1986), that Theorem 3 is no longer true if the discount rate is positive. The intuitive reason is that a positive discount rate means that both gains and losses from a path towards the normal forest are bounded. If the adjustment loss is higher than the gain from smoothness, there will be no convergence towards the normal forest. Most foresters would, however, claim that the cost function is likely to have convex segments, due to, among other things, the fact that it pays to merge cuttings of nearby stands in different age classes. This may explain why we see very few normal forests in reality.

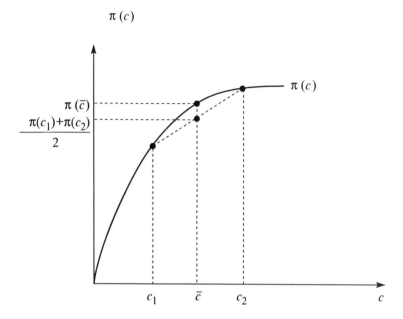

$$\pi(c)$$

$$\pi(\bar{c})$$

$$\frac{\pi(c_1)+\pi(c_2)}{2}$$

$$\pi(c)$$

$$c_1 \quad \bar{c} \quad c_2 \quad\quad c$$

Figure 9.2   Cutting pattern under a strictly concave objective function

4.   Towards empirical studies of the timber market

The above discussions have implicitly assumed that the prices of different assortments of timber, as well as the interest rate, remain constant over time. However, the typical pattern of prices and quantities in the aggregate timber market is the one shown in Figure 9.3, which means that prices and quantities might vary considerably over time.

Economists often interpret such a scatter of points as representing inter-action between a demand and a supply curve as indicated by the *DD* and *SS* curve in the diagram. However, to understand the aggregate supply and demand, it is necessary to begin by considering the behaviour of individual agents in the market.

The supply of timber

This section extends the discussion of forest management by formally introducing the concept of timber supply. A simple way to accomplish this task is to use a finite time-horizon model. We will show, among other things, that the short-run timber supply curve has a positive slope, provided that the forest owner maximizes the present value of the cut.

To formalize, let $p = (p_1 ... p_n)$ be a vector of net present-value prices (discounted to the present by the appropriate discount factor) per cubic metre

Price

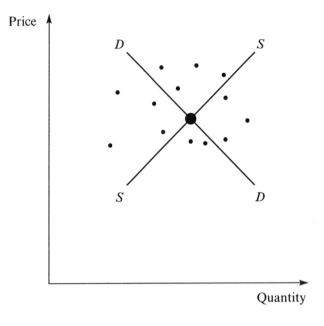

Quantity

Figure 9.3   The aggregate timber market

of timber, and let $c' = (c_1 \ldots c_n)$ be a vector of supplies from period 1 to period n. The present value of a cutting programme, Π, can now be written as the vector product $\Pi = \mathbf{p}c$. Very compactly, we can state the optimization problem of the present-value-maximizing forest owner in the following manner:

$$\underset{c}{\text{Max}}\ \mathbf{p}c$$

$$\text{subject to } c \in C \qquad\qquad (9.4)$$

Here C represents the biotechnology of the forest, which means that it contains technological restrictions, such as cutting technology, as well as information about the biological growth conditions and the initial endowment of stands. The problem of the present-value-maximizing forest owner is to choose a vector of cuts inside the feasible cutting possibilities represented by the set C, such that the present value of the cut is as large as possible. The solution to this problem is a vector of supplies from the first period to the last. The supply vector is, of course, dependent on the vector of present-value prices, and we can write:

$$c^* = c^*(p) \text{ and } \Pi^* = pc^*\,(p) \qquad\qquad (9.5)$$

where the superscript * denotes an optimal programme. The supply in period i can be written:

$$c_i^* = c_i^*(p) \tag{9.6}$$

We want to know the direction in which the supply changes in period i, when the price in period i increases. The simplest way to answer this question is to use a revealed-preference argument.

Let c^* be the optimal programme when prices are p^*, and c^{**} the optimal programme when prices are p^{**}. It is now obviously true that:

$$p^*c^* \geq p^*c^{**} \text{ and also that } p^{**}c^{**} \geq p^{**}c^*$$

In other words, the optimal programme gives at least as high a present value as a programme which is optimal at another price vector. Adding one expression to the other and rearranging yields:

$$(p^* - p^{**})(c^* - c^{**}) \geq 0$$

If the only thing that distinguishes p^* from p^{**} is the price in period i, we have:

$$(p_i^* - p_i^{**})(c_i^* - c_i^{**}) \geq 0$$

This equation tells us that if the price difference is positive (*ceteris paribus*), then it must be true that the quantity difference is non-negative. If we disregard the unlikely case when the latter is zero, we can conclude that the supply curve is upward sloping like the one drawn in Figure 9.3. The reader has, of course, already noted that the structure of the present-value-maximization problem does not differ from the standard profit-maximization problem in the theory of the firm, which also means that the present-value function:

$$\Pi(p) = \max_c pc$$

subject to $c \in C$ \tag{9.7}

shares all the properties of the profit function in the theory of the firm and, as we just have seen, the property that the supply curve is upward sloping. The reader interested in more details is referred to Johansson and Löfgren (1985).

An alternative question is what happens to the rotation period and timber supply if the price of timber is increased by a constant proportion for all future periods. To start with, if all prices, including harvesting costs, are increased by the same percentage, the rotation period remains unchanged. The intuition is that both marginal revenue and marginal cost increase by the same percentage, and they are, therefore, equalized at the original rotation period. If only the prices for wood, but not the harvesting costs, are increased, the revenues from waiting yet another year, as well as the opportunity cost of the standing trees (interest on the value of the stand), will increase. However, the opportunity cost of the bare land will increase by even more. The reason is that revenues are scaled up, while costs are kept constant. To compensate for the increased marginal cost, the rotation period is shortened to increase marginal growth and, indirectly, marginal revenue. The immediate effect of a shorter rotation period is that less wood will in the long run be supplied from the stand. On the other hand, forestry has become more profitable and it is likely that more land will be transformed into forest land. The long-run effect on wood supply is, therefore, ambiguous. Thought experiments like the one above are frequently analysed under the heading the 'long-run supply of timber' (see, for example, Binkley, 1987 or Clark, 1976). The previous more standard supply considerations are referred to as the 'short-run supply of timber' or simply the 'supply of timber'.

The long-run timber supply has also been studied by making use of both cost and engineering data. The classic paper is by Henry Vaux (1954), who constructed a 'quasi-supply curve' for sugar pine resources in California. The idea is to produce a relationship between timber prices and the number of cubic metres which can be harvested profitably. This engineering approach cannot be used to say anything about the short-run supply; rather it tells us about the size of the economically available forest resources. For a recent survey of most aspects of timber supply, readers are referred to Wear and Parks (1994).

The demand for timber
To explain the point scatter in Figure 9.3, we have to derive the demand curve and also estimate both demand and supply curves from empirical data. The derivation of the demand curve can be dealt with very quickly. Timber and pulpwood are demanded as input in the forest industry. This means that we can use the theory of the firm, and conclude that the input demand curve is downward sloping. We can derive this result formally by a simple revealed-preference argument like the one presented above.

The timber market
Econometric analyses of the timber market require us to identify and estimate both the demand and supply curves. The identification problem is

crucial. To identify the demand curve, we have to use the fact that the supply curve depends on entities such as felling costs, which do not affect the position of the demand curve. The principle is to use this shifter to cut out points along the fixed demand curve. This is illustrated in Figure 9.4, where an increase in felling costs will shift the supply curve from S_1S_1 to S_2S_2 along the demand curve D_1D_1. In the same manner, we need a variable such as the price of lumber, which shifts the demand curve but not the supply curve, to identify the latter (for example, the shift in the demand curve from D_1D_1 to D_2D_2 along the supply curve S_1S_1).

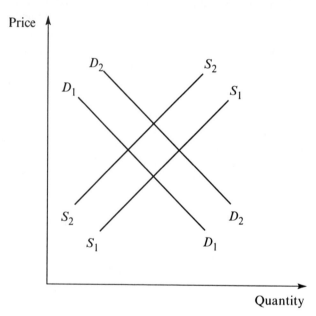

Figure 9.4   Identification of supply and demand

One of the first papers using econometric methods in the context of a timber market model was Ruist and Svennilson (1948) who, in a study of the forest industry in the northern parts of Sweden, presented results from estimation of the timber supply curve. In the US the first econometric models were 'built' and estimated in the 1950s. Among the precursors were Stan Pringle and Robinson Gregory. In 1954 Pringle, a biometrician who turned into a forest economist, wrote a thesis at Syracuse University on the demand for newsprint, computing all the regression coefficients with an electrical calculator. Gregory (1960) developed an econometric model of the market for hardwood flooring, with monthly data and recursive equations to handle the 'endogeneity problem' (that is, supply and demand are determined simultaneously, which precludes that ordinary least squares will estimate the parameters consistently). Pringle's student, William McKillop wrote a thesis at Berkeley, which may be one of the most cited studies in forest economics (McKillop, 1967), in which he developed a model which simultaneously dealt with the whole forest sector, from the supply of logs to the demand for final products.

A second generation of studies came in the 1970s. Examples are Adams (1974, 1977) and Robinson (1974), dealing with timber markets in the Douglas fir region in North America. However, the perhaps most noteworthy 'innovation' during the decade was made by Richard Haynes (Haynes, 1975), who, basing his work on a paper by the Nobel laureate Samuelson (1952), developed a model where the space and transportation costs had an essential role to play. The paper used linear programming methods to compute spatial equilibria within the US softwood market. The collaboration of Adams and Haynes led to the TAMM model (Adams and Haynes, 1980), which has been one of the most widely used models for forest policy analysis in the US. The TAMM model was designed to deal mostly with the solid wood sector, so a parallel model was built to handle the pulp and paper industry. This model was initially referred to as PAPYRUS (see Gilles and Buongiorno, 1987), and currently as the NAPAP model (see Buongiorno, 1996).

Clearly, empirical models of the forest sector can be used for many purposes. For example, some of the models mentioned above have been used in connection with the development of policy. However, leaving policy issues aside, an empirical study has at least two aims. One would be to test the theory. Is the demand curve downward sloping and the supply curve upward sloping? A second aim would be to assess how sensitive timber supply and demand are to changes in prices. Typically, this is measured by elasticities, that is, how many per cent supply (demand) is increased (decreased) when the timber price increases by 1 per cent.

To illustrate, consider a paper by Brännlund et al. (1985), which concerns the markets for sawtimber and pulpwood in Sweden. Let us begin by discussing own-price effects, that is, how the supply and demand in the sawtimber (pulpwood) market react to changes in the sawtimber (pulpwood) price. The estimates suggested an own-price elasticity of sawtimber supply equal to 0.6, meaning that a shift in demand for sawtimber, which increases the sawtimber price by 10 per cent, will increase supply by 6 per cent. Similarly, the own-price elasticity of sawtimber demand was estimated to −1.0, that is, a shift in the supply curve, which increases the timber price by 10 per cent, will reduce demand by 10 per cent. These results also imply that the sawtimber supply is upward sloping, while the demand is negatively sloped, which is what the theory predicts.

As recognized by Brännlund et al., the sawtimber market is naturally connected to the pulpwood market, since sawtimber and pulpwood are produced jointly. It is, therefore, appropriate to estimate supply and demand conditions in these markets simultaneously. Moreover, it is conceivable that the pulpwood market, due to relatively few buyers and many sellers, is more imperfect than the sawtimber market. In their analysis, Brännlund et al. treated the pulpwood market as a monopsony (many sellers and one buyer; the pulp and paper industry). The own-price elasticity of pulpwood supply was estimated to be 0.7. Turning to cross-price effects, an increased pulpwood price was found to have a negative impact on the sawtimber supply, while the reverse effect, from sawtimber price to pulpwood supply, was found to be negative but statistically insignificant.

5.   Why maximize present value?
So far we have without 'proof' used present-value maximization as the objective of the forest owner (firm or non-industrial, private forest owner). The reason is that it is, under certain conditions, possible to prove that present-value maximization gives the relevant information about how the consumption possibilities of the forest owner change as a result of the forest management decisions: for the forest owner to maximize utility, it is necessary (but not sufficient) to maximize present value. The important notion in this respect is the perfect capital market, where it is possible to borrow and lend any amount at a constant interest rate. We also require perfect certainty, and that the forest has no value to the owner other than as a source of revenue. Under a perfect capital market, it is possible to show that an investment with a positive (negative) present value unambiguously increases (reduces) the intertemporal consumption possibilities of the investor. Given that this is true, it is self-evident that it is advantageous to design the investment such that its present value is maximized. A forest is an investment in a renewable resource, and it should, therefore, be managed so that its present value is maximized.

The idea that investment and consumption decisions can be separated in a perfect capital market is frequently referred to as Fisher's separation theorem, after the American economist Irving Fisher who had the fundamental insight already at the beginning of this century. More precisely:

Theorem 4   (Fisher's separation theorem): If the capital market is perfect, investment decisions can be separated from consumption decisions, and investments can be ranked according to their present values.

Note that the theorem means that we can recommend an investment decision independently of the preferences of the investor. If the requirements on which the theorem is based are not fulfilled (for example if the market has one or many imperfections), the forest owner does not necessarily maximize utility by maximizing the present value. An analysis of timber supply requires, in this case, that the management decision be incorporated into an explicit utility-maximizing setting. This has at least two important implications. First, the properties of timber supply will, in general, reflect the theory of the consumer rather than the theory of the firm. This means, among other things, that timber price changes will involve both substitution and income (or wealth) effects. Second, differences in timber supply among individuals will not only depend on differences in prices, interest rates, biotechnology and endowments; they will also depend on demographic differences.

In the supply studies mentioned above, the supply functions are based on the validity of the present-value criterion, and they do not contain arguments other than prices and other general economic indicators. The results are, in general, consistent with the theory. However, the models cannot be set up in a way that really challenges the present-value hypothesis, since data are aggregate data. For this purpose, data on individual suppliers are necessary. In Kuuluvainen (1989) and Kuuluvainen and Salo (1991), Finnish survey data on non-industrial private forest owners are used to test the present-value hypothesis. This is done by introducing variables which should not affect timber supply under present-value maximization, such as the age, wealth and non-forest income of the owner. Most of these variables show up as strongly significant in the Tobit short-run supply equation, thus rejecting a strong version of the present-value-maximization hypothesis. Therefore, even if present-value maximization may be a reasonable microfoundation, when the analysis is concerned with aggregates (since demographic differences tend to disappear in the aggregate), it may not be a suitable basis for analysing the supply behaviour of private non-industrial forest owners.

6. Multiple-use considerations

A forest can, of course, have other values than pure timber values, both to society as a whole and to the forest owner. Virgin forests are important for the preservation of wildlife, but have, in addition, an extra value due to the irreversibility of the harvesting decision. Clearly if society's willingness to pay for preserving the virgin forest is greater than the present value from harvesting the trees, the forest should be preserved. There is no simple manner in which this willingness to pay can be estimated, but one possibility is to use the contingent valuation method. Roughly speaking, a representative sample of the population is asked for their maximum willingness to pay to preserve the forest intact. The answers are weighted together to the level of the whole population, and compared with the present value of the optimal harvesting programme. If the former is greater than the latter, the trees are not cut. An empirical study of this nature is Kriström (1990).

Even if the forest is harvested, the harvesting decision should, under multiple-use considerations, reflect the amenity values and/or other public goods properties of the stands. More specifically, the optimal rotation period will be affected by multiple-use considerations, as was shown by Hartman (1976).[3] To understand the principles involved, let us use the model in Section 2 and add an instantaneous environmental benefit in monetary terms, $g(T)$, which is assumed to be a function of the age of the trees. The social objective is now to choose a rotation period that maximizes the sum of the present value of profits from forestry and the present value of environmental benefits. The objective function is written:[4]

$$W(T) = V(T) + \frac{\int_0^T e^{-rs}g(s)ds}{1 - e^{-rT}} \tag{9.8}$$

The first term, $V(T)$, is the present value of profits from forestry as defined by equation (9.1), while the second term is the present value of the environmental benefits over all future rotation periods. The first-order condition becomes

$$a(T^v) + g(T^v) - r\frac{\int_0^{T^e} e^{-rs}g(s)ds}{1 - e^{-rT^e}} = 0, \tag{9.9}$$

where $a(T) = Pf'(T) - rPf(T) - rV(T)$, and T^v is the length of the socially optimal rotation period (for the model). The following result turns out to be true:

Theorem 5: If $W(T)$ is continuously differentiable and strictly concave in T, it follows that $T^v > T^*$, $T^v = T^*$ or $T^v < T^*$, depending on whether $g(T)$ is increasing, constant or decreasing in T.

As in Section 2, T^* refers to the Faustmann–Marshall–Pressler rotation. To see the result in the theorem, note that from strict concavity of $W(T)$, we have $T^v \geq (<)T^*$, depending on whether

$$a(T^*) + g(T^*) - r\frac{\int_0^{T^*} e^{-rs}g(s)ds}{1 - e^{-rT^*}} \geq (<) 0$$

Clearly, if $g(T)$ is constant (that is, does not vary with T) the last two terms on the left-hand side would cancel, implying that T^* is the optimal solution. Similarly, since

$$g(T^*) - r\frac{\displaystyle\int_0^{T^*} e^{-rs}g(s)ds}{1 - e^{-rT^*}} > (<) \, 0$$

if $g(T)$ is strictly increasing (decreasing) in T, we have proved Theorem 5.

The interpretation is straightforward. Suppose first that amenity values are independent of the age of the trees. Clearly, if we disregard cost considerations, this would not affect the optimal rotation period; it would just add an extra (constant) value to the forest. This means that we maximize the social objective function, $W(T)$ in the example above, by maximizing $V(T)$, and the socially optimal rotation period coincides with the Faustmann–Marshall–Pressler rotation period. On the other hand, if a forest consisting of younger trees is more valuable than the same land with older trees, the obvious way to reap the benefits from this would be to shorten the rotation period below the Faustmann–Marshall–Pressler rotation period. Finally, in the most realistic case, when old stands are more valuable than young, the optimal rotation period should, according to the same principles, be lengthened in comparison with a rotation period based solely on timber values.

The above reflections on multiple use of forests disregard, to a large extent, the implementation problems. On the other hand, these are neither more difficult nor more simple than many other public goods considerations. Direct regulations have, so far, been the most frequently used practical policy.

Notes

1. Similar, but slightly more incomplete, results are obtained by Heaps (1984) in a continuous-time optimal control model.
2. The theorem is related to the result from continuous-time optimal control theory, that the optimal control is globally asymptotically stable, that is, converges to a steady state, provided that the discount rate is sufficiently small. See Brock and Malliaris (1989), ch. 5.
3. See also Bowes and Krutilla (1993).
4. This example is based on a paper by Johansson and Löfgren (1988).

References

Adams, D. (1974), 'Forest product prices and national timber supply in the Douglas fir region', *Forest Science*, **20**, 243–59.

Adams, D. (1977), Effects of national forest timber harvest on softwood stumpage, lumber, and plywood markets: an econometric analysis', Oregon State University, *Forest Research Laboratory Research Bulletin*, **15**, Corvallis, OR.

Renewable resources: forestry 139

Renewable resources: forestry 139

Adams, D. and R. Haynes (1980), 'The 1980 softwood timber assessment model: structure projections, and policy simulations, *Forest Science Research Monograph*, no. 22.

Binkley, C. (1987), 'Economic models of timber supply', in Kallio, Dykstra and Binkley (eds), *The Global Forest Sector: An Analytical Perspective*, New York: John Wiley and Sons.

Bowes, M.D. and J.V. Krutilla (1993), 'Multiple use management of public forest lands', ch. 2 in A.V. Kneese, and J.L. Sweeney (eds), *Handbook of Natural Resource and Energy Economics*, Vol. II, Amsterdam: North-Holland.

Brännlund, R., P.O. Johansson and K.G. Löfgren (1985), 'An econometric analysis of timber supply in Sweden', *Forest Science*, **31**, 595–606.

Brock, W. and A.G. Malliaris (1989), *Differential Equations, Stability and Chaos in Dynamic Economics*, Amsterdam: North-Holland.

Buongiorno, J. (1996), 'Forest sector modeling: A synthesis of econometrics, mathematical programming, and system dynamic methods', *International Journal of Forecasting*, **12**, 329–43.

Clark, C.W. (1976), *Mathematical Bioeconomics: The Optimal Management of Renewable Resources*, New York: John Wiley and Sons.

Faustmann, M. (1849), 'Berechnung des Wertes welchen Waldboden sowie noch nicht haubare Holtzbestände für die Waldwirtschaft besitzen', *Allgemeine Forst- und Jagdzeitung*, **25**, 441–55.

Gilles, J.K. and J. Buongiorno (1987), 'Papyrus: A model of the North American pulp and paper industry, *Forest Science Research Monograph*, no. 28.

Gregory, G.R. (1960), 'A statistical investigation of factors affecting the market of hardwood flooring', *Forest Science*, **6**, 123–34.

Hartman, R. (1976), 'The harvesting decision where a standing forest has value', *Economic Inquiry*, **14**, 52–8.

Haynes, R.W. (1975), *A Dynamic Spatial Equilibrium Model of the Softwood Timber Economy with Demand Equations Specified*, PhD thesis, NC State University, Raleigh.

Heaps, T. (1984), 'The forestry maximum principle', *Journal of Economic Dynamics and Control*, **7**, 131–51.

Jevons, S. (1871), *The Theory of Political Economy*, London: Macmillan.

Johansson, P.O. and K.G. Löfgren (1985), *The Economics of Forestry and Natural Resources*, Oxford: Basil Blackwell.

Johansson, P.O. and K.G. Löfgren (1988), 'Where is the Beef? A Reply to Price', *Journal of Environmental Management*, **27**, 337–9.

Kriström, B. (1990), 'Valuing environmental benefits using the contingent valuation method: An econometric analysis', *Umeå Economic Studies*, no. 216, Umeå University.

Kuuluvainen, J. (1989), *Nonindustrial Private Timber Supply and Credit Rationing*, Swedish University of Agricultural Sciences, Department of Forest Economics, Report 85.

Kuuluvainen, J. and J. Salo (1991), 'Timber supply and life cycle harvest of nonindustrial private forest owners; an empirical analysis of the Finnish case, *Forest Science*, **37**, 1011–29.

Marshall, W. (1808), *A Review of the Reports to the Board of Agriculture: From the Northern Department of England*, London: Longman, Hurst, Rees, Orme.

McKillop, W.M. (1967), 'Supply and demand for forest products: An econometric study', *Hilgardia*, **38**, 1–32.

Mitra, T. and H.J. Wan (1985), 'Some theoretical results on the economics of forestry', *Review of Economic Studies*, **52**, 263–82.

Mitra, T. and H.J. Wan (1986), 'On the Faustmann solution to the forest management problem, *Journal of Economic Theory*, **49**, 229–49.

Pressler, M.R. (1860), 'Aus der Holzzuwachslehre', *Allgemeine Forst- und Jagdzeitung*, **36**, 173–91.

Pringle, S.L. (1954), *An Econometric Analysis of the Demand for Newsprint in the United States*, PhD dissertation, Syracuse University.

Robinson, V.L. (1974), 'An econometric model of softwood lumber and stumpage markets', *Forest Science*, **20**, 171–9.

Ruist, E. and I. Svennilson (1948), *Den norrländska skogsindustrins konjunkturkänslighet under mellankrigsperioden*, Stockholm: Industrins Utredningsinstitut.

Samuelson, P.A. (1952), Spatial price equilibrium and linear programming, *American Economic Review*, **42**, 283–303.

Scorgie, M. and J. Kennedy (1996), 'Who Discovered the Faustmann Condition?', *History of Political Economy*, **28**, 77–80.

Thünen, J.H. von (1828), *Der Isolierte Staat*, Vol 3. Published posthumously in 1863 by H. Schumacher.

Vaux, H.J. (1954), 'The economics of young growth sugar pine resources', Berkeley, University of California, Division of Agricultural Sciences, Bulletin, no. 78.

Wear, D. and P.K. Parks (1994), 'The economics of timber supply; an analytical synthesis of modeling approaches', *Natural Resource Modeling*, **8**, 199–223.

10 The economics of water use

David Zilberman and Leslie Lipper

1. Introduction

Water resources serve multiple purposes in meeting human needs and their allocation has been subject to dispute throughout man's history. Rapid population growth has resulted in increased water scarcity, and interest in the pursuit of improved productivity in water resource management. A substantial literature on the economics of water resource management and policy making has been generated, resulting in considerable advances in the field of resource and environmental economics. (See Boggess et al., 1993 and Young and Haveman, 1985 for a good review of recent literature.) This paper overviews the main research issues in the economics of water use,[1] with an emphasis on models unique to water management.

On the global level, irrigated agriculture is by far the largest consumer of water among various users, and concern over improving water use efficiency in this sector has been widely reflected in the water economics literature. The emphasis in this chapter is on water use in agriculture and its impact on the environment because much of the political debate in recent years has centred on use in this sector, and many of the conceptual and methodological issues that have been raised in addressing agricultural water issues apply in other sectors as well.

We begin our overview by looking at water use efficiency at the farm level. We present an economic model of on-farm water use incorporating environmental and technical factors which influence farmers' irrigation management choices. In Section 3 we move to the regional level and the issue of water allocation, with an analysis of the potential for institutional reform to improve efficiency. We introduce a framework for assessing when and to what extent gains can be realized by transitioning from non-market- to market-based systems of allocation.

A major source of inefficiency in water management is losses from conveyance systems. As water is moved from upstream sources through canal systems to downstream users, losses occur due to evaporation and percolation. In Section 4 we present a model of optimal conveyance management which captures the different incentives facing upstream and downstream water users. We conclude the section with a brief discussion of the necessity and basis for collective action in water management. In the following section we turn to the economic analysis of groundwater, which relies heavily on models of renewable and non-renewable resources. In the final section, we overview methodologies of water project assessment, incorporating the results of the previous sections in a combined policy framework.

2.   Farm-level water allocation decisions

One of the most important issues facing policy makers is an assessment of the response of irrigated agriculture to increased water scarcity as reflected in increased water prices or reduced aggregate supplies of water. Evidence has shown that increases in water prices and reductions in water availability result in the adoption of water conservation technologies and the reduction of water use within existing practices, as well as changes in cropping patterns (Zilberman et al., 1994). In this section we present a simple farm-level model which illustrates the interaction of economic and environmental variables in determining the choice of irrigation technologies and the rate of water use.

A key concept necessary for the analysis of farmers' water use patterns is that of 'effective water'. The water that is actually utilized by the crop is effective water and is commonly measured by crop evapotranspiration coefficients (ET) (Stewart et al., 1974; Grimm et al., 1987). The total amount of water applied to the crop comes from several sources, including water applied for irrigation, rainwater, and run-on water that is drained from other fields. The residual quantity of applied water which is not utilized by the crop becomes surface run-off or percolates to groundwater.

The distinction between applied water and effective water gives rise to the concept of water efficiency. In cases where the only source of water is applied water, water use efficiency is the ratio between effective and applied water (Caswell and Zilberman, 1985, 1986). Water efficiency is highly dependent on the ability of the soil to store water which can be utilized by the crop over time. Water efficiency is typically higher on heavier clay soils which retain applied water, in comparison with sandy soils through which water passes rapidly. Climate and water quality also affect water efficiency. Through their effect on water efficiency, these factors influence irrigation technology choices (Boggess et al., 1993; Caswell and Zilberman, 1985).

To illustrate how land quality and effective water influence farmers' choice of irrigation technology and water use, we turn to the following simple model. A farmer produces a crop with the following per acre production function:

$$y = f(e)$$

where y denotes output per acre and e is effective water. The production function $f(\cdot)$ has the regular properties of a neoclassical production function: $f(0) = 0, f'(\cdot) > 0, f''(\cdot) < 0$.

Let a_i denote applied water per acre under technology i, and α is the land quality index, assuming values from 0 to 1 from poor to good quality. For simplicity, assume two technologies: a traditional technology ($i = 0$) and a modern technology ($i = 1$). Modern irrigation technologies, which permit the application of small quantities of water over long periods of time, result in higher irrigation efficiencies – particularly on poor-quality soils which are incapable of retaining applied water. Thus, effective water under each irrigation type is a function of soil quality: $e = e_i(\alpha)$. Irrigation effectiveness is defined as:

$$h_i(\alpha) = e_i(\alpha)/a_i(\alpha)$$

and

$$1 > h_1 > h_0 > 0$$

The cost per acre associated with each technology is k_i. This cost includes annualized repayment of investment costs and annual operating costs. The modern technology is assumed to be more capital-intensive, so that $k_1 > k_0$.

The profit-maximizing choice of water application rate and irrigation technology is solved via a two-stage procedure. First the optimal amount of water for each technology is chosen and then the more profitable irrigation technology. Let $\Pi_i(a)$ denote quasi-rent (exclusive of land rent) per acre of technology i, determined according to the following choice problem:

$$\Pi_i(a) = \underset{a_i}{\mathrm{Max}} \left\{ Pf\left(h_i(\alpha) \cdot a_i\right) - wa - k_i \right\}$$

where P is the output price and w the price of applied water. The first-order condition is:

$$Pf'h_i - w = 0$$

The price of effective water is the price of applied water divided by the irrigation efficiency (w/h_i), so optimal production occurs where the marginal product of applied water is equal to the price of effective water: $Pf' = w/h_i$. The price of effective water is lower under the modern technology due to the higher irrigation efficiency; therefore higher levels of effective water will be used and higher yields may be obtained.

The optimal water application under each technology determines the quasi-rent associated with the technology (Π_i), and the technology with the highest quasi-rent is selected, assuming it is non-negative. The quasi-rent difference between the two technologies can be written as:

$$\Delta\Pi = P\Delta y - w\Delta a - \Delta k$$

The modern technology will be selected in cases where the increased profits from higher yields or lower water costs offset the higher costs associated with adoption of the technology. These results indicate that modern technology adoption will increase with increasing water or output prices. In addition, modern technology adoption is more likely to occur with poor land quality, due to the high price of effective water under the traditional technology, and the land-augmenting qualities of the modern technology. The impact of modern technology adoption on aggregate applied water use levels depends on the elasticity of the marginal productivity of water (EMP),[2] which measures how responsive the crop is to further irrigation. Under most conditions, adoption results in both a decrease in overall water use and an increase in crop yields.

This model can be extended (Caswell et al., 1990) to illustrate how irrigation technology choice affects the generation of negative environmental externalities in the form of agricultural drainage water. Irrigation water that is not used by crops is a major source of pollution, as it may result in water-logging, which injures and may eventually preclude agricultural production. By extending our simple model of technology choice and water use, we gain insight into the incentives (or lack thereof) for farmers to reduce agricultural drainage flows.

Let the pollution coefficient associated with water residuals be $g_i(\alpha)$, which is the fraction of water applied by technology i, on land of quality α, that is not utilized by the crop and which is environmentally damaging. The pollution coefficient is defined as:

$$g_i(\alpha) \le 1 - h_i(\alpha)$$

Since the modern technology is more water-efficient, it is reasonable to assume that in most cases it has a lower pollution coefficient, that is, $g_1(\alpha) < g_0(\alpha)$.

If the producer bears the costs associated with the pollution arising from water residual accumulation, the individual's profit-maximization problem becomes:

$$\Pi_i(\alpha) = \underset{\alpha_i}{\text{Max}} \left\{ Pf\big(h_i(\alpha) \cdot a_i\big) - wa_i - k_i - \big(x \cdot g_i(\alpha) \cdot a_i\big) \right\}$$

with x the cost per unit of pollution. Usually, however, this cost is a production externality, so farmers do not incorporate the effects of their water use decisions on drainage and water accumulation. Instead, x could represent a tax on the pollution associated with water residuals.

The imposition of a pollution tax increases the profitability of adopting the water-conserving technology, especially in situations where the initial costs of pollution per unit of water are large relative to water price. As land quality increases, the benefit of modern technology adoption decreases, as the quasi-rent differential between the two technologies declines.

Frequently, the imposition of a pollution tax on agricultural drainage is not feasible due to the difficulty in identifying and monitoring the polluters. An alternative policy may be to subsidize irrigation technologies, which result in reduced agricultural drainage flows. Subsidization of the modern technology will increase the quasi-rent associated with its adoption, leading to higher adoption rates and lower amounts of agricultural drainage. For an in-depth discussion of the control of non-point source pollution, see the chapter by Xepapadeas in this volume (Chapter 36).

3. Surface water allocation mechanisms
Water rights regimes determine the allocation of surface water and, in some cases, ground water. In general, there are two main types of water rights: riparian and prior appropriation. The riparian system allows individuals bordering a body of water to share the water, but disallows diversion of the water to areas further from the source. With the prior appropriation system, the rights of users are queued according to the time at which they first start diverting water. Users are allowed to divert water for 'beneficial' uses; however they are not allowed to sell it (Cuzan, 1983; Gardner, 1983).

In practice, both systems are queuing systems that set a minimal price on water use for individuals with water rights. These systems were established in response to historical conditions of abundant water supplies, allowing all rights holders to obtain sufficient supplies. However, under current conditions of increased scarcity, inefficient water allocation may result as senior rights holders can divert water for low-productivity uses, precluding higher-productivity uses among junior users. Greater productivity could be obtained if low-productivity water could be transferred from senior to junior rights holders.

Considerable research into the economic implications of queuing versus market systems for the allocation of water has been conducted, as have the conditions under which market systems may be preferable (Easter and Tsur, 1995; Saliba and Bush, 1987; Shah and Zilberman, 1992; Burness and Quirk, 1979). Water resources have several characteristics which may hamper the introduction of markets, including high transactions costs in trading, third-party impacts, non-excludability of certain water use bene-fits, natural monopoly conditions and equity issues. In this section we present a simple framework for analysing the welfare implications of a move from queuing to a market system.

In this analysis, we use Burness and Quirk's (1979) framework for analysing resource allocation under the prior appropriation system to show the welfare implications of the introduction of markets. Let i identify water users, with $i = 1$ for the most senior user and increasing for more junior users. Let $D_i(\cdot)$ be user i's demand for water, and assume that the per unit cost of diverting water is W_0. Figure 10.1 illustrates the case of two users with iden-tical demand curves, where $D_1(W)$ is the demand of the senior rights owner and $D_1(W) + D_2(W)$ is the aggregate demand of the two. Assume that there are two states of water supply: low and high. A^1 in Figure 10.1 denotes water supply in the low state and is constructed to equal the quantity demanded by senior rights owners at $W = W_0$ and thus $(D_1(W_0) = A^1)$.

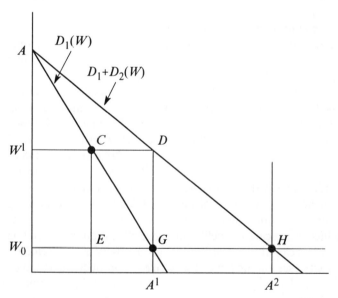

Figure 10.1   Case of two water users with identical demand curves

Let X_i^j denote water used by the user i under state of nature j. As Figure 10.1 indicates, when the supply is low, the senior rights holder will use all the available water $X_1^1 = A^1$, and the junior rights owner will not use any water $(X_2^1 = 0)$. When supply is high, the demand of both will be satisfied, given the same diversion cost of W_0. That is, $X_1^2 = X_2^2 = A^1 = (A^2/2)$.

The consumer surplus when water supply is low is equal to the area of the triangle AW_0G in Figure 10.1. When the supply is high, the surplus is AW_0H.

Suppose water trading is allowed and costless. In this case, the price of water at the low supply period will be W^1 and both users will consume $A^1/2$ units of water. The economic surplus in this period will be equal to the area AW_0GD. The transition to market will not affect the outcome of the high-supply period, since the market price will be W_0. Thus, the gains of transitioning from a prior appropriation system to one of water trading are especially high in periods of low supply.

The market-based system creates incentives for water users to conserve water, which, in turn, creates incentives for the adoption of water-conserving irrigation technologies. As discussed in the previous section, this may lead to an increase in production, as well as an increase in crop values, as high-valued crops are substituted for low-value ones. Thus, the move to a market system from the prior appropriation system may provide additional social benefits (Shah et al., 1993; Dinar and Letey, 1991).

High transactions costs may hinder the transition to a market system. The institution of a market may require the expansion and improvement of conveyance facilities (to protect against stealing and to accommodate added users), as well as the monitoring and enforcement of transactions and payments, and so on (Saliba and Bush, 1987). Water transfers in a market-based system may produce third-party impacts where beneficiaries other than the direct water users are affected by changes in water supply, but do not have access to markets, as in the case of recreational uses of in-stream flows (Colby, 1990; Gisser and Johnson, 1983). If these transactions costs are greater than the gains from trade, then the transition to market is not welfare-improving.

Political economic considerations may also prevent the establishment of a water market even when it is welfare-improving. If the water supplier (a semi-governmental agency in most cases) receives the proceeds from water sales, then senior rights owners will lose significantly from the water reform and will oppose it. When the government receives the benefits of the market reform, the economic surplus of the senior rights owners in periods of low supply will decline from AW_0G in Figure 10.1 to AW^1C. On the other hand, if the senior rights owners can hold their water rights after the introduction of a market and sell water to the junior rights owners, their welfare in a low-supply period will increase from AW_0G to AW_0GDCA, and they will gain CAD from selling low-productivity water to the junior rights owners. Thus, profit-maximizing senior rights owners will support a water reform that allows them to trade and transfer their water rights.

4.   Conveyance and spatial management of water

The uneven distribution of water over space is a major cause of inefficiency in water use. Many irrigation systems consist of long, poorly lined canals, so that conveyance losses of up to 50 per cent are experienced, resulting in low efficiency levels (Repetto, 1986). The inadequate management of water allocation over space has significant equity effects as well, since losses accrue mostly to downstream users.

In this section we present an optimal control model in order to demonstrate the determination of optimal water pricing, allocation and conveyance over space. This model captures the different incentives facing upstream and downstream water users in making conveyance investments.

Suppose a region is supplied annually with S_0 amount of water at a diversion point. The water is conveyed in a canal with the length of X (a choice variable). Let x denote distance from the water source. Let $S(x)$ denote water left in the canal at location x, and let $Y(x)$ denote water use for production at this location, with $S(x) \geq 0$, and $Y(x) \geq 0$. The monetary benefit from water use is denoted by $B(Y)$ where $B_y = \partial B / \partial Y > 0$ and $B_{YY} < 0$. The cost of conveying one unit of water one unit of distance is m.

At each location x, the change in the canal water is determined by the equation of motion:

$$\frac{dS}{dx} = -Y(x) - \delta\big(I(x)\big)S(x) \tag{10.1}$$

The water in the canal declines due to consumption and conveyance loss. The fraction of water lost at each location x is $\delta\big(I(x)\big)$, which depends on the annual cost of maintenance and improvement of the conveyance system at location x, $I(x)$. Without any investment in the conveyance system, the conveyance loss is δ_0 (natural conveyance loss), which declines with increased improvement and maintenance cost so that $\delta_I < 0 \; \delta_{II} > 0$.[3]

The optimal pattern of water use and conveyance improvement over space are determined by solving

$$\max_{X, Y(x), I(x)} \int_0^X \big[B\big(Y(x)\big) - mS(x) - I(x)\big]dx \tag{10.2}$$

             ↑   ↑   ↑

          Benefit   Conveyance Conveyance
           from   cost   improvement
       water use   cost

subject to the equation of motion of the water remaining in the canal (10.1), and given the water at the origin of the system, S_0.

This is a simplified version of the optimal control problem solved in Chakravorty et al. (1995). To characterize the optimal resource allocation, let $\lambda(x)$ be the shadow price of water at location x and λ_0 be the shadow price of water at the origin. The necessary conditions holding at the optimal solution are:

$$B_Y\big(Y(x)\big) - \lambda(x) = 0 \Rightarrow \qquad (10.3)$$

Water use at each location x should be set equal to the level where the marginal benefit from water use (value of marginal product of water) is equal to the shadow price.

$$\frac{\partial \lambda(x)}{\partial x} = \lambda \delta\big(I(x)\big) + m \Rightarrow \qquad (10.4)$$

The shadow price of water increases with distance from the source, and this increase is equal to the cost of the added conveyance loss, $\lambda\delta\big(I(x)\big)$, plus the cost of water conveyed, m.

$$-\lambda(x)\delta_I\big(I(x)\big)S(x) = 1 \Rightarrow \qquad (10.5)$$

Conveyance improvement expenditures at each location are set to a level where each additional dollar spent equals the value of the marginal benefits (in terms of reduced conveyance loss) of conveyance improvement.

$$B\big(Y(X)\big) = I(X^*) + mS(X) \Rightarrow \qquad (10.6)$$

The optimal size of the canal occurs where the benefits from water use are equal to the sum of canal improvement $\big(I(X)\big)$ and water conveyance $mS(X)$ costs.

These results suggest that under optimal conditions, water prices will increase along the canal to reflect conveyance cost and losses and, as a result, water use will decline along the canal. Investment in canal improvement will decline with distance from the source, so under reasonable conditions, conveyance loss will increase.

Improvements in conveyance facilities have the properties of a public good. Investment made by one individual to improve conveyance systems delivering water to their site will benefit downstream users by reducing their conveyance losses as well. Without intervention via regulations or an institutional mechanism to promote collective action, there will be underinvestment in conveyance facilities. The underinvestment will also result in a shorter canal than is socially optimal, lower aggregate output, over-production by users near the water source, and reduced production levels downstream.

A growing area of research is the economics of collective action in the management of public good and common-pool water resources.[4] In particular, the design of institutions which provide the incentives and conditions for the collective management of resources has received considerable attention (Ostrom, 1992; Tang, 1992; Wade, 1987). This interest has grown out of an awareness that under many circumstances, neither centralized state management nor decentralized privatization is an effective way of managing water resources (Ostrom, 1992; Wade, 1986; Evans, 1996). Localized water user groups (WUAs) which provide rules for water use, as well as their enforcement, have been found to be highly effective in managing public good and common-pool resources (Ostrom and Gardner, 1992; Lam, 1996; Tang, 1992; Wade, 1987). WUAs have been successful in the management of collective goods through their impact on reducing transaction and information costs and in increasing the capability for activity coordination (Ostrom, 1992).

Several theoretical as well as empirical studies have been conducted analysing how WUAs operate and the conditions under which they are most effective (Baland and Platteau, 1993, 1996; Tang, 1992; Lam, 1996; Ostrom, 1992; Tang, 1992; Wade, 1987). In the theoretical literature, advanced concepts of cooperative game theory, including repeated games and models of decision making under uncertainty and incomplete information are used to analyse the behaviour of WUAs (Bardhan, 1993; Baland and Platteau, 1993). These studies indicate that several factors are important determinants of the incentives for individuals to participate in group management schemes, including the relative benefits to cooperation over the alternatives, the discount rate among group participants, the size and heterogeneity of the group, the degree of communication among members and the level and variability of water supplies.

Empirical studies of WUAs have indicated that small group size, well-defined resource boundaries, close proximity of users to the resource, perceived fairness of the rules of access, clear sanction and punishment systems for trespass and good leadership are important factors of successful WUAs (Baland and Platteau, 1996). Empirical evidence has also indicated that the establishment of externally funded irrigation projects has often resulted in the destruction of local institutions, and thus a decline in the efficiency of local irrigation (Ostrom, 1992; Baland and Platteau, 1996). This evidence suggests the importance of institutional considerations in the development of new irrigation schemes or rehabilitation projects – a subject we return to in Section 6.

5. The economics of groundwater management

There is a significant literature on the economics of groundwater (Tsur and Zemel, 1995; Burt, 1964; Dixon, 1991; Gisser and Sanchez, 1980; Gisser, 1983). The optimal management of groundwater can be modelled as a non-renewable resource (for example in the case of desert regions with a closed aquifer) or as a renewable resource (when aquifers are recharged). The dynamics of optimal groundwater use depend on the price of energy, the interest rate, the efficiency of pumping, and the hydrological characteristics of the system.

In the case of non-renewable groundwater with no technological change, the level of optimal pumping follows the standard Hotelling rule. The rate of pumping declines over time with the interest rate, and the user cost of water (price minus extraction cost) rises. The introduction of technological changes which increase water use efficiency leads to a reduction in extraction levels and extends the economic life of a finite aquifer. In contrast, improvements in pumping technology that reduce extraction costs actually tend to accelerate the pumping of the aquifer.

In cases where groundwater aquifers can be recharged, the groundwater system may reach a steady state where pumping is equal to recharge. If the steady-state level is below the initial stock of water, then a decline in pumping over time will occur, until the steady state is reached. In cases where groundwater aquifers have already been significantly depleted, an initial period when replenishment exceeds pumping levels will precede the attainment of the steady state.

Groundwater resources usually exhibit characteristics of common property goods, where externalities arise because current water users do not take into account the impact of their pumping on future water users. Current pumping affects future water users primarily by lowering the depth of water, increasing pumping costs and by reducing the stock of water available for future pumping. In the absence of any common-pool management scheme, current users determine their water use levels by setting the value of the marginal product of water equal to their private pumping costs, rather than the full social cost. Correcting situations of overpumping may entail establishing a regional or local groundwater authority either by taxing pumping, forcing pumpers to pay the user, rather than the private cost of pumping, or by establishing aggregate pumping levels and introducing a system of transferable permits for pumping rights within the system (Gisser, 1983). Enactment of these situations requires monitoring of groundwater by a water agency, which may not always be feasible. Second-best solutions may include taxing groundwater users based on crop/technology choice selection where crops are be taxed in proportion to their average water use.

In many cases, the management of groundwater can be improved by removing policies which encourage overpumping, particularly the subsidization of electricity. Electricity is the major cost component in operating irrigation pumps. Lower electricity rates decrease the cost of pumping and increase the depth to which it is profitable for farmers to pump. This is a major cause of overpumping and the depletion of groundwater aquifers.

Frequently, ground- and surface-water systems can be managed conjunctively, where the optimal management of the system depends on the stocks and flows of the two water sources over time. Surface-water canals have been established in many regions to compensate or augment depleted groundwater aquifers. In other situations, groundwater reservoirs have been established as buffer stocks to supplement the use of surface-water supplies in times of low supply.

There is a growing literature on the economics of the conjunctive use of ground- and surface water (Boggess et al., 1993; Tsur, 1990; Burt, 1964). One source (in most cases, surface water) has lower extraction and conveyance costs, but its supply is subject to random variation due to climatic conditions. In most cases there is significant capacity for storage of the second resource (groundwater). The optimal management strategy involves pumping groundwater during dry years and augmenting the aquifer with extra surface water during wet years. This regime results in a more stable water supply, although water costs may vary according to the predominant source in any one year.

6.   The economic analysis of water projects

In recent years the economic analysis of water projects has come under growing scrutiny and criticism as public investment funds are increasingly scarce, and as the recognition of the environmental and social costs of such projects has increased. The primary economic tool utilized to inform policy makers on the merits of investing in such projects has been cost–benefit analysis (CBA). CBA is appealing for its simplicity and intuitive quality; however, a major flaw in the method is its reliance on the assumption of additive utility over time, which is unrealistic and may lead to flawed policy evaluations, ignoring issues of intertemporal substitution (Keen, 1990). The application of CBA to water project analysis has also been criticized because it does not account for the irreversibility of the environmental choices that project implementation entails, the costs arising from the environmental externalities which may accompany such projects, or the equity impacts of project implementation. In addition, CBA is generally focused on infrastructural and technical investments and ignores the potential for management improvements through institutional innovations.

Correction of some of the major flaws of CBA has been a major area of emphasis in water economics. Project assessment procedures are being revised to include the consideration of issues which have been ignored in the past and which have been the focus of economic research, including those listed in what follows.

Irreversibility and uncertainty
Arrow and Fisher (1974) introduced the notion of 'option value' associated with the development of water projects. In their paper, they recognized that water projects involve irreversible outcomes (for example the elimination of ecosystems) and that there may be significant uncertainty regarding preferences and technologies in the future. They argued that the correct criterion for project evaluation is the expected discounted net benefits, which are derived by computing discounted net benefits with and without the project and then applying the expectations operator to uncertain parameters. In this way, the value of waiting for future information in the face of uncertainty is incorporated into the project analysis. Taking into account irreversibility and uncertainty considerations is likely to lead to a higher frequency of project rejection or postponement than traditional CBA methods would yield. The analysis of the optimal size of water projects will be affected by the inclusion of these considerations as well, with smaller-scale projects being more likely to be constructed (Boggess et al., 1993).

Externalities and drainage
Negative environmental externalities have accompanied many water projects, generating high social costs which typically have not been accounted for in CBA. Thus water projects which appeared to be welfare-improving actually resulted in a drain on social resources. One of the major environmental externalities associated with water projects is waterlogging. In situations where impermeable barriers exist below the ground surface, percolating water from irrigation collects and begins to build up at subsurface levels, posing a threat to agricultural productivity. There are several methods for preventing or mitigating waterlogging problems, including the establishment of a drainage system which removes accumulating groundwater or a system of reusing percolated water for irrigation; however, the former is usually quite expensive and the latter results in a build-up of salts and is not sustainable. (See Dinar and Zilberman, 1991 for various perspectives on managing drainage problems in agriculture.) As discussed in the second section of this paper, the institution of farm-level incentives through the taxation of drainage or the subsidization of water-conserving technologies is another method for reducing drainage flows.

The costs of preventing or reducing environmental damage associated with drainage must be incorporated into the economic analysis of water projects in order to gain a true picture of the costs and benefits of the project to society. Similarly, the costs and benefits of other environmental externalities that may be realized through project implementation, such as loss of wilderness areas and their associated ecosystems or siltation effects, should be included. The design of the project should be such that the net benefit of all components – irrigation, drainage and other uses – should be maximized. Ignoring these externalities and their associated costs has led to overinvestment in water projects.

Institutional considerations
As has been made clear in earlier sections of this chapter, the institutional arrangements under which water is managed is a critical determinant of the efficiency and equity of water use. However, in most cases water projects are analysed solely as physical investments in equipment and technology to improve productive capacity. Institutional changes and improved management practices are not explicitly considered as a key element of project design and assessment. In most cases, the optimal management of water resources will require improvement in both physical infrastructure and management practices. The economic analysis of water projects should therefore include both these considerations, in order to provide insights on the optimal mix of institutional and technical measures.

The restoration of water resources
A major area of emphasis in water project planning is the restoration of degraded water resources, such as wetlands, fisheries, riparian and marine environments. There are two main aspects of this sort of analysis which have not traditionally been included in project economic analysis. The first is a strong interdisciplinary approach with the incorporation of biological and physical modelling into economic modelling. Braden (1989) adopts this approach by combining a spatial model of non-point pollution movement with an economic model including abatement and containment costs in order to derive a spatially optimal pollution management scheme. Antle and Capalbo (1991) and Carlson (1993) incorporate physical and biological models respectively into their analyses of groundwater contamination related to pesticide use. Keeler (1996) discusses the use of biological indicators to develop economically meaningful indicators of water quality. The second novel aspect of this sort of analysis is the estimation of society's preferences for non-market goods such as environmental amenities in order to estimate the value of restoration projects. Contingent valuation techniques which are based on the use of surveys to determine willingness to pay for environmental amenities (or the willingness to accept compensation for its loss) is a fairly recent method developed to estimate values for non-

market goods (Boggess, 1993; Carson and Mitchell, 1993). In cases where environmental amenities are associated with a traded commodity (for example land prices associated with local water contamination), hedonic pricing models may also be used (Beach and Carlson, 1993). The analysis of water restoration projects is a new area of water economic analysis, with much potential for expanding the water economics research agenda.

Equity

Traditionally the economic analysis of water projects does not include equity considerations. Project evaluation involves the aggregation of welfare over individuals, with the same weights typically given to the benefits and costs associated with each individual. The criterion for project acceptance is the potential for the gainers to compensate the losers, but not that they actually do so. Thus projects assessed with this method may cause a worsening of income distribution if the benefits are captured by wealthier members of society while the costs of the project are borne by all – or disproportionately among the poor. Since the cost of land affects the choice of project site, projects are frequently located in low-income areas, so that any negative impacts associated with such projects, including the need for relocation, fall heaviest upon the poor. One method of addressing these equity concerns is to expand the geographical scope of the analysis, so as to include all the costs which the project engenders and to investigate the potential for compensation schemes from the 'winners' to the 'losers', so that the benefits of the project are positive across all groups involved (Howe, 1996; de Janvry et al., 1995).

7. Conclusion

The emphasis in water economics research has shifted from the expansion of new sources of water towards improving the efficiency of existing uses. In this chapter we have outlined several themes dominating the water economics literature, identifying ways to improve water use efficiency at the farm, community, national and international levels of analysis. We have shown the importance of environmental factors in determining optimal technology and water use patterns. Heterogeneity in environmental conditions thus leads to diversity in optimal farm irrigation management schemes. The importance of institutions in determining water use efficiency is a theme running throughout the chapter. Two important issues have been raised: the potential for improving incentives leading to efficient water use through property rights and pricing reforms, and the important role of institutions which promote collective action in overcoming problems arising from the public good and common property characteristics of water resources. Improved economic analysis of water projects to include uncertainty, externalities and equity issues will lead to a better grasp of the real trade-offs facing society in making public investments, and thus a more efficient allocation of resources.

Notes

1. For a non-technical overview of the key issues in water resource economics and management in the American West, see Reisner (1986). Bain et al (1966) is an overview of the industrial organization of water management.
2. EMP is defined as: $\epsilon_i(e) = -f''(e_i) \cdot e_i / f'(e_i)$.
3. For simplicity, the cost of conveyance improvement is assumed not to depend on volume of water conveyed.
4. Public goods are non-excludable and non-rival while common-pool resources are non-excludable but rivalrous.

References

Antle, J. and S. Capalbo (1991), 'Physical and economic model integration for measurement of the environmental impacts of agricultural chemical use', *Northeast Journal of Agricultural and Resource Economics*, **20** (1), 68–82.

Arrow, K. and A. Fisher (1974), 'Environmental preservation, uncertainty and irreversibility', *Quarterly Journal of Economics*, **88**, 312–19.

Bain, J.S., R.E. Caves and J. Margolis (1966), *Northern California's Water Industry*, Baltimore, MD: Johns Hopkins University Press for Resources for the Future.

Baland, J.-M. and J. Platteau (1993), *A Multi-disciplinary Analysis of Local-Level Management of Environmental Resources*, Rome, Italy: Food and Agricultural Organization of the United Nations.

Baland, J.-M. and J.-P. Platteau (1996), *Halting Degradation of Natural Resources. Is There A Role for Rural Communities?* Rome, Italy: Food and Agriculture Organization of the United Nations.

Bardhan, P. (1993), 'Analytics of the institutions of informal cooperation in rural development', *World Development*, **24** (4), 633–9.

Beach, D. and G. Carson (1993), 'A hedonic analysis of herbicides: Does safety matter?', *American Journal of Agricultural Economics*, **75** (3), 612–23.

Boggess, W., R. Lacewell and D. Zilberman (1993), 'Economics of water use in agriculture', in G. Carlson, D. Zilberman and J. Miranowski (eds), *Agricultural and Environmental Resource Economics*, New York: Oxford University Press, pp. 319–84.

Braden, J.B., G.V. Johnson, A. Bouzaher and D. Miltz (1989), 'Optimal spatial management of agricultural pollution', *American Journal of Agricultural Economics*, **71** (3), 404–13.

Burness, H.S. and J.P. Quirk (1979), 'Appropriative water rights and the efficient allocation of resources', *American Economic Review*, **69**, 25–37.

Burt, O.R. (1964), 'The economics of conjunctive use of ground and surface water', *Hilgardia*, **36** (2), 31–111.

Carlson, G.A. and M. Wetzstein (1993), 'Pesticides and pest management' in G.A. Carlson et al. (eds), *Agricultural and Environmental Resource Economics*, New York: Oxford University Press, pp. 268–318.

Carson, R.T. and R.C. Mitchell (1993), 'The value of clean water: The public's willingness to pay for boatable, fishable and swimmable quality water', *Water Resources Research*, **29** (7), 2445–54.

Caswell, M. and D. Zilberman (1985), 'The choices of irrigation technologies in California', *American Journal of Agricultural Economics*, **67** (2), 224–34.

Caswell, M. and D. Zilberman (1986), 'The effects of well depth and land quality on the choice of irrigation technology', *American Journal of Agricultural Economics*, **68** (4), 798–811.

Caswell, M., E. Lichtenberg and D. Zilberman (1990), 'The effects of pricing policies on water conservation and drainage', *American Journal of Agricultural Economics*, **72** (4), 883–90.

Chakravorty, U., E. Hochman and D. Zilberman (1995), 'A spatial model of optimal water conveyance', *Journal of Environmental Economics and Management*, **29**, 25–41.

Colby, B. (1990), 'Transactions costs and efficiency in Western water allocation', *American Journal of Agricultural Economics*, **72** (5), 1184–92.

Cuzan, A.G. (1983), 'Appropriators versus expropriators: The political economy of water in the West', in T.L. Anderson (ed.), *Water Rights: Scarce Resource Application, Bureaucracy, and the Environment*, Cambridge: Ballinger, pp. 13–44.

de Janvry, A., E. Sadoulet and B. Santos (1995), 'Project evaluation for sustainable rural development: Plan Sierra in the Dominican Republic', *Journal of Environmental and Economic Management*, **28** (2), 135–54.

Dinar, A. and J. Lety (1991), 'Agricultural water marketing, allocative efficiency, and drainage reduction', *Journal of Environmental Economics and Management*, **20** (3), 210–23.

Dinar, A. and D. Zilberman (eds) (1991), *The Economics and Management of Water and Drainage in Agriculture*, Boston: Kluwer Academic Publishers.

Dixon, L.S. (1991), 'Common property aspects of ground-water use and drainage generation', in A. Dinar and D. Zilberman (eds), *The Economics and Management of Water and Drainage in Agriculture*, Boston: Kluwer Academic Publishers, pp. 677–98.

Easter, B.C. and Y. Tsur (1995), 'The design of institutional arrangements for water allocation', in A. Dinar and E. Loehman (eds), *Water Quantity/Quality Management and Conflict Resolution*, Westport, CT: Praeger, pp. 107–18.

Evans, P. (1996), 'Government action, social capital and development: Reviewing the evidence on synergy', *World Development*, **24** (6), 1119–32.

Gardner, B.D. (1983), 'Water pricing and rent seeking in California agriculture', in T.L. Anderson (ed.), *Water Rights: Scarce Resource Allocation, Bureaucracy, and the Environment*, Cambridge: Ballinger.

Gisser, M. (1983), 'Groundwater: Focusing on the real issue', *Journal of Political Economy*, **91** (6), 1001–27.

Gisser, M. and R. Johnson (1983), 'Institutional restrictions on the transfer of water rights and the survival of an agency', in T. Anderson (ed.), *Water Rights: Scarce Resource Allocation, Bureaucracy and the Environment*, Cambridge: Ballinger, pp. 137–61.

Gisser, M. and D. Sanchez (1980), 'Competition versus optimal control in ground-water pumping, *Water Resources Research*, **16** (4), 638–42.

Grimm, S., Q. Paris and A.W. Willimas (1987), 'A von Liebig model for water and nitrogen crop response', *Western Journal of Agricultural Economics*, **12** (2), 182–92.

Howe, C. (1996), 'Water resources planning in a federation of states: Equity versus efficiency', *Natural Resources Journal*, **36** (Winter), 29–36.

Keeler, A. (1996), 'The value of incorporating bioindicators in economic approaches to water pollution control', *Ecological Economics*, **19** (3), 237–45.

Keen, M. (1990), 'Welfare analysis and intertemporal substitution', *Journal of Public Economics*, **42**, 47–66.

Lam, W.F. (1996), 'Institutional design of public agencies and coproduction: A study of irrigation associations in Taiwan', *World Development*, **24** (6), 1039–54.

Ostrom, E. (1992), *Crafting Institutions for Self-governing Irrigation Systems*, San Francisco: C.S. Press, Institute for Contemporary Studies.

Ostrom, E. and R. Gardner (1992), 'Coping with asymmetries in the commons: Self-governing irrigation systems can work', *Journal of Economic Perspectives*, **7** (4), 93–112.

Reisner, M. (1986), *Cadillac Desert: The American West and Its Disappearing Water*, New York: Viking.

Repetto, R. (1986), *Skimming the Water: Rent-Seeking and the Performance of Public Irrigation Systems*, Washington, DC: World Resources Institute Research Report no. 4.

Saliba, B. and D.B. Bush (1987), *Water Markets in Theory and Practice*, Boulder, CO: Westview Press.

Shah, F. and D. Zilberman (1992), *Queuing vs. Markets*, Department of Agricultural and Resource Economics, University of California, Berkeley.

Shah, F., D. Zilberman and U. Chakravorty (1993), 'Water rights doctrines and technology adoption', in K. Hoff, A. Braverman and J. Stiglitz (eds), *The Economics of Rural*

Organization: Theory, Practice and Policy, New York: Oxford University Press, pp. 479–99.

Stewart, J.I., R.M. Hagan and W.O. Pruitt (1974), 'Functions to predict optimal irrigation programs', *Journal of Irrigation Drainage Division ASCE*, **100** (2), 179–99.

Tang, S.Y. (1992), *Institutions and Collective Action: Self-Governance In Irrigation*, San Francisco, CA: Institute of Contemporary Studies.

Tsur, Y. (1990), 'The stabilization value of groundwater when surface water supplies are uncertain: The implications for groundwater development', *Water Resources Research*, **26**, 811–18.

Tsur, Y. and A. Zemel (1995), 'Uncertainty and irreversibility in groundwater resource management', *Journal of Environmental Economics and Management*, **29** (2), 149–61.

Wade, R. (1986), 'Common property resource management in South Indian villages', in *Common Property Resource Management*, Proceedings of the Conference on Common Property Resource Management, 21–26 April 1985, Washington, DC: National Academy Press.

Wade, R. (1987), 'The management of common property resources: Collective action as an alternative to privatization or state regulation', *Cambridge Journal of Economics*, **11**, 95–106.

Young, R.A. and R.H. Haveman (1985), 'Economics of water resources: A survey', in A.V. Kneese and J.L. Sweeney (eds), *Handbook of Natural Resource and Energy Economics*, New York: North-Holland.

Zilberman, D., D. Sunding, R. Howitt, A. Dinar and N. MacDougall (1994), 'Water for California agriculture: Lessons from the drought and new water market reform', *Choices*, fourth quarter.

11 Agriculture and the environment
James S. Shortle and David G. Abler

1. Agriculture and the environment

Environmental externalities from agricultural activities, both past and present, are pervasive. Since neolithic times humans have been converting forests, wetlands and prairies into crop and grazing lands. These activities have shaped the rural landscape and the hydrology and ecology of agriculturally developed regions. Air quality, water quality and climate also influence agriculture as a bio-economic activity. Thus agriculture is both a source and receptor of environmental externalities.

Contemporary evaluations of the environmental impacts of agriculture are both positive and negative. The loss of biodiversity that occurred with the expansion of the agricultural frontier and human settlement in developed regions is now recognized as an irreversible loss of natural capital. Yet, land drainage has been an important factor in eliminating malaria in Europe and North America, and agricultural land is an important habitat for many remaining wildlife species. Moreover, rural and urban populations often value agricultural landscapes as open space. In many developing countries, traditional extensive agricultural systems cause the kinds of environmental change that agricultural development has created since ancient times, as forests and grasslands are converted to crop production and grazing. In developed countries, techniques introduced during the last century have greatly increased what can be produced from the land, removing, at least for the present, the Ricardian imperative of expansion at the extensive margin to meet the needs of growing populations. However, the pesticides, fertilizers, irrigation, mechanization, specialization and structural change that have made these (and other) social and economic gains possible have created a range of new environmental hazards.

Traditionally, agricultural policies have attempted, with varying degrees of success, to achieve objectives related to farm income, agricultural prices and agricultural trade (Gardner, 1990; Johnson, 1991). Agricultural externalities, although influenced by the scale, location and methods of agricultural production, were at most a secondary consideration. However, as this century comes to a close, a shift in priorities is evident in many countries. Agricultural policy is increasingly concerned with encouraging the supply of positive agricultural externalities, and reducing the generation of negative externalities (Ervin and Graffy, 1996; Poe, 1997).

2. Negative environmental externalities

Like any economic enterprise, farms have throughput. Energy and materials enter in purchased inputs and in environmental flows (for example, rainfall, sun), and are removed in commodities and outflows to the environment. Moreover, while soils represent a stock of productive services, they can also be a flow of pollutants in so far as wind and water carry eroded soils to off-farm locations, where they can cause significant environmental harm. Environmental outflows are in part the result of purposeful waste disposal activities, such as burning fields to remove stubble or dumping unused pesticides in streams. However, natural processes, such as run-off and volatilization of nitrogen, are important forces in the formation and fate of agricultural residuals. Below we focus on three sets of negative environmental externalities that have drawn significant attention in recent years: water pollution, air pollution and land conversion/degradation.

Water pollution
Run-off from agricultural lands can carry fertilizers, pesticides, livestock wastes, salts, pathogens and eroded soils into streams, lakes, estuaries and coastal waters. Many recent environmental assessments identify agricultural run-off as a major cause of surface-water quality problems in developed countries. For instance, the US Environmental Protection Agency (EPA) identifies agriculture as the leading contributor to US non-point source pollution and, possibly, the leading source of surface-water pollution (US EPA, 1994). While much has been done to reduce pollution from industrial and municipal point sources since the late 1960s, policy for agriculture and other non-point pollution sources has been developing slowly.[1] At the same time, structural changes in agriculture have often increased the adverse impacts of crop and livestock production on water quality (OECD, 1986, 1989). The development of extremely intensive livestock production in parts of the Netherlands, North Carolina (US) and Pennsylvania (US) are examples. Beyond limiting the extent of potential environmental quality improvements, the failure to extend pollution controls to non-point sources increases the costs of environmental protection by precluding efficient allocation of control between point and non-point sources (Freeman, 1990).

Although current knowledge of the state of groundwater is limited, there is evidence of groundwater contamination by agricultural chemicals in some areas of North America and Western Europe (OECD, 1991). Nitrates and pesticides that percolate into groundwater used to supply drinking water are of particular concern. The World Health Organization standard of 50 milligrammes per litre (mg/l) of nitrates is widely accepted and has been incorporated into law in the European Union (EU). Nitrate levels in excess of this standard have been found in certain areas of a number of EU countries. Canada and the US have an even stricter standard of 10 mg/l. Given the large safety margins included in drinking-water standards and the uncertainty about health effects from low levels of nitrate intake, the threat to public health is unclear (Bogárdi and Kuzelka, 1991). However, regardless of the true magnitude of the risk, communities are required to comply with established drinking-water standards, and this can be very costly.

The overall state of knowledge about chronic human health effects of pesticides is quite limited, but concern has been raised about the consequences of low exposures over long periods of time (Council on Scientific Affairs, 1988; World Health Organization, 1990). In addition to cancer, questions have been raised about other possible effects of pesticide exposure. For example, the US EPA cancelled two nematocides found in groundwater, EDG and DCBP, because they might cause genetic mutations and reproductive disorders, in addition to cancer.

Economic costs from agricultural water pollution include reduced productivity of sports and commercial fisheries, in-stream recreational losses, increased costs of water treatment for industrial and domestic uses, costs of illness and death when contaminated waters are consumed, materials damages and adverse impacts on the diversity and functioning of ecosystems. Although real or perceived human health rights often command the most attention, the costs associated with damages to ecosystems and non-living systems are probably much larger. The problems encountered in attempting to quantify these and other non-market costs are well known to economists (see, for example, Smith, 1997). Assessing the water-quality damage costs caused by agriculture is also complicated by problems in allocating these costs across pollution sources. The most ambitious attempt to estimate the costs of agricultural water pollution is Ribaudo's (1986, 1989) work on off-site soil erosion damages in the US. Ribaudo's (1989) 'best' estimate of the annual cost of soil erosion (in 1989 dollars) from all sources, including agriculture, is about $9 billion, with a range of estimates of about $5 billion to about $18 billion. Ribaudo estimates that agriculture accounted for about 39 per cent of gross soil erosion in the US in 1982. Agriculture's percentage of the costs of soil erosion would not necessarily be 39 per cent, but would instead depend on the percentage of erosion from agricultural sources that pollutes water resources, the uses to which those resources are put, and other factors.

Several recent studies estimate the willingness to pay for drinking water free of nitrates, pesticides, and/or other agricultural pollutants (for the US, see Crutchfield et al., 1995). Estimates of the average willingness to pay per household per year for drinking water free of one or more agricultural pollutants in the US range from less than $50 to more than $1000. Even at the lower bound, these estimates are quite large when aggregated across households.

Air pollution
Agriculture is also a source of several air pollutants. Apart from reaching surface-water or groundwater supplies, excess nitrogen in the soil can be lost to the atmosphere through denitrification and volatilization (Hidy, 1995). Volatilized forms of nitrogen such as ammonia, nitrous oxide and nitrogen dioxide can contribute to acidification of the atmosphere and, in turn, acid rain. Agriculture is a major contributor to acidifying substances in the atmosphere in several countries, including the Netherlands. Estimates for the Netherlands indicate that agriculture accounts for more than 90 per cent of total ammonia emissions and more than 60 per cent of total emissions of acidifying substances in acidification equivalents (OECD, 1995). However, ammonia emissions from Dutch agriculture have been reduced by more than one-third in the last 15 years due to faster ploughing in of manure after spreading and greater use of covered manure storage facilities (OECD, 1995).

Agriculture is a contributor to greenhouse gas emissions, with estimates suggesting that it accounts for perhaps one-fifth of global emissions (Watson et al., 1996). The conversion of tropical forests to agricultural land, which releases carbon that had been sequestered in these forests, has perhaps garnered the most attention. Agricultural practices in developed countries also contribute to climate change (van Kooten and Folmer, 1996). Methane from livestock and wet rice cultivation may be more important contributors to greenhouse gases than deforestation (Watson et al., 1996). Fossil fuels consumed in the process of using farm machinery and in the process of manufacturing inorganic fertilizers are other, albeit minor, sources of greenhouse gas emissions from agriculture.

Water and air pollution policies for agriculture
The design of cost-effective policies for controlling air and water pollution from agriculture poses large challenges (Shortle and Abler, 1997). The standard economic prescriptions for negative environmental externalities involve emissions-based policy instruments (for example, emissions standards or taxes, tradable discharge permits). However, the indirect and diffuse pathways that pollutants follow from agricultural land to air and water resources, along with large numbers of agricultural sources, make

metering individual pollution sources impractical, thereby ruling out the application of emissions-based instruments. Unobservable emissions also complicate the assignment of responsibility. How much a particular farm contributes to environmental quality problems, or even whether it contributes at all, is usually very uncertain. Other problems include the weather-driven nature of agricultural pollution processes and, in some cases, the existence of long lags between polluting events and actual contamination of surface waters or groundwater. Moreover, the feasibility, effectiveness and cost of pollution prevention and control technologies tend to vary significantly from one location to another.

While the absence of emissions-based policy instruments narrows the options, there are still many possibilities (Abler and Shortle, 1991). A voluntary compliance approach that combines public persuasion with technical assistance to encourage and facilitate adoption of environmentally friendly technologies has been used extensively to address agricultural non-point pollution in developed countries (OECD, 1989, 1993). Assessments generally indicate that these programmes have had limited impact. While there are many reasons for this, economic research suggests that costs are a significant barrier to the adoption of environmentally friendly practices (Dubgaard, 1994; Feather and Amacher, 1993; Feather and Cooper, 1995; Norton et al., 1994).

Another approach that has been taken to mitigate agricultural non-point source pollution is regulation of the supply of potentially polluting inputs. In particular, pesticide registration is the principal method for protecting the environment, workers and consumers from pesticide hazards (OECD, 1986). This policy instrument regulates which pesticides may be marketed and establishes conditions of use through labelling requirements. Pesticide registration programmes have been very effective in removing extremely hazardous pesticides in many countries, although there are some exceptions (see, for example, Thrupp, 1988). Pesticide registration can be an efficient tool when used to ban pesticides for which costs exceed benefits at any level of use. Evidence for the US suggests that it has been efficient in removing such pesticides from the market (Cropper et al., 1992). However, because labelling requirements cannot adequately account for site-specific conditions that should influence optimal management of the pesticides allowed on the market, the efficiency of registration is inherently limited (Lichtenberg, 1992; Zilberman et al., 1991).

Regulations can also be applied at the farm level. For instance, farmers in the Netherlands are subject to farm-level, tradable manure quotas (OECD, 1995). The Netherlands also imposes quantitative restrictions on phosphate and nitrogen applications from manure that vary according to crop.

Economic instruments that are used in practice include taxes on pesticides and fertilizers, subsidies for pollution control practices, and liability for environmental damages. Australia, Canada, Denmark, Sweden and the United States provide subsidies for adoption of pollution control practices in agriculture. The Netherlands taxes manure production in excess of the farm-level quotas. Taxes above and beyond the usual sales taxes are levied on fertilizers and pesticides in the state of Iowa (US). Sweden and the US offer subsidies for shifting land to activities with lower environmental hazards. A major programme in the US is the Conservation Reserve Program (CRP), which pays farmers to convert land from row crop production to grassed cover. The water-quality benefits of the CRP when fully implemented have been estimated to be within the range of $2.5 to $5.5 billion in 1989 dollars (Ribaudo, 1989). The state of Florida (US) offered a dairy herd buy-out programme as part of efforts to reduce nutrient pollution of Lake Okeechobee. Subsidies for conversion of farmland to forests in Sweden are justified in part as measures to reduce pesticide and fertilizer pollution.

Typically input taxes are levied at such low rates that they offer little incentive to reduce input usage (OECD, 1994a). The purpose seems more often to be to generate revenue for environmental programmes than to reduce input use. An exception is Sweden, which taxes fertilizers and pesticides at rates intended to have disincentive effects.

Studies of the cost-effectiveness of alternative approaches generally support the received wisdom among economists that regulations applied in a uniform way are less cost-effective than economic incentives (Shortle and Abler, 1997). Reliance on regulations rather than economic incentive mechanisms may significantly increase the costs of environmental protection in some instances (see, for example, Zilberman et al., 1991). However, there are cases in which standards make sense. One is when the expected cost of an input or process exceeds the expected benefit for essentially any level of use. Examples include extremely hazardous pesticides, especially when there are close substitutes with lesser environmental risks, spreading manure on frozen ground in hydrologically active areas of watersheds, and the use of certain types of pesticides in environmentally sensitive areas such as groundwater recharge zones. A second case is when techniques exist that have the potential to yield significant environmental gains with little cost to the user.

The extreme heterogeneity of agricultural production activities, their impacts on environmental quality, the costs of these impacts, the technical options for reducing environmental hazards, and the costs of these control options all strongly imply targeted, watershed-based approaches to managing water-quality impacts (Babcock et al., 1997; Bouzaher et al., 1990;

Braden et al., 1989; Duda and Johnson, 1985; Lee et al., 1985; Park and Shabman, 1982; Ribaudo, 1986, Lichtenberg and Zilberman, 1988; Hochman and Zilberman, 1978).

The principles of federalism suggest that policies for reducing water pollution from agriculture that are sensitive to local costs and benefits are more likely when policy choices are made by governmental authorities that serve the collective interests of the citizens who bear the costs and benefits. However, a purely decentralized approach is not optimal given pollution spillovers between jurisdictions, fiscal spillovers and the possibility of political failures in which the interests of polluters or environmentalists are over-represented in pollution policy design (Shortle, 1996). Accordingly, solving water-quality problems associated with agriculture should not be the exclusive responsibility of the national or subnational governments alone.

Technical progress
An alternative mechanism for reducing agricultural non-point source pollution that has attracted considerable attention in recent years is research and development (R&D) on 'green', 'low-input', or 'environmentally friendly' agricultural production technologies (OECD, 1993, 1994b). Various innovations designed to substitute for inputs and management practices correlated with agricultural pollution flows are currently under development or in the process of being adopted (National Research Council, 1989, 1993; OECD, 1994b). In field crop production, integrated pest management (IPM) is a major component of extension programmes in several OECD countries and has had a significant impact on pesticide usage in many cases (OECD, 1993). Other alternatives in the process of being adopted include improved crop rotations optimized for specific locations, improved manure storage and application practices, and more precise fertilizer and pesticide application techniques. Looking farther into the future, biotechnology offers the potential of significantly more effective substitutes for fertilizers and pesticides (Chrispeels and Sadava, 1994; Fransman et al., 1995).

Analyses of the environmental impacts of potential new agricultural technologies often focus on their biological, chemical and physical properties relative to existing technologies (for example, Logan, 1993; National Research Council, 1989; OECD, 1994b). These analyses typically endeavour to assess environmental externalities associated with production of a given ton of output, or production on a given hectare of land, using new technologies versus existing technologies. While analyses of this type are essential, they are incomplete because they do not take into account the economic responses of agricultural producers and consumers to new technologies.

One key economic consideration is, of course, adoption. To have an impact, new technologies must be adopted. If they are to be adopted voluntarily, they must be expected to be profitable to producers. If use is mandated by law, then political acceptability and cost-effectiveness considerations would in most situations require any negative impact on producers to be small (Abler and Shortle, 1991). However, widespread adoption is only one economic consideration (Abler and Shortle, 1995; Abler and Shortle, 1996).

Agricultural policy change
A number of economic studies provide evidence that price supports, input subsidies and other agricultural policies influence the nature, size and spatial distribution of agricultural externalities through effects on the scale and location of production, input usage and structure (for example, Abler and Shortle, 1992; Abrahams and Shortle, 1997; Laughland, 1994; Lichtenberg and Zilberman, 1988; Platinga, 1996; Swinton and Clark, 1994; Liapis, 1994; Tsai and Shortle, 1997; Weinberg et al., 1993a,b). For example, policies that increase producer prices without restricting output (such as price floors, output subsidies, import restrictions) encourage farmers to increase production. Adverse environmental impacts occur when environmentally sensitive lands are converted to agricultural production and when there is increased intensity of the use of inputs that can increase environmental harm from agricultural production (for example, pesticides, fertilizers, irrigation water, fossil fuels). Increased livestock production also means an increase in the volume of livestock wastes. Similarly, input subsidies can have adverse impacts when they encourage the use of potentially harmful inputs through either substitution or scale effects. By similar reasoning supply controls would seem to be environmentally beneficial, but this need not be the case. For example, acreage restrictions may lead to substitution of relatively harmful inputs for land. Moreover, output quotas may be environmentally harmful when the rents they create favour agricultural activities that are more harmful to the environment than those that would otherwise be pursued or when they encourage production in environmentally sensitive areas. These types of policy conflicts indicate that negative agricultural externalities can be reduced by agricultural policy reforms and have stimulated considerable interest in agricultural policy coordination (OECD, 1989, 1993).

An important recent development in the US and Western Europe is the 'decoupling' of agricultural price and income supports from agricultural production. By partially severing the link between agricultural supports and production decisions, recent policy reforms in the US and EU promise to diminish these effects, although some environmentally important distortions remain. Agricultural irrigation subsidies in the western US are an example. The US and the EU have also shifted resources into programmes that subsidize farmers for environmentally beneficial actions. Examples are the US CRP and the EU's Environmentally Sensitive Areas (ESA) programme, which offers farmers flat-rate payments for entering into land use agreements.

The presence of policies that distort agricultural product or input markets has implications for environmental policies for agriculture beyond their effects on the nature, size and location of agricultural externalities. For example, the costs of environmental policies that reduce surplus production or the excessive use of subsidized inputs will be overstated if the benefits from reducing these distortions are not counted (Lichtenberg and Zilberman, 1988). Abrahams and Shortle (1997) and Tsai and Shortle (1997) show that the relative economic performance of alternative environmental policy instruments can be affected by agricultural policy distortions; the policies that perform best with distortions may not be the same as those that perform best without. Shortle and Laughland (1994) demonstrate that the effectiveness of agricultural environmental policies can be diminished and the cost increased if distortionary agricultural policies are adjusted to compensate for the costs of compliance with environmental policies.

Land conversion and degradation
The loss of wetlands and tropical forests to agriculture has generated much controversy and environmental concern in recent years. Inefficient conversion of forests and other natural areas to agriculture can result from a number of factors. Failure of markets to reward landowners or tenants for the public goods, such as carbon sequestration, habitat, and various watershed functions that are provided by natural areas is one factor (Sandler, 1993). Failure of markets to penalize landowners or tenants for the negative externalities associated with conversion and developed uses is another. As with the water pollution externalities described above, government policies can exacerbate the consequences of missing or imperfect markets.

Another concern is degradation of agricultural land by soil erosion, soil compaction and agricultural chemicals (National Research Council, 1993; Pimentel, 1993). From an economic perspective, the essential feature of land degradation is that actions are taken to increase current agricultural production at the expense of future soil productivity and thus future production. However, unlike the negative environmental externalities discussed above, the on-farm costs of land degradation are borne first and foremost by the owners of agricultural land rather than the public at large. Provided that landowners have good information about the impacts of agricultural production decisions on land quality, and provided that agricultural output and input markets are functioning well (particularly markets for land and credit), land degradation does not present any environmental externalities. However, there may be cases where information is poor or markets are not well developed.

Agriculture in developing countries is most likely to present cases where agricultural output and input markets are missing or not functioning well. In particular, poor farmers in developing countries often lack access to credit markets, either because they lack the collateral necessary to obtain a loan or because there are few financial intermediaries in the places where they live (which is itself a result of the level of poverty in these areas). This limited ability to borrow can prevent poor farmers from obtaining loans to finance otherwise profitable investments in soil conservation activities. Empirical evidence indicates that it works in a similar manner to limit investments in schooling, health, and water and sewer facilities (Morduch, 1995; Mink, 1993).

3. Beneficial environmental externalities

Agricultural can be a source of a number of positive environmental externalities. We focus here on the positive externality that has perhaps attracted the most attention in North America and Western Europe: rural amenities. In both these regions, a major objective of land use policies is to prevent conversion of existing agricultural land to non-agricultural uses.

One argument for agricultural land conservation policies is to safeguard agricultural production capacity from urban encroachment. While this argument may have popular appeal, it lacks economic validity, at least in Western Europe and North America. First, land markets in Western Europe and the US are fairly efficient. They have long functioned well in allocating land among competing uses, including agriculture (Gardner, 1977). Second, land scarcity has not been a problem for agricultural production (Crosson, 1995). Long-term trends in production costs have been downward, which is the reverse of what should happen if land scarcity were seriously limiting agricultural production (Mitchell and Ingco, 1995).

The more cogent reason for agricultural land conservation policies, at least in countries with well-functioning land and capital markets, is to influence the supply of related public goods. In Europe and broad regions of North America, most of the land where most of the people live is in agriculture. The visual character of the landscape, outdoor recreation opportunities, wildlife habitat and agricultural output are joint products (Bromley and Hodge, 1990). Contingent valuation studies (Beasely et al., 1986; Bergstrom et al., 1985; Halstead, 1984) and revealed political preference studies (Kline and Wichelns, 1994, 1996) suggest that people are willing to pay to protect farmland from development. While markets can efficiently provide some of the uses of rural lands (for example, crop production, hunting), many others are inherently non-market goods (for example, visual amenities, habitat preservation).

A major problem for rural amenity policies is identifying preferences for existing and alternative landscapes. The 'commodity' in this case is not well defined, and because it is not traded in markets, non-market methods must be used to evaluate preferences and trade-offs that people are willing to make. Hanley and Ruffell (1993a,b) discuss the potential usefulness of non-market valuation methods for evaluating alternative rural landscapes.

Hodge (1995) identifies three broad categories of land use policy objectives: (1) preventing undesired land use changes (for example, urban containment); (2) modifying existing land uses to reduce detrimental externalities or increase beneficial externalities (for example, encouraging farming practices that preserve wildlife habitat or discouraging practices that result in water pollution); and (3) stimulating new uses that provide public or quasi-public goods (for example, wetlands). Farmland conservations policies can easily attain the first objective. However, they may conflict with the other two objectives. For instance, farmland conservation may be at odds with the second objective if existing agricultural practices are detrimental to the environment (for example, intensive livestock production). Farmland conservation may also be at odds with the third objective if other desired land uses are precluded (for example, wetlands or forests). McConnell (1989) suggests that farmland conservation policies in the US, which emphasize conservation of farmland as opposed to the supply of rural amenities, may result in too much land in agriculture as opposed to other uses. Land use policies in several European countries are more discriminating, with agricultural land conservation policies as a component part rather than the dominant feature.

Policies for modifying agricultural land use to enhance rural amenities include regulations, cross-compliance and environmental contracts. Architectural standards and other regulations can be, and are to some extent, used to control agricultural practices. However, in the provision of rural amenities, property rights and fairness considerations may reduce the feasible policy options to either voluntary action or subsidies to landowners for agricultural land use modifications (Hodge, 1989). Cross-compliance makes eligibility for government benefits in one context contingent upon satisfying environmental performance goals in some other context. The US has a cross-compliance requirement to reduce soil erosion on highly erodible lands, the carrot being eligibility for farm price and income supports (Abler and Shortle, 1989). Tax relief for compliance with environmental performance criteria would be another form of cross-compliance.

A major limitation of this approach is that the incentives for environmental performance depend on criteria unrelated to the environment. If incentives for participation vary across farmers inversely with the environmental benefits from their participation, then outcomes may be highly inefficient. Inefficiencies will also occur if incentives to participate vary inversely over time with demands for environmental performance.

With environmental contracts, a farmer agrees to farm in a particular way in return for a payment. This method has been used in a number of countries (OECD, 1989, 1993). Two examples mentioned earlier are the ESA programme in the EU and the US CRP. The design of environmental contracts is critical to the cost-effectiveness of the approach. For instance, the flat-rate payments under the ESA programme may be higher than necessary to induce farmers to participate (that is, payments in excess of participation costs), limiting the programme's cost-effectiveness. Farmers in the US CRP offer bids to the government, indicating how much they would be willing to accept to enrol land in the CRP. Contracts are awarded to the lowest bidders. However, in practice, bids in each county are rarely less than the maximum per acre rate for that county as set by the government. Thus the CRP is essentially a flat-rate programme, with rates varying by county. Moreover, environmental criteria have to date had only a small role in the spatial distribution of CRP contracts, greatly limiting the cost-effectiveness of the programme (Miranowski et al., 1989).

4.   Agriculture as a receptor

Air and water pollution have long been recognized as potential threats to agriculture. Localized cases in which agriculture has been affected by air- or water-quality degradation have been documented. However, overall understanding of the impacts is limited. Experimental research can demonstrate that exposure to a certain pollutant can have particular effects (sometimes positive) on the quality and yield of crops and livestock. However, actual impacts are not easily discerned, given the multitude of environmental and management factors influencing actual outcomes.

One problem that has received substantial attention from economists as well as plant scientists is ozone pollution (Spash, 1997). This pollutant has been shown in controlled experiments to reduce crop yields, although susceptibility varies greatly by crop type. Adams et al. (1988) estimate that ozone is responsible for 90 per cent of the vegetative damages caused by air pollution in the US. They estimate that a 25 per cent reduction in ambient ozone levels across the US would have an economic benefit of about $1.7 billion (1982 dollars) annually. This is small in comparison with agriculture's total economic value but large as a percentage of the total benefits from ozone pollution control in the US (Segerson, 1991). Most of the benefits were estimated to be passed to consumers as a result of price reductions rather than captured by producers.

An important caveat in considering these results is that they do not include changes in the economic value of agricultural externalities, both positive and negative, associated with induced changes in the scale, location and methods of agricultural production (Segerson, 1991). For example, reductions in air pollution that increase agricultural productivity may lead to increased water pollution if they lead to an increase in the land in production and the use of potentially harmful inputs. Another important point is that the magnitudes of air and water pollution control benefits are influenced by the presence of commodity programmes that distort agricultural markets (Kopp and Krupnick, 1987). Paradoxically, air and water pollution can have economic benefits in so far as they reduce agricultural production and, in turn, economic distortions from commodity programmes. Adams et al. (1988) estimated an increase in deadweight losses of about 10 per cent for the 25 per cent ozone reduction.

Acidic deposition has also received considerable attention from scientists (Spash, 1997). This case illustrates some of the physical and economic complexities of agriculture–environment interactions. Increased acidity of rainfall can cause foliar damages that reduce yields but can also increase yields through effects on soil pH. In a study of US soybeans, Adams et al. (1986) estimated a net reduction in production that reduced consumer welfare as a consequence of higher agricultural prices. However, producer welfare was increased as a result of higher prices and reduced fertilizer costs. The gain to producers exceeded the consumer loss, so the net economic effect, although modest, was positive.

More recently much attention has been given to the potential impacts of the 'greenhouse' effect on agriculture. The potential impacts depend on a number of factors that are still highly uncertain: (1) impacts on regional climates where crops and livestock are produced; (2) direct effects of climate change on crops and livestock; (3) indirect effects of climate change on soils, insects and plant diseases; (4) climate-change-induced changes in agricultural commodity demands and the prices of agricultural inputs; and (5) the feasibility and costs of economic and technological adaptation (Adams et al., 1996; Bowes and Crosson, 1993; Bruce et al., 1996; Crosson, 1989; Darwin et al., 1995; Reilly, 1995; Watson et al., 1996). Uncertainty about regional climate change is especially profound. While scientists seem largely to agree that rising greenhouse gas concentrations will lead to global climate change, there remains considerable uncertainty about exactly how, when, and where the climate will change.

The recent Intergovernmental Panel on Climate Change (IPCC) assessment of climate change concludes that projected climate change is not a significant threat to world food production (Bruce et al., 1996; Watson et al., 1996). Under some scenarios, world food production could even increase (Rosenzweig and Parry, 1994). However, effects are likely to vary greatly between countries. Reilly and Hohmann (1993) and Reilly et al. (1994) find that agricultural exporting countries may gain economically in so far as climate change leads to higher global agricultural prices, even though their agricultural production may decline. Similarly, importing countries may be economically harmed by higher global agricultural prices, even though their agricultural production may increase. Developing countries as a group were projected to experience economic losses, but within the group there were winners and losers.

A critical issue in climate change research is the ability of agriculture, as well as other ecological and economic systems, to adapt. Agricultural policies are important in this context. In particular, agricultural research and extension can enhance technological response capabilities and disseminate research findings to farmers. However, policies such as product price supports, input subsidies, agricultural trade barriers and payments for crop failures can hinder adaptation when they encourage the production of climate-sensitive crops, the use of cropping systems ill suited to the changed climate, or limit incentives for relocation or innovation (Lewandrowski and Brazee, 1993).

5. Conclusions

This review has addressed only some of the major issues related to agriculture and the environment, and has only scratched at those. However, it should be apparent that the interface between agriculture and the environment is exceptionally complex and rich with economic and policy ambiguities. Societies have many interests in agriculture, ranging from traditional economic concerns to contemporary demands for a diverse set of environmental services. Designing and implementing sound public policies in this setting is an exceptionally difficult task. The pursuit of environmental goals almost invariably conflicts with others. Many of the economic and policy ambiguities can be resolved, but it will require research integrated across the physical and social sciences. Other economic and policy ambiguities will undoubtedly be resolved only through a trial-and-error process, as policy makers experiment with alternative approaches to agriculture and the environment.

Note
1. Large point sources of pollution and manufacturers of environmentally harmful products, such as pesticides and automobiles, are the main targets of regulatory programmes. The comparative ease with which large point sources could be identified and controlled, and the political support for action against obvious polluters, made them a logical choice

for first-generation environmental programmes. Similarly, regulation of chemical and automobile manufacturers has been easier politically and administratively, at least for governments at the helm of large economies, than direct regulation of the many households and small businesses that actually cause environmental harm through their activities and use of polluting products.

References

Abler, D.G. and J.S. Shortle (1989), 'Cross compliance and water quality protection', *Journal of Soil and Water Conservation*, **44**, 453–4.
Abler, D.G. and J.S. Shortle (1991), 'The political economy of water quality protection from agricultural chemicals', *Northeastern Journal of Agricultural and Resource Economics*, **20**, 53–60.
Abler, D.G. and J.S. Shortle (1992), 'Environmental and farm commodity policy linkages in the US and EC', *European Review of Agricultural Economics*, **19**, 197–217.
Abler, D.G. and J.S. Shortle (1995), 'Technology as an agricultural pollution control policy', *American Journal of Agricultural Economics*, **77**, 20–32.
Abler, D.G. and J.S. Shortle (1996), 'Environmental aspects of agricultural technology', in J. Alston and P. Pardey (eds), *Global Agricultural Science Policy for the Twenty-First Century*, Melbourne, Australia: Conference Secretariat on Global Agricultural Science Policy for the Twenty-First Century.
Abrahams, N. and J. Shortle (1997), 'The value of information and the design of environmental policies for agriculture', paper presented at the 1997 Annual Meeting of the American Agricultural Economics Association, Toronto, July.
Adams, R.M., R.A. Fleming, C.C. Chang, B.A. McCarl and C. Rosenzweig (1996), 'A reassessment of the economic effects of global climate change on U.S. agriculture', *Climate Change*, **30**, 147–67.
Adams, R.M., J.D. Glyer and B.A. McCarl (1988), 'The NCLAN economic assessment: approach, findings and implications', in W.W. Heck, O.C. Taylor and D.T. Tingey (eds), *Assessment of Crop Loss from Air Pollutants*, London: Elsevier.
Adams, R.M., S.A. Hamilton and B.A. McCarl (1986), 'Pollution, agriculture and social welfare: the case of acid deposition', *Canadian Journal of Agricultural Economics*, **34**, 3–19.
Babcock, B.A., P.G. Lakshminarayan, J.J. Wu and D. Zilberman (1997), 'Targeting tools for purchasing of environmental amenities', *Land Economics*, **73**, 325–39.
Beasley, S.D., W.G. Workman and N.A. Williams (1986), 'Estimating amenity values of urban fringe farmland: a contingent valuation approach', *Growth and Change*, **17**, 70–78.
Bergstrom, J.D., B.L. Dillman and J.R. Stoll (1985), 'Public environmental amenity benefits of private land: the case of prime agricultural land', *Southern Journal of Agricultural Economics*, **17**, 139–49.
Bogárdi, I. and R.D. Kuzelka (eds) (1991), *Nitrate Contamination: Exposure, Consequence, and Control*, Berlin: Springer-Verlag.
Bouzaher, A., J.B. Braden and G. Johnson (1990), 'A dynamic programming approach to a class of nonpoint pollution problems', *Management Science*, **35**, 1–15.
Bowes, M.D. and P. Crosson (1993), 'Consequences of climate change for the MINK economy: impacts and responses', *Climate Change*, **24**, 131–58.
Braden, J.B., A. Bozaher, G. Johnson and D. Miltz (1989), 'Optimal spatial management of agricultural pollution', *American Journal of Agricultural Economics*, **71**, 404–13.
Bromley, D.W. and I. Hodge (1990), 'Private property rights and presumptive policy entitlements: reconsidering the premises of rural policy', *European Review of Agricultural Economics*, **17**, 197–214.
Bruce, J., H. Lee and E. Haites (eds) (1996), *Climate Change 1995 – Economic and Social Dimensions of Climate Change*, New York: Cambridge University Press.
Chrispeels, M.J. and D.E. Sadava (1994), *Plants, Genes, and Agriculture*, Boston: Jones and Barlett.
Council on Scientific Affairs (1988), 'Cancer risk of pesticides in agricultural workers', *Journal of the American Medical Association*, **260**, 959–66.

Cropper, M.L., W.N. Evans, J. J. Bernardi, M.M. Duclas Soares and P.R. Portney (1992), 'The determinants of pesticide regulation: a statistical analysis of EPA decision making', *Journal of Political Economy*, **100**, 175–97.

Crosson, P. (1989), 'Climate change and mid-latitudes agriculture: perspectives on consequences and policy responses', *Climate Change*, **15**, 51–73.

Crosson, P. (1995), 'Future supplies of land and water for world agriculture', in N. Islam (ed.), *Population and Food in the Early 21st Century: Meeting Future Food Demand of an Increasing World Population*, Washington, DC: International Food Policy Research Institute (IFPRI).

Crutchfield, S.R., P.M. Feather and D.R. Hellerstein (1995), *The Benefits of Protecting Rural Water Quality: An Empirical Analysis*, US Department of Agriculture, Report no. AER-701, Washington, DC: Government Printing Office.

Darwin, R., M. Tsigas, J. Lewandrowski and A. Raneses (1995), *World Agriculture and Climate Change: Economic Adaptation*, US Department of Agriculture, Report no. AER-709, Washington, DC: Government Printing Office.

Dubgaard, A. (1994), 'The Danish environmental programs: an assessment of policy instruments and results', in T.L. Napier, S.M. Camboni and S.A. El-Swaify (eds), *Adopting Conservation on the Farm*, Ankeny, IA: Soil and Water Conservation Society.

Duda, A.M. and R.J. Johnson (1985), 'Cost effective targeting of agricultural non-point source pollution controls, *Journal of Soil and Water Conservation*, **40**, 108–11.

Ervin, D. and E. Graffy (1996), 'Leaner environmental policies for agriculture', *Choices*, **11** (4), 27–33.

Feather, P.M. and G. Amacher (1993), 'Role of information in the adoption of best management practices for water quality improvement', *Agricultural Economics*, **11**, 159–70.

Feather, P.M. and J. Cooper (1995), *Voluntary Incentives for Reducing Agricultural Nonpoint Source Water Pollution*, US Department of Agriculture, Agriculture Information Bulletin no. 716, Washington, DC: Government Printing Office.

Fransman, M., G. Junne and A. Roobeek (eds) (1995), *The Biotechnology Revolution?* Oxford: Basil Blackwell.

Freeman, A. Myrick III (1990), 'Water pollution policy', in P.R. Portney (ed.), *Public Policies for Environmental Protection*, Washington, DC: Resources for the Future.

Gardner, B.D. (1977), 'The economics of agricultural land protection programs', *Growth and Change*, **18**, 49–61.

Gardner, B.L. (1990), *Economics of Agricultural Policies*, New York: McGraw-Hill.

Halstead, J.M. (1984), 'Measuring the nonmarket value of Massachusetts agricultural land: a case study', *Journal of the Northeastern Agricultural Economics Council*, **13**, 12–19.

Hanley, N. and R. Ruffel (1993a), 'The contingent valuation of forest characteristics: two experiments', *Journal of Agricultural Economics*, **44**, 218–29.

Hanley, N. and R. Ruffell (1993b), 'The valuation of forest characteristics', in W. Adamowicz and W. White (eds), *Forestry and the Environment: Economic Perspectives*, Oxford: CAB International.

Hidy, G. (1995), 'Acid rain', in W.A. Nierenberg (ed.), *Encyclopedia of Environmental Biology*, New York: Academic Press.

Hodge, I.D. (1989), 'Compensation for nature conservation', *Environment and Planning A*, **21**, 1027–36.

Hodge, I.D. (1995), 'Public policies for land conservation,' in D. Bromley (ed.), *The Handbook of Environmental Economics*, Oxford: Basil Blackwell.

Hochman, E. and D. Zilberman (1978), 'Examination of environmental policies using production and pollution microparameter distributions', *Econometrica*, **46**, 739–60.

Johnson, D.G. (1991), *World Agriculture in Disarray*, 2nd edn, New York: St Martin's Press.

Kline, J. and D. Wichelns (1994), 'Using referendum data to characterize public support for purchasing development rights to farmland', *Land Economics*, **70**, 223–33.

Kline, J. and D. Wichelns (1996), 'Public preferences for farmland preservation programs', *Land Economics*, **72**, 538–49.

Kopp, R.J. and A.J. Krupnick (1987), 'Agricultural policy and the benefits of ozone control', *American Journal of Agricultural Economics*, **69**, 956–62.

Laughland, A.S. (1994), *Multiple Instruments in the Regulation of Nonpoint Source Pollution*, PhD dissertation, Department of Agricultural Economics and Rural Sociology, Pennsylvania State University.

Lee, J.G., S.B. Lovejoy and D.B. Beasley (1985), 'Soil loss reduction in Finely Creek Indiana: an economic analysis of alternative policies', *Journal of Soil Conservation*, **40**, 132–5.

Lewandrowski, J.K. and R.J. Brazee (1993), 'Farm programs and climate change', *Climate Change*, **23**, 1–20.

Liapis, P.S. (1994), 'Environmental and economic implications of alternative EC policies', *Journal of Agricultural and Applied Economics*, **26**, 241–51.

Lichtenberg, E. (1992), 'Alternative approaches to pesticide regulation', *Northeastern Journal of Agricultural and Resource Economics*, **21**, 83–92.

Lichtenberg, E. and D. Zilberman (1988), 'Efficient regulation of environmental health risks', *Quarterly Journal of Economics*, **103** (1), 167–78.

Logan, T.J. (1993), 'Agricultural best management practices for water pollution control: current issues', *Agriculture, Ecosystems and Environment*, **46**, 223–31.

McConnell, K.E. (1989), 'The optimal quantity of land in agriculture', *Northeastern Journal of Agricultural and Resource Economics*, **18**, 63–72.

Mink, S.D. (1993), *Poverty, Population, and the Environment*, World Bank Discussion Paper no. 189. Washington, DC: World Bank.

Miranowski, J.A., J. Hrubovcak and J. Sutton (1989), 'The effects of commodity programs on resource use', in R.E. Just and N.E. Bockstael (eds), *Commodity and Resource Policies in Agricultural Systems*, Berlin: Springer-Verlag.

Mitchell, D.O. and M. Ingco (1995), 'Global and regional food demand and supply prospects', in N. Islam (ed.), *Population and Food in the Early 21st Century: Meeting Future Food Demand of an Increasing World Population*, Washington, DC: International Food Policy Research Institute (IFPRI).

Morduch, J. (1995), 'Incoming smoothing and consumption smoothing', *Journal of Economic Perspectives*, **9**, 103–14.

National Research Council (1989), *Alternative Agriculture*, Washington, DC: National Academy Press.

National Research Council (1993), *Soil and Water Quality: An Agenda for Agriculture*, Washington, DC: National Academy Press.

Norton, N.A., T.T. Phipps and J.J. Fletcher (1994), 'Role of voluntary programs in agricultural nonpoint pollution policy', *Contemporary Economic Policy*, **12**, 113–21.

OECD (1986), *Water Pollution by Fertilizers and Pesticides*, Paris: OECD.

OECD (1989), *Agricultural and Environmental Policies: Opportunities for Integration*, Paris: OECD.

OECD (1991), *The State of the Environment*, Paris: OECD.

OECD (1993), *Agricultural and Environmental Policy Integration: Recent Progress and New Directions*, Paris: OECD.

OECD (1994a), *Environmental Taxes in OECD Countries*, Paris: OECD.

OECD (1994b), *Towards Sustainable Agricultural Production: Cleaner Technologies*, Paris: OECD.

OECD (1995), *OECD Environmental Performance Reviews: Netherlands*, Paris: OECD.

Park, W.M. and L.A. Shabman (1982), 'Distributional constraints on acceptance of nonpoint pollution control', *American Journal of Agricultural Economics*, **64**, 455–62.

Pimentel, D. (ed.) (1993), *World Soil Erosion and Conservation*, Cambridge, UK: Cambridge University Press.

Plantinga, A.J. (1996), 'The effect of agricultural policies on land use and environmental quality', *American Journal of Agricultural Economics*, **78**, 1082–91.

Poe, G. (1977), 'Extra-market values and conflicting agricultural values', *Choices*, **12**, 4–8.

Reichelderfer, K. and R.A. Kramer (1993), 'Agricultural resource policy', in G. Carlson, D. Zilberman, and J. Miranowski (eds), *Agricultural and Environmental Resource Economics*, Oxford: Oxford University Press.

Reilly, J. (1995), 'Climate change and global agriculture: recent findings and issues', *American Journal of Agricultural Economics*, **77**, 243–50.

Reilly, J. and N. Hohmann (1993), 'Climate change and agriculture: the role of international trade', *American Economic Review: Papers and Proceedings*, **83**, 306–12.

Reilly, J., N. Hohmann and S. Kane (1994), 'Climate change and agricultural trade: who benefits, who loses?', *Global Environmental Change*, **4**, 24–36.

Ribaudo, M.O. (1986), 'Considerations of offsite impacts in targeting soil conservation programs', *Land Economics*, **62**, 402–11.

Ribaudo, M.O. (1989), *Water Quality Benefits from the Conservation Reserve Program*, US Department of Agriculture, Report no. AER-606, Washington, DC: Government Printing Office.

Rosenzweig, C. and M.L. Parry (1994), 'Potential impact of climate change on world food supply', *Nature*, **367**, 133–8.

Sandler, T. (1993), 'Tropical deforestation: markets and market failures', *Land Economics*, **69**, 225–33.

Segerson, K. (1991), 'Air pollution and agriculture: a review and evaluation of policy interactions', in R.E. Just and N.E. Bockstael (eds), *Commodity and Resource Policies in Agricultural Systems*, Berlin: Springer-Verlag.

Shortle, J.S. (1996), 'Environmental federalism and the control of water pollution from US agriculture: is the current division of responsibilities between national and local authorities about right?', in J.B. Braden, H. Folmer and T.S. Ulen (eds), *Environmental Policy with Political and Economic Integration*, Cheltenham, UK and Brookfield, US: Edward Elgar.

Shortle, J.S. and D.G. Abler (1997), 'Nonpoint pollution', in H. Folmer and T. Tietenberg (eds), *International Yearbook of Environmental and Resource Economics*, Cheltenham, UK and Lyme, US: Edward Elgar.

Shortle, J.S. and A. Laughland (1994), 'Impacts of taxes to reduce agrichemical use when farm policy is exogenous', *Journal of Agricultural Economics*, **45**, 2–14.

Smith, V.K. (1997), 'Pricing what is priceless: a status report on non-market valuation', in H. Folmer and T. Tietenberg (eds), *International Yearbook of Environmental and Resource Economics*, Cheltenham, UK and Brookfield, US: Edward Elgar.

Spash, C.L. (1997), 'Assessing the economic benefits to agriculture from air pollution control', *Journal of Economic Surveys*, **11**, 47–70.

Swinton, S.M. and D.S. Clark (1994), 'Farm-level evaluation of alternative policy approaches to reduce nitrate leaching from Midwest agriculture', *Agricultural and Resource Economics Review*, **23**, 66–74.

Thrupp, L. (1988), 'Pesticides and policies: approaches to pest-control dilemmas in Nicaragua and Costa Rica', *Latin American Perspectives*, **15**, 37–70.

Tsai, K. and J. Shortle (1997), 'Optimal differentiation of tax rates and optimal base definition in nonpoint pollution control', Working Paper, Department of Agricultural Economics and Rural Sociology, The Pennsylvania State University, University Park, PA.

US Environmental Protection Agency (EPA) (1994), 'National Water Quality Inventory: 1992 Report to Congress', EPA 841-R-94-001, Washington, DC: Government Printing Office.

van Kooten, K. and H. Folmer (1996), 'Climate change and agriculture: what can the economist say?', *Aspects of Applied Biology*, **45**, 117–31.

Watson, R.T., M.C. Zinyowera and R.H. Moss (eds) (1996), *Climate Change 1995 – Impacts, Adaptation and Mitigation of Climate Change: Scientific–Technical Analyses*, New York: Cambridge University Press.

Weinberg, M., C.L. Kling and J.E. Wilen (1993a), 'Water markets and water quality', *American Journal of Agricultural Economics*, **75**, 278–91.

Weinberg, M., C.L. Kling and J.E. Wilen (1993b), 'Analysis of policy options for the control of agricultural pollution in California's San Joaquin Basin', in C.S. Russel and J.F. Shogren (eds), *Theory, Modeling and Experience in the Management of Nonpoint-Source Pollution*, Dordrecht: Kluwer Academic Publishers.

World Bank (1992), *World Development Report 1992: Development and the Environment*, New York: Oxford University Press.

World Health Organization (1990), *Public Health Impact of Pesticides Used in Agriculture*, Geneva: World Health Organization.

Zilberman, D., A. Schmitz, G. Casterline, E. Lichtenberg and J.B. Siebert (1991), 'The economics of pesticide use and regulation', *Science*, **253**, 518–22.

12 The economics of energy
Jan Willem Velthuijsen and Ernst Worrell

1. The role of energy in society

Energy plays a crucial role in today's society. It is an essential commodity for households throughout the world, for heating, cooling, cooking, lighting, transportation and for numerous other activities. Moreover energy is a production factor of eminent importance in virtually all sectors of industry.

The need for energy has closely followed accelerated world growth in population and economic activity. Energy has obtained an enormous strategic value. The safeguarding of energy supplies has even led countries to go to war. As a consequence, energy supplies are closely and continuously watched. The price of oil is announced on the news every day. And governments throughout the world have implemented rules and regulations to monitor and control energy trade and stocks.

Since the first oil price crisis in 1973–74, awareness has increased dramatically, not only about the dependence of the world's economy on the costs of energy, but also about the exhaustion of conventional energy forms. At the same time the Club of Rome warned about 'Limits to Growth', arguing that both the exhaustion of natural resources and the pollution consequences of resource use will eventually set constraints on growth of population and the economy (Meadows et al., 1972). Energy has more and more become a scarce resource, and hence it has increasingly attracted the attention of the economist (see also Chapters 73, 74 and 75).

2. Energy and the environment

Causes and consequences

Several of the earth's crucial environmental problems originate from the energy demand to fuel human needs and economic growth. Current energy production and usage patterns rely heavily on combustion of fossil fuels. This is a key factor in the unprecedented increase in carbon dioxide (CO_2) concentrations in the earth's atmosphere that contribute to global climate change (IPCC, 1996). Key environmental problems are regional (acidification of soil and water), local (smog, urban air quality, solid wastes, effluents and thermal pollution) or indoor air pollution. Table 12.1 gives a schematic overview of the key environmental impacts of various energy carriers and

Table 12.1 Overview of environmental impacts of energy carriers and uses

	Short term	Medium term	Long term
FOSSIL FUEL Local impacts only	• Surface- and groundwater contamination	• Land, marine and coastal pollution • Ground and water contamination from heavy metals leachates from solid wastes • Air pollution from particulates SO_x, NO_x, hydrocarbons, organic material	• Land disturbance and ecosystem destruction
Mainly regional impacts		• Damage to structures, soil changes and forest degradation from SO_2, and NO_x emissions	• Marine and ocean pollution with loss of species
Global impacts			• Lake acidification and loss of communities due to acid depositions • Climate change from CO_2 and other greenhouse gas emissions (associated potential impacts include sea-level rise)

NUCLEAR

Local impacts only

- Surface- and groundwater contamination
- Land disturbance and ecosystem destruction

Mainly regional impacts

- Land and water contamination with radionuclides under accident conditions
- Radiation effects on health and land/water contamination under severe accident conditions

RENEWABLE ENERGY SOURCES

Local impacts only

- Atmospheric pollution
- Land destruction and modification to ecosystems
- Loss of species and sedimentation effects

Regional impacts

- Changes to marine life and water quality
- Changes to hydrological patterns and water quality

Source: Lazarus and von Hippel (1995).

uses; Figure 12.1 shows global primary energy consumption of energy carriers; and Table 12.2 presents the regional distribution of global primary energy use in 1971, 1980 and 1990.

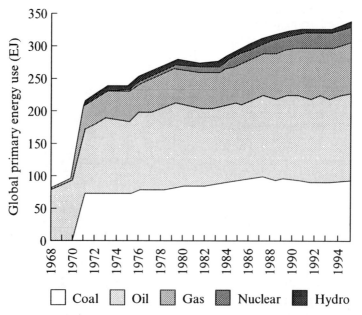

Note: The totals exclude consumption of renewable energy sources, estimated to be 41 EJ in 1995 (OECD, 1997).

Sources: British Petroleum (1988, 1996).

Figure 12.1   Global primary consumption of energy carriers, in EJ ($10^{18}J$)

Global environmental issues

The burning of fossil fuels, no matter how efficiently, inevitably produces CO_2, which is the principal cause of the greenhouse effect.[1] Although uncertainties about the impact of human-induced climate change are large (IPCC, 1996), many countries have agreed that the lack of full scientific certainty is not a reason to postpone responsive action (UNFCCC, 1992). Several countries have announced and implemented national policies to reduce greenhouse gas (GHG) emissions. Economic key issues, for example, efficiency and equity, affect the response strategy to sharing the burden of adaptation to and mitigation of climate change (King and Munasinghe, 1992).

*Table 12.2   Regional distribution of global primary energy use in 1971,
1980 and 1990 (in EJ)*

Region	1971	1980	1990
OECD	120 (63%)	142 (56%)	160 (52%)
Eastern Europe/Former Soviet Union	44 (23%)	62 (25%)	73 (24%)
Developing countries	27 (14%)	48 (19%)	75 (24%)
Total	191	253	309

Source: WEC (1995b)

Regional environmental issues
Acidification of soils and surface water is a process that increases the
acidity, resulting in damage to ecosystems. Acidification is the result of the
emissions of sulphur oxides (SO_x), nitrogen oxides (NO_x) and ammonia.
Sulphur and nitrogen oxides are emitted from combustion processes of
(fossil) fuels. As coal combustion is one of the main emitters, the highest
deposition is found in Central Europe and the UK, and in the eastern part
of the USA and Canada. Currently the use of coal is growing rapidly in
China and India, putting these areas at future risk of the effects of acidic
precipitation.

The impact of acidification depends on the vulnerability of the ecosystem. It can lead to 'dead' lakes and to reduction of nutrient availability and
fertility of the soil, affecting growth rates of forests, resilience of trees to
stress and reduction of biodiversity.

Emission reduction policies in Europe and North America include
switching to less polluting fuels (low-sulphur coals or natural gas) or flue-
gas cleaning (catalysts for automotive applications and SO_x and NO_x abatement at coal-fired power stations) (Reddy et al., 1997).

Local environmental issues
Local environmental problems affect human health. Particularly in large
cities in developing countries the health and environmental effects of the
current patterns of energy use are extreme, as abatement technologies and
policies are not always available or implemented. The best-known problem
is smog formation due to combustion of fossil fuels in traffic and stationary energy conversion. Given current patterns of population and economic
growth in the developing world, these problems will continue to worsen
(UNEP/WHO, 1992).

Other local problems include the production of solid wastes, destruction
of ecosystems and surface-water disruption in peat production (WEC,

1995a). Water quality can be negatively influenced by oil spills, effluents from energy use and thermal pollution due to using surface water as cooling water in power stations. A special problem is formed by the highly radioactive wastes from nuclear power production. Indoor air pollution can result from fuel use in buildings. The use of fuel wood in cooking is a major source of lung diseases in Africa (Dutt and Ravindranath, 1993).

Sustainability, climate change and the global political issue
The problem of climate change is regarded as one of the main environmental risks endangering sustainable development. Mankind is confronted with a global challenge, in this respect perhaps only comparable with the nuclear threat during the cold war. 'This greenhouse problem, if problem it proves to be, is truly one of the global common' (Schelling, 1992). Obviously, a global political consensus on the need to counter the problem of climate change and on the ways to do it is a prerequisite for a global policy. Such a consensus is extremely difficult to obtain, for many questions regarding welfare distribution and economic development are involved.

The present conventions, treaties and agreements are important steps, but are not sufficient to bring about the necessary changes in human use of energy. The Framework Convention on Climate Change (FCCC) of 1992 signified a beginning. At the Third Conference of Parties to the FCCC of 1997 more concrete greenhouse gas emission targets were set.

3.   Economics of energy

Energy as a production factor
Energy is used as a production factor in virtually every production process. The amount of energy necessary to produce a unit of output varies enormously among the spectrum of commodities and services. The average cost share of energy inputs in total inputs ranges from 1 per cent for certain labour-intensive services, for example, of the physician, the accountant and the lawyer, to over 30 per cent for some petrochemical and horticultural products. In a highly industrialized energy-intensive – and also energy-efficient – region like Northwest Europe, the total national cost share typically amounts to 3 per cent.

Economic theory prescribes energy demand to be determined by the optimization decision process of the firm. Given the production function, describing the production possibilities using labour, capital, energy, and other factors, a rational firm uses energy up to the point where the marginal value product (MVP) equals the energy price. In the decision process energy use is weighed against the other production factors by balancing the ratios between marginal factor productivity and factor prices. The production factor intensities are thus determined by the relative factor prices and by mutual technological substitutability or complementarity: the degree of dependence is reflected by the own- and cross-price elasticities. In short, energy demand substitutes with other production factors.

In practice, energy needs are closely connected to the installed capital equipment, at least in the short run. In fact, in most situations, energy is a close complement to capital equipment, as most equipment requires energy to function. Energy demand is therefore closely connected to the decision process the firm pursues regarding investment, installation and replacement of capital equipment. As the investment decision of the firm involves longer-term impacts, there are large differences between long-term and short-term elasticities. Empirical evidence typically locates short-term energy (own-)price elasticities in the range from 0 to −10 per cent, while long-term elasticities may reach up to −50 per cent.

Energy is not a homogeneous production factor. Energy carriers can be regarded as competing mutually: the firm selects its energy mix by equating MVPs of energy carriers to their respective prices. In practice substitution among energy carriers is often just as limited. Certainly in the short term, the installed technologies are geared to use one specific energy carrier. Cars with a switch from gasoline to LPG are a notable exception. In the longer run, substitutive adaptation to price differences becomes conceivable for a great number of applications. Yet the own-price energy elasticities are commonly less than −10 per cent (Velthuijsen, 1995).

Energy price changes trigger a third substitution mechanism, affecting the energy carrier mix. If a company has difficulties shifting energy price increases on to its domestic or international customers, it can lose market share. The intrasectoral or intersectoral market share reshuffling changes the sectoral or national energy carrier mix. The shift of the national energy mix is a long-run phenomenon that can take decades. A substantial increase in the price of energy may reduce turnover of an industrial sector that is heavily dependent on a particular energy carrier, or it may force a company to move. European aluminium smelters and basic chemicals producers have repeatedly advised relocating production to 'cheap energy havens', if energy becomes too expensive. Recent history of labour-intensive producers moving activities to Asia illustrates the potential magnitude of this effect.

A fourth mechanism relates to technological progress and innovation. High-energy prices stimulate energy conservation (See Section 4). They also stimulate further R&D into improving the efficiency of technologies. In the long run, this will lead to lower energy intensities of firms and households. This phenomenon of endogenous growth has received a lot of attention lately by economic theorists, but as yet there is virtually no empirical evidence on the order of magnitude of the effects of this kind.

Energy as feedstock

Fossil energy is a material input for several products, like plastics, fibres and fertilizers. The environmental effects of its use are in this case more indirect, and for that reason they have received less attention from politicians and economists. Eventually, at the end of the product cycle these goods are spread out on arable land, disposed to landfills or incinerated. Recently, attempts have been made to take into account the entire production cycle and design policy instruments to stimulate:

- economizing on the use of the inputs per unit of product;
- the development of clean alternatives;
- reuse, for example by means of refund systems.

As in the case of energy use as a fuel, the technical substitution opportunities of energy carriers as feedstocks determine the degree to which these goals can be achieved. The elasticities tend to be very low in the short run.

Energy as a consumer good

Energy demand by households generally breaks down into lighting, cooling, heating, cooking and transportation. Household demand for energy varies across regions in the world, and across individual households in each country. The budget shares spent on energy vary between 5 to 15 per cent. Given the preference structure of a household, a household's energy demand depends on the relative prices of the energy carriers, and on income. To a household energy is a close complement to durable equipment, and hence energy demand strongly depends on the durable goods a household wishes to possess.

Energy, being a necessary good, has a low income elasticity and a low price elasticity. The close complementarity of energy with durable equipment ties energy use to decisions with a longer-term impact. For that reason, short-term elasticities of energy demand tend to be much smaller than long-term elasticities.

Energy, exergy and economics

According to the physical sciences, energy use is restricted by the two laws of thermodynamics. The first law states that energy (or enthalpy) cannot be lost during transformation – like burning – while the second law determines the quality (entropy or exergy) of an energy carrier, or the amount of work that can be obtained at infinite speed. The second law implies that any reaction at finite speed leads to losses of the large amounts of useful energy.

Several methodologies have been developed for energy analysis (for example IFIAS, 1975; Baustead and Hancock, 1979) and exergy analysis (for example Kotas, 1985; Szargut and Morris, 1987). Analogies to the concepts of enthalpy, for example the energy-mass balance principle (Ayres and Kneese, 1969; Ayres, 1978) and entropy were introduced into economics as early as the 1970s, for example by Odum (1971), Georgescu-Roegen (1974), and Slesser (1978). The introduced theoretical principles helped to extend neoclassical economic theories to incorporate the environment and natural resources. Thermodynamics is introduced to analyse and understand the economic system, for example, production and value formation, as well as the dynamics of the economic system. On a lower aggregation level, in engineering, entropy has been used to evaluate the trade-offs between capital and energy in the design of thermodynamic processes; see, for example, Kotas (1985). See also Chapters 59 and 64.

4. Energy conservation and the efficiency gap

Structural change and dematerialization
The material content of consumption is still increasing. Studies of material consumption in industrialized countries have shown that the consumption (expressed as apparent consumption per capita or unit GDP) tends to increase in the initial development of society to a certain maximum, and eventually saturates or even declines (Williams et al., 1987). Trends in materials use in industrialized countries show saturation on a per capita basis. Expressed per unit of GDP, material intensity declines after reaching a maximum (Williams et al., 1987). The initial increase is caused by large investments required in building an industrial infrastructure. In later stages material substitution and competition between materials, as well as a shift to a more service-oriented economy, reduce the material intensity of societies (Williams et al., 1987; Bernardini and Galli, 1993). The shifts in materials and services demand change in the economic structure, leading to changes in energy intensity (Schipper and Meyers, 1992) and changes in environmental pollution (Jænicke èt al., 1997).

Rational energy efficiency improvement
Energy efficiency improvement is defined as *reducing the use of energy per unit of activity without affecting the level of this activity*. Efficiency improvement can be achieved by implementing more efficient energy technologies (for example industrial furnaces, refrigerators, compact fluorescent lamps)

and practices (such as good housekeeping, energy management, daylight sensors).

A firm or a household will invest in energy efficiency up the point where the marginal costs of conservation equal the marginal benefits. Marginal benefits equal the value of one unit of energy saved, which is equal to the unit price of energy. In other words, the firm will continue to invest in energy efficiency until the marginal cost of reducing energy use is equal to the unit price of energy.

Marginal costs, in turn, are determined by the purchasing price of the technology, the costs of financing, and the costs of operating and maintaining the technology.[2] Assuming rational behaviour, a firm will thus sequentially select the technical opportunities in the order of increasing costs per unit of energy avoided: they first select the most cost-effective option – the option with the lowest additional costs per unit of energy saved per unit of product – then the second most cost-effective option, and so on, as long as marginal benefits are higher than marginal costs.

This selection process can be displayed graphically by means of a supply curve of energy-efficient technologies. In Figure 12.2 we present such a

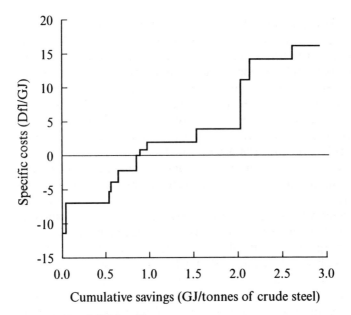

Source: Worrell (1994), p. 60.

Figure 12.2   *Supply curve for energy efficiency improvement measures: the case of steel production (discount rate of 10 per cent)*

supply curve. Generally, the supply curve is represented as a smooth line, implicitly assuming infinitesimally divisible technologies; the curve in Figure 12.2 is based on evidence from engineers' studies. On the horizontal axis we have the cumulative savings of the different technologies, ranked by ascending order of marginal costs per unit of energy saved, keeping the level of output fixed. On the vertical axis we have the *net* marginal costs of the technologies.

The net marginal cost curve is upward sloping. It is bounded to the right by the *technological potential of energy efficiency improvement*. The curve becomes steeper towards the right, indicating that additional energy savings become more expensive. The net marginal cost curve can be regarded as the abatement cost curve of CO_2 emissions.

Optimal energy efficiency improvement occurs at the intersection of the horizontal axis and the supply curve. If the energy price increases, the horizontal axis shifts upwards: efficiency improvement becomes more profitable. An energy tax thus stimulates efficiency improvement. Likewise, a subsidy or a soft loan on efficient equipment lowers marginal costs, shifting the optimum to the right.

The efficiency gap

In Figure 12.2 the curve starts at a point where net marginal costs are negative: the first not-yet-installed technological options seem profitable at current conditions. In other words, there is *economic potential of energy efficiency improvement*. According to neoclassical economists, these potentials could only exist for a short period, as rational investors would act to restore equilibrium (Nickell, 1978). However, empirical studies by engineers suggest the existence of significant and persistent economic potentials of energy efficiency improvement. This phenomenon is referred to as the *energy efficiency gap*. In the steel production case presented in Figure 12.2, the efficiency gap would amount to 5 per cent. The monetary value of the gap is equal to the surface between the marginal cost curve and the horizontal axis.

Changes in energy consumption of a nation are the result of population growth, economic growth, economic sector structure changes, and energy efficiency improvement. In many developing countries, economic growth and the expansion of the population are rapidly overtaking efficiency improvements within the economy. Yet in the near and medium term, the most effective and feasible policies for restraining energy demand growth involve improving the efficient use of energy in all sectors and encouraging the shift to a less energy-intensive economic and industrial structure (WEC, 1995b; IPCC, 1996; Worrell et al., 1997). Table 12.3 presents an overview of potentials for various sectors in various studies.

Table 12.3   Potentials for energy efficiency improvement in major energy-consuming sectors in various regions and countries

Sector	Share of 1992 world primary energy use (%)	Technical conservation potential (%)	Country/region
Industry	43		
Iron & Steel		26–50	OECD
Pulp & Paper		13–41 (25 av.)	European Union
Cement		4–36	OECD
Buildings	36		
Residential		27–48	USA
		42	Netherlands
Commercial		23–55	USA
		41	Netherlands
Transport	20		
Passenger cars		10–50	World
		18–50	USA
Trucks		10–30	World
		5–33	OECD

Source: Worrell et al. (1997).

There are serious barriers to energy efficiency improvements, including unwillingness to invest due to risk aversion or insecurity, lack of accessible information, economic disincentives and organizational or institutional barriers (Velthuijsen, 1995). A wide range or policy instruments, as well as innovative approaches, have been tried in some countries in order to achieve the desired energy efficiency improvements. These include: regulation and guidelines; economic instruments and incentives; voluntary agreements; information, education and training; and research, development and demonstration (Worrell et al., 1997). Several of these policy measures have a proven track record in various countries, and have led to successful implementation of energy efficiency measures.

5.   The energy market

The energy sector
The energy sector comprises an entire production chain, from extraction of minerals like coal, oil, uranium and gas, via production of useful fuels,

to distribution to the customers. The structure of the industry differs from country to country, mostly due to geological, technical and historic political reasons. The historical development of the energy market has been characterized by numerous government interventions, mainly motivated by attempts to safeguard strategic resources, or protect domestic industries. The historic government interventions have led to energy markets – both local and global – riddled with market imperfections (Tietenberg, 1994).

The energy market
The market for energy is complex. It is by no means a free market in the economic sense. Since the beginning of the industrial revolution, interests in the possession, production and provision of energy were considered to be too important to be left to the private domain. Natural reserves of oil, coal, uranium and gas have been under control by the states that happened to govern the parts of the earth's crust containing the resources. Consequently, the prices of carriers have been managed by the states. Institutions processing energy, controlling the distribution systems and supplying energy carriers are under tight legal, economic and administrative state governance. On a global level, the OPEC oil cartel is an example of a market imperfection with a – potentially – enormous impact.

As a consequence, the supply side of the market is far from exemplary of a free market. Even a casual look at price differences per country reveals that the price formation for an easily transportable commodity like energy is not transparent. Prices certainly do not reflect production costs, let alone other costs – such as environmental externalities.

Deregulation and privatization
Environmental concern has accelerated the current policy trends towards deregulation. In some EU states this requires more transition than in others, depending on the degree of government interest. Scandinavian countries are much more liberal than southern EU states. In the US the deregulation process of the electricity market is starting in California, soon to be followed by other states.

One step is the legal disconnection of the management of the infrastructures from the production and supply of energy. The former has still a substantial public good character; the latter is increasingly regarded as a pure market good. The European national energy markets are liberalized in controlled steps. Management of the grid is privatized by a share sale by the public authority. The public utility as the former owner commonly holds a minority share. A next step is the allowance of access of other electricity producers, that is, independent power producers (IPP).

The transition to market conditions requires preparation by the former public producer to stand a chance against powerful new entrants. This preparation involves not only the build-up of financial capital reserves sufficient to withstand takeovers or periods of underpricing, which strong outsiders can impose. It also involves the re-engineering of organizations and the re-education of managers and personnel.

6.   Economics of renewable electricity production

In order to curb emissions due to the burning of fossil fuels for electricity production, alternative means of electricity production have been contemplated. Alternatives are:

- Wind energy
- Solar energy
- Hydro power
- Biomass-fuelled power
- Nuclear power.

To the extent that the thermo-energy efficiency of power production is improved by reusing the heat generated by gas- and oil-fuelled power units – cogeneration, or combined heat and power production (CHP) – we can add CHP to the list. Obstacles of a technical nature, and economic and legal barriers,[3] prevent a swift transition towards massive use of renewable sources. The availability of sufficient natural conditions such as sun, wind or water-level changes determine to a large extent the technological feasibility of alternative electricity production.

In addition, the economic and legal system must be such that the economic feasibility is not obstructed. Generally the management of the power distribution grid is under legal control by the government, while under the liberalization trends of the day the grid is increasingly opened up to more than one licensed supplier, including the traditional state-controlled supplier.

Apart from this legal accessibility, buy-back tariff structures should be such that the installation of renewable power production becomes economically attractive. Arrangements regarding the buy-back tariff can include differentiation with respect to quantity, voltage and cycles, peak loads, timing, quality standards, and back-ups. Another potential opportunity that requires legal and tariff relaxation is the trading of power between independent private agents, virtually without interference with the grid managers, which is called 'wheeling' (Hendriks et al., 1999).

Raising the attractiveness of renewable sources is a stimulus for R&D efforts to further improvement and innovation of the existing technology.

7. Energy policy instruments

Policy instruments to affect energy use can be classified into two: non-economic and economic instruments (see Faucheux and Noël, 1995, ch. 5).

Energy use causes emissions that deteriorate the environment. This process can be regarded as utilization of the scarce assimilative capacity of the environment, off which other people live. Hence energy consumption causes negative external effects, and the victim of the emissions pays the damage (Ayres and Kneese, 1969). Conventional welfare economics states that external effects can be internalized by assigning the correct price to them. This can be achieved by a tax on the pollutive activity, or a subsidy. Scientists have argued that under normal conditions, economic instruments are less costly for society in terms of social welfare than non-economic instruments (Seskin et al., 1983; Hazilla and Kopp, 1990).

Economic instruments

Taxation The emitting agent pays a unit tax at the amount of the value of the external effects or damage the emissions cause to other agents: the polluter pays. This is the Pigouvian solution to internalizing the external effects and to obtaining Pareto optimality. Such a system can only be achieved if the marginal damage function of the emissions is known, which is rarely possible. An alternative system is the setting of standards to the environmental load, and the imposition of a set of charges sufficient to attain the standards. Such a system leads to maximum social welfare (Baumol and Oates, 1971).

In fact such a system is widely contemplated by national governments in Europe, and by the European Commission. The discussion focuses on whether it should be an energy tax or a CO_2 tax, the former taxing all energy use including nuclear, while the latter only charges fossil fuel combustion (see Chapter 34). Another issue relates to the fear of losing export revenues to other areas of the world, as companies can avoid the taxation by moving their production activities to cheaper energy sources.

Taxes are considered as a proper instrument to affect the behaviour of a large and homogeneous group of emitters that are difficult to trace, or that are easy to tax administratively, without the danger of leaving the country: households, agriculture, transport, small enterprises.

Subsidies Subsidies on abatement or avoidance efforts are also a Pigouvian solution to internalization. Various countries have schemes to subsidize energy conservation: soft loans for conservation equipment, subsidies on technical advice and information, subsidies on the purchasing price, or fiscal arrangements for green activities. Generally these schemes have a temporary nature, and frequently they are surrendered to other political priorities.

Tradable permits system   Taxation is considered in Europe, while in the USA the system of tradable permits seems to be preferred (Cropper and Oates, 1992). Tradable permits systems related to energy use are only imposed in the USA to curb SO_2 emissions.

Non-economic instruments

Voluntary agreements   A popular method of restricting large heterogenous energy-intensive industries is the voluntary agreement. A voluntary agreement is a contract between the government and an industry on emission targets. The agreement contains paragraphs on the ways and means to obtain the targets, on monitoring, and on sanctions.

Regulation, obligation and prohibition   Regulation, obligation and prohibition are used to force producers to develop more efficient or cleaner products. Examples are the emission and efficiency norms on cars.

Other instruments   Other non-economic instruments include norms and standards for products, packaging, or production and consumption processes, information programmes and know-how proliferation, and research, demonstration and development (RD&D).

Notes
1. The greenhouse effect is attributed to a particular characteristic of water vapour and some gases known as greenhouse gases (CO_2, CFC, methane, N_2O and ozone). These gases let the sun's short-wave radiation penetrate to the earth's surface, but a certain proportion of the long-wave radiation from earth into space is trapped. See further Chapters 33 and 62.
2. In fact one should calculate the present value of the benefits and costs, because capital goods tend to have a lifetime of more than a year.
3. Both compensation of back-up power generation capacity and low sell-back tariffs of excess power to the grid are prohibitive in many countries: see Hendriks et al. (1999).

References
Ayres, R.U. (1978), *Resources, Environment and Economics*, New York: J. Wiley & Sons.
Ayres, R.U. and A.V. Kneese (1969), 'Production, consumption and externalities', *American Economic Review*, **59**, 282–97.
Baumol, W.J. and W.E. Oates (1971), 'The use of standards and prices for protection of the environment', *Swedish Journal of Economics*, **73**, 42–54.
Baustead, I. and G.F. Hancock (1979), *Handbook of Industrial Energy Analysis*, Chichester, UK: Ellis Horwood.
Bernardini, O. and R. Galli (1993), 'Dematerialization: long-term trends in the intensity of use of materials and energy', *Futures*, **25**, 431–47.
British Petroleum (1988), *BP Statistical Review of World Energy*, London: British Petroleum.
British Petroleum (1996), *BP Statistical Review of World Energy*, London: British Petroleum.

Cropper, M. and W.E. Oates (1992), 'Environmental economics: a survey', *Journal of Economic Literature*, **30**, 675–740.

Dutt, G.S. and N.H. Ravindranath (1993), 'Bio-energy: direct applications in cooking', in T.B. Johansson, H. Kelly, A.N.K. Reddy and R.H. Williams (eds), *Renewable Energy: Sources for Fuels and Electricity*, Washington, DC: Island Press.

Faucheux, S. and J.-F. Noël (1995), *Économie des Ressources Naturelles et de l'Environnement*, Paris: Armand Colin.

Georgescu-Roegen, N. (1971), *The Entropy Law and the Economic Process*, Cambridge, MA: Harvard University Press.

Hazila, M. and R.J. Kopp (1990), 'Social cost of environmental quality regulation', *Journal of Political Economy*, **98**, 853–73.

Hendriks, C.A., J.W. Velthuijsen, E. Worrell and K. Blok (1999), 'The case of combined heat and power in the European Union', in F. Convery (ed.), *A Guide to Policies for Energy Conservation: the European Experience*, Cheltenham, UK, and Northampton, US: Edward Elgar.

IFIAS (International Federation of Institutes for Advanced Studies) (1975), *Report on the Workshop on Energy Analysis*, Workshop Report no. 6, Guldsmedshyttan, Sweden.

IPCC (1996), *Climate Change 1995: The Science of Climate Change*, WMO/UNEP.

Jænicke, M., M. Binder and H. Mönch (1997), 'Dirty industries: patterns of change in industrial countries, *Environmental and Resource Economics*, **9**, 467–91.

King, K. and M. Munasinghe (1992), *Global Warming: Key Issues for the Bank*, World Bank Environmental Department, Divisional Working Paper 1992–36, Washington, DC.

Kotas, T.J. (1985), *The Exergy Method of Thermal Plant Analysis*, London: Butterworths.

Lazarus, M. and D. von Hippel (1995), *A Guide to Environmental Analysis for Energy Planners*, Stockholm Environmental Institute/Boston Centre, Boston, MA.

Meadows, D.H., D.L. Meadows, J. Randers and W.W. Behrens (1972), *The Limits to Growth: A Report for the Club of Rome's Project on the Predicament of Mankind*, New York: Universe Books.

Nickell, S. (1978), *The Investment Decision of Firms*, Welwyn, Herts: James Nisbet and Co.

Odum, H.T. (1971), *Environment, Power and Society*, New York: J. Wiley & Sons.

OECD (1997), *Energy Statistics and Balances of Non-OECD Countries 1994–1995*, Paris: OECD.

Reddy, A.K.N., R.H. Williams and T.B. Johansson (1997), *Energy After Rio: Prospects and Challenges*, New York: UNDP.

Schelling, T.C. (1992), 'Some economics of global warming', *American Economic Review*, **82**, 1–14.

Schipper, L. and S. Meyers, with R. Howarth and R. Steiner (1992), *Energy Efficiency and Human Activity: Past Trends, Future Prospects*, Cambridge, UK: Cambridge University Press.

Seskin, E.P., R.J. Anderson and R.O. Reid (1983), 'An empirical analysis of economic strategies for controlling air pollution', *Journal of Environmental Economics and Management*, **10** (4), 112–24.

Slesser, M. (1978), *Energy in the Economy*, London: Macmillan.

Szargut, J. and D.R. Morris (1987), 'Cumulative exergy consumption and cumulative degree of chemical processes', *Energy Research*, **11**, 245–61.

Tietenberg, T. (1994), *Environmental Economics and Policy*, New York: HarperCollins College Publishers.

UNEP/WHO (United Nations Environment Program/World Health Organization) (1992), *Urban Air Pollution in the Mega-cities of the World*, Oxford: Blackwell Publishers.

UNFCCC (United Nations Framework Convention on Climate Change) (1992), in *Report of the Intergovernmental Negotiating Committee for a Framework Convention on Climate Change* (5th session, New York, 30 April–9 May, 1992), New York.

Velthuijsen, J.W. (1995), *Determinants of Investment in Energy Conservation*, PhD thesis, University of Groningen, The Netherlands.

WEC (1995a), *Local and Regional Energy-Related Environmental Issues*, London: World Energy Council.

WEC (1995b), *Energy Efficiency Improvement Utilising High Technology, An Assessment of Energy Use in Industry and Buildings*, London: World Energy Council.

Williams, R.H., E.D. Larson and M.H. Ross (1987), 'Materials, affluence, and industrial energy use', *Annual Review of Energy*, **12**, 99–144.

World Commission on Environment and Development (1987), *Our Common Future*, Oxford: Oxford University Press.

Worrell, E., M.D. Levine, L. Price, N.C. Martin, R. van den Broek and K. Blok (1997), *Potentials and Policy Implications of Energy and Material Efficiency Improvement*, New York: United Nations.

PART III

ECONOMICS OF ENVIRONMENTAL POLICY

13 Externalities
Erik T. Verhoef[1]

1. Introduction

External effects have been studied by economists ever since the days of Marshall and Pigou. Along with the development of the field of environmental economics, the theory of externalities has remained of great and growing importance in economic science. Indeed, it is fair to say that, starting from the traditional neoclassical economic framework, the most logical way to look at problems of environmental pollution is from the perspective of external costs (see, for instance, Baumol and Oates, 1988; Pearce and Turner, 1990; Cropper and Oates, 1992; Tietenberg, 1994). However, although economists have been investigating the concept of externalities for a long time, both theoretically and empirically, externalities still prove to be an area of slippery ice. Frequently one finds fuzzy discussions on the policy implications of external costs. This may often result from, for instance, mixing up equity and allocative efficiency arguments, from mistaking pecuniary externalities for 'true' or technological externalities, or from some sense of compassion with the victims of externalities on equity grounds, leading to pleas for 'compensation' which may often be unwarranted from the perspective of allocative efficiency.

This chapter aims at shedding some light on the concept of 'externalities'. It starts with a brief discussion of market failures in the neoclassical economic framework. It then proceeds to a definition of externalities, thereby distinguishing external effects from other sorts of 'unpriced effects'. Finally, some attention is paid to the relation, and tension, between efficiency and equity impacts of externalities. The discussion in this chapter draws heavily on earlier publications, in particular Verhoef (1994a,b; 1996a,b).

2. Paretian welfare criteria and market failures

Mainstream neoclassical micro- and welfare economic theories suggest that governments should in principle be reserved in intervening directly in the economic process. It is broadly accepted that economic science should aim at providing 'value-free' descriptions and analyses of human choice, and the associated social processes, under conditions of scarcity. As it is not possible to construct a value-free social welfare function according to some ethically objective criterion (see, for instance, Boadway and Bruce, 1984, p. 2), welfare economics has an inherent tendency to rely on quite humble welfare criteria for the evaluation of different possible outcomes of the economic process, for instance, under different possible forms of government intervention (including, of course, non-intervention). Among these, the strict and potential Pareto criteria are without doubt the ones most often employed.[2] The *strict Pareto criterion* classifies a policy (change) to be socially desirable if, as a result, everyone is made better off (in its weak version), or at least if one person is better off, while no one else is made worse off (in its strong version). For most policy choices, however, both losers and gainers will be involved, and the strict Pareto criterion becomes of limited use because it does not provide any basis for choice between the feasible alternatives. In such cases, one usually relies on well-known *potential Pareto criteria*, or compensation criteria, as suggested by Kaldor (1939) and Hicks (1939). According to these, a change is classified desirable if the winners are able to compensate the losers such that everyone could be made better off after the change has occurred (Kaldor), or if the losers are in the initial situation unable to compensate the winners such that both groups would prefer to stay in the initial situation (Hicks). Actual compensation, however, is not required according to these principles.

The related concept of *Pareto efficiency* is defined as a feasible situation, usually in terms of the allocation of goods and production factors, for which there exists no other feasible situation that is weakly preferred to it by all agents. Therefore, if an economy attains a Pareto-efficient allocation, there remain no mutually beneficial exchanges to be exploited. Unlike the strict Pareto criterion, the potential Pareto criterion will always rank any Pareto-efficient allocation above any Pareto-inefficient allocation (for a careful discussion, see Boadway and Bruce, 1984, pp. 96–102). However, neither the strict nor the potential Pareto criterion can say anything about the relative desirability of different Pareto-efficient allocations (see Atkinson and Stiglitz, 1980; Johansson, 1991).

The economists' reservation in advocating government intervention, then, is closely related to a number of basic welfare-economic theorems (see Varian, 1992, ch. 17). The first of these is known as the first theorem of welfare economics, stating that under certain conditions (see below), a competitive equilibrium, if it exists, is Pareto-efficient. In addition, the second theorem of welfare economics asserts that essentially all Pareto-efficient allocations can be supported by competitive equilibria for appropriate distributions of endowments. Next, a welfare maximum for any social welfare function that satisfies welfarism (social welfare depends only on the utility of the households) and is Paretian (it satisfies the strict Pareto criterion) is necessarily Pareto-efficient. Finally, Pareto-efficient allocations are welfare maxima under concavity assumptions for some choice of welfare weights in a welfaristic Paretian social welfare function. Varian (1992, ch. 17) presents formal derivations of these theorems.

Consequently, as it is not possible to make a value-free comparison between different Pareto-efficient market outcomes, the logical step for economists is to advocate regulation only if the 'certain conditions' necessary for the free market to attain Pareto efficiency, and hence a welfare maximum given the distribution of endowments, happen not to be fulfilled. The question of the desirability of the resulting distribution is then often left aside as an ethical one, beyond the domain of economists. Alternatively, the issue of equity is dealt with either in the light of the initial distribution of endowments, however artificial the benchmark concept of lump sum[3] distributions may be in practice, or in terms of the 'efficiency price' that has to be paid for attaining a desirable or satisfactory distribution through distortionary taxes and subsidies.

The non-fulfilment of the above-mentioned 'certain conditions' for the first theorem of welfare economics to apply is often referred to as 'market failure': markets fail to accomplish Pareto efficiency. The following forms of market failure are usually distinguished: (a) increasing returns to scale over the relevant range (falling marginal and average variable cost curves); (b) non-price-taking behaviour (market power); (c) external effects; (d) public goods; and (e) imperfect information.[4] Apart from these, two other important reasons for government intervention often mentioned are (f) distributional or equity considerations; and (g) (de-)merit good arguments when the government encourages or discourages the consumption of a certain good because it thinks this consumption is good (cultive) or bad (heroin) *per se*. In this chapter, the focus is on external effects. The next section discusses this concept in some more detail.

3.   A definition of externalities

Although the concept of external effects is widely used in economics, there seems to be some confusion about its exact definition and interpretation. This justifies a short discussion of the concept itself here. It is commonly recognized that externalities are an important form of market failure. Their existence leads to a deviation from the first-best neoclassical world, in which the price mechanism takes care of an efficient resource allocation (Pareto efficiency). In the presence of externalities, market prices do not reflect full social costs (or benefits), and, for instance, regulatory taxes (or subsidies) are called for to restore the efficient workings of the market mechanism. Furthermore, it is generally accepted that the source of externalities is typically to be found in the absence of well-defined property rights (see Baumol and Oates, 1988, p. 26). Consequently, the theory of externalities is often applied in environmental economics: environmental quality is a typical 'good' for which property rights are not defined and hence no market exists.

These commonplaces may clearly indicate the causes and consequences of external effects, but still leave the definition unclear. Such a definition can be as follows: *an external effect exists when an actor's (the receptor's) utility (or production) function contains a real variable whose actual value depends on the behaviour of another actor (the supplier), who does not take this effect of his behaviour into account in his decision-making process.* This definition is in line with, for instance, Mishan (1971). In the terminology of Viner (1931) and Scitovsky (1954), the above definition concerns 'technological' externalities, as opposed to 'pecuniary externalities'.[5] These latter, which are ruled out by considering real variables only (that is, excluding monetary variables), do not lead to shifts of production and utility functions, but merely to movements along these functions (see also the discussion of Figure 13.1 below). Consequently, externalities as defined above are, in the terminology of Buchanan and Stubblebine (1962), potentially 'Pareto-relevant' (if the costs of correcting for the market failure do not exceed the welfare gains to be obtained), whereas pecuniary externalities are not, because they do not reflect a failing market (see also Mishan, 1971). The final condition in the definition distinguishes externalities from other types of unpriced interactions, such as barter, violence, jealousy, altruism or goodwill-promoting activities (for instance, handing out samples of products as part of a commercial campaign). Such phenomena differ fundmentally from external effects, both in a theoretical and in a policy-relevance sense. According to Mishan (1971), 'the essential feature of an external effect [is] that the effect produced is not a deliberate creation but an unintended or incidental by-product of some otherwise legitimate activity' (p. 2).

The unresolved tension between the receptor, who has no direct control over the size of the effect at its source, and the supplier, who has no *a priori* interest in the magnitude of the externality, can only persist provided there is no market on which the externality is traded. This stems from a lack of well-defined property rights concerning the externality, which is in turn often related to prohibitive high transaction costs. As pointed out by Coase (1960), in the absence of transaction costs, both the supplier and the receptor of the externality can benefit from negotiations on the size of the externality. 'Corrective' Pigouvian taxation would in that case only distort the resulting Pareto-efficient outcome, as pointed out by Turvey (1963).

Within the above-defined class of technology externalities, various further distinctions can be made. One of these is between *depletable* and *undepletable* externalities, where, in the latter case, the consumption of the externality by the one receptor does not affect the consumption by other receptors. Therefore, an undepletable externality in fact exhibits two types of market failure at the same time: the external effect itself, and a public good (or bad) character. After an interesting discussion in the literature, the consensus now is that this distinction does not imply different pricing rules for each type of externality (Freeman, 1984; Bird, 1987; Peskin, 1988; Bird, 1988; Oates, 1988). Nevertheless, it has been shown elsewhere (Verhoef, 1994a) that the Coasean solution to externality optimization may easily fail for undepletable externalities due to strategic behaviour and free-riding (which is intuitively easy to understand for those who are familiar with the theory of voluntary private provision of public goods; see for instance Bergstrom et al., 1986).[6] Another specific type of technological externality that is sometimes distinguished concerns congestion externalities, where each actor is at the same time both supplier and receptor of the effect. Probably the most important form of this type of externality is road traffic congestion. This topic is studied in great depth by transport economists; for a literature review, see for instance Verhoef (1996a). It is in this respect an interesting detail that economists like Pigou (1920, p. 194) and Knight (1924) used the example of a congested highway as an illustration of the points they had to make on externality regulation.

The question of whether unpriced external relations are either external effects or other types of unpriced external relations involves important policy consequences. This is illustrated in a partial equilibrium setting in Figure 13.1 for a certain activity Q. The standard case in Figure 13.1(a) shows the optimal workings of the market mechanism in the absence of external effects. In this case, no government intervention is called for: market forces secure social walfare maximization (the bold triangle) at the market equilibrium Q^0, where marginal private cost (MPC) equals marginal private benefits (MPB). The algebraic sum of total benefits (the area under the MPB curve) minus total (variable) cost (the area under the MPC curve) is therefore maximized. MPB and MPC can be interpreted as the benefits and costs as experienced by one actor. They can also be thought of as demand and supply curves for a marketed good, in which case P^0 is the market-clearing (efficient) price.

The existence of (marginal) external costs (MEC) in Figure 13.1(b) drives a wedge between marginal social cost (MSC) and marginal private cost (the fact that both MPC and MEC are equal to 0 at $Q = 0$ and rising afterwards is an arbitrary choice, and does not in principle affect the generality of the discussion).[7] The market outcome Q^0, where private welfare is maximized, is not optimal from a social point of view. The resulting level of the external cost ($A + B + C$) is excessively large. Social welfare maximization requires the activity to be restricted to a level of Q^*, where

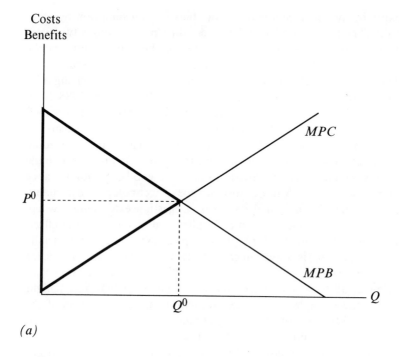

(a)

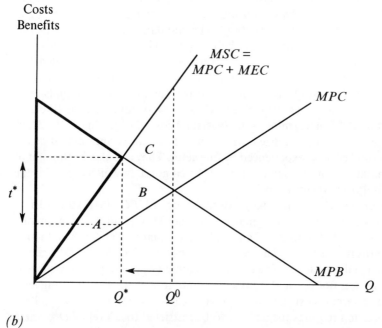

(b)

Figure 13.1   Graphical representation of a 'normal' market (a), external costs (b), external benefits (c) and pecuniary benefits (d)

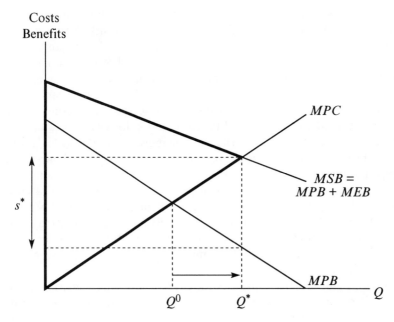

(c)

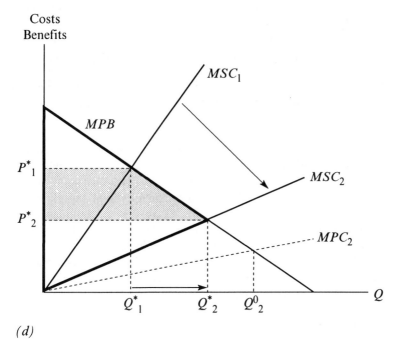

(d)

Source: Verhoef, 1994b.

the marginal social cost is equal to the marginal benefits and the dead-weight welfare loss C is avoided. This optimum can, for instance, be accomplished by means of a quantitative restriction (Q^*) or a Pigouvian tax (t^*) on the activity.[8] The triangle A gives the optimal level of the external cost. The bold triangle again represents maximum social welfare.

Two points are perhaps worth stressing here. First, it is now easy to see that, in order to be able to speak of the optimal level of an externality, it is convenient to adapt the potential Pareto criterion for welfare evaluation. According to the strict Pareto criterion, the move from Q^0 to Q^* is a welfare improvement only if accompanied by an appropriate (lump sum) compensation to the supplier of the externality. Second, the optimization of an externality clearly does not mean its minimization (or maximization).

Figure 13.1(c) shows the reverse case, where (marginal) external benefits (MEB) exist. Marginal social benefits (MSB) now exceed the marginal private benefits. In this case, social welfare maximization requires encouragement of the activity up to Q^*, for instance by means of Pigouvian subsidization (s^*).

Finally, Figure 13.1(d) illustrates the case of pecuniary beneifts. Figure 13.1(b) serves as a starting point, assuming that the activity gives rise to external costs. Suppose the private cost curve shifts downwards, perhaps due to another producer leaving the region, causing labour costs to fall. Assuming unaltered external costs, MSC will fall as well. A new social optimum Q_2^*, with a higher social welfare arises: the bold triangle is increased in comparison with Figure 13.1(b). Moreover, if Q is a traded good and MPB reflects market demand, the consumer surplus increases by the shaded area. This results from the lower market price P_2^* and the larger quantity sold, Q_2^*. This benefit, however, is not external but pecuniary: it results from a movement along – not a shift in – the MPB curve. The pecuniary benefits do not 'compensate' for the external costs: social welfare maximization still requires a restriction from the new unregulated market outcome Q_2^0 to the new social optimum Q_2^*. For the move from the old to the new social optimum (from Q_1^* to Q_2^*) itself, however – given the use of optimal Pigouvian taxes in both the old and the new situation – market forces can be relied upon, and there is no reason for stimulating the activity, unlike in the case of external benefits. Consequently, the question of whether unpriced costs and benefits of a certain activity are either external or pecuniary in nature is crucial from a policy point of view.

As mentioned in note 7, this chapter will not discuss the efficiency of various forms of the regulation of externalities in great detail. One more general point concerning the policy implications of externalities, however, deserves some attention. This is the distinction between the optimization, the compensation, the internalization and the regulation of an externality.

These concepts are often used in a rather loose way, whereas a more careful consideration reveals that they are certainly neither identical nor interchangeable. The *optimization* of an external effect can be defined as follows: an externality is optimized when its level is consistent with optimal resource allocation according to the potential Pareto criterion (see above). The *compensation* of an external effect can be defined as follows: an externality is compensated when a (financial) transaction takes place between the supplier and the receptor of the effect, which compensates for the receptor's welfare effects due to the externality. The compensation of an externality does not necessarily imply its optimization, because it may induce inefficient behaviour of the victim(s) of the effect (see also the next section). Next, the *internalization* of an external effect involves the removal of its external character, making it 'internal to the economic process' (Mishan, 1971, p. 3): an externality is internalized if a market for the effect comes into being.[9] Internalization typically involves either the creation of a market on which the externality is traded, or a gathering of interest, such as a merger in the case of a producer–producer externality, the standard example being water pollution by an upstream firm damaging the product of a downstream firm. The former requires the assignment of property rights, after which 'Coasean negotiations' between the supplier and the receptor of the effect will lead to the social optimum – at least in theory (Coase, 1960). Should such negotiations lead to compensation of the effect, in particular when the receptor of an external cost obtains the property right, then compensation need not be at odds with optimization (this is probably what Pearce and Turner, 1990, p. 61, have in mind when stating that a necessary condition for an external cost to prevail is that the loss in welfare be uncompensated). Finally, the term *regulation* can be used for direct government intervention regarding the externality, by means of, for instance, price instruments, command and control measures, tradable permits, or any other means.

4. Efficiency and equity impacts of externalities

Externalities comprise both efficiency and equity aspects. The first refer to the fact that, in the presence of externalities, the competitive market outcome is not Pareto-efficient. The second relate to the fact that the receptors of a negative (positive) externality are clearly worse (better) off at any non-zero level of the effect, unless compensation takes place. Unfortunately, there is no straightforward one-to-one mapping between the two goals of efficient allocation and 'equitable distribution', however defined. One can therefore arrive at rather different policy recommendations on the regulation of externalities, depending on the viewpoint taken.

First of all, let us consider the welfare of the receptors of an external cost. It seems reasonable that, from an equity point of view, Pigouvian tax revenues should be used to compensate the receptors of the external cost for the remaining optimal level of the externality. However, this turns out to be problematic as soon as the receptor of an externality is able to protect him- or herself by means of defensive measures (such as double glazing in the case of noise annoyance, or relocation in the case of localized external-ities). In Verhoef (1994d), this problem is investigated in several settings, and a main conclusion is that it is in general not in line with overall efficient allocation to compensate receptors for the external cost suffered, nor for any defensive measures undertaken. In some cases, in particular in the case of a localized undepletable externality, efficient allocation even requires taxation of receptors in order to secure the optimal number of receptors of an external cost. Compensation would discourage receptors of external costs from undertaking the optimal level of defensive measures. Hence, for the optimal efficient allocation, one might end up in a situation which is not very attractive from the equity point of view, namely where receptors of an external cost not only remain uncompensated for the externality they suffer, but should also be (financially) responsible for their own defensive mea-sures (see also Shibata and Winrich, 1983; Oates, 1983). A trade-off between efficiency and equity considerations is therefore unavoidable in such cases.

Related to this issue, and also unattractive from an equity point of view, is the requirement that the valuation of external costs should be based on the receptors' willingness to pay for their avoidance, or their willingness to accept their existence.[10] It is not difficult to show that this value, apart from being directly related to the marginal disutility of the effect itself, is inversely related to the marginal utility of income (for a formal derivation see Verhoef, 1994a). This means that, other things being equal, the same exposure to a negative external effect implies a higher external cost for higher-income receptors. The inequitable implications of this property are evident: an externality-generating activity should then, from the efficiency point of view, be located near low-income rather than near high-income receptors. This is closely related to the issue of 'environmental dumping'; see, for instance, Harrison (1994).

Focusing on the generators of externalities, there is often a further tension between allocative efficiency and what seems to be just from the equity point of view. For instance, consider the 'polluter pays principle'. Taking Figure 13.1(b) as an example, optimal Pigouvian taxation implies a total tax sum $Q^* \cdot t^*$, which is in the sketched case twice as large as the optimal level of the external cost (area A). Hence the question of whether the polluter should pay the total external cost, or whether marginal tax rules should be used, may often lead to different outcomes in terms of both allocative efficiency and equity – unless of course marginal external costs are constant and therefore equal to average external costs. This ambiguity in the interpretation of the polluter pays principle is, unfortunately, often overlooked.

Also relevant for the generators of externalities is the fact that people may often be opposed to price measures in the regulation of congestion type of externalities for equity reasons. For road transport, the typical statement is: 'Why should we (the road users) pay for something that only harms ourselves (congestion)?' Although it is not difficult to see that the appropriate level of aggregation at which to study optimal Pigouvian taxes is the individual (not the sector), such statements are nevertheless persistent in policy debates due to their intuitively convincing appeal to feelings of 'fairness'. Other important issues related to the public acceptance of congestion charges include its regressive incidence, the fact that most road users will be net losers if the tax revenues are not redistributed, and the allocation of the tax revenues generated (see Verhoef et al., 1997).

Given such tensions between efficiency and equity considerations, it is no surprise that mixing up equity and allocative efficiency arguments may often lead to rather fuzzy discussions about the policy implications of research findings on external costs. Table 13.1 gives an overview of the most important characteristics and implications of taking these two perspectives for the case of road transport, demonstrating the absence of a direct mapping between the two, and hence identifying some sources of confusion in the above-mentioned discussions (see Verhoef, 1996b, for a further discussion of this table).

Also in the practice of policy making, equity considerations are often at least as important as the expected efficiency of various possible instruments. This is narrowly related to the problem of the social and political feasibility of regulation. Figure 13.2, more or less repeating Figure 13.1(b), can be used to illustrate the basic issue. A certain actor, 'the producer', performs an activity Q, from which he enjoys net private benefits (private benefits minus private costs). However, he causes an external cost – say, pollution – to another actor: 'the victim'. The curves represent the marginal net private benefits ($MNPB = MPB - MPC$) and marginal external cost (MEC) of production. Without government intervention, a production level of Q^0 prevails, whereas the social optimum is again given by Q^*.

In the literature, certain 'standard' schemes can be found which yield this social optimum. Three categories of such schemes are considered below. First, two forms of regulation are distinguished: quantitative restrictions[11] and Pigouvian taxation. The third scheme is direct compensation from the producer to the victim. Finally, two forms of internalization are considered: a gathering of interest through a merger of the

Table 13.1   Characteristics and implications of the allocative efficiency versus the equity perspective for studying external costs of road transport

	Allocative efficiency perspective	Equity perspective ('unpaid bill')
Goal of the analysis	Assessment of 'optimal road mobility' and optimal regulatory taxes	Assessment of the total costs shifted to society at large
Relevant external cost measure	Marginal external cost	Total external cost *plus* induced defensive outlays
Apt level of aggregation	Individual	Sectoral
Relevant external cost categories	Intrasectoral and inter-sectoral external costs	Intersectoral external costs
Relevance of some existing financial transfers:		
Defensive outlays by receptors	Should not be accounted for in optimal taxes	Should be added to 'unpaid bill'
Insurance premiums	Very limited relevance[a]	Limited relevance[b]
Car ownership taxes	Very limited relevance[a]	Relevant[c]
Indirect taxes on fuel	Potential relevance[d]	Potential relevance[e]

Notes

[a]These transfers are usually fixed yearly payments (largely) independent of total kilometres driven. Hence they have no direct impact on road usage.

[b]A certain share of accident costs (including fatalities) are intrasectoral, and hence should not play a role in the 'unpaid bill' analysis. Neither should, therefore, a certain share of the insurance premiums. Moreover, from the perspective of the 'unpaid bill', the relevant question is whether the payments from the insurance companies to society are enough to cover the costs posed on the rest of the society.

[c]These taxes are a relevant coverage for part of the 'unpaid bill' only if they exceed government outlays on infrastructure (depreciation, maintenance, management, police, and so on).

[d]For Pigouvian taxation using fuel taxes, the tax rate on fuel needs to exceed that of indirect taxes on other goods (forgetting here about the 'optimal taxation' argument for the sake of simplicity; see for instance Sandmo, 1976).

[e]Also here, only any indirect taxes above average rates can be considered as relevant transfers from road users to society, compensating for part of the unpaid bill.

Source: Verhoef, 1996b

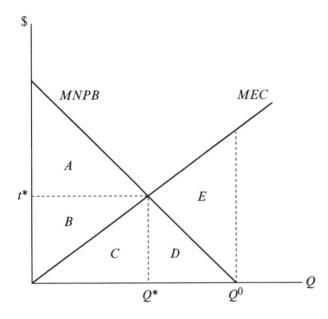

Source: Verhoef, 1994a.

Figure 13.2   Efficiency and equity implications of an external cost

victim and the producer, which will often be impossible for very practical reasons; and the assignment of property rights concerning the externality, either to the producer or to the victim, which is assumed to result in Coasean negotiations.

Table 13.2 shows the distributional impacts of these schemes. Although in this simple setting each of them yields the efficient outcome, that is, the maximum social welfare of $A + B$, they have different distributional implications. Most of the values in Table 13.2 can easily be verified with reference to Figure 13.2. However, Coasean negotiations deserve some closer attention. Here, the distributional implications depend on the distribution of property rights as well as on individual bargaining skills. The former determines the direction of the financial transfer; the latter determine its size. For both distributions of property rights, transfers between the extremes in Table 13.2 may occur. These boundary values follow from the fact that the $MNPB$ gives the producer's minimum willingness to accept (maximum willingness to pay) for decreases (increases) in production, whereas MEC represents the victim's minimum willingness to accept (maximum willingness to pay) for increases (decreases) in the production level.[12] Note that, when the property right is assigned to the producer, the

Table 13.2 The individual welfare positions associated with different schemes for optimizing externalities in a basic model

	Producer	Victim	Regulator	Social
Non-intervention	$A+B+C+D$	$-C-D-E$	0	$A+B-E$
Regulation:				
Quantitative restriction (Q^*)	$A+B+C$	$-C$	0	$A+B$
Pigouvian tax (t^*)[1]	$A+B+C-[B+C]=A$	$-C$	$[B+C]$	$A+B$
Direct compensation	$A+B+C-(C)=A+B$	$-C+(C)=0$	0	$A+B$
Internalization:				
Gathering of interest	$A+B$		0	$A+B$
Coasean negotiations[2a]	$A+B+C+(D+E)$	$-C-(D+E)$	0	$A+B$
Coasean negotiations[2b]	$A+B+C+(D)$	$-C-(D)$	0	$A+B$
Coasean negotiations[3a]	$A+B+C-(C)=A+B$	$-C+(C)=0$	0	$A+B$
Coasean negotiations[3b]	$A+B+C-(A+B+C)=0$	$-C+(A+B+C)=A+B$	0	$A+B$

Notes:

Terms between parentheses indicate financial transfers between the producer and the victim, and between square brackets between the producer and the regulator.

[1] It is assumed that the producer and the victim do not consider the allocation of Pigouvian tax revenues.

[2a] Property right lies with the producer; the producer is the extreme best bargainer.

[2b] Property right lies with the producer; the victim is the extreme best bargainer.

[3a] Property right lies with the victim; the producer is the extreme best bargainer.

[3b] Property right lies with the victim; the victim is the extreme best bargainer.

Source: Verhoef, 1994a.

associated financial transfer has the direction opposite to compensation of the external cost. Full compensation takes place when the property right is assigned to the victim, while the producer is the extreme best bargainer. As a matter of fact, direct compensation can be seen as a restricted case of Coasean negotiations. The property right is implicitly assigned to the victim, but he is not allowed to bargain over the size of the compensation.

Table 13.2 indicates that the actors have different rankings of the different schemes. The producer prefers Coasean negotiations with the property rights assigned to himself. He may then realize a welfare level above the level he enjoys with unrestricted production. His second favourite is non-intervention. Next comes a quantitative restriction, followed by direct compensation and finally either Coasean negotiations with the property rights assigned to the victim, or Pigouvian taxation, depending on the distribution of bargaining skills (the above ranking of compensation, Coasean negotiations with the property rights assigned to the victim and Pigouvian taxation in addition depends on the assumption of rising marginal external cost). The victim prefers receiving the property rights and the associated Coasean negotiations. Next comes direct compensation, followed by any form of regulation. Then comes Coasean negotiations with the property rights assigned to the producer, and finally non-intervention. The 'gathering-of-interest' possibility can for obvious reasons not be qualified on this criterion.

Of course, the above analysis is rather simplistic because it only considers one single producer of the externality and one single victim (who, in addition, is not able to defend himself). These assumptions are relaxed in Verhoef (1994a). Nevertheless, these rankings may to some extent explain why some policies are used more often than others. For example, considering regulation, the producer prefers a quantitative restriction to Pigouvian taxation, whereas the victim is indifferent, assuming he does not consider the possible allocation of the tax revenues. A vote-maximizing government may therefore prefer to use command-and-control measures rather than economic instruments, which seems to be confirmed by practical evidence[13] (see also Pearce and Turner, 1990, pp. 96–8).

5. Conclusion

This chapter provided a discussion of externalities, which is a key concept in (neoclassical) environmental economics. However, although externalities have already been studied by economists for a long time, they still prove to be an area of slippery ice. A number of potential sources of confusion and ambiguity were addressed above. These include the definition of externalities, where it is very important to distinguish between externalities and other unpriced effects. Another source of ambiguity lies in the tension between efficiency and equity impacts of externalities and their regulation. In this respect, the role of receptors of an external cost, the ambiguity of the polluter pays principle, and the distributional impacts of regulation in relation to the social feasibility were discussed. Depending on the viewpoint taken (that is, efficiency versus equity or fairness), one may often arrive at diverging policy recommendations. The aim of the above discussion was not to solve these questions, but merely to identify them, which in itself could be a first step towards a more careful treatment of externalities in scientific and policy debates.

Notes

1. This research was carried out within the NRP-II project on 'Policy Instruments for Energy Efficiency Improvement' (no. 953215). Financial support by the Netherlands' Organization for Scientific Research NWO is gratefully acknowledged.
2. For a comparison of these Pareto criteria with other social welfare criteria such as the minimal state, the egalitarian criterion, the Benthamite criterion and the Rawlsian criterion, see Atkinson and Stiglitz (1980), pp. 336–43.
3. A lump sum tax or subsidy is defined as one which is independent of the behaviour of the affected agent. It therefore induces no substitution effect. As it will usually have an income effect, it is not correct to claim that it has *no* effect on behaviour (Atkinson and Stiglitz, 1980, p. 28).
4. A somewhat different terminology may be encountered in the literature, where one speaks of 'externalities' to indicate what are called 'market failures' above. Bator (1958), for instance, uses 'technical externalities' to indicate 'scale economies'; 'public good externalities' to indicate 'public goods'; and 'ownership externalities' to indicate 'externalities' as used in this chapter. The latter only refer to 'technological externalities', as opposed to 'pecuniary externalities' (see the discussion in the main text). Conversely, the term 'market failure' is sometimes reserved solely to indicate a market's non-existence (its 'failure to exist'), which is the fundamental reason for technological externalities to occur.
5. Note that Bator's 'technical externalities' (note 3) are completely different from Viner's and Scitovsky's 'technological externalities'.
6. Another relevant sort of market failure that has been studied in joint occurrence with externalities concerns monopolistic market power (see, for instance, Buchanan, 1969; Barnett, 1980; Oates and Strassmann, 1984; and Carraro's contribution in this handbook, Chapter 16).
7. It is fair to acknowledge that in the case of a non-convex external cost function things may become a lot more complicated; see for instance Burrows (1995).
8. The present equivalence between a regulatory tax and a non-economic instrument such as a quantitative restriction is of course due to the extreme simplicity of the current setting. For instance, under uncertainty, this equivalence no longer holds (see Weitzman, 1974; and Adar and Griffin, 1976), nor does it when heterogeneity among the generators of externalities exists. However, in this rather brief contribution, I shall not focus too much on the efficiency in the regulation of externalities; Baumol and Oates (1988), Cropper and Oates (1992), and Tietenberg (1994) offer excellent analyses and reviews of this literature (see also the contributions by Helfand, and Russell and Powell in this handbook, Chapters 15 and 21).
9. Pigouvian taxation is often referred to as 'internalization' of an externality. However, such market-conforming regulation does not actually satisfy this definition of internalization.
10. In thory, these two measures should be equal at the margin. Empirical research with contingent valuation methods, however, suggests otherwise (see Mitchell and Carson, 1989, pp. 30–38).

11. Tradable permits are not considered because the model contains only one producer.
12. The maximum transfer from the victim to the producer $(D + E)$ mentioned assumes that the producer is truthful. If he pretends considering a production level above Q^0, the victim is willing to pay more than $D + E$ in order to secure Q^*. The victim does not have a comparable possibility of 'cheating'.
13. Other possible reasons for preferring either price or quantity measures have been put forward. Weitzman (1974), in his seminal paper, focuses on the relative efficiency of both types of regulation under uncertainty (see also Baumol and Oates, 1988). A bit closer to equity arguments as considered here, Buchanan and Tullock (1975) argue in another classic paper that quantity measures are preferred by producers since these can act as a barrier to entry and may therefore leave them with higher profits.

References

Adar, Z. and J.M. Griffin (1976), 'Uncertainty and the choice of pollution control instruments', *Journal of Environmental Economics and Management*, 3 (3), 178–88.
Atkinson, A.B. and J.E. Stiglitz (1980), *Lectures on Public Economics*, London: McGraw-Hill.
Barnett, A.H. (1980), 'The Pigovian tax rule under monopoly', *American Economic Review*, 70, 1037–41.
Bator, F.M. (1958), 'The anatomy of market failure', *Quarterly Journal of Economics*, 72, 351–79.
Baumol, W.J. and W.E. Oates (1988), *The Theory of Environmental Policy*, 2nd edn, Cambridge, UK: Cambridge University Press.
Bergstrom, T., L. Blume and H. Varian (1986), 'On the private provision of public goods', *Journal of Public Economics*, 29, 25–49.
Bird, P.J.W.N. (1987), 'The transferability and depletability of externalities', *Journal of Environmental Economics and Management*, 14, 54–7.
Bird, P.J.W.N. (1988), 'One more externality article: reply', *Journal of Environmental Economics and Management*, 15, 382–3.
Boadway, R.W. and N. Bruce (1984), *Welfare Economics*, Oxford: Blackwell.
Buchanan, J.M. (1969), 'External diseconomies, corrective taxes and market structure', *American Economic Review*, 59, 174–7.
Buchanan, J.M. and W.C. Stubblebine (1962), 'Externality', *Economica*, 29, 371–84.
Buchanan, J.M. and G. Tullock (1975), 'Polluters' profits and political response: direct controls versus taxes', *American Economic Review*, 65, 139–47.
Burrows, P. (1995), 'Nonconvexities and the theory of external costs', in D.W. Bromley (ed.), *The Handbook of Environmental Economics*, Oxford: Blackwell, pp. 243–71.
Coase, R.H. (1960), 'The problem of social cost', *Journal of Law and Economics*, 3 (October), 1–44.
Cropper, M.L. and W.E. Oates (1992), 'Environmental economics: a survey', *Journal of Economic Literature*, 30, 675–740.
Freeman, A.M. (1984), 'Depletable externalities and Pigovian taxation', *Journal of Environmental Economics and Management*, 8, 321–9.
Harrison, G.W. (1994), 'Environmentally sensitive industries and an emerging Mexico', *North American Journal of Economics and Finance*, 4 (1), 109–26.
Hicks, J.R. (1939), 'The foundation of welfare economics', *Economic Journal*, 49, 696–712.
Johansson, P.-O. (1991), *An Introduction to Modern Welfare Economics*, Cambridge, UK: Cambridge University Press.
Kaldor, N. (1939), 'Welfare propositions of economics and interpersonal comparisons of utility', *Economic Journal*, 49, 549–52.
Knight, F.H. (1924), 'Some fallacies in the interpretation of social cost', *Quarterly Journal of Economics*, 38, 582–606.
Mishan, E.J. (1971), 'The postwar literature on externalities: an interpretative essay', *Journal of Economic Literature*, 9, 1–28.
Mitchell, R.C. and R.T. Carson (1989), *Using Surveys to Value Public Goods: The Contingent Valuation Method*, Washington, DC: Resources for the Future.

Oates, W.E. (1983), 'The regulation of externalities: efficient behaviour by sources and victims', *Public Finance*, **38**, 362–75.

Oates, W.E. (1988), 'And one more reply', *Journal of Environmental Economics and Management*, **15**, 384–5.

Oates, W.E. and D.L. Strassmann (1984), 'Effluent fees and market structure', *Journal of Public Economics*, **24**, 29–46.

Pearce, D.W. and R.K. Turner (1990), *Economics of Natural Resources and the Environment*, Baltimore, MD: Johns Hopkins University Press.

Peskin, H.M. (1988), 'One more externality article', *Journal of Environmental Economics and Management*, **15**, 380–81.

Pigou, A.C. (1920), *Wealth and Welfare*, London: Macmillan.

Sandmo, A. (1976), 'Optimal taxation: an introduction to the literature', *Journal of Public Economics*, **6**, 37–54.

Scitovsky, T. (1954), 'Two concepts of external economies', *Journal of Political Economy*, **17**, 143–51.

Shibata, H. and J.S. Winrich (1983), 'Control of pollution when the offended defend themselves', *Economica*, **50**, 425–37.

Tietenberg, T.H. (1994), *Environmental Economics and Policy*, New York: HarperCollins College Publishers.

Turvey, R. (1963), 'On divergences between social cost and private cost', *Economica*, **30**, 309–13.

Varian, H.R. (1992), *Microeconomic Analysis*, 3rd edn, New York: Norton.

Verhoef, E.T. (1994a), 'Efficiency and equity in externalities: a partial equilibrium analysis', *Environment and Planning*, **26A**, 361–82.

Verhoef, E.T. (1994b), 'External effects and social costs of road transport', *Transportation Research*, **28A**, 273–87.

Verhoef, E.T. (1996a), *The Regulation of Road Transport*, Cheltenham, UK and Brookfield, US: Edward Elgar.

Verhoef, E.T. (1996b), 'The external costs of road transport in The Netherlands', in D. Maddison, D. Pearce, O. Johansson, E. Calthrop, T. Litman and E. Verhoef (1996), *Blueprint 5: The True Costs of Transport*, London: Earthscan.

Verhoef, E.T., P. Nijkamp and P. Rietveld (1997), 'The social feasibility of road pricing: a case study for the Randstad area', *Journal of Transport Economics and Policy*, **31**(3), 255–76.

Viner, J. (1931), 'Cost curves and supply curves', *Zeitschrift für Nationalökonomie*, **3**, 23–46.

Weitzman, M.L. (1974), 'Prices *vs.* quantities', *Review of Economic Studies*, **41**, 477–91.

14 Endogenous environmental risk

Thomas D. Crocker and Jason F. Shogren

1. Introduction

Environmental risk is defined by two elements – the *likelihood* that an unfavourable event will occur and the *severity* of the event if realized (for example, Whyte and Burton, 1980; Lowrance, 1980). Scientists increasingly acknowledge that individual choice can affect environmental risk (Starr, 1969), especially given the incomplete set of contingent claims or insurance markets that characterize environmental goods. As Marshall (1976) shows, when these markets are incomplete, risk must be endogenous: the individual might privately influence many of the environmental risks he or she confronts. Insurance would simply compensate the losses suffered by the individual who has paid the appropriate premium when an undesirable outcome is realized. Insurance alone does not alter the risk of this outcome.

Examples of endogenous risk in which the individual can choose to alter outcomes abound. People move or reduce physical activities when air pollution becomes intolerable. They buy bottled water if they suspect alternative supplies are polluted. They chelate children who have high blood-lead concentrations, and they apply sunscreen to protect their skins from UV radiation. A person invests in a water filter, moves, buys membership to a health club, jogs, eats food low in fat and high in fibre, or applies sunscreen, each choice altering his or her risk to health and welfare. How people invest resources to increase the likelihood that good things happen or bad things do not depends on both their attitudes toward risk and their technology to reduce it (Arrow, 1963; Cook and Graham, 1977; Laffont, 1980).

Hirshleifer (1970), among others, has argued for defining risk problems such that the state of nature is always independent of human action. Consider, however, a situation in which bacterial groundwater contamination threatens a household's drinking water. The probability of illness among household members can be altered if they boil the water. An analyst could define the situation as independent of the household's actions by focusing solely on groundwater contamination, over which the household probably has no control. But this definition is economically irrelevant if the question is the household's response to the risks from groundwater contamination. The household is concerned about the likelihood of illness and the realized severity, and it is able to exercise some control over those events. The household's risk is endogenous because by expending its valuable resources it influences probability and severity (Crocker et al., 1991).

2.   Theoretical foundations

Models of endogenous risk build on the seminal models of choice under uncertainty developed over the past half century (for example, von Neumann and Morgenstern, 1944, Savage, 1954; de Finetti, 1974; Drèze, 1987). A person has preferences over outcomes and preferences over the lotteries that define those outcomes, and he/she makes choices to secure those more preferred lotteries. Define *ex ante* efforts to reduce probability as self-protection, z, and *ex ante* efforts to reduce prospective severity as self-insurance, x (Ehrlich and Becker, 1972). The individual selects z and x to maximize his expected utility, EU,

$$EU = \int_a^b U\big(M - L(\varphi;x) - c(x, z)\big)dF(\varphi;z,\alpha) \tag{14.1}$$

where $W = M - L(\varphi;x) - c(x,z)$ is net wealth, M is endowed income, $L(\varphi;x)$ is the money equivalent of realized severity, φ is a random variable defined by the distribution $F(\varphi; z, \alpha)$ bounded over the support $[a, b]$, z and x are expenditures on self-protection and self-insurance against the realization of an undesirable state, $c(x, z)$ is the cost function, and α represents an index of riskiness given collective risk reduction mechanisms. Assume $U_W > 0$, $L_x < 0$, $L_\varphi < 0$, $F_z < 0$, $F_\alpha > 0$, $c_i(x, z) > 0$ ($i = x, z$), where subscripts denote the relevant derivatives. Quiggin (1992) uses a state space formulation rather than the parameterized distribution formulation of (14.1). The two formulations can be shown to be formally equivalent, suggesting that the choice between them rests upon the relative restrictiveness of the assumptions necessary to make each tractable in particular problem-specific settings.

The necessary conditions from (14.1) for a person's optimal levels of self-protection and self-insurance are

$$-\int_a^b U_W\big(M - L(\varphi;x) - c(x,z)\big)c_z(x,z)dF(\varphi;z,\alpha)$$

$$+\int_a^b U\big(M - L(\varphi;x) - c(x,z)\big)L_\varphi F_z(\varphi;z,\alpha)d\varphi = 0 \tag{14.2}$$

$$-\int_a^b U_W\big(M - L(\varphi;x) - c(x,z)\big)\big[L_x(\varphi;x) + c_x(x,z)\big]dF(\varphi;z,\alpha) = 0 \tag{14.3}$$

Equations (14.2) and (14.3) state the standard result that an individual maximizes expected utility by equating the marginal cost of influencing probability or severity to the marginal wealth acquired. The second or marginal benefit term in (14.2) embodies the distinctive feature of the endogenous risk perspective (Shogren and Crocker, 1991a). Integration by parts of the term makes clear that the marginal benefits of self-protection are realized directly in the utility function and indirectly through a first-order stochastically dominating change in outcomes induced by the risk reduction technology. Shogren and Crocker (1991a) show that a change in self-protection can be of either sign as the random variable changes because the sign of the marginal productivity of a technology is problem-specific. The endogenous risk perspective thus motivates detailed attention to the physical and biological realities that underlie environmental hazards so that one may explain *how* people prefer to reduce risk.

Individuals often prefer to substitute self-protection for collectively supplied safety programmes. Examples include the use of higher-strength building materials in response to prospective tornado, storm surge and earthquake hazards; more thorough weeding and crop storage in response to the prospect of drought; sand-bagging and evacuation in anticipation of floods; and improved nutrition and exercise regimens to cope with health threats. At the policy level, these private risk reduction choices can affect the success of collective mandates to promote safety. Use of auto seat belts reduces both the probability and the severity of injury, but their mandatory installation cannot guarantee that passengers will choose to wear them. Highway speed limits also are effective at reducing fatalities only when drivers observe them. In the workplace, initiatives involving personal protective gear (for example, hard hats) have the same problem: they protect only those workers who wear them. In each case, individual decisions about risk reduction technologies influence both the probability and the magnitude of harm. Similarly, collective actions to promote cost minimization and other narrow efficiency criteria can alter individuals' incentives to self-protect (Chapman and Hariharan, 1996; Laffont, 1995). In addition, self-protection opportunities introduce another layer of uncertainty: the individual may be uncertain about the risk-reducing productivity of a self-protection technology and may thus be willing to pay a premium to temper this source of uncertainty (Shogren, 1991).

3. Risk Assessment
The view that environmental risk is exogenous, beyond the control of normal people, is still maintained in the assessment–management bifurcation sanctified by the National Academy of Sciences (1983) and is common in scientific and policy discussions about environmental risk (Ruckelshaus,

1984; US Federal Register, 1984; Breyers, 1993). The sanctioned view is that risk assessment quantifies risk; risk management regulates risk. But endogenous risk implies that observed risks are functions of both natural science parameters and an individual's self-protection decisions. Given the relative marginal effectiveness of alternative self-protection efforts, how people make decisions about risk differs across individuals and situations, even though the natural phenomena that trigger these efforts apply equally to everyone. Therefore, assessing risk levels solely in terms of natural science can be misleading – costly self-protection is endogenous and therefore may vary systematically in the observed risk data. The sources of the systematic variation are relative prices, incomes and other economic (and social) parameters that influence any individual's self-protection decisions.

Just as good public-policy-based economics requires an understanding of the physical and natural phenomena that underpin choices, good public-policy-based natural science requires an understanding of the economic phenomena that affect risk. In the presence of endogenous risk, accurate risk assessment and effective risk management require a full accounting of the input and output substitutions that producers and consumers make when responding to environmental changes. This accounting requires an understanding of how these responses relate to the individual's risk perception and valuation, and to collective management and assessment practices (Viscusi, 1992). An attenuated description of substitution opportunities limits the means the person has to maximize gains or minimize losses and thus causes the economic gains from risk reduction to be understated. Endogenous risk implies that researchers must explicitly address the simultaneous nature of how economic decisions affect observed risk and how natural science features affect economic decisions.

4.   Risk valuation

Endogenous risk theory also spurs reconsideration of risk reduction valuation procedures. The reconsideration cuts deeper than problems of measurement. It involves acknowledgement of fundamental deficiencies in perspective. Specifically, the assumption of exogenous risk in cost–benefit analysis can lead to the undervaluation of reduced risk and the mis-identification of those who value risk reductions most highly. There are several reasons for undervaluation, all involving the inability of an exogenous risk perspective to disentangle the relative values of private and collective contributions to risk reductions. To illustrate – the valuation literature on exogenous risk characteristically assumes that the value of risk reduction declines as risk decreases. Empirical evidence that this marginal value actually increases is held to be a lapse from rational economic behaviour (for example, Tversky and Kahneman, 1981; Smith and Desvousges,

1987). An endogenous risk framework, however, can generate behaviour consistent with increasing marginal valuations of risk reductions without putting the problem at the service of the traditional practice and axioms of the exogenous risk approach (Shogren and Crocker, 1991a). If the marginal productivity effects of self-protection on probability differ from the effects on severity, increasing marginal valuations of risk reductions can occur, a result challenging the standard view that those at greater risk and with greater wealth must value a given risk reduction more highly. Poor people may have fewer and most costly opportunities to self-protect and may thus value a risk reduction more highly than do the wealthy. The result also implies that as the marginal effectiveness of collective provision declines, the relative effectiveness and therefore the value of private provision increases.

Although people have numerous ways to reduce risk privately, when researchers employ the concept of the value of a statistical life or limb in cost–benefit analyses of reduced environmental risks they implicitly dismiss the existence of substitutable risk reduction mechanisms. These researchers define the value of a statistical life as the cost of an unidentified single death weighted by a probability of death that is uniform across individuals (Cropper and Freeman, 1991). But even if individuals have identical preferences, substantial differences exist in their opportunities for or costs of altering risk. The statistical life or limb approach to collective risk reduction fails to address the differences in individual risks induced by self-protection. A complete assessment of this individual's value of a given risk reduction thus requires considering willingness to pay for self-provision as well as for collective provision. In essence, by virtue of its exclusive focus on collective provision, the statistical life or limb approach undervalues environmental threats to human health and endorses economically excessive levels of environmental degradation. For example, Agee and Crocker (1996) find that an endogenous risk approach to parents' willingness to pay to reduce their children's body burdens of lead yields estimates at least twice those of an exogenous risk treatment. By allowing the individual to reveal whether he would prefer to reduce risk privately or collectively or both, or by reducing the probability or severity or both, and by evaluating how he times his mind and minds his time, a more accurate measure of the value of risk reduction will be brought forth.

5. Risk management

Risks that are endogenous can also be transferable. Transferable risk implies that the individual protects himself by simply transferring the risk through space to another location or through time to another generation (Bird, 1987). Viewed from the materials balance perspective (Kneese et al.,

1970), most environmental programmes do not reduce environmental risks. They do not reduce the mass of materials used or cause them to accumulate in the economy. People select a technology that transfers a risk. The involuntary recipient of the transfer is uncompensated, which creates conflict and induces strategic behaviour. Transferable risk is thus motivated by intentional behaviours, not by the unintentional residuals of production. For example, in the 1970s and 1980s the mid-western industrial states reduced regional air pollution problems by building tall stacks at emitter sites where prevailing weather patterns then transfer emissions to the northeastern states and to eastern Canada. Clearly the mid-western states have lessened their regional damages by adopting abatement technologies which increase air pollution damages elsewhere. Another example occurs when some governments forbid the storage of toxins within their jurisdictions, thereby causing the toxins to be stored or dumped elsewhere.

Transferable risk implies that a person's expected utility problem in equation (14.1) must be modified to include other people's strategic self-protection expenditures. Some environmental programmes which appear desirable within an exogenous risk framework now are seen to accentuate the inefficiencies inherent in transferable risks and non-cooperative behaviour. First, environmental policies which allow unilateral transfers of risk rather than encouraging cooperative resolutions will result in excessive expenditures on self-protection (Shogren and Crocker, 1991b). Second, publicly sponsored hazard information programmes might not be efficient alternatives to direct regulation if the advice increases already excessive levels of self-protection. Third, policies that transfer risk will prompt strenuous self-protection efforts by those recipients who have an elastic damage function.

With transferable risks, regulators have a strong case for insisting upon waste reduction technologies (for example, waste prevention and recycling) rather than transfer technologies (such as waste disposal and treatment). The person who engages in prevention and recycling rather than disposal and treatment filters rather than transfers wastes. For example, the person who uses or sells recycled trash moves material flows from the environment to the economy, thus broadening the domain of efficient price signalling. Just as self-protection is excessive when transferable risks rule, it is too small when filtering governs. The person who filters provides a benefit to other people for which he/she goes unrewarded. A strong case can be made for subsidies to reduction technologies, that is, to those who practise waste prevention and recycling. Conversely, economic sense requires that programmes which encourage transfer be discouraged. That is, economic efficiency requires that waste producers be able to avoid policy prescriptions such as Pigouvian taxes only when these producers prevent or recycle rather than simply transfer their wastes.

6. Conclusions

People have choices when confronting an environmental risk. Incorporating these choices into risk assessment and reduction strategies has ramifications for environmental policy. An endogenous risk perspective can increase the precision of risk assessment, cause the benefits of risk reduction to be more accurately estimated, and temper the behaviour of those exposed to risk who spend excessively on self-protection. Failure to acknowledge the influence that individual choice has on environmental risk will result in excessive economic expenditures at no gain in environmental quality. The key is to create incentives that reward those who attempt to unify risk assessment and management into an integrated system, estimate individual preferences for alternative risk reduction strategies, and foster risk-sharing institutions that explicitly address the nature of transferable risk. Otherwise, Zeckhauser and Viscusi's (1990) demand for more 'systematic strategies for assessing and responding to risk' will fall short.

References

Agee, M.D. and T.D. Crocker (1996), 'Parental altruism and child lead exposure', *The Journal of Human Resources*, **31** (3), 677–91.

Arrow, K. (1963), Uncertainty and the welfare economics of medical care', *American Economic Review*, **53**, 941–69.

Bird, J. (1987), 'The transferability and depletability of externalities', *Journal of Environmental Economics and Management*, **14**, 54–7.

Breyers, S. (1993), *Breaking the Vicious Circle: Toward Effective Risk Regulation*, Cambridge, MA: Harvard University Press.

Chapman, K. and G. Hariharan (1996), 'Do poor people have a stronger relationship between income and mortality than the rich? Implications of panel data for wealth-health analysis', *Journal of Risk and Uncertainty*, **12**, 51–64.

Cook, P. and D. Graham (1977), 'The demand for insurance and protection: the care of irreplaceable commodities', *Quarterly Journal of Economics*, **91**, 143–56.

Crocker, T., B. Forster and J. Shogren (1991), 'Valuing potential groundwater protection benefits', *Water Resources Research*, **27**, 1–6.

Cropper, M. and A.M. Freeman III (1991), 'Environmental health effects', in J. Braden and C. Kolstad (eds), *Measuring the Demand for Environmental Quality*, Amsterdam: North-Holland, pp. 165–211.

De Finetti, B. (1974), *Theory of Probability*, New York: Wiley & Sons.

Drèze, J. (1987), *Essays on Economic Decisions under Uncertainty*, Cambridge, UK: Cambridge University Press.

Ehrlich, I. and G. Becker (1972), 'Market insurance, self-insurance, and self-protection', *Journal of Political Economy*, **80**, 623–48.

Hirshleifer, J. (1970), *Investment, Interest, and Capital*, Englewood Cliffs, NJ: Prentice Hall.

Kneese, A., R. Ayres and R. d'Arge (1970), *Economics and the Environment: A Materials Balance Approach*, Washington, DC: Resources for the Future.

Laffont, J. (1980), *Essays in the Economics of Uncertainty*, Cambridge, MA: Harvard University Press.

Laffont, J. (1995), 'Regulation, moral hazard and insurance of environmental risks', *Journal of Public Economics*, **58**, 319–36.

Lowrance, W. (1980), 'The nature of risk', in R. Schwing and W. Albers (eds), *Societal Risk Assessment. How Safe is Safe Enough?* New York: Plenum Press.

Marshall, J. (1976), 'Moral hazard', *American Economic Review*, **66**, 880–90.

National Academy of Sciences (1983), *Risk Assessment in the Federal Government: Managing the Process*. Washington, DC: National Academy Press.

Neumann, J. von and O. Morgenstern (1944), *Theory of Games and Economic Behavior*, Princeton, NJ: Princeton University Press.

Quiggin, J. (1992), 'Risk, self-protection, and ex ante economic value – some positive results', *Journal of Environmental Economics and Management*, **23**, 40–53.

Ruckelshaus, W. (1984), 'Risk in a free society', *Risk Analysis*, **4**, 157–62.

Savage, L. (1954), *The Foundation of Statistics*, New York: Wiley & Sons.

Shogren, J.F. (1991), 'Endogenous risk and protection premiums', *Theory and Decision*, **31** (2), 241–56.

Shogren, J.F. and T. Crocker (1991a), 'Risk, self-protection, and ex ante economic value', *Journal of Environmental and Economic Management*, **20**, 1–15.

Shogren, J.F. and T. Crocker (1991b), "Cooperative and noncooperative protection against transferable and filterable externalities', *Environmental and Resource Economics*, **1**, 195–214.

Smith, V.K. and W. Desvousges (1987), 'An empirical analysis of the economic value of risk change', *Journal of Political Economy*, **95**, 89–115.

Starr, C. (1969), 'Social benefit vs. technological risk', *Science*, **165**, 1232–8.

Tversky, A. and D. Kahneman (1981), 'The farming of decisions and the psychology of choice', *Science*, **211**, 453–8.

US Federal Register (1984), *Parts II, III, V, and VI: Environmental Protection Agency*, 24 September, Washington, DC.

Viscusi, W.K. (1992), *Fatal Tradeoffs*, Oxford: Oxford University Press.

Whyte, A.V. and I. Burton (1980), *Environmental Risk Assessment*, New York: John Wiley and Sons.

Zeckhauser, R. and W.K. Viscusi (1990), 'Risk within reason', *Science*, **248**, 559.

15 Standards versus taxes in pollution control

Gloria E. Helfand

1. Introduction

Much of the literature on controlling externalities focuses on efficiency. While economists have long argued that taxes on the externality provide an efficient solution, or at least a minimum-cost solution (for example, Baumol and Oates, 1988, chapters 4 and 11; Baumol, 1972), environmental legislation in the United States almost universally uses mandated standards rather than taxes (Dewees, 1983). In Europe, pollution taxes are used, though less to provide incentive for clean-up than to provide funds to subsidize abatement equipment (Howe, 1994). If taxes are generally more efficient than standards, why are standards often used?

This chapter reviews the major arguments over pollution taxes versus standards. The efficiency of each approach depends heavily on the regulatory setting; the distributional consequences and political acceptability of each approach also differ. The following discussion begins with an overview of the efficiency advantages of taxes over standards. These results are then qualified through analysis of situations where taxes may not be efficient. Uncertainty in achieving abatement goals can make combinations of instruments appear preferable to single instruments. The final section identifies additional factors affecting a policy maker's choice of regulatory instrument.

2. Efficiency advantages of taxes over standards

Externalities can be viewed as arising because of a failure of property rights: some resources are not privately owned, are not exclusive, cannot be transferred, or cannot be enforced. As a result, normal market operations do not price these resources properly, and suboptimal levels of the resource are supplied. Much of the economic research on externalities has focused on how to correct for this absence of a market at the least cost to society. Two mechanisms often discussed to solve these problems are a tax on pollution, and a standard to control the maximum level of pollution produced by firms. By charging an agent for each unit of pollution, a tax gives an incentive to a cost-minimizing agent to reduce pollution. In contrast, a pollution standard mandates a certain level of pollution that cannot be exceeded. Pollution taxes are often cited as having clear efficiency advantages over standards, because they allow firms more individual choice and thus constrain them less.

If only one firm, or a fixed number of identical firms, is being regulated in a world with no uncertainty, then taxes and standards are equally efficient at maximizing social welfare, where the level of pollution is an endogenous component of social welfare. The optimal level of pollution, the level where the marginal benefits of abatement (in reduced environmental and health damages) equal the marginal social costs of abatement, can be attained by mandating a standard set at that optimal level of pollution. Alternatively, if polluters are charged a tax per unit of pollution, they will abate pollution as long as the marginal cost of abatement is less than the tax; if the tax is set so that marginal benefits of abatement equal the marginal costs and equal the tax, the same level of pollution will be attained.

The superiority of taxes occurs when firms vary (Baumol and Oates, 1988, ch. 4). When firms have different abatement costs, and when pollution damages depend only on total emissions, abatement costs are minimized when marginal costs of abatement are equalized across firms. A pollution tax, by specifying the opportunity cost of polluting, leads a firm to reduce its pollution as long as the tax exceeds the abatement cost. If all firms face the same pollution tax, the conditions for least-cost abatement will be achieved. Firms for which abatement is not very costly will reduce pollution more than firms whose abatement is expensive. In contrast, a uniform pollution standard, which ignores differences in abatement costs across firms, requires the same environmental performance by those firms. Abatement costs will be higher with a pollution standard than with a pollution tax.

This result holds for achievement of any level of pollution. While social optimality would require marginal costs of abatement to equal marginal benefits of abatement, identifying the optimal level of pollution may be very difficult. If an abatement level is chosen through other means, a pollution tax will achieve this level with lower expenditures on abatement than will a standard (Baumol and Oates, 1988, ch. 11; Baumol, 1972).

A pollution tax also has desirable characteristics for industry structure. Spulber (1985) shows that, for identical firms in a perfectly competitive industry, a pollution tax equal to the marginal damage caused by pollution will achieve not only the correct marginal conditions for social optimality; in addition, in the long run the optimal number of firms will remain in the industry, each operating at the socially optimal scale. In contrast, a pollution standard set so that individual firms will pollute the same amount as under the tax will lead to excessive entry: because the standard does not require firms to pay a tax on remaining pollution, profits are higher, leading to entry and higher total pollution. If the pollution level is to equal that under the tax, the standard will have to be more restrictive. Spulber (1985) thus argues that a pollution tax is more efficient than a standard, even for identical firms.

Finally, a pollution tax is more effective at encouraging technological innovation to reduce abatement costs than is a pollution standard. Milliman and Prince (1989) (for the case of identical firms) and Jung et al. (1996) (for heterogeneous firms) find that pollution taxes lead to greater incentives for technological change. Since technological change reduces abatement costs (and production costs for industry output), more pollution abatement as well as greater production can be achieved through a pollution tax than through use of a standard.

In sum, efficiency gains result from the use of taxes compared to standards in this basic model. These results are premised on a number of major assumptions, such as: that an additional unit of pollution from one source causes the same marginal damage as a unit of pollution from another source; that taxes and standards are specified for emissions from producers; and that marginal benefits of abatement are decreasing, while marginal costs of abatement are increasing. When such assumptions are violated, as the following analysis discusses, the efficiency of taxes needs to be re-evaluated.

3. Qualifications to the efficiency results

The prior discussion gives a number of reasons why pollution taxes are superior to pollution standards. This result does not always hold, though. A number of factors influence the relative efficiency of these instruments and are discussed below.

If the effects of pollution from one firm differ from the effects from another firm – that is, if damages are not merely a function of summed emissions – then a uniform tax is no longer efficient (Rose-Ackerman, 1973). For example, if pollution from firm 1 directly affects a prime fishing spot, while pollution from firm 2 occurs in an area with no notable fishery, then cleaning up pollution from firm 2 cannot substitute for cleaning up pollution from firm 1. In this case, the firms should be taxed at different rates, or have individualized standards, even if they have the same marginal abatement cost curves. Rose-Ackerman suggests, but does not show, that a uniform percentage reduction in pollution may be more desirable in these cases than either a uniform tax or a uniform emissions standard. Tietenberg (1985, pp. 68–9) summarized empirical studies of emissions permits (equivalent in marginal incentive to an emissions tax) to command and control for non-uniformly mixed pollutants; in almost half the studies referenced, uniform standards had lower control costs. Since it is often true that the effect of pollutants is location-specific, a uniform tax is not clearly preferable to a uniform standard.

Care also needs to be taken in defining what exactly is taxed or regulated. As Rose-Ackerman (1973) suggests and Harford and Karp (1983), Besanko (1987), Thomas (1980), and Helfand (1991, 1993) show, regulatory standards take a number of forms, and the form in which they are specified affects their efficiency. For instance, standards specified as pollution per unit of output and mandating a minimum level of abatement are less efficient for identical firms facing fixed output price than a standard restricting pollution, but the former standards can be more efficient than the latter if firms vary or if output price changes with quantity. Helfand and House's (1995) analysis of nitrate leaching in the Salinas Valley finds that some forms of standards (such as a constant proportional reduction of pollution levels or a restriction on one polluting input) can be more efficient than some forms of taxes (such as a tax on a single input to pollution) when optimal taxes or standards are infeasible.

Changing demand and supply conditions affect the desirability of taxes as a regulatory instrument, especially if pollution control instruments are 'sticky' (Rose-Ackerman, 1973; Magat, 1978). If, for instance, demand for the product of a polluting process increases, the marginal benefits of the polluting activity increase, while the marginal costs of pollution do not move. The new optimum implies a higher level of pollution. Policy makers do not always respond rapidly to such shifts and may leave their chosen regulatory instrument unchanged. If a standard were in use, it would keep pollution at the original level. In contrast, a stable tax set at the original level of marginal benefits would lead to greater pollution, at the point where the new marginal benefits curve equals the tax. In other words, a pollution tax here leads to too much pollution, while a pollution standard leads to too little pollution.

Most of the preceding analysis assumes that the marginal benefits of abatement decrease as abatement increases, and that the marginal costs of abatement increase with additional abatement. These assumptions, also, do not always hold. Indeed, Baumol and Oates (1988, ch. 10) argued that externalities themselves lead to non-convexities in the social production set: if two activities interact with each other, a non-convexity will result if one of the activities shuts down. Non-convexities can arise from the technology of production or polluting (for instance, Repetto, 1987 found a technical non-convexity in the formation of ozone), from people's psychological responses to environmental damages (Stankey, 1972 found that the marginal cost to a wilderness user of increased congestion decreased over a range), from behaviour designed to avert damages (Starrett and Zeckhauser, 1971), and from increasing returns to scale in production

(Helfand and Rubin, 1994). Burrows (1986, 1996) argued that, in many cases, either taxes or standards will improve social welfare in the presence of non-convexities, even if they do not achieve the social optimum. Helfand and Rubin (1994), considering the case where the social optimum might involve concentrating damaging activities, argued that neither taxes nor standards will achieve a social optimum: firms will act individually, having little incentive to recognize gains due to coordination of waste reduction efforts. In contrast, a system of marketable permits will lead to an incentive for coordinated activities, since permits force firms to recognize the joint nature of their actions.

Asymmetric information also affects the advantages of taxes. Baron (1985) argued, for a regulated monopoly which has information about its abatement technology that a regulator does not, that a standard has advantages over a tax. The firm can manipulate the tax level through its announcement of abatement effectiveness. If the regulator instead uses a pollution standard coupled with regulation of output price, 'information rents' are reduced. Shortle and Dunn (1986) found, for non-point source pollution, that incentives oriented toward inputs are superior to standards on inputs, incentives to reduce effluent, or standards on effluent. In their paper, input incentives entice a farmer to make use of his specialized information, producing a better outcome than if the regulator has to make assumptions about that information. A pollution incentive instrument will not be as effective if the damage function is non-linear, since it cannot fully incorporate higher moments than the mean of the distribution of the uncertainty about pollution.

In sum, the greater efficiency of pollution taxes over pollution standards is subject to a number of qualifications. How the standards are formulated, the presence of asymmetric information, changing conditions over time, non-convexities, and differing damages across sources affect the efficiency characteristics of both taxes and standards. Choosing between the two instruments to maximize net social benefits requires careful consideration of the circumstances to be regulated.

4. The effects of uncertainty

When uncertainty is factored into the analysis, either taxes or standards may be more efficient. A regulator may not have good information either about damages caused by pollution or about benefits generated by the polluting activity. Weitzman (1974) and Adar and Griffin (1976) showed that uncertainty about damages does not affect the choice of instrument, but uncertainty about control costs does. In particular, a standard is preferable when the marginal benefits curve is highly sensitive to the actual quantity (that is, when small changes in quantity have a large effect on benefits), but that a tax is preferable when the marginal cost curve varies sharply with quantity (that is, when getting cost estimates wrong has a large effect on those costs). If there are threshold levels for damages – that is, damages increase sharply after some critical concentration of the pollutant is reached – then a standard may indeed be preferable to a tax. On the other hand, empirical studies by Morgan (1983) and Watson and Ridker (1984) generally found greater efficiency under market regimes than under standards.

A few other factors affect the choice of a tax versus a standard under uncertainty. Tisato (1994) showed theoretically that, in the typical case that marginal costs of control are higher for standards than for a tax (due to the lower cost of a tax in achieving a specified level of emissions reduction), taxes are efficient under more circumstances than Weitzman's or Adar and Griffin's analysis suggests. The potential superiority of a standard is reduced more when there are many firms with different cost functions, but it does not vanish completely. Stavins (1996) found that a positive correlation between uncertainty in damages and uncertainty in control favours a standard, while a negative correlation favours a tax. He argued that correlated uncertainty is more likely to favour a standard than a tax under realistic conditions.

When risk or uncertainty affects pollution control, a mix of instruments may be the most effective way to regulate (Baumol and Oates, 1988, ch. 13; Just and Zilberman, 1979; Roberts and Spence, 1976; Shavell, 1984). For instance, a tax may operate very effectively until a major stochastic shock occurs. In that state, a tax large enough to protect against a rare event would be unduly penalizing most of the time. If, institutionally, a tax is fairly inflexible, then 'emergency' imposition of a standard may protect the public without the need to go through a cumbersome process for revision of the tax (Baumol and Oates, 1988, ch. 13). When abatement costs are uncertain, Roberts and Spence argue that an effluent tax brings about too little clean-up when abatement costs are higher than expected, and too much clean-up when those costs are lower than expected; in contrast, marketable permits have the opposite effect. Combining these instruments reduces expected social costs. Shavell (1984) advocates joint use of quantity controls and liability rules (that is, making the one who causes damages compensate the victim) for environmental and other accidents: liability rules alone are not completely efficient, because a firm may not be sued or may go bankrupt rather than pay full damages; and regulation alone may not be completely efficient because of the regulator's lack of complete knowledge about the relative dangers posed by different firms. An optimal standard would set a minimum level of control for firms posing a small risk, and firms which posed a greater risk would increase their safety levels in response to their remaining liability.

In reality, uncertainty over the damages caused by pollution and over the costs of controlling pollution is almost impossible to avoid. Social costs of pollution control can be reduced if environmental policy instruments are designed to reflect these uncertainties. At the same time, instruments which incorporate the effects of uncertainty increase the complexity of the regulatory system; these transactions costs are not reflected in these models. Future research to examine the trade-off between the regulatory costs of improved instruments and the efficiency gains of those instruments could contribute to development of more effective pollution control measures.

5. Additional policy considerations

The choice of regulatory instrument is, ultimately, a political decision, not one made by a social planner maximizing a social welfare function. When regulators choose between pollution taxes and standards, efficiency is not the only factor they consider. Instead, factors such as distributional effects, political–economic issues and ethical perspectives are likely to play a role in the policy decision.

Pollution taxes not only induce a firm to correct its marginal behaviour; they also require the affected firm to pay taxes on the remaining pollution. A standard, in contrast, requires no payment other than for abatement. Because taxes on additional pollution hurt firm profitability, perhaps to the point where some firms may shut down (Rose-Ackerman, 1973; Gould, 1977), the distributional effects of taxes and standards can be significant. Helfand and House's (1995) empirical study finds that a uniform pollution rollback reduces farm profits less than an efficient set of pollution taxes. On the other hand, those tax revenues (which increase, rather than decrease, efficiency) can be used to offset other more distortionary taxes in the economy (Goulder, 1995, for instance), though they can also exacerbate these pre-existing distortions in labour and capital markets by further increasing production costs (Parry, 1995).

Because those affected by policy (polluters and consumers of products from polluting companies) may benefit or suffer due to the choice of regulatory instruments, they have an incentive to influence the political process in their favour; and if regulators can benefit from some acts of the agents, such as offers of political support, they can be influenced to favour the agents (Stigler, 1971; Peltzman, 1976). As a result, the instrument which most benefits affected agents could be enacted, regardless of efficiency losses. Indeed, regulation can *benefit* the regulated industry. Buchanan and Tullock (1975) show that an output tax (to reduce pollution) leads to zero economic profits for firms; in contrast, a standard in the form of output reductions for all firms acts as a government-imposed cartel, with the cartel result that price increases faster than cost, and firms make economic profits.

A barrier to entry is necessary for the cartel to hold, but environmental legislation frequently creates barriers (Maloney and McCormick, 1982) by imposing stiffer pollution control requirements on new firms than on existing firms. Firms may not be the only beneficiaries: consumers too may gain by use of a standard rather than a tax, especially if the tax revenues are not returned directly to them. Though an individual firm may produce less output under a standard than under a tax, more firms stay in the industry. As a result, total output is higher, and prices are lower (Hochman and Zilberman, 1978; Dewees, 1983) under a standard compared to a tax, to consumers' benefit.

Empirical studies by Maloney and McCormick (1982) and Pashigian (1985) lend some support to the political–economic use of pollution standards to give advantages to some firms. Leone and Jackson (1981), Bartel and Thomas (1987), and Pashigian (1984) found evidence that some existing firms, as well as potential entrants, can suffer more than others from regulations with discriminating effects, supporting the Salop and Scheffman (1983) argument that increased costs can increase profits if competitors are more adversely affected. The distributional effects of policies, and the political influence they generate, inevitably affect the policy decision of instrument choice.

Clashes between the 'economic paradigm' and the world-view of regulators or environmental activists may also affect the policy choice. Economists have a strong belief in the value of self-interest, the ability of markets to achieve social optima, preferences for voluntary exchange and free choice, an assumption that society is no more than the sum of its individuals, and a tendency to emphasize results, rather than people's attitudes or feelings about the process (Kelman, 1981, pp. 16–20). To the extent that others, especially policy makers, do not agree with these principles, market approaches may not address perceived problems and thus not provide appropriate solutions. Kelman (1981) notes four major concerns of non-economists about the use of pollution taxes: (1) the endorsement of self-interested behaviour implicit in market mechanisms is undesirable; (2) market mechanisms do not adequately stigmatize polluting behaviour; (3) bringing environmental quality into a market system cheapens it, as would making emotions marketable; and (4) wealthy firms can buy their way out of punishment for undesired behaviour, while poorer polluters have no choice but to alter their behaviour (pp. 27–8). Beder (1996) adds that institutional realities make it very unlikely (and empirically unobserved) that taxes adequate to provide an incentive for significant clean-up can be enacted; the low levels of taxes generally enacted allow polluters the ability to buy their way out of clean-up. These concerns may incline policy makers more toward standards than toward taxes.

In sum, efficiency is not the only factor that policy makers consider. Distributional effects of different policies have effects on constituents who can influence the regulatory process; and those who are regulating may distrust the market paradigm as the appropriate way to address pollution problems. From this perspective, pollution standards have advantages over taxes. Even with a higher social cost, standards might pose less direct cost to firms, and they emphasize the antisocial nature of polluting.

6. Summary

Table 15.1 summarizes the results presented here. The regulatory choice of pollution taxes versus standards depends on a number of factors. For

Table 15.1   Factors affecting the choice of taxes versus standards

Factors affecting the choice	Instrument it tends to favour
Efficiency factors	
Differences in abatement costs among firms	Taxes
Entry–exit conditions	Taxes
Effects on technological change	Taxes
Non-uniformly mixed emissions	Ambiguous
What is taxed/regulated	Ambiguous
Shifting market conditions when instruments are 'sticky'	Taxes lead to 'too much' pollution, standards to 'too little' pollution
Non-convexities	Similar effects
Asymmetric information	Ambiguous
Uncertainty factors	
Uncorrelated marginal benefits and costs	Standard for steep marginal benefits, tax for steep marginal costs
Lower social clean-up costs for tax	Tax
Correlated marginal benefits and costs	Standard
Additional policy considerations	
Distributional effects	Standard
Political–economic effect	Standard
Alternative paradigms	Standard

Note: That an instrument is 'favoured' by a cited factor does not mean that it is conclusive that the factor leads to a preference for that instrument, but rather that evidence suggests it will influence the choice of standard in that direction.

heterogeneous competitive firms in localized areas, the efficiency advantages of taxes relative to standards are likely to be large, though other considerations, such as the cost to regulated businesses of the taxes, might also loom large. When large areas are regulated, or when markets and information are imperfect, both uniform pollution taxes and standards are inefficient; whether one dominates the other on efficiency grounds must be determined empirically.

Regulators often base decisions on factors other than efficiency. By these criteria, standards have some advantages. For a given level of clean-up by a firm, a standard may be less expensive than a tax, since it does not require any transfer payments; it also appears more punitive, and more likely to give desired results, than a tax. As regulators give greater weight to these factors, the efficiency of taxes may play a lesser role in a regulator's decision.

References

Adar, Zvi and James M. Griffin (1976), 'Uncertainty and the choice of pollution control instruments', *Journal of Environmental Economics and Management*, **3**, 178–88.

Baron, David P. (1985), 'Regulation of prices and pollution under incomplete information', *Journal of Public Economics*, **28**, 211–31.

Bartel, Ann-P. and Lacy-Glenn Thomas (1987), 'Predation through regulation: the wage and profit effects of the Occupational Safety and Health Administration and the Environmental Protection Agency', *Journal of Law and Economics*, **30**, 239–64.

Baumol, William J. (1972), 'On taxation and the control of externalities', *American Economic Review*, **62**, 307–22.

Baumol, William J. and Wallace E. Oates (1988), *The Theory of Environmental Policy*, Cambridge: Cambridge University Press.

Beder, Sharon (1996), 'Charging the earth: the promotion of price-based measures for pollution control', *Ecological Economics*, **16**, 51–63.

Besanko, David (1987), 'Performance versus design standards in the regulation of pollution', *Journal of Public Economics*, **34**, 19–44.

Buchanan, James M. and Gordon Tullock (1975), 'Polluters' profits and political response: direct controls versus taxes', *American Economic Review*, **65**, 139–47.

Burrows, Paul (1986), 'Nonconvexity induced by external costs on production: theoretical curio or policy dilemma?', *Journal of Environmental Economics and Management*, **13**, 101–28.

Burrows, Paul (1996), 'Nonconvexities and the theory of external costs', in Daniel W. Bromley (ed.), *The Handbook of Environmental Economics*, Cambridge, MA: Blackwell Publishers, pp. 243–71.

Dewees, Donald N. (1983), 'Instrument choice in environmental policy', *Economic Inquiry*, **21**, 53–71.

Gould, J.R. (1977), 'Total conditions in the analysis of external effects', *The Economic Journal*, **87**, 558–64.

Goulder, Lawrence H. (1995), 'Effects of carbon taxes in an economy with prior tax distortions: an intertemporal general equilibrium analysis', *Journal of Environmental Economics and Management*, **29**, 271–97.

Harford, Jon D. and Gordon Karp (1983), 'The effects and efficiencies of different pollution standards', *Eastern Economics Journal*, **9**, 79–89.

Helfand, Gloria E. (1991), 'Standards versus standards: the effects of different pollution restrictions', *American Economic Review*, **81**, 622–34.

Helfand, Gloria E. (1993), 'The relative efficiency of different standards when firms vary', *Natural Resource Modeling*, **7**, 203–17.

Helfand, Gloria E. and Brett W. House (1995), 'Regulating nonpoint source pollution under heterogeneous conditions', *American Journal of Agricultural Economics*, **77**, 1024–32.

Helfand, Gloria E. and Jonathan Rubin (1994), 'Spreading versus concentrating damages: environmental policy in the presence of nonconvexities', *Journal of Environmental Economics and Management*, **27**, 84–91.

Hochman, Eithan and David Zilberman (1978), 'Examination of environmental policies using production and pollution microparameter distributions', *Econometrica*, **46**, 739–60.

Howe, Charles W. (1994), 'Taxes *versus* tradable discharge permits: a review in the light of the US and European experience', *Environmental and Resource Economics*, **4**, 151–69.

Jung, Chulho, Kerry Krutilla and Roy Boyd (1996), 'Incentives for advanced pollution abatement technology at the industry level: an evaluation of policy alternatives', *Journal of Environmental Economics and Management*, **30**, 95–111.

Just, Richard E. and David Zilberman (1979), 'Asymmetry of taxes and subsidies in regulating stochastic mishap', *Quarterly Journal of Economics*, **94**, 139–48.

Kelman, Steven (1981), *What Price Incentives? Economists and the Environment*, Boston, MA: Auburn House Publishing Company.

Leone, Robert A. and John E. Jackson (1981), 'The political economy of federal regulatory activity: the case of water-pollution controls', in Gary Fromm (ed.), *Studies in Public Regulation*, Cambridge, MA: MIT Press, pp. 231–76.

Magat, Wesley A. (1978), 'Pollution Control and Technological Advance: A Dynamic Model of the Firm,' *Journal of Environmental Economics and Management*, **5**: 1–25.

Maloney, Michael T. and Robert E. McCormick (1982), 'A positive theory of environmental quality regulation', *Journal of Law and Economics*, **25**, 99–123.

Milliman, Scott R. and Raymond Prince (1989), 'Firm incentives to promote technological change in pollution control', *Journal of Environmental Economics and Management*, **17**, 247–65.

Morgan, Peter J. (1983), 'Alternative policy instruments under uncertainty: a programming model of toxic pollution control', *Journal of Environmental Economics and Management*, **10**, 248–69.

Parry, Ian W.H. (1995), 'Pollution taxes and revenue recycling', *Journal of Environmental Economics and Management*, **29**, S-64–S-77.

Pashigian, B. Peter (1984), 'The effect of environmental regulation on optimal plant size and factor shares', *Journal of Law and Economics*, **27**, 1–28.

Pashigian, B. Peter (1985), 'Environmental regulation: whose self-interests are being protected?', *Economic Inquiry*, **23**, 551–84.

Peltzman, Sam (1976), 'Toward a more general theory of regulation', *Journal of Law and Economics*, **19**, 211–40.

Repetto, Robert (1987), 'The policy implications of non-convex environmental damages: a smog control case study', *Journal of Environmental Economics and Management*, **14**, 13–29.

Roberts, Marc J. and Michael Spence (1976), 'Effluent charges and licenses under uncertainty', *Journal of Public Economics*, **5**, 193–208.

Rose-Ackerman, Susan (1973), 'Effluent charges: a critique', *Canadian Journal of Economics*, **6**, 512–28.

Salop, Steven C. and David T. Scheffman (1983), 'Raising rivals costs', *American Economic Review*, **73**, 267–71.

Shavell, Steven (1984), 'A model of the optimal use of liability and safety regulation', *Rand Journal of Economics*, **15**, 271–80.

Shortle, James S. and James W. Dunn (1986), 'The relative efficiency of agricultural source water pollution control policies', *American Journal of Agricultural Economics*, **68**, 668–77.

Spulber, Daniel F. (1985), 'Effluent regulation and long-run optimality', *Journal of Environmental Economics and Management*, **12**, 103–16.

Stankey, George H. (1972), 'A strategy for the definition and management of wilderness quality', in J. V. Krutilla (ed.), *Natural Environments: Studies in Theoretical and Applied Analysis*, Baltimore, MD: Johns Hopkins University Press for Resources for the Future, pp. 106–9.

Starrett, David and Richard Zeckhauser (1971), 'Treating external diseconomies – markets or taxes?', Cambridge, MA: Harvard University John F. Kennedy School of Government Discussion Paper no. 3.

Stavins, Robert N. (1996), 'Correlated uncertainty and policy instrument choice', *Journal of Environmental Economics and Management*, **30**, 218–32.

Stigler, George J. (1971), 'The theory of economic regulation', *Bell Journal of Economics and Management Science*, **2**, 3–21.

Thomas, Vinod (1980), 'Welfare cost of pollution control', *Journal of Environmental Economics and Management*, **7**, 90–102.

Tietenberg, Thomas H. (1985), *Emissions Trading: An Exercise in Reforming Pollution Policy*, Washington, DC: Resources for the Future.

Tisato, Peter (1994), 'Pollution standards vs charges under uncertainty', *Environmental and Resource Economics*, **4**, 295–304.

Watson, William D. and Ronald G. Ridker (1984), 'Losses from effluent taxes and quotas under uncertainty', *Journal of Environmental Economics and Management*, **11**, 310–26.

Weitzman, Martin L. (1974), 'Prices vs. quantities', *Review of Economic Studies*, **41**, 477–91.

16 Imperfect markets, technological innovation and environmental policy instruments

Carlo Carraro[1]

1. Background

During the last few decades, most environmental policy analyses have focused on the development of policy instruments suitable for the regulation of perfectly competitive or monopolistic markets. However, the structure of the traditional instruments cannot be deemed appropriate when the market targeted for regulation does not possess the polar characteristics of perfect competition or monopoly. Under oligopoly, which is probably a more realistic analytical framework to describe modern industrial markets, other externalities, in addition to the environmental ones, have to be accounted for, and this drastically affects the characteristics and the effectiveness of regulatory instruments.

Emission taxes (or effluent fees), along with emission controls and tradable permits, have emerged among the most important instruments for correcting environmental externalities. Emission taxes internalize the external damages associated with polluting activities. The internalization is complete when the fees equal the marginal external damages of pollution, such as in the case of Pigouvian taxes. It has been shown, however, that the socially optimal degree of internalization depends on the market structure. Under perfect competition, the desired internalization is complete, while under imperfectly competitive conditions, optimal taxes deviate from external damages, as was first noted by Buchanan (1969) for the case of monopoly. Complete internalization of external damages created by a monopolist will impose additional social costs by restricting the suboptimal (too low) output of the monopolist more than required for attaining social optimality. In this case, the optimal effluent fee will be less than marginal external damages.

Under conditions of oligopoly, other externalities, in addition to output distortion and pollution, may be present. This could result both in drastic changes in the qualitative characteristics of the traditional environmental policy instruments used for the cases of perfect competition and monopoly, and in a need for additional instruments. The main purpose of this chapter is to examine optimal emission taxes under alternative market structures. Three cases will be considered (in Sections 2, 3 and 5 respectively):

- in the case of an oligopolistic market with a fixed number of firms, results about emission taxes under imperfect competition are presented for the cases of product diversity and of a homogeneous oligopoly;
- in the latter case, we will also account for dynamic issues, notably the entry and exit of firms;
- finally, the effectiveness of emission taxes will be discussed in the case in which environmental degradation affects market conditions, notably market demand.[2]

In addition, Section 4 will be devoted to the analysis of the role and features of tradable permits when markets are imperfectly competitive.

The last part of the chapter reviews the literature on the effects of environmental instruments on firms' innovation strategies in oligopoly. The reason is that much of the recent industrial organization literature on technological innovations (see Reinganum, 1989 for a survey) focuses on the strategic aspects of innovation choices and therefore mainly considers imperfect market structures where firms' interactions are adequately modelled. At the same time, the literature on environmental policy and imperfect markets often analyses the behaviour of firms which can decide strategically both their own production and innovation variables. Indeed the two decisions are closely linked within firms' attempts to reduce the burden of environmental regulation.

When dealing with environmental policy and imperfect markets, one may be tempted to consider market imperfections not only in product markets but also in factor markets. In particular, the role of environmental policy is crucially affected by imperfections and rigidities in the labour market. This last issue is analysed by Ruud de Mooij in Chapter 20 of this handbook, whereas the present chapter will focus on imperfections in product markets.[3]

2.   Monopoly and fixed-number oligopoly

Let us start from the simplest imperfect market structure: the monopoly. In this case, Buchanan (1969) pointed out that the use of effluent fees equal to marginal external damages of pollution, as in the case of competitive markets, will not lead to optimality and can even reduce social welfare.[4] This is because the emission tax will reduce the already suboptimal monopoly output. Thus any gain in welfare due to reduced pollution might be outweighed by the welfare loss due to reduced output. This implies that complete internalization of the external pollution damages caused by a monopolist may not be desirable, but rather that the optimal policy requires 'under-internalization', that is, an emission tax less than marginal damages. Notice that the deviation between optimal tax and marginal damage must be equal to the welfare loss from reduced output as expressed by the difference between the private value of marginal output and its private marginal cost.

In order to avoid a second-best environmental policy, that is, a policy which does not fully internalize environmental damages, it is necessary to introduce other policy instruments. As shown by Laffont (1994), the optimal policy mix is defined by three instruments:

- a Pigouvian tax which fully internalizes environmental marginal damages;
- a subsidy which ensures that the monopoly will not underproduce; and
- a lump sum tax designed to extract all the monopoly rent.[5]

A similar situation arises in a fixed-number oligopoly where n firms produce a homogeneous good with fixed and positive entry costs. According to Katsoulacos and Xepapadeas (1994), the optimal emission tax is again less than the environmental marginal damage. Moreover, the difference between tax and marginal damage is still a function of the difference between market price and production marginal cost. An additional variable influencing the optimal tax rate is the number of firms in the market (denoted by n). When $n = 1$, the optimal tax clearly coincides with the one determined under monopoly. As n increases, the optimal tax also increases and approaches the external marginal damage of pollution. When n approaches infinity, the tax rates coincides with the one derived under perfect competition, that is, the Pigouvian tax, although with positive fixed production costs there is always an upper bound for n.[6]

Therefore, when the number of firms is fixed and the product is homogenous, the oligopoly case is an intermediate one with respect to monopoly and perfect competition (Ebert, 1991). We shall see that this may not be the case when the theoretical framework is generalized (Sections 3 and 4). Moreover, as in the monopoly case, the suboptimality of environmental taxation in oligopoly can be corrected by introducing additional policy instruments. An emission tax equal to the marginal damage and an output subsidy could lead to a complete internalization of both economic and environmental externalities.

These results can be extended to the case of product diversity

(Katsoulacos and Xepapadeas, 1996a). Consider an *n*-firm oligopoly where market demand is derived under the Spence (1976) assumption that consumers prefer variety and that the outputs of various firms are imperfect substitutes for one another. It can be shown that the optimal tax is again less than marginal damages and that the difference is now a complex function of the number of firms, the degree of substitution between different products, the consumers' preferences and the emission functions.

3. Free-entry oligopoly

The above results depend crucially on the assumption that the number of firms in the market is exogenously given. This can be justified in markets with significant barriers to entry. However, more generally, the number of firms in the market should be determined endogenously (by the usual zero profit conditions). This is done in Katsoulacos and Xepapadeas (1995), where it is shown that, when the number of firms is endogenous, three effects must be accounted for in the design of the optimal tax rate. The first two were previously discussed: (1) the welfare increase induced by lower pollution levels; and (2) the welfare reduction which occurs because the already distorted imperfectly competitive output is further lowered. The third effect is related to the fact that with endogenous market structure the equilibrium number of firms exceeds the second-best socially optimal number of firms (Mankiw and Whinston, 1986). As a consequence, when an emission tax is introduced, the equilibrium number of firms in the market is reduced, with positive welfare effects.

The implications for the optimal tax rate are straightforward. As stated in the previous section, the first (environmental) effect would lead to a tax equal to the environmental marginal damage. The second (output) effect reduces the optimal tax below the marginal tax. The third (market structure) effect is such that welfare increases when the tax increases. Therefore, if the market structure effect is sufficiently strong, it may be optimal to fix the optimal tax rate above the marginal damage from polluting emissions.[7]

This 'over-internalization' is an example of the type of distortions which affect standard environmental policy instruments in the presence of more than one externality. This is typically the case of oligopolistic markets, where firms' interactions introduce economic externalities in addition to the environmental ones.

Notice again that the policy distortions described above depend crucially on the assumed restrictions on the number of instruments. If more than one policy instrument were available, then all externalities could be corrected and the optimal policy mix would achieve a first-best outcome. For example, in the case of an endogenous number of firms, a lump sum licence fee could be introduced along with the Pigouvian tax. The licence fee would restrict the number of firms to the socially optimal level and the optimal Pigouvian tax would be determined according to the results described in the previous section.

Summing up, the results of Sections 2 and 3 show that in the fixed-number case, the desired internalization is incomplete both under product homogeneity and product diversity; that is, similarly to the case of monopoly, the optimal effluent fee falls short of marginal external damages, and increases as the number of firms goes up. Under an endogenous market structure, however, internalization in excess of the external marginal damages may be the optimal policy, since it restricts the number of firms to a number closer to that corresponding to the social optimum. In this case, contrary to what might be expected under imperfect competition, the second-best emission tax exceeds marginal external damages. All the above distortions could be corrected by the use of additional policy instruments along with the emission tax.

4.   Tradable permits with imperfect markets

In the previous sections the analysis focused on the role and features of environmental taxation when markets are imperfectly competitive. If tradable permits, rather than taxation, are the environmental policy instrument, one more market, in addition to the product market, has to be considered. If both the market for emission permits and the product market are perfectly competitive, the permit system can achieve the given environmental standard at a minimum cost and without any welfare losses. Furthermore, the least-cost outcome does not depend on the initial allocation of permits.[8] The introduction of market imperfections implies three possible configurations: a competitive product market with imperfection in the permits market, an oligopolistic product market with a competitive permits market, and the case in which both markets are imperfectly competitive. The results differ in the three cases and can be summarized as follows.

In the first case – when only the permits market is imperfectly competitive – Hahn (1984) shows that the initial distribution of permits affects the efficiency of the permits market by causing deviations from the cost-minimizing solution. In particular, the price of permits increases with the share of permits allocated to the firm with market power (a competitive fringe is also considered in the model). Furthermore, the initial distribution of permits is also important in determining the level of a firm's compliance with environmental regulation. Thus the initial allocation of permits not only affects efficiency but also the enforceability of the instrument. For example, when the firm with market power is non-compliant, an increase of its initial holdings through transfers from the competitive fringe will reduce its violations (see van Egteren and Weber, 1996).

In the second case, when only the product market is imperfectly competitive, Malueg (1990) shows that the use of tradable permits may be inefficient, even with respect to command-and-control measures. In particular, an emission trading programme could reduce social welfare relative to command-and-control regulation, if permits induce a redistribution of output from low-cost firms to high-cost firms.

The final case is the most interesting. Both markets are imperfectly competitive. For the case that the product is homogeneous, Von der Fehr (1993) shows that industry profits are maximized when the industry becomes a monopoly, that is, there are gains from an asymmetric distribution of permits (all permits to one firm is the limit case). However, the consumer surplus decreases, thus making the final impact on welfare ambiguous. Notice that consumer surplus losses become larger when the products are differentiated.

When strategic interactions are considered in the context of a two-stage game where firms first compete in the permits market and then in the product market, it follows that firms tend to overinvest in emission permits if the products are strategic substitutes (as in the standard Cournot oligopoly). Moreover, if one firm has first-mover advantage in the price of permits, it will overinvest in permits in order to raise their price and subsequently raise its rivals' costs. This implies a welfare loss which can be reduced by modifying the initial allocation of permits. Again, the latter affects the efficiency of the permits market.

A general conclusion can therefore be stated as follows. Once we deviate from perfect competition in both the permits and product markets, inefficiencies arise. Thus, when comparing taxes and tradable permits one has to balance the benefits of the permits system relative to the tax (for example, fewer informational requirements) with the welfare losses (relative to those arising with the tax) induced by market imperfections. This task deserves further research (see also Chapter 18).

5.   Environmental feedbacks in oligopoly

Let us consider again a Cournot oligopoly model where firms produce a homogeneous good and where emissions are taxed. The novel features considered in this section are firms' heterogeneity and the endogenous effects of environmental damages on market demand and production costs.

First, consider market demand. It is often the case that environmental degradation affects economic agents' consumption decisions, thus modifying market demand of some industries. For example, an increase in environmental concerns and/or pollution may increase the demand for some goods (CFC-free refrigerators), and reduce the demand for others (tourism in polluted coastal zones). Let us consider this latter case. If emissions are positively related to production of certain goods, and if a higher level of environmental degradation (emissions) reduces market demand, a reduction of firms' production due to environmental regulation has a twofold effect: on the one hand, it increases the market price (through the usual movement along a downward-sloping demand curve); on the other hand, by reducing emissions, it shifts market demand upward, thus further increasing the market price. The combination of these two effects increases the slope of market demand. The increased slope can be responsible for some oligopoly-specific effects of environmental taxation. For example, a larger tax rate may increase industry profits and concentration, rather than reduce them.[9]

Second, consider a firm's cost function. If environmental taxation is introduced, a firm pays both production and environmental costs. Hence, any time a firm increases production, its costs increase progressively both because of increased factor demand, and because of proportionally increased emissions (which are taxed). Again there are two movements, one along the original cost curve, and a shift of the curve induced by environmental taxation. As in the case of market demand, the consequence of adding up these two effects is a steeper total cost function.

More importantly, interdependence among firms' decisions is modified. Usually, in oligopoly, firms' decisions are interdependent because market price depends on the production of all firms. By contrast, production costs of a given firm only depend on its own output level. By introducing environmental taxation, the cost function of a given firm will depend on the production of all other firms when the tax rate depends on the global level of environmental degradation (for example total emissions), and/or when the emission output rate of each firm depends on the total damage, that is, on total emissions (for example, because of congestion and stock depletion effects, in other words, negative externalities deriving from the other firms' production). This additional channel of interdependence increases firms' interaction, thus increasing the slope of their own reaction function (the 'degree of competitiveness' of the oligopolistic market increases). The result is a lower-equilibrium output for any given level of market demand (Carraro and Soubeyran, 1996a). This effect is obviously oligopoly-specific.

The above remarks point out that both market demand and cost function are modified by the introduction of environmental variables in an oligopoly model. These changes may have an impact on the effects that environmental taxation exerts on variables such as industry concentration, output, profits, and so on. There are indeed conditions under which a change in taxation may increase both a firm's profits and industry concentration.[10] The main intuition is that all output restrictions induced by the tax (recall that the slope of all firms' reaction functions increases) move oligopolistic firms closer to what would be a collusive output level, thus increasing profits. This result is robust with respect to different taxation schemes: from firm-specific tax rates to uniform industry taxation, and to situations in which only a subgroup of firms is taxed. This last case is relevant when firms are located in different countries. Indeed, Carraro and Soubeyran (1996a) show that even firms located in those countries which unilaterally introduce the environment tax may increase their profits.

6.   Environmental innovation and taxation

The analyses of environmental policy in imperfect markets discussed in the previous sections were undertaken under the assumption that emissions per unit of produced output are constant. This approach is common to much of the early environmental economics literature where it is assumed that once environmental policy is introduced firms either reduce their output or engage in abatement which mainly represents end-of-pipe emissions reduction.[11] Recently, however, increasing attention has been directed towards the analysis of environmental policy aimed at reducing unit emissions coefficients through the introduction of environmentally clean technology.[12] That is, firms are induced by the policy to engage in environmental innovation, or environmental R&D so as to reduce emission without introducing large output reduction or undertaking end-of-pipe abatement. As stated in Section 1, the innovative activity is usually modelled as a race towards invention in which the quantity and timing of innovation are the outcome of firms' strategic behaviour and interactions. This is why, in most cases, the literature on environmental innovation focuses on the innovation strategies of firms which compete in imperfectly competitive markets.

Notable exceptions are the seminal contributions by Downing and White (1986) and Milliman and Prince (1989), where perfect competition and complete information are assumed. The new technology, providing firms with lower abatement cost functions, is assumed to become exogenously and instantaneously available. No interactions between production and innovation are considered. Within this simplified framework, the goal of the two papers is to analyse the effectiveness of different policies in inducing environmental innovation. Their conclusions are in favour of market instruments (taxes or permits).[13]

The work by Downing and White has been extended in several directions. The timing of innovation and the role of incomplete information is analysed in Carraro and Topa (1995); the interactions between production and innovation are studied in Ulph, D. (1994). A more general framework is provided by Katsoulacos and Xepapadeas (1996b), who analyse optimal environmental policy schemes in the case of a pollution-generating duopoly, when R&D spillovers exist between firms in the process of environmental innovation, thus introducing positive externalities in addition to the negative environmental externalities. An optimal scheme of simultaneous application of taxes on emissions and subsidies on environmental R&D is developed. The government can use receipts from taxing pollution to subsidize the firms' R&D efforts, thus implementing a recycling policy which differs from the one analysed by de Mooij in this handbook (Chapter 20) where tax revenues are recycled in the labour market, and coincides with the one analysed through an econometric model in Carraro and Galeotti (1997). Further, because of the R&D spillovers, the government subsidy corrects the appropriability problem that firms face when investing in R&D, while the tax corrects the pollution externality.

Katsoulacos and Xepapadeas (1996b) show that the optimal emission tax is less than the marginal damage while the subsidy depends on three factors:

- the deviation between emission taxes and marginal pollution damages;
- the deviation between the private and the social marginal product of R&D;
- firms' strategic incentives to invest in R&D.[14]

Taxes and subsidies are also proposed by Carraro and Soubeyran (1996c) in the case in which the new technology has already been developed, but its diffusion is limited because of high fixed or variable costs. This paper analyses how environmental policy can provide the right incentives for the adoption of existing best available technologies. Two types of policy are examined and compared: a subsidy which reduces the cost of replacing old, polluting plants and a tax on polluting emissions. The firm reacts to both policies by changing the technology used in each plant, the rate of capacity utilization of its plants (producing less in more polluting plants), or both. Two types of technology are available. The less polluting one is assumed to be characterized by higher fixed and variable costs. It is shown that, under suitable conditions, both environmental policies lead the firm to operate the largest number of less polluting plants, and, in the case of environmental taxation, to reduce the rate of capacity utilization of the more polluting ones. However, in terms of social welfare, the subsidy is shown to be preferable to emission taxes if no constraint exists on the utilization of the cleaner technology, and/or if emission reductions achieved through output contractions are negligible or undesirable.[15]

A similar framework is used in Requate (1995) where the goal is a comparison of the effects of emission taxes and tradable permits on environmental innovation in the context of an *n*-firm oligopoly. Requate shows that only a subset of firms would adopt the new environment-friendly technology. Moreover, both policy instruments may lead to excess adoption or too little adoption with respect to the socially optimal rate of adoption. Taxes could cause too much adoption when little adoption is optimal and vice versa, whereas the effects of permits are the opposite of those of taxes.

The incentives to environmental innovation as a tool to bypass the cost of buying permits are also analysed in Laffont and Tirole (1996). This paper shows again that firms invest excessively in new technologies as a reaction to environmental policy. This excess adoption can be mitigated by the introduction of future markets for emission permits along with the usual spot market.

The inefficiency of using a single policy instrument is also stressed in Carraro and Topa (1995), where a dynamic model of firms' environmental innovation is proposed. Here the issue is not excess adoption but rather excess timing of adoption, that is, firms tend to delay the introduction of new environment-friendly technologies. Carraro and Topa show that an environment tax can indeed induce firms to adopt cleaner technologies, but that, without appropriate incentives, the timing of the adoption is socially sub-optimal (because firms do not fully account for the environmental benefit of their innovation even when pollution is taxed). Hence, to prevent firms from delaying innovation over time, the government should subsidise R&D costs.

Another relevant issue is the link between environmental innovation and international trade when markets are oligopolistic. There has been much debate recently about the nature of environmental policy that will be set by governments concerned about the competitive advantage their industries might obtain in a world of fierce trade competition (Barrett, 1994; Ulph, A., 1997). Some authors claim that governments will set environmental policies that are too lax (Rauscher, 1994), while others claim that policies will be excessively tough (in order to spur firms to innovate).[16] Both these claims relate to the possibility that governments may distort their environmental policies for strategic reasons (Brander and Spencer, 1985), and testing these claims requires modelling environmental policy in a world of imperfect competition where there are strategic gains to governments trying to manipulate markets through their environmental policies, and to producers trying to manipulate markets through their R&D decisions.

Ulph and Ulph (1996) provides a general treatment of the issues described above. They allow for both governments and producers to act strategically, and for producers' R&D to reduce both costs of production and emissions, but without imposing special functional forms. Their conclusions depend crucially on whether an increase in a country's environmental tax causes the costs of firms located in that country to rise or fall. In Ulph, D. (1994) it is shown that this depends on whether the increase in environmental R&D induced by the tax is more or less than enough to offset the direct effect on costs of the tax increase, and this in turn depends on the precise form of the relationship between emissions and R&D. Adding in process R&D does nothing to alter this.[17] If, ignoring process R&D, costs rise as a result of the tax, this will cause firms to lose market share. But this will lower the incentive to undertake process R&D which will just exacerbate the effect of the tax on firms' costs. Conversely, if, ignoring process R&D, firms' costs were to fall when the tax rose, this would increase market share, thus increasing the incentive for process R&D, which would simply reinforce the effects produced by the analysis in which there is only environmental R&D.

7.   Concluding remarks

Research on the effects of environmental policy instruments on firms' strategies when markets are imperfectly competitive is still developing.[18] None the less, a benchmark result can be provided. If market structure is oligopolistic, no general conclusion about the effects of environmental policy can be derived, because the presence of multiple market externalities, both positive and negative, makes the use of a single policy instrument designed to correct for the environmental externality largely suboptimal. As a consequence, environmental policy must be designed so as to take into account the characteristics of the specific market and the specific environmental phenomena to be regulated. Moreover, most works recommend the use of several instruments in order to tackle all externalities arising from the interaction among firms, between firms and the domestic government, and among governments at the international level.

Notes

1.   The author is grateful to the editor and two anonymous referees for helpful comments and remarks.
2.   This chapter focuses on theoretical analyses of the role of environmental policy instruments when markets are imperfectly competitive. Existing empirical studies are surveyed in other chapters of this handbook.
3.   Another related issue is optimal taxation in a second-best framework. See Bovenberg and de Mooij (1994, 1997); Fullerton (1997); and Chapter 20.
4.   See also Misiolek (1980, 1988) and Oates and Strassman (1984).
5.   The issue of regulation of a polluting monopoly is fully examined in Laffont (1994), where additional issues related to the introduction of asymmetric information (non-verifiable pollution level, non-point source pollution, location choices) are also discussed.
6.   The mathematical proof of this last result is obtained assuming linear demand, cost and damage functions (Katsoulacos and Xepapadeas, 1994).
7.   Note that the optimal tax may as well be lower than or equal to the environmental marginal damage.
8.   A good illustration of this result is in Xepapadeas (1997), ch. 2.

9. An example of this process is provided in Carraro and Soubeyran (1996a).
10. These results, shown in Carraro and Soubeyran (1996a, 1996b), are consistent with those contained in Levine (1985), Katz and Rosen (1985), Stern (1987), Kimmel (1992), Dung (1993) in the industrial organization literature.
11. Some examples of this latter approach are Keeler et al. (1971); Baumol and Oates (1988); Barnett (1980).
12. The seminal contribution to this literature has been provided by Downing and White (1986). Subsequent developments of the model are contained in Milliman and Prince (1989), Ulph, D. (1994), Carraro and Topa (1995), Jung et al. (1996). A different approach, where the focus is on the adoption of existing technologies rather than on R&D and the development of new technologies, is contained in Carraro and Siniscalco (1992) and Carraro and Soubeyran (1996c). A more comprehensive survey of the literature is provided by Ulph, D. (1997).
13. However, Verdier (1995), using a dynamic model, shows that there are cases in which command and control regulation may be preferable.
14. A paradoxical result is that when spillovers are sufficiently small the optimal subsidy may be negative; that is, it may be optimal to tax environmental R&D. This is to avoid over-investment in R&D, a problem also emphasized in Laffont and Tirole (1996).
15. Adopting the revenues from emission charges to subsidize firms' R&D efforts may not only be attractive for efficiency reasons, but also from a political viewpoint, because it may make the introduction of pollution charges more acceptable to firms.
16. In particular, Porter (1991) has argued that governments could provide a competitive advantage to their domestic producers by imposing environmental policies which are tougher than those faced by their rivals, since this will spur industries to innovate greener technologies ahead of their rivals, and enhance the long-run profitability of domestic industry. This view finds considerable support in the US administration, and is also commonly espoused in Germany and Japan. In its extreme form it suggests that environmental regulations are beneficial to both the environment and the economy.
17. Environmental R&D is aimed at reducing the emission–output ratio, whereas process R&D aims at lowering production costs.
18. The relationship between environmental policies and firms' location decisions is another important issue which is discussed in the chapter by James Markusen (Chapter 39 in this volume).

References

Barnett, A.H. (1980), 'The Pigouvian tax rule under monopoly', *American Economic Review*, **70** (5), 1037–41.

Barrett, S. (1994), 'Strategic environmental policy and international trade', *Journal of Public Economics*, **54**, 324–38.

Baumol, W.J. and W.E. Oates (1988), *The Theory of Environmental Policy*, Cambridge, UK: Cambridge University Press.

Bovenberg, L. and R. de Mooij (1994), 'Environmental levies and distortionary taxation', *American Economic Review*, **84**, 1085–9.

Bovenberg, L. and R. de Mooij (1997), 'Environmental levies and distortionary taxation: reply', *American Economic Review*, **87**, 252–3.

Brander, J. and B. Spencer (1985), 'Export subsidies and international market share rivalry', *Journal of International Economics*, **18**, 83–100.

Buchanan, J.M. (1969), 'External diseconomies, corrective taxes and market structure', *American Economic Review*, **59**, 174–7.

Carraro, C. and M. Galeotti (1997), 'Economic growth, international competitiveness, and environmental policies: R&D and innovation strategies with the WARM model', *Energy Economics*, **19**, 2–28.

Carraro, C. and D. Siniscalco (1992), 'Environmental innovation and international competition', *Environmental and Resource Economics*, **2**, 183–200.

Carraro, C. and A. Soubeyran (1996a), 'Environmental taxation, market share and profits in oligopoly', in C. Carraro, Y. Katsoulacos and A. Xepapadeas (eds), *Environmental Policy and Market Structure*, Dordrecht: Kluwer Academic Pubishers.

Carraro, C. and A. Soubeyran (1996b), 'Environmental feedbacks and optimal taxation in oligopoly', in A. Xepapadeas (ed.), *Economic Policy for the Environment and Natural Resources*, Cheltenham, UK and Brookfield, US: Edward Elgar.

Carraro, C. and A. Soubeyran (1996c), 'Environmental policy and the choice of production technology', in C. Carraro, Y. Katsoulacos and A. Xepapadeas (eds), *Environmental Policy and Market Structure*, Dordrecht: Kluwer Academic Publishers.

Carraro, C. and G. Topa (1995), 'Environmental taxation and innovation', in C. Carraro and J. Filar (eds), *Control and Game-Theoretic Models of the Environment*, New York: Birckauser.

Downing, P.B. and L.J. White (1986), 'Innovation in pollution control', *Journal of Environmental Economics and Management*, **13**, 18–29.

Dung, T.H. (1993), 'Optimal taxation and heterogenous oligopoly', *Canadian Journal of Economics*, **26**, 933–47.

Ebert, U. (1991), 'Pigouvian tax and market structure', *Finanz Archiv*, **49** (2), 154–66.

Fullerton, D. (1997), 'Environmental levies and distortionary taxation: comment', *American Economic Review*, **87**, 245–51.

Hahn, R.W. (1984), 'Market power and transferable property rights', *Quarterly Journal of Economics*, **99**, 753–65.

Jung, C., K. Krutilla and R. Boyd (1996), 'Incentives for advanced pollution abatement technology at the industry level: an evaluation of policy alternatives', *Journal of Environmental Economics and Management*, **30**, 95–111.

Katsoulacos, Y. and A. Xepapadeas (1994), 'Pigouvian taxes under oligopoly', mimeo, Athens University.

Katsoulacos, Y. and A. Xepapadeas (1995), 'Environmental policy under oligopoly with endogenous market structure', *Scandinavian Journal of Economics*, **97**, 411–20.

Katsoulacos, Y. and A. Xepapadeas (1996a), 'Emission taxes and market structure', in C. Carraro, Y. Katsoulacos and A. Xepapadeas (eds), *Environmental Policy and Market Structure*, Dordrecht: Kluwer Academic Publishers.

Katsoulacos, Y. and A. Xepapadeas (1996b), 'Environmental innovation, spillovers and optimal policy rules', in C. Carraro, Y. Katsoulacos and A. Xepapadeas (eds), *Environmental Policy and Market Structure*, Dordrecht: Kluwer Academic Publishers.

Katz, M. and H. Rosen (1985), 'Tax analysis in an oligopoly model', *Public Finance Quarterly*, **13**, 3–20.

Keeler, E., M. Spence and R. Zeckhauser (1971), 'The optimal control of pollution', *Journal of Economic Theory*, **4**, 19–34.

Kimmel, S. (1992), 'Effects of cost changes on oligopoly profits', *Journal of Industrial Economics*, **4**, 441–9.

Laffont, J.J. (1994), 'Regulation of pollution with asymmetric information', in C. Dosi and T. Tomasi (eds), *Non Point Source Pollution Regulation: Issues and Analysis*, Dordrecht: Kluwer Academic Publishers.

Laffont, J.J. and J. Tirole (1996), 'A note on environmental innovation', *Journal of Public Economics*, **62**, 128–40.

Levine, D. (1985), 'Taxation within Cournot oligopoly', *Journal of Public Economics*, **27**, 281–90.

Malueg, D.A. (1990), 'Welfare consequences of emission trading credit programs', *Journal of Environmental Economics and Management*, **18**, 66–77.

Mankiw, N.G. and M.D. Whinston (1986), 'Free-entry and social inefficiency', *Rand Journal of Economics*, **17**, 48–58.

Milliman, S.R. and R. Prince (1989), 'Firm incentives to promote technological change in pollution control', *Journal of Environmental Economics and Management*, **17**, 247–65.

Misiolek, S.W. (1980), 'Effluent taxation in monopoly markets', *Journal of Environmental Economics and Management*, **7**, 103–7.

Misiolek, S.W. (1988), 'Pollution control through price incentives: the role of rent-seeking', *Journal of Environmental Economics and Management*, **15**, 1–8.

Oates, W.E. and D.L. Strassman (1984), 'Effluent fees and market structure', *Journal of Public Economics*, **24**, 29–46.

Porter, M. (1991), 'America's green strategy', *Scientific American*, **264** (4), 96.

Rauscher, M. (1994), 'On ecological dumping', *Oxford Economic Papers*, **46**, 822–40.

Reinganum, J.F. (1989), 'The timing of innovation: research, development and diffusion', in R. Schmalensee and R.D. Willig (eds), *Handbook of Industrial Organisation*, Amsterdam: North-Holland.

Requate, T. (1995), 'Incentives to adopt new technologies under different pollution-control policies', *International Tax and Public Finance*, **2**, 295–317.

Spence, A.M. (1976), 'Product differentiation and welfare', *American Economic Review*, **66**, 407–14.

Stern, N. (1987), 'The effects of taxation, price control, and government contracts in oligopoly and monopolistic competition', *Journal of Public Economics*, **32**, 133–58.

Ulph, A. (1997), 'Environmental policy, strategic trade and innovation', in C. Carraro and D. Siniscalco (eds), *New Directions in the Economic Theory of the Environment*, Cambridge UK: Cambridge University Press.

Ulph, A. and D. Ulph (1996), 'Trade, strategic innovation and strategic environmental policy – a general analysis', in C. Carraro, Y. Katsoulacos and A. Xepapadeas (eds), *Environmental Policy and Market Structure*, Dordrecht: Kluwer Academic Publishers.

Ulph, D. (1994), 'Strategic innovation and strategic environmental policy', in C. Carraro (ed.), *Trade, Innovation, Environment*, Dordrecht: Kluwer Academic Publishers.

Ulph, D. (1997), 'Environmental policy and technological innovation', in C. Carraro and D. Siniscalco (eds), *New Directions in the Economic Theory of the Environment*, Cambridge, UK: Cambridge University Press.

van Egteren, H. and M. Weber (1996), 'Marketable permits, market power and cheating', *Journal of Environmental Economics and Management*, **30**, 161–73.

Verdier, T. (1995), 'Environmental pollution and endogenous growth: a comparison between emission taxes and technological standards', in C. Carraro and J. Filar (eds), *Control and Game-Theoretic Models of the Environment*, New York: Birckauser.

Von der Fehr, N. (1993), 'Tradable emission rights and strategic interactions', *Environmental and Resource Economics*, **3**, 129–51.

Xepapadeas, A. (1997), *Advanced Principles in Environmental Policy*, Cheltenham, UK and Lyme, US: Edward Elgar.

17 Environmental policy and transactions costs
Kerry Krutilla

1. Introduction

This chapter assesses the normative implications of transactions costs for the assessment of environmental policy. The topic is relatively unexplored in the environmental economics literature, notwithstanding the theoretical significance of transactions costs and their empirical relevance in many situations.

Transactions costs differ fundamentally from the conventional costs of neoclassical economics. At the proximate level, neoclassical costs arise from production activity or foregone consumption; they attach to different activity levels carried out in the context of well-specified rights. In contrast, transactions costs arise from the exchange and/or maintenance of the rights themselves (Eggertsson, 1995, p. 14); they are incurred to transfer the ownership and/or use status of the rights, and to monitor, enforce, or defend the rights.

Both neoclassical costs and transactions costs ultimately derive from tastes, technology and resource endowments – the demand for transaction services, for example, is a derived demand based on the underlying preference structure of the economy – and both are measured with reference to a pre-existing resource utilization baseline. A key difference, however, lies in the role of information. Neoclassical costs are incurred whatever the status of agents' information sets whereas many, if not all, transactions costs arise from informational imperfections and asymmetries (Eggertsson, 1995, p. 15). Hence imperfect information plays a crucial role in the transactions sector of the economy.[1]

In the traditional literature, transactions costs are typically associated with a variety of activities connected with market exchange – search and information acquisition; bargaining over price; the negotiation, monitoring and enforcement of contracts; and the protection of contractual rights from third-party encroachment (Eggertsson, 1995, p. 15). Quite naturally, this sense of the term 'transactions costs' has been adopted in the environmental field in research which examines the efficiency of market-based policy approaches, for example Coasean-style property rights assignments (Coase, 1960, 1990) and pollution allowance trading (Stavins, 1995; Munro et al., 1995).

However, transactions costs terminology has also been construed more broadly to refer to any costs associated with establishing, administering, monitoring or enforcing a government policy or regulation (Jung et al., 1995; Vollebergh, 1994, 1996). This more expansive usage can be viewed in two equivalent ways. First, it comports with a notion of 'transactions costs' as the residual category: 'not production or consumption costs'. Since 'environmental quality' is what environmental policy produces, any policy-related costs other than the costs of pollution abatement, or producer and /or consumer welfare effects arising from policy-induced output changes, would qualify under the residual transactions costs label.[2] Second, it comports with a notion of policy transactions costs as the extension of the market-based concept into the policy sphere. Whereas conventional transactions costs arise from the redistribution or maintenance of rights in the market domain, policy transactions costs arise from the redistribution or maintenance of rights in the public sector of the economy – a sector where politics and policy action, rather than market exchange, mediates the distribution of rights and the associated monitoring and enforcement activity.

This chapter employs the 'transactions costs' nomenclature in its broadest sense, and conceptualizes the policy process in a way which sharpens the focus on the normative implications of transactions costs so defined. This policy process is stylized as follows.[3] In the first stage of the process, a particular policy is chosen. In the environmental policy sphere, the policy choice implies a decision about the distribution of rights, with respect to the ownership and/or use of the environmental resource, among polluters and pollution-damaged parties. In the second stage of the process, the structure of the policy is administratively implemented. The implementation process reflects a number of factors: the way the policy has been defined in stage 1; the attributes of administrative agencies; the role of third parties with a stake in the implementation process, and so on. In stage 3, the policy operates, and is monitored and enforced.[4] The operational phase of the policy involves an adjustment process through trading if property rights are established, or agent responses to economic incentives created by regulation if the policy involves direct government control. The government will monitor and enforce the policy in the latter case, or contract these functions to the private sector, while agents themselves will conduct the monitoring when property rights are assigned and contracts will be enforced through the courts.

It is the premise of this chapter that all costs at all stages of the policy process are relevant for policy assessment. Yet, the environmental economics literature largely focuses on stage 3 of the process, for example, Baumol and Oates (1988); Hanley et al. (1997). This research orientation is attributable to the powerful influence of the Coase theorem, which treats the stage 1 property rights distribution as exogenous,[5] and to the comparative static tradition of traditional microeconomics theory which is premised on the assumption of instantaneous and/or frictionless implementation.

The stage 3 focus of the environmental economics literature is itself relatively circumscribed. With the notable exception of bargaining transactions costs, the literature has historically ignored transactions costs – although research on this subject is beginning to emerge (Malik, 1992; Stavins, 1995; Vollebergh, 1994, 1996). To date, the environmental economics literature lacks a comparative assessment of environmental policy instruments across all stages of the policy process, with transactions costs playing a role in the analysis.

It is the purpose of this chapter to take a step in the direction of outlining a more comprehensive approach to environmental policy evaluation. To that end, the next three sections review relevant transactions costs literature at each of the policy stages, and a following section offers a discussion of the transactions costs implications of between-policy-stage linkages. A final section of the chapter offers some conclusions and suggestions for future research.

2. The policy choice

The purpose of environmental policy is to establish use and/or ownership rights over environmental resources. The establishment of rights creates a distribution of rents *vis-á-vis* the pre-policy *status quo*. Rational agents have the same essential incentive to respond to this economic reality as they did to respond to the incentives they confronted in the absence of the rights definition, or to respond to the policy's incentive structure after the policy implementation.

Institutional features of representative democracy shape agents' rent-seeking incentives and the particular expression of rent-seeking activity. In their role as principals, constituents can compete over the property rights structure of alternative policy proposals by attempting to influence the votes of their representative agents. Resource commitments devoted to this end may have real economic consequences.

The behaviour of agents around a rights distribution has been formally explored in a game-theoretic setting where agents with asymmetric information and differential power can attempt to influence probabilistically the rights distribution (Jung et al., 1995; Medema, 1997). Agents will rent-seek over the rights distribution as a dominant strategy if rent-seeking costs are low enough. Unless the rights distribution is beyond the influence of affected parties, this result undermines the plausibility of the implicit Coasean assumption that agents in an undefined property rights setting will passively accept a property rights assignment as the basis for a subsequent bargaining routine. Indeed, perhaps the most relevant question is whether agents can strike a bargain to avoid a property rights dispute itself or whether a costly rights dispute is inevitable. The decades of struggle over the terms of the Law of the Sea Treaty offers an example of the degree to which agents may deploy resources in an attempt to influence a rights allocation process (Sebenius, 1986).

Buchanan (1980) and Anderson and Hill (1986) have examined a closely related issue in the context of a rights distribution motivated to ameliorate the problem of uncontrolled open access. In an open-access equilibrium, rights are undefined and all rents are dissipated; defining the rights and creating rents is the policy objective. However, if the newly defined rights are distributed through a discretionary bureaucratic process, agents have the same essential incentive to dissipate the associated rents through political competition as they had to dissipate them in the open-access situation. The policy intervention should simply shift the rent-seeking to the rights distribution itself. This result, a special case of general themes in the public choice literature, raises questions about the policy's justification (Krueger, 1990).

Buchanan recommends an auction mechanism as a means of avoiding the resource wastage associated with a politicized rights distribution process. This proposal would indeed avoid rent-seeking over the rights distribution, but would raise another potential problem – the rents associated with the property rights structure of the auction policy itself. Since auctioning the rights would deny agents the rents they would otherwise seek through the politicized distribution process, or in open-access competition, agents have the same essential incentive to lobby against the adoption of an auction mechanism as to rent-seek through any of the other channels. On the assumption that the policy choice is endogenous, the domain of the rent-seeking should simply shift to the policy decision itself.

There appears to be only one study in the literature which examines the welfare implications of rights contest explicitly in the environmental policy context (Maxwell et al., 1995). The setting is one of a potential policy conflict between pollution-impacted consumers who want stringent environmental regulation and polluting firms for whom environmental regulation is costly. In this model, firms may be able to pre-empt the political contest through quasi-cooperative behaviour, in the form of 'voluntary' abatement. Since consumer entry into the political process imposes a cost, equilibrium outcomes depend critically on that parameter. When entry costs are zero, firms cannot pre-empt entry and avoid the property rights conflict. If entry costs are positive, however, a voluntary abatement equilibrium can be achieved which avoids the rights dispute (Maxwell et al., 1995).

With respect to environmental policy evaluation, the welfare implications of stage 1 rent-seeking have not been addressed in the instrument choice literature. A body of positive literature has explored the 'political feasibility' of environmental policy instruments as a function of their property rights content (Buchanan and Tullock, 1975; Coelho, 1976; Dewees, 1983; Yohe, 1976; Mumy, 1980; Maloney and McCormick, 1982; Pezzey, 1992). However, this work has not taken the additional step of explicitly monetizing the welfare costs of the political process which produces the policy instruments.

A simple model can be used to derive some intuition about the potential normative implications of stage 1 rent-seeking. Assume we have an industry of n identical profit-maximizing firms whose production process satisfies the usual assumptions (continuity, convexity) and whose output and inputs are exchanged in perfectly competitive markets. Environmental policy restraints do not affect the price equilibria in any market. The firms generate emissions in proportion to output; environmental damages are proportional to emissions and have a one-period flow effect. In an unconstrained equilibrium, the aggregate emissions level in each period is ne^{**}, where $ne^{**} > ne^*$, and ne^* is the industry emissions level conventionally labelled as 'socially optimal', that is, the emissions level where the marginal compliance costs equal the marginal benefits of avoided damage. Environmental damages stem from the pollution impacts on n identical pollution recipients.

To highlight the relevant issue, assume that there are no transactions costs other than those associated with rent-seeking over the policy choice. Let v represent the pollution price which is conventionally defined as efficient – the pollution price which would induce each polluter to produce e^* emissions each period. Also assume that all parties know both e^* and v, and that the regulatory policy objective is to achieve the aggregate emissions level ne^*.[6]

Environmental policy consists of defining the polluters' period emissions entitlement $\underline{e}$ $[0,e^{**}]$, and requiring that the firms make unit compensation payments for emissions greater than $\underline{e}$, while receiving compensation payments for emissions less than $\underline{e}$. It is assumed that the compensation payments are directly exchanged among the polluters and the pollution-damaged parties.

The political process is assumed to be one whereby the environmental policy is offered up as a take-it-or-leave-it proposition; agents can attempt to influence the go–no-go decision by lobbying for or against the policy.[7] Alternatively, the agents can avoid the policy process altogether if the pollution-damaged party is willing to except the polluters' liberty to pollute at e^{**}, and make a Coasean compensation payment based on the administered pollution, v.

With the pollution price v and the regulatory objective e^*, $v(e^* - \underline{e}) = P$ describes each polluter's period payment schedule if the policy is adopted. Since the pollution price is v, the payment and receipt of P for any $\underline{e} \in [0, e^{**}]$ will always induce a change in the equilibrium from e^{**} to e^*, that is, the conventionally defined stage 2 efficiency effect is the same for any policy alternative/entitlement distribution. Since the only remaining difference among policy alternatives is the size and sign of P, this normalization assures that the normative effects of the policy alternatives are exclusively manifest in stage 1. This frame of reference is just the reverse of that of the Coase and standard environmental economics literatures, which assume away the welfare effects of stage 1 to focus on stage 2.[8]

Note that conventional environmental policies can be construed to represent special cases of $v(e^* - \underline{e}) = P$ (see Table 17.1), with the qualification

Table 17.1   Rank order of policy instruments: high-to-low rent-seeking incentive

Entitlement	Corresponding policy instruments
1 $e = 0$	Zero entitlement regulation plus fine = zero entitlement emissions tax
	Zero entitlement auctioned tradable permits
	Coasean property rights assignment to pollution recipient
2 $e \in (0, e^{**})$	Regulation plus fine = emissions tax with greater than zero entitlement tradable permits with some degree of grandfathering
	Coasean property rights assignment shared between polluter and pollution recipient
3 $e = e^{**}$	Conventional emissions control subsidy
	Coasean property rights assignment to polluter

that the conventional policies reflect the compensation scheme described, that is, revenue distribution among the immediately affected agents.[9] For example, an emissions tax or Coasean-style property rights assignment to the pollution-damaged parties implies that the polluter does not receive any emissions entitlement ($\underline{e} = 0$); the firms' corresponding payouts are ve^*. The other limiting extreme is where the polluters receive all the rights ($\underline{e} = e^{**}$), as in the case of an emissions reductions subsidy or explicit Coasean-style property rights assignment to the polluters. In that case, the firms' payouts are $P = v(e^* - e^{**}) < 0$, that is, they are compensated. Alternatively, policies which define $\underline{e} \in (0, e^{**})$ represents some degree of property rights sharing between the polluters and pollution-damaged parties. For policies such that

$e\epsilon(0,e^*)$, $P>0$, the firms receive some positive emissions entitlement and pay unit charges of v for emissions they produce above the entitlement. This type of policy might be viewed as a regulation with a unit charge for beyond-compliance emissions.[10] For policies such that $e\epsilon(e^*, e^{**})$, firms will end up being compensated to reduce emissions to e^*, but will receive less compensation than under the conventional emissions reduction subsidy, since $e<e^{**}$.

Under our assumptions, the payment P is a measure of period flow costs from the viewpoint of the firms, as well as a measure of period flow benefits from the perspective of pollution-damaged parties. We now ask the question: what are agents' gross rent-seeking incentives in the present context where policy is a possibility, but agents can also jointly strike a Coase bargain at the administered pollution price and avoid the policy process altogether? In game-theory terms, such a Coase bargain would be a dominant strategy equilibrium *if pollution-damaged parties were willing to accept the* status quo *emissions level e^{**}*. But note that any policy proposal other than one embodying the entitlement distribution e^{**} would allow pollution-damaged parties either to reduce their Coase compensation payments (for $e\epsilon(e^*, e^{**})$) or to receive compensation themselves (for $e\epsilon(0,e^*)$). Hence, pollution-damaged parties have a gross incentive to rent-seek for any $e\epsilon[0,e^{**})$, that is, for any policy proposal embodying an emissions entitlement less than the *status quo* emissions level e^{**}. The gross rent-seeking payoff structure which embodies this economics is:

$$G = P + v(e^{**} - e^*) \tag{17.1}$$

or

$$G = v(e^{**} - e) \tag{17.2}$$

where P in (17.1) is defined as before, and the second term in (17.1), $v(e^{**} - e^*)$, is the value of the Coase compensation payment the pollution-damaged parties avoid when a proposed policy is adopted. (Note that $G>0$ for any $e\epsilon(0,e^{**})$.) G is both the gross flow incentive for pollution-damaged parties to rent-seek and, because the described policy process is zero sum, the polluters' gross flow incentive to avoid the policy.

Not only do the pollution-damaged parties have an incentive to lobby for environmental policy but, in a representative democracy, the right to do so. In such a system, agents can request the clarification of an unspecified rights situation which personally injures them and, more generally, attempt to influence the rights distribution through the political process. Representatives have an incentive to maintain their electoral viability by responding to such constituent concerns. It is this twin combination of economic incentives and political rights which motivates policy action in this context where all policy alternatives have the same conventionally measured efficiency effect, and parties could otherwise unilaterally take care of the 'efficiency' problem via Coase bargaining.

We now let δ represent an annuity discounting factors embodying the discount rates of both firms and the pollution-damaged parties – assumed equal for convenience. We therefore have $\delta G = \delta v(e^{**} - \underline{e})$ as the firms' and pollution-damaged parties' gross rent-seeking incentive. Differentiating δG with respect to $\underline{e}$ we have: $dG/d\underline{e} = -\delta v < 0$. All else constant, the gross rent-seeking incentive will be proportional to the degree to which the rights distribution differs from the *status quo* emissions level, e^{**}. Given this relationship, the rent-seeking incentive associated with the various policy alternatives can be inferred, holding other factors constant, from the correspondence of the policy alternatives to different points on the entitlement distribution (see Table 17.1). Policy instruments such as conventional emissions taxes will elicit more rent-seeking behaviour, under our assumptions, than policies with a greater degree of emissions entitlement distributed to polluters.

Because any policy instrument can correspond to any entitlement distribution (again see Table 17.1), the policy instruments cannot be unambiguously ranked at the stage 1 level. The corollary is that policy instruments cannot be ranked independently of their property rights structure. This point raises questions about the presumptive view that incentive-based regulatory approaches, or privatization policies, are likely to yield more welfare-enhancing outcomes than command-and-control regulations. The property rights structure of the price-based policy approaches is likely to be a key variable in determining whether their stage 2 efficiency advantages hold up in an overall assessment of policy costs.[11]

Our model is quite simple and should be accordingly qualified. First, the political process is inherently uncertain. Since rational agents will base their decisions on expected payoffs which reflect the uncertainty of their actions and attitudes towards risk, actual gross rent-seeking payoffs will be less than the 'sure-thing' payoffs, δP. Second, free-rider effects and transactions costs may act as a barrier to organizing rent-seeking activity in a more realistic model with heterogeneous actors and imperfect information. Moreover, if the negotiating costs are relatively low, agents may have an incentive to negotiate a compensation scheme that avoids the political contest (Krutilla and Viscusi, 1998). This decision problem is the conceptual equivalent of that faced by agents in the legal arena who can choose to settle a dispute out of court or to engage in a legal contest. In some cases, it is more economically profitable for agents to avoid the adversarial legal proceeding by arranging a compensation scheme which settles the rights dispute (Cooter and Rubinfeld, 1989). Yet another point is that polluters' payouts are often received or paid out by an environmental authority rather than exchanged with pollution-damaged parties. All else constant, this policy structure reduces the pollution-damaged parties' incentive to rent-seek, but could conceivably inject a bureaucratic rent-seeking party into the equation (see Section 5). Another issue: if price levels in output markets are affected by environmental policy restraints, some element of monopoly rent would result from environmental regulation (Buchanan and Tullock, 1975; Coelho, 1976; Yohe, 1976). Holding other factors constant, this possibility reduces the polluters' incentive to lobby against environmental policy. Finally, some rent-seeking activity, for example, campaign contributions, may represent pure financial transfers rather than real resource costs, and thus have no welfare effect. Any of these factors would reduce the incentive to rent-seek and/or the normative import of rent-seeking activities.

These qualifications are important but do not overturn the essential conclusion that the welfare consequences of a policy's property rights structure can be normatively consequential. Since it seems likely that normative effects will be context-dependent, the appropriate evaluative stance would be to assess potential welfare ramifications in each particular circumstance.

3. Implementation

There is scant theoretical work in the environmental economies literature which addresses the implementation process, since the conventional literature assumes frictionless and/or instantaneous implementation. This is a significant omission in view of the abundance of empirical evidence suggesting the possibility of high-cost implementation. Endangered species regulation in the United States offers one illustration. The Endangered Species Act has a species-listing process which allows for public input; hence the opportunity for continuing conflict during the implementation process among agency officials, environmentalists and industry groups with different interests and viewpoints (US DOC, 1996).

Facility siting and hazardous waste clean-up are two other policy objectives which often face high implementation costs (Mitchell and Carson, 1986; Portney and Probst, 1994; US EPA, 1994). In the United States, the nuclear waste management saga offers a particularly salient example. The Nuclear Regulatory Act of 1982 established US policy for the permanent storage of domestically produced high-level nuclear waste (Parker, 1994). The Act called for the shipment of high-level nuclear waste to one of several possible storage facilities, but in the 1987 amendments, Yucca Mountain, Nevada was designated as the sole storage site. However, following the precedent of governors and congressional delegations in Alabama, Tennessee, Texas, and Washington State, who had previously blocked a variety of nuclear waste-siting proposals, the governor and the Nevada congressional delegation strenuously resisted this site selection (Miller, 1994). As a consequence, the Act's implementation again stalled, and the centralization of nuclear waste storage in the United States does not appear to be politically feasible in the near future (Parker, 1994).

From the empirical record, it is clear that the political struggle around policy implementation may represent redistributed effort on the part of agents who were not able sufficiently to define the policy in the first stage of the process. It is also possible that a policy's definition is deliberately left vague in stage 1 to facilitate agreement, a common pattern in the negotiation of international agreements (Sebenius, 1986). In this case, political activity in stage 2 represents a redirection of political effort from stage I, as agents attempt to define the policy through the implementation phase of the process.

Implementation friction is likely to be particularly significant for policies which have relatively long implementation periods and/or statutory construction, like that of CERCLA,[12] which allows for agency discretion during the implementation period. Under these circumstances, new political interests may emerge and the composition of stakeholders may change, providing the necessary conditions for a continuous re-examination of the policy.

The connection between rent-seeking around the policy choice and the implementation process is close enough for it to be possible to lump the costs of these two stages together under the rubric of 'policy establishment' costs. Rent-seeking incentives are likely to be qualitatively similar at both stages. As such, minimizing changes to the *status quo* property rights distribution and/or providing compensation is likely to reduce implementation friction, as well as stage 1 rent-seeking. Allowing communities to bid for economic assistance packages in exchange for accepting the siting of hazardous waste facilities has been proposed as one way to reduce rent-seeking costs associated with the implementation of hazardous waste policy (Mitchell and Carson, 1986).

4.   The operational phase of the policy

The Coase literature has studied extensively the role of information asymmetries and bargaining transactions costs at stage 3 of the policy process, for example, Coase (1960, 1990), Cooter and Ulen (1988); Farrell (1987). The implications of transactions costs for conventional environmental policy instruments have historically received less attention, but some research in this area is emerging.

Rent-seeking over environmental tax revenues is one research topic. The optimal level of environmental taxation is lower when agents rent-seek over the revenues (Lee, 1986), and environmental taxation may be less desirable than a Coasean-style rights assignment due to revenue-driven rent-seeking (Migue and Marceu, 1993). In another line of research, transactions costs are found to lower the volume of pollution allowance trading and yield market outcomes not necessarily independent of the initial rights distribution (Hahn, 1989; Stavins, 1995; and Munro et al., 1995).[13] Administration, monitoring and enforcement costs are also found to reduce the efficiency of emissions taxes. Conventional effluent charges may not be the first-best policy instrument in a positive transactions cost environment (Vollebergh, 1994, 1996).

The costs of enforcing environmental policy is another area of research. Incentive-based instruments allow for flexible control strategies which reduce compliance costs. Intuitively, it seems plausible that agents would have less of an incentive to evade low-cost regulation and, therefore, that incentive-based instruments would be less costly to enforce. However, the conditions for minimizing industry enforcement costs turn out to be different from the conditions for minimizing abatement costs; consequently, an allocation of control responsibility among firms which minimizes enforcement costs will not necessarily minimize abatement costs (Malik, 1992). Enforcing standards may be less costly than enforcing tradable permits or emissions taxes, or the opposite, with results being sensitive to the functional forms of enforcement and abatement cost curves (Malik, 1992).

A further distinction can be made between the economic costs of enforcement (as explored by Malik, 1992), and the costs associated with political or legal issues, which may arise in the enforcement context. The cost of contract enforcement is a potential issue when property rights are defined by a Coasean-style assignment – in contrast, for example, to the case where the property rights are embodied in an agency-enforced tradable permit system. When property rights are enforced by contract, injured rights holders must rely on court action to restrain damaging behaviour and/or determine compensation (Menell, 1991). A number of legal scholars believe that tort litigation is costly and idiosyncratic enough, at least in the United States, to render the judicial enforcement of difficult-to-define environmental property rights economically inefficient, if not prohibitively costly (Blumm, 1992; Brunet, 1992; Funk, 1992; Menell, 1992; Krier, 1992).

5. Between-stage interactions

For heuristic convenience, the previous sections have differentiated transactions costs by policy stage. Although the interconnection between the policy choice and its associated implementation costs was previously mentioned, the welfare ramifications of between-stage interactions are potentially important enough to warrant further consideration. The discussion is largely speculative since there is almost no literature on this subject in the environmental economics field.

When property rights are established through a Coasean distribution or tradable permit system, rent-seeking aimed at the policy choice should be related to the efficiency of the created market. If the created market is not efficient, agents will not be able to attenuate economic losses associated with the property rights distribution through *ex post* trading. This would probably increase the amount of rent-seeking to avoid the policy, providing an additional rationale for selecting some other policy instrument. Conversely, if the created market is efficient, there is less of an incentive to avoid the policy and rent-seeking activity should be lower – offering an additional rationale for adopting the policy. Holding the entitlement distribution constant, the same reasoning would also suggest that emissions taxes would generate relatively less stage 1 rent-seeking since they allow firms to respond flexibly after the rights are defined.[14]

In the regulatory domain, 'flexible implementation' offers an analogue to efficient markets. In this context, statutory construction which reflects unambiguous legislative standards or 'bright line rules', as opposed to general standards which allow more flexible implementation, should increase stage 1 rent-seeking. General standards and other types of flexible implementation mechanisms are likely to displace some of the rent-seeking to the implementation process. Which of these alternatives is socially preferable is hard to know *a priori*, and deserves further research in the environmental policy context.

There is an interesting interrelationship between the choice of the compensation mechanism and the probable degree of rent-seeking. For a Coasean-style property rights assignment, pollution-damaged parties receive compensation when emissions levels exceed the polluter's entitlement. As in the model of Section 2, pollution-damaged parties have as much to gain from a stringent pollution curtailment (in terms of the gross payoffs) as polluters have to lose in these particular circumstances. This economic calculus provides an additional incentive for the pollution-damaged party to lobby over the rights definition. In contrast, regulations implemented with taxes or tradable permits, or enforced by fines, transfer revenue from polluters to the government, reducing the rent-seeking incentive of the pollution-damaged parties. Whether another rent-seeking party enters the equation may well depend on whether the funds in question are earmarked for specific purposes, like the budgets of enforcement agencies, or end up in general funds. In the former case, the agents who receive the earmarked funds may have an incentive to lobby for the policy and/or to attempt to influence how funds are distributed during the policy's operational phase.

The stringency of the enforcement mechanism will also influence the degree of rent-seeking. Voluntary agreements are the least coercive instrument; unlike a contract, parties can typically 'breech' voluntary agreements without any financial consequence (Glachant, 1995). Such 'self-regulation' should reduce the transactions costs associated with both the policy's establishment and its enforcement. Although voluntary agreements do not have the desirable stage 2 efficiency properties of incentive-based instruments, and may yield higher emissions levels than direct regulation, the benefits of avoided political costs may be considerable (Maxwell et al., 1995). In a positive transactions cost world, voluntary agreements may represent a promising policy approach for achieving environmental policy objectives, in at least some situations.

6. Conclusion

Several conclusions can be drawn from this brief survey. First, it is clear that the welfare properties of policy instruments cannot necessarily be inferred from their stage 3 market impact in a zero transactions cost world. The evaluation should be expanded to consider the impact of transactions costs at all stages of the policy process. Doing so may reveal that commonly recommended incentive-based instruments are not always normatively best. Tradable permits may not be the best policy instruments in transitional economics with poorly developed market institutions and inadequate enforcement authority; assigning property rights, *à la* Coase, may not be the best environmental policy approach if court enforcement is substantially more expensive than agency enforcement; and environmental taxes may not be the least-cost policy instrument in developing countries with high tax collection costs, or if the economic cost of rent-seeking over the revenue distribution is higher than the efficiency benefits otherwise gained.

Transactions costs also have implications for the widely held premise that multiple instruments are necessary efficiently to achieve multiple policy aims. This premise does not necessarily hold if transactions costs are positive and vary across instruments. These assumptions do not necessarily hold in the environmental policy sphere. For example, even a second-best production restriction might not be feasible in some cases, such as to control pollution from widely distributed area-source emitters. In such cases, lesser-ranked instruments, such as trade taxes, may be normatively superior. Similarly, the transactions cost of enforcing such 'first-best' policy instruments as tradable permits may be prohibitively high in the context of global environmental regulation. Jurisdictional boundaries, or other international agreements, like the GATT, may also reduce the menu of feasible policy instruments in the international policy context (Krutilla, 1997).

The transactions costs literature cited in this review was produced in a number of different time periods, and covers a diverse range of topics. A more integrated treatment of the subject in future research would likely yield valuable insights. In particular, the development of a generalized instrument choice framework, incorporating transaction costs at all stages of the policy process, would be an important contribution. Additional empirical study would be helpful in identifying the magnitude of transaction costs and the various policy stages, and to offering guidance vis-á-vis the special circumstances which economically justify particular policy approaches.

Notes

1. Note that this distinction is premised on the conceptually consistent assumption that transportation is regarded as a production, rather than a transaction, sector of the economy. Transportation costs can obviously arise in a perfect information environment.
2. That is, any policy-related costs other than the conventionally measured economic adjustment responses.
3. The conceptualization is similar in spirit, though not in detail, to that of Calabresi and Melamed (1972).
4. 'The policy process' is sometimes differentiated into a number of other stages (see Noll, 1983 and Howitt, 1991), but the three-stage distinction is useful for the purposes of this analysis.
5. There is a sizeable literature in the institutional and general economics fields which explores agent behaviour in an endogenous rights setting, for example, Skaperdas (1992) and Grossman (1991).
6. ne^* is not likely to be socially optimal in a second-best transactions costs model, but because this distinction does not affect the basic point of this section, the assumption that ne^* is the policy target is maintained for expositional convenience.
7. This stylization is an obvious simplification but helps highlight the essential rent-seeking incentive I wish to examine.
8. In view of the value of property rights, assuming away stage 2 efficiency effects would probably not bias conclusions about instrument selection more than the reciprocal assumptions made in the conventional literature. However, the normalization is only for heuristic convenience, and should not be construed as a retreat from the chapter's basic premise that costs at all stages of the policy should be considered in the policy assessment.
9. I will subsequently relax this assumption.
10. An emissions tax can itself be conceptualized as a regulation prescribing zero emissions with a unit charge for beyond-compliance emissions.
11. Indeed, when $\varepsilon = 0$ or is otherwise relatively low, rent-seeking incentives can be substantially larger than the conventionally measured regulatory efficiency gain. Hence rent-seeking costs can tip the net benefits of the policy action into the negative range.
12. CERCLA stands for Comprehensive Environmental Response, Compensation, and Liability Act. It is the principal US statute dealing with hazardous waste clean-up.
13. See Chapter 18 by Koutstaal, this volume, for further discussion of the effects of transactions costs and market imperfections in permit trading markets.
14. Holding the entitlement distribution constant is crucial to this conclusion. A conventional emissions tax, with $\varepsilon = 0$, provides a relatively large rent-seeking incentive due to the property rights structure.

References

Anderson, T.L. and P.J. Hill (1986), 'Privatizing the commons: an improvement?', in C.K. Rowley, R.D. Tollison and G. Tullock (eds), *The Political Economy of Rent-Seeking*, Boston: Kluwer Academic Publishers.

Baumol, W.J. and W.E. Oates (1988), *The Theory of Environmental Policy*, Cambridge, UK: Cambridge University Press.

Blumm, M.C. (1992), 'The fallacies of free market environmentalism', *Harvard Journal of Law and Public Policy*, **15**, 371–89.

Brunet, E. (1992), 'Debunking the wholesale private enforcement of environmental rights', *Harvard Journal of Law and Public Policy*, **15**, 311–24.

Buchanan, J.M. (1980), 'Rent-seeking under external diseconomies', in J.M. Buchanan, R.D. Tollison and G. Tullock (eds), *Toward a Theory of the Rent-Seeking Society*, College Station: Texas A&M Press.

Buchanan, J.M. and G. Tullock (1975), 'Polluters' profits and political response: direct control versus taxes', *American Economic Review*, **65**, 139–47.

Calabresi, G. and A.D. Melamed (1972), 'Property rules and inalienability: one view of the cathedral', *Harvard Law Review*, **85**, 1089–128.

Coase, R.H. (1960), 'The problem of social cost', *Journal of Law and Economics*, **3**, 1–44.

Coase, R.H. (1990), *The Firm, the Market, and the Law*, Chicago: University of Chicago Press.

Coelho, P. (1976), 'Polluters' profits and political response: Direct control versus taxes: comment', *American Economic Review*, **66**, 976–8.

Cooter, R. and T. Ulen (1998), *Law and Economics*, Glenview: Scott Foresman.

Cooter, R. and D. Rubinfeld (1989), 'Economic analysis of legal disputes and their resolution', *Journal of Economics Literature*, **27**, 1067–97.

Dewees, D. (1983), 'Instrument choice in environmental policy', *Economic Inquiry*, **21**, 53–71.

Eggertsson, T.A. (1995), *Economic Behavior and Institutions*, Cambridge, UK: Cambridge University Press.

Farrell, J. (1987), 'Information and the Coase theorem', *Journal of Economic Perspectives*, **1**, 113–19.

Funk, W. (1992), 'Free market environmentalism: wonder drug or snake oil?', *Harvard Journal of Law and Public Policy*, **15**, 511–16.

Glachant, M. (1995), 'Voluntary agreements in environmental policy: a bargaining approach', paper presented at the Sixth Conference of the European Association of Environmental and Resource Economists, Umeå, Sweden, June.

Grossman, H. (1991), 'A general equilibrium model of insurrections', *American Economic Review*, **81**, 912–21.

Hahn, R.W. (1989), 'Economic prescriptions for environmental problems', *Journal of Economic Perspectives*, **3**, 95–114.

Hanley, N., J.F. Shogren and B. White (eds) (1997), *Environmental Economics: In Theory and Practice*, Oxford: Oxford University Press.

Howitt, M. (1991), 'Policy instruments, policy styles, and policy implementation: National approaches to theories of instrument choice', *Policy Studies Journal*, **19**, 1–21.

Jung, C., K. Krutilla, W.K. Viscusi and R.G. Boyd (1995), 'The Coase theorem in a rent-seeking society', *International Review of Law and Economics*, **15**, 259–68.

Krier, J.E. (1992), 'The tragedy of the commons, part 2', *Harvard Journal of Law and Public Policy*, **15**, 325–47.

Krueger, A.O. (1990), 'Government failures in development', *Journal of Economic Perspectives*, **4**, 9–23.

Krutilla, K. (1997), 'World trade, the GATT, and the environment', in L.K. Caldwell and R.V. Bartlett (eds), *Environmental Policy: Transnational Issues and National Trends*, Westport, CT: Greenwood Publishing Group.

Krutilla, K. and W.K. Viscusi (1998), 'Environmental policy and rent-seeking', Working Paper, School of Public and Environmental Affairs, Indiana University, Bloomington, January.

Lee, D.R. (1986), 'Rent-seeking and its implications for pollution taxation', in C.K. Rowley, R.D. Tollison and G. Tullock (eds), *The Political Economy of Rent-Seeking*, Boston: Kluwer Academic Publishers.

Malik, A. (1992), 'Enforcement costs and the choice of policy instruments for controlling pollution', *Economic Inquiry*, **30**, 714–21.

Maloney, M. and R.E. McCormick (1982), 'A positive theory of environmental quality', *Journal of Law and Economics*, **25**, 99–112.

Maxwell, J.W., T.P. Lyon and S.C. Hackett (1995), 'Self-regulation and social welfare: the political economy of corporate environmentalism', Indiana University Working Paper in Business Economics, 95–004.

Medema, S. (1997), 'Comment: the Coase theorem, rent seeking, and the forgotten footnote', *International Review of Law and Economics*, **17**, 177–8.

Menell, P.S. (1991), 'The limitations of legal institutions for addressing environmental risks', *Journal of Economic Perspectives*, **5**, 93–113.

Menell, P.S. (1992), 'Institutional fantasy lands: From scientific management to free market environmentalism', *Harvard Journal of Law and Public Policy*, **15**, 489–510.

Migue, J.L. and R. Marceu (1993), 'Pollution taxes, subsidies, and rent-seeking', *Canadian Journal of Economics*, **26**, 354–65.

Miller, B. (1994), 'High-level waste: view from Nevada', *Forum for Applied Research and Public Policy*, Fall, 103–5.

Mitchell, R.C. and R.T. Carson (1986), 'Property rights, protests, and the siting of hazardous waste facilities', *American Economic Review Papers and Proceedings*, **76**, 285–90.

Mumy, G.E. (1980), 'Long-run efficiency and property rights sharing for pollution control', *Public Choice*, **35**, 59–74.

Munro, A., N. Hanely, R. Faichney and J. Shortle (1995), 'Impediments to trade in markets for pollution permits', Paper presented at the Conference of the European Association of Environmental and Resource Economists, Umeå, Sweden.

Noll, R. (1983), 'The political foundations of regulatory policy', *Journal of Institutional and Theoretical Economics*, **19**, 377–404.

Parker, F.L. (1994), 'Outlook remains dim for waste solution', *Forum for Applied Research and Public Policy*, Fall, 98–102.

Pezzey, J. (1992), 'The symmetry between controlling pollution by price and controlling it by quantity', *Canadian Journal of Economics*, **26**, 983–99.

Portney, P.R. and K.N. Probst (1994), 'Cleaning up superfund', *Resources*, **114**, 2–5.

Sebenius, J.K. (1986), *Negotiating the Law of the Sea: Lessons in the Art and Science of Reaching an Agreement*, Cambridge, MA: Harvard University Press.

Skaperdas, S. (1992), 'Cooperation, conflict, and power in the absence of property rights', *American Economic Review*, **82**, 720–39.

Stavins, R.N. (1995), 'Transaction costs and tradable permits', *Journal of Environmental Economics and Management*, **29**, 133–48.

US DOC (1996), *Reference Book of Policies and Guidance for Implementing the Endangered Species Act*, US Department of Commerce, Washington, DC.

US EPA (1994), *History of PCB-contaminated superfund sites: Bloomington Indiana*, US EPA Region 5 Information Center.

Vollebergh, R.J. (1994), 'Transaction costs and European carbon tax design', in M. Faure, J. Vervaele and A. Weale (eds), *Environmental Standards in the European Union in an Interdisciplinary Framework*, Antwerp: Maklu.

Vollebergh, R.J. (1996), 'Environmental taxes and transactions costs', Paper presented at the 13th Conference of the European Association of Law and Economics, Haifa.

Yohe, G.W. (1976), 'Polluters' profits and political response: direct control versus taxes: comment', *American Economic Review*, **66**, 981–2.

18 Tradable permits in economic theory
Paul Koutstaal

1. Introduction

Since tradable emission permits first appeared in economic theory in 1968 in a book by J.H. Dales, *Pollution, Property and Prices*, a large number of articles and books have been published on tradable permits. Moreover, tradable permits have been applied in practice, mainly in the US (see Chapter 19 in this volume by Tietenberg for an overview of the experiences with tradable permits). In this chapter some of the developments in the theory of tradable permits are outlined (for a more detailed overview of the issues addressed here the reader is referred to Tietenberg, 1985, and Klaassen, 1996). In the next section the rather restrictive assumption of perfect competition on permit and product markets is relaxed and it is investigated how this will influence the performance of tradable permits. Theoretical explanations for the lack of trade which has occurred in some of the tradable permit schemes that have been put into practice is the subject of Section 3. In Section 4 the consequences of non-compliance are studied. Last, both theoretical and experimental investigations into different types of auctions are discussed.

2. Tradable permits under perfect and imperfect competition

Market power and cost-price manipulation
With perfect competition in product and permit markets, tradable pollution rights are a cost-effective means for reducing pollution. Assume an (autonomous determined) emission reduction target $\bar{E}$ and let there be N polluting firms. Let q_i be the quantity of a commodity produced by firm i for a price p_q and C_i the production costs including abatement costs. When emissions are reduced with a system of tradable permits, firm i will maximize the following profit function:

$$\max \pi_i (q_i, l_i) = p_q \cdot qi - C_i(q_i, l_i) - p_l(l_i - l_i^0)$$

$$\partial C_i / \partial q_i > 0, \ \partial^2 C_i / \partial q_i > 0, \ \partial C_i / \partial l_i < 0, \ \partial^2 C_i / \partial l_i > 0 \qquad (18.1)$$

l_i^0 is the amount of permits which the firm has received from the authorities; p_l is the price of the permit; l_i is the number of permits which source *i* will use and equals the firms' emissions. It is determined by the first-order condition with respect to l_i that

$$\partial C_i / \partial l_i + p_l = 0 \tag{18.2}$$

All sources will acquire the number of permits at which the marginal abatement costs equal the permit price. Consequently, marginal abatement costs will be the same for all sources and total abatement costs for all sources are minimized, regardless of the initial allocation of the permits.

A central assumption for the cost-effectiveness of tradable permits is that the permit market is a perfect market on which no actor has market power. Another possibility is that a source is not a price-taker but that its actions on the permit market will influence the permit price. Such a firm can use its influence on the permit price to minimize its costs, which is called cost-minimizing manipulation (CMM). Hahn (1984) has studied this issue, assuming that all firms except one (firm 1) are price-takers. Firm 1 can choose the permit price which minimizes its costs, subject to the constraint that the permit market clears:[2]

$$\min(l_2) \ C_1(l_1) + p_l(l_1 - l_1^0)$$

subject to

$$l_1 + \sum_{i=2}^{N} l_i(p_l) = \bar{E} \tag{18.3}$$

Solving equation (18.3) yields:

$$P_l = \frac{\partial C_1 / \partial l_1}{1 + \dfrac{1}{\eta} \dfrac{l_1^0 - l_1^*}{l_2^0}} \tag{18.4}$$

η is the demand elasticity for the other firms, the price-takers. l_2^0 is the initial allocation to the fringe and l_1^* is the level of permits which firm 1 will hold in the final equilibrium. Equation (18.4) shows that the cost-minimizing solution, when marginal abatement costs $\partial C_1 / \partial l_1$ equal permit price p_l, is only achieved when the number of permits which the price-taker originally receives is equal to the number of permits it will hold in equilibrium. Consequently, the distribution of the permits will matter for the cost-effectiveness of the instrument in the presence of market power.

Empirical simulations have been carried out to estimate the size of the efficiency loss which might be caused by CMM. Hahn (1984), Hahn and

Noll (1982), Maloney and Yandle (1984) and Pototschnig (1994) have examined CMM in the case of air pollution. O'Neil et al. (1983), Lyon (1982) and Hanley and Moffat (1993) have looked at CMM for controlling water pollution. The extent to which CMM reduces the efficiency of tradable permit systems depends on several factors: (1) the initial distribution of the permits; (2) the dominance which the price-taker has on the permit market; and (3) the specific form of the cost functions. Although CMM can reduce the efficiency of tradable permits, it can still increase cost-efficiency compared with command and control (see Maloney and Yandle, 1984).

Tradable permits and entry barriers: exclusionary manipulation and predatory pricing
While a firm with market power can use its influence on the permit market to minimize its abatement costs (see above), it can also use it to reduce competition from other firms on the product market, either established firms or potential entrants (called exclusionary manipulation – EM). EM has been studied by Misiolek and Elder (1989) who have applied the work done on cost-raising strategies by Salop and Scheffman (1987) and Krattenmaker and Salop (1986) to tradable permits. They assumed that there is a dominant firm (firm 1) which has market power both on the product market and on the permit market, and a fringe of firms acting as price-takers. The profit maximization problem for the dominant firm in this case is (cf. equation 18.1):

$$\max_{\{p, q_1, l_1\}} \pi_1 = p_q \cdot q_1 - C_1(q_1, l_1)$$

subject to

$$D(p_q) = \sum_{i=2}^{n} q_i(p_q, p_l) + q_1 \qquad \partial q_i/\partial p_q > 0, \ \partial q_i/\partial p_l < 0 \qquad (18.5)$$

$$p_l = p_l(l_1) \qquad\qquad\qquad \partial p/\partial l_1 > 0$$

in which $D(p_q)$ is the demand function for product q. An increase in the permit price p_l reduces the supply of the fringe; an increase in the product price p_q increase the supply of the fringe. The permit price p_i depends on the demand of the dominant firm. An increase in its demand for permit l_1 increases the price.

In contrast with the CMM case discussed above, the dominant firm buys permits to drive up the price of the permits, which increases the costs of the fringe, instead of choosing the number of permits at which his own abatement costs and permit expenditure is minimized. This will increase the product price of the fringe firms (because one of its inputs, the permits, becomes more expensive) and allows the dominant firm to raise its product price and increase profits. Whether or not EM will be attractive for the dominant firm depends on whether, at the pre-EM level of q_1, the increase in its average costs caused by the higher permit price will be offset by the higher product price (see Salop and Scheffman, 1987 and Misiolek and Elder, 1989).

Consequently, the probability that EM is profitable is larger when the dominant firm has more market power and therefore more effect on the permit price. EM is also more profitable when production of the fringe is pollution-intensive and if the demand for the product is less elastic.

Permit distribution and entry barriers
A central element in tradable permit systems is the distribution of permits. They can either be sold to polluters or they can be allocated free (grandfathered). In most permit schemes used so far the permits have been grandfathered (see Chapter 19 in this volume, by Tietenberg) to the established firms, while new firms had to buy permits. This does not necessarily raise entry barriers because the permits grandfathered to the established firms have an opportunity cost which is equal to the costs which new firms have to make to acquire permits.

However, grandfathering can raise entry barriers when capital markets do not work perfectly, as has been discussed by Bohm (1994) and Koutstaal (1997). The central assumption here is that the amount of funds which a firm can borrow on the capital market is limited by its wealth: the less capital it owns, the higher the interest it has to pay to borrow a fixed amount of money. The entrant has to borrow more than the established firm so that the interest for the entrant is higher. In this situation predatory pricing is an attractive strategy for the incumbent firm: it has larger financial resources, therefore it can outlast the entrant in a price war and drive it out of the market. This type of entry barrier occurs only when the permits are grandfathered; it will not occur in the case of auctioning of the permits or when taxes or pollution standards are used.

There is some empirical evidence that in general capital requirements can raise entry barriers (Orr, 1974; Geroski and Schwalbach, 1991). The potential effect on entry of tradable permit schemes can be evaluated by estimating by how much capital requirements of new firms rise if they have to buy permits. Koutstaal (1997) has estimated the increase in capital requirements for various Dutch industry sectors in the case of a CO_2 emission trading scheme. The additional capital requirements necessary to buy carbon permits appeared to be small, less than 2 per cent of the original capital requirements for the most affected sectors in the Dutch economy. Important factors which influence the increase in capital requirements are the price of the permits and the emission intensity of an industry sector.

Imperfect product markets and perfect tradable permit markets
In the former subsections it was assumed that the permit market was imperfect. In contrast, Malueg (1990) and Sartzetakis (1995) have looked at competitive permit markets and a non-competitive output market. Both assume that the pollutant is emitted by several sectors and that the permit market is competitive, while the output market of the sector under consideration is represented by a Cournot oligopoly model. They analyse the welfare consequences of introducing a system of tradable permits compared with a command-and-control situation in which the firms have been allotted an emissions quota. Two effects can be discerned. First, the tradable permit scheme will reduce abatement costs and therefore output and consumer surplus will increase. Second, the trade in permits will redistribute production across the firms. Firms which in the command-and-control situation are less efficient in their emission abatement will, under a tradable permit system, reduce their abatement costs and increase their output share. Profits will likewise be redistributed and there is the possibility that profits will fall. Which effect dominates is not clear. The conclusion is that under a tradable permit system total welfare may be lower than in a command-and-control situation.

3.   Lack of trade in tradable permit markets
In the early systems of tradable emission permit schemes which have been put into practice the number of trades have been below what was expected. Several explanations have been given for the gap between theory and practice (see Chapter 19 by Tietenberg). Here we shall look at the theoretical modifications to the standard model which might explain this lack of trade (for a short overview of several possible factors, see Munro et al., 1995): transactions costs on the permit market and sequential trade in permit schemes where location matters.

A number of authors have mentioned transactions costs as a reason for lack of trades (among others Hahn and Hester, 1989; Tripp and Dudek, 1989; Dwyer, 1992). Transactions costs can occur for several reasons: the costs of searching for a trading partner and the costs of acquiring information on, for example, prices; the costs of bargaining, such as broker fees and legal and insurance services. As a result of transactions costs, the optimization problem of a firm which wants to trade in permits will change (Stavins, 1995). The effect of transactions costs is 'unambiguously to decrease the volume of permit trading regardless of the specific forms that the marginal control cost functions and transaction costs function take'

(Stavins, 1995). Furthermore, total abatement costs will increase compared with the least-cost solution in the absence of transactions costs.

With transactions costs, the initial endowment of permits matters when marginal transactions costs are increasing: the more the allocation differs from the efficient allocation, the higher are total abatement costs. When marginal transactions costs are decreasing, a shift away from the efficient allocation will cause the final equilibrium to be closer to the cost-efficient solution because of positive scale effects due to the decreasing marginal costs of trading. With constant marginal transactions costs the initial allocation has no consequences for the final equilibrium.

Transactions costs can especially be a problem in cases where location matters. The theoretically optimal ambient or deposit permit system requires that a pollution source needs deposition permits for all receptors (Montgomery, 1972). If the number of receptors is high, a firm will also have to buy a large number of deposition permits, one for each receptor. This can considerably raise transactions costs and thereby limit trade. In order to overcome this problem, alternative trading rules have been proposed in which emission permits are traded instead of deposition permits (see Chapter 19). These trading rules limit the total number of trades and the cost savings which can be achieved compared to the least-cost solution.

In estimating the potential cost savings which can be realized with tradable permits, one can assume that all profitable trades will take place simultaneously, which will lead to the cost-minimizing solution, depending on the trading rule used. However, this might not be a good representation of the reality of tradable permit markets. Instead one might assume that trade is sequential instead of simultaneous. Atkinson and Tietenberg (1991) modelled sequential trading, which showed that costs savings (and total number of trades) will be less than with simultaneous trading. The reason for this is that when trade is sequential instead of simultaneous one trade can prevent another trade taking place which might yield higher cost savings, because it would violate deposition targets. With simultaneous trading, deposition targets would only have to be met when all profitable trades had taken place; therefore all profitable trades can be affected.

Trading might be further limited in the sequential trading process if one adds further constraints, as has been shown by several empirical simulation studies (see Klaassen, 1996 for an overview of these studies). One constraint is limited information, which means that traders select their partners randomly. Another restriction is to introduce transaction costs which reduce the number of profitable trades.

Kruitwagen et al. (1994) have proposed a system of so-called 'guided bilateral trade', which makes it possible to achieve the cost-efficient allocation of permits when trade is sequential. In guided bilateral trade, actors are limited in the number of permits they may trade by a 'trade vector' which is determined after the initial allocation of the permits. Deposition targets need not be met until all trades have taken place. When all trades have taken place, deposition targets will be met at the lowest possible abatement costs. However, it is not necessarily the case that all trades take place, because some of them might be unprofitable. Simulations of trade in SO_2 allowances in Europe show that some deposition targets are not met at the end of guided bilateral trade because not all the trades which were allowed by the trade vector were profitable, and therefore not all the trades took place.

4. Non-compliance

As with all other policy instruments, non-compliance will have consequences for the performance of a system of tradable emission permits, as has been shown by Malik (1990) and Keeler (1991). With the possibility of non-compliance, a firm's cost-minimization problem will change. Instead of emissions being equal to the number of permits a firm acquires, it can now choose to emit more. A profit-maximizing firm will choose an emission level at which marginal profits equal the permit price plus the expected fine for non-compliance. A sufficient condition for a firm to violate is that the expected marginal fine at a zero violation must be lower than the permit price.

A consequence of violation is that the permit demand and the permit price will be affected because violating firms will use fewer permits than they emit. The effect on the permit price of non-compliance depends on the probability that violation is detected and fined. If this audit probability increases or is constant with the number of permits and the size of emissions, non-compliance implies a lower equilibrium permit price.

When firms are non-compliant, tradable permits will not be a cost-effective instrument, except when the audit probability is independent of emissions and the number of permits a firm holds.

5. Auction of permits

One way of allocating permits is by selling them at an auction. Lyon (1986) investigates several types of auction which do not yield revenue for the government. Incentive-compatible auctions (in which bidders truthfully reveal their preferences) with lump sum refunds and grandfathering of permits followed by trade have the advantage that bidders will not behave strategically. However, incentive-compatible auctions with lump sum refunds might leave the government with a surplus or a deficit. In contrast, transfer-neutral allocation procedures do not leave a surplus or deficit for the government, but bidders will behave strategically, and consequently the allocation of the permits is not efficient.

In an experimental investigation, Franciosi et al. (1993) have looked at the so-called Hahn–Noll revenue-neutral auction (RNA). In an RNA (see Hahn and Noll, 1982 for a detailed description), permits are at first distributed among firms for free (grandfathered). Subsequently the firms have to offer all their permits for sale at the auction. They also submit a demand schedule for permits. Given the (inelastic) supply curve determined by the total number of permits available and the aggregated demand curve, the market price is determined. Permits are sold at this price, and each firm receives the value of the permits it held before the auction. In the experiment, the RNA has also been compared with a uniform price auction (UPA), in which the revenue accrues to the seller (that is, the government), in order to determine the consequences for the auction of the mechanism used for the distribution of the receipts. The conclusion of the experiments is that in terms of market efficiency, both RNA and UPA perform similarly. However, at an RNA bidders can bid very large amounts on the number of permits they received for free in order to 'hoard' permits.

Cason (1993) has shown that the auction design in the EPA Sulphur Allowance Scheme, in which the sellers with the lowest asking price receive the highest bid (for more details, see Chapter 19), causes sellers of permits to ask prices which are lower than their marginal abatement costs. This seller-incentive problem becomes worse if the number of sellers increases, because of increased competition between the sellers. The consequence is that the auction provides wrong price signals and therefore efficiency is reduced. An experimental investigation of the seller incentives of the EPA auction (Cason, 1995) supports the findings of the earlier study.

Notes
1. In the limited space available here only an outline of the theory of tradable permits can be provided. The reader is referred to other parts of this volume for issues related to the role of tradable permits in international coordination of pollution control and issues related to uncertainty in instrument choice.
2. The focus is on the minimization of abatement costs, therefore production costs $C_1(q_1)$ are left out of the analysis.

References
Atkinson, S. and T. Tietenberg (1991), 'Market failure in incentive-based regulation: the case of emission trading', *Journal of Environmental Economics and Management*, **21**, 17–31.
Bohm, P. (1994), 'Government revenue implications of carbon taxes and tradeable carbon permits: efficiency aspects', paper presented at the 50th Congress of the International Institute for Public Finance, August 22–25, Harvard University, Cambridge, MA.
Cason, T. (1993), 'Seller incentive properties of EPA's emission trading auction', *Journal of Environmental Economics and Management*, **25**, 177–95.
Cason, T. (1995), 'An experimental investigation of the seller incentives in the EPA's emission trading auction', *American Economic Review*, **85** (4), 905–22.

Dales, J.H. (1968), *Pollution, Property and Prices*, Toronto: Toronto University Press.

Dwyer, J.P. (1992), 'California's tradeable emissions policy and its application to the control of greenhouse gases', in *Climate Change – Designing a Tradeable Permit System*, Paris: OECD.

Franciosi, R., R.M. Isaac, D.E. Pingry and S.S. Reynolds (1993), 'An experimental investigation of the Hahn–Noll revenue neutral auction for emission licenses', *Journal of Environmental Economics and Management*, 24, 1–24.

Geroski, P.A. and J. Schwalbach (eds) (1991), *Entry and Market Contestability*, Oxford: Basil Blackwell.

Hahn, R.W. (1984), 'Market power and transferable property rights', *Quarterly Journal of Economics*, 99 (4), 735–65.

Hahn, R.W. and G.L. Hester (1989), 'Where did all the markets go? An analysis of EPA's Emission Trading Program', *Yale Journal on Regulation*, 6, 109–53.

Hahn, R.W. and R.G. Noll (1982), 'Designing a market for tradable emission permits', in W.A. Magat (ed.), *Reform of Environmental Regulation*, Cambridge, MA: Ballinger Publishing Company.

Hanley, N. and I. Moffat (1993), 'Efficiency and distributional aspects of market mechanisms in the control of pollution: an empirical analysis', *Scottish Journal of Political Economy*, 40, 69–87.

Keeler, A. (1991), 'Noncompliant firms in transferable discharge permit markets: some extensions', *Journal of Environmental Economics and Management*, 21, 180–89.

Klaassen, G. (1996), *Acid Rain and Environmental Degradation*, Cheltenham, UK and Brookfield, US: Edward Elgar.

Koutstaal, P.R. (1997), *Economic Policy and Climate Change: Tradable Permits for reducing Carbon Emissions*, Cheltenham, UK and Lyme, US: Edward Elgar.

Krattenmaker, T.G. and S.C. Salop (1986), 'Competition and cooperation in the market for exclusionary rights', *American Economic Review*, 76 (2), 109–13.

Kruitwagen, S., E. Hendrix and E.C. van Ierland (1994), 'Tradable SO_2 permits: guided bilateral trade in Europe', in E.C. van Ierland (ed.), *International Environmental Economics: Theories, Models and Applications to Climate Change, International Trade and Acidification*, Amsterdam: Elsevier.

Lyon, R.M. (1982), 'Auctions and alternative procedures for allocating pollution rights', *Land Economics*, 58, 16–32.

Lyon, R.M. (1986), Equilibrium properties of auctions and alternative procedures for allocating transferable permits', *Journal of Environmental Economics and Management*, 13, 129–52.

Malik, A. (1990), 'Markets for pollution control when firms are non-compliant', *Journal of Environmental Economics and Management*, 18, 97–106.

Maloney, M.T. and B. Yandle (1984), 'Estimation of the cost of air pollution control regulation', *Journal of Environmental Economics and Management*, 11, 244–63.

Malueg, D.A. (1990), 'Welfare consequences of emission credit trading programs', *Journal of Environmental Economics and Management*, 16, 66–77.

Misiolek, W.S. and H.W. Elder (1989), 'Exclusionary manipulation of markets for pollution rights', *Journal of Environmental Economics and Management*, 16, 156–66.

Montgomery, W.D. (1972), 'Market in licenses and efficient pollution control programs', *Journal of Economic Theory*, 5, 395–418.

Munro, A., N. Hanley, R. Faichney and J.S. Shortle (1995), 'Impediments to trade in markets for pollution permits', paper presented at the European Association of Environmental and Resource Economists Conference, Umeå.

O'Neil, W., M. David, C. Moore and E. Joeres (1983), 'Transferable discharge permits and economic efficiency: the Fox river', *Journal of Environmental Economics and Management*, 10, 346–55.

Orr, D. (1974), 'Determinants of entry', *Review of Economics and Statistics*, 56, 58–66.

Pototschnig, A. (1994), 'Economic instruments for the control of acid raid in Britain', in G. Klaassen and F. Førsund (eds), *Economic Instruments for Air Pollution Control*, Dordrecht: Kluwer Academic Publishers

274 *Economics of environmental policy*

Salop, S.C. and D.T. Scheffman (1987), 'Cost-raising strategies', *The Journal of Industrial Economics*, **36** (1), 19–34.

Sartzetakis, E.S. (1995), 'Interaction of competitive markets for tradeable emission permits with oligopolistic product markets', paper presented at the European Association of Environmental and Resource Economists Conference, Umeå.

Stavins, R.N. (1995), 'Transaction costs and tradeable permits, *Journal of Environmental Economics and Management*, **29**, 133–48.

Tietenberg, T.H. (1985), *Emission Trading: An Exercise in Reforming Pollution Policy*, Washington, DC: Resources for the Future.

Tripp, J. and D. Dudek (1989), 'Institutional guidelines for designing successful transferable rights programs', *Yale Journal on Regulation*, **6**, 369–91.

19 Lessons from using transferable permits to control air pollution in the United States

Tom Tietenberg

1. Introduction

Beginning in 1975, burgeoning costs associated with the rigidities inherent in its traditional, predominantly legal approach to controlling air pollution led the US Environmental Protection Agency (EPA) to begin experimenting with a limited version of a system of transferable emission permits. Since that time the transferable emission permit concept has been applied in the US to the elimination of lead in gasoline, the reduction of ozone-depleting gases in accordance with the Montreal Protocol, the elimination of 10 million tons of SO_2 emissions in connection with a programme to reduce acid rain, the reduction of pollutants in the Los Angeles area and the retirement of highly polluting vehicles. It has been proposed as a means of achieving the goals of the Climate Change Convention both domestically and internationally.

In this chapter I shall briefly describe these programmes and provide an overview of some of the major lessons we have learned about this approach.[1]

2. Pre-reform environmental policy

Since the earliest reform policies were not only motivated by the inefficiencies associated with the traditional legal approach to air pollution control, but were also shaped by it, understanding that policy provides a foundation for understanding the evolution of the reforms. Stripped to its essentials, the US pre-reform approach to pollution control relied upon a 'command-and-control' approach to controlling pollution. Ambient standards, which establish the highest allowable concentration of the pollutant in the ambient air or water for each conventional pollutant, represent the environmental targets. To reach these targets, emission or effluent standards (legal discharge ceilings) were imposed on a large number of specific discharge points such as stacks, vents, outfalls or storage tanks. Following a survey of the technological options of control, the control authority selected a favoured control technology and calculated the amount of discharge reduction achievable by that technology as the basis for setting the emission or effluent standard. Technologies yielding larger amounts of control (and, hence, supporting more stringent standards) were mandated both for emitters in areas where it is very difficult to meet the ambient standard and for new emitters. The responsibility for defining and enforcing these standards was shared in legislatively specified ways between the national government and the various state governments.

3.   The evolution of reform

The emissions trading programme
In an attempt to inject more flexibility into the manner in which the objectives of the Clean Air Act were met during the last half of the 1970s, in 1975 the US EPA created what has now become known as the emissions trading programme. The programme attempts to facilitate compliance by allowing sources a much wider range of choice in how they satisfy their legal pollution control responsibilities than is possible in the command-and-control approach. Any source choosing to reduce emissions at any discharge point more than required by its emission standard can apply to the control authority for certification of the excess control as an 'emission reduction credit' (ERC). Defined in terms of a specific amount of a particular pollutant, the certified emission reduction credit can be used to satisfy emission standards at other (presumably more expensive to control) discharge points controlled by the creating source or it can be sold to other sources. By making these credits transferable, the EPA allowed sources to find the cheapest means of satisfying their requirements, even if the cheapest means were under the control of another firm.

This early version of a trading programme was a far cry from the economist's ideal of a single market characterized by a single price (Hahn, 1989; Hahn and Hester, 1989b). Trades were normally bilateral and negotiated on a case-by-case basis; prices, which were normally treated as confidential information by the trading parties, varied and trades were sporadic (Atkinson and Tietenberg, 1991). Since the pre-existing emission standards became the trading baseline, in the absence of any trading existing sources could continue to emit what they had been allowed to emit under the conventional system; trading simply allowed them marginally to increase or reduce their emissions from these individual limits. New sources had to acquire all ERCs from existing sources. The emissions trading programme complemented the pre-reform system by attempting to increase the flexibility the sources had in meeting their assigned control responsibilities. It remains in effect.

Lead in gasoline

Following the path broken by the emissions trading programme, the government began applying the transferable permit approach more widely. In the mid-1980s, prior to the issuance of new, more stringent regulations on lead in gasoline, the EPA announced the results of a cost–benefit analysis of their expected impact. The analysis concluded that the proposed 0.01 grams per leaded gallon (gplg) standard would result in $36 billion (in 1983 dollars) in benefits (from reduced adverse health effects) at an estimated cost to the refining industry of $2.6 billion (Hahn and Hester, 1989a).

Although the regulation was unquestionably justified on efficiency grounds, the EPA wanted to allow flexibility in how the deadlines were met without increasing the amount of lead used. While some refiners could meet early deadlines with ease, others could do so only with a significant increase in cost. Recognizing that meeting the goal did not require every refiner to meet every deadline, the EPA initiated the lead phase-out programme to provide additional flexibility in meeting the regulations.

Under this programme a fixed amount of lead rights (authorizing the use of a fixed amount of lead over the transition period) were allocated to the various refiners. Refiners who did not need their full share of authorized rights (due to earlier or larger reductions) could sell their rights to other refiners. Initially the rights had to be used in the same year, but starting in 1985 refiners were allowed to bank credits for future sale or use.

Refiners had an incentive to eliminate the lead quickly because early reductions freed up rights for sale. Acquiring these credits made it possible for other refiners to comply with the deadlines, even in the face of equipment failures or acts of God; fighting the deadlines in court, the traditional response, was unnecessary. EPA analyses have suggested that the trading provisions implemented in 1982 saved the refinery industry about $65 million, while the three years of banking reduced costs by about $200 million (Nussbaum, 1992, p. 35). Designed purely as a means of facilitating the transition to this new regime, the lead banking programme ended as scheduled on 31 December 1987.

Ozone-depleting chemicals

Responding to the threat to the ozone shield, 24 nations signed the Montreal Protocol during September 1988. According to this agreement signatory nations had to restrict their production and consumption of the chief responsible gases to 50 per cent of 1986 levels by 30 June 1998. Soon after the protocol was signed, new evidence suggested that it had not gone far enough; the damage was apparently increasing more rapidly than previously thought. In response, 59 nations signed a new ozone agreement at a conference in London in July 1990. This agreement called for the complete phase-out of halons and CFCs (chlorofluorocarbons) by the end of this century. Moreover, two other destructive chemicals – carbon tetrachloride and methyl chloroform – were added to the protocol and are scheduled to be eliminated by 2000 and 2005, respectively.

The United States chose to use a transferable permit system to implement its responsibilities under the protocols.[2] On 12 August 1988 the US EPA issued its first regulations implementing a tradable permit system to achieve the targeted reductions. According to these regulations, all major US producers and consumers of the controlled substances were allocated baseline production or consumption allowances using 1986 levels as the basis for the proration. Each producer and consumer is allowed 100 per cent of this baseline allowance initially, with smaller allowances being granted after predefined deadlines.

Following the London conference, these percentage-of-baseline allocations were reduced to reflect the new deadlines and limits. These allowances are transferable within producer and consumer categories and allowances can be transferred across international borders to producers in other signatory nations if the transaction is approved by EPA and results in the appropriate adjustments in the buyer or seller allowances in their respective countries.[3] Production allowances can be augmented by demonstrating the safe destruction of an equivalent amount of controlled substances by approved means. Some interpollutant trading is even possible within categories of pollutants. (The categories are defined so as to group pollutants with similar environmental effects.) All information on trades is confidential (known only to the traders and regulators), so it is difficult to know how effective this programme has been. One estimate suggests that as of September 1993 the traded amount was roughly 10 per cent of the total permits (Stavins and Hahn, 1993).

Since the demand for these allowances is quite inelastic, supply restrictions increase revenue. By allocating allowances to the seven major domestic producers of CFCs and halons, the EPA was concerned that its regulation would result in sizeable windfall profits (estimated to be in billions of dollars) for those producers. The EPA handled this problem by imposing a tax on production to soak up the rents created by the regulation-induced scarcity.

This application was unique in two senses. It not only allowed international trading of allowances, but it involved the simultaneous application of permit and tax systems.

Acid rain
Another quite different version of the tradable permits concept was incorporated by the Clean Air Act Amendments of 1990 into the US approach

for achieving further reductions in those electric utility emissions contributing to acid rain.[4] Under this innovative approach allowances to emit sulphur oxides have been allocated to older plants; the number of allowances will be restricted to assure a reduction of 10 million tons in emissions from 1980 levels by the year 2010.[5]

These allowances, which provide a limited authorization to emit one ton of sulphur, are defined for a specific calendar year, but unused allowances can be carried forward into the next year. They are transferable among the affected sources. Any plants reducing emissions more than required by the allowances could transfer the unused allowances to other plants. Emissions may not legally exceed the levels permitted by the allowances (allocated plus acquired). An annual year-end audit balances emissions with allowances. Utilities which emit more than authorized by their holdings of allowances must pay a $2000 per ton penalty and are required to forfeit an equivalent number of tons in the following year (Kete, 1992, 1994; Rico, 1995).

Spurred by the desire to ensure both the availability of information to the public on prices and sufficient supply of allowances to accommodate new sources, an innovative auction market was established. Each year the EPA withholds 2.24 per cent of the allocated allowances to go into an auction run by the Chicago Board of Trade. These withheld permits are allocated to the highest bidders, with successful buyers paying their bid price. The proceeds are refunded to the utilities from whom the allowances were withheld on a proportional basis. Trades can also take place between private parties any time of year; they must be reported to the allowance tracking system (ATS) so that the EPA can keep track of the allowances.

Not all allowances sold at the auction are those withheld from utilities. Any allowance holder may choose to offer allowances for sale at these auctions. Potential sellers specify minimum acceptable prices. Once the withheld allowances have been disbursed, the EPA matches the highest remaining bids with the lowest minimum acceptable prices on the private offerings and matches buyers and sellers until all remaining bids are less than the remaining minimum acceptable prices. This auction design unfortunately is not particularly efficient because it provides incentives for inefficient strategic behaviour (Hausker, 1992; Cason, 1993).

Despite lower prices and somewhat less trading volume than initially expected (Conrad and Kohn, 1996; Burtraw, 1996), the programme has brought about more emissions reductions sooner than expected. As of 1997, SO_2 emissions from electric power plants were more than 4 million tons below their 1980 levels. Overall, SO_2 emissions from all sources were more than 6 million tons below their 1980 levels and compliance costs are apparently about half those originally projected. Since 1993, the number of allowances bid for in the auctions tripled from 600000 to 1.9 million, even though the amount available has only doubled. Also, the spread between the highest bid and the clearing price dropped considerably from $319 to $14, indicating the effect of public knowledge of price information.

Though the annual auctions provide a reliable price signal to the allowance market, they are by no means the only place in which trading is occurring. The volume of allowances transferred reported to the allowance tracking system (ATS) grew from less than 900000 in 1994 to almost 4.5 million in 1996. By the end of 1996, the ATS had recorded over 3100 public and private transactions involving over 51 million allowances.[6]

RECLAIM
While all the above programmes were initiated and promoted by the federal government, the newest programmes have arisen from state initiatives. Faced with the need to reduce pollution concentrations (normally, but not exclusively ozone) considerably in order to come into compliance with the ambient standard, states have chosen to use trading programmes as a means of facilitating rather drastic reductions in emissions.

One of the most ambitious of these programmes is California's Regional Clean Air Incentives Market (RECLAIM), established in 1994 by the South Coast Air Quality Management District, the district responsible for the greater Los Angeles area (Robinson, 1993; Johnson and Pekelney, 1996; Hall and Walton, 1996). Under RECLAIM, each of the almost 400 participating industrial polluters are allocated an annual pollution limit for nitrogen oxides and sulphur, which will decrease by 5 per cent to 8 per cent each year for the next decade.[7] Polluters are allowed great flexibility in meeting these limits, including purchasing credits from other firms which have controlled more than their legal requirements.

The RECLAIM programme shares with the sulphur allowance programme the characteristic that it sets a cap on total emissions from the controlled group rather than on emissions from each source: this cap ensures that expansion must be accommodated within the cap (by cutting back a compensating amount somewhere else) rather than by allowing emissions to increase.

From its inception in January 1994 to 1 January 1996, participating firms traded more than 100000 tons of nitrogen and sulphur oxide emissions for more than $10 million, according to an audit by the agency. During the programme's first year, trading prices for NO_x credits ranged from an average of $24 per ton for 1994 to $1529 for 1998. SO_x prices ranged from $13 per ton for 1994 to $960 in 1998.[8]

Mobile sources

Due in part to the emission reductions achieved from stationary sources, in many regions of the United States mobile sources now account for a high percentage of the remaining pollution. Though individual new vehicles have also been controlled for many years, an increase in both the number of vehicles and the amount of mileage the average vehicle is driven has offset to a large degree the gains achieved from the production of cleaner vehicles.

The desire to reduce mobile source pollution beyond what can be achieved with traditional emissions standards has motivated recent attempts to include them in emissions trading programmes designed to reduce ozone. Because remote sampling of in-use vehicles has confirmed that in many cases a substantial proportion of the mobile source pollution is coming from a relatively small number of vehicles (Bishop et al., 1993), one approach specifically targets those vehicles for early retirement[9] (Boyd, 1993; Kling, 1994).

In this approach, credits can be created by any source which acquires and retires high-emission vehicles. In California, for example, the UNOCAL Corporation, in cooperation with the California Air Resources Board, initiated a vehicle scrappage programme. Offering $700 for each pre-1971 vehicle, the programme was ultimately responsible for retiring some 8000 vehicles (Dudek, Goffman et al., 1992).

Vehicle retirement strategies are not the only way to include mobile sources within an emissions trading programme. A credit system can be used to provide manufacturers with an incentive to produce cleaner cars than required by law (Rubin and Kling, 1993) or to reward fleet operators for driving cleaner cars than required by law.

4. Analysing the evolution

Substituting for versus complementing traditional regulation

Whereas the early programmes complemented traditional regulation by making it more flexible, later programmes represent a more radical departure from traditional regulation. They are beginning to substitute for traditional regulation.

The earliest use of this concept, the emissions trading programme, overlaid credit trading on an existing regulatory regime and was designed to facilitate implementation of that programme. Trading baselines were determined on the basis of already-determined, technology-based standards and created credits could not be used to satisfy a number of these standards. The requisite technology had to be installed.

More recent programmes, such as the sulphur allowance and RECLAIM programmes, replace rather than complement traditional regulation. Allowance allocations for these programmes were not based on pre-existing technology-based standards. In the case of RECLAIM the control authority (the South Coast Air Quality Management District) could not have based allowances on predetermined standards even if they had been inclined to do so. Defining a complete set of technologies which offered the necessary environmental improvement and yet were feasible in both an economic and engineering sense proved impossible. Traditional regulation was incapable of providing the degree of reduction required by the Clean Air Act.

The solution was to define a set of allowances which would meet the environmental objectives, leaving the choice of methods for living within the constraints imposed by those allowances up to the sources covered by the regulations. This approach fundamentally changes the nature of the control process. The historical approach involved making the control authority responsible not only for defining the environmental objectives and performing the monitoring and enforcement activities necessary to ensure compliance with those objectives, but it was also assigned the responsibility for defining the best means for reaching those objectives. The allowance programme transfers the last of these responsibilities to the private sector, while retaining for the public sector both the responsibility for defining the environmental target and performing the monitoring and enforcement function.

Pursuing cost-effectiveness
A vast majority, though not all, of the relevant empirical studies in the United States have found the control costs to be substantially higher with the regulatory command-and-control system than the least-cost means of allocating the control responsibility (Tietenberg, 1985). This is an important finding because it provides the motivation for introducing a reform programme; the potential social gains (in terms of reduced control cost) from breaking away from the *status quo* are sufficient to justify the trouble. Although the estimates of the excess costs attributable to a command-and-control system presented in the numerous studies overstate the cost savings that would be achieved by even a completely unrestricted permit market (Tietenberg, 1990), the general conclusion that the potential cost savings from adopting economic incentive approaches are large seems accurate even after correcting for overstatement (Burtraw, 1996).

On the other hand, the earliest application, the emissions trading programme, has not produced the magnitude of cost savings that was anticipated by most proponents at its inception. The fraction of the permits that were traded was smaller than expected. Part of this failure to fulfil expectations can be explained as the result of unrealistically inflated expectations. More restrictive regulatory decisions than expected and higher than expected transaction costs also bear some responsibility (Hahn and Hester, 1989b).

The theoretical presumption that tradable permit markets are cost-effective assumes that all trades are multilateral and are simultaneously consummated. In practice in the emissions trading programme actual trades were usually bilateral and sequential. The amount of potential cost savings that is sacrificed in bilateral, sequential trading of non-uniformly mixed pollutants is apparently quite large (Atkinson and Tietenberg, 1991).

It also assumes that transactions costs of trading are low (Stavins, 1995). In the presence of significant transactions costs fewer trades are consummated and not all of the possible cost savings are exploited. Fortunately the magnitude of transactions costs can be reduced by incorporating appropriate design features into the programme.

Reducing transactions costs with programme design
Since the earliest experiment with transferable permits (the emissions trading programme) resulted in fewer trading opportunities than had been anticipated, it fell far short of achieving full cost-effectiveness. Yet, as revealed by later programmes, those shortfalls are not inevitable. Some of the high transactions costs which characterized the emissions trading programme can be reduced with proper programme design. One element, providing better information to participants, can be accomplished by ensuring that prices are public knowledge and that buyers and sellers can meet and contract easily.

One of the specific problems with the early system was that prices were determined in private during bilateral negotiations. Since the results of those negotiations were typically not publicly revealed, the prices associated with emission reduction credits (ERCs) were not generally known.

Inadequate knowledge about prices not only makes negotiations more complicated than necessary for the parties involved, but it makes pollution control investment planning more difficult for all sources. Since equilibrium prices should reflect marginal control costs, knowing these prices and how they are changing over time provides a great deal of information on the desirability of future control investments.

The sulphur allowance programme rectifies this deficiency by initiating both spot and future auctions for sulphur allowances. One of the side benefits of this action is that it reveals both current and future prices to everyone, thereby improving information considerably.

Another strategy for lowering transactions costs is providing a clearing-house for all buyers and sellers to learn about trading possibilities. 'One-stop shopping' for allowances represents a considerable improvement over the previous practice of hiring brokers to ferret out possible sources. While brokers were a market response to high transactions cost, providing a clearing-house makes it easier, quicker and cheaper for all parties.

Shifting the payoff
The demonstration that the traditional regulatory policy was not cost-effective had two mirror-image implications. It either implied that the same air-quality goals could be achieved at lower cost or that better air quality could be achieved at the same cost. While the earlier programmes were designed to exploit the first implication, later programmes attempted to produce better air quality and lower cost.

Trading programmes were used to produce better air quality in many ways. The lower costs offered by trading were used in initial negotiations to secure somewhat more stringent pollution control targets (acid rain programme and RECLAIM) or earlier deadlines (lead phase-out programme). Offset ratios for trades in non-attainment areas were set at a ratio greater than 1.0 (implying that a portion of each acquisition would go for better air quality). Environmental groups are allowed to purchase and retire sulphur allowances at the auction.

This shift toward sharing the benefits has had two consequences. The cost savings are lower than they would have been without this benefits sharing, but the public support, and particularly the support from environmental organizations, has been increased a great deal. Politically this means that it is now easier to implement trading programmes because the potential common ground has been expanded.

Coping with spatial issues
Transferable permits seem to have worked particularly well for trades involving uniformly mixed pollutants (those for which only the level of emissions matters) and for trades of non-uniformly mixed pollutants (those for which emission location also matters) involving contiguous discharge points. The plurality of consummated trades in the emissions trading programme have involved uniformly mixed pollutants. Since dispersion modelling is not required for uniformly mixed pollutants, even when the trading sources are somewhat distant from one another, trades involving these pollutants are cheaper to consummate. Additionally, trades involving uniformly mixed pollutants need not worry about local air-quality deterioration since the location of the emissions is not a matter of policy consequence.

But how about when emission location matters? When it does, the dominance of economic instruments over traditional command-and-control strategies is less clear-cut in practice than it might appear from theory.

Although the fully cost-effective system is relatively easy to define in this circumstance (Montgomery, 1972), implementing such a system imposes a large administrative burden. Since the economic and environmental benefits from allowing trading both in the short run and the long run (particularly their ability to stimulate technological progress and pollution prevention) are so large, attempts to implement 'second-best' designs are justified. (Second-best designs are those which attempt to solve the spatial problems with administratively simple rules.) While all second-best designs necessarily involve an element of compromise with the cost-effectiveness goal, they can still represent an improvement, sometimes a substantial improvement, over more traditional approaches.

The menu of promising second-best strategies is growing (Atkinson, 1994; Tietenberg, 1995; Klaassen, 1996). While the most commonly discussed second-best strategies all have problems, slight modifications of those approaches as embodied in this new generation of approaches do appear to offer the prospect of significant reductions in compliance costs, while ensuring environmental improvement.

While space does not permit an elaboration of all the possibilities here, one approach can be illustrated. The starting point for this approach is the assumption that it is better to implement a basic system built around standard emission permits, dealing individually with those trades which would result in hot spots or excess pollution at the most severely affected receptors, rather than establishing wholesale restrictions on trades.

One illustration of how this type of constrained trading could be implemented has surfaced in the United States in the trading rules developed by a new entity for controlling tropospheric ozone – the Ozone Transport Commission (OTC). Attempting to implement a truly regional strategy which deals realistically with the spatial elements of the problem, the one operating commission (with jurisdiction over the northeastern United States from Washington, DC to Maine) has allowed regional trading of NO_x offsets subject to some specific trading constraints.

Since the ozone plume typically moves in a particular direction and not all emissions in the region affect non-attainment status equally, without any constraints it would be possible for offset trades actually to worsen the degree of non-attainment. To allow interstate trading while ensuring environmental improvement in the most severely affected areas, the OTC plan imposes two restrictions on trading: (1) offsets must come from an area with equal or more severe non-attainment,[10] and (2) offsetting reductions must have contributed to violations of the ambient standard in the area of the new emissions. The first rule offers protection against trades which worsen pollution in the most severely affected areas, while the second rule in effect creates trading zones which conform to wind flow patterns.

Compared to an unrestricted trading area, these rules have the effect of reducing the size of trading areas and, hence, the number of possible trades. However, they do allow trades across large distances, while offering better environmental protection than an unrestricted system.

Sharing the risk

Risk sharing can be achieved even for very limited versions of transferable entitlement systems. In the United States, for example, some sulphur oxide control equipment manufacturers have indicated a willingness to install the pollution control equipment free of charge, taking only the sulphur oxide allowances in return.[11] In this way the recipient utility incurs neither a financial burden nor a financial risk. When the equipment supplier is willing to accept both by accepting the allowances as payment, his chances of making a sale are enhanced. In this way the price risk associated with allowances can be shifted to the party most willing and able to accept that risk.

Encouraging technological progress

Transferable permits encourage more technological progress in pollution control than the command-and-control system[12] (Milliman and Prince, 1989; Jung, Krutilla et al., 1996). The anecdotal evidence, and so far it is only that, seems to suggest that it not only bolsters the rate of change in pollution control, but also influences the direction and structure of control approaches.

In particular, allowances have facilitated the transition to new areas of pollution control, most notably pollution prevention. Whereas under traditional regulation firms saw their role as merely adopting the end-of-pipe technology suggested by the federal or state control authority, now they have begun to scrutinize their entire production process. Strategies which prevent pollution (such as process changes) free up valuable allowances and, hence, become more attractive to the adopting source.

Combining policy instruments

Should raising revenue become an important component in the coalition-building strategy followed by negotiators, revenue could be raised, even while using a grandfathered entitlement system, by levying a low annual fee on each entitlement. This revenue could be used for financing the monitoring and enforcement system, retained by the community or dedicated to other worthy purposes without jeopardizing the cost-effectiveness of the system.

Although an annual fee is not a necessary component of a transferable entitlement system, it can be added if so desired. This combined system would leave the control of emissions to the quantity-based entitlements, while using the fee to raise revenue.

Coupling a low annual fee with a free distribution of permits provides an attractive alternative to both auctioned entitlements and an emissions charge. Due to the political reluctance to establish rates as high as would be required to achieve conventional emission reduction targets, emission charges have traditionally not been very effective in producing the desired level of emission reduction. They have, however, been effective in raising revenue for environmental purposes, particularly in Europe (OECD, 1989). Conversely, while grandfathered entitlements have been effective in producing the desired level of control, they produce no revenue. The combined system provides more assurance of sufficient emission reduction, while raising revenue.

Since per unit annual fees applied to the emissions authorized by the allowances do not affect the cost-effectiveness of the system, the fee can be as low or as high as necessary to achieve the desired revenue result. While the fees do lower the entitlement price, they do not affect the incentive to trade. Although the entitlement price is lowered by the existence of a fee, the incentive to trade is preserved by the fact that a seller not only receives the price for the entitlement, but is able to avoid paying the annual fee any longer on the transferred entitlements. The buyer is exactly compensated by the lower price for the fact that he now has to pay the fee.

Merging equity with cost-effectiveness
Because transferable entitlement systems allow the issue of who will pay for control to be separated from who will undertake control, they allow distributional and cost-effectiveness goals to be pursued simultaneously.[13] Distributional issues can, in principle, be handled by the initial permit allocation, while the subsequent trading produces cost-effectiveness.

Regardless of the initial allocation of permits, gains from trade would continue to exist until the unique cost-effective allocation was achieved. This is a particularly important feature when concerns about fairness and affordability preclude simple solutions such as equal proportional reductions.[14] Even very complex allocations of the control responsibilities which are sensitive to a host of individual fairness concerns can be fully compatible with achieving the desired emission target at the lowest possible cost.

Application to developing countries?
While no definitive answer can be given to this question because developing-country implementation experience is limited, some grounds for optimism exist. To start with, it certainly appears that attempts to use this

type of system in a developing-country context are merited if the regulatory infrastructure is sufficient. In developing countries, where the opportunity cost of capital is high, it makes especially good sense to ensure that investments (including pollution control investments) are made wisely. The cost-effectiveness properties of tradable permits are especially important in capital-scarce economies. Furthermore, the powerful incentive effects provided by transferable permits could stimulate much more rapid development and implementation of new, innovative control technologies and strategies such as pollution prevention. By stimulating technological progress, a transferable permits approach can contribute to the lowering of long-run, as well as short-run, costs. These potential costs savings should provide considerable motivation to adapt the strategy for use in developing countries.

Transferable permits also offer the possibility of raising revenue for environmental protection in countries where government revenue is a serious constraint. Combining fees with transferable permits allows an additional source of funding. In the United States at the moment much of the financial responsibility for funding the monitoring and enforcement system has been transferred from the taxpayers to the pollution sources by means of fees on permits.

The most serious concerns about the transferability of this approach to developing countries have to do with whether developing countries have sufficient organizational resources to run this approach (Lyons, 1989). When this question is raised, the questioner is usually making the implicit assumption that the organizational resources in developing countries are homogeneous and insufficient. They are not homogeneous, of course. Some countries have sufficient resources now, while others could use a programme such as this to begin the process of accumulating sufficient resources over time, little by little.

My experience in the United States leads me to believe that the infrastructure which would be necessary to run a transferable permit programme is not, over the long run, greater than that necessary to run an equally effective traditional regulation system, but the nature of the infrastructure may differ.

One misleading myth about conventional regulation holds that merely verifying (1) that the correct control equipment has been acquired by the source, and (2) that it has been installed correctly, is a sufficient enforcement strategy. While it is possible to set up a regulatory system where enforcement takes this form, those systems are rarely effective (Russell et al., 1986). Initial compliance does not ensure continuing compliance. Installing the right equipment certainly does not guarantee that it is operated and maintained correctly; effective enforcement requires continuous monitoring of some form. In this respect transferable permits and traditional regulation share the same requirements.

As a practical matter, however, reasonable monitoring systems are not very burdensome for the control authority. Most emissions monitoring is based upon a system of self-reporting (Russell et al., 1986). Though self-reporting systems immediately raise concerns about possible abuse, in practice they work remarkably well, particularly when complemented by an effective system of criminal penalties for falsification.

Furthermore, it is possible to design limited-resource enforcement systems which can be quite effective (Harrington, 1988; Russell et al., 1986). The secret to this design is to target more resources on repeat offenders. Among other characteristics, this approach discourages sources from becoming repeat offenders, so that they can avoid the hassle of intense scrutiny.

But the skills involved in running these two types of programmes are rather different. Under traditional regulation the responsibility for defining appropriate control technologies falls on the regulatory authority. With transferable permits it falls on the private sources. Therefore with transferable permits the control authorities need fewer staff trained in environmental engineering. The remainder could be dedicated to the monitoring and enforcement functions.

Finally, the public monitoring and enforcement infrastructure can be bolstered by allowing some degree of private enforcement (Naysnerski and Tietenberg, 1992). Allowing private enforcement to complement public enforcement increases the amount of resources dedicated to monitoring and enforcement and allows public resources to be used more effectively. And an effective self-reporting system, as described above, makes this private enforcement possible. Some forms of private enforcement have already made inroads in Latin America (Tietenberg, 1996).

It will probably not be long before we have implementation experience from developing countries. Chile has recently passed an Environmental Framework Law which requires the use of transferable permits (O'Ryan, 1996). In its effort to implement this law Santiago is likely to become the world leader in crafting versions of this approach which are appropriate in a developing-country context. At that point we will thankfully be able to replace speculation with experience.

Notes

1.   In the limited space permitted in this chapter only a few highlights can be illustrated. All the details of the proofs and the empirical work can be found in the references. For a comprehensive summary of this work see Tietenberg (1985); Dudek and Palmisano (1988); Hahn (1989); Hahn and Hester (1989a and b); Tietenberg (1990); Klaassen (1996).

2. The interested reader can find the details of the system at 40 Code of Federal Regulations 82.
3. Note that this approach does not require that both trading countries have implemented a transferable permit system. It does require both countries to adjust their production and consumption quotas assigned under the protocols to ensure that the overall global limits on production and consumption are not affected by the trades. The European Union has also implemented a tradable permits scheme for ozone-depleting chemicals. See Council Regulation (EEC) No. 594/91 of 4 March 1991 on substances that deplete the ozone layer, *Official Journal of the European Communities*, 14.3.91.
4. This statute became law on 15 November 1990. See 104 Stat § 2584. For an analysis of the application of the emissions trading concept to acid rain see Atkinson (1983); Oates and McGartland (1985); Feldman and Raufer (1987); Tietenberg (1989); Klaassen and Førsund (1994); Klaassen (1995; 1996).
5. The details of the acid rain programme can be found in 40 Code of Federal Regulations 73.
6. The data in this section came from the EPA web site located at: (http://www.epa.gov/acidrain/auctions/auc97tlk.html
7. For further details on RECLAIM, consult the South Coast Air Quality Management web site at: http://www.aqmd.gov/
8. These data are from the RECLAIM web site located at: http://www.aqmd.gov/news/recaudit.html (28 March 1997).
9. Interim EPA guidance for mobile source crediting can be found in 58 Federal Register 11134 (23 February 1993).
10. Non-attainment areas are further classified into one of five categories depending on current ozone concentration levels (marginal, moderate, serious, severe and extreme). These designations affect both the deadlines for achieving the ambient ozone standards and the rules affecting offset trading.
11. I am indebted to Dan Dudek of the Environmental Defense Fund for pointing this out.
12. The analysis also suggests, however, that a grandfathered permit system produces less of an incentive for technological progress than either an emission charge or a system where all permits are auctioned off (Jung, Krutilla et al., 1996).
13. To be more precise, as long as transactions costs are low under normal convexity assumptions for uniformly mixed pollutants in perfectly competitive markets, the cost-effective allocation of control responsibility will be reached regardless of how the fixed number of permits is allocated among the sources in a grandfathered system. However, when transactions costs are high, this ability simultaneously to pursue both goals may not hold (Stavins, 1995).
14. Consider an example of how this feature can be used. Suppose a source is in such a financially precarious position that installing any control will force its prices to a non-competitive level. Traditional systems of control usually protect existing jobs by exempting this source from anything more than nominal control. With transferable permits this source could sell its permits, using the revenue from the sale to finance the control investment. It could install the control without having to raise prices because the cost of control is actually borne by the source which acquires its newly freed-up permits. In this case the jobs are still protected, but control costs are lowered by bringing this source under control as an alternative to ratcheting up control on other, already heavily controlled sources.

References

Atkinson, S.E. (1983), 'Marketable pollution permits and acid rain externalities', *Canadian Journal of Economics*, **16** (4), 704–22.

Atkinson, S.E. (1994), 'Tradable discharge permits: restrictions on least cost solutions', in *Economic Instruments for Air Pollution Control*, G. Klaassen and F.R. Førsund, Boston: Kluwer Academic Publishers, pp. 3–21.

Atkinson, S.E. and T.H. Tietenberg (1991), 'Market failure in incentive-based regulation: the case of emissions trading', *Journal of Environmental Economics and Management*, **21** (1), 17–31.

Bishop, G.A., D. Stedman et al. (1993), 'A cost-effectiveness study of carbon monoxide emissions reduction utilizing remote sensing', *Air and Waste*, **43**, 978–85.

Boyd, J.D. (1993), 'Mobile source emissions reduction credits as a cost-effective measure for controlling urban air pollution', in F. Kosobud, W.A. Testa and D.A. Hanson (eds), *Cost-Effective Control of Urban Smog*, Chicago: Federal Reserve Bank of Chicago.

Burtraw, D. (1996), 'The SO_2 emissions trading program: cost savings without allowance trades', *Contemporary Economic Policy*, **14** (2), 79–94.

Cason, T.N. (1993), 'Seller incentive properties of EPA's emission trading auction', *Journal of Environmental Economics and Management*, **25** (2), 177–95.

Conrad, K. and R.E. Kohn (1996), 'The US market for SO_2 permits – policy implications of the low price and trading volume', *Energy Policy*, **24** (12), 1051–9.

Dudek, D.J. and J. Palmisano (1988), 'Emissions trading: why is this thoroughbred hobbled?', *Columbia Journal of Environmental Law*, **13** (2), 217–56.

Dudek, D., J. Goffman et al. (1992), *Mobile Emissions Reduction Crediting*, New York: Environmental Defense Fund and General Motors.

Feldman, S.L. and R.K. Raufer (1987), *Emissions Trading and Acid Rain: Implementing a Market Approach to Pollution Control*, Totawa, NJ: Rowman & Littlefield.

Hahn, R.W. (1989), 'Economic prescriptions for environmental problems: how the patient followed the doctor's orders', *The Journal of Economic Perspectives*, **3** (2), 95–114.

Hahn, R.W. and G.L. Hester (1989a), 'Marketable permits: lessons from theory and practice', *Ecology Law Quarterly*, **16**, 361–406.

Hahn, R.W. and G.L. Hester (1989b), 'Where did all the markets go? An analysis of EPA's emission trading program', *Yale Journal of Regulation*, **6** (1), 109–53.

Hall, J.V. and A.L. Walton (1996), 'A case study in pollution markets: dismal science vs. dismal reality', *Contemporary Economic Policy*, **XIV** (2), 67–78.

Harrington, W. (1988), 'Enforcement leverage when penalties are restricted', *Journal of Public Economics*, **37**, 29–53.

Hausker, K. (1992), 'The politics and economics of auction design in the market for sulfur dioxide pollution', *Journal of Policy Analysis and Management*, **11** (4), 553–72.

Johnson, S.L. and D.M. Pekelney (1996), 'Economic assessment of the regional clean air incentives market: a new emissions trading program for Los Angeles', *Land Economics*, **72** (3), 277–97.

Jung, C.H., K. Krutilla et al. (1996), 'Incentives for advanced pollution abatement technology at the industry level: an evaluation of policy alternatives', *Journal of Environmental Economics and Management*, **30** (1), 95–111.

Kete, N. (1992), 'The U.S. acid rain control allowance trading system', in T. Jones and J. Corfee-Morlot (eds), *Climate Change: Designing a Tradeable Permit System*, Paris: OECD, pp. 69–93.

Kete, N. (1994), 'Air pollution control in the United States: a mixed portfolio approach', in G. Klaassen and F.R. Førsund (eds), *Economic Instruments for Air Pollution Control*, Boston: Kluwer Academic Publishers, pp. 122–44.

Klaassen, G. (1995), 'Trade-offs in sulfur emission trading in Europe', *Environmental and Resource Economics*, **5** (2), 191–219.

Klaassen, G. (1996), *Acid Rain and Environmental Degradation: The Economics of Emission Trading*, Cheltenham, UK and Brookfield, US: Edward Elgar.

Klaassen, G. and F.R. Førsund (eds) (1994), *Economic Instruments for Air Pollution Control*, Boston: Kluwer Academic Publishers.

Kling, C.L. (1994), 'Emission trading vs rigid regulations in the control of vehicle emissions', *Land Economics*, **70** (2), 174–88.

Lyon, R.M. (1989), 'Transferable discharge permit systems and environmental management in developing countries', *World Development*, **17** (8), 1299–1312.

Milliman, S.R. and R. Prince (1989), 'Firm incentives to promote technological change in pollution control', *Journal of Environmental Economical Management*, **17** (3), 247–65.

Montgomery, W.D. (1972), 'Markets in licences and efficient pollution control programs', *Journal of Economic Theory*, **5** (3), 395–418.

Naysnerski, W. and T. Tietenberg (1992), 'Private enforcement of environmental law', *Land Economics*, **68** (1), 28–48.

Nussbaum, B.D. (1992), 'Phasing down lead in gasoline in the U.S.: mandates, incentives, trading and banking', in T. Jones and J. Corfee-Morlot (eds), *Climate Change: Designing a Tradeable Permit System*, Paris: OECD, pp. 21–34.

Oates, W.E. and A.M. McGartland (1985), 'Marketable pollution permits and acid rain externalities: a comment and some further evidence', *Canadian Journal of Economics*, **18** (3), 668–75.

OECD (1989), *Economic Instruments for Environmental Protection*, Paris: OECD.

O'Ryan, R. (1996), 'Cost-effective policies to improve urban air quality in Santiago, Chile', *Journal of Environmental Economics and Management*, **31** (3), 302–13.

Rico, R. (1995), 'The U.S. allowance trading system for sulfur dioxide: an update on market experience', *Environmental and Resource Economics*, **5** (2), 115–29.

Robinson, K. (1993), 'The regional economic impacts of marketable permit programs: the case of Los Angeles' in R.F. Kosobud, W.A. Testa and D.A. Hanson (eds), *Cost-Effective Control of Urban Smog*, Chicago: Federal Reserve Bank of Chicago.

Rubin, J. and C. Kling (1993), 'An emission saved is an emission earned: an empirical study of emission banking for light-duty vehicle manufacturers', *Journal of Environmental Economics and Management*, **25** (3), 257–74.

Russell, C., W. Harrington et al. (1986), *Enforcing Pollution Control Laws*, Washington, DC: Resources for the Future Inc.

Stavins, R.N. (1995), 'Transaction costs and tradable permits', *Journal of Environmental Economics and Management*, **29** (2), 133–48.

Stavins, R. and R. Hahn (1993), *Trading in Greenhouse Permits: A Critical Examination of Design and Implementation Issues*, Cambridge, MA: John F. Kennedy School of Government, Harvard University.

Tietenberg, T.H. (1985), *Emissions Trading: An Exercise in Reforming Pollution Policy*, Washington, DC: Resources for the Future.

Tietenberg, T.H. (1989), 'Acid rain reduction credits', *Challenge*, **32** (2), 25–9.

Tietenberg, T.H. (1990), 'Economic instruments for environmental regulations', *Oxford Review of Economic Policy*, **6** (1), 17–33.

Tietenberg, T.H. (1995), 'Tradable permits for pollution control when emission location matters: what have we learned?', *Environmental and Resource Economics*, **5** (2), 95–113.

Tietenberg, T.H. (1996), 'Private enforcement of environmental regulations in Latin America and the Caribbean: an effective instrument for environmental protection?', report written for the Inter-American Development Bank, Washington, DC (February).

20 The double dividend of an environmental tax reform

Ruud A. de Mooij[1]

1. Introduction

Recently, environmental tax reforms have received increasing attention from economists. The question is whether a shift from ordinary taxes on income towards pollution taxes can improve the quality of the environment and, at the same time, enhance the efficiency of taxation as a revenue-raising device. This is called the double-dividend hypothesis. This chapter sheds some light on this debate by discussing the theoretical and empirical literature on the double-dividend hypothesis. Furthermore, it elaborates on some political-economy aspects that have as yet received little attention in this literature.

2. Theory of second-best environmental taxation

In his seminal book, Pigou has shown that pollution taxes are able to internalize the adverse externalities associated with polluting activities (Pigou, 1947). Indeed, in a first-best world without other distortions it is optimal to set the pollution tax equal to the marginal environmental damage from pollution. The revenue of this so-called Pigouvian tax is assumed to be returned to economic agents in a lump sum fashion.

In a second-best world with pre-existing tax distortions things are different. In particular, public finance theory tells us that replacing distortionary taxes on labour or capital by lump sum taxes yields an improvement in the efficiency of the tax system as a revenue-raising device. This is because lump sum taxes do not drive a wedge between producer and consumer prices and thus leave the allocation of goods unchanged. Some authors have used this result to argue that raising pollution taxes and using the revenues to cut other distortionary taxes – rather than lump sum taxes as in the world of Pigou – improves welfare on both environmental and non-environmental grounds. This claim is referred to as the double dividend of an environmental tax reform (ETR), that is, it exerts two dividends: an environmental (or *green*) dividend and a non-environmental (or *blue*) dividend.

Broadly speaking, the literature distinguishes three definitions of the double dividend (see Table 20.1). All versions define the green dividend as follows: environmental welfare after the ETR is higher than before the ETR. The three versions of the double dividend differ with respect to

Table 20.1   Three definitions of the double dividend

DOUBLE DIVIDEND	= GREEN DIVIDEND	+ BLUE DIVIDEND
Weak double dividend	Environmental welfare higher than before ETR	Non-environmental welfare higher than with lump sum recycling
Strong double dividend	Environmental welfare higher than before ETR	Non-environmental welfare higher than before ETR
Employment double dividend	Environmental welfare higher than before ETR	Employment higher than before ETR

the blue dividend. First, a *weak double dividend* is obtained if recycling the revenues from the environmental tax through lower distortionary taxes yields higher non-environmental welfare than recycling the revenues in a lump sum fashion. Second, a *strong double dividend* occurs if non-environmental welfare in the equilibrium after the ETR is higher than before the ETR. Finally, an *employment double dividend* is obtained if employment after the ETR is higher than before the ETR.[2]

In general, economists agree about the green dividend, that is, an ETR will improve the quality of the environment. Furthermore, there is broad support for the weak version of the double dividend. Hence economists tend to prefer using the revenues from environmental taxes to reduce distortionary taxes rather than recycling them in a lump sum fashion.[3] The strong double dividend and the employment double dividend, however, have been heavily debated in recent economic literature. To illustrate, Pearce (1991) and Repetto et al. (1992) have argued that we can clean up the environment and improve the tax system by imposing a reform from labour towards pollution taxation. Bovenberg and de Mooij (1994a), however, show that this is typically not true because environmental taxes are more likely to exacerbate, rather than alleviate, pre-existing tax distortions. How can this disagreement between the proponents and opponents of the double dividend be understood?

Parry (1995a) explains the difference in views by the use of different methodologies, namely, partial versus general equilibrium approaches. In particular, Parry shows that partial equilibrium models – used by the proponents of the double dividend – ignore the interactions between environmental taxes and pre-existing tax distortions. These so-called 'tax-interdependence' effects are responsible for the failure of the double dividend in general equilibrium models. Indeed, Bovenberg and de Mooij use a general equilibrium framework to show that an ETR may reduce employment and blue welfare (in the strong sense). The reason is that environmental taxes interact with the labour market. Intuitively, the incidence of environmental taxes is borne by labour incomes. Accordingly, labour taxes and environmental taxes distort labour-supply decisions in a similar way. The direct labour tax, however, is more efficient from a revenue-raising perspective than the environmental tax because the latter tax also changes the composition of consumption over clean and polluting commodities, thereby eroding the tax base. Hence, viewed from a non-environmental perspective, environmental taxes involve a higher excess burden. The presence of distortionary labour taxes thus makes it less attractive for the government to rely on environmental taxes for revenue-raising purposes. Hence the strong (employment) double dividend fails. For a survey on the double-dividend literature, see Bovenberg (1995 and 1997), Goulder (1995), Oates (1995), de Mooij (1996) and de Mooij and Vollebergh (1995).

The second-best optimal environmental tax
An alternative approach to the double dividend is the second-best optimal-tax literature. The optimal environmental tax – first derived by Sandmo (1976) and later used by Bovenberg and van der Ploeg (1994a) – can be written as follows:

$$T^* = \left(1 - \frac{1}{\eta}\right)T^R + \frac{1}{\eta}T^P \qquad (20.1)$$

Expression (20.1) reflects the twofold task of the tax system. It reveals that the optimal environmental tax, T^*, is determined by two terms. First, the so-called Ramsey component, T^R, which denotes the revenue-raising task of environmental taxes. The second term on the right-hand side of (20.1) represents the so-called Pigouvian component, T^P, related to the externality-correcting task of the environmental tax. The term η stands for the so-called marginal cost of public funds (MCF). The MCF measures how scarce public funds are relative to private funds. In particular, if the government requires distortionary taxes to raise revenues, public funds are scarcer than private funds, so that the MCF lies above unity.

Expression (20.1) reveals that the weights the government assigns to its revenue-raising task and the environmental task depend on the MCF. In particular, a more distortionary tax system – reflected by a higher value of η – increases the weight of the Ramsey component and reduces the weight of the Pigouvian component. Intuitively, a more distortionary tax system makes it less attractive for the government to use taxes aimed at correcting externalities and makes it more urgent to use taxes that raise revenues with lowest cost to private incomes. This result from the optimal-tax literature is consistent with the results from the tax-reform literature discussed above. For a discussion about the optimal environmental tax in relation to the double dividend, see Fullerton (1997) and Bovenberg and de Mooij (1997a).

Opportunities for an employment double dividend
The conclusion that the employment double dividend and the strong double dividend fail is not a general result, however. Indeed, the literature provides several general equilibrium channels through which an ETR can yield a strong double dividend or an employment double dividend. The channels that may be favourable for an employment double dividend include the following:

1. An ETR may alleviate non-tax labour market distortions associated with union power or efficiency wages. Indeed, in models with an imperfect labour market, wages are too high from a pure efficiency point of view. If a shift between different taxes induces wage moderation – for example because unions bid for lower wages in return for a cleaner environment – it boosts employment (see Brunello, 1996; Carraro et al., 1996) and improves non-environmental welfare. Note that ETRs can also exacerbate these non-tax labour market distortions. Indeed, some empirical models suggest that labour market imperfections have unfavourable implications for the double-dividend opportunities (see, for example, Proost and van Regemorter, 1995).
2. In an open economy, an ETR may induce a shift in tax incidence from the home country towards foreigners through changes in the terms of trade. In particular, if the price of export goods rises due to an ETR, foreigners will share in the tax burden imposed by the home country. This may be beneficial for the home country but comes at the cost of foreigners (see, for example, de Mooij et al., 1997). Note that the terms-of-trade effect is irrelevant for a small open economy that supplies homogeneous goods to the world market. Indeed, a small open economy cannot influence world market prices and is thus unable to shift the tax burden to foreigners (Bovenberg and de Mooij, 1994c).
3. In the case where an ETR towards energy taxes is internationally co-ordinated, a reduction in energy demand in the participating countries may induce a fall in pre-tax world energy prices. In this way, part of the tax burden is shifted on to energy suppliers through an effect on the terms of trade. Note that lower world energy prices may induce so-

called carbon leakage effects because non-participating countries will use more energy if energy prices fall. This may reduce the environmental dividend.

4. The environment may not only act as a consumption good (that is, as an element in the utility function), but also as a capital good that determines production possibilities in the economy. In that case, an ETR may boost the productivity of private factors of production because it raises the supply of the public investment good of the environment (see Bovenberg and de Mooij, 1997b).

5. An ETR may boost labour supply if environmental quality is a much better substitute for leisure than for consumption commodities. In contrast, if environmental quality is a poorer substitute for leisure, a cleaner environment induces people to enjoy more leisure and thus to reduce labour supply (see Bovenberg, 1997).

6. An ETR may boost employment if it shifts the tax burden from labour towards immobile capital. Indeed, with more than one immobile factor of production, it is efficient to share the tax burden among the various production factors. The initial tax system is inefficient if it overtaxes labour. A shift from labour taxes towards pollution taxes then amounts to a shift in tax incidence from labour towards the other immobile factor, thereby improving the efficiency of taxation (see Bovenberg and van der Ploeg, 1996; de Mooij and Bovenberg, 1998).

7. Environmental taxes may be borne by incomes that are raised in the informal economy, that is, activities that are not taxed by direct income taxes. A swap of environmental taxes for income taxes then shifts the tax burden towards the incomes from informal activities. This may improve the efficiency of the tax system and boost employment (see Bovenberg and van der Ploeg, 1998).

8. The revenues from environmental taxes can also be employed to reduce other taxes than those on labour income. To illustrate, de Mooij and Bovenberg (1998) show that an ETR away from capital taxes, rather than labour taxes, may boost employment. The reason is that the initial tax system may be inefficient from a revenue-raising point of view by overtaxing (mobile) capital. An ETR is then able to correct for these inefficiencies by shifting the burden of taxation from the overtaxed factor (capital) towards the undertaxed factor (labour). Other recycling options that are potentially favourable for the double dividend involve investment subsidies or positive R&D incentives (see, for example, Grubb et al., 1993).

All the channels mentioned here suggest that an ETR may yield a double dividend through several economic mechanisms. These insights can be helpful in understanding the results from larger empirical models employed in the double-dividend debate which are discussed below.

3.   Empirical studies on the double dividend

Empirical macroeconomic models for economic policy analysis have been used extensively to investigate whether an ETR can yield a double dividend, in particular an employment double dividend. These empirical/simulation studies yield several interesting insights, both in qualitative and quantitative terms. This section discusses these insights. The numerical outcomes from some macroeconomic models are reported in Table 20.2. This table presents the long-run effects on employment and welfare of several policy proposals. They mainly apply to Europe because European economies in particular suffer from severe labour market problems.

The CPB Netherlands Bureau for Economic Policy Analysis has explored the consequences of three types of environmental tax reform (CPB, 1992): an OECD-wide tax on all energy use; a unilateral tax in the Netherlands on all energy use; and a unilateral tax in the Netherlands on small-scale energy use. To analyse these policies, CPB adopted the Athena model – a multisectoral econometric model – linked to an energy submodel called CENECA. The effects of a 100 per cent energy tax (implying a doubling of the user price of energy) recycled through lower taxes on labour are presented in the first row of Table 20.2. We see that the first two simulations indicate a large drop in employment in the Netherlands. The fall in employment in the second experiment is more substantial than in the first. In the third experiment, employment remains more or less constant.

Two important conclusions can be drawn from these outcomes. First, a unilateral tax in the Netherlands implies a larger reduction in employment than a coordinated tax reform in all OECD countries. The reason is that a coordinated tax is less detrimental to the competitive position of Dutch industries, relative to its competitors in the OECD. Second, exempting large-scale users mitigates the fall in employment. Hence, whereas a shift from labour taxes towards energy taxes on households is almost neutral with respect to employment, a shift towards taxes on energy-intensive industries involves the destruction of a large number of jobs. The main reason for this is that firms relocate to other regions if a unilateral tax on Dutch industries is imposed.

Environmental taxes on industries

The conclusion that unilateral energy taxes deteriorate the competitive position of domestic industries has been widely discussed in empirical models. Some studies find that these effects are substantial, such as the CPB study above. Other studies, however, predict much smaller effects. To illustrate, simulations with the OECD's GREEN model suggest that an EU-wide energy tax of $10 on all energy use would imply a boost in energy use elsewhere – caused by relocation of firms – of only 11 per cent. Besides, the macroeconomic effects for the EU are small (see Burniaux et al., 1992).[4] Simulations with CPB's WorldScan model also indicate that the macroeconomic effects of an energy tax in the EU are small. However, sectoral shifts can be substantial. In order to prevent such sectoral shifts, governments might introduce border-tax adjustments, such as import tariffs or export subsidies. Accordingly, sectoral shifts are mitigated, the competitive position of participating countries is maintained, and carbon leakage can be prevented (see de Mooij et al., 1997).

Another important element that may support the double-dividend hypothesis of an ETR is technological progress. In particular, den Butter et al. (1995) find positive effects on employment in a model for the Netherlands with endogenous energy-saving technology. The reason is that an ETR stimulates energy-saving technological progress at the cost of labour-saving technologies. Accordingly, an employment double dividend can be obtained, although the strong double dividend fails. The role of technological progress is also emphasized in the WARM model (Brunello, 1996) and in simulations for the Austrian Economy (Köppl et al., 1995).

Experiments with the WARM model and also the calculation from CPB (1992) suggest that the short-term effects of environmental tax reforms may differ from the long-term consequences. Indeed, lower taxes on labour may reduce wage costs in the presence of real wage resistance, which is typically relevant in the short run for some European countries (Brunello, 1996). In the long run, wage resistance tends to be less important. Hence, by reducing wage costs, an ETR may stimulate employment, especially in the short term (see Carraro et al., 1996).

Environmental taxes on households
An ETR towards pollution taxes on households suffers less from the adverse consequences for the competitive position of industries. Accordingly, most studies that have analysed this tax find smaller effects on employment (see, for example, CPB, 1992 and 1993). The QUEST model even predicts a rise in employment of about 0.1 per cent if an EU-wide tax on small-scale energy use is introduced and at the same time the labour tax is cut (CEC, 1992). In a more recent study, QUEST predicts an even larger boost in employment, namely by 2 per cent. In this latter study, the revenues of the energy tax are targeted at reducing the labour costs for low-skilled workers. This is found to be a more effective way of revenue recycling than a general tax cut (EC, 1994). Indeed, shifting the burden of taxation from low-skilled workers towards high-skilled workers may boost

Table 20.2 Effects of an ETR on employment in different models

Study	Energy tax design	Revenue recycling	Green welfare (energy use)	Blue welfare (private income or NNI)	Blue welfare (employment)
CPB (1992)	1. 100% general tax in OECD	Income tax	−35% in NL	−7%	−3.0% in NL
	2. 100% general tax in NL		−50% in NL	−6%	−5.0% in NL
	3. 100% household tax in NL		−5.5% in NL	−0.7%	−0.2% in NL
De Mooij and Bovenberg (1998)	10% tax on firms in NL	1. Labour tax 2. Capital tax	−6.5% in NL −5.7% in NL	−0.2% in NL +0.6 in NL	−0.1% in NL +0.1% in NL
Den Butter et al. (1995)	1. 50% general tax in NL	Social security premiums of employers	−22.3% in NL	−0.7% in NL	+1.0% in NL
	2. 50% household tax in NL		−9.7% in NL	+0.1% in NL	+0.1% in NL
Brunello (1996)	General tax of 19 ECU per ton CO_2 in EU	Payroll tax			+1% short run +3% long run
Köppl et al. (1995)	General tax, c.f. Austrian CO_2 committee proposal	1. Payroll tax 2. Idem + tech-nology stimulus	−4.6% in Aus. −5.4% in Aus.	0.1% in Aus. −0.3% in Aus.	−0.2% in Aus. +0.4% in Aus.

CEC (1992)	$10 tax per barrel on EU households	Labour tax			+0.1% in EU
EC (1994)	CO_2 tax of 1.1% GDP in EU	Tax on low-paid			+2.0% in EU
Bovenberg and de Mooij (1994b)	100% household tax in NL	1. Tax on labour	−10.5% in NL	+0.01% in NL	+1.0% in NL
		2. Tax on income (labour + social benefits)	−11.6% in NL	−0.7% in NL	−0.1% in NL

Note: Aus. = Austria; NL = Netherlands.

employment because it reduces the inefficiencies associated with the poverty trap. This argument, however, ignores the negative consequences of high marginal tax rates for middle- and high-income workers (see, for example, Bovenberg and van der Ploeg, 1994b; Lindbeck, 1994).

In the case of an ETR on households, Bovenberg and de Mooij (1994b) show that there is a close relationship between the effect on employment and the consequences for the income distribution between workers and inactive people. For instance, an energy tax on households bears on both workers and people receiving a social benefit. If the revenues from the environmental tax are used to compensate only workers through lower labour taxes, the ETR amounts to a shift in the tax burden from workers towards transfer recipients. Such a shift will be beneficial for employment and for the efficiency of taxation, but comes at the expense of a less equitable income distribution. Indeed, a rise in employment in the Bovenberg and de Mooij model is typically associated with a shift in incomes from outsiders – such as unemployed or elderly people – towards people inside the labour force. Once the government also compensates transfer recipients for the loss in purchasing power, the rise in employment vanishes (see also CPB, 1993). An ETR thus seems to be able to alleviate initial inefficiencies associated with the redistributive device of the tax system, thereby producing an employment double dividend. One should keep in mind, however, that inefficiencies associated with the redistribution of income are present for non-economic reasons such as equity. This brings us to the debate on the political economy of the double dividend.

4.   Political-economy issues and the double dividend

Coase has argued that a market economy is – even in the presence of environmental externalities – able to arrive at the optimal allocation of goods (Coase, 1960). A crucial condition in Coase's theorem is that the property rights of environment are well defined. In that case, polluters negotiate with victims about the amount of pollution and a financial transfer to the owner of the property rights. In reality, transactions costs impede direct negotiations between polluters and victims. Therefore, the government usually represents the interests of the victims in negotiations with polluters.

In Coase's theorem, the distribution of property rights is irrelevant for environmental quality. For the distribution of incomes and wealth between polluters and victims, however, the distribution of property rights matters. The current distribution of property rights in most European countries is determined by a continuous process of negotiations between polluters and governments (representing the victims). This merely translates into a political discussion about the choice of environmental policy instruments used by the government. In particular, by deciding about the environmental policy instrument, the government implicitly determines the distribution of property rights. To illustrate, if the government imposes environmental taxes, the government owns the property rights. In that case, polluters transfer money to the victims (represented by the government) to compensate for the welfare loss caused by the pollution.

One should keep in mind that distributional issues, rather than efficiency, often dominate the political discussions about environmental policy instruments. Environmental taxes are unattractive instruments in this respect because they assign all property rights to the government. Indeed, compared to the *status quo* – in which most polluters do not have to pay for emissions – an environmental tax would amount to a redistribution of property rights from polluters towards the government. This is against the interest of polluters. Even if the revenues from environmental taxes are recycled through reductions in other taxes, shifts in incomes often cannot be prevented so that particular agents will be worse off. To illustrate, an ETR away from taxes that bear on labour income but not on transfer income will benefit workers at the expense of jobless or elderly people.

Such changes in the income distribution are at the heart of the double-dividend debate. The fundamental reason why the government adopts distortionary taxes is equity. Indeed, without equity considerations, a government that strives for efficiency should rely on non-distortionary lump sum taxes, rather than distortionary taxes. Hence there is a fundamental trade-off between equity and efficiency: improving efficiency by shifting from distortionary taxes towards lump sum taxes is difficult because it reduces equity. An ETR can also reduce the inefficiencies associated with the redistributive device of the tax system. However, this boils down to an indirect way to change the efficiency/equity trade-off. Such a double dividend ignores the social welfare related to society's aversion to income inequality. If these values are incorporated into the analysis, the welfare implications of environmental tax reforms may change (see, for example, Proost and van Regemorter, 1995; Mayeres and Proost, 1997).

Political feasibility related to equity can sometimes be reconciled with the pure efficiency argument of the tax instrument. Shifts in incomes can be minimized, for instance, if tax recycling is targeted at the polluters, for example through tax exemptions or targeted subsidies.[5] Alternatively, the introduction of environmental taxes can be part of a package of reducing tax levels so that everyone benefits from the total tax reform. In general, the government should focus on minimizing the political barriers associated with the redistribution of property rights. This means that it should not concentrate on the blue dividend when recycling the revenues from environmental taxes. Rather, it should emphasize the green dividend – a cleaner environment.

Unfortunately, the role of the green dividend often takes second place in policy debates on ETRs. Nevertheless, these benefits can be a crucial element for the political feasibility of an ETR and for the double dividend. To illustrate, Bovenberg and van Hagen (1996) show that the distribution of environmental benefits over heterogeneous agents may increase the possibility of a double dividend. Indeed, if poor households feature a relatively high concern for the environment and consume relatively little of the polluting commodity, an environmental tax that is recycled through lower labour taxes may produce a double dividend (that is, reduce inefficiencies associated with the redistributive device of the tax system) while still maintaining the distribution of welfare in a broad sense – including environmental welfare. Intuitively, the environmental tax itself acts as a second-best redistributive device. The study by Bovenberg and van Hagen thus shows that the environmental benefits are perhaps the core dividend that deserves much more attention than in previous discussions.

5. Conclusions
An ETR is unlikely to improve the quality of the natural environment and, at the same time, boost employment or enhance welfare from a non-environmental point of view. Indeed, such a double dividend is only possible if shifts in the income distribution between people is allowed for. However, for political reasons such shifts are not acceptable because they harm equity. Therefore, it may be wise for governments not to concentrate on the non-environmental dividend of an ETR but to put more emphasis on the welfare improvements associated with a cleaner environment.

Notes
1. The author is grateful to Jeroen van den Bergh, Gilbert van Hagen and two anonymous references for helpful comments on an earlier draft.
2. Yet another version of the double dividend compares environmental taxes with non-revenue-raising environmental policy instruments. That version is similar to the weak double dividend. Indeed, the economic consequences of non-revenue-raising instruments are comparable with those of environmental taxes that are recycled in a lump sum fashion (see, for example, Parry, 1995b).
3. The weak double dividend has sometimes been criticized because it does not take distributional considerations into account (see also the section about political-economy issues below).
4. The GREEN model does not provide effects on employment and is thus not reported in Table 20.2. This also holds for de Mooij et al. (1997).
5. A good example of such an environmental tax proposal was implemented in January 1996 in the Netherlands. Indeed, for political reasons, the effects on the income distribution are minimized by introducing a tax-free allowance for unavoidable energy use. Besides, the revenues from the energy tax are recycled in such a way that those groups who pay the taxes are compensated as much as possible. Also in January 1996, Denmark imposed an energy tax on firms. The revenues of this tax are recycled through targeted subsidies for polluting industries in order to make the tax politically acceptable.

References

Bovenberg, A.L. (1995), 'Environmental taxation and employment', *De Economist*, **143**, 111–40.
Bovenberg, A.L. (1997), 'Environmental policy, distortionary labour taxation, and employment: pollution taxes and the double dividend', in C. Carraro and D. Siniscalco (eds), *New Directions in the Economic Theory of the Environment*, Cambridge, UK: Cambridge University Press.
Bovenberg, A.L. and R.A. de Mooij (1994a), 'Environmental levies and distortionary taxation', *American Economic Review*, **94**, 1085–9.
Bovenberg, A.L. and R.A. de Mooij (1994b), 'Environmental policy in a small open economy with distortionary labour taxes: a general equilibrium analysis', in E.C. van Ierland (ed.), *International Environmental Economics*, Amsterdam: Elsevier.
Bovenberg, A.L. and R.A. de Mooij (1994c), 'Environmental taxes and labour-market distortions', *European Journal of Political Economy*, **10**, 655–83.
Bovenberg, A.L. and R.A. de Mooij (1997b), 'Environmental tax reform and endogenous growth', *Journal of Public Economics*, **63**, 207–37.
Bovenberg, A.L. and F. van der Ploeg (1994a), 'Environmental policy, public finance and the labour market in a second-best world', *Journal of Public Economics*, **55**, 349–90.
Bovenberg, A.L. and F. van der Ploeg (1994b), 'Effects of the tax and benefit system on wage formation and unemployment', mimeo, University of Tilburg.
Bovenberg, A.L. and F. van der Ploeg (1996), 'Optimal taxation, public goods and environmental policy with involuntary unemployment', *Journal of Public Economics*, **62**, 59–83.
Bovenberg, A.L. and F. van der Ploeg (1998), 'Tax reform, structural unemployment and the environment', *Scandinavian Journal of Economics*, **100**, 593–610.
Bovenberg, A.L. and G.H.A. van Hagen (1996), 'Environmental levies, pre-existing tax distortions and distributional concerns', mimeo, Tilburg University.
Bovenberg, A.L. and R.A. de Mooij (1997a), 'Environmental levies and distortionary taxation: reply', *American Economic Review*, **87**, 252–53.
Brunello, G. (1996), 'Labour market institutions and the double dividend hypothesis: an application of the WARM model', in C. Carraro and D. Siniscalco (eds), *Environmental Fiscal Reform and Unemployment*, Dordrecht: Kluwer Academic Publishers.
Butter, F.A.G. den, R.B. Dellink and M.W. Hofkes (1995), 'Energy levies and endogenous technology in an empirical simulation model for The Netherlands', in A.L. Bovenberg and S. Cnossen (eds), *Public Finance and the Environment in an Imperfect World*, Dordrecht: Kluwer Academic Publishers.
Carraro, C., M. Galeotti and M. Gallo (1996), 'Environmental taxation and unemployment: some evidence on the double dividend hypothesis in Europe', *Journal of Public Economics*, **62**, 141–81.
CEC (Commission of the European Communities) (1992), 'The climate challenge – economic aspects of limiting CO$_2$ emmissions', *European Economy*, no. 51, September.
Coase, R.H. (1960), 'The problem of social cost', *Journal of Law and Economics*, **3**, 1-44.
CPB (1992), 'Long term economic consequences of energy taxes' (in Dutch: 'Economische gevolgen op lange termijn van heffingen op energie'), Working Paper no. 43, The Hague.
CPB (1993), 'Effects of an energy tax on small-scale users at low and high price levels' (in Dutch: 'Effecten van een kleinverbruikersheffing op energie bij lage en hoge prijsniveaus'), Working Paper no. 64, The Hague.
EC (European Commission) (1994), 'Taxation, employment and environment: fiscal reform for reducing unemployment', *European Economy*, no. 56, Part C, Analytical study no. 3, March.
Fullerton, D. (1997), 'Environmental levies and distortionary taxation: Comment', *American Economic Review*, **87**, 245–51.
Goulder, L.H. (1995), 'Environmental taxation and the double dividend: A reader's guide', *International Tax and Public Finance*, **2**, 155–82.
Grubb, M., J. Edmonds, P. ten Brink and M. Morrison (1993), 'The costs of limiting fossil-fuel CO$_2$ emissions', *Annual Review of Energy and Environment*, **18**, 397–478.

Köppl, A., K. Kratena, C. Pichl, F. Schebeck, S. Schleicher and M. Wuger (1995), 'Macro-economic and sectoral effects of an environmentally motivated energy taxation in Austria', WIFO, Vienna.
Lindbeck, A. (1994), 'Overshooting, reform and retreat of the welfare state', *De Economist*, **142**, 1–20.
Mayeres, I. and S. Proost (1997), 'Optimal tax and public investment rules for congestion type of externalities', *Scandinavian Journal of Economics*, **99**, 261–80.
Mooij, R.A. de (1996), 'Environmental taxes and unemployment in Europe', *Transfer European Review of Labour and Research*, **2**, 481–92.
Mooij, R.A. de and A.L. Bovenberg (1998), 'Environmental taxes, international capital mobility and inefficient tax systems: tax burden vs. tax shifting', *International Tax and Public Finance*, **5**, 7–39.
Mooij, R.A. de and H.R.J. Vollebergh (1995), 'Prospects for European environmental tax reform', in F.J. Dietz, H.R.J. Vollebergh and J.L. de Vries (eds), *Environment, Incentives and the Common Market*, Dordrecht: Kluwer Academic Publishers.
Mooij, R.A. de, P.J.G. Tang and R. Nahuis (1997), 'European energy taxes and border-tax adjustments: simulations with WorldScan', OCFEB Research Memorandum 9705, Erasmus University, Rotterdam.
Oates, W.E. (1995), 'Green taxes: Can we protect the environment and improve the tax systems at the same time?', *Southern Economic Journal*, **61**, 915–22.
Parry, I.W.H. (1995a), 'Pollution taxes and revenue recycling', *Journal of Environmental Economics and Management*, **29**, S64–77.
Parry, I.W.H. (1995b), 'Environmental policy in a second-best world', mimeo, Resources for the Future, Washington, DC.
Pearce, D.W. (1991), 'The role of carbon taxes in adjusting to global warming', *Economic Journal*, **101**, 938–48.
Pigou, A.C. (1947), *A Study in Public Finance*, 3rd edn, London: Macmillan.
Proost, S. and D. van Regemorter (1995), 'The double dividend and the role of inequality aversion and macroeconomic regimes', *International Tax and Public Finance*, **2**, 205–17.
Repetto, R., R.C. Dower, R. Jenkins and J. Geoghegan (1992), 'Green fees. How a shift can work for the environment and the economy', World Resources Institute document, Washington, DC.
Sandmo, A. (1976), 'Optimal taxation in the presence of externalities', *Swedish Journal of Economics*, **77**, 86–98.

21 Practical considerations and comparison of instruments of environmental policy

Clifford S. Russell and Philip T. Powell

1. Introduction

'Environmental policy' is a phrase with a very wide range of possible meanings, potentially encompassing any policy that impinges directly, or even indirectly, on the natural world. For example, one does not need to stretch to file each of the following under this label: mining law; water law; policies on the acquisition and management of local, regional and national parks; highway design and construction rules; policies concerning the control of disease vectors such as mosquitoes and rodents; and urban and regional planning.

Perhaps the most obviously environmental policies, however, are rules for the control of point and non-point sources of air, water and solid waste pollution and standards for ambient environmental quality at every geographic level from the local creek to the global shield of stratospheric ozone.

Similarly, the range of possible environmental policy instruments is fully as wide as the range of concerns they might be used to address – from mining royalties for public lands, through irrigation water pricing, park access fees and permits, highway tolls and traffic rules – to the roughly ten policy instrument types commonly mentioned with respect to the management of pollution and resulting ambient environmental quality. (These are discussed and listed below. See, for example, US OTA, 1995.) To make this brief chapter manageable, some limits have to be imposed on what will be discussed. And the most straightforward limits are those separating pollution concerns from the rest of the spectrum. This approach has the advantage of focusing attention on the set of problems and approaches most frequently discussed in the environmental economics literature, though it necessarily leaves undiscussed many fascinating and difficult issues for environmental and resource economists.

2. Instruments and settings for their application

To see that there is still plenty to discuss, even after limiting the chapter to pollution-type problem settings, note first, in Table 21.1, how many different kinds of situations fall under the pollution control heading, where

Table 21.1   Examples of pollution management settings

	Discharge location(s)	
	Fixed	Movable by source
Type of discharge		
Point	Municipal sewage	Containerized toxics
	Industrial process	(solvents, acids and
	waste water	so on)
	Combustion wastes from	Batteries, tyres, car
	boilers and process units	bodies
	Irrigation return flow	
	via drainage tiling	
Non-point: area or	Farm and forest run-off	Spray-can emissions
line	Home heating	Auto exhaust
	Highway construction	
	run-off	

we take account of only two distinctions: point versus non-point and fixed location versus location movable by the responsible party. Both these features help to define which policy instrument types are most likely to be relevant to which problem, in particular because these distinctions are key to defining the relevant monitoring task (see below, Section 3). Second, consider Table 21.2 in which are listed ten instrument types that among them span the range of possibilities we have found in the economics and policy literatures.

Now, the prospect of slogging through the 40 cells of the implied options table to try to identify happy matches of instrument and problem is a daunting one, because behind each judgement would necessarily lie considerations on multiple dimensions of comparison (see Table 21.5 below). A substantial fraction of the literature in this area, especially the less formal and mathematical part, has tended to simplify the task in two ways:

- by dividing the instruments into two blocks, one referred to as 'command and control' (CAC) and the other as 'economic incentives' or 'market-based instruments' (EI or MBI);
- by minimizing the importance of some of the distinctions in Table 21.1 by assuming that perfect monitoring (usually implicitly costless as well) is possible.

Table 21.2   Instruments of environmental policy

---

1 Prohibition (of inputs, processes or products)
2 Technology specification (for production, recycling or waste treatment)
3 Technological basis for discharge standard[a]
4 Performance specification (discharge permits)[b]
5 Tradable performance specification (tradable permits)
6 Pollution charges
7 Subsidies
   (i) Lump sum for capital cost
   (ii) Marginal for desired results[c]
8 Liability law provisions
9 Provision of information
   (i) To polluters (technical assistants)
   (ii) To investors, consumers, activists (e.g. US Toxics Release Inventory)
   (iii) To consumers (green product or process)
10 Challenge regulation and voluntary agreements

Notes:
[a]In a technology-based standard setting, the amount of allowed pollution is determined via an engineering study in which a legally designated technology is applied on paper to a particular polluting operation with known uncontrolled pollution load (raw load). The result of this exercise is an achievable discharge amount.
[b]Performance specification can be based on any of a number of rules or methods from uniform percentage reduction by all sources to modelling that determines the cheapest way to attain a given ambient quality standard.
[c]The deposit-refund system, for example for drinks containers, is a self-financed marginal study for container return.

Generally, the definition of the MBI class of instruments takes in tradable permits, pollution charges, liability provisions and subsidies – or four of the ten instrument types in Table 21.2. Thus, implicitly, the phrase 'command and control' is taken to include approaches as disparate as product prohibitions, technology-based discharge standards and the provision of information about what regulated parties ('polluters' or 'sources' for this chapter's purpose) are doing. Now, any label that is this inclusive is unlikely to be useful. But at least as important as its imprecision is the connotational baggage carried by 'command and control', for the phrase harks back to descriptions of the centrally planned economies of Eastern Europe and the Soviet Union. Production quotas were commands, and price signals lost any meaning because of controls over every phase of production and distribution, from choice of technology to quotas for 'retail' outlets. The result was, at best, dismal economic performance. The implication seems clear: command and control is no way to run a railroad, or a steel mill – or an environmental policy. Arguments about the best choice of policy instruments therefore begin with the conclusion prefigured if not absolutely set in stone. (As an aside, we note that there is a dispute brewing in the literature over whether information provision should be classified as 'market-based'. We return to this in Section 4 below.)

However, returning to the problem of the imprecision of the single label for all the non-MBI options, it will be worthwhile to sharpen up the distinctions among those and, indeed, to look more carefully beneath the CAC label itself. To that end, consider the following pair of choices that designers of policy must make, implicitly or explicitly, in crafting a strategy for managing an environmental problem caused by the actions of a group of economic actors, the 'sources':

1. Those parties may or may not be ordered to achieve particular *results* relevant to the problem (for example, to discharge no more than some fixed amount of pollution per period of time).
2. The parties may or may not be told *what* exactly to do – *how to achieve* whatever it is that they do achieve (for example installing equipment type x or burning fuel type y).

Together, these choices imply a two-by-two matrix table (Table 21.3), into which the instruments from Table 21.2 can be placed. Several features of that table are worth stressing. First, only the upper left-hand cell, in which parties are told both *what* to achieve and *how* to achieve it seems to qualify as 'command and control' in any useful sense. Second, a very important instrument in US environmental policy, technology-based standards (on discharges of water pollution) specifies *what* is to be achieved but not *how*. The distinction between technology-based and technology specification has often been lost sight of in critiques of existing policy choices. Third, even some instruments commonly included under the MBIs can be used in ways that involve specifying how to proceed if not what to achieve. This is true of liability law when a standard of care is specified and can be used as a defence. It is also true of subsidies, when these are tied to particular technologies, for example. Thus, while the economist's enthusiasm for MBIs rests heavily on the range of choices they generally leave to regulated parties, it is necessary to be careful and to recognize that not every way of structuring instruments that involve exchanges of money rather than the issuing of bureacratic 'licences' need involve both freedoms – to choose what and how.[1]

Table 21.3   An alternative taxonomy of environmental policy tools
(numbers refer to Table 21.2)

	Specifying *what* is to be achieved	Not specifying *what* is to be achieved
Specifying *how* to achieve whatever is achieved	1 Prohibitions 2 Combining technology specification with 4 Performance standards (this combination is used for auto exhaust regulation in the US)	7(i) Subsidies (lump sum for particular equipment 8 Liability provision (with minimum standard of care) 9(i) Technical assistance (focused on particular technology)
Not specifying *how* to achieve whatever is achieved	3 Design (technology-based) standards 4 Performance standards 10 Voluntary agreements and challenge regulation	5 Tradable permits 6 Pollution charges 7(ii) Subsidies (marginal, open-ended) 8 Liability provisions (without minimum standards of care) 9(i) Technical assistance (not focused on particular technology) 9(ii),(iii) Information reporting

3.   Some general observations setting the stage for proposed criteria for judging among policy instruments

Static efficiency
Economists have been impressed, since the earliest work of Kneese and his fellow enthusiasts for MBI (especially charges), with the argument that this class of instruments promotes static efficiency, either by equating marginal

costs to marginal damages, if marginal damages by source are known, or by equalizing marginal clean-up costs across sources if the goal of the policy is to meet a politically chosen ambient quality standard (for example, Kneese, 1964; Baumol and Oates, 1971). To put this property in perspective, however, two things should be borne in mind. First, if the target or standard really does involve ambient quality, then it is not in general the marginal costs of discharge reduction that must be equalized; rather it is the costs of changing the sources' impact on the environment at the ambient quality monitoring point(s) established by the agency. Sources differ in location, and the natural processes between sources and monitoring points dilute, transform and transport discharged material to create the ambient pollution levels found at those points. Thus efficiency (lowest cost) in general will require that the charge per unit of discharge will be different for each source.

This, in turn, means that:

- trial-and-error setting of charges is most unlikely to be feasible;
- marketable *discharge* permit systems will not produce static efficiency in general because the single market price cannot be efficient.[2]

A temptation at this point may be to say: Well, even granting the argument above, it is still likely to be better to have a uniform emission charge than some arbitrary regulatory rule. That is, aren't uniform charges that induce the meeting of ambient standards (or their duals, single market, tradable discharge permits) second-best instruments? Unfortunately, the answer is no. There is no general rule that a uniform marginal cost beats an arbitrary assignment of discharge reduction responsibility. In Russell (1986), the result is proved for a uniform charge and a roll-back rule – one in which each source is required to reduce discharges by the same percentage. Which instrument produces lower costs of meeting a given ambient standard depends on the details of cost functions, and locations relative to the monitoring point. See Tietenberg (1995) for a summary of modelling results that demonstrate the same effect numerically. The models whose results are summarized there are examples of those that would be required to calculate and set optimal charges (or standards). They all involve cost functions for discharge reduction at individual sources, and models capturing the actions of the natural systems (air or water or both) that transform, transport and dilute discharges in the process of producing ambient quality. Before leaving the static case, it is worth noting that there are two potentially very important pollution problems for which equal marginal costs of discharge reductions *are* efficient: greenhouse gases and chemicals that ultimately deplete stratospheric ozone. This is because the effects of concern involve global average pollutant concentrations, after full mixing by global meterological processes can be assumed to have taken place. This observation helps explain the enthusiasm for MBI in these settings (see, for example, Fisher et al., 1996).

Contrasting the static and dynamic cases
The ability to say *a priori* anything at all about static efficiency rests on a generally persuasive and accepted model of the static situation. This model usually includes the following central assumptions:

- that each source knows its static marginal-cost-of-discharge reduction function;
- that the impact of the source on the relevant policy target is known (in the general case this means that transformation functions, mapping discharges into ambient conditions, are assumed to be known);
- that the policy instrument is understood by the source as it is by the analyst;
- that monitoring and enforcement are costless, but sufficient effort is expended to ensure compliance with permits or perfect reporting of discharges for effluent charge billing.

None of this stretches credulity, at least the credulity of environmental economists, very far. It is worth noting, however, that the optimality or otherwise of any particular set of charges, or other instruments, is not something straightforwardly observable in monitoring data. To show that a particular instrument choice induced the static optimum would require either 'experiments', in which instruments were varied and removal costs and remaining damages observed at all the levels (a search of the regional response surface), or collection of sufficient information on cost and damage functions as well as on the regional natural systems so that a regional optimizing model could be constructed and solved to find the optimum (assuming only one exists, to avoid an even longer digression).

Things look quite different when the setting is dynamic and the goal is to produce even roughly analogous efficiency results that would involve the *paths* of alternative instrument values (charges, permit terms) over time. Instead of an unchanging set of sources producing a fixed output level, we confront, in general, a changing set, with sources entering and leaving the region, varying in size and in location, and changing both production and pollution control technology. These changes can be both endogenous (reactions to environmental policy) and exogenous (reactions to changes in tastes, incomes, factor availability and technology that have nothing to do with that policy). Optimal instrument paths can in principle be determined for particular assumptions about the standards to be met and about the nature, size and timing of the shifts; about the costs of adding increments of capacity; and, indeed, about how the sources see the problem they have to solve – whether they anticipate change or treat each instrument value as if it would be unchanging.

This is a complicated problem, with many possible sets of assumptions and, almost certainly, with many possible different orderings of instrument efficiencies, even ignoring endogenous technological change. Rather than create the dynamic models, perform the calculations and assess the results, economists have tended to content themselves with observing (with more or less sophistication – see below) that marketable permits have an advantage in the dynamic setting because the permit prices do automatically adjust, rising if the number or size of sources grows, falling if capacity disinvestment is going on, or if marginal costs of discharge reduction are falling. The mention of changing marginal costs of discharge reduction brings up the second dynamic problem, one even more difficult for the profession to deal with in a convincing way: endogenous technical change – change driven by the path and level of the policy instruments themselves. To deal convincingly with instrument comparisons in this setting would require a convincing model of the process of induced technical change. This model would have to allow the determination of an optimal path of instrument values for particular assumptions about standards, sources, and so on, as above. But it would also have to reflect the costs of searching for successful innovations, including the costs of failures.

Given these challenges, it is not surprising that no one has done a fully satifactory job on the dynamic problem. Table 21.4 summarizes the characteristics of 11 published studies dating back to 1972 and including two that have appeared as recently as early 1996. One can see in this table two broad lines of attack on the dynamic problem. The first concentrates on determining the relative size of the incentive created by the instruments to develop and adopt innovations that reduce the marginal cost of achieving any particular level of pollution discharge that is less than the source's unconstrained (zero shadow-price) level. Examples, in increasing order of sophistication, of this approach are Wenders (1975); Mauleg (1989); Downing and White (1986); Milliman and Prince (1989); and Jung et al (1996). Roughly speaking, these all conclude that charges create a greater incentive than non-marketable discharge permits. Those that look at marketable permits find that the relative incentive effects of marketable versus unmarketable permits depends on the situation of the particular firm (for example, Mauleg, 1989). But the most recent results, applying to an industry of heterogeneous firms (Jung et al., 1996), provide an unambiguous ranking:

1. permits auctioned each year
2. emission taxes and subsidies
3. permits issued free but marketable
4. performance standards (non-marketable permits).

The other line of the literature is not only broad but diverse. Thus the earliest piece in the table (Smith, 1972) concerned itself only with incentive direction. One of the most sophisticated (Magat, 1978) dealt with the comparison of paths of output, waste and the size and 'bias' of technology R&D spending, given myopic firm decision making in the face of emission charges and of performance standards. Mendelsohn (1984) is concerned with exploring the effect of the possibility of endogenous technical change on the conclusions of Weitzman (1974) on the relative desirability of pollution charges and standards when cost curves are not known with certainty. He finds that the endogenous technical change makes standards relatively more desirable than they are in its absence. Wiersma (1991) presents a modelling case study of Dutch SO_2 control policy, comparing abatement costs over 1985–2000 using market and non-market instruments, with and without endogenous 'learning by doing' – a variant of technical change that lowers marginal cost curves over time. He assumes that the rate of learning depends on the amount of reduction achieved in any time period. Because after the first reduction in costs, a constant charge leads to more reduction than does a constant standard, learning accelerates under a charge relative to a standard. So the charge approach, when used in the model, results in cost savings relative to the standard. These amount to about 25 per cent over 15 years. Jaffe and Stavins (1995) examine the prospective effects of building codes, energy taxes and insulation subsidies on the adoption of more energy-efficient housing construction in the US based on data from 1979–88. They conclude that building codes had no significant effects during the period of data generation while prices and subsidies did.

In a recent paper, Gottinger (1996) creates a very rich but also somewhat eccentric (by the standards of the literature) model of production, pollution and technological advance in both areas, that leaves him saying: 'In summary, there is no policy regime [instrument choice] that is optimal for all situations. The optimal policy regime will depend on the characteristics of the social damage, treatment function, and production function.' A final observation is that none of the work referred to in the table is really dynamic in the sense that the decision maker acts on the perception that current decisions affect future decision *possibilities*. Some look over time under the assumption of myopic decisions, while others use comparative static techniques.[3]

Table 21.4 Twenty-five years of studies that go beyond static efficiency in the examination of environmental policy instruments

	Character of technical change			Motivating question(s)			Character of decision problem			Instruments considered				
	Exog.	Quasi-endog. (1)	Endog.	Incent. size	Effect on welfare	Other (3)	Dynamic	Quasi-dyn. (2)	Static	Qtystd permit	Mktble permit	Charge	Auction permit	Other(s)
Smith '72			x			(3a)			x			x		
Wenders '75		x		x				x		x		x		
Magat '78		x	x		x	(3b)		x		x		x		
Mendelsohn '84			x			(3c)			x	x		x		
Downing and White '86		x		x				x		x	x	x		subsidies
Mauleg '89		x		x				x		x	x			
Milliman and Prince '89		x		x				x		x	x	x	x	subsidies
Wiersma '91	x			Assumed		(3d)		x		x		x		
Jaffe and Stavins '95		x				(3e)		x		x		x		subs's; tech'y std
Jung et al. '96		x		x				x		x	x	x	x	subsidies
Gottinger '96	x				x			x		x		x		

Notes:

(1) Quasi-endogenous. Technologies are not sought by the firm and no R&D expenses are part of the firm's decision problem. But the choice of whether or not to adopt a new technology is considered open.

(2) Quasi-dynamic. Time is considered but only as the period over which the results of decisions play themselves out.

(3) Other motivating questions:

   (a) direction of incentive

   (b) paths of output and waste under constant charge, constant standard and shifting charge

   (c) comparison of charges and standards under uncertainty *with* technical change available

   (d) effect on cost of technology adoption

   (e) Jaffe and Stavins are interested in the technology-adoption decision and allow in their model for several instruments to be used at the same time. They do not, however, derive comparative results symmetric with those of other sources in the table.

Monitoring and enforcement

One or another version of the following proposition is surprisingly common in the literature on environmental policy instruments: charges (sometimes MBI more generally) are 'self-enforcing' because they 'harness the commercial self-interest of [the regulated parties]'. The quoted phrase is from Deutsche Gesellschaft für Technische Zusammenarbeit, 1995, p. 1.)

The thinking behind this generic proposition appears to run along the following lines: given that regulated parties face a particular negative incentive (such as a charge per unit discharge) and given that they are rational, they will react in a way that the charger (the environmental agency) intends. And nothing has apparently been said about the agency having to do any monitoring. This is implicitly or explicitly contrasted with a discharge limit (standard, permit) which can be violated and will be in the absence of monitoring and enforcement. The problem with this reasoning is the word 'face'. As used in the logic of those sentences it must mean not just that the parties know what the charge per unit is, but in addition that the agency can, with some probability, know what the party actually discharges and hence its correct bill for the period. In the absence of such a capability on the agency's part, the source is free to set its own bill by declaring its own discharge level. And the charge becomes merely a penalty for telling the truth rather than announcing falsely low numbers. In short, the agency's chore of monitoring and enforcing a charge is the same as the chore it would face under any choice of policy tool that involves quantity discharged per unit of time, whether as a limit or as the basis for a bill.

This does not mean that there are no differences among the instruments of Table 21.2 in terms of the relative difficulty of the monitoring jobs they imply. Nor does it mean that in a particular setting there is no way to change the monitoring chore. For example if the problem to be addressed is litter (solid waste 'emissions' from autos and pedestrians), monitoring is made difficult by the sheer number of 'sources' and the fact that the emissions are ephemeral, infrequent and random events. But a subsidy per item turned in to a 'proper' place in effect puts the burden of proof on the 'sources', who must show, in order to claim the reward, that they did not jettison bottles or cans. If this subsidy is self-financed it becomes the refund in a deposit-refund system. Something similar may be achieved by using a 'presumptive charge' – a charge that will be of a particular size unless the charged party can prove it deserves a lower one (for example, Eskelund and Devarajan, 1996).

Prices, ethics and politics in environmental policy

For economists, prices are signalling devices through which decentralized actors on the economic stage communicate about tastes and desires, capabilities and sacrifices. The information efficiency of the market economy resting on these signals is a thing of beauty to many, if not all, in the profession. But the world at large does not necessarily share this view. For many, it seems that prices symbolize greed and the exclusionary aspects of markets. These people observe that those ideals and conditions that are valued most are not priced – for example, freedom, religious expression, the everyday glories of the ambient environment. For these people, prices may be a necessary part of reality, but they are not a part to try to expand. Applying them in environmental management may be compared to putting a price on a sunset – free marketeering run amok. Indeed, the notion of pollution prices strikes some of the extreme opponents as analogous to selling licences to murder. This connotation is one part of the overall political problem faced in trying to bring MBI into use in actual policy. In the early days of this argument, the opponents used the phrases 'licence to pollute' to condemn the charging idea. Economists were understandably baffled, for permits, given away free, seem more deserving of that label than charges. It appears in retrospect that the word 'licence' in this context was intended to be thought of in terms of a different one of its definitions: 'excessive or undue freedom or liberty'. (Still one of the best, if not the best, statement of this general position, as well as other arguments against the environmental use of emission charges, is to be found in Kelman, 1981. A more recent political and philosophical attack on MBI may be found in Beder, 1996.)

Another political dimension that cannot be ignored arises from the transfer payments that are at the heart of the much-praised incentive effects of charges and marketable permits. Simply put, the actual charge payments are for economists 'mere transfers', not real resource costs. But for the payers – polluters – they are real, out-of-pocket expenses. (Similarly for payments for marketable or periodically auctioned permits.) Anyone who stands to pay more for a given result under a charge system than under a performance standard, for example, can be expected to oppose the introduction of MBI.[4]

Institutional demands
The discussions above of monitoring and enforcement, and of the data and computation requirements to achieve static efficiency, together suggest a broader consideration – the total demand on the institutional capacity of the government and regulated parties made by any particular policy instruments. Thus, for example, a charge system generates money flows that in turn create incentives for corrupt behaviour by sources and agency employees. Marketable permits also involve money flows, but in the usual case these are among sources, so that the institutional demand is on the ability

of the sources to understand and function in markets. If the sources are state-owned monopolies, with no experience in having to respond to price signals, permit markets may not function at all as theory assumes.

As suggested by these examples, worrying about institutional capacity may be particularly relevant in the settings of developing countries or of 'economies in transition' as the economies of Eastern Europe and the former Soviet Union are being labelled. (For an extended discussion of phases of institutional development and corresponding recommendations for instrument choices, see Russell and Powell, 1996. For more about institutional development, albeit in the slightly narrower setting of water resource management in Latin American countries, see Lord and Israel, 1996.)

4.   Criteria on which to compare instruments of environmental policy

The above observations suggest some ways of thinking about comparisons among environmental policy instruments that go beyond the most familiar – the assertions about static efficiency results. Let us therefore consider a set of criteria that take account of such features of the world as exogenous economic change and the political reaction to the implicit message some see in administered prices.

The list of a dozen criteria in Table 21.5 reflects an effort to synthesize the concerns of the literature, starting with Bohm and Russell (1985). Thus, even after narrowing the chapter topic to pollution control situations and instruments, we find ourselves, in principle, looking at 10 instrument types, to be compared along 12 dimensions in 4 different settings – inevitably a tedious chore if the discussion is required to cover each cell of the implied matrix. To avoid that tedium and maintain a reasonable chapter length, we confine ourselves to a few general comments based on the points made above and the more formal, if necessarily narrower, arguments to be found in Bohm and Russell (1985), the appendix to Russell and Powell (1996), and in such other key sources at Tietenberg (1995 – on marketable permits); and Dewees (1992) and Tietenberg (1989 – on liability rules).

First, as a general rule, instruments that allow for the possibility of attaining static efficiency have attached to them heavy institutional demands, both general and specific (information gathering, computation and monitoring). Those same instruments also tend to exhibit more political problems than other options, except that they are not particularly risky from the point of view of the regulated parties (though some of them seem risky for the responsible agency because of the possibility that less will be achieved in environmental terms than is desired and has been politically promised). Second, the instruments that exhibit the smallest political problems and lowest institutional demands are the least likely to produce low

Table 21.5   A synthesis of criteria against which to judge policy instruments

---

Static concerns

  1 Efficiency
  2 Information/computation demands
  3 Relative ease of monitoring and enforcement

Dynamic concerns

  4 Flexibility in the face of exogenous changes
  5 Incentive for environment-saving technical change

General institutional demands

  6 Agency: honesty, technical capabilities (including data gathering, model building and solving, monitoring and enforcement, and revenue handling)
  7 Regulated parties: experience in markets, reliance on government regulations to protect markets, technical skills (including controlling discharges via production and treatment processes and making decisions about processes, products and inputs)

Political dimensions

  8 Distributional implications
  9 Perceived ethical message
 10 Perceived fairness

Perceived *a priori* risks

 11 To agency: failure to achieve goals, freezing current technology for too long, possible perverse responses
 12 To regulated parties: false convictions, 'ratcheting down' of requirements

---

aggregate costs of meeting ambient quality standards. These include product prohibitions, technology specification, information provision and technical assistance. In between, we have the mixed bag associated with design standards, challenge regulation and liability law.

Given the trade-offs that seem to exist, the characteristics of actual environmental policies seem far less perverse than they do when viewed through the single lens of static efficiency – or even through the dual lens of static efficiency and dynamic incentive for innovation. Thus, in the US, early policy for air pollution control focused on performance standards based (albeit usually in crude ways) on ambient quality targets where existing sources were concerned; while new sources faced technology specification. In water, the standards were of the design variety (technology-*based* discharge standards) with different words describing the technological bases for existing and new sources. Alongside the permit systems there have been efforts at technical assistance, such as funding of research into better treatment methods. Subsidies of the lump sum, capital-cost-reducing variety have also been a feature of US policy, especially on the water pollution side. These were designed to redistribute the costs of municipal compliance with federal requirements.

As knowledge and experience have accumulated and institutional capacity has grown, the permits in which discharge standards were embodied have been made tradable (under many restrictions). And the acid rain provisions of the Clean Air Act Amendments of 1990 created a new system of tradable permits designed to help tackle a new problem in a politically acceptable way. Also in the late 1980s experiments began with challenge regulation and information provision. For example, EPA created the 33/50 programme to challenge industry to reduce toxic emissions (Arora and Cason, 1995). And the Emergency Planning and Community Right-to-Know Act of 1986 created the Toxic Release Inventory, reporting discharges by firms of several hundred toxic but unregulated compounds.

Liability law has been a feature principally of the method of dealing with problems created by disposition of toxic wastes in ways, legal when done, but posing long-term problems. Thus, under Superfund (Comprehensive Environmental Response, Compensation, and Liability Act of 1980, as amended in 1986), 'dischargers' to old landfills or other toxified sites become potentially responsible parties from whom clean-up costs may be sought on a joint and several liability basis. In addition, provisions in several other statutes give natural resource 'trustees' (the National Oceanic and Atmospheric Agency (NOAA), the Department of Interior, and state governments most often) the obligation and ability to act to recover 'natural resource damages' from parties responsible for current spills or deliberate disposal. Damage claims of this sort are possible under the Clean Water Act, the Oil Pollution Act and the Resource Conservation and Recovery Act. The public provision of information about the behaviour of sources is discussed below.

Thus one can see the US experience as a long experiment with instruments, in the context of perceived political constraints, rather than as a record of political perversity in the face of overwhelming economic rationality.

5. Two newer concerns of the instrument literature

The potential importance of 'mere transfers'
The static efficiency results for economic incentive instruments refer, of course, to resource costs. When economic incentives are used, other costs are involved for the regulated parties. With marketable permits distributed free, for existing sources those other costs are opportunity costs, not out-of-pocket cash flows. But for emission charges there will be actual money changing hands – from source to agency. The amounts involved can be enormous when the charge applies to every unit of discharge. For example, work on refinery and steel-mill pollution control in the 1970s suggested that, at least at that stage of the clean-up process, the charge payments could be as large as the costs of clean-up themselves (Russell, 1973; Russell and Vaughan, 1976). For a similar result in a very different setting (the impact of a fertilizer tax designed to achieve particular reductions in application rates) see Quiroga et al. (1995). This can be a half-full or a half-empty glass, depending on other assumptions about reductions in other taxes and the elasticities that relate to those taxes. See Chapter 20 by de Mooij in this handbook. In any case, if one is sceptical about the possibility that other taxes will be reduced, enthusiasm for this new source of environmental funding has to be at least somewhat tempered by the realization that, to the regulated party, the cost of the 'least-cost' solution could be doubled, unless some other way of full or partial 'recycling' can be arranged. Farrow (1995) suggests a 'lump sum tax credit' based on some amount of discharge not subject to current control by the source. (He uses a 'base year' quantity.) The same effect could be achieved by combining a standard and a charge, with the charge applying only to amounts discharged above the standard. Any such approach weakens the double-dividend argument and reduces the incentive for the source to find ways of shifting down its marginal costs of discharge reduction. It does, on the other hand, reduce the potential political objections to a charge. Even in the double-dividend case, there will be differential impacts across firms and regions in any but a most unlikely case: that in which the sources of payments of the reduced taxes happen to mimic those for the new emission charge.

The public provision of information as a regulatory strategy
While economists, psychologists and others with environmental interest have long been curious about how citizens respond to information provided on risks, it does not appear that the emergence of information as a regulatory tool owes much to prior research. Rather a major impetus seems to have been frustration with the pace of environmental change on the part of

certain key players. Thus, in the US, the advent of the Toxic Release Inventory (TRI) has been linked by some observers to Congress's dissatisfaction with the EPA's failure to get putatively toxic chemicals listed officially under laws that would then allow restrictions to be placed on discharges. Other efforts, such as official and unofficial 'green labelling' approaches, target products rather than discharges from production facilities and attempt to influence consumers toward products judged less environmentally harmful. These exercises seem to appeal to environmentalists who believe that well-informed consumers will go further faster than governments in the direction of forcing 'greener' behaviour by firms. In Europe, enthusiasm for 'green labelling', referring to either product or production process, is widespread. When such a system is put in place voluntarily and unofficially it can be seen as substituting for or supplementing government policies, such as those common in Europe governing, for example, recyclability of consumer products (OECD, 1991).

Thus one major reason for thinking that information may be used to influence polluter behaviour is that information may influence consumers to shift purchases to products (or services) that are found by some trusted institution to be more environmentally benign. (For a highly stylized but interesting analysis of when such information can improve collective welfare in the presence of consumption-related externalities, see Kennedy et al., 1994.)

But it is a bit of a leap of faith to see *discharge* information as influencing consumer purchase decisions. Most fundamentally, there is not a good match between facility discharges and products. Indeed, consumers may find it hard even to match facilities and companies. But discharge information may be seen by investors as indicative of future problems for the emitters. These future problems could include stepped-up enforcement of other regulations as they apply to large emitters; possible increased liability under regulations applying to existing toxic waste sites; and greater expense to respond to likely future regulation, as mere information is replaced by mandatory limits on discharges. This version of the information provision mechanism was tested in a preliminary way by Hamilton (1995) and Laplante and Lanoie (1995). They found some evidence that the release of TRI data by the EPA did lead to some firms taking stock price hits, though why some firms were hit and others not is not well explained by the data. (The tautological 'explanation' is that for some firms the data constituted a surprise while for others stock prices already reflected the equivalent knowledge.) More recently, Konar and Cohen (1997a and b) have established an important link in the regulatory-tool reasoning by showing that firms taking the largest stock price hits after release of TRI data were more likely to cut down those discharges, both absolutely and relative to other firms in their industries, than were either the largest emitters (in pounds per dollar of sales) or a randomly chosen sample of firms from the same industries.

None the less, there remains a great deal to do in understanding and harnessing the power of information as an environmental policy tool. The work can usefully be divided into two broad areas. One is refining the information provided and understanding its impact on consumers and investors. The other is characterizing in a reasonably systematic way (as begun by Kennedy et al., 1994, but more generally), the circumstances under which information will actually be helpful from the aggregate welfare perspective.

The information currently provided under TRI, for example, in principle involves facility-by-facility annual emissions of several hundred compounds to air, water and land. Media stories and environmentalist reports on TRI results, however, tend to aggregate across chemicals to get facility, company or political jurisdiction totals. None of these aggregation efforts are helpful as ways of summarizing the risk implications of the reported discharges (and controlling risk is, after all, what this is ultimately about). In the longer run, it would be desirable to work at ways of mechanizing the provision of the risk implications of the TRI data for citizens in particular places. But along with such efforts, it will be necessary to explore how lay individuals, activists and public officials actually react to such inherently more complex information. In the meantime, such responses as the data do produce are as likely to be efficiency-harming as helping since there is no necessary correlation between the size of discharges, particularly aggregated over chemicals, and the magnitude of ecological or human risks. Similar comments apply to green labelling, for this is also a rather crude yes–no signal but is often based on multiple considerations and even complex 'life cycle' calculations of environmental impact (OECD, 1991). In order better to understand the normative impacts of information provision we need not only to understand how consumers, investors and regulators respond, but how those responses drive, in turn, polluter responses – and where these complex interactions take the system. One thing, however, is clear even now: although information released by regulators acts on polluters via consumer and investor markets, it is quite misleading to try to wrap this instrument in the flag of 'market-based-instruments', by implication claiming something about static efficiency potential, dynamic incentives, and so forth.

6. Concluding comments

The basis for choice among environmental policy instruments has long been an important part of the environmental economics literature. Early on the emphasis was on the desirability of economic incentive (market-based) instruments, especially emission charges, principally because of their potential for bringing about (static) regional situations in which given ambient standards are met at least-resource costs. Later, enthusiasm built up for marketable permits because they appeared to maintain some of the efficiency advantages of charges while being consistent with the prior existence of actual permits.

Along the way, the earliest oversimplifications, such as those about relative monitoring and enforcement difficulties, and about flexibility in the face of exogenous change, have been examined and corrected.

More recently, interest in instrument choice has exploded in the environment and development literature. Unfortunately, a distressingly large amount of the resulting material ignores the scepticism of the instruments literature of the 1980s, where MBIs are concerned, and returns to quite unqualified enthusiasm based on static efficiency, an assumed but non-existent second-best attribute, and the double-dividend revenue argument.

The other directions of the new literature seem more promising if no more important in the real-world scheme of things. These include, specifically: developing a better understanding of the dynamic incentive properties of alternative instruments; working out the extent to which the public provision of information about discharges or products (or both) is really promising; and further exploring the potential for a double dividend from charges.

Notes
1. It is worth noting, anticipating later comments about risks for bureaucrats in instrument choice, that tradable permits do involve an aggregate specification of *what* is to be achieved. This sets an upper limit on the aggregation of discharge rights by any single source and thus puts a limit on how bad quality can be made at any point. But the facts that total allowed discharges are limited and that dischargers are very likely to have different marginal costs for reducing discharges strongly suggest that any single discharger faces an upward-sloping supply curve for rights. This differentiates a tradable rights scheme from a pure emission charge instrument, in which 'supply' will be completely elastic.
2. Zoned systems or systems using 'trade-off' ratios that force a difference between the price per pound obtained and the price per pound relinquished can make marginal costs differ in equilibrium (for example, Tietenberg, 1995). But only by luck would the requirements imposed be the 'right' ones to produce the statically efficient set of marginal costs – unless the trading ratios were set on the basis of the information that would have allowed efficient charges to have been set in the first place.
3. Parry (1996) attempts to bring in a more sophisticated model of the R&D process as another step on the road to a dynamic 'solution'. His conclusions are consistent with those summarized in the text.
4. Some MBI enthusiasts will point out here that the increase in efficiency achieved by use of charges could leave room for charge payments with everyone still better off. This assertion is empirical and cannot be dismissed on *a priori* grounds. But as a political matter, not only would polluters in the aggregate have to be better off; this aggregate result would have to be achieved via making most individual sources better off, not by having one or two of many sources benefit immensely and all others lose out.

References

Arora, Seema and Timothy N. Cason (1995), 'An experiment in voluntary environmental regulation: participation in EPA's 33/50 Program', *Journal of Environmental Economics and Management*, **28** (3), 271–86.

Baumol, W.J. and W.E. Oates (1971), 'The use of standards and prices for protection of the environment', *Swedish Journal of Economics*, **73** (March), 42–54.

Beder, Sharon (1996), 'Charging the earth: the promotion of price-based measures for pollution control', *Ecological Economics*, (16), 51–63.

Bohm, Peter and Clifford S. Russell (1985), 'Comparative analysis of alternative policy instruments', in Allen V. Kneese and J.L. Sweeney (eds), *Handbook of Natural Resource and Energy Economics*, Amsterdam: North-Holland.

Deutsche Gesellschaft für Technische Zusammenarbeit (GTZ) (1995), *Market-based Instruments in Developing Countries*, Eschborn, Germany.

Dewees, Donald (1992), 'Tort law and the deterrence of environmental pollution', in T. Tietenberg (ed.), *Innovation in Environmental Policy*, Aldershot, UK and Brookfield, US: Edward Elgar.

Downing, Paul B. and Lawrence J. White (1986), 'Innovation in pollution control', *Journal of Environmental Economics and Management*, **13** (1), 18–29.

Eskelund, Gunnar and Shantayanan Devarajan (1996), *Taxing Bads by Taxing Goods: Pollution Control with Presumptive Charges*, Directions in Development Series, Washington, DC: World Bank.

Farrow, Scott (1995), 'The dual political economy of taxes and tradable permits', *Economic Letters*, **49**, 217–20.

Fisher, B.S., S. Barrett, P. Bohm, M. Kuroda, J.K.E. Mubazi, A. Shah and R.N. Stavins (1996), 'An economic assessment of policy instruments for combating climate change', in J.P. Bruce, H. Lee and E.F. Haites (eds), *Climate Change 1995: Economic and Social Dimensions of Climate Change*, Cambridge, UK: Cambridge University Press.

Gottinger, Hans W. (1996), 'A model of principal–agency control of wastes under technological progress', *Environmental and Resource Economics*, **7** (3), 263–86.

Hamilton, J. (1995), 'Pollution as news: media and stock market reactions to the Toxics Release Inventory data', *Journal of Environmental Economics and Management*, **28** (1), 98–113.

Jaffe, A.B. and R.N. Stavins (1995), 'Dynamic incentives of environmental regulations: the effects of alternative policy instruments on technological diffusion', *Journal of Environmental Economics and Management*, **29** (3), part 2, S43–S63.

Jung, Chulho, Kerry Krutilla and Roy Boyd (1996), 'Incentives for advanced pollution abatement technology at the industry level: an evaluation of policy alternatives', *Journal of Environmental Economics and Management*, **30** (1), 95–111.

Kelman, Steven (1981), *What Price Incentives: Economists and the Environment*, Boston: Auburn House.

Kennedy, P.W., B. Laplante and J. Maxwell (1994), 'Pollution policy: the role for publicly provided information', *Journal of Environmental Economics and Management*, **26** (1), 31–43.

Kneese, Allen V. (1964), *The Economics of Regional Water Quality Management*, Baltimore, MD: Johns Hopkins University Press for Resources for the Future.

Konar, Shameek and Mark A. Cohen (1997a), 'Information as regulation: the effect of community right-to-know laws on toxic emission', *Journal of Environmental Economics and Management*, **32**, 109–24.

Konar, Shameek and Mark A. Cohen (1997b), 'Why do firms pollute (and reduce) toxic emissions?', Working Paper, Vanderbilt Center for Environmental Management Studies, Nashville, TN.

Laplante, B. and Paul Lanoie (1995), 'The market response to environmental incidents in Canada: a theoretical and empirical analysis', *Southern Economic Journal*, **62** (1), 657–72.

Lord, Wm B. and Morris Israel (1996), *A Proposed Strategy to Encourage and Facilitate Improved Water Resources Management in Latin America and the Caribbean*, Washington, DC: the Interamerican Development Bank.

Magat, W.A. (1978), 'Pollution control and technological advance: a dynamic model of the firm', *Journal of Environmental Economics and Management*, **5** (1), 1–25.

Mauleg, David A. (1989), 'Emission credit trading and the incentive to adopt new pollution abatement technology', *Journal of Environmental Economics and Management*, **16** (1), 52–7.

Mendelsohn, R. (1984), 'Endogenous technical change and environmental regulation', *Journal of Environmental Economics and Management*, **11**, 202–7.

Milliman, S.R. and R. Prince (1989), 'Firm incentives to promote technological change in pollution control', *Journal of Environmental Economics and Management*, **17**, 247–65.

OECD, (1991), *Environmental Labelling in OECD Countries*, Paris: OECD.

Parry, Ian W.H. (1996), 'The choice between emission taxes and tradeable permits when technological change is endogenous', Discussion Paper 96–31, Washington, DC: Resources for the Future. Published (1998) as 'Pollution, regulation and the efficiency gains from technological innovation', *Journal of Regulatory Economics*, **14**, 229–54.

Quiroga, Ricardo, Jorge Fernandez-Cornejo and Utpal Vasavada (1995), 'The economic consequences of reduced fertilizer use: a virtual pricing approach', *Applied Economics*, **27**, 211–17.

Russell, Clifford S. (1973), *Residuals Management in Industry: A Case Study of Petroleum Refining*, Baltimore, MD: Johns Hopkins University Press for Resources for the Future.

Russell, Clifford S. (1986), 'A note on the efficiency ranking of two second-best policy instruments for pollution control', *Journal of Environmental Economics and Management*, **13** (1), 13–17.

Russell, C.S. and P.T. Powell (1996), *Choosing Environmental Policy Tools: Theoretical Cautions and Practical Considerations*, Washington, DC: Interamerican Development Bank, June, ENV-102.

Russell, Clifford S. and William J. Vaughan (1976), *Steel Production: Processes, Products, and Residuals*, Baltimore, MD: Johns Hopkins University Press for Resources for the Future.

Smith, V. Kerry (1972), 'The implications of common property resources for technical change', *European Economic Review*, (3), 469–79.

Tietenberg, T.H. (1989), 'Indivisible toxic torts: the economics of joint and several liability', *Land Economics*, **65** (4), 305–19.

Tietenberg, T.H. (1995), 'Tradeable permits for pollution control when emission location matters: what have we learned?', *Environmental and Resource Economics*, **5** (2), 95–113.

US Office of Technology Assessment (OTA) (1995) *Environmental Policy Tools: A User's Guide*, OTA-ENV-634, Washington, US GPO, September.

Weitzman, M.L. (1974), 'Prices vs. Quantities', *Review of Economic Studies*, **41**, 477–91.

Wenders, John T. (1975), 'Methods of pollution control and the rate of change in pollution abatement technology', *Water Resources Research*, **11** (3), 393–6.

Wiersma, Doede (1991), 'Static and dynamic efficiency of pollution control strategies', *Environmental and Resource Economics*, **1** (1), 63–82.

22 Public economics and environmental policy
Stef Proost

1. Introduction

Public economics has evolved as an economics discipline on its own since the pioneering textbook of Atkinson and Stiglitz (1980). It studies, using mainly microeconomic theory, the allocation functions of the 'state', as it is there that the optimal design of taxes and the allocation of public goods are located. It has had mainly a normative orientation: how can a decision maker who is equipped with a welfare function use traditional government instruments to improve the economic equilibrium? Although environmental economics is a discipline on its own, it has borrowed many insights from the public economics tradition and there are still many parallel developments. In this chapter we survey this interaction between disciplines and discuss the parallel developments. The emphasis is on the use of public economics insights for environmental policy. A recent survey of the public economics literature can be found in Myles (1995) and a historical view on its development can be found in Drèze (1994).

The first link between the two disciplines runs via the *concept of public good* and the definition of externalities. A public good (say a public concert) is generally considered as a good that, once provided for one consumer, can be made available for other consumers or firms at no extra cost. It is often also characterized by the non-rivalness or non-depletable property, to which one can add the non-excludability of beneficiaries. Pollution generated by one agent is a public bad in the sense that, once created, it affects all agents within its reach negatively. Similarly, natural areas preserved by one agent will benefit all other agents that can access the area. When there is no compensation for this negative or positive effect on the utilities of the other agents, there are external effects. The main difference between both types of environmental goods and the traditional public goods has to do with the production of the goods. For public goods it is generally assumed that they are produced in an efficient way by a private or public production sector: concerts, defence and so on. Environmental goods are mostly a by-product of many different activities and there is no guarantee that they are produced efficiently, that is, that abatement of pollution takes place in those activities where the abatement cost is the lowest.

The second link between both disciplines runs via the *use of public funds*. The public economics tradition has developed a whole theory about the optimal use of public revenue instruments to achieve simultaneously allocation objectives (public goods supply) and distributional objectives. This theory has been the major source of inspiration for second-best types of arguments about environmental policy design: double-dividend arguments, distributional consequences of standards versus taxes and the like.

We shall discuss three types of contributions from public economics that have recently interesting insights relevant for environmental economics. First we discuss the private provision of public goods. This is of particular relevance for international pollution control where, in the absence of a world government, environmental improvements have many characteristics of a public good that is privately supplied. A second long-standing issue in public economics and in environmental economics is the revelation of preferences for public goods. In this context we examine the recent use of cooperative mechanisms to address international environmental problems. A third issue is the integration of income distribution considerations and public goods supply. Here we analyse the close parallel with the literature on environmental tax reform.

Many other interesting contributions from public economics to environmental economics will not be discussed here. One could refer to the contribution of the tax enforcement literature to the environmental policy enforcement problems: the importance of social custom, the use of a dynamic auditing mechanism, (Harrington, 1988). Another interesting parallel is the fiscal federalism theory (Oates, 1972), and its application to the design of environmental policy in federal countries (Braden and Proost, 1997). Another example is the behavioural theory of executive government institutions (bureaucracies *à la* Niskanen, 1971) that also applies to environmental agencies. Finally, insights could be gained from the public choice and constitutional approach to public economics. In the public choice approach (Mueller, 1990) the actual government decisions are explained as a function of the design of the decision mechanism. Recently this has been applied to the choice of instruments for environmental policy (Boyer and Laffont, 1996). In the constitutional approach to public economics, the design of the public decision mechanism is a contract with incomplete information between groups with different interests.

2.   The non-cooperative provision of public goods

In the absence of government intervention it is up to the individual agents to organize the supply of public and environmental goods. There are several reasons why such a private provision exists. A government is not always fully aware of the needs of its citizens and there may be institutional barriers to the supply of some public goods. It is therefore of interest to study how a private mechanism performs. For public goods on a world scale, there simply is no world government that can enforce contributions, and the spontaneous contributions of the different country governments may be the only important mechanism by which some world environmental problems are addressed.

In order to analyse the private provision by individual households in an economy, assumptions are necessary about the behaviour of each contributor. The most common assumption used is *Nash behaviour*: in planning their contribution, every household takes the contributions of the others as given. In the application to traditional public goods the marginal cost is taken as constant and equal for everybody. The quantity of public goods contributed by each individual will be determined by the equality between the individual marginal willingness to pay and the marginal cost where the individual marginal willingness to pay is measured, taking the other individual contributions as given (Nash equilibrium). This condition stands in sharp contrast to the traditional Samuelson condition for an efficient supply of public goods where the level of supply is increased until the sum, over all the beneficiaries of the public good, of the marginal willingness to pay equals the marginal cost. How inefficient the private provision equilibrium will be depends on several factors. One expects that, the more individuals there are, the greater the inefficiency because everybody expects all others to contribute (known as the free-rider problem). This is not necessarily true and the divergence between efficient and private levels of supply can increase or decrease. However Andreoni (1988) has shown that when everybody has identical preferences but different endowments, then an infinite population leads to an equilibrium where *only the households with the highest endowments contribute*, total contributions increase to a finite value and the average contribution decreases to zero. Bergstrom et al. (1986) proved a second strong result of general interest. They showed that the total private provision of public goods is *unaffected by any income redistribution among the contributors*. The basic reason is that the source of provision is irrelevant for every individual. This would imply that any exogenous increase of public provision would be completely compensated by (would 'crowd out') an equivalent reduction in the provision of private supply.

The Andreoni (1988) result implies that the level of voluntary provision of environmental goods is inefficient but that it does not decrease when the population becomes large. The Bergstrom et al. (1986) result implies that the introduction of public supply of environmental goods causes the private supply to decline. The empirical analysis of charitable donations has shown that this crowding out of private provision by public provision is not entirely satisfactory in explaining behaviour. The private provision theory performs much better when a 'warm glow' effect is added to the preference structure. This 'warm glow' effect (Andreoni, 1990) means that individuals generate utility by the level of private goods, by the total quantity of public goods supplied but also by the act of giving itself. The individual contribution gives some utility on its own even if it does not lead to a larger total quantity of public goods provided.

There have not been many *applications* of these theories to the actual private supply of environmental goods (contributions to foundations for nature preservation). However, the warm glow effect has also been recognized in the literature on the valuation of environmental quality as one of the potentially important explanatory factors behind the willingness to pay for environmental quality (see Kriström, Chapter 54, this volume). There have been more applications of the theory of the private provision of public goods in the domain of international environmental problems. Take the climate change problem. There are international agreements but like most international agreements they have not been enforced. However, we observe efforts by different countries. These efforts can be seen as voluntary contributions by countries (individuals) to the world environmental problem (public good). Eyckmans et al. (1993) used a simple numerical world model with 11 independently acting regions with abatement costs and damage costs estimates taken from the literature to examine the private provision equilibrium for greenhouse gas reduction. They found that instead of the efficient level (MC_i = sum of MB) of carbon emission reduction of 16 per cent, private provision (Nash behaviour with $MC_i = MB_i$) would result in a reduction of only some 2 to 3 per cent of world carbon emissions. The inefficient level results from two sources: the inefficient level of supply of greenhouse gas reduction and the inefficient production of abatement (marginal abatement costs differ). Eyckmans and Proost (1996) tested the removal of the second inefficiency by assuming that countries could, via tradable permits, produce abatement efficiently. They found a total abatement level of the order of 4 per cent where only the region with the largest willingness to pay contributes to the environmental good. In fact, by separating the production of abatement and the financing of the abatement, the environmental problem has all the characteristics of a traditional public good and the results can be seen as an application of Andreoni's (1988) result.

Buchholz and Konrad (1995) and Ihory (1996) studied another application of private provision of a public good to international environmental problems. They look at the problem where *high-cost countries can transfer income to low-cost countries* in the hope that they will increase their supply of pollution abatement to a common environmental problem. In the first stage of the game one country can give a lump sum transfer of income to another country. In the second stage, each country decides on its emission abatement efforts. It is shown that it can be beneficial to give unconditional transfers of income to low-cost countries and that the transfer can be so big that the donor countries reduce their own pollution abatement to zero. Another interesting application of this framework is the analysis of Hoel (1992). He studies the effect on total abatement of an international pollution problem of an extra effort beyond the Nash voluntary contribution equilibrium mechanism by one country. He finds that the ultimate effect on total abatement efforts may be negative and that the welfare effect of the extra effort is likely to be negative.

3. The use of cooperative mechanisms in the provision of public goods
Since the early 1970s (Drèze and de la Vallée Poussin, 1971), mechanisms have been studied that lead to an efficient supply of public goods and that include sufficient incentives for all partners to cooperate and, if possible, also to reveal their preferences honestly. In this way they can escape from the prisoner's dilemma. As international pollution problems are probably among the most relevant examples of a public good problem where only voluntary cooperation is possible, there has been a renewed interest in these mechanisms. The extra difficulty in the case of international pollution is that the abatement costs differ among the countries so that an efficient solution requires a sufficient level of overall abatement and an efficient distribution of abatement efforts.

Chander and Tulkens (1995) propose a procedure that leads to a Pareto-optimal solution where all participants in the process are sure to be better off than in the non-cooperative solution. Moreover, *the cost-sharing rule and the international transfer system proposed are also strategically stable*: it is not in the interest of partners to form coalitions in order to improve their position. An important property of the proposed solution is that it is part of the gamma core. This means that the resulting allocation cannot be improved upon by a coalition of countries ('core' concept), where it is moreover assumed that the players not belonging to the coalition of countries behave rationally ('gamma' core). This procedure has been illustrated in the case of acid rain cooperation between Finland, Russia and Estonia by Kaitala et al. (1995). In fact, in this application, a more sophisticated mechanism has been used. As only marginal benefit and marginal abatement cost information are known, rather than the complete cost and damage functions of all countries, a stepwise mechanism is used that generates a succession of emission abatement programmes. The series of emission abatement programmes converges to an economic optimum where the traditional efficiency properties for public goods (MC_i = sum over MB for all i) are verified.

4. The traditional public economics model and its lessons for policy design
One of the major achievements of public economics is the integration of
equity and efficiency considerations in the second-best models of taxation
and public goods. In public economics, *equity* is mostly defined by using a
Bergson–Samuelson social welfare function (SWF) as objective function
for the government. This welfare function is a weighted sum of individual
utility functions. The relative weight of an individual will depend on the
degree of income inequality aversion of the government. This degree of
income inequality can be parametrized by attributing the same utility function to all individuals that can be represented by real income. The social
welfare function is then defined as the sum of real incomes; and all the individual real income levels have the same exponent epsilon. By varying
epsilon, one can cover the whole range of income inequality aversion cases,
varying from complete indifference to income inequality (epsilon = 1) to
the Rawlsian case (epsilon tends to 1/infinity) where only the utility of the
least well-off counts.

In the *first-best model* the redistribution problem is always solved in the
background by using individualized lump sum taxes and transfers. To illustrate what is an individualized lump sum tax, take the example of two individuals, one with a high innate productivity and one born with a very low
productivity. An individualized lump sum tax system means that the
government can redistribute income by forcing the one with a high productivity to pay a fixed but high tax per year and giving a fixed subsidy to
the low-productivity individual. The work–leisure choice of both individuals is not distorted because the amount of the individual taxes is fixed.

The major advantage of this type of instrument is that the traditional
efficiency properties for an economy (MRS in consumption for all consumers = MRT in production for all firms) remain unaffected. With
individualized lump sum transfers the marginal social utilities of income
(the derivative of the SWF with respect to the income of one individual)
are always equalized over individuals. In the first-best models, the quantity
of public goods supplied satisfies the Samuelson condition and the
necessary government revenue is collected via lump sum taxes; in a
world without income inequality aversion this is done via a head tax.
Environmental problems are solved via Pigouvian taxes because any equity
effect of imposing these taxes is corrected by using the individualized lump
sum taxes and subsidies.

In *second-best models*, individualized lump sum taxes and subsidies are
ruled out because of the incentive compatibility problems this creates when
they are used to redistribute income. Indeed, in order to escape a high individual lump sum tax, all highly productive individuals have an incentive to
hide their productivity and to pretend they are of low productivity by

working fewer hours and declaring a low income. In second-best models, the government can redistribute income and collect sufficient government revenue only via instruments that rely on observable market behaviour rather than on innate productivity. This means that taxes will be levied on income earned and on commodities consumed or produced and that the efficiency properties of a first-best market economy will be lost. This is the basic trade-off between efficiency and equity. The higher the degree of income inequality aversion of the government, the more the trade-off will be tilted against efficiency and the higher will be the tax distortions introduced. Of course this trade-off is also present in any environmental problem. Public economics offers different suggestions to make this trade-off between equity and efficiency in an optimal way. Three guidelines are of particular interest for environmental economics: how to deal with market imperfections in production; how to design optimal Pigouvian taxes; and how to determine the optimal level of supply of environmental goods.

A first very important result is that, when indirect consumption and income taxes are available as instruments, *production efficiency* is in general desirable (Diamond and Mirrlees, 1971). This means that taxes on transactions between firms (or on imports and exports) are inefficient except if there are interfirm externalities in the production sector (one firm affecting negatively the production of another). These should be corrected via standards or Pigouvian taxes so as to regain the production possibilities frontier. Environmental taxes on interfirm externalities should only be based on the marginal environmental damage and should not be increased or reduced because of government revenue considerations or because of income distribution concerns. This forms the basis for much of the theory of the choice of environmental policy instruments on the production side of the economy.

Optimal commodity and income tax policies that aim to raise government revenue and distribute income always contain a mix of efficiency and distributional considerations. The efficiency goal calls for lower distortions between producer and consumer prices by taxing the less price-elastic consumer goods. The distributional goal requires taxes to be lower for those commodities that are proportionally more consumed by the poor. Under certain conditions a pure income tax can be sufficient; sometimes consumption taxes on certain commodities need to be added to have an optimal tax mix of direct and indirect taxes. This framework can be readily applied to the design of environmental taxes. The first to realize this was Sandmo (1975) who showed that, in a second-best framework, it is sufficient to address an externality problem that is caused at the consumption side by adding an extra tax to the consumption of the externality-generating good and by readjusting all other taxes in function of the revenue needs and the

distributional considerations. There is no need to subsidize clean substitutes or to tax complements of the dirty good if taxes on all commodities are available. This is called the 'additivity' property.

The double role of Pigouvian taxes as both environmental policy instrument and as raisers of government revenue has been rediscovered in the
1990s in the *double-dividend debate* (see de Mooij, Chapter 20, this volume).
The income distribution concern has been largely left out of this debate.
This debate was about the 'second' benefit of using the revenue of
Pigouvian taxes to reduce existing distortionary taxes. There were two
questions: should one use the environmental tax revenue to lower existing
distortionary taxes and, second, does this call for a Pigouvian tax that is
larger than the traditional sum of marginal environmental damages? In the
double-dividend debate the answer to the first question is yes: there is a
preference for using the Pigouvian tax revenue to lower existing distortionary taxes rather than to redistribute it as a lump sum. The answer to the
second question is in general no: a Pigouvian tax normally erodes the existing more efficient tax base and this means that it is in general not appropriate to increase the Pigouvian tax beyond the sum of the marginal damages.
In general it is rather the reverse that holds. Mayeres and Proost (1997) integrate distributional concerns in the double-dividend discussion by using
the Sandmo (1975) approach. First they point out that the distributional
concern is at the origin of the distortionary taxes so that the double-dividend issue is in theory irrelevant in an economy with identical individuals
where all revenue can be raised by a head tax. With non-identical individuals and a concern for equity, the introduction of an optimal Pigouvian tax
requires a simultaneous reoptimization of the whole tax system. The
optimal Pigouvian tax will combine three considerations. First the marginal damages of all the victims of the externality are weighted by their
social marginal value of income; the social marginal welfare weights are not
equalized as in the first-best model because of the imperfect tax instruments. The second consideration is the distributional weight of the
consumption that is taxed: the more the good is consumed disproportionally by lower-income individuals the lower should be the tax burden
imposed on that good. The final consideration is the marginal cost of
public funds, which is higher than 1 because raising revenue in an equitable
way implies inefficiency losses. The reoptimization of the rest of the tax
system can be complex. When extra tax revenue becomes available via the
Pigouvian tax it may be optimal for equity purposes to spend part of the
revenue to increase a lump sum subsidy to all households. This contradicts
the simple double-dividend prescription.

In the second-best models, the optimal levels of supply of public goods
is determined via the Samuelson condition that is amended in three ways:

one takes into account the socially weighted sum of marginal damages to consumers; the marginal cost of public funds is taken into account; and finally, one takes into account the feedback of the environmental quality on the consumption of taxed goods, as the level of the public good can lower or raise the inefficiencies proper to the tax system. The same considerations apply to the supply of environmental goods.

The foregoing discussion has been cast in terms of a reoptimization of a full set of commodity and income taxes. Of course when only the Pigouvian tax, or other environmental instruments, can be controlled, the determination of the optimal instrument calls for complex rules in which distributional weights and existing tax distortions come into play. General equilibrium cost–benefit rules can be found in Drèze and Stern (1987) and, more specifically for the environment, in Johansson (1993).

References
Andreoni, J. (1988), 'Privately provided public goods in a large economy: the limits of altruism', *Journal of Public Economics*, **35**, 57–73.
Andreoni, J. (1990), 'Impure altrusim and donations to public goods: a theory of warm-glow giving', *Economic Journal*, **100**, 464–77.
Atkinson, A.B. and J.E. Stiglitz (1980), *Lectures on Public Economics*, New York: McGraw-Hill.
Bergstrom, T., L. Blume and H. Varian (1986), 'On the private provision of public goods', *Journal of Public Economics*, **29**, 25–49.
Boyer, M. and J.J. Laffont (1996), 'Toward a political theory of environmental policy', *Nota di Lavoro* 56.96, Fondazione ENI Mattei, Italy.
Braden, J. and S. Proost (eds) (1997), *The Economic Theory of Environmental Policy in a Federal System*, Cheltenham, UK and Lyme, US: Edward Elgar.
Buchholz, W. and K.A. Konrad (1995), 'Strategic transfers and private provision of public goods', *Journal of Public Economics*, **39**, 157–76.
Chander P. and H. Tulkens (1995), 'A core theoretic solution for the design of cooperative agreements on transfrontier pollution', *International Tax and Public Finance*, **2**, 279–96.
Diamond, P.A. and J.A. Mirrlees (1971), 'Optimal taxation and public production I: Production efficiency and II: Tax rules', *American Economic Review*, **61**, 8–27 and 261–78.
Drèze, J.J. (1994), 'Forty years of public economics: a personal perspective', *CORE discussion paper*, no. 9478.
Drèze, J. and N. Stern (1987), 'The theory of cost–benefit analysis', in A.J. Auerbach and M. Feldstein (eds), *Handbook of Public Economics*, vol. II, Amsterdam: North-Holland.
Drèze, J.J. and D. de la Vallée Poussin (1971), 'A tâtonnement process for public goods', *Review of Economic Studies*, **38**, 133–50.
Eyckmans, J. and S. Proost (1997), 'Voluntary supply of greenhouse gas abatement and emission trading equilibria', in E. van Ierland and K. Gorka (eds), *The Economics of Atmospheric Pollution – Theories, Models and Applications to Central and Eastern Europe*, Berlin: Springer-Verlag.
Eyckmans, J., S. Proost and E. Schokkaert (1993), 'Equity and efficiency in greenhouse negotiations', *Kyklos*, **46**, 363–97.
Harrington, W. (1988), 'Enforcement leverage when penalties are restricted', *Journal of Public Economics*, **37**, 29–53.
Hoel, M. (1992), 'Global environmental problems: the effects of unilateral action taken by one country', *Journal of Environmental Economics and Management*, **20**, 55–70.
Ihory, T. (1996), 'International public goods and contribution productivity differentials', *Journal of Public Economics*, **61**, 139–54.

Johansson, P.-O. (1993), *Cost Benefit Analysis of Environmental Change*, Cambridge, UK: Cambridge University Press.

Kaitala, V., K.-G. Maler and H. Tulkens (1995), 'The acid rain game as a resources allocation process with an application to the international cooperation among Finland, Russia and Estonia', *Scandinavian Journal of Economics*, 325–43.

Mayeres, I. and S. Proost (1997), 'Optimal tax and public investment rules for congestion type of externalities', *Scandinavian Journal of Economics*, **99** (2), 255–73.

Mueller, D.C. (1990), *Public Choice II*, Cambridge, UK: Cambridge University Press.

Myles, G.E. (1995), *Public Economics*, Cambridge, UK: Cambridge University Press.

Niskanen, W.A. (1971), *Bureaucracy and Representative Government*, Chicago: Aldine.

Oates, W. (1972), *Fiscal Federalism*, New York: Harcourt Brace Jovanovich.

Sandmo, A. (1975), 'Optimal taxation in the presence of externalities', *Swedish Journal of Economics*, **77**, 86–98.

23 Explaining instrument choice in environmental policies

Frank J. Dietz and Herman R.J. Vollebergh[1]

1. The Dominance of command-and-control instruments

Current environmental policies in industrialized countries are dominated by command-and-control (CAC) instruments (Downing and Hanf, 1983; Opschoor and Vos, 1989; Opschoor et al., 1994). Regulatory techniques, such as uniform reduction percentages across pollution sources, input restrictions, product requirements and technology-specific prescriptions, adjust the behaviour of individual economic agents corresponding to particular environmental goals, usually emission standards.

In contrast, the economics literature is dominated by the view that environmental goals could be achieved at lower costs if economic or market-based instruments were more often used.[2] Instruments such as emission charges, product charges, tax differentiation, subsidies, deposit-refund systems and tradable pollution rights change the (price) incentive structure economic agents face. These more indirect interventions leave room for a flexible response to environmental demands of society, mobilizing the (search for) knowledge of technological feasibilities and local physical constraints of individual economic agents to accommodate their polluting activities to particular environmental policy goals. In turn, flexibility creates cost-efficiency, as has been shown in the influential work of Baumol and Oates (1971; 1988, pp. 159–76).

Looking at the dominance of the CAC approach in environmental policies, the question arises why the frequent pleas for the application of market-based instruments have had so little impact on (the design of) environmental policies in the last two decades? Ignorance is not a valid explanation, as both Kelman (1981) and Hanley et al. (1990) have shown for quite different periods. Those involved in the process of policy design appear familiar with the core of the argument in favour of market-based instruments: improving cost-effectiveness by allowing a non-uniform, that is, flexible response to environmental demands. But if unfamiliarity is not the main reason, what, then, explains the back seat of market-based instruments in environmental policies?

This chapter reviews the contributions in the economics literature providing *economic* explanations for this observable fact. The aim here is to explain why some instruments have actually been chosen over others. Studies in line with this approach are scarce. By far the major part of economics is part of the so-called 'normative' tradition in welfare economics. According to this tradition the choice of instrument is guided by optimization procedures for a given objective or criterion for choice (usually economic efficiency).[3] Dealing with explanations for the dominance of regulatory instruments in environmental policies, however, this chapter fits into the positive approach to instrument choice, which is primarily based on interest identification, conflict resolution and analysis of political pressure.

As noted, only a few contributions in the economics literature explicitly aim to explain the dominance of CAC instruments in practical environment policy design.[4] Although these attempts have a common (methodological) basis, they are usually rather *ad hoc*, focusing on one particular agency or interest group while at the same time neglecting the role of others. In some studies the influence of interest groups on environmental policy design is emphasized, while in others special attention is paid to the interests of politicians and bureaucrats. To our knowledge, the role of interest groups such as environmentalists is not even seriously studied at all. Next, we discuss the literature explaining the dominance of the regulatory approach in environmental policies by distinguishing explicitly between the role of two major interest groups on the one hand and the role of the central agents in the policy process on the other.

2. Political pressure from interest groups

As noted, we only distinguish two categories of interest groups in the context of environmental policy design. First, various polluting branches or industries which are supposed to focus on the impact of environmental policy on their profits. Second, those agents who are thought to be more concerned with the impact of policy on the environment, for simplicity called 'environmentalists'. Environmentalists not only represent a variety of ecological groups (including victims of pollution), but also others, such as consumer organizations, which demonstrate great care for the environment in addition to their main objective of promoting consumer interests.

Polluters
In their seminal paper Buchanan and Tullock (1975) have shown why polluting industries can be expected to prefer CAC regulation over emission taxes. From the viewpoint of a firm, taxes increase costs more than equivalent emission standards. Because a tax must be paid on top of the abatement costs, the incentive to seek for rents is not only higher for the polluter, but also for those who have a stake in the distribution of the collected rev-

enues.[5] In addition, quota regulation with quotas assigned to existing firms might increase firm profits due to the *de facto* entry barrier created. Aversion of polluters will not be less if the alternative of auctioned tradable pollution permits is introduced as, in equilibrium, the costs of obtaining permits would be equal to the costs of the emission tax (Pezzy, 1992).

The reason why polluting industries would prefer CAC regulation to protect their interests against new competitors can be illustrated easily. In the case of product-specific regulation, for example, established firms enjoy the advantage of negotiating product specifications and the compliance period. Another example is the aim of industries to keep pollution permits inalienable, offering only the inframarginal firms, which remain in the industry, the opportunity to capture rents from regulation (Maloney and McCormick, 1982; Dietz and Termeer, 1991). Such negotiated agreements also favour the regulator, because the monitoring and enforcement costs are relatively low once inalienable permits, industry-specific standards or product-specific regulations are obtained (Maloney and McCormick, 1982; Verbruggen, 1994).

As far as the *intra*firm interests are concerned, Dewees (1983) notes that both shareholders and employees of a polluting firm also have a stake in instruments which affect profits least. In general, both suffer from any reduction in a firm's profits and therefore might prefer regulation with the lowest additional transfer of pollution rights. Hence firms and those who are dependent on their performance can be expected to resist emission taxes and auctioned tradable permit proposals more strongly than direct regulation.

Having an interest, however, does not explain political influence. Nevertheless, firms are also quite effective in exerting pressure in favour of particular instruments. One likely explanation might be their small number compared to the general public. As explained in the seminal contributions of Stigler (1971) and Peltzman (1976) on the role of interest groups in public decision making, the transactions costs of mobilizing and coordinating individual firms into one (lobbying) voice are relatively modest. At the same time, the willingness to contribute financially by individual firms will be high because the choice of instrument has a substantial impact on the financial performance of individual firms. Furthermore, the regulator is easily tempted to satisfy the preferences of existing firms, because the (social) costs of introducing environmental regulation reducing competition and creating rents for vested firms can be dispersed over a large number of taxpayers or consumers. The additional costs for the individual taxpayer or consumer are usually too small to constitute an incentive to organize resistance. But even if such costs are substantial, high transactions costs might prevent the development of sufficient countervailing power.

Cost shifting to taxpayers and consumers only partly explains the success of the rent-seeking efforts of polluting industries. An additional explanation mentioned in the literature is asymmetric information between polluters and regulator (Frey, 1983, pp. 242–3; Verbruggen, 1991 and 1994; Ogus, 1994; Faure and Ruegg, 1994). The regulating agency needs information from polluting industries on marginal and average costs of production processes and cleaner technologies available, for example in order to judge whether a specific firm really applies the Best Available Techniques at No Excessive Costs (BATNEC) as required by existing environmental law. To gather such information and to obtain cooperation instead of obstruction, the regulator has hardly any other choice but to go for a consultation with the industry involved. Usually this consultation results in a negotiating process, offering existing industries ample rent-seeking opportunities.

It is sometimes suggested that asymmetric information would equally apply to market-based instruments. However, this is not the case as far as the cost-minimizing property of market-based instruments is concerned. The crucial element of the Baumol–Oates theorem is that information on cost curves and technological potentials is not required if market-based instruments are used (Baumol and Oates, 1971, 1988, pp. 159–76). The decision to abate the emissions or to pay the tax is decentralized and left to the polluter. Such information is only necessary if the regulator aims at maximizing social welfare, that is, weighting the (marginal) benefits of avoided environmental damage versus the (marginal) abatement costs. Without this information a process of trial and error can be used to approach the social optimum. Only if trial and error is perceived inappropriate, for instance because it dramatically increases uncertainty in society, has the regulating agency any other option than to consult the polluting industries creating opportunities to capture rents from their monopoly on information.

The introduction of market-based instruments is not always avoidable for polluters. In such cases distributional issues tend to dominate negotiations with the regulating agency. Apart from negotiating exemptions, industries usually claim earmarking of the revenue from charges as if fairness demanded the benefit approach to environmental taxation. For instance, in water quality management it is claimed that those who have to pay tax for water discharges also should get subsidies on equipment to abate water pollution (Hahn, 1989). Hence, instead of interpreting regulatory charges as shadow prices for using particular environmental resources, industries see charges as ordinary fund raising by government, which justify earmarking of the revenues.

Indeed, this kind of rent-seeking behaviour is what one would expect from the economic point of view. Although, in general, taxes and tradable permits leave less room for discretion at the individual level, sufficient possibilities for rent-seeking still remain for polluters as they can try to influence the *design* of the tax or permit system itself.[6] In the case of a tax or tradable permit system, polluters can be expected to minimize the financial impact of this instrument by struggling over their distributional effects (Buchanan, 1980). For instance, the choice of an environmental tax can be used to argue for other specific tax bases, exemptions or reduced rates. Moreover, the frequent claims for earmarking of the revenues of this tax point to the importance of the existing distribution of property rights as existing firms would reap the benefit here at the expense of the less polluting newcomers to the market.

The opposition to auctioning of pollution rights which can be observed in practice also shows the importance of the existing distribution of property rights. In those cases in which markets in pollution rights are created, 'grandfathering' of pollution rights to existing firms based on the current distribution of rights appears to be an important focal point (Welch, 1983). All existing tradable permit systems applied in the US, for instance, 'grandfather' pollution rights as this precludes the additional transfer to the government (Hahn, 1989). Here the distributional issue as to who has the right to pollute is clearly solved in favour of the existing polluters as they receive their rights without any payment. The current distribution of rights is further consolidated by the fact that newcomers on the market usually face a stricter environmental regime than established firms. Such a different treatment of firms undoubtedly facilitates the introduction of environmental measures, because the resistance of vested polluting sources is reduced at the expense of new sources who cannot vote.

Environmentalists
As victims of pollution one would expect environmentalists to be clearly in favour of economic instruments as they force polluters to pay a price for any amount of pollution. Traditionally, however, environmentalists have firmly opposed market-based instruments and only recently have some environmentalists changed their opinion and started to defend the use of taxation in environmental policies, although tradable permits are still met with scepticism (Weale, 1992, pp. 154–85). Explicit attempts to explain this opposition by environmentalists in the economics literature are lacking, as well as a positive theory of the role of environmental interest groups in general.[7] We do not aim to fill this gap here, but instead present some ideas which might be helpful as a starting point for such a theory.

One important issue related to differences in consequences between instruments is the role of uncertainty. As Weitzman (1974) has shown, uncertainty might explain why, in general, quantity-based environmental regulation might be preferred to price-based regulation, because the risk of missing the reduction target might be higher in the case of price-based regulation. Therefore, if environmentalists were risk-averse with respect to the effectiveness of policy instruments, inefficient use of social means in quantity-based regulation would have a much lower weight. In this perspective, social benefits are higher the more effectively an instrument constrains the acts of polluters with the optimum equal to zero pollution. Direct interventions in polluting activities serve this aim better than the indirect method of price manipulation. In the same vein, the flexibility of tradable permit systems might therefore be considered as a higher risk compared to traditional CAC regulation. None the less, it remains somewhat surprising that environmentalists do not embrace economic instruments, including auctioned tradable permits, as they force polluters to pay a price for any use of the environment, while regulation through legal standards leaves the right to pollute unaffected, without costs below this standard.

Probably the most fundamental reason for opposing market-based instruments has a moral basis. Environmentalists fear that these instruments may give a certain legitimacy to the act of polluting (Kelman, 1981, pp. 45–6). For most environmentalists a charge or a tradable permit is a licence to pollute: if you pay, polluting is allowed. In their view, polluting, even if monetary compensation is paid, is morally just as improper as robbery. Society does not sanction robbing a bank if you are 'willing to pay' the penalty of, say, five year in prison for it. On the contrary, the penalty is a signal of society's disapproval. People should not rob banks, even if it can be demonstrated that the money would mean more to the robber than to the depositors. In the same way as most people do not accept the utilitarian idea of an 'optimal amount of bank robberies', environmentalists reject the concept of an optimal amount of pollution. Similarly, a firm with high abatement costs – being the equivalent of the desperately poor man robbing a bank – should not be exempted from its duty on utilitarian grounds.

A closely related objection by environmentalists to market-based instruments is their concern that pricing natural assets may erode the level of environmental quality society desires to attain (Kelman, 1981, pp. 69–77). This concern is based on the feeling that natural assets are debased if a monetary value is assigned to, for example, the assimilative capacity of a marine estuary. In other words, the absence of a price for unspoiled nature expresses its special status, just as human beings, liberty and health are not for sale. Indeed, empirically there is certainly evidence that people are reluctant to place money values on natural resources (Sagoff, 1988, pp. 68–9; Hanley, 1989; Stevens et al., 1991; Blamey et al., 1995).[8]

Summarizing, although the motives differ, both polluting firms and environmentalists show a distinct preference for direct regulation in environmental issues. Therefore it is not surprising that they have cooperated in several cases in order to influence environmental policy (design) in the desired direction (see, for example, Ackerman and Hassler, 1981; Maloney and McCormick, 1982). In general, environmentalists have provided political support on the side of the polluting industry to seek direct regulation, because both expect to benefit from output reductions at the expense of potential newcomers on the market as well as consumers.

3.   The regulator

So far we have implicitly assumed that environmental policies are designed and implemented by a single, or representative, decision maker. This is obviously an oversimplification. Again, however, the economics literature explaining the choice of environmental policy instruments, in view of the specific interests agents have in the political process, is remarkably scarce. Although more categories or roles of actors in the public sector could be distinguished (see, for example, Nentjes and Dijkstra, 1994), this section is confined to the role of politicians and bureaucrats.

Politicians

Compared to market-based instruments, CAC instruments offer politicians better opportunities to present an image as caring for the environment. As, according to public choice theory, politicians seek maximum electoral support, such an image is important as long as environmental quality matters for the electorate at large. Advocating measures such as emission reduction percentages, prescribed technical adaptions, input restrictions and product requirements shows the public politicians who apparently stand firm against environmental degradation. The inefficiencies of these measures attract much less attention and are, according to suspicious minds, better to hide (Dietz and van der Straaten, 1992). After all, without sufficient information on (aggregated) abatement costs and dose–effect relations, the environmental gain of market-based instruments is rather uncertain.

The worst-case scenario for a politician is, not surprisingly, the example of implementing a charge which hardly has environmental effects but generates substantial costs. Then, the responsible politicians will receive criticism from all parties involved:

- from environmentalists, because the promised environmental improvement has failed to materialize;
- from employers, who accuse the government of ordinary fund raising using the environment as an excuse;
- from employees, being afraid of losing their jobs in industries which are to a large extent established on pollution and have to compete on

world markets (for example, intensive agriculture, transportation by air and by road);
- from citizens, because their financial sacrifices (for example, through an increased excise duty on petrol) have no (visible) environmental effects, generating the perception of politicians who sneakily raise taxes.

If strictly maintained, regulatory instruments avoid this twofold risk. Moreover, politicians prefer the efficiency risk of regulatory instruments over the environmental effectiveness risk of market-based instruments since society expects, above all, physical environmental results from environmental policies (de Savornin Lohman, 1994).

Economists usually consider abatement cost minimization as the most important criterion for selecting instruments to attain environmental goals once they are determined. However, political processes are often dominated by other values, especially equity, more or less reflecting the 'value hierarchy' in society. For electoral reasons, politicians are highly sensitive to (substantial) redistributions of income due to their decisions, which may easily mobilize 'hurt interests' (Rolph, 1983; Welch, 1983). Indeed, the increasing attention to environmental taxes and their assumed double dividend have been linked with the requirement of 'revenue neutrality': new environmental taxes are only considered if the revenue raised is used to reduce other taxes (de Mooij and Vollebergh, 1995; Pearson, 1995).

As distributional impacts are inescapable, politicians prefer smaller redistributions to larger ones. This 'distributional inertia' (de Savornin Lohman, 1994) appears to be an additional force pushing the use of regulatory instruments in environmental policies, while holding back economic instruments. Under a regime of regulatory instruments polluters only pay for abatement. Applying economic instruments means, in principle, payment for both abatement costs and residual emissions. Hence, if politicians seek to minimize social unrest – which is generated by each substantial redistribution of income – 'furnishing' environmental policies with regulatory instruments offers the least distributional impacts at the expense of the cost-minimizing allocation.

Apart from minimizing distributional impacts of environmental policies, politicians might be constrained for constitutional reasons in their abilities to choose a specific type of instrument (Boyer and Laffont, 1996). Such a constitutional constraint is optimal if it prevents politicians from distributing rents towards, for example, interest groups. Hence Boyer and Laffont argue that economists' comparison of instruments on some cost-efficiency criterion is questionable if one recognizes the inefficiencies of the political process.[9]

Bureaucrats

In interviews bureaucrats show a considerable degree of satisfaction with the environmental results of the current regulatory system through CAC instruments. They demonstrate little interest or even a blind spot for improving the cost-efficiency of environmental policies (Hanley et al., 1990). Assuming bureaucrats are concerned with the size of their department or budget available, executive bureaucrats have vested interests in the *status quo*, that is, they have several reasons to thwart initiatives for applying more market-based instruments in environmental policies. First of all and also mentioned in the literature, CAC regulation creates more jobs and influence for bureaucrats than allowing the market to perform some of the regulation (Frey, 1983, pp. 237, 240, 246; Rees, 1988). A switch to a market-based approach, especially in the case of environmental taxes, inevitably means sharing responsibilities with the Treasury, which is usually in charge of collecting taxes but lacks an explicit environmental mission (Kelman, 1981, p. 134).

Second, the vested agency on environmental affairs would bear the brunt of the organizational learning that a switch to a new system would imply. As people usually have a conservative attitude towards change, they perceive new trends as threatening to the 'easy life' of the present. Those individual employees who are sympathetic to new approaches, including using market-based instruments, therefore need 'outside pressure' to have a fair chance of changing the attitude of the agency from resistance to cooperation (Kelman, 1981, p. 135).

An additional observation which might explain the hostile attitude of bureaucrats towards economic instruments is departmental compartmentalization, which has paralysing effects on environmental policies. Usually two, three, and sometimes more departments are involved in the formulation of a particular environmental policy. As regulatory instruments offer the best opportunity to protect the share of a particular sector in overall reduction programmes, they can be used for pacification purposes in the 'struggle' between departments. Indeed, each of these departments pays special attention to the economic interests of 'their industry', although they scrupulously avoid speaking of representing the interests of these industries in the policy-making process.

The abatement of acidifying emissions in the Netherlands is only one interesting example as acid rain policy here requires the cooperation of at least the following departments:

- the Ministry for Environmental Affairs, as the architect of the abatement strategy;
- the Ministry of Agriculture, 'representing' the livestock sector whose

spreading of manure on land generates substantial acidifying emissions of ammonia;
- the Ministry of Transport and Public Works, which is in charge of the infrastructure and has a special eye for the interests of truckers and the largest part of the population as confirmed motorists, contributing considerably to the acidification by their NO_x emissions;
- the Ministry of Economic Affairs, being in charge of, among other things, employment and the climate for investment, which could deteriorate due to a strict abatement policy.

Not surprisingly, conflicts on 'how much the environment can bear', the distribution of residual emissions among sectors and the costs of environmental protection dominate this cooperation. Consequently, regulatory instruments are preferred, offering the best opportunity to protect the share of a particular sector in the allowable emissions.

4. Concluding remarks

The preceding discussion of the positive analysis of instrument choice in environmental policies is, of course, not exhaustive. Additional thwarting institutions and forces can result from existing legislation which does not (yet) permit the adoption of market-based instruments for the control of pollution (see, for example, Hanley et al., 1990, Pearson, 1995), or the resistance generated by the asymmetrical geographical distribution of the impacts of alternative instruments (see, for example, Segerson, 1996).

Such additional elements and refinements in the analysis, however, would not radically change the overall picture: despite the diversity of interests of most economic agents involved in the formulation of environmental policies – both officially (politicians, executive bureaucrats) and unofficially (polluting industries, environmentalists) – all these interests appear to be best served by CAC regulation, which might explain its widespread application in practice. Even though agreement on the goals of pollution control might be missing, most forces in the policy-making process seem to be satisfied by using the same tool, that is, using regulatory instruments while neglecting the use of market-based instruments. Now that CAC instruments are 'locked into' current environmental policy practices in most countries, this creates – usually tacitly and often unconsciously – an additional barrier to the introduction of a market-based policy approach.

As far as the positive economics literature is concerned, we found relatively few explicit contributions which aim to explain the preferences of particular agents for the use of specific instruments in environmental policy. It seems that only recently are theorists beginning to explore this area in more detail. For instance, Boyer and Laffont (1996) provide an explanation for a preference of politicians for CAC if they face a constitutionally constrained choice of mechanism. Another interesting new contribution is Jung et al. (1995) who explore the behaviour of agents around rights or entitlements distributions in a game-theoretic setting, where agents with asymmetric information and differential power can attempt to probabilistically influence the rights distribution. However, as our chapter has shown, considerable work remains to be done in explaining the role and preferences of other interest groups, such as environmentalists, as well as apparent changes in preferences over time. It is somewhat unsatisfactory if the explanation were simply that only a few of those involved in the formulation of environmental policies have backgrounds in economics, which hinders perceiving things through the organizing principles of the microeconomic paradigm (Kelman, 1981, p. 148; Hanley et al., 1990). In that case one has to wonder what relevance this paradigm might have after all.

Notes
1. We would like to thank D.J. Wolfson, two referees and the editor for comments on an earlier draft of this chapter.
2. Not all economists share this view. Frey et al. (1985) find this conviction held mainly with university-employed and theoretically inclined professional economists living in a market-oriented country, while public sector employed and policy-oriented professional economists living in a country with a long tradition of government intervention often prefer the use of regulatory instruments.
3. A well-known summary of the theoretical literature is Bohm and Russell (1985) and the review in this book (notably Chapters 15 and 21). A recent example of translating these theoretical ideas into more practical policy proposals is Dietz et al. (1995).
4. By focusing on environmental policy design we implicitly assume policy intervention by governments with the existing distribution of property rights taken as given. Thus we neglect (voluntary) transactions between agents without government intervention (Coase, 1960), as well as issues of rent-seeking behaviour over entitlements (see Buchanan, 1980; Jung et al., 1995). For the latter see Chapter 17.
5. Rent-seeking in this context refers to the resource-using activities of regulated agents with the intention to influence environmental policy controls, implying artificially contrived transfers (see Tollison, 1982; Mueller, 1989, pp. 229–46).
6. Only so-called 'pure' economic instruments do not allow for any infringement of the general structure of the tax or (auctioned) permit system, for example, through exemptions or reduced rates. As Vollebergh et al. (1997) argue, such infringements can also be used by the government to attain overall political acceptability without sacrificing the cost-minimizing character of these instruments.
7. As suggested by a referee, one might think here of individual citizens with an above-average preference for environmental quality compared to other goods and apply the usual theory of the (expected) benefits of collective action.
8. Obviously, this perception on prices is rather different from their role as indicators for relative scarcity adopted by most economists (see also chapters on valuation in Part VII of this book).
9. The (normative) implication of this line of thought is, however, that politicians might even optimize social welfare by preferring less sophisticated incentive instruments, such as CAC instruments.

350 Economics of environmental policy

References

Ackerman, B.A. and W.T. Hassler (1981), *Clean Coal/Dirty Air*, New Haven, CT: Yale
University Press.
Baumol, W.J. and W.E. Oates (1971), 'The use of standards and prices for protection of the
environment', *Swedish Journal of Economics*, **73**, 42–54.
Baumol, W.J. and W.E. Oates (1988), *The Theory of Environmental Policy*, Cambridge, UK:
Cambridge University Press.
Blamey, R., M. Common and J. Quiggin (1995), 'Respondents to contingent valuation
surveys: consumers or citizens?', *Australian Journal of Agricultural Economics*, **39** (3),
263–88.
Bohm, P. and C.S. Russell (1985), 'Comparative analysis of alternative policy instruments', in
A.V. Kneese and J.L. Sweeney (eds), *Handbook of Natural Resource and Energy Economics*,
vol. I, Amsterdam: North-Holland, pp. 395–460.
Boyer, M. and J.-J. Laffont (1996), '*Toward a political theory of environmental policy*', *Nota di
Lavoro* 56.96, Fondazione ENI Mattei, Italy.
Buchanan, J.M. (1980), 'Rent-seeking under external diseconomies', in J.M. Buchanan, R.D.
Tollison and G. Tullock (eds), *Toward a Theory of the Rent-seeking Society*, Texas: A&M
Press.
Buchanan, J.M. and G. Tullock (1975), 'Polluters' profits and political response: direct con-
trols versus taxes', *American Economic Review*, **65**, 139–47.
Coase, R. (1960), 'The problem of social cost', *Journal of Law and Economics*, **3**, 1–44.
Dewees, D. (1983), 'Instrument choice in environmental policy', *Economic Inquiry*, **21**, 53–71.
Dietz, F.J. and K.J.A.M. Termeer (1991), 'Dutch manure policy: the lack of economic instru-
ments', in D.J. Kraan and R.J. in 't Veld (eds), *Environmental Protection: Public or Private
Choice*, Dordrecht: Kluwer Academic Publishers, pp. 149–63.
Dietz, F.J. and J. van der Straaten (1992), 'Rethinking environmental economics: missing links
between economic theory and environmental policy', *Journal of Economic Issues*, **26** (1),
27–51.
Dietz, F.J., H.R.J. Vollebergh and J.L. de Vries (eds) (1995), *Environment, Incentives and the
Common Market*, Dordrecht: Kluwer Academic Publishers.
Downing, P.B. and K. Hanf (1983), *International Comparisons in Implementing Pollution
Laws*, Boston: Kluwer Academic Publishers.
Faure, M. and M. Ruegg (1994), 'Environmental standard setting through general principles
of environmental law', in M. Faure, J. Vervaele and A. Weale (eds), *Environmental Standards
in the European Union in an Interdisciplinary Framework*, Antwerp: MAKLU, pp. 36–60.
Frey, B.S. (1983), *Democratic Economic Policy*, Oxford: Martin Robertson.
Frey, B.S., F. Schneider and W.W. Pommerehne (1985), 'Economists' opinions on environmen-
tal policy instruments: Analysis of a survey', *Journal of Environmental Economics and
Management*, *12*, 62–71.
Hahn, R.W. (1989), 'Economic prescriptions for environmental problems: how the patient fol-
lowed the doctor's orders', *Journal of Economic Perspectives*, **3** (2), 95–114.
Hanley, N. (1989), 'Valuing non-market goods using contingent valuation', *Journal of
Economic Surveys*, **3** (3), 235–52.
Hanley, N., S. Hallett and I. Moffatt (1990), 'Why is more notice not taken of economists' pre-
scriptions for the control of pollution?', *Environment and Planning A*, **22**, 1421–39.
Jung, C., K. Krutilla, W.K. Viscusi and R.G. Boyd (1995), 'The Coase theorem in a rent-
seeking society', *International Review of Law and Economics*, **15**, 259–68.
Kelman, S. (1981), *What Price Incentives? Economists and the Environment*, Boston: Auburn.
Maloney, M.T. and R.E. McCormick (1982), 'A positive theory of environmental quality reg-
ulation', *Journal of Law and Economics*, **25**, 99–123.
Mooij, R. de and H.R.J. Vollebergh (1995), 'Prospects for environmental tax reform', in F.J.
Dietz et al. (1995), pp. 139–59.
Mueller, D.C. (1989), *Public Choice II*, Cambridge, UK: Cambridge University Press.
Nentjes, A. and B. Dijkstra (1994), 'The political economy of instrument choice in environ-
mental policy', in M. Faure, J. Vervaele and A. Weale (eds), *Environmental Standards in the
European Union in an Interdisciplinary Framework*, Antwerp: MAKLU, pp. 197–216.

Ogus, A. (1994), 'Standard setting for environmental protection: principles and processes', in M. Faure, J. Vervaele and A. Weale (eds), *Environmental Standards in the European Union in an Interdisciplinary Framework*, Antwerp: MAKLU, pp. 25–37.

Opschoor, J.B. and H. Vos (1989), *Economic Instruments for Environmental Protection*, Paris: OECD.

Opschoor, J.B., A.F. de Savornin Lohman and H.B. Vos (1994), *Managing the Environment: The Role of Economic Instruments*, Paris: OECD.

Pearson, M. (1995), 'The political economy of implementing environmental taxes', *International Tax and Public Finance*, **2** (2), 357–74.

Peltzman, S. (1976), 'Towards a more general theory of regulation', *Journal of Law and Economics*, **19**, 211–400.

Pezzey, J. (1992), 'The symmetry between controlling pollution by price and controlling it by quantity', *Canadian Journal of Economics*, **25** (4), 983–99.

Rees, J. (1988), 'Pollution control objectives and the regulatory framework', in R.K. Turner (ed.), *Sustainable Environmental Management. Principles and Practice*, Boulder, CO: Westview Press, pp. 170–89.

Rolph, E. (1983), 'Government allocation of property rights: who gets what?', *Journal of Policy Analysis and Management*, **3** (1), 45–61.

Sagoff, M. (1988), *The Economy of the Earth*, Cambridge, UK: Cambridge University Press.

Savornin Lohman, L. de (1994), 'Economic incentives in environmental policy: why are they white ravens?', in J.B. Opschoor and R.K. Turner (eds), *Economic Incentives and Environmental Policies: Principles and Practice*, Dordrecht: Kluwer Academic Publishers, pp. 55–67.

Segerson, K. (1996), 'Issues in the choice of environmental policy instruments', in J.B. Braden, H. Folmer and T.S. Ulen (eds), *Environmental Policy with Political and Economic Integration*, Cheltenham, UK and Brookfield, US: Edward Elgar, pp. 149–74.

Stevens, T.H., J. Echeverria, R.J. Glass, T. Hager and T.A. More (1991), 'Measuring the existence value of wildlife: what do CVM estimates really show?', *Land Economics*, **67** (4), 390–400.

Stigler, G.J. (1971), 'The theory of economic regulation', *Bell Journal of Economics*, **2**, 3–21.

Tollison, R.D. (1982), 'Rent seeking: a survey', *Kyklos*, **35**, 575–602.

Verbruggen, H. (1991), 'Political economy aspects of environmental policy instruments', in F.J. Dietz, F. van der Ploeg and J. van der Straaten (eds), *Environmental Policy and the Economy*, Amsterdam: North-Holland, pp. 77–93.

Verbruggen, H. (1994), 'Environmental policy failures and environmental policy levels', in J.B. Opschoor and R.K. Turner (eds), *Economic Incentives and Environmental Policies: Principles and Practice*, Dordrecht: Kluwer Academic Publishers, pp. 41–54.

Vollebergh, H.R.J., J.L. de Vries and P.R. Koutstaal (1997), 'Hybrid carbon incentive mechanisms and political acceptability', *Environmental and Resource Economics*, **9** (1), 43–63.

Weale, A. (1992), *The New Politics of Pollution*, Manchester, UK: Manchester University Press.

Weitzman, M.L. (1974), 'Prices vs. quantities', *Review of Economic Studies*, **41** (4), 477–91.

Welch, W.P. (1983), 'The political feasibility of full ownership property rights: the cases of pollution and fisheries', *Policy Sciences*, **16**, 165–80.

24 Equity in environmental policy with an application to global warming
Adam Rose and Snorre Kverndokk[1]

1. Background

A hallmark of political economy, as economics was known in the nineteenth century because of its policy emphasis, was the co-equal status of aggregate and distributional analysis, often translating into co-equal concern with efficiency and equity. It was clear from the beginning, however, that the latter term defied universal agreement as to its precise definition, though it was generally held to be synonymous with the concept of fairness.[2] It was acknowledged that equity had deeper and more profound philosophical roots than did efficiency. To some this became a stigma. The combination of philosophical depth and competing definitions led critics to focus on the value judgements underlying equity, and to conclude that equity in particular and the current status of welfare economics (the twentieth-century synonym for political economy in the mainstream of the profession) in general were inherently subjective and therefore on shaky ground. This attitude reached its peak in the work of Robbins (1935), who recommended that for economics to become more scientific it must be purged of all value judgements.

Little (1957), Nath (1969), and others have pointed out that even some aspects of economic efficiency are value-laden. However, the immediate response to Robbins by much of the economics profession was to rally around the welfare criteria of Pareto, which focused on efficiency as the sole objective of welfare. Analysts soon pointed out the inherent conservativeness and policy paralysis associated with the Pareto rule: a policy should only be implemented if no one is made worse off by it.[3] Obviously very few policies can meet this test in the real world. However, even the major resolution, as offered by Hicks (1939) and Kaldor (1939), of winners compensating losers in the policy process, was only put forth in terms of potential. That is, whether compensation was actually to be granted was not a matter for economists to decide (or even to evaluate), but rather up to the discretion of policy makers, because it was a matter of equity.

At about the same time, however, another branch of mainstream economics found a way of salvaging equity considerations. The dominant approach to policy analysis before Robbins was characterized by the work of Pigou (1932), and vulnerable to criticism because equity and efficiency considerations were often intertwined unnecessarily. For example, the assumptions of diminishing marginal utility of income (measured in cardinal numbers), together with the explicit or implicit assumption of equivalent or near-equivalent utility functions, always implied that the total welfare of society could be improved by transfers of income from the rich to the poor, and thus pre-ordained many policy outcomes. In response, Bergson (1938) and Samuelson (1947) formalized the concept of a social welfare function (SWF), in which it was possible to separate efficiency and equity considerations, though trade-offs between the two objectives still prevail (as illustrated below). This construct kept intact most of the Paretian welfare economics structure, which in part was a formalization of Adam Smith's main doctrine that, in a market economy, each individual pursuing his or her own self-interest would lead to the attainment of the highest overall level of (a solely efficiency-based definition of) well-being for society. This has come to be known as the first fundamental theorem of welfare economics in the specialized form that a competitive equilibrium implies Pareto optimality. But the Bergson–Samuelson formulation clearly emphasized that, while the market could ensure an efficient allocation of resources, it was blind to equity, and hence by itself could not ensure a maximum of welfare (if welfare is defined beyond efficiency to include equity, or, more generally, if welfare also includes public goods, such as environmental quality).

Today mainstream economics offers a framework to include equity (mainly in relation to work on social welfare functions), or to ignore it (adherence to strict interpretations of Pareto's work). There are also heterodox views from the Left and the Right, as well as from another dimension, the Green, to further highlight, downplay or redefine equity. The focus of this chapter is on more mainstream, humanistic theories in a static (intragenerational) context.[4] We begin with welfaristic theories based on social welfare functions, and then consider several alternatives. The reader is referred to the chapter by Martínez-Alier and O'Connor in this volume (Chapter 25) for a broader set of distributional issues including aspects of time-discounting and sustainability; the chapter by Glasser (Chapter 66) for naturalist and non-humanist philosophies; and the chapter by Blamey and Common (Chapter 56) on ethics and valuation.

Equity is of no less importance in environmental and natural resource economics than it is in economics in general. One reason is that both environmental catastrophes and chronic problems have disproportionate impacts across socioeconomic groups and regions (see, for example, Bryant and Mohai, 1992). Moreover, disadvantaged groups have fewer resources or political clout to protect themselves (for example, inner city residents, Bhopal villagers, Alaskan fishermen, or Amazon peoples). At the same time, the relatively well-to-do have greater access to environmental amenities. Finally, much of the natural resource base in the US and other countries is owned by the government, and the question of resource allocation raises equity issues. Even the most ardent conservative who suggests that the first fundamental theorem does take equity into account because the market outcome is the 'fair' outcome (see, for example, Lane, 1986) cannot appeal to this viewpoint in cases where a market does not exist (such as mining, grazing, or logging on public lands).

Probably the most interesting new aspects of equity pertain to transboundary pollution and the fairness of policies across regions or nations. Most of the examples in this chapter will address spatial equity in the context of global warming issues. In many cases, equity principles used in interpersonal comparisons can be extended to this realm with only minor modification. However, some interesting subtleties, pitfalls and opportunities arise. Finally, in these contexts, equity has not only a normative context, but a positive one. That is, equity is worthy of pursuit not only because of fairness, but because it may enhance the likelihood of agreement between parties. Also, a great amount of recent attention to the subject has focused on dynamic, or intergenerational, equity; here again the reader is referred to other work in this volume for a more extensive treatment, most notably the chapter by Goodland on sustainability (Chapter 48) and the chapter by van den Bergh and Hofkes on sustainable development models (Chapter 72).

2. Basic principles in welfare economics

Simple analytics of welfare maximization
We can illustrate the discussion thus far with the aid of a simple diagram containing two major constructs. First is a utility possibility frontier, or UPF, which traces the maximum combination (m) of the utility (U) two individuals or groups (1,2) can attain, given all the efficient allocations of finite resources in society (see curve $U^1_m U^2_m$ in Figure 24.1). Interestingly, all of the points on the UPF are Pareto-optimal, that is, one person cannot be made better off without another person being made worse off.

Note that there are an infinite number of Pareto-optimal points on the UPF.[5] We can be assured, under ideal conditions, that the market will lead to a point on the UPF, thus illustrating the first fundamental theorem of welfare economics. but, from the standpoint of efficiency alone, the points on the UPF cannot be ranked.

However, if we introduce equity, then we have a way of preferring some

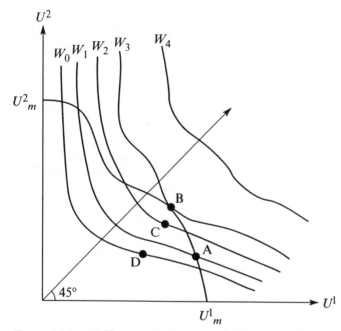

Figure 24.1   Welfare maximization and efficiency–equity trade-offs

to others. In fact that is the essence of the definition of a social welfare function – a complete ranking of all states of the economy.[6] Although many
alternative equity concepts exist (see below), the one most used in welfare
economics is 'vertical' equity, which holds that equity increases as utility (or
income) disparities between individuals decrease. (Note that this relationship need not be monotonically increasing and can reach a plateau, that is,
even most ardent supporters of this concept would not insist that everyone
should have the same utility or income.) Generally, however, equity is
enhanced as joint utility allocations in Figure 24.1 move closer to the 45°
line.

A social welfare function can be superimposed on Figure 24.1 that
embodies both efficiency and equity. The welfare contours (W_0, W_1, W_2,
W_3, W_4) are analogous to indifference curves (that is, they are horizontal
slices of a three-dimensional surface). The shape of these contours reflects
equity; the more bent toward the centre, the greater the emphasis on
equity.[7]

The welfare optimum, or *optimum optimorum* (see Bator, 1957), is given
by point B. Again, there is no guarantee that a market economy will lead
to this outcome, and, in fact, given the infinity of possible Pareto-optimal
outcomes, it is likely that it will not. Moreover, while theoretically society

can move from a competitive equilibrium but not maximum welfare outcome, such as A, to point B through the use of various types of transfers, there may be some limitations in practice, as discussed in the following section.

Efficiency–equity trade-off
For some, one major justification for downplaying equity is the efficiency–equity trade-off. This refers to the possibility that transfers to promote equity will create a work disincentive to the transferring party (usually the well-to-do), with the ensuing inefficiency limiting society to a lower level of welfare even when utilities (or incomes) are equal or made more equal. In effect, this is an empirical question, though most studies indicate that the effect is rather small (see, for example, Danziger et al., 1986).

We can use Figure 24.1 to illustrate this potential problem. Previously we noted that the ideal transfer would move society from point A to point B. However, if the disincentive effect exists, and is weak, the move would be from point A to point C, whereby there is an efficiency–equity trade-off but an unequivocal welfare gain. But it is also possible that the disincentive is strong and will result in a move from point A to point D, whereby overall welfare is even lower than in the original state. The threat of moving to point D, and even the possibility of moving to point C (note the discussion of cost-benefit analysis below) causes many economists to be nervous about pursing equity goals. We can be more certain of achieving equity with the minimum of efficiency loss if we utilize 'lump sum' transfers, or if we avoid price-distorting policies. The difficulty is that there are few lump sum transfers, that is, transfers that are not based on effort.[8] Examples of price-distorting policies are a ceiling on natural gas or oil prices, such as have been in place in the US and elsewhere, and which have typically caused a misallocation of resources, even when they have the good intentions of helping the poor cope with high energy bills. The preferred alternative is to offer an energy tax credit to low-income households. However, while most are quick to acknowledge the existence of market failure, there is a strong likelihood of 'political failure' in policy making. That is, resolutions of problems such as the ones just discussed often require coordination by two arms of government, which makes implementation all the more difficult.

The Coase theorem
One way out of this dilemma is offered by the Coase theorem (Coase, 1960), which states that in the case of externalities the delineation and assignment of property rights will lead, through market exchange, to an efficient allocation of resources, irrespective of how the rights are distributed.[9] For

years, the secondary clause of this theorem was used as a justification to ignore equity. Ironically, it now offers a reason to address it. For example, there is no supranational authority to force countries to mitigate greenhouse gases, and an agreement will only come about through voluntary compliance. Such an agreement is more likely to take hold if it is perceived to be fair. (Appeal to overall global efficiency is unlikely to win the day because it will result in such large disparities in welfare gains and losses.) Thus equity can be a unifying principle, since countries are likely to be concerned with how they are impacted alone and in relation to others. Moreover, by way of the Coase theorem, one can address equity head on in good conscience without undercutting efficiency, through a system of marketable permits for greenhouse gas emissions.

3. Extensions and alternatives

So far we have discussed the concept of equity within the framework of a social welfare function, which is the mainstream approach in economic theory. These welfaristic theories (meaning theories that focus on welfare outcomes) are in the tradition of utilitarianism. We shall take a further look at this theory as a humanistic justice theory, and also consider some nonwelfaristic approaches.

A theory of justice is, as are theories of rationality and ethics, a normative theory. Such a theory has two aspects. First, it will regulate individual rights (and duties), and second, it will propose or evaluate a distribution of goods (and burdens). Different theories of justice may weight these two aspects differently. They are, for instance, given equal weight by utilitarians, while Rawls (1971) gives political freedom and rights a lexicographical priority over economic distribution.

We shall consider global justice theories as opposed to local justice. According to Elster (1991), a 'local justice' problem is characterized by decentralized decisions, where the distribution is not contingent on compensation and the distribution consists of goods other than money. In contrast, 'global justice' problems are centrally designed, intended to compensate people for various sorts of bad luck, and typically take the form of cash transfers. The study of local justice is the normative study of how institutions allocate their scarce resources. Justice is local if the institutional distribution cannot be derived from a comprehensive redistributive scheme of society-wide or global justice, where global does not necessarily mean international. Examples of local justice problems are who shall perform military service, who shall receive organs for transplantation, and so on, while income distribution and wage determination enter into the global redistributive system and may therefore be classified as global justice problems. The rules that are chosen are independent of decisions made in other spheres of society. In fact, most institutional decisions are taken at an autonomous and separate level. However, important environmental problems such as transboundary pollution are hard to isolate as pure autonomous problems, and we therefore consider the global philosophical theories of justice (see also Elster, 1992, for an overview).

Utilitarianism

The utilitarian aim is to distribute goods so as to maximize the total utility of members of society, where 'goods' are interpreted broadly to include economic goods, rights, freedom and political power. Even though utilitarianism does not explicitly address equity, its welfare maximization objective does have distributional implications. Different versions of the theory exist. One important distinction is the difference between 'act utilitarianism' and 'rule utilitarianism' (for example, see Harsanyi, 1985). The former enjoins us to perform the act that will maximize the utility on every single occasion, while the latter tells us to act so that we will maximize total utility over time. These two forms of utilitarianism may conflict, as many actions provide immediate pleasure but long-run costs. For example, a high level of fossil fuel consumption today may maximize current welfare, but, due to the accumulation of greenhouse gases, will cause a reduction of maximum attainable welfare in the future (see Kneese and Schulze, 1985, for a more extensive discussion of utilitarian theory and its applications).

The theory of John Rawls

The theory of John Rawls (1971) can basically be seen as a critique of utilitarianism. According to Rawls, utilitarianism has no respect for individuals. A person is not seen as valuable and worth protecting in his/her own right. A classical but grotesque example is if you kill a healthy person and use his/her organs to save the life of five other human beings. This may increase the utility of society, but it does not respect individual rights. Rawls argues that a theory of justice should respect the individuals as ends in themselves.[10]

The methodological starting point of Rawls's theory is the 'original position'. Most people would argue for what is just or unjust depending on their own position in society. Therefore, as a starting point to decide the basic structure of the society, which according to Rawls is the primary subject of justice, we have to think about a hypothetical and idealized world where all individuals sit behind a veil of ignorance – the original position. They do not know their abilities, sex, race or position in society. All they know is that they are going to live in the society about which they are going to decide the basic structure. In this hypothetical situation, Rawls argues that they will agree on certain principles:

First Principle: Each person is to have an equal right to the most extensive total system of equal basic liberties compatible with a similar system of liberty for all (Rawls, 1971, p. 250).

Second principle: Social and economic inequalities are to be arranged so that they are both:

(a) to the greatest benefit of the least advantaged, and
(b) attached to offices and positions open to all under conditions of fair equality of opportunities (Rawls, 1971, pp. 302–3).

The first principle, the 'principle of greatest equal liberty', is about individual rights. As this principle has a lexicographic priority, none of the basic liberties should be traded against material advancement. However, it is the first part of the second principle, the 'difference principle', that is mostly referred to. One common misinterpretation in economics is that Rawls argues for maximizing the utility of the least advantaged. However, Rawls's theory is not utilitarian; rather an alternative theory, and Rawls argues for distributing 'primary goods', that is goods everybody needs to realize their plan of life, independent of what the plan is. While the first principle distributes one subset of the total set of primary goods, the basic liberties, the difference principle distributes another subset including wealth, income, power and authority. The last part of the second principle, the 'principle of fair equality of opportunity', requires that we go beyond formal equality of opportunity to ensure that persons with similar skills, abilities and motivation enjoy equal opportunities.

As mentioned in Section 1, the most interesting new aspects of equity in environmental policy pertain to transboundary pollution and the fairness of policies across regions and nations. However, Rawls's theory is basically a theory of justice within a nation. To obtain international principles, Rawls again considers an original position, where the individuals are supposed to protect the interests of their regions or nations. However, the decisions of international principles are taken after the agreement of national principles, that is, we have a two-step decision making framework, and the international principles are decided in an idealized world where each nation has established a just basic structure of the society. If all countries were independent of each other, there would be no need for international principles. Also, the national principles would be international if all economies were totally open and the world were a fully integrated system. In Rawls's theory, it is assumed that the countries are mainly self-contained, and only marginal contact is necessary. However, while Rawls does not analyse the international problem explicitly, several authors have addressed the problem within his theory.

Beitz (1985) argues that even if Rawls's assumptions about an idealized world and self-containment hold, there is still a need for principles to distribute natural resources. He also argues that the self-containment assumption does not hold, so that we need distributional principles. One should first try to obtain international justice before studying principles for the national state. The appropriate global principle should be something like Rawls's 'general conception', which is a generalization of Rawls's two principles, defined as 'All social primary goods – liberty and opportunity, income and wealth, and the bases of self-respect – are to be distributed equally unless an unequal distribution of any or all of these goods is to the advantage of the least favored' (Rawls, 1971, p. 303). There should be only one original position where all principles should be decided. This is also supported by Pogge (1989). In this original position, Pogge argues that the principles will be similar to Rawls's original principles.

Libertarian theory
Probably the most widely used criterion in economic theory is the Pareto criterion, which is most often applied to efficiency and political feasibility (for example, in bargaining theory). It has also been applied to equity, for instance by a common-sense conception of justice (see, for example, Elster, 1992). In libertarian theory, the baseline is that individual freedom should prevail except where others may be harmed. Thus, the ethic is in the same line as Pareto superiority, saying that there is an improvement in welfare if one or more persons are made better off due to change in resource use as long as the other persons are at least as well off as before. A strict interpretation of libertarian theory is that an act is only immoral if anyone is worse off because of it.

Robert Nozick's work (Nozick, 1974) is the best-known statement of libertarian thought.[11] The theory can be summarized in three principles: justice in appropriation, justice in transfer, and justice in rectification. A distribution of goods is just if it is the end result of an unbroken chain of just transfers, beginning from a just original appropriation. If these conditions are not satisfied, justice in rectification requires that we should establish the distribution that would have occurred if all unjust links in the chain had been replaced by just ones.

The first principle is essentially a 'finder's keepers' principle, where the basic idea is that anyone has the right to appropriate, exploit and enjoy the fruits of any unowned piece of nature. The principle of just transfers says that the outcome of any voluntary transaction between two or more individuals is just. It is assumed that there is no coercion. If individuals agree on a contract that will benefit all, there is no reason to stop the contract. The only reason to invalidate the contract is if anyone uses its power to make the non-agreement state worse for other parties than it would otherwise have been. The last principle is probably the main weakness of the theory, as identifying the point in time when the earliest violation occurred and thereafter the counterfactual chain of just transfers may be rather indeterminate.

Assume an agreement which all parties accept without any coercion. In general, may anybody have a moral right to block an agreement that will favour everybody? There are several answers to this. First, not all Pareto-optimal outcomes are equally preferred, as discussed in Section 2. Second, the Pareto criterion is related to distribution. The most efficient outcome may not be preferred if redistribution or compensation is not possible. Finally, due to unfair background conditions, an agreement where all parties gain is not necessarily just. Nozick argues that a distribution is just only if it is the end result of an unbroken chain of just transfers that has begun with a just original appropriation. Rawls is also concerned about background conditions. According to his theory, interpersonal agreements can carry moral weight only if they are freely entered into under conditions that are fair, that is, when some participants' basic rights, opportunities, or economic positions are not grossly inferior. An agreement is only morally appealing if the differences in bargaining powers do not exceed certain limits (see Pogge, 1989, p. 248). Agreements that are not based on a certain background justice may make the society even more unjust. For criticism of libertarian theory relating to sustainability issues, see, for example, Dragun and O'Connor (1993).

4. Principles of equity and justice
One possible distinction is between equity and justice principles. 'Equity principles' may be defined as normative criteria for how a society should be organized, how goods or burdens should be distributed, and so on (see, for example, Rose, 1990). On the other hand, 'principles of justice' are basic rules underlying theories of justice, as most theories of justice are quite coarse-grained. Thus they can be interpreted as side constraints to these theories. Several principles of justice may be in accordance with one equity principle, and vice versa.

Several global theories of justice give different equity principles for the distribution of goods and rights.[12] Moreover, intuitions about particular cases may be compatible with more than one theory of justice. However, there may be common denominators in theories of distributive justice. Meta-principles are principles implicit in all global theories of justice. Elster (1992, 1993) claims two such meta-principles to be 'ethical individualism' and 'ethical presentism'.

The view of *ethical individualism* (EI) is that justice is attached to individual human beings. It is a denial of supra-individual and non-human justice, the first treating groups, and the second organic or inorganic nature, as subjects of justice. There are two claims of EI: (i) theories of justice should allocate goods among individuals, and (ii) this allocation should be made on the basis of information about individuals (Elster, 1993).

In general, a ranking of societies based on individual measures (for each society) will be compatible with EI, while a ranking of societies based on, for instance, a comparison of average income for different groups within a society will violate EI. This can be explained by establishing a function $F(v_s)$ which ranks societies, S, according to justice. EI states that only information about individuals can enter as inputs, v, in the function. Assume that the function is based on the income of groups of individuals. Then assume that the individuals are regrouped such that the average income in some groups changed, while each individual's income remained the same. If this regrouping changes the value of the function, then EI is violated. That is, the ranking of justice has changed, but the individuals' situations are unchanged.

The basis of *ethnical presentism* (EP) is 'that past practices are irrelevant to distribution in the present, except to the extent that they have left morally relevant and causally efficacious traces in the present' (Elster, 1992, p. 200). A few examples may clarify this meta-principle. First, no one should have to suffer from crimes committed by his or her parents; one cannot choose one's parents. Nevertheless, if people are worse off today than they otherwise would have been because of discrimination against their parents, a claim for compensation is compatible with EP. Compensation does not follow from EP, since meta-principles are only constraints in a justice evaluation. However, you cannot claim to discriminate against somebody today on the grounds that your parents were discriminated against in the past. A general morally accepted principle is that nobody can claim stolen wealth left in a will from their parents.[13] Inheritance is, however, compatible with, but not an implication of EP as long as the inherited wealth has been legally and fairly acquired. For an application of meta-principles to global warming policy, see Section 6 below.

5.   Cost–benefit analysis

The role of equity

Equity inherently plays a role in cost–benefit analysis (CBA). Unlike a market situation where the individual group that benefits from a good or service is one that pays for it, CBA is used in situations where there are no markets and where it is likely that someone other than those benefiting actually provide funding (typically via taxation). The *benefits principle* of public finance (that is, that a person should pay taxes in proportion to the benefits received from public expenditures) is an attempt to eliminate this divergence, but is rarely applied for two reasons. First, it is often not considered to be a paramount definition of equity. Second, even if it were, it is difficult to determine individual benefits empirically, especially when environmental values are involved.

Distributional considerations and equity have, however, typically played a minor role in cost–benefit analysis. The mainstream view is that projects should only be implemented that pass the positive net benefits test, irrespective of equity implications. Alternatively, Herfindahl and Kneese (1974) and others state that inefficient projects should never be accepted, even for reasons of promoting equity. Most analysts, however, are not necessarily saying that equity is unimportant, but just that project selection is a rather blunt instrument for promoting it. As in the discussion of distortionary policies above, they suggest that there are more finely tuned instruments that should be used. Again, however, there is the matter of coordinating policy implementation between two arms of government, as for example, a department of natural resources and a department of treasury.

Evaluations of social welfare
The shadow price of a good is defined as the net impact on social welfare of a unit increase in the supply of that good. To find the shadow price, an SWF (social welfare function) has to be specified. But which function should be chosen? When choosing an SWF, ethical views and other specific assumptions are made at the same time. All SWFs can in principle be used in a cost–benefit analysis, but different choices will give different rankings of projects. The most common approach is to use an SWF with equal weights. This function is consistent with utilitarianism and the assumption that everybody has the same marginal utility of income, but is not generally consistent with other ethical views.

The problem arises if the analyst uses a different SWF from that of the policy makers. Will the shadow price calculated by the analyst provide a useful information for the policy maker? Probably not. It will not be useful if the analysis is intended as input to a political debate, and there are many policy makers with diverging views. Similarly, if an analysis suggesting a Pareto-improving project is based on costless redistribution of income, and decision makers find this assumption implausible, the results may seem irrelevant to them if they are concerned about distributional issues. Assume that there is disagreement on the weighting of individuals in an SWF, and also no costless redistribution of income exists. What information is useful for decision makers with a variety of ethical and political views? One approach frequently suggested in the literature is to identify a range of SWFs thought to reflect policy makers' different opinions (see, for example, Drèze and Stern, 1987). Another approach is to provide 'sufficient welfare indicators', that is, information that can be used as input to an arbitrary SWF (see Brekke et al., 1996; Nyborg, 1996). Thus, instead of providing information that is the output from a certain SWF, the analyst can provide factual information about different population groups (such as their social state, size, characteristics, as well as their changes in income and access to public goods). Also, if some decision makers are concerned about intrinsic value variables (non-welfaristic concerns), as for instance rights and duties, the project's effects on these values can be reported separately.

One example of disagreement on ethical views and weights attached to damage in cost–benefit analyses is the discussion of the value of a statistical life in global warming analyses, for instance in the context of the 'social cost' chapter of the IPCC Second Assessment Report (Pearce et al., 1996). The studies by Fankhauser (1995) and Tol (1995) form the basis for the cost estimates published in this chapter, and have received widespread attention and caused considerable debate since they have used lower values for climate-related death in a poor country than in a rich. One answer to the debate has been to provide different weight factors to the damages in poor and rich countries (see, for example, Azar and Sterner, 1996; Azar, 1997; Fankhauser et al., 1997).

Positive analysis
A certain irony arises from ignoring distributional considerations in cost–benefit analysis. For example, most economists are nervous about considering altruistic behaviour. However, presenting a voter with a single net benefit number requires a certain degree of altruism if this is to be the sole basis for his or her decision to support a project. All that it conveys is how the community as a whole is affected; it does not provide much indication of how the voter is affected himself or herself (a self-interest motivation), or in relation to others (an equity-oriented altruistic consideration).

For the case where the decision on resource allocation is up to a single decision maker, these other points are less relevant, but, with the greater emphasis on public participation in the use of natural resources stemming from the current emphasis on sustainable development, they are important. We are not saying that individual decision making should be based only on self-interest, but that how the individual voter is affected is important. To this extent, information is required on the distribution of impacts both from normative and positive standpoints (see also the discussion on sufficient welfare indicators above). One can justify providing an equity evaluation, as well as individual impact information to create a more enlightened citizenry. To this end, Rose et al. (1988) have proposed three positive measures of distributional impacts in the context of CBA: (1) a distributional impact matrix, (2) a community impact index, and (3) a political articulation index. These are intended to facilitate the public participation process and to gauge any bias in its actual implementation.

6. Application to global warming

Philosophical considerations
If a tradable permit system is introduced in a global warming treaty, one important problem of equity is the initial distribution of carbon dioxide (CO_2) emissions permits.[14] We use as an example the study of Kverndokk (1995) that proposes one way to solve this problem, namely by using the meta-principles introduced in Section 4 together with a generally accepted principle in global theories of justice of avoiding distributions based on moral arbitrariness. An analysis using these principles of justice requires a list of competing allocation rules, since the force of these principles is exclusionary rather than determinative, that is, we can say which rules from a given list violate the principles, but we cannot determine the 'best' allocation rule. The weakness of this type of analysis is that the conclusion depends on which allocation rules are included in the list. Therefore, the list should be extensive. In the literature, the following simple allocation rules have been suggested:[15]

- A distribution proportional to current CO_2 emissions.
- A distribution inversely proportional to accumulated CO_2 emissions.
- A distribution proportional to gross domestic product (GDP) or to GDP adjusted by purchasing power parities.
- A distribution proportional to land area.
- A distribution proportional to population (POP).

The first claim of ethical individualism (EI) is *prima facie* violated under an international agreement since the permits are distributed among countries. However, if each country distributes the income from permits among its citizens, the claim is satisfied. All allocation rules will at first sight be compatible with the second claim of EI. The first four rules are distributions based on average measures (the GDP rule distributes permits to each country according to *GDP/POP × POP*, which means that population is taken into account), and the last allocation rule means an equal per capita distribution of permits. Thus, in the strict interpretation, EI seems to be a rather coarse-grained or indeterminate principle. One answer to this is that

EI requires theories of justice to be concerned with individuals in an 'essential way'.

A discussion of essential information promotes a consideration of morally relevant information (see below). Here we consider the weaker claim that the number of people living in a country should matter. Consider a distribution proportional to land area. There is no direct proportionality between a country's land area and its population. Even if the land area is the sum of land area per capita across the individuals, land area is constant, and we do not need information about the individuals to calculate it. Thus it can be argued that land area per capita does not incorporate essential information about individuals in this distribution problem.[16] The same argument can be used if GDP and, therefore, also CO_2 emissions, as most anthropogenic CO_2 emissions are connected to GDP-producing activities, is mainly based on a rent from natural resources. For example, Saudi Arabia's and Kuwait's GDPs and CO_2 emissions are relatively independent of their populations, as they are based mainly on oil production and OPEC production quotas. Thus the allocation rules based on land area, GDP and CO_2 emissions (current and accumulated) may under certain conditions be excluded on the grounds that they violate EI.

Next, consider the principle of ethical presentism (EP). If an allocation rule gives advantages to countries based on their present superior position that has been achieved by these countries' past discrimination and exploitation of other countries, then EP is violated. On the other hand, if the countries' present superior position has been achieved because they have previously used their resources more efficiently than other countries, EP may not be violated. In the first case the worse-off countries can claim compensation but they cannot in the second one.

One argument in the greenhouse policy debate is that 'the bucket is full', mainly filled up by the developed West, and that they have a moral obligation to 'clean it up'. Following this argument, it would not be 'fair' if developing countries have to restrict their consumption of fossil fuels, as it may reduce their possibilities of attaining higher standards of living. Accordingly, it has been suggested that they receive compensation from industrialized countries. A natural means for the compensation is the distribution of tradable permits and a distribution based on accumulated CO_2 emissions is relevant since compensation is due to past practices. The question of compensation is, however, complicated. For instance, emissions of CO_2 in the past have created positive externalities; not only the emitting countries have benefited from the combustion of fossil fuels. Thus the argument that the developed world is totally liable for past emissions, and that these emissions only harmed developing countries, is hard to support.

Consider the distributions of permits based on current CO_2 emissions and GDP. As most CO_2 emissions are connected to GDP-producing activities, we only consider GDP. The crucial question is then whether GDP is only a function of the present situation. If it is, then a distribution proportional to GDP does not violate EP. However, it is hard to argue that current CO_2 emissions and GDP are independent of the past. If GDP depends on history, countries' present economic and social positions are, at least partially, attributable to their inheritances. If the present superior position of some countries is the result of these countries' exploitation of other countries in the past, then the GDP and CO_2 allocation rules are not compatible with EP. In summary, none of the allocation rules can be clearly excluded on grounds of EP, but the rules based on GDP and on current and accumulated CO_2 emissions can be excluded under certain conditions.

Finally, we analyse the principle of avoiding distribution based on moral arbitrariness. There seems to be a widespread understanding of this principle. One exception is, however, the first chain in the theory of Nozick (1974), that is, the original appropriation. Two elements are often claimed to contribute to the material advancement of societies (see Beitz, 1985, pp. 288–9): one is the human cooperative activity, and the other is called the natural component. The second element consists of components present on the earth's surface that are not due to human production, for example, natural resources or assets. 'Natural assets' are arbitrarily distributed on the earth's surface and are in the literature (Beitz, 1985; Pogge, 1989) compared to the distribution of 'natural endowments', defined as contingencies that are inescapable and present from birth, and may contribute to material advancement because of the implications for human cooperative activity (for example, nationality, genetic endowments, race, gender and social class). According to Rawls (1971, p. 102), natural endowments are 'neither just nor unjust; nor is it unjust that men are born into society at any particular position. These are simply natural facts. What is just and unjust is the way that institutions deal with these facts'. The distribution of natural assets and endowments is, in general, assumed to be morally arbitrary and unacceptable as a standard for distribution, since it is beyond the control of human beings. Nobody should have to suffer from the pain of inequality due to morally arbitrary factors, if the sacrifices cannot be shown to advance equality in other or more important fields.[17] Justifications for basing distributions on morally arbitrary factors may be to eliminate existing inequalities or to distribute necessary burdens to those who best can handle them.

Morally arbitrary components may be non-essential information in this distributive problem (see the discussion of EI) for three main reasons. First, land area is a natural component and should not be used as a standard for distributing permits if it cannot be proven that this allocation rule actually eliminates existing inequalities (see note 15). Second, continuing the analysis of EP, inheritance may be defined as a morally arbitrary component. Thus, even if the better position of a country is dependent on the past but cannot be claimed to be the result of past exploitation and discrimination, a distribution based on GDP (or CO_2 emissions) can be rejected by reason of moral arbitrariness. Such a distribution would give disadvantages to people already suffering from inequalities for morally arbitrary reasons. Third, nationality is a natural endowment. People cannot choose their nationality, at least not at birth. An allocation rule giving preference to one nationality compared to others can only be advocated if there are morally relevant characteristics of all individuals of the nationality which are not present for any individuals of other nationalities. Given that there are no such relevant characteristics for this distribution problem, the only way of avoiding a morally arbitrary distribution is a distribution of permits proportional to population.

To conclude from the analyses of justice principles, a distribution of permits proportional to population appears to be the only rule from the list of alternative allocation rules that is in accordance with all the three principles of justice.

Policy simulations
Several equity principles, a general operational rule emanating from each, and a corresponding rule applicable to the allocation of marketable permits for CO_2 emissions are presented in Table 24.1. The reader is referred to Rose (1992) for a discussion of conceptual underpinnings of each criterion. Note that, although the discussion below is presented in the context of marketable permits, the criteria apply equivalently to redistributing carbon tax revenues (see, for example, Pezzey, 1992; Rose and Stevens, 1999). An important distinction is whether a given equity criterion applies to the *process* by which a criterion is chosen, the *initial allocation* of permits, or to the *final outcome* of the implementation of the policy instrument, that is, to net welfare impacts following trading and greenhouse gas mitigation. For example, the sovereignty criterion refers to the right to emit greenhouse gases (GHGs), so it applies directly to permit allocations, while horizontal equity applies to welfare changes, that is outcomes. Other criteria do not have any predetermined rules at either end (for example consensus equity and market justice), but apply more to the manner in which decisions are made (see, for example, Thompson et al., 1997). We can thus divide the criteria into three categories as denoted in Table 24.1.

Outcome-based criteria are more in keeping with the 'welfarist' orientation of equity in terms of much of traditional welfare economics. However, some equity concepts are based on inherent rights (for example, egalitarian) that tie them to initial allocations. Others relate to the fairness of the process of allocating/trading the rights, though emphasis on the process begs the question of what rule will be chosen and what its equity implications are. In the case of global warming, the allocation stage is more immediate and more certain than the final outcome, and hence might receive more attention, but this would be short-sighted. At the same time, concerns about the eventual outcome are compounded by actual or perceived uncertainties about potential benefits, economic and emissions growth rates, permit prices and the competitiveness of the permits markets. Still, these considerations are too important to ignore, and improving knowledge of them will enable all nations to make more informed judgements about bottom-line impacts. Also, we emphasize the difference between formal equity criteria and the use of *reference bases*, which are merely implementation indices (see Rose, 1992). Examples of reference bases are GDP, population, energy use, emissions and land area; some have an obvious equity criterion counterpart (for example, population), others apply to more than one criterion (for example, emissions), and still others have no obvious equity counterpart (land area). Reference bases do have the desirable properties of focal points, a term Schelling (1960) coined to represent a key facilitating feature of negotiation processes. Toman and Burtraw (1991, p. 12) suggest that 'negotiators will seek out rules of thumb' but also note that because of strategic considerations, it is unlikely that 'simple rules of thumb alone can successfully guide the negotiation process'. Morrisette and Plantinga (1991, p. 6) have likewise stated: 'Success, however, will depend on how the different stakes of nations can be dealt with in the negotiation process in an equitable manner.' We thus ascribe primacy to equity principles. If global warming were an uncomplex issue that could be settled in a short time, we would endorse the more pragmatic 'rule-of-thumb' approach. Since the issue is complex, negotiations likely to take years, and to go through several stages, it is important to have a solid foundation. It is likely that equity principles will need to be thoroughly articulated and their full implications understood before a lasting agreement can be reached.

Several analysts claim that objective criteria exist for distributing the cost burden across countries (examples include: grandfathering, 'no harm to developing countries', 'avoiding worsening the income gap between rich and poor nations', and the Kantian imperative). From a normative standpoint, some claim that only a 'no harm' criterion applied to all countries would qualify, since it is consistent with the concept of Pareto optimality. From a positive economic standpoint, other analysts have suggested that some criteria are more likely to be acceptable than others to the majority of nations, and are therefore more likely to lead to global agreement. However, their acceptability seems to be more dependent on implicit

Table 24.1 Alternative equity criteria for global warming policy

Criterion	Basic definition	General operational rule	Operational rule for CO_2 permits
Allocation-based			
Sovereignty	All nations have an equal right to pollute and to be protected from pollution	Cut back emissions in a proportional manner across all nations	Distribute permits in proportion to emissions
Egalitarian	All people have an equal right to pollute or to be protected from pollution	Allow emissions in proportion to population	Distribute permits in proportion to population
Ability to pay	Mitigation costs should vary directly with national economic well-being	Equalize abatement costs across nations (gross cost of abatement as proportion of GDP equal for each nation)[a]	Distribute permits to equalize abatement costs (gross cost of abatement as proportion of GDP equal for each nation)[a]
Outcome-based			
Horizontal	All nations should be treated equally	Equalize net welfare change across nations (net cost of abatement as proportion of GDP equal for each nation)[b]	Distribute permits to equalize net welfare change (net cost of abatement as proportion of GDP equal for each nation)[b]
Vertical	Welfare changes should vary inversely with national economic well-being	Progressively share net welfare change across nations (net cost proportions inversely correlated with per capita GDP)[b]	Progressively distribute permits (net cost proportions inversely correlated with per capita GDP)[b]
Compensation	No nation should be made worse off	Compensate net losing nations	Distribute permits so that no nation suffers a net loss of welfare

Process-based Maximin	The welfare of the worst-off nations should be maximized	Maximize the net benefit to the poorest nations	Distribute largest proportion of net welfare change to poorest nations
Consensus	The international negotiation process is fair	Seek a political solution promoting stability	Distribute permits in a manner that satisfies the (power-weighted) majority of nations
Market justice	The market is fair	Make greater use of markets	Distribute permits to highest bidder

Notes:
[a] Gross cost refers to abatement cost only.
[b] Net welfare change (cost or benefit) is equal to the sum of mitigation benefits − abatement costs + permit sales revenues − permit purchase costs.

371

notions of equity than some natural or inherent characteristics (for example, most of the acceptability criteria call for some favourable treatment for developing countries). Currently, many industrialized countries are pleading special circumstances to receive favourable treatment in meeting mitigation targets being negotiated as part of the Framework Convention on Climate Change. Still, these 'differentiation' proposals now on the table are either a matter of individual country self-interest or appeals to fairness, while trying to avoid the use of the latter term (for fear it will open the floodgates for even more formidable appeals from developing countries). Thus, as with other areas of economics, there are no criteria free of value judgements.

The welfare effects of utilizing four distinct equity criteria for distributing CO_2 emission permits are presented on Table 24.2 (see Rose and Stevens, 1996, for a more extensive presentation and a broader set of criteria; those presented here have received a great deal of attention in the policy debates and cover a broad range of philosophical viewpoints). The results pertain to a 20 per cent reduction in projected CO_2 emissions in the year 2000, which in effect fixes the global supply of CO_2 entitlements at 80 per cent of projected year 2000 emissions. Our analysis is undertaken for eight countries or country groupings, representative of various levels of development. Estimates of individual country benefits (environmental damage avoided) from mitigation of 20 per cent of CO_2 emissions in the year 2000 are adapted from Nordhaus (1991) and listed in column 1. At this stage of scientific inquiry, the numbers are of course crude, but are still able to indicate the relative policy impacts. For example, benefits are relatively small for Canada and the Former Soviet Union (FSU), since a warming of their climate would increase agricultural productivity and would offset considerably the damage due to sea-level rise and loss of recreational benefits and tourist revenues. At the same time, some of the more populated areas of Western Europe and Indonesia could be inundated by a fairly modest melting of the polar ice caps. Mitigation costs are evaluated in terms of actual direct expenditures from a synthesis of the literature. Equilibrium (post-trading) mitigation costs are listed in column 2, and, consistent with the Coase theorem, are the same for all permit distributions. The current reliance of China on its coal resources and the cost of fuel switching, for example, are the main reasons for its relatively high mitigation costs in relation to other developing countries.

Permit trading will take place under any distribution criterion as long as some countries have marginal abatement costs greater than the world market price of permits, and some countries have marginal costs less than this price. It is usually assumed, and generally borne out by cost studies, that abatement costs are relatively higher in industrialized countries than

Table 24.2 Summary of permit trading and net welfare change associated with various equity criteria[a]

Country (area)	All cases		Sovereignty		Horizontal		Vertical		Egalitarian	
	Gross benefit of mitigation	Equilibrium mitigation cost	Value of permit trading	Net benefit post-trade[b]	Value of permit trading	Net benefit post-trade[b]	Value of permit trading	Net benefit post-trade[b]	Value of permit trading	Net benefit post-trade[b]
United States	16.98	3.64	4.19	9.15	4.90	8.44	10.87	2.48	35.15	-21.81
Canada	1.07	0.30	0.43	0.34	0.01	0.76	-1.70	2.48	2.95	-2.18
Western Europe	10.27	2.08	3.24	4.95	0.90	7.29	5.71	2.48	13.93	-5.74
FSU	2.28	7.72	-6.14	0.70	-7.22	1.78	-7.92	2.48	17.43	-22.87
Brazil	1.52	0.53	-0.63	1.62	0.40	0.59	-1.49	2.48	-8.19	9.18
Central Africa	0.14	0.02	-0.00	0.12	0.06	0.06	-2.36	2.48	-5.23	5.35
Indonesia	0.47	0.30	-0.36	0.53	0.01	0.16	-2.30	2.48	-10.88	11.05
China	5.38	3.72	0.73	2.39	0.94	0.71	-0.82	2.48	-45.16	46.82
Total[c]	38.11	18.31	7.86[d]	19.80	7.22[d]	19.80	16.58[d]	19.80	69.46[d]	19.80

Notes:
[a]All figures in billions of 1990 dollars
[b]Net welfare change (cost or benefit) is equal to the sum of mitigation benefits − abatement costs + permit sales revenues − permit purchase costs.
[c]Totals may not add up due to rounding.
[d]Sum of absolute value of either permit purchases (positive entries; additions to cost) or sales (negative entries; offsets to cost).

in developing ones (see Haites and Rose, 1996). Trading will thus lower the total abatement costs to the former and provide a transfer to the latter, which in effect also lowers the net costs of developing countries.

The net change in national welfare (benefit or cost), before permit trading, from a 20 per cent global reduction in CO_2 when permits are initially allocated according to the sovereignty criterion (equal percentage emission reductions) is $15.31 billion (not shown). All eight countries/regions would stand to reap positive net benefits except the FSU. The effect of trading, as determined by a formal non-linear programming model, is presented in columns 3 and 4 of Table 24.2. The results indicate that the US, Canada and Western Europe would be permit buyers, and the other five countries/regions would be permit sellers. Nearly 205 million permits would be traded with a total value of $7.86 (sum of column 3) billion at the equilibrium price of $38.35 per ton of CO_2. The revenues from the sale of permits more than offset the increased costs of abatement incurred by the sellers, raising global net benefits to $19.80 billion (sum of column 4).

Trading has several implications for the viability of a treaty protocol. First, the equalization of marginal abatement costs across countries saves this global group $4.49 billion, or almost 20 per cent of the $22.80 billion of abatement costs associated with a uniform emission reduction requirement. The net cost savings (including expenditures on permits) to the three Western industrialized countries/regions is $2.80 billion, or about 17 per cent of their original costs. In addition, trading is estimated to be a source of revenue for developing and transitional economies. In fact, for Brazil and Indonesia, the permit revenues more than offset their total abatement costs (compare country entries in columns 2 and 3). Finally, all of the countries examined receive positive net benefits from a 20 per cent CO_2 emission reduction policy (see again column 4), though it is important to note that the US and Western Europe received the highest net change overall and the greatest gains from trading.

For the case of horizontal equity, the proportion of net benefits to GDP is equalized across all nations at the global average of approximately 0.19 per cent. As Table 24.2 shows, slightly less than half of global net benefits go to the United States, and together the US and Western Europe would receive almost 80 per cent of global net benefits. Note, however, that all nations are projected to have positive net benefits from the use of this criterion (see column 6). Interestingly, the FSU would be the only permit seller, with approximately two-thirds of these sales being to the US (see column 5).

For vertical equity, the requirement that individual country net benefits bear a directly inverse relationship to GDP means that global net benefits must be distributed in equal shares, or $2.48 billion for each country (see column 8 of Table 24.2). Global net benefits after trading are again $19.80

(sum of column 8), and total abatement costs are $18.31 billion, with individual country/region equilibrium (post-trading) abatement costs the same across all criteria (not shown). In this case, however, six of the country groupings are permit sellers, and only the US and Western Europe are buyers (see column 7).

In the egalitarian case, the global supply of permits is distributed according to the projected year 2000 population in each region. For some developing countries, the initial stock of permits even substantially exceeds year 2000 emissions. The resulting total trades are much greater (by at least a factor of five) than under the sovereignty criterion, and large monetary transfers from industrialized nations to these countries occur (see column 7). The net welfare changes of this allocation prior to trading (not shown) would result for the US in an astounding $144 billion *loss* (per year) with abatement costs of $161 billion (not shown). The net welfare effects for Western Europe and the FSU would also be strongly negative. Trading significantly reduces the negative impacts, though they remain in the sizeable $20 billion range for both the US and the FSU (see column 10). These large negative net benefits for industrialized countries, even with trading, imply that the egalitarian rule is likely to receive formidable opposition.

These results, as well as results for the five other criteria listed in Table 24.1 (see Rose and Stevens, 1996), indicate two major groupings of outcomes.[18] The individual country net welfare (benefit) impacts for the sovereignty, horizontal, vertical (as well as for the ability to pay, maximin and compensation) criteria, fall within a reasonable range of outcomes. The egalitarian (and consensus) criteria indicate rather extreme outcomes. We can draw two important conclusions. Although several criteria may differ significantly on philosophical grounds, their welfare effects are quite similar, a fact that will probably ease tensions at the bargaining table. Also, even though a valid theoretical argument was presented in the previous subsection for the egalitarian (population-based) criterion, its implementation might be opposed on practical grounds.

7. Conclusion

Environmental issues have and are likely to continue to grow in prominence. As such, the stakes in the policy process are becoming enormous. The impacts of pollution and of pollution abatement are becoming so widespread that they affect virtually everyone on the planet. Moreover, the size of the damages (and benefits of preventing them), as well as the costs of mitigation, are no longer trivial to the vast majority. As everyone becomes affected, there is a tendency for each individual (or nation) to ask: Am I being treated fairly by environmental policy? Often this question and its answer are viewed in terms of how one entity is affected in relation to others.

This chapter has endeavoured to provide a framework for analyzing the intragenerational equity implications of environmental policy. The extensive literature and, more importantly, operational tools now available mean that we need not shy away from addressing equity issues for lack of decision-making expertise. The increasing awareness that all of economics is fraught with value judgements is also slowly removing the stigma attached to equity, so that we can no longer be diverted from addressing the issue on philosophical grounds. Perhaps the major obstacle to progress on this front is the need for more empirical work on linking income distribution impacts with economic activity at a fine level of delineation in terms of socioeconomic groups, economic sectors, pollutants and regions.[19]

Finally, we acknowledge that this chapter has only presented part of the picture (again, the reader is referred to other chapters in this volume for insight into other aspects of intragenerational equity and for an analysis of intergenerational equity and its broader implications). In some cases, intragenerational equity considerations can be isolated from more dynamic concerns, while in other cases some modifications are needed. Our intent has been to provide an initial framework for analysis upon which the reader can build.

Notes

1. We would like to acknowledge the very helpful comments of Agnar Sandmo, the editor and two anonymous referees.
2. Distinguishing between the related concepts of equity, fairness and justice may in general be difficult, and we do not attempt to make extensive distinctions. However, fairness often has a specific meaning in economic theory and philosophical theories of justice. One example is to define fairness as non-envy (see, for example, Feldman and Kirman, 1974). Equity seems to be a broader concept than fairness, while justice is sometimes taken to be an umbrella term, incorporating all dimensions of evaluation besides efficiency (see, for example, Hausman and McPherson, 1993).
3. Economists often refer to this rule as having universal appeal and therefore able to rise above ethical choices. However, it is based on the value judgement that more is better, even if this means more inequality, thus posing an immediate conflict with equity. For a discussion of the historical basis for efficiency and some of its limitations as a criterion for public policy see Bromley (1990).
4. Theories have also been put forth that consider organic or inorganic natural environment as subjects of justice.
5. The UPF is similar to the concept of the production possibility frontier (PPF). However, while the PPF is usually drawn as a strictly convex set, the irregular boundary of the UPF stems from the fact that it is measured in ordinal numbers rather than cardinal numbers, as well as from the presence of comparability problems between the two individuals.
6. Social welfare functions are often distinguished according to the strengths, or restrictiveness, of the assumptions underlying them with respect to measurability and comparability (see, for example, Boadway and Bruce, 1984).
7. The reader can verify this by contrasting linear social welfare contours, which denote no concern for equity, with right-angle welfare contours, which make equity paramount. Also, the social welfare contours are not drawn as perfectly convex to the origin, as in the case of indifference curves, again because the addition of two people's (ordinal) utility functions are involved in a social welfare function.

8. Even income-related transfers violate this non-distortionary requirement in that they affect the labour–leisure choice.
9. Additional qualifiers to this theorem are that transactions costs and income effects be negligible. In the case of global warming policy to be discussed below, both of these conditions are likely to hold (for example, Rose and Stevens, 1996 and Chao and Peck, 1997 both find that revenues from selling permits are less than 1 per cent of GNP in nearly all cases).
10. Rawls's theory is a theory of intragenerational distributive justice, and the principles cannot easily be extended to intergenerational concerns. In contrast, social welfare functions are often used in analyses of intertemporal equity; see, for example, Howarth and Norgaard (1992, 1993).
11. Nozick is often called a 'natural rights Libertarian' as he is defending private property on moral grounds as a natural right. In contrast, 'empirical Libertarians' defend private property on empirical bases out of the belief that such institutions maximize total welfare (see, for example, Hayek, 1960; Friedman, 1962).
12. For instance studies of different international equity criteria applied to the global warming problem (see Rose, 1990, 1992), give no unique allocation rule for carbon dioxide permits. One equity criterion can have more than one allocation rule and one allocation rule can be consistent with more than one criterion. See also the discussion in Section 6 (policy simulations).
13. The problem is more complex if the wealth was stolen by ancestors several centuries ago. Examples of this can be both on an individual and group level. For example in Australia it is not generally accepted that Europeans have no moral right to land ownership. It is, however, generally accepted that the transfers of control of land from the Aboriginals to Europeans were not voluntary. One answer may be found in Nozick's theory, where a distribution based on stolen inheritance is unjust.
14. The reader is also referred to the chapters on tradable permits by Koutstaal (Chapter 18) and by Tietenberg (Chapter 19) in this volume.
15. Kverndokk (1993) shows the distributional consequences of several of these rules.
16. This allocation rule could, however, be advocated by referring to the consequences to individuals. Living in a rural area may require more resources than living in a densely populated and smaller area. Distributing the resources according to land area could, therefore, reduce inequality.
17. Natural endowments may be relevant for distribution in problems such as who shall perform military service and who shall be members of the South African Parliament.
18. The results are based on cost and benefit functions developed by Nordhaus (1993). Similar results have been obtained with a cost-side model developed by Edmonds et al. (1995), as presented in Rose et al. (1998).
19. The reader is referred to Rose et al. (1988) and Kilkenny and Rose (1995) for a discussion of some of the issues involved.

References

Azar, C. (1997), 'Weight factors in cost–benefit analysis of climate change', paper presented at the Eighth Annual Conference of The European Association of Environmental and Resource Economists, Tilburg, 26–28 June.
Azar, C. and T. Sterner (1996), 'Discounting and distributional considerations in the context of global warming', *Ecological Economics*, **19**, 169-85.
Bator, F. (1957), 'The simple analytics of welfare maximization', *American Economic Review*, **72**, 351–79.
Beitz, C.R. (1985), 'Justice and international relations', in C.R. Beitz, M. Cohen, T. Scanlon and A.J. Simmons (eds), *International Ethics: A Philosophy and Public Affairs Reader*, Princeton, NJ: Princeton University Press.
Bergson, A. (1938), 'A reformation of certain aspects of welfare economics', *Quarterly Journal of Economics*, **52**, 310–34.
Boadway, R. and N. Bruce (1984), *Welfare Economics*, Oxford: Basil Blackwell.

Brekke, K.A., H. Lurås and K. Nyborg (1996), 'Allowing disagreement in evaluations of social welfare', *Journal of Economics*, **63**, 303–24.

Bromley, D. (1990), 'The ideology of efficiency: searching for a theory of policy analysis', *Journal of Environmental Economics and Management*, **19**, 86–107.

Bryant, B. and P. Mohai (1992), *Race and the Incidence of Environmental Hazards: A Time for Discourse*, Boulder, CO: Westview Press.

Chao, H. and S. Peck (1997), 'Pareto optimal environmental control and income distribution with global climate change', Discussion Paper, Electric Power Research Institute.

Coase, R. (1960), 'The problem of social cost', *Journal of Law and Economics*, **3**, 1–44.

Danziger, S., R. Haveman and R. Plotnick (1986), 'How income transfer programs affect work, savings, and income distribution', *Journal of Economic Literature*, **19**, 1–36.

Dragun, A.K. and M. O'Connor (1993), Property rights, public choice and Pigovianism', *Journal of Post Keynesian Economics*, **16**, 127–52.

Drèze, J. and N. Stern (1987), 'The theory of cost–benefit analysis', in A.J. Auerbach and M. Feldstein (eds), *Handbook of Public Economics*, vol. II, Amsterdam: North-Holland.

Edmonds, J., M. Wise and D. Barns (1995), 'Carbon coalitions: the cost and effectiveness of energy agreements to alter trajectories of atmospheric carbon dioxide emissions', *Energy Policy*, **23**, 309–35.

Elster, J. (1991), 'Local justice: how institutions allocate scarce goods and necessary burdens', *European Economic Review*, **35**, 273–91.

Elster, J. (1992), *Local Justice*, New York: Russell Sage Foundation.

Elster, J. (1993), 'Ethical individualism and presentism', *The Monist*, **76**, 333–48.

Fankhauser, S. (1995), *Valuing Climate Change: The Economics of the Greenhouse*, London: Earthscan.

Fankhauser, S., R. Tol and D. Pearce (1997), 'The aggregation of climate change damages: a welfare theoretic approach', *Environmental and Resource Economics*, **10**, 249–66.

Feldman, A. and A. Kirman (1974), 'Fairness and envy', *American Economic Review*, **64**, 995–1005.

Friedman, M. (1962), *Capitalism and Freedom*, Chicago: University of Chicago Press.

Haites, E. and A. Rose (eds) (1996), 'Energy and Greenhouse Gas Mitigation: The IPCC Report and Beyond', *Energy Policy (Special Issue)*, 10–11.

Harsanyi, J.C. (1985), 'Rule utilitarianism, equality and justice', in E. F. Paul, J. Paul and F.D. Miller Jr (eds), *Ethics and Economics*, Oxford: Basil Blackwell.

Hausman, D.M. and M.S. McPherson (1993), 'Taking ethics seriously: economics and contemporary moral philosophy', *Journal of Economic Literature*, **31**, 671–731.

Hayek, F.A. (1960), *The Constitution of Liberty*, London: Routledge and Kegan Paul.

Herfindahl, O. and A.V. Kneese (1974), *Economic Theory of Natural Resources*, Columbus, OH: Merrill Publishers.

Hicks, J.R. (1939), 'The foundations of welfare economics', *Economic Journal*, **69**, 696–712.

Howarth, R. and R.B. Norgaard (1992), 'Environmental valuation under sustainable development', *American Economic Review*, **82**, 473–7.

Howarth, R. and R.B. Norgaard (1993), 'Intergenerational transfers and the social discount rate', *Environmental and Resource Economics*, **3**, 337–58.

Kaldor, N. (1939), 'Welfare comparisons of economics and interpersonal comparisons of utility', *Economic Journal*, **69**, 549–52.

Kilkenny, M. and A. Rose (1995), 'A social accounting matrix for modeling transboundary flows of capital-related income', in G. Hewings and M. Madden (eds), *Social and Demographic Accounting: Papers in Honor of Sir Richard Stone*, New York: Cambridge University Press.

Kneese, A.V. and W.D. Schulze (1985), 'Ethics and environmental economics', in A.V. Kneese and J.L. Sweeney (eds), *Handbook of Natural Resource and Energy Economics*, vol. 1, Amsterdam: North-Holland.

Kverndokk, S. (1993), 'Global CO_2 agreements: a cost-effective approach', *The Energy Journal*, **14**, 91–112.

Kverndokk, S. (1995),'Tradeable CO_2 emission permits: initial distribution as a justice problem', *Environmental Values*, **4**, 129–48.

Lane, R. (1986), 'Market justice, political justice', *American Political Science Review*, **80**, 383–402.

Little, I.M.D. (1957), *A Critique of Welfare Economics*, 2nd edn, Oxford: Clarendon Press.

Morrisette, P. and A. Plantinga (1991), 'The global warming issue: viewpoints of different countries', *Resources*, **103**, 2–6.

Nath, S.K. (1969), *A Reappraisal of Welfare Economics*, London: Routledge.

Nordhaus, W. (1991), 'The cost of slowing climate change: a survey', *Energy Journal*, **12**, 35–67.

Nordhaus, W. (1993), 'Rolling the DICE: the optimal transition path for controlling green-house gases', *Resource and Energy Economics*, **15**, 27–50.

Nozick, R. (1974), *Anarchy, State and Utopia*, New York: Basic Books.

Nyborg, K. (1996), 'Information requirements for environmental policy making', PhD thesis, University of Oslo.

O'Connor, M. and E. Muir (1995), 'Endowment effects in competitive general equilibrium: a primer for Paretian policy analysts', *Journal of Income Distribution*, **5**, 147–75.

Pearce, D.W., W.R. Cline, A.N. Achanta, S. Fankhauser, R.K. Pachauri, R.S.J. Tol and P. Vellinga (1996). 'The social costs of climate change: greenhouse damage and benefit of control', in J.P. Bruce, H. Lee and E.F. Haites (eds), *Climate Change 1995: Economic and Social Dimensions of Climate Change* (Second Assessment of the Intergovernmental Panel on Climate Change), Cambridge: Cambridge University Press.

Pezzey, J. (1992), 'The symmetry between controlling pollution by price and by quantity', *Canadian Journal of Economics*, **25**, 983–91.

Pigou, A.C. (1932), *The Economics of Welfare*, London: Macmillan.

Pogge, T.W. (1989), *Realizing Rawls*, London: Cornell University Press.

Rawls, J. (1971), *A Theory of Justice*, Oxford: Oxford University Press.

Robbins, L.C. (1935), *An Essay on the Nature and Significance of Economic Science*, London: Macmillan.

Rose, A. (1990), 'Reducing conflict in global warming policy: the potential of equity as a uni-fying principle', *Energy Policy*, **18**, 927–35.

Rose, A. (1992), 'Equity considerations of tradeable carbon emission entitlements', in S. Barrett et al. (eds), *Combating Global Warming: Study on a Global System of Tradeable Carbon Emission Entitlements*, New York: United Nations.

Rose, A. and B. Stevens (1996), 'Equity aspects of the marketable permits approach to global warming policy', Working Paper, Department of Energy, Environmental, and Mineral Economics, The Pennsylvania State University.

Rose, A. and B. Stevens (1999), *The Marketable Permits Approach to Global Warming Policy*, Chicago: University of Chicago Press (forthcoming).

Rose, A., B. Stevens and G. Davis (1988), *Natural Resource Policy and Income Distribution*, Baltimore, MD: Johns Hopkins University Press.

Rose, A., B. Stevens, J. Edmonds and M. Wise (1998), 'International equity and differentia-tion in global warming policy', *Environmental and Resource Economics*, **12**, 25–51.

Samuelson, P.A. (1947), *Foundations of Economic Analysis*, Cambridge, MA: Harvard University Press.

Schelling, T. (1960), *The Strategy of Conflict*, Cambridge, MA: Harvard University Press.

Thompson, M., S. Rayner, L. Gerlach, M. Grubb, D. Lach, S. Ney, M. Paterson and A. Rose (1997), 'Cultural discourses', in S. Rayner et al. (eds), *Human Choice and Climate Change: An International Social Science Assessment*, Columbus, OH: Battelle Press.

Tol, R.S.J. (1995), 'The damage cost of climate change: towards more comprehensive calcu-lations', *Environmental and Resource Economics*, **5**, 353–74.

Toman, M. and D. Burtraw (1991), 'Resolving equity issues: greenhouse gas negotiations', *Resources*, **103**, 10–13.

25 Distributional issues: an overview
Joan Martínez-Alier and Martin O'Connor

1. Distribution of property rights, income and power

The main issue of this chapter is whether or not allocative and distributional issues can be dealt with independently. The economic values which non-traded and traded environmental goods and services, or negative externalities, might be given depend (in different ways) on the endowment of property rights and on the distribution of power and income. Consequently, since environmental and resource economics is concerned with the economic valuation of negative externalities and of environmental goods and services, then the question of *rights* and of *power* and *income distribution* has central importance in environmental and resource economics, both at the level of theory and for policy applications. Lawrence Summers (1992) emphasized the theoretical and policy importance of income distribution for valuation when he wrote:

> the measurement of the costs of health impairing pollution depends on the foregone earnings from increased morbidity and mortality. From this point of view a given amount of health impairing pollution should be done in the country with the lowest cost, which will be the country with the lowest wages.

In other words, 'the poor sell cheap', and their best chance of addressing 'externalities' will not be in the market or in 'surrogate' markets (where damages are valued in terms of willingness to pay (WTP) or willingness to accept compensation (WTAC)), but through other types of social action (cf. the 'environmentalism of the poor' analysed in Guha and Martínez-Alier, 1997). In effect, in neoclassical equilibrium theory, a zero price for an environmental good would signal non-scarcity of that good relative to the demands on it over the time horizon considered, for example, abundant air, water and genetic resources, or carbon sinks. Changed perceptions that the good is scarce should result in a positive price. But alternatively, we may choose to look directly at the power relations that underlie pricing. A zero price may then signal not non-scarcity *per se*, but a relation of power in a situation of conflict. For example, a good may be plundered by an act of an invasive force, or may be appropriated by a dominant social group who define for themselves the terms of 'legitimate' possession. Similarly, pollutants or toxic wastes may be discharged in ways that degrade the living habitat of others who are unable to stop the event. Although such situations may be interpreted as *de facto* rights or liability inequalities, it is more lucid to offer an interpretation directly in terms of *power*, that is, *might rather than right*, namely the capacity of the dominant social group(s) to ignore or discount the 'demands' of the other group(s) who claim an interest in the resources or services in question but who cannot give practical effect to this claim.

In particular, the measures of sustainability offered in recent work adopting a neoclassical perspective (the so-called 'weak sustainability test') are critically sensitive not only to assumptions about substitutability between 'natural' and economic capitals, but also to the prices used for the measure of depreciation of 'natural capital'. The relative prices for measure of 'natural capital' will depend, in various ways, on the endowment of property rights, and on the distribution of income and power. So the use of existing prices, or of willingness-to-pay estimates (WTP) based on existing distribution, for indicators relating to 'sustainability', is theoretically incoherent as well as empirically wrong. (Faucheux, Muir and O'Connor, 1997)

2. Ecological distribution and externality valuation
Starting from the recognition that most natural resources and environmental services are not in the market, the concept of 'ecological distribution' is introduced (cf. Martínez-Alier and O'Connor, 1996). Political economy is the name frequently given to the study of economic distribution conflicts. Political ecology studies ecological distribution conflicts. *Ecological distribution* refers to the social, spatial and temporal asymmetries or inequalities in the use by humans of environmental resources and services (whether traded or not), for example, in the depletion of natural resources (including the loss of biodiversity), and in the burdens of pollution. An example: unequal distribution of land, and pressure of agricultural exports on limited land resources, may cause land degradation by subsistence peasants pushed up into mountain slopes. The field of political ecology has been developed in such rural contexts by anthropologists and geographers (Blaikie and Brookfield, 1987; Little and Horowitz, 1987; Painter and Durham, 1995; Peet and Watts, 1996). Some other types of ecological distribution conflicts are listed below:

- the territorial asymmetries between SO_2 emissions and the burdens of acid rain have given rise in Europe and elsewhere to the concept of 'transboundary pollution';
- 'environmental racism' in the US is a contentious notion, which means locating polluting industries or toxic waste disposal sites in areas of poor and black, hispanic or Indian population, with

consequent disproportionately high environmental and health effects. Correspondingly we find a movement for 'environmental justice' in the United States, reacting against such 'environmental racism' (Bullard, 1993; Szasz, 1994; Schwab, 1994; Bryant, 1995);

- conflicts over health and safety in or around factories, mines and plantations, sometimes led by labour unions ('red' outside, 'green' inside), pre-date in many countries the birth of the nature conservation movement;

- the appropriation of genetic resources ('wild' or agricultural) without payment or recognition of peasant or indigenous knowledge and ownership, has given rise to the notion of 'biopiracy';

- 'ecologically unequal exchange' (similar to the notion of *Raubwirtschaft* in nineteenth-century German geography) refers to the imports of commodities from poor regions or countries at prices which do not take into adequate account either local externalities or the exhaustion of such resources;

- Azar and Holmberg (1995) quantify the intergenerational 'ecological debt' as the costs of absorbing excessive emissions of carbon dioxide through reforestation. 'Ecological debt' has been used to designate the claims for damages from rich countries on account of past excessive emissions of carbon dioxide (for instance) or because of previous plundering of natural resources (Borrero, 1994; Robleto and Marcelo, 1992);

- research has been done on the environmental space or on the ecological footprint effectively 'occupied' by some economies, both for procuring resources and for disposal of emissions (for instance, Wackernagel and Rees, 1996).

Some ecological distribution conflicts are acquiring well-known names, but the transfers of burdens or resources to which the names refer have no agreed prices. Therefore we view externalities not so much as 'market failures' as '*cost-shifting* successes' (Kapp, 1983). For instance, Europeans, Japanese and North Americans pay nothing for the use of the carbon sinks they are using outside their own territories in order to dispose of emissions of CO_2. In this case, such countries act as owners of environmental services outside their own territories (Agarwal and Narain, 1991), but (almost) nobody is yet complaining, or trying to charge them a fee. As emphasized by Samuels (1991), Bromley (1989), Nijkamp (1986) and Beckenbach (1989), the measure of external costs will depend on the concrete attribution of property rights and the distribution of income and power. The outcomes of such ecological distribution conflicts will greatly influence the pattern of prices in the economy.

In the intragenerational context, the shifting of environmental burdens or the use of natural resources to the detriment of some groups of people will sometimes give rise to environmental protest movements outside the market and also outside the 'surrogate' markets which are sometimes used for economic valuation. This point was made by Leff (1994) with a play on words: 'from the marginalist analysis of externalities to the actions of "marginal" environmental groups'. A similar idea (the 'second contradiction' of capitalism) has been put forward by James O'Connor (1988).

One can then think of the exploitation of nature by modern industry and consumer society as having two complementary senses – first, as predations, and second as impositions of unwanted burdens. Other things being equal, competitive enterprises may be expected to seek lower input costs and to impose burdens on other parties such as government, the community at large, and future generations. The social, ideological and technical mechanisms for achieving a shifting of social and environmental burdens may vary a great deal. Some of the mechanisms are quite subtle. For instance, Schultz (1993) described how women in particular were being coerced or coopted, as the care-givers in the household, to increase their everyday unpaid labours in sorting and recycling of materials under the Duales System Deutschland. These gestures of environmental concern constitute a sort of gender-biased social subsidy (that is, a social free gift) to commercial waste management and to the recycling of materials for the benefit of industry. Waring (1989) indicates the general parallel between the invisibility of 'women's work' in conventional national income statistics, and the non-inclusion of 'environmental costs' of resource depletion and pollution damages. (See also O'Connor, 1994b, and Salleh, 1994.) At a general level, we are dealing then with problems of *cost-shifting*, but typically in the *absence of prices*, so that natural resources and services can be formally treated as 'free gifts' and 'free disposals' (O'Connor, 1993a). Here the word 'cost' is misleading since it seems to imply an economic numeraire. What is really at stake is the redistribution of burdens and benefits, short and long term, immediately tangible or speculative and uncertain, across and within societies, spatially and through time. Economic price theory and formal mathematical models cannot be expected to have high explanatory power in these respects. They can, however, still help sharpen insight into the character of such economic and ecological distribution conflicts.

3. Non-separability of efficiency and distribution in general equilibrium models

Much work in environmental economics and environmental policy is concerned with the 'internalization' of negative external effects – that is, *cost-shifting success* from the point of view of those parties benefiting from the

'non-internalization'. The usual norm for 'correction' is to achieve allocative efficiency in resource use, so that the marginal costs of the activity in
question are equal to the marginal benefits obtained. It is often proposed
that the effect of a 'correction' of the market failure is that the size (in value
terms) of the 'economic pie' is maximized, and that questions of the cost/
benefit distribution can be dealt with (separately from such 'wealth maximization') in terms of political decisions about how the gains from the
internalization come to be shared out. But this formulation is fundamentally flawed.

First, although much rhetoric in policy circles is about efficiency of
resource use and opportunity cost, in most policy calculations we are
dealing, at best, only with cost-effectiveness – and in this respect, only with
effectiveness in relation to those environmental and resource objectives for
which policy impacts can reasonably be predicted and physically quantified
by expert advice. Attempts at quantifications are often controversial. This
is why the negotiation of environmental norms and standards should itself
be subject to scrutiny in environmental economics.

Second, even in the very restrictive world of 'first-best', as expressed
within a general equilibrium framework, for a given production possibility
frontier the 'wealth-maximizing' output mix (and hence the input resource-
use pattern) is a function of the relative prices; and the vector of 'correct'
prices (signalling relative opportunity costs) is a function of consumers'
preferences in conjunction with the distribution of ownership (property
rights). The decisive question is: allocative efficiency relative to what underlying wealth, rights or income distribution?

Neoclassical economics focuses on the efficiency of the allocation of
scarce resources to alternative present and future ends, with opportunity
costs supposed to be signalled through the price system. The *simultaneous
determination of relative prices and output mix in general competitive equilibrium* means that, within the logic of the model, welfare distribution (in
the sense of relative and absolute purchasing power of consumers) can be
determined (or decided) only simultaneously with equilibrium prices and
output levels. Consumers' welfare levels depend on their respective income
levels and relative prices of goods. In general equilibrium, a vector of equilibrium-relative prices for inputs and outputs will be determined simultaneously with a Pareto-efficient output mix; the consumer-efficient output
mix will, in general, depend on the *relative income distribution across consumers*; and these relative incomes will in turn depend on the distribution
of input endowments amongst consumers-as-owners *and* the relative prices
of inputs (O'Connor and Muir, 1995). In particular, when preferences are
non-homothetic or differ across social groups, a change in distribution of
income would influence prices, from the demand side, jointly with the tech-

nical determinants of opportunity cost on the production margins. The demand for different environmental goods and services thus varies according to the distribution of income, or the relative levels of income between distinct social groups (Martínez-Alier, 1995a). By deciding distribution of property rights and/or income, we are simultaneously deciding output mix; by determining output mix we determine opportunity costs (and thus equilibrium relative prices), and vice versa.

It follows that there is no unique determination possible of 'correct' prices for doing a cost–benefit calculation. The 'correct' prices will depend on distributional choices, including rights of future generations, as we shall see below. If the question of the income redistribution effects of a policy change (say, a new ecotax) is addressed when equilibrium-relative prices depend significantly on the distributional situations, it is logically invalid to utilize pre-change prices to calculate post-change effects. These costs and benefits cannot be 'correctly' evaluated without knowing the redistributions of wealth and income that are to take place, and the new prices producers and consumers will face. In other words, the distribution of property rights and incomes matters for the valuation of opportunity costs associated with resource use, including the valuation of externalities. (O'Connor and Muir, 1995, present the simplest possible case, with two inputs, two goods, two consumers; and it follows by extension that valuation is sensitive not just to input endowments but also to decisions about rights and liability *vis-à-vis* the damages imposed by the externality.)

4. Neo-Ricardian and Sraffian modelling of economic and ecological distribution

Amongst economists, valuation usually means relative prices. The proposition that prices depend on the distribution of income is, in fact, common ground between conventional neoclassical economics and neo-Ricardian, Sraffian economics, although for different reasons. In neoclassical economics, the distribution of income is a by-product of the formation of the prices for the services of production factors. If the distribution of income is changed, for instance by fiscal redistribution, or if the distribution of ownership of production is changed, for instance by land reforms or CO_2 emissions permit regimes, then the pattern of demand and therefore the pattern of prices will change. For the Sraffian political economy, distribution (between wages and profits, and sometimes also land rent) determines from the supply side (jointly with the technical specificities of the production) the 'prices of production'. The Sraffian approach is relevant, in an environmental context, for the analysis of the valuation of so-called natural capital which is in turn relevant for the measurement of both 'weak sustainability' and 'strong sustainability' (when 'strong sustainability' means the maintenance of some kinds of so-called natural capital, not assessed by physical indicators but in economic terms).

The Sraffian political economy has a 'reproductive' approach to the economy instead of an 'allocative' approach. In the Sraffian system, demand plays no role. This system has a 'reproductive' approach in economic terms – but not a fully fledged 'biophysical' approach (Christensen, 1989). It studies the formation of 'production prices' from the supply side, and it shows that they depend on distribution. A Sraffian system is a system of 'production of commodities by means of commodities', or an input–output system, the analytical objective of which is to ascertain how much it costs to produce the different commodities (the 'prices of production'), and the political objective of which is precisely to show that such prices depend on the distribution of income (as between wages and profits). Therefore the values of the capital stocks depend on the 'class struggle', so to speak. The remuneration to the owners of capital has nothing to do with the marginal productivity of capital as in neoclassical economics, because 'capital' is a heterogeneous collection of items, the produced means of production, the value of which depends on the results of the distributional conflict between wage-workers and capital-owners.

This idea of 'capital' as a heterogeneous collection of produced means of production, the valuation of which *in toto* presents some difficulties, was a main ingredient in debates of the 1960s and 1970s on capital theory and income distribution. So-called natural capital is still more heterogeneous than human-made capital (see Victor, 1991). Most of it is not in the market, yet we might ask what sorts of insights the Sraffian approach can give concerning valuation of natural capital stocks and flows. In a classical Sraffian economy, so-called natural capital appears only as Ricardian land, and there is no analysis of whether it is in open access and therefore unpriced, or in communal property and therefore perhaps administered outside the market, or already privately owned and in the market. However, it is readily possible to 'ecologize' the Sraffian approach, through a generalization of joint production theory, to include ecological production and economy–ecosystem exchanges of natural resources, environmental services and waste products. (See work by Perrings, 1985, 1986, 1987, and by O'Connor, 1993a, 1993b). Nevertheless, we remain sceptical of the use of terms like 'natural capital' or 'ecological capital', which inevitably mean 'nature as capital' (cf. O'Connor, 1993c; Sachs, 1993). First, nature itself cannot really be dealt with as capital which can be appropriated (for instance, unknown biodiversity, or the water cycle). Second, the money value of such 'natural capital' as there is will depend on the endowment of property rights, on the distribution of income (in a Sraffian manner, and also from the demand side), and more particularly on the distribution of power.

For a Sraffian–ecological economics, we need first to decide how to make environmental stocks and flows appear in the production–reproduction picture, and in what terms the identified items belong to 'natural capital' (that is, are appropriated for what purposes and by whom). We may then proceed to explore how their valuation depends, in one way or another, on the distribution of income. The distributional conflicts may be between different societies and between groups within society, over access to depletable resources, or concerning reproduction versus destruction of ecological necessities or life-support systems or environmental amenities. They may also be conflicts concerning which cultural projects will or will not be served by appropriation of environmental services and resources such as biodiversity (O'Connor, 1993a). This opens up a range of questions about institutional forms and so on. However, we should emphasize that Sraffian economics (even if 'ecologized' in this way) is still economics, and as such it still attempts to explain economic values in 'classical' terms of prices of re/production (see also Erreygers, 1996). It does not specifically investigate the physical embeddedness of the economy nor the wider social or cultural issues such as political arrangements and incommensurability of values and systems of legitimacy, although it is aware of these.

5. Sustainability, the time-discount rate, and future generations
The general equilibrium methodology, although useless in analysing the real march of the economy and its impact on ecosystems, can nevertheless be put to good counterfactual or paradoxical use, as we have seen in Section 3. Let us now pursue this line further, introducing future generations. The problem of 'market failure' or 'missing markets' is central to the externality problem as treated in the equilibrium methodology. As no prices exist for the benefits or disservices provided, these latter go unheeded by actors in the market. If future interests are regarded as having standing, then there are 'missing markets', meaning, *prima facie*, a source of Pareto inefficiency or market failure. The alternative is to assert that 'the future' has no rights, hence no demand of its own, and simply receives whatever (much or little) we, the present, see fit to pass on to them. For instance, there are intergenerational distributional conflicts between the enjoyment of nuclear energy (or emissions of CO_2), and the burdens of radioactive waste (or global warming).

The traditional remedy to market failure has been to augment the market through defining appropriate tradable rights, or through a Pigouvian tax. If creating new or pseudo-markets is problematic enough for many static or localized spillover problems, it is insuperable in regard to intertemporal choice problems. Hahn (1973, pp.14–16) made the following pertinent remarks:

The Arrow–Debreu equilibrium is very useful when for instance one comes to argue with someone who maintains that we need not worry about exhaustible resources because they will always have prices which ensure their 'proper' use. Of course there are many things wrong with this contention but a quick way of disposing of the claim is to note that an Arrow–Debreu equilibrium must be an assumption he is making for the economy, and then to show why the economy cannot be in this state.

So, in this counterfactual spirit, let us momentarily set aside real uncertainty and historical time, and examine the construct of intertemporal general equilibrium. In the intergenerational context, we obtain again the result that the relative prices supporting an efficient equilibrium will depend on the endowments of property rights (and the distribution of income) between social groups with differing preferences. Central to the contemporary debates on sustainability are questions of the 'rights' of future generations and of intertemporal equity in endowments of environmental necessities and amenities.

Work by Howarth and Norgaard (1990, 1992, 1993) and Muir (1996) has shown, in overlapping generations (OLG) general equilibrium models, how the relative valuation of an externality, and the relative price of a good from one period to the next (that is, the 'interest rate' from one period to the next), will be functions of the endowment of property rights across generations (and, hence, of the income distribution), and also a function of the preferences of each generation. Moreover, since any policy to 'internalize' environmental spillover effects involves a redistribution of entitlements, the externality valuation and the time-discount rate from period to period will also be functions of the way in which rights and liabilities (for example, pollution taxes paid and received) are distributed across the affected generations.

This recent theoretical work casts light on some old debates about the discount rate and intertemporal valuation. In principle, within neoclassical theory, the 'sustainability' rate of time-discount would be the marginal productivity of capital, or the intertemporal opportunity costs of investment, along a sustainable time-path. We accept this argument (within the neoclassical theory), and therefore we do not, here, go along with a fundamentalist zero rate of discount. It may be admitted that investment sometimes increases productive capacity. The rate of discount appropriate for an ecological economy should be a rate at which investment maintains or increases *sustainable* production capacity. The problem is whether or in what sense this 'sustainability' interest rate can be defined and measured. When 'investment' in economic capital does not mean simple accumulation on the basis of an indestructible environment (as in Ricardo's view of economic growth), but consists, as is really the case with industrial societies, not in a simple increase of *productive* capacity but in a mixture of production and destruction (some of the destruction being irreversible), then the basis for defining the appropriate rate of discount is very unclear. Of course, 'natural capital' may be enhanced (soil conservation measures, for instance) as well as destroyed. We focus here on irreversible destruction. The appropriate discount rate should, one might suppose, be the sustainable rate of growth of the economy, but we are then trapped in circular reasoning because, in order to ascertain this sustainable rate of growth which would yield the appropriate discount rate, we need first to subtract from observed growth the present value of the irreversible destruction of some natural capital (for instance, biodiversity), and in order to do this we must not only put a price on such natural capital (which is problematic enough), but we also need a discount rate.

6. Conclusions

We have discussed how, in theory and in reality, valuations of today's externalities and also valuations of future externalities (and of environmental resources and services) will depend on the distribution, not only of property rights, but also of income, and also of power in social–institutional terms. The absence of future generations and of other species from markets has often been remarked upon. In this contribution we have emphasized the social background to the valuation of negative externalities and environmental resources and services, both in a general equilibrium framework and in neo-Ricardian analysis, and in both intragenerational and intergenerational contexts.

We may conclude that there is no such thing as a set of ecologically right prices because, first, values of environmental resources and services, and of externalities, always depend on the property rights endowment and on the distribution of income and power; and second, these real valuations cannot plausibly be reconciled within an 'equilibrium' system of value. Rather, the existence of conflicts and indeterminacies about economic *and* ecological distribution has, for a practical result, the incommensurability (or at least, incomplete commensurability) between different dimensions of the economic and ecological goods and bads. In fact, the feature of incommensurability of values has been recognized in the tradition of institutional and ecological economics for some time. Thus Otto Neurath (analytical philosopher of the Vienna Circle), writing in the late 1910s and 1920s in the context of the 'socialist calculation debate', had already pointed out that, as a consequence of distributional conflicts, decisions could not be taken based on only one single type of value. He compared different situations, asking whether the economy should use more coal, and less human labour, or vice versa. The answer depends on whether one thinks that hydro-electric power may be sufficiently developed or that solar heat might come to be better used, etc. If one believes the latter, one may 'spend' coal more freely and will hardly waste human effort where coal can be used. If however one is afraid that when one generation uses too much coal thousands will freeze to death in the future, one might use more human power and save coal. Such and many other non-technical matters determine the choice of a technically calculable plan ... we can see no possibility of reducing the production plan to some kind of unit and then to compare the various plans in terms of such units.

The increased greenhouse effect, and the long-term problems of nuclear power, can be readily brought into this framework. Comparability need not presuppose commensurability (O'Neill, 1993; Martínez-Alier, 1995b, 1995c). We can rationally discuss sources of energy, transport systems, agricultural practices, patterns of industrialization, and the preservation of tropical forests, taking into account both monetary costs and benefits, and socio-environmental burdens and benefits, as they impinge on different groups of people and on other species, now and in the future, without appealing to a single numeraire (Funtowicz and Ravetz, 1994). Help in decision making could come instead from non-compensatory multi-criteria evaluation (Munda, 1995; Faucheux and O'Connor (eds), 1998). Economic incommensurability also opens up a broad social and political space for environmental movements, and for what has sometimes been called 'discursive democracy'.

References
Agarwal, A. and S. Narain (1991), *Global Warming in an Unequal World*, Delhi: Center for Science and Environment.
Azar, Christian and John Holmberg (1995), 'Defining the generational environmental debt', *Ecological Economics*, **14** (1), 7–19.
Beckenbach, Frank (1989), 'Social costs of modern capitalism', *Capitalism, Nature, Socialism*, no. 3 (Fall). Revised and reprinted as ch 6 in M. O'Connor (ed.) (1994), *Is Capitalism Sustainable? Political Economy and Politics of Ecology*, New York: Guilford Publications.
Blaikie P. and H. Brookfield (eds) (1987), *Land Degradation and Society*, London: Methuen.
Borrero, José M. (1994), *La deuda ecológica. Testimonio de una reflexión*, Cali: FIPMA.
Bromley, D. (1989), *Economic Interests and Institutions. The Conceptual Foundations of Public Policy*, Oxford: Blackwell.
Bryant, B. (ed.) (1995), *Environmental Justice: Issues, Policies and Solutions*, Washington, DC: Island Press.
Bullard, R. (1993), *Confronting Environmental Racism: Voices from the Grassroots*. Boston: South End Press.
Christensen, Paul (1989), 'Historical roots for ecological economics: biophysical versus allocative approaches', *Ecological Economics*, **1**, 17–30.
Erreygers, G. (1996), 'Sustainability and stability in a classical model of production', in Sylvie Faucheux et al. (eds), *Models of Sustainable Development*, Cheltenham, UK and Brookfield, US: Edward Elgar.
Faucheux, S.E. Muir and M. O'Connor (1997), 'Neoclassical theory of natural capital and "weak" indicators for sustainability', *Land Economics*, **73** (4), 528–52.
Faucheux, S. and M. O'Connor (eds) (1998), *Valuation for Sustainable Development: Methods and Policy Applications*, Cheltenham, UK and Northampton, MA, USA: Edward Elgar.

Funtowicz, S. and J. Ravetz (1994), 'The worth of a songbird: ecological economics as a post-normal science', *Ecological Economics*, **10**, 197–207.

Guha, R. and J. Martínez-Alier (1997), *Varieties of Environmentalism*, London: Earthscan.

Hahn, Frank (1973), *On the Notion of Equilibrium in Economics*, Inaugural Lecture, Cambridge, UK: Cambridge University Press.

Howarth, R.B. and R.B. Norgaard (1990), 'Intergenerational resource rights, efficiency, and social optimality', *Land Economics*, **66**, 1–11.

Howarth, R.B. and R.B. Norgaard (1992), 'Environmental valuation under sustainable development', *American Economic Review Papers and Proceedings*, **80**, 473–7.

Howarth, R.B. and R.B. Norgaard (1993), 'Intergenerational transfers and the social discount rate', *Environmental and Resource Economics*, **3**, 337–58.

Kapp, K.W. (1983), *Social Costs, Economic Development, and Environmental Disruption*, edited and introduced by John E. Ullman, Lanham: University Press of America.

Leff, E. (1994), *Ecology and Capital*, New York: Guilford Publications.

Little, P.D. and M. Horowitz (eds) (1987), *Lands at Risk in the Third World*, Boulder, CO: Westview Press.

Martínez-Alier, J. (1995a), 'The environment as a luxury good or "too poor to be green"?', *Economie Appliquée*, **48** (2), 215–30.

Martínez-Alier, J. (1995b), 'Political ecology, distributional conflicts, and economic incommensurability', *New Left Review*, **211**, 70–88.

Martínez-Alier, J. (1995c), 'Distributional issues in ecological economics', *Review of Social Economy*, **53** (4), 511–28.

Martínez-Alier, J. and M. O'Connor (1996), 'Ecological and economic distribution conflicts' in R. Costanza, O. Segura and J. Martínez-Alier (eds), *Getting Down to Earth. Practical Applications of Ecological Economics*, Washington, DC: ISEE/Island Press.

Muir, E. (1996), 'Intra-generational wealth distribution effects on global warming cost benefit analysis', *Journal of Income Distribution*, **6** (2).

Munda, G. (1995), *Multicriteria Evaluation in a Fuzzy Environment. Theory and Applications in Ecological Economics*, Heidelberg: Physika Verlag.

Nijkamp, Peter (1986), 'Equity and efficiency in environmental policy analysis: separability versus inseparability', in A. Schnaiberg, N. Watts and K. Zimmerman (eds), *Distributional Conflicts in Environmental Resource Policy*, Aldershot: Gower.

O'Connor, James (1988), 'Introduction', *Capitalism, Nature, Socialism*, no. 1.

O'Connor, Martin (1993a), 'Value system contests and the appropriation of ecological capital', *The Manchester School*, **61** (4), 398–424.

O'Connor, Martin (1993b), 'Entropic irreversibility and uncontrolled technological change in economy and environment', *Journal of Evolutionary Economics*, **3** (December), 285–315.

O'Connor, Martin (1993c). 'On the misadventures of capitalist nature', *Capitalism Nature Socialism*, **4** (3), 7–40. Reprinted as ch. 7 in O'Connor (1994a).

O'Connor, Martin (ed.) (1994a), *Is Capitalism Sustainable? Political Economy and the Politics of Ecology*, New York: Guilford Publications.

O'Connor, Martin (1994b), 'The material/communal conditions of life', *Capitalism Nature Socialism*, **5** (3), 95–104.

O'Connor, Martin and Eliot Muir (1996), 'Endowment effects in competitive general equilibrium: a primer for policy analysts', *The Journal of Income Distribution*, **5** (2).

O'Neill, John (1993), *Ecology, Policies, Politics*, London: Routledge.

Painter, M. and W. H. Durham (eds) (1995), *The Social Causes of Environmental Destruction in Latin America*, Ann Arbor: University of Michigan Press.

Peet, R. and M. Watts (eds) (1996), *Liberation Ecologies. Environment, Development, Social Movements*, London and New York: Routledge.

Perrings, C. (1985), 'The natural economy revisited', *Economic Development and Cultural Change*, **33**, 829–50.

Perrings, C. (1986), 'Conservation of mass and instability in a dynamic economy–environment system', *Journal of Environmental Economics and Management*, **13**, 199–211.

Perrings, C. (1987), *Economy and Environment: A Theoretical Essay on the Interdependence of Economic and Environmental Systems*, Cambridge, UK: Cambridge University Press.

392   Economics of environmental policy

Robleto, María Luisa and Wilfredo Marcelo (1992), *Deuda Ecológica*, Santiago de Chile: Instituto de Ecología Política.

Sachs, Wolfgang (ed.) (1993), *Global Ecology: A New Arena of Political Conflict*, London: Zed Books.

Salleh, Ariel (1994), 'Nature, woman, labor, capital: living the deepest contradiction', ch. 6 in O'Connor (1994a).

Samuels, W. (1991), *Essays on the Economic Role of Government, Vol. 1 Fundamentals; Vol. 2 Applications*, London: Macmillan.

Schultz, Irmgard (1993), 'Women and waste', *Capitalism Nature Socialism*, **4** (2), 51–63.

Schwab, J. (1994), *Deeper Shades of Green: The Rise of Blue-Collar and Minority Environmentalism in America*, San Francisco: Sierra Club Books.

Summers, Lawrence (1992), internal World Bank memo, as reported in *The Economist*, 8 February.

Szasz, A. (1994), *EcoPopulism: Toxic Waste and the Movement for Environmental Justice*, Minneapolis: University of Minnessota Press.

Victor, Peter (1991), 'Indicators of sustainable development: some lessons from capital theory', *Ecological Economics*, **4**, 191–213.

Wackernagel, M. and W. Rees (1996), 'Our ecological footprint: reducing human impact on the earth', *The New Catalyst Bioregional Series*, Vol. g, Gabriola Island, BC: New Society Publications.

Waring, Marilyn (1989), *Counting for Nothing*, Sydney: Unwin.

PART IV

INTERNATIONAL ASPECTS OF ENVIRONMENTAL ECONOMICS AND POLICY

26 Environmental policy in open economies
Michael Rauscher*

1. Introduction

In the 1970s and early 1980s, environmental economics was concerned mainly with the regulation of environmental externalities in closed economies. At that time, only very few authors looked at the interactions of environmental policies and international trade, for example, Baumol (1971), Markusen (1975), Pethig (1976), Siebert (1977, 1979), Siebert et al. (1980), and McGuire (1982). Recently, the interest in this area of research has been revived, for at least two reasons. On the one hand, the rapid growth of international trade and the ratification of new trade agreements (for example NAFTA) and the deepening of existing ones (such as the Maastricht Treaty) have increased the economic interdependences of countries. Industry lobbies fear that tight environmental standards undermine the competitiveness of their products in international markets. Environmentalists are worried that pollution-intensive industries might migrate to pollution havens and that a race for the bottom in environmental regulation will be started. On the other hand, the global dimension of environmental disruption has become an issue of increasing concern and this had not been considered in most of the early models. The revival of the trade-and-environment debate has produced a large number of publications. Major contributions are Merrifield (1988), Krutilla (1991), Anderson and Blackhurst (1992), Esty (1994), Copeland and Taylor (1994), Ulph (1996), and Rauscher (1994, 1995, 1997). See also Chapters 27–30.

This survey is organized as follows. The next section discusses how environmental policies affect the patterns of trade. Then I shall address the issue of using environmental policies to achieve trade-policy objectives. Afterwards I shall discuss trade interventions that are implemented to achieve environmental goals. The problem of regulatory capture of environmental policies in open economies will be addressed in Section 5. Section 6 will deal with international agreements on trade and the environment and the final section will raise some questions that still remain to be answered by trade and environmental economists. In this chapter, the term

* I am indebted to Karl Steininger and Jeroen van den Bergh for helpful suggestions. The usual disclaimer applies.

'openness' will be used merely in the sense of openness to foreign trade in goods but not to foreign direct investment. Foreign direct investment and the location of economic activities are addressed in Markusen's contribution in this book (Chapter 39).

2.   Environmental policies and the patterns of trade

According to the results of Heckscher–Ohlin trade theory, a country exports the goods that use relatively intensively the factors of production with which the country is well endowed. Besides the traditional factors of production (capital, labour and land), environmental resources enter the arena. Environmental resources are air and water quality, soil purity, the capacity of nature to assimilate wastes and toxic substances and so on. One can interpret emissions as that part of environmental resources which is used up during the production process and returned to the environment in the form of waste and pollutants. A country well endowed with environmental resources is expected to be an exporter of environmentally intensively produced goods. When is a country well endowed with environmental resources?

- One determinant is the degree of physical scarcity of environmental resources. Its components are, among others, assimilative capacity and population density. In a densely populated country, the endowment of environmental resources per capita is relatively small. Or, to put it the other way round: in a densely populated country the same level of deterioration of environmental resources affects a larger number of people than in a country with low population density.
- The second determinant is the willingness of the population to pay for conservation of environmental resources. The larger the environmental concern, the less abundant is the environmental resource and the more likely that the environmentally intensive good will be imported.
- Demand for final goods is the third determinant of factor abundance. A high level of domestic demand for an environmentally intensive good makes environmental resources relatively scarce and forces the country to import these goods after the move from autarky to free trade.

Physical availability and environmental concern are translated by the political process into the environmental regulation which ultimately determines a country's relative abundance of environmental resources and its position in the international division of labour. Of course, the political process may lead to a biased representation of environmental scarcity, in particular when there are strong lobbies or if a high level of inequality leads to a large difference between the will of the median voter and that of the average individual in society. To make a distinction between the scarcity determined by physical factors and preferences on the one hand and by the political process on the other, Rauscher (1997, ch. 2) uses the terms 'true endowment' and 'de facto endowment'.

Additional considerations become relevant (i) if there are many goods and factors, (ii) if emissions have external effects on production, (iii) if consumption externalities are considered, and (iv) if trade in pollutants, for example toxic waste, is possible. In the case of many goods and factors, the prediction of the standard two-good, two-factor Heckscher–Ohlin model holds only on average: a country with scarce environmental resources may export some environmentally intensively produced goods, but not most of them; see Deardorff (1982). If environmental damages affect production, then a Ricardian productivity argument needs to be added. Productivity losses due to environmental disruption may differ across industries. Thus a country with stringent environmental policies tends to export goods whose production is particularly sensitive to pollution. If domestic use of a particular commodity is restricted for environmental reasons, domestic demand is low and the commodity will be exported. An example is the production of toxic herbicides in countries where their use is prohibited. Finally, as regards exports of hazardous waste, producers in countries with stringent environmental policies are willing to pay for the possibility to export pollutants. Thus tight regulation tends to induce waste exports.

How important is the impact of environmental regulation on international trade empirically? Not much evidence has been found up to now. The literature is reviewed in Rauscher (1997, ch. 1) and the conclusion is that there is not much evidence of a close relationship between trade and environmental regulation. See also Steininger's contribution to this volume (Chapter 28). The recent paper by van Beers and van den Bergh (1997) is a notable exception and it shows that more empirical research is necessary. The main reason for the insignificant results in many studies is that the costs of environmental regulation are rather modest in most sectors of the economy: about 2 per cent of total production costs. However, this may change if local and global pollution become increasingly severe and environmental standards are tightened in the future.

Should environmental standards be harmonized internationally? The general answer is no. Differences in endowments constitute the basis of mutual gains from trade and they should not be eliminated artificially. Harmonization is necessary only in cases where the impact of pollution is independent of the location of the source of pollution, that is, in the case of global pollutants such as greenhouse gases or substances that deplete the ozone layer.

The catchword of 'environmental dumping' has been used in the public discussion to describe situations in which a country uses laxer environmental policies than its trading partners. Used in this sense, environmental dumping represents something which is regarded as a non-problem from the point of view of trade economists. It appears to be more useful to define environmental dumping as an environmental policy which, for the sake of achieving trade-policy objectives, internalizes domestic social costs only incompletely; see Rauscher (1994). This is the subject of the following section.

3. Environmental policies as trade policies

In a first-best world, trade–policy instruments such as import tariffs and export subsidies should be used to achieve trade-related policy objectives. However, these instruments are not always available to the policy maker. Regional and international trade agreements restrict their use. Therefore, policy makers may think about alternative instruments and one candidate is environmental regulation. The most interesting questions in this context are (i) whether there will be environmental dumping and (ii) whether a race for the bottom is started when other countries retaliate. The following policy objectives may be thought of.

Terms-of-trade considerations

A large country can improve its terms of trade by reducing the domestic demand for the import good and increasing its demand for the export good. The first-best instrument is the optimal tariff. If this is not available, environmental policies may be used. If production is environmentally harmful, the country exporting the 'dirty' good should use a stringent environmental policy since this increases the scarcity and the relative price of its export good. This is just the opposite of environmental dumping. The importer of the 'dirty' good should relax its standards and choose an environmental dumping strategy in order to reduce the price of its import good. In a Nash equilibrium where both countries choose their optimal responses, there is no race to the bottom: one country benefits from lax standards, but the other one prefers stringent environmental policies. Similar results are obtained if consumption is environmentally harmful. Laxer environmental standards increase the demand for and the relative price of the environmentally harmful good. This is beneficial to the exporter of this commodity and bad for its importer. Again, there is no race to the bottom since one country strives for tight environmental standards. If external effects on production are considered, anything can happen, depending on how these externalities are modelled; see Rauscher (1997, ch. 5).

Industrial policies
Environmental policies can be used to support particular industries in an economy. There are two motives for doing this. The first one is welfare maximization and the literature is surveyed in Ulph's paper on strategic environmental policy in this volume (Chapter 29). See also Rauscher (1997, ch. 6). It is seen that no unambiguous policy implications concerning the stringency of environmental policy can be derived. The second motive is the protection of idiosyncratic interest groups from foreign competition. This can be achieved by indirect subsidies to domestic producers by means of lax environmental policies or by raising rivals' costs, for example through discriminative product standards. There is a tendency towards lax environmental regulation at home and too-strict requirements for foreign goods; see Rauscher (1997, ch. 7).

Leakage effects and transfrontier pollution
Changes in environmental policies lead to changes in comparative advantage and specialization. If a country uses tighter standards, then environmentally intensive industries abroad become more competitive and tend to expand their outputs. This results in higher emission levels and tends to dilute the intended effects of the domestic policies. Since the net benefits from stringent environmental policies are reduced by the increase in foreign emissions, the optimal emission taxes will not internalize the social costs of pollution. In the Nash equilibrium emission taxes tend to be too low in all countries.

The terms-of-trade argument is probably of minor relevance since the impact of environmental policy on international trade is rather small empirically. However, the other arguments remain valid.

4. Green trade interventions
Should trade be restricted for environmental reasons? As long as environmental damages are purely national and transport externalities are neglected, the answer is no. It can be shown, however, that in second-best situations with non-optimal environmental policies a country may benefit from trade restrictions but the first-best solution would be to correct the environmental policies.

Transport externalities require the environmental regulation of transport activities, for example the taxation of transportation fuels. Of course this is a barrier to trade but a beneficial one since it removes indirect subsidies to transportation. There are other cases where trade is very close to the source of the environmental problem, for example the cases of toxic-waste exports and trade in endangered species. In these cases, trade interventions are close to first best from an economic-theory point of view.

Leakage problems constitute a second motive for trade interventions. If domestic environmental standards change the patterns of specialization such that domestic production is substituted by imported goods that are produced environmentally intensively abroad, then restrictions on imports are welfare-improving. If the domestic economy is an exporter of these goods, export subsidies are required to avoid an increase in foreign emissions. Matters are different if primary rather than final goods are traded. Probably the most severe leakage problems arise in international energy markets. CO_2 taxes imposed unilaterally by a large country reduce the world demand for energy and the decline in prices leads to an increase in energy use elsewhere. The appropriate accompanying measures of an environmental policy that restricts domestic energy use are subsidies for imports of energy or taxes on energy exports. These instruments raise world energy demand or reduce world energy supply and thus partially offset the adverse effects of the reduction of domestic energy demand. It should be noted that trade interventions designed to deal with leakage effects are optimal only from the point of view of a single country. They reduce leakage at the cost of distorting international trade. A globally optimal solution would be a combination of free trade and cooperative environmental policies involving higher emission taxes and, possibly, side payments.

Finally, trade restrictions may be used as sanctions to stabilize international environmental agreements. An example is the Montreal Protocol on Substances that Deplete the Ozone Layer.

5. Regulatory capture

Particularly in open economies, environmental regulation is subject to regulatory capture. Interest groups striving for protection from international competition lobby for lax environmental standards, for environmental tariffs, and for discriminatory product standards. Thus environmental protection may be turned into environmental protectionism rather easily. How can this be avoided?

One component of a solution is the use of market-oriented environmental policy instruments instead of command-and-control solutions. The command-and-control approach usually regulates polluters. Polluters then have strong incentives to negotiate favourable conditions, often on the basis of information to which the regulator has limited access, for example concerning the best available technology. Market-based instruments usually address polluting substances rather than polluters. Thus the group of regulatees is larger and more heterogeneous than in the command-and-control scenario. This raises the costs of creating a lobby. Moreover, the required information is marginal environmental damage and there are no inherent informational advantages on the part of the regulatees.

The other major component is monitoring. The protectionist content of environmental regulations should be documented. Supranational bodies such as the World Trade Organization (WTO) or the European Court of Justice can play a significant role in this process.

Finally, environmental trade restrictions should probably not be used unilaterally by a single country but, if they are, this should only be as a means of last resort. An international negotiation process links green trade interventions to mutually agreeable conditions and procedures and it is to be expected that the influence of national protectionist lobbies on the decision process is less than in the case of unilateral interventions.

6. International agreements on trade and the environment

The policy debates of the recent past have led to the impression that international trade agreements and environmental agreements are in conflict. See Esty (1994) for a comprehensive inquiry of the issues and Rauscher (1997, ch. 9) for a shorter discussion.

It is widely argued that trade agreements are generally pro free trade and tend to restrict their signatory parties in their choice of environmental policies. An example is the General Agreement on Tariffs and Trade (GATT), which in its Article XX states that measures to protect human, animal or plant life or health can be adopted or enforced as long as they do not constitute a means of unjustifiable discrimination or a disguised trade restriction. Similar articles can be found in other agreements such as the Treaty of Rome and the North American Free Trade Agreement (NAFTA). Recent GATT panel decisions interpreted this article in a way which, environmentalists argue, gives precedence to free trade over environmental concerns. It should, however, be noted that this article does not explicitly prohibit green barriers to trade, nor does it say that the humans, animals or plants to be protected have to be located in the territory of the country adopting the measures. Thus extraterritorialism, albeit in conflict with some interpretations of Article XX, is not excluded generally. The NAFTA, being the most recent major trade agreement, has been influenced more than any other trade agreement by environmental concerns. It explicitly allows for green barriers to trade if these are implemented on the basis of an international environmental agreement. Moreover, it states that signatory parties should not use lax environmental standards to attract foreign direct investment. None the less, there are still restrictions on the use of environmental policies. They may not be unjustified or discriminatory barriers to trade or a means of disguised protection.

Many international environmental agreements allow for or even require trade restrictions. Examples are the Convention on International Trade in Endangered Species (CITES), the Montreal Protocol on Substances that Deplete the Ozone Layer, and the Basel Convention on the Control of Transboundary Movements of Hazardous Wastes and their Disposal. The trade restrictions contained in these agreements are in conflict with the pro free-trade interpretations of the GATT. They are discriminating in that non-signatory parties are treated differently from signatory parties and one may argue that some of these measures are unjustified because there exist alternative policy instruments that are less distorting.

Can these conflicts be resolved? A less restrictive interpretation of the GATT rules may be a step in the right direction. The WTO expresses the desirability of sustainable development in its preamble and places environmental issues on its agenda. None the less, one should keep in mind that, though far from perfect, the GATT has functioned rather well over half a century in removing barriers to trade and improving the global division of labour. These gains should not be gambled away by opening a Pandora's box of green protectionism.

As far as international transport is concerned, the WTO may be the right forum to negotiate an agreement on the internalization of transport externalities. In particular, an appropriate taxation of aviation fuels is difficult to implement on a unilateral basis, and an international agreement appears to be necessary to internalize the environmental costs of airborne transportation.

7.   Summary and some open questions

What can be learnt from the literature on environmental policies in open economies? The best of all possible worlds is characterized by free trade and a tight environmental regulation which internalizes all environmental costs of production, transportation and consumption – including those costs that occur across the border. However, the real world is still far from the first best. Depending on the type of distortion prevailing, any kind of results can be derived. In second-best worlds (and in nth-best worlds, too, of course), environmental policies do not correctly internalize the social costs, and trade interventions become justifiable. From the empirical results, however, one can infer that most of the effects of foreign trade on environmental quality are probably rather small.

Although much has been achieved in the recent research on trade and the environment, there are still some areas where future research will offer valuable new insights. First, most of the models used in the literature are based on the assumption of atomistic competition or of oligopolies with a fixed number of firms. This is not particularly satisfying and models with endogenous market structure are desirable. Second, the problems of capture of environmental policies in open economies by idiosyncratic interest groups is not yet understood well enough and future research should be directed to the search for 'capture-proof' institutions. Third, there is a need to combine trade models with game-theoretic approaches to analyse international environmental agreements. The tying of issues, which is so relevant in practice, has not yet been analysed in depth by economic theorists. Last but not least, additional empirical research is necessary to assess the magnitude and relevance of the effects derived in theoretical models.

References

Anderson, K. and R. Blackhurst (eds) (1992), *The Greening of World Trade Issues*, New York: Harvester Wheatsheaf.

Baumol, W.J. (1971), *Environmental Protection, International Spillovers, and Trade*, Stockholm: Alqvist and Wicksell.

Copeland, B.R. and M.S. Taylor (1994), 'North–South trade and the environment', *Quarterly Journal of Economics*, **109**, 755–87.

Deardorff, A.V., (1982), 'The general validity of the Heckscher–Ohlin theorem', *American Economic Review*, **72**, 683–94.

Esty, D.C. (1994), *Greening the GATT: Trade, Environment, and the Future*, Washington, DC: Institute for International Economics.

Krutilla, K. (1991), 'Environmental regulation in an open economy', *Journal of Environmental Economics and Management*, **10**, 127–42.

Markusen, J.R. (1975), 'International externalities and optimal tax structures', *Journal of International Economics*, **5**, 15–29.

McGuire, M.C. (1982), 'Regulation, factor rewards, and international trade', *Journal of Public Economics*, **17**, 335–54.

Merrifield, J.D. (1988), 'The impact of abatement strategies on transnational pollution, the terms of trade, and factor rewards: a general equilibrium approach', *Journal of Environmental Economics and Management*, **15**, 259–84.

Pethig, R. (1976), 'Pollution, welfare, and environmental policy in the theory of comparative advantage', *Journal of Environmental Economics and Management*, **2**, 160–69.

Rauscher, M. (1994), 'On ecological dumping', *Oxford Economic Papers*, **46**, 822–40.

Rauscher, M. (1995), 'Environmental legislation as a tool of trade policy', in G. Boero and Z.A. Silberston (eds), *Environmental Economics: Proceedings of a Conference held by the Confederation of European Economic Associations at Oxford, 1993 CEEA Conference*, Basingstoke: Macmillan, pp. 73–90.

Rauscher, M. (1997), *International Trade, Factor Movements, and the Environment*, Oxford: Oxford University Press.

Siebert, H. (1977), 'Environmental quality and the gains from trade', *Kyklos*, **30**, 657–73.

Siebert, H. (1979), 'Environmental policy in the two-country case', *Zeitschrift für Nationalökonomie*, **39**, 259–74.

Siebert, H., J. Eichberger, R. Gronych and R. Pethig (1980), *Trade and the Environment: A Theoretical Enquiry*, Amsterdam: North-Holland.

Ulph, A. (1996), 'Environmental policy and international trade: a survey of recent economic analysis', in H. Folmer (ed.), *International Yearbook of Environmental Economics*, Cheltenham, UK and Brookfield, US: Edward Elgar, pp. 205–42.

van Beers, C. and J.C.J.M. van den Bergh (1997), 'An empirical multi-country analysis of the impact of environmental regulations on foreign trade flows', *Kyklos*, **50**, 29–46.

27 Partial equilibrium models of trade and the environment
Kerry Krutilla

1. Introduction

In recent years, research exploring the nexus between environmental policy evaluation and non-strategic trade theory has increasingly relied on general equilibrium analysis (see Chapter 28 by Steininger, this volume). None the less, partial equilibrium modelling affords an efficient means of policy evaluation in an open-economy setting if the effects of policy actions on factor incomes are not of interest and outcomes do not differ substantively from those of general equilibrium analysis.[1] In the 'trade-and-environment' context, partial equilibrium models are particularly useful for studying the consequences of terms-of-trade effects, and for indicating how such factors as a country's commodity trade balance, and the type of the externality problem, affect the normative properties of environmental policy actions.

This chapter reviews partial equilibrium modelling to assess the impact of trade liberalization on the environment, and to determine the structure of optimal environmental policy in an open-economy setting. For most of the chapter, pollution is assumed to be local, but the effects of environmental regulation in the transboundary context are also briefly considered.

A number of standard assumptions underlie the analysis. First, in keeping with the orthodox trade literature, the 'rest of the world' does not respond strategically when a country initiates environmental regulation or trade-policy reform (see Chapter 29 by Ulph, this volume, for a discussion of strategic trade policy). Second, the environmental distortion in question is the only distortion in the economy, except when other distortions are explicitly addressed within the modelling framework.[2] Finally, the production process is one in which emissions are proportional to output. This assumption is stronger than necessary to ensure that economic adjustments to environmental policy actions influence commodity prices and international trade flows, but it is maintained in this form for expositional convenience.[3]

The following two sections of the chapter focus on environmental policy in the case where pollution is local and economic adjustment responses in the international trade system exclusively determine the open-economy welfare ramifications. Section 4 extends the analysis to consider the effects of transboundary pollution, in which the direct environmental impact channel, as well as trade linkages, influence the results. Section 5 offers some brief concluding remarks.

2.   Trade liberalization and the environment[4]

Environmentalists have frequently expressed concerns about the environmental impact of trade liberalization (Charnovitz, 1992; Wathen, 1993; Esty, 1994). However, the relationship between trade liberalization and environmental consequences is not straightforward, even in the simplest cases. Consider a small country with one polluting commodity sector such that $e = K_q$, where e are emissions, K is a proportionality constant, and q is the sector's output. For expositional convenience, the country is assumed not to trade in the start-point equilibrium; P, q and e are the price, quantity and emissions equilibria in autarky (Figure 27.1). Assume first that the production side of the economy produces pollution yielding a social cost curve (SC) which is above the private supply curve (S) (drawn linearly in Figure 27.1 for convenience).[5] Now the country eliminates the prohibitive trade barrier, allowing unrestricted trade at the world price (which, by

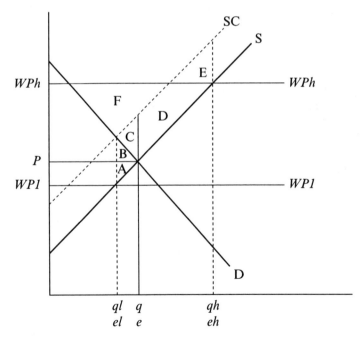

Figure 27.1   Welfare impact on small countries from trade liberalization – production externality

assumption, the country is too small to influence). If the country is economically positioned to be a net exporter of the product – $P < WPh$, where *WPh* is the high world price – production and emissions will increase, all else constant (to qh and eh, respectively, in Figure 27.1). Without environmental policy to redress the environmental damages, the conventionally measured welfare benefit of the trade liberalization $(F + C + D)$ is attenuated by additional environmental damages $(D + E)$ and could be negative (if $E > C + F$). Conversely, if the country is economically positioned to be a net importer – $P > WPl$, where *WPl* is the low world price – opening the country to trade will reduce emissions (from e to el) as the dirty import-competing sector contracts (from q to ql) (again see Figure 27.1). In this case, the environmental side effect increases the welfare gain of the trade policy (by $A + B + C$).

When the externality is generated by the product's consumption, so that the marginal social benefits are lower than the market demand curve (DSB < D in Figure 27.2), the welfare effects of trade liberalization, in relation to the commodity trade balance, are just the reverse. With the country positioned to be a net exporter, the commodity price rise associated with

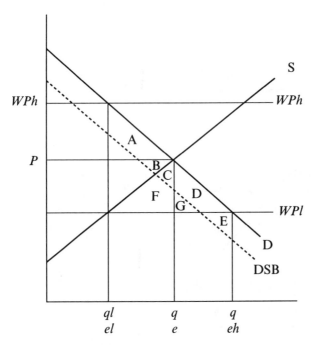

Figure 27.2   Welfare impact on small countries from trade liberalization –
consumption externality

the trade liberalization reduces domestic consumption and pollution (to ql and el respectively in Figure 27.2). The environmental impact of the lower emissions $(A + B + C)$ augments the welfare gains of the trade liberalization. On the other hand, when the country is positioned to be a net importer, the domestic price decline associated with the trade liberalization increases consumption and pollution (to qh and eh in Figure 27.2), reducing the welfare benefits of trade liberalization (into the negative range if $E > C + F + G$). These results are summarized in Table 27.1.

Table 27.1   Environmental impact of trade liberalization – small-country case

	Direction of welfare effect	
	Net exporter	Net importer
Production externality	−	+
Consumption externality	+	−

Trade liberalization is unambiguously welfare-enhancing in all cases when paired with an optimal environmental policy instrument (Anderson, 1992a). The analytics in this case do not differ in any important way from those in the case where environmental policy is implemented in a competitive closed economy. Assuming that the transactions costs of employing the appropriate environmental policy instrument are not too costly, this reality underlies the usual view of economists that environmental side effects associated with trade liberalization pose an environmental-policy problem, rather than a trade-policy problem, *per se* (see Bhagwati, 1993).

It is possible that the transactions costs of using the environmental policy instrument are prohibitive in some cases, for example, to ameliorate area source water pollution (Krutilla, 1997). In this circumstance, some degree of trade restraint may be theoretically justified as a second-best policy approach for the two out of four cases where trade liberalization worsens environmental damage (Anderson, 1992a).

Environmentalists have also expressed concern about the impact on small countries when larger countries liberalize trade (Charnovitz, 1992; Wathen, 1993). What happens to the environment and welfare of a small country, or a group of small countries, when their trading partners initiate environmental policy? Assume that the block of countries which regulate, at least taken together, is large enough to influence the world price. Further assume that the externality is on the production side of the same commodity market for all countries in the trade system. Given these assumptions, the environmental regulation will reduce production in the regulating countries, thereby reducing global excess supply and raising world price (Krutilla, 1991a). The transmission of the price effect will shift the production locus of the pollution, with some of the production displaced from the regulating countries to the countries which do not regulate. That is, the price effect will boost domestic output and pollution in the non-regulating countries – whether the polluting industry is export-oriented or import-competing.

The environmental regulation will also affect the terms of trade. The price increase will boost profits to exporters in the small country, which at least partially offsets the negative impact of the environmental damage. Conversely, if the country is a net importer, the increase in the cost of imports imposes a negative welfare loss which reinforces the consequences of the increased environmental damage (Krutilla, 1991a).

If the externality is on the consumption side, there is the same environmental damage impact but the terms-of-trade effect is in the opposite direction. Consumption restraints in the other countries will reduce global demand, increase global excess supply, and reduce world price (Krutilla, 1991a). Whether the non-regulating countries are net exporters or importers, the lower world price will increase consumption, worsening environmental damage. However, lower prices hurt exporters but provide a welfare gain if the country is a net importer. Thus countries which are net exporters unambiguously lose in this case, while terms-of-trade effects attenuate the environmental damages when the country is a net importer. The results of these permutations are summarized in Table 27.2.

There is a certain irony to these conclusions. In two of the four cases, the

Table 27.2   Welfare effect on a small country when larger countries regulate

| | Direction of welfare effect | | | |
| | Net exporter | | Net importer | |
	ED	TOT	ED	TOT
Production externality	–	+	–	–
Consumption externality	–	–	–	+

ED = environmental damage effect
TOT = Terms-of-trade effect

terms-of-trade effects attenuate the welfare loss on the environmental side which, in any event, may be addressed with an environmental policy instrument. Thus the environmental side effect may not be a major issue in these cases. However, terms-of-trade deterioration adds to the welfare losses associated with increased environmental damage in the other two cases. Again, domestic environmental policy can be used to address the environmental side effect, but small countries have no policy instrument with which to cope with an exogenous deterioration in their terms of trade. Consequently, the terms-of-trade effects may have more of a significant impact on the welfare of small countries than additional environmental damages. This possibility does not appear to have received much notice by environmentalists and policy makers in the trade and environment area.

3. Optimal environmental policy making in an open economy

In the large-country case, the terms of trade becomes a variable under the country's control. In this case, it becomes difficult to separate the welfare effects of a country's trade policies from the welfare effects of its environmental policy making. Thus we now turn to the subject of optimal environmental policy in the large-country context and its relationship to the terms of trade.

In theory, environmental impacts and terms-of-trade effects can be handled directly by using both trade and environmental policy instruments (first-best), or indirectly by using either an environmental policy instruments or tariff to address both effects (second-best). The following formulae (from Krutilla, 1991a) are useful for sorting out the permutations:

$$ts^* = \epsilon(qs) + \alpha(qs - qd) + \alpha X_p T \qquad (27.1)$$

$$td^* + \epsilon(qd) + \gamma(qs - qd) + \gamma X_p T \qquad (27.2)$$

where ts^* is a welfare-maximizing environmental tax on producers, holding constant the tariff T; td^* is a welfare-maximizing environmental tax on consumers, given T; qs and qd are the level of domestic production and consumption, respectively; $\epsilon(qs)$ is the marginal environmental damage cost of production; $\epsilon(qd)$ is the marginal damage cost of consumption; $(qs - qd)$ is excess supply; $X_p < 0$ is the slope of the rest of the world's excess demand schedule, $(X(P))$, where $P =$ the world price; and $\alpha \geq 0$, $\gamma \leq 0$ are terms-of-trade parameters reflecting the slopes of the behavioural equations in the system (Krutilla, 1991a).[6,7] There is a sign convention reflected in equations (27.1) and (27.2) that $T < 0$ when $qs < qd$, while $T > 0$ when $qs > qd$. We now consider some special cases.

Case 1. Small-country case: $X_p = -\infty$, $\alpha = 0$, $\gamma = 0$, $T = 0$.
This may be taken as a benchmark. With no terms-of-trade effects or tariffs, equations (27.1) and (27.2) reduce to $ts^* = \epsilon(q_s)$ and $td^* = \epsilon(q_d)$ for the production and consumption cases respectively, that is, the standard Pigouvian taxes. This result is consistent with the earlier statement that small countries can dichotomize trade and environmental policy making by levying the optimal environmental tax, ts^* or td^*, as $T \to 0$ with trade liberalization.

Case 2. Large-country case: $X_p \neq -\infty$; $\alpha > 0$, $\gamma < 0$.
Maintaining for the moment the assumption that $T = 0$ – perhaps, for political reasons, the country has implemented a total trade liberalization – equations (27.1) and (27.2) show that the optimal (second-best) environmental taxes are:

$$ts^* = \epsilon(qs) + \alpha(qs - qd) \tag{27.3}$$

$$td^* = \epsilon(qs) + \gamma(qs - qd) \tag{27.4}$$

for the cases of production- and consumption-side externalities, respectively. These formulae differ from the classic Pigouvian tax by the presence of the terms-of-trade terms, α $(qs - qd)$ and γ $(qs - qd)$. With $T = 0$, equations (27.3) and (27.4) indicate the formulae for a country optimally to recapture terms-of-trade losses via second-best environmental policy instruments. To do so, equation (27.3) shows that, in the production externality case, $ts^* > \epsilon(qs)$, when $qs - qd > 0$, and vice versa. That is, environmental regulation should be higher than the Pigouvian tax level, $\epsilon(qs)$, when the large country is a net exporter, and lower than the Pigouvian tax level when the large country is a net importer. The intuition follows from the discussion in the previous section: an environmental production restriction lowers world excess supply and raises world price, a terms-of-trade change which provides extra profits to exporters but increases the cost and volume of imports when the country is a net importer. The optimal environmental tax should be raised in the first instance to allow domestic producers to capture the additional rents, but lowered in the second instance to reduce the impact on consumers of higher-cost imports.

Since the terms-of-trade effect works in the opposite direction when consumption is taxed, the consumption tax (equation 27.2) will be higher (lower) than the Pigouvian level when excess supply is negative (positive). These results are summarized in Table 27.3.

When $T \neq 0$, equations (27.1) and (27.2) show that the tariff terms work in the opposite direction of the terms-of-trade term. Effectively, the tariff instrument handles some of the terms-of-trade effect which the terms-of-

Table 27.3 Welfare effect of environmental regulation in large countries

	Direction of welfare effect			
	Net exporter		Net importer	
	ED	TOT	ED	TOT
Production externality	+	+	+	−
Consumption externality	+	−	+	+

Abbreviations as for Table 27.2.

Source: Krutilla (1991a).

trade term would otherwise address. This relationship obtains as long as the existing tariff is lower than the optimal tariff of international trade theory (see Krutilla, 1991a). In that case, the environmental tax can again revert to the Pigouvian tax level, and trade and environmental policy can again be dichotomized.

Now consider the case where the environmental policy instrument is not available, so that a second-best tariff must be used to address both terms-of-trade and environmental effects. Letting ts^* and td^* equal zero in equations (27.1) and (27.2) and solving for T we have:

$$T^* = -P/\eta - \epsilon(qs)/\alpha X_p \qquad \text{(net exporter)} \qquad (27.5a)$$

$$-T^* = P/\eta + \epsilon(qs)/\alpha X_p \qquad \text{(net importer)} \qquad (27.5b)$$

$$T^* = -P/\eta - \epsilon(qd)/\gamma X_p \qquad \text{(net exporter)} \qquad (27.6a)$$

$$-T^* = P/\eta + \epsilon(qd)/\gamma X_p \qquad \text{(net importer)} \qquad (27.6b)$$

Equation (27.5) shows the formulae for a production externality, while equation (27.6) shows the formulae for consumption.[8] Note that η is the elasticity of world excess demand, $\eta = X_p(P/X) = X_p(P/(qs - qd))$; $\eta < 0$ when $qs > qd$; $\eta > 0$ when $qs < qd$. It can be seen that the first terms in equations (27.5) and (27.6) are the standard optimal tariffs of international trade theory (see Krutilla, 1989). The second term adjusts the optimal tariff for environmental damage. For the production externality, the environmental damage term is positive when the country is a net exporter – increasing the optimal tariff (equation 27.5a).[9] In this case, production should be restricted more than in the standard case to reduce environmental damages;

thus raising the optimal export tariff when it is the second best means accomplishing the environmental policy objective. When the country is a net importer, environmental damages lower the optimal tariff (second-term equation 27.5b is negative). In this case the level of imports should be increased, relative to the usual situation absent the environmental externalities, to reduce environmentally damaging domestic production. This requires a lower second-best optimal tariff.

The opposite relationship obtains when the externality is on the consumption side; the optimal tariff should be lower in the net export case in order to export more of the polluting product abroad, and higher in the net import case to restrain more domestic consumption.

Note that because subsidies have the opposite effects of taxes, all the results in this section would hold with reverse sign for positive externalities (Krutilla, 1991a). If there is a positive externality on the production side, for example, the optimal tariff would be lower when the country is a net exporter to induce more domestic production, and higher when the country is a net importer to induce more domestic production.

In reality, the GATT significantly constrains the active use of tariffs as policy instruments, and trade liberalization appears to be the widely held policy goal (Bhagwati, 1993). Hence equations (27.1) and (27.2) are probably the most empirically relevant for assessing second-best environmental policy making in the open-economy context.

4.   Trade and transboundary pollution

When pollution spills over national boundaries, the international transmission of welfare effects occurs through an environmental impact channel as well as through price effects (see Baumol and Oates, 1988). Adopting a strictly local perspective, the stringency of a country's environmental policy should be lower, all else constant, to the degree that pollution falls out on other countries. The limiting case is when all pollution is exported and local environmental policy becomes unnecessary.

The distinction between purely local and global effects blurs when pollution produced by trading partners mutually falls out on all players in the trade system. In this case, an incentives-compatible cooperative agreement, rather than unilateral regulation, becomes the first-best policy approach (see Ostrom et al., 1993, and Carraro, Chapter 31 in this volume). Since cooperative agreements involving all the relevant players may be difficult to achieve in practice, however, it is worth examining the factors which determine the effectiveness of less-than-comprehensively implemented environmental policy.

Consider a global pollution problem and two subsets of nations: a group which has agreed collectively to curtail emissions (which may be referred to as the 'home' countries) and a group which refuses to cooperate to reduce emissions (which may be referred to as the 'abroad' countries). Imagine that the world's supply capacity of the polluting product is exclusively located abroad, and exclusively consumed by the home countries. In this case, the home countries could reduce emissions entirely by phasing out imports of the polluting product. Using an import tariff as the policy instrument would transfer rents to the home countries during the initial phase-out period, providing compensation to home countries for the environmental regulation while penalizing abroad countries for non-compliance (Krutilla, 1991b).[10]

If the market dichotomy between home consumers and abroad producers is less than total, but the additional supply capacity in the home countries is still small enough so that home countries maintain their status as net importers, $(qs - qd < 0)$, a home consumption tax becomes the best instrument to reduce emissions. Such a consumption restraint would increase excess supply on the world market (see Sections 2 and 3), and the resulting price signal would reduce emissions production abroad, reinforcing the policy objective. The regulating countries will ultimately phase out all consumption at home, reducing production abroad to the point where it is determined exclusively by the size of the residual domestic market. If the residual market is small, the erosion of the policy through non-participation would be relatively slight – as was the case with the Montreal Protocol.[11] On the other hand, if the residual market is large, the recalcitrant nations, through their non-participation, could significantly diminish the policy's effectiveness. The size of the domestic market for coal consumption in India and China offers a good example; these countries, unilaterally or in combination, have the capacity significantly to undermine international efforts to restrain carbon emissions.

Imagine now that there is enough supply capacity of the polluting product at home so that the home countries are in fact net exporters $(qs - qd > 0)$. Interestingly, this situation diminishes the effectiveness of less-than-comprehensive policy during the implementation period (Krutilla, 1991b). A production tax or other restraint will reduce excess supply on the world market and raise world price (see Sections 2 and 3), initially providing an incentive to increase production and pollution abroad. This side effect undermines the policy objective during the implementation period. However, as the production restriction in the home market continues, the home and abroad markets will ultimately become dichotomized, and the volume of emissions production abroad will again be determined by the size of the residual market.

5. Conclusion

Partial equilibrium modelling yields diverse and interesting results with respect to trade and environmental policy outcomes. Trade liberalization will always be beneficial for small countries when paired with the appropriate environmental policy instrument. Without associated environmental policy, however, liberalizing trade will improve the environment in two out of four special cases, while worsening it in two others. Terms-of-trade effects in an open-economy setting are potentially significant, both for small countries which are passively subject to world price shocks when larger countries initiate environmental regulation, and for larger countries which can strategically manipulate the world price as a part of their environmental policy making. The former issue has not received much attention in the trade and environment literature.

Price signals transmitted through the world trade system have the potential to undermine or reinforce the objectives of less-than-comprehensively implemented global environmental policy during the implementation period. The direction of price signals is determined by whether the regulating block of countries are net importers or net exporters of the environmentally damaging product in the pre-regulation *status quo*. In either case, the size of the residual markets in the non-regulating countries will ultimately determine the degree of policy erosion through non-participation. Since fundamental economic factors shape the size of the residual markets, policy makers ultimately have limited scope unilaterally to influence the global consequence of less-than-comprehensively implemented environmental agreements.

Notes

1. In fact, the partial analysis employed in this chapter can easily be translated into a simple two-good, two-factor general equilibrium framework (see Corden, 1980, p. 23).
2. See Anderson (1992b) and van Beers and van den Bergh (1997) for empirical studies of environmental policy levied in distorted markets.
3. It is only necessary to assume that emissions and other inputs into production or consumption are never completely substitutable, so that there is always some degree of linkage between the volume of output or consumption and the level of pollution (Krutilla, 1991a).
4. The first part of this section draws significantly on insights in Anderson (1992a).
5. I refer to this case as a 'production externality', while a 'consumption externality' will refer to demand-side-generated pollution. This usage contrasts with a typology which, independently of the source of the pollution, labels externalities in terms of whether they impact utility or production functions.
6. Specifically, $\alpha = -[X_p + qd_{pd}]^1$, and $\gamma = [X_p - qs_{ps}]^{-1}$ where $qd(pd)$ is domestic demand; $qs(ps)$ is domestic supply; ps and pd are the domestic demand and supply prices; and qd_{pd} and qs_{ps} are the first partial derivatives of demand and supply with respect to the supply and demand prices, $qd_{pd}<0$; $qs_{ps}>0$.
7. In the model from which (27.1) and (27.2) are derived, emissions are directly proportional to output, as has been assumed in this chapter. Hence production and consumption taxes are the relevant environmental policy instruments.

8. Given the sign convention previously noted, equations 27.5a and 27.6b are multiplied by -1 to yield positive magnitudes when countries are net importers (See Krutilla, 1991a).
9. The term is positive because $\alpha > 0$ while $X_p < 0$.
10. This policy could possibly be justified under the GATT as a consumption tax which happens to strike imports only, because there is no domestic production.
11. When the agreement was ratified, roughly 85 per cent of the world's CFC (chlorofluorocarbon) production capacity was located in the signatory countries, leaving a residual 15 per cent that was unconstrained (Krutilla, 1991b).

References

Anderson, K. (1992a), 'The standard welfare economics of policies affecting trade with the environment', in K. Anderson and R. Blackhurst (eds), *The Greening of World Trade Issues*, Ann Arbor: University of Michigan Press.

Anderson, K. (1992b), 'Effects on the environment and welfare of liberalizing world trade: the cases of coal and food', in K. Anderson and R. Blackhurst (eds), *The Greening of World Trade Issues*, Ann Arbor: University of Michigan Press.

Baumol, W.J. and W.E. Oates, (1988), *The Theory of Environmental Policy*, Cambridge, UK: Cambridge University Press.

Beers, C. van and J. van den Bergh (1997), 'An empirical multi-country analysis of the impact of environmental regulations on foreign trade flows', *Kyklos*, **50**, 29–46.

Bhagwati, J. (1993), 'Trade and the environment, false conflict?' in D. Zaelke, P. Orbusch and R.F. Housman (eds), *Trade and the Environment: Law, Economics, and Policy*, Washington, DC: Island Press.

Charnovitz, S. (1992), 'GATT and the environment: examining the issues, *International Environmental Affairs*, **4**, 213–14.

Corden, W.M. (1980), *Trade Policy and Economic Welfare*, Oxford: Oxford University Press.

Esty, D.C. (1994), *Greening the GATT: Trade, the Environment, and the Future*, Washington, DC: Institute for International Economics.

Krutilla, K. (1989), 'Tariff burdens and optimal tariffs under alternative transportation costs and market structures', *Economics Letters*, **31**, 381–6.

Krutilla, K. (1991a), 'Environmental regulation in an open economy', *Journal of Environmental Economics and Management*, **20**, 127–42.

Krutilla, K. (1991b), 'Unilateral environmental policy in the global commons', *Policy Studies Journal*, **19**, 126–39.

Krutilla, K. (1997), 'World trade, the GATT, and the environment', in L. Caldwell and R.V. Bartlett (eds), *Environmental Policy: Transnational Issues and Environmental Trends*, Greenwood, CT: Greenwood Publishing.

Ostrom, E., R. Gardner and J. Walker (eds), *Rules, Games, and Common-Pool Resources*, Ann Arbor: University of Michigan Press.

Wathen, T. (1993), 'The guide to trade and the environment', in D. Zaelke, P. Orbusch and R.F. Housman (eds), *Trade and the Environment: Law, Economics, and Policy*, Washington, DC: Island Press.

28 General models of environmental policy and foreign trade

Karl W. Steininger

1. Introduction

The path towards answering environmental policy and foreign trade questions lies between – and draws upon – two subfields of economics, namely international and environmental economics. Both are very rich areas in their own right, and a survey of their interlinkage cannot but be selective. This chapter seeks to provide a link between a categorization of the issues on the research agenda, and the body of general equilibrium theory as well as a link to empirical research to shed light on these areas. Some of the links have already been explored; others point to areas of future work. Interest in the field has increased dramatically since the early 1990s. The aim of this survey is to give the flavour of a subject which remains a vibrant and fruitful source of theoretical insight, of testable hypotheses and of illuminating quantification.

The rapid integration of the world economy puts questions such as the following high on the agenda:

- Which countries export goods the production of which is pollution-intensive?
- Can a country unilaterally introduce an energy or CO_2 tax without significant implications for its trade flows or for industry migration?
- How does trade liberalization affect the environment?

Each of these questions represents one key area in a threefold classification of trade and environment issues within economics: (a) in terms of positive theory, the objective of international economics is to explain the manifestation of the international division of labour and resulting trade flows (the pattern of trade). This increasingly needs to take into account factor endowment and use of environmental and natural resources. Further, the subject of (positive and normative) analysis is policy evaluation for the following linkages: (b) the effect of environmental policy on trade flows and (c) the effect of trade policy on the state of the environment.

We can ask which modelling approach is the appropriate one, or, more specifically for this chapter, when do we need a general model? With respect to (a), explaining the patterns of trade is a task which by its very nature requires a general model, that is, a model covering the full range of products (the exported goods and the imported goods they are exchanged for) and all factors of production available within a country. Partial models as covered in Chapter 27 by Krutilla (this volume) are not sufficient to determine in what range of produced goods a country specializes. With respect to (b) and (c), that is, in the area of policy evaluation, the specific nature of the question asked determines whether a partial or a general model is appropriate. A general model covers the interlinkages among sectors, between agents' incomes and expenditures, among factor markets and thus also the feedback effects of policy. The use of a general model is required where the following aspects are concerned:

- *type of policy* examined: when trade liberalization concerns either the whole economy or crucial sectors of it, or when environmental policy produces economy-wide impacts, as is the case with energy policy or CO_2 policy;
- *type of effects* analysed: when the distribution of impacts across agents within one country (under any grouping), or when the impact distribution among countries is of concern;
- *importance of net balances*: when the structure of the balance of payments (for example a balanced current account) is of relevance, or, on the environmental side, the net (for example, global) environmental impact is of importance (leakage effect).

The structure of this chapter is as follows. Section 2 focuses on the underlying theoretical basis. This has developed primarily as environmental extensions to the theory of international trade. Empirical evaluation is surveyed thereafter, split into past experience (section 3) and simulation analysis (section 4). The outlook for future research concludes the chapter.

2.   Environmental extensions in trade theory

Environmental application of standard trade theorems
A natural first step in analysing the trade and environment interlinkage is to expand the existing body of trade theory by including environmental considerations. The foundation for explaining trade patterns laid by Ricardo focuses on the notion of comparative cost advantage as opposed to absolute cost advantage. The Ricardian model identifies (i) differences in the productivity of one factor (labour) as the source of differences in relative pre-trade (costs and) prices, and (ii) the comparative pre-trade prices as explaining trade patterns. As far as environmental questions are

concerned, with respect to (i), environmental factors are of insignificant importance in explaining intercountry differences in labour productivity. However, with respect to (ii), which became the core of international economics, environmental expansion of its multi-factor representation, the Heckscher–Ohlin (H–O) model, is more fruitful.

The H–O model (for an exposition see, for example, Bhagwati and Srinivasan, 1983, chs 5–7) is an application of neoclassical general equilibrium theory to international economics. It focuses on differences between countries in their relative factor endowments, and generates results primarily in three areas:

1. *Patterns of trade (Heckscher–Ohlin theorem)*   A country will specialize in the production (and export) of the good intensive in that factor which is in abundant supply at home, which for a country with high assimilative environmental capacity, for example, will be the pollution-intensive good. The introduction of an environmental policy (such as a tax) will cause a shift toward or – given a sufficient level – even establish a comparative advantage in the 'clean' good (Pethig, 1976; Siebert et al., 1980; Siebert, 1995, p. 171ff.). The H–O model, however, rests on quite restrictive assumptions, for example, same technology across countries, constant returns to scale, only two goods and two factors. For the multi-good, multi-factor case a weaker version of the patterns-of-trade conclusion holds in terms of factor content of goods: a country tends to import those factors that are relatively expensive pre-trade (Heckscher–Ohlin–Vanek (H–O–V) theorem). For local and regional environmental resources, for which the assumption of international factor immobility is highly valid, this implies that the higher the pre-trade resource price relative to prices of additional production factors, the more this resource will be imported, in the form of goods whose production is intensive in these resources.

2. *Factor prices (factor-price equalization theorem)*   Free trade is shown to equalize factor prices such that trade in goods (or international mobility of some factors) substitutes for migration of immobile factors (for example labour, environment). It implies that environmental shadow prices (environmental taxes) will equalize across countries (Siebert, 1987, p. 169 and 1995, p. 177). Intuitively, the country with less assimilative capacity will focus on the production of goods which are cleaner and thus raise pollution abroad until shadow prices are equal. Note that this does not imply the same environmental quality in the trading partner countries. However, this result does not hold whenever mobility of the factor labour depends on environmental quality. Labour will then migrate to the cleaner area and further increase the

demand for environmental goods in that area, implying higher pollution taxes (and a segmented labour market) (Siebert as cited).

As with the traditional version focusing on wage equalization, the importance of the theorem lies in its ability to explain the sources of real world *deviation* from environmental factor-price equalization as each of its rather rigid assumptions are lifted (cf. Haberler, 1961, p. 18). Deviations occur

- with increasing rather than constant returns to scale (country size differences become decisive – Markusen and Melvin, 1981);
- with imperfect rather than perfect competition (bargaining power of factor owners becomes the relevant factor; for a survey of imperfect competition models see Jones and Neary, 1984, p. 50ff. and Krugman, 1995);
- with internationally non-identical production functions (differences in technological progress across industries and/or countries become decisive); and
- with complete specialization (factor endowment becomes decisive, for example Bhagwati and Srinivasan, 1983, p. 61ff.).

3. *Income distribution (Stolper–Samuelson theorem)* The protection of an industry, if it raises the domestic goods price, will cause the owners of the factor intensively used in producing that good to gain absolutely. When environmental property rights are allocated in a country and the use of the factor environment is rewarded, protection of environmentally intensive industries thus benefits the owners of environmental resources absolutely. However, in general, for the 'more than two goods and more than two factors case' only a weaker version holds true: a given (policy-induced) range of changes in commodity prices gives rise to a larger range of changes in factor prices (what Jones, 1965 has called the 'magnification effect'), implying only that 'there is some factor' whose real return goes up, but not necessarily the one intensively used (see Ethier, 1984, p. 165).

Summarizing, the application of the standard trade theorems in models including environmental and natural resource factors does allow us to advance to some extent. While partial equilibrium analysis of environmental policy only allows welfare conclusions to be made once knowledge is available on whether the good prior to policy is imported or exported (for a comprehensive exposition see Anderson, 1992), the H–O model specifies exactly this prerequisite knowledge, that is, which country exports and which country imports the environment-intensive good. Further, this approach also identifies why environmental shadow prices (for example taken as environmental taxes) do not equalize across countries. Also, the international income distribution effects of environmental policy can be derived.

However, the multitude of interdependences within a general equilibrium model implies that in order to reach definite conclusions quite restrictive assumptions are required. The H–O model itself, focusing on factor endowment differences, is considered a particular case of the neoclassical general equilibrium model in which internationally identical production functions and tastes are assumed. Neoclassical trade theory beyond the H–O approach finds the determinants of trade simultaneously in three areas: in the differences between technologies, factor endowments and tastes of different countries.[1] Considering such simultaneous interactions entails an extremely high degree of complexity and often prevents clearcut analytical solutions. Numerical solutions have thus increasingly gained importance, with the results of the class of computable general equilibrium simulations being covered here in Section 4. Theory deals with this complexity in a different way. Beyond the environmental results of the standard trade theorems stated above, the contribution of theory is to alter a (rather basic) H–O model regarding generally just one aspect at a time, which is considered the most relevant for a particular trade and environment question.

Issue-specific environmental extensions to trade theory
This line of research turned out to focus on the environmental effects of international economic liberalization. The approaches differ on two grounds: (a) the aspect of liberalization and (b) the primary causality determining environmental quality.

Rauscher (1991) abandons the assumption of factor immobility of capital in a model with no goods trade, and Rauscher (1995, 1997) additionally includes consumption externalities (pollution) and external effects on production (production is influenced by environmental quality). He finds that increased capital mobility (increased 'openness') leads to pollution reduction in at least one country, but has ambiguous welfare effects, especially for the large-country case, due to transfrontier pollution spillover. Overall, international environmental problems may be aggravated by international capital mobility.

Chichilnisky (1994) allows for endogenous factor supply (namely of the environmental resource), governed by the degree of establishment of a system of property rights. The 'North' has a well-established system, in contrast to the 'South', where resources are subject to open access. International trade simply increases the problem of overexploitation, with the definition of private property rights as the only feasible policy response in the model.[2]

Copeland and Taylor (1994) endogenize the level of environmental policy. They allow for intercountry differences in the endowment of effective labour (human capital), which results in income differences. The demand for the environment, which is taken to be a normal good, increases with income. Considering only local pollution, they find that free trade shifts pollution-intensive production to the country where human capital is relatively scarce (the poor South) and raises world pollution. The impact in any one country can be separated into the scale effect (increasing pollution), the composition effect (reflecting different international specialization in more or less dirty products) and the technology effect (indicating the move towards cleaner technology).

Copeland and Taylor (1995) enlarge the analysis to cover the global commons (as well as the multi-country case). They find that if world distribution of income is highly skewed, free trade will harm the environment, but also that international trade in emission permits can reduce this negative impact, that lower-income countries have an incentive to delay international pollution agreements until after multilateral trade liberalization has been achieved, and that income transfers – only if tied directly to pollution reduction – can be welfare-enhancing.

3. Analysing past experience: statistical and econometric approaches

Looking at empirical evidence, statistical and econometric approaches have been used to analyse quantitatively the question of whether environmental policy has influenced trade flows and industry location. This is done to determine the significance of political concerns which vary according to the environmental policy instrument chosen. The use of environmental *economic instruments* (taxes, permits, subsidies) raises *domestic* concerns regarding industry competitiveness, whereas *product or production process regulation* (binding or voluntary, for example eco-labelling) raises *foreign* concerns with respect to market access.

Ideally, one would like to test empirically the effects of environmental policy on competitiveness by identifying the effect that the policy would have on net exports, holding real wages and exchange rates constant. In an open economy, however, the fall in net exports in one industry will be balanced quickly by the rise of net exports in another industry, an industry which, if the change is solely brought about by exchange rate changes (or a fall in real wages) should not be thought of as having gained competitiveness.[3] Noting that this ideal form of the empirical text is essentially impossible to implement in practice, Jaffe et al. (1995) categorize the three alternative indicators of competitiveness used in empirical studies as follows:

(i)   changes in net exports of heavily regulated industries relative to the net exports in more lightly regulated industries
(ii) changes in the share of world production in heavily regulated industries indicating shifts in the loci of production
(iii) changes in the geographic destination of foreign direct investment flows of heavily regulated industries.[4]

Most research to date has focused on the first indicator, with two surveys available: Ugelow (1982) reviews the studies of the 1970s and Dean (1992) those up to 1990. The broad overall finding was that the effects of environmental regulation on trade patterns have been rather small, where noticeable at all. Dean (1992, p. 16) concludes:

> The methodologies are quite varied, making comparisons between studies difficult. However, some generalizations can be drawn. First, estimates of total environmental control costs (ECC) by industry tend to be very low – abatement costs are a very small portion of industry costs on average. Second, reductions in output caused by ECC are also small and insignificant on average, though they can be significant for some individual sectors. Third, there is little evidence of any significant impact of ECC on the pattern of trade.

Environmental control cost data can be used in two types of analyses. For quantifying direct ECC effects, time-series and/or cross-industry data are used in a regression framework. Control costs, however, can be passed on to intermediate input users further along in the production sequence. To cover both direct and indirect ECCs (price increases of intermediate inputs) a model on an input–output basis must be employed. With a general equilibrium model being the most comprehensive representative of this second type, the incidence of upstream costs changes can be determined to a degree sufficient for most analyses by combining the input–output table with direct ECC (Kalt, 1988). While the time-series/cross-industry approach neglects indirect costs, it is applicable at a very disaggregated industry level. For the second approach, which includes indirect costs, the effort involved in constructing the input–output table limits the possible degree of disaggregation.

That the trade impact of direct and indirect ECC data is not significant is reconfirmed by the studies of the early 1990s. Grossman and Krueger (1993) employ a regression framework and, even though they focus on US–Mexico trade, and thus on two countries that experience both a large volume of trade due to geographical proximity and significant historical differences in environmental laws, they find that the coefficient of pollution abatement control cost is not significant in explaining US imports. They regress imports on factor shares, the effective tariff rate and pollution abatement control costs. Tobey (1990, 1993), focusing on 24 pollution-intensive agricultural and manufacturing industries and data from 23 countries in a cross-section H–O–V model, similarly does not find any significant influence of environmental regulation stringency on trade flows.

The central limitation of these studies can be seen in the representation of environmental policy stringency. First, there are no internationally comparable ECC data available. Second, data from firm surveys are likely to under-report ECCs if respondents do not have full knowledge of all costs. Also, determination of costs is increasingly difficult, the more integrated environmental technology becomes. Finally, ECCs need to be related correctly, that is, direct ECCs are to be expressed as a ratio of value added, and direct plus indirect ECCs as a ratio of total costs (Kalt, 1988). Tobey's analysis, for example, has been criticized by the Office of Technology Assessment (1992, p. 101) on the second count. For a detailed survey on the studies and their limitations see Steininger (1995, pp. 82–92).

When van Beers and van den Bergh (1997) eliminate both the above-mentioned as well as a further potential drawback of Tobey's analysis by selecting the environmental policy indicator better to reflect private environmental production costs, and by focusing on bilateral instead of multilateral trade flows, they do find significant export effects of environmental policy on total trade flows and on 'dirty' industries' trade flows. For the latter, however, their results hold only for the subgroup of footloose (non-resource-based) industries. For imports the impact is negative as well, that is, import barriers may have been installed, together with stricter environmental regulations.

With respect to the second indicator of competitiveness, that is, shifts in the locus of production of pollution-intensive goods, Low (1992) contains a number of empirical studies, while the standard comprehensive earlier reference is Leonard (1988). A number of studies do find evidence that pollution-intensive industries have shifted to low-income countries in the South (for example Low and Yeats, 1992, Lucas et al., 1992, Birdsall and Wheeler, 1992). This result is open to interpretation, however. Beghin et al. (1994) consider the contrast between the findings that the South specializes in dirty industries and that environmental regulations have only modest effects on competitiveness to signal measurement problems (under-reporting of environmental costs). Jaffe et al. (1995), in their survey of the empirical evidence, regard this firm migration as being small, when seen in the overall context of economic development (for example the share of pollution-intensive products in Southeast Asia rising from 3.4 to 8.4 per cent in the period 1965–88 (Low and Yeats, 1992), while the lion's share of the world's exports of 'dirty' products is still accounted for by industrialized countries). Also, the move of production may simply be due to increased

demand in those countries. Finally, natural resource endowments significantly contribute to explaining the patterns of pollution-intensive exports.
They conclude that it is 'by no means clear that the changes in trade patterns were caused by increasingly strict environmental regulations in developed countries. [The observed changes]... are consistent with the general
process of development in the Third World.'

Where environmental regulation can indeed play a significant role
causing location shifts in production, is in individual (sub)sectors of the
economy. Several case studies do exist; for example Lesperance (1991)
studied the wood product coatings industry, which is heavily regulated in
California, and found that employment shifted to Mexico.

With respect to the third indicator, foreign direct investment, the impact
of environmental regulation on complex investment decisions is even more
difficult to isolate. Of the very few studies available, Leonard (1988) documents that there is no systematic pattern of foreign direct investment in polluting industries. Also, more recent empirical work has not been able to
establish a systematic pattern that is beyond doubt.[5] This finding may
reflect the fact that weak environmental standards often go hand in hand
with other factors that deter investment, such as political instability, uncertainty about future regulation, and corruption. Such factors are of equal
or greater importance than low environmental regulation costs.

With respect to all three classes of studies, one criticism mentioned above
and relevant for many other empirical evaluations is the determination of
environmental control costs. The backward-looking perspective of these
studies must also be considered a limiting factor as the importance of environmental control costs is likely to increase in the future (OTA, 1992, p. 97).
While in such backward-looking analysis the first limitation is difficult and
the second impossible to overcome, they can both be dealt with in prospective simulation studies.

4. Simulation analysis: the computable general equilibrium (CGE) approach

Computable general equilibrium modelling provides a suitable tool for
empirical analysis when it is the general, economy-wide effects of policy
which are of concern. CGE modelling is an approach that builds upon one
of the most fundamental ideas of economics, namely that of grasping the
complex interdependence among the different markets in an economy by
taking the outcome to represent a 'general equilibrium'. Dating back to
Walras, it was formally analysed by Arrow and Debreu, and has subsequently been extended – parallel to the development of solution algorithms
– for practical empirical policy analysis. A CGE model contains explicit
modelling of (i) the behaviour of individual agents (households, produc-

ers), (ii) market clearing of factor and goods markets, (iii) budget constraints for agents, institutions, as well as macroeconomic balances (based on the Social Accounting Matrix), and (iv) sectoral interlinkages in production (based on the input–output table). See Chapter 69 by Conrad (this volume) for further details on environmental CGE modelling.

Two of the main classes of applications for CGE models are international trade on the one hand and energy and environment on the other. The interlinkage of the two fields has also been seen to lend itself naturally to this type of analysis. In addition to the modelling characteristics relevant for environmental CGE models (such as description of taxes/permits, abatement technology, and revenue recycling modelling), for the trade and environment interlinkage the type of trade flow modelling is crucial.

It is the assumption on the degree of substitutability between imported and domestic goods that most importantly govern the range of the quantitative environment and trade results. CGE modelling originally started with the traditional trade theory assumption (Heckscher–Ohlin) of perfect interchangeability of imported and domestic goods. Two important real-world trade features are inconsistent with such modelling: two-way trade and pervasive violation of the law of one price. Modellers reacted with a multi-stage specification of the demand structure. In the first stage, total expenditure is allocated between all the production sectors. In the second stage, expenditure for each industrial sector is allocated between imports and competing domestic production. The most widely used form for this second stage is *national* product differentiation combined with the constant elasticity of substitution (CES) functional form ('Armington assumption', Armington, 1969). This delinks the domestic and international price level and avoids complete specialization. Generally, however, elasticities of substitution between varieties of goods will vary over time and in addition be unequal between pairs (country A and B; country A and C) of varieties (on the latter see Winters, 1984). The specification of the second stage has thus been generalized to account for these two features by using flexible functional forms for the demand specification, such as AIDS (almost ideal demand system). An alternative, chosen by other modellers, is to switch to firm-level, rather than national product differentiation. Finally, one can also return to perfect substitutability between domestic and foreign products, at least for some sectors modelled (small open economy). In this case, with constant returns to scale, however, there will only be as many goods produced domestically as there are primary factors (Samuelson, 1953); if there are more goods, complete specialization will occur. Complete specialization can also be avoided by limiting sectoral factor mobility, by introducing sectorally specific capital vintages subject to an explicit depreciation process (as in Bergman, 1991).

The reaction of (sectoral) domestic production to environmental policy in general is largest in models that assume high or perfect substitutability between domestic and foreign (varieties of) products. The same holds for the reverse policy link: trade liberalization moves domestic prices closer to the international price level the higher international competition in the sector is, with the larger quantity adjustments triggered implying a stronger environmental quality change. Many of the CGE models on environment and trade seek to establish upper bounds of potential impacts and thus include at least some sectors modelled as price-taking. Usually the sectors best characterized as price takers are also those of highest pollution intensity (basic industries).

CGE modelling conclusions

A major concern with the introduction of environmental policy is the competitive position of exposed industries in small open economies. Bergman (1991), in a seven-sector model of the Swedish economy, distinguishes two exposed sectors as price takers. For rather significant emission reduction targets (in a 15-year period), compared with unconstrained development, emissions of SO_x are reduced by 44 per cent, NO_x by 57 per cent and CO_2 by 28 per cent, and while the aggregate impacts on production are comparatively small, the output in one of the exposed sectors (Steel and Chemicals) is cut to below half. As mentioned above, this model distinguishes sectoral capital vintages. Assumptions about the depreciation rate and technological change in emission intensity relevant for these vintages have a strong influence on the result. In a 19-sector Armington specification for Austria designed to estimate the cost of meeting the Toronto objective, Breuss and Steininger (1998) find a similar result for the sector Base Metals, with the sectors Paper and Wood, Mining, and Petroleum following successively in output reduction. They also show that choosing sectoral differentiation in emission-revenue recycling as a means of temporarily slowing sectoral adjustment can strongly mitigate sector-specific production losses, although this is achieved at the cost of up to 50 per cent higher environmental tax rates. While there is more long-term experience with environmental policy in the US, sectoral foreign trade concerns are not at the centre of analysis for the large-country case (for example Boyd and Krutilla, 1992; Jorgenson and Wilcoxen, 1995).

How strongly do the costs of environmental policy differ for unilateral and multilateral policy implementation? Multi-country modelling provides the appropriate framework for answering this question and has primarily been applied to issues of the global commons (the greenhouse effect). As a yardstick for measuring and comparing costs we are used to GDP figures. Such figures are, however, only a partial indicator of welfare, as they fail to take into account, *inter alia*, changes in the terms of trade and the consumption losses due to environmental taxes (as noted by, for example, Dean and Hoeller, 1992). Most recent studies thus prefer to use real income changes. Representing the results in terms of equivalent variations would be more revealing, but is not yet common in multi-country modelling. The OECD GREEN (GeneRal Equilibrium ENvironment) model, distinguishing 12 world regions, has been employed to analyse unilateral versus coordinated greenhouse policy (Burniaux et al., 1992). It was found, for example, that unilateral OECD emission stabilization comes at a real income loss of 0.6 per cent for the period 1995–2050, while a worldwide Toronto-type agreement implies a sixfold reduction of global emissions and causes a 1.2 per cent real income loss for the OECD. When this higher worldwide emission reduction is achieved in cost-effective terms (equalizing marginal costs across regions) the real income loss for the OECD is reduced to 0.5 per cent.

Similarly, when the EC acts unilaterally within the OECD, costs are above the case of overall OECD action, but only slightly. When comparing unilateral German greenhouse policy action with EC-wide action in a three-region model, Welsch and Hoster (1995) find that the impacts on German output are much *smaller* for unilateral action, due to German dependence on export to other EC countries.

For the distribution of welfare impacts across countries, CGE models indicate that it is not only the choice of the base of the tax (for example production or consumption) that is important (Piggot and Whalley, 1992), but also that terms-of-trade effects are significant. In the context of greenhouse policy this is particularly true for oil exporters and oil-importing LDCs (GREEN model, Burniaux et al., 1992).

Considering policy effectiveness, a central issue for *global* environmental problems is leakage, that is, unilateral emission reduction increasing emissions abroad due to changed trade structures. For unilateral greenhouse policy, leakage can occur through three channels of international trade: (i) emission-intensive manufacturing relocating abroad; (ii) demand-induced reduction of world oil prices increasing oil use abroad; and (iii) substitution of oil by natural gas which is less greenhouse-effective and induces the reverse substitution effect aboard. Manne (1994) identifies the energy-intensive manufacturing link as the largest, and the gas link as substantial, but primarily in the medium term. The quantification, however, is crucially dependent on the foreign trade modelling chosen. The leakage rates resulting from 'Armington' models of imperfect goods substitutability (Burniaux et al., 1992) are much smaller than those derived from models that use the Heckscher–Ohlin assumption of perfect substitutability (Rutherford, 1992; Felder and Rutherford, 1993). Manne (1994) offers an intermediate approach by allowing for perfect substitutability but imposing quadratic penalties for deviations from base-year trade flows, thus moderating the Armington assumption. For a unilateral OECD 20 per cent emission cutback he quantifies leakage rates, that is, foreign emission increase as a percentage of domestic reduction, of up to 30 per cent. However, the long-term potential is higher: when Manne allows for energy-intensive production to be completely phased out in the OECD by the time today's workers retire, imports of energy-intensive production rise fivefold, implying a substantial leakage increase.

5.   Current trends and prospects

Space matters
Environmental and natural resource considerations offer a strong potential for supplying missing building blocks in trade-theory development. The significance of geographical distance in trade theory and policy has been largely neglected since Marshall. Its importance has only recently been pointed out again by Krugman (for example, Krugman, 1991). Within this new development in trade theory, geography and trade, there is still some '"mystery" ... [left on] the origins of economically meaningful regions'. The role of environmental services could help to explain these origins (Smith and Espinosa, 1996). Environmental sciences emphasize the spatial dimension and interactions of environmental impacts in physical terms (acknowledged in a trade and environment analysis by Perroni and Wigle, 1994). Also the demand for goods is found to be dependent on environmental preferences present in a region. Regions can thus be defined based on simultaneous acknowledgement of natural science and social science dimensions.

Environmental innovation
Innovation is acknowledged as a major force in economic development at both the firm level (industrial organization) and at the aggregate level (endogenous growth). Hall (1994) and Kwašnicki (1996) give recent surveys of the field; the collection by Carraro (1994) links innovation to trade and environment for both positive analysis and policy design. It focuses on policy coordination for solving global commons issues. However, several questions remain open. What market and social forces beyond fiscal policies enhance the environmental efficiency of innovations? What market structures and policy approaches best foster their international distribution? Adequate answers to these and related questions have yet to be found. In both theoretical and empirical terms this area remains an ample field for future research.

Focusing on the developing world

In the modelling of global environmental problems, developing countries represent one or more country blocks within both theoretical and numerical approaches, as covered above. These analyses leave unanswered, however, the extent to which changes in trade and/or environmental policy in an open economy affect local environmental problems. We know that open trade systems magnify the effect of environmental externalities (see Munasinghe and Cruz, 1995), but how large these effects are, and how policies interlink, must remain the subject of further analysis. The CGE model by Munasinghe and Persson (1995) for analysing deforestation in Costa Rica indicates that quite distinct modelling features are required, for example the introduction of property rights in a numerical model formulation and the interlinking of the markets for logs and cleared land.

Overall it can be said that the building of general models of trade and the environment, along the lines of the respective subfields, benefits greatly from findings in these areas, but in the future is itself likely to be a source of feedback in turn, that is, it may become a source of conceptual and methodological input for both the theoretical and empirical literature. Aside from analytical rigour, however, in a world exhibiting such a rapid pace of economic integration and environmental change as ours, it is to be hoped that researchers will not only select the most crucial issues, but, what is of equal importance, allow their results to be translated into the world of politics.

Notes

1. The first two areas are touched on in this chapter. Linder (1961) should be consulted for details of the last area.
2. While Chichilnisky (1994) relies on positive factor supply elasticity, van Beers and van den Bergh (1996) further point out technological differences and production externalities as alternative means to introduce environmental considerations by changing the production function assumptions of the H–O model.
3. The term competitiveness in the environment-policy context mainly focuses on competitiveness of particular industries, which is related to but different from competitiveness of a country as a whole (for a trenchant criticism on common but misguided statements on the latter see Krugman, 1994). The concern with the loss of individual industry competitiveness from a national perspective is fourfold (see Jaffe et al., 1995): trade-imbalance-caused devaluations lead to a deterioration in the terms of trade and thus in the domestic standard of living; the loss is likely to concern specific industries of mainly low-skilled labour with distributional consequences; it may concern sectors that are important for national security; and finally, the adjustment process of sectoral shifts will be connected to a broad set of social costs – irrespective of the final international division of labour which represents an equilibrium again.
4. Beyond these relationships Jaffe et al. also point out a fourth and more fundamental (especially long-term) competitiveness link: environmental policy and productivity. See the chapters on growth and the environment in Part VI for a detailed discussion of this issue.

5. In a draft paper, Xing and Kolstad (1995) find that SO_2 emissions (used as an indicator of environmental laxness) significantly explain inflows of foreign direct investment. The causality, however, may also be running in the opposite direction, from investment to pollution (Jaffe et al., 1995). For strictly regulated Germany, the OECD (1993, p. 112) concludes that 'environmental policy does not deteriorate its attractiveness as a location for industry to any decisive degree', while Bouman (1998) finds some evidence that German outward direct investment is indeed affected by domestic environmental costs, though, as he also states, 'the results are not always unambiguous'.

References

Anderson, K. (1992), 'The standard welfare economics of policies affecting trade and the environment', in K. Anderson and R. Blackhurst (eds), *The Greening of World Trade Issues*, New York: Harvester Wheatsheaf.

Armington, P. (1969), 'A theory of demand for products distinguished by place of production', *International Monetary Fund Staff Papers 16*, Washington: IMF, pp. 159–78.

Beers, C. van and J.C.J.M. van den Bergh (1996), 'An overview of methodological approaches in the analysis of trade and environment', *Journal of World Trade*, **30** (1), 143–67.

Beers, C. van and J.C.J.M. van den Bergh (1997), 'An empirical multi-country analysis of the impact of environmental regulations on foreign trade flows', *Kyklos*, **50**, 29–46.

Beghin, J., D. Roland-Holst and D. van der Mensbrugghe (1994), 'A survey of the trade and environment nexus: global dimensions', *OECD Economic Studies*, **23**, Winter, Paris: OECD, pp. 167–92.

Bergman, L. (1991), 'General equilibrium effects of environmental policy: a CGE-modeling approach', *Environmental and Resource Economics*, **1**, 43–61.

Bhagwati, J.N. and T.N. Srinivasan (1983), *Lectures on International Trade*, Cambridge, MA: MIT Press.

Birdsall, N. and D. Wheeler (1992), 'Trade policy and industrial pollution in Latin America: where are the pollution havens?', in Low (1992), pp. 159–67.

Bouman, M. (1998), *Environmental Costs and Capital Flight*, Tinbergen Institute Research Series 177, University of Amsterdam: Thesis Publishers.

Boyd, R. and K. Krutilla (1992), 'Controlling acid depositions: a general equilibrium assessment', *Environmental and Resource Economics*, **2**, 307–22.

Breuss, F. and K. Steininger (1998), 'Biomass energy use to reduce climate change: a general equilibrium analysis for Austria', *Journal of Policy Modeling*, **20** (4), 513–35.

Burniaux, J.-M., J.P. Martin, G. Nicoletti and J. Oliveira Martins (1992), 'The costs of reducing CO_2 emissions: evidence from Green', Economics Department Working Paper 115, Paris: OECD.

Carraro, C. (1994), *Trade, Innovation, Environment*, Dordrecht: Kluwer Academic Publishers.

Chichilnisky, G. (1994), 'North–South trade and the global environment', *American Economic Review*, **84**, 851–75.

Copeland, B.R. and M.S. Taylor (1994), 'North–South trade and the environment', *Quarterly Journal of Economics*, **109**, 755–87.

Copeland, B.R. and M.S. Taylor (1995), 'Trade and transboundary pollution', *American Economic Review*, **85**, 716–37.

Dean, J. (1992), 'Trade and the environment: a survey of the literature', in Low (1992), pp. 15–28.

Dean, A. and P. Hoeller (1992), 'Costs of reducing CO_2 emissions: evidence from six global models', Economics Department Working Paper 122, Paris: OECD.

Ethier, W.J. (1984), 'Higher dimensional issues in trade theory', in R.W. Jones and P.B. Kenen (eds), *Handbook of International Economics* Vol. 1, Amsterdam: North-Holland, ch. 3.

Felder, S. and T. Rutherford (1993), 'Unilateral CO_2 reductions and carbon leakage: the consequences of international trade in oil and basic materials', *Journal of Environmental Economics and Management*, **25**, 162–76.

Grossman, G.M. and A.B. Krueger (1993), 'Environmental impacts of a North American Free Trade Agreement', in P. Garber (ed.), *The U.S.–Mexico Free Trade Agreement*, Cambridge, MA: MIT Press, pp. 13–56.
Haberler, G. (1961), 'A survey of international trade theory', *Special Papers in International Economics* 1, International Finance Section, Department of Economics, Princeton University, 78pp.
Hall, P. (1994), *Innovation, Economics and Evolution*, New York: Harvester Wheatsheaf.
Jaffe, A.B., S.R. Peterson, P.R. Portney and R. Stavins (1995), 'Environmental regulation and the competitiveness of U.S. manufacturing', *Journal of Economic Literature*, 33, 132–63.
Jones, R.W. (1965), 'The structure of simple general equilibrium models', *Journal of Political Economy*, 73, 557–72.
Jones, R.W. and J.P. Neary (1984), 'Positive theory of international trade' in R.W. Jones and P.B. Kenen (eds), *Handbook of International Economics*, Vol. 1, Amsterdam: North-Holland, ch. 1.
Jorgenson, D.W. and P.J. Wilcoxen (1995), 'Intertemporal equilibrium modelling of energy and environmental policies' in P.-O. Johansson, B. Kriström and K.-G. Mäler (eds), *Current issues in environmental economics*, Manchester: Manchester University Press.
Kalt, J. (1988), 'The impact of domestic environmental regulatory policies on U.S. international competitiveness', in A.M. Spence and H.A. Hazard (eds), *International Competitiveness*, Cambridge, MA: Ballinger, pp. 221–62.
Krugman, P. (1991), *Geography and Trade*, Cambridge, MA: MIT Press.
Krugman, P. (1994), 'Competitiveness: a dangerous obsession', *Foreign Affairs*, 73, March/April, 28–44.
Krugman, P. (1995), 'Increasing returns, imperfect competition and the positive theory' in G.M. Grossman and K. Rogoff (eds), *Handbook of International Economics*, Vol. 3, Amsterdam: North-Holland, ch. 24.
Kwaśnicki, W. (1996), *Knowledge, Innovation and Economy*, Cheltenham, UK and Brookfield, US: Edward Elgar.
Leonard, J. (1988), *Pollution and the Struggle for World Product: Multinational Corporations, Environment and International Comparative Advantage*, Cambridge, UK: Cambridge University Press.
Lesperance, A.M. (1991), 'Air quality regulations and their impacts on industrial growth in California: a case study of the South Coast Air Quality Management District Rule 1136 and the wood products coatings-industry, Master's thesis, University of California, Los Angeles.
Linder Burenstam, S. (1961), *An Essay on Trade and Transformation*, Upsala: Almquist and Wiksell, and New York: John Wiley and Sons.
Low, P. (ed.) (1992), *International Trade and the Environment*, World Bank Discussion Paper 159, Washington, DC: World Bank.
Low, P. and A. Yeats (1992), 'Do dirty industries migrate?', in Low (1992), pp. 89–103.
Lucas, R.E., D. Wheeler and H. Hettige (1992), 'Economic development, environmental regulation and the international migration of toxic industrial pollution: 1960–1988', in Low (1992), pp. 67–86.
Manne, A.S. (1994), 'International trade: the impact of unilateral carbon emission limits', in OECD, *The Economics of Climate Change*, Paris: OECD, pp. 193–205.
Markusen, J.R. and J.R. Melvin (1981), 'Trade, factor prices and the gains from trade with increasing returns to scale', *Canadian Journal of Economics*, 14, 450–69.
Munasinghe, M. and W. Cruz (1995), 'Economywide policies and the environment, lessons from experience, *World Bank Environment Paper* 10, Washington, DC: World Bank.
Munasinghe, M. and A. Persson (1995), 'Natural resource management and economywide policies in Costa Rica: a computable general equilibrium (CGE) approach', *The World Bank Economic Review*, 9, 259–85.
OECD (1993), *Environmental Policies and Industrial Competitiveness*, Paris: OECD.
Office of Technology Assessment (OTA) (1992), *Trade and Environment: Conflicts and Opportunities*, Washington, DC: US Congress, OTA-BP-ITE-94.
Perroni, C. and R.M. Wigle (1994), 'International trade and environmental quality: how important are the linkages?', *Canadian Journal of Economics*, 27 (3), 551–67.

Pethig, R. (1976), 'Pollution, welfare, and environmental policy in the theory of comparative advantage', *Journal of Environmental Economics and Management*, **2**, 160–69.

Piggott, J. and J. Whalley (1992), 'Economic impacts of carbon reduction schemes: some general equilibrium estimates from a simple global model', Center for Economic Studies Working Paper 17, Munich: University of Munich.

Rauscher, M. (1991), 'National environmental policies and the effects of economic integration', *European Journal of Political Economy*, **7**, 313–29.

Rauscher, M. (1995), 'Environmental policy and international capital mobility: an aggregate view', presented to the Workshop on Environmental Capital Flight, Wageningen University, October.

Rauscher, M. (1997), 'Environmental policy and international capital movements', *International Trade, Factor Movements and the Environment*, Oxford: Oxford University Press, ch. 3.

Rutherford, T. (1992), 'Welfare effects of carbon dioxide restrictions', OECD Working Paper 112, Paris: OECD.

Samuelson, P.A. (1953), 'Prices of factors and goods in general equilibrium', *Review of Economic Studies*, **21**, 1–20.

Siebert, H. (1987, 1995), *Economics of the Environment*, 2nd and 4th edn, Berlin: Springer.

Siebert, H., J. Eichberger, R. Gronych and R. Pethig (1980), *Trade and Environment: A Theoretical Inquiry*, Amsterdam: Elsevier/North-Holland.

Smith, V.K. and J.A. Espinosa (1996), 'Environmental and trade policies: some methodological lessons', *Environment and Development Economics*, **1**, 19–40.

Steininger, K. (1995), *Trade and Environment. The Regulatory Controversy and a Theoretical and Empirical Assessment of Unilateral Environmental Action*, Heidelberg: Physica.

Tobey, J.A. (1990), 'The effects of domestic environmental policies on patterns of world trade: an empirical test', *Kyklos*, **43**, 191–209.

Tobey, J.A. (1993), 'The impact of domestic environmental policy on international trade', in H. Giersch (ed.), *Economic Progress and Environmental Concerns*, Berlin: Springer, pp. 181–200.

Ugelow, J. (1982), 'A survey of recent studies on costs of pollution control and the effects on trade', in S. Rubin (ed.), *Environment and Trade*, New Jersey: Allanheld, Osmun and Co.

Welsch, H. and F. Hoster (1995), 'A general equilibrium analysis of European carbon/energy taxation', *Zeitschrift für Wirtschafts- und Sozialwissenschaften*, **115**, 275–303.

Winters, L.A. (1984), 'Separability and the specification of foreign trade functions', *Journal of International Economics*, **17**, 239–63.

Xing, Y. and C. Kolstad (1995), 'Do lax environmental regulations attract foreign investment?', Working Paper in Economics 6–96, University of California, Santa Barbara.

29 Strategic environmental policy and foreign trade

*Alistair M. Ulph**

1. Introduction – the issues

To understand what is meant by strategic environmental policy in the context of international trade, note that much economic analysis of a specific environmental problem is of a partial nature. For example, if a firm is discharging pollution to a river, then the usual economic policy advice would be to impose an emission tax equal to marginal damage costs or an emission standard such that marginal abatement costs equal marginal damage costs. Such a policy may have quite widespread effects: the firm may have to raise its prices, which will affect consumer demand for other products; the firm may have to buy special pollution abatement equipment and lay off some of its production workers, who must find employment in other sectors. If the firm is involved in international trade some of these effects may be felt in other countries – the firm may lose market share to international competitors, or the pollution abatement equipment it uses may be imported. However, from the welfare maximization perspective that underlies much economic policy advice, these effects of the original policy can be ignored as long as in all other sectors there are either no distortions or any distortions have been corrected by appropriate policies; these effects are just the normal effects of resources being correctly reallocated in response to the original policy. In particular, provided each government corrects the environmental externalities in its own country, it can ignore the effects of its environmental policy on other countries.

There are three reasons why this simple partial approach to environmental policy may be inadequate, and why individual governments may act strategically in setting their environmental polices with respect to the environmental policies of other countries. The first is that the pollutant may be transboundary, so that, as is well known, if an individual country sets its environmental policies based only on the damage caused domestically and ignoring damage to other countries, then the environmental policies set by individual governments acting independently do not maximize collective

* The author is grateful to two anonymous referees and the editor, Dr Jeroen van den Bergh, for comments on an earlier version of this paper. The usual disclaimer applies.

welfare. The second reason is that international trade may be imperfectly competitive. It is well known that in such circumstances governments have incentives to set trade or industrial policies in a strategic fashion to try to give their domestic firms some competitive advantage (Brander and Spencer, 1985; Helpman and Krugman, 1989); if governments are forbidden from using trade or industrial policies strategically (for example because of trade liberalization agreements), they may resort to using environmental policies strategically. These two cases are examples where there are market distortions which have not been corrected and so the caveat about when it is appropriate to use a partial approach to policy making does not apply. The third reason is that governments may not be concerned with welfare maximization but are concerned rather with objectives like preserving domestic share of world markets. In this chapter I shall be concerned primarily with the second of these issues. Thus I shall ignore problems of transboundary pollution. For analysis of environmental policy when governments pursue objectives other than welfare maximization see Hillman and Ursprung (1992).

The interaction between environmental policy and trade policy has been the focus of considerable debate in recent years, sparked by the moves towards further trade liberalization in the Single European Market, the Uruguay Round of the GATT and, particularly, NAFTA (see, for example, the debate between Bhagwati and Daly in *Scientific American*, 1993 and the contributions in Low, 1992). In this debate, a number of environmentalists argued that any gains from trade liberalization would be substantially outweighed by the damage trade liberalization would do to the environment. As I have noted, the particular concern which will be the focus of this chapter was that in the absence of traditional trade policy instruments governments might seek to distort their environmental policies as a form of strategic trade policy. In the case of environmental damage related to 'production and process methods' it was thought that all governments would relax their environmental policies in a process of legislative competition, resulting in what has been called 'ecological dumping' (see Rauscher, 1994 for a useful discussion of different concepts of ecological dumping).To counter ecological dumping various policies have been proposed – the use of countervailing tariffs on products from countries with lower environmental standards, the harmonization of environmental standards or at least the setting of minimum environmental standards. Throughout this chapter I shall deal only with the case where pollution is caused by production.

Standard trade theory based on welfare-maximizing governments and competitive markets provides no support for the concern about 'ecological dumping' and the policy proposals that stem from it. In the 'small-country' case, governments have no incentive to distort their environmental policies from the first-best rule (equating marginal damage costs and marginal abatement costs), since by assumption they cannot influence their terms of trade and failure to internalize environmental externalities is welfare-reducing (Markusen, 1975b; Long and Siebert, 1991, among many). Allowing countries to have market power will give governments an incentive to manipulate terms of trade in their favour, but the first-best policies will again involve trade taxes to manipulate the terms of trade and environmental policies to address the environmental distortion (Markusen, 1975a, b; Panagariya et al., 1993, among many). In the absence of trade instruments governments may well use environmental policies to address both sets of distortion, in which case environmental policies will not be set using the simple first-best rule outlined above. But there is no presumption that this will involve *relaxing* environmental policies by all governments.

A country which is a net importer will wish to set too weak an environmental policy in order to encourage domestic production and so reduce its demand for imports and hence the price it pays for its imports. But a country which is a net exporter of a good whose production causes pollution will wish to set too tough environmental policies, essentially as a proxy for the optimal export tax (Anderson, 1992; Krutilla, 1991; Rauscher, 1994).

So conventional economic analysis based on welfare-maximizing governments and competitive markets provides no support for the concern that all governments will engage in ecological dumping. But what happens when producers themselves exploit market power? In the rest of this chapter I review a number of recent studies which have taken the framework of strategic trade theory and applied it to the analysis of environmental policy. As I shall show, this can produce an argument supporting 'ecological dumping' though, as I shall also show, this argument is by no means robust. The introduction of strategic behaviour by governments will also allow me to address another claim, known as the 'Porter hypothesis' (Porter, 1991), that governments acting strategically would set policies which are too tough (relative to the first-best rule) as a way of inducing their producers to innovate new 'green technologies' ahead of their rivals and thus gain a long-term competitive advantage.

In the next section I shall set out a very simple model to explain what is meant by strategic environmental policy, and show how this can support a claim that governments may engage in ecological dumping. I shall also show why neither this claim nor the 'Porter hypothesis' is robust. In the third section I shall discuss briefly the policy implications of this research.

2. A simple model of strategic environmental policy

I consider a partial equilibrium analysis of a homogeneous good industry. I consider a particular country, call it the home country, and suppose that there is a single firm belonging to this industry located in the home country. To keep things simple at this stage, there are no consumers of this good located in the home country, so the firm is selling on the world market. Production of this good causes pollution, and again for simplicity assume that one unit of the good produces one unit of pollution, there is no abatement technology, and the pollution generated damages only the inhabitants of the home country, so there is no transboundary pollution. In Figure 29.1 I draw the marginal private cost curve (MPC) and the marginal social cost curve (MSC) for production of this good, where the difference between the two curves represents the marginal damage cost of the pollution caused by production of the good.

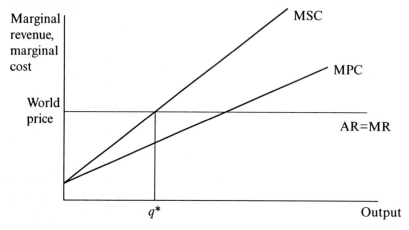

Figure 29.1   Competitive market

There are two stages of decisions. In the first stage the government of the home country sets its environmental policy for the firm in this industry. For what follows I do not need to be very explicit about environmental policy, and shall characterize it simply by the extent to which the policy causes the firm to internalize the damage costs of pollution; in the absence of any environmental policy the firm would operate with its private marginal cost curve. I shall call a *first-best* environmental policy one which causes the firm to operate as if its marginal cost curve were the marginal social cost curve; a *lax* environmental policy is one which would make the firm operate as if its marginal cost curve were below the social marginal cost curves, while a *tough* environmental policy is one which would make the firm operate as if its marginal cost curve were above the marginal social cost curve. In the second stage the firm chooses how much output to produce, and it will do this so as to maximize profits, setting marginal revenue equal to whatever marginal cost curve the government has faced it with. In the first stage, the government knows how its environmental policy will determine the output of the firm, and will choose its environmental policy (implicitly the output of the firm) so as to maximize welfare, which in this simple model is just the profits of the firm minus the costs of the damage caused by the firm's pollution.

To see whether the government has any incentive strategically to manipulate its environmental policy, I consider three possible structures for the world market.

Perfect competition
Suppose the firm in the home country is one of many competing in the world market for this product, so that, as shown in Figure 29.1, the firm faces a perfectly elastic world price for this good. It is clear that in this case the government has no incentive to distort its environmental policy away from the first-best. It should choose its environmental policy so that the firm produces output level q^* where price (marginal revenue) equals marginal social cost of production, or equivalently the marginal loss of profit to the country from the last unit of output (price minus marginal private cost) just equals the marginal damage caused by the last unit of output. If the government relaxed its environmental policy, to allow the firm to produce a bit more output, the marginal damage from the extra output would be greater than the marginal private profit from the extra output. Neither the government nor the firm can affect the world price; the firm is acting to maximize profits, so the only role for government policy is to internalize the externality from pollution and make the firm produce where price equals marginal social cost. There is no role for any *strategic* environmental policy. This is the conventional analysis I summarized in the introduction.

Pure monopoly
Now consider the polar opposite case where the firm in the home country serves the entire world market for this good. Figure 29.2 shows the marginal revenue curve for the firm derived from the world demand curve. Just as in the perfectly competitive case, the optimal policy for the government is to impose the first-best environmental policy and get the firm to produce output level q^* where marginal revenue equals marginal social cost, or equivalently, the marginal cost of pollution damage caused by the last unit of output just equals the marginal private profit earned on the last unit of output. Unlike the competitive case, it is now possible for the firm to affect the price it receives, and it is clearly in the interests of the firm and the government that the firm exploit this market power. But given that the firm

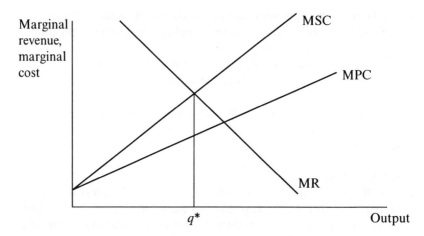

Figure 29.2   Pure monopoly

is acting to maximize profits, the only need for government intervention is
again to ensure that the firm internalizes the external costs of its pollution.
Once that is done, the firm should be left free to set the profit-maximizing
level of output. In particular, if the government were to relax its environmental policy, that would encourage the firm to produce more output, but
the marginal cost of the extra pollution produced would outweigh the marginal private profit from the increased output.

Oligopoly
Finally, suppose that there is imperfect competition, which, for the sake of
simplicity I shall take to be duopoly. So suppose that there is another firm
located in some other country, called the foreign country. I shall assume for
the moment that this other firm produces no pollution, so that it just operates with its marginal private cost curve. Output is determined by means of
Cournot competition, that is, each firm takes as given the output of its rival
and chooses its own output to maximize profits. Assuming for the moment
that the government in the home country sets first-best environmental policy,
then the situation is as shown in Figure 29.3. Given the output of the foreign
firm, Q^*, the firm in the home country is faced with the marginal revenue
curve MR(Q^*); and produces output level q^*. There is a similar analysis for
the foreign firm which shows that given the output q^* of the home firm, the
optimal output of the foreign firm is Q^*. But is it the case that the optimal
policy is for the government to impose the first-best environmental policy? *If
the government also operates on the Cournot assumption that the output of
the rival firm is fixed at Q^*, then it is again the case that the government's*

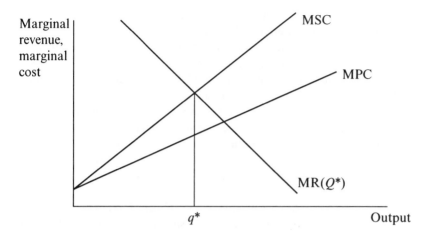

Figure 29.3 Oligopoly

optimal policy is to impose the first-best environmental policy, for exactly the same reasons as were given for the monopoly case.

But suppose the government relaxes its environmental policy from first-best. That will induce its firm to expand output above q^*. There will be three effects. As in the previous analysis the extra output will generate additional profits and additional pollution; starting from q^*, the costs of the additional pollution will, to the second order, just outweigh the additional profits. But there will be a third effect: the expansion of output will reduce the marginal revenue of the foreign firm, and so it will cut its output; that will in turn increase the marginal revenue faced by the home firm, raising its profits. Starting from q^*, this latter effect must dominate (since the two previous effects were self-cancelling), so that government welfare is unambiguously higher if it relaxes its environmental policy from the first-best. If the government realizes that its environmental policy will have this impact on the output of the foreign firm, then it has a *strategic* reason to relax its environmental policy. There is no strategic element in competitive markets, since the world price cannot be manipulated, nor in the pure monopoly case, since there are no rivals whose output can be manipulated.

What I have shown is that, starting from the first-best environmental policy, the government would be better off relaxing its environmental policy. However, this does not mean that the government will set no environmental policy at all. There will be an optimal degree of relaxation, for as the output of its domestic firm expands and the output of the rival firm contracts, the gain in terms of additional profits to the domestic firm will decline, and the cost in terms of additional pollution will increase. Another way of thinking of the optimal environmental policy in this context is to assume that the environmental policy consists of an emission tax. Then the optimal emission tax will have two elements: one which reflects the environmental externality and equals marginal social cost, and one which reflects the strategic trade interaction and would be equivalent to the optimal export subsidy. The optimal emission tax is then the sum of these two elements. Only in special cases would it be zero, and it will be negative if marginal social costs are low relative to strategic trade gains.

I want first to draw out a number of points from this analysis, then analyse the effect of dropping some of the simplifying assumptions, and finally analyse the effect of changing or extending the model.

1. I have considered the case where there is only one foreign firm and only the home firm pollutes, and I have shown that the government's optimal environmental policy would be to relax its environmental policy relative to the first-best rule. If the foreign firm also generates pollution and its government sets an environmental policy, and if both governments act non-cooperatively, taking as given the environmental policy set by the other country, then the above analysis shows that each government will have an incentive to relax its environmental policy relative to the first-best. This analysis can be generalized to many countries, so it provides some justification for the concern about 'ecological dumping' – all governments of exporting countries will wish to relax their environmental policies. Note that this is the opposite of the prediction for competitive markets where countries have market power, where the governments of net exporting countries would set too tough environmental policies.

   But notice that while each individual government has an incentive to expand its domestic firm's output in the expectation that other firms will reduce their output, when all governments act this way the aggregate effect is to drive up total output, which reduces total industry profits and also increases pollution in each country. The countries would be better off if they could agree collectively not to engage in ecological dumping. Indeed, there is a stronger conclusion to be drawn. For it is in the collective interests of the producing governments to *reduce* industry output, since imperfect competition yields industry output above the monopoly level. Thus if governments were able to act cooperatively, the optimal policy would be for governments to set environmental policies which were *tougher* than first-best (see, for example, Barrett, 1994).

2. Notice that the argument that governments acting non-cooperatively will have an incentive to relax their environmental policies depends crucially on the assumption that the only policy instrument available to

governments is environmental policy. In particular, if governments were able to use trade policies, such as export subsidies, then the non-cooperative choice of policies would be to use export subsidies to achieve strategic trade objectives and first-best environmental policies to achieve the internalization of externalities. Thus a necessary condition for ecological dumping is a problem of missing instruments; hence the concern that ecological dumping may be a consequence of trade liberalization.

3. I have not been very specific about the nature of environmental policies (emission taxes, emission standards, tradable permits). The conclusion that governments acting non-cooperatively have an incentive to relax their environmental policies does not depend on the nature of environmental policy, but the size of the strategic effect can depend on it. This also means that the choice of policy instrument has a strategic element. To understand this, return to the two-country example, and consider the situation where there is no technology for abating pollution, so that the only way to reduce pollution is to reduce output. Suppose now that the foreign government sets an emission standard, and this emission standard is effective. This means that the level of output of the foreign firm is effectively determined by the environmental policy of the foreign government, irrespective of the output produced by the domestic firm. This implies that in the first-stage game between governments, where the domestic government takes as given the emission standard set by the foreign government, there can be no strategic incentive for the domestic government to distort its environmental policy from first-best (whatever environmental policy the domestic government uses), because it cannot affect the output level of the foreign firm. On the other hand if the foreign government uses an emission tax, then the output of the foreign firm will respond to variations in the output of the domestic firm, and in the first-stage game between governments there will be an incentive for the domestic government to distort its environmental policy, since by affecting the output of the domestic firm it can indirectly affect the output of the foreign firm. For further details see Ulph (1992, 1996c).

4. The analysis has assumed that there are no consumers located in the producing countries and no transboundary pollution. Relaxing these assumptions will reinforce the conclusion that non-cooperative governments will engage in ecological dumping. Imperfect competition means that firms produce less output than they would under perfect competition and this harms consumers; to counteract this effect, governments wish to encourage their firms to expand their output. When there is transboundary pollution, governments have an additional incentive to

reduce foreign production since that reduces the pollution damage caused by the foreign production. Both these arguments reinforce the incentive for governments acting non-cooperatively to relax environmental policy. The conclusions are more ambiguous when governments act cooperatively. Transboundary pollution means that all governments should set environmental policies which are tougher than simple first-best since they should take account of the pollution damage caused by their domestic production to foreign countries as well as to themselves. But the desire to protect consumers by raising output conflicts with the desire to raise profits by restricting output. Again, these issues arise because of missing instruments: ideally governments would deal with protection of consumers through industrial policy, leaving environmental policy to address externalities (see Conrad, 1993a, b; Kennedy, 1994; Ulph, 1996c for further discussion).

5. The simple analysis with no consumers assumed that there was a single firm in each country. If there are several domestic firms then the government has a conflicting objective. Because the domestic firms compete with each other, they collectively produce too much output for any *given* output from foreign firms, and this should lead government to toughen its environmental policy relative to the first-best. However, the government has the same strategic incentive to expand domestic output at the expense of foreign output. So even when governments act non-cooperatively, it can no longer be concluded that they will have an incentive to set environmental policy which is laxer than simple first-best (Barrett, 1994). Indeed, as noted in Section 1, in the limit, as the market becomes perfectly competitive, the incentive is for the government to set environmental policies tougher than first-best as a proxy for the optimal export tax.

6. A crucial assumption of the duopoly model outlined above was that the product was homogeneous and that firms competed taking as given the *output* of their rivals (Cournot competition). If the model is changed to allow for the products of the firms to be imperfect substitutes and for firms to compete by taking the *prices* of their rivals as given, then the conclusion about ecological dumping is overturned: if governments act non-cooperatively they will set environmental policies which are tougher than first-best. In the case of Cournot competition firms took as given the output of their rivals, while each government realized that if its domestic firm expanded its output, then rival firms would cut their output, assuming foreign governments did not change their environmental policies. In the case of Bertrand competition each firm takes as given the *prices* set by their rivals. But if one firm raised its price, that will increase the demand for its rivals' products, and they

will respond by also raising their prices. So in this case the strategic incentive is to induce domestic firms to raise their prices so that foreign firms will also raise their prices, and if environmental policies are the only weapons available to governments, then governments achieve their strategic objectives by setting environmental policies which are tougher than first-best. It remains the case that if governments act cooperatively they will set tougher environmental policies than if they act non-cooperatively, for the same reason I gave for Cournot competition. For further discussion see Barrett (1994), Ulph (1996d). Obviously other oligopolistic concepts could be used, and the general point is that the form of market interaction between firms affects the direction that strategic distortions of environmental policy will take. An important question is which oligopolistic concept is appropriate for any particular market – a question which is the subject of much debate amongst industrial economists. The implication for policy making, discussed briefly in Section 3, is whether governments could know which form of oligopolistic interaction would be used in any particular market where they may seek to set their environmental policies strategicaly.

7. An important structural feature of all the models of strategic environmental policy discussed so far is the assumption that governments set their environmental policies *prior* to firms setting their outputs or prices. It is implicit that governments can *commit* themselves to an environmental policy, and it is this commitment that allows them to influence the outcome of the subsequent market game and hence provides the basis for strategic behaviour. This raises two obvious issues. First, is it reasonable to suppose that governments can make such commitments? This has more force in conjunction with the second issue – since if governments can make such commitments to influence markets, so too can firms. The obvious mechanisms available to firms are investments in plant capacity or R&D which are designed to lower operating costs (including costs of emissions of pollution) and hence give a competitive advantage in the subsequent competition for market share. This raises the question whether, if firms can make such strategic investments, this eliminates the incentive for governments to distort their environmental policies for strategic reasons. Ulph (1996a) shows that to the extent that firms' strategic behaviour is a substitute for government strategic behaviour, then indeed this will reduce the incentive for governments to distort their environmental policies. However, this is not the end of the story, for governments' environmental policies will also affect the incentives for firms to act strategically, and the important question is the direction of this effect. The 'Porter

hypothesis' referred to in the introduction assumes that tougher environmental regulations will *increase* the incentives for firms to invest in R&D. But, as shown by D. Ulph (1993) and Ulph and Ulph (1996), this need not be the case. There are two effects of tougher environmental policy on incentives to invest in R&D. First, to the extent that R&D reduces emissions per unit of output, then tougher environmental policies will stimulate R&D. But tougher environmental policies also reduce the profits earned by firms, and this reduces the incentives to undertake R&D. It is not clear which of these effects will dominate. But it is clear that for R&D which is designed only to reduce costs, not emissions of pollution, only the second effect applies, and so tougher environmental policies will *reduce* domestic producers' incentives to invest in R&D. Under these circumstances, the incentive is for governments to relax their environmental policies. Thus theoretical analysis cannot provide unambiguous support for the 'Porter hypothesis'. For further discussion of this issue see Oates et al. (1994), Palmer et al. (1995) and Porter and van der Linde (1995).

8.   The analysis so far has assumed that the number and location of firms is fixed. It is possible to extend the models to allow for the possibility that firms can respond to tough environmental policies in one country by relocating plants to countries with laxer environmental policies (we can think of location decisions by firms as another form of strategic investment). The same broad conclusion can be drawn that governments will have an incentive to manipulate their environmental policies in order to influence where firms locate, but this can mean governments setting policies which are tougher or laxer than first-best. Having firms located in a country has benefits and costs. For example: the government may be able to tax either the pollution generated by production or the profits of firms; consumers may benefit from lower prices because goods do not have to be transported from other countries; there are costs of the damage caused by pollution. Simplifying, if there are positive net benefits from having plants located in a country, then governments will have incentives to relax environmental policies to attract inward investment. On the other hand if there are net costs to having plants located in a country, then governments will compete to deter inward investment by setting environmental policies which are too tough ('nimbyism'). There can be more subtle aspects of environmental policy with endogenous location, such as hysteresis effects, but space precludes a detailed dicussion. For further analysis of environmental policy and plant location see the chapter by Markusen in this handbook (Chapter 39).

I began this section by setting out a very simple model designed both to illustrate what was meant by strategic environmental policy and to show that it was possible to use some models to support the fears of environmentalists that trade liberalization might lead to governments engaging in 'ecological dumping'. But while this conclusion has been robust to some relaxations and extensions of the basic model, it is not robust to all variations, so that it is possible to construct equally plausible models where the strategic incentives are for governments to set environmental policies which are tougher than simple first-best policies. By the same token, the 'Porter hypothesis' that governments will set too tough environmental policies to stimulate investment in R&D aimed at reducing pollution cannot be supported as a general theoretical proposition.

3. Policy implications

The previous section has established that, under certain assumptions, trade liberalization could induce governments to distort their environmental policies, though this need not be in the form of ecological dumping. I briefly consider the policy implications, under two headings. First, how likely is it that governments will actually distort their environmental policies, and second, if they do, is there anything supranational organizations such as WTO or the EU can do to reduce such distortions?

On the first point, the analysis suggests a number of reasons why governments may not distort environmental policies. First, for governments to act strategically in their environmental policies they must be able to commit themselves to a particular level of emission tax or emission standard, and it is not obvious that governments can do this. This has even more force when governments are trying to influence very long-term decisions by firms such as R&D investment or plant location. Second, the analysis has shown that there are a number of different factors affecting how governments might wish to distort their environmental policies and these can go in different directions, so that even if governments carefully took account of all these factors the net effect could be that the optimal policy differs very little from first-best. Third, the analysis shows that the direction of distortion can depend sensitively on factors such as the nature of product market competition or how responsive R&D is to environmental policies, which governments could have great difficulty in finding out about. This difficulty could be compounded when it is recognized that any particular environmental policy is likely to have an impact on many industries, each with different characteristics. Finally, the argument that in the absence of trade instruments governments will have incentives to distort environmental policies applies equally to other areas of government policy which affect production costs of firms, and these other policy areas may have much larger impacts on costs than environmental policies. The obvious example is labour market policies, with associated claims about 'social dumping'. (See Ulph, 1996b for elaboration of these points.)

Even if it could be established that governments acting non-cooperatively would engage in significant distortions to their environmental policies, and supposing this took the form of ecological dumping, what could be done about it? Now the first point to note is that if there is a difference between the policies that governments adopt if they act cooperatively compared to those they adopt when they act non-cooperatively, then there is a set of policies which will make all governments better off. The point I wish to emphasize is that the policies often suggested to tackle ecological dumping – harmonization and minimum standards – may not lie in that set. Harmonization may be inappropriate for the obvious reason that countries may differ significantly in the damage caused by the same pollutant (because of differences in the natural environment or local preferences) so that first-best policies would differ significantly across countries. (Note that this depends on the assumption that pollution is local. If pollution were global, then efficiency would require all countries to set emission taxes equal to world marginal social costs.) Imposing harmonized environmental policies could leave a country with low environmental damage costs worse off than if it had no policy reform at all. Ulph (1995) shows that countries do not have to differ very significantly in their damage costs (less than 50 per cent) for this argument to apply. .

The argument behind minimum standards is that if countries with the laxest environmental policies can be forced to raise their environmental standards, then other countries will respond by toughening their policies, and there will be a 'ratcheting up' of environmental standards, while still allowing for differences in environmental policies to reflect differences in damage costs. Kanbur et al. (1994) provide an analysis of NAFTA which shows that minimum standards could make all governments better off. The difficulty, as shown by Ulph (1995), is that toughening the environmental policy of the country with the lowest environmental standards does not always induce other countries to raise their environmental standards. This depends on factors such as the nature of product market competition and the environmental policy instrument used by governments. For example, if firms compete in terms of output (Cournot competition) and governments use emission standards as their policy instruments, then government reaction functions in terms of emission standards are downward-sloping, that is, if one government toughens its emission standard other governments will relax theirs. The reason is that when the first government toughens its emission standards, its domestic firms will reduce output and foreign firms will find it profitable to expand their output; but if emission standards in these countries are unchanged, all the extra output must be matched by extra abatement, and it will be optimal to allow some of this extra output to result in extra pollution, so emission standards must be relaxed. As Ulph (1995) showed, this must make the country that had been required to raise its emission standards worse off than in the non-cooperative outcome. Thus, even if one could be sure that ecological dumping was a significant problem, designing policies to tackle it is by no means straightforward.

4. Conclusions

In this brief survey I have argued that traditional economic analysis based on competitive markets provides no support for the claims of environmentalists that trade liberalization will lead to ecological dumping. Allowing for imperfect competition implies that governments may engage in strategic environmental policy – distorting their policies to try to obtain a trade advantage – but this need not always take the form of ecological dumping. I have given reasons why it may be unlikely in practice that governments would distort their environmental policies for strategic trade reasons, and argued that, even if it were clear that governments were engaging in ecological dumping, there are difficulties in designing policies to counter it, and certainly the remedies frequently suggested – harmonization and minimum standards – may be quite inappropriate.

References

Anderson, K. (1992), 'The standard welfare economics of policies affecting trade and the environment', in K. Anderson and R. Blackhurst (eds), *The Greening of World Trade Issues*, Hemel Hempstead: Harvester Wheatsheaf.

Barrett, S. (1994), 'Strategic environmental policy and international trade', *Journal of Public Economics*, **54** (3), 325–38.

Bhagwati, J. and H. Daly (1993), 'Debate: does free trade harm the environment?', *Scientific American*, November, 17–29.

Brander, J. and B. Spencer (1985), 'Export subsidies and international market share rivalry', *Journal of International Economics*, **18**, 83–100.

Conrad, K. (1993a), 'Taxes and subsidies for pollution-intensive industries as trade policy', *Journal of Environmental Economics and Management*, **25**, 121–35.

Conrad, K. (1993b), 'Optimal environmental policy for oligopolistic industries in an open economy', *Department of Economics Discussion Paper 476–93*, University of Mannheim.

Helpman, E. and P. Krugman (1989), *Trade Policy and Market Structure*, Cambridge, MA: MIT Press.

Hillman, A. and H. Ursprung (1992), 'The influence of environmental concerns on the political determination of trade policy', in K. Anderson and R. Blackhurst (eds), *The Greening of World Trade Issues*, Hemel Hempstead: Harvester Wheatsheaf.

Kanbur, R., M. Keen and S. van Wijnbergen (1994), 'Industrial competitiveness, environmental regulation and direct foreign investment', in I. Goldin and A. Winters (eds), *The Economics of Sustainable Development*, Paris: OECD.

Kennedy, P.W. (1994), 'Equilibrium pollution taxes in open economies with imperfect competition', *Journal of Environmental Economics and Management*, **27**, 49–63.

Krutilla, K. (1991), 'Environmental regulation in an open economy', *Journal of Environmental Economics and Management*, **20**, 127–42.

Long, N.V. and H. Siebert (1991), 'Institutional competition versus ex-ante harmonisation – the case of environmental policy', *Journal of Institutional and Theoretical Economics*, **147**, 296–312.

Low, P. (ed.) (1992), *International Trade and the Environment*, Washington, DC: World Bank.

Markusen, J. (1975a), 'Cooperative control of international pollution and common property resources', *Quarterly Journal of Economics*, **89**, 618–32.

Markusen, J. (1975b), 'International externalities and optimal tax structures', *Journal of International Economics*, **5**, 15–29.

Oates, W., K. Palmer and P.R. Portney (1994), 'Environmental regulation and international competitiveness: thinking about the Porter hypothesis', *Discussion Paper 94–02* Washington, DC: Resources for the Future.

Palmer, K., W. Oates and P. Portney (1995), 'Tightening environmental standards: the benefit – cost or no-cost paradigm?', *Journal of Economic Perspectives*, **9** (4), 119–32.

Panagariya, A., K. Palmer, W. Oates and A. Krupnick (1993), 'Toward an integrated theory of open economy environmental and trade policy', *Working Paper No 93–8*, Department of Economics, University of Maryland.

Porter, M.E. (1991), 'America's Green strategy', *Scientific American*, **264**, 168.

Porter, M.E. and C. van der Linde (1995), 'Toward a new conception of the environment – competitiveness relationship', *Journal of Economic Perspectives*, **9** (4), 97–118.

Rauscher, M. (1994), 'On ecological dumping', *Oxford Economic Papers*, **46**, 822–40.

Ulph, A. (1992), 'The choice of environmental policy instruments and strategic international trade' in R. Pethig (ed.), *Conflicts and Cooperation in Managing Environmental Resources*, Berlin: Springer-Verlag.

Ulph, A. (1995), 'International environmental regulation when national governments act strategically', in J. Braden and S. Proost (eds) (1997), *The Economic Theory of Environmental Policy in a Federal System*, Cheltenham, UK and Lyme, US: Edward Elgar.

Ulph, A. (1996a), 'Environmental policy and international trade when governments and producers act strategically', *Journal of Environmental Economics and Management*, **30**, 265–81.

Ulph, A. (1996b), 'Strategic environmental policy, international trade and the Single European Market', in J. Braden, H. Folmer and T. Ulen (eds), *Environmental Policy with Political and Economic Integration: The European Union and the United States*, Cheltenham, UK and Brookfield, US: Edward Elgar, pp. 235–56.

Ulph, A. (1996c), 'Environmental policy instruments and imperfectly competitive international trade', *Environmental and Resource Economics*, **7** (4), 333–55.

Ulph, A. (1996d), 'Strategic environmental policy and international trade – the role of market conduct', in C. Carraro, Y. Katsoulacos and A. Xepapadeas (eds), *Environmental Policy and Market Structure*, Dordrecht: Kluwer Academic Publishers, pp. 99–130.

Ulph, A. and D. Ulph (1996), 'Trade, strategic innovation and strategic environmental policy – a general analysis', in C. Carraro, Y. Katsoulacos and A. Xepapadeas (eds), *Environmental Policy and Market Structure*, Dordrecht: Kluwer Academic Publishers, pp. 181–208.

Ulph, D. (1993), 'Strategic innovation and strategic environmental policy', in C. Carraro (ed.), *Trade Innovation and the Environment*, Dordrecht: Kluwer Academic Publishers, pp. 205–28.

30 Environment, international trade and development
Harmen Verbruggen

1. Introduction

The environment, trade and development nexus is approached here from the perspective of the pursuit of a global sustainable development, with special emphasis on the North–South dimension. Whereas the other authors in this part of this book deal with various international aspects of environmental policy, and the chapter by Barbier (Chapter 50 in Part VI) discusses environment and development, the focus of this chapter is on the interface between environment, trade and development. Sections 2 and 3 attempt to conceptualize this interface by emphasizing the fundamental question of the intra- and intergenerational attribution of the earth's environmental capital between the North and the South. It will become clear that equity and development aspirations are at the heart of this distributional problem. Alternative distributions will lead to differences between the North and the South regarding the extent to which the scarcity value of environmental goods is priced. Changing comparative advantages will, in turn, be the result. Hence trade is pivotal, at least at a conceptual level (Anderson and Blackhurst, 1992; Verbruggen and Kuik, 1997).[1] Section 4 tries to shed light on the possible directions of these changing comparative advantages. Section 5 briefly discusses two of the currently most debated environment-and-trade issues, notably in the WTO circuit, namely trade measures pursuant to multilateral environmental agreements (MEAs) and eco-labelling schemes. Finally, Section 6 touches upon the design of an international system of environmental governance.

2. Conceptualizing the environment, trade and development nexus

Inherent to the concept of sustainable development is the notion that the earth's environmental capital, comprising all the stocks of renewable and non-renewable environmental resources which provide us directly or indirectly with goods and services, is limited. Many have tried to grasp the exhaustibility, and hence scarcity, of environmental goods, be it by referring to the physical laws of thermodynamics and entropy (Boulding, 1966; Daly, 1987), to the concepts of carrying capacity and ecosystem resilience (Arrow et al., 1995; van den Bergh, 1993), or in terms of given stocks, and the environmental utilization space (Siebert, 1982; Opschoor, 1995). Denoting this limitedness simply as environmental capital, two issues come to the fore. First, the establishment of the sustainable stocks of the various components of environmental capital, and second, the attribution of property and user rights for these components to countries and economic agents. From the viewpoint of economic efficiency, both issues need to be resolved. A strictly scientific determination of the sustainable size of environmental capital is virtually impossible, given the uncertainty that surrounds ecological–economic interactions, the scope of substitution possibilities between environmental capital, man-made capital, human capital and social capital and among different components of environmental capital, and the prospects for size-enlarging technological developments (Serageldin and Steer, 1994). This means that risk assessments and, hence, societal valuations and political trade-offs are inevitable (den Butter and Verbruggen, 1994).

Hence the level of conservation and the attribution of the earth's environmental capital between countries of the North and the South is predominantly of a political nature. It may sound rather abstract to consider the distribution of the (use of the) global commons between (groups of) countries. But that is indeed exactly under negotiation at international conferences on, for instance, climate change, biological diversity and exploitation of the oceans (Pearce, 1992). It is about CO_2 emission reduction targets per country group, the protection of ecosystems and foregone alternative uses, and territorial waters and fishing rights. Also in the North–South debate on environment and trade, this global distributional question figures prominently. Here the central issue is to what extent international harmonization of environmental standards is required. This issue refers to the Northern perception of 'fair' trade and a level playing field versus the Southern views on the sovereign rights of countries to exploit their own environmental goods and not to be confronted with Northern environmental regulations and standards. In other words, lower environmental standards and hence compliance costs of Southern competitors are perceived 'unfair' by Northern industry, and call for border adjustment measures. Also, environmentalists often oppose the idea of 'double standards'. By contrast, countries of the South fear that if harmonization instead of environmental diversity, that is, cross-country differences in environmental standards and objectives, becomes the internationally accepted principle, Northern standards will be forced upon them. This could thwart their development aspirations in various ways (see Sections 4 and 5).

This North–South controversy on harmonization versus diversity constitutes the interface between environment, trade and development. To place this interface in a proper context, it has to be established that an open trading system can only lead to a sustainable North–South trade if prices on the world market reflect full environmental and resource costs. Through environmental policies, countries pursue more sustainable production methods, consumption patterns and trade relations. In general, the level of environmental protection or sustainability each country aims at is the outcome of an interplay between the availability and quality of environmental endowments, actual environmental pressures and preferences for environmental quality. Countries preferring higher levels of environmental quality could set more stringent standards, and pay the price of a reduced competitiveness of some sectors and products, and vice versa. Hence, at least from a static and a short-term perspective, a trade-off between environmental protection and competitiveness is conceived.

To reconcile the North–South tensions on environment, trade and development, the relative intensity of the use of the earth's environmental capital by the North and the South has to be established. This means that in one way or another, property and user rights have to be defined and attributed, explicitly or implicitly. It is then important to distinguish between different types of environmental problems and the related components of environmental capital. Not all of the vast range of environmental problems that confront us today necessarily require international coordination. A distinctive criterion to decide whether and to what extent policy coordination between countries is needed can be found in the so-called optimal policy level. In economic terms, the optimal policy level is the level beyond which no externalities occur any more (cf. Tinbergen, 1954). In environmental terms, this policy level refers to the ecological scale of the externalities; it encompasses the scale at which the cause–effect chains are manifest (Mäler, 1990; Siebert, 1992, ch. 10; Verbruggen and Jansen, 1995). The subsidiarity principle of the European Union recognizes the merits of the optimal policy level. It states that the scope for Union policy is limited to those cases in which policy objectives, by reason of the scale or effects of a problem or action, can be better attained at Union level.

Thus the optimal policy level can be global in the case of the global commons, like the earth's atmosphere, the ozone layer, the oceans, unique ecosystem and (endangered) plant and animal species. Environmental resources that extend over at least two countries, but are not global, can be denoted as international components of environmental capital. They may be either ecological subsystems, shared fishing grounds, or they may be pollution deposition patterns that extend over two or more countries. International policy coordination can take the form of MEAs (Multilateral Environmental Agreements), where countries allocate property and use rights for global and international environmental resources, in connection with other modalities as to responsibilities, transfer of financial resources and technology, instruments and monitoring and enforcement provisions (Mäler, 1990; Lloyd, 1992). The optimal policy level is national where there are no environmental linkages with other countries. Local environmental resources have the smallest spatial scale.

The current allocation of the earth's environmental capital leaves much to be desired: it is either imperfectly distributed or not distributed at all. There are also wide differences between North and South. Global environmental goods, for instance, are subject to practically no management arrangements whatsoever, with the exception of the phasing out of CFCs under the Montreal Protocol, the regulation of trade in endangered species under CITES (Convention on International Trade in Endangered Species of Wild Fauna and Flora), the protection of Antarctica and a framework convention on the Law of the Sea. The regulation of international environmental goods is at a more advanced stage, especially among countries of the North. Here, numerous agreements have been made to do, for instance, with the distribution of fishing grounds, the management of international river basins and acidification, though these agreements are not always as effective as they might be. In the South, however, attribution of international goods has hardly begun.

The most glaring differences between North and South concern the management of local and national environmental goods. The advanced countries of the North have brought the use of their most important goods under some form of regulation. This is not the case in developing countries. Many developing countries are even displaying a sort of regression in which traditional, community-based environmental management systems are collapsing under the pressures of population growth, migration and institutional change. In short, the allocation of the earth's environmental capital has yet to be effected; this applies especially to the South's environmental goods and to the environmental capital allocation between North and South. All these non-allocated environmental assets therefore have an open-access character (cf. the chapter by Pearce in this book – Chapter 33), the best possible guarantee of their non-sustainable exploitation.

Siebert (1977) has already indicated that if a country specializes in the export of a pollution-intensive commodity, whose world market price does not reflect the use of environmental goods in its production, the welfare gains from trade are offset by a deterioration in environmental quality. Placed in a North–South context, Chichilnisky (1994b) argues that a form of unequal exchange arises between North and South as a result of the different degrees to which property and user rights of environmental resources are accorded on the one hand, and the open-access character of global and international goods themselves on the other. In this unequal exchange, the developing countries export more of their environmental capital, at whatever price, than would be the case if property rights were well defined and well allocated. The developed countries therefore consume too much of the South's environmental goods at too low a price, and sometimes entirely unpriced. By contrast, the South ends up paying for those of the North's environmental costs which are passed on in its export prices. A mutually beneficial trade, then, between North and South does not exist. In fact, due to differences in property rights, exports of underpriced environmental goods lead to welfare losses in the South.

3.   Common but differentiated responsibilities

In order to make North–South trade sustainable and more gainful for the South, property and user rights for global and international goods have to be properly allocated between North and South, whereas the South has to take its reponsibility for managing its own environmental resources. Policy coordination at the optimal policy level in the context of an MEA does not necessary imply equal environmental standards across countries. On the contrary, for that, the differences between the North and the South in their preferences for and perceptions of environment and development are too far-reaching (Verbruggen and Opschoor, 1994; Chichilnisky, 1994a). Generally, in interpreting the concept of sustainable development, the North weighs the importance of sustainability, whereas the South emphasizes its own economic development. Where developing countries do consider sustainability an important issue, they concentrate on local and national environmental problems. Examples include air and (drinking) water pollution in Third World metropolis and industrial sites, overexploitation of renewable resources, soil degradation, desertification, low commodity prices and the environment–poverty trap. The North, by contrast, argues for an international approach to transboundary and global environmental problems. These differences are amplified by divergent perceptions of global problems in particular. The North dreads the idea that by the year 2050 the world's population will be nearing 10 billion. Almost all these extra 4 billion inhabitants will be born and live in the most underprivileged part of the world, the South, and will rightly be calling for improvements in their living standards. The South has a historical perspective that includes the past and the present. Not only is the North largely responsible for these global environmental problems, but the developed countries, with only a small fraction of the world's population, lay claim to a disproportionally large share of the earth's environmental capital (WRI, 1994, ch. 1). Developing countries feel that it is absurd that the developed countries should demand their loyal cooperation in dealing with problems that the North itself created. Above all, the South sees this as an obstruction of its prospects of economic development for its own, growing population.

The North–South divide is most clearly expressed in Principle 7 of the Rio Declaration on Environment and Development. Principle 7 reads, after having established that countries have the duty to cooperate in protecting the earth's environmental capital:

> In view of the different contributions to global environmental degradation, States have common but differentiated responsibilities. The developed countries acknowledge the responsibility that they bear in the international pursuit of sustainable development in view of the pressures their societies place on the global environment and of the technologies and financial resources they command.

The phrase 'common but differentiated responsibilities' is central to this principle. It instructs developed countries to take the lead in the pursuit of sustainable development. Translated into the environment, trade and development nexus, it means that (parts of) the earth's environmental capital has to be attributed in favour of the South. Economically, it can be inferred that in allocating property and user rights, the South is afforded relatively more environmental capital. This will result in a relatively lower marginal valuation of the environment in the South. In turn, this lower valuation will be expressed in either generally lower environmental standards, more time to comply with higher, that is, Northern standards, or that developing countries are afforded financial compensation and technological assistance in the framework of MEAs. Hence, that policies are internationally coordinated at the level of MEAs does not necessarily mean equal standards across countries.

As regards national and local environmental resources, it should be acknowledged that developing countries are amply endowed with natural and environmental resources, except for a number of newly industrializing countries like South Korea, Taiwan, Hong Kong and Singapore. And given developing countries' priority for economic development and employment generation, both factors will lead to a generally lower revealed environmental preference in the South than in the North. Thus the extent to which the scarcity value of global, international and national environmental goods is priced will vary between the North and the South. Diversity rather than harmonization in environmental standards and objectives in a free trade context has to become the guiding principle. This is in line with traditional trade theory and the literature that shows that international coordinated policies need side payments (transfers from North to South) to become more equitable and better enforceable (Oates, 1996; Barrett, 1994).

4. Changing North–South comparative advantages

Environmental diversity will change the pattern of comparative advantages. The South may improve its competitive position for environment-intensive products. However, there are factors and developments that might inhibit the developing countries from taking advantage of their new competitive edge. A number of these are briefly indicated (cf. Verbruggen and Opschoor, 1994).

First of all, from a global perspective, a relative abundance of environmental endowments in a particular country may very well turn into a relative scarcity. A case in point is tropical rainforest with which countries like Brazil, Malaysia and Indonesia are richly endowed. From a global point of view, however, the tropical rainforest has become scarce. MEAs to combat climate change and protect biodiversity will be geared towards preservation of forest, thus preventing these countries from taking advantage of their abundance of environmental endowments. This may occur more generally, and illustrates that environmental comparative advantages can easily be reduced.

Second, it can be questioned anyway to what extent an environmental preference can really be freely chosen. Is it at the people's discretion to let species become extinct and to deliberately overexploit the environment for the sake of short-term revenues at the expense of future development? There is also the concern that large differences among countries as to environmental standards might cause distinctly dirty industries to relocate to pollution havens in developing countries, although the empirical evidence for that to happen is scant (Low and Yeats, 1992). Both these questions lead to the introduction of minimum international environmental standards, to be concluded in MEAs, and this, too, makes the realization of new environmental comparative advantages by developing countries only partly possible.

Third, the introduction of clean technologies changes the factor intensity of a sustainable economy. Process-integrated clean technologies not only economize on the use of environmental resources, but also on capital and labour. Clean technology improves productivity and the quality of the products produced, which strengthens competitiveness. The North has a decisive lead in this respect. As a result, the competitive position of the South for clean sectors and products may structurally deteriorate as a sustainable economy seems to be relatively more capital- and knowledge-intensive. The North–South technology gap may widen, brought about by accelerated technological development in the North in response to stringent environmental regulation.

Fourth, policies in the North are increasingly being implemented to increase material efficiency, reuse of materials, shifts to renewable resources and increased use of secondary materials through recycling. All this weakens already sluggish primary commodity exports of developing countries, especially the least developed ones. It is important to realize that dematerialization as currently formulated and practised is primarily dictated by waste control policies in the North, and has little to do with a comprehensive sustainable management of resources through cooperation between consuming and producing countries. Developing countries are not consulted and involved in these policies. The adverse effects on their export prospects could be mitigated if developing countries could attract part of the recycling market. And indeed, there is evidence that such a specialization pattern is emerging. Whereas developed countries are the major importers of primary plastics, metals and paper, secondary flows of these recyclable materials increasingly find their way to developing countries. Recovery and recycling are growing industries, especially in South Korea, China, India, Indonesia and Mexico (van Beukering and Curlee, 1998).

Finally, in the South it is feared that the proliferation of trade-related environmental measures in the North, together with the (implicit) pursuit of international harmonization of environmental standards, will thwart their development aspirations. Developing countries fear that the strict environmental standards of the North will be imposed on them, resulting in relatively higher compliance and transaction costs and/or reduced market access for their export products. There is only circumstantial evidence to fuel such fear, of which the tuna–dolphin dispute between Mexico and the US is the most discussed case (Thaggert, 1994). Just to give an idea of the problem, Table 30.1 provides an indication of the frequency of incidence and coverage of trade-related environmental measures for exports from developing countries to the EU market in 1992. The incidence index indicates the ratio of the number of products (according to 6-digit Harmonized System tariff lines) subject to at least one environmental measure and the total number of products imported from developing countries. In the coverage index, these product numbers are weighted by the value of corresponding trade flows. Trade-related environmental measures comprise (i) economic instruments like product changes, tax differentiation and deposit-refund schemes, (ii) technical regulations and standards, among which are product standards, packaging requirements and eco-labelling schemes, and (iii) quantity import controls. The German trade-related environmental measures were taken to be representative of the entire EU.

Table 30.1 shows that of all products that developing countries export to the EU, 23 per cent are facing whatever trade-related environmental measures are in force, covering 20 per cent of the value of trade. By far the majority of these measures are directed towards manufactures, and pre-

Table 30.1   *Frequency and coverage indices for export products from developing countries to the EU market subject to environmental measures, 1992*

Exports	Frequency index (all measures)	Coverage index (all measures)
All products	0.23 (0.21)[1]	0.20 (0.16)[1]
Commodities	0.01	0.04
Manufactures	0.22	0.16
Per selected HS product group[2]		
3 Pharmaceutical and chemical products	0.40	0.56
4 Rubber, leather, wood, paper	0.26	0.20
5 Silk, wool, cotton, fibres	0.18	0.23
6 Clothing, garments, shoes, ceramic	0.80	0.83

Notes:
[1] Indices between brackets only refer to technical regulations and standards.
[2] HS = Harmonized System classification of traded goods.

Source: Calculated after TRAINS, including GREENTRADE, UNCTAD, Geneva and H. Verbruggen, O, Kuik, M. Bennis, H. Hoogeveen and R. Mollerus, *Environmental Product Measures: Barriers for South–North Trade?*, CREED Working Paper Series No. 18, IIED, London/IVM-VU, Amsterdam.

dominantly take the form of technical regulations and standards. It should be borne in mind that food safety measures, relevant for commodities, are not considered as environmental measures and not included in the indices. These indices indeed reveal that a relatively large share of manufactured exports from developing countries to the EU might be affected by environmental measures. To what extent these measures increase the cost for exporters and/or reduce market access can only be assessed on the basis of case studies.

5. Trade measures pursuant to MEAs and eco-labelling

Two issues are briefly dealt with that can be considered exemplary in the international policy debate, namely trade measures pursuant to MEAs and eco-labelling (Verbruggen and Kuik, 1997). A relevant distinction for this policy debate is between products, and processes and production methods (PPMs). PPMs concern the way in which products are manufactured or processed and natural resources are extracted and harvested. This distinction goes back to the GATT Articles 1, 3 and 11 that do not allow unequal treatment of like products, be they domestic or foreign. In principle, GATT rules are directed towards (traded) products and leave PPMs undisturbed. In the WTO circuit, the current understanding is that a country cannot take trade measures against another country on the basis of PPM differences. In WTO jargon, unilateral measures with an extraterritorial impact are not allowed (GATT Secretariat, 1992; Esty, 1994, chs 2 and 5; Thaggert, 1994).

However, trade measures pursuant to MEAs are considered an important tool for both implementation and enforcing MEAs. Such complementary trade measures should then have the same effect on the international market as environmental regulations have on the domestic market. Also, MEAs legitimize these complementary trade measures, if they are directed at PPMs, and cannot be considered trade distortions. More controversial is the (potential) use of trade measures to initiate an MEA at the optimal policy level, that is to say if trade provisions in an MEA are directed towards free-riding non-parties. Nevertheless, for MEAs to be efficient and effective, (potential) trade measures may indeed be necessary. But although developing countries fear this stick, it seems advisable not to leave this matter unsettled. Well-defined criteria on the legitimacy of the use of these trade measures should be included in international trade rules, taking due account of the principle of common but differentiated responsibilities.

Interference with PPMs is also at the heart of the eco-labelling discussion. Eco-labelling is increasingly used as an instrument to provide consumers with environmental information on products on which they can base their consumption decisions. As such, these schemes are not trade-distorting. The reason for developing countries' distrust is that eco-labels may *de facto* discriminate. This has to do with the fact that these labelling schemes are based on a life cycle or integrated chain management concept. Production and consumption chains are often spread over different countries. This means that a balance has to be found between the minimization of environmental impacts along the chain according to the environmental endowments and preferences of the importing country *vis-à-vis* similar trade-offs in the exporting countries where parts of the chain are performed. As it is unlikely that identical trade-offs are made in all the supplying countries, and as usually the importing country in the North formulates the criteria to be awarded an eco-label, developing countries may have Northern standards imposed upon them.

This tension seems to be in principle insoluble, unless through international coordination of policies. International consensus should be sought on the openness and criteria of eco-labelling schemes, taking due account of environmental circumstances and preferences in exporting developing countries, and on a system of mutual recognition of eco-labels. Then, developing countries may indeed create new export opportunities for relatively environmentally intensive products and realize a market premium as well.

6. International environmental governance

A global sustainable development which promotes simultaneous achievement of environmental and trade goals, meets the development aspirations of the South, as well as manages global and international environmental goods more effectively, requires an international system of environmental governance. Opinions differ as to how such a system should be shaped. Frequently, pleas are made to create a genuine global environmental institution with supranational authority, either under the umbrella of the United Nations or as an independent organization (Harris, 1991; Esty, 1994). Others question the functionality and political feasibility of a global authority. Instead, a multitude of limited, concomitant environmental agreements is proposed as a more flexible tool to manage particular environmental goods, and so that the sum of these limited coverage agreements would form a decentralized alternative to a supranational, all-embracing regulator (Dorfman, 1991). This alternative is more in line with the conclusion of MEAs at the optimal policy level. In either case, the WTO system of trade rules should incorporate environmental considerations more fully into international trade policy, as well as faciliate international environmental governance. Such a synergy between environment, trade and development constitutes one of the most important challenges of the coming decades.

Note
1. It should be acknowledged that, up to now, there is hardly any empirical evidence to substantiate the supposed relationship between stringency of environmental policy and changing comparative advantages and competitiveness for traded products (Tobey, 1990; Low and Yeats, 1992; van Beers and van den Bergh, 1997). This relationship, however, remains a controversial question.

References

Arrow, K. et al. (1995), 'Economic growth, carrying capacity, and the environment', *Ecological Economics*, 15 (2), 91–5.

Anderson, K. and R. Blackhurst (1992), 'Trade, the environment and public policy', in K. Anderson and R. Blackhurst (eds), *The Greening of World Trade Issues*, New York: Harvester Wheatsheaf.

Barrett, S. (1994), 'The biodiversity supergame', *Environmental and Resource Economics*, 4, 111–22.

Beers, C. van and J.C.J.M. van den Bergh (1997), 'An empirical multi-country analysis of the impact of environmental regulations on foreign trade flows, *Kyklos*, 50 (1), 29–46.

Bergh, J.C.J.M. van den (1993), 'A framework for modelling economy–environment–development relationships based on dynamic carrying capacity and sustainable development feedback', *Environmental and Resource Economics*, 3, 395–412.

Beukering, P. van and T.R. Curlee (1998), 'Frontiers in recycling', in P. Vellinga, J. Gupta and F. Berkhout (eds), *Substantial Sustainability*, Dordrecht: Kluwer Academic Publishers.

Boulding, K.E. (1966), 'The economics of the coming spaceship Earth', in H. Jarrett (ed.), *Environmental Quality in a Growing Economy*, Washington, DC: Resources for the Future.

Butter, F.A.G. den and H. Verbruggen (1994), 'Measuring the trade-off between economic growth and a clean environment', *Environmental and Resource Economics*, 4, 187–208.

Chichilnisky, G. (1994a), 'Sustainable development and North–South trade', *FEEM Newsletter*, **3**, 15–22.
Chichilnisky, G. (1994b), 'North–South trade and the global environment', *American Economic Review*, **84** (4), 851–74.
Daly, H.E. (1987), 'The economic growth debate: what some economists have learned but many have not', *Journal of Environmental Economics and Management*, **14** (4), 323–36.
Dorfman, R. (1991), 'Protecting the global environment: an immodest proposal, *World Development*, **19** (1), 103–10.
Esty, D.C. (1994), *Greening the GATT: Trade, Environment, and the Future*, Washington, DC: Institute for International Economics.
GATT Secretariat (1992), *Trade and Environment Report*, Geneva: GATT.
Harris, J.M. (1991), 'Global institutions and ecological crisis', *World Development*, **19** (1), 111–22.
Lloyd, P.J. (1992), 'The problem of optimal environmental policy choice', in K. Anderson and R. Blackhurst (eds), *The Greening of World Trade Issues*, New York: Harvester Wheatsheaf, pp.49–72.
Low, P. and A. Yeats (1992), 'Do "dirty" industries migrate?', in P. Low (ed.), *International Trade and the Environment*, Discussion Paper 159, Washington, DC: World Bank.
Mäler, K.G. (1990), 'International environmental problems', *Oxford Review of Economic Policy*, **6**, 80–108.
Oates, W.E. (1996), 'Global environmental management: towards an open economy environmental economics', in W.E. Oates, *The Economics of Environmental Regulation*, Cheltenham, UK and Brookfield, US: Edward Elgar.
Opschoor, J.B. (1995), 'Ecospace and the fall and rise of throughput intensity, *Ecological Economics*, **15** (2), 137–40.
Pearce, D. (1992), 'Economics and the global environmental challenge', in A. Markandya and J. Richardson (eds), *The Earthscan Reader in Environmental Economics*, London: Earthscan.
Serageldin, I. and A. Steer (eds) (1994), *Making Development Sustainable: From Concepts to Action*, Environmentally Sustainable Development Occasional Paper Series No. 2, Washington, DC: World Bank.
Siebert, H. (1977), 'Environmental quality and the gains from trade', *Kyklos*, **30** (4), 657–73.
Siebert, H. (1982), 'Nature as a life support system: renewable resources and environmental disruption', *Journal of Economics*, **42**, 133–42.
Siebert, H. (1992), *Economics of the Environment*, Berlin/New York: Springer-Verlag.
Thaggert, H.L. (1994), 'A closer look at the Tuna–Dolphin case: "Like product" and "extra-jurisdictionality" in the trade and environment context', in J. Cameron, P. Demaret and D. Geradin (eds), *Trade & the Environment: the Search for Balance*, London: Cameron May.
Tinbergen, J. (1954), *International Economic Integration*, Amsterdam: Elsevier.
Tobey, J.A. (1990), 'The impact of domestic environmental policies on patterns of world trade: an empirical test', *Kyklos*, **43** (2), 191–209.
Verbruggen, H. and H. Opschoor (1994), 'Environmental policy and changing North–South comparative advantage', in J.W. Gunning, H. Kox, W. Tims and Y. de Wit (eds), *Trade, Aid and Development, Essays in Honour of Hans Linnemann*, New York: St Martin's Press, pp. 99–119.
Verbruggen, H. and H.M.A. Jansen (1995), 'International coordination of environmental policies', in H. Folmer, H.L. Gabel and J.B. Opschoor (eds), *Principles of Environmental and Resources Economics*, Aldershot, UK and Brookfield, US: Edward Elgar, pp.228–52.
Verbruggen, H. and O. J. Kuik (1996), 'Environmental standards in international trade', in P. van Dijck and G. Faber (eds), *Challenges to the New World Trade Organization*, The Hague/London/Boston: Kluwer Law International.
Verbruggen, H. and O. Kuik (1997), 'WTO Ministerial Conference in Singapore: environmental diversity versus harmonization', *Environmental and Resource Economics*, **10** (4), 405–12.
World Resources Institute (WRI) (1994), *World Resources 1994–95*, New York/Oxford: Oxford University Press.

31 Environmental conflict, bargaining and cooperation

Carlo Carraro[1]

1. Background

Most of the new environmental phenomena have an intrinsic international dimension due to transnational or global spillovers. The depletion of the ozone layer and climate change depend on global aggregate emissions. Acid depositions and marine pollution usually cross the borders of the polluting country. Even deforestation is an international problem as forests are a sink for CO_2 and provide important support for biodiversity.

The international dimension of the environment is a source of substantial interdependence among nations: each country benefits from using the environment as a receptacle of emissions and is damaged by environmental deterioration. While the benefit for any country is primarily related to domestic pollution alone, the environmental damage is related to both domestic and foreign emissions. This problem is not new to economists, and has been analysed in the area of externalities and public goods. What is new is the context where these problems take place. Currently, the atmosphere and the waters are managed as global common-property goods, and there is no institution which possesses powers to regulate their use by means of supranational legislation, economic instruments, or by imposing a system of global property rights. Hence the difficulty in achieving large environmental agreements and the necessity to design negotiation mechanisms leading to self-enforcing outcomes.

Environmental agreements among sovereign countries have been widely advocated and debated in the last few years, following the Montreal Protocol on CFCs (chlorofluorocarbons), to protect the ozone layer, and the UN Conference on the Environment and Development, organized in Rio de Janeiro in 1992. In the recent history of international agreements to protect the global environment, one can observe different attempts to achieve cooperation among countries.

The first attempt has been to design worldwide agreements to cut emissions by bargaining solely on emissions. The result of these attempts has usually been frustrating. The conventions, whenever signed by a great number of countries, are rather empty in terms of quantitative targets and /or deadlines. Precise commitments, on the other hand, are signed by small

461

groups of 'like-minded' countries. Examples are provided by the 1992 Climate Change Convention, which is widely signed but notoriously empty, and by the EC proposal on CO_2 emission control, which is rather binding and precise but, whenever signed, confined to a small number of countries. The early outcome of the Montreal Protocol provides another example of a small group of signatories, *vis-à-vis* a global phenomenon, with many other countries in the position of free-riders.

The dissatisfaction with such an outcome, and in particular with small environmental coalitions, has been followed by attempts to expand the agreements by bribing reluctant countries by means of transfers (as in the follow-up of the Montreal Protocol, or in the plans for financial implementation of Agenda 21). Alternatively, but with the same goal, the negotiating process is trying to link environmental protection to other international agreements: on technological cooperation (as in the case of the Climate Change Convention) and trade (as in the environmental clause in GATT/WTO).

There are probably two reasons which explain the difficulty in achieving self-enforcing agreements with a large number of signatories. The first one is the large economic and environmental asymmetries across world regions. Less developed countries, for example, are quite reluctant to adopt measures to control global pollution because this could slow down their growth, with high economic costs which are evaluated as larger than the environmental benefits resulting from emission reduction. In other words, signing an environmental agreement may not be profitable for all countries involved in the negotiation process.

The second problem is the intrinsic instability of environmental agreements. In other words, some countries may prefer to free-ride, that is, to profit from the emission reduction achieved by the signatory countries (because the environmental benefit is not excludable). This phenomenon is not related to the presence of asymmetries, even if asymmetries can strengthen it, and it occurs even if countries are identical. Therefore, even when all countries are conscious that gains from environmental cooperation are above the economic costs of abating pollution, that is, that cooperation is profitable, most of them may not sign the environmental agreement because of the possibility of achieving the environmental benefit without paying the costs (that is, cooperation is unstable).[2]

2. Theoretical framework

Let us provide a more formal description of the above two problems and of the solutions proposed in the environmental literature. Let $P_i(s)$ denote the value of country i's welfare when it decides to join the coalition s, whereas $Q_i(s)$ is the value of its welfare when country i does not join the coalition s.

The only argument of the payoff functions is the identity and number of cooperating countries. However, it is implicit that all other relevant variables, including emissions and policy decisions in other countries, enter country i's welfare function.

Let $P_i(\emptyset) = Q_i(\emptyset)$, $i = 1,2, \ldots, n$, be a country's payoff when there is no coalition (the non-cooperative Nash equilibrium payoff), whereas $P_i(S)$ is country i's payoff when all countries decide to cooperate (the grand coalition S is formed). Then, an environmental coalition is profitable, that is, each country $i \in s$ gains from joining the coalition, with respect to its position when no countries cooperate, iff $P_i(s) \geq P_i(\emptyset)$, $\forall i \in s$. The coalition is also stable when, for all $i \in s$, $P_i(s)$, the country's payoff for belonging to the coalition s, is larger than $Q_i(s \setminus i)$, the country's payoff when it exits the coalition, and lets the other countries sign the cooperative agreement.[3] Therefore, an environmental agreement is self-enforcing when it is profitable and stable.

A first difficulty arises with this definition of stability, which coincides with the one used in the oligopoly literature on cartel stability (D'Aspremont and Gabsewicz, 1986; D'Aspremont et al., 1983; Donsimoni et al., 1986). Indeed, this definition excludes the possibility of group deviations and assumes that free-riders behave as singletons and have no incentive to form another coalition. Moreover, this definition assumes that countries conjecture that no reaction follows a change of their move. For example, this implies that when a country leaves the coalition it assumes that the other countries will not follow, and remain in the coalition.[4] Some criticisms have been raised against this definition (see Le Breton and Weber, 1993; Konishi et al., 1997; Ray and Vohra, 1997; Yi 1997; Chew, 1994; Bloch, 1994, 1997). For example, the notion of far-sighted stability implies that a country, when deciding to leave a coalition, takes into account the other countries' incentives to stay or leave. An application of the concept of far-sighted stability to the emergence of environmental coalitions is contained in Echia and Mariotti (1997).[5] However, the research on the consequences for the existence of self-enforcing agreements of a more general definition of stability is still in its early stages.

Most papers in the theoretical literature on environmental cooperation and conflict (Hoel, 1991, 1992; Carraro and Siniscalco, 1992, 1993; Barrett, 1994, 1997b; Heal, 1994) adopt the standard definitions of stability and self-enforcing agreements provided above. There is a result which is common to most of this literature. The presence of asymmetries across countries and the incentive to free-ride makes the existence of self-enforcing agreements quite unlikely. When they exist they are signed by a limited number of countries (Hoel, 1991; Carraro and Siniscalco, 1992; Barrett, 1994). When the number of signatories is large, the difference between the cooperative behaviour adopted by the coalition and the non-cooperative one is very small (Barrett, 1997b). These results, which are robust with respect to different specifications of countries' welfare function, and with respect to the burden-sharing rule[6] used in the asymmetric case (Barrett, 1997a; Botteon and Carraro, 1997a), suggest that the attempt to negotiate on emission reductions is unlikely to be successful, unless more complex policy strategies, in which environmental policy interacts with other policy measures, are adopted. This is why in the environmental economics literature two main sets of instruments have been proposed to expand environmental coalitions, that is, to increase the number of signatories of an environmental agreement. These instruments are 'transfers' and 'issue linkage'.

3.   Environmental cooperation and transfers

Let us consider transfers first. It is quite natural to propose transfers to compensate those countries which may lose by signing the environmental agreement. In other words, a redistribution mechanism among signatories, from gainers to losers, may provide the basic requirement for a self-enforcing agreement to exist, that is, the profitability of the agreement for all signatories. Therefore, if well designed, transfers can guarantee that no country refuses to sign the agreement because it is not profitable. Formally, this implies $P_i(S) + T_i \geq P_i(\emptyset)$, for all $i \in S$, where T_i denotes the transfer given or received by country i and where a budget constraint requires T_i to be self-financed (compensated Pareto criterion). Chander and Tulkens (1993, 1995) show that there exist transfers such that not only is each country better off with full cooperation than it is with no cooperation, but it is also better off with full cooperation than it is in any sub-coalition, provided the remaining countries behave non-cooperatively. This result is important because it implies that no country or group of countries has an incentive to exclude other countries from the environmental coalition, that is, the grand coalition is optimal (but it may not be stable).

Transfers also play a major role with respect to the stability issue. Indeed it is not sufficient to guarantee the profitability of the environmental agreement. Incentives to free-ride must also be offset. The possibility of using self-financed transfers to stabilize environmental agreements is analysed in Carraro and Siniscalco (1993) and Hoel (1994), which show that transfers may be successful only if associated with a certain degree of commitment. For example, when countries are symmetric, only if a group of countries is committed to cooperation can another group of uncommitted countries be induced to sign the agreement by a system of transfers.[7] Suppose that s is the largest stable coalition when no transfer system is implemented. The joint additional benefit for countries belonging to s when an additional country j enters the coalition is $\Sigma_{i \in s}[P_i(s \cup j) - P_i(s)] > 0$ (where it is assumed that the environmental benefit increases monotonically with the number of cooperators). The incentive for country j to free-ride on the $s \cup j$ coalition is $Q_j(s) - P_j(s \cup j) > 0$, because the coalition $s \cup j$ is not stable. Hence, the coalition $s \cup j$ can be stabilized by a system of transfers if the joint benefits from cooperation are larger than the incentive to free-ride, that is, (i) $\Sigma_{i \in s}[P_i (s \cup j) - P_i(s)] > Q_j(s) - P_j(s \cup j)$, and if: (ii) there exists a sharing rule such that $P_i(s \cup j) - P_i(s) \geq 0$ for all $i \in s$; (iii) countries belonging to the coalition s are committed to cooperation.[8] However, these conditions are difficult to meet for the case in which j is replaced by $S \backslash s$, that is, in the case in which transfers are used to achieve the grand coalition.[9]

Three types of partial commitment that could serve as possible blueprints for environmental cooperation can be proposed (of course, other types of institutional mechanisms could be proposed as well): stable coalition commitment when only the j countries belonging to the stable coalition commit to cooperation; sequential commitment when the j countries are committed to cooperation and any new signatory, as soon as it enters the expanded coalition, must commit to cooperation as well; external commitment when a subset of non-cooperating countries commits to transfer welfare in order to induce the remaining non-signatories to cooperate, and to guarantee the stability of the resulting coalition. Assuming these alternative commitment schemes, Carraro and Siniscalco (1993) analyse the formal conditions to expand coalitions.[10]

A general conclusion emerges from their analysis: both the existence of stable coalitions, and the possibilities of expanding them, depend on the pattern of interdependence among countries. If there is leakage, that is, a non-cooperating country expands its emissions when the coalition restricts them, thus offsetting the effort of the cooperating countries, then environmental benefits from cooperation are low, the incentive to free-ride is high, and conditions for transfers to be effective are unlikely to be met. If, on the contrary, there is no leakage, that is, the free-riders simply enjoy the cleaner environment without paying for it, but do not offset the emission reduction by the cooperating countries, then environmental benefits are larger, free-riding is less profitable and transfers may achieve their goal to expand the coalition.

The stability issue has been often analysed within a theoretical framework in which all countries are identical (symmetric). However, there are a few attempts to analyse the existence of self-enforcing agreements and the role of transfers in the case of asymmetric or heterogeneous countries. This is done both in Barrett (1997a) and in Botteon and Carraro (1997a). These papers show that asymmetries may increase the effectiveness of transfers rather than reducing it. For example, a commitment may not be necessary (in this case an agreement with transfers would also be self-enforcing). Moreover, they address the issue of burden sharing by showing that the way in which gains are redistributed affects both profitability, as previously stressed, and stability of the agreement, thus modifying the effectiveness of transfers and the role of commitment. In other words, there are two types of transfers: those which make the agreement profitable to all countries and those which make it stable. There are therefore two objectives (profitability and stability) with a single instrument (transfers), a situation that economists immediately recognize as inefficient.

4. Issue linkage

This is why a second approach to address the profitability and stability problems has been proposed. The basic idea is to design a negotiation mechanism in which countries negotiate not only on the environmental issue, but also on another interrelated (economic) issue. For example, Barrett (1995) proposes to link environmental negotiations to negotiations on trade liberalization, whereas Carraro and Siniscalco (1995, 1997) and Katsoulacos (1997) propose to link them to negotiations on R&D cooperation.

Again we must distinguish the profitability from the stability problem. The idea of 'issue linkage' was originally proposed by Folmer et al. (1993) and Cesar and de Zeeuw (1994) to solve the problem of asymmetries among countries. The intuition is that some countries gain on a given issue, whereas other countries gain on a second one. By 'linking' the two issues it may be possible that the agreement in which the countries decide to cooperate on both issues is profitable to all of them. Formally, if $P_{i1}(s)$ is the payoff of country i when it joins coalition s on issue 1, and $P_{i2}(s)$ denotes country i's payoff when it joins the same coalition on issue 2, then 'issue linkage' solves the profitability problem if $P_{i1}(s) + P_{i2}(s) \geq P_{i1}(\emptyset) + P_{i2}(\emptyset)$ for all $i \epsilon s$, where for some $i \epsilon s$ we may have $P_{i1}(s) \leq P_{i1}(\emptyset)$ or $P_{i2}(s) \leq P_{i2}(\emptyset)$.[11]

The idea of 'issue linkage' can also be used to achieve the stability goal. Suppose there is no profitability concern (either because countries are symmetric or because a transfer scheme is implemented to make the agreement profitable to all countries). Consider the case in which it is Pareto-optimal to link the environment to another economic issue (see Carraro and Siniscalco, 1995 for a formal definition). Then, if stable, the linked agreement is also self-enforcing (no commitment is necessary).

Let us consider the stability of the linked agreement. Formally, there is no incentive to leave the linked coalition (that is, the coalition is internally stable) if $P_{1i}(s) + P_{2i}(s) \geq Q_{1i}(s \backslash i) + Q_{2i}(s \backslash i)$ for all $i \epsilon s$, where for some $i \epsilon s$ we may have $P_{1i}(s) \leq Q_{1i}(s \backslash i)$ or $P_{2i}(s) \leq Q_{2i}(s \backslash i)$. In words, the mechanism can be explained through the following example.[12] Suppose the environmental negotiation is linked to the negotiation on R&D cooperation, which involves an excludable positive externality and increases the join coalition welfare. In this way, the incentive to free-ride on the benefit of a cleaner environment (which is a public good fully appropriable by all countries) is offset by the incentive to appropriate the benefit stemming from the positive R&D externality (which is a club good fully appropriable only by the signatory countries). The latter incentive can stabilize the joint agreement, thus increasing its profitability because countires can reap both the R&D cooperation and the environmental benefit (this second benefit would be lost without the linkage).

This idea is also exploited in Katsoulacos (1997). This paper, which accounts for information asymmetries, provides additional support for the conclusion that 'issue linkage' can be very effective in guaranteeing the stability of an environmental agreement.[13] However, the benefit function which relates gains from cooperation on the issue characterized by excludable benefit with the number of cooperating countries is generally humpshaped. In other words, the grand coalition is not optimal when the negotiation takes place on this issue. By contrast, negotiations on the environmental issue lead to a monotonically increasing function (this is an implication of Chander and Tulkens, 1995). The behaviour of the benefit function for the joint coalition depends on the relative weight of the two issues. There are cases in which the optimal number of countries in the joint coalition is lower than the number of countries belonging to the stable group of signatories of the joint agreement. Hence three groups of countries may emerge (three roles): those which cooperate, those which would like to cooperate but are excluded from the agreement (and are therefore forced to non-cooperation) and those which prefer not to cooperate. This conclusion holds both when countries are symmetric (Carraro and Siniscalco, 1997) and when they are asymmetric (Botteon and Carraro, 1997b). In the asymmetric case a further result arises. A given country *i* may prefer some countries, say *j* and *h*, as partners in the cooperating group, but these countries may want to sign the agreement with country *k*, rather than with *i*. And *k* may prefer *i* and *h* rather than *j*. In this case, an equilibrium may not exist, that is, a stable international environmental agreement may not be signed (Carraro and Siniscalco, 1998).

These latter insights lead to the conclusion that issue linkage may damage environmental protection rather than benefit it. This is the case whenever the incentives to exclude some countries from the linked agreement or the possible political economy problem that undermines the emergence of an equilibrium dominate the benefits of linking two synergetic (in terms of profitability and stability) issues.

5.   Conclusions and further research directions

Even if the literature on the international environmental negotiations and cooperation is likely to develop further in the next year and to provide new results on the existence and features of self-enforcing agreements, there are a few conclusions that can be drawn. First, the attempt to achieve an agreement signed by all countries is likely to be unsuccessful if the negotiation is restricted to emissions only. Second, even when the negotiations are broadened to include transfers and/or they are linked to negotiations on other international issues, the outcome may not be the grand coalition, because of lack of commitment (in the case of transfers) or because of the conflict between optimality and stability of the coalition (in the case of issue linkage).

There are several directions for further research that deserve additional efforts. The strategic dimension of environmental negotiations, both at the international and domestic levels (voters may be asked to ratify an environmental agreement), opens interesting political economy problems. The lack of a supranational authority calls for an analysis of new international institutions (Compte and Jehiel, 1997 propose an international arbitrator). The possibility of expanding coalitions by linking environmental and trade negotiations requires further theoretical and empirical analyses. The stability concept used in the existing literature may be replaced by a more satisfactory one, thus modifying the results on the existence of large self-enforcing agreements (Bloch, 1997; Echia and Mariotti, 1997). Finally, a dynamic framework may be more appropriate to deal with environmental issues in which the stock of pollutants, rather than the flow (emissions) is the crucial variable to monitor (see Mäler, 1990; van der Ploeg and de Zeeuw, 1992).

More empirical work is also necessary. The existing empirical literature is large (two good examples are Fankhauser and Kverndokk, 1992; Kverndokk, 1993) but it assumes the exogenous formation of environmental coalitions, and assesses the effects of countries' decisions to sign the agreement on the main economic and environmental variables. However, an empirical analysis of the incentives to sign the agreement and of the negotiation process that leads to the endogenous formation of the coalition is still missing.

Notes
1.   The author is grateful to Domenico Siniscalco, with whom many of the ideas contained in this chapter have been developed, and to Jeroen van den Bergh and two anonymous referees for helpful comments on the first draft.
2.   This argument is well described in the early works on environmental cooperation. See Hardin (1968), Hardin and Baden (1977), and Ostrom (1990).
3.   This condition is known as internal stability. It is usually coupled with a condition of external stability which says that the payoff of a country which does not belong to the

coalition is larger than its payoff when it joins the coalition ($P_j(s \cup j) \leq Q_j(s), j \notin s$), that is, no additional country has an incentive to join the coalition. However, there are cases in which members of the coalition may want to exclude some countries from those which sign the agreement (see Carraro and Soubeyran, 1999, for an example). The exclusive-membership stable coalitions have been proposed in Yi (1997).

4. The opposite assumption is contained in Chander and Tulkens (1993, 1995) where a country leaving a coalition expects all other countries to leave the coalition. This is the source of their results which prove the stability of the coalition formed by all countries.

5. An analysis of international environmental agreements with symmetric and far-sighted countries was already contained in Bauer (1993). However, this paper does not provide any explicit reference to a new stability concept or a new definition of coalitional equilibrium.

6. In the asymmetric case, the rule which is chosen to divide the gains from cooperation among the countries in the coalition (usually called the burden-sharing rule) plays a crucial role because it affects the likelihood that each country decides to sign the agreement. The burden-sharing rule is usually taken from cooperative game theory and those of Nash and Shapley are the most used. By contrast, in the symmetric case different rules lead to the same outcome (equal shares).

7. This condition is less stringent when countries are asymmetric. See Botteon and Carraro (1997a).

8. See Carraro and Siniscalco (1993) where the result is shown for symmetric countries.

9. When j is replaced by $S \backslash s$, conditions (i)–(iii) are met if the net benefit for the marginal country in s is large. This cannot be the case when all countries are identical (symmetric) because the net benefit of the marginal country is approximately zero (when the number of countries is large), but it is more likely when countries are asymmetric (see Botteon and Carraro, 1997a).

10. However, recall that the idea of commitment, albeit partial, that is, confined to a group of countries, cannot be entirely consistent with the concept of self-enforcing agreement stressed in the previous sections.

11. Here we assume the payoffs on the two issues to be additive. More generally, it should be $P_{iu}(s) \geq P_{iu}(\emptyset)$ for all $i \in s$, where $P_{iu}(.)$ denotes country i's payoff when the two issues are linked (see Carraro and Siniscalco, 1995).

12. See Carraro and Siniscalco (1997) for a full presentation of the model.

13. Information asymmetries are also dealt with in Petrakis and Xepapadeas (1996) and in Chillemi (1997). These papers design implementation mechanisms which can induce countries to sign an environmental agreement even when emission levels are not observable.

References

Barrett, S. (1994), 'Self-enforcing international environmental agreements', *Oxford Economic Papers*, **46**, 878–94.

Barrett, S. (1995), 'Trade restrictions in international environmental agreements', CSERGE Working Paper 94–13, London Business School.

Barrett, S. (1997a), 'Heterogeneous international environmental agreements', in C. Carraro (ed.), *International Environmental Negotiations: Strategic Policy Issues*, Cheltenham, UK and Lyme, US: Edward Elgar.

Barrett, S. (1997b), 'Towards a theory of international cooperation' in C. Carraro and D. Siniscalco (eds), *New Directions in the Economic Theory of the Environment*, Cambridge, UK: Cambridge University Press.

Bauer, A. (1993), 'International cooperation over environmental goods', paper presented at the Oslo seminar on Environmental Economics', 15–17 September.

Bloch, F. (1994), 'Sequential formation of coalitions in games with externalities and fixed payoff division', presented at the CORE–FEEM Conference on Non-Cooperative Coalition Formation, Luvain, 27–28 February.

Bloch, F. (1997), 'Noncooperative models of coalition formation in games with spillovers', in C. Carraro and D. Siniscalco, *New Directions in the Economic Theory of the Environment*, Cambridge: Cambridge University Press.

Botteon, M. and C. Carraro (1997a), 'Burden-sharing and coalition stability in environmental negotiations with asymmetric countries', in C. Carraro (ed), *International Environmental Negotiations: Strategic Policy Issues*, Cheltenham, UK and Lyme, US: Edward Elgar.

Botteon, M. and C. Carraro (1997b), 'Strategies for environmental negotiations: issue linkage with heterogeneous countries', in H. Folmer and N. Hanley (eds), *Game Theory and the Global Environment*, Cheltenham, UK and Lyme, US: Edward Elgar.

Carraro, C. and D. Siniscalco (1992), 'Transfers and commitments in international environmental negotiations', forthcoming in K.G. Mäler (ed.), *International Environmental Problems: an Economic Perspective*, Dordrecht: Kluwer Academic Publishers.

Carraro, C. and D. Siniscalco (1993), 'Strategies for the international protection of the environment', *Journal of Public Economics*, **52**, 309–28.

Carraro, C. and D. Siniscalco (1995), 'Policy coordination for sustainability: commitments, transfers, and linked negotiations', in I. Goldin and A. Winters (eds), *The Economics of Sustainable Development*, Cambridge, UK: Cambridge University Press.

Carraro, C. and D. Siniscalco (1997), 'R&D cooperation and the stability of international environmental agreements', in C. Carraro (ed.), *International Environmental Negotiations: Strategic Policy Issues*, Cheltenham, UK and Lyme, US: Edward Elgar.

Carraro, C. and D. Siniscalco (1998), 'International environmental agreements: incentives and political economy', *European Economic Review*, **42**, 561–72.

Carraro, C. and A. Soubeyran (1999), 'R&D cooperation, innovation spillovers and firms' location in a model of environmental policy' in E. Petrakis, E. Sartzetakis and A. Xepapadeas (eds), *Environmental Regulation and Market Structure*, Cheltenham, UK and Northampton, MA, USA; Edward Elgar.

Cesar, H. and A. de Zeeuw (1994), 'Issue linkage in global environmental problems', in A. Xepapadeas (ed.) (1996), *Economic Policy for the Environment and Natural Resources*, Cheltenham, UK and Brookfield, US: Edward Elgar.

Chander, P. and H. Tulkens (1993), 'Strategically stable cost-sharing in an economic–ecological negotiations process', forthcoming in K.G. Mäler (ed.), *International Environmental Problems: an Economic Perspective*, Dordrecht: Kluwer Academic Publishers.

Chander, P. and H. Tulkens (1995), 'A core-theoretical solution for the design of cooperative agreements on trans-frontier pollution', *International Tax and Public Finance*, **2**, 279–94.

Chew, M.S. (1994), 'Farsighted coalitional stability', *Journal of Economic Theory*, **63**, 299–325.

Chillemi, O. (1997), 'International environmental agreements and asymmetric information', in C. Carraro (ed.), *International Environmental Negotiations: Strategic Policy Issues*, Cheltenham, UK and Lyme, US: Edward Elgar.

Compte, O. and P. Jehiel (1997), 'International negotiations and dispute resolution mechanisms: the case of environmental negotiations', in C. Carraro (ed.), *International Environmental Negotiations: Strategic Policy Issues*, Cheltenham, UK and Lyme, US: Edward Elgar.

D'Aspremont, C.A. and J.J. Gabszewicz (1986), 'On the stability of collusion', in G.F. Matthewson and J.E. Stiglitz (eds), *New Developments in the Analysis of Market Structure*, New York: Macmillan Press, pp. 243–64.

D'Aspremont, C.A., A. Jacquemin, J.J. Gabszewicz and J. Weymark (1983), 'On the stability of collusive price leadership', *Canadian Journal of Economics*, **16**, 17–25.

Donsimoni, M.P., N.S. Economides and H.M. Polemarchakis (1986), 'Stable cartels', *International Economic Review*, **27**, 317–27.

Echia, G. and M. Mariotti (1997), 'The stability of international environmental coalitions with farsighted countries: some theoretical observations', in C. Carraro (ed.), *International Environmental Negotiations: Strategic Policy Issues*, Cheltenham, UK and Lyme, US: Edward Elgar.

Fankhauser, S. and S. Kverndokk (1992), 'The global warming game: simulation of a CO_2 reduction agreement', GEC Working paper 92–10, CSERGE, University College of London.

Folmer, H., P. van Mouche and S. Ragland (1993), 'Interconnected games and international environmental problems', *Environmental Resource Economics*, 3, 313-35.
Hardin, G. (1968), 'The tragedy of the commons', *Science*, 162, 1243-8.
Hardin, G. and J. Baden (1977), *Managing the Commons*, New York: Freeman & Co.
Heal, G. (1994), 'The formation of environmental coalitions', in C. Carraro (ed.), *Trade, Innovation, Environment*, Dordrecht: Kluwer Academic Publishers.
Hoel, M. (1991), 'Global environmental problems: the effects of unilateral actions taken by one country', *Journal of Environmental Economics and Management*, 20, 1, 55-70.
Hoel, M. (1992), 'International environmental conventions: the case of uniform reductions of emissions', *Environmental and Resource Economics*, 2, 141-59.
Hoel, M. (1994), 'Efficient climate policy in the presence of free-riders', *Journal of Environmental Economics and Management*, 27, 259-74.
Katsoulacos, Y. (1997), 'R&D spillovers, R&D cooperation, innovation and international environmental agreements', in C. Carraro (ed.), *International Environmental Negotiations: Strategic Policy Issues*, Cheltenham, UK and Lyme, US: Edward Elgar.
Konishi, H ., M. Le Breton and S. Weber (1997), 'Stable coalition structures for the provision of public goods', in C. Carraro and D. Siniscalco (eds), *New Directions in the Economic Theory of the Environment*, Cambridge, UK: Cambridge University Press.
Kverndokk, S. (1993), 'Global CO_2 agreements: a cost-effective approach', *Economic Journal*, 14, 91-112.
Le Breton, M. and S. Weber (1993), 'Stability of coalition structures and the principle of optimal partitioning', mimeo, GREQE, Aix-Marseille.
Mäler, K.G. (1990), 'International environmental problems', *Oxford Review of Economic Policy*, 6, 80-108.
Ostrom, E. (1990), *Governing the Commons*, Cambridge, UK: Cambridge University Press.
Petrakis, E. and A. Xepapadeas (1996), 'Environmental consciousness and moral hazard in international agreements to protect the environment', *Journal of Public Economics*, 60, 95-110.
Ploeg, F. van der and A.J. de Zeeuw (1992), 'International aspects of pollution control', *Environmental and Resources Economics*, 3, 117-39.
Ray, D. and R. Vohra (1997), 'Equilibrium binding agreements', *Journal of Economic Theory*, 73, 30-78.
Yi, S.S. (1997), 'Stable coalition structures with externalities', *Games and Economic Behavior*, 20, 201-37.

32 Transboundary environmental problems
Michael Hoel

1. General description

We have a transboundary environmental problem whenever the environment in one country is directly affected by actions taken in one or more other countries. Notice that the term 'directly affected' excludes any indirect effects via prices, incomes, and so on, making actions in one country affect actions in other countries. Transboundary environmental problems have received large attention in the literature; early contributions include OECD (1976), d'Arge (1975).

Typical examples of transboundary environmental problems are: (i) several countries polluting a river, a lake or an ocean; (ii) acid rain caused by emissions of SO_2 and NO_x; (iii) global warning caused by emissions of CO_2 and other greenhouse gases; (iv) depletion of the ozone layer caused by emissions of CFCs and other ozone-depleting substances. In the next section, the examples of acid rain and global warming are treated in more detail.

In the examples above the environmental problem is caused by emissions of some physical substances from the countries involved. However, if 'environment' in each country is broadly defined, transboundary environmental problems may be of a non-physical kind. Perhaps the most obvious example is biodiversity (see, for example, Barrett, 1992). If a country is concerned about worldwide (or region-wide) loss of biodiversity, then any action in another country which contributes directly to this loss (for example, through deforestation) has a negative 'environmental' impact on the first country. Formally, this is very similar to the case in which one country is harmed by physical emissions from another country.

In the subsequent formalization I shall interpret variables as if it is physical emissions which are causing environmental damage. However, with suitable reinterpretations the analysis is also valid for non-physical environmental problems.

To formalize the analysis of transboundary environmental problems, consider n countries with emissions $(e_1, ..., e_n)$. For each country j there is an environmental variable z_j which depends on emissions from all the n countries. The variable z_j is defined so that an increase in z_j gives a deterioration of the environment in country j. For pollution of a river or a lake,

z_j would be a measure of the pollution in that part of the river or lake which country j is concerned about. For acid rain, z_j could measure the amount of sulphur and nitrogen deposited in country j. For global environmental problems such as climate change and ozone depletion, z_j could be a measure of the quality of the atmosphere. As will shortly be seen, all z_js will be equal for the latter case.

For simplicity I assume that the relationships between emissions and depositions are linear, that is,

$$z_j = \sum_i e_i a_{ij} \qquad (32.1)$$

where the element a_{ij} gives the amount of depositions in country j per unit emission in country i.

For many environmental problems, it is not the *flow* of depositions of the pollutant which matters for the environment, but the accumulated *stock*. When this is the case, one should specify the link between the z_js and the stocks of pollutants in each country. However, for the purpose of the present discussion the distinction between flows and stocks is not a major concern, I shall therefore stick to the simple specification in which the z_js measure the environmental quality in the countries.

Country j's welfare, u_j, depends positively on its own emissions, e_j (because it is costly to reduce emissions), and negatively on its environmental variable, z_j. In the subsequent discussion it is useful to allow for the possibility of money transfers between countries. I therefore denote I_j as the net transfer to country j. Naturally, country j is better off the higher I_j is (*ceteris paribus*). We thus have

$$u_j = u_j(\underset{+}{e_j}, \underset{-}{z_j}, \underset{+}{I_j}) \qquad (32.2)$$

This function is a relatively general measure of welfare. As shown more formally in Hoel (1991a), a function of the type shown in (32.2) is a relevant measure of welfare even if there are several domestic market failures, political preferences which include far more variables than the 'utility of a representative consumer', limitations on feasible policies, and so on.

In several studies one uses less general functions than (32.2). It is quite common to assume that each country's welfare is measured in money. This corresponds to the special case in which the u_j functions in (32.2) take the special form

$$u_j = I_j + R_j(e_j) - D(z_j) \qquad (32.3)$$

In (32.3), $I_j + R_j(e_j)$ is the income of country j, which is lower the lower this country's emissions, while $D(z_j)$ is a monetary measure of the environmental damage in country j, which is larger the larger z_j.

The general description (32.1)–(32.2) includes several special cases. Consider, for example, the pure unidirectional case in which a river runs through several countries which all pollute the river (for a recent discussion, see, for example, Rogers, 1997). Clearly, an upstream country cannot be polluted by a country which is further downstream. For the three-country case, this gives the following transportation matrix, when the countries are indexed so that their index is higher the further downstream the country is.

$$\mathbf{A} = \begin{bmatrix} a_{11} & a_{12} & a_{13} \\ 0 & a_{22} & a_{23} \\ 0 & 0 & a_{33} \end{bmatrix} \tag{32.4}$$

Climate change and depletion of the ozone layer are examples of environmental problems for which it is only the sum of emissions from all countries which matters for the environment. For this special case we thus have $a_{ij} = 1$ for all i,j, implying from (32.1) that

$$z_1 = \ldots = z_n = \sum_i e_i \tag{32.5}$$

Notice that even if the physical measure z_j of the environment is the same for all countries, the countries may differ in their evaluation of the environment, that is, the u_j functions may differ across countries.

2.   Two important examples of transboundary pollution

In this section, I shall discuss the problems of global warming and acid rain in more detail. Consider first the case of global warming. As mentioned above, it is only the sum of emissions which is of importance in this case. However, the relationship between emissions and the environmental variable z (equal for all countries) is slightly more complex than in (32.5). The environmental variable z is some measure of the global climate, and is non-indexed since the global climate is common to all countries. This variable changes gradually over time, depending (with quite a long time lag) on the development of the atmospheric concentrations of a large number of greenhouse gases (of which CO_2 is the most important). The development of each of these atmospheric concentrations in turn depends on the emissions of the greenhouse gas from all countries. Any applied analysis of the climate problem must start with a model of these two first steps, in order to obtain a specification of the connection between emissions ($\sum_i e_i$ for *all* greenhouse gases) and a description of the climate (z). There have been a number of analyses of this relationship; perhaps the best known are the IPCC studies (see Houghton et al., 1990, 1992, 1996 and Watson et al., 1996). Simpler versions of these scientific models are sometimes used as parts of economic models containing also the welfare functions (32.2) for all countries (or group of countries); see, for example, Nordhaus (1992) and Peck and Teisberg (1992).

In most applied economic models used for analysing the climate problem, it is assumed that the welfare functions of the countries are of the form (32.3). With this specification, a large number of studies have tried to give numerical estimations of the functions $R_j(e_j)$ (or abatement cost functions $R_j(e_j^0) - R_j(e_j)$, where e_j^0 represent 'business as usual emissions' for country j). Overviews of these studies are given by Cline (1992) and Bruce et al. (1996). There have also been a number of studies trying to estimate the environmental damage functions $D_j(z)$, although it is broadly agreed that the exact nature of this function is very uncertain (see Cline, 1992 and Bruce et al., 1996 for an overview). Notice that this latter uncertainty comes in addition to the scientific uncertainty regarding the relationship between emissions and the development of the climate.

Consider next the problem of acid rain. Acid rain is caused by the discharge of sulphur and nitrogen oxides into the air. The problem of acid rain is transboundary because these oxides remain in the air long enough to be transported across national boundaries. Unlike the climate problem, the transportation matrix A in the problem of acid raid for a particular region (for example Europe) does not have a specific and simple structure. Typically, all or most coefficients in the matrix differ, and are positive. Estimates of transportation matrix for Europe are given in, for example, the RAINS model (see Alcamo et al., 1990), and for subgroups of European countries by Tahvonen et al. (1993).

Also for the acid rain problem, it is the accumulation of pollution which is important, and not the flow; see, for example, Mäler (1991). However, in many studies of acid rain there is no specific explicit damage function of the type $D_j(z_j)$ in (32.3). Instead , studies such as Klaasen (1996) have specified critical levels which depositions should not exceed.

3. The non-cooperative equilibrium[1]

In the absence of any coordination between countries, it is usually assumed that each country chooses its own level of emissions so that its own welfare is maximized, taking emission levels of other countries (and transfers) as given. Formally, this Nash equilibrium is given by emission levels $e_1^*, ..., e_n^*$ such that

$$\frac{\partial u_j(e_j^*, z_j^*, I_j)}{\partial e_j} = -a_{jj} \frac{\partial u_j(e_j^*, z_j^*, I_j)}{\partial z_j} \qquad (32.6)$$

$$z_j^* = \sum_i e_i^* a_{ij}$$

holds for all j.

The Nash equilibrium (32.6) is illustrated in Figure 32.1 for the two-country case in which all $a_{ij} > 0$. In this figure, $_j IC'$ and $_j IC''$ are iso-welfare curves for country j, with IC'' representing a higher welfare level than IC'_j (since $\partial u_j / \partial z_j < 0$). $r_1(e_2)$ is country 1's response function, giving its optimal emission level for any given emission level of country 2. It will be downward sloping as in Figure 32.1 for a wide class of welfare functions u_1, including the special case (32.3) provided r_1 is strictly concave and D_1 is strictly convex. The interpretation of this is that an increase in emissions from country 2 will increase z_1, which will increase the marginal environmental cost in country 1, thus making it optimal to reduce emissions from country 1. Notice that this reason for a downward-sloping response function (discussed in more detail in, for example, Hoel, 1991b) is different from the reason often given for 'carbon leakage' for the climate problem. Carbon

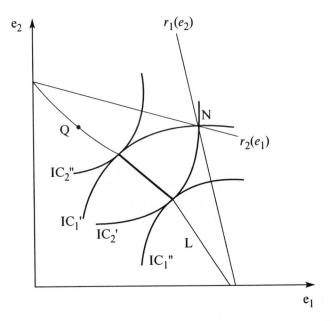

Figure 32.1   Nash equilibrium (point N) for the two-country case in which $\alpha_{ij} > 0$

leakage is discussed by, for example, Pezzey (1992), Bohm (1993), Golombek et al. (1995) and Hoel (1996), and is the result of changes in world market prices of energy and energy-intensive goods caused by one or several countries introducing a carbon tax or other policies to reduce the demand for fossil fuels in these countries.

The curve $r_2(e_1)$ in Figure 32.1 is country 2's response function. It will be downward sloping under corresponding assumptions as for country 1. The Nash equilibrium is given at point N in Figure 32.1.

4. Pareto optimality with and without side payments

It is clear from Figure 32.1 that N is not a Pareto-optimal point. Ignoring any side payments (that is, keeping $I_1 = I_2 = 0$), the Pareto-optimal points in Figure 32.1 are all points along the line L connecting the tangency points of iso-welfare curves. Among these Pareto-optimal points, all curves on the heavily drawn portion of L are Pareto-preferred (that is preferred by both countries) to the Nash equilibrium, N.

Formally, the Pareto-optimal emission levels follow from maximizing

$$W = \sum_k \alpha_k u_k \left(e_k, \sum_{i,} e_i \, a_{ik} \right) \tag{32.7}$$

with respect to all emission levels, taking all I_js as given (as long as side payments are ignored). The outcome, given by

$$\frac{\partial u_j}{\partial e_j} = -\sum_k a_{jk} \frac{\alpha_k}{\alpha_j} \frac{\partial u_k}{\partial z_k} \quad \text{for all } j \tag{32.8}$$

of course depends on the weights $(\alpha_1, \ldots, \alpha_n)$. The set of all Pareto outcomes is given by (32.8) for the set of non-negative α_is satisfying $\sum_i \alpha_i = 1$.

If side payments are permitted, the set of Pareto-optimal outcomes changes. In this case, (32.7) is maximized with respect to all emission levels and all transfer payments with the constraint that the transfers add up to zero. It is straightforward to see that this gives the following conditions:

$$\frac{\dfrac{\partial u_j}{\partial e_j}}{\dfrac{\partial u_j}{\partial I_j}} = -\sum_k a_{jk} \frac{\dfrac{\partial u_k}{\partial z_k}}{\dfrac{\partial u_k}{\partial I_k}} \quad \text{for all } j \tag{32.9}$$

The term on the left-hand side of (32.9) is the marginal cost of emission abatement, measured in terms of money. The fractions on the right-hand side of (32.9) are the marginal environmental costs, measured in terms of money. The interpretation of (32.9) is thus that the marginal abatement cost in country j should be equal to the sum of marginal environmental costs its emissions cause in all countries. The levels of emissions implied by (32.9) will in general depend on the I_js, which in turn will depend on the vector of α_is used in (32.7). For the special case in which the cross-derivatives between I_j on the one hand and e_j and z_j on the other hand are zero for all j, as is the case for (32.3), emission levels follow uniquely from (32.9). For most environmental problems, the effect from the level of transfer to the optimal emission levels is probably quite weak, so that a utility function of the type (32.3) is in most cases a good approximation.

For the case when the emissions following from (32.9) are independent of the I_js, the unique level of emissions is the point on the L curve in Figure 32.1 which maximizes W for all $\alpha_j = 1$. If the welfare functions are given by (32.3), the Pareto-optimal emission levels thus maximize $\Sigma_j \left[R_j(e_j) - D_j(e_j) \right]$, giving

$$R_j'(e_j) = \sum_k a_{jk} D_k'(z_k) \text{ for all } j \qquad (32.10)$$

which of course also follows from (32.9) when the u_js are given by (32.3). Notice that the Pareto-optimal point in this case may very well be given by a point such as Q in Figure 32.1. Without side payments, country 1 would be worse off under this equilibrium than it was under the Nash equilibrium. With side payments, however, any distribution of welfare between the countries is possible to achieve. In particular, a continuum of equilibria with welfare levels higher than under the Nash equilibrium are possible to achieve with suitable side payments.

Mäler's (1989) study of acid rain in Europe is an example of the case in which a unique Pareto-optimal point Q is worse for some countries than the Nash equilibrium (in the absence of side payments). Mäler's study includes 26 European countries, with linear transportation functions as in (32.1), and with utility functions of the type (32.3). The Pareto-optimal allocation of emissions is thus given by (32.10). Although the total gain to the countries is substantial, four of the countries are worse off than under the Nash equilibrium (in the absence of transfers).

It is also useful to consider the case of a pure unidirectional transboundary problem. Consider the two-country case, and assume that country 1 is the upstream country, that is, $a_{21} = 0$. Moreover, assume that the welfare functions are of the type (32.3). This case is illustrated in Figure 32.2. Country 2's iso-welfare curves and response function are the same as in Figure 32.1. However, for country 1, the iso-welfare curves are now vertical, forming a ridge at e_1^*. At this ridge $r_1'(e_1^*) = 0$, and the iso-welfare curve on the top of this ridge is also the response function of country 1. The Nash equilibrium is now given by N, and in the absence of side payments the

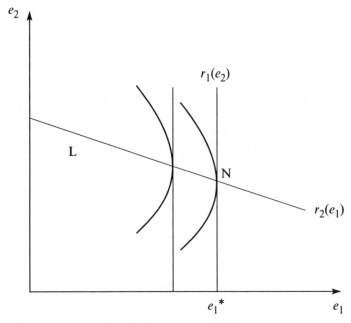

Figure 32.2   Nash equilibrium (point N) for the two-country case in which
$\alpha_{ij} = 0$

Pareto-optimal outcomes are on the line L. Notice in particular that for this case the Nash equilibrium is Pareto-optimal and that no other Pareto-optimal outcomes are Pareto-preferred to the Nash equilibrium. These properties of the Pareto-optimal outcomes are of course only valid when side payments are ignored. With side payments, the Pareto-optimal outcomes must satisfy (32.10), which gives a particular level of emissions somewhere on the L line to the left of N (since 32.10 implies that $r_1'(e_1) > 0$).

Consider next the special case in which the environment in each country depends only on the sum of emissions from all countries (such as the climate problem and the problem of ozone depletion). As mentioned previously, this special case corresponds to all a_{ij} being equal to one. When side payments are permitted, it thus follows from (32.9) that

$$\frac{\frac{\partial u_j}{\partial e_j}}{\frac{\partial u_j}{\partial I_j}} = -\sum_k \frac{\frac{\partial u_k}{\partial z_k}}{\frac{\partial u_k}{\partial I_k}} \text{ for all } j \quad (32.11)$$

or, for the utility function (32.3), it follows from (32.10) that

$$R_j'(e_j) = \sum_k D_k'(z_k) \text{ for all } j \qquad (32.12)$$

The important property of (32.11) and (32.12) is that the right-hand side is independent of j. This implies that the marginal abatement cost (in money terms) should be equalized across countries. This equalization of marginal abatement costs across countries is necessary and sufficient for cost-effectiveness for this type of environmental problem. Cost-effectiveness means that the environmental goals, whatever they are, are reached at as low costs as possible. When side payments are permitted, cost-effectiveness is obviously a necessary (but not sufficient) condition for Pareto optimality.[2] If side payments are ruled out, cost-effectiveness as defined above is not a particularly interesting concept, since total costs are of limited interest when there are restrictions on the distribution of the costs between countries.

Notice that is only for the special case of all $a_{ij} = 1$ that equalization of marginal abatement costs across countries is a necessary condition for Pareto optimality. Conditions for cost-effectiveness can also be derived for the more general transboundary problem (that is, for the a_{ij}s depending on i and j). As mentioned above, some studies specify critical levels which depositions should not exceed (see, for example, Klaasen, 1996). More precisely, in these studies one has specified limits of depositions for each country (that is, for all z_js), and calculated the Pareto optimum subject to these constraints. When side payments are permitted, this gives optimum conditions of the type (32.9) or (32.10), except that one gets shadow prices λ_k instead of marginal environmental costs D_k'. These shadow prices are non-negative, and for a country h we have $\lambda_h = 0$ if the constraint on deposition for country h is not binding. Given the constraints on emissions, these conditions give a specific allocation of sulphur emissions across countries.

5.   International cooperation

It is clear from the discussion above that without cooperation between countries, the outcome will generally not be Pareto-optimal. The only exception is the case of a unilateral transboundary environmental problem. In this case, the Nash equilibrium is Pareto-optimal, provided side payments are ruled out. It is, however, difficult to find good reasons for ruling out side payments. When side payments are allowed, there are always outcomes which are Pareto-preferred to the Nash equilibrium. This follows directly from (32.6) and (32.9): an emission vector $(e_1^*, ..., e_n^*)$ satisfying (32.6) cannot satisfy (32.9), whatever the transfer payments $(I_1, ..., I_n)$ are (that is, whatever the weights $(\alpha_1 ... \alpha_n)$ are), as long as $a_{ij} > 0$ for some $i \neq j$.

Even if there were only two countries, cooperation might be difficult to achieve. The reason is that there are several outcomes which are Pareto-optimal and Pareto-preferred to the Nash equilibrium. One of the problems of reaching an agreement between the countries is that it may be difficult to agree on which of these outcomes to implement. If the two countries were equal in all respects, it is likely that the countries would quickly agree upon a symmetric agreement, with equal emissions and no transfer payments. When countries differ, as they do in reality, it is likely to be more difficult to reach an agreement.

For most transboundary environmental problems, there are more than two countries involved. This is likely to increase the difficulties of reaching an agreement, due to the free-rider problem: if a country stays outside an agreement between all other countries, it can enjoy (almost) the same benefits of reduced emissions as if it participates in the agreement, while it doesn't bear any of the costs of reducing emissions. This free-rider incentive remains even if the agreement is such that all countries are better off with the agreement than without: a country may be better off participating in an agreement than it would be without any agreement. But it will usually be even better off if the other countries cooperate, while it itself stays outside the agreement and pursues its self-interest.

The issue of free-riding, and the possibility of creating stable coalitions, is discussed in more detail by Carraro in Chapter 31 of this volume.

6.   The design of an international agreement

Assume now that the difficulties of reaching an agreement between countries affected by a transboundary environmental problem have been 'solved', in the sense that some or all countries involved agree to cooperate. The next issue is how an international environmental agreement between these countries ought to be designed.

There are two main types of international environmental agreements for transboundary environmental problems. The first, and probably most common, focuses directly on emissions in each country. The second type of agreements focuses on environmental policies in each country. An obvious example of the second type would be an agreement which specified the emission tax rates to be used by each country.

An international agreement focusing directly on emissions from each country would have to specify emissions according to (32.11) in order to be Pareto-optimal. More or less arbitrary emission allocations, such as cutting back emissions by some uniform percentage rate in all countries (compared with a specified base year) would not be Pareto-optimal. Moreover, even if one succeeded in designing an agreement specifying emissions in accordance with (32.11), it would in many cases be necessary to supplement this agreement with a set of transfers in order to make all countries better off with the agreement than without (see the discussion above of Mäler's 1989 study on acid rain).

The Sulphur Protocols of several European countries are examples of international environmental agreements. The aim of these agreements has been to reduce acid rain cased by the emission of SO_2. The First Sulphur Protocol is from 1985, and was signed by 20 countries. This protocol was an example of a simple 'uniform percentage reduction' type: each country was required to reduce its annual emissions of SO_2 by 30 per cent as rapidly as possible, and no later than 1993, using 1980 as a base year. This protocol was followed up with the Second Sulphur Protocol in 1994, which was signed by 26 countries, and had a more sophisticated design than the First Protocol. In the Second Protocol, the required emission reductions differ between countries. A starting point for the emission reductions agreed upon is the cost-effective emissions, given specific limits on depositions in various regions; cf. the discussion at the end of Section 4. See Klaasen (1996, ch. 8) for a further discussion of the details of the Second Sulphur Protocol.

For the special case in which it is only the sum of emissions which matters for the environment in each country, there is a good case for allowing initial emission allocations to be tradable between countries. If this is allowed, and a competitive market for emission permits is established, cost-effectiveness is achieved no matter how emissions are initially allocated between countries. To see this, consider country j, which is allocated the right to emit an amount E_j. Assume that the market price of permits is q. Ignoring other transfers, I_j will be equal to country j's net revenue from selling excess permits, that is, $I_j = q(E_j - e_j)$ (which will be negative if country j emits more than its initial entitlement). Maximization of (32.2), given this expression for I_j and taking $z_j = \Sigma_i e_i$, E_j and q as given, gives

$$\frac{\dfrac{\partial u_j}{\partial e_j}}{\dfrac{\partial u_j}{\partial I_j}} = q \qquad (32.13)$$

Since this holds for all j, we thus get an equalization of marginal abatement costs across countries. If total emissions are suitably chosen, the equilibrium price q will be equal to the right-hand side of (32.11), so that we obtain Pareto optimality. Since we do so no matter how the initial emission entitlements are allocated, this allocation can be based entirely on distributional considerations.

The result above implies that, for example, for the climate problem, an international agreement based on some scheme of CO_2 emission permits which are tradable between countries has desirable properties. This result holds under quite general conditions, since the u_j functions are quite general; see the discussion after (32.2). However, an important assumption in the reasoning above is that all countries take the price of emission permits as given. If some countries have market power on the emission market, first-best optimality will not be obtained (see, for example, Hoel, 1997).[3] However, a numerical analysis by Westskog (1996) indicates that the loss resulting from some countries not being price-takers on the emission market may be quite small.

For a more general transboundary problem, that is, with the a_{ij}s depending on i and j, tradability of emission permits does not guarantee cost-effectiveness or Pareto optimality. On the contrary, equalization of marginal abatement costs is normally in conflict with Pareto optimality for this general case (see 32.9). Emission trading may also, however, have desirable effects for these more general types of transboundary problems. For instance, Klaasen (1996) and Klaasen et al. (1994) have shown that a system of emission trading may improve efficiency under an international agreement of reducing sulphur emissions in Europe. In these studies it is assumed that trading must take place at particular 'exchange rates' specified in the international agreement. To see how such emission trading works, assume that if country 1 trades with country 2, then country 2 must reduce its emissions by w_{12} for each unit that country 1 increases its emissions. If country 1 and 2 act jointly to minimize their abatement costs (that is, maximize $R_1(e_1) + R_2(e_2)$), given the constraint that $(e_2^0 - e_2) = w_{12}(e_1 - e_1^0)$, their emissions will satisfy

$$\frac{R_1'(e_1)}{R_2'(e_2)} = w_{12} \tag{32.14}$$

Comparing with (32.10), we see that the relative marginal abatement costs will be the same as they are in the first-best optimum if the exchange rate w_{12} is chosen so that

$$w_{12} = \frac{\sum_k a_{1k} D_k'(z_k)}{\sum_k a_{2k} D_k'(z_k)} \tag{32.15}$$

The problem with a scheme of trading with exchange rates of this type is that the correct exchange rates depend on the equilibrium values of the marginal environmental costs. Unless environmental costs are linear in the environmental variables z_j, that is, all D_js are constant, these equilibrium values will generally not be observable for the regulator. In particular, in the problem discussed in the end of Section 4 (minimizing total abatement costs given exogenous limits on the depositions in each country), the equilibrium shadow prices are not observable before trading has taken place.

As mentioned above, an alternative to agreements focusing directly on emissions is an agreement specifying the use of policy instruments, for example, emission taxes. For the general transboundary problem, an agreement, specifying equal taxes or equal use of any other policy instrument will usually not give a Pareto-optimal outcome. For the greenhouse gas problem, or other problems where it is only the sum of emissions from all countries that affects the environment, an emission tax which is equalized across countries makes more sense. Given that households and producers respond to the tax so that marginal abatement costs in equilibrium are equal to the emission tax rate, marginal abatement costs will be equalized across countries. There are, however, problems with this type of agreement. Consider, for example, a carbon tax which is equalized across countries. One problem is the associated distribution of cost between countries. Even if *marginal* costs are equalized across countries, *total* costs of reducing emissions will generally differ between countries. An analysis by Kverndokk (1993) suggests that the cost as a percentage of GDP differs sharply between countries when CO_2 emissions are allocated in a cost-efficient manner. Moreover, Kverndokk's analysis suggests that it is the richest countries in the world which would have the smallest total costs of reducing emissions (relative to GDP). An international climate agreement with such distributional properties will be unacceptable to a large group of countries, and will therefore in practice be infeasible unless it is supplemented with some kind of transfer payments between countries.

Another problem associated with harmonizing carbon taxes is related to the free-rider issue. The free-rider incentive implies that it is in each country's interest to have little or no restrictions on its own CO_2 emissions, given the emissions from other countries, or given the policies of other countries. If a country is required to have a specific carbon tax through an international agreement, it is therefore in the interest of that country to try to render this tax as ineffective as possible. As argued in, for example, Hoel (1992), there are several ways in which a country can reduce the effect of an imposed carbon tax on the country's consumption and production pattern, and thereby reduce the cost for the country, even though it is in a formal sense adhering to the international agreement to tax CO_2 emissions. To eliminate evasions of this type, the agreement would have to be more complex than simply specifying a uniform carbon tax to be used by all countries. Even if one restricted oneself to existing fossil fuel taxes in the narrow sense, it would be difficult to specify exactly what each country can and cannot do with these domestic taxes. Expanding an agreement to include more or less detailed instructions on how each country can use other policy instruments which strongly affect CO_2 emissions would make the agreement very complicated. Moreover, it seems likely that most countries would consider detailed specifications and restrictions on their use of various domestic policy instruments over time an unacceptable restriction on their sovereignty.

7. Transboundary environmental problems and international trade

There are at least two important ways in which international trade interacts with transboundary environmental problems. The first is related to the free-rider issue: the threat of trade sanctions may make it less tempting for a country to be a free-rider. The problem with using this kind of threat to deter free-riding is that trade sanctions may also hurt the countries imposing them, that is, the countries which participate in the international environment agreement. A threat of trade sanctions may therefore not be credible. This issue is discussed further by Barrett (1994), who shows that within the context of imperfect competition a perfect equilibrium may exist with all countries participating in an international agreement, and with the threat of trade sanctions against defectors supporting the equilibrium.

In many cases it will not be possible to achieve cooperation between all countries that contribute to the transboundary environmental problem. A subset of all of the countries may nevertheless cooperate to increase the welfare of this smaller group of countries. In such a situation, the cooperating countries are affected by the emissions in the non-cooperating countries. These emissions may depend on international prices, which in turn may depend on policies in the cooperating countries. The cooperating countries may thus have an indirect way to affect emissions in the non-cooperating countries. The first-best policy of the cooperating countries is to have the same environmental policy as would be optimal for the case in which all countries cooperated, and supplement this with tariffs (positive or negative) on trade flows between the group of cooperating countries and the non-cooperative countries (see, for example, Hoel, 1996). An obvious candidate for this policy in respect of the greenhouse gas problem would be for the group of cooperating countries to have a positive tariff on the group's imports of goods from the non-cooperating countries which are relatively fossil-fuel-intensive in their production. Such a tariff contributes to discouraging the production of such goods in the non-cooperating countries, and thus gives lower CO_2 emissions from these countries than there would have been without such a tariff.

If tariffs for some reason are ruled out, the best environmental policy for the cooperating countries will typically differ from what would be optimal if countries cooperated. This is analysed in detail by Golombek et al. (1995) and Hoel (1996) for the greenhouse gas problem, where it is shown that the second-best (that is, restricting the use of tariffs) optimal policy implies a carbon tax which is differentiated both across fuels and across different users.

Notice the tariffs of the type above are optimal even if the partition of countries in a cooperating and a non-cooperating group is given. Trade sanctions of this type are therefore credible threats, and may thus have the additional advantage of making it less tempting for countries to be free-riders.

Notes

1. The analysis in this section is closely related to the analysis by Markusen (1975).
2. Cost-effectiveness means that all R'_js are equal. This common value of R'_j must equal the right-hand side of (32.12) in order to have full Pareto optimality.
3. Some countries may also have market power on markets for energy or energy-intensive products. This may remove the outcome even further away from the first-best optimum. A general discussion of tradable emission permits in the presence of market power is given by Koutstaal in Chapter 18 of this volume.

References

Alcamo, J., L. Hordijk and R. Shaw (1990), *The RAINS Model of Acidification: Science and Strategies in Europe*, Dordrecht: Kluwer.

Barrett, S. (1992), 'Some economics of the convention on biological diversity', CSERGE GEC Working Paper GEC 92–33.

Barrett, S. (1994), 'Trade restrictions in international environmental agreements', mimeo, London Business School.

Bohm, P. (1993), 'Incomplete international cooperation to reduce CO_2 emissions: alternative policies', *Journal of Environmental Economics and Management*, **24**, 258–71.

Bruce, J.P., H. Lee and E.F. Haites (eds) (1996), *Climate Change 1995 – Economic and Social Dimensions of Climate Change, Contribution of Working Group III to the Second Assessment Report of the IPCC*, Cambridge, UK: Cambridge University Press.

Cline, W. (1992), *The Economics of Global Warming*, Washington, DC: Institute for International Economics.

D'Arge, R.C. (1975), 'On the economics of transnational environmental externalities', in E. Mills (ed.), *Economic Analysis of Environmental Problems*, New York: Columbia University Press, pp. 397–434.

Golombek, R., C. Hagem and M. Hoel (1995), 'Efficient incomplete international climate agreements', *Resource and Energy Economics*, **17**, 25–46.

Hoel, M. (1991a), 'Principles for international climate cooperation', in T. Hanisch (ed.), *A Comprehensive Approach to Climate Change*, Oslo: CICERO.

Hoel, M. (1991b), 'Global environmental problems: the effects of unilateral actions taken by one country', *Journal of Environmental Economics and Management*, **20**, 55–70.

Hoel, M. (1992), 'Carbon taxes: an international tax or harmonized domestic taxes?', *European Economic Review*, **36**, 400–406.

Hoel, M. (1996), 'Should a carbon tax be differentiated across sectors?', *Journal of Public Economics*, **59**, 17–32.

Hoel, M. (1997), 'CO_2 and the greenhouse effect: a game-theoretical exploration', in P. Dasgupta and K.G. Mäler (eds), *The Environment and Emerging Development Issues*, Vol. 2, Oxford: Clarendon Press.

Houghton, J.T., G.J. Jenkins and J.J. Ephraums (eds) (1990), *Climate Change, The IPCC Scientific Assessment*, Cambridge, UK: Cambridge University Press.

Houghton, J.T., B.A. Callander and S.K. Varney (eds) (1992), *Climate Change 1992, The*

Supplementary Report to the IPCC Scientific Assessment, Cambridge, UK: Cambridge University Press.

Houghton, J.T., L.G. Meiro Filho, B.A. Callander, N. Harris, A. Kattenberg and K. Maskell (eds) (1996), *Climate Change 1995 – The Science of Climate Change, Contribution of Working Group I to the Second Assessment Report of the IPCC*, Cambridge, UK: Cambridge University Press.

Klaassen, G. (1996), *Acid Rain and Environmental Degradation. The Economics of Emission Trading*, Cheltenham, UK and Brookfield, US: Edward Elgar.

Klaassen, G., F. Førsund and M. Amann (1994), 'Emission trading in Europe with an exchange rate', *Environmental and Resource Economics*, **4** (4), 305–30.

Kverndokk, S. (1993), 'Global CO_2 agreements: a cost-effective approach', *The Energy Journal*, **14** (2), 91–112.

Markusen, J.R. (1975), 'Cooperative control of international pollution and common property resources', *Quarterly Journal of Economics*, **89**, 618–32.

Mäler, K.G. (1989), 'The acid rain game', in H. Folmer and E. van Ierland (eds), *Valuation Methods and Policy Making in Environmental Economics*, Amsterdam: Elsevier.

Mäler, K.G. (1991), 'Critical loads and international environmental cooperation', in P. Rüdiger (ed.), *Conflicts and Cooperation in Managing Environmental Resources*, Berlin /Heidelberg: Springer-Verlag.

Nordhaus, W. (1992), 'The "DICE" model: background and structure of a dynamic integrated climate model of the economics of global warming', Yale University, New Haven, mimeo.

OECD (1976), *Economics of Transfrontier Pollution*, Paris: OECD.

Peck, S.C. and T.J. Teisberg (1992), 'CETA: a model for carbon emissions trajectory assessment', *The Energy Journal*, **13**, 55–77.

Pezzey, J. (1992), 'Analysis of unilateral CO_2 control in the European Community', *The Energy Journal*, **13**, 159–72.

Rogers, P. (1997), 'International river basins: pervasive unidirectional externalities', in P. Dasgupta, K.G. Mäler and A. Vercelli (eds), *The Economics of Transnational Commons*, Oxford: Clarendon Press.

Tahvonen, O., V. Kaitala and M. Pohjola (1993), 'A Finnish–Soviet acid rain game: noncooperative equilibria, cost efficiency, and sulphur agreements', *Journal of Environmental and Resource Economics*, **24**, 87–100.

Watson, R.T., M.C. Zinyowera and R.H. Moss (eds) (1996), *Climate Change 1995 – Impacts, Adaptions and Mitigation of Climate Change, Contribution of Working Group II to the Second Assessment Report of the IPCC*, Cambridge, UK: Cambridge University Press.

Westskog, H. (1996), 'Market power in a system of tradeable CO_2 quotas', *The Energy Journal*, **17**, 85–103.

33 Economic analysis of global environmental issues: global warming, stratospheric ozone and biodiversity

David Pearce

1. Earth economy and environment

Earth as an entire ecosystem operates so as to sustain life in all its forms. How far human activity in the form of homogenized use of natural resources can impair those major functions is open to debate. It seems barely conceivable that just one species, albeit a dominant one at the top of the food chain, could bring about the very demise of such global ecological functions as temperature regulation and nutrient cycling (both with enormous implications for biomass productivity). Yet the past decades have witnessed events which some feel contain just such threats, in various degrees of uncertainty. Stratospheric ozone depletion, climate change, the loss of coastal ecosystems, deforestation, and the impairment of the oceans themselves, testify to the potential for mankind's interference with such global biogeochemical cycles. On one interpretation of the Gaia hypothesis, humans will eliminate themselves before they eliminate the earth's self-regulating and self-repairing functions: Gaia as an integrated life and environment system is pretty well immortal (Joseph, 1990). On another interpretation, they stand at least a good chance of taking many, but far from all, of those functions with them to their demise (Lovelock, 1979, 1987). Even as a basic hypothesis, Gaia is disputed and likely to remain so. But it provokes not just fresh looks at the science, but at the economics of global environmental issues as well.

Human activity and the ecological context for the successful functioning of that activity are interrelated and mutually dependent. Where there are environmental problems, their cause may, often as not, be found in the workings (or the misworkings) of the economic system. The reverse interaction is more complex: when economic systems fail, environmental factors may be at work. The link from 'economic failure' to environmental problem is now well established. The second link, from environmental degradation to unsuccessful economic performance, is only now emerging in the literature on sustainable development. Given these general economy–environment linkages, it should hardly be surprising that they extend to the global economy and the global environment. Four main features of global issues can be discerned.

First, a great many externalities spill over from one country to another, even from one world region to another. Examples include the long-range transport of acidic pollutants in Europe, North America and the Far East, and the transmission of waste and pollutants through international watercourses such as the Rhine and the Nile. These 'transboundary externalities' are addressed in the previous chapter by Hoel (Chapter 32).

Second, economic systems are intricately interlinked through trade and financial flows: the phenomenon of 'globalization'. This means that international trade becomes a medium for the transmission of externalities, although the extent to which restrictions on trade should be seen as part of the solution to such problems is questionable. Examples include the welfare losses in importing countries due to contamination of exported goods and, more importantly, welfare losses arising from concerns about production processes used to generate exports, for example, unsustainable timber logging and indiscriminate fishing technology (see Pearce, 1995 and various chapters in Part II of this volume).

Third, economic systems tend to be entropic as they evolve. They become entropic because the production processes themselves use more and more materials in more and more dissipative ways. Obvious examples include lead in gasoline or the many different but bonded materials in a modern-day motor vehicle. An entropic activity in country 1 therefore tends to be mirrored by the same activity in country 2: production processes become globalized in the sense that uniform processes are used. Thus country 1 adopts high-yielding wheat varieties and country 2 does the same. Production processes are homogenized because the high-yielding varieties require the same inputs – artificial fertilizers, pesticides, uniform genetic varieties. These processes themselves contribute to entropy because of the fact that, once used, the inputs dissipate into the environment. Increasing *process homogenization* therefore characterizes global economic systems. Such homogenization places sustainability at severe risk: shocks or stresses on economic systems have the capacity to deplete large proportions of output, rather than being limited to a few activities among a diverse portfolio of activities (Swanson, 1994). Clear examples exist with the increasing output variability of crops through time. This variability shows up as increasing coefficients of variation through time as output expands, and one factor in this increasing variability is the homogeneous production processes which place crops at higher risk from pests or weather events. As is well known, wider portfolios limit the susceptibility of output to damage from such events.

Finally, and linked to process homogenization and the loss of diversity, global life support functions have come under threat because of the aggregate effects of modern technology and economic activity.

2.   The economic characteristics of global problems

The owner of a property has an incentive to look after and care for that property. If the property is neglected, it will fail to yield a continued flow of services (or 'rents') and may ultimately not sustain the owner's lifestyle, or even the owner's very existence. One of the features of global environmental problems is that they occur in contexts where there are no owners, or where there are owners who have only limited rights to the property in question. Lack of ownership, or 'property rights', gives rise to neglect and over-use. Because the atmosphere belongs to no one (at least until recently), it is treated as a free resource and hence one for which no one individual or nation has responsibility. Free resources tend to be abused. Thus the atmosphere has become a dumping ground for the waste gases of fossil fuel combustion and for other gases – the 'greenhouse gases'. The same is true of the stratosphere – it too became the dumping ground for chlorofluorocarbons (CFCs), just as the oceans are also dumping grounds for ship waste, oil pollution, nuclear waste, sewage sludge and other waste. Much of the recent development of international environmental agreements can be seen as an effort to confer property rights on these resources, to make them owned by someone rather than leaving them as owned by no one.

A useful distinction is between 'open access' and 'common property' resources, the terms referring to the way the resources are managed (or not managed). Garret Hardin's famous essay 'The tragedy of the Commons' (Hardin, 1968) did much to confuse the two. An open-access resource has no owner. A common property resource does have an owner: it may be a local community or a community of nations. The distinction is crucial because, while common property does have some inbuilt risks of overexploitation, it is often a perfectly viable and sustainable form of resource management. This is because the common owners mutually agree to limit use of the resource. Under open access, there is no such agreement on limiting use. Common property regimes also tend to have defined management groups, individuals or institutions with a special responsibility for caring for the resource. Hardin's 'tragedy' is really the tragedy of open access. The risks of overexploitation are very much less with common property (Bromley, 1991; Berkes 1989).

A third property regime is private property. If common property is confused with open access it is easy to jump to a false conclusion, namely that private property is the only solution to environmental problems. And there are many who believe that, perhaps because they have confused communal management with no management at all. Private property will often be a good solution, but often it will not be. The reason is that the single owner has no incentive to take account of the costs that his activities impose on other private owners – he has no incentive to account for the externality. Under common property, however, the externality generated by A is suffered by B who is a member of the same community. The managers of common property then invoke the mutual rules of behaviour governing the common property. The externality is 'internalized' within the community. 'Conferring property rights' is widely advocated as a prerequisite for managing environmental problems. Communal management tends to be fairer and may avoid the externalities, but it also has some risks in the face of forces such as rapid population growth. Indeed, many communal management schemes have broken down precisely because rapid population growth has led to repeated subdivision of the asset. Finally, assets may be taken under state control – nationalization. While nominally internalizing the externality issue by common ownership, nationalization invariably worsens the situation since governments and government agencies often do not have maximization of community welfare as their objective. Bureaucracies emerge with their own goals, including the maximization of the extent of the bureaucracy. Even where governments may seek to maximize community well-being, they often lack the monitoring and enforcement mechanisms to be successful.

The 'global commons' – the atmosphere, oceans outside of territorial waters, the stratosphere – should therefore be better classified as the global open-access resources. When nations come together to agree on limits to the abuse of these resources they are effectively turning those open-access resources into global common property resources. And they also establish a global management regime by setting up monitoring and sanctioning devices. These might range from specific threats – trade sanctions, perhaps – against those who seek not to fulfil their obligations under the agreement (as is the case with the Montreal Protocol which regulates the production and consumption of chlorofluorocarbons), or they may be less well defined. Nations experience regular occasions on which they need to speak to other nations and secure favours. Breaking one agreement may therefore mean that they are denied what they want in some future agreement. In other words, no international agreement can be seen in isolation. It is always part of a wider set of bargains and deals, 'repeated games' that act as sanctions against breaking a single agreement (see Chapter 31 by Carraro).

Global resources have other important features apart from the way they tend to be managed. The nature of global resources also matters, for they tend to have the characteristics of *public goods*. A public good may be contrasted with a private good. A private good is a good such that, if A buys it, B cannot buy the same unit of the good. A and B are said to be 'rivals' in the market-place. One of the features of a public good, however, is that A's consumption of the good does not diminish B's consumption of the same good. It is said to be 'non-rival'. Clean air is a public good because the benefit A gets from breathing clean air does not diminish the benefit B gets as well. Many global resources have this 'non-rival' feature: the ozone layer protects A against ultraviolet radiation as well B. Global warming control also has the features of a public good but with some qualifications. If global warming is likely to lead to major disruptions in, say, ocean currents, then the whole world is likely to suffer the disruptive effects. If, on the other hand, global warming results in shifts in crop productivity and local climate, some may actually gain while others lose (Parry, 1990). Global warming control is then an ambiguous good in that it will have public good characteristics for some groups and public 'bad' characteristics for others. Controlling ozone layer depletion, on the other hand, tends to benefit everyone since effects on skin cancers and cataracts appear to be ubiquitous, and potential impacts on ocean biomass could threaten food supplies in many areas. The ozone layer is closer to a 'pure' public good.

There is a second feature of public goods and bads. With private goods it is usually possible to devise a mechanism whereby others can be excluded from their benefits. Price is a common exclusion mechanism. With a public good, however, exclusion is difficult and may be impossible. Accordingly, it may be difficult to prevent people enjoying the benefits of reduced global warming without paying – the so-called 'free-riders'. Of course, we could argue that those who are responsible for the pollution should be the ones who pay for its control. Rather than have an agreement based on the 'beneficiary pays' principle, the agreement should be based on the 'polluter pays' principle. This is exactly how the Rio Framework Convention on Climate Change was formulated: rich countries contribute most of the greenhouse gas control. The fact that many other nations benefit from the control explains why they are party to the agreement but why they do not bear any of the burden of cost. This issue of responsibility makes the analysis of global public goods more complex than the usual public good analysis.

Why does the private/public good distinction matter in the context of global environmental issues?

First, given the public-good characteristics of global environments, no individual nation has an incentive to 'go it alone' to correct the over-use of a global resource exhibiting public-good characteristics, even if that country is a 'big player' in terms of its contribution to the global problem in question. The reason for this lies in the 'free-rider' phenomenon: others will reap the benefit but will not bear the cost. This explains why it is necessary to have an international agreement and why special incentives have to be designed.

Second, if the problem lies with the open access nature of the resource, then what has to be done is to confer property rights through either 'privatization' – turning the public good into a private good in the way that beaches or game parks might be converted (single ownership) – or through communal management. Single ownership of the atmosphere or stratosphere has no obvious meaning, so that global communal management of the atmosphere and the stratosphere becomes the solution. This is how the issue has been approached under the Montreal Protocol (concerning the ozone layer) and the Framework Convention on Climate Change (concerning global warming). Biological diversity is somewhat more complex and is discussed below.

Third, communal management can be, and often is, extremely effective. While there may be a 'tragedy of open access', there need be no 'tragedy of the commons'. But there are risks with communal management. Unless the sanctions for breaking the communal agreement are strong, the incentive remains for any one individual to break the agreement. This is why the analysis of international agreements is so important. The Rio agreements on climate and biodiversity are particularly complex in this respect.

3. Biological diversity
How does biological diversity fit into this picture? It can be questioned whether biological diversity – the diversity of living things – is a public good. In many respects it is. For example, without it, it would not be possible to cross-breed plants to ensure their resistance to diseases. Repeated cross-breeding between cultivated and wild species, for example, is the way that crop breeders 'race against time' to overcome the emergence of new threats to crops as their resistance to disease is weakened. Genetic diversity, then, is rather like information and it is very difficult to exclude others from the benefits of information. On the other hand, diversity resides in biological resources, and the richest sources of those resources are confined to certain areas of the world, especially the tropical forests. This means that individual countries can try to 'own' the information value of the biodiversity. This is essentially what securing 'intellectual property rights' means. In the Convention on Biological Diversity, much is made of the need for the rich countries to pay the poor countries for the diversity in the resources they extract and which may then be processed into valuable products such as medicinal drugs. Here we have an example of a resource with public-good characteristics that begins as an open access resource but which becomes the subject of property rights regimes.

Biodiversity is a public good in a much grander sense, however. For many ecologists argue that it is the very basis of life on earth. Without biodiversity we would not have ecological processes that process wastes, recycle

494   *International aspects*

nutrients and regulate the environments in which we all live. By reducing diversity the argument is that we expose everyone – the entire global population – to increasing risks of some form of 'collapse'. That collapse need not be the end of life itself. Collapses could (and do) take the form of greater risks of disease, fewer amenities to enjoy (for example, disappearing coral reefs) and so on. Again, the Gaian debate is partly characterized by the disputes between those who see biodiversity as essential to ecological stability and hence to sustainability, and those who see no particular links between complexity and stability (Joseph, 1990).

But a considerable part of the benefits of the conservation of biodiversity accrue not to the world as a whole, but to the individual nations in which those resources reside. Countries with diverse species, for example, can usually gain from eco-tourism and from sales of diverse products. In effect, biodiversity becomes a 'mixed good', yielding benefits that have many of the characteristics of a private good, and other benefits that accrue as public goods.

A major problem arising from assessments of the benefits of biodiversity lies in the fact that many of those benefits are non-realizable in the absence of created markets. Thus, unless there are mechanisms whereby richer countries can not only reveal their willingness to pay to conserve biodiversity in poorer countries, but also translate those stated preference into actual resource flows, biodiversity is unlikely to be conserved. Newly created markets have begun to emerge, such as debt-for-nature swaps, and some markets have existed for some time but in incomplete form, as with royalty payments for plant and other genetic material. The necessity of 'capturing' these values is underlined in the context of land-based biodiversity, in contrast to marine-based biodiversity where solutions lie in resolving open access and failed common property arrangements. For in the land-based case, the 'base resource', land itself, has an alternative use. This may be contrasted with the oceans, where alternative uses are few, so that the ocean itself has a low or even zero opportunity costs. The fact that land can be used to support biodiversity or agriculture and other developments means that conservation has to 'do better' than the rate of return to the developmental use of the land. Whilst many conservation campaigns have focused on illegal trade in biodiversity (rhinoceros horn, elephant ivory and so on), they have typically failed to understand the need to demonstrate and capture the full range of biodiversity values in order to compete with the opportunity cost of conservation on land (Swanson, 1994).

4. The economic value of global environmental assets

Part VIII of this volume deals with the economic approach to assessing the value of environmental assets. Applications of these techniques to global issues have been fairly limited. This section briefly surveys the results.

Global warming control
Global warming can give rise to costs and benefits. Typical examples of costs include flooding of land from sea-level rise, potential crop losses, and changed incidence of disease, for example, malaria spreading into newly warm areas. Benefits tend to include increased amenity, that is, people tend to value a warmer climate. Table 33.1 summarizes some damage estimates. These estimates are based on the limited information available from impact models, for example, the link between temperature change and crop output, and between sea-level rise and land inundation. Monetary values are

Table 33.1   *Monetary $2 \times CO_2$ damage in different world regions*

	Fankhauser (1995)		Tol (1995)	
	$bn	%GDP[1]	$bn	%GDP[1]
European Union	63.6	1.4		
United States	61.0	1.3		
Other OECD	55.9	1.4		
OECD America			74.2	1.5
OECD Europe			56.5	1.3
OECD Pacific			59.0	2.8
Total OECD	*180.5*	*1.3*	*189.5*	*1.6*
E. Europe/Former USSR	18.2[2]	0.7[2]	−7.9	−0.3
Centrally planned Asia	16.7[3]	4.7[3]	18.0	5.2
South and South East Asia			53.5	8.6
Africa			30.3	8.7
Latin America			31.0	4.3
Middle East			1.3	4.1
Total non-OECD	*89.1*	*1.6*	*126.2*	*2.7*
World	*269.6*	*1.4*	*315.7*	*1.9*

Notes:
[1]Note that the GDP base may differ between the studies.
[2]Former Soviet Union only.
[3]China only.

Sources: as shown.

assigned either from market data (as with crop prices) or by assuming that some impacts will be mitigated through expenditures on flood control. Health impacts are translated into premature mortality which is then monetized through conventional values for the willingness to pay to reduce risk (the so-called 'value of statistical life'). The largest uncertainty relates to non-market impacts, particularly to biological diversity change. It is important to understand that the estimates relate to a doubling of CO_2 concentrations ('2 × CO_2 equivalent warming'), that is, they are point estimates of future damage, expressed in present-value terms, for the period in which this doubling is likely to occur, say 2040 or 2050. Warming will not stop at this point since concentrations will continue to increase in the absence of strong control measures.

In the developed world losses from CO_2 doubling lie in the range 1–2 per cent of GDP. Regional differences can be substantial. For the former Soviet Union damage could be as low as 0.7 per cent of GNP or even negative (that is, climate change is beneficial). The negative figure estimated by Tol (1995) mainly stems from large beneficial impacts in the agricultural sector. In the Fankhauser study (1995), on the other hand, possible beneficial yield impacts are more than offset by the adverse impact of increased world prices on food imports. The region will also suffer from particularly high health and air pollution costs. The extremely high estimates for the Asian regions and Africa, on the other hand, are predominantly due to the severe life/morbidity impacts. Of course, significant uncertainty attaches to all the estimates. Damage is also likely to be more severe in developing countries. Table 33.1 reports damages in non-OECD countries of about 1.6–2.7 per cent of GDP, some 50 per cent higher than the OECD average. The main causes for this high estimate are health impacts and the high proportion of natural habitats and wetlands found in developing countries. Although the data for the non-OECD estimates are significantly weaker, they provide a clear indication that global warming will have its worst impacts in the developing world, with a damage of probably at least 2 per cent of GNP for 2 × CO_2. In addition, damage from extreme events, such as reversal of ocean currents, is excluded from the damage studies.

Total damage can be related back to the damage done by one tonne of greenhouse gases emitted now and cumulating in the atmosphere over time. Table 33.2 summarizes the available estimates. The most sophisticated of these estimates are those by Fankhauser, who suggests a damage estimate of around $20 per tonne of carbon. This allows for much of the uncertainty of estimates, but not for all of it. 'Surprises' could add significantly to such average damage estimates.

The benefits of greenhouse gas abatement will not be limited to reduced climate change costs alone, but are likely to spill over to other sectors. This

Table 33.2   *The social costs of CO_2 emissions (current value (1990)$/tC)*

Study	Type	1991–2000	2001–2010	2011–2020	2021–2030
Nordhaus (1991)	MC		7.3 (0.3–65.9)		
Ayres and Walter (1991)	MC		30–35		
Nordhaus (1994)	CBA				
– certainty/ best guess		5.3	6.8	8.6	10.0
– uncertainty/ expected value		12.0	18.0	26.5	n.a.
Cline (1992)	CBA	5.8–124	7.6–154	9.8–186	11.8–221
Peck and Teisberg (1992)	CBA	10–12	12–14	14–18	18–22
Fankhauser (1995)	MC	20.3 (6.2–45.2)	22.8 (7.4–52.9)	25.3 (8.3–58.4)	27.8 (9.2–64.2)
Maddison (1994)	CBA/MC	5.9–6.1	8.1–8.4	11.1–11.5	14.7–15.2

Notes:
MC = marginal social cost study.
CBA = shadow value in a cost–benefit study.
Figures in parentheses denote 90 per cent confidence intervals.

Sources: as indicated.

is why greenhouse damage is different from the benefits of greenhouse gas abatement. For example, efforts to halt deforestation in order to reduce the emission of CO_2 will contribute to the conservation of the world's biological diversity. Other ancillary benefits could occur in the form of local and regional air quality improvements, a reduction in traffic-related externalities like accidents or congestion, and the reduced risk of tanker accidents and oil spills. These problems are tied to global warming in that they are caused by largely the same activities, in particular the consumption of fossil fuels. Because no economic CO_2 removal technologies currently exist, attempts to limit CO_2 emissions will by and large concentrate on reducing the use of fossil fuels. A reduction in CO_2 emissions will therefore also reduce other environmental problems related to fuel combustion. These effects are called the *secondary benefits* of carbon abatement.

The secondary benefits from air quality improvements may be quite large. Various studies suggest that they vary widely, from about $2 per tonne of carbon abated to over $500/tC. In absolute terms secondary benefits offset about 30–50 per cent of the initial abatement costs in the case of Norway (Alfsen et al., 1993) and over 100 per cent in the UK (Barker, 1993).

Explicit attempts to measure the direct *benefits* of global warming have been made. Leary (1994) reports on various studies which show how climate influences migration, wages and property values. He concludes that climate definitely influences all three variables (migration is higher, wages are lower and property prices are higher the 'better' the climate). This is because workers trade off climate against lower wages, being prepared to move to areas with better climates even though wages are correspondingly lower. House prices also tend to internalize the benefits of a better climate. But Leary suggests that the precise quantitative relationship is not known. Enough is known, however, to suggest that the amenity value of climate is high, offsetting, to some extent, the damage estimates in Tables 33.1 and 33.2.

How do the benefits and costs of climate change control compare? The report of Working Group III of the Intergovernmental Panel on Climate Change (1996) offers some clues, although they are scattered among a welter of confusing chapters and statements. One way to determine the requisite action is to compare *marginal* benefits and costs. IPCC (1996) gives estimates of marginal *damages* ranging from $5–125/tC. Suppose a fairly low figure of $20/tC is taken as the estimate, consistent with the Fankhauser (1995) estimate above. This is still not the marginal *benefit* of control. To get benefits we need to add the 'secondary' benefits of carbon control, and these come to perhaps another $20/tC, taking a low figure from the ranges reported in Chapter 6 of IPCC (1996), producing a fairly conservative $40/tC of benefits from preventing the emission of one tonne of carbon.

Chapter 9 of IPCC (1996) reports that there are many investments that can be made in fuel switching and energy conservation a long way below $40/tC, and many below $20/tC. This suggests that climate change control has a strong economic justification quite independently of the other arguments that might be marshalled in its favour, for example, 'equity' arguments relating to the dominance of the rich countries as the main emitters of greenhouse gases and to the relatively higher suffering of the poor countries from the damages arising from global warming.

Not all analyses of global warming suggest action now. There is a school of thought that stresses the role of deferring decisions until better information is available. The emphasis in this model is on the research that is needed to improve information and, hence, the probabilities to be attached to what are initially highly uncertain outcomes. In short, information itself may have high economic value (Manne and Richels, 1992; Peck and Teisberg, 1992; Hourcade and Chapuis, 1994). While this argument is persuasive in the climate change context it cannot be used to argue that no emission reduction activities take place now. This is because so many of those activities have clearly defined benefits (for example, reduced local air pollution) regardless of whether climate change turns out to be 'real' or not.

Biological diversity
While there have been numerous attempts to place economic values on biological resources from a 'local' standpoint, very few exercises have been conducted which attempt to place economic values on the global dimensions of biological diversity. Only one study exists of the willingness to pay of one country to conserve a global environmental asset – the tropical forests. A number of studies exist on the commercial value of tropical forests as 'storehouses' of genetic material for pharmaceutical drugs. While the final product – a commercial drug – appears as a private good, the genetic information tends to be closer to a public good (Sedjo, 1992). What is owned and patented is the drug rather than the original source material.

Kramer et al. (1996) suggest that the average US household would be willing to pay between $24 and $31 as a one-off payment to protect 5 per cent of the world's remaining rainforests (in addition to 5 per cent already protected). Summed across 91 million households in the US this would amount to a once-for-all total willingness to pay of $2.2 billion to $2.8 billion. To get a broader view, we might extend the valuation to all OECD households (around 400 million) to get a global willingness to pay of $9.7–12.3 billion. Annuitized at, say, 10 per cent, this would produce an annual fund of some $1–1.2 billion.

The values of pharmaceutical material are disputed. Mendelsohn and Balick (1995) suggest that tropical forests have undiscovered drugs that are worth some $147 billion to world society as a whole, or about $48 per hectare of forest in present-value terms. This is somewhat lower than a previous estimate by Pearce and Puroshothaman (1995) of some $420 billion. The Mendelsohn and Balick estimates nets out more of the development costs of drugs than does the Pearce and Puroshothaman estimate. As several writers have pointed out, however, care has to be taken in using such *avarage* values. Marginal values are more relevant, that is, what is needed is the incremental contribution to the probability of making a commercial discovery, allowing for the fact that new discoveries can easily be redundant in the face of the availability of other sources of chemicals. On this basis, Aylward (1993) finds a marginal value of $44 per untested plant species *in situ*, while Simpson et al. (1994) suggest that the marginal value is negligible.

What limited evidence there is suggests that the global value of biological diversity, as inferred through the value of ecosystems themselves, could be high. Minimum estimates based on an analysis of debt-for-nature swaps, the available contingent valuation work, and willingness to pay for endangered species conservation suggest perhaps $1.5 billion per annum for tropical forests alone (Pearce, 1995). This might be compared with the budget of the Global Environment Facility which exists in part to 'capture' some of this global biodiversity value. Its triennial budget is about $2 billion, or, say $0.7 billion p.a., and this in turn has to be allocated to issues besides biodiversity conservation. A tentative conclusion is that the world is willing to pay more than the GEF's implicit biodiversity budget to conserve biodiversity.

A further focus on the biodiversity issue lies in the governance of conservation projects. All too many projects have failed because of the neglect of incentives to involve local communities. Conservation of wilderness and specific species, or restrictions on land use, inevitably results in losses of well-being for local communities who see conservation as conflicting with their chosen land uses. Examples of incentive structures that overcome this problem now abound. Among the more famous is the CAMP-FIRE programme in Zimbabwe where local communities secure a stake in conservation by sharing in the profits from game viewing and other wildlife use.

Stratospheric ozone
The US Environmental Protection Agency (1988) produced an analysis of the benefits to the US alone of controls on chlorofluorocarbon (CFC) emissions. They estimated that health and environmental benefits from an 80 per cent reduction in emissions would, in present-value terms, amount to a staggering $3.5 trillion (in 1985 prices). While such estimates appear barely credible, they reflect the estimates of substantial numbers of lives lost from skin cancer in the absence of controls: in the US alone these have been put at some 3 million people alive today or to be born up to the year 2075. Taking a 'value of statistical life' as being some $3 million (which is low compared to values used in many US studies), this automatically gives $9 trillion (undiscounted).

How valuable are the 'global commons'?
As can be seen, studies of the economic value of global common resources are few and far between. Nor is it easy to aggregate the values that do exist. The available estimates exclude the many local values that such assets may have, for example. Also, the values for global warming are point estimates for a single year, around 2050, corresponding to $2 \times CO_2$ concentrations. Damages are less before this year and greater afterwards. None the less, the present value of the services from the ozone layer, the global atmosphere and the tropical forests clearly runs into trillions of dollars rather than billions, justifying considerable effort to protect them.

5. Dealing with uncertainty

While the global commons are immensely valuable as assets, considerable uncertainty surrounds that value. Global climate change is, for example, still the subject of extensive scientific debate. How should the uncertainty surrounding these global issues be addressed?

If there is extensive uncertainty about the true social costs of global environmental degradation, and if the negative payoff to being wrong about environmental choices is potentially high, perhaps because of irreversibilities, then conventional economic theory would dictate a risk-averse strategy. Such strategies have been propounded in several guises – 'safe minimum standards' (SMS) (Bishop, 1978), the 'precautionary principle' (PP) (and 'sustainability constraints' (SC) (Pearce et al., 1989). In these cases there is a presumption to conserve unless the social costs of conservation are 'very high', even though the nature of the costs attached to the risks may not be known. In a risk context this would be translated as a presumption to reduce risks to the highest level achievable unless the social costs of doing so are very high. Unfortunately, none of these approaches has defined what is meant by 'very high' costs, while some interpretations of the PP neglect to mention cost at all. A reason for this neglect lies in the failure to understand the elementary concept of opportunity costs. If risks can be reduced costlessly, then there is no issue to be debated: they should be reduced. But invariably risks are costly to reduce and the money used up in reducing those risks could have been used elsewhere, even to reduce other risks. It might make little sense, for example, to reduce the risks from global warming beyond a certain level if the resources could have been used to save lives through, say, increased primary health care, or reducing water pollution. The essential point is that money is not 'just' money. It is a real command over real resources and, in a finite world, those resources *always* have an alternative use, including the reduction of risks elsewhere. If the objective is to reduce risks, then the cost of reducing a risk needs to be translated into potential lives saved. This is the essence of 'risk–risk' analysis, in which given resource budgets are allocated across different risk reduction programmes so as to maximize risk reduction in terms of lives saved. The basic condition that emerges is that risk per unit of resource spent should be equalized at the margin.

How far does risk–risk assessment take us in addressing the global environmental issues? For ozone layer damage avoidance the answer is fairly straightforward. Per dollar spent, reducing damage to the ozone layer appears to have a very high cost-effectiveness ratio. Taking the US EPA study referred to earlier, 3 million (undiscounted) lives saved at the cost of $22 billion would amount to saving a life for about $7000. For global warming the issues are far more complex. No one really knows how much it will cost to combat global warming to varying levels of reduced temperature increase. Nor are the estimates of lives at risk reliable. On the other hand, it might be argued that avoiding a risk from global warming is conferring a risk reduction benefit on all future generations, making 'lives saved' a substantial number. If so, cost-effectiveness would be high. Once the context becomes one of biodiversity, the calculations appear to be impossible since there are no estimates at all of lives at risk from reduced species and ecosystem diversity. Such contexts are ones of pure uncertainty and decision analysis offers no real guidance on how to behave.

6. Instruments

The issues surrounding the choice of economic instruments are addressed in Chapter 21. Given the uncertainty about some of the problems and the potentially high cost of addressing them, choice of instruments could be important for global concerns. For example, use of a carbon tax would help reduce global warming by encouraging energy conservation and the switch to non-carbon fuels. But carbon taxes also have the potential to be huge revenue raisers, changing the very basis of tax systems away from income towards polluting goods and resources. In addition, as was noted above, carbon taxes could yield many secondary benefits. These additional benefits could render the cost of tackling such problems more acceptable. The role of uncertainty as a factor militating against global pollution control should therefore be reduced. The policy implication is one of always searching for 'multiple benefit' instruments, ones that yield a number of benefits. Then, if the problem turns out not to be real after all, little is lost and a great deal may still be gained.

Tradable permit systems exist for sulphur emissions in the US. It is perhaps less widely appreciated that an incipient international carbon-trading system already exists in the form of 'joint implementation' (JI) (Pearce, 1996). Under JI, a carbon-emitting source in country A can secure relaxation of any controls it may face by reducing carbon emissions in country B. Such 'carbon offsets' already exist and have been formalized, for example, in the US Initiative on Joint Implementation. In a similar fashion, the state electricity utility in the Netherlands reduces carbon emissions in a number of other countries to offset its own increases. JI can be thought of as a carbon-trading system in which the credits for carbon emission reduction are not (yet) saleable. JI represents one of a number of 'global bargains' that need to be exploited. JI deals that combine biodiversity conservation with carbon emission reduction are also beginning to emerge – for example, through forest conservation which both sequesters carbon and conserves forest wildlife.

7. Conclusion

This brief survey of global environmental issues has touched on the main issues. The analysis might be summarized by asking the main questions. First, how important is degradation of the 'global commons'? The answers vary according to the issue. For ozone layer depletion there seems no question that the benefits of preventing ozone layer depletion are enormous and the benefit–cost ratio is over 100 to 1. For global warming the issues are complex, but if it can be shown that significant numbers of lives are at risk, then preventing many future lives from being lost could justify strong action on global warming. As it is, even an orthodox cost–benefit test suggests much stronger action than the world has taken so far. Probably the most perplexing issue is biodiversity loss. Some would argue that it is the most important issue, but demonstrating why this is so remains a major challenge. In the meantime, recourse to precautionary rules has its attractions, but fails to avoid the central issue that, in a world of scarce resources, some efficient allocation of effort between the many risks facing humankind is still needed.

References

Alfsen, K., H. Birkelund and M. Aaserund (1993), *Secondary Benefits of the EC Carbon/Energy Tax*, Research Department Discussion Paper No. 104, Statistics Norway, Oslo.

Aylward, B. (1993), 'A case study of pharmaceutical prospecting', in B. Aylward, J. Echeverria, L. Fendt and E. Barbier, *The Economic Value of Species Information and its Role of Biodiversity Conservation*, Stockholm: Swedish International Development Authority.

Ayres, R.U. and H. Walter (1991), 'Global warming: abatement policies and costs', *Environmental and Resource Economics*, **1** (3), 237–70.

Barker, T. (1993), *Secondary Benefits of Greenhouse Gas Abatement: the Effects of a UK Carbon/Energy Tax on Air Pollution*, mimeo, Department of Applied Economics, Cambridge University.

Berkes, F. (1989), *Common Property Resources: Ecology and Community Based Sustainable Development*, London: Belhaven Press.

Bishop, R. (1978), 'Endangered species and uncertainty: the economics of a safe minimum standard', *American Journal of Agricultural Economics*, **60**, 10–13.

Bromley, D. (1991), *Environment and Economy: Property Rights and Public Policy*, Oxford: Blackwell.

Cline, W. (1992), *The Economics of Global Warming*, Cambridge, UK: Cambridge University Press.

Fankhauser, S. (1995), *Valuing Climate Change*, London: Earthscan.

Hardin, G. (1968), 'The tragedy of the commons', *Science*, **162**, 1243–8.

Hourcade, J.C. and T. Chapuis (1994), 'No-regret potentials and technical innovation: a viability approach to integrative assessment of climate policies', in N. Nakikenovic, W. Nordhaus, R. Richels and F. Toth (eds), *Integrative Assessment of Mitigation Impacts and Adaptations to Climate Change*, Laxenburg, Austria: International Institute for Applied Systems Analysis.

Intergovernmental Panel on Climate Change (1996), *Working Group III: Second Assessment Report*, Cambridge, UK: Cambridge University Press.

Joseph, L. (1990), *Gaia: the Growth of an Idea*, London: Arkana.

Kramer, R., E. Mercer and N. Sharma (1996), 'Valuing tropical rainforest protection using the contingent valuation method', in V. Adamovicz, P. Boxall, M. Luckett, W. Phillips and W. White (eds), *Forestry, Economics and the Environment*, Reading: CAB International.

Leary, N. (1994), *The Amenity Value of Climate: a Review of Empirical Evidence from Migration, Wages and Rents*, mimeo, US Environmental Protection Agency – Climate Change Division, Washington, DC.

Lovelock, J. (1979), *Gaia: a New Look at Life on Earth*, Oxford: Oxford University Press.

Lovelock, J. (1987), 'Gaia: a model for planetary and cellular dynamics', in W. Thompson (ed.), *Gaia: a Way of Knowing. Political Implications of the New Biology*, Hudson, NY: Lindisfarne Press, pp. 83–97.

Maddison, D. (1994), *The Shadow Price of Greenhouse Gases and Aerosols*, Centre for Social and Economic Research on the Global Environment, University College London.

Manne, A. and R. Richels (1992), *Buying Greenhouse Insurance*, Cambridge, MA: MIT Press.

Mendelsohn, R. and R. Balick (1995), 'The value of undiscovered pharmaceuticals in tropical forests', *Economic Botany*, **49** (2), 223–8.

Nordhaus, W. (1991), 'To slow or not to slow: the economics of the greenhouse effect', *Economic Journal*, **101** (407), 938–48.

Nordhaus, W. (1994), 'Expert opinion on climate change', *American Scientist*, Jan–Feb.

Parry, M. (1990), *Climate Change and World Agriculture*, London: Earthscan.

Pearce, D.W. (1995), 'International trade and the environment', ch. 6 of D.W. Pearce, *Blueprint 4: Capturing Global Environmental Value*, London: Earthscan, pp. 74–105.

Pearce, D.W. (1996), *Joint Implementation*, Report to the European Bank for Reconstruction and Development, London.

Pearce, D.W. and S. Puroshothaman (1995), 'The economic value of plant-based pharmaceuticals', in T. Swanson (ed.), *Intellectual Property Rights and Biodiversity Conservation: an Interdisciplinary Analysis of the Values of Medicinal Plants*, Cambridge, UK: Cambridge University Press.

Pearce, D.W., A. Markandya and E. Barbier (1989), *Blueprint for a Green Economy*, London: Earthscan.

Peck, S. and T. Teisberg (1992), 'Global warming uncertainties and the value of information: an analysis using CETA', *Resource and Energy Economics*, **15** (1), 71–97.

Sedjo, R. (1992), 'Property rights, genetic resources and biotechnological change', *Journal of Law and Economics*, **35**, 199–215.

Simpson, D., R. Sedjo and J. Reid (1994), 'Valuing biodiversity: an application of genetic prospecting', *Resources for the Future Discussion Paper 94–20*, Washington, DC: Resources for the Future.

Swanson, T. (1994), *The International Regulation of Extinction*, London: Macmillan.

Tol, R. (1995), 'The damage costs of climate change: towards more comprehensive calculations, *Environment and Resource Economics*, **5**, 353–74.

US Environmental Protection Agency (1988), *Regulatory Impact Analysis – Protection of Stratospheric Ozone*, Washington, DC: US EPA.

34 Tax instruments for curbing CO_2 emissions

Stephen Smith

1. Introduction

At the Earth Summit in Rio in June 1992 more than 150 countries signed the UN Framework Convention on Climate Change. This commits the industrialized countries, in particular, to take actions to bring carbon dioxide emissions down to 1990 levels by the year 2000. This commitment responds, as Chapter 30 has discussed, to the accumulating scientific evidence, drawn together by the Intergovernmental Panel on Climate Change, that human activity has been responsible for a substantial rise in the concentration of greenhouse gases in the atmosphere (IPCC First Assessment Report, 1990), and that this has had a discernible influence on global climate (IPCC Second Assessment Report, 1995).

The policy instruments employed by countries in taking measures to meet these international commitments have been extremely varied:

- regulations on fuel efficiency of vehicles, appliances, and so on, and other policy measures to stimulate greater energy efficiency;
- energy pricing measures, including carbon taxes in at least five European countries – Finland, Sweden, Norway, Denmark and the Netherlands;
- voluntary agreements between industry and government;
- policies to stimulate research, development and diffusion of low-carbon energy technologies (through R&D subsidies for renewables, and so on);
- joint implementation deals, to support emissions reductions in other countries where abatement is less costly.

Not all countries may in practice meet the Rio target; some have not made the necessary policy effort, whilst adverse factors may prevent the attainment of the target in other countries, despite substantial effort. Analysis of the effectiveness of different policy instruments for curbing CO_2 emissions may help assess the policies needed, both to correct existing policy failures, and to develop policies for the even more stringent emissions control that will be needed to prevent renewed growth in emissions after 2000.

The desirability of using tax instruments to control CO_2 emissions has been controversial both among policy makers and in the research literature. Carbon and energy taxes have, in practice, become a focal point of the more general debate concerning the relative merits of 'command-and-control' regulation and market mechanisms in environmental policy. The economic theory relevant to this debate is reviewed in Part III of this volume. This chapter confines its attention to those aspects which are particular to the CO_2 control problem. How should a carbon tax be designed and implemented to achieve efficient control of CO_2 emissions, especially when there are various constraints on policy which may impede straightforward, first-best, solutions?

The remainder of this chapter is in four main sections. The first defines precisely what would be involved in using carbon or energy taxes to control CO_2 emissions, and discusses the possible ways in which a carbon tax might be implemented. The second considers issues relating to the determination of the first-best carbon tax rate. Since control of CO_2 emissions is designed to deal with a global environmental problem, the policies appropriate in individual countires will depend on what other countries are prepared to do. Whilst general issues of international coordination of global environmental policy are discussed in other chapters, the third section discusses the specific question of the extent to which coordination interacts with instrument choice in the CO_2 tax case. The fourth section considers the implications of the conclusion of Section 2 that efficient policy could involve high carbon tax rates, and looks at issues of adjustment efficiency, international competitiveness and distributional effects which may arise when energy is subject to heavy taxation.

2.   What is a carbon tax? Efficient specification of the tax base

Ideally, a tax to control atmospheric emissions of carbon dioxide would be levied directly on the individuals or firms who are responsible for the emissions, and would be based directly on the amounts of carbon dioxide emitted. In practice, there are too many sources of emissions for direct measurement of emissions to be practicable. In practice, therefore, carbon taxes take the form of a tax on the carbon content of fuels, intended to proxy for the carbon emission which results from the combustion of these fuels. The relationship between carbon content and eventual carbon emissions is very close, partly because no viable end-of-pipe emissions-cleaning technologies are available. Many of the problems that might, in principle, arise from the taxation of inputs as a proxy for emissions (Holterman, 1976; Sandmo, 1976) are not likely to be of great significance for the carbon tax case.

Nevertheless, there are some practical issues about how a carbon or carbon/energy tax should be structured and administered which might have implications for economic efficiency.

In the European countries (Sweden, Norway, Finland, the Netherlands and Denmark) which have actually introduced carbon taxes, these have taken the form of extended systems of fuel excises. Rates of tax are defined separately for each fuel, in terms of fuel quantities, and relative tax levels on different fuels are set so as to equate the implicit rate of tax per unit of carbon across fuels. This requirement is not, however, always observed; in Denmark and Norway, for example, some fuels are not subject to the carbon tax. Also, the level of tax can vary across types of energy user; in Sweden and the Netherlands, for example, much lower rates of tax apply to industrial energy users than to energy use by private households. Most of the carbon taxes actually implemented in these countries have provisions which exempt firms or sectors which are particularly exposed to international competition.

The presumption that a carbon tax should naturally be implemented as an extension of existing fuel excises has been questioned by Pearson and Smith (1991). They contrast two schemes – a 'primary' carbon tax, levied on primary fuels (for example crude oil, coal, and gas) where they are mined, extracted or imported, and a 'final' carbon tax, levied on final fuel products (such as coke, anthracite, four-star petrol) sold to industrial users or households (Figure 34.1). The latter corresponds to the current approach of extending existing fuel excises. They argue that, although there are advantages and disadvantages associated with each, a primary carbon tax would have some advantages compared to the excise duty route.

A 'primary' carbon tax would involve fewer taxable individuals than a 'final' tax, and no need for fiscal supervision of the energy chain beyond the first point; administrative costs would be expected to be low, and there would be scope for tight supervision to prevent evasion.

The fact that a primary carbon tax would be applied at an earlier stage in the production chain would not necessarily imply that it would have different economic or economic effects from an equivalent tax levied on final fuel products. The incidence, for example, of the carbon tax on fuel consumers could be largely invariant to the stage at which tax is formally incident; some part of the burden of a primary carbon tax would be passed on in the prices of fuel products according to their carbon content, so that the prices of fuels purchased by industry and consumers would be much the same as if an equivalent final carbon tax had been levied.

However, Pearson and Smith point out that this equivalence can only be achieved if the tax authorities have comprehensive information about the carbon 'history' of final fuel products. To calculate the carbon tax to be applied to a final fuel product requires information not only about the

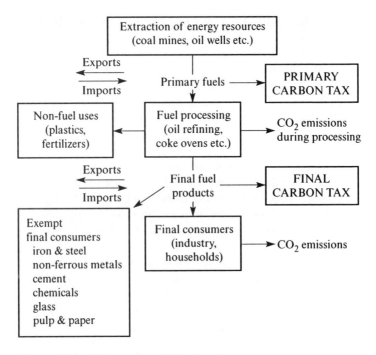

Figure 34.1   'Primary' and 'final' carbon taxes

actual carbon content of the fuel, but also about the carbon emissions associated with its processing. This means that the amount of tax to be applied to a particular final fuel product can no longer be determined simply by reference to its physical characteristics (which would provide a straightforward and uncontroversial basis for administration of the tax) but requires in addition that these measurements be supplemented by assumptions about the carbon emissions associated with its past history. Where different processing technologies are used, with different emissions during processing, a final carbon tax levied on the basis of average carbon emissions during processing will be liable to lead to inefficient technology choices. In principle, therefore, a primary carbon tax might be expected to be more efficient, in both static and dynamic terms (though this greater efficiency of a primary tax may be partly undermined if carbon tax refunds then have to be made on processed energy which is exported or used as inputs to exempt activities). Whether there is any significant efficiency gain from using a primary carbon tax is essentially an empirical matter; it will be greater the more variation there is in intermediate emissions across different technologies of fuel processing. The quantitative significance of these issues for the choice of carbon tax type has not, to date, been assessed.

Developing this line of argument, Poterba and Rotemberg (1995) have considered the case where joint production of final fuel products take place, and where the output mix is a choice variable. In other words, they consider a process of fuel refining or processing where a single primary fuel is processed into more than one final fuel product, and where the mix of final fuels produced can, to some extent, be varied. In this case they show that it may be impossible to define any objective basis to estimate the intermediate carbon emissions associated with the production of particular final fuels.

One implication of these arguments is that environmental and economic efficiency is unlikely to be fully attainable with a carbon tax levied on final fuel products (that is, an excise tax). Further implications, however, are that arrangements for refund of past carbon tax on fuel exports, and on fuel supplies to any exempt sectors and non-fuel uses, cannot be done in a way which accurately reflects their total (potential and past) carbon emissions; likewise, levying the carbon tax on imported processed fuels can only approximate the past carbon emissions involved in their processing.

3. Setting the carbon tax rate

Dynamics
In the most straightforward formulation of the Pigouvian tax problem, that of a single-period externality, the efficient externality tax (in the absence of any wider fiscal considerations) would be set equal to the level of marginal pollution damage at the socially optimal level of emissions. Determining an appropriate rate for a carbon tax is, however, considerably more complex than in this simple case, because the CO$_2$ control problem involves significant multi-period, or dynamic, elements. These make the assessment of marginal pollution damage more difficult, and also mean that the policy maker may need to consider the optimal time path of carbon tax rates, rather than a single optimal tax rate.

First, the problem of global warming is a function of the accumulated stock of CO$_2$ and other greenhouse gases in the atmosphere. Since the rate of decay of any addition to the stock of atmospheric CO$_2$ is slow, current emissions have an effect which extends into many future periods. Likewise, policy measures taken now potentially confer benefits on future generations as well as the current one. Given the length of the time horizon involved, balancing the interests of present and future generations in climate change policy raises unusually difficult philosophical issues (Broome, 1992) concerning the treatment of large gains and losses in the distant future, which conventional discount rates could render of negligible current value.

Second, there may be a substantial adjustment lag to any climate change policy based on energy-pricing measures, since the level of energy use in the economy will be partly governed by the speed at which the existing capital stock is replaced. The scope for changing the energy intensity of production using existing capital equipment is likely to be much lower than when existing machinery is being replaced. As Ingham et al. (1990) show, the average life of plant and machinery may be of the order of 15 years. Even if the introduction of a heavy new tax on energy led to some acceleration of the replacement of the most energy-inefficient capital equipment, a considerable proportion of existing capital would be likely to continue in use for a decade or more, and full adjustment of energy use to higher energy prices would thus take many years to complete. At the same time, there may be scope for policy to exploit announcement effects, in which the announcement of future carbon taxes may affect current investment decisions and lead to the adoption of low-emission technologies, even before the carbon tax is actually imposed.

Third, using taxes on fossil fuels to control CO_2 emissions has a further dynamic aspect, due to the fact that the tax would be levied on a non-renewable natural resource with a finite stock. If a tax is levied at a constant *ad valorem* rate (that is, a constant percentage of price) on an exhaustible resource (with a zero cost of extraction), it will have no impact on the time profile of resource extraction and use (Dasgupta and Heal, 1979). Following this line of argument, Sinclair (1992) suggests that a high carbon tax would be liable to be ineffective if it is constant over time, and a rising carbon tax over time would be even less attractive, because it would accelerate the depletion of the energy stock, and hence lead to higher carbon emissions in the initial years of the policy than if no carbon tax were levied. To reduce current carbon emissions it is necessary to shift depletion of the finite energy stock to future periods, which would require that the carbon tax should fall as a percentage of the energy price over time.

The implications of the above for the carbon tax that should be levied per unit of carbon are, as Ulph et al. (1991) note, not immediately apparent. The Hotelling rule would imply that the price of the finite energy resource would be rising, and though the optimal *ad valorem* tax rate might be falling, the tax rate per unit of carbon need not necessarily also be falling. In addition, there are other factors which may also be relevant in assessing the optimal dynamic profile of tax rates, including the effect of natural decay in the stock of atmospheric CO_2, and of discounting of future costs. Ulph et al. (1991) show that the optimal time profile for a carbon tax may be quite complex, and the optimal tax per unit of carbon may initially be low, and might subsequently rise. For a period, the optimal tax may even rise in *ad valorem* terms.

Interaction between CO_2 taxes and other taxes

A further source of complexity in determining the optimal carbon tax is the existence of other energy taxes, and other energy-related pollution problems which might be tackled using taxation. How should these be taken into account in setting the carbon tax rate? There are a number of separate issues.

First, what in principle should be the relationship between a carbon tax and other taxes levied on energy, either for revenue-raising purposes or to correct other externalities? Newbery (1992) considers the relationship between the optimal rate of a carbon tax and the rates of any existing externality taxes on energy. He concludes that in some circumstances the relationship may not simply be additive. For example, introduction of a carbon tax may increase the optimal rate of a tax on motor fuel levied to reflect other traffic externalities. The reason for this is that in the long run the carbon tax will increase fuel efficiency of motor vehicles, and hence will increase the non-carbon externality costs per litre of fuel.

Second, how should interactions between different pollution problems (for example CO_2 and acid rain) be treated in the design of the tax structure? Pearce (1991) has argued that carbon taxes in excess of the marginal damage from CO_2 emissions may be appropriate to reflect the 'secondary benefits' of carbon abatement in the form of reductions in sulphur dioxide and other energy-related emissions, if other instruments do not provide appropriate and more specific incentives for control of these pollutants.

Third, in international discussion of coordinated carbon taxes, how much 'credit' – if any – should be given to countries which already levy high rates of tax on energy? Also, should any restriction be placed on their ability to reduce other taxes on energy when the carbon tax is imposed by international agreement? It is possible to interpret existing taxes on energy as implicit carbon taxes (Hoeller and Wallin, 1991; Hoeller and Coppel, 1992), and it may then be argued that any new carbon tax should be imposed at different rates, in order to equalize the overall tax burden on carbon in different countries (see the discussion in Cnossen and Vollebergh, 1992, for example). The issue has a number of subtleties – how to avoid discouraging countries from introducing carbon taxes in advance of any agreement, and how to avoid countries gaining credit for simply renaming existing energy taxes. It also relates to the question, discussed at more length in Section 4 below, of whether the efficient pattern of carbon taxes across countries would be uniform, or whether optimal carbon tax rates would vary across countries.

Impact on carbon emissions of particular tax rates

How high would carbon tax rates need to be to meet a given quantitative target to reduce carbon dioxide emissions? Although practical experience of carbon taxation is too recent to provide much, if any, guide to likely behavioural responses, variations in energy taxes and prices (both across time and across countries) can provide a broad indication of the likely size of the effect on aggregate energy use.

It may be possible to gauge some of the effects of a carbon tax on aggregate energy consumption from the experience of past changes in energy prices. In particular, the two OPEC oil prices hikes of the 1970s provide considerable time-series variation in energy prices, allowing the price elasticity of energy demand to be estimated with much greater precision than if energy prices had been more stable. In some respects, however, the effects of a carbon tax would be likely to differ from those of the OPEC price rises; in particular, an important element in the effect of a carbon tax may be the incentive to substitute from high-carbon to low-carbon fuels, whilst the OPEC experience raised the price of all energy, and oil in particular. Also, expectations of future prices (which will be crucial in determining the impact on investment decisions) may differ between the two cases; individuals could have anticipated the instability of the OPEC cartel, or might expect that political opposition would lead to quick abolition of the carbon tax, and might then respond less than if they expected the higher price to be sustained. A further difference between the OPEC episodes and the imposition of a carbon tax is in the macroeconomic context; one important effect of higher prices for oil supplies was a massive transfer of resources from the industrialized countries to the oil producers, and this led to macroeconomic instability as the world economy adjusted. With a carbon tax levied by consuming countries, the effects would be different, and with a coordinated carbon tax, it is conceivable that there would be some welfare shift away from the producing countries through an optimal oil import tariff effect, counterbalancing the OPEC cartel.

The cross-section differences between countries in existing energy prices, arising from tax and other factors, might also provide some information on the price elasticity of energy demand. However, this evidence needs to be interpreted with considerable caution, and may, in particular, be a poor guide to the quantitative impact of a coordinated increase in energy prices across all countries. Where energy prices differ between countries, one source of differences in energy use may be the relocation of energy-intensive activities to locations where the energy price is low. If this effect is strong, substantial differences between countries in the level of energy consumption could arise through changes in the composition of activity, without any change in the level of global emissions. Without correction for this effect, energy price elasticities estimated on the basis of international cross-section data could therefore be liable to overestimate the likely behavioural response to an internationally coordinated carbon tax.

Scale

Policies to control carbon dioxide emissions could have much larger impacts on private sector production and consumption activities than many other environmental policy measures, because of the central importance of carbon-based energy in both industrial production and household consumption, and because large behavioural adjustments may be required.

Using the OECD 'GREEN' model, Burniaux et al. (1991) estimate that a carbon tax averaging $215 per tonne of carbon across all countries ($308 per tonne in the OECD countries) would be needed to keep aggregate global emissions at 1990 levels over the period until the year 2020. To achieve longer-term targets for emissions reduction or for stabilization of atmospheric concentrations of carbon dioxide, more substantial carbon taxes would be required, although their level will depend critically on the prices at which new sources of non-fossil fuels eventually become available. Thus, for example, Manne and Richels (1991) estimate that in order to reduce carbon dioxide emissions by the US to a long-run level 20 per cent below current emissions, a long-run carbon tax of $250 per tonne of carbon would be needed; over the first few decades of the policy the tax would have to be even higher, peaking at $400 in the year 2020. These estimates perhaps lie towards the upper end of the likely range, and other studies have suggested that emissions might be more responsive to a carbon tax, and the required tax rates correspondingly lower than indicated by Manne and Richels. Cline (1992) summarizes the results of four key studies in terms of the marginal carbon tax required to achieve a one percentage point reduction in year 2050 emissions below their level in the absence of policy intervention. His analysis shows that the marginal tax rates required for a one-point reduction range from $5.9 per tonne of carbon (Manne and Richels, 1991), $4.9 (Edmonds and Reilly, 1983), $2.8 (Nordhaus and Yohe, 1983), to $1.2 (Jorgenson and Wilcoxen, 1991). A considerable part of the variation in tax rates has to do with different assessments of the likely backstop technologies which will become available, and which will govern the long-term prices of non-fossil fuels, and hence the costs of substitution away from fuels which give rise to carbon dioxide emissions.

Rates of carbon tax as high as these would raise important policy issues concerning the distributional incidence of the tax, and possibly also of abatement cost burdens (Section 5, below). High rates of carbon tax also mean that the revenues from environmental tax measures might conceivably be sufficiently large to facilitate major tax reform elsewhere in the fiscal system. This has given rise to a debate over the scope for a 'double dividend', discussed in more detail in another chapter.

4.   International bargaining and coordination of carbon tax policies

Given the global nature of the climate change problem, effective policy will need to involve international coordination. The impact that an individual country can make on climate change through independent action is negligible, whilst national policies incur appreciable costs of abatement. Another chapter in this volume has discussed many of the issues in achieving efficient bargains for the control of international environmental phenomena, including the distribution of the costs of CO_2 control, the achievement of a stable coalition of signatories to an international agreement, and so on.

There are some interesting interactions between the issue of instrument choice and the feasibility, credibility and/or efficiency of international agreements. In particular, is bargaining over tax rates likely to lead to a better or worse outcome than bargaining over quantitative emissions reductions? And if countries agree on coordinated tax measures, how far should carbon tax rates be harmonized?

In some circumstances it would, in principle, be desirable for international negotiations to go further than simply specifying quantitative targets for emissions reductions in individual countries, and to determine the form of policy measures to be taken.

One is that negotiating over tax rates rather than over quantitative emissions targets may in certain circumstances achieve a more efficient pattern of abatement across countries. For example, where global pollutants are concerned, agreement on a uniform tax rate to apply in all countries may be more efficient than agreeing that all countries implement the same percentage reduction in pollution. Indeed, in some circumstances involving uniformly mixed global pollutants a uniform tax rate on emissions across countries would constitute the optimal policy. Hoel (1994) considers whether a carbon tax, levied to control climate change problems arising from the accumulation of global carbon dioxide emissions, should be uniform across countries. Ideally, he finds, the tax should be uniform. But there are two sets of circumstances in which non-uniformity across countries could be appropriate. One is where side payments are ruled out, a case which Hoel, however, argues is unlikely to be a major constraint in practice. In this case, agreements must confer net benefits on all signatories, and non-uniform carbon taxes could then be Pareto-optimal. Another group of circumstances concerns the availability of other tax instruments which can be deployed to tackle other energy-related externalities, and to tax energy within a structure of optimal revenue-raising taxes on commodities. Typically, the efficient rates to be set for these energy taxes will vary across countries: in the first case to reflect differences in abatement costs, the assimilative capacity of the national environment, and citizens' preferences for environmental quality; and in the second case to reflect the range of factors underlying optimal tax structures. If separate taxes on energy were not available, and the carbon tax had to perform these functions as well as reducing carbon emissions, uniformity in the carbon tax rate across countries would be unlikely to be optimal. However, since all countries already levy substantial taxes on at least some types of energy, Hoel argues that the case for uniformity across countries in a new coordinated carbon tax would appear to be strong.[1]

As Smith (1995) discusses, another reason for specifying the form of policy, rather than simply emission reduction targets, may be the credibility of any agreement. Agreeing to introduce a tax at a particular rate may make it easier for countries to verify that the bargain was being implemented, than where the agreement was simply to undertake unspecified measures to achieve a quantitative target for emissions reduction at some future date. It may be particularly difficult for other countries to judge whether a package of non-fiscal measures is sufficient to achieve a country's commitments to carbon abatement, or whether it is simply an attempt at window-dressing. It may then be relatively easy for countries to free-ride without detection, and this will reduce the incentive for any country to undertake costly abatement measures.

5. Policy implications of high carbon tax rates

Section 3 has indicated that first-best carbon tax rates could be high, leading to a substantial increase in energy prices, a heavy carbon tax burden on energy-intensive activities, and significant carbon tax revenues. The scale of taxation required may lead to a number of problems which have concerned policy makers. Three are discussed below: the requirements for efficient adjustment to increased energy prices, and the impact of the carbon tax burden on industrial competitiveness and on income distribution.

Adjustment efficiency

If high carbon taxes are imposed, the efficiency of market adjustment to higher energy prices becomes a matter of considerable importance.

The aggregate economic cost of adjustment to higher energy prices will be higher, where energy consumers are prevented by market failures from making optimal adjustments in energy use. An efficient pattern of adjustment to higher energy prices might include both reductions in energy consumption and greater levels of investment by both household and industrial energy users in various measures to increase the efficiency with which energy is used. In the domestic sector, measures which households can take to improve domestic energy efficiency may include such things as loft insulation, double glazing and wall insulation. Similar measures may be undertaken by industrial energy users, who may also seek to develop new, more energy-efficient, products and technologies. It has been suggested that markets for these investments may be subject to various forms of market failure, possibly including credit market failures, informational failures, and certain market failures related to housing tenure (Sutherland, 1991; Brechling and Smith, 1994; Levene et al., 1995). Where these market failures prevent efficient adjustment to higher energy prices, reductions in energy consumption in response to higher energy prices will tend to be smaller, and more 'painful' in terms of their welfare cost.

Impact of a carbon tax on 'competitiveness'
The impact of carbon taxes on the international competitiveness of industry has, in practice, been a major source of political opposition in many of the countries which have introduced carbon taxes. In Sweden, in particular, it has led to substantial modifications of the initial carbon tax system, which had the effect of reducing sharply the level of carbon tax on industry. The issues are most significant where countries introduce a carbon tax through unilateral action.

The impact on competition could, of course, be offset, on average, by exchange rate movements; a devaluation by a country imposing a carbon tax could offset the impact of the higher taxation on industrial competitiveness. Much the same effect could be achieved by returning the revenues from the tax to the industrial sector through reductions in other taxes (such as corporate profits or payroll taxes). In each case, the net impact of the carbon tax would be to worsen the relative position of carbon-intensive sectors, whilst improving the competitiveness of sectors of industry with low carbon intensity.

In the long run, some contraction of carbon-intensive sectors might be one of the desired outcomes from policies to reduce carbon emissions. However, whilst other countries do not impose the tax, these sectors may be liable to contract too much, in the countries which do impose the tax, relative to the final desired equilibrium where all countries impose similar carbon taxes. Part of this contraction may represent 'carbon leakage' – international displacement of carbon-intensive production when a carbon tax is implemented without full international coordination – and this may impose adjustment costs and loss of profits, without any corresponding environmental gain.

One possible way of limiting this would be by exempting particular sectors in the tax structure. This was proposed for the six most energy-intensive sectors in the European Commission's 1991 plans for a carbon tax (Commission of the European Communities, 1991) and has been a feature in most of the countries which have so far introduced carbon taxes.

An alternative approach which might reduce the extent of international displacement to countries which do not impose the carbon tax would be to make compensatory border tax adjustments on traded goods to reflect the tax treatment of the carbon used in their manufacture. Thus it would be possible in principle (though perhaps less straightforward in practice) to levy tariffs on goods imported from countries which do not impose a carbon tax, at a level reflecting the carbon used in their manufacture, and to make corresponding refunds of tax to reflect the carbon embodied in exported goods. There has been some debate amongst policy makers as to whether such border tax adjustments would be compatible with WTO rules.

Hoel (1996) discusses the circumstances in which sectoral differentiation of carbon tax rates (either in the form of exemptions for some sectors, or differential tax rates) would be efficient. He observes that if countries are not able to levy tariffs on trade with non-signatories to an international agreement to restrain carbon dioxide emissions, it may be appropriate to levy differentiated taxes across sectors. Informally, these taxes would aim to offset the competitive advantage that firms in energy-intensive sectors would receive in non-signatory countries, although the efficient pattern of carbon tax differentiation across sectors would be complex. However, if countries are able to determine tariff rates without restriction, then tariffs should be employed for this purpose, and the optimal pattern of tax rates across sectors will be uniform.

Distributional impact, and possible offsetting policy measures
The distributional impact across household groups of a carbon tax has been a focus of policy concern in some countries, and is discussed, for example, by Poterba (1991), Smith (1992), OECD (1995, 1996), and Cornwell and Creedy (1996). The distributional impact will reflect the impact of the carbon tax on the prices of household energy (for heating, light, and so on), motor fuels, and other industrial goods and services (through the higher cost of energy inputs to production). The distributional issues are most acute in the case of the additional tax on domestic energy, which in Northern Europe at least has the character of a necessity, forming a much larger part of the budgets of poorer households than of the population as a whole. Smith (1992) shows that in the UK domestic energy accounts for some 16 per cent of the non-durable spending of the bottom decile group of households, but only 7 per cent of household spending on average. Additional taxes on domestic energy will thus tend to have a regressive distributional incidence, in the sense that the extra energy tax payments will be a higher percentage of income (or of total spending) for poorer households than for the better off. However, once the use of the

additional revenues from energy taxation is considered, a revenue-neutral package of measures, including higher energy taxes combined with higher transfers to poorer households, could be designed which, overall, would on average leave poorer households better off.

Smith (1992) shows that in the UK the EC's proposed carbon tax would probably also have had a regressive distributional impact; the regressive effect of higher taxation of domestic energy would have outweighed the progressive distributional incidence of higher taxes on motor fuels. However, in many other EC countries this would not have been the case, because the domestic energy component of the tax is either smaller relative to the motor fuels component, or less regressive, than in the UK.

In addition to the burden of extra taxation, a second issue has been the distribution of the burden of reductions in energy consumption in response to higher energy prices. In the case of the UK it appears likely that the reduction in energy consumption induced by the imposition of higher taxes on domestic energy is greater amongst poorer households; Pearson and Smith (1991) estimate that the energy spending of the bottom quintile would have fallen in response to a $10 per barrel carbon tax by 12 per cent in volume terms, whilst the average reduction in the volume of household energy consumption would be of the order of 7 per cent.

The social and distributional costs of higher energy prices may be exacerbated if market failures in energy efficiency investment are particularly concentrated amongst low-income households, or other vulnerable groups (Smith, 1992). Thus, for example, income-related market failures, such as those related to the credit market, or to housing tenure, may tend to amplify the distributional cost of reducing energy consumption through pricing instruments. Measures (such as building regulations or home energy audits) to rectify the underlying market failures would then have the twin merits that they would tend to reduce the aggregate economic cost of achieving a given reduction in consumption, and at the same time would also help to reduce the social and distributional cost of higher energy taxation.

6. Present trends and prospects for future research

The case for a carbon tax as a cost-effective instrument to reduce greenhouse gas emissions continues to be actively debated in a number of countries. In addition, although the European Commission's proposals for a Community-wide coordinated regime have, so far, been rebuffed by member states, the general issues continue to be discussed in a number of related policy contexts, including a possible coordinated restructuring of existing energy taxes to reflect climate change objectives. This continuing policy debate about methods of implementing national or EU commitments to emissions limits will presumably intensify as the international community moves on to consider the level and pattern of emissions restraint that will be required beyond the start of the next century.

A number of areas for research may be prompted by these policy developments. First, *ex post* evaluation of the effects and cost-effectiveness of the existing carbon taxes may help to shed some light on aspects central to the policy debate, such as the effects on industrial competitiveness of unilateral measures, and the size of the behavioural response. Second, research on monitoring and compliance strategies will be given added emphasis if, as seems likely, a considerable number of countries fail to achieve the targets to which they are currently committed. How far is this failure due to a half-hearted commitment to implement effective measures, and how can this reason for non-compliance be disentangled from the impact of adverse country-specific shocks, which may have derailed even well-intentioned policy? What more can be done to ensure that signatories to a future agreement can have confidence that other signatories are fulfilling their part of the bargain?

Third, it may be useful to explore the impact of the threat of a carbon tax in countries which considered such a measure but, ultimately, decided against it. How far has the threat of a carbon tax been successful in inducing so-called 'voluntary agreements', under which parts of the private sector may have undertaken commitments to abatement measures, in exchange for non-introduction of a carbon tax? Have these commitments genuinely achieved the abatement promised, and more abatement than would have been undertaken anyway in the absence of any policy? What problems might they have raised, for example, in ensuring compliance, and how do they affect the long-term development of the sectors concerned?

Note

1. There would, of course, be a risk that countries might seek to avoid their obligations to contribute to international action to control carbon dioxide emissions by, at the same time, reducing their other taxes on energy to offset the effects of the agreed carbon tax. Essentially, the test of whether countries are making their contribution to global climate change policy requires a comparison with what they would have done otherwise, and this is impossible to observe.

References

Brechling, V. and S. Smith (1994), 'Household energy efficiency in the UK', *Fiscal Studies*, **15** (2), 44–56.

Broome, J. (1992), *Counting the Cost of Global Warming*, Cambridge, UK: The White Horse Press.

Burniaux, J.M., J.P. Martin, G. Nicoletti and J.O. Martins (1991), *The costs of policies to reduce global emissions of CO$_2$: initial simulation results with GREEN*, OECD Economics and Statistics Department Working Papers no. 103, Paris: OECD.

Cline, W.R. (1992), *The Economics of Global Warming*, Washington, DC: Institute for International Economics.

Cnossen, S. and H.R.J. Vollebergh (1992), 'Towards a global excise on carbon', *National Tax Journal*, **45**, 23–36.

Commission of the European Communities (1991), *A Community Strategy to Limit Carbon Dioxide Emissions and to Improve Energy Efficiency*, communication from the Commission to the Council, SEC(91)1744, 14 October 1991, Brussels.

Cornwell, A. and J. Creedy (1996), 'Carbon taxation, prices and inequality in Australia', *Fiscal Studies*, **17** (3), 21–38.

Dasgupta, P. and G. Heal (1979), *Economic Theory and Exhaustible Resources*, Cambridge, UK: Cambridge University Press.

Edmonds, J. and J. Reilly (1983), 'Global energy and CO_2 to the year 2050', *The Energy Journal*, **4** (3), 21–47.

Hoel, M. (1994), 'International co-ordination of environmental taxes', FEEM Working Paper 41.94. Milan: Fondazione ENI Enrico Mattei.

Hoel, M. (1996) 'Should a carbon tax be differentiated across sectors?', *Journal of Public Economics*, **59** (1), 17–32.

Hoeller, P. and M. Wallin (1991), *Energy Prices, Taxes and Carbon Dioxide Emissions*, OECD Working Papers no. 106, Paris: OECD.

Hoeller, P. and J. Coppel (1992), *Energy Taxation and Price Distortions in Fossil Fuel Markets: Some Implications for Climate-Change Policy*, OECD Working Papers no. 110, Paris: OECD.

Holterman, S. (1976), 'Alternative tax systems to correct for externalities and the efficiency of paying compensation', *Economica*, **43**, 1–16.

Ingham, A., J. Maw and A. Ulph (1990), 'Energy conservation in the UK manufacturing sector – a vintage approach', in D. Hawdon (ed.), *Energy Demand – Evidence and Expectations*, Guildford: University of Surrey Press.

Jorgenson, D.W. and P.J. Wilcoxen (1991), *The Cost of Controlling US Carbon Dioxide Emissions*, mimeo, Harvard University.

Levene, M.D., J.G. Koomey, J.E. McMahon and A.H. Sanstad (1995), 'Energy efficiency policy and market failures', *Annual Review of Energy and the Environment*, **20**, 535–55.

Manne, A. and R. Richels (1991), 'Global CO_2 emission reductions: the impacts of rising energy costs', *The Energy Journal*, **12** (1), 88–107.

Newbery, D.M.G. (1992), 'Should carbon taxes be additional to other transport fuel taxes?', *The Energy Journal*, **13** (2), 49–60.

Nordhaus, W.D. and G.W. Yohe (1983), 'Future carbon dioxide emissions from fossil fuels', in National Research Council, *Changing Climate*, Washington: National Academy Press, pp.87–153.

OECD (1995), *Climate Change, Economic Instruments and Income Distribution*, Paris: OECD.

OECD (1996), *Implementation Strategies for Environmental Taxes*, Paris: OECD.

Pearce, D. (1991), 'The role of carbon taxes in adjusting to global warming', *The Economic Journal*, **101** (407), 938–48.

Pearson, M. and S. Smith (1991), *The European Carbon Tax: An Assessment of the European Commission's Proposals*, IFS Report Series, London: Institute for Fiscal Studies.

Poterba, J.M. (1991), 'Tax policy to combat global warming: on designing a carbon tax', in R. Dornbusch and J.M. Poterba (eds), *Global Warming: Economic Policy Responses*, Cambridge, MA: MIT Press, pp.71–98.

Poterba, J.M. and J.J. Rotemberg (1995), 'Environmental taxes on intermediate and final goods when both can be imported', *International Tax and Public Finance*, **2** (2), 221–8.

Sandmo, A. (1976), 'Direct versus indirect Pigouvian taxation', *European Economic Review*, **7**, 337–49.

Sinclair, P. (1992), 'High does nothing and rising is worse: carbon taxes should keep declining to cut harmful emissions', *The Manchester School*, **60**, 41–52.

Smith, S. (1992), 'The distributional consequences of taxes on energy and the carbon content of fuels', *European Economy*, special edition no. 1/1992: 'The economics of limiting CO_2 emissions', pp.241–68.

Smith, S. (1995), 'The role of the European Union in environmental taxation', *International Tax and Public Finance*, **2**, 375–87.

Sutherland, R. (1991), 'Market barriers to energy-efficiency investments', *Energy Journal*, **12**, 15–34.

Ulph, A., D. Ulph and J. Pezzey (1991), *Should a carbon tax rise or fall over time?*, University of Bristol, Department of Economics, Discussion Paper no. 91/309.

PART V

SPACE IN ENVIRONMENTAL ECONOMICS

35 Environment and regional economics
Peter Nijkamp

1. Regional economics and environmental economics

Regional economics – as an established discipline – dates back to the 1950s, when it was recognized that the economy does not operate in a wonderland of no geographical dimensions. Regional economics aims to study the spatial patterns and processes of human activity from an economic perspective.

A search for linkages – theoretical, methodological or empirical – between regional economics and environmental economics may start from two different though complementary departures. One may try to identify environmental aspects in spatial economic theories, models or applications. Alternatively, one may seek for clear spatial dimensions in existing environmental economic analyses. In the present chapter we shall adopt a blend of these two research explorations. The first section of this contribution sets out to present some main features of both regional and environmental economics with a view to identifying linkages between these two subdisciplines in economics. We start with regional economics, followed by environmental economics.

Although the origin of *regional economics* dates back to the nineteenth century (mainly von Thünen) and the first part of the twentieth century (Weber, Hotelling, Christaller, Lösch), the real genesis took place in the 1950s (see, for a historical survey, Paelinck and Nijkamp, 1975 and Ponsard, 1983). One of the pioneers in regional economics, Walter Isard, recognized that distance friction and transportation costs on the one hand and agglomeration economies on the other were largely responsible for the heterogeneity in location patterns of both firms and households (see Isard, 1956). The awareness of spatial frictions and opportunities in the behaviour of economic actors also induced a profound interest in urban economics, housing market economics, regional labour market economics, and transportation economics. Next to regional economics in a strict sense, we may also distinguish *regional science* as a broader interdisciplinary approach to spatial phenomena, including geography, planning, architecture, political science and so forth. It is evident that in this broader framework environmental issues also find a 'natural niche'.

Environmental economics has followed a slightly different development pace. Despite the early recognition of the existence and the implications of external effects in a market economy (Marshall, Pigou, Hotelling), it was mainly the widespread concern with the observed decay in our quality of life and in ecosystem conditions which prompted, as of the 1960s, a broad interest in the economics of the environment (see, for example, Boulding, 1969; Mishan, 1967; Kneese, 1965; Krutilla, 1972). The Club of Rome studies generated, especially in the 1970s, a further interest in environmental economics, but – with a few exceptions – it lasted until the 1980s before an extensive package of environmental economics journals and (hand)books entered the academic market. This is not the right place to dwell extensively on the history of environmental economics. For more details see Crocker (Chapter 2, this handbook).

Clearly, the concept of a region is central in regional economics. However, there is a multitude of regional demarcations: administrative regions, economic regions, natural resource regions and the like. A clear feature of a system of regions is its openness, which means the possibility of free trade, free movement of people and goods, as well as transport of pollutants. The clear geographical focus in regional systems also means a close connection with the resource base and the pollution in a certain area.

In an early stage of the development of both regional and environmental economics several intricate links can already be observed. In regional economics, for example, we saw the application of (multiregional) input–output models to environmental and pollution issues (see, for example, Cumberland, 1966; Isard, 1969, 1972; Leontief, 1970; and Muller, 1979), while the presence of environmental externalities was also analysed in a spatial–economic welfare context (see, for example, Nijkamp, 1977). In environmental economics, on the other hand, the intricate relationship between environmental assets and spatial economic behaviour was also clearly realized, as is witnessed by the great many valuation studies on natural parks, where travel costs methods become a popular analytical tool (see, for example, Burton, 1971), and studies on urban pollution valuation, where revealed preference methods showed a great scientific potential.

One may thus conclude that there are many analytical connections between regional and environmental economic phenomena. These relationships may be unidirectional in nature, but may also show complicated feedback structures of modularly or hierarchically operating environmental–economic systems in space and time. The nature of such interactions is dependent on ecosystem and human behaviour as well as on spatial–environmental policy. Clearly, environmental policy has a direct bearing on regional and urban development, while regional and urban policies have immediate implications for environmental quality (see, for example, Schnaiberg et al., 1986). This holds for command-and-control policies (such as prohibitions), but also for market-oriented policies (such as user pay strategies).

The twin character of space and environment is a direct result of the fact that environmental externalities – unpaid burdens imposed by polluters on other actors (see Verhoef, Chapter 13 in this volume) – are usually transmitted through the medium of space. In other words, environmental externalities are likely to show up as unpaid spatial spillovers (at various geographical scales, ranging from local to global). Such spillovers may manifest themselves in the form of, for example, water pollution of downstream areas, or ambient concentrations of pollutants in areas depending on prevailing wind directions, but also as environmental stress on the commons (such as ocean pollution, or ozone layer destruction). On the other hand, all space-related activities (such as residential locations, industrial development, transportation, and the like) are closely connected with environmental changes. For example, it has in this context become quite common to make a distinction between fixed (point) sources of pollution and mobile sources such as vehicles. The previous considerations can be further substantiated by the following observations on the twin nature of space and environment (see also Nijkamp, 1981):

- Space is the *geographical medium* (or 'physical market') for environmental externalities in a broad sense; this applies to global environmental change, but also to local issues like noise annoyance, soil pollution, and so on.
- Space is of a *heterogeneous nature*, with the consequence that environmental externalities have geographically discriminating, distributive impacts (for example recreational visits to attractive areas may pose an excessive burden on such areas).
- Space is a *scarce good* whose consumption (for example land use) has environmental implications and welfare effects for other members of society, now or in the future, here or elsewhere (such as environmental degradation processes in a global space–time context).

In conclusion, the space–environment relationship manifests itself as a complex nexus at the interface of regional economics and environmental economics. In the next sections we shall pay more attention to the linkages between these subdisciplines by addressing their mutual connections from a theoretical, modelling and policy perspective.

2. Integration of spatial–economic and environmental–economic theory
The main reason for the intricate linkage between regional economics on the one hand and environmental (and resource) economics on the other is

the fact that both disciplines have a clear geographical focus, as both human activities and environmental (and resource) issues manifest themselves at a given point (or area) in space. This also explains why these two disciplines have many elements in common with other economic disciplines.

Regional economics has built up a significant body of explanatory theoretical and operational frameworks for the analysis of the geographical dispersion and coherence of economic activities. Location theory (partial or general) may be regarded as the heart of regional economics. Its main aim is to identify the optimal spatial position of economic actors, based on cost or welfare criteria (see for an extensive survey of the literature Thisse et al., 1996).

The recognition of environmental externalities in industrial location theory may take place along several lines:

- The adoption of a 'polluter pays' principle. This implies that the costs of environmental damage caused by a producer have to be charged to the polluting firm. In a locational context this means that the social costs of environmental decay have to be incorporated in the locational costs of the private firm, so that the ultimate location decision would respect environmental quality conditions (see Markusen, Chapter 39 in this book).
- The adoption of a regulatory regime, based, for example, on zoning conditions. Although such environmental regulations are second-best solutions, they have in practice become rather popular, as their implementation is easier to exercise. Consequently, industrial environmental policy is often based on land-use restrictions, at best supplemented by taxation schemes for environmental spillovers. Only more recently has a combination of the two approaches, based on tradable emission permits within a set of prespecified environmental quality conditions in a given area, gained more popularity (see Klaassen, 1995 and Verhoef et al., 1997; see also Koutstaal, Chapter 18 and Tietenberg, Chapter 19 in this book).

The theory of residential location decisions runs more or less parallel to the above description of industrial location analysis. Environmental externalities may either be included in the prices or rents of dwellings (so that locational choices will internalize environmental externalities) or be taken into consideration on the basis of physical planning and zoning principles (see, for example, Guldmann and Shefer, 1980). A particular case of spatial externalities may show up in the form of (positive or negative) neighbourhood effects. Such effects may also have an impact on the price levels (or rents) of dwellings and may be measured by using, for example, valuation studies based on hedonic prices or contingent valuation methods (see Part III of the present book).

At this stage, it ought to be added that a related discipline, that is, urban economics, investigates the agglomeration forces of human activities, by addressing issues of economic concentration and the development of core–periphery areas. Clearly, human and industrial settlement patterns also have drastic implications for the environmental quality of an area (including its biophysical environment). In this context, issues like urban sustainability also play a role (see Nijkamp and Perrels, 1993).

Moreover, it should be recognized that a spatial system is usually not a closed system, but faces various spatial economic and environmental interactions. Economic interactions may relate to trade flows, migration, transport and so on, while environmental interactions may concern diffusion of pollutants or water flows, but also migratory birds or animals. This means that an open regional system is permanently in a state of flux, so that integrating the spatial interactions between different variables in different regions is fraught with many problems (see Braat and van Lierop, 1987). In the past many models in the area of integrated economic–environmental analysis were static in nature, but we observe nowadays a rapid emergence of spatial dynamic models, where the dynamics of a regional economy (for example, based on investments, R&D, innovation, and so on) is linked to the dynamics of the ecosystem (for example, based on predator–prey evolution).

Seen from an open spatial systems' perspective, it is clear that a situation of global environmental sustainability is difficult to achieve (see also Giaoutzi and Nijkamp, 1993; Pezzey, 1989). Therefore it seems more promising to address environmental sustainability issues at a *meso* (that is, regional) level, as then it may be possible to achieve a more practical and operational environmental policy and management strategy. Another reason why spatial dimensions are directly connected with sustainability issues is that the geographical subdivision has far-reaching implications for the type of sustainability (for example, weak or strong) that can be attained. Environmental externalities often imply a spatial transfer of environmental burdens to other areas, so that a situation of strong sustainability in an open system of (small) regions is not likely to be reached (see also van den Bergh and Nijkamp, 1997).

We now turn to the way environmental economics has managed to include spatial(–economic) aspects in its framework of analysis. Implicitly, the spatial dimensions of environmental externalities are abundantly present in many studies, ranging from transport externalities analysed by Coase (1960) to general ecosystem degradation analysed by van den Bergh

(1996). Two major streams of analysis may be identified which pay explicit attention to geographical space.

First, a major part of the literature in the early days of environmental economics has been devoted to valuation studies, for example, of tourist areas, national parks, historical monuments and so on. Past studies in this area can be found in Nourse (1967) and Wieand (1973). The main aim was to derive from actual behaviour or from the perceived importance regarding these assets their implicit socioeconomic value in a situation where the presence of external effects prevented a straightforward market evaluation (cf. Randall and Castle, 1985). Most of these studies were based on spatially discriminating externalities as a result of the geographical spread of pollutants or the geographical distribution of environmental assets. Although several valuation studies have been undertaken in an a-spatial context, it should be recognized that the economic value of any asset (such as a dwelling, a park, a monument) is site-specific, so that spatial–economic aspects do implicitly or explicitly play a role. Common approaches were travel cost methods or willingness-to-pay methods for assessing a monetary value for the environmental asset concerned, an approach which has set the stage for the current popularity of contingent valuation studies and hedonic price studies, which have become a dominant stream in economic valuation analysis of environmental externalities (see Part VII of this book). Such analyses may also offer a foundation for Pigouvian taxation schemes in a spatial setting. Such methods were often also included in social cost–benefit analyses of environmental policies, for example in relation to agricultural, infrastructural or urbanization plans (see van Pelt, 1993).

Another major spatial orientation in the environmental economics literatures was concerned with the analysis of interactions between different regions, sectors or groups, for example, trade, transport, emission of pollutants and so on. Well-known examples of studies with a clear spatial connotation are noise annoyance studies, water pollution studies, and multiregional input–output studies (including resources and pollutants). For policy assessment and predictive purposes the latter approach in particular appeared to be very useful. Many interesting examples and spatial–economic theoretical contributions can be found in Schnaiberg et al. (1986). In the next section some further remarks on this approach will be offered.

This concise overview has clearly demonstrated that the space–environment linkage is multifaceted and calls for research into various difficult analytical issues, such as the distributional impacts of policy (witness the NIMBY phenomenon), the analysis of environmental options in space, the management of common resources in a given area, or the establishment of spatial compensation schemes for environmental decay. Optimization models seeking to identify shadow prices for spatially discriminating environmental standards are good examples of innovative research in this area (see, for example, Hafkamp, 1984). Other interesting concepts are the shadow project approach seeking for real-world compensation for the loss of environmental goods (see Klaassen and Botterweg, 1976). Thus there are many new perspectives for analysing the linkages between the space–economy and the environment, in which land use and spatial behaviour are closely connected with environmental externalities.

3. Modelling the spatial–economic and environmental–economic nexus

The element of space in environmental economics and the position of the environment in regional economics have been modelled in various ways in the past decades. Environmental–economic modelling has become a broad research area (see also Madsen et al., 1996). The analysis of the space–environment nexus provokes various questions on the interaction between land use and the environment, for example, on the role of the environment as a productive resource or as a consumption item to be included in a welfare function, on the trade-off between unpriced and priced goods, on the interest of new generations (here or elsewhere); see van Pelt (1993). He claims that environmental policy has to be region-specific in light of distributional issues and site-specific attributes and human perceptions of environmental decay. But the modelling of such phenomena is fraught with a number of difficulties, partly of a methodological nature, partly of an empirical nature. There is not an unambiguous research tradition on spatial and environmental economic issues, but there are different research methodologies which will be concisely reviewed here.

First, there are several attempts to analyse formally – by means of partial statistical models or integrated equilibrium models – spatial–environmental externalities, in the form of social costs incurred in the form of pollution (air, water, soil) emerging from the regional–industrial structure of a given area. Such studies started as a generalization of 'space-less' economic models, but focused increasingly on broader environmental issues such as land use, nature conservation, quality of life or even urban monument conservation. Empirically they also achieved a much more concrete focus, for example on cities, islands, lakes, mountainous areas, or agricultural regions. In the 1980s a wide variety of scientific efforts has been made to design operational planning and forecasting models for such issues (see, for an overview, Giaoutzi and Nijkamp, 1993; see also Banister, Chapter 38, this book). Later on, there was also growing interest in the environmentally disruptive impacts of tourism, recreation, intensified land use, development conflicts and extractive activities. It is increasingly recognized that effective policy measures must be taken to reduce or eliminate the environmental externalities of such activities. Here the issue of sustainable development for ecologically vulnerable areas – with a focus on local and regional conditions – is at stake (see also Section 2). In this context, the notion of *regional* sustainable development is an important one (see Giaoutzi and Nijkamp, 1993).

A second class of modelling contributions at the interface of regional and environmental economics – mainly of an applied nature – can be found in the field of spatial interactions. Such interactions may concern the distribution of pollutants over various regions or cities, such as transboundary air pollution, pollution of rivers crossing different areas, transport of solid waste as part of a materials chains, and so on. Modelling such flows already has a long tradition, starting from the materials balance model which is essentially based on the law of conservation of materials and energy (see Ayres and Kneese, 1969). In addition, the large number of transportation models with environmental decay components should be mentioned here (see Verhoef, 1996; see also Button and Rietveld, Chapter 40, this book). In a multiregional context, this issue provokes various distributional concerns which may have important policy implications. Examples are spatial compensation schemes for damage caused by environmental externalities from different regions, tradable emission permits for pollution from different areas of a spatial system, and so forth (see also Folmer and Thijssen, 1996). Such models are often used for spatial–environmental policy assessment. It is clear that the nature of policy solutions is in general dependent on the reciprocity of pollution effects and on the separability of the external (social) costs (in terms of marginal costs).

A complementary way of depicting economic–environmental interdependences is the use of multiregional input–output models already alluded to above. In this approach the focus is on economic intersectoral linkages between different regions, represented in a closed form. Pollution, resource and energy implications of such interregional flows are then added through a balanced physically oriented model, often based on an integration of materials balance notions and fixed input–output linkages. Important questions to be answered by using such models may be the regional implications of (possibly regional discriminatory) taxation schemes on environmental externalities, or the environmental implications of new industrial developments in one region on all other regions. Interesting empirical examples of such approaches can be found in Lakshmanan and Nijkamp (1983) and Hafkamp (1984). All such attempts offer a consistent and comprehensive picture of spatial, environmental and economic interwovenness. Clearly, this approach requires an extensive database, which is in many cases unavailable, so that the actual potential of this approach is often rather limited.

A more recent class of integrated spatial, economic and environmental models can be found in spatial–economic (price) equilibrium analysis and in applied (or computable) general equilibrium analysis (see van den Bergh et al., 1996 and Takayama, 1996). Such models describe spatially disaggregated, economy-wide equilibrium patterns, in terms of commodity (freight) flows or passenger flows. Spatial price equilibrium models are based on flexible prices clearing spatial excess demands and supplies for given transport costs structures (see also Takayama and Labys, 1986). An extension of such models with spatial environmental externalities (for example environmental decay caused by pollution) is contained in Verhoef and van den Bergh et al. (1996) and van den Bergh and Nijkamp (1997). It is noteworthy that a similar approach can not only be found in the area of regional economics, but also at a wider scale of international trade theory (see, for example, Verbruggen, 1996). Spatial dynamic environmental models with an evolutionary perspective are also increasingly coming to the fore, although most of these attempts are still rather theoretical (see Nijkamp and Reggiani, 1997).

In the light of the previous concise overview, we may conclude that the modelling of environmental–economic phenomena in a spatial context has no doubt generated a wealth of inspiring scientific contributions which in many cases also have a clear policy relevance. Challenging tasks can, however, still be found in the following research fields:

- Design of spatial–dynamic models with non-linear feedback loops so as to map out the complex environmental–economic linkages in a space–time setting including endogenous growth issues (see also Nijkamp and Reggiani, 1997).
- Development of common areal classification principles for spatial–economic and environmental phenomena, using varying scale methods based on, for example, geographic information systems (GIS) (see, for example, Douven, 1997).
- Development of a proper spatial–environmental indicator system which may be helpful in assessing plausible environmental parameter values in spatial–economic models.
- Establishing critical threshold values (safe minimum standards, carrying capacity and so on),which may be site-specific and which may also be helpful in risk (perception) studies often characterized by a strong geographical component (for example, distance decay).
- Integration of analytical modelling results with spatial–environmental policy issues which may map out the complicated trade-offs of economic and environmental welfare components in a spatial context (including, for example, land-use zoning or protected environmental areas).

Needless to say, progress at the interface of regional and environmental economics is contingent upon the availability of proper spatial information systems (such as geographic information systems).

4.   Spatial–environmental policy studies

Spatial–environmental policies cover a wide range of government measures, such as (local and regional) taxation schemes or subsidies, land-use zoning initiatives, regional environmental standards, industrial location strategies, infrastructure investments and the like. Such measures may be market-oriented or just be based on second-best principles; they may be of a control-and-command type or of a stimulating (or discouraging) nature; they may be strictly environmental in nature or address broader issues related to regional sustainable development. It is clear that different economic policies in an open economic system of regions have immediate implications for the environmental quality in each of the regions. Furthermore, different environmental policies in a spatial system of regions have consequences for the well-being in each area. Thus, both regional–economic and environmental–economic policies may become competitive weapons in an open regional system.

Spatial–environmental policy studies are normally based on analytical frameworks as described in the previous sections, but have also their distinct intrinsic merits and features. In general, such studies may be subdivided into two main categories: *impact studies* and *decision support studies*. We shall briefly describe both classes.

Impact studies normally deal with 'what if' questions. The analytical tools have already been described in Section 3 (input–output models, spatial equilibrium models and so on). Such studies are particularly important, as in an open spatial–economic and environmental system interregional flows (for example, goods, services, migration, pollution) may lead to spatially discriminating distributive effects which may form the root of many conflicts. Clearly, both industrial policies and environmental policies may generate complicated spatial spillovers which may affect the welfare position of the regions at hand. For instance, public investment programmes, physical planning and infrastructural measures, land-use zoning principles, establishment of regional environmental standards and the like will all affect the environmental quality of regions in an open spatial system (see for a broad review Schnaiberg et al., 1986). Interesting recent illustrations of such spatial–environmental policy studies can be found in a study by Gørtz (1996) on the regional consequences of environmental taxes, of Jensen and Stryg (1996) on the spatially distributive impacts of a taxation of fertilizers, and of Jensen-Butler and Madsen (1996) on the spatial–economic impacts of environmental measures in the transport sector. The results of such studies may also form an operational input for decision support studies in a multiregional context.

Decision support studies aim to map out the trade-offs between different policy options, including distributional conflicts and environmental quality consequences. In a spatial context, these trade-offs are also reflected in different development opportunities of regions or places in a spatial system (see, for example, Nijkamp et al., 1992; Forslund and Lindberg, 1996). There is in general a multiplicity of actors, of regions, of regional environments and of policy objectives, which may be depicted by an operational spatial–environmental economic model as described above. In several cases, however, research has to rely on *ad hoc* information, expert opinion and so on, so that a precise assessment of the (socio)economic and environmental implications of spatial–environmental policies is fraught with uncertainties.

In this context, the results of valuation and modelling studies are often fed into decision support analysis which may comprise various analysis frameworks. They may pertain to social cost-benefit analysis (for example, for infrastructure network programmes or regional environmental taxation schemes), to multiple objective programming models (especially in the case of a continuous modelling representation with conflicting policy objectives), or to multi-criteria analysis (in the case of the evaluation of a discrete number of environmental–economic policy choices). In a situation of qualitative or fuzzy information, specific qualitative multi-criteria decision support techniques are available (see Janssen, 1992, Munda, 1995 and Chapter 58 in this book). These decision support methods have been used extensively in spatial–environmental policy studies, for instance, land reclamation projects, location policies on nuclear power plants, evaluation of new industrial sites and so on (for a survey see Nijkamp et al., 1992).

We may conclude that in the field of environmental policy support a wide variety of different operational methods does exist, which have proven their feasibility in the past decades.

5. Prospect

The methodology for the integration of socioeconomic variables (depicting the pattern and evolution of a local or regional economy) and of ecological variables (mirroring the development of ecosystems in the study area concerned) is usually fraught with many difficulties. In order to map out such complex interactions in a consistent way, it is often appropriate to design a cohesive economic–ecological structure model on the basis of the so-called 'satellite' principle (cf. Brouwer, 1988). This principle means that the core of interactions between the economy and the environment in a regional system is described in a compact but comprehensive system model.

All other (non-core) phenomena are not represented in full depth and without all their complex dynamic interactions, but are only depicted in terms of their main linkages to the core. All satellite modules may also have a distinct spatial scale (for example, for ecosystems, for recreational behaviour, for system-wide efficiency and so on). This core–satellite design ensures a consistent, concise and structured presentation of a compound multidimensional system for a spatial economy, based on a hierarchical modular structure.

Several variables (like landscape or ecological data) can be spatially differentiated, whereas others (like socioeconomic data) are often only used in an aggregate manner. This means that the spatial component has to be dealt with carefully in the empirical analysis, which is also the reason why GIS (geographical information systems) is an indispensable element in modern environmental planning studies.

In general, systems theory offers a fruitful background and frame of reference for assessing various effects in a compound spatial–economic and environmental system. In order to develop a practical research methodology for sustainability planning at the local or regional level, various scientific methods may be helpful. Examples are: dynamic systems analysis; spatial impact analysis; spatial–environmental scenario analysis; geographical information systems modelling; multi-criteria decision support analysis; spatial simulation studies, and so forth.

It is evident that effective and accessible information systems are vital to spatial–economic and environmental decision making. The rapid development of digital and electronic technologies, for instance, in the form of digital recording and transmission of sound and pictures, optical fibres for the high speed of transmission of information, super-fast computers, satellite broadcasting and video transmission, offer a new potential for sophisticated voice, data and image transmission. All such information systems may be highly important for the planning of our scarce space, not only on a global scale (for example, monitoring of rainforest development), but also on a local scale (for example, physical planning). Within this framework, spatial information systems are increasingly combined with geographic pattern recognition, spatial systems theory, topology and spatial simulation analysis.

Finally, it is important to stress that the degree of sophistication in spatial–environmental systems modelling should keep pace with the needs of decision makers and stakeholders. Thus there is a clear need for an increase in user-friendliness of regional–environmental models. Clearly, making a complex system more user-friendly may narrow its range of applications and may make the system more rigid. Proper user support tools, amongst others, are: accessible source programme documentations;

user-oriented scenario visualization; inclusion of sample runs with graphical results, and so on. There is no doubt that, seen from a regional economic and land-use perspective, a formidable research challenge still lies ahead of us.

References
Ayres, R.U. and A.V. Kneese (1969), 'Production, consumption and externalities', *American Economic Review*, **59**, 282–97.
Bergh, J.C.J.M. van den (1996), *Ecological Economics and Sustainable Development*, Cheltenham, UK and Brookfield, US: Edward Elgar.
Bergh, J.C.J.M. van den and P. Nijkamp (1997), 'Growth, trade and sustainability in the spatial economy', *Studies in Regional Science*, **25** (2), 67–87.
Bergh, J.C.J.M. van den, P. Nijkamp and P. Rietveld (eds) (1996), *Recent Advances in Spatial Equilibrium Modelling*, Berlin: Springer-Verlag.
Boulding, K.E. (1969), 'Economics as a moral science, *American Economic Review*, **59**, 1–2.
Braat, L.C. and W.F.J. van Lierop (eds) (1987), *Economic Ecological Modelling*, Amsterdam: North-Holland.
Brouwer, F.M. (1988), *Integrated Environmental Modelling*, Dordrecht: Kluwer Academic Publishers.
Burton, T.L. (1971), *Experiments in Recreation Research*, London: Allen university.
Coase, R.H. (1960), 'The problem of social cost', *Journal of Law and Economics*, **3**, 1–44.
Cumberland, J.H. (1966), 'A regional inter-industry model for analysis of development objectives', *Papers of the Regional Science Association*, **17**, 65–95.
Douven, W. (1997), *Improving the Accessibility of Spatial Information for Environmental Management*, Ph.D. dissertation, Free University, Amsterdam.
Folmer, H. and G. Thijssen (1996), 'Interaction between the agricultural economy and the environment', in Madsen et al. (1996), pp. 12–36.
Forslund, U.M. and G. Lindberg (1996), 'Multicriteria assessments of national road programs', in Madsen et al. (1996), pp. 239–58.
Giaoutzi, M. and P. Nijkamp (1993), *Decision Support Models for Regional Sustainable Development*, Aldershot, UK: Avebury.
Gørtz, M. (1996), 'Regional consequences of environmental taxes', in Madsen et al. (1996), pp. 93–116.
Guldmann, J.M. and D. Shefer (1980), *Industrial Location and Air Quality Control*, New York: John Wiley.
Hafkamp, W.A. (1984), *Economic–Environmental Modelling in a National Regional System*, Amsterdam: North-Holland.
Isard, W. (1956), *Location and the Space-Economy*, Cambridge: MIT Press.
Isard, W. (1969), 'Some notes on the linkage of ecologic and economic systems', *Papers of the Regional Science Association*, **22**, 85–96.
Isard, W. (1972), *Ecologic–Economic Analysis for Regional Development*, New York: Free Press.
Janssen, R. (1992), *Multi-Objective Decision Support for Environmental Management*, Dordrecht: Kluwer.
Jensen, T. and P.E. Stryg (1996), 'The regional economic consequences of taxation on commercial fertilizers', in Madsen et al. (1996), pp. 187–209.
Jensen-Butler, C. and B. Madsen (1996), 'Modelling the regional economic consequences of environmental policy instruments applied to the transport sector', in Madsen et al. (1996), pp. 308–30.
Klaassen, G.A.J. (1995), *Trading Sulphur Emission Reduction Commitments in Europe*, Ph.D. thesis, Free University, Amsterdam.
Klaassen, L.H. and T.H. Botterweg (1976), 'Project evaluation and intangible effects: a shadow project approach', in P. Nijkamp (ed.), *Environmental Economics*, vol. 1, The Hague, pp. 35–49.

Kneese, A.V. (1965), 'Rationalizing decisions in the quality management of water supply in urban–industrial areas', in J. Margolis (ed.), *The Public Economy of Urban Communities*, Baltimore, MD: Johns Hopkins University Press, pp. 170–91.

Krutilla, J.V. (ed.) (1972), *Natural Environments*, Baltimore, MD: Johns Hopkins University Press.

Lakshmanan, T.R. and P. Nijkamp (eds) (1983), *Systems and Models for Energy and Environmental Analysis*, Aldershot, UK: Avebury.

Leontief, W. (1970), 'Environmental repercussions and the economic structure', *The Review of Economics and Statistics*, **52** (3), 262–71.

Madsen, B., C. Jensen-Butler, J. Birk Mortensen and A.M. Brown Christensen (eds), *Modelling the Economy and the Environment*, Berlin: Springer-Verlag.

Mishan, E.J. (1967), *The Costs of Economic Growth*, London: Staples Press.

Muller, F. (1979), *Energy and Environment in Interregional Input–Output Models*, The Hague: Martinus Nijhoff.

Munda, G. (1995), *Multicriteria Evaluation in a Fuzzy Environment*, Heidelberg: Physica-Verlag.

Nijkamp, P. (1977), *Theory and Application of Environmental Economics*, Amsterdam: North-Holland.

Nijkamp, P. (1981), *Environmental Policy Analysis*, New York: John Wiley.

Nijkamp, P. and A. Perrels (1993), *Sustainable Cities in Europe*, London: Earthscan.

Nijkamp, P. and A. Reggiani (1997), *The Economics of Complex Spatial Systems*, Amsterdam: Elsevier.

Nijkamp, P., P. Rietveld and H. Voogd (1992), *Multicriteria Analysis for Physical Planning*, Amsterdam: North-Holland.

Nourse, H.O. (1967), 'The effect of air pollution on house values', *Land Economics*, **43**, 181–9.

Paelinck, J.H.P. and P. Nijkamp (1975), *Operational Theory and Method in Regional Economics*, Aldershot, UK: Saxon House.

Pelt, M.J.F. van (1993), *Ecological Sustainability and Project Appraisal*, Aldershot, UK: Avebury.

Pezzey, J. (1989), *Economic Analysis of Sustainable Growth and Sustainable Development*, Washington, DC: World Bank.

Ponsard, C. (1983), *History of Spatial Economic Theory*, Berlin: Springer-Verlag.

Randall, A. and E.N. Castle (1985), 'Land resources and land markets', in A.V. Kneese and J.L. Sweeney (eds), *Handbook of Natural Resource and Energy Economics*, Amsterdam: North-Holland, pp. 571–620.

Schnaiberg, A., N. Watts and K. Zimmermann (eds), *Distributional Conflicts in Environmental Resource Policy*, Aldershot, UK: Gower.

Takayama, T. (1996), 'Thirty years with spatial and intertemporal economics', in J.C.J.M. van den Bergh, P. Nijkamp and P. Rietveld (eds), *Advances in Spatial Equilibrium Modelling*, Berlin: Springer-Verlag, pp. 3–45.

Takayama, T. and W.C. Labys (1986), 'Spatial equilibrium analysis' in P. Nijkamp (ed.), *Handbook of Regional and Urban Economics*, vol. 1, Amsterdam: Elsevier, pp. 171–99.

Thisse, J.F., K. Button and P. Nijkamp (eds) (1996), *Location Theory*, Cheltenham, UK and Brookfield, US: Edward Elgar.

Verbruggen, H. (1996), 'Environmental standards in international trade', in P. van Dijck and G. Faber (eds), *Challenges to the World Trade Organization*, The Hague: Kluwer Law International, pp. 265–90.

Verhoef, E.T. (1996), *The Economics of Regulating Road Transport*, Cheltenham, UK and Brookfield, US: Edward Elgar.

Verhoef, E.T. and J.C.J.M. van den Bergh (1996), 'A spatial price equilibrium model for environmental policy analysis of mobile and immobile sources of pollution', in J.C.J.M. van den Bergh, P. Nijkamp and P. Rietveld (eds), *Recent Advances in Spatial Equilibrium Modelling: Methodology and Applications*, Heidelberg: Springer-Verlag, pp. 201–20.

Verhoef, E.T., J.C.J.M. van den Bergh and K.J. Button (1997), 'Transport, spatial economy and the global environment', *Environment and Planning A*, **29B**, 1195–1213.

Wieand, K.F. (1973), 'Air pollution and property values', *Journal of Regional Science*, **13** (1), 91–5.

36 Non-point source pollution control
Anastasios Xepapadeas

1. Introduction

In contrast to point source (PS) pollution problems where the source, the size and the distinctive characteristics of the discharges can be identified with sufficient accuracy at a non-prohibitive cost, in non-point source (NPS) pollution problems neither the source nor the size of the individual emissions can be observed by an environmental regulator seeking to implement a given environmental policy. Both in theoretical and applied environmental economics, PS pollution problems have traditionally been associated with large industrial or municipal emissions, while NPS pollution problems relate mostly to emissions by small sources like farmers or households, or mobile sources such as vehicles. The pollution that these sources generate mainly includes nutrient pollution, pesticide pollution, sedimentation, vehicle pollution, and hazardous and solid wastes.

The significance of NPS type pollution is indicated by the fact that part of the degradation of many of the world's lakes and reservoirs can be traced to this type. Degradation is due to a number of factors, including eutrophication, which results from accelerated nutrient loading due to expanded farming practices; toxic substances entering the water bodies as agricultural runoff along with forestry drainage, which includes a range of toxic pesticides and herbicides; accelerated sedimentation caused by farming on fragile soils and steep slopes, forestry activities, construction activities and urban drainage; acidification of aquatic systems from emissions of sulphur dioxide and nitrous oxides due to acid rain or through leaching from affected land. In all of these cases monitoring of the individual emissions which are associated with farming or forestry activities, with acid rain, or with urban drainage, and which are responsible for environmental degradation, is not possible due to the number of sources and the diffused character of the pollution. In many cases critical pollution-generating inputs are not always observable while weather conditions introduce stochastic elements into the pollution dispersion process, making identification of the polluting source and its contribution to the ambient pollution in the specific receiving body practically impossible. Thus in an NPS problem an environmental regulator can measure the ambient pollution at specific 'receptor points', but cannot attribute any specific portion of the pollutant concentration to a specific discharger. Therefore the problems that characterize an NPS pollution problem are mainly informational, and have been distinguished by Braden and Segerson (1993) into two broad classes: problems related to monitoring and measurement, and problems related to natural variability.[1] Monitoring problems are associated with the inability directly to observe individual emissions or to infer them from observable inputs or from the ambient concentration of the pollutant. Natural variability is associated mainly with weather conditions or technological uncertainty and results in stochastic pollution processes.

The informational asymmetries between the regulator and individual dischargers in an NPS problem could take the form of moral hazard characterized by hidden actions or/and adverse selection. Inability to observe the emissions of each potential polluter is associated with moral hazard, while inability to know the specific characteristics or type of each potential polluter – which is private information known only to the polluter – is associated with adverse selection. In a situation characterized by these informational asymmetries, the environmental regulator cannot use standard instruments of environmental policy such as Pigouvian taxes, tradable emission permits and emission standards as a means of inducing dischargers to follow socially desirable policies. The potential dischargers will choose higher than socially desirable emission levels if by doing so they can increase their profits, since their emissions cannot be observed and the standard environmental policy instruments cannot be used to internalize external damages and to obtain the Pareto-optimal outcome. Policy schemes capable of dealing with this situation are summarized in the following section.

2.   Environmental policy for NPS pollution

The inadequacy of the standard instruments of environmental policy to deal with NPS problems has resulted, in recent years, in increasing attention being given to the development of policy schemes appropriate for NPS problems. These schemes can be divided into two broad categories: ambient taxes where the scheme is based on the observed ambient pollution; and input-based schemes, where the policy scheme consists of taxes applied to observable polluting inputs. In the former category collective penalty schemes and schemes that constitute menus of ambient taxes and effluent fees, which are based on incomplete observability of individual emissions and self-reporting by potential polluters, can also be included.

Imperfect observability and ambient taxes
When individual emissions are not observed then the problem is characterized by moral hazard with hidden actions. A prototype model of imperfect

observability of individual emissions that can be used as a basis for the development of policy instruments can be described as follows (Xepapadeas, 1995).

A perfectly competitive market of $i = 1, ..., n$ firms producing a homogeneous output is considered, where output production generates pollution that can be abated by using additional resources. The benefit function of each firm can be defined as a function of emission levels when the firm chooses the profit-maximizing level of output, $B_i = B_i(e_i)$, $B_i'' < 0$, where $e_i \in E_i \in \Re_+$ denotes the emissions of the ith firm.

Damage from total emissions is defined as a convex function of total emissions, with pollution regarded as a flow externality, $D = D(X)$, $D' > 0$, $D'' \geq 0$, $X = \Sigma_i e_i$. As is well known, an environmental regulator seeking to maximize total benefit less environmental damages will choose the socially optimum emission level for each firm, such that marginal benefit equals marginal damages for all i, or $B'_i(e_i^*) = D'$. Then the optimal level of ambient pollution is $X^* = \Sigma_i e_i^*$.

Let s_i represent the observed part of emissions by firm i, that is, $s_i \in [0, e_i]$. It is assumed that firm i's observed emissions depend on a parameter m_i, and is determined according to the function: $s_i = f_i(m_i)$. The parameter m_i can be interpreted in different ways. It can be regarded as reflecting monitoring effort to determine physical characteristics of the firm (for example, location, soil constitution, types of inputs used, production practices) that permit the quantification of emissions, or as information provided by the firm itself that can lead to a quantification of a certain part of its own emissions, or as the amount of installed monitoring equipment.

Assume that the environmental regulator tries to formulate a policy that will induce firms to emit at the socially desirable level, e_i^*. Consider two possible policy instruments:

1. A Pigouvian tax or effluent fee, τ_i, that is imposed on firm i per unit of observed emissions.
2. An ambient tax which firms are liable to pay if measured total ambient emissions, X, at some receptor point exceed the desired cutoff level, X^*. The ambient tax is specified as a function of the observed emissions of each firm. That is, for firm i, the ambient tax is defined as: $g_i(s_i) \equiv g_i(f_i(m_i)) \equiv h_i(m_i)$.

If the firm faces a tax scheme consisting of both ambient and effluent taxes, its profit function will be:

$$\Pi(e_i, m_i) = B_i(e_i) - h_i(m_i)(X - X^*) - \tau_i f_i(m_i) \qquad (36.1)$$

The environmental regulator must choose the tax parameters $h_i(m_i)$ and τ_i to maximize total benefits less total damages. Furthermore, if firms follow the regulator's instructions about the environmental policy to be adopted, they should maximize their profits. The last requirement implies that in the regulator's problem the constraint that (36.1) is maximized for $e_i = \hat{e}_i$, given the emission policies of the rest of the firms, should be imposed. This means that the regulator's problem takes the form:

$$\max_{\substack{e_1, \dots, e_n \\ m_1, \dots, m_n \\ \tau_1, \dots, \tau_n}} \sum_i B_i(e_i) - D(X) \qquad (36.2)$$

$$X = \sum_i e_i,\ m_i \in M_i,\ \tau_i \in T_i \qquad (36.2a)$$

$$e_i \in \operatorname{argmax} B_i(e_i) - h_i(m_i)\left(e_i + \sum_{j \neq i}\hat{e}_j - X^*\right) - \tau_i f_i(m_i) \forall\ i \quad (36.2b)$$

$$\text{subject to } f_i(m_i) \leq e_i \qquad (36.2c)$$

Solving this problem,[2] the optimal ambient and effluent fees in the two polar cases of non-observability and complete observability are determined as follows:

(i)   If there is no observability of individual emissions, that is for all i, $m_i = 0$, then $a_i = D'$, $\tau_i = 0$.
(ii) If there is full observability of individual emissions, then $a_i = 0$, $\tau_i = D'$.

When there is no observability, the producers are liable for an ambient tax equal to marginal damages per unit deviation from the cut-off level. The producer facing this scheme will adjust its production and abatement process such that marginal benefits from emissions equal marginal damages, adopting therefore the socially desirable emissions levels. Under the ambient tax, as can be easily shown by substituting a_i and τ_i from (i) into (36.1), profit-maximizing firms equate marginal benefits from emissions with the *full* marginal damages of emissions. Thus the socially optimal emission level is chosen and moral hazard is eliminated.[3] Under full observability the polluter discharges the socially desired emissions when the tax per unit of its own emissions is equal to marginal damages, which is the usual Pigouvian tax.

In an NPS pollution problem the regulator has no incentive to increase observability by increasing m_i since it can achieve the social optimum by setting the ambient tax at the optimal level. Furthermore, there is no incentive from the firm's point of view to reveal information about its emissions and as a result of this pay an effluent fee in exchange for a low ambient tax rate (Xepapadeas, 1995). Thus if the ambient tax is set at the level of marginal damages and there is no uncertainty, the firms that have adjusted their emissions to the desirable emission level are not willing to pay any effluent fee, by having their emissions measured or by revealing some information to the regulator, in order to be liable for a lower ambient tax rate. Since neither the regulator nor the firm has any incentive to increase m_i from zero, it is socially optimal to have individual emissions remain unmonitored (or unobserved) in an NPS pollution problem and use ambient taxes.

Ambient taxes can also be defined in a dynamic set-up where the pollution has stock characteristics. That is, it is the accumulated amount of the pollutant that causes damages. This amount increases by the adding up of individual emissions and is reduced to the extent of the environment's self-cleaning capacity. In this context it can be shown (Xepapadeas, 1992) that an ambient tax determined by the dynamic shadow cost of the accumulated pollutant and applied to the observed deviations per unit time between the observed pollution stock and the desired cut-off stock can achieve the long-run socially optimal pollution accumulation.

Uncertainty issues can be incorporated into the definition of ambient taxes. As has been shown by Segerson (1988), ambient taxes can be defined in terms of expected marginal damages. The same methodology can be extended to include spatial considerations by examining a multiple-zone system with stochastic transport of pollutants among zones and with ambient measurements at specific zones (Cabe and Herriges, 1991). Again the ambient taxes which are zone-specific depend on expected marginal damages as well as on possible discrepancies between the regulator's and the polluters' beliefs about the probability distributions of factors influencing the ambient pollution level in each zone.

It is very likely, however, that the introduction and implementation of ambient taxes will be difficult. While individual dischargers might accept the idea of paying an effluent fee based on their own emissions, they may very well resent the idea of being liable for a tax which will strongly depend on other dischargers' actions, along with random factors, after they have internalized the social costs by adjusting their emissions to the socially desirable level. There might also exist a legal problem in enforcing the ambient tax scheme, especially when random penalties are involved in cases of balancing-budget schemes for NPS pollution (Xepapadeas, 1991).

These factors suggest that any increase in observability of individual emissions in an NPS pollution problem might be desirable. The argument can be made more precise by considering the case where the ambient concentration of the pollutant as measured at some receptor point is stochastic. In this case, the polluting firm might be liable for the payment of the ambient tax, even if it has adjusted its emissions to the optimal level, because the measured pollutant level could exceed the expected cut-off level due to random shocks.

On the other hand, the ambient tax liability would have been zero if individual emissions had been observed. So observability of individual emissions might be regarded as some type of insurance for individual dischargers when the ambient pollutant level is stochastic. As shown in Xepapadeas (1995) the environmental regulator is able, by measuring ambient pollution at a receptor point and by choosing appropriate levels of effluent fees and ambient taxes, to induce individual profit-maximizing polluters to reveal a part or even all of their emissions without any need to incur any further individual monitoring cost, and at the same time to secure the socially desirable emission levels. Thus this fundamental complementarity between Pigouvian taxes and ambient taxes can be used to introduce a combined instrument without any extra costs that could be more implementable than pure ambient taxes.[4]

Collective penalties and budget-balancing schemes   When ambient taxes are used as an instrument, the payment by all potential polluters is triggered when measured ambient pollution levels at a receptor point exceed some desired or cut-off level. This gives ambient taxes the characteristic of a collective penalty. The collective penalty of the ambient tax is further intensified by adding to the scheme a fixed penalty that is independent of the deviation between observed and desired pollution levels (Meran and Schwalbe, 1987; Segerson, 1988). The purpose of the penalty, which can also be used as a single instrument and not in combination with an ambient tax, and is paid by all potential polluters if deviations are observed, is to counterbalance any gains from free-riding which result if individual polluters emit unobserved more than the desirable level.

Collective penalty schemes consisting of some combination of ambient taxes and fixed penalties are referred to as non-budget-balancing (NBB) contracts, which implies that the total payment of the polluters, or the total subsidy given to polluters to abate pollution under the contract, exceeds the social cost of pollution or the social value of abatement. On the other hand under budget-balancing (BB) contracts the potential polluters receive exactly the net social value of abatement after deducting the social cost of any excess emissions.[5] BB contracts introduced by Xepapadeas (1991) in the field of environmental policy are based on penalties imposed randomly on one or more potential polluters and subsidies given to the rest so that the budget is always balanced; that is, the total subsidy for abating pollution equals the net social value of abatement. As shown by Herriges et al. (1994), if the polluters are sufficiently risk-averse, then the BB contract provides the correct incentives for optimal abatement in the case of NPS pollution. Although BB contracts can reduce the informational requirements of the regulator since the contract does not require information about individual abatement but only measurements at receptor points, the introduction of random penalties could undermine its acceptability as an instrument of environmental policy.

Input-based incentive schemes
Input-based incentive schemes, also called indirect schemes, were first suggested by Griffin and Bromley (1982). In its simplest form this approach states that if unobservable emissions are perfectly correlated with an observed input and if there are no informational problems associated with the type of the potential polluters, then the first-best policy can be obtained by appropriately taxing the observed input.

Assume, using the model in Section 2.1, that the emissions generated by each polluter are defined as a deterministic function of one observable input x used by the polluter. This function is known to the regulator and is defined as $e_i = h(x_i)$, $h_x > 0$, $h_{xx} < 0$. Then the tax on input x is defined as $\tau_x = D'(X^*)h_x(x^*)$, where x^* is determined by the relationship $e^* = h(x^*)$. In this case the polluter solves the problem:

$$\max_{x_i} B_i\big(h(x_i)\big) - \big(D'(X^*)h_x(x_i^*)\big)x_i$$

choosing again emissions according to the usual optimality condition that marginal benefits equal marginal damages.

However, the implementation of such an input tax is most likely to be impeded by informational asymmetries due to imperfect correlation between individual emissions and the observed variables. In such a case the approach is basically to build models describing the interactions between production technologies and environmental pollution. These combined economic–biophysical models can be used to estimate individual emissions, by relating observable inputs used by the potential polluters and measured ambient concentration of pollutants (Shortle and Dunn, 1986; Dosi and Moretto, 1990, 1993; Weaver, 1996). Provided that the models can be granted 'political legitimacy', they can be used as a basis for designing incentive schemes, such as economic instruments based on the individual emissions estimated by the biophysical models, taxes on the use of observed polluting inputs or management practice standards. The indirect approach can be extended to cover stochastic changes in 'site quality', which is an important parameter in the estimation of individual emissions through biophysical models (Dosi and Moretto, 1994).

Input-based schemes can also be extended to cover adverse selection cases, in which the informational asymmetries correspond to the specific polluters' characteristics which are private information. Spulber (1988) derives an incentive scheme wherein the effluent tax and the effluent level depend on the combined announcement cost parameters of the firm. Shortle and Abler (1994), in a framework where individual emissions are stochastic and unobservable and the polluters' profits depend on private information, derive input taxes and mixed schemes, consisting of input-based taxes/subsidies and permits for the use of polluting inputs, which can be used to control NPS pollution. Weaver and Thomas (1996), on the other hand, discuss an input-based tax when the regulator cannot observe private characteristics associated with efficiency in the use of polluting inputs. In a comparable set-up, Xepapadeas (1996) considers a simultaneous moral hazard and adverse selection problem, that is, unobservability of individual emissions and private knowledge of the polluters' characteristics. In this model emissions are defined as $e_i(\beta) = h(x_i(\beta)) - \beta + \epsilon$, where β is the type of the polluter reflecting efficiency in emission generation. The higher β is, the better the emission characteristics of the polluter are, and ϵ is a random variable with zero mean reflecting observational errors. Since β is unobservable by the regulator, emissions cannot be inferred from the observed input use as in the case of the deterministic emission function. In this model emissions is the moral hazard variable, while the type β is the adverse selection variable. By using the mechanism design approach to regulation,[6] linear taxes on observable polluting inputs are derived, which can be used to control the unobservable emissions.[7]

3.   Applied policy issues

NPS pollution problems in practice relate mainly to water pollution due to agricultural, industrial or household activities. Actual policies against water pollution which are common in many countries (OECD, 1994) include user charges for sewerage and sewage treatment, water effluent charges and charges in agriculture, along with a number of more specific policies. These are general policies that do not readily conform to the stylized characteristics of the NPS pollution instruments discussed here; nevertheless there are features that attempt to address the non-observability of individual emissions.

User charges for sewerage and sewage treatment when measurement of the pollution load is not possible are based on water usage which provides an indirect indicator of waste-water generation. This policy can be regarded as a type of input-based incentive scheme. In fact from 18 countries surveyed by the OECD (1994) only in nine countries were firms charged on the basis of metered pollution load, while on the other hand all households were charged for water use.

Water effluent charges are mainly based on metered pollution loads, thus resembling more closely a point source instrument. In France, according to a charge administered by 'Agence de l'Eau', firms can lower their effluent bill if they can prove that their emissions are lower than those estimated by the Agence. This is a case of individual emission revelation in order to reduce payment. Thus this instrument can be regarded as having some similarities, regarding the private revelation process, to the combined instrument scheme discussed at the end of the second section. The Dutch water pollution charge has ambient tax characteristics for households and small firms, since they pay a fixed amount independent of their actual emissions. On the other hand large firms are metered. In this case we have a transformation of an NPS problem to a PS problem through metering.

Charges in agriculture are a more profound case of input-based schemes. Charges on fertilizers as applied in many countries, are based on the nitrogen and phosphorus content of fertilizers which are the main contributors to NPS pollution in surface water. A number of off-farm management methods also exist for reducing phosphorus runoff such as vegetation buffer strips, riparian zones, and dredging of the lake sediment.

There are also more specific policies aimed at addressing NPS pollution problems, especially in relation to agriculture. For example, in Austria there are groundwater protection zones in which if the water quality is reduced, farmers have to comply with certain management practices or change land use. In Spain there are zonal programmes for reducing fertilizers; in Holland there is a 'manure and mud ammonia policy'; in England and Wales codes exist which give farmers guidance on maintaining good agricultural practices, while in Ireland there is a voluntary scheme for farmers to follow a specific nutrient management plan.

4. Summary and conclusions
Efficient environmental regulation in an NPS pollution problem is not possible by using the conventional policy instruments derived for PS pollution problems. Direct and indirect approaches have been developed which determine incentive schemes based on ambient concentration of the pollutants and the use of observable polluting inputs.

Empirical work in the field has concentrated mainly on the development of combined economic–biophysical models which can be used for the determination of input-based taxes.[8] In contrast to these approaches,

Thomas (1995) estimates an emission tax based on an asymmetric information model where the efficiency of the polluter with respect to abatement is private knowledge.

Because of the complexity of the problem, the informational requirements for the application of the incentive schemes for NPS pollution regulation are formidable and their political feasibility, especially for some collective penalty schemes, is not always guaranteed. Policies aimed at increasing the informational basis of the regulator regarding emission observability[9] could transform an NPS pollution problem into a PS one and allow the use of more conventional and acceptable policy instruments.

Instruments used in practice to address NPS pollution problems are not close enough to the stylized theoretical instruments, as is the case of the PS instruments applied in practice, such as emission taxes or tradable emission permits. This is due to the complexity of the problem and the informational requirements necessary for the application of some of the more refined input-based schemes which seem to be the most common instrument in practice. However, the structure and the incentive characteristics of some policies applied can be associated with those of theoretical NPS pollution instruments.

The modelling of learning processes and optimal monitoring and enforcement of NPS pollution, along with the further development of empirical models, the elaboration of input-based incentive schemes under asymmetric information, and the development of multiple-instrument incentive schemes constitute areas for further research in NPS pollution problems.

Notes

1. For a survey of issues related to NPS pollution problems see also Tomasi et al. (1994).
2. For the solution to this problem see Xepapadeas (1995).
3. Of course since each polluter pays the full marginal damages, total payments exceed total damages. This characteristic exemplifies the collective penalty nature of ambient taxes.
4. The combined use of ambient taxes and Pigouvian taxes can be regarded as an intermediate case between full observability and no observability.
5. NBB contracts have been introduced by Holmstrom (1982) while BB contracts have been introduced by Rasmusen (1987) in the context of the theory of teams.
6. See for example Laffont and Tirole (1993); Laffont (1994a).
7. See also Laffont (1994b) for the regulation of pollution under asymmetric information. Laffont's model considers several cases such as monopoly regulation, regulation of industry, location issues and also examines one case of NPS pollution. In general regulation is achieved by several schemes that include linear or non-linear transfers, and Pigouvian taxes, personalized or uniform.
8. See DeCoursey (1985), Vatn et al. (1996), Weaver (1996), Weaver et al. (1996).
9. See Xepapadeas (1994) for a model incorporating optimal investment policies in monitoring equipment along with the combined use of Pigouvian taxes and emission taxes.

References

Braden, J. and K. Segerson (1993), 'Information problems in the design of nonpoint-source pollution policy', in C. Russel and J. Shogren (eds), *Theory, Modeling and Experience in the Management of Nonpoint-Source Pollution*, Dordrecht: Kluwer Academic Publishers.

Cabe, R. and J. Herriges (1992), 'The regulation of nonpoint source pollution under imperfect and asymmetric information', *Journal of Environmental Economics and Management*, **22**, 134–46.

DeCoursey, D. (1985), 'Mathematical models for nonpoint source pollution control', *Journal of Soil and Water Conservation*, **40**, 408–13.

Dosi, C. and M. Moretto (1990), 'Incentives for nonpoint source water pollution control under asymmetric information', mimeo, University of Padua, Italy.

Dosi, C. and M. Moretto (1993), 'NPS pollution, information asymmetry and the choice of time profiles for environmental fees', in C. Russel and J. Shogren (eds), *Theory, Modeling and Experience in the Management of Nonpoint-Source Pollution*, Dordrecht: Kluwer Academic Publishers.

Dosi, C. and M. Moretto (1994), 'Nonpoint source externalities and polluter's site quality standards under incomplete information', in T. Tomasi and C. Dosi (eds), *Nonpoint Source Pollution Regulation*, Dordrecht: Kluwer Academic Publishers.

Griffin, R. and D. Bromley (1982), 'Agricultural runoff as a nonpoint externality', *American Journal of Agricultural Economics*, **64**, 547–52.

Herriges, J., R. Govindasamy and J. Shogren (1994), 'Budget-balancing incentive mechanisms', *Journal of Environmental Economics and Management*, **27**, 275–85.

Holmstrom, B. (1982), 'Moral hazard in teams', *Bell Journal of Economics*, **13**, 323–40.

Laffont, J.-J. (1994a), 'The new economics of regulation ten years after', *Econometrica*, **62**, 507–37.

Laffont, J.-J. (1994b), 'Regulation of pollution with asymmetric information', in C. Dosi and T. Tomasi (eds), *Nonpoint Source Pollution Regulation: Issues and Analysis*, Dordrecht: Kluwer Academic Publishers.

Laffont, J.-J. and J. Tirole (1993), *A Theory of Incentives and Procurement in Regulation*, Cambridge, MA: MIT Press.

Meran, G. and U. Schwalbe (1987), 'Pollution control and collective penalties', *Journal of Institutional and Theoretical Economics*, **143**, 616–29.

OECD (1994), 'Managing the environment: the role of economic instruments', Paris: OECD.

Rasmusen, E. (1987), 'Moral hazard in risk-averse teams', *RAND Journal of Economics*, **18**, 428–35.

Segerson, K. (1988), 'Uncertainty and incentives for nonpoint pollution control', *Journal of Environmental Economics and Management*, **15**, 87–98.

Shortle, J.S. and D.G. Abler (1994), 'Incentives for nonpoint pollution control', in T. Tomasi and C. Dosi (eds), *Nonpoint Source Pollution Regulation*, Dordrecht: Kluwer Academic Publishers.

Shortle, J. and J. Dunn (1986), 'The relative efficiency of agricultural source water pollution control policies', *American Journal of Agricultural Economics*, **68**, 668–77.

Spulber, D.F. (1988), 'Optimal environmental regulation under asymmetric information', *Journal of Public Economics*, **35**, 163–81.

Thomas, A. (1995), 'Regulating pollution under asymmetric information: the case of industrial wastewater treatment', *Journal of Environmental Economics and Management*, **28**, 357–73.

Tomasi, T., K. Segerson and J. Braden (1994), 'Issues in the design of incentive schemes for nonpoint source pollution control', in T. Tomasi and C. Dosi (eds), *Nonpoint Source Pollution Regulation*, Dordrecht: Kluwer Academic Publishers.

Vatn, A., L. Bakken, M. Azzaroli Bleken, P. Botterwg, H. Lundeby, E. Romstad, P. Rørstad and A. Vold (1996), 'Policies for reduced nutrient losses and erosion from Norwegian agriculture', *Norwegian Journal of Agricultural Sciences*, Supplement no. 23.

Weaver, R. (1996), 'Prosocial behavior: private contributions to agriculture's impact on the environment', *Land Economics*, **72**, 231–47.

Weaver, R., J. Harper and W. Gillmeister (1996), 'Efficacy of standards vs. incentives for managing the environmental impact of agriculture', *Journal of Environmental Management*, **46**, 173–88.

Weaver, R. and A. Thomas (1996), 'Regulation of nonpoint source pollution with factor augmentation of polluting inputs', 17th Annual Conference of The European Association of Environmental and Resource Economists, Lisbon.

Xepapadeas, A. (1991), 'Environmental policy under imperfect information: incentives and moral hazard', *Journal of Environmental Economics and Management*, **20**, 113–26.

Xepapadeas, A. (1992), 'Environmental policy design and nonpoint-source pollution', *Journal of Environmental Economics and Management*, **23**, 22–39.

Xepapadeas, A. (1994), 'Controlling environmental externalities: observability and optimal policy rules', in T. Tomasi and C. Dosi (eds), *Nonpoint Source Pollution Regulation*, Dordrecht, Kluwer Academic Publishers.

Xepapadeas, A. (1995), 'Observability and choice of instrument mix in the control of externalities', *Journal of Public Economics*, **56**, 485–98.

Xepapadeas, A. (1997), 'Regulation of mineral emissions under asymmetric information', in Eirik Romstad, Jesper Simonsen and Arild Vatn (eds), *Policy Measures to Control Environmental Impacts from Agriculture in the European Union–Volume 2: Mineral Emissions*, Reading: CAB International Publishers.

37 Land use and environmental quality
William B. Meyer

1. Introduction

The term 'land use' refers to a set of human activities that exploit the varied resources offered by the biophysical features of land cover. Because all human activities require the land resources of horizontal space and vertical support, 'land use', interpreted generously, could become an unmanageably inclusive term. Traditionally, and more usefully, it has been reserved for a set of activities whose connections with the biophysical character of the land cover are particularly direct and intimate: agriculture, livestock rearing, forestry. These activities are of interest to environment–society researchers in many ways, ranging from the constraints placed on crop production by environmental variables of climate, soil, and pests and diseases to the impacts on water quality, atmospheric composition, and global climate of emissions from farms and feedlots and from forest clearance and thinning.

Within the framework of this volume, these linkages between land use and environment are covered under other headings. The present section will discuss very briefly the current state of inquiry into non-residential land use, especially at the global level. The focus of the chapter thereafter will instead be on the best-studied and most salient remaining form of land use related to environment–residential settlement.

Inasmuch as residential settlement always competes with other possible uses of the land, it and they cannot be fully understood outside of a unifying framework that incorporates them all. The development of such a framework at the global scale is one of the aims stated in the recent science plan for a joint International Geosphere–Biosphere Programme and Human Dimensions of Global Environmental Change Programme core project, and is now in the early stages of implementation. The LUCC (Land-Use and Land-Cover Change) plan (Turner et al., 1995) recognizes the need to integrate the social and natural sciences and their different disciplines; the different possible land (and water) uses that compete in any situation; and the various temporal and spatial scales at which processes and patterns may be studied. It seeks a better understanding of the driving forces (for example, population, technological change, political–economic institutions) and consequences (for example, greenhouse gas emissions, biodiversity loss, agricultural sustainability) of land-cover change through three main research foci. The activities within these foci will be coordinated towards the ultimate goal of building regional and global models that will make projections of change possible. Economic analysis will be an integral part of the analysis and modelling. It will be supplemented by approaches from other fields to make understanding and projections more realistic: addressing, for example, the effects on land use and cover of political interventions and cultural and lifestyle changes.

A second valuable product of LUCC's efforts will be the development of more standardized classifications and sets of data on both land use and land cover. The proliferation of data on both in recent decades that has come with the steady development of techniques of remote sensing and with the increase in collection and dissemination of statistics has been far less useful than it might because of great disparities in the quality and organization of the data. Increasingly sophisticated techniques of analysis are used on figures whose validity is at best doubtful. Progress in analytical tools such as geographic information systems (GIS) promises to aid immensely in exploiting the available data and laying down guidelines for the collection of useful knowledge in the future. In the area of residential land use, too, remote sensing and GIS have already proved their usefulness as tools of data acquisition and analysis, respectively. As in the field of global land use, though, they can be profitably used only in concert with theories and concepts defining the problems at hand.

2.   Residential land use

Residential land use and environmental quality are related in two important ways. The first is the influence of the biophysical environment (whether natural or modified by human action) on patterns and processes of settlement. The second is the influence on the biophysical environment of settlement patterns and processes. They are discussed here in that order. A comprehensive review of the literature at the time of writing is not possible within this chapter; what is offered rather is a discussion of the key relationships, the key concepts underpinning empirical research, and the various policy tools available to put those concepts into action so as to influence patterns in desired ways.

The effects of environment on land use

The aspects of the biophysical environment influencing residential land use can be distinguished as amenities and disamenities. Amenities are aspects of the environment judged pleasant, and measured as such by their ability to command a premium in the market for residential land. Disamenities are aspects unpleasant enough to lower detectably the value of affected sites in the housing market; hazards, such as exposure to floods, earthquakes and other environmental stresses are a subset of disamenities. There are, of course, many amenities and disamenities affecting residence that are not part of the biophysical environment (for example, quality of the schools, characteristics of residents); they are not dealt with here, but are often studied by the same methods and in the same studies as those discussed below.

The amenities, disamenities and hazards of the biophysical environment have not been given much attention in the chief economic and geographical theories of the location and patterns of residence (Mueller-Wille, 1990; Palm, 1990). Such theories emphasize space rather than environment as the key variable, in particular the trade-off between accessibility to the centre or the place of employment and the price of land for living space (Alonso, 1964) or, when treating migration at wider scales, regional wage and employment levels.

Yet the role of environmental amenities, especially climate, in national-level migration patterns has been a topic of sporadic interest since the pioneering discussion by Ullman (1954). Migration research has not consistently taken the amenity factor into account. Yet those studies that have done so have generally found it to be significant in drawing population to certain regions in the developed world, particularly those characterized by moderate temperatures in both summer and winter, low rainfall, and varied topography including hills and proximity to lakes or the ocean (Svart, 1976; Kritz, 1990; Perry, 1993; Mueger and Graves, 1995). In seasonal (as opposed to permanent) migration, which grades into tourism, the amenity factor is still more pronounced. It, like tourism, may create economic problems by increasing the seasonality of demand for labour and services, unless compensating off-season uses can be created.

Elements of environmental quality have likewise received some attention in studies of housing and land prices. Most studies are based on the concept of hedonic prices (among recent reviews containing details on methodological issues are Palmquist, 1991; Freeman, 1993; McConnell, 1993). In the hedonic approach, the price of a house is interpreted as reflecting the prices of the various structural and environmental characteristics – or the 'dwelling-specific' and the 'location-specific' attributes (Wilkinson, 1973) – that are bundled together in the given building in its given location.

The structural or dwelling-specific characteristics have been and still are studied more closely and systematically. None the less, the past two decades have brought forth a large literature examining the contribution to house prices of environmental and other neighbourhood characteristics. A seminal article by Ridker and Henning (1967) explored the contribution of air quality levels to house prices in St Louis, Missouri, US; a recent review article (Smith and Huang, 1993) could cite well over a hundred studies of the role of air quality. While 'the inclusion of land, location and a realistic and relatively full range of location-specific characteristics is virtually unknown in the literature' even today (Cheshire and Sheppard, 1995, p.262), marked effects on house prices have been sought – and generally, though not uniformly, have been found – of wide arrays of environmental amenities including views, water frontage, tree cover, and park space; of such disamenities as airport and freeway noise, air pollution, and proximity to waste sites and nuclear power plants; and of hazards of, for example, flooding, earthquakes and landslides.

A potentially serious problem of biased estimations in all such studies is introduced by the fact that the factors examined will often be only a fraction of all those that might be at work. The range of possible factors will inevitably differ from one setting to another. Moreover, Atkinson and Crocker (1992) find that while price functions for dwelling-specific characteristics have proven moderately transferable across housing markets of submarkets, those for neighbourhood-specific characteristics have not. They argue that such is to be expected on theoretical grounds as between produced goods and non-produced externalities. Smith and Huang (1995) find a wide range in marginal willingness-to-pay values for air quality among studies conducted in different American cities. They warn against the simple transfer of estimates from one locality to another, but suggest that a meta-analysis explaining the differences as the result of economic and physical differences between cities might permit values for one city to be derived from those obtained elsewhere.

Less has been done toward formulating generalizations about how the overall patterns of amenities and disamenities in the urban environment affect urban form, although their evidently growing importance will surely require modification of the classical theories (Hoch and Waddell, 1993; Waddell et al., 1993). An important exception is the idea of the positive rent gradient advanced by Richardson (1977). He suggested that land, at least for residential purposes, might increase rather than decrease in value with distance from the city centre as a result of an overall increase in amenities and decline in disamenities, including environmental ones, towards the urban fringe. The suggestion remains controversial both theoretically and empirically. A recent article tested under near-ideal circumstances the classical predictions of a negative rent gradient and a negative density gradient. It upheld both, while finding that the decline in housing prices closely approximated, as theory also predicted, the increased cost of transportation (Coulson, 1991). The setting examined, though, was a small city in which disamenity levels, a key reason for positive rent gradients, were unlikely to have been pronounced. Richardson's positive rent gradient and his suggested basis for it offer a new foundation for the concentric-zone model of urban social geography proposed by the American sociologist E.W. Burgess in the 1920s. The model has often received empirical support, but the theoretical basis Burgess gave it is too tied to its time and place of origin to remain adequate today (Marchand, 1986). That environmental and other amenities should indeed have assumed a steadily greater role in residential location as transportation improvements have lessened the friction of distance has been asserted at least since the work of Ullman (1962) and Webber (1963).

The principal policy problems in this area have to do with the efficiency and equity implications of externalized costs and benefits of land-use changes. Where high transaction costs, as explained by Coase (1960), forbid market internalization, measures requiring state intervention may be tried, but with possible costs and inefficiencies of their own. Neighbours may be compensated for losses from the siting of noxious facilities, and they may be taxed for their gains from the provision of amenity benefits from land-use changes. In both cases, though, the sums involved are difficult to calculate and politically fraught. Siting of noxious facilities on the basis of willingness to pay may lead to their inequitable concentration in poorer neighbourhoods, though so too may any other means of siting them.

One tool particularly relevant to recurrent environmental hazards is insurance. Private provision of residential insurance against hazards may be hampered by the problem of adverse selection, while government or subsidized insurance poses problems of moral hazard, and may also represent a significant wealth transfer among social groups (for example, Shilling et al., 1989).

The effects of land use on environment

Residential land use has innumerable effects externalized in time and space. It can significantly alter micro-climate, open space and farmland availability, atmospheric emissions, vegetation cover, faunal habitat, hydrology upstream (for water supply) and downstream (through waste emissions and flow modification) (for a review, see Douglas, 1994). All these effects have received some study. The prevailing view among academics and policy makers has been that low-density sprawl is the least desirable form of urban settlement because it consumes land and raises energy demand for transportation, thus raising emissions of carbon dioxide, a greenhouse gas (GHG), and of such atmospheric pollutants as carbon monoxide, sulphur dioxide, and oxides of nitrogen. An influential study by Newman and Kenworthy (1989) showed an inverse relation between city density and per capita gasoline consumption, with very low-density cities exhibiting extremely high levels. Land-use controls and other measures to encourage urban containment and higher-density, compact-city development, with

GHG emissions reductions as one of the stated goals, have in the past few years been adopted by a number of European government agencies (Breheny, 1995) and widely touted elsewhere.

These findings and policies have been questioned on a number of grounds (for example, Gomez-Ibanez, 1991; Gordon et al., 1991; Levinson and Kumar, 1994). The differences in gasoline consumption identified by Newman and Kenworthy may in large part be the result of income and gasoline price levels, strongly correlated with urban density, rather than of land-use patterns *per se*; moreover, studies in the US indicate that the process of sprawl does not markedly raise gasoline consumption, inasmuch as residents and workplaces decentralize together. Breheny (1995) and Anderson et al. (1996) conclude that understanding of the density–emissions relationship is still weak, but that the current literature offers little support for the idea that land-use controls, direct or indirect, can make a significant difference in greenhouse gas emissions.

They note, however, that considering other factors, ranging from other pollutant emissions to farmland and habitat preservation to the enhancement of community, might change that assessment, or might reinforce it. Full and integrated assessment of the overall costs and benefits of sprawl versus concentration has yet to be undertaken. It is evident in any case that the overall effects of high- versus low-density settlement are mixed and that any policy to restrain the latter would involve costs of its own. So much is apparent from the history of zoning and kindred forms of land-use control. Such regulation of land uses may enhance welfare by forestalling the externality problems created by disamenities in residential areas. It may also both inefficiently and inequitably distort the allocation of land to serve narrow interests, raising housing prices to the detriment of lower-income residents. The main bodies neither of theory (Pogodzinski and Sass, 1990) nor of empirical work (Pogodzinski and Sass, 1991; see also Evans, 1996) adequately integrate the many considerations that must be addressed to judge the overall impact of land-use controls in the aggregate or in particular settings.

3.   Conclusion

The study of residential land use/environment relations has suffered from a number of pressures that have unduly restricted its achievement to date. Hedonic studies of house prices have been pursued largely with the goal of finding market valuations for environmental interventions of various sorts rather than in developing a fuller understanding of the general relations between housing and the biophysical environment in their own right. The superior availability of data, moreover, has confined most studies to the developed countries, although Third World cities may display far sharper intra-urban contrasts in environmental amenity, disamenity and hazard levels (see Main and Williams, 1994), and their rapid growth both raises especially urgent issues of environment–settlement relationships and offers unusually large opportunities for intervention to shape the future. Ideally, rather than developing *ad hoc* models for particular purposes, social scientists would have developed an understanding of the various factors in the residence–environment connection and of how they vary over time and space, which could be drawn upon to clarify any number of issues.

Such an understanding cannot be developed without cross-disciplinary work on, for example, why (and when, and where) amenities are amenities and disamenities are disamenities (and phenomena that can be either one or the other, such as coastal or hillside location). In economic investigations of amenity and disamenity values, there is always an element of circularity: amenities are identified by the premiums paid for them, and the premiums are explained by the amenity character of the attributes in question. How attributes become and cease to be amenities and disamenities in different parts of the world is a question that must be addressed with other tools. Exposure of skin to the sun, now a valued amenity in the developed world, was a disamenity a century ago. Possession of a view has generally been found in developed-world studies to raise the value of a house, but to understand why views are an important amenity one has to go outside the usual bounds of economics. Appleton's (1975) 'prospect and refuge' theory of landscape perception offers an explanation with a strong biological element, implying substantial commonalities across time and space, while others insist on the cultural and historical specificity of aesthetic preferences. In Accra, Ghana, proximity to the ocean, an amenity in most developed-world studies, appears to be interpreted as a hazard and lowers land values (Asabere, 1981). In many Western European cities, the centre is still seen as the most desirable residential location, inverting the Burgess–Richardson model and implying either a different spatial pattern of amenities or different judgements of what phenomena constitute amenities. Hedonic models of housing prices in Seoul, South Korea require quite different variables than in North America and Western Europe (Huh and Kwak, 1997). Likewise, risk analysis has made it clear that the public's perceptions of risks and hazards are not identical to those of experts; McConnell (1993) urges more attention to such subjective judgements and their own determinants as determinants of hedonic price functions. The tools that have been and could be developed within economics cannot by themselves solve the problem of why these differences and others exist, but will be essential parts of the solution.

558   *Space in environmental economics*

References

Alonso, W. (1964), *Location and Land Use: Toward a General Theory of Land Rent*, Cambridge, MA: Harvard University Press.
Anderson, W.P., P.S. Kanaroglou and E.J. Miller (1996), 'Urban form, energy and the environment: A review of issues, evidence, and policy', *Urban Studies*, **33**, 7–35.
Appleton, J. (1975), *The Experience of Landscape*, London: Wiley.
Asabere, P.K. (1981), 'The determinants of land values in an African city: The case of Accra, Ghana', *Land Economics*, **57**, 385–97.
Atkinson, S.E. and T.D. Crocker (1992), 'The exchangeability of hedonic property price studies', *Journal of Regional Science*, **32**, 169–83.
Breheny, M. (1995), 'The compact city and transport energy consumption', *Transactions of the Institute of British Geographers*, n.s., **20**, 81–101.
Cheshire, P. and S. Sheppard (1995), 'On the price of land and the value of amenities', *Economica*, **62**, 247–67.
Coase, R. (1960), 'The problem of social cost', *Journal of Law and Economics*, **3**, 1–44.
Coulson, N.E. (1991), 'Really useful tests of the monocentric model', *Land Economics*, **67**, 299–307.
Douglas, I. (1994), 'Human settlements', in W.B. Meyer and B.L. Turner II (eds), *Changes in Land Use and Land Cover: A Global Perspective*, Cambridge: Cambridge University Press, pp.149–69.
Evans, A.W. (1996), 'The impact of land use planning and tax subsidies on the supply and price of housing in Britain: A comment', *Urban Studies*, **33**, 581–5.
Freeman, A.M. III (1993), 'Property value models', in *The Measurement of Environmental and Resource Values: Theory and Methods*, Washington, DC: Resources for the Future, ch. 11, pp.367–420.
Gomez-Ibanez, J.A. (1991), 'A global view of automobile dependence', *Journal of the American Planning Association*, **57**, 376–9.
Gordon, P., H.W. Richardson and M.-J. Jun (1991), 'The commuting paradox: Evidence from the top twenty', *Journal of the American Planning Association*, **57**, 416–20.
Hoch, I. and P. Waddell (1993), 'Apartment rents: Another challenge to the monocentric model', *Geographical Analysis*, **25**, 20–34.
Huh, S. and S.-J. Kwak (1997), 'The choice of functional form and variables in the hedonic price model in Seoul', *Urban Studies*, **33**, 989–98.
Kritz, M. (1990), 'Climate change and migration adaptations', Working Report 2.16, Population and Development Program, Department of Rural Sociology, Cornell University.
Levinson, D.M. and A. Kumar (1994), 'The rational locator: Why travel times have remained stable', *Journal of the American Planning Association*, **60**, 319–32.
Main, H. and S.W. Williams (eds) (1994), *Environment and Housing in Third World Cities*, London: Wiley.
Marchand, B. (1986), *The Emergence of Los Angeles: Population and Housing in the City of Dreams, 1940–1970*, London: Pion.
McConnell, K.E. (1993), 'Indirect methods for assessing natural resource damages under CERCLA', in R.J. Kopp and V.K. Smith (eds), *Valuing Natural Assets: The Economics of Natural Resource Damage Assessment*, Washington, DC: Resources for the Future, pp. 153–96.
Mueger, P.R. and P.E. Graves (1995), 'Examining the role of economic opportunity and amenities in explaining population redistribution', *Journal of Urban Economics*, **37**, 176–200.
Mueller-Wille, C. (1990), *Natural Landscape Amenities and Suburban Growth: Metropolitan Chicago, 1970–1980*, Chicago: University of Chicago Department of Geography Research Paper no. 230.
Newman, P.W.G. and J.R. Kenworthy (1989), 'Gasoline consumption and cities: A comparison of U.S. cities with a global survey', *Journal of the American Planning Association*, **55**, 24–37.
Palm, R. (1990), *Natural Hazards: An Integrative Framework for Research and Planning*. Baltimore, MD: Johns Hopkins University Press.

Palmquist, R.B. (1991), 'Hedonic methods', in J.B. Braden and C.D. Kolstad (eds), *Measuring the Demand for Environmental Improvement*, Amsterdam: Elsevier, pp. 77–120.

Perry, A. (1993), 'Climate, greenhouse warming and the quality of life', *Progress in Physical Geography*, **17**, 354–8.

Pogodzinksi, J.M. and T.R. Sass (1990), 'The economic theory of zoning: A critical review', *Land Economics*, **66**, 294–314.

Pogodzinski, J.M. and T.R. Sass (1991), 'Measuring the effects of municipal zoning regulations: A survey', *Urban Studies*, **28**, 597–621.

Richardson, H.W. (1977), 'On the possibility of negative rent gradients', *Journal of Urban Economics*, **4**, 60–68.

Ridker, R.G. and J.A. Henning (1967), 'The determinants of residential property values with special reference to air pollution', *Review of Economics and Statistics*, **49**, 246–57.

Shilling, J.D., C.F. Sirmans and J.D. Benjamin (1989), 'Flood insurance, wealth redistribution, and urban property values', *Journal of Urban Economics*, **26**, 43–53.

Smith, V.K. and J.-C. Huang (1993), 'Hedonic models and air pollution: Twenty-five years and counting', *Environmental and Resource Economics*, **36** (1), 23–36.

Smith, V.K. and J.-C., Huang (1995), 'Can markets value air quality? A meta-analysis of hedonic property value models', *Journal of Political Economy*, **103**, 209–27.

Svart, L.M. (1976), 'Environmental preference migration: A review', *Geographical Review*, **66**, 314–30.

Turner, B.L. II et al. (1995), 'Land-use and land-cover change: Science/Research Plan', IGBP Report no. 35/ HDP Report no. 7. Stockholm and Geneva: IGBP and HDP.

Ullman, E.L. (1954), 'Amenities as a factor in regional growth', *Geographical Review*, **44**, 110–32.

Ullman, E.L. (1962), 'The nature of cities reconsidered', *Papers and Proceedings of the Regional Science Association*, **9**, 7–23.

Waddell, P., B.J.L. Berry and I. Hoch (1993), 'Housing price gradients: The intersection of space and built form', *Geographical Analysis*, **25**, 5–19.

Webber, M.M. (1963), 'Order in diversity: Community without propinquity', in L. Wingo Jr (ed.) *Cities and Space: The Future Use of Urban Land*, Baltimore, MD: Johns Hopkins University Press for Resources for the Future, pp. 23–54.

Wilkinson, R.K. (1973), 'House prices and the measurement of externalities', *Economic Journal*, **83**, 72–86.

38 Urban sustainability
David Banister

1. Introduction

Urban sustainability is not just about making towns and cities more efficient in terms of their use of resources. The main objective is to improve the quality of life by providing affordable housing, employment opportunities, a wide range of facilities and services, with a high-quality environment in safe and secure surroundings. It also aims to provide quality through open space, green space, and it could include cultural, leisure and recreational resources, as well as the dynamics of cities as users of resources and producers of waste. The discussion here will be focused on three of the key elements which contribute to that quality – land, energy and transport – and the range of decisions which have to be made (Banister and Button, 1993). The main question is, how can we reverse the movement of employment and people out of our cities as this is reducing the already high levels of urban sustainability? The answer must be a combination of factors as suggested here to enhance the quality, attractiveness, distinctiveness and opportunities which urban areas are uniquely able to offer (see Haughton and Hunter, 1994; Nijkamp and Perrels, 1994).

Some 70 per cent of the population of developed countries live in urban areas (over 25000 population), but development patterns have become increasingly car-dependent, land-hungry and energy-intensive – urban sustainability is being reduced. The consequences are now being felt in terms of environmental pollution, congestion, loss of countryside and the use of all forms of non-renewable resources. Many factors have contributed to this situation: demographic change, economic restructuring, rising car ownership, improved transport links, aspirations to move out of cities, a general dissatisfaction with urban living, and greater flexibility and complexity in lifestyles and patterns of movement. In short, all the indicators would suggest a substantial and permanent move towards patterns of unsustainability.

The actual situation is less bleak. Urban sustainability will be examined along three dimensions – land, energy and transport. Each of these components contributes towards the overall use of resources and levels of emissions within urban areas, and the aim for urban sustainability would be to improve the efficiency in the use of each of these three components.

This means that decisions relating to new development, decisions relating to the reuse of existing sites, decisions relating to transport, and decisions relating to increasing the energy efficiency within urban areas all need to be addressed. The first two relate to land, the third to transport, and the final one to energy. At the same time, concerns over quality of life within urban areas must be addressed as the aim of urban sustainability strategies must be to enhance the attractiveness of urban areas, and to prevent and reverse the continued movement of population out of these areas. The arguments presented here on urban sustainability refer only to developed countries. Contrasting trends can be observed in developing countries where there is still substantial in-migration to cities, whilst in other countries (for example Central and East European countries and the Commonwealth of Independent States) there is stability in urban population.

2. Decisions relating to new development

The pressure for new housing is generating the largest demand for land, and the decisions facing many urban planning authorities is whether that demand can be accommodated with minimal environmental damage, whilst at the same time providing high-quality living environments. Fundamental demographic change is taking place as traditional family structures are being broken down and as new types of social structures emerge – single-parent families, cohabitation, increasing numbers of elderly people – much of the new housing is required to meet these new demands.

However, in many urban areas the availability of sites for housing is limited, so the tendency has been for urban infill and extensions to urban areas to allow development to be clearly related to existing transport services with mixed land uses. In this way urban development densities can be maintained or increased. A second option would be to develop expanded towns, so that existing settlements over 25 000 population can be promoted as the availability of existing services and facilities, together with local jobs, means that locally based travel patterns can develop – there would be high level of self-containment.

The high-risk strategy would be to develop new settlements. If new settlements are to be sustainable, they would have to be large (a minimum of 50 000 population) with a high level of self-sufficiency in employment, shopping, and social and recreational activities. The difficulty here is that large new settlements are unacceptable politically and the rate of build-up is often slow. It may take 20 years to reach the target size and by that time travel patterns based on the car will have evolved. Planning must allow for local facilities and services, together with public transport provision, to be in place before residents move in. In the Netherlands, this problem has been overcome through planned new settlements with phased development (for example Almere; see Box 38.1), but even here there is substantial out-commuting (such as from Almere to Amsterdam).

Box 38.1   Almere – urban sustainability through new town development

Almere in the Netherlands provides an example of a new settlement (population 85000) which has a fully integrated transport and land-use system, with the emphasis clearly on public transport and cycling. The transport network is planned to maximize the use of sustainable forms of transport, whilst land-use planning has provided services in locations accessible to the residential neighbourhoods. The town is centred on three railway stations which provide a fast and frequent connection to central Amsterdam 20 miles away, where many of the residents work. The main commercial and business centres, which have an element of mixed use and residential, are located around each station. A comprehensive network of bus-only streets leads away from the stations to serve the rest of the town. Cycle and pedestrian routes connect each of the neighbourhoods and provide direct connections both to the central areas and the industrial estates on the outskirts. At every external link to the town there is a car pool area (for both cars and cycles) for those both arriving and leaving the town. Housing density is designed to be high but there are large attractive recreational areas surrounding the town and open spaces within each neighbourhood. Each district lies within a radius of about one mile from its centre which offers a wide range of retail and service facilities. Local neighbourhoods contain a primary school and a more limited range of shops. The town makes no attempt to prohibit car ownership or use, but the availability of alternative modes, set within pleasant surroundings, encourages a high usage of non-car modes. Most importantly, the town is designed so that nobody needs to have or use their own car. From limited surveys, car ownership is lower than elsewhere in the Netherlands at about one car per household. The modal split is: car 35 per cent; bike 28 per cent; walk 21 per cent, and public transport 16 per cent (TEST, 1991). But improvements in the road and rail infrastructure have increased commuting out of the new town, particularly by car (Hofstra Verkeeradviseurs, 1991).

In all the debate over urban sustainability and new development, size and density emerge as key determinants (Banister, 1996; Newman and Kenworthy, 1989). A concentration of population in the compact city can help support a better range of local facilities and reduce the dependence on the car (Breheny, 1995). In the UK at densities over 50 persons per hectare, 40 per cent of all trips are made on foot. At densities between 15 and 50 persons per hectare this reduced to 30 per cent of all trips, and at low densities only 20 per cent of all trips are made on foot (ECOTEC, 1993). Higher densities also allow better-quality access to district/local centres or a public transport facility – the key threshold distance here would be about 800 metres or a 10-minute walk. Higher density result in less land being used, greater efficiency in the supply of energy, and shorter journey lengths. It also maximizes the potential for higher proportions of travel by 'green modes', such as walking, cycling, bus and tram.

Many of the trends in urban areas suggest that development pressures are concentrated at greenfield sites on the periphery of urban areas at low densities with greater land requirements and longer journeys, often by car. This type of new development has been particularly apparent in retailing and warehouse location, together with high-technology, business and science parks. More recently, new forms of recreation and leisure activities have also tended to be developed in peripheral locations. The implications of these new developments on sustainability are clear, with land, energy and transport costs all being increased. If urban sustainability is to be encouraged, then clear guidance needs to be given to developers to concentrate new development in corridors and near to interchanges which are accessible to public transport and the car. Examples include zoning of particular areas for specific types of development (GB: Departments of the Environment and Transport, 1995), the Dutch ABC policy (Priemus, 1995), and the Almere case (see Box 38.1), where development and transport principles can be combined to reduce car dependence. Authorities should designate areas for development which minimizes the need to travel. Consistency in approach between urban authorities is necessary so that decisions taken on sustainability criteria can be made without losing out on development opportunities.

3. Decisions relating to the reuse of existing sites

Derelict, contaminated and vacant land represents a substantial under-utilized urban resource. This brownfield land within urban areas must be brought back into positive use in preference to the development of greenfield land. Apart from reducing pressure on the countryside, the reuse of brownfield sites can assist local area renewal and the provision of housing and employment for local people. It can contribute to the maintenance of local facilities and services by raising levels of demand, and it can reduce travel demand and encourage the use of public transport. On the land, energy and transport criteria it scores well, and will help to reduce the use of resources and promote urban sustainability.

However, it is often expensive to redevelop these brownfield sites, particularly if the land has been contaminated. Provisions must be made for the polluter to pay for restoration work on land which they have polluted, perhaps requiring some form of restoration bonds from developers undertaking activities which could result in land becoming polluted. Investors and developers require greater certainty about the possibility of future liability arising from brownfield land they acquire and develop.

The existing building stock provides considerable potential to accommodate new and different uses, to increase density and provide diversity so that urban sustainability objectives can be met. Houses can be transformed into flats, offices into houses and surplus upper-floor space into housing – living over the shop. This spatial mixing may provide opportunities to increase density of development and diversity.

4.   Decisions relating to transport

Transport is a critical issue, but urban transport policies continue to favour the car over other forms of transport. Fragmentation of public transport services and the separation of responsibilities between operators and local authorities means that integrated and coordinated services are difficult to provide. Sustainable urban transport must be based on the best combination of modes, with environmentally friendly transport being given clear priority within towns. This means that walking, cycling, bus and tram should be given preference within the city, with rail and car providing passengers from outside the city. Priority includes vehicle-actuated lights, bus-only routes and lanes, and exclusive access for buses to the central area. Cars and rail need to be seen as complementary to the bus, providing an essential part of the integrated service by supplying passengers at park-and-ride locations. Trams complement the bus services in large cities, but most towns will only have bus-based public transport systems.

Similarly, cycle routes are often fragmented and not available where most needed. It is only with a network of routes, together with appropriate safe storage, particularly at interchange points, that substantial increases in cycle use will take place. Freight transport distribution is also organized on a company basis so that only limited coordination can take place. Regulations may be imposed on size of vehicle and timing of delivery, but little attention has been given to reducing the number of freight movements through coordinated transhipment or through reductions in empty running.

With any set of proposals, the overall efficiency of the transport system must be balanced against the need to reduce trip lengths and to reduce the use of the car, particularly for short journeys within urban areas. It is here that the car is operating at its most inefficient, with slow speeds resulting from congestion, and with high levels of fuel consumption and emissions caused by the engine operating from cold and in congested conditions. The closer jobs, houses, facilities and services are to each other, the greater the likelihood that the car will not be used. Restrictions on the use of the car in urban areas is central to achieving the best combination of modes, to providing an efficient transport service and to enhancing quality of life. It is here that market forces and planning actions can work together to obtain optimality in the use of scarce urban space through investment in public transport and local facilities, and control on development, as well as through substantially raising the costs of using the car in urban areas. Pricing strategies include increases in fuel prices, road pricing and parking pricing.

5.   Decisions relating to increasing energy efficiency within urban areas

An energy-efficient settlement gives high priority to recycling, to district heating and combined heat and power (CHP), to housing design and insulation standards, and to energy-efficient offices and buildings. It may also explore the possibilities of using renewable energy sources (such as biomass). Energy use in industry has declined over the last 30 years, but this has been matched by increases in energy use in domestic and commercial sectors. The real growth has come in the transport sector which has more than doubled its use of energy (1960–93) in most Western countries, with most of this increase coming from longer car-based journeys made across cities or to destinations outside the urban area.

The opportunities to improve energy efficiency in urban areas are substantial. At the urban scale, combined heat and power and district heating schemes can increase thermal efficiency to 80 per cent, as compared with the 38 per cent efficiency obtained from a conventional power station. Their efficiency and cost advantage are very sensitive to location and density of development, as thermal losses increase with distance. The potential is enhanced if refuse-based systems can combine recycling with heating. Comprehensive waste management systems for both liquid and solid waste must form an integral part of any strategy to reduce waste production, to help conserve valuable resources, and to reduce the risk of environmental contamination and health hazards.

Opportunities are also available at the neighbourhood scale to reduce energy use through the built form. Here, layout considerations and high thermal insulation standards in housing, with higher densities and smaller units (terraced and flats), all increase energy efficiency. Passive solar design allows the siting, design, orientation, layout and landscaping aspects to be calculated, so that the solar gain can be maximized with reduced requirements for space and water heating (or cooling). Micro-climatic factors are important in reducing heat loss from buildings by controlling wind speed and raising external ambient temperatures, principally through the use of shelter belts and other forms of planting, which in turn helps improve the local environment.

Underlying the argument here is the necessity to attract people back to the city as this enhances possible economies of scale in energy provision, reduces travel distances and provides opportunities to promote energy-efficient public transport. Experiments are being carried out with non-polluting public transport with electric buses and natural-gas-powered buses to match the energy efficiency of trams and trolley buses which have been in use for many years. All of this depends upon critical thresholds for demand. The urban area provides the opportunity for the greatest efficiency in the use of resources, yet people in many cities are now choosing to leave. Out-migration from cities and reductions in density of development are two key reasons why the sustainability of cities is being reduced. This is the compact city paradox where greater levels of sustainability can be achieved through greater densities, but as a result of this, the perceived quality of life is reduced, and the reverse is actually occurring. The paradox can only be resolved if density and perceived quality of life in cities are both improved at the same time (Jenks et al., 1996).

6. The next steps

Considerable action has already taken place through national and international agencies (for example, Commission of the European Communities, 1992; EU Expert Group on the Urban Environment, 1995; and Local Government Management Board, 1993), but clear guidance, together with the means to overcome barriers to implementation, is still required. At the city-wide level, environmental strategies and statements, together with action plans, need to be set up. These statements can and should be set within the statutory planning process so that issues of sustainability become a central consideration in policy making at the city level. To implement these broad policy and environmental statements, a series of lower-level plans and management systems is required (Breheny, 1992). One possibility here is integrated environmental plans which explicitly involve community consultation and participation – this idea is central to Local Agenda 21 and the EU's Fifth Environmental Action Plan 'Towards Sustainability'.

Environmental budgeting and environmental management systems

(Eco-Management and Auditing Scheme – EMAS) help establish levels of resource use, facilitate the monitoring of progress towards sustainability targets, and provide a regular audit of the total urban environment. For new projects it is essential to have both a full environmental impact assessment of the individual project and a complementary assessment of how it fits into the city as a whole – a strategic environmental assessment (Glasson et al., 1994).

Urban sustainability is a 'creative, local, balance seeking process extending to all areas of local decision making' (City Charter, 1994, para. 107). This Charter suggests that by building the management of a city around the information collected through this process, the city can be understood as an organic whole, and this in turn will allow citizens to make informed choices. Through a management process rooted in sustainability, decisions can be made which not only represent the interests of current stakeholders, but also of future generations.

In addition to actions at all levels, two other important issues need to be addressed. Urban sustainability relates to long-term development and the dynamics of cities. Competitive forces, new technologies and knowledge will all change the nature of cities over time. Consequently, the notion of urban sustainability must also change over time. Second, the process of change is complex and requires agreement from decision makers at all levels, together with support from the general public. New institutional structures may be required plus a greater active involvement of actors if urban sustainability is to move from being an ideal to a reality.

References

Banister, D. (1996), 'Energy, quality of life and the environment: The role of transport', *Transport Reviews*, **16** (1), 23–35.

Banister, D. and K. Button (1993) (eds), *Transport, the Environment and Sustainable Development*, London: Spon.

Breheny, M. (ed.) (1992), *Sustainable Development and Urban Form*, London: Pion.

Breheny, M. (1995), 'The compact city and transport energy consumption', *Transactions of the Institution of British Geographers*, n.s. **20**, 81–101.

City Charter (1994), 'Charter of European cities and towns towards sustainability', signed at the European Conference on Sustainable Cities and Towns, Aalborg, Denmark, 27 May.

Commission of the European Communities (1992), 'Towards sustainability: A European Community programme of policy and action in relation to the environment and sustainable development', COM 92(23), CEC, Brussels.

ECOTEC (1993), *Reducing Transport Emissions Through Planning*, Report for the Department of the Environment, London: HMSO.

EU Expert Group on the Urban Environment (1995), 'European sustainable cities – sustainable city project', Brussels, June.

GB: Departments of the Environment and Transport (1995), *PPG13 A Guide to Better Practice: Reducing the Need to Travel Through Land Use and Transport Planning*, London: HMSO.

Glasson, J., R. Therivel and A. Chadwick (1994), *Introduction to Environmental Impact Assessment*, London: UCL Press.

Haughton, G. and C. Hunter (1994), *Sustainable Cities*, Regional Studies Association, Regional Policy and Development Series 7, London: Jessica Kingsley.

Hofstra Verkeersadviseurs (1991), 'Almere perspectief 2015 (Deelstudie Verkeer en Vervoer)', Groningen.

Jenks, M., E. Burton and K. Williams (1996) (eds), *The Compact City: A Sustainable Urban Form?*, London: Spon.

Local Government Management Board (1993), 'The UK's Report to the UN Commission on Sustainable Development: An initial submission by the UK Local Government', London, May.

Newman, P. and J. Kenworthy (1989), *Cities and Automobile Dependence – An International Sourcebook*, Aldershot: Gower.

Nijkamp, P. and A. Perrels (1994), *Sustainable Cities in Europe*, London: Earthscan.

Priemus, H. (1995), 'Reduction of car use: Instruments of national and local policies – a Dutch perspective', *Environment and Planning B*, **22** (4), 721–37.

TEST (1991), 'Changed travel, better world?', London. Available from Transport 2000, Walkden House, 10 Melton Street, London NW1.

39 Location choice, environmental quality and public policy

James R. Markusen

1. Introduction

Much of the literature in environmental economics and indeed in public finance and international trade abstracts from the location decisions of individual firms. Yet the possibility that individual plants may relocate in response to environmental costs has clearly been a concern of public policy. Often these concerns are expressed at a relatively local level, where a single plant can be a major employer. But in the last few years, these concerns have been expressed at a national level in the US and Europe. The possibility of US plants relocating Mexico was an issue in the NAFTA debate, and possible relocations by European firms to Eastern Europe concern the EU.

The purpose of this chapter is to consider the location decisions of footloose firms in response to environmental costs imposed by regulatory standards or taxes. To accomplish this purpose we require a conceptual and modelling approach that includes several elements. First, in so far as the model requires that individual firms can be identified and plant location decisions are meaningful, production technology must be characterized by increasing returns to scale. In traditional neoclassical general equilibrium trade theory with constant returns to scale, only 'industries' can be identified and a firm's plant location decision is not a meaningful concept. Increasing returns to scale in turn implies that market structure will be characterized by imperfect competition. Second, in so far as the policy debate frequently mentions multinationals, we must include features that support multinational firms in equilibrium. This will permit a comparison of intrafirm location decisions within the multinational with interfirm reallocations by market mechanisms in the absence of multinationals.

Severe space constraints mean that the chapter does not address topics which are treated elsewhere in this volume or in recent high-quality surveys. First, I shall not deal with the location of industries in competitive models, as I suggest in the previous paragraph. This is a straightforward Ricardian problem (generally combined with Heckscher–Ohlin factor-intensity effects) and is relatively well understood. Second, I shall not deal with 'capital flight' in the sense of a regional or international movement of homogeneous capital in a competitive model. Indeed, I shall assume that factors of production *per se* are immobile. Third, I shall not be able to review the important and substantial literature on tax competition, but rather review some results only in the context of discrete plant location decisions.[1]

2.   Increasing returns, imperfect competition, and plant location decisions
How do environmental costs affect the types and locations of firms and plants active in equilibrium? I shall frame the discussion in terms of a fairly specific general equilibrium model, which is a simplified version of Markusen (1997).[2]

1.   There are two countries (h and f), and two goods (X and Y). Sector Y is competitive and produces with constant returns to scale.
2.   There are two factors of production, L ('labour') used in both sectors, and R ('land') used only in the Y sector. The existence of the fixed factor R means that the X sector must draw L from the Y sector at increasing cost (preventing a small policy from catastrophically shifting all production to the other country).
3.   The X sector produces with increasing returns to scale, and is imperfectly competitive. Firms are Cournot competitors.
4.   There are fixed costs to producing X at both the firm level (F) and at the plant level (G). A second plant can be opened for the additional cost of G only, reflecting the notion of multiplant economies of scale due to the joint-input nature of knowledge capital. For example, blueprints can be supplied relatively cheaply to foreign plants.
5.   There is a constant unit labour requirement in X production (but the wage rate is endogenous). Single-plant firms can export to the other country for a transport cost t (also in units of L).
6.   There is free entry and exit, and any potential firm can choose whether to be a single-plant or two-plant (multinational) firm and choose in which country to locate its headquarters (firm-specific capital F) and plants. I make one restrictive assumption, which is that single-plant firms must locate their headquarters and plant in the same country.
7.   Assume that the two countries are absolutely identical initially, so as to remove elements of comparative advantage from consideration.

In this model, there is a tension between the added fixed costs of a second plant versus the added costs of serving the other market by exports. In the symmetric-country case (assumption 7), we shall have an equilibrium with single-plant national firms producing X in each country in equilibrium if transport costs (t) are low relative to plant-level scale economies (G). These X firms are referred to as type h and type f firms depending on which country they are located in. Multinationals (type *m* firms) dominate in equilibrium if transport costs are moderately high relative to plant scale economies.

The introduction of any asymmetries, such as environmental policies, will obviously shift production. But they will also shift the composition of firms and may create mixed regimes of national and multinational firms.

I want to focus on the interesting issues that arise in this type of model that are distinct from those that would arise in a competitive, constant returns model. First, we would expect that in either the model just outlined or in a competitive model environmental restrictions or taxes which raise the cost of *X* production in one country (henceforth country *f*) will shift production to the unregulated country (henceforth country *h*). However, the degree of production shifting might be different depending on whether there are multinational firms in existence. The regime-shifting effects of policy might in turn be of interest in their own right. Perhaps more interesting, the welfare effects here might be very different from a competitive model. In the present case, there is a direct connection between production levels and welfare since price exceeds marginal cost. There is no such connection in the standard competitive model.

Second, in so far as multinationals are often named in the policy debate, it is interesting to contrast results with endogenous multinationals with results that occur when multinational firms are suppressed. This question was important in the US–Canada–Mexico free trade debate: do production and/or welfare respond more sensitively to environmental policies if multinationals rather than national firms dominate production?

Third, there are interesting issues connected to the dreaded word 'competitiveness'. Because of the direct link between production and welfare just noted, policies that cause domestic firms to 'lose competitiveness' may be very harmful. The model can be used in this context to note that restrictions that fall on marginal costs (for example, cleaner fuels) have a very different effect from restrictions that fall on fixed costs (for example, designing more efficient machinery and processes to consume less fuel and other inputs).

Consider results derived from the numerical general equilibrium model of Markusen (1997). Figure 39.1 plots the equilibrium regime (the types of firms active in equilibrium) as a function of the marginal cost of production in country *f* on the vertical axis (country $h = 1.00$), and transport costs on the horizontal axis (measured in terms of country *h*'s marginal production cost). Each cell in the diagram is a solution to a numerical version of the model outlined above, involving 41 non-linear inequalities. In the top row of the table, there is no environmental policy and the countries are identical. For transport costs less than 10 per cent, there are type *h* and type

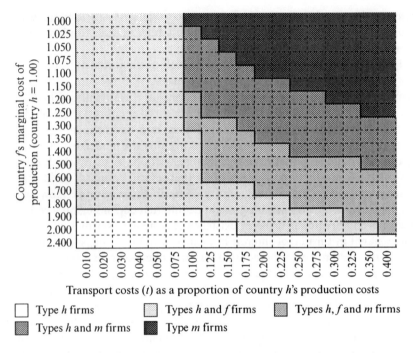

*Figure 39.1   Equilibrium regime as a function of environmental cost
increases and trade costs*

f firms active in equilibrium. At a transport cost of 10 per cent or higher,
the regime is composed solely of two-plant type *m* firms.

Moving down a column of Figure 39.1 (higher environmental costs) such
as *t* = 0.05, there is an eventual shift of regime to type *h* firms only.
Production of *X* is too expensive in country *f* and all production is by
single-plant firms in country *h*.

At higher transport costs, the sequence of regime shifts is much more
complicated. Consider the column *t* = 0.20. Only type *m* firms are active in
equilibrium when the cost in country *f* is not too high. But high costs in
country *f*, impacting on both type *m* firms and potential type *f* firms, eventually allow the entry of type *h* firms with their production in country *h*
only. Further cost increases in country *f*, somewhat paradoxically, permit
the entry of type *f* firms. This is connected to general equilibrium effects, in
that the exit of type *m* firms lowers labour demand in country *f*, permitting
a smaller number of type *f* firms to enter (for example, one exiting type *m*
firm is replaced by $n_h > 1$ type *h* firms and $n_f < 1$ type *f* firms. But we see that
at the bottom of column *t* = 0.20 in Figure 39.1 that the type *f* firms are
forced out and all production is carried on by type *h* firms. In spite of the

complicated regime shifting moving down a column like $t = 0.20$ of Figure 39.1, production and the number of plants in country f falls monotonically, moving down a column. The volume of production in country f moving down column $t = 0.20$ of Figure 39.1 is shown in the lower panel of Figure 39.3 (excuse the forward reference).

Figure 39.2 plots quantitative results in order to address two of the questions noted above. First, for a given environmental cost increase, do transport or other trade costs protect production and welfare? Second, does the existence of multinationals make production and welfare more sensitive to the cost increase? The 'diamonds' in Figure 39.2 trace out the effects of trade costs on welfare (top panel) and production (bottom panel) for country f moving across row 1.20 of Figure 39.1 (20 per cent cost increase in country f). The 'squares' plot the same variables with multinationals suppressed. 'Welfare' is defined as arising from consumption only, ignoring any benefits of environmental policy.[3]

The results of Figure 39.2 indicate that transport or trade costs protect production from the cost increase, but not welfare (welfare is given as a proportion of the no-cost-increase level). As we noted above, the volume of production is important in so far as the industry is characterized by price in excess of marginal cost. It is well known from the 'strategic trade-policy literature' that protection might be beneficial because of this. However, in the present case, potential gains are outweighed by the fact that protection forces consumers to buy the costly product rather than import it from a low-cost source. This is important from a policy point of view, because it suggests that there is no second-best argument for protecting production following the imposition of an environmental policy.

Figure 39.2 also reveals that there is no second-best argument for banning multinationals. Indeed, results show that intrafirm reallocation of production by multinationals is less than the market-mediated interfirm reallocation of production by national firms (bottom panel, $t > 0.075$). The notion that multinationals are adept at reallocating production ignores that fact that markets are as well. Welfare is similarly reduced by a ban on multinationals (top panel of Figure 39.2).

Figure 39.3 plots country f's welfare (diamonds, top panel) and production of X (diamonds, bottom panel) moving down column $t = 0.20$ of Figure 39.1. In spite of the complicated regime shifting, both welfare and production are monotonically decreasing in the level of marginal costs. For the sake of comparison, I then recalculated these solutions by assuming that fixed costs are increased by an equivalent amount instead of marginal costs.[4] We see from Figure 39.3 that the effects of the fixed-cost increase are much smaller than the effects of the variable-cost increase. Intuitively, the X industry in country f can 'absorb' a fixed-cost increase in equilibrium by

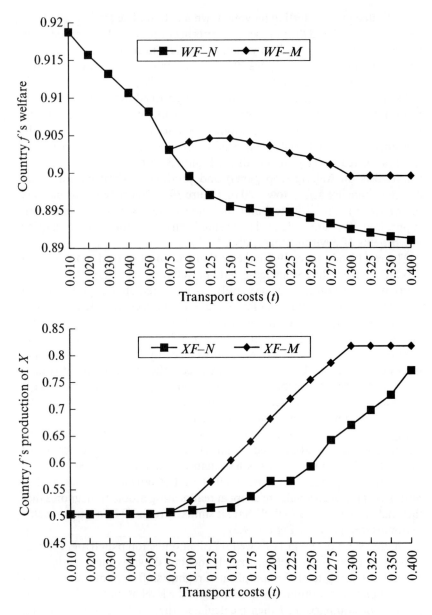

Note: WF and XF refers to country *f*'s welfare and X production respectively. *M* denotes multinationals permitted; *N* denotes multinational firms excluded by assumption.

Figure 39.2   Effect of trade costs on country f's welfare and production (cost increase: 20 per cent)

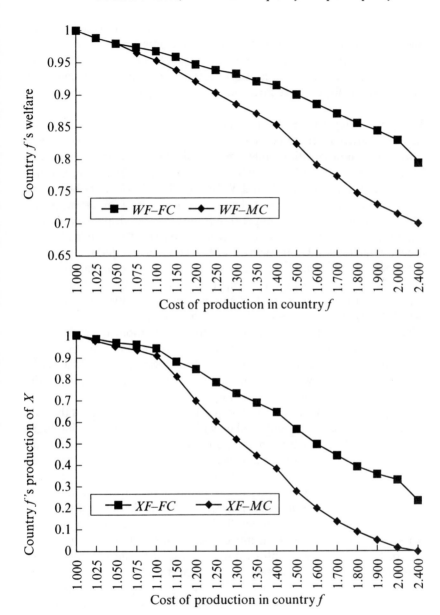

Note: WF and XF refer to country *f*'s welfare and *X* production respectively. *MC* and *FC* are regulations impacting on marginal and fixed costs respectively.

Figure 39.3   Contrast between restrictions that impact on marginal costs (MC) versus fixed costs (FC) (trade cost: 20 per cent)

firm exist (so fewer fixed costs are incurred), with the surviving firms producing larger outputs per firm. With increasing returns to scale, output per firm has a direct connection to welfare. The fact that the marginal-cost and fixed-cost restrictions have opposite effects on output per firm accounts for their different effects on welfare, shown in the top panel of Figure 39.3.

3. Public policy with footloose firms

As noted earlier, there exists a substantial literature on 'tax competition' in competitive models with mobile capital. I shall not be able to review that literature here, but readers are referred to extensive references in Cropper and Oates (1992), Jinoungh and Wilson (1994), Rauscher (1995b), and Markusen et al. (1995). Also, I shall not review several important papers which adopt an imperfect-competition framework, but deal with policy for a single country only. The interested reader is referred to Motta and Thisse (1994), Ulph (1994), Ulph (1995), and Markusen et al. (1993).

Instead, I shall focus on two issues which I believe to be the essence of the problem added to the tax-competition literature by footloose firms. First, does it make any sense for regions or municipalities to compete in plant location decisions? Second, if such incentives do exist, how do they affect equilibrium standards or taxes relative to situations where firm locations are fixed? This second question compares non-cooperative taxes/ standards under the assumptions that firm locations are fixed versus endogenous. A somewhat different question is how these non-cooperative rates compare with jointly optimal rates across regions.

The point of departure for the first question is to note again that the issue of footloose firms is inherently tied up with increasing returns technologies and imperfectly competitive market structures. These elements generally imply that local production is valuable, in that it raises the real wage of local fixed factors of production. But at the same time, these elements suggest an incentive for local governments to tax plants if their locations are fixed, quite apart from environmental issues. This is a basic rent-shifting argument from the 'strategic trade-policy' literature. Given an oligopolistic market structure, there is an incentive to shift rents from the firm to the taxpayers if indeed the latter only own small shares of the firm's equity. If two municipalities or regions engage in non-cooperative tax setting under the assumption that plant locations are fixed (assume that each has one plant), the Nash equilibrium rates may actually be jointly optimal for the two regions if firm profits accrue to owners outside the region (Markusen et al., 1995).[5] But they are too high if the firm's profits accrue entirely to owners inside the two regions (Hoel, 1997; Levinson, 1997). In the latter case, each region is ignoring the negative impact of its tax on the profit earnings of the other region's residents.

Now consider endogenous location decisions and assume that a single X-sector firm is choosing a production location or locations. Hoel (1997) and Rauscher (1995a) present analyses in which there are no transport costs between regions, so that the firm will always choose a single plant. This formulation makes the trade-off between attracting and repelling the firm quite clear. On the one hand, a government wants the firm to locate the plant in its region because of the tax revenue that generates. On the other hand, that region then absorbs all the pollution (assuming that pollution is local), in a sense providing a free 'public good' for the other region: the latter region enjoys consuming the good and has a clean environment. If the disutility of pollution is relatively small, such that the tax effect dominates, the two regions will compete down their tax rates to Nash equilibrium rates that are below the cooperative optimum. If the disutility of pollution is large relative to the tax gains, then the opposite occurs and tax competition raises rates above the optimum as neither region wishes to provide the public good. Nash equilibrium may involve no production, the NIMBY phenomenon (not in my backyard).

Markusen et al. (1995) have a somewhat richer model with positive transport costs, although this makes the analysis more complicated and the results less clear. Transport costs imply that the firm might choose two plants, one in each region. In addition, if there is only one plant then product prices (or alternatively real wages) will differ across regions, creating a consumer-surplus motive for attracting the plant in addition to the tax motive. In many parametrizations, each region would like to have the only plant because it can earn tax revenue on export sales. Thus regardless of whether the firm chooses one or two plants at the initial (fixed-location) Nash tax rates, a tax-cutting competition ensues, resulting in equilibrium taxes below the fixed-location rates. The endogenous-location rates are generally below the jointly optimal rates if profits largely accrue outside the region, but may actually move the regions toward joint optimality if profits are owned within the two regions, as noted by Levinson (1996).

Endogenizing the plant location decision can lead to tax increases if the disutility of pollution is sufficiently high, as in Hoel (1997) and Rauscher (1995a). In such a situation, each region wants to be able to consume the good, but wants it produced in the other region. Non-cooperative behaviour can then lead to an increase in taxes until, in equilibrium, the firm is driven out of the market. The outcome is inferior to a cooperative agreement in which one region accepts the plant and receives a side payment from the other region. In any case, all four of the papers noted here emphasize that it is not at all clear that regional competition for mobile plants leads to lower standards in equilibrium.

4.   Empirical relevance

In spite of the rather substantial theoretical literature and significant public policy concern, the weight of empirical evidence suggests that plant location decisions are not very sensitive to environmental costs. A great deal of empirical evidence on international and intra-US location decisions is reviewed in a recent article by Levison (1994), and many other studies are reviewed by Cropper and Oates (1992), and Rauscher (1995b). Many methodological approaches have been used involving many different data sources. The latter range from survey evidence to very formal econometric approaches. Levinson's reading of the literature is that there is scant support for the notion that plant location decisions are very sensitive to differing environmental standards (or, more correctly, other factors are far more important). Important studies using establishment-level data include Bartik (1988), McConnell and Schwab (1990), Freidman et al. (1992) and Levinson (1996).

Rauscher's reading of the evidence (quite a different set of studies) is similarly that there is not much support for the hypothesis that environment regulation affects trade and international capital movements (also the view of Cropper and Oates). Tests of the reverse relationship by Rauscher, that of trade on the environment, receives somewhat more support. A recent study by van Beers and van den Bergh (1997) finds some support for the impact of environmental policy on production and trade if industries are disaggregated into resource-based (non-footloose) and more footloose industries. The latter do seem to respond to regulation. Kaderjak (1996) finds some support for 'capital flight' if industries are disaggregated by types of pollution. Industries creating simple air pollution seem to be sensitive to regulation, but industries involving hazardous wastes are not. He speculates that the latter finding is due to perceived risk on the part of firms: they are not going to move to discharge hazardous wastes somewhere else.

Levinson (1994) then asks why there is the puzzling gap between the public perception and the weak/mixed empirical evidence. Alternatively, why are environmental costs unimportant? Several suggestions have been advanced. One is that it is most cost-effective to use the same technology everywhere, and therefore to operate everywhere according to the most stringent regulations. A second argument is that environmental compliance costs are too small relative to other costs to weigh heavily in location decisions. The figure of 2 per cent is often mentioned as an appropriate one for environmental costs as a percentage of all costs in manufacturing on average, implying that if a firm could cut its environmental costs in half by relocating to a low-standard country, it would only be saving 1 per cent of total costs. A third argument follows from some evidence for the US, that the US has a comparative advantage in pollution-intensive industries relative to Mexico, for example. Following trade liberalization, the environmental regulation effect (pulling firms in these industries to Mexico) is largely or completely offset by the comparative advantage effect (pulling these industries to the US). Existing studies have had difficulty isolating these two effects. A related idea is that countries with low environmental standards are also countries with poor physical, legal and institutional infrastructure, factors which discourage firms from locating in them. The latter are inevitably not held constant in empirical studies.

Further empirical work is desirable, particularly with firm- and plant-level data. Liberalizations within North America and in Eastern Europe should help provide the 'shock' from which to study the effects. From a theoretical point of view more work on the possibility and sustainability of cooperative agreements would be desirable, and the study of linking environment issues to negotiations on trade issues (linked games) would be interesting.

Notes

1. For extensive discussion and literature reviews, see Jinoungh and Wilson (1994), and Rauscher (1995b). Papers incorporating various dimensions of imperfect competition are noted in Markusen et al. (1993, 1995), Motta and Thisse (1994), Hoel (1997), and Rauscher (1995b). Levinson (1994) provides an excellent review of empirical studies, while Cropper and Oates (1992) present a much broader view.
2. For the interested reader, Markusen (1995) reviews many papers which attempt to endogenize multinational firms in general equilibrium trade models. Beckman and Thisse (1986) present an excellent but far broader review of location theory. Unfortunately, these two literatures are largely disjoint at this time. Location theory has had limited interest in the traditional trade formulation: two or more distinct and exogenous markets (that is, countries) between which there are positive trade costs and zero factor mobility, but within which there are no transport costs and perfect factor mobility. The present chapter will follow traditional trade theory, which is not to argue that it is the best approach.
3. The welfare results shown should thus be interpreted as the most pessimistic outcome, in which no environmental benefits are realized.
4. This is a tricky business, since endogenous changes in outputs make the fixed-cost increase that is equivalent to some marginal-cost increase dependent on firm scale. I solved for a multiple of base fixed cost that is equivalent to a 10 per cent marginal cost increase, and then used that (constant) multiple to convert marginal-cost increases to fixed-cost increases.
5. There is implicitly a third region (rest of world) if profits accrue to outside owners. Thus I avoid the term 'Pareto-optimal', using 'jointly optimal' to refer to just the two regions in question.

References

Bartik, Timothy J. (1988), 'The effects of environmental regulation on business location in the United States', *Growth and Change*, Summer, 22–44.

Beckman, Martin J. and Jacques-François Thisse (1986), 'The location of production activities', in P. Nijkamp (ed.), *Handbook of Regional and Urban Economics*, Amsterdam: Elsevier Science Publishers, pp. 21–95.

Cropper, Maureen and Wallace Oates (1992), 'Environmental economics: a survey', *Journal of Economic Literature*, **30**, 675–740.

Freidman, Joseph, Daniel A. Gerlowski and Jonathan Silberman (1992), 'What attracts foreign multinational corporations? Evidence from branch plant location in the United States', *Journal of Regional Science*, **32**, 403–18.

Hoel, Michael (1997), 'Environmental policy with endogenous plant locations', *Scandinavian Journal of Economics*, **99**, 241–59.

Jinoungh, Kim and John Douglas Wilson (1994), 'Capital mobility and environmental standards: racing to the bottom with multiple tax instruments', *Japan and the World Economy*, **9**, 537–51.

Kaderjak, Peter (1996), 'Cheap environmental services of Hungary: How attractive they are for foreign investors', working paper.

Levinson, Arik (1994), 'Environmental regulations and industry location: international and domestic evidence', University of Wisconsin Working Paper.

Levinson, Arik (1996), 'Environmental regulations and manufacturers' location choices: evidence from the Census of Manufacturers', *Journal of Public Economics*, **62**, 5–29.

Levinson, Arik (1997), 'A note on environmental federalism: interpreting some contradictory results', *Journal of Environmental Economics and Management*, **33**, 359–66.

Markusen, James R. (1995), 'The boundaries of multinational enterprises and the theory of international trade', *Journal of Economic Perspectives*, **9**, 169–89.

Markusen, James R. (1997), 'Costly pollution abatement, competitiveness, and plant location decisions', NBER Working Paper no. 5490, *Resource and Energy Economics*, **19**, 299–320.

Markusen, James R., Edward Morey and Nancy Olewiler (1993), 'Environmental policy when market structure and plant locations are endogenous', *Journal of Environmental Economics and Management*, **24**, 69–86.

Markusen, James R., Edward Morey and Nancy Olewiler (1995), 'Competition in regional environmental policies with endogenous plant location decisions', *Journal of Public Economics*, **56**, 55–77.

McConnell, Virginia D. and Robert M. Schwab (1990), 'The impact of environmental regulation on industry location decisions: the motor vehicle industry', *Land Economics*, **66**, 67–81.

Motta, Massimo and Jacques-François Thisse (1994), 'Does environmental dumping lead to delocation?', *European Economic Review*, **38**, 563–76.

Rauscher, Michael (1995a), 'Environmental regulation and the location of polluting industries', *International Tax and Public Finance*, **2**, 229–44.

Rauscher, Michael (1995b), 'Environmental policy and international capital allocation', University of Kiel and CEPR Working Paper.

Ulph, Alistair (1994), 'Environmental policy, plant location and government protection', in Carlo Carraro (ed.), *Trade, Innovation, Environment*, Rotterdam: Kluwer, pp. 123–63.

Ulph, David (1995), 'Globalisation and environmental dumping: firm location and environmental policy', University College London Working Paper.

van Beers, Cees and Jeroen C.J.M. van den Bergh (1997), 'An empirical multi-country analysis of the impact of environmental regulations on foreign trade flows', *Kyklos*, **50**, 29–46.

40 Transport and the environment
Kenneth J. Button and Piet Rietveld

1. Environmental impacts of transport

Modern transport poses particular problems for the environment (Banister and Button, 1993; Button, 1993). It is a significant generator of many atmospheric pollutants, a serious contributor to noise nuisance, its infrastructure can be visually dominant and there are major safety considerations. The environmental intrusions extend through local effects, inflicted on those living and working adjacent to transport infrastructure, to transboundary effects, such as transport's contribution to gas emissions contributing to acid rain, on through to global effects including the emission of greenhouse gases (Hughes, 1990).

While there is some dispute about the exactitude of the valuation methods used, it is generally agreed that these transport-induced environmental intrusions impose considerable economic costs on society. Table 40.1 provides estimates of these for the main industrial countries expressed in terms of their importance as a percentage of GDP.

In contrast to many other sectors, motorized transport is particularly intrusive because the demands for its services are often such that people want transport services to be delivered physically close to human habitation and economic activities. This means it is difficult to isolate people from the local environmental problems of transport such as visual intrusion, and noise and air pollution from fuel additives such as benzene and lead. The very mobility of transport poses further problems for initiating remedial actions.

Different modes of transport affect the environment in different ways. Generally, the main problems of maritime transport centre around the potential spillage from ships and from the pollution and shoreline damage found around ports. Aircraft are particularly intrusive. The issues surrounding surface transport are manifestly different. In terms of passenger transport, public transport modes are often seen as environmentally more benign than the private motor vehicle, but the calculus is complex, depending on such things as load factors, the extent to which multimodal transport is used and types of geographical areas involved.

Table 40.2 offers an indication of the energy consumption of main passenger transport modes which provides a proxy for their associated levels

Table 40.1   Estimated costs of transport in OECD countries as a
percentage of GDP*

Environmental problem	Costs	
	Road (%)	Other modes (%)
Noise	0.10	0.01
Pollution	0.40	
Accidents	2.00	
Time	6.80	1.70
User expenditure (including infrastructure management)	9.00	3.00
Total	18.30	4.71

Source: Quinet (1994).

of atmospheric pollution. However, the correlation is sometimes not perfect and, for instance, the same mode can have different implications for the environment according to the forms of technology used – the cocktail of pollutants given out by diesel-engine cars, for example, is not the same as that for gasoline-engine vehicles. Traffic conditions, the vintage of individual vehicles and the level of vehicle maintenance also affect the link between energy use and pollution. The table is also incomplete in that it does not include the energy embodied in the physical assets used in transport. If one includes the energy used over the lifetime of transport equipment and infrastructure, then car transport becomes even less energy-efficient.

2. Transport demand features

The problems associated with the environment are growing mainly because the worldwide demand for transport services is expanding – a fact which holds true for both passenger and freight transport. Further, a doubling of car ownership is foreseen over the next 25 years (Darmstadter and Jones, 1990). While the environmental damage done by individual vehicles is often decreasing as technology improves, this is being overshadowed in many cases by the sheer growth in the aggregate amount of transport.

A major determinant of passenger transport demand is income. The income elasticity of demand for car ownership, for instance, which is closely linked to that of car use, is high and this is particularly so in the expanding newly industrializing countries. It can be anticipated, therefore, that the present large global share of car ownership in regions such as North America (30 per cent of cars but only 5 per cent of the world's

Table 40.2   Energy efficiency of transport modes

	Number of persons carried (% laden)	Energy (MJ) per passenger mile	Energy (MJ) per passenger mile (fully laden)
Petrol car			
<1.4 litre	1.5	2.79	1.05
1.4–2.0 litre	1.5	3.21	1.20
2.0 litre	1.5	4.96	0.87
Diesel car			
<1.4 litre	1.5	2.42	0.91
1.4–2.0 litre	1.5	2.96	1.11
2.0 litre	1.5	3.93	1.47
Rail			
InterCity	338(60)	0.77	0.46
InterCity 225	289(60)	1.04	0.62
InterCity 125	294(60)	0.95	0.57
Super Sprinter	88(60)	0.89	0.53
Electric suburban	180(60)	0.70	0.42
Bus			
Double-decker	25(25)	0.83	0.28
Single-decker	16(33)	1.40	0.47
Minibus	10(50)	1.15	0.57
Express coach	30(65)	0.61	0.40
Air			
Boeing 737	100(60)	3.90	2.34
Motorcycle	1.2	3.13	1.80
Moped	1	1.31	1.31
Bicycle	1	0.10	0.10
Walk	1	0.25	0.25

Source: Hughes (1990).

population) will gradually diminish. This trend will be reinforced by demographic factors because most of the industrialized countries appear to be approaching saturation levels of car ownership as population growth slows, the level of female participation in the labour force is high and further significant reductions in family size are unlikely to occur.

The quality and range of transport services enjoyed by users have increased as technology has improved quality and more transport infrastructure has become available. These supply features are likely to facilitate and encourage more transport in the future as local and national govern-ments and international bodies, such as the European Union, improve existing infrastructure, particularly inter-urban roads, and invest in new networks, such as high-speed rail. At the local level, however, the scope for expanding transport networks is, for cost and physical reasons, more limited. This is leading to high concentrations of environmental damage within many urban areas, combined with a trend in suburbanization where this is physically possible. The latter, however, often only adds to the environmental problems as it induces an increase in overall travel demand.

Public policies, including those relating to transport pricing, also influ-ence transport demand and, *ipso facto*, are a key influence on environ-mental intrusion (Verhoef, 1996). Recent years have seen a trend towards less government regulation of transport industries and towards a greater reliance on market forces to achieve economic objectives. The economic evidence is that generally this has brought down the fares charged for public transport and, given relatively high price elasticities, with this has come a rise in the quantity of transport services demanded.

There are also important technical developments which may affect future transport levels and patterns. Advances in electronic communication are continually improving the way transport services can be delivered to the customer (for example, the computer reservation systems used by airlines) and offer more efficient methods of infrastructure management (such as computerized traffic light systems). These enhance demand. Other advances offered, for instance, scope for teleworking, teleconferencing and teleshopping, may affect the pattern of travel demand but, since they free up time for other travel or in some cases themselves stimulate new trips, the implications for overall transport demand are uncertain.

An almost identical picture emerges regarding freight transport. In most countries, freight transport has grown faster than GDP, reflecting the greater relative input of transport in the production process. The cause of this is, in part, a reflection of lower real freight transport costs due to such things as deregulation of markets, which allows suppliers to exploit economies of scale, and reduction in international trade barriers. It is also a reflection of demand changes and, particularly, an increase in demand for product variety by final consumers. Producers have also developed new management strategies, including 'just-in-time' production, which are transport-intensive.

The traffic-associated problems of developing countries are posing new types of challenges. The infrastructure in many of these countries is often inadequate for the growth of traffic which is taking place, leading to noise and safety problems, while the vehicle parks tend to be old, because used-car imports are high, and maintenance is generally very poor. With much of the economic growth in these countries concentrated in urban areas, the environmental implications for cities are becoming particularly acute.

3. Transport policies

As with all environmental issues, the underlying cause of the problems associated with transport is the existence of negative externalities. Because of the lack of fully allocated property rights, there are no effective markets for the environmental attributes involved or, if they do exist, markets are partial and do not function efficiently. Environmental problems are often compounded because other aspects of transport costs are not fully reflected in user charges due to the existence of subsidies or because of the way prices are imposed. Lack of appropriate road user fees, for instance, means that excessive traffic congestion in cities is rife and, while not strictly an environmental problem *per se*, this exacerbates levels of atmospheric pollution and noise.

A variety of policy instruments is available to contain the environmental damage associated with modern transport (Table 40.3 offers a listing) and the policy response to the problem has varied across countries and has also changed with time.

The standard externality diagram (Figure 40.1) provides a simple way of comparing the implications of the various policy options. The potential users of transport will use transport services up to the point where the benefits they derive, as represented by their demand schedule, is equated with the additional costs they have to incur (that is, to traffic volume Q_d). What they do not take into account are the environmental costs that they impose on others, but if they did so, they would limit their travel to the traffic volume Q_o. This latter, optimal volume can theoretically be reached in a number of ways. Traffic could, for instance, simply be limited to Q_o by law; regulations could be imposed to clean up vehicles, leading to convergence of the private and social cost curves; the monetary or other costs of transport could be adjusted to reflect the full, including environmental, costs of making a trip; or travel demand could be influenced by policies affecting substitutes or complements to travel.

The conventional approach to limiting the environmental damage associated with transport is through the use of command-and-control instruments. The range of regulatory controls is substantial. Measures such as the compulsory fitting of catalytic converters to reduce gas emissions contributing to acid rain, for example, and the establishment of maximum permitted engine-noise levels, including aircraft engines, are standard policies in most industrialized countries. Equally, speed limits are used both to reduce accident risk and to assist in the economical use of fuels. In cities, central areas are increasingly being reserved for pedestrians. More recently

Table 40.3 Policy instruments for containing the environmental intrusion of transport

	Market-based incentives		Command-and-control regulations	
	Direct	Indirect	Direct	Indirect
Vehicle	• Emissions fees	• Tradable permits • Differential vehicle taxation • Tax allowances for new vehicles	• Emissions standards	• Compulsory inspection and maintenance of emissions control systems • Mandatory use of low-polluting vehicles • Compulsory scrappage of old vehicles
Fuel		• Differential fuel taxation • High fuel taxes	• Fuel composition • Phasing out of high-polluting fuels	• Fuel economy standards • Speed limits
Traffic		• Congestion charges • Parking charges • Subsidies for less polluting modes	• Physical restraint of traffic • Designated routes	• Restraints on vehicle use • Bus lanes and other priorities

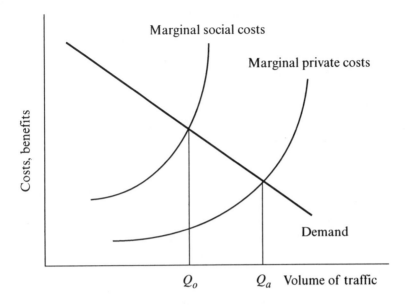

Figure 40.1   Externality diagram

a number of cities, such as Athens, have established limits for certain types of pollution which, when exceeded, result in traffic bans. In relation to maritime transport there are international codes concerning the cleaning of tanks and the discharge of oil waste.

Controls over where and when particular types of transport may be used also serve environmental ends. Traffic management measures such as one-way streets, junction priorities and so on in cities can take vehicles away from residential areas while flight paths of aircraft around airports are usually controlled to protect noise-sensitive areas. There are also often night curfews at airports.

The provision of new transport infrastructure is generally the subject of planning regulations and additional capacity is generally only permitted after a full social impact appraisal which embraces some form of environmental assessment. Urban planning is also often forced to play considerable attention to the interaction of motorized traffic and those living and working in cities with the intention of limiting local pollution, visual intrusion and noise problems. Where major new structures are built, this may involve separation of major transport arteries from residential areas, but in older cities, where this is often not possible, it may mean careful consideration in design of transport infrastructure and possibly insulation.

The use of economic instruments to achieve environmental targets has been limited. Several countries have employed fuel taxation premia to contain the use of carbon-based fuels, some have differential taxation structures favouring less environmentally intrusive vehicles while yet others have deployed fiscal incentives to encourage maximum recycling of vehicular components. The use of differential taxation on leaded and unleaded fuel has been particularly useful in reducing the use of the fuel additive. While these, and similar measures, are important instruments in containing particular transport-associated environmental problems, perhaps more important are fiscal measures, such as the area licensing scheme in Singapore, which act to reduce the overall levels of car use.

Finally, there are policies aimed at making less environmentally intrusive transport options more attractive. The use of subsidies to stimulate the use of public transport modes in urban areas is one widely used approach, although the evidence is that the cross-elasticity of demand is such that only limited transfers take place in practice. More recently there has been discussion of the use of electronic modes of communicating information replacing personal movements – concepts such as teleworking, video-conferencing and teleshopping come within this debate. Again, the evidence is of limited transfer, although as technology has advanced there has been some substitution, and in some cases there has even been evidence of increased travel as electronic communications have stimulated new patterns of contacts. Where improved information systems seem at present to be more important from an environmental perspective is in reducing the amount of 'wasted' transport due to such things as aircraft stacking at airports and empty running by trucks. Information systems are improving the match between demands for transport services and their supply.

In practice, social and political feasibility are factors which influence governments in the way they treat transport and the environment. Social feasibility can limit the types and intensities of policies since all effective policies have distributional as well as efficiency attributes. These redistributive effects are neglected in standard cost–benefit analysis and, therefore, policy makers often prefer solutions which appear less attractive than those supported by narrow welfare-economic considerations. For instance, interest groups affected by transport policies often aim at minimizing transfer effects from the private to the public sector and this can imply a preference for command-and-control measures rather than the use of fiscal instruments.

A promising instrument to reduce gross financial transfers from the private sector to the public sector while improving economic efficiency is that of the tradable permit. This involves the distribution of a limited number of pollution permits which can then be bought and sold to ensure their efficient utilization. Another option which may improve social and political acceptance is to adopt a package of measures (Jones, 1991). For instance, this may combine the use of both fiscal and regulatory measures coupled with explicit commitments on how any revenues collected are to be used.

References

Banister, D. and K.J. Button (1993), *Transport, the Environment and Sustainable Development*, London: Spon.

Button, K.J. (1993), *Transport, the Environment and Economic Policy*, Aldershot, UK and Brookfield, US: Edward Elgar.

Darmstadter, J. and A. Jones (1990), 'Prospects for reducing CO_2 emissions in automobiles transport', Washington, DC: Resources for the Future.

Hughes, P. (1990), *Transport and the Greenhouse Effect*, Energy and Environmental Research Unit, Open University, Milton Keynes.

Jones, P. (1991), 'Gaining public support for road pricing through a package approach', *Traffic Engineering and Control*, **32**, 194–6.

Quinet, E. (1994), 'The social costs of transport: evaluation and links with internalisation policies', in ECMT/OECD, *Internalising the Social Costs of Transport*, Paris: ECMT/OECD.

Verhoef, E.T. (1996), *The Economics of Regulating Road Transport*, Cheltenham, UK and Brookfield, US: Edward Elgar.

PART VI

ENVIRONMENTAL MACROECONOMICS

41 Environment in macroeconomic modelling

Ekko C. van Ierland

1. Introduction

Macroeconomic theory traditionally focuses on the development of national income and its constituent expenditure categories. Targets of macroeconomic policy include economic growth, full employment, balance of payments equilibrium and a stable price level. The main emphasis is on wage and price formation, its implications for the labour market, stability in the monetary sphere and adjustment of disequilibria in the markets. For many years macroeconomic textbooks have neglected environmental issues, including the use of natural resources, emissions of pollutants and their environmental impacts (Daly, 1991).

Today, macroeconomic theory gives more attention to the basic interactions between the economic process and the environment. Both theoretical and applied macroeconomic studies analyse how macroeconomic development results in exploitation of natural resources and affects the environment. In the same way economists analyse how environmental and energy policies influence macroeconomic performance. This reminds us of the famous '*Tableau Economique*' (Quesnay, 1758), which was developed to describe how economic activity is the result of interactions between nature and agricultural production, which was considered to be the basis of economic prosperity.

Following the publication of the Report to the Club of Rome, *Limits to Growth* (Meadows et al., 1972), new developments in macroeconomic theory and modelling have taken place. New models have been developed to analyse the macroeconomic impacts of environmental policy measures, to study the characteristics of sustainable development in macroeconomic growth models and to analyse the economic aspects of global warming in integrated dynamic climate and economy models (Nordhaus, 1991; Kolstad, 1994, 1996; Manne and Richels, 1992, 1997; van Ierland, 1994, 1996).

Gradually, natural resources and emissions are taken into account in macroeconomic models, not only in those addressing national economic problems, but also in those addressing international trade and global issues, such as global warming and impacts on biodiversity. Because energy consumption is one of the main sources of greenhouse gases and acidifying compounds, macroeconomic models are often (directly or indirectly) linked to energy demand and supply models. They describe options and macroeconomic effects of various energy policies, including changes in fossil fuel mix and introduction of renewables, such as solar, wind and biomass.

This chapter deals with some of the relevant macroeconomic theories and models for the environment. Section 2 starts with a discussion of macroeconomic analysis of the environment and its main purposes. Section 3 deals with neoclassical growth models and their applications in environmental economics. The section also briefly discusses uncertainty and learning in macroeconomic models for climate change. Section 4 focuses on empirical regionalized world models, mainly in the area of climate change. Section 5 indicates how input–output analysis is applied to environmental issues. It also deals with integrated economy–energy–environment models. Section 6 pays attention to the qualitative macroeconomic study *Scanning the Future* (CPB, 1992b), which deals with various coordination perspectives and their implications for macroeconomic development in a number of world regions. Section 7 explains how better availability of environmental data and improved computer facilities have stimulated progress in macroeconomic modelling for the environment. Section 8 contains conclusions and suggestions for further research.

2. Macroeconomic analysis for the environment
Macroeconomic analysis for the environment takes place for a large number of reasons, such as:

1. To identify future environmental problems by means of macroeconomic scenario studies.
2. To analyse macroeconomic impacts of environmental policies.
3. To analyse energy strategies, related emissions of air pollutants and their macroeconomic impact.
4. To identify efficient solutions to environmental problems.
5. To suggest 'optimal' policies on the basis of formal optimization.
6. To analyse impacts on personal and intergenerational income distribution.
7. To analyse coalitions and reasons for non-cooperation of various stakeholders in international environmental problems.

Daly (1991) shows in a challenging analysis that macroeconomic theory has not, until recently, given much attention to the fundamental relations between macroeconomic activity and the environment. He notes that many macroeconomic textbooks do not even include environment or natural resources as entries in the subject index. However, it is widely recognized that the circular flow of income can only be maintained by intensive use of natural resources, intensive use of agricultural land and high levels of emissions of pollutants related to economic activity. Daly considers the question of which level of macroeconomic activity can be maintained by the ecological system as one of the key questions in the macroeconomic theory of the environment. He argues that the optimal scale of economic activity should be studied by economists.

In mainstream macroeconomics an extensive debate between Keynesians and monetarists has taken place, which was followed by the theory of rational expectations. Nowadays, in most macroeconomic models of the environment both the supply and the demand side of the economy are included. For the short-run analysis typical Keynesian issues like unemployment, capacity utilization and cyclical movements are relevant. For the long run, attention particularly focuses on supply factors, like the availability of natural resources, the accumulation of capital, the development of technological progress and the long-run rate of growth of the labour supply.

In environmental economics discussion focuses not so much on the different schools of thought in macroeconomic theory. Instead discussion centres on the questions of how economic growth affects the environment and vice versa, and how technological development and production are influenced by environmental policies.

In analysing these macroeconomic issues, an infinite number of models can be developed, depending on theoretical axioms, the time and regional scale of analysis, and the quest for sectoral details. The literature provides highly aggregated and stylized models, and very detailed models for sectoral policies, energy planning and policies for specific pollutants. Some models include an extensive set of equations for modelling ecological aspects; others include only a few equations on emissions and concentrations of pollutants. In some integrated assessment models a detailed regional specification is included, such as in the RAINS models (Alcamo et al., 1990; Hordijk, 1995), the IMAGE 2.0 model (Alcamo, 1994) or TARGETS (Tool to Assess Regional and Global Environmental and Health Targets for Sustainability) (Rotmans et al., 1994).

Models are specified as *simulation* models for answering 'what if' questions, or as an *optimization* framework for analysing 'optimal' solutions under specific constraints. Optimization models can be based on optimal control and similar analytical tools (Chiang, 1992; Feenstra et al., Chapter 71 in this book), or optimization can be performed numerically by linear or non-linear dynamic optimization programmes. In some cases a simple comparative static analysis will be sufficient, but in general the development over time, the dynamics of convergence, stability and robustness of dynamic systems are studied (Nordhaus, 1991; Smulders, 1994; Kolstad, 1994). Dynamic models are essential for studying environmental issues, since the dynamics of pollutants (stock or flow pollutants), the regeneration capacity of the environment and the depletion of renewable and non-renewable resources are typically dynamic processes. Also capital accumulation and population growth have typically dynamic characteristics. Both the long-run development and short-term adjustments should therefore be analysed in a dynamic setting (van den Bergh, 1991).

Simulation and optimization models can be used in a framework of *neoclassical cost–benefit analysis* of environmental impacts. In the neoclassical cost–benefit approach it is necessary that environmental effects are valued and expressed in *monetary terms* to be compared with the economic costs of environmental policies. If this is not possible the analysis confines itself to the economic efficiency of policies to reach prespecified environmental targets expressed in *physical units*. The latter approach is typically chosen in the RAINS model (Alcamo et al., 1990) in which critical loads for acidification can be used as environmental constraints.

In *ecological economic analysis* the relation between economic activity and the ecological process is described in more detail on the basis of the laws of thermodynamics (cf. Georgescu-Roegen, 1971) and by means of materials balance models (see the chapters by Ruth and Ayres, Chapters 59 and 60 in this book). In some of the ecological economic models extensive attention is given to detailed modelling of ecological processes, including the stability and resilience of ecosystems. Specific attention is given to the various functions of ecosystems, such as production functions, carrier functions, information functions and regeneration functions (cf. de Groot, 1995). In models for the analysis of global warming detailed attention is paid to the accumulation of greenhouse gases in the atmosphere, the resulting radiative forcing and the interactions between the ocean and atmosphere in the exchange of greenhouse gases.

In the past decades new developments have taken place in *computable general equilibrium models* (CGE models) (see Chapter 69 by Conrad in this book). Although large differences traditionally existed between CGE models and macroeconomic models, they are now starting to converge. With the study of the microeconomic foundations of macroeconomic models, the underlying microeconomic theory, which plays a dominant role in CGE models, is also included in macroeconomic models. With the extension of CGE models to the theory of public finance and taxation, the difference between macroeconomic models and CGE models is also becoming less clear. A key characteristic of some classes of macroeconomic models is the specific attention to disequilibrium in some of the markets (for example labour or capital markets). However, in CGE models possible distortions in these markets are also analysed (see the chapter on the double dividend of an environmental tax reform by de Mooij, and on public economics and the environment by Proost, Chapters 20 and 22 in this book). An important difference between CGE models and macroeconomic models is that in the former investment is explained by the level of savings in the economy. In macroeconomic models more attention is paid to the explanatory variables for *ex ante* investment of firms, for example on the basis of profits, the rate of interest or the rate of return on capital and the short-term dynamics related to it. In this regard macroeconomic models may be better suited to explain some of the short-term cyclical developments in the economy, and the short-run impacts of environmental and resource policies.

3. Macroeconomic models based on the neoclassical growth model

For analysing the relation between economic growth, technological progress, the use of natural resources and the emissions and accumulation of pollutants, the neoclassical growth model as developed by Solow (1956) has been widely used. The basic structure of the model includes a Cobb–Douglas or CES production function, a function for capital accumulation over time, an exogenous rate of growth of technological progress and an exogenous rate of growth of the stock of labour. The model explains per capita economic growth and is capable of generating Phelps's famous 'golden rule of accumulation' (Phelps, 1961), which indicates that optimal per capita consumption can be reached by 'consuming your wages and investing your profits'. Recent developments in modern growth theory, including the theory of endogenous growth, are discussed in the chapter by Smulders in this book (Chapter 42).

Neoclassical growth models are particularly suited to analyse sustainability issues, such as the relationship between the level of GDP and the level of emissions of pollutants, as expressed in the environmental Kuznets curve (discussed in the chapter by de Bruyn and Heintz – Chapter 46). This curve indicates that at low income levels the level of emissions of pollutants increases more than proportionally, while after reaching a certain maximum the emissions start to decline, because at higher income levels more environmental policies will be imposed (Opschoor, 1995; Arrow et al., 1995). The environmental Kuznets curve can be *empirically* established for a number of compounds (at least for a certain number of countries for a specific period of time). The theoretical conditions for combining economic growth with declining emissions can be analysed in neoclassical growth models with extensions for the use of natural resources and the emissions of pollutants. (See also the chapters by Beckerman, by Daly, and by van den Bergh and de Mooij in this volume – Chapters 43, 44 and 45.)

The neoclassical model has also been extended for the integrated economic analysis of energy issues and global warming. The most straightforward and elementary specification is Nordhaus's DICE model (Nordhaus, 1991). This model includes a Cobb–Douglas production function for the specification of gross world product (GWP) and exogenous (and declining) growth of technological progress and labour. The basic neoclassical framework is used in which the capital stock increases per period on the basis of investment that is equated to total savings, in combination with a fixed percentage of depreciation per period. The model is extended to include emissions of greenhouse gases by means of an emission factor, which is exogenously declining over time, related to gross world product. The model also includes an emission reduction function, which makes it possible to reduce emissions by sacrificing a part of gross world production (GWP). At the same time a climate module is included that calculates the average change of temperature as compared to the pre-industrial level on the basis of the stock of greenhouse gases and the resulting radiative forcing. Finally, the model includes a quadratic damage cost function, which relates the monetary damages of climate change to the average increase of atmospheric temperature. The model is capable of calculating the optimal time path of emission reduction by maximizing the discounted utility obtained from per capita consumption.

Nordhaus's model is a very interesting illustration of how the macroeconomic heritage of the neoclassical growth model has been used for integrated macroeconomic environmental analysis. Although the uncertainty about the parameter values is widely recognized, and despite its aggregated character, the model provides a very strong analytical framework for studying the key questions in this area of environmental economics.

Uncertainty about climate change and the process of learning have been analysed by Kolstad (1994, 1996) who includes in the DICE model various states of the world that express the possibilities that climate change turns out to be a minor or a major problem. The damage function is adjusted to express high damage when climate change is serious and low damage when climate change turns out to be a minor problem. By attaching a probability distribution to the various states of the world and by changing this probability distribution on the basis of learning over time, Kolstad studies the impact of learning on the optimal emission reduction level, in a setting of uncertainty about the impacts of climate change. This type of analysis also makes it possible to calculate the value of perfect information by calculating how much additional consumption per capita can be obtained if full information on the 'real state of the world' is obtained in an early stage. This type of analysis has also been carried out by means of the CETA model (Peck and Teisberg, 1993) and the SLICE model (Nordhaus and Yang, 1997).

Integrated assessment models for climate change in which microeconomic development plays an important role are briefly summarized in Table 41.1 with a number of their key characteristics. DICE, SLICE and CETA have already been mentioned. The regionalized models will be discussed in Section 4, which focuses on regionalized world models.

4. Regionalized world models

An interesting class of macroeconomic models consists of regionalized macroeconomic world models. These models are widely applied in the analysis of climate change (see also the chapters on environmental policies in an international context in part IV of this book). Typical examples are RICE (Nordhaus and Yang, 1995, 1996), CETA (Peck and Teisberg, 1993), MERGE (Manne and Richels, 1992, 1997), MERGE/DIALOGUE (Mensink and Hoekstra, 1997), the IMAGE models (Rotmans, 1990; Alcamo, 1994), the FUND model (Tol, 1994, 1996) and the OECD Green model (Burniaux et al., 1992); see also Table 41.1.

The RICE model (Nordhaus and Yang, 1995, 1996) is based on the DICE model, which has been regionalized to study the macroeconomic costs of various emission reduction strategies in regions of the world. This makes it possible to analyse the emission reduction that will occur in a full cooperative setting and the emission reduction strategies for the various regions if these pursue policies maximizing the regional benefits, assuming that all other regions follow the same strategy of maximizing local benefits. The Nash equilibrium that is calculated in this way shows very modest emission reductions for all regions. This type of analysis falls in the class game-theoretical models that analyse the various strategies that the economic actors can choose in optimizing their payoff. In the setting of transboundary air pollution Mäler (1989, 1994) illustrated that a noncooperative Nash strategy would result in underabatement of sulphur emissions in Europe as compared to full cooperation. He stresses that large cost savings could be obtained if a fully cooperative solution were chosen. The same result is obtained by Nordhaus and Yang (1996), who show that also in the case of global warming a Nash strategy would result in very low emission reduction strategies for the various regions in the world.

The CETA model is a regionalized world model that includes explicit specification of energy carriers, like coal, oil, natural gas, nuclear and a carbon-free backstop technology. This concise model is capable of analysing uncertainty and has been used to calculate the expected value of perfect information.

Manne and Richels developed the MERGE model, which explicitly pays

Table 41.1 A number of integrated assessment models for climate change

Name	Author(s)	Economic characteristic	Energy characteristic	Climate characteristic	Simulation/ optimization
DICE	Nordhaus, 1991, 1993	Cobb–Douglas	Implicit	Carbon accumulation	Optimization
RICE	Nordhaus and Yang, 1995, 1996	Cobb–Douglas; Multiregion	Implicit	Carbon accumulation	Optimization; Negishi weights
SLICE	Nordhaus and Yang, 1997	Cobb–Douglas; uncertainty analysis; learning	Implicit	Carbon accumulation	Optimization
CETA	Peck and Teisberg, 1993	Cobb–Douglas Multiregion; uncertainty analysis	Explicit energy carriers	Carbon accumulation	Optimization
MERGE	Manne et al., 1995	Nested CES; multiregion; international trade	Explicit energy carriers and technologies	Carbon accumulation; other greenhouse gases	Optimization; Negishi weights
MERGE/DIALOGUE	Mensink and Hoekstra, 1997	Idem; climate impacts; specified in Dialogue	Idem	Carbon accumulation; other greenhouse gases	Simulation; optimization Linked models, forward/ backward

IMAGE 1.0	Rotmans, 1990	Economic scenarios; land use	Explicit energy carriers	Carbon accumulation; other greenhouse gases	Simulation; linked models
IMAGE 2.0	Alcamo, 1994	Economic scenarios; land-use modelling	Explicit energy carriers	Carbon accumulation; other greenhouse gases	Simulation; optimization; linked models
FUND	Tol, 1994, 1996	Exogenous economic growth; Multiregion	Implicit	Carbon accumulation	Optimization
OECD Green	Burniaux et al, 1992	CES production function; multiregion; International trade; carbon leakage	Detailed modelling of energy markets	Not detailed	Simulation

Note: For a more exhaustive listing of integrated assessment models for climate change see Nakicenovic et al. (1994, 1996) and van der Sluijs (1997).

attention to the availability of energy resources, their exploitation and international trade. The model is developed to analyse global warming issues and has gradually developed into a macroeconomic general equilibrium model for five regions of the world. The model includes a detailed climate module and an elaborated module for damage assessment. Production factors are combined in a nested Cobb–Douglas production function in which capital and labour are combined into a composite input, that is combined with a composite energy input for each of the five regions. Global welfare is maximized by optimizing welfare of the regions in the world, weighted by means of Negishi weights. These weights are calculated on the basis of the original factor endowments of the regions, valued at the appropriate shadow prices in the optimal solutions (Manne and Rutherford, 1994; Rutherford, 1998).

The MERGE model is a very interesting illustration of how macroeconomic modelling is evolving over time toward the full integration of energy economics, emissions of pollutants and greenhouse gases, their resulting effects on average atmospheric temperature, and the various policy instruments to mitigate environmental impacts. It also is a clear illustration of how macroeconomic modelling and CGE modelling are starting to be further integrated.

Whereas the studies by Meadows et al. (1972, 1992) were based on simulation models in a systems dynamics setting, the more elaborated MERGE model is now specified in a non-linear optimization framework, for multi-regions, multi-commodities and multi-emissions. The basic foundations of the models of Meadows et al. have always been criticized for a lack of technological progress and insufficient substitution possibilities. The MERGE model is more flexible and better founded on a solid empirical basis for the availability of natural resources. The MERGE model also explicitly calculated emissions, not measured as an obscure index (as is the case in Meadows et al., 1992), but clearly expressed in physical units.

The MERGE model of Manne and Richels has been linked to the DIA-LOGUE model, which describes the climate system and the impacts of climate change in a detailed manner (Mensink and Hoekstra, 1997). The advantage of linking the two models is that more detailed analysis of regional impacts of climate change becomes possible. A drawback, however, is that complete optimization to calculate the 'optimal path of emissions reduction' on the basis of costs and damages is no longer possible.

The IMAGE model is an integrated assessment model that includes a very detailed analysis of land use on the basis of a macroeconomic analysis of future demands for various food products in 13 world regions. The model also includes a detailed analysis of future energy demands and emissions of greenhouse gases. IMAGE 1.0 started with a highly simplified world model. IMAGE 2.0 is much more elaborated and contains combined simulation and optimization procedures for constructing scenarios on future land use. IMAGE 2.0 is an interesting model in the class of integrated assessment models. It integrates many aspects of economic growth and energy consumption with detailed analysis of land-use development in 13 world regions for analysing the causes and impacts of climate change. For analysing emissions of greenhouse gases and their impacts on agriculture and ecosystems a detailed analysis of changes in land use and land cover is desirable. The IMAGE model provides a simulation model for analysing the emissions of greenhouse gases related to land use, such as N_2O and CH_4. It also analyses carbon sequestration in forests or the release of carbon through deforestation. In addition to the IMAGE model the TARGETS model has been specified (Rotmans et al., 1994). TARGETS focuses in particular on the interactions between the cultural, the socioeconomic and the ecological systems.

The FUND model (Tol, 1994, 1996) is based on Nordhaus's DICE model, but it contains a regional specification, interregional capital flows and a detailed specification of the functions for assessing the damage costs of climate change. It also focuses on the international trade issues related to climate change policies.

The OECD Green model (Burniaux et al., 1992) focuses on macroeconomic development and energy consumption at the international level. It is a general equilibrium model that deals with energy consumption and the related emissions of CO_2. In this context it analyses the impacts of carbon taxes on energy consumption, on emissions of CO_2 and on carbon leakage, that is, the shifting of carbon emissions towards regions in which no carbon taxes are imposed.

Other models that focus on these issues are models such as Minicam, Page, DGEM and ICAM (for an excellent overview see Nakicenovic et al., 1994 and 1996).

5. Environmental input–output models

A different class of macroeconomic models is based on an extended version of input–output analysis (see Chapter 68 by Duchin and Steenge). Leontief (1966, 1970) extended his famous input–output system for studying the sectoral development of economies to include emissions of pollutants, and to analyse the sectoral impacts of policies to reduce emissions by abatement sectors. His seminal work has led to many applied models in which an input–output structure was included. Many studies have elaborated on Leontief's basic system by combining it with vintage models for the specification of the capital stock and labour demand, and linear expenditure systems for endogenizing consumer demand (CPB, 1992a; van Ierland,

1993). In some cases technical coefficients, which are assumed to be constant in Leontief's original input–output analysis, were also made endogenous on the basis of price development. National input–output models include equations for imports and exports that are generally specified on the basis of price and income elasticities for imports. For exports the sectoral export volumes are generally linked to the relevant volume of world imports and competitiveness as expressed by the distributed lag function of the difference between the export prices of the relevant sector and the prices of its competitors on the world market. The input–output structure for intermediate deliveries is also often included in CGE models for analysing environmental policies and impacts.

The input–output structure is at present used for further analysing the system of national accounts, and for the elaboration of detailed statistics on emissions per sector of industry, in order to provide the database for detailed modelling of materials flows and emissions in macroeconomic (sectoral) models. The National Accounting Matrix including Environmental Accounts (NAMEA) system (de Boo et al., 1993) focuses on very detailed data on emissions per sector or class of economic activity, not only providing insight into the present levels of emissions and their sources but also into their development over time. Also the depletion of natural resources receives full attention in the composition of these statistics. Input–output models have also been used to estimate the share of the output due to abatement activities (in a way that avoids double counting, for example, Schafer and Stahmer, 1989; Nestor and Pasurka, 1995).

A special class of environmental models combines the input–output framework with optimization. WRR (1987) has applied this seminal approach to analyse the scope for growth in the Netherlands under specific constraints for energy consumption and emissions of acidifying pollutants. More recently the DEOS study by IvM (1996) used a similar approach employing the emission coefficients that are now available for a large number of pollutants for the various branches of industry.

Input–output models have the general drawback of focusing on the demand side of the economy, in many cases neglecting the supply side. Also the monetary aspects of the economic process are in most cases neglected or only specified in a very elementary way in the models. However, this omission may be less serious if the studies focus on long-run economic development in which stable monetary policies are assumed.

Given the large impact of the energy system on emissions of pollutants for acidification, eutrophication, smog and global warming, many macroeconomic models are focusing on macroeconomic development, energy demand, energy supply and related emissions of pollutants (see also Chapters 12 and 73 in this volume). A typical example of a fully applied and empirical model is the Markal Macro model (Manne, 1992) which originated as a bottom-up energy supply model, but which was extended to include the macroeconomic feedback of increasing energy prices on energy demand.

At the European level the HERMES models (cf. Mot et al., 1989) have been developed to analyse economic development in the various member states. The HERMES models are characterized by nested CES and Cobb–Douglas production functions at the sectoral level that include capital, labour, energy and (in most cases) materials. The HERMES models include a full specification of wage and price formation, employment and expenditure categories. Imports and exports for the various European countries are linked in the project to analyse the balance of payments position of the various countries. The specification of energy demand in the HERMES project was rather elementary and no specific attention was paid to emissions of pollutants. Another example of a linked economy–energy model is Markal-Macro (Manne, 1992).

At present the PRIMES model (Capros and Kokkolakis, 1996) is used for a large number of European countries to build scenarios for macroeconomic development, energy consumption and emissions of pollutants. PRIMES is conceived for forecasting, scenario construction and policy impact analysis. It covers a medium- to long-term horizon but it is not designed for the very long term. The PRIMES model contains a detailed specification for energy consumption of various fuel types and for the emissions of the main categories of air pollutants such as SO_2, NO_x and CO_2 for several categories of economic activities, including industrial production, housing and transportation.

6. A qualitative macroeconomic scenario study

That macroeconomic analysis can not only be based on model calculations, but also on profound qualitative analysis is demonstrated in the study *Scanning the Future*, published by the Central Planning Bureau (CPB, 1992b). The study provides an in-depth analysis of future developments of the world economy till the year 2020. It pays extensive attention to the problems that will arise and the various coordination mechanisms to overcome these problems. The scenarios that are distinguished are European Renaissance, Global Shift, Global Crisis and Balanced Growth. These scenarios are based on different perspectives on economic development: the equilibrium perspective, the coordination perspective and the free market perspective. An important environmental element in the study is the development of CO_2 emissions in the various scenarios for the regions of the world, including the USA, Japan, Western Europe, dynamic Asian economies, other less developed economies, the Commonwealth of

Independent States and Central Europe. The study is challenging but from a scientific point of view it contains some obscure elements, particularly on how the quantitative results of the economic, energy and environmental variables have been obtained. The study *Scanning the Future* is recommended for those interested in qualitative scenario studies and Delphi methods.

7. Data availability

Better availability of data has contributed to a rapid development in the past two decades of empirical macroeconomic models addressing the environment. Whereas at the beginning of the 1970s very little information was available on emissions of pollutants and their impact on the environment, nowadays extensive databases are available for emissions of greenhouse gases, acidifying pollutants and many other environmental statistics. Also databases for costs of emission reduction and costs of new energy technologies have been established. This expansion of data collection and documentation is essential for making further progress in applied environmental economic analysis. On the basis of improved data it can be expected that applied modelling of economy–energy and environment interactions will make much progress towards policy relevant applications.

8. Conclusions

Macroeconomic modelling plays a central role in the analysis of environmental policies, from the national (sometimes even regional) level to the global level. Basic macroeconomic models and theories such as the neoclassical growth model and the theory of endogenous technical progress are relevant today, with extensions to the exploitation of natural resources, emissions of pollutants and climate change. Particularly the further development of macroeconomic models towards integrated general equilibrium models with international trade and the analysis of tradable emission permits is very challenging.

The results of both relatively small analytical models and large computer-based numerical models are clarifying complex issues in environmental economics. The small analytical models can be applied for analysing complicated issues like decision making under uncertainty, learning and irreversibility. The larger empirical models provide insight into the actual quantitative relations that are highly relevant in policy analysis. A key role will be played by the analysis of technological progress, which does not come as 'manna from heaven', but which is clearly induced by economic incentives and policies, such as environmental and energy policies.

Macroeconomic theory and modelling plays, and will play, a dominant role in the preparation of environmental policy. Environmental issues will be further integrated, both in macroeconomic theory and in theoretical and applied models. A large variety of theories and models, though confusing to policy makers, is an essential element in the scientific debate on how economic activity and the environment are related.

The answers to the questions of whether economic growth can be combined with high environmental quality, and whether there are limits to growth, depend to a large extent on technologies that will be developed for energy conservation, for dematerialization and for sustainable energy supply. The willingness to support environmental policies plays a key role in answering the question of whether the environmental Kuznets curve is relevant for the future. Environmental policies should particularly be directed towards stimulating clean and sustainable technologies. To the extent that technologies for protecting the environment are not available at present (and may not be available in the future), human consumption and production patterns should be adjusted in order to avoid irreversible damage to the natural environment and ecosystems. It is definitely a challenge for macroeconomic theory to develop a consistent framework for analysing the interactions between the economic system and the ecological system, searching for optimal policies under uncertainty.

References

Alcamo, J. (ed.) (1994), *Image 2.0, Integrated Modeling of Global Climate Change*, Dordrecht: Kluwer Academic Publishers.

Alcamo, J., R. Shaw and L. Hordijk (1990), *The RAINS Model of Acidification: Science and Strategies in Europe*, Dordrecht: Kluwer Academic Publishers.

Arrow, K., B. Bolin, R. Costanza, P. Dasgupta, C. Folke, C.S. Hotelling, B.-O. Jansson, S. Levin, K.-G. Mäler, Ch. Perrings and D. Pimentel (1995), 'Economic growth, carrying capacity and the environment', *Science*, **268**, 520–21.

Boo, A.J. de, P.R. Bosch, C.N. Gorter and S.J. Keuning (1993), 'An environmental module and the complete system of national accounts', in A. Franz and C. Stahmer (eds), *Approaches to Environmental Accounting*, Heidelberg: Physica Verlag.

Burniaux, J.M., G. Nicoletti and J. Oliveira Martins (1992), 'Green: A global model for quantifying the costs of policies to curb CO_2 emissions', *Economic Studies*, Special Issue: 'The economic costs of reducing CO_2 emissions', no. 19, pp.49–92.

Capros, P. and E. Kokkolakis (1996), *Energy Efficiency and Conversion Decentralisation: Evidence from the Primes Model*, Athens: National Technical University of Athens.

Chiang, A. (1992), *Elements of Dynamic Optimisation*, New York: McGraw-Hill.

CPB (Central Planning Bureau) (1992a), *FKSEC, A Macro-econometric Model for the Netherlands*, Leiden: Stenfert Kroese.

CPB (Central Planning Bureau) (1992b), *Scanning the Future*, The Hague: Sdu Publishers.

Daly, H.E. (1991), 'Elements of environmental macroeconomics', in R. Costanza (ed.), *Ecological Economics, The Science and Management of Sustainability*, New York: Columbia University Press.

de Groot, R. (1995), *Functions of Nature*, Groningen: Wolters Noordhoff.

Georgescu-Roegen, N. (1971), *The Entropy Law and the Economic Process*, Cambridge, MA: Harvard University Press.

Hordijk, L. (1995), 'Integrated assessment models as a basis for air pollution negotiations', *Water, Air and Soil Pollution*, **85**, 249–60.

IvM (Institute for Environmental Studies) (1996), *DEOS*, Vrije Universiteit, Amsterdam.

Kolstad, C.D. (1994), 'The timing of CO_2 control in the face of uncertainty and learning', in E.C. van Ierland (ed.), *International Environmental Economics*, Amsterdam: Elsevier Science Publishers.

Kolstad, C.D. (1996), 'Uncertainty, learning, stock externalities and capital irreversibilities', in E.C. van Ierland and K. Gorka (eds), *Economics of Atmospheric Pollution*, Berlin: Springer Verlag.

Leontief, W. (1966), *Input–output Economics*, New York: Oxford University Press.

Leontief, W. (1970), 'Environmental repercussions and the economic structure: an input approach', *Review of Economics and Statistics*, **52** (3), 262–71.

Mäler, K.-G. (1989), 'The acid rain game', in H. Folmer and E.C. van Ierland, *Valuation Methods and Policymaking in Environmental Economics*, Amsterdam: Elsevier Science Publishers.

Mäler, K.-G. (1994), 'Acid rain in Europe: A dynamic perspective on the use of economic incentives', in E.C. van Ierland (ed), *International Environmental Economics*, Amsterdam: Elsevier Science Publishers.

Manne, A.S. (1992), 'Markal Macro: a linked model for energy-economic analysis', Stanford University, Stanford, CA.

Manne, A.S. and R.G. Richels (1992), *Buying Greenhouse Insurance, The Economic Costs of Carbon Dioxide Emissions Limits*, Cambridge, MA: MIT Press.

Manne, A.S. and R.G. Richels (1997), 'On stabilising CO_2 concentrations–Cost-effective emission reduction strategies', Stanford University, Stanford, CA.

Manne, A.S. and T. Rutherford (1994), 'International trade, capital flows and sectoral analysis: formulation and solution of intertemporal equilibrium models', in W.W. Cooper and A.B. Whinston (eds), *New Directions in Computational Economics*, Dordrecht: Kluwer Academic Publishers.

Manne, A.S., R. Mendelsohn, R. Richels (1995), 'MERGE, A model for evaluating regional and global effects of GHG reduction policies', *Energy Policy*, **23** (1), 17–34.

Meadows, D.H., D.L. Meadows and J. Randers (1992), *Beyond the Limits, Global Collapse or a Sustainable Future*, London: Earthscan.

Meadows, D.H., D.L. Meadows, J. Randers and W. Behrens (1972), *Limits to Growth*, New York: Universe Books.

Mensink, P. and J. Hoekstra (1997), 'Notes on simulations with the linked Dialogue–Merge model', KEMA Environmental Services, report no. 83434.SP.1496P11, Arnhem.

Mot, E., P.J. van den Noord, D. van der Stelte-Scheele, M. Koning and M. Couwenberg (1989), 'Hermes–The Netherlands', Foundation for Economic Research (SEO), University of Amsterdam.

Nakicenovic, N., W.D. Nordhaus, R. Richels and F.L. Toth (eds) (1994), *Integrative Assessment of Mitigation, Impacts and Adaptation to Climate Change*, Laxenburg, Austria: IIASA.

Nakicenovic, N., W.D. Nordhaus, R. Richels and F.L. Toth (eds) (1996), *Climate Change: Integrating Science, Economics and Policy*, Laxenburg, Austria: IIASA.

Nestor, D. and C. Pasurka (1995), 'Environment–economic accounting and indicators of the economic importance of environmental protection activities', *Review of Income and Wealth*, **41** (3), 265–87.

Nordhaus, W.D. (1991), 'To slow or not to slow?: the economics of the greenhouse effect', *Economic Journal*, **101**, 920–37.

Nordhaus, W.D. (1993), 'Rolling the "DICE": An optimal transition path for controlling greenhouse gases', *Resource and Energy Economics*, **15**, 27–50.

Nordhaus, W.D. and Z. Yang (1995), *RICE: A Regional Dynamic General Equilibrium Model of Optimal Climate-Change Policy*, Yale University.

Nordhaus, W.D. and Z. Yang (1996), 'A regional dynamic general equilibrium model of alternative climate-change strategies', *American Economic Review*, **86** (4), 741–65.

Nordhaus, W.D. and Z. Yang (1997), 'Slice: Stochastic Learning Integrated Climate Economy Model, research paper, Yale University.

Opschoor, J.B. (1995), 'Ecospace and the fall and rise of throughput intensity', *Ecological Economics*, **15**, 137–40.

Peck, S. and Th. Teisberg (1993), 'Global warming uncertainties and the value of information: an analysis using CETA', *Resource and Energy Economics*.

Phelps, E.S. (1961), 'The golden rule of accumulation: A fable for growth men', *American Economic Review*, September, 638–43.

Quesnay, F. (1758), 'Analyse des formules arithmethique du tableau économique de la distribution des dépenses annuelles d'une nation agricole', Versailles.

Rotmans, J. (1990), *IMAGE: an Integrated Assessment Model to Assess the Greenhouse Effect*, Dordrecht: Kluwer.

Rotmans, J., M.B.A. van Asselt, A.J. de Bruijn, M.G.J. den Elzen, J. de Greef, H. Hilderink, A.Y. Hoekstra, M.A. Janssen, H.W. Köster, W.J.M. Martens, L.W. Niessen and H.J.M. de Vries (1994), *Global Change and Sustainable Development: A Modelling Perspective for the Next Decade*, Bilthoven: RIVM.

Rutherford, T. (1997), 'Sequential joint maximization', in J. Weyant (ed.), *Energy in Environmental Policy Modeling*, Dordrecht: Kluwer.

Schafer, D. and C. Stahmer (1989), 'Input–output model for the analysis of environmental protection activities', *Economic Systems Research*, 1 (2), 203–28.

Smulders, S. (1994), 'Growth, market structure and the environment, essays on the theory of endogenous economic growth', Ph.D. thesis, Catholic University Brabant, Tilburg.

Solow, R.M. (1956), 'A contribution to the theory of economic growth', *Quarterly Journal of Economics*, 65–94.

Solow, R.M. (1970), *Growth Theory*, Oxford: Oxford University Press.

Tol, R.S.J. (1994), 'The climate fund–optimal greenhouse gas emission abatement', W94/08, Institute for Environmental Studies, Vrije Universiteit, Amsterdam.

Tol, R.S.J. (1996), 'A decision-analytic treatise of the enhanced greenhouse effect', Ph.D. thesis, Vrije Universiteit, Amsterdam.

van den Bergh, J.C.J.M. (1991), *Dynamic Models for Sustainable Development*, Amsterdam: Thesis Publishers.

van Ierland, E.C. (1993), *Macroeconomic Analysis of Environmental Policy*, Amsterdam: Elsevier Science Publishers.

van Ierland, E.C. (ed.) (1994), *International Environmental Economics: Theories, Models and Applications to Climate Change, International Trade and Acidification*, Amsterdam: Elsevier Science Publishers.

van Ierland, E.C. and K. Gorka (eds) (1996), *Economics of Atmospheric Pollution*, Berlin: Springer.

van der Sluijs, J. (1997), 'Anchoring amid uncertainty: On the management of uncertainties in risk assessment of anthropogenic climate change', Ph.D. thesis, University of Utrecht, Utrecht.

WRR, (Dutch Scientific Council for Government Policy) (1987), *Scope for Growth*, The Hague: Sdu.

42 Endogenous growth theory and the environment

Sjak Smulders[1]

1. Introduction

Economic growth and changes in the environment seem to be inseparable over most of the economic history of the world. The invention of agriculture and subsequent agricultural improvements not only dramatically altered land use but also freed part of the labour force to engage in a growing volume of non-agricultural production activities. Especially since the industrial revolution, an endless stream of product and process innovations stimulated the exploitation of more and more natural resources, thereby satisfying ever expanding new wants but also creating unknown pollution problems. Shortages of vital fuels or other natural resources during various periods in history made society aware of the fact that the economy depends on energy and ecological services provided by the natural environment. However, environmental and natural resource constraints did not turn the historical growth process into stagnation. Instead, accumulation of human knowledge (how to plough, forge, or build a combustion engine; how to grow crops, exploit other fuels) allowed the economy to expand within the fixed physical system of the earth. While no energy or material can be created by man, he continually creates new knowledge to derive more value from a given amount of physical resources. The new knowledge is embodied in new skills (human capital), tools, structures and public infrastructure (physical capital), as well as in institutions and norms (social capital). Therefore, from the most fundamental perspective, the study of the interaction between economic growth and environmental problems requires thinking about the creation of human knowledge.

Until recently, the interaction between knowledge creation and natural resources use only rarely played a fundamental role in models of aggregate economic growth. Malthus's dismal predictions for economic development were based on one-sided attention to natural resource constraints. At the other extreme, the standard neoclassical growth model focuses on capital and labour, ignoring natural resources and confining knowledge creation to exogenous technological progress. In the 1970s, exhaustible natural resources and pollution have been incorporated into neoclassical growth models. However, long-run economic growth was still either absent in these models, or driven by exogenous factors (for example, technological progress and population growth).

Modern growth theory (called new or endogenous) explicitly deals with endogenous technological progress, public investment, human capital and other forms of knowledge creation as the driving force behind economic growth. This chapter surveys how environmental issues can be examined in models of endogenous growth. It will be shown how these models shed light on the conditions under which economic growth and environmental preservation are compatible in the long run, on the relation between optimal growth and sustainability, and on the consequences of environmental policy for growth. To this end, the key elements of environmental endogenous growth models and their results are discussed.[2] The chapter ends with a critical evaluation and suggestions for further research.

2. Models
From the early 1990s onwards, the 'endogenous growth literature'[3] has led to general equilibrium growth models that incorporate environmental variables and allow the aggregate economic growth rate to be determined endogenously.[4] The models try to formalize and link (or reconcile) two main ideas that are already present in earlier literature. First, knowledge creation is the ultimate source of growth in a physically bounded environment, as stressed by, for example, Simon (1981). Second, growth can be sustained only if the economy maintains constant rates of energy and material throughput, as in Daly's (1973) 'steady state economy'.

2.1 Building blocks of the models
Economic growth and physical conditions of the environment interact. Economic activity may be the cause of environmental problems, but so also might a deterioration in physical conditions hamper economic processes. In order to model these interactions, ecology and economy have to be treated as conceptually different spheres and have to be appropriately linked.

Models of economic growth and the environment therefore connect the following building blocks: the *technology* block and the *preference* block model form together the economic sphere in which production and allocation are determined; the *ecology* block models how environmental variables evolve. In particular, the elementary model structure can be represented by a production function, a utility function and a natural resource growth function.

The environment–economy links (the connections among the model blocks) are manifold. First, the environment is a *sink* for wastes and, second, a source of resources for the economy. Third, the environment may enter the utility function, because environmental quality has an *amenity* value. Fourth, the environment exhibits a *productive* value, so that it enters the production function. Finally, part of economic activity may be directly devoted to cleaning up spoilt parts of the environment, that is, *abatement* and recycling may take place.

2.2   An illustrative archetypical model

The simplest model one could think of consists of three equations, one for each of the building blocks discussed above.

$$\dot{N} = E(N) - R \qquad\qquad \text{natural resource growth} \quad (42.1)$$

$$\dot{H} = Y(N, R, H) - C \qquad\qquad \text{knowledge production} \quad (42.2)$$

$$W = \int_{0}^{\infty} U(C, N) \exp(-\theta t)\, dt \qquad \text{(intertemporal) utility} \quad (42.3)$$

where N is an indicator of environmental quality, R is the use of services from the environment in production, Y is aggregate economic activity (production), H is the stock of (man-made) knowledge, and C is consumption of man-made goods, $U(\cdot)$ is instantaneous utility, and θ is time preference; all variables depend on the time index t. The *a priori* restrictions on (42.1)–(42.3) are as follows (subscripts attached to function symbols denote partial derivatives). All inputs in the production and utility function have a positive contribution: $Y_N \geq 0$, $Y_R > 0$, $Y_H > 0$, $U_C > 0$, $U_N \geq 0$. All inputs are essential: $Y(0, R, H) = Y(N, 0, H) = Y(N, R, 0) = 0$; $U(0, N) = U(C, 0) = -\infty$, $E(0) \leq 0$, $E_{NN} < 0$. The non-negativity constraints are: $N \geq 0$, $R \geq 0$, $C \geq 0, H \geq 0, Y \geq 0$; the initial values $N(0)$ and $H(0)$ are given.

Ecological processes are modelled as growth and depletion of a renewable resource.[5] Nature has a capacity to renew itself, as captured by the term $E(N)$. Both extraction of natural resources (where the environment acts as a source) and the disposal of wastes (where it acts as a sink) are represented by R, since both activities diminish the stock of available natural resources. As long as the economy uses less environmental services than are provided ecological processes, that is, $R < E(N)$, environmental quality improves over time. Nature is able to absorb a constant amount of pollution without deteriorating, $R = E(N)$, so that $E(N)$ represents the absorption capacity of the environment. An ecological equilibrium (defined by $\dot{N} = 0$) can only be maintained if pollution R is constant and does not exceed the maximum absorption capacity.

The technology block is given by equation (42.2). Production (Y) uses natural resources and man-made knowledge to produce valuable consumption goods (C) and new knowledge ($\dot{H}$). At this stage, we do not distinguish between different kinds of man-made capital, for example, physical capital and human capital are included in H. N enters the production function because a higher environmental quality renders the economy more productive. This might happen because the health of workers is improved, which boosts labour productivity, or because a richer biodiversity provides a larger pool of knowledge (genetic information), which boosts productivity in research and development (for example, pharmaceutical research or the search for new resistant crop varieties).

The preference block is modelled by the utility function in (42.3) with produced consumption (C) and environmental amenities (measured by N) as the arguments. The latter also allows us to take into account the existence value of the environment.

So far, the model resembles very much the standard renewable resource model (Clark, 1990). However, two features are different. First, man-made capital H is called knowledge, rather than merely capital, to indicate that it is a much broader concept. More detailed models consider issues like learning and R&D. Second, the production function no longer features the Inada conditions. In particular, what distinguishes endogenous growth models from Solow-type neoclassical growth models is that the long-run marginal productivity of capital is bounded from below. Hence, in the long run, decreasing returns with respect to man-made capital (broadly defined) are absent. Investment in man-made capital not only encompasses physical capital investment (as in older growth models), but also knowledge creation, for which diminishing returns are less likely. If social interaction, economic activity, investment and problem solving yield new ideas and if knowledge spillovers inspire others, diminishing returns may be absent in the creation of knowledge. In the model above we lumped together all man-made inputs in the variable H.

If we assume that there are constant returns in production with respect to the man-made knowledge input, holding fixed other inputs (which implies that the Inada conditions are violated), and that a fraction of production S_H is devoted to investment (knowledge creation), we may write:

$$Y(N, R, H) = y(N, R) \cdot H, \qquad \text{constant returns to scale in } H \quad (42.4)$$

$$C = (1 - S_H) \cdot Y(\cdot) \qquad\qquad \text{consumption} \quad (42.5)$$

As explained above, ecological processes allow for an equilibrium level of environmental quality in the long run and a sustainable (constant) pollution level that exactly matches the absorption capacity of the environment $R = E(N)$. Taking this into account and substituting (42.4) and (42.5) into (42.2), we can derive the following expression for the feasible long-run growth rate of knowledge:

$$\dot{H}/H = S_H \cdot y\big(N, E(N)\big) \qquad \text{long-run feasible growth rate} \quad (42.6)$$

Equation (42.6) reveals the feasibility of a balanced growth path with non-deteriorating environment. If economic activity allows ecosystems to reach and sustain a stable environmental quality N by restricting pollution to nature's absorption capacity, $E(N)$, and if investment ratio S_H is constant, the sufficient conditions are satisfied for which the growth rate of knowledge $\dot{H}/H$ is constant and positive. Moreover, the growth rates of consumption (C) and economic activity (Y), both measured in economic terms, are equal to $\dot{H}/H$ and hence constant and positive. In sum, knowledge creation fuels economic growth without deteriorating the environment.

Equation (42.6) is derived without reference to the utility block of the model. Preferences – in interaction with institutional features like externalities and the type of policy intervention – ultimately determine how much is invested in knowledge and in environmental preservation, that is, they determine S_H and N. Examination of the role of institutions and preferences requires more detailed models, to which I now turn.

2.3 Structural model features: behaviour and policy

The model in equations (42.1)–(42.6) can be considered as an archetypical form of many of the environmental endogenous growth models, and only served as an illustration of the basic mechanisms at work. The models found in the literature are typically much more detailed.

First of all, the typical model explicitly considers how market behaviour and government intervention affect investment and pollution. Firms maximize profits and consumers maximize utility, but both take as given the level of environmental quality and the amount of generally applicable knowledge. Firms choose their pollution levels and invest in physical capital, in knowledge capital (via R&D activities), and in abatement activities. The government implements environmental policy (through pollution charges, emission standards, public abatement) and may be involved in technology programmes (through R&D subsidies, or infrastructural projects).

Second, the ecological side of the model is modelled in a variety of ways. Pollution may be modelled as an inevitable side-product of economic activity, rather than of a particular input as in the model above. In this approach, the flow of pollution is a by-product of economic activity, that is, pollution is directly related to total production (Y) (for example, Huang and Cai, 1994; Verdier, 1993). Since the flow of pollution involves extractive use of the environment (that is, the environment provides rival services in absorbing or assimilating pollution, denoted by R), this approach is equivalent to the assumption of a fixed natural-resource input coefficient. Substitution possibilities are introduced in this approach by assuming that pollution can be abated by giving up some part of production (for example, Gradus and Smulders, 1993; Ligthart and van der Ploeg, 1994; den Butter and Hofkes, 1995; Hofkes, 1996; Smulders and Gradus, 1996).

Many models include the stock of pollution as an argument in the utility and ecology function, rather than environmental quality. However, an obvious transformation from pollution stocks to environmental quality is possible because the stock of wastes is equivalent to the complement (or the reciprocal or a similar transformation) of the stock of valuable environmental resources. Many other models only incorporate a flow variable to represent the environment. Thus ignoring the accumulation of wastes and the irreversibility of environmental damage, these models are not able to examine the possible conflict between short-run and long-run consequences of economic growth on the environment, but they prove to be a useful simplification to examine, for instance, the effects of different environmental tax issues (for example, Ligthart and van der Ploeg, 1994; Bovenberg and de Mooij, 1997).

3. Results

The growth models outlined above are developed with the purpose of shedding light on three main questions. Are economic growth and environmental preservation compatible? Is sustainable growth optimal? What is the effect of environmental policy on economic growth? This section reviews what kind of answers and arguments modern growth theory has provided and discusses the empirical relationship between economic growth and environment.

3.1 Are economic growth and environmental preservation compatible?

As the discussion of equation (42.6) revealed, unlimited growth is possible through the steady accumulation of new knowledge without relying on increasing extraction of natural resources. In the language conventional in growth theory, compatibility of economic growth and environmental preservation requires the existence of a balanced growth path along which economic variables grow at a constant positive rate, but environmental variables remain constant. This growth path can be called sustainable, either in the narrow ecological sense (ecosystem does not deteriorate over time) or in the economic sense (utility is non-declining over time; see Pezzey, 1992).

A sustainable balanced endogenous growth path is feasible if the economy exhibits constant returns to scale with respect to the factors of production that can be reproduced by the economy itself (cf. Rebelo, 1991). Knowledge is man-made and reproducible but, by definition, environmental factors are not. Hence, in the model of subsection 2.2, sustainability requires that the production function $Y(\cdot)$ exhibits constant returns with respect to the man-made factor H (and this was indeed imposed above). In the more detailed structural models, knowledge may be available in the form of blueprints or may be embodied in various kinds of capital: physical, human, infrastructural capital, and also abatement capital. The returns to investment will not fall if the economy's aggregate production function exhibits constant returns to scale with respect to all these factors taken together, and if the economy is investing in all of these factors but is using non-increasing amounts of material, energy or other services from the environment. If investment took place only in one kind of capital, for example physical capital, the economy would run into diminishing returns. This would cause growth to slow down. However, if this investment is matched by investment in new technologies and infrastructure, the diminishing returns may be offset. This offsetting knowledge growth may be brought about as a side-effect of production or investment through learning-by-doing (for example, Michel, 1993) or it may result from deliberate investment in R&D (for example, Hung et al. 1993; Bovenberg and Smulders, 1995, 1996; Verdier, 1993) and infrastructure (for example, van Marrewijk et al., 1993).

3.2 Is sustainable growth optimal?

Although sustainable growth may be feasible, it is not necessarily a market outcome, nor always socially optimal. Sustainability requires both the right investment strategy and appropriate treatment of the environment: pollution should not exceed absorption capacity and new technologies have to be developed to offset diminishing returns. The market may fail in both respects. Private incentives to develop cleaner technologies may be too small, in particular when such technologies have a public good character. Producers do not take into account the ecological effects and other externalities of pollution and natural resource use.

Even in a first-best economy in which all such effects are internalized, society might prefer a non-sustainable growth path or a sustainable path without growth (Michel and Rotillon, 1995). For example, Bovenberg and Smulders (1995) show that a society that regards produced (material) consumption goods and environmental amenities as poor substitutes will optimally choose to invest more and more in the environment when the economy grows larger, thereby reducing economic growth in the end. The reason is that demand for environmental quality improvements increases if production grows, thus diverting investment from production to abatement. In general, while feasibility of sustainable growth depends on properties of the production function, its optimality depends on the utility function. Optimality of non-sustainable growth is studied by Baranzini and Bourguignon (1995).

3.3   How does environmental policy affect economic growth?

The most frequently addressed issue is the impact on growth of a tightening of environmental standards. The theoretical models indicate that growth may fall or increase, depending on the relative strength of the following opposing forces. On the one hand, improving environmental quality requires investment (abatement expenditures or reductions in polluting output) so that less resources are available for growth-generating investment activities (*crowding-out effect*). On the other hand, improvement of the environment may have positive *productivity effects*, which increases the incentive to invest. Higher environmental quality improves the productivity of ecosystems so that in the long run the economy might benefit from more environmental services (see Smulders, 1995a), but also productivity of human capital and other man-made assets might increase through health effects or less physical depreciation. If crowding-out effects are small relative to productivity effects, long-run growth rates may be permanently higher. In the short run, however, the costs are likely to outweigh the benefits as it takes time for ecosystems to improve (Bovenberg and Smulders, 1996).

If the economy is distorted not only because of environmental externalities but also by distortions in factor markets, environmental policy may affect economic growth by a *tax-interaction effect*. Consider the situation in which public expenditure is financed by distortionary taxes. When pollution taxes are raised, taxes on capital can be lowered which may stimulate rates of return on investment and economic growth (Bovenberg and De Mooij, 1997). Alternatively, labour income tax rates can be lowered, which may stimulate labour supply and economic growth (Nielsen et al., 1995, Hettich, 1998).

3.4   Empirical results

None of the empirical studies that examine the relationship between growth and environmental policy are explicitly based on the theoretical models discussed so far. Earlier research did focus on the crowding-out issue, though. Christainsen and Tietenberg (1985) conclude in their review article that environmental regulation has had negative but small effects on productivity growth. Jorgenson and Wilcoxen (1990) used a dynamic sectoral econometric model to simulate the US economy with and without environmental regulation. They found a significant cost in terms of production and consumption levels associated with regulation but did not touch on the link between productivity changes and improvements in environmental quality.

Other empirical studies find evidence for a 'Kuznets curve' characterizing the relation between pollution and economic development: pollution first increases if economic development proceeds, but, after some threshold, decreases (Grossman and Krueger, 1995; Shafik, 1994; Selden and Song, 1994; Ansuategi et al., 1998). Although this research does not study growth rates of income, it suggests that higher income *levels* are compatible with lower pollution, probably because richer countries are willing to spend more on investments in a clean environment.

4.   Future research themes and conclusions

Up to now, the environmental branch of endogenous growth theory has focused on conceptual issues and general (abstract) questions. To derive further theoretical results, the link between economic growth theory and ecological modelling principles have to be strengthened and made more rigorous. The basic laws of thermodynamics can provide a solid foundation for this avenue. Starting with Georgescu-Roegen (1971), many have attempted to introduce these laws in economics (for an overview and contribution, see Ruth, 1993).[6] The approach seems particularly useful because the entropy law can be applied both to ecological change and to the concept of information or knowledge, the two key factors in environmental endogenous growth models.

A second direction for future research involves the operationalization of the growth models for more practical purposes. This requires the introduction of exhaustible resources as essential inputs for the economy and population growth, which are both ignored in endogenous environmental growth models so far. It also requires a more elaborate consideration of the private incentives for abatement (most existing models rely on publicly financed pollution control or technology development). In order to shift attention from the normative character of most of the existing models to a more positive approach, the political economy of environmental regulation has to be considered. The introduction of overlapping generations may improve our insight into the concept of sustainability and intergenerational equity in a growth context (cf. John and Pecchenino, 1994, 1997; and Jones and Manuelli, 1995).

At least as important is empirical testing and calibration. The theoretical analysis yields conditions for feasibility and optimality of sustainable growth. Are they empirically relevant? The theory also raises new empirical questions, in particular how large crowding-out effects are relative to productivity effects of environmental policy. Existing empirical research tends to overlook or underestimate the benefits in terms of improved productivity of investment.

New growth theory explains why growth and environmental preservation might be compatible in the long run by stressing the interaction between the accumulation of knowledge and the physical limits that energy and material impose on the economy. New growth models are not necessarily 'pro-growth'. They provide the appropriate framework to study under what conditions sustainable long-run growth is feasible and how knowledge may be developed to establish sustainable policies and to introduce technologies that rely on renewable resources.

Notes

1. This chapter was written when the author was visiting scholar at Stanford University. He would like to thank Edward Barbier, Jeroen van den Bergh, Dafne Reymen and an anonymous referee for useful comments.
2. Space limitations prevent me from classifying and comparing all the existing models. Instead, I present the common elements and some variations (in subsections 3.2 and 3.3, respectively). For a more detailed survey, see Smulders (1995b).
3. This literature was initiated by Romer (1986) and Lucas (1988); see Grossman and Helpman (1991) and Barro and Sala-í-Martin (1995) for comprehensive overviews.
4. For a list of models that fall in this category, see the asterisked references at the end of this chapter.
5. Up to now, the link between endogenous growth theory and *non*-renewable resource models is largely ignored (exceptions are Schou, 1999; Scholz and Ziemes, 1996; Aghion and Howitt, 1998, Chapter 5). Note, however, that in the neoclassical models developed in the 1970s (for example, Stiglitz, 1974) the growth rate does not solely depend on exogenous technological progress, but also, for example, on intertemporal preferences. Hence these models are endogenous growth models *avant la lettre*. The combination of endogenous technological change and non-renewable resources is an important area for future research.
6. Elsewhere (Smulders, 1995b) I have pointed out how some environmental endogenous growth models can be reconciled with this approach.

References

Publications marked with an asterisk deal with environmental endogenous growth models.

*Aghion, Ph. and P. Howitt (1998), *Endogenous Growth Theory*, Cambridge: MIT Press.
Ansuategi, A., E. Barbier and C. Perrings (1998), 'The environmental Kuznets Curve', in J.C.J.M. van den Bergh and M. Hofkes (eds), *Theory and Implementation of Economic Models for Sustainable Development*, Dordrecht: Kluwer.
*Baranzini, A. and F. Bourguignon (1995), 'Is sustainable growth optimal?', *International Tax and Public Finance*, **2**, 341–56.
Barro, R.J. and X. Sala-í-Martin (1995), *Economic Growth*, New York: McGraw-Hill.
*Bovenberg, A.L. and R.A. de Mooij (1997), 'Environmental tax reform and endogenous growth', *Journal of Public Economics*, **63**, 207–37.
*Bovenberg, A.L. and S. Smulders (1995), 'Environmental quality and pollution-augmenting technological change in a two-sector endogenous growth model', *Journal of Public Economics*, **57**, 369–91.
*Bovenberg, A.L. and S. Smulders (1996), 'Transitional impacts of environmental policy in an endogenous growth model', *International Economic Review*, **37**, 861–93.

620   Environmental macroeconomics

*Butter, F.A.G. den and M.W. Hofkes (1995), 'Sustainable Development with extractive and non-extractive use of the environment in production', *Environmental and Resource Economics*, **6**, 341–58.

Christainsen, G. and T. Tietenberg (1985), 'Distributional and macroeconomic aspects of environmental policy', in A. Kneese and J. Sweeney (eds), *Handbook of Natural Resource and Energy Economics*, vol. I, Amsterdam: Elsevier, pp. 345–93.

Clark, C.W. (1990), *Mathematical Bioeconomics, The Optimal Management of Renewable Resources*, 2nd edn, New York: Wiley.

Daly, H.E. (ed.) (1973), *Economics, Ecology, Ethics: Towards a Steady-State Economy*, San Francisco: Freeman.

Georgescu-Roegen, N. (1971), *The Entropy Law and the Economic Process*. Cambridge, MA: Harvard University Press.

*Gradus, R. and S. Smulders (1993), 'The trade-off between environmental care and long-term growth; pollution in three proto-type growth models'. *Journal of Economics*, **58**, 25–51.

Grossman, G.M. and E. Helpman (1991), *Innovation and Growth in the Global Economy*, Cambridge, MA: MIT Press.

Grossman, G. and A. Krueger (1995), 'Economic growth and the environment', *Quarterly Journal of Economics*, **110**, 353–77.

Hettich, F. (1998), 'Growth effects of a revenue-neutral environmental tax reform', *Journal of Economics*, **67**, 287–316.

*Hofkes, M.W. (1996), 'Modelling sustainable development: an economy–ecology integrated model', *Economic Modelling*, **13**, 333–53.

*Huang C. and D. Cai (1994), 'Constant returns endogenous growth with pollution control', *Environmental and Resource Economics*, **4**, 383–400.

*Hung, V.T.Y., P. Chang and K. Blackburn (1993), 'Endogenous growth, environment and R. and D..', in C. Carraro (ed.), *Trade, Innovation and Environment*, Dordrecht: Kluwer Academic Publishers, pp. 241–58.

*John, A. and R. Pecchenino (1994), 'An overlapping generations model of growth and the environment', *Economic Journal*, **104**, 1393–410.

John, A. and R. Pecchenino (1997), 'International and intergenerational environmental externalities', *Scandinavian Journal of Economics*, **99**, 37–87.

*Jones, L.E. and R.E. Manuelli (1995), 'A positive model of growth and pollution controls', *NBER working paper* 5205.

Jorgenson, D.W. and P.J. Wilcoxen (1990), 'Environmental regulation and US economic growth', *Rand Journal of Economics*, **21**, 314–40.

*Ligthart, J.E. and F. van der Ploeg (1994), 'Pollution, the cost of public funds and endogenous growth', *Economics Letters*, **46**, 351–61.

Lucas, R.E. (1988), 'On the mechanics of economic development', *Journal of Monetary Economics*, **22**, 3–42.

*Marrewijk, C. van, F. van der Ploeg and J. Verbeek (1993), 'Pollution, abatement and endogenous growth: is growth bad for the environment?', Working Paper, World Bank, Washington.

*Michel, Ph. (1993), 'Pollution and growth towards the ecological paradise', Fondazione Eni Enrico Mattei, working paper 80.93.

*Michel, Ph. and G. Rotillon (1995), 'Disutility of pollution and endogenous growth', *Environmental and Resource Economics*, **6**, 279–300.

*Nielsen, S.B., P.B. Sørensen and L.H. Pedersen (1995), 'Environmental policy, pollution, unemployment, and endogenous growth', *International Tax and Public Finance*, **2**, 185–205.

Pezzey, J. (1992), 'Sustainability: an interdisciplinary guide', *Environmental Values*, **1**, 321–62.

Rebelo, S. (1991), 'Long-run policy analysis and long-run growth', *Journal of Political Economy*, **99**, 500–521.

Romer, P.M. (1986), 'Increasing returns and long-run growth', *Journal of Political Economy*, **94**, 1002–37.

Ruth, M. (1993), *Integrating Economics, Ecology and Thermodynamics*, Dordrecht: Kluwer Academic Publishers.

*Scholz, C. and G. Ziemes (1996), 'Exhaustible resources, monopolistic competition, and endogenous growth', forthcoming in *Environmental and Resource Economics*.

*Schou, P. (1999), *Endogenous Growth, Nonrenewable Resources and Environmental Problems*, Ph.D. thesis, University of Copenhagen.

Selden, T. and D. Song (1994), 'Environmental quality and development: is there a Kuznets curve for air pollution emissions?', *Journal of Environmental Economics and Management*, **27**, 147–62.

Shafik, N. (1994), 'Economic development and environmental quality: an econometric analysis', *Oxford Economic Papers*, **46**, 757–73.

Simon, J.L. (1981), *The Ultimate Resource*, Princeton, NJ: Princeton University Press.

*Smulders, S. (1995a), 'Environmental policy and sustainable economic growth; an endogenous growth perspective' *De Economist*, **143**, (2) 163–95.

*Smulders, S. (1995b), 'Entropy, environment and endogenous economic growth', *International Tax and Public Finance*, **2**, 319–40.

*Smulders, S. and R. Gradus (1996), 'Pollution abatement and long-term growth', *European Journal of Political Economy*, **12**, 505–32.

Stiglitz, J.E. (1974), 'Growth with exhaustible natural resources: efficient and optimal growth paths', *Review of Economic Studies*, Symposium, 123–37.

*Verdier, T. (1993), 'Environmental pollution and endogenous growth: a comparison between emission taxes and technological standards', Fondazione Eni Enrico Mattei, working paper 57.93.

43 A pro-growth perspective
Wilfred Beckerman

1. Economic growth versus the environment: sources of concern

Economists see environmental problems as arising primarily because the environment is a scarce resource which tends to be used up more than is socially optimal on account of various types of market failure. So whilst they will differ on details, almost all economists would be in favour of policies designed to minimize these market failures and to give due weight to environmental protection in policy formation.

But many non-economists (and a few economists) believe that there are additional reasons for concern about the environment, and that the main environmental problems facing us today call for far more drastic action – and of a different character – than most economists would advocate. This is often based on the view that the environment has more than purely instrumental value, and that it also has some intrinsic value of one kind or another, such as a spiritual or ethical value, or some 'higher' value that is not commensurate with the monetary values entering into standard economic analysis (Anderson, 1993). A closely related view is that continued economic growth is undesirable, on the grounds that it does not increase welfare (defined one way or the other). Indeed, it is often argued that growth reduces welfare and that the 'costs' of economic growth include a deterioration in the 'quality of life'.

As well as scepticism about the desirability of continued economic growth, doubts have frequently been expressed concerning its feasibility. This is much more a technical economic issue. For it is widely believed that economic growth of the kind that we have been experiencing for decades is now 'unsustainable' on the grounds that it will sooner or later come up against the limits set by 'finite' supplies of resources or the capacity of the ecosystem to absorb harmful pollutants (such as carbon dioxide) or the loss of biodiversity.

2. Economic growth and welfare: the conceptual relationship

As regards the relationship between GNP and 'welfare', all economists know that GNP is simply one component of welfare, namely that part of total welfare which, in the classic phrase of one of the greatest economists of the twentieth century, A.D. Pigou, 'can be brought directly or indirectly into relation with the measuring rod of money.'[1] Furthermore, in the same book, Pigou actually used the now fashionable term 'quality of life' in the course of his enumeration of the various ways in which a rise in *economic* welfare (which is more or less what a rise in GNP is supposed to measure) may fail to lead to a corresponding rise in *total* welfare.

Similarly, economists are not in favour of maximizing the rate of economic growth. The usual objective is to maximize the present value of the future stream of consumption over whatever time period is believed to be relevant. Absurd assumptions would have to be made to equate this with maximum economic growth. Nevertheless, reasons will be given below for assuming that, in most countries and at most periods of time, economic growth does both add to welfare at the time and help maximize the sum of consumption over whatever time period is believed to be relevant.

3. Economic growth and welfare: the facts
Of course, there can never be any scientific demonstration of the relationship between income levels and welfare. For the concept of 'welfare' is not one that can be scientifically established. Different people can hold different views as to what constitutes welfare. The best one can do is to take a balanced view of the changes that have taken place in people's living standards as a result of economic growth and let the reader make up his own mind.

There is no doubt that, over the last two or three decades, some ingredients of the quality of life have deteriorated, particularly in advanced societies. These include the rise in violence and other forms of crime such as those associated with the spread of drugs, and, during the last decade, increased job insecurity, as well as certain forms of environmental damage, notably air pollution in many cities, and the emergence of global environmental problems, such as climate change and the threat to biodiversity. And it is true that none of these developments is captured fully, if at all, in national income statistics. On the other hand there have been many improvements in the quality of life that are also excluded from national income estimates.

For example, one might want to include the increase over the course of this century in the amount of social capital available (libraries, hospitals, schools, and so on) and other benefits for the ordinary person in the more advanced countries that are not included in national accounts estimates, such as a great improvement in housing conditions, a reduction in domestic drudgery for the housewife, and increased freedom to travel and to discover new horizons and new lands.

And whilst there has been a decline in job security over the last few years, in a longer-term perspective there has been a substantial improvement in working conditions, as in many other aspects of life that are most important for the large majority of the population, such as hours of work, holidays with pay, environmental conditions inside places of work, social security benefits, legislation preventing unfair dismissal or sexual discrimination, the provision of redundancy pay and severance allowances, improved mandatory maternity arrangements, and so on.

Health is another major area of life that most people would put at the top of their welfare concerns, and it has steadily improved over the last few decades. True, AIDS is a new and serious threat to health, but, at the same time, other killer diseases have been more or less eradicated in the course of this century. To take just a few specific examples, deaths or serious illness associated with respiratory tuberculosis, polio, whooping cough, scarlet fever and diphtheria have been greatly reduced or eliminated under the combined impact of medical advances and improved sanitary conditions. And the great advances made in surgery have brought relief to millions of people.

At a more general level, the downward trend in infant mortality has continued in the past 30 years. For example, in low- and middle-income countries infant mortality has fallen by about one half between 1965 and 1988, and in high-income countries the rate fell, over the same period, from 26 per 1000 to only 9.[2] And because of improvements in health and in the treatment of disease at all ages, there has been a remarkable rise in life expectancy throughout the world. For example, in more developed regions average life expectancy at birth has risen from about 66 years to about 74 years over the last four decades, and in less developed regions it has risen even more dramatically from just over 40 years to just over 60 years over the same period (UN, 1995). In the last 15 years life expectancy has fallen in only two countries, Sierra Leone and Uganda (UNDP, 1991, p.27). Income may not be the only thing in life, but when a life is snuffed out there isn't even the income.

These improvements in life expectancy, particularly in developing countries, are not surprising given the close relationship between income levels and what are probably the most important environmental factors in such countries. These are lack of decent drinking water and sanitation, which are the major causes of disease and infant mortality in developing countries. And there is a close correlation between income levels and improvements in these two environmental items (Beckerman, 1995a, chs 2 and 3).

Nor is the reason for this difficult to see. As people get richer their priorities change and the environment moves up in the hierarchy of human needs. When their basic needs for food, water, clothing and shelter are satisfied they can begin to attach importance to other ingredients in total welfare, including, eventually, the environment. As public perceptions and concerns move in the environmental direction and societies become richer, so they become both more willing and able to allocate resources to this purpose. Of course, countries differ with respect to the speed with which rising incomes lead to increased protection of the environment. And some forms of domestic pollution tend to become worse even in very environmentally conscious countries. One of these is urban air conditions in big cities, where traffic congestion is rarely satisfactorily tackled. But this is not because of some unavoidable technical relationship between traffic congestion in cities and rising incomes. It is because governments believe, probably mistakenly, that measures to reduce urban traffic congestion by means of proper road and congestion pricing would, on balance, be politically unpopular.

But in many countries, even if rising incomes lead to a temporary worsening of the environment, this does not necessarily imply a decline in overall welfare. Other components of welfare usually still improve, such as those determining health and longevity. As a result, various statistical studies confirm that incomes per head are highly correlated with both important individual ingredients of the quality of life and with so-called 'composite' indices that combine many major ingredients of welfare together. For example, a recent Dasgupta and Weale (1992) analysis shows positive correlations between per capita national income and individual indicators, such as life expectancy at birth, the adult literacy rate, and even with indices of political and civil liberties (though the direction of causation here is open to question). A similar study by Dasgupta (1990), covering 50 developing countries with per capita GNP of only US$1000 per annum or less, examined the relationship between these income levels and life expectancy at birth, literacy, infant mortality and indices of political and civil liberty, in 1970 and 1980. The main finding was that, with the exception of literacy rates, all these components of welfare were positively and significantly correlated with growing per capita income levels.

More recently sophisticated attempts have been made, under the auspices of the United Nations Development Programme, to combine together these and other components of welfare, or of 'human development', into a 'composite' index, known as the 'Human Development Index'. This shows a strong positive correlation between income per head and an index that gives equal weight to incomes, life expectancy and literacy. As the *Human Development Report 1991* says, 'Human development requires economic growth – for without it, no sustained improvement in human well-being is possible ... The best way to promote human development is to increase the national income and to ensure a close link between economic growth and human well-being.' So even if some components of the environment may get worse at certain stages in a country's economic development, there seems little doubt that, on the whole, welfare still increases.

But perhaps the simplest and most decisive refutation of the view that GNP is not very well correlated with welfare, however much it may lead to environmental deterioration for many years, is that there is enormous pressure from people living in countries with low GNP per head to emigrate to countries with high GNP per head. And there is not much evidence of any great desire by anybody to move in the opposite direction, or even of any sign that many of the people who had moved have decided that they had made a mistake or had been badly informed and hence moved back again.

4. Global environmental problems

It may be objected that although all the above is true, it merely demonstrates that, as countries become richer, their inhabitants are able to ensure that local or national pollution problems are tackled more effectively. But it may not guarantee that international action is taken to deal with the growing problem of *global* environmental damage. This is so, but the situation is not as alarming as many would have us believe.

For example, there was widespread concern in the 1970s over the damage to the ozone layer with the alleged consequent rise in the amount of ultraviolet radiation (UVB) which could lead to increased skin cancer or harm plant and animal life in other ways. But within about ten years an international agreement was reached (the Montreal Convention) which entailed a gradual phasing out of production of the CFCs (chlorofluorocarbons) that attack the ozone layer. And this has been achieved in spite of major differences of interest between the contracting parties and in spite of the fact that there has not yet been any recorded rise in the amount of UVB reaching the earth's surface or any increase in skin cancer that can be attributed to it.

Considerable progress has also been made over the past two decades in reaching international agreement to check destruction of certain species of whales, to limit trade in 'endangered species', and to reduce oil spillages at sea. None of these agreements is perfect, but the lesson is fairly clear, namely that in spite of considerable differences between countries concerning their national interests, when the existence of any serious common threat is beyond dispute the international community is capable of reaching agreement to meet the threat.

It is in this context that one has to view the problem of global warming. Here there are far greater differences between countries with respect to the impact of global warming, if any, and of the costs of preventing it. For example, some regions – notably vast areas of North American and Russia – might benefit from global warming in so far as it means shorter and milder winters and hence longer growing periods. There are also major differences between them as regards their production of fossil fuels. Some

Middle Eastern countries, for example, depend almost entirely on them. Others, such as China and India, are likely to rely heavily on coal to meet the vast increase in their energy demands that their economic growth will entail. Thus the chances of early agreement to curtail world emissions of carbon are very slight and, as Cooper (1994) has authoritatively demonstrated, the most one can expect is that, if and when individual countries find that they are seriously threatened by global warming, they will gradually take adaptive action (building sea walls, changing agricultural patterns or techniques, and so on).

The best countries can probably be expected to do now – and there is evidence that it is being done – is to take the possibility of global warming seriously and carry out substantial research into the climate change phenomenon. For there is still much uncertainty about the global warming predictions, largely because of lack of understanding in many areas, for example, the role of increased water vapour and hence of feedback effects, such as those arising from increased cloud cover, or the effect on the extent to which carbon can be absorbed in the oceans at different depths, or the precise role of increased concentrations of sulphate particulates, and so on. On account of these and other uncertainties, it will be many years before it is clear just how much, and where exactly, temperatures will rise.

Meanwhile, the fact that very little effective action will be taken for many years to check total global carbon emissions is not necessarily a cause for alarm. For during that time (i) the scientific evidence will accumulate and it will become clearer how far there is really any case for drastic action; (ii) there will be further substantial technological progress in the development of alternative sources of energy, so that the costs of any switch away from fossil fuels will be far less, thereby increasing the chances of international agreement over the burden sharing needed in the interests of reducing global carbon emissions; and (iii) there will have been time to implement sensible no-cost policies to reduce undesirable and uneconomic emissions, such as those resulting from subsidized output of coal or old-fashioned coal-intensive industries, or excessive deforestation encouraged by lack of property rights or by government subsidies to bad land-use activities.

5. Is continued economic growth 'sustainable'?

The concept of sustainable development
As well as questioning how far continued economic growth is desirable, many critics of growth have also proclaimed that economic growth will shortly come up against sheer physical constraints of one kind or another. These include, notably, the exhaustion of 'finite' resources, such as minerals, or the impossibility of feeding the projected increase in world

population. These fears have given rise to the very widespread concept of 'sustainable development'.

Again, there are two aspects to the problem of 'sustainable development': conceptual and factual. It would be out of place here to dwell on the former, and it must suffice to say that, while there is no clear agreed interpretation of the concept, one feature of most definitions is that we should ensure that there is no decline in the welfare of future generations. But the rationale of this is not as obvious as many of its proponents seem to believe. For example, if one accepted that society's proper objective should be to maximize the total welfare of society over whatever time period is thought to be relevant, it is difficult to see why some feasible time path of welfare that could achieve this objective should be rejected simply because it may include some period – possibly in the middle or the end – of declining welfare. If that is the way that total social welfare over the whole period is maximized, why should it be rejected?[3] It is true that the later generations whose welfare is assumed to be reduced will not be compensated by the higher welfare that the earlier generations have achieved at their expense. But this is a question of how far one is prepared to trade off the sum of total welfare over all the generations in question against inequality of welfare between generations. There is room for legitimate differences of opinion as regards this trade-off, reflecting different degrees of inequality aversion. But there does not seem to be much case for disregarding it altogether and assuming that any sacrifice of total welfare over the whole period is acceptable in the interests of avoiding any inequality between generations.

The facts
There is space here to mention only three examples.

Minerals   The first is the widespread assertion that there is a problem of 'finite resources'. One of the best known of relatively modern predictions that economic growth would soon come up against resource constraints is the famous 1972 report to the Club of Rome, entitled *The Limits to Growth*. By comparing estimates of known reserves of many minerals with annual rates of consumption, the Club of Rome's computer showed that, at current rates of consumption, the existing reserves would soon all be used up. We are now in a position to see what actually happened.

Table 43.1 compares the 1970 estimates of reserves of key metals and primary fuels as given in the Club of Rome's *Limits to Growth* with the 1989 figures and estimates of how much of the metals in question have been consumed in the 19 years that have elapsed since. It can be seen that the 1989 reserves are much greater than those reported in 1970, for all the items covered, in spite of the fact that cumulative consumption during the intervening years has been large relative to initial 1970 reserves. Indeed, for two of the items listed, namely lead and oil, more has been consumed in the period 1970–89 than had been recorded in 'known reserves' in 1970, so we ought to have run out of supplies already. Consumption of natural gas and zinc during the period 1970–89 was also just about as great as the initial level of known reserves of these products, yet for both of these products we have more now in known reserves than we had when we started.[4]

Table 43.1   *How we used up all the resources we had and still finished up with more than we started with*[a]

	Reserves (tonnes $\times 10^6$ unless otherwise stated)		Cumulative consumption, 1970–89
	1970	1989	
Aluminium	1170	4918	232
Copper	308	560	176
Lead	91	125	99
Nickel	67	109	14
Zinc	123	295	118
Oil[b]	550	900	600
Natural gas	250	900	250

[a] For details of sources, see Beckerman (1995a), p. 53.
[b] Billions of barrels of oil equivalent.

Clearly, it is inappropriate to use estimates of 'known reserves' in the way that the Club of Rome and others have done, since these represent only those reserves that have been found worthwhile seeking out, given the prices of the minerals in question. If there were a long-run failure of supply to meet demand the price would rise and this would set in a whole chain reaction of a shift to substitutes, exploration for more reserves, improved extraction technologies, and so on. Throughout the course of human history the demands and supplies of materials have followed varying trends with accompanying changes in relative prices, and there is no reason to believe that this mechanism will not work in the future.

Food and population   In 1968 the distinguished biologist Paul Ehrlich published a book which began by saying that 'The battle to feed all of humanity is over. In the 1970s the world will undergo famines – hundreds of millions of people are going to starve to death in spite of any crash programs embarked upon now' (Ehrlich, 1968, p. i). During the following two decades, in fact, world food supply grew faster than population, as it has done consistently since Malthus made his famous predictions of unavoidable starvation 200 years ago.

It is true that the upward trend in world per capita food output levelled off around the mid-1980s. But this does not indicate any 'watershed' year in which the forces of Malthusian pessimism were at last vindicated. The break in the upward trend in per capita food production was inevitable given the emergence of huge surpluses of some food products in many parts of the world and the problems this created of disposing of them without disrupting established markets and with minimum cost to the taxpayers of the countries.

The long upward trend in food output per head was, unsurprisingly, accompanied by a steep fall in the relative price of food. For example, between 1953–55 and 1983–85 the price of rice fell by 42 per cent, wheat by 57 per cent, sorghum by 39 per cent, and maize by 37 per cent (Sen, 1994). Thus, as Amartya Sen points out,

> When we take into account the persistent cheapening of food prices, we have good grounds to suggest that food output is being held back by a lack of effective demand in the market. The imaginary crisis in food production, contradicted as it is by the upward trends of total and regional food output per head, is thus further debunked by an analysis of the economic incentives to produce more food. (Sen, 1994)[5]

This desirable and normal operation of market forces is further confirmed by noticeable regional difference in food output. Between 1979–81 and 1991–93 food output per head rose by 3 per cent for the world as a whole. But it rose by only 2 per cent in Europe and fell by about 5 per cent in the US – that is, the two regions where surpluses had been a major problem.[6] By contrast, it rose by 22 per cent in Asia as a whole, including 23 per cent in India and 39 per cent in China – that is, in countries where there have been large population increases (Sen, 1994; Dyson, 1995).

The one major exception to this is, of course, Africa, where food production per head fell by 6 per cent over the same period. But in Africa the food problem has not been the result of population pressures. It has been the result mainly of wars (including civil wars and ethnic conflicts), dictatorship and political chaos. This was the case, for example, with the mass starvation in Ethiopia and the Sudan in the 1980s or in Somalia at the end of the 1980s and early 1990s, and, more recently, in Ruanda. In other words, the main cause of recent famines – as with the Soviet famine of 1934 or the Chinese famine of 1958–61 – was human evil and stupidity, not environmental catastrophe. Man versus man, as always, has been the culprit, not man versus the environment.

Biodiversity Space does not permit a full discussion of the ethics or economics of preserving biodiversity.[7] We shall limit ourselves here, therefore, to the question 'How fast is biodiversity being destroyed?' The answer is probably 'fast, but nothing like as fast as some environmentalist pressure groups claim'. One product of the great concern with the threat of mass extinction of species was that the International Union for Conservation of Nature and Natural Resources (IUCN, also known as the World Conservation Union) commissioned a survey of the state of knowledge concerning species extinctions. All the contributors to this survey were biologists specializing in this topic and all expressed considerable concern at the dramatic rate of species extinction that was taking place. At the same time, all of them stressed the vast deficiencies in the available estimates (Whitmore and Sayer, 1992).

For example, one of the contributors was Daniel Simberloff, a distinguished professor of ecology, who pointed out that

> Forests of the eastern United States were reduced over two centuries to fragments totalling, 1–2% of their original extent ... during this destruction, only three forest birds went extinct ... Why, then, would one predict massive extinction from similar destruction of tropical forest? (Simberloff, 1992)

Two other contributors wrote that

> the IUCN, together with the World Conservation Monitoring Centre, has amassed large volumes of data from specialists around the world relating to species decline, and it would seem sensible to compare these more empirical data with the global extinction estimates. In fact, these and other data indicate that the number of recorded extinctions for both plants and animals is very small. (Heywood and Stuart, 1992)

The same authors stated that, on certain reasonable assumptions based on available data,

> the annual rate of extinction would be some 2,300 species per year. This is a very significant and disturbing number, but it is much less than most estimates given over the last decade ... Despite extensive enquiries we have been unable to obtain conclusive evidence to support the suggestion that massive extinctions have taken place in recent times as Myers and other have suggested. On the contrary, work on projects such as Flora Meso-Americana has, at least in some cases, revealed an increase in abundance in many species.

And, more specifically, they write that 'There are many reasons why recorded extinctions do not match the predictions and extrapolations that are frequently published.' On the other hand, more recent work suggests that, although the methods that have to be used are still subject to enormous uncertainties, the three main methods do seem to lead to the same conclusion, namely that the rate of species extinction may be accelerating and that predictions of future high rates may be greater than had hitherto been warranted (May et al., 1995).

On the other hand, a major element in all such estimates of species extinction is, as indicated above, an estimate of the rate of destruction of habitats, which refers mainly – but by no means exclusively – to deforestations. But here, too, the estimates are by no means firm. This is emphasized in estimates of total world forest area by the UN Food and Agriculture Organization and estimates by Marion Clawson (the pre-eminent student of forest economics for many decades) and Roger Sedjo that were made for Resources for the Future, a widely respected research institute that has always been very concerned with sustainable development and related issues. Sedjo and Clawson concluded that 'there is certainly nothing in the data to suggest that the world is experiencing significant net deforestation', although they do point out that 'A hard look at the available data supports the views that some regions are experiencing rapid deforestation.' In other words, it may well be true that, say, Brazilian rainforests are being rapidly depleted, as are those in Thailand and other countries, but they conclude that 'the view that this is a pervasive phenomenon on a global level is questionable' (Simon, 1986).[8]

In any case, it is not clear exactly how much loss of species is significant for human welfare. If, for example, it is a question of preserving species on account of their possible future medicinal value, then one has to ask how far investments by pharmaceutical companies in exploration and preservation in various tropical areas are inadequate and why they should be doing more of this rather than, say, spending more on research into biotechnology and genetic engineering or even genetic preservation of endangered species (Cooper, 1994).

6. Future prospects

The determinants of economic growth are not fully understood. They include a wide range of economic variables and institutional and political variables, all of which interact in complex and barely understood ways. It is unwise, therefore, to make precise predictions. Nevertheless, those factors which are fairly well understood all point to a sustained increase in world output per head. One of the most important of these factors is technical progress which, in turn, is a function of levels of education and research. And we are witnessing a great increase in the proportion of the population in most countries of the world that is obtaining an education that, until relatively recently, was the exclusive privilege of a small minority of the world population. This is being accompanied by vast increases in the resources devoted to research that, sooner or later, add to our command over the environment and our capacity to satisfy human needs and aspirations. The prospects for sustained economic growth are, therefore, better than at any previous time in human history. And, whilst one cannot rule out changes in the social and political environment that could bring this process to an end, one type of constraint can be confidently ruled out, namely the environmental doomsday scenario that is so widely proclaimed by the 'Greens'.

Notes

1. Pigou (1932), ch. 1, para. 5.
2. World Bank (1991), p. xiv.
3. For detailed discussion of the conceptual issue, see Beckerman (1995a), ch. 9 and Beckerman (1995b).
4. For details of definitions and methods see Beckerman (1995a), ch. 4.
5. The same point is made in Dyson (1994).
6. For example, during the 1980s the US undertook numerous steps to reduce food output, such as reducing cereal support costs, and withdrawing large areas of cropland under the Conservation Reserve Program and under various commodity schemes (Dyson, 1994).
7. For a somewhat fuller discussion of these topics see Beckerman (1995a). The outstanding work on the ethics of conservation is Passmore (1974).
8. A rather sceptical survey of the whole species extinction problem is contained in Simon and Wildavsky (1994).

References

Anderson, E. (1993), *Value in Ethics and Economics*, Cambridge, MA: Harvard University Press.

Beckerman, W. (1995a), *Small is Stupid*, London: Duckworth.

Beckerman, W. (1995b), 'How would you like your 'sustainability', sir? Weak or strong? A reply to my critics', *Environmental Values*, **4**, 169–79.

Cooper, R.N. (1994), *Environmental and Resource Policies for the World Economy*, Washington, DC: Brookings Institution.

Dasgupta, P. (1990), 'Well-being and the extent of its realisation in poor countries', *Economic Journal*, **100**, Supplement, 1–32.

Dasgupta, P. and M. Weale (1992), 'On measuring the quality of life', *World Development*, **20** (1), 119–31.

Dyson, T. (1994), 'Population growth and food production: recent global and regional trends', *Population and Development Review*, **20** (2), 397–411.

Dyson, T. (1995), 'World food demand and supply prospects', paper to the International Conference of the Fertiliser Society, Cambridge, December.

Ehrlich, P. (1968), *The Population Bomb*, New York: Sierra Club, Ballantine.

Heywood, V.H. and S.N. Stuart (1992), 'Species extinction in tropical forests', in Whitmore and Sayer (1992).

May, R.M., J.H. Lawton and N.E. Stark (1995), 'Assessing extinction rates', in J.H. Lawton and R.M. May (eds), *Extinction Rates*, Oxford: Oxford University Press.

Passmore, J. (1974), *Man's Responsibility for Nature*, London: Duckworth.

Pigou, A.C. (1932), *The Economics of Welfare*, London: Macmillan.

Sen, Amartya (1994), 'Population: delusion and reality', *New York Review of Books*, 22 September.

Simberloff, D. (1992), 'Do species-area curves predict extinction in fragmented forests?', in Whitmore and Sayer (1992).

Simon, J. (1986), 'Disappearing species, deforestations and data', *New Scientist*, 15 May.

Simon, J. and A. Wildavsky (eds) (1994), *The State of Humanity*, Oxford: Blackwell.
United Nations (1995), *World Population Prospects: The 1994 Revision*, New York: UN.
United Nations Development Programme (1991), *Human Development Report*, Oxford: Oxford University Press.
Whitmore, T.C. and J.A. Sayer (eds) (1992), *Tropical Deforestation and Species Extinction*, New York: Chapman and Hall.
World Bank (1991), *Social Indicators of Development*, Washington, DC: World Bank.

44 Steady-state economics: avoiding uneconomic growth

Herman E. Daly

> *'That which seems to be wealth may in verity be only the gilded index of far-reaching ruin . . .'*
> John Ruskin, *Unto this Last,* 1862

How is the economy related to its environment, the ecosystem? The economy, in its physical dimensions, is a subsystem of the earth's ecosystem. The ecosystem is finite, non-growing and materially closed. In the earth's ecosystem solar energy enters and exits and it is this throughput of energy (itself finite and non-growing) that powers the material biogeochemical cycles on which life depends. Within the earth's ecosystem the economy exists as an open subsystem. That means that both matter and energy enter from the larger system, and that both matter and energy exit back to the larger system. All physical processes of life and production are maintained by this metabolic flow-through (throughput) of matter–energy from and back to the environment. The economy lives off the environment in the same way that an animal does – by taking in useful (low-entropy) raw material and energy, and giving back waste (high-entropy) material and energy. The rest of the ecosystem, the part that is not within the economic subsystem (that is, natural capital), absorbs the emitted wastes, and through biogeochemical cycles powered by the sun, reconstitutes much of the waste into reusable raw materials (Figure 44.1).

As the economic subsystem expands in its physical dimensions, it assimilates into itself a larger and larger proportion of the total matter–energy of the earth's ecosystem. More and more of total life space is converted into economic space – that is, living space for expanding populations and space taken over to provide sources of our raw materials and sinks for our waste materials. Consequently less and less life space remains outside the economy to provide the vital function of carrying out the biogeochemical cycles at the rates and through the pathways to which we are adapted (Figure 44.1, bottom). The planet earth develops without growing – that is, it evolves qualitatively without expanding quantitatively. The economy, as a subsystem of the earth, must at some scale adapt itself to this same pattern of 'development without growth' – which is what should be

Empty world

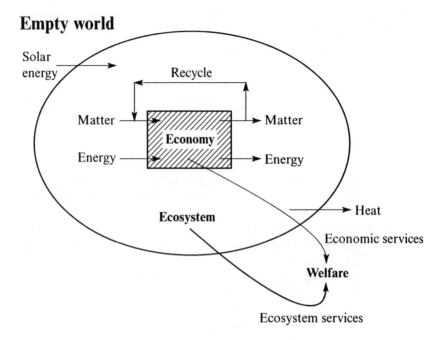

Full world

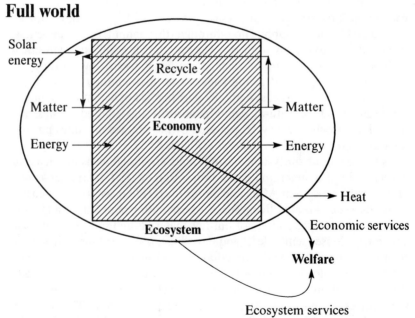

Figure 44.1   A 'macro' view of the macroeconomy

understood by the popular term 'sustainable development'. That is the paradigm or pre-analytic vision of steady-state economics.

If GNP growth resulted only from increments in value added to a non-growing resource throughput, then it would probably remain *economic* growth for much longer. But that is not yet what happens in today's world. According to the World Resources Institute, and others, per capita resource requirement rose, albeit slowly, over the period 1975–93 in Germany, Japan and the Netherlands.[1] It also rose in the US if one does not count reductions in erosion. Population growth in these countries is low, but not zero, giving a further boost to total throughput growth. Since current levels of resource use in these countries range from 45 to 85 thousand kilograms per person per year, a level already causing severe environmental degradation, it seems a bit premature to herald the advent of the 'dematerialized economy', however much we remain committed to it as a goal.

In sharp contrast, the pre-analytic vision underlying standard economics (the neoclassical–Keynesian synthesis) is that the economy is an isolated system: a circular flow of exchange value between firms and households (Figure 44.2). An 'isolated' system is one in which neither matter nor energy

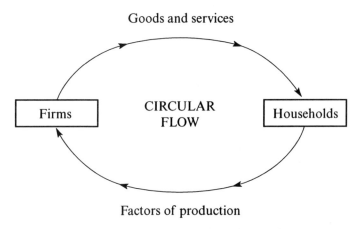

Figure 44.2   Economy as isolated system

enters or exits – it has no relation with its environment, and for all practical purposes has no environment. While this vision is useful for analysing exchange between producers and consumers, and related questions of price and income determination, it is quite useless for studying the relation of the economy to the environment. It is as if a biologist's vision of an animal contained only a circulatory system, but no digestive tract. The animal would be an isolated system. It would be completely independent of its environment.

If it could move it would be a perpetual motion machine. As long as the economic subsystem was small relative to the Earth's ecosystem it was acceptable to abstract from the larger system since its services were not scarce. But now 'full world' economics must replace 'empty world' economics.

The isolated system, the pre-analytic vision that supports most economic analysis today, takes the economy as the total system, unconstrained in its growth by anything. Nature may be finite, but it is just a sector of the economy, for which other sectors can substitute, without limiting overall growth of the economy in any important way. This seems to be the view of neoclassical resource and environmental economists – they do not neglect the role of natural resources, but consider natural resources as no different from other factors of production, and as highly substitutable by them. Therefore the economy is still seen as an isolated system (containing a natural subsystem, the extractive sector), but with no environment to constrain its continual growth (see Figure 44.3). If the economy is the whole,

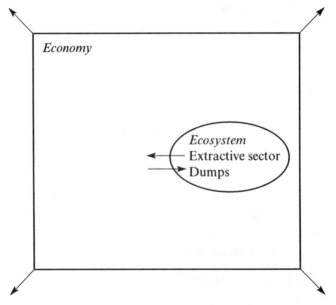

Figure 44.3   Ecosystem as subsystem of macroeconomy

then its expansion is not at the expense of anything else because there is nothing else. But if we see the economy not as the whole, but as a subsystem of a larger, but finite and non-growing ecosystem, then obviously its growth is at the expense of something else. There is an opportunity cost to its expansion, as well as an ultimate physical limit. The economy may continue to develop qualitatively, just as the planet Earth does, but it cannot continue to grow – that is, beyond some point it must approximate a steady state in its physical dimensions.

An economy in sustainable development, a steady-state economy, is one whose scale (or resource throughput, equal to population times per capita resource use) remains constant at a level that neither depletes the environment beyond its regenerative capacity, nor pollutes it beyond its absorptive capacity. Such an economy adapts and improves in knowledge, organization, technical efficiency and wisdom; and it does this without assimilating or accreting an ever-greater percentage of the matter–energy of the ecosystem into itself, but rather stops at a scale at which the remaining ecosystem (the environment) can continue to function and renew itself year after year. The non-growing economy is not static – it is being continually maintained and renewed as a steady-state subsystem in dynamic equilibrium with its environment.

If we accept the pre-analytic vision of steady-state economics (economy as subsystem), then the first analytic questions that come to mind are: how big *is* the subsystem relative to the total system? How big *can* it be? How big *should* it be? Since these questions do not arise under the standard growth paradigm, we have no good answers for them. That is why we need steady-state economics. The answers to the first two questions are basically empirical–factual. The third requires a value criterion, but that should be no surprise to economists. What is surprising is that there is so much disagreement over answers to the empirical questions. Some think we are very far from any limits; others think we have already overshot critical limits and will soon face a collapse. We debate about time horizons, dematerialization possibilities, ecosystem resilience, size of reserves, degree of toxicity of wastes, and so on. We often expect agreement on the facts, and disagreement over norms. In this case there seems to have been an inversion – most people accept the norm of sustainability, while disagreeing intensely about the factual question of whether our economy is or is not sustainable. This disagreement seems more a function of basic paradigm differences than of empirical knowledge regarding the issues mentioned above.

Growth of the subsystem is further limited by the complementary relation between man-made and natural capital. If the two forms of capital were good substitutes, then natural capital could be totally replaced by man-made, and the only limit to expansion of man-made capital would be the finitude of the containing system. But in fact man-made capital loses its value without a complement of natural capital. What good is the man-made capital of fishing boats without the natural capital of fish populations? Sawmills without forests? And even if we could convert the whole ocean into a catfish pond, we would still need the natural capital of solar energy, photosynthetic organisms, nutrient recyclers, and so on.

The neoclassical economists' emphasis on substitution to the eclipse of complementarity in technical relations among factors of production seems really quite extreme when one takes a hard look at neoclassical production functions used in growth theory. Usually production has been taken as a function only of labour and capital. Resources are excluded. One wonders how the labour of the cook and the capital of his kitchen can produce a cake with no flour, eggs, milk, sugar, and so on. Substitution is one thing; breaking the law of conservation of mass is something else. More recently we find resources sometimes stuck in the Cobb–Douglas functions as a third factor multiplied with labour and capital, and therefore assumed to be substitutable by them. We now need some greater-than-zero amount of eggs, flour, sugar and the like to make our cake, and that seems a big step forward until we realize that the function says we could make our cake a thousand times bigger if the cook simply stirred faster and used a bigger oven.

Such absurdities reflect a strong animus in neoclassical economics to deny any significant role to nature in the generation of wealth. In fact, the large statistical residual of around 50 per cent (the Solow residual), the variation in production unexplained by variations in labour and capital, is attributed to technology – another human factor. The idea that natural resources could have been responsible is ruled out by the dogma that only human factors – labour, capital and (residually) technology – add value. There is no consideration of 'that to which value is added' and its differing receptivities to receiving the value added by labour and capital. Nature is thought to contribute only inert, abundant, passive, indestructible building blocks to which labour and capital add whatever value the final product has. Ecological economists consider that nature does make a contribution – they agree with the view expressed long ago by William Petty that while labour is the father of value, nature is the mother. Of course, if nature is thought to add value, then we can no longer maintain the fiction that the total value added is distributed to the two factors that added it. Who gets nature's value added – labour or capital?

In the view of steady-state or ecological economics there is a limit to nature's ability to contribute value – a *maximum* scale of the economic subsystem – a point beyond which the total system collapses under the demands of its too-large subsystem. Before that point there is an *optimal* scale – a point beyond which further physical growth, while possible, costs more than it is worth. The logic is entirely analogous to that of microeconomics – finding the optimal scale of a part relative to the whole on which its expansion inflicts an opportunity cost – the familiar equating of marginal costs with marginal benefits. Figure 44.4 applies this logic to the macroeconomy by adapting a diagram that William Stanley Jevons (1871)

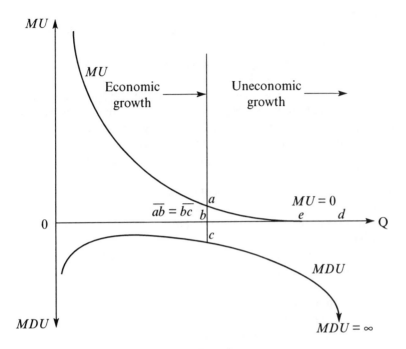

Note: MU = marginal utility from consuming produced goods and services (Q). MU
declines because, as rational beings, we satisfy our most pressing wants first.
MDU = marginal sacrifices made necessary by growing production and consumption, for
example, disutility of labour, sacrifice of leisure, depletion, pollution, environmental
destruction, congestion.
Marginal sacrifice eventually increases, assuming we sacrifice least important values first.
b = economic limit; MU = MDU; (maximum net positive utility)
e = futility limit; MU = 0; (consumer satiation)
d = catastrophe limit; MDU = ∞; (ecological disaster)

Figure 44.4   Jevonian view of limits to growth of macroeconomy

used in analysing a microeconomic problem. It allows a rather clear distinction between economic and uneconomic growth.

An optimal scale exists even if we think of the non-human part of
Creation as having only instrumental value to humans and no intrinsic
value in its own right. If we recognize intrinsic value of other sentient creatures, in addition to their instrumental value to us, then the optimal scale
of the human niche would be smaller than if we recognized only instrumental value. A man is worth many sparrows, but a corollary is that a
sparrow's worth cannot be zero. Since growth beyond the optimal scale
increases ecological costs faster than production benefits, it makes us
poorer, not richer, thereby reducing our ability to cure poverty, and even

creating more poverty. The belief that growth is the cure for poverty is an evasion of the real, but politically unpopular cures, namely sharing and population control, and improvement in resource productivity.

The frequent call for more growth, so that we can afford to pay the costs of environmental repair and poverty alleviation, simply assumes that growth in GNP is making us richer, when that is the very question at issue. No one doubts that all our problems would be easier to solve if we were truly richer – the issue is, does growth as currently measured and from the present margin really make us richer, or is it making us poorer?[2] In John Ruskin's terms how do we know that growth is not increasing 'illth' faster than wealth?

Some quantitative idea of the present size of the economy relative to the earth's ecosystem is given by the estimate that we humans currently pre-empt about 40 per cent of the net primary product of solar energy captured by land-based ecosystems.[3] There is abundant evidence that even the present scale of the economic subsystem is unsustainable by the remainder of the ecosystem, and that further physical expansion of the economy (current doubling time is about 40–50 years) is diminishing the capacity of the earth to support life. This destruction of carrying capacity means a reduction in the cumulative number of lives ever to be lived over time in conditions of material sufficiency for a good life. Once 'economic' growth increases ecological costs faster than production benefits, it becomes in truth uneconomic growth, impoverishing rather than enriching, and its measure, GNP, indeed becomes 'a gilded index of far-reaching ruin'.[4]

Notes

1. See *Resource Flows: The Material Basis of Industrial Economies*, 1997, Washington, DC, World Resources Institute (USA), Wuppertal Institute (Germany), Netherlands Ministry of Housing, Spatial Planning and Environment, and National Institute for Environmental Studies (Japan).
2. For evidence that GNP growth in the US over the past decade has indeed been associated with declining welfare, see Appendix on the Index of Sustainable Economic Welfare, in Herman Daly and John Cobb, *For the Common Good*, Boston: Beacon Press, 1994, second edition. For further evidence from other countries, see Manfred Max-Neef, 'Economic growth and quality of life: a threshold hypothesis', *Ecological Economics*, **15** (1995), 115–18.
3. Peter Vitousek et al., 'Human appropriation of the products of photosynthesis', *BioScience*, **34** (6), May 1986, pp. 368–73.
4. Readers interested in pursuing further steady-state or ecological economics should consult the following: H. Daly, *Steady-State Economics, Second Edition with New Essays*, Island Press, Washington, DC, 1991; Robert Costanza (ed.), *Ecological Economics: The Science and Management of Sustainability*, New York: Columbia University Press, 1991; Herman Daly and Kenneth Townsend (eds), *Valuing the Earth: Economics, Ecology, Ethics*, Cambridge, MA: MIT Press, 1993; Robert Goodland, et al. (eds), *Population, Technology, and Lifestyle*, Island Press, Washington DC, 1992; issues of the journal *Ecological Economics* (Elsevier Publishers); and *A Survey of Ecological Economics*, edited by Rajaram Krishnan, Jonathan M. Harris and Neva R. Goodwin, Island Press, Washington, DC, 1995.

45 An assessment of the growth debate
Jeroen C.J.M. van den Bergh and Ruud A. de Mooij

1. Introduction

The relationship between growth and environment has been controversial for a long time. Some economists and many non-economists have argued that a rise in gross domestic product (GDP) will harm natural environments without any doubt (see Daly, Chapter 44 in this book, for an anti-growth perspective). Indeed, during the last few decades economic growth has gone along with a substantial increase in energy use, congestion and transformation of land cover. Other economists have maintained that the economy can grow for ever without harming the quality of the environment. Technical progress is then considered as a critical factor for reconciling growth and environment (see Beckerman, Chapter 43 in this book, for a pro-growth perspective).

These different views on growth and the environment often give rise to debates between advocates and opponents of growth (for a unique account of this, see Myers and Simon, 1994). The aim of this chapter is to provide some clarification about these debates, and in particular to assess the economic (contra-)arguments. The standard economics perspective is essentially welfare-based, or even more restricted, namely GDP-based, where environmental destruction is only regarded as a problem in so far as it affects the present value of market exchange (or welfare in welfare/externality theory). Alternative non-anthropocentric (ecocentric or biocentric) views exist, such as based on intrinsic values in nature (see Blamey and Common, Chapter 56, and Glasser, Chapter 66 in this book), and these can explain some of the perspectives on growth versus environment discussed in Section 4 (notably the first one).

We pay attention to both the old 'growth debate' and the recent literature. Indeed, the introduction of the concept 'sustainable development' can to some extent be regarded as a reopening of the growth debate (see Pezzey, 1993; van den Bergh, 1996). Reference to the broad literature on sustainable development will be minimized, however, as this is addressed in other contributions in this book (Chapters 3, 38, 48, 49 and 72). Although the various publications on the conflict between economic growth and environmental conservation together offer a range of perspectives, a systematic comparison of these is usually lacking. Here such a comparison is aimed for, based on a general framework and carefully chosen criteria.

2.   A static view on economy and environment

Standard economic theory distinguishes the following exogenous factors that characterize a market economy at each moment in time:

(b1)   Institutions and conventions
(b2)   Population
(b3)   Preferences
(b4)   Technology and knowledge
(b5)   The stock of man-made capital.

Note that not only the market mechanism, but also the social cohesion and community structure, and public policies and institutions are included under (b1). Environmental economists usually distinguish two important links in relation to the interaction between the economy and the ecological system. First, the environment serves as a factor of production, in terms of natural resource supply, availability of space, provision of production conditions for agriculture, forestry and fishery, supply of basic human needs such as fresh air and fertile soil, and storage and assimilation of waste. Second, the environment is a consumption good in terms of its direct impact on the well-being of people. In both respects, the environment amounts to a basic economic factor. Consequently, we add it as a sixth element to the set of basic factors:

(b6)   The stock of environmental capital.

The market mechanism is an institution (b1) which generates prices for goods and factors that reflect relative scarcities in the economy. Scarcity of some good is determined by household preferences (b3) and technology (b4). Together with the stocks (b5) and (b6) and the size of the population (b2), these determine the *scale* on which economic activity takes place. However, the *composition* of economic activities is also the result of market behaviour. This composition can be characterized by the following three structures:

(r 1)   The input mix of production, that is, the use of labour, capital, energy, virgin materials, recycled materials and abatement technology.
(r 2)   The composition of demand, that is, commodities, services, environmental goods, leisure.

(r 3)   The output mix of production, that is, commodities, services, pollution.

The basic factors (b1)–(b6), that underlie the economic framework, and the resulting economic structure defined by (r 1)–(r 3) describe, in a nutshell, the basic context in which the relationship between economic growth and environmental preservation can be discussed.

3.   Growth and the environment

Section 2 provides a static view of the relation between the economy and the environment. Economic growth, however, is a dynamic concept. It is generally defined as the increase in the total value added of marketable, man-made goods and services in the economy. In our model, dynamics can be introduced by exploring changes in the basic factors (b1)–(b6). In particular, developments in factors (b1)–(b3) are usually considered to be more or less exogenous to the market economy. These factors depend, for instance, on cultural change (b3) and public policy (b1). The latter is important in the present context as it allows us to study the influence of environmental regulation on the relationship between growth and environment. Of course, if policy is regarded as an endogenous process, this means that (b1) will also have to be endogenized. For a long time, economists have also treated technical change (b4) as an exogenous trend. However, since the development of endogenous growth theory, technology is generally considered to be an endogenous factor which depends on economic decisions such as education and R&D activities. The stock of physical capital increases in time through investments. We consider knowledge as a factor determining technical change. Alternatively, it may be considered as a human capital good, similar to physical capital (see Smulders, Chapter 42 of this book). Note that economists do not generally take the impact of technological change on behaviour and preferences into account. The stock of environmental capital is linked to economic activity in such a way that it deteriorates due to extraction of natural resources and emissions from production and consumption processes. However, nature has some regenerative and assimilative capacity through which the stock of environmental capital may recover.

Traditionally, an important question for economists is how development with respect to basic factors affects, on the one hand, the value added of marketable goods and services as measured by (real) GDP and, on the other hand, the quality of the natural environment as measured by the physical stock of environmental capital. The difference between *economic value* terms which relate to economic activity and *physical* measures associated with the environment is crucial here. If development implies a continuous increase in value added, the crucial issue is whether this can be reconciled with an environmental sustainability constraint, such as a constant or non-decreasing stock of environmental capital. It should, however, be noted that the economic valuation based on individual preferences – either via prices, indirect market-based assessment or stated preferences – has been much criticized (see Bromley, 1995; Gowdy, 1997).

A second important note to the above conceptual framework is that it is not meant to imply only an equilibrium perspective on growth. Standard growth theory has focused most attention on growth in equilibrium. Ayres (1997) regards this as an oxymoron, because all incentives to individual agents to buy, to sell, to invest, to invent or to innovate arise only and directly as result of some disequilibrium. One might even conjecture that the further away from equilibrium, the more strongly these incentives will push agents to react in a destructive or constructive way. As opposed to traditional and modern neoclassical growth theories, alternative models of technological progress and economic evolution focus attention on disequilibrium conditions as essential for, and inherently linked to, economic and technological change. Gowdy (Chapter 65 in this book) gives a broad entrance to this literature. van den Bergh and Hofkes (Chapter 72) offer a survey of models supporting the various perspectives on growth and environment. The discussion here will focus attention on assumptions, interpretations and implications of alternative perspectives, in the context of the above sketched framework, and skip further reference to formal models.

4.   Five perspectives on growth and environment
Below, we consider five different views on the potential for reconciling growth and environmental preservation, and relate these to the above discussion of changes in basic factors $(\Delta b1)$–$(\Delta b6)$, as well as changes in economic structure as represented by $(\Delta r1)$–$(\Delta r3)$. In addition, we pursue an explicit treatment of the interdependence between environmental quality and long-run growth. This distinguishes our classification from other ethical or basic views on environment and nature, often presented in introductions to environmental science and ecological economics (see, for example, van den Bergh, 1996). In particular, the taxonomy 'technocratic' ('cornucopian' and 'accommodating') and 'ecocentric' ('communalist' and 'deep ecology') is often used (see Turner et al., 1994, p.31). Here we are more focused on the *long run*, both in terms of economic and environmental time scales. Clearly, any view on the relation between these will affect one's perspective on growth and environment. For instance, some people believe that the market, if appropriately guided by environmental policies – notably price-oriented – can take long-run goals and values into

account. Others are more pessimistic, pointing at myopic behaviour on the part of both economic agents and policy makers or politicians.

The first perspective mainly questions the desirability of growth. The other four perspectives deal with the technical ability (perspectives (ii) and (iii)), the socioeconomic endogenous resolution potential (perspectives (iv) and (v)), and the capability of nature itself (perspective (ii)), to harmonize economic growth and environmental conservation and preservation.

(i)   The immaterialist (moralist): growth is undesirable
The first perspective addresses the issue of whether economic growth is desirable or, in other words, whether growth contributes to the goals we strive for as individuals or communities. Several authors have pointed out that economic growth in general does not coincide with a rise in welfare or well-being. In contrast, if economic growth is associated with degradation of the natural environment we should evade growth (see for example, Mishan, 1967, 1977; Schumacher, 1973; Daly, 1991. An overview is given in Daly and Townsend, 1993, and an unequivocal dismissal by Beckerman, 1976, 1995; see also the previous two chapters.)

Some of these authors indicate that there is a distinction between limited absolute needs – like food, clothing, shelter, clean water, health care – and relative desires – that is, relative to the perceptible (material) welfare or consumption of other individuals in the community (see Daly, 1991, p. 40). For the first category boundless growth is not required. For the second category it cannot give rise to continuing improvements in individual welfare for everyone. From a completely different angle, a non-anthropocentric ethic based on intrinsic values in nature (deep ecology) can also provide strong support for this perspective.

(ii)   The pessimist: growth is impossible in the long run
The pessimist states that economic growth will inevitably lead to an irrevocable depletion of natural resources and to an irreversible degradation or destruction of natural and environmental constituents. Hence, perspective (ii) is pessimistic about the technological potential (Δb4) to prevent further environmental damage with continuing economic expansion. As the economy requires a minimal availability of environmental quality and resources, there are limits to growth. This perspective has been elaborated in studies by the Club of Rome (see Meadows et al., 1972, 1992; reactions to the first report are summarized in Lecomber, 1975; on the second report, see Nordhaus, 1992). A recent study by Duchin and Lange (1994) used an extended and updated version of the well-known Leontief multi-region multi-sector input–output world model to test the Brundtland Commission's statement that growth and sustainability can go together.

Their conclusion is strongly negative, and they argue that we should rethink how to integrate development of rich and poor countries with environmental sustainability.

An important motivation for perspective (ii) is the second law of thermodynamics. This law states that, in order to sustain or develop a system, low-entropy materials and energy should be imported, while high-entropy materials and energy should be exported (see Boulding, 1966; Georgescu-Roegen, 1971). The traditional economic approach is incomplete here because it examines relative scarcity and optimal allocation based on relative prices. No price system can reflect absolute scarcity. A related critique is that economists only deal with allocation, and not with (optimal) scale and size of an economy (Daly, 1991). A shift in the use of energy and materials in production and consumption can thus be regarded as a way to relax the limits to growth until the point is reached where all thermodynamic potential improvements have been exhausted. Georgescu-Roegen (1971) has demonstrated that a distinction between actors ('funds') and material and energy inputs ('flows') is of the utmost importance in performing a correct calculation of substitution options. Substitution among different types of materials should be regarded in terms of 'replacement' (for example, metal by plastics), and is different from substitution between labour (or capital) and materials which can be characterized by 'saving' of materials or energy (see, for example, Ruth, 1993, and Chapter 59 in this book; see also Smulders, 1995, and van den Bergh, 1999).

A second reason why economic growth in the long run is impossible is that it exerts a negative impact on *living* organisms and systems. Once the carrying capacity of life on Earth is severely degraded, economic growth and perhaps even survival of mankind are jeopardized (see Clark and Munn, 1986). Concrete focal points are the greenhouse effect, tropical deforestation and loss of habitats and biodiversity around the world (see, for example, Arrow et al., 1995 and *Ecological Economics*, 1995). Worrying in this context is the often-mentioned approximate figure of 40 per cent of the natural products of photosynthesis that humans have presently appropriated (Vitousek et al., 1986). Furthermore, ecologists worry about the stability of ecosystems on a larger scale, including systems not directly used by humans, and wider life-support functions. In the context of this particular reasoning, one may regard the debate as mainly one between concerned biologists and optimistic economists, with the first group tending to focus on precautionary and the second on optimization strategies.

(iii)   The technocrat: growth and environmental quality are compatible
The technocrat argues that there is no unique relation between economic growth, in the sense of an increasing valuation of man-made goods and

services, and an expansion of the physical size of production and consumption, in the sense of use of materials and energy ('throughput' in the terminology of Daly, 1991). Indeed, we not only add value to products and services by means of physical flows, but also via labour, knowledge and technology. In other words, just like a labour theory of value, a materials or energy theory of value will be incomplete. Therefore, the question should be whether an economy can realize an ever-growing value added on the basis of a finite amount of natural resources and environmental capacity for storage and assimilation of waste.

The technocrat shows a positive attitude to this issue, as opposed to the pessimist of perspective (ii). According to the technocrat there are options permanently to relax the limits to growth via three channels. First, there are substitution options replacing non-renewable resources or polluting factors in production by renewable capital ($\Delta b5$) and cleaner factors. Substitution will be encouraged if the environment as a production factor becomes scarcer. In that case, prices of resources increase, other prices will rise, and producers and consumers will search for inputs, goods and services that are less environmentally damaging or less resource-intensive. Second, investments ($\Delta r 1$) and technological progress ($\Delta b4$) may imply the same level of production with less resource use and environmental damage. Third, recycling of materials and reuse of products ($\Delta r 1$) can give rise to a lower level of environmental pressure. All three mechanisms emphasize the significance of 'environmental technology' for harmonization of growth and environment (see Goeller and Weinberg, 1976; Dasgupta and Heal, 1979; Simon and Kahn, 1984). Even the 'Factor 4' notion can be regarded as contributing to such technological optimism (Von Weizsäcker et al., 1997).

(iv) The opportunist (carpe diem): growth and environmental degradation are inevitable

Suppose technical possibilities can reconcile growth and environment: will mankind be capable of turning economic development in a way that is sustainable? The answer depends on one's confidence in the adaptive capacity of people, society, government and policy. The fourth perspective shows little of such confidence, and also states that the economic development path can hardly be influenced. Both the rate and the direction of growth are the result of economic decisions by households and firms at the micro-level, largely beyond the control of any planner. Besides, the aspirations of governments regarding economic and social stability are nowadays restricted by international relations and institutions. The evolution of the natural environment is in this perspective not open to discussion: it merely depends on individual actions and public support for environmental policy.

According to perspective (iv), preferences will not adequately affect changes in technology and knowledge (Δb4), so that economic development will be disastrous for the environment. Just as individuals do not have eternal life, mankind may become extinct some day (see, for example, Aalbers, 1995).

(v)   The optimist: growth is necessary for environmental conservation
Changes in preferences (Δb3) and institutions (Δb1) are important for environment and economy. When people care more about the environment – for example, because specific environmental problems become pressing, or more information becomes available – the demand for polluting goods may drop (Δr 2). Furthermore, the consumer may behave more consciously regarding environmental impacts of his/her actions, and become more supportive of stricter environmental policies. This can lead to a changed, 'cleaner' structure of production activity (Δr 3) and consumption.

Optimists have a positive attitude towards such changes in preferences. Some optimists even think that these, as well as institutional transformations, occur in response to economic growth. In other words, optimists highlight the luxurious-good character of the natural environment: growth is an imperative for environmental preservation as it encourages public support as well as financial means for stringent environmental policy.

5. Evaluation
The five perspectives are summarized and systematically compared in Tables 45.1 and 45.2. The first table shows which elements from the theoretical framework of Section 2 are emphasized in the various perspectives. It is clear that this table implies that each perspective can be regarded in terms of a specific weighting of the various factors, and changes therein, as outlined in Sections 2 and 3. This may give an indication of the completeness of the models that implicitly underlie the perspectives. Table 45.2 contains a summary of the previous section. The perspectives are seen mainly to differ in the following ways: they (implicitly) adopt distinct time horizons; they evaluate differently the technical capacity to harmonize growth and environmental quality; and they start from different views of mankind.

An evident question is whether it is possible to indicate which perspective receives most support from facts. The immaterialist perspective (i) may be considered as the most critical on the conventional economic analysis of growth. It criticizes fundamentally the assumptions and implications of standard (neoclassical) economic theory. In a concrete sense, it argues that it is certainly incorrect to think that we increase our welfare as long as the GDP rises, even if environmental quality remains unchanged.

The pessimist perspective (ii) directs the attention mainly on to the physical and biological–ecological dimension of the economy. Most economists

Table 45.1   A comparison of the five perspectives based on the framework

Perspective	Basic factors	Outcomes	Changes
(i) Immaterialist	b3: preferences	r2: composition demand	Δb3, volume material welfare
(ii) Pessimist	b4: technology b5: capital b6: environment	r1: input mix r3: sector structure	Material/energy use, depletion
(iii) Technocrat	b4: technology b5: capital	r1: input mix r3: sector structure	Δb4, Δr1, Δr3, appraisal of 'man-made goods'
(iv) Opportunist	b1: institutions b3: preferences	r2: composition demand r3: sector structure	Δb2, Δb3, volume economy, depletion, pollution
(v) Optimist	b1: institutions b3: preferences	r2: composition demand r3: sector structure	Δb3, Δb4, Δr2, Δr3, environment as luxurious good

nowadays admit that there are physical limits to the size of production, i.e. that infinite physical growth is not possible. In addition, there is much uncertainty about the natural resilience and stabilizing capacity of the biosphere, among other things, with respect to the increase of greenhouse gases in the atmosphere. Nevertheless, the physical scale of the economy is still increasing, both in terms of materials and energy use. The dilemma of perspective (ii) is that there is no straightforward and universal relationship between the value added, and the physical requirements for production and consumption. In principle, the economy can grow without physical growth. Service sectors may have a large growth potential, although physical capital, materials and energy are required. For the moment, however, efficiency seems to be increasing, especially due to modern information technology. In response to this, many supporters of perspective (ii) emphasize that complementarity prevails over substitution as a relationship between, on the one hand, environmental capital – provision of production and consumption conditions and goods – and material/energy use, and, on the other hand, production factors like labour and man-made capital. To support this, differential characteristics of environmental capital are often stressed, notably uniqueness, irreversibility and multifunctionality. In other words, perspective (ii) adheres to the concept of strong sustainability, that is, limited substitution of environmental by economic capital (see Daly and Cobb, 1989; Pearce et al., 1990). The main problem may be caused by

Table 45.2 Characteristics of the five perspectives

Perspective	Time horizon	Ideology	Prediction	Policy implication
(i) Immaterialist	Short–long	Ethical–psychological	Happiness via non-material items	Reconsider goals
(ii) Pessimist	Long	Physical–material–biological	Lower material welfare	(Selective) contraction
(iii) Technocrat	Short–medium	Technological–human-ingenuity	Hyper-technological world	Encourage technological progress
(iv) Opportunist	Short–long	International–social–political	Catastrophe scenario	Present more important than future
(v) Optimist	Short	Market–welfare–financing	Responsible man, transition to other vision	Support of market and democracy

absolute scarcity of non-renewable resources. Although this seems something amenable for empirical research, economists are not in agreement on how to come to an objective measure of scarcity (Smith, 1980; Cleveland and Stern, in Chapter 7 in this book).

The *carpe diem* perspective (iv) is rather cynical and leaves us little hope and room for discussion. To counter it, some authors note the fact that 'economic growth has been a relatively episodic phenomenon in human history' (Ayres, 1997, p.2). Furthermore, some confidence in mankind is necessary to be able to find solutions to pressing economic–environmental conflicts. Both the technocrat and the optimist show such confidence. Both believe that growth is certainly feasible without further degradation of environmental capital. In the past, mankind has shown many times that it has plenty of ingenuity and flexibility to react adequately to large-scale environmental transformation and threatening resource scarcity. Perspectives (iii) and (v) are therefore optimistic regarding technological options, adaptive preferences, and changes in behaviour and institutions. Perspective (iii) contrasts mostly with the thermodynamically motivated perspective (ii). However, it is difficult to come up with an absolute limit to the economic output in value terms that can be obtained from a given material/energy resource input (Ayres, 1997, p.28; Stern, 1997). Optimists go one step further, and believe that the environment has many characteristics of a luxurious good. Hence economic growth is considered as necessary for increasing consciousness regarding nature and environment. Indeed, empirical research indicates that for a specific class of environmental problems the relationship between income and the level of environmental pressure shows an inverted U curve (see de Bruyn and Heintz, Chapter 46 of this book). This curve indicates that if the income level is low, people care little about the environment. Beyond a certain turning point, however, economic growth no longer goes along with further environmental degradation. Growth may even motivate such an increase in environmentally supportive and enhancing activities that it becomes compatible with an improvement of environmental quality. The conclusions of these empirical studies can, however, be criticized on several grounds. First, results obtained from cross-section data (various countries) cannot simply be translated to (future) time-series for specific countries. Second, the existence of international trade and reallocation of activities generate problems of interpretation because a complete account of interactions between the spatial distribution of economic activities causing high environmental pressure is missing. Finally, empirical studies only focus on particular aspects of environmental pressure that are not representative of categories of environmental problems that are related to the carrying capacity and natural resilience of ecosystems (see Arrow et al., 1995; Ayres, 1995).

654   *Environmental macroeconomics*

6. Conclusion

In general, it is difficult to conclude unequivocally about the reconciliation of environmental conservation and preservation and growth objectives. Moderate optimism characterizes many individuals and policy documents, largely based the argument that we have solved similar problems in the past. An important objection against optimism is that one cannot simply extrapolate historical trends, certainly not in the long run. Instead, trends should be questioned, based on theoretical and empirical approaches covering all relevant issues related to ecosystem resilience and destruction, unique and scarce resources and serious pollution and health risks.

Different perspectives have created a situation in which people do not talk the same language. This can be rather confusing. Our framework offers some insights to explain differences and place different perspectives in a consistent framework. Primarily the choice of a time horizon and the subjective evaluation of technical potential, the flexibility of social preferences and institutions, and the stability and resilience of natural systems explain differences between the perspectives. Confrontation between disciples of the different perspectives, as well as between social and natural sciences, may perhaps provide more consensus some day.

References

Aalbers, R. (1995), 'Extinction of the human race: Doom-mongering or reality?', *De Economist*, **143**, 111–40.
Arrow, K.J., B. Bolin, R. Costanza, P. Dasgupta, C. Folke, C.S. Holling, B.-O. Jansson, S. Levin, K.-G. Mäler, C. Perrings and D. Pimentel (1995), 'Economic growth, carrying capacity, and the environment', *Science*, **268**, 520–21.
Ayres, R.U. (1995), 'Economic growth: politically necessary but *not* environmentally friendly', *Ecological Economics*, **15**, 97–9.
Ayres, R.U. (1997), 'Theories of economic growth', working paper 97/13/EPS, Centre for the Management of Environmental Resources, INSEAD, Fontainebleau, France.
Beckerman, W. (1976), *In Defence of Economic Growth*, London: Jonathan Cape.
Beckerman, W. (1995), *Small is Stupid*, London: Duckworth.
Bergh, J.C.J.M. van den (1996), *Ecological Economics and Sustainable Development: Theory, Methods and Applications*, Cheltenham, UK and Brookfield, US: Edward Elgar.
Bergh, J.C.J.M. van den (1999), 'Materials, capital, direct/indirect substitution and mass balance production functions, *Land Economics*, **74**, November (forthcoming).
Boulding, K.E. (1966), 'The economics of the coming spaceship earth'. in H. Jarret (ed.), *Environmental Quality in a Growing Economy*. Baltimore, MD: Johns Hopkins University Press.
Bromley, D.W. (1995), 'Property rights and natural resource damage assessments', *Ecological Economics*, **14**, 129–36.
Clark, W.C. and R.E. Munn (eds) (1986), *Sustainable Development of the Biosphere*, Cambridge, UK: Cambridge University Press.
Daly, H.E. (1991), *Steady-State Economics*, 2nd edn, Washington, DC: Island Press.
Daly, H.E. and W. Cobb (1989), *For the Common Good: Redirecting the Economy Toward Community, the Environment and a Sustainable Future*, Boston: Beacon Press.
Daly, H.E. and K.N. Townsend (eds) (1993), *Valuing the Earth: Economics, Ecology, Ethics*, Cambridge, MA: MIT Press. (1980 edition: *Economics, Ecology and Ethics: Essays Toward a Steady-State Economy*, San Francisco: Freeman and Co.)

Dasgupta, P. and G.M. Heal (1979), *Economic Theory and Exhaustible Resources*, Cambridge, UK: Cambridge University Press.
Duchin, F. and G.M. Lange, in association with K. Thonstad and A. Idenburg (1994), *The Future of the Environment: Ecological Economics and Technical Change*, Oxford: Oxford University Press.
Ecological Economics, Vol. 15, (1995), Forum on 'Economic growth, carrying capacity, and the environment', with reactions from 14 economists and ecologists to Arrow et al. (1995).
Georgescu-Roegen, N. (1971), *The Entropy Law and the Economic Process*, Cambridge, MA: Harvard University Press.
Goeller, H. and A. Weinberg (1976), 'The age of substitutability', *Science*, **191**, 683–9.
Gowdy, J.M. (1997), 'The value of biodiversity: markets, society, and ecosystems', *Land Economics*, **73**, 25–41.
Lecomber, R. (1975), *Economic Growth versus the Environment*, London: Macmillan.
Meadows, D.H., D.L. Meadows, J. Randers and W.W. Behrens III (1972), *The Limits to Growth*, New York: Universe Books.
Meadows, D.H., D.L. Meadows and J. Randers (1992), *Beyond the Limits: Confronting Global Collapse; Envisioning a Sustainable Future*, Post Mills: Chelsea Green.
Mishan, E.J. (1967), *The Cost of Economic Growth*, London: Staples Press.
Mishan, E.J. (1977), *The Economic Growth Debate: An Assessment*. London: George Allen & Unwin.
Myers, N. and J.L. Simon (1994), *Scarcity or Abundance? A Debate on the Environment*, New York: W.W. Norton & Co.
Nordhaus, W.D. (1992), 'Lethal Model 2: The limits to growth revisited', *Brooking Papers on Economic Activity*, **2**, 1–59.
Pearce, D.W., E.B. Barbier and A. Markandya (1990), *Sustainable Development: Economics and Environment in the Third World*, Aldershot, UK and Brookfield, US: Edward Elgar.
Pezzey, J. (1993), 'Sustainability: an interdisciplinary guide', *Environmental Values*, **1**, 321–62.
Ruth, M. (1993), *Integrating Economics, Ecology and Thermodynamics*, Dordrecht: Kluwer Academic Publishers.
Schumacher, E.F. (1973), *Small is Beautiful: Economics as if People Mattered*, New York: Harper and Row.
Simon, J.L. and H. Kahn (1984), *The Resourceful Earth*, Oxford: Basil Blackwell.
Smith, V.K. (1980), 'The evaluation of natural resource adequacy: elusive quest or frontier of economic analysis?', *Land Economics*, **65**, 257–98.
Smulders, S. (1995), 'Entropy, environment and endogenous economic growth', *International Tax and Public Finance*, **2**, 319–40.
Stern, D.I. (1997), 'Limits to substitution and irreversibility in production and consumption: a neoclassical interpretation of ecological economics', *Ecological Economics*, **21**, 197–215.
Turner, R.K., D.W. Pearce and I. Bateman (1994), *Environmental Economics*, London: Harvester-Wheatsheaf.
Vitousek, P. et al. (1986), 'Human appropriation of the products of photosynthesis', *Bioscience*, **34**, 368–73.
Weizsäcker, E. von, A.B. Lovins and L.H. Lovins (1997), *Factor Four: Doubling Wealth – Halving Resource Use, A Report to the Club of Rome*, London: Earthscan.

46 The environmental Kuznets curve hypothesis

Sander M. de Bruyn and Roebijn J. Heintz[1]

1. Introduction

One particular aspect in the growth-versus-environment debate that has evoked much discussion in the 1990s has been the finding of a so-called 'environmental Kuznets curve' (EKC) between certain types of pollutants and per capita income. According to the EKC, environmental quality declines during early stages of economic development but improves in later stages. Graphically, this visualizes to the inverted U curve between pollutants and economic development, similar to the 'bell-shaped' relationship which Simon Kuznets (1955) suggested exists between income inequality and per capita income.

Acceptance of an EKC as a descriptive pattern for various types of environmental pressure would suggest that environmental deterioration is only a temporary phenomenon, associated with a particular stage of development. Holtz-Eakin and Selden (1995, p. 3) remarked that the EKC 'raises the tantalising possibility that instead of there being a *trade-off* between greenhouse gases and economic growth, faster growth could serve as a part of the *solution* to the world-wide emissions dilemma' (original italics). Hence if the EKC adequately describes the patterns of environmental deterioration during the course of economic development, economic growth may be beneficial and not harmful to the state of the environment.

The benefits of economic growth for environmental protection had earlier been hypothesized by growth 'optimists' such as Beckerman (1972) and Simon (1981), who argued that due to income growth people are willing to spend a larger share of their budget on environmental protection. With the finding of an EKC, this hypothesis seems to be empirically supported. The inverted U relationship between income and environmental pressure is nowadays regarded by some as a 'stylized fact', a generally applicable notion asserting that environmental pressure decreases after a particular level of income has been reached (cf. World Bank, 1992; Beckerman, 1992). But the question is whether things are as simple as that. To accept the EKC as a stylized fact, empirical evidence must be convincing and explanations for the phenomenon must be unambiguous.

This chapter investigates the evidence and explanations that may support the EKC hypothesis. Section 2 provides a background to the empirical growth-versus-environment debate related to the older body of research on patterns of resource consumption. Section 3 gives an overview of studies that have identified empirical regularities in the relationship between environmental pressure and income. In Section 4 the mechanisms explaining EKCs will be investigated and Section 5 explores in more detail the policy relevance of the EKC hypothesis. Discussion and conclusions will be dealt with in Section 6.

2. Background

Until the late 1960s, the consumption of raw materials, energy and natural resources was believed to grow almost at the same rate as economic growth. This development gave rise to a growing concern for the Earths' natural resource availability, which was firmly put forward by the Club of Rome's *Limits to Growth* (Meadows et al., 1972). This report assumes a positive and rather deterministic relationship between economic output and material input.

The work by the Club of Rome has been criticized on both theoretical and empirical grounds. Empirical work by Malenbaum (1978), for example, showed that the ratio of consumption of certain metals to income was declining in developed economies during the 1970s, which conflicts with the predictions set out in the *Limits to Growth*. This induced Malenbaum to derive an inverted U-shaped relationship between the intensity of metal use and income, which became later known as the 'intensity-of-use hypothesis' (Auty, 1985). The inverted U curve thus derived reveals that intensity of materials use decreases after a particular level of income has been reached. Other studies have subsequently found a general tendency after 1973 of an absolute decline in consumption of several materials, a tendency that is most pronounced in the developed economies (Williams et al., 1987; Jänicke et al., 1989; Tilton, 1990).

Since the beginning of the 1990s empirical data on various pollutants became available through the Global Environmental Monitoring System on air and water quality (GEMS), the Toxic Release Inventory (TRI) on toxic emissions from US manufacturers, the environmental data compendium by the OECD, as well as the CO_2 emissions estimates from the Oak Ridge National Laboratory (ORNL). These data have facilitated testing of whether the inverted U curve hypothesis also holds for output-based indicators of environmental pressure. Empirical evidence for an inverted U-shaped relationship between certain types of pollutants and income was first generated by Grossman and Krueger (1991), followed by a number of other studies. The observed inverted U curve has been labelled by Panayotou (1993) as the environmental Kuznets curve (EKC), which has become a common catchword in the literature. The analogy with the 'bell-shaped' relation between income inequality and income levels found by Kuznets in the discussion about income growth and environmental pressure is the following (see Figure 46.1). During the first stage of income growth (economic development) environmental pressure grows faster than GDP (phase 1). This is followed by a period in which environmental pres-

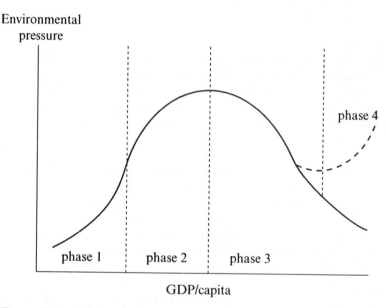

Figure 46.1   Relation between income growth and environmental pressure

sure increases, but slower than the rate of economic growth (phase 2). After a particular level of income has been reached, environmental pressure declines despite the growth in GDP (phase 3). In fact, income growth is then 'de-linked' from environmental pressure. If this trend of de-linking is continued, then there is a genuine EKC. If, however, the de-linking is not persistent and followed by a period of 're-linking' (phase 4), we speak of N-shaped curves (de Bruyn and Opschoor, 1997). What does empirical evidence teach us in this respect?

3.   Empirical evidence on the EKC

The empirical evidence for the existence of an EKC has been gathered in a number of studies that share common characteristics with respect to the data and methods employed. The data used in these kinds of studies are typically a 'panel' of observations in various countries for some moments in time. The common method to test for the various possible relationships between environmental pressure *EP* and income *Y* is to fit the following regression or basic reduced-form model to the available panel of data:

$$EP_{i,t} = \alpha_{i,t} + \beta_1 Y_{i,t} + \beta_2 Y_{i,t}^2 + \beta_3 Y_{i,t}^3 + \beta_4 Z_{i,t} + e_{i,t} \qquad (46.1)$$

Here the subscript *i* stands for a country index, *t* is a time index, α is a constant (or the average level of *EP* when income has no significant influence on environmental pressure), β_k indicates the relative importance of the *k* explanatory variables, $Z_{i,t}$ relates to other variables of influence on environmental degradation, and $e_{i,t}$ is the normally distributed error term. Model (46.1) allows us to test seven distinguished forms of environmental–economic relationships:

1. $\beta_1 > 0$ and $\beta_2 = \beta_3 = 0$ reveals a monotonic increasing relationship indicating that rising incomes are associated with rising levels of emissions.
2. $\beta_1 < 0$ and $\beta_2 = \beta_3 = 0$ reveals a monotonic decreasing relationship indicating that rising incomes are associated with declining levels of emissions.
3. $\beta_1 > 0$, $\beta_2 < 0$ and $\beta_3 = 0$ reveals an inverted U-shaped quadratic relationship, representing the EKC.
4. $\beta_1 < 0$, $\beta_2 > 0$ and $\beta_3 = 0$ reveals a U-shaped quadratic relationship opposite the EKC.
5. $\beta_1 > 0$, $\beta_2 < 0$ and $\beta_3 > 0$ reveals a cubic polynomial, representing the N-shaped figure.
6. $\beta_1 < 0$, $\beta_2 > 0$ and $\beta_3 < 0$ reveals a cubic polynomial opposite the N-shaped curve (first declining, then rising and subsequently declining levels of *EP*).
7. $\beta_1 = \beta_2 = \beta_3 = 0$ reveals a flat pattern, indicating that emissions are not influenced by the level of income.

The foregoing indicates that the EKC relation is only one of the possible outcomes of model (46.1). The turning point of the EKC relation is obtained by setting the derivative of (46.1) equal to zero, which yields $Y_t = -\beta_1/2\beta_2$.

A large number of econometric studies have used model (46.1) or a log-linear transformation of (46.1) to test for the emergence of an EKC in a wide variety of output-based environmental pressure indicators. Among the most cited studies are Shafik and Bandyopadhyay (1992), Lucas et al. (1992), Panayotou (1993), Selden and Song (1994), Grossman and Krueger (1995) and Holtz-Eakin and Selden (1995). Overviews of these (and some other) studies can be found in Stern et al. (1996), Ekins (1997), Ansuategi et al. (1997) and Stern (1997). Interpretations and (political) implications of the alleged EKCs have been discussed by the World Bank (1992, 1995) and critically reviewed by Arrow et al. (1995). Their publication in *Science* has provoked widely diverging reactions (see the collections of short contributions in *Ecological Economics*, 1995; *Environment and Development Economics*, 1996, and *Ecological Applications*, 1996). The search for empirical evidence in support of the EKC and its policy implication is ongoing (both *Environment and Development Economics*, 1997, and *Ecological Economics*, 1996 have devoted special issues on empirical estimates of EKCs).

Table 46.1 summarizes the empirical work of studies that have investigated the relation between specific indicators of environmental pressure and levels of income based on model (46.1). Only those studies have been included that: (i) are published, and (ii) employ model (46.1) without major modifications so that the results are comparable.[2] Only those pollutants for which at least two estimates were available have been included in Table 46.1. For each pollutant at least one study has confirmed an EKC, although the per capita income turning point for CO_2 emissions lies outside the sample range. But the most remarkable result when comparing these studies is that there is no consensus on how the various pollutants develop along economic development. Except for NO_x emissions, conflicting patterns have been found for all pollutants. This is especially striking in the case of water quality indicators such as the amount of faecal coliform or dissolved oxygen in rivers. For these indicators, Grossman and Krueger reported an EKC, but Shafik and Bandyopadhyay and Torras and Boyce found either N-shaped, monotonically increasing or flat patterns. Most studies have investigated atmospheric sulphur and particulate pollutants and these pollutants often reveal an EKC, but the turning points found differ considerably among the studies. Table 46.1 confirms an earlier result by Ekins (1997, p. 812) who remarked that 'none of the pollutants unequivocally shows an inverse U relationship where studies have been done by more than one group of researchers'.[3]

The wide variety in discovered patterns puts serious doubts on the validity of the EKC hypothesis. A general explanation for the differences is that data and methods employed vary among the studies. More specifically, the differences can be ascribed to: (i) the use of emissions or concentrations as indicators of environmental pressure; (ii) different estimations methods that have been used; (iii) different sets of countries that have been included in the panel; (iv) different methods employed to transfer the national per capita income data to comparable monetary units; and (v) the use of variables other than income that have been included in the regressions in order to explain some of the variation in environmental pressure. These five characteristics explain to a large extent the different findings among various studies and will be discussed below in more detail.

Emissions or concentrations as indicators
Most of the empirical evidence on EKCs deals with indicators of water and air pollutants.[4] These can be measured in terms of emissions or concentrations, which matters for the estimated turning points. The studies that investigated ambient air concentrations found, for example, lower turning points than those that investigated emissions (see Table 46.1). Ambient air quality is often measured within cities and the lower turning points can be explained with reference to the relative importance of urban air quality over national emissions, and by the rise in land rents in urban cities which have stimulated industries to move out (Selden and Song, 1994, p. 148). The process of economic development seems to be associated with de-urbanization and dispersal of industries after particular income levels (cf. Shukla and Parikh, 1992; Stern et al., 1996).

Estimation methods
Different studies based on model (46.1) have employed different econometric techniques to determine the values and significance of the coefficients. This makes the results only weakly comparable. For example, some studies have simply pooled the data, while others have corrected for country-specific differences using fixed or random effects. The importance of country-specific effects in a panel of countries has been highlighted by Liddle (1996). This favours the use of fixed and random effects estimates that capture country-specific effects such as latitude. Stern et al. (1996) have argued in favour of generalized least squares (GLS) methods to correct for heteroscedasticity that may be present in the errors.[5] For example, pollution data may be more accurately measured in higher-income countries, or large countries may average out variations in emissions within their economies.

In comparing several methods, Selden and Song (1994) show that different econometric techniques may have a considerable impact on the results. In the case of SO_2 emissions, for example, their pooled cross-section estimates point at a U-shaped curve (though not significant), while both the fixed and random effects models showed an EKC (with different turning points at \$8700 and \$10 300 respectively).

Sample of countries
The outcomes of the studies may be highly influenced by the sample of countries and by the exchange rates that have been used to compare the per

Table 46.1 *Overview of empirical studies that have used model (46.1) for estimating the relationship between pollutants and income*

Authors	Methods[a] (effects)	SO2 (peak) (through) type[b]	Part.[c] (peak) type	NOx emis. (peak)	CO2 emis. (peak)	Faecal coliform (peak)	1/Dissolved oxygen (peak)[d]	De-forestation rates	Exch. rates	Additional variables
Grossman and Krueger, 1995	GLS (re)	N (4100) (13000) conc.	EKC (6200) conc.			EKC (8000)	EKC (2700)		PPP	Lagged income
Shafik and Bandyopadhyay, 1992	OLS (fe)	EKC (3700) conc.	EKC (3300) conc.		MI	N (1200) (11400)	MI	flat	PPP	Variety of other variables
Panayotou, 1993	OLS (pcs)	EKC (3000) emis.	EKC (4500) emis.	EKC (5500)				EKC (1200)	MER	
Selden and Song, 1994[e]	GLS (re, fe)	EKC (10300) emis.	EKC (10300)	EKC (11200)					PPP	Population density
Torras and Boyce, 1998	OLS (pcs)	N (3400) (14000) conc.	flat			Flat	N (5100) (19900)		PPP	Inequality variables

Holtz-Eakin and Selden, 1995	OLS (fe)	EKC (35400)	PPP

Notes:

N = N-shaped curve, U = U-shaped curve, EKC = inverted U-shaped curve, MI = monotonically increasing curve, flat = all parameters except intercept insignificant. Peaks rounded at US$100.

[a]GLS = generalized least squares, OLS = ordinary least squares, re = random effects, fe = fixed effects, pcs = pooled cross-section.

[b]Conc = concentrations, emis = emissions, PPP = purchasing power parity, MER = market exchange rate.

[c]Particles differ with respect to how these are being measured.

[d]Dissolved oxygen is an indicator for environmental quality, not degradation, and for these reasons we take the inverse of dissolved oxygen. Hence an EKC in fact reflects a U-shaped curve and the monotonically decreasing pattern found by Shafik and Bandyopadhyay reflects continuous deterioration.

[e]Turning points for models with population density, for SO_2 using random effects, for particles and NO_x using fixed effects.

Other studies not included in the table deal with:

Study	Method	Pollutants
De Bruyn et al. (1998)	Time-series	SO_2, NO_x, CO_2 emissions
De Bruyn (1997)	Various	SO_2 emissions
Ekins (1997)	Various	Multidimensional indicator
Horvath (1996)	OLS (fe, pcs)	Energy consumption
Kaufmann et al. (1998)	GLS (fe, re)	SO_2 concentrations
Liddle (1996)	OLS (fe)	SO_2 NO_x emissions
Lucas et al. (1992)	OLS (fe)	Toxic intensities
Suri and Chapman (1998)	OLS (fe)	Energy consumption
Xepapedeas and Amri (1995)	Probit	SO_2 concentrations, dissolved oxygen

capita incomes of these countries. When two different databases with a different sample of countries are used, the outcomes may contradict each other. For example, Grossman and Krueger have explored the GEMS database for dissolved oxygen and faecal coliform in rivers. In both cases an EKC was found with turning points of near $2700 and $8000 respectively. Shafik and Bandyopadhyay, however, used for these two indicators the database from the Canadian Center for Inland Waters and found an N-shaped form for faecal coliform, while dissolved oxygen diminished monotonically with income.

The position of the countries with economies in transition in particular deserves attention. During the late 1980s, the emissions of sulphur and particulates per unit of GDP in countries like Poland and the Czech Republic were about 20–30 times higher than in OECD economies. Hence these countries should be recognized as outliers in the sample and should be removed from the analysis. Unfortunately, most studies do not mention which countries have been used in the sample, but we suspect that most studies included observations from former communist countries.

Exchange rates
If a certain sample of countries has been chosen, the type of income data is another important feature that explains why the results of empirical studies differ so much. Income data from individual countries have to be brought under a common denominator using exchange rates. The exchange rates that have been used are either market exchange rates (MER) or purchasing power parities (PPP). The common argument in favour of using purchasing power parities is that these data more adequately reflect the 'wealth of nations', as they reflect what consumers can buy domestically with their incomes.

The divergence between MER and PPP income data is substantial, especially for countries with various import barriers, as was the case in the former communist countries. It is therefore not surprising that the studies that found EKCs for emissions of sulphur and particulates peak near the per capita income levels of the former communist countries (about US$3000 in market exchange rates (cf. Panayotou, 1993) and about US$8000 in purchasing power parities (cf. Selden and Song, 1994)). Hence the different turning points between the Panayatou (1993) and Selden and Song (1994) studies could be entirely attributable to the different exchange rates that have been used.

The use of other explanatory variables
Some studies have added variables other than income to the regressions; these are also listed in Table 46.1. The inclusion of other variables in the

regressions aims to improve the fit of the estimations and to provide additional explanations for the patterns of pollutants along economic development or income growth. Variables that have been added include: population density (Selden and Song, 1994), lagged income (Grossman and Krueger, 1995); trade variables (Shafik and Bandyopadhyay, 1992; Suri and Chapman, 1998), variables representing the structure of the economy (Lucas et al., 1992; Suri and Chapman, 1998, Kaufmann et al., 1998), and variables for capturing political and civil rights (Shafik and Bandyopadhyay, 1992; Torras and Boyce, 1998). When such variables are related to income, they capture part of the income-related effects and may result in different turning points than in estimates without such variables. Some authors explicitly show that the inclusion of the variables indeed has a considerable impact on the estimated turning points of the EKC (cf. Suri and Chapman, 1998).

Although the addition of explanatory variables other than income both improves the fit of the estimations and provides some explanations, this approach has some disadvantages as well. For example, if $Z_{i,t}$ represents civil rights or the share of international trade and is related to income, multicollinearity can be expected between $Z_{i,t}$ and the various orders of $Y_{i,t}$. This makes the regression estimates difficult to interpret since the individual effects of the variables cannot be disentangled.

4. Explanations for the EKC

The previous section has shown that various studies do not unambiguously point at the EKC as an adequate description of the pollutant–income relationship for a number of substances. In addition, the various studies have not yet reached agreement on the explanations of an eventual EKC. Confusion about the driving forces of the relationship between environmental pressure and income is due to the use of a reduced-form model for estimation. The single equation (46.1) that is used in most studies is supposed to capture the structural model in which income influences technology, the composition of economic output and environmental policy, and changes in these factors in turn influence both environmental pressure and income. Thus in the structural model income relates only indirectly to environmental pressure. By the assumption of a direct link between income and environmental pressure and the omission of variables relating to technological innovation, composition of economic output and environmental policy, the model *reduces* to (46.1). The advantage of working with a reduced-form model lies in the fact that the total, direct and indirect, influence of income on environmental pressure is estimated. A disadvantage, as pointed out by Grossman and Krueger (1995), is that it is not unambiguously clear why the estimated relationship exists and especially what kind of interpretation should be given to the estimated coefficients of the model in (46.1).

Since the model itself does not provide insight into the factors that can explain the EKC, explanations offered by various authors are nothing more than propositions, derived either from theory, from other empirical work, or from intuitive notions. The following explanations have been proposed for the EKC.

Behavioural changes and preferences

The most common explanation for the shape of the EKC is the notion that when a country achieves a sufficiently high standard of living, people attach increasing value to environmental amenities (cf. Pezzey, 1989; Selden and Song, 1994; Baldwin, 1995). Environmental quality is thus regarded as a luxury good, that is, the income elasticity of demand for environmental goods is higher than one. In other words, after a particular level of income, the willingness to pay for a clean environment rises by a greater proportion than income. This will be reflected in people's susceptibility to devoting a larger part of the budget to a clean environment, such as through defensive expenditures, donations to environmental organizations, or the selection of less environmentally damaging products.

Despite the attractiveness of behavioural changes as an explanation of the EKC, most (contingent) valuation studies have found an income elasticity of demand for environmental services smaller than unity (see Flores and Carson, 1995; Kriström and Riera, 1996). A study by Komen et al. (1996), analysing public R&D expenditures for environmental protection in OECD countries at different income levels, finds an income elasticity of demand that is positive, albeit significantly lower than one.

Institutional changes

The steepness of the EKC in stage 1 is often attributed to policy distortions, such as the subsidization of energy consumption, and to market failures such as ill-defined property rights for natural resources and the lack of payment for environmental externalities (Panayotou, 1993). The second stage of the EKC is associated with the removal of subsidies and other distortions, establishment of property rights for natural resources, and the initiation of policies to internalize environmental externalities. The subsequent stages of the EKC are then ascribed to the introduction of stricter environmental policies, the raising of public awareness, education, protection of intellectual property and so on. Indirectly, people may increase their support for environmental policies via elections and referenda, which fuels institutional changes. Along with economic development, societies advance their social, legal and fiscal infrastructures essential to enforce environmental regulation.

Institutional changes triggered by citizens' demand for cleaner environments are more likely to occur in democratic countries. Empirical evidence for the influence of democracy on pollutants exists but is scarce and contradictory. Shafik and Bandyopadhyay (1992) test for the influence of political and civil rights on, among others, ambient sulphur concentrations, and find that these are higher in more democratic countries. However, Torras and Boyce (1998) find opposite results when dividing the sample into a subset of high- and low-income countries. Most of the pollutants investigated in their study are substantially lower in more democratic low-income countries.

Technological and organizational changes
As countries develop over time, industry and government replace their capital stock with new capital which is usually more efficient. The vintage of technology is a crucial determinant of the environmental consequences of economic growth, and replaced capital is typically more efficient and environmentally benign. Technological innovation can benefit or harm the environment, but on balance innovation in technology and organization may increase efficiency to the benefit of the environment. Government policy may provide an important impetus for environmentally benign innovation. In the past the focus of both governments and business has been primarily on the development and application of 'end-of-pipe technology' but, as remarked in the environmental management literature, today there is a growing trend among industries to reconsider their production processes and thereby take environmental consequences of production into account (cf. Steger, 1996). This concerns not only 'traditional' technological aspects but also the organization of production as well as the design of products. Companies slowly become accustomed to 'green thinking', which may result in dematerialization of products and increased possibilities for recycling of waste products, with the potential to reduce the environmental intensity of GDP. The overall environmental success provided by (voluntary) corporate strategies such as 'pollution prevention', 'closing the loop' and 'design for the environment' is difficult to estimate empirically (Hertwich, 1997). Technological changes associated with the production process may also result in changes in the input mix of materials and fuels. Material substitution may be an important element of advanced economies (cf. Labys and Wadell, 1989) that may result in lower environmental impacts.

Structural changes
Changes in consumer behaviour, institutional changes and changes in international competitiveness may result in changes in the composition of

economic activities that take place in a country, with associated changes in environmental pressure. Typically, countries pass through a number of stages of development, from subsistence farming, to more intensive agriculture, to industrialization, and ultimately to a more service-sector-based economy (Baldwin, 1995). When agriculture and heavy industry make up the largest share of the economy, environmental pressure grows with increasing production. But when heavy industry gives way to light consumer products industry, the growth in environmental pressure decreases. When finally the service sector accounts for the dominant share of the economy, environmental pressure may decline.

Although structural change is a very intuitive notion, empirical evidence is scarce. Lucas et al. (1992) found evidence for the impact of differences in the structure of production on toxic manufacturing emissions.[6] Suri and Chapman (1998) include in their regressions a variable $Z_{i,t}$, representing the share of manufacturing in GDP and find this variable to have a significantly positive influence on the levels of energy consumption, indicating that a higher industrial share of GDP is associated with more energy use. de Bruyn (1997), however, comes to opposite conclusions when applying decomposition analysis to the development of sulphur emissions in the Netherlands and Western Germany. Structural changes have not been a dominant factor in the reduction of SO_2 emissions in either country, at least not during the 1980s.

International reallocation
The alleged emergence of structural change in production has been linked with consumption and international trade by, among others, Arrow et al. (1995), Stern et al. (1996), Ekins (1997) and Rothman (1998). If changes in the structure of production in developed economies are not accompanied by equivalent changes in the structure of consumption, the EKC may simply record displacement of dirty industries to less developed economies.[7] An attractive feature of this 'displacement hypothesis' is that the reallocation of dirty industries can explain the inverted U curve effectively: decreases of pollutants in developed and increases in developing countries.

Empirical evidence on displacement is almost absent because both emissions and concentration indicators of water and air pollutants relate to the production side of the economy and information on the pollution intensity of international trade is lacking. Among the few exceptions is Rothman (1998), who investigated the role of consumption in determining the EKC. His results suggest that displacement may provide an important explanation for the reduction of pollutants in developed economies. Others have investigated the role of international trade on the patterns of emissions by including in model (46.1) a variable $Z_{i,t}$ representing the trade volume of the economy. Shafik and Bandyopadhyay (1992) found mixed evidence for the effects of trade on the various indicators they have used. In the case of ambient sulphur concentrations, more trade seems to result in lower concentrations, which may reflect efficiency improvements in resource use due to increasing competition. Suri and Chapman (1998), however, came to opposite conclusions for energy consumption when taking into consideration the composition of international trade. Countries that export more manufactured goods tend to have a higher energy consumption, which may be seen as evidence for the 'displacement hypothesis'.

Balancing the arguments
Which of the (combination of) factors proposed above dominates the EKC? This is difficult to determine since different factors are not independent. For example, behavioural changes may have technological, structural and institutional implications and may influence trade patterns as well. But, as explained above, the use of reduced-form models hampers any insight into the underlying causes of the EKCs. Different authors have therefore been able to emphasize dissimilar explanations and there is no consensus on the dominating factor. It could be argued that the lack of insight into the process that causes pollution to curve downwards after particular income levels have been reached makes it difficult to draw specific policy implications from an (alleged) EKC. For it is unclear which elements effective environmental policies should encompass to reduce pollution. Yet virtually all of the studies that investigated EKCs have hinted at the important policy implications of their work. The question of which valid policy implications may follow from the EKC will be discussed in the next section.

5. What are the policy implications of an alleged EKC?
An extreme policy implication of EKCs is that policies promoting economic growth are a sufficient criterion to safeguard the environment. Beckerman (1992, p. 491), for example, states that 'the strong correlation between incomes and the extent to which environmental protection measures are adopted demonstrates that, in the longer run, the surest way to improve your environment is to become rich'. Others, such as Shafik and Bandyopadhyay (1992) are more cautious and acknowledge the importance of environmental policies that may or may not be implemented when economies develop. According to the framework outlined in the present chapter, it can be argued that statements such as that by Beckerman, are both preliminary and superficial: preliminary, given the lack of clear unambiguous evidence on the patterns of emissions during the course of economic development and economic growth (see Section 3); and

superficial, given the lack of consensus about the process driving the ECK (see Section 4). In addition, there are several points that impede a clear policy conclusion derived from the EKCs, related to unclear answers to the following questions:

1. Is the EKC valid for all types of environmental pressure?
2. Is the EKC valid for all countries, individually and collectively?
3. Is the EKC permanent?
4. Is the EKC optimal?

Positive answers to these questions would grant the EKC policy relevance. Negative answers would indicate that the validity and policy relevance of EKCs is partial at best – partial with respect to countries, indicators, time and cost-effectiveness.

Is the EKC relation valid for all types of environmental pressure?
Evidence that environmental problems are solved at higher levels of income only exists for a few selected indicators of environmental pressure and degradation. This is particularly true when there is a direct link between environmental quality and human welfare or health impacts; pollutants generate local short-term costs and there are substantial private and social benefits of abatement (such as in the case of local air pollution, water contamination and acidification). In short, the EKC applies only to environmental problems that are easy to solve and which are well documented and well known. The air pollutants that have been investigated are all energy-related: sulphur oxides, nitrogen oxides, various types of particulates[8] and carbon oxides (both CO and CO_2). Particulates and sulphur oxides show lower turning points than nitrogen and especially carbon dioxide. An explanation may be related to the lower costs of removing dust and sulphur from exhaust gases and the well-documented human health impacts from high ambient air concentrations of these pollutants (cf. World Bank, 1993). Carbon dioxides, on the other hand, represent environmental problems that have impacts far away both in space and time (Perrings and Hannon, 1996). In this respect, O'Neill et al. (1996) remark that 'a subset of pollutants in a limited number of places cannot be accepted as surrogates for the complex interactions between economic growth and the environment on which that growth depends'.

Only a few attempts have been made to investigate a more comprehensive set of indicators that represent overall environmental pressure. Ekins (1997) compared the evidence from a number of selected EKC studies with the state of environment as evaluated by the OECD and the European Commission, and concluded that these latter studies almost completely negate the EKC hypothesis for rich countries: 'Despite improvements in some indicators, notably of some air pollutants, these countries seem to be experiencing continuing, serious environmental degradation on all fronts' (Ekins 1997, p. 815). Similar conclusions have been arrived at by de Bruyn and Opschoor (1997) using an indicator of throughput, and Rothman (1998) using the concept of 'ecological footprint' (cf. Wackernagel and Rees, 1996). Both studies concluded that aggregated environmental pressure rises when countries become richer. Also attempts to use energy consumption as an indicator of overall environmental pressure point at higher turning points (if any) than in EKC studies based on other indicators (cf. Nakicenovic, 1993; Nilsson, 1993; Suri and Chapman, 1998). Hence there exists virtually no evidence that *overall* environmental pressure is decreasing as income grows.

A related problem is associated with the question of whether the focus on a few pollutants has resulted in displacement of environmental pollution to other compartments or substances. The collection of dust and sulphur from exhaust gases or heavy metal particles from waste-water discharges indeed results in improved air and water quality but increases (toxic) solid wastes that may be difficult to dispose of. Moreover, due to material substitution, new substances may enter the environment, some of which are not even represented in statistical data compendia.[9] In line with this, new patterns of pollutants may emerge with still unknown environmental consequences.

Is the EKC relation valid both for individual countries and worldwide?
Due to limited data on the patterns of pollutants over time, the EKC is typically estimated in a cross-section panel of countries. But such estimates do not guarantee that over time individual countries will move along the estimated relationship of the panel of countries (cf. de Bruyn et al., 1998).[10] For some developed countries longer time-series data are available for pollutants such as SO_2 and NO_x, and these data show decreasing levels of emissions and concentrations over time. However, this may not be due to economic growth, as has been supposed by the EKC, since higher growth rates in developed economies are often associated with lower emission reductions (cf. de Bruyn et al., 1998).

Also, for developing economies, in which environmental pressure is still increasing over time, the prospects are unclear. Developing countries have not yet reached income levels high enough to be able to derive their (hypothetical) turning points. Whether pollution will decrease after these countries have reached the per capita income turning points remains speculative. Moreover, if translocation of dirty industries is the driving force behind the EKC, the reduction of environmental impacts will be less and less available the more developing countries move to higher income levels (Low and Yeats, 1992; Arrow et al., 1995). Also, for emissions worldwide, the prospects are not as optimistic as might be expected on the basis of the EKC results. Stern et al. (1996) have emphasized that the improvements in environmental quality according to the EKC hypothesis are not attainable for the majority of world population that have standards of living sub-stantially below the estimated turning points. Emissions worldwide are therefore expected to continue to increase due to economic growth (cf. Selden and Song, 1994), even for the pollutants for which an inverted U curve has been estimated, such as for SO_2.

Is the EKC relation permanent?

The EKC hypothesis assumes that the initial increases in environmental pressure are temporary, but that the subsequent decreases in environmental pressure are permanent. Only a few authors have questioned whether these observed decreases could also be a temporary phenomenon. The result would be an 'N'-shaped curve (including phase 4 in Figure 46.1). Grossman and Krueger (1995) found for some pollutants such an N curve, but they state without further elaboration that they mistrust these results. However, an upswing of the EKC can be explained by the difficulty of keeping up efficiency improvements (innovation) with continuing growth of produc-tion. At an institutional level it may be difficult to introduce increasingly strict environmental standards, the more so when marginal costs of com-pliance increase. Also, if there exists a thermodynamic lower bound on reductions in materials and energy use per unit of GDP, emissions may rise once these boundaries are approached. Empirical results by de Bruyn and Opschoor (1997) on an aggregated indicator of material and energy throughput suggest that since the second half of the 1980s most developed economies have gone through a phase of re-linking their throughput with economic growth.[11] The fact that re-linking cannot be found for pollutants such as SO_2 and particulate matter may reflect the continuing importance of end-of-pipe solutions over more fundamental changes in the economy, such as reducing throughput. Pollutants for which the end-of-pipe solution is costly may follow a similar N-shaped pattern. For example, between 1973 and 1985 the CO_2 emissions of OECD countries declined by 3.8 per cent, but from 1985 to 1990 the emissions increased again by 8.6 per cent (CPB, 1993).

Is the EKC relation optimal?

The EKC only indicates the patterns of pollution, without reference to environmental impacts. EKCs represent the patterns of flows of pollutants whereas environmental impacts are often characterized as a stock problem (Arrow et al., 1995). Hence the EKC does not necessarily reflect a sustainable time-path of pollution. But it need not reflect an optimal time-path of pollution as well. Optimal levels of pollution, as defined in (neoclassical) economics, depend on costs and benefits of pollution abatement, which differ among countries. Differences in absorptive capacities, social preferences and discount rates give rise to different costs/benefits structures, which implies different optimal levels of pollution among countries (Low and Safadi, 1992). This limits the policy relevance of an estimated collective turning point for a whole sample of countries. Moreover, there is no guarantee that the rising part and top of the EKC does not bypass ecological thresholds and sustainability constraints beyond which environmental deterioration is irreversible (Panayotou, 1993; Arrow et al., 1995). Restructuring the environment may then become unnecessarily expensive, that is, it may be less costly to prevent or abort today than in the future (Schindler, 1996).

6.   Conclusions and directions for future research

This chapter has investigated a number of studies on the environmental Kuznets curve hypothesis. Results, methods, explanations and policy implications of the studies that have found empirical evidence for EKCs have been discussed and this discussion lends evidence to refute the EKC hypothesis that economic growth can be at the benefit of the environment. Given the conflicting patterns that have been found for the pollutants under investigation, the lack of insight into the mechanisms through which pollution may curve downwards and questions concerning the policy relevance of the estimated results, it can be safely asserted that the EKC remains an unproven hypothesis so far.

   The critical evaluation of the EKC literature in this chapter implies that various points require elaboration in future research. First, it is necessary to examine a wider range of environmental issues. The indicators chosen could be more closely related to established work in the field of environmental indicators (cf. Adriaanse, 1993). This implies that indicators selected should be related to specific environmental problems, such as the enhanced greenhouse effect or acidification. Analyses of these problems require more substances to be included in empirical work than CO_2 or SO_2 emissions only. Second, the methods employed in EKC analyses should be reconsidered in more detail. A comparison of various methods, such as in Selden and Song (1994), provides a good background for a discussion of the advantages and disadvantages of the methods employed. In addition to panel data analysis, efforts should be devoted to time-series analysis that may provide a better picture of the development of pollution associated with specific phases of development in individual countries. Third, identification of the dominant factors that explain the EKC should have a high priority in future research. Only when the (combination) of factors underlying the EKC have been properly identified can one design policies that affect the course of the EKC. Estimation of structural models, instead of the current reduced-form models, may be needed for this purpose. Such structural models can be based on recent efforts to describe the EKC from a theoretical perspective (cf. Lopez, 1994 and McConnell, 1996). Moreover, decomposition analysis (as elaborated by Ang and Rose – Chapters 74 and 75 in this book) can provide more insight into which combination of explanations is dominant, such as technological improvements and structural changes.

Notes

1   The authors would like to thank Jeroen van den Bergh, Jos Boelens, Joyeeta Gupta, Peter Mulder, David Stern and one anonymous reviewer for useful comments on an earlier draft. The usual disclaimer applies.

2.   Many other empirical studies exist that have not been published at the moment of writing or that use different indicators or models to estimate the relationship between pollutants and income. Some of these studies are mentioned below Table 46.1.

3.   Ekins (1997) not only compares the results between various studies but also between different estimates within the various studies. For that reason, his quotation is not inconsistent with our finding for NO_x, since the results from the pooled cross-section estimates by Selden and Song (1994) suggest monotonically increasing patterns of emissions. In Table 46.1 we have only selected those regressions of the various studies that were preferred by the authors based on test statistics, for example, the NO_x results by Selden and Song are based on their fixed-effects estimates.

4.   A few other environmental indicators have been investigated, such as deforestation (Shafik and Bandyopadhyay, 1992; Panayatou, 1993), toxic emission intensities (Lucas et al., 1992), municipal waste (Shafik and Bandyopadhyay, 1992), lack of clean water and urban sanitation (Shafik and Bandyopadhyay, 1992; Torras and Boyce, 1998), and energy consumption (Suri and Chapman, 1998; Horvath, 1996).

5.   When heteroscedasticity is ignored while applying conventional estimation methods, the variances are biased, which may result in wrong conclusions concerning the significance of the estimates.

6.   It should be noted, however, that Lucas et al. (1992) calculated emissions for developing countries based on emission coefficients of the US. Hence the difference in emissions between countries can only be attributed to differences in the production structure because the emission characteristics of production are assumed to be similar for all countries in their sample.

7.   Although displacement is generally not regarded as a 'solution' to environmental problems, there can be a rationale for displacement when resulting in a more even spatial distribution of environmental pollution with local impacts. For pollutants with global impacts, however, total environmental impacts remain the same (or even increase if production is less efficient in the recipient countries).

8.   Measured differently as dark matter, suspensible particulate matter or smoke.

9.   Labys and Wadell (1989) have suggested that the use of materials typically follows a Schumpeterian life-cycle stage from introduction, via growth and maturity, to saturation and decline. Whereas the intensities of copper and iron ore in the US economy typically peaked during the 1940s, new peaks are currently recorded for polyethylene, platinum and ceramics. Labys and Wadell therefore argue that 'dematerialization' inadequately

describes materials demand because of material substitution. They argue that the observed 'dematerialization' may be better described as 'transmaterialization'.
10. Stern et al. (1996) also seem to point at this when they remark: 'We believe that a more fruitful approach to the analysis of the relationship between economic growth and environmental impact would be the examination of the historical experience of individual countries, using econometric and also qualitative historical analysis.'
11. This study extends a previous study by Jänicke et al. (1989) that found declining throughput levels between 1970 and 1985 for most developed economies.

References

Adriaanse, A. (1993), *Environmental Policy Performance Indicators*, The Hague: SDU.
Ansuategi, A., E. Barbier and C. Perrings (1997), 'The environmental Kuznets curve', forthcoming in J.C.J.M. van den Bergh and M. Hofkes (eds), *Theory and Implementation of Sustainable Development Modelling*, Dordrecht: Kluwer Academic Publishers.
Arrow, K., B. Bolin, R. Costanza, P. Dasgupta, C. Folke, C.S. Holling, B. Jansson, S. Levin, K. Mäler, C. Perrings and D. Pimentel (1995), 'Economic growth, carrying capacity, and the environment" *Ecological Economics*, **15**, 91–5.
Auty, R. (1985), 'Materials intensity of GDP: research issues on the measurement and explanation of change', *Resources Policy*, **11**, 275–83.
Baldwin, R. (1995), 'Does sustainability require growth?' in I. Goldin and L.A. Winters (eds), *The economics of sustainable development*, Cambridge, UK: Cambridge University Press, pp. 19–47.
Beckerman, W.B. (1972), 'Economic development and the environment: a false dilemma', *International Conciliation*, **586**, 57–71. Reprinted in W.B. Beckerman (1992), *Growth, the Environment and the Distribution of Incomes: Essays by a Sceptical Optimist*, Aldershot, UK and Brookfield, US: Edward Elgar.
Beckerman, W. (1992), 'Economic growth and the environment: whose growth? Whose environment?', *World Development*, **20**, 481–96.
Centraal Plan Bureau (CPB) (1993), *Scanning the Future: A Long Term Scenario Study of the World Economy 1990–2015*, The Hague: SDU.
de Bruyn, S.M. (1997), 'Explaining the environmental Kuznets curve: structural change and international agreements in reducing sulphur emissions', forthcoming in *Environment and Development Economics*, **2**, 485–503.
de Bruyn, S.M. and J.B. Opschoor (1997), 'Developments in the throughput–income relationship: theoretical and empirical observations', *Ecological Economics*, **20**, 255–68.
de Bruyn, S.M., J.C.J.M. van den Bergh and J.B. Opschoor (1998), 'Economic growth and emissions: reconsidering the empirical basis of environmental Kuznets curves', *Ecological Economics*, **25**, 177–94.
Ekins, P. (1997), 'The Kuznets curve for the environment and economic growth: examining the evidence', *Environment and Planning A*, **29**, 805–30.
Flores, N.E. and R.T. Carson (1995), 'The relationship between income elasticities of demand and willingness to pay', discussion paper 95–3, University of California, San Diego.
Grossman, G.M. and A.B. Krueger (1991), 'Environmental impacts of a North American Free Trade Agreement', NBER working paper 3914, National Bureau of Economic Research (NBER), Cambridge.
Grossman, G.M. and A.B. Krueger (1995), 'Economic growth and the environment', *Quarterly Journal of Economics*, **112**, 353–78.
Hertwich, E.G. (1997), 'Eco-efficiency and its role in industrial transformation', Working Paper IHDP-IT, no. 4, Institute for Environmental Studies/Human Dimensions of Global Environmental Change, Amsterdam/Bonn (IVM).
Holtz-Eakin, D. and T.M. Selden (1995), 'Stoking the fires? CO_2 emissions and economic growth', *Journal of Public Economics*, **57**, 85–101.
Horvath, R.J. (1996), 'Environmental quality and economic development: the environmental Kuznets curve debate', paper presented at the 4th biennial conference of the International Society for Ecological Economics, Boston University, Boston, MA.

Jänicke, M., H. Monch, T. Ranneberg and U.E. Simonis (1989), 'Economic structure and environmental impacts: East–West comparisons', *The Environmentalist*, **9**, 171–82.
Kaufmann, R.K., B. Davidsdottir, S. Garnham and P. Pauly (1998), 'The determinants of atmospheric SO_2 concentrations: reconsidering the environmental Kuznets curve', *Ecological Economics*, **25**, 209–20.
Komen, R., S. Gerking and H. Folmer (1996), 'Income and environmental protection: empirical evidence from OECD countries', Department of Economics and Finance, University of Wyoming, Laramie, WY.
Kriström, B. and P. Riera (1996), 'Is the income elasticity of environmental improvements less than one?', *Environmental and Resource Economics*, **7**, 45–55.
Kuznets, S. (1955), 'Economic growth and income inequality', *American Economic Review*, **49**, 1–28.
Labys, W.C. and L.M. Waddell (1989), 'Commodity lifecycles in US materials demand', *Resources Policy*, **15**, 238–52.
Liddle, B.T. (1996), 'Environmental Kuznets curves: revisited for regional pollutants', paper presented at the 4th biennial conference of the International Society for Ecological Economics, Boston University, Boston, MA.
Lopez, R. (1994), 'The environment as a factor of production: the effects of economic growth and trade liberalization', *Journal of Environmental Economics and Management*, **27**, 163–84.
Low, P. and R. Safadi (1992), 'Trade policy and pollution', in P. Low (ed.), *International Trade and the Environment*, World Bank discussion paper 159, Washington, DC: The World Bank, 29–52.
Low, P. and A. Yeats (1992), 'How do differences in national environmental control measures influence industry location decisions and patterns of trade?', in P. Low (ed.), *International Trade and the Environment*, World Bank discussion paper 159, Washington, DC: World Bank.
Lucas, R.E.B., D. Wheeler and H. Hettige (1992), 'Economic development, environmental regulation and the international migration of toxic industrial pollution: 1960–88', in P. Low (ed.), *International Trade and the Environment*, World Bank discussion paper 159, Washington, DC: World Bank.
Malenbaum, W. (1978), *World Demand for Raw Materials in 1985 and 2000*, New York: McGraw-Hill.
McConnell, K.E. (1996), 'Income and the demand for environmental quality', paper presented at the Seventh Annual Conference of the EAERE, Lisbon, Portugal.
Meadows, D.H., D.L. Meadows, J. Randers and W. Behrens III (1972), *The Limits to Growth*, New York: Universe Books.
Nakicenovic, N. (1993), 'Decarbonization: doing more with less', IIASA working paper 93–076, Laxenburg, Austria.
Nilsson, L.J. (1993), 'Energy intensity trends in 31 industrial and developing countries 1950–1988', *Energy*, **18**, 309–22.
O'Neill, R.V., J.P. Kahn, J.R. Duncan, S. Alliot, R. Efroymson, H. Cardwell and D.W. Jones (1996), 'Economic growth and sustainability: a new challenge', *Ecological Applications*, **6**, 23–4.
Panayotou, T. (1993), 'Empirical tests and policy analysis of environmental degradation at different stages of economic development', discussion paper 1, Geneva: International Labour Office.
Perrings, C. and B. Hannon (1996), 'A sense of time and place: an introduction to spatial discounting', paper presented at the conference 'Ecology, Society, Economy', 23–25 May, Université de Versaille, Paris.
Pezzey, J. (1989), 'Economic analysis of sustainable growth and sustainable development', Environment Department Working Paper no. 15, World Bank.
Rothman, D.S. (1998), 'Environmental Kuznets curves – real progress or passing the buck?: A case for consumption-based approaches', *Ecological Economics*, **25**, 177–94.
Schindler, D.W. (1996), 'The environment, carrying capacity and economic growth', *Ecological Applications*, **6**, 17–19.

Selden, T.M. and D. Song (1994), 'Environmental quality and development: is there a Kuznets curve for air pollution emissions?', *Journal of Environmental Economics and Management*, **27**, 147–62.

Shafik, N. and S. Bandyopadhyay (1992), 'Economic growth and environmental quality: time series and cross-country evidence', World Bank Background Papers, Washington, DC.

Shukla, V. and K. Parikh (1992), 'The environmental consequences of urban growth: cross-national perspectives on economic development, air pollution and city size', *Urban Geography*, **12**, 422–49.

Simon, J.L. (1981), *The Ultimate Resource*, Princeton, NJ: Princeton University Press.

Steger, U. (1996), 'Organization and human resource management for environmental management', in P. Groenewegen, K. Fischer, E.G. Jenkins and J. Schot (eds), *The Greening of Industry Resource Guide and Bibliography*, Washington, DC: Island Press.

Stern, D.I. (1997), 'Progress on the environmental Kuznets curve?', *Working Papers in Ecological Economics*, 9601, CRES, Australian National University, Canberra.

Stern, D.I., M.S. Common and E.B. Barbier (1996), 'Economic growth and environmental degradation: a critique of the environmental Kuznets curve', *World Development*, **24**, 1151–60.

Suri, V. and D. Chapman (1998), 'Economic growth, trade and the environment: implications for the environmental Kuznets curve', *Ecological Economics*, **25**, 195–208.

Tilton, J.E. (1990), 'The OECD countries: demand trend setters', in J.E. Tilton (ed.), *World Metal Demand: Trends and Prospects*, Washington, DC: Resources for the Future, pp. 35–76.

Torras, M. and J.K. Boyce (1998), 'Income, inequality and pollution: a reassessment of the environmental Kuznets curve', *Ecological Economics*, **25**, 147–60.

Wackernagel, M. and W.E. Rees (1996), *Our Ecological Footprint: Reducing Human Impact on the Earth*, Gabriola Island: New Society Publishers.

Williams, R.H., E.D. Larson and M.H. Ross (1987), 'Materials, affluence and industrial energy use', *Annual Review Energy*, **12**, 99–144.

World Bank (1992), *World Development Report*, New York: Oxford University Press.

World Bank (1993), 'Environmental action programme for Central and Eastern Europe', Lucerne, Switzerland.

World Bank (1995), 'Monitoring environmental progress: a report on work in progress', Environmentally Sustainable Development Series, Washington, DC.

Xepapedeas, A. and E. Amri (1995), 'Environmental quality and economic development: empirical evidence based on qualitative characteristics', Nota di Lavoro 15.95, Fondazione Eni Enrico Mattei, Italy.

47 Growth-oriented economic policies and their environmental impacts

Mohan Munasinghe[1]

1. Introduction

Sustainable development has become an important policy goal for most nations and the international development community – because of the increasing evidence that failure to account for environmental degradation erodes the capital base for future development. Moreover, governments have accepted the responsibility for promoting the sustainability of development, in response to the Agenda 21 programme – following the United Nations Conference on Environment and Development. In this context, the role of country-wide or economy-wide policies (both macro-economic and sectoral) have come under increasing scrutiny, because of their powerful and pervasive impacts.

The concept of sustainable development has evolved to encompass three major points of view: economic, social and environmental (Munasinghe, 1992). While the balanced treatment of all these three elements is desirable, this chapter focuses mainly on economic–environmental linkages. Some discussion of associated social issues such as poverty, income distribution and resettlement is also included. Other key social objectives such as popular participation, empowerment and the rights of indigenous peoples fall outside the scope of this discussion. Nevertheless, the generic findings and the approach presented here would also be useful in systematically identifying a wider range of social impacts, and analysing them.

Country-wide policies consist of both sectoral and macroeconomic policies which have widespread effects throughout the economy; therefore it is not surprising that their environmental and social consequences could be both positive and negative. Table 47.1 summarizes some of the main economy-wide policy instruments and strategies, and the broad objectives of decision makers. Sectoral measures mainly involve a variety of economic instruments, including pricing in key sectors (for example, energy or agriculture) and broad sector-wide taxation or subsidy programmes (for example, agricultural production subsidies, and industrial investment incentives). Macroeconomic policies and strategies are even more sweeping, ranging from exchange rate, interest rate, and wage policies, to trade liberalization, privatization, and similar programmes. Such economy-wide

Table 47.1 Typical examples of economy-wide concerns and policy tools to address them

Issues	Policy tools and strategies
1. Macroeconomic concerns	
Trade imbalance (usually a deficit)	Exchange rate adjustment
Inflation	Monetary policy (changes in money
Government budget deficits	supply, interest rate, etc.)
Unemployment	Reductions in government spending
Poverty	Fiscal policy (e.g., increased taxes)
	Economic liberalization (trade,
	prices, etc.)
	Privatization/decentralization
2. Broad sectoral concerns	
Low productivity	Pricing policy reforms
Unprofitability and chronic deficits	Economic incentives
Inefficient use of resources	Building human resource capacity
Institutional weaknesses	Strengthening institutions
	Liberalization/privatization
	/decentralization

policies are often packaged within programmes of structural adjustment and sectoral reform, aimed at promoting economic stability, efficiency and growth, and ultimately improving human welfare. Although the emphasis is on economic policies, other non-economic measures (such as social, institutional and legal actions), are also relevant.

The next section provides a brief summary of the main links between country-wide policies and issues of sustainability, as well as key elements of the underlying analytical basis for these findings. Section 3 contains a brief review of selected recent studies that illustrate the analysis presented in Section 2. Finally, some concluding remarks and directions for future work are presented in Section 4.

2. Some stylized results and analysis

It is difficult to generalize about the environmental and social impacts of economy-wide policies, because the linkages tend to be extremely complex and country-specific. For example, a recent study indicated that even the purely economic impacts of structural adjustment programmes are difficult to trace comprehensively (Tarp, 1993). Nevertheless, we attempt to

680 Environmental macroeconomics

summarize below some stylized results concerning the impacts of country-wide policies on various indicators of sustainability, in three broad categories – beneficial, harmful and unknown effects. In the first group are the so-called 'win–win' policies, where it is possible to achieve simultaneous gains in all three areas of sustainable development (that is, economic, social and environmental) when economy-wide reforms are implemented. The second category recognizes important exceptions where such potential gains cannot be realized unless the macro-reforms are complemented by additional environmental and social measures which protect both the environment and the poor. The third and final category consists of impacts that are less predictable, mainly because of the complexity of the linkages involved, and the long-run time perspective. This section ends with a theoretical analysis of the various linkages between economy-wide policies and the environment.

Impacts of economy-wide policies on sustainability

Beneficial impacts Several studies (see Section 3 for details) indicate that liberalizing reforms which seek to make desirable alterations in the structure of the economy often contribute to both economic and sustainability gains. Such changes include the removal of price distortions, promotion of market incentives, and relaxation of trade and other constraints (which are among the main features of adjustment-related reforms). For example, reforms which improve the efficiency of industrial or energy-related activities could reduce economic waste, increase the efficiency of natural resource use and limit environmental pollution. Similarly, improving land-tenure rights and access to financial and social services not only yields economic gains but also promotes better environmental stewardship and helps the poor.

In the same vein, there is evidence to show that shorter-run policy measures aimed at restoring macroeconomic stability will generally yield economic, social and environmental benefits, since instability undermines sustainable resource use and especially penalizes the poor. For example, price, wage and employment stability encourage a longer-term view on the part of firms and households alike. Lower inflation (and discount) rates not only lead to clearer pricing signals and better investment decisions by economic agents, but also protect fixed-income earners.

Avoiding harm A number of researchers have pointed out how economy-wide structural reforms have had adverse environmental and social side effects. Such negative impacts are invariably unintended and occur when some broad policy changes are undertaken while other hidden or neglected policy, market or institutional imperfections persist. The remedy does not generally require reversal of the original reforms, but rather the implementation of additional complementary measures (both economic and non-economic) that remove such policy, market and institutional difficulties. These complementary measures are not only socially and environmentally beneficial in their own right, but also help to broaden the effectiveness of economy-wide reforms. Typical examples of potential environmental damage caused by remaining imperfections include:

- *Policy distortions* Export promotion measures that increase the profitability of natural resource exports might encourage excessive extraction or harvesting of this resource if it were underpriced or subsidized (for example, low stumpage fees for timber). Similarly, trade liberalization could lead to the expansion of wasteful energy-intensive activities in a country where subsidized energy prices persisted.
- *Market failures* Economic expansion induced by successful adjustment may be associated with excessive environmental damage – for example, if external environmental effects of economic activities (such as air or water pollution), are not adequately reflected in market prices that influence such activities.
- *Institutional constraints* The benefits of country-wide reforms could be negated by unaddressed institutional problems, such as the poor accountability of state-owned enterprises (which would allow them to ignore efficient price signals), weak financial intermediation, or inadequately defined property rights. Such issues tend to undermine incentives for sustainable resource management and worsen equity.
- *Stabilization* The shorter-term stabilization process also may have unforeseen adverse environmental and social impacts. For example, general reductions in government spending are often required to limit budgetary deficits and bring inflation under control. However, unless such cutbacks are carefully targeted, they may disproportionately penalize expenditures on environmental protection or poverty safety nets. Another important linkage is the possible short-term adverse impact of adjustment-induced recession on poverty and unemployment, whereby the poor are forced to increase their pressures on fragile lands and 'open access' natural resources – due to the lack of economic opportunities elsewhere. As before, complementary measures to limit the adverse consequences of adjustment would be justified – on both social and environmental grounds.

Less predictable and longer-term effects   Economy-wide policies will have additional longer-term effects on sustainability, whose net impacts are often unpredictable. Some of these effects need to be traced through a general equilibrium framework that captures both direct and indirect links. For example, several studies confirm that adjustment-induced changes often succeed in generating new economic opportunities and sources of livelihood, thereby alleviating poverty and helping to break the vicious cycle of environmental degradation and poverty. However, while such growth is an essential element of sustainable development, it will necessarily increase the overall pressures on environmental resources. At the same time, properly valuing resources, increasing efficiency and reducing waste will help to reshape the structure of economic growth and limit undesirable environmental impacts. Finally, environmental policies themselves could have impacts on income distribution and employment.

Up to now, we have focused on the use of complementary policies to limit environmental and social harm, without interfering with the economy-wide reforms themselves. However, it is prudent to recognize that if the threat to long-term sustainability is great enough, the country-wide policy reform process itself may need to be modified directly.

Analysing and addressing the causes of environmental harm

Magnitude of growth   Some linkages between growth-inducing economy-wide policies and the environment that illustrate the interplay of both price and income effects are summarized briefly below (see Munasinghe, 1995, for details). Consider a relatively stagnant economy which has open access forest areas, as depicted in Figure 47.1. Initially, the demand for timber is given by the usual downward-sloping curve D_o in the figure, where the demand is assumed to be a function of both price p and income Y (that is, $D = D(p, Y)$). At the effective (subsidized) price p_S which represents the marginal cost of logging, the initial rate of deforestation is Q_o. Suppose Q_L is the safe limiting rate of deforestation beyond which serious ecological damage occurs.[2] As long as $Q_o < Q_L$, the situation may continue undetected and uncorrected.

Next, suppose an economic reform package stimulates growth and shifts the timber demand curve outward to D_1. This 'income effect' could be the result of increased domestic demand (for example, timber required by a construction boom), and/or higher timber exports (for example, due to trade liberalization and devaluation that make such exports more profitable). Now the deforestation rate could quickly shift to Q_s, greatly exceeding the safe limit Q_L and causing serious environmental harm.

Clearly, the remedy is not to stop growth (especially in a poor country),

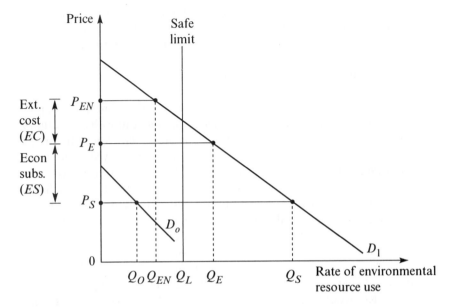

Source: Munasinghe (1995).

Figure 47.1 Environmental damage due to economic imperfections

but rather to introduce complementary measures that establish a proper market price for timber. As a first step, property rights may need to be re-established in open access areas and an 'efficient' stumpage fee imposed – to eliminate the economic subsidy (*ES*) and correctly reflect the opportunity cost of the timber. The resulting efficient price (p_E) would reduce the logging rate to Q_E, which still exceeds Q_L. The next step might be to impose an additional externality cost (*EC*) that reflects the loss of biodiversity or damage to watersheds, and thereby establish the full environmentally adjusted price (p_{EN}). The deforestation rate would now fall to $Q_{EN} < Q_L$.

Exactly analogous reasoning would apply if we considered fuel prices and polluting emissions from urban transport or industry. In this case, p_S might be a subsidized diesel price, p_E the equivalent import (or export) opportunity cost, P_{EN} the full price including a tax to cover the externality cost of air pollution, and Q_L the health-determined safety standard.

This rather simple example based on comparative statics helps to clarify how the expansionary effects of economic reform policies could combine with hitherto neglected economic distortions to cause environmental harm. It also indicates that environmental damage need not be inextricably linked to economic growth (see the discussion on the structure of growth, below), but might be moderated by sound policy measures.[3] Thus the parallel introduction of complementary measures that address the specific distortions would allow the broader reforms to go forward without adverse environmental (or social) impacts. These additional measures would need to be built (*ex ante*) into the macroeconomic reform package, rather than introduced as an afterthought.

Structure and stage of growth   Over a period of time, economy-wide policies also influence the structure and stage of economic growth of a country, which could, in turn, also affect the state of the environment. In this context, the recent concern for the environment has revived interest in a generic concept proposed by Kuznets (1955, 1963) over 30 years ago – that as countries develop and incomes rise, certain measures of the quality of life (for example, income distribution) might initially deteriorate before improving. More specifically, several authors have presented evidence that the level of environmental degradation and per capita income (conventionally measured) might obey the inverted U-shaped relationship shown in Figure 47.2 – dubbed the 'environmental Kuznets curve' or EKC (see de Bruyn and Heintz, Chapter 46 in this volume, and Munasinghe, 1996).

The EKC hypothesis is intuitively appealing. Thus, at the low levels of per

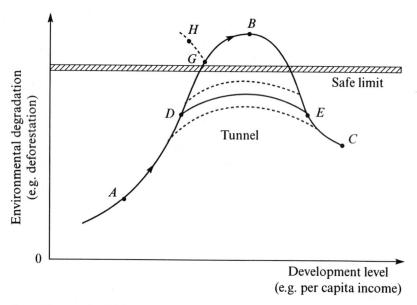

Source: Munasinghe (1995).

*Figure 47.2   Tunnelling through the environmental Kuznets curve using
sustainable strategies*

capita income associated with pre-industrial and agricultural economies, one might expect rather pristine environmental conditions relatively unaffected by economic activities at the subsistence level. As development and industrialization progressed, the increasing use of natural resources and emission of pollutants, less efficient and relatively 'dirty' technologies, high priority given to increases in material output, and disregard for or ignorance of the environmental consequences of growth, would all have contributed to increasing environmental damage. This argument might be relevant for middle-income or newly industrializing countries (NICs) – especially where growth rates of GNP exceeding 5 per cent per annum are commonplace. In the final post-industrial stage (corresponding to the mature Western economies), cleaner technologies and a shift to information- and service-based activities, the growing ability and willingness to pay for a better environment, improved internalization of environmental externalities, and greater financial surpluses that could be used to pay for a more pre-emptive approach to environmental protection, might be expected to result in reduced environmental degradation. A basic analytical model which examines the elements underlying the EKC, and how economy-wide policies could influence the path of economic development and environmental damage in the framework of the EKC, is presented in Munasinghe (1996).

There are many other factors which tend to complicate the simple and stylized description of the links between economic development and environmental conditions discussed above. In particular, the choice of meaningful indicators for the X and Y axes of the EKC raises several issues (see Munasinghe, 1996, for details). In this context, one serious criticism raised in the 'green' national accounting literature is that the currently used measures of national well-being (especially conventionally measured national income) do not adequately reflect either the depletion of natural resource stocks or environmental damage (for example, due to pollution) – see the chapter by El Serafy in this volume (Chapter 77). Such an approach suggests that if the system of national accounts (SNA) correctly reflected the status of the environment, then any increases in such a measure of 'green' income per capita would be related with monotonically decreasing environmental degradation. In other words, the EKC might be an artifact of incorrect measurement of economic output or income – due to the neglect of environmental impacts. Nevertheless, to the extent that the practical measurement of environmentally adjusted national accounts has proved rather problematic, we may conclude that for policy-making purposes it would still be worthwhile to analyse the EKC phenomenon using conventional measures of income and environmental degradation that are presently available. The key issue is whether appropriate economic policies can be devised to influence the structure of growth in the various stages of development, and thereby limit the environmental and social harm (see the section on 'Tunnelling through the EKC', below).

Timing and sequencing of policy reforms   Up to now we have not seriously considered altering economy-wide policies merely to achieve sustainability objectives, but instead have relied on specific complementary measures to mitigate environmental and social harm. For illustrative purposes, however, suppose that the environmental damage due to an economic reform programme is likely to be rather large. In such a case, is it possible to adjust the timing and sequencing of macroeconomic and sectoral policy tools, to avoid the worst environmental consequences? In fact, Mäler and Munasinghe (1996) have shown, theoretically, that in the presence of economic imperfections that affect the use of environmental resources, first-best policies aimed at macroeconomic growth and stability could well be suboptimal, and therefore, it would be advisable for decision makers to consider second-best approaches. In this same vein, there is a growing body of literature that seeks to examine the pros and cons of timing and sequencing stabilization and adjustment measures – to achieve economic goals (see for example, Edwards, 1992), but not environmental ones. One may adapt some of this past work to obtain basic insights that help to deal with environmental issues.

Consider Figure 47.3, in which the X axis indicates aggregate expenditure in a national economy (for example, government expenditure) and the Y axis reflects the effects of domestic currency appreciation (for example, the ratio of domestic goods prices to foreign goods prices weighted by the exchange rate). Suppose that the initial state of the economy is at point A (within the shaded quadrant) – below the line of internal balance IN (along which the economy is producing at the full employment level Y_F), and above the line of external balance EX (along which the current account balance CA is zero). In this situation, economy-wide policy reforms would seek to move the economy towards the equilibrium point B by reducing both the current account deficit (since $CA<0$), and the excess demand (since $Y>Y_F$).

A movement in the (downward) direction AD could be achieved by a currency devaluation and removal of trade barriers. A shift in the (leftward) direction AL would occur if the government budget deficit were reduced by eliminating public sector subsidies (for example, by raising subsidized energy prices). Suppose that the reforms affecting AD could be achieved first, and those underlying AL somewhat later – due to powerful vested interest (for example, transport or industrial lobbies). In this case, the opening up of the economy represented by AD alone might lead to greater foreign investment and expansion of energy-intensive industries which

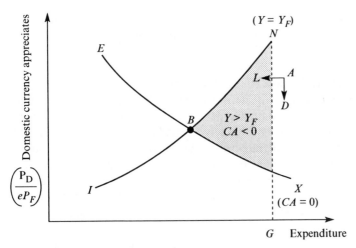

P_D = price of domestic goods Y = income
P_F = price of foreign goods Y_F = full employment income
e = exchange rate CA = current account
IN = internal balance equilibrium G = government expenditure
EX = external balance equilibrium

Source: Munasinghe (1995).

Figure 47.3   *Timing and sequencing of economic policies to reduce environmental damage*

were attracted by the low energy prices. However, this apparent gain would also result in wasteful use of (the still subsidized) energy and more environmental pollution.

Clearly, the foregoing analysis is limited by its simple, static and short-term nature. None the less, some environmentally related arguments such as the above could be used fruitfully to re-examine (and perhaps modify) the timing and sequencing of policy reforms. Since hardly any work has been carried out in this area, and country circumstances vary widely, it would not be possible to generalize. At the same time, restraint and good judgement are required to avoid the temptation of making major changes in economy-wide policies merely to achieve minor environmental (and social) gains. Once again, policy options that achieved 'win–win' gains would be the most desirable.

Some policy aspects

Learning from experience – tunnelling through the environmental Kuznets curve A major motivation for more systematically examining the links between economy-wide policies and the environment, based on analysis of past growth patterns, is the search for environmentally sustainable development paths in the future. The EKC diagram (Figure 47.2) provides a convenient framework to represent some of the lessons of experience.

First, if the EKC hypothesis holds true, the early to middle stages of economic growth could be quite detrimental from both the environmental and social viewpoints of sustainable development. In particular, low-income groups might be even more adversely affected than Kuznets had originally predicted on the basis of income inequality alone, to the extent that the poor also suffer more due to environmental degradation. This would require appropriate policy responses, especially on the social side. Second, the extent to which decision makers ought to devote their limited time and resources towards designing and implementing policies for sound environmental management could well depend on the extent to which the driving forces underlying the EKC are susceptible to such policies. In other words, if environmental damage is a structurally determined and inevitable consequence of economic growth, then attempts to avoid such damage in the early stages of development might be futile.

In contrast, this chapter recommends a more proactive approach whereby the developing countries could learn from the past experiences of the industrialized world – by adopting sustainable development strategies and measures which would permit them to build a strategic 'tunnel' through the EKC, as shown in Figure 47.2 (Munasinghe, 1995). Thus the emphasis is on identifying policies that will help de-link environmental degradation and growth, so that environmental harm will be reduced along the development path. With such a focus, the EKC becomes useful mainly as a metaphor or organizing framework for policy analysis, while other issues become less important – such as the exact shape of the EKC,[4] or whether the empirically estimated EKCs which tend to be based on cross-section or pooled data (rather than a time-series of observations) can adequately capture the growth characteristics of any single country.

A basic model developed by Munasinghe (1997) shows how economic imperfections (which make private decisions deviate from socially optimal ones) could lead to the high peak *B* in the path *ADBEC* in Figure 47.2. Thus the adoption of corrective policies that reduce such divergences and thereby reduce environmental damage would permit movement through the tunnel *ADEC*. Avoiding the peak of environmental damage at *B* would be especially desirable to prevent irreversible environmental harm (for example, loss of biodiversity).

In other words, the tunnel would enable developing countries to short-circuit more conventional development paths (such as *ABC* in the figure), which merely mimicked the evolution of the Western market economies. This approach is quite consistent with the fundamental insight provided by the theoretical analysis presented earlier – that imperfections in the economy could combine with growth-inducing economy-wide policies to cause environmental harm. Therefore, complementary policies that removed such imperfections would be needed to protect the environment. The same conclusion is a principal result of the empirical work summarized in Section 3.

Figure 47.4 encapsulates the above results. For a country at point *I* in its development path, what is of immediate policy relevance is not necessarily

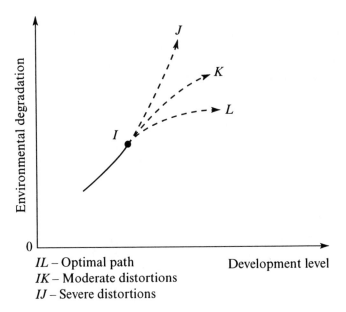

IL – Optimal path
IK – Moderate distortions
IJ – Severe distortions

Figure 47.4   Alternative development paths under different policy regimes

the actual shape of the complete EKC, but rather the direction of future change. Thus, *IL* is the theoretically ideal path, if the economy were functioning optimally. A path like *IJ* might result if there were severe economic imperfections. In actual practice, some intermediate path such as *IK* could emerge if the following policy elements could contribute to successful 'tunnelling':[5]

1. Every effort should be made to adopt 'win–win' policies that provide simultaneous economic, environmental and social gains – in particular, this will require more systematic analysis to identify the environmental

and social impacts of economy-wide policies (see next section on the action impact matrix).

2. Unintended but harmful environmental and social impacts should be addressed through complementary measures, rather than by reversing successful economic reforms.

3. If the threat to sustainability is serious enough, even economy-wide policies might be reshaped appropriately – for example, by modifying the timing and sequencing of reforms.

Action impact matrix (AIM): a tool for policy analysis, formulation and coordination   In the context of the foregoing discussion, economic–environmental–social interactions may be identified and analysed, and effective sustainable development policies formulated, by linking and articulating these activities explicitly. Implementation of such an approach would be facilitated by constructing an action impact matrix (AIM) – a simple example is shown in Table 47.2, although an actual AIM would be very much larger and more detailed (Munasinghe, 1993b). Such a matrix helps to promote an integrated view, meshing development decisions with priority economic, environmental and social impacts. The far left column of the table lists examples of the main development interventions (both policies and projects), while the top row indicates some of the main sustainable development issues. Thus the elements or cells in the matrix help to: (a) identify explicitly the key linkages; (b) focus attention on valuation and other methods of analysing the most important impacts; and (c) suggest action priorities. At the same time, the organization of the overall matrix facilitates the tracing of impacts, as well as the coherent articulation of the links between a range of development actions – that is, policies and projects.

A stepwise procedure, starting with readily available data, has been used effectively to develop the AIM in several country studies that have been initiated recently (for instance, Ghana, the Philippines and Sri Lanka). This process has helped to harmonize views among those involved (economists, environmental specialists and others), thereby improving the prospects for successful implementation (see Munasinghe and Cruz, 1994, for details).

One of the early objectives of the AIM-based process is to help in *screening and problem identification* – by preparing a preliminary matrix that identifies broad relationships, and provides a qualitative idea of the magnitudes of the impacts. Thus the preliminary AIM would be used to prioritize the most important links between policies and their sustainability impacts. For example, in the top row of Table 47.2, a currency devaluation aimed at improving the trade balance may make timber exports more profitable and lead to deforestation of open access forests. The appropriate remedy might involve complementary measures to strengthen property rights and restrict access to the forest areas.

A second example might involve increasing energy prices closer to marginal costs – to improve energy efficiency and reduce pollution (second row of Table 47.2). A complementary measure involving the addition of pollution taxes to marginal energy costs will further reduce pollution. Increasing public sector accountability will reinforce favourable responses to these price incentives, by reducing the ability of inefficient firms to pass on cost increases to consumers or to transfer their losses to the government. In the same vein, a major hydroelectric project is shown lower down in the table as having two adverse impacts – inundation of forested areas and villages – as well as one positive impact – the replacement of thermal power generation (thereby reducing air pollution). A re-afforestation project coupled with adequate resettlement efforts may help address the negative impacts.

This matrix-based approach therefore encourages the systematic articulation and coordination of policies and projects to achieve sustainable development goals. Based on readily available data, it would be possible to develop such an initial matrix for many countries. Furthermore, a range of social impacts could be incorporated into the AIM, using the same approach.

The process may be developed further to assist in *analysis and remediation*. For example, more detailed analyses and modelling may be carried out for each matrix element in the preliminary AIM which represented a high-priority linkage between economy-wide policies and environmental impacts that had already been identified in the cells of the preliminary matrix. This, in turn, would lead to a more refined and updated AIM, which would help to quantify impacts and formulate additional policy measures to enhance positive linkages and mitigate negative ones.

The types of more detailed analyses which could help to determine the final matrix would depend on planning goals and available data and resources. These may range from the application of conventional sectoral economic analysis methods (appropriately modified in scope to incorporate environmental impacts), to fairly comprehensive system or multi-sector modelling efforts – including CGE models that include both conventional economic, as well as environmental or resource variables. Sectoral and partial equilibrium analyses are more useful to trace details of direct impacts, whereas CGE modelling provides a more comprehensive but aggregate view, and insights into indirect linkages.

3.   Evidence from recent studies

A large number of papers and several volumes have attempted to present the results of case studies of the environmental and social impacts of

Table 47.2 Example of an action impact matrix (AIM)

Activity/policy	Main objective	Impacts on key sustainable development issues			
		Land degradation	Air pollution	Resettlement	Others
Macroeconomic and sectoral policies	Macroeconomic and sectoral improvements	Positive impacts due to removal of distortions. Negative impacts mainly due to remaining constraints			
Exchange rate	Improve trade balance and economic growth	(−H) (deforest open access areas)			
Energy pricing	Improve economic and energy use efficiency		(+M) (energy efficiency)		
Others					
Complementary measures[1]	Specific/local social and environmental gains	Enhance positive impacts and mitigate negative impacts (above) of broader macroeconomic and sectoral policies			
Market-based	Reverse negative impacts of market failures, policy distortions and institutional constraints		(+M) (pollution tax)		

692

Non-market-based	(+H) (property rights)	(+M) (public sector accountability)	
Investment projects	Improve efficiency of investments Use of project evaluation (cost–benefit analysis, environmental assessment, multi-criteria analysis, etc.)	Investment decisions made more consistent with broader policy and institutional framework	
Project 1 (Hydro dam)	(–H) (inundate forests)	(+M) (displace fossil fuel use)	(–M) (displace people)
Project 2 (Re-afforest and relocate)	(+H) (replant forests)		(+M) (relocate people)
Project N			

Notes:
A few examples of typical policies and projects as well as key environmental and social issues are shown. Some illustrative but quantitative impact assessments are also indicated: thus + and – signify beneficial and harmful impacts, while H and M indicate high and moderate intensity. The AIM process helps to focus on the highest priority environmental issues and related social concerns.
[1] Commonly used market-based measures include effluent charges, tradable emission permits, emission taxes or subsidies, bubbles and offsets (emission banking), stumpage fees, royalties, user fees, deposit-refund schemes, performance bonds, and taxes on products (such as fuel taxes). Non-market-based measures comprise regulations and laws specifying environmental standards (such as ambient standards, emission standards, and technology standards) which permit or limt certain actions ('dos' and 'don'ts').

Source: Munasinghe (1993b).

693

country-wide policies, including structural adjustment programmes (see, for example, Nyang'oro and Shaw, 1992; Reed, 1992; Munasinghe and Cruz, 1994; Abaza, 1995; Young and Bishop, 1995; Munasinghe, 1996; Opschoor and Jongma, 1996; Cruz et al., 1997; Warford et al., 1997). In this section, we briefly review selected studies within the three impact categories (beneficial, harmful, and longer term) discussed in the previous section, and then summarize a framework for understanding the relevant linkages – using the action impact matrix (AIM) approach.

Beneficial impacts

Macroeconomic reforms   Two recent studies highlighted in Munasinghe and Cruz (1994) illustrate win–win situations. In a case involving Zimbabwe, currency devaluation would help economic adjustment efforts, while also promoting wildlife management activities that are environmentally beneficial. More indirect or systemic effects of economic policies on the environment have been analysed using a computable general equilibrium (CGE) model for Morocco, which showed that a combination of trade liberalization and water-pricing reforms would not only increase economic growth rates, but also conserve water and help limit emerging water deficits. Similarly, an earlier CGE model of Thailand showed that combined economic and environmental gains would be possible with adjustment policies coupled with complementary measures, including the clear delineation of property rights in rural areas, and use of regulatory or economic instruments to limit urban pollution (Panayatou and Susangkarn, 1991). Although the quantitative results of CGE models should be interpreted with care, the qualitative results provide valuable insights and highlight the kinds of information needed to be able to anticipate with greater accuracy the environmental consequences of policy reform (Devarajan, 1990; Robinson, 1990).

Other illustrative examples of the role of macroeconomic policies include the investigation of links between adjustment policy and environment in the agriculture sector in Sub-Saharan Africa (Stryker et al., 1989). Important contributions have also been made by environmental organizations through studies on the environmental impact of the adjustment process in Thailand, the Ivory Coast, Mexico and the Philippines (Reed, 1992; Cruz and Repetto, 1992). Another study suggests that trade policies which encourage greater openness in Latin America have tended to be associated with a better environment, primarily due to environmentally benign characteristics of modern technologies (Birdsall and Wheeler, 1992).

Sectoral reforms More specific or restricted policies affecting key resources like energy and water, or major sectors such as industry and agriculture, are also addressed in programmes of economy-wide policy reforms.

First, with *energy:* Meier et al. (1995) demonstrate that raising subsidized energy prices closer to the long-run marginal cost of electricity supply will not only improve the efficiency of power use and accelerate GNP growth, but also reduce both in-country air pollution and CO_2 emissions that contribute to global greenhouse warming (for details, see Munasinghe, 1996). More generally, the World Bank (1993a) estimates that developing countries spend more than $250 billion annually on subsidizing energy. The countries of the former USSR and Eastern Europe account for the bulk of this amount ($180 billion), and it is estimated that more than half of their air pollution is attributable to such price distortions. Removing all energy subsidies could produce large gains in efficiency and in fiscal balances, and also sharply reduce local pollution and cut carbon emissions by as much as 20 per cent in some countries, and by about 7 per cent worldwide.[6]

Experience in *water and sanitation* show that both targeting and reducing subsidies would have beneficial economic, social and environmental impacts. It would help to reduce wasteful use of water, improve cost recovery in a resource-scarce sector, eliminate the large subsidies that are captured mainly by the wealthy, expand facilities to low-income areas, and reduce water pollution. A number of recent projects illustrate these points, including the Water Quality and Pollution Control Project in Brazil (World Bank, 1992b), the Karnataka Rural Water Supply and Environmental Sanitation Project in India (World Bank, 1993c), and the Changchun Water Supply and Environmental Project in China (World Bank, 1992c).

The negative environmental effects of *industrial protection policies* in Mexico also suggest the potential for 'win–win' industrial policy reforms (for details, see Munasinghe and Cruz, 1994). From 1970 to 1989, when energy was heavily subsidized, the energy intensity of industry increased by almost 6 per cent. Not surprisingly, industrial pollution intensity (per unit of value added) in Mexico also increased by 25 per cent in the same period, induced by government investments and subsidies in the petrochemical and fertilizer industries. Broad subsidies for fuels and electricity absorbed $8–13 billion, or 4 to 7 per cent of GDP, from 1980 to 1985. Studies indicate that removing such subsidies and distortionary incentives to energy-intensive industries would result in both large economic savings and reductions in pollution.

The negative effects of underpricing resources can also be seen in the *agricultural sector* of Tunisia, where the government's concern with ensuring sufficient supply and affordability of livestock products resulted in a web of pricing and subsidy interventions which have encouraged farmers to attempt to maintain herds much larger than the rangelands' carrying capacity (for details, see Munasinghe and Cruz, 1994). Thus removal of livestock subsidies would produce significant economic gains and also improve the sustainable use of rangelands. Studies done for the Zambia Marketing and Processing Infrastructure Project (World Bank, 1992d) show that restructuring public expenditures for agriculture by eliminating maize, fertilizer and transport subsidies would improve the efficiency of food production, increase farm output, and encourage more sustainable farming practices. In the past few years, several additional examples have emerged of how eliminating perverse subsidies would simultaneously yield economic, environmental and social benefits. In the Amazon region, Mahar (1988) and Binswanger (1989) have analysed the role of subsidies to agricultural and livestock expansion as the key factor leading to deforestation. Schneider (1993) focuses on institutional barriers at the economic frontier that prevent the emergence of land-tenure services, such as titling and property rights enforcement, and thus undermine the potential for sustainable land use. Other studies have addressed similar adverse impacts of agricultural policies on the environment in Indonesia (on soil erosion), Sudan (on deforestation), and Botswana (on pasture-land degradation) (Barbier, 1988; Larson and Bromley, 1991; Perrings, 1993).

Stabilization   The critical link between inflation and sustainability is illustrated in a case study of Costa Rica, using a CGE model to examine the deforestation implications of various macroeconomic factors (Persson and Munasinghe, 1995). The results demonstrate that lower interest rates associated with a stable economy allow the logging sector correctly to anticipate greater benefits from future returns to forestry, thereby leading to more sustainable logging practices. Similarly, the establishment of better tenurial security over the resource (and better assurance of realizing future benefits from it) also promotes more sustainable logging. This corresponds to the well-known result in renewable resource exploitation models, that the effects on economic behaviour of open access resource conditions are formally equivalent to those of having secure property rights with very high discount rates.

Other studies have indicated that low and stable discount rates favour the choice of sustainable farming rather than short-term cultivation practices (Southgate and Pearce, 1988). This is important since 'mining' of agricultural land resources is often the prevailing form of resource use in many tropical areas. Frontier farmers have to choose between a sustainable production system with stable but low yields and unsustainable practices which initially have high yields. Using farm models and data from Brazil, a recent study found that if interest rates are very high, farmers tend to use less sustainable methods (Schneider, 1994). The critical macroeconomic implication of this result is that attempts to resolve the land-degradation problem solely by focusing on providing better agricultural technologies would probably be ineffective. To arrest land degradation, macroeconomic reforms which reduce the real interest rate would be needed.

Harmful impacts
The results of a recent UNEP/World Bank workshop (Abaza, 1995) concluded that two major outcomes of structural adjustment programmes may have adverse consequences. First, strong substitution effects in favour of exports could lead to environmental harm – for example, due to the increased profitability of export crops that may be more soil-erosive in the long run, or through the deforestation of open access areas caused by export-oriented logging. Second, changes in both public expenditures and relative prices have often hurt the poor, and in turn led to further environmental degradation – especially when the landless poor have had no other alternative but to overexploit fragile lands. In this context, a typical economy-wide reform programme is handled in stages, with the initial adjustment package aimed at the most important macroeconomic issues. Often, some distortions that policy makers intend to address later, or other constraints that have passed unnoticed in the initial screening, are the cause of environmental or social harm (Munasinghe et al., 1993). As mentioned earlier and elaborated further below, additional complementary measures (including both market- and non-market-based policies, as well as specific investment projects) may be required to avoid such an outcome.

Policy distortions   Environmental gains can be realized by addressing remaining policy failures. In Poland, initial country-wide adjustments, including increases in energy prices, contributed to some improvements in energy use and pollution (Bates et al., 1995). However, both environmental harm and economic losses persisted, because of the remaining policy distortions resulting from the entire system of state ownership which placed little emphasis on financial discipline and managerial accountability. This means that price responsiveness is blunted, since financial losses are simply absorbed by the public budget, or passed on to consumers in the form of higher output prices. Similar challenges face the Former Soviet Union (FSU) and other countries of Central and Eastern Europe as they attempt to restructure their economies and make a rapid transition to a market-oriented system (see for example, World Bank, 1993a). Basically, the reform of regulations and institutions should not be allowed to lag too far behind economic restructuring.

Market failures   In the case of Indonesia, liberalization policies and industrial promotion have accelerated growth in the modern sector, expanded employment opportunities and contributed to reduced pollution through the use of more efficient production and better pollution control techniques (for details, see Munasinghe and Cruz, 1994). In addition, industry expanded rapidly outside densely populated Java, reducing the potential health impacts of industrial concentration. However, there are signs that polluting discharges would increase due to the sheer scale of expansion coupled with market failures – because of inadequate price signals to address the pollution externalities. Clearly, the introduction of complementary measures in the form of pollution taxes and environmental regulations is warranted to correct this emerging problem.

Institutional constraints   In Ghana, as in many regions of Africa, agricultural lands are governed by traditional institutions with communal ownership by the village or tribe. These common property regimes may have been sufficient in the past – allowing sustainable use of agricultural lands when populations were much smaller, and adequate fallowing periods could allow land to regain its fertility. However, recent policy reforms including trade liberalization (by reducing the taxation of agricultural exports) lead to increased production of export crops, while efforts to reduce the government wage bill increase unemployment. Such economy-wide forces tend to overwhelm the traditional land-use arrangements, resulting in reduced fallowing, loss of soil fertility and environmental decline. Thus complementary measures in the form of better-defined rural property rights may help to resist externally induced pressures on land resources, encroachment on to marginal lands, and soil erosion.

Relevant laws and regulations governing resource access should be reviewed when economy-wide reforms are planned, especially when there is evidence that key resource sectors such as land, forests, minerals or marine resources will be affected. In a recent adjustment operation in Peru, it was determined that economy-wide reforms to promote economic recovery could potentially increase harvesting pressures on Peru's overexploited fisheries (World Bank, 1993b). Accordingly, complementary new fishing regulations to protect various fishing grounds were incorporated directly into the adjustment programme.

Stabilization, government deficit reduction and recession   Early views on the social aspects of adjustment were motivated by the concern that adjustment programmes would focus on growth at the expense of distributional objectives (Cornia et al., 1992). A major issue was that the poor, who would be most vulnerable to the effects of macroeconomic contraction, also might be deprived of 'safety nets' – especially if governments cut social services disproportionately. In this same vein, reduced government spending and its potential adverse impact on environmental protection services have been the subject of criticism from environmental groups. In a study performed by ECLAC (1989), it was concluded that adjustment policies pursued in Latin America during the 1980s led to cutbacks in current expenditure allotments for managing and supervising investment in sectors such as energy, irrigation, infrastructure and mining. This limited the funds available for environmental impact assessments and the supervision of projects to control their environmental impacts. Miranda and Muzondo (1991), in an IMF survey, recognized this problem and suggested that high levels of government expenditure in other areas may lead to reduced funding of environmental activities. Recent case studies attributed increases in air pollution problems in Thailand and Mexico to reductions in expenditures for adequate infrastructure (Reed, 1992). Severe adverse impacts of stabilization programmes on low-income groups in Africa (especially women and children) have been noted by Nzomo (1992) – typically due to reduced government spending in areas like health.

By contrast, a study of the social consequences of adjustment lending in Africa found that although there have been declines in government expenditures, the budget proportion going to social expenditures and agriculture actually increased during the adjustment period (Stryker et al., 1989). The results of similar studies focusing on social safety nets during adjustment programmes confirm that pursuing fiscal discipline and macroeconomic stability need not take place at the cost of increased hardship for the poor. In much the same way, specific environmental concerns can be incorporated in stabilization efforts. For example, it has been reported that in many countries in Sub-Saharan Africa, forestry departments and their activities have always been severely underfunded (World Bank, 1994). Thus targeted efforts to support forestry management activities could, with modest costs, by included in reform packages as part of a proactive environmental response. In brief, both critical environmental and social expenditures could be protected if government budget cuts are made judiciously.

Longer-term and less predictable effects
In addition to the short- to medium-term concerns discussed earlier, the crucial long-term links between poverty and environmental degradation in developing countries are increasingly being recognized (see, for example, World Bank, 1992a). The need to break the 'cycle' of poverty, population growth and environmental degradation has been identified as a key challenge for sustainable development. Unfortunately, such longer-term impacts are less predictable.

An important result of examining the general equilibrium effects of macroeconomic policy is that indirect resource allocation effects are important and may dominate the more direct effects of some price or income policy changes. In the Costa Rica study, the economic and environmental implications of wage restraints in structural adjustment are examined with the use of a CGE model which highlights the economic activities and factors affecting deforestation (Persson and Munasinghe, 1995). Because the role of intersectoral resource flows is incorporated in the CGE model, the effects of changes in wages are different from partial equilibrium results. If the wage of unskilled labour were increased (for example, due to minimum wage legislation), the model predicts that deforestation could rise rather than decline. Although logging declines due to increased direct costs, this is more than made up for by the indirect effect of intersectoral flows since the industrial sector (where minimum wage legislation is more binding) is much more adversely affected by the higher labour costs. Labour and capital thus tend to flow from industry to agriculture, leading to greater conversion of forest land for farming. This simulation exercise suggests the need for caution in attempting to 'legislate' income improvements by increasing minimum wages. Introducing higher wages initially improves labour incomes but a resulting contraction of industrial and agricultural employment leads not only to more unemployment but to environmental degradation as well. The increase in unemployment results in greater pressures to expand shifting cultivation in forest lands.

Beyond pricing and intersectoral environmental linkages that can be identified in general equilibrium approaches, another set of studies has looked at the environmental implications of rural poverty and unemployment within the broader context of the social and demographic problems of inequitable land access and rapid population growth (Feder et al., 1988; Cruz and Gibbs, 1990; Lele and Stone, 1989). Import substitution, industrial protection and regressive taxation are some economy-wide policies that have historically been associated with lagging employment generation, income inequality and poverty. Unequal distribution of resources and inappropriate tenure are institutional factors that also contribute to the problem. In the context of inequitable assignment of endowments and rapid population growth, the resulting unemployment and income inequality force the poor to depend increasingly on marginal resources for their livelihood. The result is pressure on fragile environments. This effect can be analysed in conjunction with the assessment of large migration episodes. These may occur as part of direct resettlement programmes or may be induced by inappropriate policies, such as land colonization programmes.

With regard to sustainable agriculture concerns, recent work explicitly links the related problems of rapid population growth, agricultural stagnation and land degradation in Africa (Cleaver and Schreiber, 1991). The study found that shifting cultivation and grazing in the context of limited capital and technical change cannot cope with rapid population growth. At the same time, the traditional technological solution of relying on high-yielding crop varieties is not available. Thus the study identified the need for a mix of responses in terms of reforms to remove subsidies for inappropriate land uses, improve land-use planning, recognize property rights, provide better education, and construct appropriate rural infrastructure to promote production incentives. The importance of long-term links between adjustment programmes, trade and agriculture, and the difficulties of analysing them, have also been emphasized by Goldin and Winters (1992).

A Philippines case study evaluates the policy determinants of long-term changes in rural poverty and unemployment that have motivated increasing lowland to upland migration, and led to the conversion of forest lands to unsustainable agriculture (for details, see Munasinghe and Cruz, 1994). The inability of the government to manage forest resources is an important direct cause of deforestation, but the study also links deforestation induced by lowland poverty to agricultural taxation, price controls and marketing restrictions. At the same time, trade and exchange rate policies (dominated by an urban consumer and industrial sector bias) have played important roles in the Philippines. The agricultural sector was implicitly taxed by an average of about 20 per cent for several decades, worsening rural incomes and poverty, and forcing migration into environmentally fragile lands.

The foregoing evidence suggest that country-wide policy reforms may have counter-intuitive environmental and social impacts, through longer-term and indirect mechanisms. Considerable new work will be required more accurately to trace these complex linkages and improve the long-run sustainability of economic policies.

4. Conclusions

A wide range of economy-wide policy reform programmes has been undertaken to address macroeconomic and sectoral problems. Although these policies are not directed explicitly towards addressing sustainability issues, they may, none the less, have significant environmental and social impacts. While such impacts are often too diverse to be traced comprehensively with precision, many key economy-wide reforms have specific, identifiable impacts on a much smaller subgroup of high-priority environmental and social problems. Some of these impacts may be intuitively obvious, and many of them may be traceable on the basis of country-specific analysis.

Even modest progress in this regard is helpful because the proper recognition of the environmental and social benefits of county-wide policies will clearly help build support for economic reforms. At the same time, broader recognition of the underlying economic and policy causes of environmental and social problems can enhance support for sustainable development initiatives – in terms of both environmental and social policies and projects.

Analytical findings

The stylized results indicate that economy-wide reforms, including removal of price distortions, promotion of market incentives, and relaxation of other constraints will generally contribute simultaneously to economic, social and environmental gains. However, unintended adverse side effects occur when such reforms are undertaken while other neglected policy, market or institutional imperfections persist. The remedy does not generally require reversal of the original economy-wide reforms, but rather the implementation of additional complementary measures (both economic and non-economic) that remove such policy, market and institutional difficulties.

Measures aimed at restoring macroeconomic stability will also generally yield economic, social and environmental benefits. However, the stabilization process may have unforeseen adverse short-term impacts on sustainability issues. Once again, specific complementary measures designed to address the possible adverse environmental and social consequences of stabilization policies would be justified.

Economy-wide policies will have additional (and often unpredictable) longer-term effects on the environment through employment and income distribution changes. Often, adjustment-induced changes generate new economic opportunities and sources of livelihood, thereby alleviating poverty and reducing pressures on the environment due to overexploitation of fragile resources by the unemployed. However, while growth is an essential element of sustainable development, it will necessarily intensify pressures on environmental resources. Increasing efficiency, reducing waste and properly valuing resources will help reshape the structure of growth and reduce undesirable environmental impacts.

Policy implications

In general, some past economy-wide reforms have been implemented without adequate consideration of their environmental and social, as well as economic, impacts. In the case of structural adjustment policies implemented to address the debt crisis faced by many developing countries in the 1980s, partial or piecemeal reforms sometimes pressured countries to adopt methods of increasing economic production which were not only socially harmful, but also environmentally damaging. Nevertheless, despite short-term sacrifices, properly managed adjustment facilitates long-term growth without which environmental damage could be worse. More specifically, non-growth scenarios tend to give rise to worse results than growth situations, because of the linkages between poverty and both environmental and social sustainability.

Hence the best approach seems to be the successful implementation of sound economic policies aimed at the recovery or maintenance of growth, combined with the adoption of specific remedial environmental and social programmes. The availability of appropriate sustainability indicators is a crucial prerequisite for improving all such development decisions. Most importantly, sustainable development strategies must be devised on a country-by-country basis, with due regard for local conditions, resource endowments and social needs.

This chapter indicates how the analytical process may be strengthened by developing a more general framework based on the concept of an action impact matrix (AIM), which more clearly identifies a country's environmental problems in relation to its programme of economy-wide policy reforms and major projects. Such a stepwise approach focuses initially on the links among a relatively small subset of priority environmental and social concerns and a few key economic policy reforms. In subsequent stages, the analysis may be made much more comprehensive. The AIM-based analysis helps to avoid environmental and social damage by identifying, prioritizing and analysing the most serious economic-sustainability linkages. Ideally it would be desirable to devise specific *ex ante* complementary measures to limit environmental and social harm, whenever economy-wide reforms are contemplated. Where data and resource constraints preclude the accurate tracing of such links (*ex ante*), the preliminary screening and prioritization of environmental and social issues could be followed by establishing contingency plans and carefully monitoring these problems of sustainability, to deal with them if they worsen *ex post*. In cases involving more severe environmental and social harm (especially where *ex ante* analysis has carefully prepared the ground), special care may be required to orchestrate the timing and sequencing of various economy-wide policies and complementary measures to minimize environmental and social damage.

These findings also suggest that developing countries seeking sustainable development paths might be well advised to learn from the experience of the industrialized countries, in order to avoid repeating the same mistakes. In particular, income growth and poverty alleviation have the highest priority in low-income countries. If such growth is to take place on a sustained basis, the following points provide useful guidance in the context of tunnelling through the environmental Kuznets curve – by adopting 'win–win' policies that provide simultaneous economic, environmental and social gains; using complementary measures to address harmful impacts on sustainability; and even reshaping economy-wide policies in cases where the threat to sustainability was serious enough.

Further work
More in-depth work is required in tracing the sustainability implications of economy-wide policies that will seek to relate comprehensive packages of country-wide policy reforms to a range of priority environmental and social concerns in different countries. Some areas of current interest such as trade reform and privatization policies should receive early attention. At the same time, there ought to be more emphasis on developing practical models and analytical tools that can be applied in a variety of situations.

Distributional, political economy and institutional issues also need to be addressed in future work. The nature of environmental and social problems is heavily dependent on the allocation of political and institutional power, and policy reforms may have substantial implications for redistributing income and wealth. Thus there are obvious obstacles to overcoming what might be very powerful vested interests when environmental and social reforms are recommended, and implementation problems such as asymmetries in the incidence of costs and benefits, and the timing of reforms, will have to be studied.

Finally, the need for a more systematic way of monitoring the impacts of policies and projects suggests that better environmental and social indicators should be developed. Thus far, the more successful attempts to value environmental impacts in the macroeconomic context have been based on their effects on conventional economic output which are priced in the marketplace (supplemented sometimes with shadow-pricing corrections). This approach may be linked more easily with commonly used market measures of well-being like GNP. For example, the new United Nations handbook for the System of National Accounts (SNA) includes a proposal to supplement the conventional SNA with a set of satellite accounts that reflect pollution damage and depreciation of natural resource stocks (UNSO, 1993).

Some environmentally and socially crucial impacts (for example, loss of biodiversity or human health hazards) are often important, and may require the extension or adaptation of conventional economic techniques. One step would be to improve environmental valuation by using a wider range of methods which employ both market and non-market information to estimate indirectly the economic value of environmental assets (for example, travel cost or contingent valuation methods). Such techniques have been used quite widely in project-level applications in the industrial countries (see the chapter by Hanley in this volume – Chapter 57 – or Freeman, 1993). There is a growing body of case studies on the environmental valuation of project impacts in the developing countries (Munasinghe, 1993a). However, considerable work is required to extend this experience to cover economy-wide impacts.

Other (non-economic) indicators of environmental and social well-being (both micro and macro) also would be helpful in decision making, especially in cases where economic valuation of environmental and social impacts was difficult. Techniques such as multi-criteria analysis (MCA) may be used to trade off among different economic, social and environmental indicators, as a supplement to conventional cost–benefit analysis (see Chapter 58 by Janssen and Munda in this volume). The essential point is that even when valuation of environmental and social impacts is not possible, techniques like MCA exist that will help to better prioritize such impacts, thereby improving development actions (see for example, Munasinghe 1996, ch. 8).

Severe data constraints are likely to limit the applicability of methods requiring comprehensive data requirements in many developing countries. Therefore, 'short-cut' methods need to be developed. For example, easily applicable rules of thumb (calibrated by well-chosen national studies) could be used to devise baseline estimates of national wealth in the form of natural resources, human capital and produced assets (see, for example, Atkinson et al., 1997). Environmental indicators of land use, soil, water and air quality could supplement economic measures, in the same way as social indicators – such as education and health status.

Notes

1. The author is grateful to Jeroen van den Bergh as well as two anonymous referees for their helpful comments. Thanks are also owed to Arati Belle for assistance in putting the paper together.
2. We recognize that normal ecosystem dynamics will result in safe limits that are time-varying, although this does not affect the essential result of the arguments presented above.
3. Note that further outward shifts in the demand curve (due to income growth) will require even greater price increases in subsequent years.
4. In the case of some forms of environmental degradation and pollution, the EKC is more S-shaped, rather than bell-shaped.
5. Given that policy regimes vary widely across countries and over time, an EKC estimated using cross-section (or pooled) data is likely to be a composite of many paths such as IK. Even an EKC based on time-series data for one country will reflect the effects of a range of time-varying policies.
6. A more general equilibrium-based approach suggests that energy price increases would need to be introduced gradually and in harmony with the tempo of wider liberalization efforts throughout the economy.

706   Environmental macroeconomics

References

Abaza, H. (1995), 'UNEP/World Bank workshop on the environmental impacts of structural adjustment programs – New York, 20–21 March 1995', *Ecological Economics*, **14** (1), 1–5.

Atkinson, G., R. Dubourg, K. Hamilton, M. Munasinghe, D. Pearce and C. Young (1997), *Measuring Sustainable Development*, Cheltenham, UK and Lyme, US: Edward Elgar.

Barbier, Edward (1988), 'The economics of farm-level adoption of soil conversation measures in the uplands of Java', Environment Department Working Paper 11, Environment Department, World Bank, Washington, DC.

Bates, R., J. Cofala and M. Toman (1995), 'Alternative policies for the control of air pollution in Poland', Environment Paper 7, World Bank, Washington, DC.

Binswanger, Hans (1989), 'Brazilian policies that encourage deforestation in the Amazon', Environment Working Paper 16, Environment Department, World Bank, Washington, DC.

Birdsall, Nancy and D. Wheeler (1992), 'Trade policy and industrial pollution in Latin America: where are the pollution havens?', in P. Low (ed.), *International Trade and the Environment*, World Bank Discussion Paper 159, World Bank, Washington, DC.

Cleaver, Kevin and G. Schreiber (1991), 'The population, environment, and agriculture nexus in Sub-Saharan Africa', Africa Region Technical Paper, World Bank, Washington, DC.

Cornia, G.A., R. Jolly and F. Stewart (1992), *Adjustment with a Human Face*, Vol. 1, *Protecting the Vulnerable and Promoting Growth*, Oxford: Clarendon Press.

Cruz, Wilfredo and C. Gibbs (1990), 'Resource policy reform in the context of population pressure, and deforestation in the Philippines', *American Journal of Agricultural Economics*, **72** (5), 1264–8.

Cruz, Wilfredo and Robert Repetto (1992), *The Environmental Effects of Stabilization and Structural Adjustment Programs: The Philippines Case*, Washington, DC: World Resources Institute.

Cruz, Wilfredo, Mohan Munasinghe and Jeremy Warford (1997), *The Greening of Economic Policy Reform*. Vol. 2 (Case Studies), Washington, DC: World Bank.

Devarajan, Shantayanan (1990), 'Can computable general equilibrium models shed light on the environmental problems of developing countries?', paper prepared for WIDER conference, 'The Environment and Emerging Development Issues', Helsinki.

ECLAC (Economic Commission for Latin America and the Caribbean) (1989), 'Crisis, external debt, macroeconomic policies, and their relation to the environment in Latin America and the Caribbean', paper prepared for the meeting of high-level government experts on Regional Co-operation in Environmental Matters in Latin America and the Caribbean, United Nations Environmental Programme, Brasilia.

Edwards, Sebastian (1992), 'Structural adjustment and stabilization: issues on sequencing and speed', EDI Working Papers, Economic Development Institute, World Bank, Washington, DC.

Feder, Gershon, T. Ochan, Y. Chalamwong and C. Hongladarom (1988), *Land Policies and Farm Productivity in Thailand*, Baltimore, MD: Johns Hopkins University Press.

Freeman, A. Myrick (1993), *The Measurement of Environmental and Resource Values: Theory and Methods*, Washington, DC: Resources for the Future.

Goldin, I. and A. Winters (1992), *Open Economies: Structural Adjustment and Agriculture*, London: Cambridge University Press.

Kuznets, Simon (1955), 'Economic growth and income inequality', *American Economic Review*, **49**, 1–28.

Kuznets, Simon (1963), 'Quantitative aspects of the economic growth of nations, VIII: The distribution of income by size', *Economic Development and Cultural Change*, **11**, 1–92.

Larson, B. and Daniel Bromley (1991), 'Natural resource prices, export policies, and deforestation: the case of Sudan', *World Development*, **19**, 1289–97.

Lele, U. and S. Stone (1989), 'Population pressure, the environment, and agricultural intensification: variations on the Boserup hypothesis', MADIA Discussion Paper 4, World Bank, Washington, DC.

Mahar, Dennis (1988), 'Government policies and deforestation in Brazil's Amazon region', Environment Working Paper 7, Environment Department, World Bank, Washington, DC.

Mäler, Karl G. and Mohan Munasinghe (1996), 'Macroeconomic policies, second-best theory, and the environment' in M. Munasinghe (ed.), *Environmental Impacts of Macroeconomic and Sectoral Policies*, Washington, DC: World Bank.

Meier, Peter, Mohan Munasinghe and Tilak Siyambalapitiya (1995), 'Energy sector policy and the environment: a case study of Sri Lanka', in M. Munasinghe (ed.), *Environmental Impacts of Macroeconomic and Sectoral Policies*, Washington, DC: World Bank.

Miranda, K. and T. Muzondo (1991), 'Public policy and the environment', *Finance and Development*, **28** (2), 25–7.

Munasinghe, Mohan (1992), *Water Supply and Environmental Management*, Boulder, CO: Westview Press.

Munasinghe, Mohan (1993a), *Environmental Economics and Sustainable Development*, Washington, DC: World Bank.

Munasinghe, Mohan (1993b), 'The economist's approach to sustainable development', *Finance and Development*, **30** (4), 16–19.

Munasinghe, Mohan (1995), 'Making economic growth more sustainable', *Ecological Economics*, **15**, 121–4.

Munasinghe, Mohan (1996), 'An overview of the environmental impacts of macroeconomic and sectoral policies', in M. Munasinghe (ed.), *Environmental Impacts of Macroeconomic and Sectoral Policies*, Washington, DC: World Bank.

Munasinghe, Mohan (1997), 'The long term sustainability of growth in developing countries: a review of selected issues', Environmental Department, World Bank, Washington, DC.

Munasinghe, Mohan and Wilfredo Cruz (1994), *Economywide Policies and the Environment: Lessons from Experience*, Washington, DC: World Bank.

Munasinghe, Mohan, Wilfredo Cruz and Jeremy Warford (1993), 'Are economywide policies good for the environment?', *Finance and Development*, **28**, 25–7.

Nyang'oro, J. and T. Shaw (eds) (1992), *Beyond Structural Adjustment in Africa - The Political Economy of Sustainable and Democratic Development*, New York: Praeger.

Nzomo, M. (1992), 'Beyond structural adjustment programs: democracy, gender, equity, and development in Africa, with special reference to Kenya', in J. Nyang'oro and T. Shaw (eds), *Beyond Structural Adjustment in Africa - The Political Economy of Sustainable and Democratic Development*, New York: Praeger.

Opschoor, J.B. and S.M. Jongma (1996), 'Structural adjustment policies and sustainability', *Environment and Development Economics*, **1**, 183–202.

Panayotou, T. and C. Susangkarn (1991), 'The debt crisis, structural adjustment and the environment: the case of Thailand', paper prepared for the World Wildlife Fund Project on the Impact of Macroeconomic Adjustment on the Environment, Washington, DC.

Perrings, Charles (1993), 'Pastoral strategies in Sub-Saharan Africa: the economic and ecological sustainability of dryland range management', Environment Working Paper 57, Environment Department, World Bank, Washington, DC, February.

Persson, Anika and Mohan Munasinghe (1995), 'Natural resource management and economywide policies in Costa Rica: a computable general equilibrium (CGE) modeling approach', *World Bank Economic Review*, **9** (2), 259–85.

Reed, David (ed.) (1992), *Structural Adjustment and the Environment*, Boulder, CO: Westview Press.

Robinson, S. (1990), 'Pollution, market failure, and optimal policy in an economywide framework', Working Paper 559, Department of Agricultural and Resource Economics, University of California at Berkeley.

Schnieder, R. (1993), 'Land abandonment, property rights, and agricultural sustainability in the Amazon', LATEN Dissemination Note no. 3, World bank, Washington, DC.

Schneider, R. (1994), 'Government and the economy on the Amazon frontier', Latin America and the Caribbean Technical Department, Regional Studies Program, Report no. 34. World Bank, Washington, DC.

Southgate, Douglas and David W. Pearce (1988), 'Agricultural colonization and environmental degradation in frontier developing economies', Environment Working Paper 9, Environment Department, World Bank, Washington, DC.

Stryker, J.D. et al. (1989), 'Linkages between policy reform and natural resource management in Sub-Saharan Africa', Fletcher School, Tufts University, Bedford, MA, and Associates for International Resources and Development.

Tarp, Finn (1993), *Stabilization and Structural Adjustment: Macroeconomic Frameworks for Analyzing the Crisis in Sub-Saharan Africa*, New York: Routledge.

United Nations (1993), *Integrated Environmental and Economic Accounting*, Series F, no. 61, United Nations, New York.

United Nations Statistics Office (UNSO) (1993), *System of National Accounts 1991*, New York: United Nations.

Warford, Jeremy, Mohan Munasinghe and Wilfredo Cruz (1997), *The Greening of Economic Policy Reform*, Vol. 1 (*Principles*), Washington, DC: World Bank.

World Bank (1992a), *World Development Report 1992: Development and the Environment*, New York: Oxford University Press.

World Bank (1992b), *Water Quality and Pollution Control Project in Brazil.* Staff Appraisal Report, World Bank, Washington, DC.

World Bank (1992c), *The Changchun Water Supply and Environmental Project in China.* Staff Appraisal Report, World Bank, Washington, DC.

World Bank (1992d), *The Zambia Marketing and Processing Infrastructure Project.* Staff Appraisal Report, World Bank, Washington, DC.

World Bank (1993a), *Energy Efficiency and Conservation in the Developing World.* A World Bank Policy Paper, Washington, DC.

World Bank (1993b), *Peru: Privatization Adjustment Loan*, Report no. P-5929-PE, Washington, DC.

World Bank (1993c), *The Karnataka Rural Water Supply and Environmental Sanitation Project in India.* Staff Appraisal Report, World Bank, Washington, DC.

World Bank (1994), *Adjustment in Africa: Reforms, Results and the Road Ahead.* A World Bank Policy Research Report, Washington, DC.

Young, C.E.F. and J. Bishop (1995), *Adjustment Policies and the Environment: A Critical Review of the Literature*, CREED Working Paper Series No. 1, IIED, London.

48 The biophysical basis of environmental sustainability

*Robert Goodland**

1. Introduction

This chapter seeks to define environmental sustainability (ES) partly by sharply distinguishing it from social sustainability and, to a lesser extent, from economic sustainability (see Table 48.1). While overlap exists among the three, economic sustainability and ES have especially strong linkages.

If the term 'development' is introduced, discussion becomes more ambiguous. This chapter is not focused on sustainable development, here assumed to be development that is socially, economically and environmentally sustainable, or 'development without throughput growth beyond environmental carrying capacity and which is socially sustainable'.

Environmentally sustainable development implies sustainable levels of both production (sources), and consumption (sinks), rather than oxymoronic sustained economic growth. The priority for development should be improvement in human well-being – the reduction of poverty, illiteracy, hunger, disease and inequity. While these development goals are fundamentally important, they are quite different from the goals of environmental sustainability, the unimpaired maintenance of human life-support systems – the environmental sink and source capacities.

Historians of future generations may well be interested in the social constructs we devised with respect to biophysical reality, but those generations will be confronted primarily with the reality and not with whatever contemporary social construct we made of it. It makes no difference for actual climate change due to greenhouse gas accumulation whether societies or governments 'believe' in it or not (Hueting and Reijnders, 1997); it is a biophysical reality.

2. A potted history of sustainability

If one addresses only the last century or so, some notion of economic sustainability was firmly embodied in the writings of J.S. Mill ([1848] 1900) and Malthus ([1798] 1970). J.S. Mill emphasized that environment

* I warmly appreciate the many years of help, including comments on the manuscript, generously given by Herman Daly and Salah El Serafy.

Table 48.1 Comparison of social, economic and environmental sustainability (after Goodland, 1995, 1997)

Social sustainability	Economic sustainability	Environmental sustainability (ES)
This can be achieved only by systematic community participation and strong civil society. Cohesion of community, cultural identity, diversity, sodality, comity, tolerance, humility, compassion, patience, forbearance, fellowship, fraternity, institutions, love, pluralism, commonly accepted standards of honesty, laws, discipline, etc., constitute the part of social capital least subject to rigorous measurement, but essential for social sustainability.	Economic capital should be stable. The widely accepted definition of economic sustainability is 'maintenance of capital', or keeping capital intact. Thus Hicks's definition of income – 'the amount one can consume during a period and still be as well off at the end of the period' – can define economic sustainability, as it devolves on consuming interest, rather than capital.	Although ES is needed by humans and originated because of social concerns, ES itself seeks to improve human welfare by protecting the *sources* of raw materials used for human needs, and ensuring that the *sinks* for human wastes are not exceeded, in order to prevent harm to humans.
This 'moral capital', as some call it, requires maintenance and replenishment by shared values and equal rights, and by community, religious and cultural interactions. Without such care it depreciates as surely as does physical capital.	Economics has rarely been concerned with natural capital (e.g. intact forests, healthy air). To the traditional economic criteria of allocation and efficiency must now be added a third, that of scale (Daly, 1992). The scale criterion would constrain throughput growth – the flow of material and energy (natural capital) from environmental sources to sinks.	Humanity must learn to live within the limitations of the biophysical environment. ES means natural capital must be maintained, both as a provider of inputs (sources), and as a sink for wastes. This means holding the scale of the human economic subsystem to within the biophysical limits of the overall ecosystem on which it depends. ES needs sustainable consumption by a stable population.

Human or social capital – investments in education, health, and nutrition of individuals – is now accepted as part of economic development, but the creation and maintenance of social capital as needed for social sustainability is not yet adequately recognized.

Economics values things in money terms, and is having major problems in valuing natural capital, intangible, intergenerational and especially common access resources, such as air. Because people and irreversibles are at stake, economics needs to use anticipation and the precautionary principle routinely, and should err on the side of caution in the face of uncertainty and risk.

On the sink side, this translates into holding waste emissions within the assimilative capacity of the environment without impairing it.

On the source side, harvest rates of renewables must be kept within regeneration rates.

Non-renewables cannot be made sustainable, but quasi-ES can be approached for non-renewables by holding their depletion rates equal to the rate at which renewable substitutes can be created.

711

('Nature') needs to be protected from unfettered growth if we are to preserve human welfare before diminishing returns set in: people should be content to be stationary (steady-state), for the sake of posterity, long before necessity compels them to it. Malthus emphasized the pressures of exponential population growth on the finite resource base. The modern version (neo-Malthusianism) is exemplified by Ehrlich and Ehrlich (1989a, 1989b, 1991) and by Hardin (1968, 1993).

Daly's *Toward a Steady State Economy* (1972, 1973, 1974) and *Steady State Economics* (1977, 2nd edn 1991) synthesized the impacts of population and resources. Daly's steady-state economics is the seminal work in which population and consumption pressures on environmental sources and sinks are integrated and extended into the single critical factor of scale – the throughput of matter and energy from the environment, used by the human economy, and released back into the environment as wastes. This is the basis for defining sustainability.

Neither Mill's nor Malthus's views on the relationship between the environment and the economy are held in great esteem by today's economists who follow the technological optimism of David Ricardo ([1817] 1973). Ricardo rightly believed that human ingenuity and scientific progress would postpone the time when population would overtake resources or 'the niggardliness of nature'. As the absolute numbers of poor are increasing worldwide (World Bank, 1992, 1997), that postponement seems to have ended.

The definition of environmental sustainability hinges on distinguishing between throughput growth and development. The 'growth debate' started becoming mainstream two decades after World War II. Boulding (1966, 1968, 1973, 1992), Mishan (1967, 1977) and Daly (1972, 1973, 1974), in particular, seriously questioned the wisdom of infinite throughput growth in a finite earth. Toman (1994) claims that the *World Development Report 1992* basically treats sustainability as another way of espousing economic efficiency in the management of services derived from the natural endowment. Throughput growth is defended by most economists, including Beckerman (1974, 1992, 1994, 1995), who still reject the concept of sustainability (but see Daly, 1995 and El Serafy, 1996). *The Limits to Growth* (Meadows et al., 1972) and *Beyond the Limits* (Meadows et al., 1992) concluded that 'it is possible to alter these growth trends and establish a condition of ecological and economic stability that is sustainable into the future'. Barney's (1980) US Global Report to the President amplified and clarified the limits argument. Large populations, their rapid growth and increasing affluence or consumption, are unsustainable.

The optimistic Ricardian tradition still dominates conventional economics and is exemplified by the cornucopians Simon and Kahn in their 1984 response to the Global 2000 report (Barney, 1980). Panayotou (1993), Summers (1992) and Fritsch et al. (1994) find growth compatible with sustainability, and even necessary for it. The 1980 World Conservation Strategy by IUCN and WWF (IUCN, 1980) and Clark and Munn's 1987 IIASA report *Sustainable Development of the Biosphere* reinforced the 'limits to growth' conclusions. Daly and Cobb's (1989) prizewinning *For the Common Good* estimated that GDP growth in the US has become decoupled from all measures of well-being over the last two decades. Daly and Cobb's seminal findings that growth is not at all improving well-being has subsequently been shown for most OECD nations, and for an increasing number of low-consumption nations too. The growth debate and sustainability are usefully synthesized by Korten (1991) and Max-Neef (1995).

The most consensualist definition of sustainable development is that of the UN Brundtland Commission: 'Development that seeks to meet the needs and aspirations of the present without compromising the ability to meet those of the future (WCED 1987).' Part of the success of the Brundtland Commission's definition stems from its opacity (Hueting, 1990); sustainability was defined in a growth context. But when WCED (1992) reconvened five years later, calls for growth were striking by their absence. Prince Charles commended WCED in the same publication (WCED, 1992), on dropping their 1987 tolerance of huge '5- to 10-fold increases in economic growth'. They also elevated the population issue higher on the agenda to achieve sustainability (WCED, 1992).

Few economics Nobel prizewinners write on sustainability. Haavelmo and Hansen (1992) and Tinbergen and Hueting (1992) repudiate throughput growth and urge the transition to sustainability. Solow's earlier writings (1974) questioned the need for sustainability, but recently he has modified that position (1993a, 1993b). The World Bank adopted environmental sustainability in principle rather early on in 1984 and then promoted it actively (Ahmad et al., 1989; Serageldin et al., 1995). Daly and Cobb (1989) is the most influential and durable of these publications because it shows that more growth has started to do more harm than good. It outlines pragmatic operational methods to reverse environmental damage and reduce poverty. Goodland et al. (1992), supported by two economics Nobel prizewinners, Tinbergen and Haavelmo, advanced the case that there are indeed limits, that the human economy has reached them in many places, that it is impossible to grow into sustainability, that source and sink capacities of the environment complement human-made capital which cannot substitute for their environmental services, and that it is highly unlikely that the South can ever catch up with the North's current consumerist lifestyle. Thus redistribution has become more urgent (Daly, 1992, 1996).

Since the late 1980s there has been a substantial corpus of literature on 'ecological economics' (Costanza, 1991; Costanza et al., 1997), largely espousing stronger types of sustainability, as outlined below (Hueting, 1974; Collard et al., 1987; Archibugi and Nijkamp, 1989; Tisdell, 1992; IIASA, 1992; Barbier, 1993; Turner, 1993; Netherlands, 1994; Jansson et al., 1994).

Intergenerational and intragenerational sustainability
Most people in the world today are either impoverished or live barely above subsistence; the number of people living in poverty is increasing. Developing countries can never be as well off as today's OECD average. Future generations seem likely to be larger and poorer than today's generation. Even if the human population starts to decline after *c.* 2050, it will inherit and have to make do with damaged life-support systems. How damaged it may be, is up to us of today's generation. Sustainability includes an element of not harming the future (intergenerational equity), as well as not harming society today (intragenerational equity). If the world cannot move toward intragenerational sustainability during this generation, it will be that much more difficult to achieve intergenerational sustainability sometime in the future. This is because the capacity of environmental services is being impaired, so will probably be lower in the future than it is today. In addition, the demand for such services from the world's higher population will be much greater.

3. What should be sustained?
Environmental sustainability seeks to maintain environmental services indefinitely, especially those maintaining human life. Source capacities of the global ecosystem provide raw material inputs – food, water, air, energy. Sink capacities assimilate outputs or wastes. These source and sink capacities are large but finite; sustainability requires that they be maintained rather than run down. Overuse of a capacity impairs its provision of life-support services. For example, accumulation of CFCs (chlorofluorocarbons) is damaging the capacity of the atmosphere to protect humans and other biota from harmful ultraviolet radiation. UN conventions then promoted sustainability by conserving sink capacity or assimilation rates by severely restricting the production of CFCs.

Protecting human life is the main reason that anthropocentric humans seek environmental sustainability. Human life depends on other species for food, shelter, breathable air, moderate rainfall, plant pollination, waste assimilation, and other environmental life-support services. The huge instrumental value of non-human species to humans is grossly undervalued by economics. The vast number of species with apparently no 'use' to humans, and the even bigger number of species as yet unknown to science, are largely unaccounted in economics. Non-human species of no present value to humans have intrinsic worth, but this also is almost entirely excluded in economics.

Although biodiversity conservation is becoming a general ideal for nations and development agencies, there is no agreement on what and how much should be conserved, nor at what cost. Leaving aside the important fact that we have not yet learned to distinguish useful from non-useful species, agreeing on how many other species to conserve is not central to the definition of environmental sustainability. Reserving habitat for other species to divide among themselves is important; let evolution select the mix of species, not us. But reserving a non-human habitat requires limiting the scale of the human habitat. 'How much habitat should be conserved?', while an important question to ask, is moot; the answer is probably 'no less than today's remnants'. Sustainability suggests that we should seek to reduce human-induced species extinctions to zero, to conserve as much remaining habitat as possible, and to restore degraded lands.

This brings us to the precautionary principle: in cases of uncertainty and in view of the possibility of irreversibility, sustainability mandates that we err on the side of caution. Because survival of practically all the global life-support systems is uncertain and non-linear we should be very conservative in our estimate of various input and output capacities, and particularly of the role of unstudied, apparently 'useless', species.

The dictionary distinguishes between growth and development. 'To grow' means 'to increase in size by the assimilation or accretion of materials'; 'to develop' means 'to expand or realize the potentialities of; to bring to a fuller, greater or better state'. As Daly and Cobb (1989) emphasize, growth implies quantitative physical or material increase; development implies qualitative improvement or at least change. Quantitative growth and qualitative improvement follow different laws. Our planet develops over time without growing. Our economy, a subsystem of the finite and non-growing earth, must eventually adapt to a similar pattern of development without throughput growth. The time for such adaptation is now. Historically, an economy starts with quantitative throughput growth as infrastructure and industries are built, and eventually it matures into a pattern with less throughput growth but more qualitative development. While this pattern of evolution is encouraging, qualitative development needs to be distinguished from quantitative throughput growth if environmental sustainability is to be approached. For sustainability, development needs to replace throughput growth to the fullest extent possible.

4. The definition of environmental sustainability

The definition of ES as the 'maintenance of natural capital' (Table 48.1) is expanded as input–output rules in Table 48.2. By definition, the two funda-

Table 48.2   The definition of environmental sustainability

---

1. Output rule:
   Waste emissions from a project or action being considered should be kept within the assimilative capacity of the *local* environment without unacceptable degradation of its future waste absorptive capacity or other important services.

2. Input rule:
   (a) Renewables: Harvest rates of renewable resource inputs must be kept within regenerative capacities of the natural system that generates them.

   (b) Non-renewables: Depletion rates of non-renewable resource inputs should be set below the rate at which renewable substitutes are developed by human invention and investment according to the Serafian quasi-sustainability rule, outlined below. An easily calculable portion of the proceeds from liquidating nonrenewables should be allocated to the attainment of sustainable substitutes.

Note on the Serafian quasi-sustainability of non-renewables (El Serafy, 1989; Daly and Cobb, 1989; Hueting et al., 1995): The Serafian rule pertains to non-renewable resources, such as fossil fuels and other minerals, but also to renewables to the extent they are being 'mined'. It states that their owners may enjoy part of the proceeds from their liquidation as income, which they can devote to consumption. The remainder, a user cost, should be reinvested to produce income that would continue after the resource has been exhausted. This method essentially estimates income from sales of an exhaustible resource. It has been used as a normative rule for quasi-sustainability, whereby the user cost should be reinvested, not in any asset that would produce future income, but specifically to produce renewable substitutes for the asset being depleted. The user cost from depletable resources has to be invested specifically in replacements for what is being depleted in order to reach sustainability, and must not be invested in any other venture – no matter how profitable. Hueting et al. (1995) take this further, especially for non-renewable energy, by basing a future acceptable rate of extraction of the non-renewable resource on the historic rate at which improved efficiency, substitution and reuse became available. These calculations show the folly of relying on technological optimism, rather than on some historic track record.

Sources: Daly (1973, 1974, 1992, 1996); Daly and Cobb (1989).

mental environmental services – the source and sink functions – must be maintained unimpaired during the period over which sustainability is required. ES is a set of constraints on the four major activities regulating the scale of the human economic subsystem: the use of (a) renewable and (b) non-renewable resources on the source side, and (c) pollution and (d) waste assimilation on the sink side. This short definition of ES is the most useful so far and is gaining adherents. The fundamental point about this definition is that ES is a natural science concept and obeys biophysical laws (Table 48.2). This general definition seems to be robust irrespective of country, sector or future epoch (Goodland and Daly, 1996).

5. Causes of unsustainability

When the human economic subsystem was small, the regenerative and assimilative capacities of the environment appeared infinite. We are now learning painfully that environmental sources and sinks are finite. Originally, these capacities were very large, but the scale of the human economy has exceeded them. Source and sink capacities have now become limited. As economics deals only with scarcities, in the past source and sink capacities of the environment did not have to be taken into account. Conventional economists still hope or claim that economic growth can be infinite or at least that we are not yet reaching limits to growth; hence the fierce recent repudiation of *Beyond the Limits* (Meadows et al., 1992), and the endorsement of Brundtland's view that '5- to 10-fold more growth will be needed' (WCED, 1987).

The scale of the human economy is a function of throughput – the flow of materials and energy from the sources of the environment, used by the human economy, and then returned to environmental sinks as waste. Throughput growth is a function of population growth and consumption. Throughput growth translates into increased rates of resource extraction and pollution, or the use of sources and sinks. The definition of unsustainability is that the scale of throughput has exceeded environmental source and sink capacities. The evidence is pervasive: greenhouse gases are accumulating, the ozone shield is being damaged, scarcely a drop of seawater can be found free of human pollution, anthropically induced species extinction rates are high and rising, oceanic fish catches and natural forests are declining fast – as a few examples. In addition, that the number of poor people is increasing suggests that low-cost extractive or harvested foods have become scarce or unobtainable.

There is little admission yet that consumption above sufficiency, however defined, is not an unmitigated good. The scale of the human economy has become unsustainable because it is living off inherited and finite capital (for example, fossil fuels, fossil water); because we do not account for losses of natural capital (for example, extinctions of species), nor do we adequately count the costs of environmental harm.

6. The time for environmental sustainability

Approaching sustainability is urgent. Three examples of this follow. First, consider that if release were halted today of all substances that damage the ozone shield, it may need as much as one century to return to pre-CFC effectiveness. Second, the world has only a brief 25 years or so to make the fundamental transition from fossil fuels to hydro and other renewable energy, unless we accept perilous risks of climatic instability (Goodland and El Serafy, 1997). Third, the rates of topsoil erosion, depletion of fossil aquifers and species extinctions are high and soaring. These pervasive examples of unsustainability are exacerbated because every passing year means sustainability has to be achieved for the extra 80 million people who are added to world's population. Technology seems highly unlikely to produce substitutes for the ozone shield, stable climates, topsoil, readily available water, and species. Though environmental sources and sinks have been providing humanity with their free services for the last million years, and until recently have seemed vast and resilient, we have now begun to exceed their capacities and to damage them worldwide. That is why environmental sustainability is so urgent.

7.   Sustainability and substitutability

Where environmental services are substitutable, the substitution achieved has been marginal. Most natural capital or environmental services cannot be substituted for, and their self-regenerating properties are slow and cannot be significantly hastened. Conventional economics and technological optimists claim that substitutability is the rule, rather than an exception. The extent of substitutability between natural and human-made capital, although marginal, is rarely discussed by neoclassical economists, yet it is central to the issue of sustainability. Substitutability is the ability to offset a diminished capacity of environmental source services to provide healthy air, water, and so on, and of environmental sink services to absorb wastes.

The importance of substitutability is that if it prevails, then there can be no limits, because if an environmental good is destroyed, it is argued, a substitute can replace it. When white pine or sperm whales became scarce, there were acceptable substitutes. When easily gathered surficial oil flows were exhausted, drilling technology enabled very deep deposits to be tapped. In Europe, when the native forest was consumed, timber for houses was replaced with brick. If bricks did not substitute for timber, then timber was imported.

The realization that substitutability is the exception, rather than the rule, is not yet widespread. Once limits of imports cease to mask substitutability (for example Northwestern America timber controversies show the limits of imports), then it becomes plain that many, if not most, forms of capital are more complementary or neutral, and are less substitutable.

Ecologists attach great importance to Baron Justus von Liebig's Law of the Minimum – the whole chain is only as strong as its weakest link. The factor in shortest supply is the limiting factor in a process because factors are complements, not substitutes. If scarcity of phosphate is limiting the rate of photosynthesis, then photosynthesis would not be enhanced by increasing another factor such as nitrogen, light, water, or CO_2. If one wants faster photosynthesis, one must ascertain which factor is limiting and then invest in that one first, until it is no longer limiting. More irrigation and fertilizer cannot increase crop yield if day length is limiting. More nitrogen fertilizer cannot substitute for lack of phosphate, precisely because they are complements.

Environmental sustainability is based on the conclusion that most natural capital is a complement for human-made capital, and not a substitute. Complementarity is profoundly unsettling for conventional economics because it means there are limits to growth, or limits to environmental source and sink capacities. Human-made capital is a very poor substitute for most environmental services. Substitution for some life-support systems is impossible. The sooner economics internalizes these facts, the sooner the world can start to approach environmental sustainability.

References

Ahmad, Y., S. El Serafy and E. Lutz (eds) (1989), *Environmental Accounting for Sustainable Development*, Washington, DC: World Bank.

Archibugi, F. and P. Nijkamp (eds) (1989), *Economy and Ecology: Towards Sustainable Development*, Dordrecht: Kluwer.

Barbier, E. (ed.) (1993), *Economic Ecology: New Frontiers and Sustainable Development*, London: Chapman and Hall.

Barney, G.O. (ed.) (1980), *The Global 2000 Report to the President of the USA*, 2 vols., Harmondsworth, UK: Penguin.

Beckerman, W. (1974), *In Defense of Economic Growth*, London: Jonathan Cape.

Beckerman, W. (1992), 'Economic growth: Whose growth? Whose environment?', *World Development*, **20**, 481–92.

Beckerman, W. (1994), 'Sustainable development: Is it a useful concept?', *Environmental Values*, **3**, 191–209.

Beckerman, W. (1995), *Small is Stupid: Blowing the Whistle on the Greens*, London: Duckworth.

Boulding, K.E. (1966), 'The economics of the coming spaceship earth' in H. Jarret (ed.), *Environmental Quality in a Growing Economy*, Baltimore, MD: Johns Hopkins University Press, pp. 3–14.

Boulding, K.E. (1968), *Beyond Economics*, Ann Arbor: University of Michigan.

Boulding, K.E. (1973), 'The economics of the coming spaceship earth' in H.E. Daly (ed.), *Toward a Steady State Economics*, San Francisco: Freeman, pp. 121–32.

Boulding, K.E. (1992), *Towards a New Economics: Ecology and Distribution*, Aldershot, UK and Brookfield, US: Edward Elgar.

Clark, W.C. and Munn, R.E. (eds) (1987), *Sustainable Development of the Biosphere*, Cambridge, UK: Cambridge University Press.

Collard, D., D.W. Pearce and D. Ulph (eds) (1987), *Economics, Growth and Sustainable Environments*, New York: St Martin's Press.

Costanza, R. (ed.) (1991), *Ecological Economics: The Science and Management of Sustainability*, New York: Columbia University Press.

Costanza, R., J. Cumberland, H. Daly, R. Goodland and R. Norgaard (1997), *An Introduction to Ecological Economics*, Boca Raton, FL: St Lucie Press (CRC Press).

Daly, H.E. (1972), 'In defense of a steady-state economy', *American Journal of Agricultural Economics*, **54** (4), 945–54.

Daly, H.E. (ed.) (1973), *Toward a Steady State Economy*, San Francisco: Freeman.

Daly, H.E. (1974), 'The economics of the steady state', *American Economic Review, Papers and Proceedings* (March), 15–21.

Daly, H.E. ((1977) 1991), *Steady-State Economics*, 2nd edn, Washington, DC: Island Press.

720   Environmental macroeconomics

Daly, H.E. (1992), 'Allocation, distribution and scale: towards an economics that is efficient, just and sustainable', *Ecological Economics*, **6** (3), 185–93.

Daly, H.E. (1995), 'On Wilfred Beckerman's critique of sustainable development', *Environmental Values*, **4**, 49–55.

Daly, H.E. (1996), *Beyond Growth: the Economics of Sustainable Development*, Boston, MA: Beacon Press.

Daly, H.E. and J. Cobb (1989), *For the Common Good*, Boston, MA: Beacon Press.

Ehrlich, P.R. and A. Ehrlich (1989a), 'Too many rich folks', *Populi*, **16** (3), 3–29.

Ehrlich, P.R. and A. Ehrlich (1989b), 'How the rich can save the poor and themselves', *Pacific and Asian Journal of Energy*, **3**, 53–63.

El Serafy, S. (1989), 'The proper calculation of income from depletable natural resources', in Y. Ahmad et al. (eds), *Environmental Accounting for Sustainable Development*, Washington, DC: World Bank, pp. 10–18.

El Serafy, S. (1996), 'In defence of weak sustainability: a response to Beckerman', *Environmental Values*, **5**, 75–81.

Fritsch, B., S. Schmidheiny and W. Seifritz (1994), *Towards an Ecologically Sustainable Growth Society: Physical Foundations, Economic Transitions and Political Constraints*, Berlin: Springer.

Goodland, R. (1995), 'The concept of environmental sustainability', *Annual Review of Ecology*, **26**, 1–24.

Goodland, R. (1997), 'Biophysical and objective environmental sustainability', in A. Dragun and K. Jakobsson (eds), *Sustainability and Global Environmental Policy*. Cheltenham, UK and Lyme, US: Edward Elgar, pp. 63–95.

Goodland, R., H.E. Daly and S. El Sarafy (1992), *Population, Technology, Lifestyle: The Transition to Sustainability*, Washington, DC: Island Press.

Goodland, R. and H.E. Daly (1996), 'Environmental sustainability: universal and non-negotiable', *Ecological Applications*, **6**, 1002–17.

Goodland, R. and S. El Serafy (1998), 'The urgent need to internalize CO$_2$ emission costs', *Ecological Economics*, **27**, 79–90.

Haavelmo, T. and S. Hansen (1992), 'On the strategy of trying to reduce economic inequality by expanding the scale of human activity', in R. Goodland, H.E. Daly and S. El Serafy (eds), *Population, Technology, Lifestyle: The Transition to Sustainability*, Washington, DC. Island Press, pp. 38–51.

Hardin, G. (1968), 'The tragedy of the commons', *Science*, **162**, 1243–8.

Hardin, G. (1993), *Living Within Limits: Ecology, Economics and Population Taboos*, New York: Oxford University Press.

Hueting, R. (1974) (English edition 1980), *New Scarcity and Economic Growth: More Welfare through Less Production*, Amsterdam, North-Holland.

Hueting, R. (1990), 'The Brundtland report: A matter of conflicting goals', *Ecological Economics*, **2**, 109–17.

Hueting, R., P. Bosch, and B. de Boer (1995), 'The calculation of sustainable national income', The Hague: Netherlands Organization for International Cooperation and New Delhi, Indian Council of Social Science Research.

Hueting, R. and L. Reijnders (1997), 'Sustainability is an objective concept', ms, The Hague: Netherlands Bureau of Statistics.

IIASA (1992), *Science and Sustainability*, Laxenburg, Vienna: International Institute of Applied Systems Analysis.

IUCN (1980), *The World Conservation Strategy*, Gland, Switzerland: IUCN, WWF, UNEP, FAO and UNESCO.

Jansson, A., M. Hammer, C. Folke and R. Costanza (1994), *Investing in Natural Capital: The Ecological Economics Approach to Sustainability*, Washington, DC: Island Press.

Korten, D.C. (1991), 'Sustainable development', *World Policy Journal* (Winter), 156–90.

Malthus, T.R. ([1798] 1970), *An Essay on the Principle of Population*, Harmondsworth, UK: Penguin.

Max-Neef, M. (1995), 'Economic growth and the quality of life', *Ecological Economics*, **15**, 115–18.

Meadows, D., D. Meadows, J. Randers and W. Behrens III (1972), *The Limits to Growth*, New York: Universe Books.
Meadows, D.H., D.L. Meadows and J. Randers (1992), *Confronting Global Collapse: Envisioning a Sustainable Future*, Post Mills, VT: Chelsea Green.
Mill, J.S. ([1848] 1900), *Principles of Political Economy*, 2 vols., New York: Collier.
Mishan, E.J. (1967), *The Costs of Economic Growth*, London: Staples Press.
Mishan, E.J. (1977), *The Economic Growth Debate: An Assessment*, London: Allen and Unwin.
Netherlands (1994), *The Environment: Towards a Sustainable Future*, Dordrecht: Kluwer Academic Publishers.
Panayotou, T. (1993), *Green Markets: The Economics of Sustainable Development*, San Francisco: International Center for Economic Growth.
Ricardo, D. ([1817] 1973), *Principles of Political Economy and Taxation*, London: Dent.
Serageldin, I., H.E. Daly and R. Goodland (1995), 'The concept of sustainability', in W. Van Dieren (ed.), *Taking Nature into Account*, New York, Springer Verlag, pp. 99–123.
Simon, J. and H. Kahn (eds) (1984), *The Resourceful Earth: a Response to Global 2000*, Oxford: Blackwell.
Solow, R. (1974), 'The economics of resources or the resources of economics', *American Economic Review*, **15**, 1–14.
Solow, R. (1993a), 'An almost practical step toward sustainability', *Resources Policy*, **19**, 162–72.
Solow, R. (1993b), 'Sustainability: an economist's perspective', in R. Dorfman and N.S. Dorfman (eds), *Selected Readings in Environmental Economics*, New York: Norton, pp. 179–87.
Summers, L. (1992), 'Summers on sustainable growth', *The Economist*, 30 May, p. 191.
Tinbergen, J. and R. Hueting (1992), 'GNP and market prices: wrong signals for sustainable economic success that mask environmental destruction', in R. Goodland, H.E. Daly and S. El Serafy (eds), *Population, Technology, Lifestyle: The Transition to Sustainability*, Washington, DC: Island Press, pp. 52–62.
Tisdell, C. (1992), *Environmental Economics: Policies for Environmental Management and Sustainable Development*, Aldershot, UK and Brookfield, US: Edward Elgar.
Toman, M.A. (1994), 'Economics and sustainability: balancing trade-offs and imperatives', *Land Economics*, **70** (4), 399–413.
Turner, R.K. (ed.) (1993), *Sustainable Environmental Economics and Management; Principles and Practice*, London: Belhaven.
World Bank (1992), *World Development Report 1992: Development and the Environment*, New York: Oxford University Press.
World Bank (1997), *World Development Report 1997: The State in a Changing World*, Washington, DC: World Bank.
World Commission on Environment and Development (WCED) (1987), *Our Common Future* (The Brundtland Commission's report), Oxford: Oxford University Press.
World Commission on Environment and Development (WCED) (1992), *Our Common Future Reconvened*, Geneva: Centre for Our Common Future.

49 Indicators of sustainable development
Onno J. Kuik and Alison J. Gilbert

1. Introduction

In the last decade sustainable development has become an important policy objective for many governments and other decision-making bodies across the world. A question that logically follows the adoption of sustainable development as a policy objective is how to measure its achievement. Sustainable development has been described as a *meliorative* concept: it offers a general direction to policy making, but it is not very precise in its *operational* guidance. Although the concept of sustainable development may be clear enough at a sufficiently high level of abstraction, not so clear are its practical, day-to-day, policy implications. In the preparations for UNCED this was clearly understood. The action programme of UNCED, Agenda 21, thus calls for the development of *indicators* for sustainable development, rather than for precise measurement. In fact, Agenda 21 argues that 'Indicators of sustainable development need to be developed to provide solid bases for decision-making at all levels and to contribute to a self-regulating sustainability of integrated environment and development systems' (UNCED, 1992).

Indicators are bits of information that highlight what is happening in the large system; they are small windows that provide a glimpse of the 'big picture' (Sustainable Seattle, 1996). Clearly, sustainable development is such a 'big picture'. Indicators of sustainable development should highlight, or provide a glimpse of, the sustainability of development. The primary functions of indicators are simplification and communication. They are a compromise between scientific accuracy and the demand for concise information. The purpose of their use may be planning (for example, problem identification, allocation of resources, policy assessment) and/or communication (for example, warning, mobilization, legitimization). The basic challenge of indicator development is: '[how] to reduce a large quantity of data down to its simplest form, retaining essential meaning for the questions that are being asked of the data' (Ott, 1978).

Several desired features of indicators have been identified in the literature, for example Liverman et al. (1988), Kuik and Verbruggen (1991), OECD (1994), Gilbert and Feenstra (1994), Nilsson and Bergström (1995) and Azar et al. (1996). One of these features is that indicators should represent some part of the cause–effect chain in the processes being assessed. This is discussed briefly in the context of sustainable development in the section below. Sustainability indicators differ from other indicators in that they are derived by measuring the gap between existing conditions (either pressure or state) and a reference condition which is taken to reflect sustainability (Opschoor and Reijnders, 1991).[1] Issues related to this reference condition are also discussed in Section 2 below. Section 3 offers a glimpse of current indicator development, and distinguishes between three different approaches. Section 4 describes some trends and prospects for future research.

2. A conceptual framework for indicator development

Cause–effect chain
The cause–effect chain of economy–environment interactions has been summarized in various ways for indicator development. Figure 49.1 offers one example of a cause–effect chain of economic activities and their effects on the environment. It is based on the pressure–state–impact–response framework initially used by the OECD. Production and consumption lead to pressures on the environment. Pressures lead to an environmental state

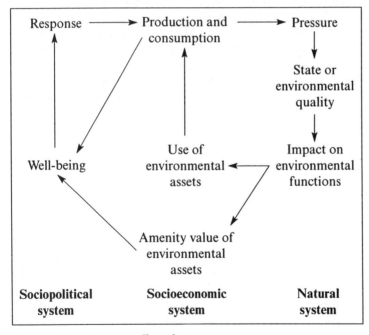

Figure 49.1   A cause–effect chain

or quality. Environmental quality may feedback within natural systems to impact their performance of environmental functions and their users. Human well-being may be affected, either because of a reduction in the natural systems' ability to supply inputs for the production of goods and services or directly through a loss of amenities. These effects may trigger a response from the sociopolitical system.

Environmental indicators and indicators of sustainable development can focus on different aspects of the cause–effect chain. They can focus on the pressures from the socioeconomic system on the natural system (pressure indicators), on the state of the natural system (state indicators), its capacity to provide goods and services to society (impact indicators), and on the sociopolitical system's response to environmental problems (response indicators). Factors such as uncertainty, irreversibilities, non-linearities, time lags and diverging spatial scales mean that pressure, state and response indicators may not be closely linked to each other. Therefore the choice of focus is very important.

The reference condition

Indicators of sustainable development measure the gap between actual societal (including economic) development and development that may be called sustainable. In thinking about reference conditions for sustainable development it is useful to distinguish between necessary and sufficient conditions. For development to be sustainable it is necessary that the capital stock on which this development depends does not diminish over time. The capital stock that is relevant to development includes both human-made and natural capital.[2] Pearce et al. (1997) have used the notion of a non-decreasing capital stock (per capita) in their indicator of sustainability which they call the 'genuine savings' indicator. Genuine savings is a measure of net savings which accounts for the depreciation of man-made capital, the depletion of natural resources and the accumulation of pollutants. Pearce et al. (1997) argue that persistent negative savings rates must lead to non-sustainability, in the sense that the level of welfare of a country must eventually decline. Thus a non-negative genuine savings rate is a necessary condition for sustainable development.

Just because a country has a positive genuine savings rate does not mean that it is on a sustainable path. A positive genuine savings rate may not be sufficient if certain types of natural capital are 'essential' or 'critical' to development and human well-being, in the sense that they cannot be substituted by human-made capital.[3] Green plants provide a case in point: their capacity to produce oxygen would seem essential to human life and it is difficult to imagine how the loss of this capacity through the eradication of plant cover could be realistically compensated by a human-made artefact.

As yet, there is no consensus on the sufficient conditions for sustainable development, although many attempts have been made in defining such conditions. Conditions based on considerations of multifunctionality of use, historically sustainable states, and most sensitive receptor have been proposed. The following are offered as joint principles for sustainable development (adapted from Azar et al., 1996; Moffatt, 1996):

1. lack of full scientific certainty should not be a reason for postponing cost-effective measures to prevent environmental degradation – the Precautionary Principle (UNCED, 1992);
2. environmental problems should be solved as near to the source as possible – the Proximity Principle;
3. substances extracted from the lithosphere or produced by society should not systematically accumulate in the ecosphere;
4. the vigour, organization and resilience of ecosystems (ecosystem 'health' – Costanza et al., 1992) should not become systematically deteriorated;
5. access to and value derived from the use of natural resources should be equitable in both space and time; and,
6. the use of resources must be economically efficient.

3. Recent developments

Three alternative approaches to indicators of sustainable development can be distinguished. The first approach is to summarize all information on sustainable development into one aggregate indicator. The indicator is expressed in one common metric: the most likely candidates are monetary and energy units. Examples of such efforts include a wide variety of monetary indicators, the most familiar being the 'Green GDP' that, although existing as a concept, has not yet been assessed by any statistical office. Green GDP and its many variants aim at correcting some existing measure of national economic activity (GDP, GNP, NI, NNP) for the degradation and depletion of the natural environment. Related indicators are developed or proposed by Daly and Cobb (1990), Hueting (1989), Repetto et al. (1989), and the already-mentioned genuine savings indicator by Pearce et al. (1997). In terms of the cause–effect chain in Figure 49.1 above, these indicators are located in the socioeconomic and sociopolitical systems. Because it is difficult or impossible to value in a credible way each element of environmental degradation in monetary units, the monetary indicators are either not comprehensive of all facets of sustainable development (Repetto, Pearce) or they are built on strong and controversial assumptions (Hueting). Slesser et al. (1994) have tried to develop a set of indicators in energy units. However, apart from anything else, indicators exclusively expressed in energy units do not communicate easily and are therefore not very powerful in changing the behaviour of decision makers in our society who are familiar with money but not with 'Joules'.

In the second approach, information on sustainable development is not reduced to one common metric, but the environmental and natural resource (sub)indicators are nevertheless closely linked to the economic system. In terms of the cause–effect chain in Figure 49.1, these indicators address pressures from the economy to the natural system and the impact of environmental change on the socioeconomic system. Den Butter and Verbruggen (1994) argue that separate economic and environmental indicators, in contrast to one aggregate 'Green GDP' indicator, are more transparent and useful to policy makers for making trade-offs between economic growth and environmental quality. This approach is taken by the UN Statistical Office (Bartelmus and van Tongeren, 1988) and by the European Commission's Pressure Indicator project (EC, 1994). Several national statistical offices also work along these lines (see, for example, Keuning, 1993).

In the third approach, there is no close link between the indicators and the system of national accounts. Indicators can address all elements of the cause–effect chain and even beyond. We could call these indicators 'free-form' indicators of sustainable development. Examples of the development of these indicators include the 'Sustainable Seattle' project, the UN Commission on Sustainable Development (UN, 1996), the indicator of cadmium accumulation in the Netherlands (Gilbert and Feenstra, 1994) and various other initiatives. There are obvious costs in breaking the connection between the economy and the environment in these 'free-form' indicators even though these indicators could capture information missing in the system of national accounts. Further, it is unclear how to come to some conclusion regarding the sustainability of development if three indicators suggest that things are going well while two suggest the opposite. However, 'free-form' indicators could be valuable to governmental agencies responsible for environmental, rather than economic, management.

4.   Trends and prospects for future research

Section 3 showed that a variety of approaches to sustainable development indicators coexist. In a field of research that is so new and dynamic, it is difficult to discern definite trends in one or the other direction. The science or art of developing indicators of sustainable development faces many technical problems that require the cooperation of a variety of scientific disciplines, including natural sciences, economics and communication science. Problems that have to be faced in indicator development include indicator needs, the weighing and aggregation of indicators with different dimensions, the scope and boundaries of indicators and questions regarding the timeliness and spatial coverage of indicators.

Indicator needs

Indicators of sustainable development have been and are being developed in a diversity of contexts and for a variety of purposes. Policy has a strong influence on indicator selection and development. That indicators of sustainable development should be relevant to policy is unarguable, but policy is a fickle driver for their development. The last 20 years of environmental policy have demonstrated considerable dynamics in terms of policy goals and priorities. It is not unusual for considerable effort to be devoted to one urgent problem, but, once results become available, other problems with greater urgency take over the stage. A strategic approach to indicator development is required. Indicator selection and development should be based on a scientific and comprehensive analysis of the relevant cause-and-effect chains, not on the fashions of the day. The pressure–state–impact–response framework has potentially much to offer.

Aggregation

One of the main difficulties and challenges of the development of indicators of sustainable development is to reduce the complexity of the question without sacrificing its essential meaning. Sustainable development is a multifaceted issue; aggregate indicators should weigh and aggregate its many facets into one clear message. There are a number of ways to deal with multidimensional information.

First, the information can be scaled into one common metric, for example, monetary or energy units. Scaling all information into one common metric has the advantage that aggregation is straightforward. The question is whether it is possible to reduce all information on sustainable development to one metric without loss of meaning. It is, for example, not always obvious how changes in essential biogeochemical cycles or biological diversity can be valued in money terms.

Second, multi-criteria techniques can be used to weigh and evaluate information with different dimensions. Their advantages lie in that no information is lost in the scaling operation. Disadvantages are that different multi-criteria techniques may produce different answers and that these techniques depend on a certain level of subjectivity in the weighting of the various aspects of sustainable development.

Third, visual images can sometimes be used for easy interpretation of multidimensional information. The advantage is that images can contain much of the original information in an accessible form ('one picture can say more than a thousand words'). Disadvantages include underestimation of their ease of interpretation given that the information density can be high (for example, maps produced by simulation models). It is known that people are able to process no more than seven stimuli at once and that the interpretation of images is strongly dependent on, for example, the colours used (Miller, 1956; Bertin, 1981). Further, visual images are easily manipulated to the point where they can become very misleading.

Scope and boundaries

Indicators of sustainable development are intended to provide a window on the big picture. In order to do this, specification of scope and boundaries are needed. In the assessment of environmental (and other) problems, there is a strong need for bounding so that the analysis does not get out of hand. However, inappropriate bounding may also lead to analytical distortions and false information.

An excellent example of this is provided by spatial scale. The sustainable development of a country can be understood in terms of the sustainability of its activities within its own national borders, but also in terms of its relations with the rest of the world. A national indicator that neglected the possible negative impacts of the country's economic development on the possibilities for sustainable development of other countries would clearly be inappropriate. In general, the problem of bounding is common to the assessment of sustainable development of all open systems (van den Bergh, 1991).

Closing remarks

In the final analysis the development of indicators of sustainable development cannot be considered merely a scientific or a technical exercise. In essence it is also a political exercise. The concept of sustainable development itself is to a large degree a political concept. The different approaches to indicator development reflect not only alternative scientific views, they also reflect alternative political views. To paraphrase Ott: different questions are being asked of the data. Because of the political nature of much of the sustainable development debate, it is highly unlikely that a common and widely accepted set of indicators will be developed in the near future. Therefore, different sets of indicators of sustainable development and different approaches to indicator development will, in all likelihood, remain coexisting, reflecting the different societal concerns that underlie the concept of sustainable development.

Notes

1. Note that this chapter only discusses indicators of *sustainable development*. It does not discuss any other type of indicators, such as environmental policy indicators or ecosystem indicators.

2. Serageldin and Steer (1994) argue that (at least) four types of capital can be recognized:
   1. Human-made or 'fabricated' capital such as machines, factories, buildings and infrastructure. Most economic analysis focuses on this category. Consistent with human tendency to 'treasure what we measure', more efforts have gone into increasing the volume of this stock than of the other three. Consequently, the discussion of sustainable development tends to focus on the remaining capital forms since it is there that remedial analysis and action are needed. These other capital forms are:
   2. Natural capital, consisting of renewable (ecosystems and their components) and non-renewable natural resources (e.g. oil and subsoil minerals).
   3. Human capital. Investment in people – for example in their health, education and nutrition – is now seen to be a very high return investment, particularly in developing societies.
   4. Social capital, because a society is more than just the sum of its individuals. The existence of civic community is not only the precursor and guarantor of good governance but also the key to sustained socio-economic development.
3. The difference between necessary and sufficient conditions is central to the debate on weak versus strong sustainability. A lively debate was held in the journal *Environmental Values*, starting from a critical contribution of Beckerman in 1994. Our approach deliberately plays this debate down and argues for a spectrum between the two within which sustainable development could lie.

References

Azar, C., J. Holmberg and K. Lindgren (1996), 'Socio-ecological indicators for sustainability', *Ecological Economics*, **18**, 89–112.
Bartelmus, P., J.W. van Tongeren (1988), *SNA Framework for Satellite Accounting*, Washington, DC: World Bank/UNSO.
Beckerman, W. (1994), 'Sustainable development: is it a useful concept?', *Environmental Values*, 3, 191–209.
Bergh, J.C.J.M. van den (1991), *Dynamic Models for Sustainable Development*, Ph.D. thesis, Tinbergen Institute; Amsterdam: Thesis Publishers.
Bertin, J. (1981), *Graphics and Graphic Information Processing*, Berlin: Walter de Gruyter.
Butter, F.A.G. den and H. Verbruggen (1994), 'Measuring the trade-off between economic growth and a clean environment', *Environmental and Resource Economics*, 4, 187–208.
Costanza, R., B. Norton and B.J. Haskell (eds) (1992), *Ecosystem Health: New Goals For Environmental Management*, Washington, DC: Island Press.
Daly, H.E. and J.B. Cobb (1990), *For the Common Good: Redirecting the Economy Toward Community, the Environment and a Sustainable Future*, Boston: Beacon Press.
EC (1994), *Directions for the European Union on Environmental Indicators and Green National Accounting* (COM(94) 670 final), Brussels.
Gilbert, A.J. and J.F. Feenstra (1994), 'A sustainability indicator for the Dutch environmental theme "diffusion": cadmium accumulation in soil', *Ecological Economics*, 9, 253–65.
Hueting, R. (1989), 'Correcting national income for environmental losses: toward a practical solution', in Y.J. Ahmad, S. El Serafy and E. Lutz (eds), *Environmental Accounting for Sustainable Development*, Report of a UNEP – World Bank Symposium, Washington, DC: World Bank.
Keuning, S.J. (1993), 'An information system for environmental indicators in relation to national accounts', in W.F.M. de Vries et al. (eds), *The Value Added of National Accounting: Commemorating 50 Years of National Accounts in the Netherlands*, Voorburg: Netherlands Central Bureau of Statistics, pp. 287–305.
Kuik, O.J. and H. Verbruggen (ed) (1991), *In Search of Indicators of Sustainable Development*, Dordrecht: Kluwer Academic Publishers.
Liverman, D.M., M.E. Hanson, B.J. Brown and R.W. Meredith Jr (1988), 'Global sustainability: towards measurement', *Environmental Management*, 12 (2), 133–43.
Miller, G.A. (1956), 'The magical number seven plus or minus two: some limits on our capacity for processing information', *Psychological Review*, **63**, 81–97.

Moffatt, I. (1996), 'An evaluation of environmental space as the basis for sustainable Europe', *International Journal of Sustainable Development and World Ecology*, **3**, 49–69.

Nilsson, J. and S. Bergström (1995), 'Indicators for the assessment of ecological and economic consequences of municipal policies for resource use', *Ecological Economics*, **14**, 175–84.

OECD (Organization for Economic Cooperation and Development) (1994), *Environmental Indicators: OECD Core Set*, Paris: OECD.

Opschoor, J.B. and L. Reijders (1991), 'Towards sustainable development indicators', in O.J. Kuik and H. Verbruggen (eds), *In Search of Indicators of Sustainable Development*, Dordrecht: Kluwer Academic Publishers.

Ott, W.R. (1978), *Environmental Indices: Theory and Practice*, Ann Arbor, MI: Ann Arbor Science Publishers.

Pearce, D.W., G. Atkinson and K. Hamilton (1997), 'The measurement of sustainable development', in J.C.J.M. van den Bergh and M.W. Hofkes (eds), *Theory and Implementation of Sustainable Development Modelling*, Dordrecht: Kluwer Academic Publishers.

Repetto, R., W. Magrath, M. Wells, C. Beer and F. Rossini (1989), *Wasting Assets: Natural Resources in National Income Accounts*, Washington, DC: World Resources Institute.

Serageldin, I. and A. Steer (1994), *Making Development Sustainable: From Concepts to Action*, Environmentally Sustainable Development Occasional Papers no. 2, World Bank, Washington, DC.

Slesser, M., J. King, C. Revie and D. Crane (1994), *Non-Monetary Indicators for Managing Sustainability*, Report to EC-DGXII, CHE Edinburgh University, Edinburgh.

Sustainable Seattle (1996), *The 1995 Indicator Report* (http://www.scn.org-sustainable/susthome.html).

UN (United Nations) (1996), *Indicators of Sustainable Development: Methodology Sheets*, Commission on Sustainable Development, United Nations, New York.

UNCED (United Nations Conference on Environment and Development) (1992), *Rio Declaration and Agenda 21*, Report on the UN Conference on Environment and Development, Rio de Janeiro, 3–14 June 1992, UN doc. A/CONF.151/26/Rev.1 (Vols I–III).

50 Development, poverty and environment
Edward B. Barbier[1]

1. Introduction
Since the 1980s, substantial progress has been made in economic research of natural resource degradation problems in developing countries. Global support for such research was strongly endorsed by the UN Conference on Environment and Development (UNCED) held in Rio de Janeiro, Brazil in June 1992. For example, in its Agenda 21 pre-conference declaration, the UNCED Secretariat made the following statement:

> In the last two decades, there has been some progress through conventional economic policy applied in parallel with environmental policy. It is now clear that this is not enough, and that environment and development must be taken into account at each step of decision making and action in an integrated manner. (UNCED, 1992)

As a result, post-Rio a 'new' subdiscipline of *economics of environment and development* has quickly emerged, and there is an even more rapidly expanding demand for policy analysis that applies environmental economics to development problems.[2] An overriding feature of recent economic analysis in environment and development has been to treat the environment as an 'asset', or form of 'natural capital', that must be managed to 'sustain' economic development (Barbier, 1994). The crucial decision is how much economic rent can be gained through exploiting stocks of natural capital and reinvesting in other economic assets, that is, reproducible (man-made) capital, foreign assets and human resources, in order to meet both current and future economic opportunities. This decision is of paramount importance to many low-income developing countries, as they are usually characterized as having an abundance of natural capital and too little human and man-made capital. Similarly, poor people within developing countries are considered to be overly dependent on natural resources and primary production, because of the lack of economic opportunities in other sectors of the economy and insufficient (man-made) capital formation.

In short, the interrelationship between economic development, poverty and environment has become a critical factor in understanding the conditions and constraints determining whether developing countries can attain sustainable economic development and growth. The present chapter briefly examines this interrelationship, focusing in particular on the problem of resource dependence in low-income countries; the tendency of poor households within low-income economies to be concentrated within 'ecologically fragile' zones; and the myth of a unidirectional poverty–environment 'trap'.

2.   Resource dependence in low-income countries

The recent debate in economics over the role of innovation in economic growth has fostered empirical investigations across countries and regions to investigate the factors underlying long-term economic growth (Barro and Sala-í-Martin, 1995; Mankiw et al., 1992; Pack, 1994; Romer, 1994). Unexpectedly, these cross-country comparisons of growth rates have pointed to an important but unresolved issue for analysts: why is it that the long-term economic growth rates of poor countries as a group are not catching up with those of rich countries? Conventional explanations suggest that the inability of poor countries to 'take off' economically 'can be attributed to failed policies and weak institutions' (Pack, 1994). The lack of stable economic policies and institutions in poor countries in turn inhibits the generation or use of new technological ideas to reap greater economic opportunities, thus constraining economic growth and development. Other factors that may also explain the comparatively poor growth performance of low-income countries include the lack of well-defined property rights, insecurity of contracts and general social instability (World Bank, 1992).

Although such arguments are persuasive, they may be only half correct. Institutional and policy failures in poor economies are important determinants of their inability to innovate sufficiently to achieve higher long-term growth rates. However, an equally important factor overlooked in conventional analysis and explanations is the structural economic dependence of poor economies on their natural resource endowments.

Barbier (1994) shows that many low-income and lower middle-income economies – especially those displaying low or stagnant growth rates – are highly *resource-dependent*. Not only do these economies rely principally on direct exploitation of their resource bases through primary industries (for example, agriculture, forestry, fishing, and so on) but also over 50 per cent or more of their export earnings come from a few primary commodities (see Table 50.1). These economies tend to be heavily indebted and are experiencing dramatic land-use changes – especially conversion of forest area to agriculture – as well as problems of low agricultural productivity, land degradation and population-carrying-capacity constraints. A recent cross-country analysis by Sachs and Warner (1995) has confirmed that resource-abundant countries, that is, countries with a high ratio of natural resource

Table 50.1 Poor economies with high export concentration in primary commodities[a]

	Contribution of primary commodities to total exports[b]	Export share in 1980/81	Export share in 1965	Main export commodities[b] 1		Main export commodities[b] 2	
	over 90%				%		%
Uganda ($280)	100	100	100	Coffee	95.6	Tea	0.3c
Eq. Guinea ($410)	100	91	NA	Cocoa	34.4	Coffee	3.1
Sao Tome & Pr. ($490)	99	100	NA	Cocoa	95.5	Copra	1.8
Ethiopia ($120)	99	99	99	Coffee	53.8	Hides	15.3
Rwanda ($320)	99	99	100	Coffee	75.5	Tea	10.8c
Yemen PDR ($430)	99	NA	94	NA		NA	
Zambia ($290)	98	99	100	Copper	83.0	Cobalt	5.4
Burkina Faso ($210)	98	85	95	Cotton	32.6	Livestock	26.8e
Nigeria ($290)	98	99	97	Petroleum	87.3	Cocoa	4.7
Liberia ($450)c	98	98	97	Iron Ore	63.4	Rubber	16.1e
Ghana ($400)	97	98	98	Cocoa	51.1	Gold	20.3
Mauritania ($480)	97	99	99	Fish	65.8	Iron Ore	33.3
Bolivia ($570)	97	100	95	Gas	40.1	Tin	13.9
Niger ($300)	96	98	95	NA		NA	
Somalia ($170)	95	99	86	Meat	39.7	Banana	34.5
Papua N.G. ($810)	95	100	90	Gold	37.7	Copper	28.9
Zaire ($170)	93	94	92	Copper	35.8	Coffee	11.2e
Sudan ($480)	93	99	99	Cotton	30.3	Livestock	24.4
Ecuador ($1120)	93	93	98	Petroleum	44.8	Fish/Shrimp	19.0
Togo ($370)	92	85	97	Phosphate	36.2	Cotton	12.6

Table 50.1 (cont.)

	Contribution of primary commodities to total exports[b]	Export share in 1980/81	Export share in 1965	Main export commodities[b] 1	%	Main export commodities[b] 2	%
Comoros ($440)	92[c]	86[e]	NA	Cloves	41.7	Vanilla	33.3[c]
Lao PDR ($180)	90	100[e]	NA	Timber	51.7	Electricity	19.0
over 80%							
Chad ($160)	89[c]	96[e]	97	Cotton	69.4	Hides/Skins	3.8[e]
Myanmar ($210)[c]	89	81[d]	NA	Rice	32.7	Teak	32.2[e]
Yemen A.R. ($640)	89	49	100	Oil	93.7		
Honduras ($860)	89	89	96	Bananas	39.0	Coffee	21.0
Congo ($910)	89	94	37	Oil	71.6	Timber	15.6
Cote d'Ivoire ($770)	88	90	95	Cocoa	25.7	Coffee	13.1
Cameroon ($1010)	88	97	94	Petroleum	48.9	Coffee	12.2
Paraguay ($1180)	88	NA	92	Cotton	10.3	Timber	2.5
Guinea-Bissau ($190)	87[c]	71[d]	NA	Cashewnut	73.3	Groundnut	6.7[c]
Guyana ($420)	87[c]	NA	NA	NA		NA	
Madagascar ($190)	84	92	94	Coffee	26.6	Cloves	5.7
Malawi ($170)	83	93	99	Tobacco	62.8	Tea	10.3
Burundi ($240)	83	96	95	Coffee	82.6	Tea	5.0
Kenya ($370)	83	88	94	Coffee	26.2	Tea	21.9[c]
Tanzania ($160)	81	86	87	Coffee	31.4	Cotton	12.7
over 70%							
Peru ($1300)	78	83	99	Copper	12.9	Zinc	8.8

Country				Commodity	Value	Commodity	Value
Maldives ($410)	77c	70e	NA	Fish	57.1c	Groundnut	14.8
Senegal ($650)	75	81	97	Fish	26.9	Oil	17.0
Colombia ($1180)	75	72	93	Coffee	30.2	Fuel	9.4
Benin ($390)	74	96	95	Cotton	13.4		
Egypt ($660)	74	92	80	Oil	64.4	Cotton	6.5
Dominican Rep. ($720)	74	81	98	Nickel	31.2	Sugar	20.5
Indonesia ($440)	71	96	96	Petroleum	40.0	Rubber	5.0
El Salvador ($940)	71	63	83	Coffee	60.6	Fish	3.5c
Mali ($230)	70	83	97	Cotton	36.9	Livestock	29.0
over 60%							
Guatemala ($900)	62	71	86	Coffee	34.8	Bananas	7.6
C.A.R. ($380)	60	74	46	Diamonds	40.9	Coffee	18.9
Zimbabwe ($650)	60	63	85	Tobacco	21.5	Gold	13.1
over 50%							
Sri Lanka ($420)	57	79	99	Tea	25.9	Rubber	7.0c
Jordan ($1500)	53	57	81	Minerals	38.6	Food	10.2
Morocco ($830)	50	72	95	Ph. Acid	16.8	Phosphate	13.3

Notes:

a Poor economies are those with per capita incomes of $1500 or less in 1988. US dollar figure after each country listed indicates GNP per capita in 1988.

b Contributions to the value of total merchandise exports in 1988, unless indicated.

c 1987 value.

d 1981–83 average value.

e 1984 value.

Source: Barbier (1994), based on various editions of the following World Bank documents: *World Development Report; Trends in Developing Countries; Commodity Trade and Price Trends; African Economic and Financial Data.*

exports to GDP – have tended to grow less rapidly than countries that are relatively resource-poor.

Recent explanations as to why resource dependence may be a factor in influencing economic growth point to a number of possible fundamental linkages between environment, innovation and long-term growth relevant to poor economies. For example, Barbier (1998a) demonstrates the possible influences of depletion in a resource-dependent economy on innovation and growth, which vary depending on the feedback effects between resource scarcity and innovation. The limitations of resource-based development have also been examined by Matsuyama (1992) and Sachs and Warner (1995). Matsuyama shows that trade liberalization in a land-intensive economy could actually slow economic growth by inducing the economy to shift resources away from manufacturing (which produces learning-induced growth) towards agriculture (which does not). Sachs and Warner extend the Matsuyama model to allow for full 'Dutch disease' influences of a mineral or oil-based economy, that is, when an economy experiences a resource boom, the manufacturing sector tends to shrink and the non-traded goods sector tends to expand. The authors' theoretical and empirical analyses support the view that a key factor influencing endogenous growth effects is the relative structural importance of tradable manufacturing versus natural resource sectors in the economy.

Thus the continuing dependence of most of the world's poorest economies on their resource base suggests that environmental management should be given a higher priority as a development concern. This is particularly the case given that past economic policies and investments have led to rapid changes – frequently with adverse economic consequences – in resource stocks and patterns of use. Demographic trends have often worsened the relationship between population and resource-carrying capacity in many regions. Continuing agricultural extensification into marginal lands has increased the susceptibility of economic systems and livelihoods to environmental degradation.[3]

In short, the available physical indicators suggest that the natural asset base of the poorest, resource-dependent economies is being rapidly run down. Yet these economies remain in a fundamental state of 'underdevelopment' and cannot generate sufficient long-term economic growth to 'take-off'. That is, development remains essentially 'unsustainable' in poor economies because the net depreciation of their natural asset base (and any increase in population) is not being compensated by investment in renewable human and physical capital. Clearly, then, a major factor affecting the long-term development prospects of poor economies is their failure to place a higher priority on policies for efficient and sustainable management of the natural resource base to maintain the 'capital' required for the transition to and achievement of long-term sustainable economic development goals.

There is also evidence that in many poor economies depletion and degradation of natural resources – such as croplands, forests, freshwater and fisheries – may be a contributing factor in social processes that destabilize the institutional and economic conditions necessary for innovation and growth (Barbier and Homer-Dixon, 1996; Homer-Dixon, 1995). Despite the relative abundance of natural resource endowments in many low-income countries, incidences of resource scarcity and conflicts over resource use and allocation can be sufficiently severe to cause widespread social unrest, friction and even violent conflict. The result is continual disruption of the stable institutional and policy environment necessary for these countries to generate sufficient human capital, develop R&D capacity, utilize existing technological knowledge available domestically and internationally, and produce and disseminate new technologies throughout the economy. In short, while resource scarcity often induces market and endogenous technological responses that in turn mitigate scarcity, it can also disrupt the stable policy and social environment necessary for these responses to occur automatically.

For example, in Bangladesh increasing scarcities of land and water have aggravated social struggles over the distribution of power and wealth, which have in turn limited innovations to control flood and irrigation necessary for boosting productivity (Golleti, 1994; Boyce, 1987). In Haiti, depletion of forest and soil resources has led to significant rent-seeking behaviour by powerful élites such as wealthy landowners, who have blocked reforestation projects, land improvements and other innovations in rural areas that would have threatened their highly profitable monopoly of forest and arable land resources (Wallich, 1994). Finally, Deacon (1994) has found evidence that across a wide cross-section of low- and middle-income countries social and political instability is highly correlated both with low levels of productive investments generally and with resource scarcity (in this case deforestation). Thus Deacon suggests that the overall results of his analysis 'are broadly consistent with the hypotheses that deforestation results both from population growth – and the increased competition for land and natural resources that accompany it – and from political environments that are not conducive to investment'.

3.   The concentration of the poor in marginal areas.

A worrying trend in developing economies is the concentration of the poorest groups in 'ecologically fragile' zones – areas where environmental degradation or severe environmental hazards constrain and even threaten economic welfare. As indicated by Leonard et al. (1989), around 470 million, or 60 per cent, of the developing world's poorest people live in rural or urban areas that can be classified as 'ecologically fragile'.[4] Around 370 million of the developing world's poorest people live in 'marginal' agricultural areas. These less favourable agricultural lands, with lower productivity potential, poorer soils and physical characteristics, and more variable and often inadequate rainfall, are easily prone to land degradation due to overcropping, poor farming practices and inadequate conservation measures.

The result is that the economic livelihoods and welfare of the poorest income groups in low-potential areas are at greater risk from increasing environmental degradation. It is this risk, combined with the impact of public policies, institutions and investments on the economic incentives, that the poorest face that may have the most profound – and often perverse – effects on the willingness and ability of the poorest groups to counteract degradation.

Another major 'poverty reserve' in developing countries is peripheral urban areas, or 'squatter' settlements. Recent evidence from West Java and Nigeria confirms that the informal employment sector and settlements around urban and semi-urban settlements are often the preferred 'open access' resource for the poor (Jagannathan, 1989). Although precise estimates of how many of the 1.3 billion urban dwellers in developing countries live in 'squatter' settlements are scarce, it is common for between 30 and 60 per cent of the population in large cities to live either in illegal settlements or in tenements and cheap boarding houses. In smaller urban centres of less than 100000 inhabitants – which contain about three-quarters of the developing world's urban population – the proportion of people living in illegal settlements may be smaller than in the large cities. However, the proportion living in areas with inadequate infrastructure or services may be as high or even higher in small as compared to larger urban centres (Cairncross et al., 1990). As a consequence, the economic welfare of a substantial, and growing, number of the poorest urban dwellers is threatened by the environmental hazards and health risks posed by pollution, inadequate housing and poor sanitation, water and other basic infrastructure services.[5]

The concentration of the poorest groups in developing countries in 'ecologically fragile' areas suggests that it is the welfare of the poorest in developing economies that is at the greatest risk from continued environmental degradation. As argued by Kates (1990), throughout the developing world the poor often suffer from three major processes of *environmental entitlement* loss:

- the poor are *displaced* from their traditional entitlement to common resources by development activities or by the appropriation of their resources by richer claimants;

- the remaining entitlements are *divided* and reduced by their need to share their resources with their children or to sell off bits and pieces of their resources to cope with extreme losses (crop failure, illness, death), social obligations (marriages, celebrations) or subsistence; and
- the resources of the poor are *degraded* through excessive use and by failure to restore or to improve their productivity and regeneration – a process made worse by the concentration of the poor into environments unable to sustain requisite levels of resource use.

As a result of these processes, the economic livelihoods of the poor become even more vulnerable to the risks posed by environmental degradation, and their ability and willingness to manage resources sustainably may become even more constrained. Moreover, statistics indicate that the poorest groups in the relatively more affluent developing regions of Latin America and Asia are even more concentrated in ecologically fragile areas than the poorest groups in Africa (Leonard et al., 1989). This suggests that the problem does not easily disappear with economic growth and rising national income.

4. The poverty–environment trap

It is often assumed that the effectiveness of public policies and economic incentives in controlling environmental degradation in developing economies is limited by the existence of a poverty–environment 'trap'. Given the presence of both high levels of poverty and environmental degradation in developing countries, it is tempting to conclude that poverty *causes* environmental degradation. However, poverty and environmental degradation may be positively correlated, but correlation does not imply causation. If anything, recent evidence suggests that poverty–environmental linkages cannot be reduced to simple unidimensional cause–effect relationships.[6]

There are numerous complex factors that influence poor people's perceptions of the environment and their behaviour towards natural resource management. These range from the economic distortions arising from policy and market failures, to underlying labour and capital endowments and constraints (including pressures to increase family size), to access to alternative employment and income-earning opportunities, to institutional and legal factors such as tenure or access security, property rights and delivery systems. Public policies and other factors often affect the incentive structures and redirect capital and labour flows between sectors and regions, with adverse consequences for the poor and their ability or willingness to manage resources sustainably (Jagannathan, 1989).

As poor people have little or no access to capital and must rely on family or low-skilled labour to earn income, it would seem economically perverse that they would degrade any 'natural' capital at their disposal. Many studies have revealed that poor people and communities are often acutely aware of the essential role of natural resources in sustaining their livelihoods, and equally, of the costs and impacts of environmental degradation.[7] This would suggest that, *ceteris paribus*, there exist tremendous *incentives* for the poor to manage and sustain the stock of natural capital at their disposal in order to maintain or enhance both their immediate and future livelihood options. Where they choose to degrade their environment – and there may be rational grounds for doing so under certain circumstances – it is because changing economic and social conditions have altered the incentive structures of the poor, including perhaps their control over or access to essential resources.

Thus from an economic perspective, simply observing that poor people are 'driven' to degrade the environment – even when this appears to be the case – is not helpful. Designing appropriate policy responses to alleviate problems of poverty and environmental degradation therefore requires careful analysis of the *determinants* of individual behaviour. Such an analysis would clarify the factors leading them to degrade their environment, their responses to environmental degradation and the incentives required to induce conservation.

Where further analysis reveals that poverty is not the direct 'cause' of environmental degradation, designing appropriate policy responses will nevertheless be affected by poverty's indirect role. The response of poor people and communities to incentives encouraging sustainable resource management may be affected by special factors influencing their behaviour, such as high rates of time preference induced by greater risk and uncertainty over livelihood security, labour and capital constraints, insecure tenure over and access to resources, imperfect information and access to marketed inputs and a variety of other conditions and constraints.[8] For example, in a recent review of farmer adoption of agroforestry systems in Central America and the Caribbean, Current et al. (1995) conclude that 'poorer farmers may find agroforestry profitable, but their rate and scale of adoption is often constrained by limited land, labor, and capital resources and their need to ensure food security and reduce risks'.

Moreover, the poor are not a homogeneous group. The work of Lipton (1983, 1988) highlights how the 'ultra' or 'core' poor, other poor and the non-poor in developing countries all differ in terms of demographic, nutritional, labour-market and asset-holding characteristics.[9] A recent study in Malawi illustrates how the poor and the 'core' poor face different incentives and constraints in combating declining soil fertility and erosion, which are serious problems afflicting smallholder agriculture (Barbier and Burgess, 1992).

In Malawi, female-headed households make up a large percentage (42 per cent) of the 'core-poor' households. They typically cultivate very small plots of land (<0.5 ha) and are often marginalized on to the less fertile soils and steeper slopes (>12 per cent). They are often unable to finance agricultural inputs such as fertilizer, to rotate annual crops, to use 'green manure' crops or to undertake soil conservation. As a result, poorer female-headed households generally face declining soil fertility and lower crop yields, further exacerbating their poverty and increasing their dependence upon the land. Thus policies to alleviate poverty and control land degradation must take into account the labour, land and cash constraints faced by poor female-headed households, or these households may not respond fully to policy measures and incentives that ignore such constraints on their land management decisions.

In fact, inappropriate policies are often at the heart of many poverty–environment linkages, which on a large scale create serious development problems. For example, in Colombia poor rural households are increasingly migrating to both marginal upland areas and equally fragile land in the forested Amazon–Orinoco basin (Heath and Binswanger, 1996). The result is continued unsustainable farming of both the Andean slopes and the Amazonian basin, followed by land abandonment as yields decline and further expansion of farming on frontier and marginal lands. The problem is exacerbated less by failures in rural labour markets or policies than by the failure of agricultural and land policies to provide adequate rural labour absorption, efficient land-use patterns and, most importantly, higher returns to existing smallholder agricultural land.

5. Conclusion

Recent advances in the economics of environment and development have improved our understanding of the key interrelationships between poverty, environment and economic development in low-income countries. First, these countries are heavily dependent on their natural resource base as the basic 'capital' for economic development. Efficient and sustainable management of this 'natural' capital is essential for these countries to achieve long-term growth and development. Problems of environmental degradation and resource scarcity in developing countries may further impede long-term growth prospects by undermining the institutional stability and policy environment necessary for social and technical innovation.

Another major concern for developing countries is the increasing concentration of the poorest groups in marginal urban and rural areas. This results in the economic livelihoods of the poor becoming even more vulnerable to the risks posed by environmental degradation, further constraining their ability and willingness to manage resources sustainably. Whether poverty is directly or only indirectly the 'cause' of environmental degradation seems a less relevant concern when compared to the implications of pervasive environmental degradation for the livelihoods of the poor. This is the real 'poverty–environment' link that should be the focus of development efforts. Although poverty alleviation is an ultimate aim of economic development, past economic policies and investments in developing countries have led to rapid changes in resource stocks and patterns of use – frequently with adverse economic consequences for the poor. Clearly, designing policies and investments to improve the efficient and sustainable management of natural resources must take into account the poverty–environment linkages outlined in this chapter if the sustainable economic development of low-income countries is to be achieved.

Notes
1. I am grateful to Jeroen van den Bergh, Sjak Smulders, Harmen Verbruggen and an anonymous reviewer for helpful comments on earlier drafts of this chapter. However, the usual caveat applies.
2. One indicator that a new subdiscipline in economics has 'arrived' is the launching of its own specialist journal. This occurred in March 1996 with the publication by Cambridge University Press of the first volume and issue of *Environment and Development Economics*. For various recent overviews and surveys of research in environment and development economics see Barbier (1991, 1994); Böjo, et al. (1990); Dasgupta (1996); Pearce et al. (1990); and Pearce and Warford (1993).
3. Statistical evidence of these trends for resource-dependent poor economies can be found in Barbier (1994). For a theoretical exploration of how poor initial resource endowments can lead to unsustainable growth paths, see Barbier and Markandya (1990).
4. The 'poorest people' are defined by Leonard et al. (1989) as the poorest 20 per cent of the population in developing countries. In commenting on the data presented by Leonard, Kates (1990) argues that it is too simplistic to equate all land of low agricultural potential and squatter settlements with 'areas of high ecologically vulnerability'. Thus, 'while there is good reason to expect an increasing geographic segregation of the poor onto the threatened environments, both the purported distribution of the hungry and the actual state of environmental degradation needs to be examined much more carefully'.
5. Further examples of the impact of urban environmental problems and sub-standard living conditions on the welfare of the urban poor can be found in Hardoy et al. (1990) and Hardoy et al. (1992).
6. See, for example, Barbier (1997, 1998b); Conway and Barbier (1990); Dasgupta (1992, 1995); Hardoy et al. (1992); Jagannathan (1989); Pearce and Warford (1993); and Pretty et al. (1992).
7. On indigenous knowledge and views of the role of natural resources in the livelihood security of the poor, see Chambers (1987), Gadgil et al. (1993) and Pretty et al. (1992).
8. For further discussion, see Barbier (1990, 1997, 1998b); Binswanger (1980); Pender and Walker (1990).
9. The exact numbers and composition of poor and ultra-poor will obviously vary by country and region; however, as an approximate indication Lipton (1988) suggests that the ultra-poor can be defined as those at significant risk of income-induced caloric under-

nutrition and the poor as those with sufficiently low income to be at risk of hunger but not undernutrition, with the former usually falling in the bottom 10–20 per cent income category (the 'poorest quintile'). For an up-to-date comprehensive analysis of rural poverty, see López and Valdés (1998).

References

Barbier, E.B. (1990), 'The farm-level economics of soil erosion: the uplands of Java', *Land Economics*, **66** (9), 199–211.

Barbier, E.B. (1991), 'Natural resource degradation: policy, economics and management', ch. 6 in J.T. Winpenny (ed.), *Development Research: The Environmental Challenge*, London: Overseas Development Institute, pp. 43–57.

Barbier, E.B. (1994), 'Natural capital and the economics of environment and development', in A.M. Jansson, M. Hammer, C. Folke and R. Costanza (eds), *Investing in Natural Capital: The Ecological Economics Approach to Sustainability*, Washington, DC: Island Press.

Barbier, E.B. (1997), 'The economic determinants of land degradation in developing countries', *Philosophical Transactions of the Royal Society*, Series B, **352**, 891–9.

Barbier, E.B. (1998a), 'Endogenous growth and natural resource scarcity', *Environmental and Research Economics*, forthcoming.

Barbier, E.B. (1998b), 'Rural poverty and natural resource degradation', in R. López and A. Valdés (eds), *Rural Poverty in Latin America*, Washington, DC: World Bank.

Barbier, E.B. and J.C. Burgess (1992), *Malawi – Land Degradation in Agriculture*, Divisional Working Paper no. 1992–37, World Bank, Washington, DC.

Barbier, E.B. and T. Homer-Dixon (1996), 'Resource scarcity, institutional adaptation, and technical innovation: can poor countries attain endogenous growth?', Occasional Paper, The Project on Environment, Population and Scarcity, American Association for the Advancement of Science, Washington, DC.

Barbier, E.B. and A. Markandya (1990), 'The conditions for achieving environmentally sustainable development', *European Economic Review*, **34**, 659–69.

Barro, R.J. and X. Sala-i-Martin (1995), *Economic Growth*, New York: McGraw-Hill.

Binswanger, H.P. (1980), 'Attitudes toward risk: experimental measurement in rural India', *American Journal of Agricultural Economics*, **90**, 395–407.

Böjo, J., K.-G. Mäler and L. Unema (1990), *Environment and Development: An Economic Approach*, Amsterdam: Kluwer.

Boyce, J. (1987), *Agrarian Impasse in Bengal: Institutional Constraints to Technological Change*, Oxford: Oxford University Press.

Cairncross, S., J.E. Hardoy and D. Satterthwaite (1990), 'The urban context', in J.E. Hardoy, S. Cairncross and D. Satterthwaite (eds), *The Poor Die Young: Housing and Health in Third World Cities*, London: Earthscan.

Chambers, R. (1987), 'Sustainable livelihoods, environment and development: putting poor rural people first', Discussion Paper 240, Brighton: Institute of Development Studies, University of Sussex.

Conway, G.R. and E.B. Barbier (1990), *After the Green Revolution: Sustainable Agriculture for Development*, London: Earthscan.

Current, D., E. Lutz and S. Scherr (eds) (1995), *Costs, Benefits and Farmer Adaption of Agroforestry: Project Experience in Central America and the Caribbean*, World Bank Environment Paper no. 14, World Bank, Washington, DC.

Dasgupta, P.S. (1992), 'Population, Resources and Poverty', *AMBIO*, **21** (1), 95–101.

Dasgupta, P.S. (1995), 'The population problem: theory and evidence', *Journal of Economic Literature*, **33** (4), 1879–1902.

Dasgupta, P.S. (1996), 'The economics of the environment', *Environment and Development Economics*, **1** (4), 387–428.

Deacon, R.T. (1994), 'Deforestation and the rule of law in a cross-section of countries', *Land Economics*, **70** (4), 414–30.

Gadgil, M., F. Berkes and C. Folke (1993), 'Indigenous knowledge for biodiversity conservation', *AMBIO*, **22** (2–3), 151–6.

Golleti, F. (1994), *The Changing Public Role in a Rice Economy Approaching Self-Sufficiency: The Case of Bangledesh*, IFPRI Research Report 98, International Food Policy Research Institute, Washington, DC.

Hardoy, J.E., S. Cairncross and D. Satterthwaite (eds) (1990), *The Poor Die Young: Housing and Health in Third World Cities*, London: Earthscan.

Hardoy, J.E., D. Mitlin and D. Satterthwaite (1992), 'The future city', in J. Holmberg (ed.), *Policies for a Small Planet*. London: Earthscan.

Heath, J. and H. Binswanger (1996), 'Natural resource degradation effects of poverty and population growth are largely policy-induced: the case of Colombia', *Environment and Development Economics*, **1**, 65–83.

Homer-Dixon, T.F. (1995), 'The ingenuity gap: can poor countries adapt to resource scarcity?', *Population and Development Review*, **21** (3), 1–26.

Jagannathan, N.V. (1989), *Poverty, Public Policies and the Environment*, Environment Working Paper no. 24, Washington, DC: World Bank.

Kates, R.W. (1990), 'Hunger, poverty and the environment', paper presented at the Distinguished Speaker Series, Center for Advanced Study of International Development, Michigan State University, Lansing, 6 May.

Leonard, H.J. with M. Yudelman, J.D. Stryker, J.O. Browder, A.J. De Boer, T. Campbell and A. Jolly (1989), *Environment and the Poor: Development Strategies for a Common Agenda*, New Brunswick, NJ: Transaction Books.

Lipton, M. (1983), *Labour and Poverty*, World Bank Staff Working Papers no. 616, World Bank, Washington, DC.

Lipton, M. (1988), *The Poor and the Poorest: Some Interim Findings*, World Bank Discussion Paper no. 25, World Bank, Washington, DC.

López, R. and A. Valdés (eds) (1998), *Rural Poverty in Latin America*, Washington, DC: World Bank.

Mankiw, N.G., D. Romer and D.N. Weil (1992), 'A contribution to the empirics of economic growth', *Quarterly Journal of Economics*, **107**, 407–37.

Matsuyama, K. (1992), 'Agricultural productivity, comparative advantage, and economic growth', *Journal of Economic Theory*, **58**, 317–34.

Pack, H. (1994), 'Endogenous growth theory: intellectual appeal and empirical shortcomings', *Journal of Economic Perspectives*, **8** (1), 55–72.

Pearce, D.W. and J.J. Warford (1993), *World Without End: Economics, Environment and Sustainable Development*, Oxford: Oxford University Press for World Bank.

Pearce, D.W., E.B. Barbier and A. Markandya (1990), *Sustainable Development: Economics and Environment in the Third World*, Aldershot, UK and Brookfield, US: Edward Elgar.

Pender, J.L. and T.S. Walker (1990), 'Experimental measures of time preference in rural India', Draft paper, Food Research Institute, Stanford University and ICRISAT, Stanford.

Pretty, J., I. Guijt, I. Scoones and J. Thompson (1992), 'Regenerating agriculture: the agro-ecology of low-external input and community-based development', in J. Holmberg (ed.), *Policies for a Small Planet*, London: Earthscan.

Romer, P. (1994), 'The origins of endogenous growth', *Journal of Economic Perspectives*, **8** (1), 3–22.

Sachs, J.D. and A.M. Warner (1995), 'Natural resource abundance and economic growth', Development Discussion Paper no. 517a, Harvard Institute for International Development, Cambridge, MA.

UNCED Secretariat (1992), *Integration of Environment and Development in Decision Making*, Report to the Preparatory Committee for UNCED, New York: UNCED.

Wallich, P. (1994), 'The analytical economist: the wages of Haiti's dictatorship', *Scientific American*, **271** (6), 36.

World Bank (1992), *World Development Report 1992*, Washington, DC: World Bank.

PART VII

ECONOMIC VALUATION AND EVALUATION

51 Theory of economic valuation of environmental goods and services

Per-Olov Johansson

1. Ordinary and compensated money measures

The literature that deals with the theory and measurement of the *consumer's surplus* is both large and growing. The concept of consumer surplus was first introducted by Dupuit ([1844] 1933), who was concerned with the benefits and costs of constructing a bridge. Marshall (1920) introduced the concept to the English-speaking world. As a measure of consumer surplus, Marshall used the area under the demand curve less actual money expenditure on the good. At least this is a common interpretation. Marshall's measure, like that of Dupuit, was an all-or-nothing measure: 'The excess of the price which he would be willing to pay rather than go without the thing, over that which he actually does pay is the economic measure of this surplus of satisfaction' (Marshall, 1920, p.124). Adding to this amount actual money expenditure on the good yields the total *willingness to pay* (WTP) for a particular quantity of the good.

Measuring the consumer surplus as an area to the left of an ordinary or Marshallian demand curve yields what is known as the ordinary or uncompensated or Marshallian consumer surplus. Later Hicks (1940/41) and Henderson (1940/41) demonstrated that consumer surplus could be interpreted in terms of amounts of money that must be given to/taken from an individual. The Hicksian or income-compensated consumer surplus is measured as an area to the left of a compensated or Hicksian demand curve where the individual, through adjustments in his income, is held at a prespecified level of utility. The best-known Hicksian money measures are the *compensating variation* and the *equivalent variation*. In the former case, the individual remains at his initial or pre-change level of utility. In the latter case, he is held at the level of utility he would attain with the considered change in, say, a price (or any other parameter, for example, environmental quality). The reader should note that some of the terminology in this area is confused. Many authors use the terms 'compensating variation' and 'equivalent variation' when prices change and the terms 'compensating' and 'equivalent' surplus (or 'quality-compensating variation' and 'quantity-equivalent variation') when quantities change. When a price changes, the magnitude of the differences between different consumer surplus measures turn out to depend on the income elasticity of the demand for the good in question and the size of the consumer surpluses in relation to income. These facts have been used by Willig (1976) and others to derive bounds on the difference between different consumer surplus measures.

2.   The path-dependence issue

An analysis of the welfare foundations of different WTP measures and the conditions under which they coincide began with the work by Samuelson (1942) and Patinkin (1963). The debate centred around the interpretation of the constancy of the *marginal utility of income* or money; some kind of constancy assumption is needed for the area to the left of a demand curve to be proportional to the underlying change in utility. In recent years, much attention has been devoted to the more general question of how to evaluate money measures in the multiple price change case. Although the basic problem, which is known as the *path-dependence* issue, was introduced by Hotelling (1938), the main stream of papers on this issue have appeared in the 1970s and the 1980s. (See, however, Samuelson's 1950 historical survey of the integrability issue.) The basic problem is that the sum of the changes in consumer surpluses (and/or WTPs) in general depends on the order in which prices are changed. However, conditions for path-independence have been established, and these conditions turn out to be closely related to the aforementioned constancy of the marginal utility of income; see, for example Johansson (1987) for details and references. The ordinary consumer surplus measure turned out to suffer from the path-dependence problem, unless strong restrictions were placed on the individual's utility function (assuming it to be quasi-linear or homothetic; see, for example, Johansson, 1987, for details). On the other hand, the compensated or Hicksian consumer surplus (or WTP) measures do not suffer from this problem, that is, the sum of compensating variations and the sum of equivalent variations are both independent of the order in which prices (and other parameters) are changed. Moreover, the compensated measures are sign-preserving in the sense that they also have the same sign as the underlying change in utility in the multiple-price change case; the properties of different money measures are further explored below.

The previously mentioned literature is generally confined to situations in which the only constraint facing the consumer is the size of his budget. The compensated money measures have been generalized so as to cover changes in rationed goods, discrete choices and public goods (externalities). Thus it is possible to define money measures for complex projects involving changes in relative prices, incomes, quantity constraints and public goods. For such money measures, the reader is referred to Braden and Kolstad (1991), Freeman (1993), Johansson (1987, 1993) or Mäler (1985). There is also an emerging literature on the evaluation of changes in health (risks) due to pollution and other environmental hazards; see, for example, Johansson (1995), Jones-Lee (1989) and Viscusi (1993).

3. Using market prices to value environmental goods

The conditions under which the demand curve for a private good can be used to value changes in an unpriced environmental (public) good have also been explored; see, for example, Mäler (1985) and Bockstael and McConnell (1993). There are two conditions which must hold for this approach to work. First, the private commodity must be non-essential in the sense that there exists a choke price (possibly approaching infinity) at which its demand becomes zero; basically, you must be able to survive without consuming the commodity. Second, the private commodity and the environmental commodity must be weak complements. Weak complementarity means that the marginal utility of the environmental commodity is zero whenever the consumption of the private commodity is equal to zero. To illustrate, this condition holds if you don't value changes in the quality of a national park if the travel cost is so high that you do not visit the park. Provided these assumptions hold, the area to the left of a compensated demand curve for the private good above its price provides a measure of the consumer surplus associated with a particular quality of the environmental commodity, say a park. If one repeats the experiment for another quality level, one obtains a new surplus measure (since the demand curve shifts as the quality level is altered). The difference in surplus can be attributed to the change in environmental quality.

Alternatively, if the two goods are perfect substitutes, the price of the marketed good can be used to value the unpriced environmental commodity; for example, installing a water filter may (but need not) be a perfect substitute for improved groundwater quality. In other words, sometimes household-defensive expenditures can be used to infer the value of a public (environmental) good. However, in addition to use values, environmental assets may yield values, for example, altruistic values or existence values, which are not reflected in market prices. Such non-use values cannot be evaluated using market-based valuation techniques, in general.

4. Properties of money measures

As mentioned earlier, the compensated or Hicksian money measures are money measures of a change in utility. This also holds true for complex projects causing changes in all relative prices, incomes and environmental quality; see, for example, Johansson (1987) or Mäler (1985). However, unless the underlying utility function is quasi-linear, the compensating variation and the equivalent variation impute different dollar values to a utility change. This is because the monetary valuation of a good depends on the utility level attained, and the two measures keep people at different levels of utility. If the commodity under investigation is normal in the sense that the marginal willingness to pay for the commodity increases with income, then the equivalent variation exceeds the compensating variation. The reason is that the equivalent variation (EV) is evaluated at the final utility level and the compensating variation (CV) at the initial utility level. (If the project decreases utility, both measures take on negative values but EV is closer to zero than CV and hence larger. However, once again, the terminology is confused; some authors define their money measures in such a way that CV exceeds EV when the project decreases utility.)

Even though theory, as indicated above, tells us that CV and EV of the same change should differ in magnitude in general, empirical comparisons reveal unexpectedly large differences between willingness to pay and willingness to accept compensation; see, for example, Bishop and Heberlein (1979), Coursey et al. (1987) and Knetsch and Sinden (1984). No simple and completely convincing explanation of these large differences is available. However, an interesting idea put forward by Hanemann (1991) for environmental goods is that the substitution possibilities between environmental goods and other goods (money) play a crucial role. The more difficult it is to replace a loss of environmental goods with other goods, the higher the compensation needed in order for the individual to accept the loss. In turn, this tends to create a large difference between the compensation measure (the willingness to accept compensation – WTA) and the willingness to pay (WTP) for more environmental goods. On the other hand, if there is a high degree of substitutability between environmental goods and ordinary market goods, then the compensation measure and willingness to pay should be close in value. A recent experiment with real payments/compensations by Shogren et al. (1994) reveals a convergence of WTP and WTA for a market good. However, for a non-market good (reduced health risk) with imperfect substitutes, they record a persistent difference between the WTP and the WTA. The reader is referred to Morrison (1997) and Shogren and Hayes (1997) for further discussion of these results. Several other possible explanations for the often observed large differences between the WTP and WTA measures have also been suggested. In particular, the conventional utility theory has been questioned. For example, in terms of prospect theory, the value function is assumed to be steeper for losses than for gains, so that an unpleasant change in status will elicit a more extreme response than will a seemingly equivalent desirable change. The reader is referred to Gregory (1986) and Harless (1989) for a detailed discussion of these and other explanations.

The next question is whether our money measures can be infinitely large.

With regard to an increase in environmental quality, the compensating variation is a payment and is hence bounded by income. In the case of a decrease in environmental quality, the equivalent variation becomes the WTP measure and cannot exceed income. Apparently, however, nothing ensures that a compensation requirement falls short of income or even infinity. Suppose, though, that the good under examination is non-essential in the sense that any bundle including the good can be matched by a bundle excluding the good. This is a necessary and sufficient condition for the good always to have a finite consumer's surplus regardless of whether the surplus measure is the compensating variation or the equivalent variation or some uncompensated money measure; see Johansson (1987) for details. Health and many environmental services such as air to breathe and water to drink are, however, ultimately essential, that is, it does not make sense to compensate for the complete loss of these goods. Meaningful money measures can be defined for changes in the availability/quality of such goods and services provided that we do not pass critical levels.

Sometimes the investigator is interested in ranking several different projects (assuming here a single initial commodity bundle or point of reference). It can be shown that the equivalent variation measure ranks any three (any number of) bundles in the same order as the underlying utility function. The compensating variation measure, on the other hand, may fail to rank complex projects (unless the underlying utility function happens to be quasi-linear). The reason for this potential failure is the fact that the compensating variation compares projects at the levels of utility which will be attained with the different projects. Thus the reference level of utility (and hence also the marginal utility of income used in translating monetary units into units of utility) will vary across projects. In contrast, the equivalent variation compares all projects at one and the same level of utility. In closing, it should be stressed that both money measures are suitable for binary comparisons, for example for a comparison of a particular air quality improvement with no improvement at all. The ranking problem appears if we want to compare, that is, rank, several different kinds of complex projects improving air quality.

5. Intertemporal issues

It is straightforward to extend single-period models to cover optimization for T-period horizons, at least provided the world is perfectly competitive. Such models have been used by, for example, Boadway and Bruce (1984) to derive overall or *lifetime* consumer surplus measures. However, such measures require huge amounts of information and may hence be difficult to calculate and estimate. Recently, Blackorby et al. (1984) did show that the present value of *instantaneous* consumers' surpluses can be a sign-preserving measure of the overall utility change. These findings probably simplify calculations in many cases.

6.   Altruism and other non-use values

In a recent paper, Milgrom (1993), drawing on results derived by Bergström (1982), has argued forcefully that one can ignore *altruistic* components, that is, concerns for the welfare of others living now and/or in the future, in a social cost–benefit analysis. In terms of a project affecting people's health, such as improved groundwater quality, Milgrom thus implicitly claims that one should consider only a person's willingness to pay for changes in his/her *own* health (welfare). Moreover, in two recent papers Jones-Lee (1991, 1992) has derived a set of results on the valuation of a statistical life in the presence of different kinds of altruism; the value of a statistical life is the aggregate WTP for a project expected to save one life. In particular, Jones-Lee shows that one should take full account of people's willingness to pay for the safety of others if and only if altruism is (paternalistic or) exclusively safety-focused in the sense that people care about the safety of others but ignore other dimensions of their welfare. If altruism is pure in the sense that people care about the overall level of welfare attained by others, one can simply ignore a person's WTP for the project's impact on others. The intuition behind this result is that the pure altruist values both benefits and costs that accrue to others (the overall change in utility). Thus, if the pure altruist assumes that others (just like him/herself) will pay so as to remain at their initial levels of utility, he/she finds that their welfare remains unchanged by the project under consideration. This explains the fact that the pure altruist's total WTP is equal to his/her WTP for the project's impact on him/herself (on his/her own health, say).

However, this result assumes that people pay according to their WTP. Assume instead that they pay a uniform amount of money for the public (safety) project. In this case a pure altruist's *total* WTP for such a project can exceed or fall short of his WTP for a change in his/her own safety depending on whether he/she believes his/her own WTP falls short of or exceeds the WTP of others. Let us assume that he/she is willing to pay \$t for a *ceteris paribus* increase in his/her own safety. His/her total WTP for a uniform public risk reduction of the same magnitude will fall short of \$t if he/she believes that others are willing to pay less than \$t. This is because those other individuals, for whom he/she cares, will experience a lower utility if the programme is implemented and they have to pay more (that is, \$t) for the programme than they are willing to. This decrease in the utility of others has an offsetting impact on the pure altruist's WTP for the public safety project. In contrast, the paternalistic altruist values only one particular aspect of the welfare of others (say, their access to an environmental asset or their wealth) without paying any attention to the project's impact on their overall welfare. Hence, provided others gain from the project in this particular respect, the pure paternalistic altruist's total WTP will exceed his/her WTP for the project's direct impact on his/her own welfare. From a strict valuation perspective, pure existence values, say, concern for an endangered species, function just like paternalistic altruism; see Chapter 56 by Blamey and Common for more on existence values.

7. Present trends

Empirical studies of the value of environmental quality have shown that simple models of utility maximization are unable fully to reflect an individual's behaviour. We don't know how individuals form their expectations and if they have preferences in the way a simple well-behaved utility function prescribes. It is likely that we shall see a lot of research, probably interdisciplinary, on these fundamental issues. In a sense, stating the WTP for an environmental good is like participating in a game. The WTP is stated conditional on one's expectations about the WTP (or payment) of others. Similarly, people may have views on what games (or distributions) are fair, that is, they may refuse to participate (cooperate) if the benefits and the costs are distributed in a way which is considered to be too unfair. We shall probably see much more game-theoretic approaches to valuation in the future. Similarly, evolutionary game theory may be a useful tool in examining what kinds of behavioural strategies (say, altruistic versus selfish) will survive in the long run. Also, as is pointed out by Smith and Van Houtven (1998), non-market valuation has largely ignored the collective nature of household decision-making. To the extent that a collective framework is adopted, then recovery of individual preferences from household behaviour requires distinguishing how preference and within household income allocations affect choices.

References

Bergström, T.C. (1982), 'When is a man's life worth more than his human capital?', in M.W. Jones-Lee (ed.), *The value of life and safety*, Amsterdam: North-Holland.

Bishop, R.C. and J.A. Heberlein (1979), 'Measuring values of extra market goods: are indirect measures biased?', *American Journal of Agricultural Economics*, **61**, 926–30.

Blackorby, C., D. Donaldson and D. Moloney (1984), 'Consumer's surplus and welfare change in a simple dynamic model', *Review of Economic Studies*, **51**, 171–6.

Boadway, R.W. and N. Bruce (1984), *Welfare Economics*, Oxford: Basil Blackwell.

Bockstael, N.E. and K.E. McConnell (1993), 'Public goods as characteristics of non-market goods', *Economic Journal*, **103**, 1244–57.

Braden, J.B. and C.D. Kolstad (eds) (1991), *Measuring the Demand for Environmental Quality*, Amsterdam: North-Holland.

Coursey, D.L., J.L. Hovis and D.W. Schulze (1987), 'The disparity between willingness to accept and willingness to pay measures of value', *Quarterly Journal of Economics*, **102**, 679–90.

Dupuit, J. ([1844] 1933), *De l'utilité et de la mesure*, La Riforma Sociale, Turin. Reprints of works published in 1844 and the following years.

Freeman, A.M. (1993), *The Measurement of Environmental and Resource Values*, Washington, DC: Resources for the Future.

Gregory, R. (1986), 'Interpreting measures of economic loss: evidence from contingent valuation and experimental studies', *Journal of Environmental Economics and Management*, **13**, 325–37.

Hanemann, M.W. (1991), 'Willingness-to-pay and willingness-to-accept: How much can they differ?', *American Economic Review*, **81**, 635–47.

Harless, D.W. (1989), 'More laboratory evidence on the disparity between willingness to pay and compensation demanded', *Journal of Economic Behavior and Organisation*, **11**, 359–79.

Henderson, A. (1940/41), 'Consumer's surplus and the compensating variation', *Review of Economic Studies*, **8**, 117–21.

Hicks, J.R. (1940/41), 'The rehabilitation of consumers' surplus', *Review of Economic Studies*, **8**, 108–15.

Hotelling, H. (1938), 'The general welfare in relation to problems of taxation and of railway and utility rates', *Econometrica*, **6**, 242–69.

Johansson, P.-O. (1987), *The Economic Theory and Measurement of Environmental Benefits*, Cambridge, UK: Cambridge University Press.

Johansson, P.-O. (1993), *Cost–benefit Analysis of Environmental Change*, Cambridge, UK: Cambridge University Press.

Johansson, P.-O. (1995), *Evaluating Health Risks: An Economic Approach*, Cambridge, UK: Cambridge University Press.

Jones-Lee, M.W. (1989), *The Economics of Safety and Physical Risk*, Oxford: Basil Blackwell.

Jones-Lee, M.W. (1991), 'Altruism and the value of other people's safety', *Journal of Risk and Uncertainty*, **4**, 213–19.

Jones-Lee, M.W. (1992), 'Paternalistic altruism and the value of a statistical life', *Economic Journal*, **102**, 80–90.

Knetsch, J.L. and J.A. Sinden (1984), 'Willingness to pay and compensation demanded: experimental evidence of an unexpected disparity in measures of value', *Quarterly Journal of Economics*, **98**, 507–21.

Mäler, K.-G. (1985), 'Welfare economics and the environment', in A.V. Kneese and J.L. Sweeney (eds), *Handbook of Natural Resource and Energy Economics*, Amsterdam: North-Holland.

Marshall, A. (1920), *Principles of Economics*, 8th edn, London: Macmillan.

Milgrom, P. (1993), 'Is sympathy an economic value? Philosophy, economics, and the contingent valuation method', in J.A. Hausman (ed.), *Contingent Valuation: A Critical Assessment*, Amsterdam: North-Holland.

Morrison, G.C. (1997), 'Resolving differences in willingness to pay and willingness to accept: Comment', *American Economic Review*, **87**, 236–40.

Patinkin, D. (1963), 'Demand curves and consumer's surplus', in C.F. Christ et al. (eds), *Measurement in Economics, Studies in Mathematical Economics and Econometrics in Memory of Yehuda Grunfeld*, Stanford, CA: Stanford University Press.

Samuelson, P.A. (1942), 'Constancy of the marginal utility of income', in O. Lange, F. McIntyre and T.O. Yntema (eds), *Studies in Mathematical Economics and Econometrics in Memory of Henry Schulz*, Chicago: University of Chicago Press.

Samuelson, P.A. (1950), 'The problem of integrability in utility theory', *Economica*, **30**, 355–85.

Shogren, J.F. and D.J. Hayes (1997), 'Resolving differences in willingness to pay and willingness to accept: Reply', *American Economic Review*, **87**, 241–4.

Shogren, J.F., S.Y. Shin, D.J. Hayes and J.B. Kliebenstein (1994), 'Resolving differences in willingness to pay and willingness to accept', *American Economic Review*, **84**, 255–70.

Smith, V.K. and G. Van Houtven (1988), 'Non-market valuation and the household', Duke University: *Duke Economics Working Paper*, no. 98–04.

Viscusi, W.K. (1993), 'The value of risks to life and health', *Journal of Economic Literature*, **31**, 1912–46.

Willig, R.D. (1976), 'Consumers' surplus without apology', *American Economic Review*, **66**, 589–97.

52 Recreation demand models for environmental valuation
Catherine L. Kling and John R. Crooker

1. Introduction

Empirical models of the demand for environmental services using observations on the cost of accessing an environmental site have commonly been referred to as 'travel cost models' (as the costs of travel to the site are often a major component of acquiring environmental services). The origin of the term and methodology are credited to Hotelling in a now much-heralded letter to the Park Service. The first empirical work is due to such pioneers as Clawson (1959), Clawson and Knetsch (1966) and Cesario and Knetsch (1976). Whereas the use of the term 'travel cost' once implied a standard model, there is now a diverse array of alternative modelling approaches that use travel costs as the price. 'Indirect methods', 'recreation demand models' and 'travel cost models' have all been used to describe this set.

In a review of approaches to valuing recreational goods, Bockstael et al. (1991) reserve the term 'travel cost model' to mean continuous demand models where the number of trips a recreationist takes in a season is modelled to depend on price and possibly income, quality of the recreation sites, and other socioeconomic characteristics.[1] In contrast to continuous models which focus on the decision of how often to visit a particular site each season are the discrete choice approaches. These models follow the tradition of McFadden's random utility models which focus on the individual's decision of which recreation site to visit on any given choice occasion. The individual visits the site that achieves the highest utility and the probability that a particular site is chosen is a function of the difference between the utilities associated with each site choice and their random components. Thus the discrete and continuous choice models both employ the same type of data; the main difference between them is whether they focus on the number of visits to a particular site or set of sites or whether the focus is on modelling which site the individuals will choose from among a number of alternatives.

Here, we adopt a nomenclature somewhat different from the Bockstael et al. definitions. All models that estimate the demand for environmental services using the cost of access as the price are termed 'recreation demand models', regardless of whether they employ a discrete or continuous model for analysis. Whereas the commonly used 'travel cost models' is equally descriptive, we prefer the use of 'recreation demand' to highlight the fact that these models can be considered a subset of the microeconomic demand literature. In fact, recreation is one of the most broadly studied goods using micro-level data. Within the broad category of recreation demand, we differentiate between continuous recreation demand models, discrete recreation demand models and various combinations.

In this chapter, we provide a brief survey of the empirical recreation demand literature focusing primarily on recent advances and current approaches to modelling.[2] We also provide an assessment of the current state of the art and try our hand at predicting the future directions of this work.

2.   Outlining the approaches to recreation demand modelling

To begin our discussion, we start with continuous models that consider only the use of a single recreation site, earning them the label 'single-site models'. These were the first of the recreation demand models. Initially, these models were estimated with aggregate data from zones where visits per capita from each zone of residence were regressed on the travel cost from that zone to the site. Examples of this approach are Brown and Nawas (1973), Wetzstein and McNeely (1980), Sutherland (1982), Smith and Kopp (1980), Bowes and Loomis (1980) and Huppert and Thomson (1984). Most current studies use individual observations as the unit of measurement rather than zonal aggregates, although Hellerstein (1995) argues that zonal models may in some cases yield less biased welfare estimates than individual observations and Hellerstein (1991) employs zonal data in a study of the boundary waters canoe area.

Once individual observations became the norm as the unit of measurement, several econometric problems became transparent. First, many recreation data sets are on-site surveys that result in truncated samples (only observations with positive numbers of trips are reported). Second, even if a random population survey is employed to collect the data, these samples suffer from censoring at zero trips since it is not possible for recreationists to consume negative trips. A third econometric problem yielded by the use of individual observations is the requirement that trips can only be taken in integer values, thus suggesting the use of count-data models.

A variety of estimators have been used to correct for censoring of the data including the Tobit, Heckman, and Cragg estimators (Bockstael et al., 1990; Smith, 1988; and Shaw, 1988). Haab and McConnell (1996), Hellerstein and Mendelsohn (1993), and Hellerstein (1992) focus on the theoretical foundations and appropriate welfare measurement for these models. Further, numerous authors have addressed the problem of counts either solo or in conjunction with censoring or truncation problems by adopting Poisson or binomial regression models (Creel and Loomis, 1990; Smith, 1988; Shaw, 1988). Englin and Shonkwiler (1995) consider count models that also correct for endogenous stratification.

Several other issues independent of sample selection problems have engaged researchers. Ziemer et al. (1980), Kling (1989), Adamowicz et al. (1989), and Ozuna et al. (1993) have examined the implications of alternative functional forms on welfare measures, finding, not surprisingly, that different forms can yield large differences in consumer surplus. Models that focus on incorporating environmental quality into single-site recreational models have been estimated by Vaughan and Russell (1982), Smith et al. (1983) and Smith and Desvousges (1985), among others.

A drawback of the single-site studies is the difficulty of adequately modelling the effects of substitute prices and qualities in this framework. In these cases, it may be desirable to recognize the existence of a system of recreation demand sites and to model the system accordingly. One of the first such models of systems of demands applied to recreation is a study of the value of introducing an additional set of lakes in southern Missouri by Burt and Brewer (1971). In addition to estimating a system of demands, they also tested for and imposed symmetry of the cross-price effects to assure the path-independence of their consumer surplus measures. Cichetti et al. (1976) also provide an early application of systems of demands. A recent application of demand systems by Ozuna and Gomez (1994) estimates count models using seemingly unrelated regression techniques. An alternative approach is taken by Morey (1981, 1984, 1985) who, in a series of papers, specifies and estimates share equations. Although commonly estimated in the general demand literature, systems of share equations have seen little application in recreation demand.

In attempting more accurately to model recreation goods, analysts have introduced models to deal with counts, truncated and censored data sets, and systems to account for substitutes. In so doing, they have altered the simple continuous models to reflect some of the discrete components of the recreation site choice decision.

Now, we turn our attention to the models that are motivated explicitly by the discreteness of the choice facing recreationists. As noted earlier, these models are based on McFadden's work (see for example McFadden, 1981). Early applications used multinomial logit models (Hanemann, 1978; Caulkins et al., 1986; Kling, 1988a, 1988b; Bockstael et al., 1989; and Morey et al., 1991). Welfare estimates are computed from the coefficient estimates using results of Small and Rosen (1981) and Hanemann (1982).

A well-understood limitation of the simple multinomial logit model is its imposition of the property of independence of irrelevant alternatives (IIA).[3] The undesirability of this condition prompted a move towards the use of nested multinomial logit models. These models allow for the partial relaxation of the IIA property while still retaining the relatively simple structure of logit models to ease estimation. Examples include papers by Morey et al. (1993) and Milon (1988).

Whether the site selection model is estimated assuming a logit or nested logit structure, there is still the problem of estimating the relationship between price, quality and the number of recreation trips individuals take over a season. To accomplish this, a variety of authors have estimated separate demand equations that predict the number of trips taken in a season as a function of inclusive values computed from the site selection model as well as socioeconomic characteristics. This strand of work began with Bockstael et al. (1987a) and has been followed with papers by Creel and Loomis (1992a), Morey et al. (1991), Yen and Adamowicz (1994), and Hausman et al. (1995). An alternative approach is suggested by Feather et al. (1995) and Parsons and Kealy (1996). These models provide intuitive approaches to tying together the discrete and continuous decisions; none are completely utility-theoretic (see the argument in Smith, 1997b).

A substantive effort has been devoted in this literature to examining the implications on welfare estimates of aggregating or randomly sampling from numerous recreation sites to simplify estimation (Parsons and Needelman, 1992; Parsons and Kealy, 1992; Kaoru et al., 1995; and Feather, 1994), with various degrees of success reported. Other empirical issues that have been treated include consistency of model estimates with utility maximization (Borsch-Supan, 1990; Herriges and Kling, 1995; and Kling and Herriges, 1995), implications of alternative nesting structures (Kling and Thomson, 1996), and the use of a multinomial probit distributions (Chen and Cosslett, 1996).

Two themes emerge from our brief description of the recreation demand literature of the recent past. First, much of the theoretical and empirical work has been devoted to providing solutions associated with data problems. The quality and quantity of data available for analysis have driven the research agenda. Second, viewing the discrete choice models as one end of a continuum and the continuous models as the other end, recent advances have moved the state of the art in both areas towards the centre. Discrete choice models have added continuous components by specifying aggregate demands whereas the continuous models have recognized the discrete component of the problem by investigating count models.

There are several issues that face analysts whether discrete or continuous models are adopted. Notable among these is the treatment of time costs. This has been a perplexing problem since the issue was first identified by Cesario (1976) where he valued time at a fixed ratio of the wage rate.

More sophisticated treatments of this issue are provided by McConnell and Strand (1981) who estimate the implicit value of time directly from the data and by Bockstael et al. (1987b) who investigate the issue when individuals face fixed work weeks, thus suggesting that the wage rate does not represent the opportunity cost of time. Larson (1993a) argues that a long-run view makes the full wage the appropriate opportunity cost of time even in this case. A related issue is the treatment of on-site time (Kealy and Bishop, 1986; McConnell, 1992; and Larson, 1993b).

Bockstael and Strand (1987) were among the first to recognize that welfare measures were random variables since they depend on estimated coefficients. On recognizing the randomness of the welfare measures, it was natural to investigate ways to compute standard errors and/or confidence intervals for the estimators of interest. Due to the non-linearity of the welfare measures arising from either the continuous or discrete type recreation demand models, this is non-trivial. Several methods have been investigated including bootstrapping (Adamowicz et al., 1989; Kling and Sexton, 1990), simulation approaches and Taylor's approximations (Kling, 1991). On a related theme, Smith (1990) considers estimation criteria in terms of consumer surplus.

Other issues that affect both discrete and continuous models include welfare measures under uncertainty (Larson and Flacco, 1992; Kling, 1993), congestion (McConnell, 1988), bag limits (Creel and Loomis, 1992b), habit formation (Adamowicz et al., 1990, and Adamowicz, 1994), benefits transfer[4] (Parsons and Kealy, 1994; and Downing and Ozuna, 1996) and the accuracy of the price measure based on travel costs (Randall, 1994).

3. Recent developments and future directions

As noted above, continuous and discrete recreation demand models have become more similar, with each approach attempting to capture elements of the other. Both approaches have made important strides in capturing the most salient features of the problem, but neither has been completely successful. In contrast, an appealing approach is the discrete continuous choice model of Wales and Woodland (1983) and Hanemann (1984), discussed in Bockstael et al. (1986) and Morey et al. (1995). In this model, individuals are assumed to choose both the number of recreation trips to the available sites and whether to participate at all. Two empirical applications of this approach to recreation demand are Phaneuf et al. (1997) and Morey et al. (1990).

Discrete choice models could continue to be improved with further relaxation of restrictions on the structure of the models. The estimation of the models employing a normal distribution would allow both the relaxation of the IIA assumption and avoid the need for the analyst to make arbitrary grouping decisions as necessitated in the nested logit approach. Further improvements might come with the use of non-parametric approaches which further relax assumptions regarding the distribution of the error term.

Another intriguing recent development in recreation demand models is the combining of these models with contingent valuation models and data. Many previous studies have employed the alternative methods as validity checks of one another (Smith et al., 1986 provide a nice example). In contrast, instead of treating recreation demand and contingent valuation data as mutually exclusive approaches to estimating welfare measures of environmental goods, this alternative approach suggests that both types of data be combined in a single model to estimate welfare. Cameron (1992) first suggested and implemented this approach in a continuous demand model setting. A growing number of refinements and applications have now made their way into the literature including papers from an AERE conference on the topic in 1996 and Larson (1990), McConnell et al. (1992), Adamowicz et al. (1994), Niklitschek and Leon (1996), and Kling (1997). Further development of these models will provide important advances in this literature.

Notes
1. Other valuable reviews are provided by Ward and Loomis (1986), Freeman (1993), and Smith (1989, 1993, 1997a).
2. Space prevents us from discussing the theoretical underpinnings for welfare analysis. Interested readers are referred to Just et al. (1982), Bockstael and McConnell (1983, 1993), Morey (1994), and various chapters in Part III of this volume for a sampling of the literature.
3. IIA is an outcome of the logit distribution and it results in the ratio of any two choice probabilities being independent of the probability of selecting any other alternative.
4. See the December 1992 issue of *Water Resources Research* for a special section on this topic and van den Bergh and Button in this volume (Chapter 55).

References
Adamowicz, W. (1994), 'Habit formation and variety seeking in a discrete choice model of recreation demand', *Journal of Agricultural and Resource Economics*, **19**, 9–31.
Adamowicz, W., J. Fletcher and T. Graham-Tomasi (1989), 'Functional form and the statistical properties of welfare measures', *American Journal of Agricultural Economics*, **71**, 414–21.
Adamowicz, W., S. Jennings and A. Coyne (1990), 'A sequential choice model of recreation behavior', *Western Journal of Agricultural Economics*, **15**, 91–9.
Adamowicz, W., J. Louviere and M. Williams (1994), 'Combining revealed and stated preference methods for valuing environmental amenities', *Journal of Environmental Economics and Management*, **26**, 271–92.
Bockstael, N.E. and K.E. McConnell (1983), 'Welfare measurement in the household production function for wildlife recreation', *American Economic Review*, **73**, 806–14.

Bockstael, N.E. and K.E. McConnell (1993), 'Public goods as characteristics of non-market commodities', *The Economic Journal*, **103**, 1244–57.

Bockstael, N.E. and I.E. Strand (1987), 'The effect of common sources of regression error on benefit estimates', *Land Economics*, **63**, 11–20.

Bockstael, N.E., W.M. Hanemann and I.E. Strand (1986), 'Measuring the benefits of water quality improvements using recreation demand models,' EPA Cooperative Agreement CR-811043–01–0.

Bockstael, N.E., W.M. Hanemann and C.L. Kling (1987a), 'Measuring recreational demand in a multiple site framework', *Water Resources Research*, **23** (May), 951–60.

Bockstael, N.E., I.E. Strand and W.M. Hanemann (1987b), 'Time and the recreational demand model', *American Journal of Agricultural Economics*, **69**, 293–302.

Bockstael, N.E., K.E. McConnell and I.E. Strand (1989), 'A random utility model for sportfishing: some preliminary results for Florida', *Marine Resource Economics*, **6** (Fall), 245–60.

Bockstael, N.E., K.E. McConnell and I.E. Strand (1991), 'Recreation', in J. Braden and C. Kolstad (eds), *Measuring the Demand for Environmental Quality*, Amsterdam: North-Holland.

Bockstael,N.E., I.E. Strand, K.E. McConnell and F. Arsanjani (1990), 'Sample selection bias in the estimation of recreation demand functions: an application to sportfishing', *Land Economics*, **66**, 40–49.

Borsch-Supan, A. (1990), 'On the compatibility of nested logit models with utility maximization', *Journal of Econometrics*, **43**, 373–88.

Bowes, M.D. and J.B. Loomis (1980), 'A note on the use of travel cost models with unequal zonal populations', *Land Economics*, **56**, 465–70.

Brown, W.G. and F. Nawas (1973), 'Impact of aggregation on the estimation of outdoor recreation demand functions', *American Journal of Agricultural Economics*, **55**, 246–9.

Burt, O.R. and D. Brewer (1971), 'Estimation of net social benefits from outdoor recreation', *Econometrica*, **39**, 813–28.

Cameron, T. (1992), 'Combining contingent valuation and travel cost data for the valuation of nonmarket goods', *Land Economics*, **68**, 302–17.

Caulkins, P., R. Bishop and N. Bouwes (1986), 'The travel cost model for lake recreation: a comparison of two methods for incorporating site quality and substitution effects', *American Journal of Agricultural Economics*, **68** (May), 291–7.

Cesario, F. (1976), 'Value of time in recreation benefit studies', *Land Economics*, **52**, 32–41.

Cesario, F. and J. Knetsch (1976), 'A recreation site demand and benefit estimation model', *Regional Studies*, **10**, 97–104.

Chen, H.Z. and S.R. Cosslett (1996), 'Heterogeneous preference of environmental quality and benefit estimation in multinomial probit models: a simulation approach', manuscript.

Cichetti, C., A. Fisher and V. Smith (1976), 'An econometric evaluation of a generalized consumer surplus measure: the mineral king controversy', *Econometrica*, **44**, 1259–76.

Clawson, M. (1959), *Methods of Measuring the Demand for and Value of Outdoor Recreation*, Washington, DC: Resources for the Future, reprint 10.

Clawson, M. and J. Knetsch (1966), *Economics of Outdoor Recreation*, Washington, DC: Resources for the Future.

Creel, M.D. and J.B. Loomis (1990), 'Theoretical and empirical advantages of truncated count data estimators for analysis of deer hunting in California', *American Journal of Agricultural Economics*, **72**, 434–41.

Creel, M. and J. Loomis (1992a), 'Recreation value of water to wetlands in the San Joaquin Valley: linked multinomial logit and count data trip frequency models', *Water Resources Research*, **28** (October), 2597–606.

Creel, M. and J. Loomis (1992b), 'Modeling hunting demand in the presence of a bag limit with tests of alternative specifications', *Journal of Environmental Economics and Management*, **2**, 99–113.

Downing, M. and T. Ozuna (1996), 'Testing the reliability of the benefit function transfer approach', *Journal of Environmental Economics and Management*, **30**, 316–22.

Englin, J. and J. Shonkwiler (1995), 'Estimating social welfare using count data models: an application to long-run recreation demand under conditions of endogenous stratification and truncation', *Review of Economics and Statistics*, **77**, 104–12.

Feather, P. (1994), 'Sampling and aggregation issues in random utility model estimation', *Journal of Environmental Economics and Management*, **28**, 772–80.

Feather, P., D. Hellerstein and T. Tomasi (1995), 'A discrete-count model of recreational demand', *Journal of Environmental Economics and Management*, **29**, 214–27.

Freeman, M. (1993), *The Measurement of Environmental and Resource Values*, Washington, DC: Resources for the Future.

Haab, T.C. and K.E. McConnell (1996), 'Count data models and the problem of zeros in recreation demand analysis', *American Journal of Agricultural Economics*, **78**, 89–102.

Hanemann, W.M. (1978), 'A methodological and empirical study of the recreation benefits from water quality improvement', Ph.D. dissertation, Department of Economics, Harvard University.

Hanemann, W.M. (1982), 'Applied welfare analysis with qualitative response models', California Agricultural Experiment Station, October.

Hanemann, W.M. (1984), 'Discrete-continuous models of consumer demand', *Econometrica*, **52**, 541–61.

Hausman, J.A., G.K. Leonard and D. McFadden (1995), 'A utility-consistent, combined discrete choice and count data model: assessing recreational use losses due to natural resource damage', *Journal of Public Economics*, **56** (Winter), 1–30.

Hellerstein, D. (1991), 'Using count data models in travel cost analysis with aggregate data', *American Journal of Agricultural Economics*, **73**, 860–66.

Hellerstein, D. (1992), 'Estimating consumer surplus in the censored linear model', *Land Economics*, **6**, 83–92.

Hellerstein, D. (1995), 'Welfare estimation using aggregate and individual-observation models: a comparison using Monte Carlo techniques', *American Journal of Agricultural Economics*, **77**, 620–30.

Hellerstein, D. and R. Mendelsohn (1993), 'A theoretical foundation for count data models', *American Journal of Agricultural Economics*, **75**, 604–11.

Herriges, J.A. and C.L. Kling (1995), 'Testing the consistency of nested logit models with utility maximization', *American Journal of Agricultural Economics*, **77**, 875–84.

Huppert, D.D. and C.J. Thomson (1984), 'Demand analysis of partyboat angling in California using the travel cost method', Southwest Fisheries Center Administrative Report, NOAA.

Just, R., D. Hueth and A. Schmitz (1982), *Applied Welfare Economics and Public Policy*, Englewood Cliffs, NJ: Prentice-Hall.

Kaoru, Y., V.K. Smith and J.L. Liu (1995), 'Using random utility models to estimate the recreational value of estuarine resources', *American Journal of Agricultural Economics*, **77** (February), 141–51.

Kealy, M.J. and R.C. Bishop (1986), 'Theoretical and empirical specifications issues in travel cost demand studies', *American Journal of Agricultural Economics*, **68**, 660–67.

Kling, C.L. (1988a), 'The reliability of estimates of environmental benefits from recreation demand models', *American Journal of Agricultural Economics*, **70**, 892–901.

Kling, C.L. (1988b), 'Comparing welfare estimates of environmental quality changes from recreation demand models', *Journal of Environmental Economics and Management*, **15**, 331–40.

Kling, C.L. (1989), 'The importance of functional form in the estimation of welfare', *Western Journal of Agricultural Economics*, **14**, 168–74.

Kling, C.L. (1991),'Estimating the precision of welfare measures', *Journal of Environmental Economics and Management*, **21** (November), 244–59.

Kling, C.L. (1993), 'An assessment of the empirical magnitude of option values for environmental goods', *Environmental and Resource Economics*, **3**, 471–85.

Kling, C.L. (1997), 'The gains from combining travel cost and contingent valuation data to value nonmarket goods', *Land Economics*, **73**, 428–39.

Kling, C.L. and J.A. Herriges (1995), 'An empirical investigation of the consistency of nested logit models with utility maximization', *American Journal of Agricultural Economics*, 77, 875–84.

Kling, C.L. and R.J. Sexton (1990), 'Bootstrapping in applied welfare analysis', *American Journal of Agricultural Economics*, 69, 406–18.

Kling, C.L. and C. Thomson (1996), 'The implications of model specification for welfare estimation in nested logit models', *American Journal of Agricultural Economics*, 78, 103–14.

Larson, D. (1990), 'Testing consistency of direct and indirect methods for valuing nonmarket goods', University of California, Davis, draft manuscript, December.

Larson, D. (1993a), 'Separability and the shadow value of leisure time', *American Journal of Agricultural Economics*, 75, 572–7.

Larson, D. (1993b), 'Joint recreation choices and implied values of time', *Land Economics*, 69, 270–86.

Larson, D. and P. Flacco (1992), 'Measuring option prices from market behavior', *Journal of Environmental Economics and Management*, 22, 178–98.

McConnell, K.E. (1988), 'Heterogeneous preferences for congestion', *Journal of Environmental Economics and Management*, 15, 251–88.

McConnell, K.E. (1992), 'On-site time in the demand for recreation', *American Journal of Agricultural Economics*, 74, 918–25.

McConnell, K.E. and I.E. Strand (1981), 'Measuring the cost of time in recreation demand analysis: an application to sport fishing', *American Journal of Agricultural Economics*, 63, 153–6.

McConnell, K.E., Q. Weninger and I.E. Strand (1992), 'Testing the validity of contingent valuation by combining referendum responses with observed behavior', Department of Agricultural and Resource Economics, University of Maryland.

McFadden, D.L. (1981), 'Econometric models of probabilistic choice', in C.F. Manski and D.L. McFadden (eds), *Structural Analysis of Discrete Data*, Cambridge, MA: MIT Press.

Milon, J.W. (1988), 'A nested demand shares model of artificial marine habitat choice by sport anglers', *Marine Resource Economics*, 5 (Fall), 191–213.

Morey, E. (1981), 'The demand for site-specific recreational activities: a characteristics approach', *Journal of Environmental Economics and Management*, 8, 345–71.

Morey, E. (1984), 'The choice of ski areas: estimation of a generalized CES preference ordering with characteristics, quadratic expenditure functions and non-additivity', *Review of Economics and Statistics*, 66, 584–90.

Morey, E. (1985), 'Characteristics, consumer's surplus and new activities: a proposed ski area', *Journal of Public Economics*, 26, 221–36.

Morey, E. (1994), 'Two RUMs UnCLOAKED: nested-logit models of site choice and nested-logit models of participation and site choice', Discussion paper, Department of Economics, University of Colorado, Boulder, February.

Morey, E.R., W.D. Shaw and R.D. Rowe (1991), 'A discrete choice model of recreational participation, site choice, and activity valuation when complete trip data are not available', *Journal of Environmental Economics and Management*, 20, 181–201.

Morey, E., D. Waldman, D. Assane and D. Shaw (1990), 'Specification and estimation of a generalized corner solution model of consumer demand: an Amemiya–Tobin approach', Department of Economics, University of Colorado, Boulder, manuscript.

Morey, E.R., R.D. Rowe and M. Watson (1993), 'A repeated nested-logit model of Atlantic salmon fishing', *American Journal of Agricultural Economics*, 75 (August), 578–92.

Morey, E., D. Waldman, D. Assane and D. Shaw (1995), 'Searching for a model of multiple-site recreation demand that admits interior and boundary solutions', *American Journal of Agricultural Economics*, 77, 129–40.

Niklitschek, M. and J. Leon (1996), 'Combining intended demand and yes/no responses in the estimation of contingent valuation models', *Journal of Environmental Economics and Management*, 31, 387–402.

Ozuna, T. and I. Gomez (1994), 'Estimating a system of recreation demand functions using a seemingly unrelated Poisson regression approach', *Review of Economics and Statistics*, 76, 356–9.

Ozuna, T., L. Jones and O. Capps (1993), 'Functional form and welfare measures in truncated recreation demand models', *American Journal of Agricultural Economics*, **75**, 1030–35.

Parsons, G.R. and M.J. Kealy (1992), 'Randomly drawn opportunity sets in a random utility model of lake recreation', *Land Economics*, **68** (February), 93–106.

Parsons, G.R. and M.J. Kealy (1994), 'Benefits transfer in a random utility model of recreation', *Water Resources Research*, **30**, 2477–84.

Parsons, G.R. and M.J. Kealy (1996), 'A demand theory for number of trips in a random utility model of recreation', *Journal of Environmental Economics and Management*, **29**, 357–67.

Parsons, G.R. and M.S. Needelman (1992), 'Site aggregation in a random utility model of recreation', *Land Economics*, **68** (November), 418–33.

Phaneuf, D.J., C.L. Kling and J.A. Herriges (1997), 'Estimation and welfare calculations in a generalized corner solution model with an application to recreation demand', draft manuscript, Iowa State University.

Randall, A. (1994), 'A difficulty with the travel cost method', *Land Economics*, **70**, 88–96.

Shaw, D. (1988), 'On-site samples' regression: problems of non-negative integers, truncation, and endogenous stratification', *Journal of Econometrics*, **37**, 211–23.

Small, K.A. and H.S. Rosen (1981), 'Applied welfare economics with discrete choice models', *Econometrica*, **49**, 105–30.

Smith, V.K. (1988), 'Selection and recreation demand', *American Journal of Agricultural Economics*, **70**, 29–36.

Smith, V.K. (1989), 'Taking stock of progress with recreation demand models: theory and implementation', *Marine Resource Economics*, **6**, 279–310.

Smith, V.K. (1990), 'Estimating recreation demand using the implied properties of the consumer surplus', *Land Economics*, **66**, 111–20.

Smith, V.K. (1993), 'Nonmarket valuation of environmental resources: an interpretive appraisal', *Land Economics*, **69**, 1–26.

Smith, V.K. (1997a), 'Pricing what is priceless: a status report on non-market valuation', in H. Folmer and T. Tietenberg (eds), *The International Yearbook of Environmental and Resource Economics, 1997/1998*, Cheltenham, UK and Lyme, US: Edward Elgar.

Smith, V.K. (1997b), 'Combining discrete choice and cost data models: A comment', unpublished manuscript.

Smith, V.K. and W.H. Desvousges (1985), 'The generalized travel cost model and water quality benefits: a reconsideration', *Southern Economic Journal*, **51**, 371–81.

Smith, V.K. and R.J. Kopp (1980), 'The spatial limits of the travel cost recreational demand model', *Land Economics*, **56**, 64–72.

Smith, V.K., W.H. Desvousges and M.P. McGiveney (1983), 'Estimating water quality benefits: an econometric analysis', *Southern Economic Journal*, **50**, 422–37.

Smith, V.K., W. Desvousges and A. Fisher (1986), 'A comparison of direct and indirect methods for estimating environmental benefits', *American Journal of Agricultural Economics*, **68**, 280–90.

Sutherland, R.J. (1982), 'The sensitivity of travel cost estimates of recreation demand to the functional form and definition of origin zones', *Western Journal of Agricultural Economics*, **7**, 87–98.

Vaughan, W.J. and C.S. Russell (1982), *Fresh Water Recreational Fishing: The National Benefits of Water Pollution Control*, Washington, DC: Resources for the Future.

Wales, T.J. and A.D. Woodland (1983), 'Estimation of consumer demand systems with binding non-negativity constraints', *Journal of Econometrics*, **21**, 263–85.

Ward, F. and J. Loomis (1986), 'The travel cost demand model as an environmental policy assessment tool: a review of literature', *Western Journal of Agricultural Economics*, **11**, 164–78.

Wetzstein, M.E. and J.G. McNeely (1980), 'Specification errors and inference in recreation demand models', *American Journal of Agricultural Economics*, **62**, 798–800.

Yen, S.T. and W.L. Adamowicz (1994), 'Participation, trip frequency and site choice: a multinomial Poisson hurdle model of recreation demand', *Canadian Journal of Agricultural Economics*, **42**, 65–76.

Ziemer, R., W. Musser and R. Hill (1980), 'Recreation demand equations: functional form and consumer surplus', *American Journal of Agricultural Economics*, **62**, 136–41.

53 Hedonic models
Raymond B. Palmquist

1. Introduction

Hedonic models were developed to deal with markets for differentiated products. A differentiated product is one where there can be significant differences between various units of the product yet consumers consider them all to be members of the same general product class. The market for such a product can be perfectly competitive, and yet the prices for the models of the differentiated product will differ depending on the specific characteristics or attributes that the model contains. In its simplest form the hedonic model seeks to explain the price for which a model sells by the quantities of the characteristics it contains. For example, some of the earliest applications (Court, 1939; Griliches, 1971) sought to explain the price of automobiles by characteristics such as horsepower, weight and so on, and the techniques have been useful in developing quality-adjusted price indexes.

In environmental economics hedonic models have been used extensively in efforts to estimate willingness to pay for environmental improvements. Most environmental goods are not traded on markets, so their valuation is typically done by stated preference methods such as contingent valuation, or by revealed preference methods such as travel cost models. Hedonic methods are revealed preference methods, and they represent one of the few instances where environmental quality is traded in actual markets. This is so because environmental quality is one of the characteristics of some differentiated products. Housing markets are the most frequently used example of this. In buying or renting a house, the consumer considers characteristics such as square feet of living space or number of bathrooms, but also environmental characteristics such as air quality or ambient noise. Hedonic models seek to extract information on the value of the environmental characteristics from the market for houses. They are also applied to labour markets because the equilibrium wage for a job in a particular location may be influenced by the environmental quality in that location.[1] Markets for differentiated factors of production such as farmland also can be modelled using hedonics.[2]

2. Theoretical hedonic models

The theoretical model of the market for a differentiated product developed by Rosen (1974) is still extremely influential, although there have been significant modifications and improvements in the implementation of that model. In addition to the original Rosen article, the theoretical model is covered in detail in Bartik and Smith (1987), Epple (1987), and Palmquist (1991).[3] Because of this, only a brief summary of the most relevant parts of the model will be provided here.[4]

The price of a differentiated product, P, is explained by the vector of characteristics, z, that it contains: $P = P(z)$. This hedonic function represents a market equilibrium schedule of prices. As such, it is a type of reduced-form equation that does not represent a behavioural equation for any of the market participants.[5] The theoretical model says nothing about the functional form of the price equation except that it is monotonically increasing in desirable characteristics. If it were possible costlessly to unbundle and repackage the characteristics of the product, arbitragers would do so until the hedonic function was linear. In the case of housing and most other differentiated products where hedonic techniques have been applied, such costless repackaging is not possible and cannot force the function to be linear. Neither does the theory preclude the linearity of the hedonic function. It is strictly an empirical question.

The hedonic equation results from the market interaction of consumers and those firms or individuals supplying the goods.[6] Consumers derive utility from the characteristics of the differentiated product and other goods. For this reason they are willing to bid different amounts for products containing different characteristics. The amount they would bid also depends on their income and level of utility. The suppliers of the differentiated product have offer prices that depend on, among other things, the quantities of the characteristics in the product. Rosen's original model dealt in some detail with the supply side of the market. However, since the quantities of the characteristics in existing houses are predetermined and costly to alter, the equilibrium price schedule is completely demand-determined, just as the price of vacant land in a specific location is demand-determined. Also, in environmental economics most applications need not be concerned with the supply side because disaggregate data are used. Just as we say that consumers in a competitive market are price-takers (they cannot influence the price by their individual actions), the individuals in a competitive market for a differentiated product are price-schedule-takers (they cannot influence the hedonic price schedule by their individual actions). Thus the hedonic price equation and the behavioural equations of the consumers are the relevant components of the model.[7]

The estimation strategy for the complete hedonic model involves two steps.[8] First, the hedonic price equation is estimated. The resulting parameters are used to calculate marginal prices for the characteristics. Second, these marginal prices are used with the socioeconomic attributes of the consumers and some measure of income, wealth, or expenditure on non-housing goods to estimate the parameters of the behavioural equations of the consumers.[9] These equations may be demand or inverse demand equations or the utility function, depending on the application.

There are important and complex econometric issues in the estimation of the second stage. Two of the most important are identification and endogeneity. Identification is a problem because the researcher must find a way to distinguish the demand equation from the hedonic equation that has already been estimated.[10] Most researchers believe that the best solution is to use data from a number of different markets (urban areas). Separate hedonic regressions are run for each urban area and the marginal prices differ in each market. For the second stage, the data from the different cities are aggregated, and the demands or utility parameters are estimated. This assumes that once the researcher controls for socioeconomic variables, there is no systematic differences between individuals living in different locations. An alternative strategy for obtaining identification of the demand or utility parameters is to place restrictions on the specifications of the hedonic equation and the equations of interest. The endogeneity problem arises because the marginal prices and quantities of the characteristic are determined simultaneously by the consumer's choice of a house. Typically, instruments for the endogenous variables are used to overcome this estimation problem.[11]

Useful information for environmental economics can be gained at both stages in the estimation process. This is fortunate because the data requirements for the second-stage estimation are quite extensive and are not always met. For this reason, most studies are only able to estimate the hedonic price equation. It has long been known (Freeman, 1974) that the hedonic equation yields information on the *marginal* willingness to pay for the environmental improvement because the consumers optimize by equating their marginal rate of substitution between the characteristic and the numeraire to the marginal price which is estimated by the hedonic price equation. Polinsky and Shavell (1976) showed that the benefits of amenities (air quality improvements) can be estimated from the hedonic equation in an urban model of a small, open city. In Palmquist (1992a) it is shown that the willingness to pay for an environmental change can be determined from the hedonic estimation in the case of a 'localized' externality.[12] A localized externality affects only a relatively small number of properties within the market, so the equilibrium price equation is unaffected by the change. Some important environmental issues meet these requirements. For example, a hazardous waste site typically affects only the properties in the immediate vicinity (unless a major aquifer becomes polluted). Similarly, the noise from a major highway only affects adjoining properties.

If the environmental change is not localized, so that the price schedule changes due to the policy, the second-stage estimation is necessary to determine non-marginal willingness to pay. This is the case with some important policy issues. For many air pollutants, for example, air quality improvements will affect properties throughout an urban area and policies are often designed to achieve significant (that is, non-marginal) changes. The estimation of the demand for air quality or the parameters of the utility function will be necessary to evaluate such policies. There is also interest in transferring results estimated for one location to address policy questions in another area because of the expense of doing a new study in each area. The hedonic results cannot be transferred because they represent a reduced-form equilibrium equation. However, the structural parameters estimated in the second stage could be transferred. Even with the second-stage estimation, it is only possible to provide lower bounds for the *ex ante* willingness to pay for an environmental policy because the shift in the equilibrium price schedule cannot be forecast accurately (Palmquist, 1988).

3.   Recent developments in hedonic price equation estimation

The very first environmental application of hedonic techniques (Ridker and Henning, 1967) was concerned with air quality. Since that time there have been more hedonic studies of air quality than any other environmental problem, although the proportion of hedonic studies applied to air quality has fallen substantially in recent years. This decline can probably be attributed to two factors. First, even though the damages due to air quality are still substantial in many areas, research funding and public interest in this environmental problem have decreased. Second, since air quality is not a localized problem within an urban area, it is necessary to do the second-stage estimation to determine non-marginal willingness to pay. The necessary data are often not available. Recently there has been more interest in issues like hazardous wastes because of the high profile and localized nature of the problem.

None the less, it is interesting to examine what we have learned from hedonic studies of air quality. Recently, Smith and Huang (1993, 1995) conducted an exhaustive search for published and unpublished hedonic studies of the effect of air pollution on property values. They then used the studies to conduct a meta-analysis of what common insights can be gleaned from these studies. Meta-analysis is discussed in detail in chapter 55 of this book. Here only the implications for hedonic research are considered.

In the first article, Smith and Huang (1993) used a probit model to determine what factors account for a negative and significant coefficient on any pollution variable and specifically on particulate matter. They did not find a significant relationship between whether or not the work had been published and whether or not a negative and significant coefficient was found. Interestingly, they found that disaggregate data were less likely to reveal a negative and significant coefficient than census data. They attribute this to the greater variability in individual sales even though such data are theoretically preferable. The use of a linear functional form also reduces the probability. Cropper et al. (1988) found the linear Box–Cox functional form performed best, although they did find linear to be the next best. Smith and Huang also found that studies with more air pollutants included were less likely to find a negative and significant effect for *any* pollutant. They attribute this to collinearity of the air pollutant measures. However, in Palmquist (1983) the Belsley et al. (1980) diagnostics revealed almost no collinearity among the pollutants, so the explanation of this result is still open to question.

In their second paper Smith and Huang (1995) use meta-analysis to study the marginal willingness-to-pay estimates in the various studies and evaluate the prospects of benefits transfer from these first-stage hedonic models. Using mean absolute deviation models (to reduce the weight given to outliers) as well as OLS, they find some (but not conclusive) evidence that higher-income communities have higher willingness to pay and that higher pollution levels reduce willingness to pay. This latter result may seem puzzling until one considers that individuals with the highest willingness to pay will locate in areas with better air quality. Their experiments with benefits transfer lead them to be somewhat pessimistic about its prospects. The meta-analysis of hedonic studies may provide some insights into designing studies in the future, and it certainly synthesizes what we have learned so far.

The recent hedonic literature has also carefully examined the timing of the adverse impacts on property values from environmental problems. Many of these studies have been of hazardous wastes sites. In most such cases there is initially little public awareness of the existence of the site. Then the publicity begins and gradually increases until the site is officially listed as a hazardous wastes site. Still later the clean-up begins and, after a period of time, is officially concluded. Once again there is a period of stability in the expectations about the hazard, although the level of the expectations may differ from that in the initial period. In other cases it is not a pre-existing site but rather a new site for handling hazardous wastes. There are similar phases, although the final stage has to do with an ongoing operation rather than a site that has been declared to be cleaned up. How are property values affected during these stages?

Possibly the most interesting of such studies is Kiel and McClain (1995). They track the effects on property values of a waste incinerator through five stages: pre-rumour, rumour, construction, on-line, and ongoing operation.

They find that the distance of a house from the site of the incinerator does not have a statistically significant effect on price in either the pre-rumour or rumour stage. However, in the construction phase there was a significant negative effect, and when the site came on-line the effect was even larger. However, by the time the site had been operating for four years, the impact was reduced to about the level it had been during construction, and was still significant. Apparently as residents got more information about the incinerator, they revised downward (but did not eliminate) their concerns.

Kask and Maani (1992) do a similar study of the effects of a high-pressure natural gas pipeline. Their theoretical model is more ambitious, although their empirical work is perhaps less successful. Noble (1993) does a similar analysis of the timing of the impacts of the construction of a major highway using repeat sale techniques. The repeat sale method for studying environmental effects on property values was developed by Palmquist (1982) as an alternative to hedonic techniques. Data on houses that have sold two or more times in an area where there has been an environmental change are used. This eliminates the need to control for all the characteristics of the houses that do not change between sales (some of which may not be observable by the researcher).

A final area where some recent research has been done is on the functional form of the hedonic equation. As mentioned above, Cropper et al. (1988) did Monte Carlo experiments on functional form. The most general functional form that they used was the quadratic Box–Cox. The Box–Cox transformation of any variable x is $(x^\theta - 1)/\theta$ if $\theta \neq 0$ and $\ln x$ if $\theta = 0$, where θ is an estimated parameter. If the Box–Cox parameters for the dependent and independent variables (and for the cross-products of the independent variables in the quadratic case) take on particular values (for example, 0, 0.5, 1, or 2), the functional form is restricted to a wide variety of the most common functional forms in the hedonic literature (see Halvorsen and Pollakowski, 1981). Cropper et al. (1988) found that, in realistic circumstances where there may be some misspecification, a linear Box–Cox (that is, with no cross-product terms) functional form[13] produced the least error in estimating marginal characteristics prices and the ordinary linear form may be an acceptable alternative in some circumstances. A study that was published somewhat later, Rasmussen and Zuehlke (1990), comes up with different recommendations. Based on specification tests and a single data set, they advocate the use of the log transform of price and a quadratic form for the characteristics. Since this is almost the exact opposite of the results of Cropper et al. (1988), work on functional form will probably continue.

Most environmental research is interested in the effects of changes in the environmental variables. Studies such as the ones discussed above use the same transformation (value of θ) for all independent variables. Variables such as the number of square feet of living space have the greatest effect on price and therefore the appropriate transformation for those variables has the greatest influence on the estimated value for θ. The same transformation is being applied to the environmental variables even though this may not be the most appropriate transformation. Cassel and Mendelsohn (1985) suggest that the use of simpler forms (for example, linear) may be preferable to Box–Cox forms when the interest is in the environmental variable. On the other hand, Palmquist (1991) recommends allowing different Box–Cox parameters for the variables of interest. With recent innovations in estimation, allowing different transformations for all characteristics is no longer infeasible. Another part of the functional form debate where some progress is being made is the use of new forms (for example, sigmoid functions) for the environmental variables (Palmquist et al., 1997). For example, when the level of some externality is quite low, the marginal effect on house price of an increase in the externality also may be quite small. As the externality increases, the marginal impact on price may become considerably larger as the externality becomes a serious problem. However, at some point the externality may become so serious that homeowners elect to take mitigating steps (for example, air conditioning). The mitigating behaviour causes the marginal effect of an increase in the externality when the externality is at high levels to become smaller once again.

4. Recent developments in second-stage estimation

There has also been some interesting recent research on estimating the underlying demand for the environmental characteristics or the parameters of the underlying utility function. In addition, some comparisons of the two-stage hedonic model and the discrete choice model as means of estimating these underlying parameters have been done.

A study by Zabel and Kiel (1994) made use of proprietary data from the American Housing Survey to study individual houses and owner estimates of house price in four cities in five different years. These markets that were separated by time and/or space allow them to use the multiple-market techniques discussed earlier to identify the demands for four air pollutants. They find negative and significant coefficients for price in the demand equations for air quality with respect to three of the four pollutants, and the demands are quite inelastic with respect to own price. Income does not have a statistically significant effect on demand. There is evidence of increasing demand over time for air quality with respect to suspended particulates and ozone.

Chattopadhyay (1999) follows an alternative strategy using data from a single city and time period. He achieves identification with functional form restrictions rather than multiple markets. He experiments with the usual array of functional forms, but finds that the quadratic and quadratic Box–Cox yield implausible willingness-to-pay results. He estimates the parameters of Diewert and translog utility functions and uses these in developing estimates of willingness to pay for non-marginal environmental improvements.

A different question is addressed by Cropper et al. (1993) in a second Monte Carlo study. They simulate the performance of a two-stage hedonic model for a single city and the multinomial logit model of the discrete choice that consumers make in selecting a house. A discrete choice model for housing assumes that consumers make a decision between distinct models of houses. A random utility model is used to represent that decision. This modelling strategy is in contrast to the continuous range of housing choices assumed in the hedonic model. They find that the two models have similar success in estimating marginal willingness to pay, but that the discrete model outperforms the hedonic for non-marginal willingness to pay. It would be interesting to do a Monte Carlo study comparing the multiple-market hedonic model with the discrete choice model.

A final comparison of the hedonic and discrete choice models is Israngkura (1994), where data from multiple markets are used to estimate the two models. There are four air pollutants and 16 cities. Various forms for the utility function were used, and the compensated own-price elasticities for the pollutants were consistently negative and the coefficients of the price variables were uniformly statistically significant. The willingness to pay for a 20 per cent reduction in an air pollutant varied little with the form of the utility function. It ranged from \$52.79 to \$292.78 depending on the pollutant and the form of the utility function. The discrete choice model was less successful. Particulates were the only pollutant with statistically significant coefficients. However, for particulates the willingness to pay was larger than with the hedonic model. Such comparisons deserve further research.

5. Conclusions

Hedonic techniques can be applied in any situation where the price of a good or factor of production is influenced by environmental factors. They are most commonly applied with residential housing. Early applications considered air pollution, and this still is the most common environmental issue in hedonic studies. However, studies of hazardous wastes sites, waste incinerators, and other locally undesirable land uses are becoming more and more prevalent. Hedonic studies have been used repeatedly to study highway noise and airport noise. They have also been used for earthquake risk, hazardous water quality, visibility, non-residential land use, hog operations, public housing programmes, and congestion. Still other hedonic studies have been applied to beach proximity, shoreline, views, coastal land-use restrictions, neighbourhood quality and energy efficiency.

For factors of production, hedonics have been applied to farmland erosion, drainage issues, wetland preservation, and amenity uses of timberlands. Wage hedonics consider climate issues such as rainfall, humidity, temperature, as well as some of the environmental issues in the previous paragraph, particularly air pollution. Finally, many wage studies have considered job risks, and the results are widely used to approximate the value of a statistical life for environmental policy considerations.

The link between market goods and the environmental goods in hedonic models is both the strength and the weakness of the technique. It is a strength because the environment goods are actually traded as part of a differentiated product. Thus there are fewer assumptions that must be imposed in determining their marginal value. For example, with the various travel cost models the researcher must decide on the appropriate value for travel time and on-site time and decide what the substitute sites should be. Contingent valuation faces all the survey design issues and questions about strategic or ill-considered answers. On the other hand, hedonics can only value environmental goods that are linked to market goods and even then only certain aspects of the environmental goods are considered. For example, a hedonic study can estimate the value of an air quality improvement to consumers during their time at the residence but would miss the value of the improvement while the individuals are at work.[14] Other techniques, such as travel cost and contingent valuation, clearly dominate when the environmental good is not part of a differentiated product that is traded on markets.

Since the major reviews of the hedonic literature were written (for example, Bartik and Smith, 1987; Palmquist, 1991; Freeman, 1993), hedonics have continued to be applied to an ever-increasing range of environmental problems. The applications have become more sophisticated, and there has been further research on the important methodological questions raised by the second-stage estimation. The usefulness of hedonic techniques should continue, and the methods will be refined. At the same time, newer techniques such as the random utility models show promise as well.

Notes

1. Cropper and Arriaga-Salinas (1980) and Smith (1983) are good early examples of hedonic wage studies. More recently researchers have combined hedonic wage and property values (for example, Roback, 1982 and Hoehn et al., 1987).
2. The theoretical model for differentiated factors of production was developed by Palmquist (1989). Empirical applications are common in agricultural economics.

3. Mäler (1977) provided an early critique of hedonic techniques. He raised interesting issues, some of which have been addressed or discussed in subsequent literature. However, in the 20 years since the article was published, the widespread use of hedonic techniques seems to indicate that many researchers do not agree with his conclusion that the difficulties he raises 'show conclusively, that there is no real possibility of estimating willingness to pay for environmental quality from property value studies' (p. 368).
4. There is a related literature in urban and spatial economics that considers land values in a general equilibrium framework. There is not space to discuss them here, but they are summarized in Palmquist (1991).
5. The only exceptions to this statement are if all customers are identical (so the hedonic function and the bid function common to all consumers coincide) or if all firms are identical (so the hedonic function and the offer function common to all firms coincide). Neither of these cases is relevant in empirical work.
6. With houses, only a small fraction of the homes in a given market sell within a particular time period. None the less, people do move for a variety of reasons (new job location, changed wealth, new family status, and so on). In the buying and selling of houses in connection with such moves, equilibrium prices for environmental characteristics are established. There seems to be no reason to believe that this price schedule would differ systematically if all houses were traded.
7. The assumption of a competitive market implies that buyers and sellers have easy access to information about the prices and characteristics of houses. While this assumption probably does not cause major problems in many cases, it is true that brokers and consultants are common in the markets for differentiated products and search costs can be important. Recently, the hedonic literature has begun to address these issues using stochastic frontier analysis and duration modelling.
8. Estimating the two parts of the model simultaneously has been suggested by Epple (1987) and others. This strategy has not yet been implemented, probably because the specification of the hedonic equation cannot be determined theoretically and the form of the marginal prices depends on the form of the hedonic. Also, there are a large number of characteristics (and thus a large number of equations to be estimated simultaneously) in a typical hedonic study.
9. In estimating the demand for a typical product with observations on the actions of individuals, the researcher observes the market price as well as the quantity purchased and the socioeconomic attributes of the individual. The estimation can immediately proceed to the demand equation. This is analogous to the hedonic second stage, but with a differentiated product the price of the characteristic is not observed. Its estimation is the reason for the first step (estimating the hedonic price equation).
10. See Brown and Rosen (1982) or Palmquist (1984) for a discussion of this issue.
11. See Epple (1987), Bartik (1987), and Palmquist (1984) on this issue.
12. If there are significant transactions and moving costs, these must be incorporated in the welfare measurement, and upper bounds for the willingness to pay and required compensation are available rather than exact measures (see Palmquist, 1992b).
13. Both the dependent variable (price) and all strictly positive and continuous independent variables (characteristics) were transformed. All independent variables (and the cross-products in the quadratic case) were transformed by the same Box–Cox parameter, although it was allowed to differ from the one for the dependent variable.
14. One could invoke an assumption such as weak complementarity and assume that the benefits measured at the house exhausted all benefits. However, such an assumption seems inappropriate.

References

Bartik, T.J. (1987), 'The estimation of demand parameters in hedonic price models', *Journal of Political Economy*, **95**, 81–8.

Bartik, T.J. and V.K. Smith (1987), 'Urban amenities and public policy', in E.S. Mills (ed.), *Handbook of Regional and Urban Economics*, vol. 2, pp.1207–54, Amsterdam: North-Holland.

Belsley, D., E. Kuh and R. Welsch (1980), *Regression Diagnostics: Identifying Influential Data and Sources of Collinearity*, New York: Wiley.

Brown, J.N. and H.S. Rosen (1982), 'On the estimation of structural hedonic price models', *Econometrica*, **50**, 765–8.

Cassel, E. and R. Mendelsohn (1985), 'The choice of functional forms for hedonic price equations: comment', *Journal of Urban Economics*, **18**, 135–42.

Chattopadhyay, S. (1999), 'Estimating the demand for air quality: new evidence based on the Chicago housing market', *Land Economics*, **75**, 22–38.

Court, A.T. (1939), 'Hedonic price indexes with automotive examples', in *The Dynamics of Automobile Demand*, New York: General Motors.

Cropper, M.L. and A.S. Arriaga-Salinas (1980), 'Intercity wage differentials and the value of air quality', *Journal of Urban Economics*, **8**, 236–54.

Cropper, M.L., L.B. Deck and K.E. McConnell (1988), 'On the choice of functional form for hedonic price equations', *Review of Economics and Statistics*, **70**, 668–75.

Cropper, M.L., L. Deck, N. Kishor and K.E. McConnell (1993), 'Valuing product attributes using single market data: a comparison of hedonic and discrete choice approaches', *Review of Economics and Statistics*, **75**, 225–32.

Epple, D. (1987), 'Hedonic prices and implicit markets: estimating demand and supply functions for differentiated products', *Journal of Political Economy*, **95**, 59–80.

Freeman, A.M. III (1974), 'Air pollution and property values: a further comment', *Review of Economics and Statistics*, **56**, 554–6.

Freeman, A.M. III (1993), *The Measurement of Environmental and Resource Values*, Washington, DC: Resources for the Future.

Griliches, Z. (1971), 'Hedonic price indexes for automobiles: an econometric analysis of quality change', in his *Price Indexes and Quality Change*, Cambridge, MA: Harvard University Press.

Halvorsen, R. and H.O. Pollakowski (1981), 'Choice of functional form for hedonic price equations', *Journal of Urban Economics*, **10**, 37–49.

Hoehn, J.P., M.C. Berger and G.C. Blomquist (1987), 'A hedonic model of interregional wages, rents, and amenity values', *Journal of Regional Science*, **27**, 605–20.

Israngkura, A. (1994), *Environmental Benefit Measures: A Comparison between Hedonic and Discrete Choice Models*, Ph.D. dissertation, North Carolina State University.

Kask, S.B. and S.A. Maani (1992), 'Uncertainty, information, and hedonic pricing', *Land Economics*, **68**, 170–84.

Kiel, K.A. and K.T. McClain (1995), 'House prices during siting decision stages: the case of an incinerator from rumor through operation', *Journal of Environmental Economics and Management*, **28**, 241–55.

Mäler, K.G. (1977),'A note on the use of property values in estimating marginal willingness to pay for environmental quality', *Journal of Environmental Economics and Management*, **4**, 355–69.

Noble, B. (1993), 'Efficiency in the housing market: implications for hedonic analysis', working paper, University of Washington.

Palmquist, R.B. (1982), 'Measuring environmental effects on property values without hedonic regressions', *Journal of Urban Economics*, **11**, 333–47.

Palmquist, R.B. (1983), *Estimating the Demand for Air Quality from Property Value Studies: Further Results*, Report to the Environmental Protection Agency, October.

Palmquist, R.B. (1984), 'Estimating the demand for the characteristics of housing', *Review of Economics and Statistics*, **66**, 394–404.

Palmquist, R.B. (1988), 'Welfare measurement for environmental improvements using the hedonic model: the case of nonparametric marginal prices', *Journal of Environmental Economics and Management*, **5**, 297–312.

Palmquist, R.B. (1989), 'Land as a differentiated factor of production: a hedonic model and its implications for welfare measurement', *Land Economics*, **65**, 23–8.

Palmquist, R.B. (1991), 'Hedonic methods', in J. B. Braden and C.D. Kolstad (eds), *Measuring the Demand for Environmental Quality*, Amsterdam: North-Holland, pp.77–120.

Palmquist, R.B. (1992a), 'Valuing localized externalities', *Journal of Urban Economics*, **31**, 59–68.

Palmquist, R.B. (1992b), 'A note on transactions costs, moving costs, and benefit measurement', *Journal of Urban Economics*, **32**, 40–44.

Palmquist, R.B., F.M. Roka and T. Vukina (1997), 'Hog operations, environmental effects, and residential property values', *Land Economics*, **73**, 114–24.

Polinsky, A.M. and S. Shavell (1976), 'Amenities and property values in a model of an urban area', *Journal of Public Economics*, **5**, 119–29.

Rasmussen, D.W. and T.W. Zuehlke (1990), 'On the choice of functional form for hedonic price functions', *Applied Economics*, **22**, 431–8.

Ridker, R.G. and J.A. Henning (1967), 'The determinants of residential property values with special reference to air pollution', *Review of Economics and Statistics*, **49**, 246–57.

Roback, J. (1982), 'Wages, rents, and the quality of life', *Journal of Political Economy*, **90**, 1257–78.

Rosen, S. (1974), 'Hedonic markets and implicit prices: product differentiation in pure competition', *Journal of Political Economy*, **82**, 34–55.

Smith, V.K. (1983), 'The role of site and job characteristics in hedonic wage models', *Journal of Urban Economics*, **13**, 296–321.

Smith, V.K. and J.C. Huang (1993), 'Hedonic models and air pollution: twenty-five years and counting', *Environmental and Resource Economics*, **3**, 381–94.

Smith, V.K. and J.C. Huang (1995), 'Can markets value air quality? A meta-analysis of hedonic property value models', *Journal of Political Economy*, **103**, 209–27.

Zabel, J.E. and K.A. Kiel (1994), 'Estimating the demand for clean air in four United States cities', International Institute of Public Finance.

54 Contingent valuation
Bengt Kriström*

1. Introduction
This chapter provides a brief outline of the contingent valuation method (CVM). We begin, in Section 2, by describing some key developments of the method, including some brief historical notes. The third section provides a discussion of key issues in the development of an actual experiment, where we divide an experiment into four different phases. Section 4 comments on some of the issues that are at the forefront of the current discussion. Section 5 offers some concluding remarks on fruitful future research directions.

2. From esoteric toy to multibillion dollar assessment tool
The contingent valuation method is a practical survey technique, designed to shed empirical light on matters of resource allocation. Survey techniques are the main tool for generating data within the social sciences. Household expenditure surveys, employment surveys, health surveys, opinion polls and surveys used to compile the national accounts are examples of data-generating processes in the social sciences. Indeed, surveys are the life-blood of empirical studies for economists, psychologists, sociologists and for vast number of other researchers.

At first blush the CVM is straightforward; simply ask a set of people how much they would be willing to pay (WTP) for obtaining a particular good. As is now well understood, this is only a caricature of a state-of-the-art application, which needs input not only from economic theory, but also from several other disciplines, including sociology, psychology, statistics and survey research.

Historical notes
It might be useful to recount some of the historical highlights in the development of the CVM. Readers interested in extensive surveys should consult Braden and Kolstad (1992) or Mitchell and Carson (1989).

It was probably the Berkeley economist Ciriacy-Wantrup (1947) who

* I thank the editor, Glenn Harrison, Giovanni Signorello and two referees for much help in preparing the manuscript. I feel a little bit like Zsa Zsa Gabor's fifth husband. I know what's expected of me, but I'm not sure if I still can make it interesting (Al Gore).

first alerted economists to the simple fact that information about people's preferences can be obtained by appropriately constructed interviews. As Hanemann (1994) points out, Ciriacy-Wantrup never followed up his idea and we had to wait a number of years until the first application. The first contingent valuation study appears to have been undertaken by a consulting company in 1958, where people visiting the Delaware Basin (US) were asked their willingness to pay (WTP) for entering national parks (Mack and Myers, 1965). Robert K. Davis's (1963) Harvard dissertation was the first significant academic application of the CVM. The study by Alan Randall and co-workers (1974) in the first issue of *Journal of Environmental Economics and Management* is a well-known application of the method. A number of other studies appeared in the 1970s; see Mitchell and Carson (1989) for a detailed survey.

Bishop and Heberlein (1979) presented the subjects with a particular price to accept/reject – the binary valuation question ('take-it-or-leave-it', 'referendum approach' are other common names of this approach). Hanemann (1984) asked if Bishop and Heberlein's (1979) approach could be couched in welfare-theoretic terms, where the theory would address the individual response mechanism. Using the random utility maximization model, he provided a theoretical foundation that has since then remained the basis for further explorations of the CVM. Cameron and James (1987) and later Cameron's (1988) paper provided a different technique for computing welfare measures as compared to Hanemann's (1984) suggestion.

Extensions first focused upon the statistical aspects. Kriström (1990) and Duffield and Patterson (1991) provided non-parametric approaches, arguing that the distributional assumption is essential when a mean (and to a lesser extent the median) is estimated from data. Further developments of non-parametric approaches are found in Carson et al. (1996) and for a semi-parametric approach, which handles covariates in a straightforward way, see Li (1996).

A second set of extensions involves the way binary valuation questions are asked and a third literature develops optimal designs of such experiments. These issues are discussed below.

Returning now to the general situation in the 1980s, this decade was marked by the fact that the CVM was being extensively employed in some countries outside the US. The Scandinavian countries appear to have been particularly active, as evidenced by the recent survey in Navrud (1992). However, the approach is quickly spreading to southern Europe. There has also been considerable activity in Australia and New Zealand; see Jakobsson and Dragun (1996). The World Bank has also commissioned several studies in Africa.

In the 1990s, the CVM reached public debate and even the first pages of the *New York Times*, spurred by the intensive controversy following the grounding of the tanker *Exxon Valdez* in Prince William Sound, Alaska. The subsequent litigation process led to involvement of several well-known economists, serving on different sides.

A key issue came to circle around the notion of non-use values, which arises independently of the use of a resource, for example for altruistic reasons. Non-use values had only appeared to a limited extent in US litigation and their legal standing was quite unclear at the time. An earlier ruling (often known as the 'Ohio Court ruling') suggested that non-use values should be included in the damage assessment. See Cummings and Harrison (1994, 1995) for a survey of this particular issue.

The sometimes acrimonious debate in the aftermath of the *Exxon Valdez* eventually led the responsible authority to establish a special 'Blue-Ribbon' panel (the NOAA panel (*Federal Register*, 1993)) for guidance. The panel included some of the best-known economists (for example, Nobel prizewinners Robert Solow of MIT and Kenneth Arrow of Stanford). In its final report, the panel issued a number of detailed recommendations on how to carry out a contingent valuation study. Most importantly, the panel were quite sympathetic to the use of the CVM, although the recommendations that they advanced have been subject to some debate.

In summary, the CVM has marched from a place in the opaque back alleys of applied welfare economics to being the most widely applied method for welfare measurement when markets do not exist. From being considered an exotic cousin to well-established methods for valuing non-market goods, the CVM is enjoying a popularity and influence in the 1990s that few would have considered possible. The number of applications was and still is growing rapidly, as is the range of the goods being valued. A recently compiled survey shows that articles in the major journals of environmental economics have been dominated by discussions related to the CVM. NRDA (1996) has collected a bibliography of more than 2000 papers that deal with the CVM.

3. Characteristics of an experiment

We turn now to some of the details of carrying out a particular experiment. Because the acronym CVM relates to the method *per se*, it is more convenient to discuss a contingent valuation experiment (CVE), even though it introduces another acronym. A CVE involves a number of different, but closely related steps. A number of key issues must be resolved before proceeding with the details of each step. The four phases are:

1. Developing the study
2. Crafting and administration

3.   Collecting the data
4.   Data analysis and reporting.

The most important aspect of these phases is that they are not independent. A CVE must be very carefully planned. For example, when generating the data via binary valuation questions, one must generally decide in phase 1 what it is one wants to measure. For example, an optimal design of an experiment is not necessarily independent of whether one wants to measure the mean or the median WTP. There are many similar, sometimes subtle, links between the different stages. We illustrate some of them in the sequel.

Phase 1   Developing the study
The first step in a CVM experiment is (or should be) construction of a conceptual model. Ideally, a set of cost–benefit rules are derived, as outlined in, for example, Johansson (1993). Cost–benefit rules make clear how benefits and costs should be counted to, for example, avoid double-counting.

To illustrate, consider the following example. Assume that a government body wants some information on the benefits and costs of expanding an existing city airport. An expansion involves social costs in terms of additional noise and pollution. It also involves benefits, such as reduced transportation time and so on. Property owners may be affected through changes in property values, as may be firms that lose or gain by the expansion. A cost–benefit rule makes clear how these benefits and costs should be aggregated. Most importantly, it gives much help when constructing the valuation question *per se*. Johansson (1993) gives many excellent examples of how cost–benefit rules are useful for the CVM practitioner.

It is important to note that we need more research on how these cost–benefit rules work in the context of hypothetical choices in non-arbitrage environments. This is an important research agenda and we shall comment briefly on it at various points in this chapter.

The extent of the market   The cost–benefit rule may also highlight the 'extent of the market'. That is, what subset of the population is to be included in the survey? The target population could – in principle – consist of every living person. The problem of global warming (resulting from excessive emissions of 'greenhouse gases' like carbon dioxide) is a case in point.

The extent of the market issue is related to the distinction between non-use and use values. The introduction of non-use values complicates the choice of market boundary, because non-use values arise independent of the person's participation in a particular market.

Nevertheless, choosing the extent of the market is often less difficult in practice than in theory. There are typically characteristics of the underlying resource allocation problem that make the choice of target population natural. A simple rule of thumb is to include those who have a legal and economic standing in the matter. This approach was used in the *Exxon Valdez* study by Carson et al. (1992).

Information issues   The scenario conveys the information about the good to be delivered in a CVE. We call this abstractly the *information set*. A fundamental question concerns the structure of this information set: how much information should be given? What kind of information should be given and how should the information be conveyed? These questions have been the subject of extensive research in the literature on the CVM.

It should be expected that the values obtained are sensitive to the amount of information provided. Randall and Stoll (1983, p. 270) noted this in the case of snail-darter (a small fish thought to live only in a Tennessee river, downstream of a proposed dam). Bergstrom et al. (1990) provided different amounts of information to different groups of respondents, finding that values did indeed depend on the information sets. Similar results appear in Samples et al. (1986).

The Cummings et al. (1986) volume brought the notion that values from a CVE are more reliable if: subjects are given 'time to think'; if they are familiar with the good and, finally, if they are made aware of substitutes and complements. These three conditions are called reference operating conditions (ROC) and can be thought of as a restriction on the information set.

Because information is costly to collect and process, there is typically some point when the marginal benefit of additional information is equal to the marginal cost of acquiring it. This is the only sense in which one can speak of the correct size of an information set, although the marginal benefit (and cost) is typically unknown in any given experiment.

Developing the scenario   The CVM derives its name from the idea that subjects are asked to evaluate a change contingent on two (or more) states of the world. These states are described in the questionnaire. Harrison (1996) holds that one could as well ask respondents about states of the world that are not certain.

Typically, an initial state of the world is described, followed by a portrait of a second state of the world. It is not necessary that, say, the second state has occurred; the subject is often asked to evaluate hypothetical changes.

The scenario describes the good the individual is supposed to 'buy' in the hypothetical market. A number of criteria for creating an effective scenario have been developed by, for example, psychologists such as Fischoff and Furby (1988).

Description of the good to be valued   There are various ways of portraying the good to be valued in the experiment. Written explanatory text along with some relevant drawings and, in some cases, photographs, are typical ways of describing the good. Visual displays have proven helpful in conveying the scenarios, as evidenced by Mitchell and Carson's (1995) review. Sophistication varies; some studies include only a rudimentary description, while others contain elaborate visual displays. Navrud (1994) provides encouraging results of using videos to present the scenario.

Questioning modes   The *binary valuation question* is now, to some extent, dominating the theoretical and applied literature. The respondent in subsample k is presented with a price A_k for the good under consideration. A recent extension of this approach is to ask the respondent to consider a second price, where the value of the second price depends on the reaction to the initial price. Thus the respondent in subsample k is first asked to consider a price $A_{k,0}$. If he accepts to pay this amount, he is asked to consider $A_{k,up}$, where $A_{k,up} > A_{k,0}$. Conversely, if he rejects to pay $A_{k,0}$ he is presented with a lower price $A_{k,down}$. See Hanemann et al. (1991) for detailed exposition of the so-called double-bounded approach.

Another version of the double-bounded approach is developed in Kriström (1997), following Johansson et al. (1992), where respondents are allowed to have a zero WTP. This is called the spike model, because the distribution is allowed to have a spike at zero (the proportion of respondents with zero WTP).

A key issue is if the second question affects the individual's WTP in some unwanted ways. As Harrison and Kriström (1995) argue, it could be the case that the individual anchors on the first price, in the sense of a contract. If you have agreed to pay $A_{k,0}$ for the good, it may be psychologically difficult to pay more than this (presumably since delivery has been 'promised' at $A_{k,0}$). Thus there is some risk that the second question distorts information about WTP in the sample. See, for example, Herriges and Shogren (1996) for a recent test of this hypothesis.

Cameron and Quiggin (1994) explicitly attempted to model the fact that the answer to the second question may depend on the first, by using a so-called bivariate probit model. This approach allows one to test for the presence of distortionary effects. For additional suggestions on similar tests, see the review by Hanemann and Kanninen (1996).

The potential 'surprise effect' of the second valuation question has led Cooper and Hanemann (1995) to introduce what they call the *one-and-a-*

half bounded valuation question. In this model, the respondent is informed by the interviewer that the cost of the project is expected to fall in the range $\{Cost_{low}, Cost_{high}\}$. The interviewer picks one of these at random. If, for example, the respondent accepts paying $Cost_{high}$, no second question is asked. Similarly, if the respondent rejects paying $Cost_{low}$, the respondent is not asked a second question. This approach reduces the potential for inconsistency between answers.

It can be noted that this approach is quite similar to the *spike model*. One can arrange this question so that the respondent is first asked if he wants to contribute anything at all to the project. If he says no, there is obviously no need for further question about benefits (although one may want to explore the reasons why the respondent did not want to pay). Thus it may be argued that there is less risk of contaminating the data by introducing a second valuation question, when using the spike model.

A further variation, which is called the *triple-bounded* approach (or trivariate binary valuation question in our terminology), has been used by Bateman et al. (1996). Here, the respondent is asked to respond yes or no to three different amounts. Theoretically, this will yield more information about the distribution of WTP, but runs the same (possibly higher) risk of distorted answers.

The *payment card* provides the respondent with a range of possible WTP, including figures on actual spending (or costs) for certain publicly provided goods. For example, the card can give information about how much the state is spending on fire brigades, liming of lakes, hospitals and so on, in order to put the values in some perspective. For illustrations, see Mitchell and Carson (1989).

The *bidding game* is an iterative bidding process. The individual is given a starting point (a 'bid') and then asked whether he would like to revise it upwards or downwards. It is hoped that the process converges to the respondent's WTP. Starting-point bias arises if the value of the first bid affects the finally reported WTP in some systematic way. Because empirical research has revealed that starting-point bias is a common tendency, the bidding game has lost appeal.

Optimal design When using the binary question, one needs to decide which prices to present to the respondent. The sample is divided in to k subsamples and one uses a different bid A in each subsample. The prices $[A_1, A_2, \ldots A_k]$ is often called the bid-vector. The practical problem that arises is, of course, the structure of this vector. How many bids should one use? How does one decide the lowest/highest bid? How does one decide the spacing of the bids? These questions are difficult to answer in general, although there is some statistical theory that sheds light on them. There is now a substantial literature on the choice of bids; see, for example, Kanninen (1993a, 1993b) and Nyquist (1992). It is important to note that the criteria used to derive a statistically optimal design (for example, the one that minimizes the variance of the used estimator) may be rather restrictive from an economic point of view.

The *contingent ranking* technique is relatively new in the contingent valuation literature, but has been used extensively in market research and transportation economics. The approach is also known as conjoint analysis (see Louviere, 1988). Here, one asks the respondent to rank a set of alternatives describing environmental qualities obtainable at certain costs. For example, a respondent could be asked to rank three different programmes: {save 100 ha of forest area X, cost US$30}, {save 200 ha of forest area Y, cost US$60}, {save 400 ha of forest Z, cost US$120}. To estimate WTP from these kinds of data, one uses econometric techniques similar to those used for binary valuation questions. See also Smith and Desvouges (1986).

Provision rules   The valuation question should state under what conditions the good becomes available to the respondent. It is vitally important that the provision rule is explicitly stated in the questionnaire. Without any clear notion of how his answer is going to affect the supply of the good, one cannot expect that the respondent will refer to the intended resource allocation problem. It is rather more likely that the respondent's answer reflects some general sympathy towards the issue, and that he is responding to a much more general good than was intended in the survey.

Provision rules and the free-rider problem   When a private good is traded, then (under perfect information) the provision rule is not controversial and there is no doubt that the buyer will eventually pay the seller. A contract will be reached only if both parties find it to their advantage. In this sense, markets for private goods are incentive-compatible. But in a hypothetical context involving hypothetical payments it is clear that the individual has an incentive to hide his true WTP (or WTA). If the provision rule states that the public good is delivered if the sum of WTP covers the cost, there is an incentive for an individual simply to state that he is willing to pay the whole cost of the project. In this way, he will be certain that the good is delivered and he assumes (quite correctly!) that he is not going to have to pay the amount he stated. Thus a hypothetical approach to eliciting preferences may not be incentive-compatible.

How serious this theoretical problem is for the CVM is ultimately an empirical question. What is needed are detailed tests of the *free-rider hypothesis*. At this point we state only that this issue is a subject of much current research (for a pessimistic view, see Diamond and Hausmann, 1994, and for a more optimistic, see Hanemann, 1994).

It is an interesting question whether incentives to free-riding vary across elicitation modes. There are several claims in the literature to the effect that there is a difference between questioning modes in terms of incentive effects, even though the situation is hypothetical. One of the first papers to provide a theoretical argument in support of this claim is the contribution by Hoehn and Randall (1987). They argued that the binary response approach is incentive-compatible, a claim that generated several responses from experimental economists (see, for example, Cummings et al., 1995; see also Cummings et al., 1997).

The provision rules might vary between elicitation modes. If an *open-ended* question is used, the provision rule might be that the good is delivered if the sum of money obtained covers the costs of delivery. In the *closed-ended* case, a referendum interpretation can be used; for example, the good will be delivered if more than 50 per cent of the 'voters' accept paying the stated sum. It is not necessary always to use a 50 per cent majority type of provision rule. Knut Wicksell argued, for example, that important decisions should require a much larger proportion of agreement. Such super-majority rules and other voting issues have been extensively discussed and, indeed, used in many countries since long ago.

Phase 2   Crafting and administration
The second phase of a CVE involves constructing the actual survey instrument and developing the logistics of the experiment. This phase also includes building the sampling frame. Perhaps the most important practical issue to be resolved is the choice of delivery modes, to which we now turn.

Delivery modes   The typical experiment either employs personal interviewers (in-person/telephone) or uses mail. Either approach has various advantages/disadvantages. A significant disadvantage with the in-person interview is that it is costly. This disadvantage is often a decisive factor, despite the many advantages offered by in-person interviews.

Cheapest among the three approaches is to use a mailed questionnaire. This approach permits less feedback from the investigator and becomes much more clumsy for certain types of valuation questions. The in-between approach, telephone interview, can be combined with a mailed questionnaire. Such an approach has much to recommend it, but there are as yet not many applications.

There has been much debate in the literature on the appropriateness of each delivery mode. Some researchers, such as Mitchell and Carson (1995) argued strongly in favour of personal interviews. Dillman (1993) provides a staunch defence of mail delivery. The US legislation and the NOAA panel on contingent valuation advocate the use of personal interviews, if the approach is used to assess large damages from oil spills.

Yet another approach has been suggested by Harrison and Lesley (1996). They argue that good results can be obtained by using a convenience sample (for example, students) and then expanding the results to the population of interest by regression methods. The main argument of Harrison and Lesley is that the cost of a large-scale survey has to be weighed against the benefits of obtaining a representative sample.

Thus there is no consensus in the literature on the choice of delivery mode. The key parameter seems to be the budget of the study. Roughly, mail delivery is not more than 10 per cent of the cost of using interviews. This explains why the large majority of applications have been based on mail surveys.

Phase 3   *Collecting the data*
The third phase of the study is to collect the actual data. It is often helpful to begin this data-collection process by using a small focus group, as we argued above. Here a small sample of individuals discuss a number of aspects of the questionnaire. Some of these can be revised before a draft questionnaire is completed. This draft can then be delivered to sponsors and critics for scrutiny.

A vital next step is to complete a pilot study, using a sample of 10–20 per cent of the final sample size. The pilot study is used to improve understanding of how well the survey instrument performs and to obtain some information about underlying key characteristics of the population.

If the binary valuation question is used, this is the time for testing a particular choice of bid-vector. Because of the uncertainty that typically exists regarding people's preferences, the bid-vector may be a 'shot in the dark'.

The pilot study is the only way of discovering that the subjective assessment of the distribution of WTP is badly wrong. Obviously, if every subject accepts paying the suggested costs in the survey, not much information has been obtained; the only aspect revealed is that WTP apparently exceeds the lowest amount used. Such sparse information is probably not of much value. Consequently, the pilot study is of paramount importance. Some extremely expensive mistakes have been made, when the investigator has selected to jump directly to the main sample.

Having assessed the results from the pilot study, one can now proceed to delivering the survey to the main sample. The assessment may involve formal procedures for updating the bid-vector and removing or adding other information based on the reactions from the sample.

Phase 4   Data analysis and reporting
Once the data set has been obtained, the final phase of the study is to analyse
the data and to report the results. It is in this stage that the investigator also
knows the response rate, a key ingredient in the statistical analysis.

Response rates   A discussion of what constitutes 'acceptable' response
rates is complicated. The complexity of the issue is enhanced by the fact
that it is not only the response rate itself that is important. More likely, it
is the properties of the received sample that are crucial. Thus a biased
sample, where a particular subset of the population is over-represented in
the final data set, can be more serious than a 'low' response rate. Whitehead
(1991) provides an example, where he finds that environmental interest
groups have much higher response rates than a control group (a general
population sample).
    In its recommendations, the NOAA panel on contingent valuation rec-
ommends a response rate of 70 per cent. It is unclear if the process of
obtaining this 'high' response rate may affect the quality of the responses
obtained. Indeed, it might be very costly to obtain the 'last percentage' if
the issue under scrutiny does not interest the population in the study. If the
respondents are repeatedly pressed to answer, it is not clear that the quality
of the information obtained sufficiently justifies the cost of obtaining it.

Reporting the results   The final stage involves dissemination of the results.
It might seem rather trivial and uninteresting to discuss this matter in this
book. But if an outsider is to be able to assess the results obtained, it is
imperative that high standards are obeyed in the matter of reporting. Thus
the survey instrument should be readily available for inspection. If this is
not possible for reasons of space, the full valuation question must at least
be reproduced. It is also consistent with high scientific standard to store
electronically the data for ease of replication.

4.   Current issues
This section provides a sampler of some current issues in the literature. The
choice reflects, to an important extent, personal biases, and space limitations prevent an extended coverage of many other interesting issues.

Exxon Valdez and the NOAA panel
At 12:04 a.m. 24 March 1989, the tanker *Exxon Valdez* ran aground on
Bligh Reef in Alaska's Prince William Sound. The resulting 11 million
gallons of crude oil affected about 1000 miles of shoreline and killed thousands of animals. It is believed that the spill may affect marine plants,
micro-organisms, fish, marine mammals and also birds in the long run. The

State of Alaska sued the Exxon Corporation (and other potentially responsible parties) shortly after the spill. A team of CVM researchers was hired
to conduct a study of the lost 'passive use values'. At about the same time,
the Exxon Corporation hired a number of economists, including CVM
researchers, to conduct studies of their own. A third research team was
coordinated by the Federal government of the US; their results remain
unpublished, however.

Predictably, the two main contestants came to widely different conclusions regarding the ultimate damage assessment. Because only a small fraction of the American population visits Prince William Sound, much of the
damages were thought to be in the form of lost passive use values.

The Exxon consultants published a critical account of the CVM, arguing
that the method cannot be used to estimate such values; see Hausman
(1993). By contrast, the Alaska team produced a conservative assessment
of 2.8 billion dollars of lost passive use values (Carson et al., 1992).

The National Oceanic and Atmospheric Administration (NOAA)
requested information and comments on appropriate procedures for
damage assessment, beginning in December 1990. Included in this process
was the establishment of a panel (the NOAA panel on contingent valuation) 'to evaluate the use of CVM in determining nonuse values and
provide comments to NOAA' (*Federal Register*, 1993, p.4602).

The panel concludes that the CVM can be used as a starting point in a
judicial process, provided the experiment meets certain conditions. It also
devised a number of guidelines for an experiment. Of these, we pick three
for discussion. By 'conservative design' the panel means that one should use
the option that is likely to underestimate WTP. 'Generally, when aspects of
the survey design and the analysis of the responses are ambiguous, the
option that tends to underestimate willingness to pay is preferred. A conservative design increases the reliability of the estimate by eliminating
extreme responses that can enlarge estimated values wildly and implausibly' (NOAA, 1993, p.4608). Alas, this recommendation does not square
with the suggestion to use the binary valuation question, because the
general findings in the literature on open versus closed valuation questions
suggest that the latter give higher values, see below. The panel also recommended that the valuation question should be expanded to offer explicitly
an 'I would not vote' response. The objective is to mimic the practice of
voting in which people can decide not to participate in the referendum. This
issue has recently been analysed by Carson et al. (1996).

Altruism and CVM
The economic significance of altruism has become a focus of discussion.
Altruism appears to be an important component of lost passive use values.

The issue of altruism and its proper place in cost–benefit analysis is certainly not new in the economics literature. The early literature came to the conclusion that altruistically motivated values should not be counted in the cost–benefit analysis, because there will be some kind of double-counting. Milgrom (1992) contends that altruism should not be considered in a CVM study, supplying a model to verify his claim. Milgrom (1992) also makes the interesting argument that a person cannot be considered to suffer a loss if he or she is unaware of an environmental disaster.

Following Johansson (1993), assume that the economy consists of two persons, each of whom is an altruist. Assume now that an environmental disaster occurs and that the sums of money that will restore each person's utility level is (somehow) found. What is the meaning of the sum of these two numbers, when the two people care about each other's utility level? The answer turns out to be the form of altruism. In one form of altruism, an individual cares about the other individual's welfare (that is, his utility function). In another, he cares only about a certain attribute of welfare (that is, environmental quality). The important conclusion is, however, that independent of how altruism is modelled, it is always correct to ask the individual about his WTP; the individual will state a number that has the usual interpretation as a money equivalent of the welfare change involved. In this sense, altruism poses no particular problem for the CVM. It also remains the only currently known method where such values can be estimated, although there seems to be little reason to estimate them *per se*. The important issue is whether such values are included in the welfare measures one seeks and if the empirical method includes them.

Comparative analysis of elicitation formats
In recent years, a series of papers have addressed an apparent disparity between different elicitation formats (for example, Desvousges et al., 1993; Kriström, 1993; Li and Fredman, 1994; Brown et al., 1996; Boyle et al., 1996; and Ready et al., 1996). From economic theory alone, we do not expect to find any differences between open-ended and closed-ended formats. Empirically, a number of studies show that there might exist a large disparity here. While the evidence is not conclusive, it seems as if binary response questions generate higher mean WTP. Brown et al. (1996, p. 153, table 1) show that mean WTP is about twice as high on the average for the closed-ended format compared to the open-ended.

Kahnemann et al. (1982) argue that choices under uncertainty are affected by the existence of anchors. If the participant in a contingent valuation experiment is considered to be making a choice under uncertainty, it is possible that cost information provided by the researcher serves as an anchoring point. This hypothesis, incidentally, is rejected in a formal test for the Kriström (1993) data.

Embedding and sequencing
The embedding hypothesis has been popularized by Kahneman and Knetsch (1992). It holds that people are insensitive to the level of the public good. Thus people may report the same WTP for preserving a particular bird as they are WTP for preserving all endangered species. This empirically based hypothesis finds support in the studies reported by Kahneman and Knetsch (1992) and Desvousges et al. (1993). Other studies fail to find embedding, for example, Imber et al. (1991), Carson and Mitchell (1995) and Smith (1996).

A related hypothesis, explored in the Hausman (1994) volume, is that if an environmental good C can be decomposed into A and B, then WTP(C) is not equal to WTP(A) + WTP(B). Assume now that we could somehow decompose a valuation question in two parts, so that we first ask about A and then B. It is apparent from this formulation that the hypothesis can only be tested if the valuation questions are asked conditionally. We cannot ask two unconditional questions and then sum the two in order to get WTP(C). In a more general setting, when several parameters are changing, the valuation questions will be path-dependent (in general). That is, the sum of WTP(A) and WTP(B) will be different, depending on which order the valuation questions are asked.

The WTA/WTP disparity
According to conventional economic theory, your maximum willingness to pay for obtaining an extra unit of private good is approximately the same as the minimum amount of money you would accept for abstaining from having this extra unit, provided that the income effect is small. If this were true for environmental goods, we could ask the allegedly simpler willing-ness-to-pay (WTP) question rather than the more unfamiliar willingness-to-accept compensation question (WTA). According to Randall and Stoll (1980), this is a theoretically consistent procedure, provided a (slightly different) income effect is also 'small' for public goods. Empirically, one often finds large disparities between WTP and WTA, the latter typically being three or more times larger than the former (Knetsch and Sinden, 1984 and others).

In a paper by Hanemann (1991b) it is shown that the disparity involves more than the income effect; a substitution effect is also involved. The fundamental result Hanemann (1991) arrives at is that the difference between WTA and WTP is the ratio between an income elasticity and a substitution elasticity. The lower the substitution elasticity (the less willing the individual is to trade off environmental quality with private goods), the larger the disparity. Shogren et al. (1994) verify Hanemann's (1991) theoretical results in a controlled experiment, although the results have recently been challenged by Harrison (1996). MacDonald and Bowker (1994) find, however, no support for Hanemann's (1991) theoretical explanation in their experiment.

Mean versus median

There has been some debate on the choice of mean versus median. The debate may have begun with Johansson et al. (1989), who argued that the mean is the correct welfare measure, if the Pareto criterion is used. This critique arose from an observation that CVM studies invariably seem to use the median as the preferred measure. Hanemann (1984) had argued that a purely statistical argument favours the median over the mean, since the median is much more robust towards small perturbations of the data in the tails. In his rebuttal, Hanemann (1989) argued that the choice between the mean and the median reflects a deeper choice related to what one believes is the correct social welfare function. A similar argument is made in Harrison and Kriström (1995).

Suppose that the true WTP in a three-individual society is {1,2,99}. According to the Pareto rule a project should be passed if the total costs are less than 102. Using the median, one finds a value of 2, or an aggregate of 6. This simple example shows that the key issue is distributional.

The statistics of the problem of which welfare measure to use has several dimensions. One is related to the problem of describing a probability distribution. Hanemann and Kanninen (1996, p. 19) argue that the answer is related to the properties of the loss function. If a sum-of-squares loss function is used, the mean is the optimal measure of tendency, while the median is optimal under a sum-of-absolute-errors loss function.

5. Concluding remarks

This chapter has painted a rough picture of the CVM, leaving many issues aside and only scratching the surface of many others. It might still be useful to end this chapter by discussing some avenues for future research. We have seen a significant expansion of the econometric and statistical techniques that are being applied to the data. It is not in this area that the marginal product will be highest in the near future. We have also seen many issues being scrutinized in laboratory settings, using the tools of experimental economics. There remains much work to do in this area as well, although it is maturing quite quickly. My personal belief is that there will be a high return on research that focuses on the scope of applicability. Theoretically, there is no limit to the scope of the CVM, much as there is no limit on the number of planets and stars we can theoretically visit. One can envision a situation where universally accepted principles lead one to reject the CVM for a particular resource allocation problem. As of today, there is no lack of ideas of where to use the CVM, even though it seems intuitively obvious that there is a limited scope for applying the method to 'everything'. There has been some exploratory work comparing the CVM with real payments in realistic environments, but much more remains to be done (see Cummings et al., 1997 for a recent attempt). Experiments typically focus on objects like coffee mugs or candy bars and we have no way of knowing that the results of such experiments maps one-to-one into conclusions about the effectiveness of the CVM. Several papers in the experimental economics literature propose that such inferences are not fragile, but we need additional research on this key issue.

To end where we began: the CVM is at first blush the simplest of techniques – it only involves asking people a simple question. But, as we have seen, there is more to this than meets the eye. Many challenges lie ahead and it is only through meticulous research based on received theory that we can forge ahead and shape the CVM into an even more powerful tool.

References

Bateman, I.J., I.H. Langford and J. Rabash (1996), 'Elicitation effects in contingent valuation studies', in I.J. Bateman and K.G. Willis (eds), *Valuing Environmental Preferences: Theory and Practice of the Contingent Valuation Method*, Oxford: Oxford University Press.

Bergström, J., J.R. Stoll and A. Randall (1990), 'The impact of information on environmental valuation decision', *American Journal of Agricultural Economics*, 72 (3), 614–21.

Bishop, R.C. and T.A. Heberlein (1979), 'Measuring values of extra-market goods: are indirect measures biased?', *American Journal of Agricultural Economics*, 61, 926–30.

Boyle, K.J., F.R. Johnson, D.W. McCollum, W.H. Desvouges, R.W. Dunford and S.P. Hudson (1996), 'Valuing public goods: discrete versus continuous contingent value responses', *Land Economics*, 72 (3), 381–96.

Braden, J. and J. Kolstad (1992), *The Demand for Environmental Quality*, Amsterdam: North-Holland.

Brown, T.C., P.A. Champ, R.C. Bishop and D.W. McCollum (1996), 'Which response format reveals the truth about donations to a public good?', *Land Economics*, 72 (2), 152–66.

Cameron, T.A. (1988), 'A new paradigm for valuing non-market goods using referendum data: maximum likelihood estimation by censored logistic regression', *Journal of Environmental Economics and Management*, 15, 355–79.

Cameron, T.A. and M.D. James (1987), 'Efficient estimation methods for "closed-ended" contingent valuation surveys', *Review of Economics and Statistics*, 69, 269–76.

Cameron, T.A. and J. Quiggin (1994), 'Estimation using contingent valuation data from a "dichotomous choice with follow-up" questionnaire', *Journal of Environmental Economics and Management*, 27 (3), 218–34.

Carson, R.T. and R.C. Mitchell (1995), 'Sequencing and nesting in contingent valuation surveys', *Journal of Environmental Economics and Management*, 28 (2), 155–73.

Carson, R.T., W.M. Hanemann, R.J. Kopp, S. Presser and P. Ruud (1992), 'A contingent valuation study of lost passive use values resulting from the *Exxon Valdez* oil spill', Anchorage: Attorney General of the State of Alaska, November.

Carson, R.T., W.M. Hanemann, R.J. Kopp, J.A. Krosnick, R.C. Mitchell, S. Presser, P.A. Rudd and V.K. Smith, with M. Conaway and K. Martin (1996), 'Referendum design and contingent valuation: the NOAA Panel's no-vote recommendation', Discussion paper 96–05, Resources for the Future, Washington, DC.

Ciriacy-Wantrup, S.V. (1947), 'Capital returns from soil-conservation practices', *Journal of Farm Economics*, **29**, 1181–96.

Cooper, J. and W.M. Hanemann (1995), 'Referendum contingent valuation: how many bids are enough?', USDA Research Service, Food and Consumer Economics Division, Working Paper, May.

Cummings, R.G., S. Elliott, G.W. Harrison and J.H. Murphy (1997), 'Are hypothetical referenda incentive compatible?', *Journal of Political Economy*, **105** (3), 609–21.

Cummings, R.G. and G.W. Harrison (1994), 'Was the Ohio Court well informed in their assessment of the accuracy of the contingent valuation method?', *Natural Resources Journal*, **34**, 1–36.

Cummings, R.G. and G.W. Harrison (1995), 'The measurement and decomposition of nonuse values: a critical review', *Environmental and Resource Economics*, **5**, 225–47.

Cummings, R.G., D.S. Brookshire and W.D. Schulze (eds) (1986), *Valuing Environmental Goods: An Assessment of the Contingent Valuation Method*, Totowa, NJ: Rowman and Littlefield.

Cummings, R.G., G.W. Harrison and E.E. Rutström (1995), 'Homegrown values and hypothetical surveys: do dichotomous choice questions elicit real economic commitments?', *American Economic Review*, **85**, 260–66.

Davis, R.K. (1963), 'The value of outdoor recreation: an economic study of the Maine Woods', Ph.D. dissertation, Harvard University.

Desvousges, W.H., F.R.Johnson, R.W. Dunford, K.J. Boyle, S.P. Hudson and K.N. Wilson (1993), 'Measuring natural resource damages with contingent valuation: tests of validity and reliability', in J.A. Hausman (ed.), *Contingent Valuation: A Critical Assessment*, Amsterdam: North-Holland.

Diamond, P.D. and J.A. Hausman (1994), 'Contingent valuation: is some number better than no number?', *Journal of Economic Perspectives*, **8** (4), 45–66.

Dillman, D.A. (1993), 'Letter to Alan Carlin, Director of Policy, Planning and Evaluation', US-EPA, 31 March.

Duffield, J.W. and D.A. Patterson (1991), 'Inference and optimal design for a welfare measure in dichotomous choice contingent valuation', *Land Economics*, **67** (2), 225–39.

Federal Register (1993), **58** (10), 11 January 4602–14.

Fischoff, B. and L. Furby (1988), 'Measuring values: a conceptual framework for interpreting transactions with special reference to contingent valuation of visibility', *Journal of Risk and Uncertainty*, **1**, 147–88.

Hanemann, W.M. (1984), 'Welfare evaluations in contingent valuation experiments with discrete responses', *American Journal of Agricultural Economics*, **66**, 332–41.

Hanemann, W.M. (1989), 'Welfare evaluations in contingent valuation experiments with discrete responses: reply', *American Journal of Agricultural Economics*, **71**, 1057–61.

Hanemann, W.M. (1991), 'Willingness-to-pay and willingness-to-accept: how much can they differ?', *American Economic Review*, **81**, 635–47.

Hanemann, W.M. (1994), 'Valuing the environment through contingent valuation', *Journal of Economic Perspectives*, **8** (4), 19–43.

Hanemann, W.M. and B. Kanninen (1996), 'The statistical analysis of CV-data', Working Paper 798, Giannini Foundation, DARE, UC Berkeley.

Hanemann, W.M., J. Loomis and B. Kanninen (1991), 'Statistical efficiency of double-bounded dichotomous choice contingent valuation', *American Journal of Agricultural Economics*, **73**, 1255–63.

Harrison, G.W. (1996), 'Experimental Economics and Contingent Valuation', Economics Working Paper 96–10, University of South Carolina: College of Business Administration.

Harrison, G.W. and B. Kriström (1995), 'On the interpretation of responses to contingent valuation questionnaires', in P.-O. Johansson, B. Kriström and K.-G. Mäler (eds), *Current Issues in Environmental Economics*, Manchester: Manchester University Press.

Harrison, G.W. and J.C. Lesley (1996), 'Must contingent valuation surveys cost so much?', *Journal of Environmental Economics and Management*, **30**, 79–96.

Hausman, J.A. (ed.) (1994), *Contingent Valuation: A Critical Assessment*, Amsterdam: North-Holland.

Herriges, J.A. and J.F. Shogren (1996), 'Starting point bias in dichotomous choice valuation with follow-up questioning', *Journal of Environmental Economics and Management*, **30** (1), 112–31.

Hoehn, J. and A. Randall (1987), 'A satisfactory benefit–cost estimator from contingent valuation', *Journal of Environmental Economics and Management*, **14**, 226–47.

Imber, D., G. Stevenson and L. Wilks (1991), 'A contingent valuation survey of the Kakadu Conservation Zone' Canberra: Austrialian Government Publishing Service for the Resource Assessment Commission.

Jakobsson, K.M. and A.K. Dragun (1996), *Contingent Valuation and Endangered Species*, Aldershot, UK and Brookfield, US: Edward Elgar.

Johansson, P.-O. (1993), *Cost–Benefit Analysis of Environmental Change*, Cambridge, UK: Cambridge University Press.

Johansson, P.-O., B. Kriström and K.-G. Mäler (1989), 'A note on welfare evaluations with discrete response data', *American Journal of Agricultural Economics*, **71**, 1054–6.

Johansson, P.-O., B. Kriström and H. Nyquist (1992), 'Bid vectors, spikes and uncertainty', mimeo, Stockholm School of Economics.

Kahneman, D. and J.L. Knetsch (1992), 'Valuing public goods: the purchase of moral satisfaction', *Journal of Environmental Economics and Management*, **22** (1), 57–70.

Kahneman, D., P. Slovic and A. Tversky (1982), *Judgments under Uncertainty: Heuristics and Biases*, New York: Cambridge University Press.

Kanninen, B.J. (1993a), 'Optimal experimental design for double-bounded dichotomous choice contingent valuation', *Land Economics*, **69** (2), 138–46.

Kanninen, B.J. (1993b), 'Design of sequential experiments for contingent valuation studies', *Journal of Environmental Economics and Management*, **25** (1), 2–20.

Knetsch, J.K. and J.A. Sinden (1984), 'Willingness to pay and compensation demanded: experimental evidence of an unexpected disparity in measures of value', *Quarterly Journal of Economics*, **99**, 507–21.

Kriström, B. (1990), 'A non-parametric approach to the estimation of welfare measures in discrete-response contingent valuation studies', *Land Economics*, **3**, 135–9.

Kriström, B. (1993), 'Comparing continuous and discrete choice valuation questions', *Environmental and Resource Economics*, **3**, 63–71.

Kriström, B. (1997), 'Spike models in contingent valuation', *American Journal of Agricultural Economics*, **79** (3), 1013–23.

Li, C.-Z. (1996), 'Semi-parametric estimation of the binary choice model for contingent valuation', *Land Economics*, **72** (4), 462–73.

Li, C.-Z. and P. Fredman (1994), 'On reconciliation of the discrete choice and open-ended responses in contingent valuation experiments', in C.-Z. Li, *Welfare Evaluations in Contingent Valuation*, University of Umeå, Umeå Economic Studies 241.

Louviere, J.J. (1988), 'Conjoint modeling of stated preferences: a review of theory, methods, recent developments and external validity', *Journal of Transport Economics and Policy*, **10**, 93–119.

MacDonald, H.F. and J.M. Bowker (1994), 'The endowment effect and WTA: a quasi-experimental test', *Journal of Agricultural and Applied Economics*, **26** (2), 545–51.

Mack, R.P. and S. Myers (1965), 'Outdoor recreation' in R. Dorfman (ed.), *Measuring Benefits of Government Investments*, Washington, DC: The Brookings Institution.

Milgrom, P. (1992), 'Is sympathy an economic value? Philosophy, economics and the contingent valuation method', in *Contingent Valuation: A Critical Assessment*, Cambridge Economics, Inc.

Mitchell, R.C. and R.T. Carson (1989), *Using Surveys to Value Public Goods: The Contingent Valuation Method*, Washington, DC: Resources for the Future.

Mitchell, R.C. and R.T. Carson (1995), 'Current issues in the design, administration and analysis of contingent valuation surveys', in P.-O. Johansson, B. Kriström and K.-G. Mäler (eds), *Current Issues in Environmental Economics*, Manchester: Manchester University Press.

Navrud, S. (ed.) (1992), *Pricing the Environment: The European Experience*, Oxford: Oxford University Press.
Navrud, S. (1994), 'Does the presentation of information matter in contingent valuation studies?', presented at the workshop 'Determining the value of non-market goods: economic, psychological, and policy relevant aspects of contingent valuation methods', Bad Homburg, Germany, 27–29 July.
NRDA (Natural Resource Damage Assessment, Inc.) (1996), 'A bibliography of contingent valuation studies and papers', San Diego, CA.
Nyquist, H. (1992), 'Optimal designs of discrete response experiments in contingent valuation studies', *Review of Economics and Statistics*, **74** (3), 559–6.
Randall, A. and J.R. Stoll (1980), 'Consumer surplus in commodity space', *American Economic Review*, **70**, 449–55.
Randall, A. and J.R. Stoll (1983), 'Existence value in a total value framework', in R.D. Rowe and L.G. Chestnut (eds), *Managing Air Quality and Scenic Resources at National Parks and Wilderness Areas*, Boulder, CO: Westview Press.
Randall, A., B.C. Ives and C. Eastman (1974), 'Bidding games for valuation of aesthetic environmental improvements', *Journal of Environmental Economics and Management*, **1** (1), 132–49.
Ready, R.C., J.C. Buzby and D. Hu (1996), 'Differences between continuous and discrete contingent value estimates', *Land Economics*, **72** (3), 397–411.
Samples, K.C., J.A. Dixon and M.M. Gowen (1986), 'Information disclosure and endangered species valuation', *Land Economics*, **62** (3), 306–12.
Smith, V.K. (1996), 'Can contingent valuation distinguish values for different public goods?', *Land Economics*, **72** (2), 139–51.
Smith, V.K. and W.H. Desvousges (1986), *Measuring Water Quality*, Boston, MA: Kluwer & Nijhoff.
Shogren, J., S.Y. Shin, D.J. Hayes and J.B. Kliebenstein (1994), 'Resolving differences in willingness to accept and willingness to pay', *American Economic Review*, **84** (1), 255–70.
Whitehead, J.C. (1991), 'Environmental interest group behavior and self-selection bias in contingent valuation mail surveys', *Growth and Change*, **22** (1), 10–21.

55 Meta-analysis, economic valuation and environmental economics

Jeroen C.J.M. van den Bergh and Kenneth J. Button[1]

1. Introduction

When the characteristics and results of distinct empirical studies are similar, especially in terms of the problems considered and the methodological approaches used, a logical question is whether these can be systematically processed to generate comprehensive and concise conclusions. If this is so, then rather than performing an additional in-depth study to gain new insight, it may be possible to elicit relevant information by a formal analysis of earlier studies. This procedure is generally referred to as meta-analysis (for example, Cooper and Hedges, 1994). It can broadly be defined as the formal synthesis of results and findings of scientific studies, possibly including summarizing, assessing, comparing, averaging, evaluating, and apprehending common elements in impact studies. It has been widely used in the natural sciences but its uptake has been slower in the social sciences (Stanley and Jarrell, 1989). Here we focus on the use of meta-analysis in environmental economics, in particular in the context of empirical valuation studies. A more extensive discussion of meta-analysis in environmental economics is offered by van den Bergh et al. (1997).

Section 2 discusses important characteristics of meta-analysis. Particular objectives and techniques are presented in Section 3, and applications in environmental economics are reviewed in Section 4. Next, Section 5 discusses the main limits of meta-analysis. Section 6 concludes.

2. Characteristics of meta-analysis

Meta-analysis, and its focus on rigorous synthesis, contrasts with more conventional literary review procedures (Cook and Leviton, 1980). It moves away from the taxonomies of findings that often characterize literary reviews, and provides a basis for reducing the level of subjectivity inherent in any reviewing activity. The approach circumvents the common problem that literary reviews often have of handling and then presenting a large number of findings in a succinct and comprehensible way.

Meta-analysis can delve beneath the elaborate combinations of statistical procedures used in the modern sciences to isolate core assumptions or parameters. Appropriate application of meta-analysis can help to improve our understanding of economic analysis. It can enable us to make better use of prior information and knowledge. It can also help remove some of the subjectivity from analysis and from forecasting, or at least make judgements more transparent. It can provide more focused valuations of economic costs and benefits. Furthermore, by inclusion of appropriate indicators, meta-analysis can help to pinpoint scientific, ethical and political biases in existing studies. Finally, it may offer initial insights into phenomena for which no specific study has yet been conducted, and lead to greater clarity as to where future efforts in environmental economic analysis can most usefully be deployed.

Differences and similarities between case studies are both important. Seldom do two studies differ in only one significant feature. It is always difficult to compare them in terms of only one or a very limited number of features. To give an idea of the factors that contribute to the originality and specificity of particular case studies, the following elements may be considered. With regard to data characteristics, the size of a sample, the quality of the data, and their time or period and cross-section properties are relevant. In addition, exogenous or omitted factors are important, and these may include socioeconomic, political, cultural, geographical, environmental or temporal ingredients. Methodological and theoretical characteristics can often be critical. Furthermore, the differing output of specific case studies should be considered, which may embrace estimated numbers, statistical indicators, optimized values of a goal function and control variables, or the confirmation or refutation of hypotheses. Finally, output quality indicators may be provided in the case study, such as statistical indicators of output quality, or uncertainty and sensitivity analysis results.

These various elements can be used to obtain a quick insight into the essential characteristics of a case study, and allow for a systematic comparison with similar studies. In some cases this can then be used as a preliminary procedure for deciding whether a particular case study is in any way suitable for inclusion in a meta-analysis.

3. Particular objectives and techniques of meta-analysis
Meta-analysis is applied to many different questions and problems. It may seek to gain insights in a variety of ways, focusing on one or more of the following objectives:

1. Summarizing over a collection of similar studies, relationships, indicators and so on.
2. Averaging, possibly using weights, for collections of values obtained in similar studies.

3. Comparing, evaluating and ranking studies on the basis of well-defined criteria or goal functions.
4. Aggregating studies, by taking complementary results or perspectives.
5. Identifying common elements in different studies.
6. Comparing different methods applied to similar questions.
7. Tracing factors that are responsible for differing results across similar studies.

There are a variety of techniques that can be employed in the conduct of a meta-analysis to address these objectives. The adoption of any one will be influenced by the particular types of insight being sought as well as by the nature of the evidence presented in the set of case studies under review.

There are conventional statistical methods which have the advantages that they are well understood by economists, can make use of existing computer software, and have been extensively used in meta-analytical work in the natural sciences. These techniques can play useful roles when concern is with purposes 1, 2, 4 and 7. The problem is that they require information to be presented in a manner that is amenable to statistical analysis and this may limit both the range of topics that can be treated and the types of effects that can be considered across a variety of case studies. Discrete modelling procedures have enhanced the degree of standardization in recent years and reduced this type of problem, but it still remains.

The statistical techniques used in traditional meta-analyses are diverse. This is in part because of the differing nature of the topics addressed and the range of statistical issues that emerge when looking at heterogeneous, quantitative works. A first category of methods is based on counting studies with a significant result, which allows for construction of a confidence interval for the assumed common-effect size. Even if not every research report mentions the estimated value of the effect size, it is possible to estimate an assumed common-effect size by means of the method of 'vote counting' (for an explanation of the statistical procedure, see van den Bergh et al., 1997, section 5.3). Second, there are non-parametric methods for combining significance levels. A third group of methods allows for combining the effect sizes into one single estimate of the supposed common-effect size. If the assumption that there exists a common-effect size is refuted by a homogeneity test, this can give rise to the use of a random instead of a fixed-effects model. A fourth group consists of methods to analyse variations in effect sizes found by different studies. Rejecting the hypothesis that the real-effect sizes are equal in all studies gives rise to the question of what causes the variations between the found effect sizes. Meta-analysis may explain these variations, for instance, by estimation of a linear regression model with 'effect size' as the dependent variable and a number of variables, commonly referred to as moderator variables, characterizing the different studies as independent variables (for more details, see Cooper and Hedges, 1994).

The formal statistical techniques developed for traditional meta-analysis of strict experiments, however, can seldom be directly applied to studies in which 'quasi-scientific' methods are used (Bryant and Wortman, 1984). Other methods, for data analysis and evaluation, may be useful here. These may include techniques which provide less specific statistical information but offer more general insights from less precise case-study material. Rough set analysis is an example in case, which offers a method for data analysis with the potential to handle a much more diverse and less immediately quantifiable set of factors. It can be useful for dealing with the objectives mentioned at the opening of this section. This technique allows for transforming a data set – which may, for instance, comprise past examples or a record of experience – into knowledge, in the sense of ability to classify objects (van den Bergh et al., 1997). In such a situation it is not possible to distinguish objects on the basis of given information descriptors. The imperfection of this information prevents precise assignments to sets (referred to as 'indiscernibility'). In this case the only sets which can be precisely characterized are lower and upper approximations to the set of objects. Rough set theory can often deal in an effective way with problems of explanation and prescription of a decision situation where knowledge is imperfect. It can help to evaluate the importance of particular attributes, to eliminate redundant ones from the decision table, and to generate sorting rules.

Another alternative approach is based on multi-criteria analysis to evaluate different case studies based on a number of criteria, or on more qualitative indicators. This type of analysis can be very useful for objectives 3 and 6 set out above, especially where multiple criteria, or objectives, underlie a comparison of similar studies. This is especially relevant when studies do not offer a simple estimation of an important indicator or when the interest lies in looking at a number of indicators.

4. Applications of meta-analysis in environmental economics

The application of meta-analysis to issues concerning the environment, regional, urban and transport economics has been relatively limited. This is not to say that there has been no good work but rather that, either because of a lack of interest or because of technical difficulties, the number of meta-analyses has remained comparatively small. The work that has been done has tended to rely heavily on meta-regression techniques or variants of it. Table 55.1 offers a summary of some of the main areas where work has been published.

Table 55.1   *Studies in environmental, regional, urban and transport*
            economics using meta-analysis

Subject area	Meta-analysis studies
Urban pollution valuation	Smith (1989), Smith and Huang (1993), Smith and Huang (1995), Schwartz (1994), van den Bergh et al. (1997)
Recreation benefits	Smith and Kaoru (1990a), Walsh et al. (1989a, 1989b)
Recreation fishing	Sturtevant et al. (1995)
Water quality	Magnussen (1993)
Valuation of life estimates	van den Bergh et al. (1997)
Contingent valuation vs revealed preference	Carson et al. (1996)
Wetlands contingent valuation	Brouwer et al. (1997)
Noise nuisance	Nelson (1980), Button (1995), Schipper (1998)
Congestion	Waters (1996)
Visibility improvement	Smith and Osborne (1996)
Transport issues	Button (1995), Button and Kerr (1996)
Multiplier effects of tourism	Nijkamp and Baaijens (1997)
Price elasticity of demand and travel cost	Smith and Kaoru (1990b)
Price elasticity of gasoline demand	Espey (1996)
Valuing morbidity	Johnson et al. (1996)

Some of the key features of this emerging literature may be highlighted.

Urban pollution valuation studies
In the context of urban environmental issues attention has focused mainly
on hedonic property value models for estimating individuals' marginal willingness to pay for a reduction in the local concentration of specified air pollutants. Smith and Huang (1995) reviewed 50 studies between 1967 and
1988, and identified 37 studies offering hedonic price function estimations
including air pollution measures. These studies deal in particular with
large cities. Pooling estimated relationships across studies and model
specifications resulted in 167 hedonic model estimations, from which 86
were selected as suitable for the meta-analysis. The marginal willingness to
pay (MWTP) for reducing total suspended particulates was measured as
the change in the asset value of the property. When an imputed rent was

used in the primary hedonic price relationships, the estimate was converted into a measure of housing price change. The median MWTP for the sample is $22.40 (1982–84 US$); however, the range of estimated values is relatively wide (the extreme values are − $239.8 and $1807.8).

The variables deployed in the meta-analysis are of four types: characteristics of the subjects concerned, characteristics of the model estimation procedures, characteristics of the data, and characteristics of source. The latter covers, for example, whether a study was published.

The results show that, although the ordinary least squares and MAD estimates[2] are similar in sign and magnitude, their statistical significance levels are quite different for the various meta-analysis variables – the moderator variables. The differences are most pronounced with respect to the number of neighbourhood variables in the original studies, the actual price and the publication bias indicator. Variables relating to neighbourhood indicators, dummies for (linear and semi-log) regression equation specification, and variables relating to the year of the data are highly significant in both cases. The last can be explained by the fact that more recent studies use improved model specifications. Another conclusion is that smaller MWTP estimates are found for published studies, which may be consistent with the phenomenon of publication bias often mentioned in the meta-analytical literature.[3]

Comparison of methods: contingent valuation vs revealed preference
An important question with respect to the choice of an economic valuation method is whether one method leads generally to upward- or downward-biased estimates of monetary values of environmental amenities. Meta-analysis seems particularly useful in addressing this issue, as it allows for a pairwise comparison of methods, often using large samples of past studies. At a general level it is often possible, by pooling methods, to construct a large meta-analysis sample by including valuation estimates for various types of environmental goods or bads.

Carson et al. (1996), for example, used 83 studies to render 616 comparisons of contingent valuation (CV) and revealed preference (RP) estimates, with the latter based on applications of travel cost and hedonic pricing techniques, expenditure and household production function models, and simulated or actual market creation. The estimates cover a variety of environmental issues that fall in the class of quasi-public goods, and include recreation benefits, water quality improvements, fishing, mining impacts, forest harvesting, preservation, and job-related risk reduction. These were coded into three broad classes named recreation, environmental amenities (air and water quality) and health risks. It was found that CV estimates are generally, though not always, smaller but only slightly smaller than their RP counterparts. In other words, this provides support for convergent validity of the two basic approaches to non-market valuation. This is indicated by all the statistical tests applied to CV/RP ratios, RP/CV ratios, (CV–RP) difference, and vote counting, and for all of the following subsets: the complete data set; a 5 per cent trimmed data set (to ameliorate the large influence of gross outliers); and a weighted data set giving equal weight to each case study rather than each single CV/RP comparison within case studies, effectively using the mean CV/RP ratio for each study as that study's observation. Although each approach leads to unique statistical indicators, the qualitative conclusions are identical.

Judging internal consistency of contingent valuation estimates
Recently there has been much debate on whether contingent valuation can be relied on to generate indicators for values. Since the *Exxon Valdez* oil spill and the subsequent evaluation of the contingent valuation method by the National Oceanic and Atmospheric Administration (NOAA) panel (Arrow et al., 1993), a number of respected economists outside the circle of environmental economics have focused their attention on this method (Hausman, 1993). Their main concern is that when non-use values dominate, willingness to pay (WTP) functions do not necessarily comply with properties that economic theory implies. An internal validity test is necessary. The NOAA panel proposed a scope test, requiring the contingent valuation WTP estimates to be responsive to the amount that is available of the environmental amenity (for more details, see Chapter 54 by Kriström, this volume). Smith and Osborne (1996) perform such a test based on a meta-analysis of studies estimating the marginal willingness to pay for improved or maintained visibility in natural parks. The underlying idea is that to trace how the WTP reacts to various changes in relevant observable factors, sufficient variation of observations is required. For this purpose past case-study estimates can be used. Using estimated relationships from five main studies, together rendering between 88 and 115 meta-analysis observations, various models were estimated, based on omitting specific observations, and dealing with a number of specifications and different sets of independent variables. In all meta-analysis estimations a significant, positive relationship is found between WTP and the proportionate improvement in the visibility range. For a specific quasi-linear, indirect utility function, Diamond (1996) showed that a scope test requires the ratio of two WTP estimates for two different physical indicators to be greater than the ratio of these physical indicators. The meta-analysis results are consistent with this requirement. In other words, the contingent valuation method passes the scope test, as argued by Smith and Osborne (1996).

Meta-analysis of ecosystem valuation studies

Valuations of ecosystem change have been based on a framework of processes and functions linked to particular use and non-use values. Individual ecosystem valuation studies provide limited insights about this. A meta-analysis of such studies can enhance understanding of the links between functions and values and provide additional quantitative information. It may suggest which values and functions are the more important. Brouwer et al. (1997) have performed a meta-analysis along these lines employing 30 contingent valuation studies of wetlands. These were categorized according to wetland type, main functions, country, type of value estimated, and selected characteristics of the contingent valuation survey design. Four wetland functions were examined in detail, and it was found that the average willingness to pay was highest for flood control, followed by the supply of water, water quality, and provision and maintenance of biodiversity.

Meta-regression and panel data

Many meta-analysis studies focus on non-parametric density estimates for the meta-analysis data set, or use statistical correlation measures to examine whether estimates are significantly different between studies, estimated relationships or techniques. Other studies have used regression methods to understand the factors causing differences between estimates among studies or estimated relationships. These factors may include case characteristics (for example, according to resource, region, time), study characteristics (such as method used, sample size) or characteristics of the source (whether published study or not).

Sturtevant et al. (1995) argue that some meta-analysis data sets can be regarded as panel data, and illustrate the usefulness of using panel estimation techniques in the context of fishery recreational demand studies. The underlying idea is that regression based on ordinary least squares does not deal adequately with the correlated error structure of the data and that modified estimation procedures are needed. Correlation occurs among multiple estimates from single studies, resulting from the use of subsets of the complete data set available, different model specifications, different indicators or other assumptions.

To deal with systematic effects on estimates obtained within single studies, panel models are suggested. Sturtevant et al. report the results of three such models: fixed-effects, random-effects and separate variances models. Panel data allow for distinguishing groups, and in the context of a meta-analysis groups can be defined based on the criteria that estimates belong to a single case study, or relate to a similar problem or resource. The various panel models can deal with different phenomena, for example, the intercept or the error term varying across studies. In the analysis of Sturtevant et al. the best-fit panel model leads to the lowest predictions of all the models estimated, which means that sufficient variation among groups is required to be able to predict for new cases.

Benefits transfer and meta-prediction
Meta-analysis has been used for benefit transfer, notably in cases where time or money for in-depth studies is limited, or when application of results obtained for one case to another seems evident. Basic benefits transfer can be performed, where the estimate from the best study extracted from the relevant literature is transferred to the new case under consideration (Sturtevant et al., 1995). One can also take the mean of the estimates extracted from case studies that have been conducted on similar types of problem. Alternatively, a regression model derived from the closest study can be used to predict for other cases using appropriate values for the variables in the model. Finally, a meta-analysis model can be used for prediction. Comparisons of such predictions can, among others, be found in Sturtevant et al. (1995) and Smith and Huang (1995). Both find that basic transfer based on mean values obtained from similar studies leads to higher estimates than various meta-analysis models. Whether this is generally true is to be examined by further studies.[4]

5. Limits to meta-analysis
Meta-analysis has its advantages, but equally it has limitations in terms of its overall approach and in relation to how it can be and is used in environmental economics. While meta-analysis can reduce the degree of subjectivity relative to conventional literature reviews, it cannot remove it. For instance, one has to decide what type of approach to adopt in a meta-analysis. Perhaps a more serious practical problem is the possible bias that results from the nature of the studies that are included. Looking across a range of social science meta-analyses, a variety of reasons has been given for excluding some studies from the analysis. Linked to this in the particular case of academic literature, is the prevailing tendency only to achieve publication of work containing positive results. This makes it difficult to incorporate quite legitimate negative results in any overview analysis.

Meta-analysis is limited by the aggregate character of its inputs. The information loss or interpretation bias resulting from the meta-analysis of aggregate (that is, case-study estimates and characteristics) rather than disaggregate data (that is, the combined sets of individual observations used in the original case studies) may be examined. This type of test of reliability of meta-analysis in synthesizing information is in principle possible. The problem is that it requires that all original data sets be available and combined in a single, quantitative analysis (see Brouwer et al., 1997).

This inclusion issue is linked to the broader assumption of meta-analysis about the separability of studies, and the fact that each study examined should be clearly distinct from others. In practice, though, human nature leads to adaptation rather than revolution and the first reaction of any researcher is to look at the previous literature. Of more direct relevance, the possibility of research work being published and encapsulated in a meta-analysis tends to rise if it has strong links with an established literature.

While many of the above arguments can be seen to relate to the more general problems of adopting meta-analysis reviews in the social sciences, there are a number of particular problems in its application to environmental research. Perhaps the main problem is related to the nature of most economic research on environmental topics. The empirical method is usually one of quasi-experimentation rather than strict experimentation. It is still virtually impossible to conduct well-controlled laboratory experiments in environmental economics, although the situation is now improving. A guide to experimental economics is provided by Shogren and Hurley in this book (Chapter 76).

Furthermore, anyone who has looked at the literature in environmental economics discovers very rapidly that individual academic researchers have their own styles of presentation. Quite simply, and unlike strict experimental results, the reporting of assumptions, error distributions, data idiosyncrasies and so on are not standardized. This point is made in a slightly different way by Goodwin (1992), when he discusses the differing nature of the dissemination cultures as between the academic, refereed journal route and the official or consultancy report channel. There are important differences in the pre-release evaluations they endure.

A somewhat different problem arises in the context of synthesizing results from the increasing number of stated preference studies of microeconomic behaviour which are being conducted – for instance contingent valuation methods used in evaluating environmental impacts. Unlike revealed preference analysis, where past actions are reviewed, stated preference analysis involves hypothetical, *ex ante* assessments, often based on questionnaires and interviews. The implication for conducting meta-analysis is that each example involves not only variations in the way results are reported, but also that the results relate to a particular set of unique questions and possible responses. These cases are difficult to handle although some efforts have been made in non-economic fields such as social psychology. These have only tended to be successful, though, where similar types of analytical procedures are adopted in each study.

6.   Concluding remarks

Meta-analysis is a potentially useful way of supplementing our knowledge in a relatively speedy and cost-effective way. It also combines well with the rapid advance of information systems which is now taking place and which is making it increasingly convenient to access existing bodies of analysis. It seems possible, by adopting a variety of statistical and other, softer, procedures, to extend and develop meta-analysis in ways which make it a powerful tool to supplement conventional, primarily literary, methods of reviewing existing bodies of work in environmental economics. This extends beyond the more conventional types of application found in the natural sciences, paralleled by point estimates of such things as elasticities and externality valuations in economics, to the consideration of policy options and policy instruments (Phillips and Goss, 1995). Finally, in the area of economic valuation, and particularly contingent valuation, meta-analysis may be useful as valuation surveys are expensive both financially and in terms of the manpower involved.

In addition to the examples of meta-analysis presented here, one can easily design a list of suitable areas for further application of this method. Some examples of topics which may have scope for examination by meta-analysis include: global warming issues and the cost of climate change (see Pearce, Chapter 33 in this book); production functions in resource-based activities such as agriculture and fisheries; inverted U or environmental Kuznets curves (see de Bruyn and Heinz, Chapter 46 in this book); and behavioural responses to policies, in terms of response elasticities (Kriström and Riera, 1995).

Application of traditional statistical meta-analysis to case studies in the field of environmental economics is potentially more intricate than many other areas of economics where data collection has been more standardized and developed, such as in labour economics and economics of financial markets. Good environmental, ecological and economic data are often scarce. This is, in part, because the interaction between economic activities and environmental degradation has only been intensively studied for a relatively short time, and systematic observation and data collection has started only recently (for example, national resource accounting). Furthermore, there is a fundamental problem because many environmental effects are often delayed or do not occur in simple cause–effect loops but are embedded in a complex network of ecological, hydrological and physical processes. Additionally, there is only limited experience with implementing policies and management scenarios at various administrative levels, so that little systematic and long-standing information about environmental policy effects is available.

The result is that, although it seems extremely useful to apply meta-analysis methods to relevant categories of environmental policy studies, directly transferring meta-analytical techniques from long-established sciences, such as medicine, to environmental economics is extremely problematic and, in some instances, may be inappropriate. Instead, it is probably more useful to start from a general meta-analytical framework in designing and applying various types of formal and less formal meta-analytical tools and techniques.

Notes
1. This chapter has benefited from comments by Mick Common, Raymond Palmquist, Raymond Florax, Frans Bal and Peter Nijkamp.
2. Two estimation approaches were adopted (Smith and Huang, 1995). The first is based on a minimum absolute deviation (MAD) estimator to address the feature of outlying observations, which make the assumption of normally distributed errors doubtful. The second approach is an OLS estimation with a Huber-consistent covariance matrix to deal with potential correlation between observations and with heteroscedasticity.
3. A rough set analysis of the same data set confirms some of these results, but also produces some differences (van den Bergh et al., 1997).
4. For more information on benefit transfer studies, see Parsons and Kealy (1994), Loomis et al. (1995), Bergland et al. (1995), Downing and Ozuna (1996), and a special issue of *Water Resources Research* (1992, vol. 28, no. 3).

References
Arrow, K.J., R. Solow, P. Portney, E. Leamer, R. Radner and H. Schuman (1993), 'Report of the NOAA Panel on contingent valuation', Federal Register, **58**, 4601–14.
Bergh, J.C.J.M. van den, K.J. Button, P. Nijkamp and G.C. Pepping (1997), *Meta-analysis in Environmental Economics*, Dordrecht: Kluwer Academic Publishers.
Bergland, O., K. Magnussen and S. Navrud (1995), 'Benefit transfer: testing for accuracy and reliability', Discussion Paper no. D-03/1995, Department of Economics and Social Sciences, Agricultural University of Norway, Oslo.
Brouwer, R., I.H. Langford, I.J. Bateman, T.C. Crowards and R.K. Turner (1997), 'A meta-analysis of wetland contingent valuation studies', CSERGE Working Paper GEC 97–20, Centre for Social and Economic Research on the Global Environment, University of East Anglia, Norwich, UK.
Bryant, F. and P.M. Wortman (1984), 'Methodological issues in meta-analysis of quasi-experiments', *New Directions in Program Evaluation*, **24**, 25–42
Button, K.J. (1995), 'Evaluation of transport externalities: what can we learn using meta-analysis?', *Regional Studies*, **29**, 507–17.
Button, K.J. and J. Kerr (1996), 'Effectiveness of traffic restraint policies: a simple meta-regression analysis', *International Journal of Transport Economics*, **23**, 213–25.
Carson, R.T., N.E. Flores, K.M. Martin and J.L. Wright (1996), 'Contingent valuation and revealed preference methodologies: comparing the estimates for quasi-public goods', *Land Economics*, **72**, 80–99.
Cook, T.D. and L.C. Leviton (1980), 'Reviewing the literature: a comparison of traditional methods with meta-analysis', *Journal of Personality*, **48**, 449–72.
Cooper, H. and L.V. Hedges (eds) (1994), *The Handbook of Research Synthesis*, New York: Russell Sage Foundation.
Diamond, P.A. (1996), 'Testing the internal consistency of contingent valuation surveys', *Journal of Environmental Economics and Management*, **30**, 337–47.
Downing, M. and T. Ozuna Jr (1996), 'Testing the reliability of the benefit function transfer approach', *Journal of Environmental Economics and Management*, **30**, 316–22.
Espy, M. (1996), 'Explaining the variation in elasticity estimates of gasoline demand in the United States: a meta-analysis', *The Energy Journal*, **17**, 49–60.

Goodwin, P.B. (1992), 'A review of the new demand elasticities with special reference to short and long run effects of price changes', *Journal of Transport Economics and Policy*, **26**, 155–70.

Hausman, J.A. (ed.) (1993), *Contingent Valuation: A Critical Assessment*, Amsterdam: North-Holland.

Johnson, F.R., E.E. Fries and H.S. Banzhaf (1996), 'Valuing morbidity: an integration of the willingness-to-pay and health-status index literatures', TER Technical Working Paper no. T-9601, Triangle Economic Research, Durham, NC.

Kriström, B. and P. Riera (1995), 'Is the income elasticity of environmental improvements less than one?', *Environmental and Resource Economics*, **5**, 1–11.

Loomis, J.B., B. Roach, F. Ward and R. Ready (1995), 'Testing transferability of recreation demand models across regions: a study of Corps of Engineer reservoirs', *Water Resources Research*, **31**, 721–30.

Magnussen, K. (1993), 'Mini meta-analysis of Norwegian water quality improvements valuation studies', unpublished manuscript.

Nelson, J.P. (1980), 'Airports and property values: a survey of recent evidence', *Journal of Transport Economics and Policy*, **19**, 37–52.

Nijkamp, P. and S. Baaijens (1997), 'A comparative analysis of multiplier effects in tourist regions', *Journal of Policy Modelling* (forthcoming).

Parsons, G.R. and M.J. Kealy (1994), 'Benefits transfer in a random utility model of recreation', *Water Resources Research*, **30**, 2477–84.

Phillips, J.M. and E.P. Goss (1995), 'The effect of state and local taxes on economic development: a meta-analysis', *Southern Economic Journal*, **62**, 320–33.

Schipper, Y.J.J. and P. Rietveld (1998), 'Why do aircraft noise value estimates differ? A meta-analysis', *Journal of Air Transport Management*, **4**, 117–24.

Schwartz, J. (1994), 'Air pollution and daily mortality: a review and a meta analysis', *Environmental Economics*, **64**, 36–52.

Smith, V.K. (1989), 'Can we measure the economic value of environmental amenities?', *Southern Economic Journal*, **56**, 865–78.

Smith, V.K. and J.-C. Huang (1993), 'Hedonic models and air pollution: twenty-five years and counting', *Environmental and Resource Economics*, **3**, 381–94.

Smith, V.K. and J.-C. Huang (1995), 'Can markets value air quality? A meta-analysis of hedonic property values models', *Journal of Political Economy*, **103**, 209–27.

Smith, V.K. and Y. Kaoru (1990a), 'Signals or noise: explaining the variation in recreation benefit estimates', *American Journal of Agricultural Economics*, **72**, 419–33.

Smith, V.K. and Y. Kaoru (1990b), 'What have we learned since Hotelling's letter? A meta-analysis', *Economics Letters*, **32**, 267–72.

Smith, V.K. and L. Osborne (1996), 'Do contingent valuation estimates pass a "scope" test? A meta analysis', *Journal of Environmental Economics and Management*, **31**, 287–301.

Stanley, T.D. and S.B. Jarrell (1989), 'Meta-regression analysis: a quantitative method of literature surveys', *Journal of Economic Surveys*, **3**, 161–70.

Sturtevant, L.A., F.R. Johnson and W.H. Desvousges (1995), 'A meta-analysis of recreational fishing', Triangle Economic Research, Durham, NC.

Walsh, R.G., D.M. Johnson and J.R. McKean (1989a), 'Market values from two decades of research on recreational demand', in A.N. Link and V.K. Smith (eds), *Advances in Applied Economics Volume 5*, Greenwich, CT: JAI Press.

Walsh, R.G., D.M. Johnson and J.R. McKean (1989b), 'Issues in nonmarket valuation and policy application: a retrospective glance', *Western Journal of Agricultural Economics*, **14**, 178–88.

Waters, W.G. (1996), 'Values of travel time savings in road transport project evaluation' in D. Hensher, J. King and T. Oum (eds), *World Transport Research, Vol. 3, Transport Policy*, Oxford, Pergamon.

56 Valuation and ethics in environmental economics

Russell K. Blamey and Mick S. Common

1. Introduction

Economists have, in the last 30 years or so, developed a range of techniques for the valuation of unpriced environmental attributes: see the other chapters in this part of the book. In this chapter we restrict our attention mainly to contingent valuation, CV, which is commonly used to elicit existence values for cost–benefit analysis, CBA, purposes. It is in this context that ethical issues are generally seen as most pertinent.

'Ethics' is relevant in two ways here. First, ethics as the study of morally correct behaviour has been used to argue that CV in extended CBA is the wrong way for society to make decisions which impact upon the natural environment. We briefly review some of the main issues in Section 2. Second, it has been suggested that the ethical attitudes held by individuals will influence their responses in CV surveys, with implications for the usefulness of the survey results in CBA. We consider this in Section 3. The chapter concludes, in Section 4, with some brief remarks on alternatives to CBA.

We do not in this chapter consider the ethics, in either sense, of intertemporal valuation, that is, discounting. The ethical foundations of environmental economics are discussed in, for example, Chapter 2 of Perman et al. (1996) and Chapter 66 in this volume; see also the chapter on CBA in this handbook (Chapter 57).

2. Ethics and environmental economics

Competing ethical theories can be classified in several ways: see, for example, Popkin and Stroll (1986). According to motivist theories, the rightness or wrongness of an action depends solely upon its motivation. Consequential theories assign rightness or wrongness on the basis of the effects that follow from the action. Deontological theories hold that rightness or wrongness depends solely upon the nature of the action. Ethical theories can also be classified as subjectivist or objectivist. According to the former, to say that an action is wrong is simply to say that one disapproves of it, or dislikes it, whereas the latter claim that, in accord with 'common sense', rightness and wrongness are more than matters of taste and that ethical statements are factual.

Welfare economics is based on a particular form of utilitarianism, which is consequentialist and subjectivist in nature. In it, it is the consequences for human individuals, and only human individuals, that are of interest – only humans have 'moral standing'. The measure of what is good for a human individual is that human individual's own assessment. The individual's assessment is to be ascertained from his/her preferences as revealed in behaviour. It is assumed that individual preferences satisfy the conditions for the existence of 'well-behaved' ordinal utility functions: see, for example, Chapter 2 of Deaton and Muellbauer (1980). For aggregation across individuals, applied welfare economics as CBA generally relies on the potential Pareto improvement test according to which a 'project' should go ahead if the beneficiaries could compensate the losers and still be better off. Actual compensation is not required. A project which adversely affects the environment should go ahead if $B_d - C_d \geq EC$, where B_d and C_d are the (discounted) non-environmental benefits and costs and EC is the (discounted) environmental, or external, cost arising from the utility losses suffered by individuals, which can be expressed in monetary terms if the environmental impacts appear as arguments in well-behaved utility functions.

If it is assumed that individuals do have preferences over ordinary commodities and environmental attributes that satisfy the conditions for the existence of utility functions, there remain two classes of ethical objection to this way of proceeding.

The first rejects consumer sovereignty, arguing that individual preferences are a poor guide to individual human interests. Following Penz (1986), four particular arguments can be distinguished:

1. Individuals may be inadequately informed as to the consequences for themselves of the alternatives they face.
2. Individuals may be insufficiently deliberative in assessing the consequences of alternative choices.
3. Individuals may lack self-knowledge in the sense that they cannot properly relate the consequences of alternative choices to their preferences.
4. Individuals' preferences may not reflect their true interests due to 'preference shaping' arising from socialization processes and advertising.

These arguments are not restricted to the environmental context, but have been argued to have special force there: see, for examples, Sagoff (1994), Vatn and Bromley (1995), Norton (1994).

A second class of argument is that the scope of ethical concern should not be restricted to humans, that animals and plants (and in some versions non-living entities) should have 'moral standing': see, for examples, Naess

(1973), Goodpaster (1978), Regan (1981), Singer (1979, 1993). Booth (1994) argues that 'cost–benefit analysis cannot be legitimately applied where non-human natural entities are viewed as morally considerable' (p. 241), and that the ethically correct principle for social decision making is that:

> Destruction of the natural environment shall not be undertaken unless absolutely necessary to maintain the real incomes of all human individuals at a level required for the living of a decent human life. (p. 251)

This clearly has affinities with the safe minimum standard approach, see Bishop (1978) and Randall and Farmer (1995), which is based upon a consequentialist theory restricted to human interests, but which recognizes the uncertainties that attend predicting the future costs of current environmental damage. Similarly, while one could argue that future human interests require that life-supporting environmental processes be protected, and that this may require limiting the domain of consumer sovereignty (see Common and Perrings, 1992), one could arrive at much the same position by arguing that those processes themselves be 'viewed as morally considerable'.

Altruism
Most ethical theories accord other humans moral standing. Concern for others, human and non-human, may alternatively be founded in altruism. In the environmental economics literature, concern for others is frequently referred to as 'altruism' without consideration of the basis for it. This is unhelpful and can cause confusion. Sen (1977) uses the terms 'sympathy' and 'commitment'. Sympathy is where my concern for others exists on the basis that what happens to others affects my utility. Commitment is where my concern for others is based on my ethical principles. In the latter case, I may act for others even though so doing reduces my own utility. Some argue that commitment in this sense must be a conceptual nullity, in that observing an individual performing an act that benefits others simply reflects the fact that the individual is acting so as to improve his/her own utility. Given that human individuals are observed to, for example, die for others, this position appears, at the general level, to reveal a circularity in the definition of utility. This is not to say that it is not, in many less extreme circumstances, difficult in any particular case to distinguish between sympathy and commitment as the basis of action for others.

Altruism as sympathy has received some attention in the CV/existence value literature, on the basis that existence, as opposed to option, value must involve altruism. Randall (1986), for example, distinguishes between three different objects of altruistic, that is, sympathetic motives in valuing environmental goods. Philanthropic motives involve altruism directed toward members of the current generation who may want to use the good, bequest motives involve future generations who may want to use it, and Q-altruism motives involve concern for non-human components of the ecosystem.

It is also worth noting here that altruism as sympathy is seen in the literature as possibly taking two distinct forms. Here we shall refer to 'utility altruism' as distinct from 'commodity altruism': an alternative terminology is 'individualistic' as opposed to 'paternalistic'. In the former case, what appears as an argument in the altruistic individual's utility function is the utility of some other individual(s). In the latter case, it is the level of consumption of some commodity by the individual of concern that is an argument in the altruist's utility function. As discussed in Collard (1978), with utility altruism the standard economic results derived from the assumption of pure self-interest are unaffected, while for commodity altruism they break down.

There is a dimension of the distinction between sympathy and commitment that is important here. Those who have considered sympathy in relation to CBA; see, for example, Johansson (1992), have assumed that the extended – over others' utility levels or consumption levels – preference orderings of altruists satisfy the conditions for the existence of well-behaved utility functions. On the other hand, consideration of commitment on the basis of ethical attitudes has led to suggestions that it will give rise to preferences which do not satisfy those conditions. We discuss the implications of this for responses to CV surveys in the next section.

Some authors have argued against including altruistically motivated willingness to pay, WTP, for environmental preservation in extended CBA. Milgrom (1993), for example, argues that WTP associated with altruism toward members of the current generation results in double counting. Johansson (1992), on the other hand, and consistently with Collard (1978), argues that where utility altruism is involved, CV in extended CBA will not involve double counting: see also Madariaga and McConnell (1987). Johansson also considers commodity altruism, and finds that it requires modification to current practice for CV in extended CBA. Whether the procedure recommended by Johansson could be effectively operationalized remains to be seen.

3. Ethical attitudes and CV responses

It is recognized that there are problems in the use of CV for the elicitation of existence values for use in CBA. As revealed in, for example, Hausman (1993), those problems include:

- the incidence of protest responses
- 'implausibly high' estimates of average WTP
- low sensitivity of yes/no responses to price variation (in dichotomous choice formats)
- low sensitivity of WTP to the extent of the environmental commodity ('embedding')
- large differences between willingness to pay for preservation and willingness to accept compensation for development.

Some of these problems may be interrelated in particular CV studies. For example, if in a dichotomous choice format CV study responses are not price-sensitive, this may itself be the source of a high estimated average WTP.

Reactions to these problems among those interested in environmental valuation vary considerably, but for present purposes we can distinguish two broad groups. One takes the position that the problems with extant studies are explainable in terms of the standard theory, which assumes that CV responses are formulated on the basis of well-behaved utility functions, and that further refinements to CV survey practice can reduce the problems so that CV can provide useful inputs to CBA: see, for example, Arrow et al. (1993). The other view is that CV responses cannot be properly understood solely in terms of the standard theory, from which it follows that their use in CBA may, even after further refinement of CV technique, be of questionable validity. One basis for this view derives from the influence of individuals' ethical attitudes on their responses to CV questions designed to elicit existence values.

The relevant ethical attitudes can be seen to fall within two categories. Perceptions of *distributive justice* are concerned with the fair allocation of scarce resources, and hence outcomes. Perceptions of *procedural justice*, on the other hand, are concerned with the fairness of procedures by which decisions are made (see Lind and Tyler, 1988; Mellors and Baron, 1993). Examples of the objects of distributive concern are the incidence of:

- benefits to current and future human generations
- benefits to other species
- opportunity costs of preservation
- financial costs of preservation.

Examples of the objects of procedural concern include:

- desirability of government involvement
- desirability of community input

- role of economics in environmental decision making
- desirability of monetary evaluation
- appropriateness of institutional basis of elicitation format (referendum or trust fund, for example).

We now provide an overview of some of the contributions to the literature concerning ethical attitudes, relating them to identified problems with CV, and to the distributive/procedural classfication.

Citizen responses

Some writers, such as Sagoff (1988), deny that individuals typically have utility functions that include ordinary commodities and environmental attributes as arguments. He argues that a significant proportion of individuals will be unable, or unwilling, to make trade-offs across the two classes, and that there is a consumer self which deals with trade-offs between commodities, and a citizen self which deals with environmental (and other) matters. The claim here is that, where existence values are at issue, responses are not typically on the basis of a single utility function. Sagoff's arguments appear to relate to both distributive and procedural matters. He sees individuals as being ethically concerned in relation to both environmental outcomes and the institutional settings used for social choices where the environment is at issue. Sagoff further claims that citizen preferences tend to be less self-centred and more impartial than standard consumer preferences. At the impartiality extreme of this continuum, the individual would effectively respond in terms of what he or she perceives to be in the best interests of society overall, irrespective of outcomes for self and family.

If CV responses do reflect citizen behaviour, then there is an argument that one would expect to find a lack of price sensitivity in them, where the dichotomous choice format is used, with respondents behaving as voters largely disregarding the price information contained in the question. Blamey et al. (1995) report results from a re-examination of price-insensitive response data in regard to forest preservation that they interpret as support for the Sagoff hypothesis; see also Blamey (1996). Blamey and Common (1994) report results from some classroom experiments where the majority of subjects offered the choice, before being presented with any price information, between a political and a market-based approach to social decision making about preservation, opted for the former. See also Common et al. (1997). In this case, the subjects were, after committing to one or the other institutional setting, presented with a cost, which varied across subjects, and asked if they would be willing to meet it. Subjects opting for the political institutional framework were asked dichotomous choice questions regarding reallocations of government expenditure. The proportion answering 'yes' declined as the amount to be taken away from other government programmes increased. This suggests that individuals as citizens may be 'price'-sensitive.

Lexicographic preferences
Cognitive psychologists have observed the use by individuals of non-compensatory, or conflict-avoiding, strategies for choice (Hogarth, 1987; Payne et al., 1992). To understand the implications of non-compensatory decision rules in the context of CV, the underlying motives for such behaviour need to be considered. Individuals who appeal to duty-based moral theories, for example, may give intrinsic species rights trump status over other more homocentric considerations (Randall, 1991). One form of non-compensatory decision rule is the lexicographic preference ordering, in which alternatives are compared on the most important dimension only, unless equal scores are obtained, in which case scores on the second most important dimension are considered, and so on until a decision is reached. If individuals have lexicographic preferences, well-behaved utility functions do not exist in the sense that indifference curves cannot be drawn: the continuity condition is violated.

Edwards (1986) suggested that individuals' ethical attitudes could give rise to lexicographic preference orderings of ordinary commodities and environmental attributes, based on a moral commitment in favour of environmental protection. Edwards (1992) considered bounded lexicographic preferences where, for example, species preservation is always preferred to more income, so long as income is above some threshold level. Lexicographic preferences would imply a lack of price sensitivity, and could give rise to high estimates of average WTP for preservation. Spash and Hanley (1995) identified lexicographic preferences in an open-ended CV study as corresponding to respondents who stated a zero WTP for the reason that biodiversity should be protected by law, and respondents who stated that animals/ecosystems/plants should be protected irrespective of the costs, and who refused to give a WTP amount. Common et al. (1997) conducted some experiments to investigate the possibility of lexicographic preferences with respect to environmental goods and obtained results consistent with lexicographic preferences for approximately a quarter of respondents.

Ethical commitments are not the only possible source of lexicographic preference orderings. It appears consistent with work in psychology that they may reflect a rule-of-thumb strategy adopted to deal with information-processing difficulties, or with uncertainty as to the consequences of choice. In the study reported in Common et al. (1997), an additional quarter reported preferences that were incomplete or intransitive. Faced with a dichotomous choice CV question in a postal survey, individuals do not have the option of reporting such difficulties. They must answer yes or no, or not respond at all.

Responsibility considerations

Distributive justice concerns may have an important influence on how individuals react to the payment information contained in a CV survey. Individuals are likely to think that treatment of problems is the responsibility of those who caused them in the first place, and/or those who stand most to benefit from their solution (Schwartz 1968; Brickman et al., 1982). In discussing how citizens think about national issues, for example, Iyengar (1989) found that individuals' attributions of responsibility for both the cause of a problem and its treatment were significant determinants of their opinions. Since most CV questions implicitly or explicitly imply that the respondent has some responsibility to help protect the environment, thereby justifying some sort of payment, the extent to which this aligns with the individual's own perception of responsibilities regarding the issue in question has an important influence on both the likelihood of payment and the likelihood of protest. Harris and Brown (1992) stress the important influence responsibility ascriptions may have on CV responses. Peterson et al. (1996) investigated the effects of different levels of moral responsibility on CV responses and concluded that:

> when in a role of agency for the public interest, people tend to use a different utility function than when in the role of individual consumer. When compared with shared responsibility, sole responsibility for choices among public circumstances tends to increase the relative value of public goods and services, with the effect being greatest for environmental goods. (p. 156)

An important question that arises is whether 'no' responses to the question 'would you be willing to pay $x?' that are motivated by denial of responsibility can be considered legitimate from a CBA standpoint. Denial of responsibility is likely to result in protest responses and outliers, which are not generally considered legitimate CV responses for CBA. In fact, CV surveys frequently do not investigate the basis for 'no' or 'yes' responses. If a proportion of 'no' responses are motivated by protests denying responsibility, and if it is accepted that such responses are not valid for CBA, then including such responses in the estimation of average WTP will produce results that are biased with respect to the desired outcome. Stevens et al. (1991) found that the majority of respondents would not pay any money for the existence of bald eagles or wild turkeys in New England, or for salmon restoration. In this study response motivations were investigated. In the case of bird preservation, 40 per cent of zero WTP responses protested against the payment vehicle used in the CV question on responsibility grounds, stating that 'these species should be preserved but that the money should come from taxes or license fees'. Stevens et al. also report that 'Twenty-five percent protested for ethical reasons, claiming that wildlife values should not be measured in dollar terms' (p. 397).

Procedural concerns
Behaviour is always contextual, and procedures and institutions are part of context. However, in the case of CV-respondent behaviour, the procedures in respect of the postulated payment vehicle are often simply an artefact of the CV scenario, intended to enhance its 'face validity'. Thus, for example, respondents may be asked about willingness to pay 'higher taxes' where, in fact, this is not what would necessarily follow from a social decision in favour of environmental preservation. Given that individuals have ethical attitudes concerning such procedural matters, it would be expected that the payment vehicle adopted could influence CV responses. The empirical status of these issues appears to have received little attention in the literature. Blamey (1995) reports results that support the hypothesis that general-level ethical attitudes influence CV responses in relation to a particular environmental preservation issue, and that respondents see different payment vehicles as more or less appropriate. In particular, the respondents in this study found tax increases a less appropriate payment vehicle than redirections of government expenditure.

The purchase of moral satisfaction
A controversial paper by Kahneman and Knetsch (1992a) sought to explain embedding in CV studies relating to existence-value-type issues in terms of respondents using their participation in a CV to get a 'warm inner glow' from the (hypothetical) purchase of moral satisfaction. According to Kahneman and Knetsch an important feature of the warm inner glow hypothesis is that the 'warm glow of moral satisfaction . . . increases with the size of the contribution: for this unusual good, the expenditure is an essential aspect of consumption' (p. 64). The hypothesis is claimed to explain embedding in that the 'moral satisfaction associated with contributions to an inclusive cause, extends with little loss to any subset of that cause'. This claim is disputed in a number of papers: see, for examples, Smith (1992) and Harrison (1992). Kahneman and Knetsch (1992b) is a response to some of the criticism that their work attracted. Subsequent contributions to this debate are Diamond et al. (1993), Plott (1993) and Kemp and Maxwell (1993). One of the issues raised in the debate is that the warm glow hypothesis itself has moral satisfaction attaching to actual donations to good causes, whereas responses to CV questions do not entail

actual expenditure. We consider a behavioural hypothesis for CV respondents which has affinities with the Kahneman and Knetsch hypothesis, but is not subject to this difficulty, below.

Schkade and Payne (1993, 1994) used verbal protocol analysis to investigate the thought processes driving CV responses, and found that 23 per cent of respondents 'suggested a desire to signal concern for larger or more inclusive issues (than those covered in the CV question), such as preserving the environment or leaving the planet for their progeny' (parentheses added). They interpret this as support for the Kahneman and Knetsch hypothesis. Given our remarks above, it is not clear that it is, though it clearly is consistent with an influence from ethical attitudes to CV responses for some individuals.

Expressive benefits and decisiveness discounting
Public choice theory seeks to explain voting behaviour in terms of the instrumental pursuit of self-interest. However, in purely instrumental terms, it is difficult to see why any individual should incur the costs of voting given the low probability that his/her vote will be decisive. Brennan and Lomasky (1993) offer an explanation of voting behaviour in terms of, on the one hand, the benefits that individuals derive from the act of expressing what we have called ethical attitudes, and on the other the fact that whereas the instrumental benefits of voting are discounted by the low probability of being decisive, these expressive benefits are not so discounted.

Blamey (1998) argues that the Brennan and Lomasky argument applies to CV responses, which are more like casting a vote than buying a commodity in relation to the likely salience of ethical attitudes and the decisiveness discounting of any instrumental personal benefits. This hypothesis can explain both a lack of price responsiveness and embedding-type phenomena in CV studies. Blamey also argues that this hypothesis about CV responses can explain seemingly lexicographic preference revelation there: see also Blamey and Common (1995).

Willingness to pay and willingness to accept
If environmental deterioration is at issue, individuals might be asked either what they would be willing to pay to prevent it, or what they would require as compensation for accepting it – willingness to accept, WTA. At one time it was generally understood that, for a given environmental change, it should make little difference to the resulting monetary valuation whether individuals were asked about WTA or WTP, if they behaved in accordance with well-behaved utility functions. In the event, CV studies revealed order of magnitude differences in the monetary valuations arising: see, for example, Knetsch (1990). It was also observed that WTA questions tended

to produce more protest responses, refusals to accept any amount. The large empirical WTP/WTA discrepancies led to some re-examination of the standard theory, and a large discrepancy between WTP and WTA is not now regarded as necessarily discomforting for that theory: see Hanemann (1991). These are somewhat complex matters, and here we simply wish to note that if we step outside the bounds of the standard theory, large discrepancies between WTP and WTA may be explainable in terms of ethical attitudes.

To develop this point, recall the Sagoff distinction between the citizen and consumer self. Requested to pay for environmental preservation as a consumer, the citizen will find the question inappropriate, but not wildly so. Asked to accept individual compensation for damage to a collective asset such as the natural environment, and to say how much, the citizen will find the question wildly inappropriate. Consider an analogy. An individual might believe that poverty relief is properly a matter for the state, yet have few qualms about making a contribution, when asked, to a charity engaged in helping the poor. Now consider such an individual asked the question: how much would you need to be paid to compensate you for the abolition of all state-financed poverty relief? For many, but not all, such individuals there is likely to be a very large, but non-infinite answer to such a question, some price at which the prospective consumer gain will compensate for the mental costs of acting against an ethical attitude.

It appears that most CV practitioners now consider that where an environmentally damaging project is involved, the best way to proceed is to ask about WTP and to treat it as a lower bound on what is the proper measure, WTA, given the potential Pareto improvement criteria and the *status quo*.

4. Social choice and the environment
The question of environmental valuation methodology cannot be separated from the purpose for which environmental values are required. One such purpose, which explicitly or implicitly informs most of the environmental valuation literature, is to provide inputs to CBA for social decision making on projects entailing environmental damage. Hence arguments about ethics and environmental valuation raise questions about CBA and the environment. Such questions raise other questions. If the ethical position adopted is that individuals' views should count, if dictatorship or expert rule is rejected, then the question is how to bring those views to bear on social decision making as it affects the natural environment. CBA is one, but not the only possible, answer to this question.

If the ethical foundations of CBA are accepted, and the arguments reviewed in Section 2 here discounted, then the operative question is: can

CV provide useful inputs to CBA? Answering this question where it is existence values that are at issue is a matter of judgement rather than science, since there is no independent source of measurements of such values against which to test CV results. The extent to which ethical attitudes affect CV responses is surely relevant to such a judgement, and it seems clear that the lack of interest in respondent motivations evident in much of the literature to date is an impediment to informed judgement. This is an important area for future research. An interesting question is whether it would be possible to design and run a CV survey such that those individuals who might otherwise respond on the basis of ethical attitudes could be treated (manipulated?) so as to respond as the standard theory requires. The question has ethical as well as practical dimensions. If it were possible to induce, for example, citizens in Sagoff's sense to respond as consumers in his sense, would this be ethical? Kohn (1993) argues that the problem can, in principle, be avoided by a two-part CV approach which would seek to elicit separately consumer and citizen WTPs, which could then be jointly utilized in project appraisal by exploiting the concept of an individual social welfare function. This argument, and its practical implications and possibilities, clearly warrants further investigation.

If the ethical foundations of welfare economics and CBA are rejected where the environment is at issue, then the question is: how else to inform social decision making which respects individuals' views. Given the importance of the question that they raise, those who reject the ethical foundations of extended CBA have had surprisingly little to say about possible answers to this question. Frequently the implicit answer appears to be that these matters should be left to the existing system of representative democracy. However, one of the driving forces for the interest in CBA, CV and related methods and techniques has been the demand of that system for the sort of information that some have claimed those methods and techniques are able to supply. It appears that another important area for future research is the question of alternative, to CBA, means of supplying the political system with useful and appropriate information.

One possibility would be the use of surveys as sample referenda. The directions in which some CV practice is moving – dichotomous choice with taxation payment vehicles, for example – would be consistent with this reorientation of principle. Some commentators advocate the use of multi-criteria analysis (see Janssen, 1992) for the appraisal of projects with environmental impacts. While this approach is more flexible than CBA, it still requires, as input, weights for the various impacts arising. In most applications these weights are derived from the preferences of 'the decision maker', though they could, in principle, be based on the preferences of individuals comprising the affected community. In this case, the problem of meaningful elicitation of those preferences would remain. A possible means of addressing this problem is the idea that decisions should be made, or at least advice offered, on the basis of jury-like deliberation by a panel of citizens, which would have available to it decision support systems such as multi-criteria analysis.

References

Arrow, K., R. Solow, E. Leamer, P. Portney, R. Radner and H. Schuman (1993), 'Report of the NOAA Panel on contingent valuation', *Federal Register*, **58** (10), 4601–14, Washington, DC.

Bishop, R.C. (1978), 'Endangered species and uncertainty: the economics of a safe minimum standard', *American Journal of Agricultural Economics*, **60**, 10–18.

Blamey, R.K. (1995), *Citizens Consumers and Contingent Valuation: an Investigation into Respondent Behaviour*, Ph.D. thesis, Australian National University, Canberra.

Blamey, R.K. (1996), 'Citizens, consumers and contingent valuation: clarification and the expression of citizen values and issue-opinions', in W.L. Adamowicz, P. Boxall, M.K. Luckert, W.E. Phillips and W.A. White (eds), *Forestry, Economics and the Environment*, Wallingford: CAB International, pp. 103–133.

Blamey, R.K. (1998), 'Decisiveness attitude expression and symbolic responses in contingent valuation surveys', *Journal of Economic Behaviour and Organization*, **34**, 577–601.

Blamey, R.K. and M. Common (1994), 'Sustainability and the limits to pseudo market valuation', in J.C.J.M. van den Bergh and J. van der Straaten (eds), *Towards Sustainable Development: Concepts, Methods and Policy*, Washington, DC: Island Press.

Blamey, R.K. and M. Common (1995), 'Symbols and attitude expression in contingent valuation responses', Australia New Zealand Society for Ecological Economics, Coffs Harbour NSW, November.

Blamey, R.K., M. Common and J. Quiggin (1995), 'Respondents to contingent valuation surveys: consumers or citizens?', *Australian Journal of Agricultural Economics*, **39**, 263–88.

Booth, D.E. (1994), 'Ethics and the limits of environmental economics', *Ecological Economics*, **9**, 241–52.

Brennan, G. and L. Lomasky (1993), *Democracy and Decision: The Pure Theory of Electoral Preference*, Cambridge, UK: Cambridge University Press.

Brickman, P., V.C. Rabinowitz, J. Karuza Jr, D. Coates, E. Cohn and L. Kidder (1982), 'Models of helping and coping', *American Psychologist*, **37**, 368–84.

Collard, D. (1978), *Altruism and Economy: A Study In Non-Selfish Economics*, Oxford: Martin Robertson.

Common, M. and C. Perrings (1992), 'Towards an ecological economics of sustainability', *Ecological Economics*, **6**, 7–34.

Common, M., I. Reid and R. Blamey (1997), 'Do existence values for cost benefit analysis exist?', *Environmental and Resource Economics*, **9**, 225–38.

Deaton, A. and J. Muellbauer (1980), *Economics and Consumer Behaviour*, Cambridge, UK: Cambridge University Press.

Diamond, P.A., J.A. Hausman, G.K. Leonard and M.A. Denning (1993), 'Does contingent valuation measure preferences? Experimental evidence', in J.A. Hausman (ed.), *Contingent Valuation: A Critical Assessment*, Amsterdam: North-Holland, pp. 31–85.

Edwards, S.F. (1986), 'Ethical preferences and the assessment of existence values: does the neoclassical model fit?', *Northeastern Journal of Agricultural Economics*, **15**, 145–59.

Edwards, S.F. (1992), 'Rethinking existence values', *Land Economics*, **68**, 120–22.

Goodpaster, K.E. (1978), 'On being morally considerable', *Journal of Philosophy*, **75**, 168–76.

Hanemann, M. (1991), 'Willingness to pay and willingness to accept: how much can they differ?', *American Economic Review*, **81**, 635–47.

Harris, C.C. and G. Brown (1992), 'Gain loss and personal responsibility: the role of motivation in resource valuation decision-making', *Ecological Economics*, **5**, 73–92.

Harrison, G.W. (1992), 'Valuing public goods with the contingent valuation method: a critique of Kahneman and Knetsch', *Journal of Environmental Economics and Management*, **23**, 248–57.
Hausman, J.A. (ed.) (1993), *Contingent Valuation: A Critical Assessment*, Amsterdam: North-Holland.
Hogarth, R. (1987), *Judgement and Choice*, Chichester, UK: John Wiley and Sons.
Iyengar, S. (1989), 'How citizens think about national issues: a matter of responsibility', *American Journal of Political Science*, **8**, 878–900.
Janssen, R. (1992), *Multiobjective Decision Support for Environmental Management*, Dordrecht: Kluwer Academic Publishers.
Johansson, P.-O. (1992), 'Altruism in cost-benefit analysis', *Environmental and Resource Economics*, **2**, 605–13.
Kahneman, D. and J.L. Knetsch (1992a),'Valuing public goods: the purchase of moral satisfaction', *Journal of Environmental Economics and Management*, **33**, 57–70.
Kahneman, D. and J.L. Knetsch (1992b), 'Contingent valuation and the value of public goods: reply', *Journal of Environmental Economics and Management*, **22**, 90–94.
Kemp, M.A. and C. Maxwell (1993), 'Exploring a budget context for contingent valuation estimates', in J.A. Hausman (ed.), *Contingent Valuation: A Critical Assessment*, Amsterdam: North-Holland, pp. 218–65.
Knetsch, J.L. (1990), 'Environmental policy implications of disparities between willingness to pay and compensation demanded measures of values', *Journal of Environmental Economics and Management*, **18**, 227–37.
Kohn, R.E. (1993), 'Measuring the existence value of wildlife: comment', *Land Economics*, **69**, 304–8.
Lind, E.A. and T.R. Tyler (1988), *The Social Psychology of Procedural Justice*, New York: Plenum Press.
Madaragia, B. and K.E. McConnell (1987), 'Exploring existence value', *Water Resources Research*, **23**, 936–42.
Mellers, B.A. and J. Baron (eds) (1993), *Psychological Perspectives on Justice: Theory and Applications*, New York: Cambridge University Press.
Milgrom, P. (1993), 'Is sympathy an economic value? Philosophy, economics, and the contingent valuation method', in J.A. Hausman (ed.), *Contingent Valuation: A Critical Assessment*, Amsterdam: North-Holland, pp. 417–35.
Naess, A. (1973), 'The shallow and the deep, long-range ecology movement', *Inquiry*, **16**, 95–100.
Norton, B.G. (1994), 'Economists' preferences and the preferences of economists', *Environmental Values*, **3**, 311–32.
Payne, J.W., J.R. Bettman and E.J. Johnson (1992), 'Behavioural decision research: a constructive processing perspective', *Annual Review of Psychology*, **43**, 87–131.
Penz, C.P. (1986), *Consumer Sovereignty and Human Interests*, Cambridge, UK: Cambridge University Press.
Perman, R., Y. Ma and J. McGilvray (1996), *Natural Resource and Environmental Economics*, London: Longman.
Peterson, G.L., T.C. Brown, D.W. McCollum, P.A. Bell, A.A. Birjulin and A. Clarke (1996), 'Moral responsibility effects in valuation of WTA for public and private goods by the method of paired comparisons', in W.L. Adamowicz, P. Boxall, M.K. Luckert, E.E. Phillips and W.A. White (eds), *Forestry Economics and the Environment*, Wallingford: CAB International, 134–59.
Plott, C.R. (1993), 'Contingent valuation: a view of the conference and associated research', in J.A. Hausman (ed.), *Contingent Valuation: A Critical Assessment*, Amsterdam: North-Holland, pp. 468–78.
Popkin, R.H. and A. Stroll (1986), *Philosophy Made Simple*, 2nd edn, London: W.H. Allen.
Randall, A. (1986), 'Human preferences, economics and the preservation of species', in B.G. Norton (ed.), *The Preservation of Species*, Princeton, NJ: Princeton University Press.
Randall, A. (1991), 'The value of biodiversity', *Ambio*, **20**, 64–8.

Randall, A. and M. Farmer (1995), 'Benefits, costs, and the safe minimum standard of conservation', in D.W. Bromley (ed.), *The Handbook of Environmental Economics*, Oxford: Blackwell.

Regan, T. (1981), 'On the nature and possibility of an environmental ethic', *Environmental Ethics*, **3**, 19–34.

Sagoff, M. (1988), *The Economy of the Earth*, Cambridge, UK: Cambridge University Press.

Sagoff, M. (1994), 'Should preferences count?', *Land Economics*, **70**, 127–44.

Schkade, D.A. and J.W. Payne (1993), 'Where do the numbers come from? How people respond to contingent valuation questions', in J.A. Hausman (ed.), *Contingent Valuation: A Critical Assessment*, Amsterdam: North-Holland, pp.271–93.

Schkade, D.A. and J.W. Payne (1994), 'How people respond to contingent valuation questions: a verbal protocol analysis of willingness to pay for an environmental regulation', *Journal of Environmental Economics and Management*, **26**, 88–109.

Schwartz, S.H. (1968), 'Words, deeds and the perception of consequences and responsibilities in action situations', *Journal of Personality and Social Psychology*, **10**, 232–42.

Sen, A.K. (1977), 'Rational fools: A critique of the behavioural foundations of economy theory', *Philosophy and Public Affairs*, **16**, 317–44.

Singer, P. (1979), 'Not for humans only: the place of non-humans in environmental issues', in K.E. Goodpaster and K.M. Sayes (eds), *Ethics and Problems of the Twenty First Century*, Notre Dame: University of Notre Dame Press.

Singer, P. (1993), *Practical Ethics*, 2nd edn, Cambridge, UK: Cambridge University Press.

Smith, V.K. (1992), 'Arbitrary values, good causes and premature verdicts', *Journal of Environmental Economics and Management*, **22**, 71–89.

Spash, C.L. and N.D. Hanley (1995), 'Preferences information and biodiversity preservation', *Ecological Economics*, **12**, 191–208.

Stevens, T.H., J. Echeverria, R.J. Glass, T. Hager and T.A. More (1991), 'Measuring the existence value of wildlife: what do CVM estimates really show?', *Land Economics*, **67**, 390–400.

Vatn, A. and D. Bromley (1995), 'Choices without prices without apologies', in D. W. Bromley (ed.), *The Handbook of Environmental Economics*, Oxford: Blackwell.

57 Cost–benefit analysis of environmental policy and management

Nick Hanley[1]

1. Introduction

In many contexts of environmental policy making and management, it seems desirable to develop decision-making aids which have a number of characteristics. These include the ability to handle a wide range of problems; the ability to capture many important aspects of these problems; and the ability to judge how far a policy/project moves society towards some socially defined and accepted goal. Cost–benefit analysis (CBA from now on) has been claimed to be just such a methodology. CBA can be applied to any decision which involves a reallocation of resources within society, from constructing a new bridge to expanding the number of heart operations in our hospitals. CBA also captures many important aspects of such resource allocations. Specifically, it identifies and measures the costs and benefits of such actions to all members of society. These costs and benefits are expressed in a limiting language, it is true (in monetary units), and are also confined to 'relevant effects'. 'Relevance' is accorded to any action which impacts, directly or indirectly, on utility. However, this language allows CBA to express both the intensity and direction of preferences for a resource allocation, as well as allowing the comparison of many different aspects of projects/policies, such as wetland losses with tons of concrete used in constructing a marina. However, this common language is also a weakness of CBA, since aspects of a project/policy which cannot be so measured must perforce be ignored. These include, for example, the equity implications of the project/policy, its impacts on sustainable development, political acceptability, and the degree to which the policy/project fits into existing institutional arrangements.

CBA can thus be compared with alternative decision-making aids. In the environmental field, three commonly cited alternatives are multi-criteria analysis (MCA), environmental impact analysis (EIA) and public referenda. MCA, as discussed in the next chapter, is a body of techniques which allow multiple objectives to be considered, as opposed to the single objective of relevance in CBA, namely efficiency. CBA is thus a much narrower technique. However, MCA relies on a subjective specification of weights by the decision maker/analyst, whilst it does not have the welfare economics foundation of CBA (although see Romero and Rehman, 1987; Zeleny, 1982). EIA avoids the need to express all environmental impacts in a single numeraire, and so can provide much more detailed and disaggregated information on the environmental effects of a policy/project. However, it is not capable of incorporating non-environmental impacts, so is very limited in its scope and inclusiveness. Finally, referenda are not common as means of decision making in all countries, and may be argued to have higher trans-actions costs than CBA. In addition, referenda can only express the direction of preferences, whilst CBA can also measure their intensity (although see van den Doel and van Velthoven, 1993).

Economists claim that CBA informs policy makers about the social desirability of a project/policy. This claim can be traced to the link between CBA and neoclassical welfare economics, alluded to above. Within welfare economics, the Pareto principle has been well accepted as a criterion for assessing whether a resource allocation improves social welfare. The Pareto principle states that if at least one person in society feels better off as a result of a change and no one feels worse off, then the change improves social welfare. However, very few projects/policies have no costs, so the alternative principle proposed separately by Kaldor and by Hicks seems more useful: that a project improves social welfare if gainers *could* compensate losers and still be better off (Boadway and Bruce, 1984; Johansson, 1991), Note that this criterion, known as the potential Pareto improvement criterion, implies two things: (i) that gains are comparable to losses, that is, both are expressed in the same units; and (ii) that all losses are compensatable (both of these assumptions turn out to cause problems in environmental applications of CBA). However, it does not imply that losers are *actually* compensated for losses, merely that they could be.

An excess of aggregate benefit over aggregate cost in CBA (a positive net present value) is assumed to be equivalent to satisfying the Kaldor–Hicks criterion. This also assumes that the gains and losses to all individuals are equally weighted in the implied social welfare function.[2] It also assumes the possibility of transferring gains and losses over time (in other words, that losers in later generations can somehow be compensated by gainers in early generations). The possibility of substituting utility changes across time, albeit in discounted form, is a key feature of CBA and, some would say, a key weakness.

2. The practicalities of CBA
The steps involved in carrying out a CBA are as follows. First, the project/policy is defined, along with the 'relevant population' (that is, those individuals whose welfare will be considered relevant). For example, suppose a new amenity woodland near a city is being planned. The relevant

population would include all those likely to benefit from this new recreational facility. Second, the relevant impacts of the project are identified, using the criterion of whether they constitute a change in resource availability or a change in prices. Changes which increase resource availability, in terms of either quantity or quality, are termed benefits, as are price reductions to consumers. Changes which reduce resource availability or which reduce its quality, or which increase prices to consumers, are counted as costs. In the woodland example, a new recreational resource is being created, but the land which the wood will be planted on will not be available to alternative uses such as house building (an opportunity cost). Also, labour and capital resources will be used up in establishing the wood.

Third, relevant costs and benefits are valued in money terms. Where price changes are involved, this necessitates calculation of changes in consumers' and producers' surplus. In many cases of environmental impacts, price changes are not relevant, since we are faced with changes in unpriced goods. However, if, for example, a reduction in wetland changes production possibilities for fishermen, and shifts local prices, then surplus changes are relevant (see, for example, Ellis and Fisher, 1987). For changes in the supply of public goods, such as clean air, estimates of compensating or equivalent surplus are required. This is the maximum amount of money that individuals would be willing to pay to have the improvement, or alternatively, the minimum compensation payment they would accept to go without it. This, for a public good, is equal to the area under a marginal willingness to pay function for the good bounded by the 'with' and 'without' quantities of the good (Johansson, 1993). For the woodland, for example, we could estimate the willingness to pay of prospective users for the creation of this new resource.

Benefits, generally, are measured using consumers' effective demand, typically expressed in market demands and prices. Note that this involves an implicit weighting of preferences according to people's purchasing power in the marketplace. Where no market prices exist to value costs and benefits, as will often be the case in environmental projects/policies, non-market valuation techniques must be used: we return briefly to this subject below. Costs are measured as social opportunity costs. Thus the cost of the land which the forest is planned for would be valued using the social net benefits which that land could generate in its next best use. Where market imperfections (such as monopoly) or market interventions such as guaranteed minimum prices or tariffs drive a wedge between market prices and marginal social costs or benefits, then shadow prices should be calculated. In practice, however, extensive use of shadow pricing is typically reserved for developing-country applications of CBA by external funding bodies such as the World Bank (Irvin, 1978). Such shadow prices represent the analyst's estimate of either the marginal social cost or marginal social benefit of the relevant input/output.

Fourth, benefits and costs are aggregated over time by discounting. The correct discount rate to use in CBA is a matter of great dispute (see, for example, Lind, 1982 and Hanley, 1992), as capital market imperfections drive a wedge between the social time-preference rate (the rate at which society is prepared to trade off present against future utility) and the social opportunity cost of capital (that is, the social return on investment). The Arrow–Lind theorem (1970) suggests that the cost of risk is lower for the public sector than the private sector, since greater risk spreading is possible, so that the social discount rate should be reduced accordingly. We return to the issue of the choice of discount rate in environmental appraisal below. The fifth stage in CBA involves a comparison of total discounted benefits with total discounted costs, to produce a net present value (NPV). If the NPV is positive, then the project is said to have passed the CBA test. Alternatively, information may be presented in terms of benefit–cost ratios (the ratio of the present value of benefits to that of costs); or as an internal rate of return, which is the discount rate which yields a zero NPV (Zerbe and Dively, 1994). The final stage involves conducting a sensitivity analysis on important parameters such as the discount rate, project life-span, and cost and benefit estimates, noting the impact of changes in these parameters on predicted net benefits.

It should be noted here that any CBA exercise, whether applied to environmental issues or not, faces considerable problems in terms of data collection. These include, for example, difficulties in predicting responses by consumers or producers due to price changes brought about by a project/policy, problems in calculating the *net* effect of the project/policy on output (in terms of possible displacement and crowding out), and difficulties in deciding the relevant population. However, the data collection problem is likely to be exacerbated, on the whole, when environmental effects are considered, simply because a wider view is now being taken of impacts.

CBA has a relatively short history in its application to environmental impacts, although the earliest large-scale applications of the technique were to water resource development projects in the US in the 1950s (Hanley and Spash, 1993). Such projects clearly had major environmental impacts, yet these were not included in early CBAs. In the UK, a major early application was to the siting of a third airport for the London region, and this exercise saw the partial incorporation of environmental effects (principally noise impacts on property values), although the treatment of cultural impacts did a great deal to damage CBA in non-economists' eyes. For example, the loss of a Saxon (tenth-century) church was valued using the costs of building a modern replacement! Institutional use of CBA in the

UK in the 1970s and 1980s to evaluate major drainage projects led to accusations of institutional capture of the technique (Bowers, 1988). In the US, high-profile conservation issues, such as forest development and the protection of the spotted owl in the Pacific Northwest, and the enforcement of the Endangered Species Act, have highlighted unease over basing conservation decisions on a technique which seeks to reduce all values to monetary ones. The use of CBA in the context of the Endangered Species Act also shows, in the case of an obscure fish known as the snail darter (*Percina tanasi*) how governments and their agencies can easily ignore the results of a CBA if it gives the 'wrong answer' from their political perspective (Davis, 1988). Sagoff (1988) has argued that CBA was used as a device by the Reagan administration in the 1980s as a means of forestalling new regulatory initiatives in environment and safety originating from bodies such as the US Environmental Protection Agency.

3. Environmental problems for CBA

CBA would appear, on the face of it, to be a useful tool for guiding environmental management, and decisions over other projects/policies which impact on the environment, *if* the environmental impacts of projects/policies can be included to a satisfactory degree in the analysis. However, the application of CBA to environmental management encounters several major problem areas (Hanley, 1992). These are: (i) how to place monetary values on environmental resources, such as wildlife or clean water; (ii) how to cope with irreversible changes in environmental quality; (iii) how to incorporate ecosystem complexity; and (iv) whether environmental issues pose special problems for the choice of discount rate.

3.1 Environmental valuation

The subject of environmental valuation has been dealt with elsewhere in this volume (see Chapters 55–61). In summary, one might say that many methods now exist for valuing non-market environmental resources, and that great strides have been made in increasing the rigour of these methods. However, there are still many areas of methodological debate and empirical uncertainty (for example, in connection with the issue of part–whole bias in contingent valuation,[3] and in the value of leisure time in travel-cost-type models), which mean that the degree of confidence that can be placed on estimates of environmental values are often only of the 'order-of-magnitude' variety. Thus estimating the benefits of creating a new amenity woodland for public use may be problematic.

Sometimes, order-of-magnitude estimates will be sufficient from a CBA perspective. As Krutilla and Fisher (1985) noted in an early application of CBA to environmental management (in their case, a decision over whether to allow a series of dams to be built on a wilderness river), so long as the lower-bound estimate of environmental preservation benefits exceeds the present value of net development benefits, then no attention need be given to other points in the probability distribution of benefits. However, where the lower-bound estimate for environmental benefits is not large enough to outweigh net development benefits, then some other point estimate must be chosen, and here the precision of benefits estimation becomes important. Typically, though, mean values from contingent valuation studies tend to have rather large confidence intervals.

3.2 Irreversibility

The environmental effects of certain policies or projects are irreversible. By this we mean that such effects cannot be undone, or the initial condition returned to, either at all, or within a time frame thought relevant to individuals (say less than 1000 years). Draining wetlands for forestry, felling rainforests so that soils are eroded, and species extinction are all examples of irreversibilities. In the specific context of species loss, Vatn and Bromley (1994) have referred to a 'functional transparency' of environmental resources, in that the contribution a species makes to an ecosystem is not known until it is removed (when it may be too late to do anything with this new knowledge). Irreversibilities may be thought of as violating an assumption in CBA that utility is capable of being transferred across time, since perpetual losses are involved: whilst the perpetuities formula used below would in principle provide a financial flow over time equal to the present value of the permanent loss, we have no way of committing succeeding generations to keep up these payments, nor do we know that future generations would accept monetary compensation for a loss, say, in species diversity or of some unique natural feature. The *possibility of compensation for losses* assumption implicit in the Kaldor–Hicks principle is thus potentially violated.

The principle approach in CBA[4] to irreversibilities involves the Krutilla–Fisher (KF) model (1985). This model treats irreversible costs as a financial perpetuity. As is well known, the present value of such a perpetuity is found by multiplying it by the inverse of the discount rate. Thus preservation benefits foregone into perpetuity are included in the net present value expression, alongside development benefits (such as the value of timber) and any initial development costs. The net present value of an irreversible development with initial costs C, development benefits D_t and preservation benefits foregone of P_t is given as:

$$NPV_d = -C + \frac{D_t}{(i-g)} - \frac{P_t}{(i-r)} \tag{57.1}$$

where *i* is the discount rate, *g* is the growth (decay) rate of development benefits and *r* is the growth (decay) rate of preservation benefits foregone. For example, in a decision over whether to allow afforestation of a wetland area, *r* represents the annual rate of change in the real value of preservation benefits (estimated, perhaps, from a contingent valuation study), and *g* represents the annual rate of growth in the real price of timber.

However, the KF model requires two pieces of information which are impossible to know for sure. These are:

1. The preferences of future generations for environmental goods relative to other goods. These are needed in order to value the infinite stream of foregone preservation benefits. In practice, the preferences of the present generation (or some subset of it) are used instead, since only these preferences are capable of being valued at the time of the study.
2. The rates of change for the real values of both the development and preservation alternatives. A possible asymmetry between the real rate of change in preservation versus development benefits was explicitly recognized by Krutilla and Fisher, who include estimates of these growth (or decay) rates in their empirical applications of the technique. Such estimates may also be found, for example, in Hanley and Craig (1991). Yet forecasting the rate of change of the relative prices of preservation and development into the infinite future is a far from simple task!

3.3   Environmental complexity and uncertainty

The application of CBA to environmental management is complicated in many cases by uncertainty over the long-term environmental effects of current actions. Examples include pesticide leaching from farmlands to water courses, the health effects of low-level radiation from nuclear power stations, the effects of depleting biological diversity on ecosystem resilience (and thus on sustainability), and the environmental impacts of dumping at sea. Frequently this uncertainty is of a non-probabilistic nature, in that we do not know all states of the world that could occur, nor the probability with which each state will occur. Scientific uncertainty is made more likely if threshhold effects or discontinuities (non-linearities) occur. Examples here include some dose-response functions, such as critical loads for acid deposition, or dissolved oxygen levels in a river. In the absence of probabilistic information, CBA analysts are reduced to sensitivity and scenario analysis (for example, looking at best and worst cases), which clearly reduces the extent to which CBA can inform decisions.

As Gowdy (1997) has noted, ecosystems 'may be seen as hierarchical layers of processes operating at different levels of complexity, each level operating on vastly different time scales' (O'Neil et al., 1986, quoted in Gowdy, op. cit.). This feature makes the prediction of impacts intrinsically different. What is more, several authors in the ecological economics field (Norgaard, 1984; Perrings, 1987; Common and Perrings, 1992) have argued that dynamic interdependencies between economic and ecological systems imply that strict economic optimizing may lead to a decrease in the stability of ecosystems, producing undesirable feedbacks on the economic system. This world-view sees the parameters of both systems (economic and ecological) co-evolving, so that decision making based on one system only (the economic, if CBA is used) is unlikely to be a sufficient stand-alone decision mechanism.

3.4   Discount rates and discounting

A large literature exists on the choice of discount rate for CBA. An outrageous simplification of the majority view evolving from this literature is that discounting can be justified on grounds of intertemporal efficiency but not on grounds of intertemporal equity (Howarth and Norgaard, 1993). Given the long-term nature of many environmental costs and benefits (such as the costs of global warming, benefits from deciduous forest planting, or irreversible species losses), the outcome of CBA analyses of projects with environmental impacts can often be highly sensitive to the choice of discount rate.

But at what rate should the discount rate be set for environmental projects? Jungermann and Fleischer (1988) show that discount rates for an individual can vary (from positive to negative) according to whether a pleasure or a pain is in prospect, implying that different discount rates should be used for environmental gains or losses. Luckert and Adamowicz (1993) showed that on average individuals hold lower discount rates for environmental goods than other goods, implying that the government should reduce the discount rate on projects having environmental impacts relative to all other projects. Much controversy also exists over whether the Arrow–Lind theorem should hold for the social discounting of environmental effects. As will be recalled, this theorem states that as the number of individuals sharing a risk goes to infinity, the amount of risk premium demanded by each goes to zero. This depends on the extent to which environmental risk spreading is possible; for Fisher (1973) it is not, since for environmental risks with the characteristic of non-rival consumption, such as nuclear accidents, the number of people sharing the risk does not affect the risk borne by each individual. This implies that the Arrow–Lind theorem does not hold for environmental costs.

Discounting has traditionally been partly defended on the grounds that capital is productive. Natural capital is not always capable of reproduction, however. Whilst fisheries and forests can grow, and can be reinvested in, in terms of increasing growth rates and/or stock sizes, non-renewable resource deposits cannot grow (although additional resources can be expended to increase the economically available portion of a non-renewable deposit). Finally, the social rate of discount for environmental effects may be lower than private rates due to the weight attached by individuals to 'citizenship' motives regarding the environment. Individuals may have lower time-preference rates in their roles as 'citizens' as compared to their roles as consumers, to use the distinction put forward by Sagoff (1988).

4.   Recent developments and applications

There have been a very large number of recent (post-1985) developments in this area, but for brevity only three are mentioned here. These are the areas of links with sustainable development; environmental valuation; and uncertainty.

4.1   Sustainable development

Before 1985, sustainable development (SD from now on) was a relatively obscure concept. However, since the publication by the UN of *Our Common Future* in 1987, and the UN Rio conference on the environment in 1992, SD has become the main buzzword of environmental policy. An obvious question is whether CBA is consistent with SD: more precisely, whether a government following a CBA rule in project/policy selection is likely to move closer to a sustainable path. The answer depends on how one defines sustainability. If SD is defined as non-declining per capita welfare, then CBA could contribute to achieving this goal, since all projects passing the CBA test are potential Pareto improvements. However, CBA addresses neither the intertemporal nor the intratemporal distribution of resources, and thus cannot guarantee that future welfare is not depleted at the expense of present welfare, nor that the poor of the current generations are not further impoverished to benefit the rich. This failure of CBA to guarantee SD so defined should be obvious from the fact that whilst SD is mainly an equity issue, CBA addresses only the efficiency of project/policy selection. Howarth and Norgaard (1993), for example, have shown that incorporating environmental values into CBA cannot guarantee sustainability.

SD has also been defined as a non-declining stock of natural capital, somehow measured. On this definition CBA offers no guarantee of sustainability, since the CBA process explicitly allows the running down of one stream of potential benefits (such as environmental benefits) so long as the offsetting stream of realized benefits is large enough (Pearce et al., 1989). A suggestion by Pearce et al. (1990) is to make use of 'shadow projects' to replace depleted natural capital, as a constraint on the CBA process.

However, few practical or theoretical steps have been taken to developing this concept. Thus, to summarize, passing the CBA test cannot be seen as a sufficient condition for sustainability under two popular definitions of that concept: under the non-declining per capita utility over time definition, CBA explicitly allows the trade-off of (discounted) future utility against present utility, so cannot guarantee a non-declining path; under the constant natural capital stock definition, CBA explicitly allows the running down of environmental capital so long as the offsetting utility gain is big enough.

4.2 Environmental valuation
Within the field of environmental valuation, the principal advances since 1985 have come in two areas: stated preferences and revealed preference approaches. In stated preference approaches, continued refinements of the contingent valuation technique have occurred, particularly in the design and analysis of dichotomous choice versions, in the area of preference uncertainty, and in the context of establishing tests of reliability and consistency (see, for example, Hanemann, forthcoming). A new approach to stated preference valuation which has been developed in the 1990s is choice experiments (Adamowicz et al., 1994; Boxall et al., 1996). This has allowed researchers to identify the marginal value of changes in the characteristics of environmental resources, such as fishing streams, which is potentially much more useful than knowing their total value (that is, the welfare loss if access to them is denied). In revealed preference analysis, the use of random utility models to predict site choice and marginal attribute values (Bockstael et al., 1987; Coyne and Adamowicz, 1992), and the use of count models to predict total recreational demand (Englin and Shonkwiler, 1995) have greatly increased the potential for better recreational demand modelling as an input to CBA.

4.3 Uncertainty
Finally, CBA has traditionally had a big problem in coping with uncertainty, unless expected values could be calculated. However, in few if any environmental policy problems do sufficient data exist to calculate expected values (because all states of the world are now known and/or their probabilities are now known). Alternative approaches to uncertainty are therefore being pursued (Faucheux and Froger, 1995). This includes use of the 'precautionary principle', whereby actions are taken to avoid potentially irreversible and catastrophic environmental damages before sufficient information has been gathered to exactly estimate their costs. Examples would include cutting CO_2 emissions to limit global warming, or banning pesticides which are potentially carcinogenic. Elsewhere, useful work on

uncertainty has included attempts to better categorize different situations of risk and uncertainty (for example, Vercelli, 1991); and alternative analytical treatments of the types of uncertainty (known as ignorance and strong uncertainty) which typify, for example, the costs of biodiversity losses (that is, alternative to the neoclassical approach based on expected utility theory). These alternatives have sought to develop the ideas of Shackle (1955), and include the work of Katzner (1989) and Vickers (1994).

5.   Conclusions

CBA has emerged as a powerful tool for helping decision makers consider a wide range of environmental management problems in a rational, ordered and potentially open manner. In addition, CBA has the advantage of being linked to a well-developed body of theory that can say something about the social desirability of projects. These attractions have led to a greatly increased use of CBA in environmental policy making, for example in the UK (Department of the Environment, 1991) and US (Sagoff, 1988). However, it is undoubtedly true that the application of CBA to environmental management confronts us with many problems (outlined above), whilst the criterion which CBA uses (that of economic efficiency) is a very narrow one. The CBA process can also lead to the validation of decisions which might be viewed as very unfair since it does not explicitly take equity issues into account, unless a 'revisionist' approach is taken (Pearce and Nash, 1978): for example, a CBA could recommend the preservation of tropical rainforest for the benefit of rich foreign tourists at the expense of very poor local people who are denied development opportunities.

For these reasons, it is very unlikely and also highly undesirable that CBA should ever be used as the sole deciding mechanism in policy/project selection. CBA should be part of a whole suite of decision-aiding methods, including environmental impact analysis, local economic multiplier analysis, citizen juries and public referenda. Information relevant to a CBA could also be used as part of a wider multi-criteria analysis, which is capable of addressing far more social goals than the single goal addressed by CBA. Analysts and policy makers should also keep in mind all the environmental problems with CBA when interpreting the results of CBA exercises. However, it seems likely that the use of CBA and CBA techniques (such as environmental valuation) will continue to increase in both policy making and academic circles into the foreseeable future.

Notes
1. I thank two anonymous referees for comments on an earlier draft of this chapter.
2. Although it is possible to specify non-uniform weightings (weighted by relative income, for example). This 'revisionist' approach is outlined in Pearce and Nash (1978) and Zerbe and Dively (1994).

3. The phenomenon whereby an individual's bid to preserve an environmental resource, for example, is biased by his/her valuation of some more inclusive set.
4. The precautionary principle is an alternative approach to both uncertainty and irreversibilities, but it is not part of the CBA paradigm, and so is not discussed here.

References

Adamowicz, W., J. Louviere and M. Williams (1994), 'Combining revealed and stated preference methods for valuing environmental amenities', *Journal of Environmental Economics and Management*, **26** (3), 271–92.

Arrow, K. and R. Lind (1970), 'Uncertainty and the evaluation of public investment decisions', *American Economic Review*, **60**, 364–78

Boadway, R. and N. Bruce (1984), *Welfare Economics*, Oxford: Basil Blackwell.

Bockstael, N., M. Hanemann and C. Kling (1987), 'Estimating the value of water quality improvements', *Water Resources Research*, **23**, 951–60.

Bowers, J. (1988), 'Cost benefit analysis in theory and practice: agricultural land drainage projects', in R.K. Turner (ed.), *Sustainable Environmental Management*, London: Belhaven.

Boxall, P., W. Adamowicz, J. Swait, M. Williams and J. Louviere (1996), 'A comparison of stated preference methods for environmental valuation', *Ecological Economics*, **18**, 243–53.

Common, M. and C. Perrings (1992), 'Towards an ecological economics of sustainability', *Ecological Economics*, **6**, 7–34.

Coyne, A. and W. Adamowicz (1992), 'Modelling choice of site for hunting bighorn sheep', *Wildlife Society Bulletin*, **20**, 26–33.

Davis, R. (1988), 'Lessons in economics and politics from the snail darter', in V.K. Smith (ed.), *Essays in honour of John V Krutilla*, Washington, DC: Resources for the Future.

Department of the Environment (1991), *Policy Appraisal and the Environment*, London: HMSO.

Doel, H. van den and B. van Velthoven (1993), *Democracy and Welfare economics*, Cambridge, UK: Cambridge University Press.

Ellis, G. and A. Fisher (1987), 'Valuing the environment as an input', *Journal of Environmental Management*, **25**, 149–56.

Englin, J. and J. Shonkwiler (1995), 'Estimating social welfare using count data models', *The Review of Economics and Statistics*, **77**, 104–12.

Faucheux, S. and G. Froger (1995), 'Decision making under environmental uncertainty', *Ecological Economics*, **15**, 29–42.

Fisher, A.C. (1973), 'Environmental externalities and the Arrow–Lind public investment theorem', *American Economic Review*, **63**, 722–5.

Gowdy, J. (1997), 'The value of biodiversity', *Land Economics*, **73** (1), 25–41.

Hanley, N. (1992), 'Are there environmental limits to cost–benefit analysis?', *Environmental and Resource Economics*, **2**, 33–59.

Hanley, N. and S. Craig (1991), 'Wilderness preservation and the Krutilla Fisher model: the case of Scotland's Flow Country', *Ecological Economics*, **4**, 145–64.

Hanley, N. and C. Spash (1993), *Cost–Benefit Analysis and the Environment*, Cheltenham, UK and Brookfield, US: Edward Elgar.

Hanemann, M. (forthcoming), 'Econometric issues in contingent valuation', in K. Willis and I. Bateman (eds), *The Contingent Valuation Method: Theory and Application*, Oxford: Oxford University Press.

Howarth, R. and R. Norgaard (1993), 'Intergenerational transfers and the social discount rate', *Environmental and Natural Resource Economics*, **3** (4), 337–58.

Irvin, G. (1978), *Modern Cost–Benefit Methods: an Introduction to the Appraisal of Development Projects*, Basingstoke, UK: Macmillan.

Johansson, P.-O. (1991), *An Introduction to Modern Welfare Economics*, Cambridge, UK: Cambridge University Press.

Johansson, P.-O. (1993), *Cost–Benefit Analysis of Environmental Change*, Cambridge, UK: Cambridge University Press.

Jungermann, H. and F. Fleischer (1988), 'As time goes by: psychological determinants of time preferences', in G. Kirsch, P. Nijkamp and K. Zimmerman (eds), *The Formulation of Time Preferences in Multidisciplinary Perspective*, Berlin: WZB Publications.

Katzner, D. (1989), 'The Shackle–Vickers approach to decision making in ignorance', *Journal of Post Keynsian Economics*, **12**, 237–59.

Krutilla, J. and A. Fisher (1985), *The Economics of Natural Environments*, Washington, DC: Resources for the Future.

Lind, R. (1982), 'A primer on the major issues relating to the discount rate' in R. Lind (ed.), *Discounting for Time and Risk in Energy Policy*, Baltimore, MD: Johns Hopkins Press.

Luckert, M. and W. Adamowicz (1993), 'Empirical measures of factors affecting social rates of discount', *Environmental and Resource Economics*, **3**, 1–22.

Norgaard, R. (1984), 'Co-evolutionary development potential', *Land Economics*, **60**, 160–73.

O'Neil, R., D. DeAngelis, J. Waide and T. Allen (1986), *A Hierarchical Concept of Ecosystems*, Princeton, NJ: Princeton University Press.

Pearce, D. and C. Nash (1978), *The Social Appraisal of Projects*, Basingstoke, UK: Macmillan.

Pearce, D., A. Markandya and E. Barbier (1989), *Blueprint for a Green Economy*, London: Earthscan.

Pearce, D., A. Markandya and E. Barbier (1990), *Sustainable Development*, Cheltenham, UK and Brookfield, US: Edward Elgar.

Perrings, C. (1987), *Economy and Environment*, Cambridge, UK: Cambridge University Press.

Romero, C. and T. Rehman (1987), 'Natural resource management and the use of multi-criteria decision making techniques', *European Review of Agricultural Economics*, **14**, 61–89.

Sagoff, M. (1988), *The Economy of the Earth*, Cambridge, UK: Cambridge University Press.

Shackle, J. (1955), *Uncertainty in Economics*, Cambridge, UK: Cambridge University Press.

Vatn, A. and D. Bromley (1994), 'Choices without prices without apologies', *Journal of Environmental Economics and Management*, **26**, 129–48.

Vercelli, A. (1991), *Methodological foundations of macroeconomics: Keynes and Lucas*, Cambridge, UK: Cambridge University Press.

Vickers, D. (1994), *Time, Uncertainty and Choice in Economic Theory*, Ann Arbor: University of Michigan Press.

Zeleny, M. (1982), *Multiple Criteria Decision Making*, Quantitative methods in management series, New York: McGraw-Hill.

Zerbe, R. and D. Dively (1994), *Benefit–Cost Analysis in Theory and Practice*, New York: HarperCollins.

58 Multi-criteria methods for quantitative, qualitative and fuzzy evaluation problems
Ron Janssen and Giuseppe Munda

1. Introduction
It has become more and more difficult to see the world around us in a uni-dimensional way and to use only a single criterion when judging what we see. Multiple and conflicting objectives, for example, to minimize costs, to maximize environmental quality and to make sure that everybody gets a fair share are key issues in most projects. The importance of negative external effects of economic growth and the emergence of equity issues in economic development have shown limitations of cost–benefit analysis as a tool to deal with conflicts between policy objectives. Cost–benefit analysis essentially follows the priorities of the market: prices are derived directly or indirectly from market prices or are assessed from the willingness of individuals to pay (contingent valuation). To maximize economic efficiency is the central policy objective.

Multi-criteria methods revolve around preferences of decision makers. These methods try to consider simultaneous multiple conflicting criteria. Environmental decision making usually involves competing interests groups, conflicting objectives and different types of information. This may explain the increasing popularity of multi-criteria methods in environmental decision making. In the Netherlands, for example, many environmental impact statements use a multi-criteria method to compare alternatives. Recent examples include decisions on routing of new highways and rail links, decisions on location of waste storage and waste-processing facilities, decisions on housing and wind power projects (Bonte et al., 1997). Reviews of applications in other countries can be found in Faucheux and O'Connor (1997), Munda (1995) and Paruccini (1994).

A typical multi-criteria problem may be described in the following way: A is a finite set of n feasible actions (or alternatives) $a_j (j = 1,2, ..., n)$; G is the set of evaluation criteria $g_i (i = 1,2, ..., m)$ considered relevant in a decision problem. An action a_1 is evaluated to be better than action a_2 (both belonging to the set A) according to the ith criterion if $g_i(a_1) > g_i(a_2)$. In this way a decision problem may be represented in a tabular or matrix form. Given the sets A (of alternatives) and G (of evaluation criteria) and assuming the existence of n alternatives and m criteria, it is possible to build an

$n \times m$ matrix **P** whose typical element $g_i(a_j)$ $(i = 1, 2, \ldots, m; j = 1, 2, \ldots, n)$ represents the evaluation of the jth alternative according to the ith criterion. This matrix is called an evaluation table (Table 58.1). The evaluation table may include quantitative evaluation criteria (measured on an interval or ratio scale), qualitative evaluation criteria (measured on a nominal or ordinal scale) or both types of evaluation criteria.

Table 58.1   An evaluation table

Criteria	Units	Alternatives			
		a_1	a_2	a_3	a_4
g_1		$g_1(a_1)$	$g_1(a_2)$	.	$g_1(a_4)$
g_2		.	.	.	.
g_3		.	.	.	.
g_4		.	.	.	.
g_5		.	.	.	.
g_6		$g_6(a_1)$	$g_6(a_2)$	.	$g_6(a_4)$

Ideally, the criterion scores are precise, certain, exhaustive and unequivocal. But in reality, these scores can be uncertain. If uncertainty can be expressed using probabilities, sensitivity analysis based on Monte Carlo analysis can be applied (see Janssen, 1992). Fuzzy uncertainty arises if uncertainty does not concern the occurrence of an event but the event itself and cannot be described unambiguously. Fuzziness is linked to the nature of the event and not to its probability. The problem is not to predict a future state, but to describe correctly the event in the present (Zadeh, 1965). This sort of situation is readily identifiable in complex systems. Spatial–environmental systems in particular, are complex systems characterized by subjectivity, incompleteness and imprecision. Fuzzy set theory is a mathematical theory useful for modelling situations of this kind, that is, it aims to portray in terms of fuzzy uncertainty some of the indeterminacies of the socio-ecological system under study (Munda, 1995).

This chapter is organized as follows. A classification of different types of evaluation methods is presented in Section 2. This is followed by a short discussion of different types of multi-criteria methods (Section 3). An overview of fuzzy evaluation methods is presented in Section 4. An example illustrating the concepts used on an environmental management problem is included in Section 5. Finally conclusions and recommendations on the use of methods can be found in Section 6.

2. Classification of evaluation methods

Evaluation methods differ as to the characteristics of the set of alternatives and measurement scales they can handle, the decision rule they apply, and the way scores are standardized. A typology of evaluation methods is presented in Figure 58.1. For each class a representative, but certainly not exhaustive, set of methods is included. These methods are described in the remainder of this chapter. It is simply impossible to include all methods that make up the enormous array of available methods. A selection is made from various classes of methods with particular relevance to environmental problems. Extensive reviews are given in Nijkamp et al. (1990), Janssen (1992) and Janssen et al. (1999). The typology in Figure 58.1 is based on the following four distinctions:

1. *The set of alternatives: discrete versus continuous problems*   All multi-objective decision problems can be represented in *J*-dimensional space. Discrete decision problems involve a finite set of alternatives. Continuous decision problems are characterized by an infinite number of feasible alternatives. The selection of a nuclear plant site from nine possible sites is an example of a discrete choice problem. The allocation of nuclear, coal and natural gas resources for the production of electricity is an example of a continuous decision problem.

2. *The measurement scale: quantitative versus qualitative attribute scales*   Most environmental problems include a mixture of qualitative and quantitative information. Qualitative and mixed multi-criteria methods such as the regime method, permutation method, evamix method and expected value method can process this type of information. If available information is not exact, fuzzy evaluation methods can be applied. Evaluation by graphics can be used on quantitative, qualitative and mixed decision problems.

3. *The decision rule: priorities or prices*   The decision rule is specific to each method. Examples include: maximize total utility (decision analysis), maximize the ratio of benefits over costs (cost–benefit analysis), minimize the distance to the ideal solution (ideal point method) and a visual impression (evaluation by graphics). In cost–benefit analysis prices can be derived directly or indirectly from market prices or can be assessed from the willingness of individuals to pay (contingent valuation). In multi-criteria analysis priorities reflect the trade-offs or relative importance given by decision makers among criteria.

4. *The valuation function* f: *standardization versus valuation*   Quantitative scores can be measured in a variety of measurement units. To make these scores comparable, they must be transformed into a common dimension or into a common dimensionless unit. Scores can be

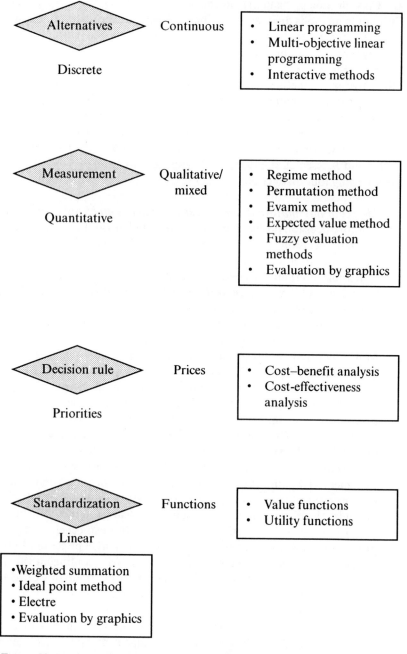

Figure 58.1   A typology of evaluation methods

transformed into standardized scores using a linear standardization function, or by using value or utility functions. Value and utility functions transform information measured on a physical measurement scale to a value or utility index.

3. Multi-criteria methods

Multi-criteria methods can be divided in quantitative and qualitative methods. Quantitative methods include weighted summation, value and utility analysis, the ideal point method, outranking methods and the analytical hierarchy process (AHP). These methods require quantitative information about scores of each criterion. Qualitative methods can be used if only qualitative information on scores is available or if a mixture of quantitative and qualitative scores is available. Examples are the regime method, the permutation method and the evamix method. A short description of all methods is included. Fuzzy evaluation methods are described in the next section.

Weighted summation

Weighted summation is a simple and often used evaluation method. An appraisal score is calculated for each alternative by first multiplying each value by its appropriate weight and then summing the weighted scores for all criteria. If the scores for the criteria are measured on different scales, they must be standardized to a dimensionless scale before weighted summation can be applied.

Value and utility functions

An important element in utility analysis is the use of value or utility functions. In contrast to weighted summation where a fixed, usually linear, function is used to transform scores on all criteria into standardized scores, in utility analysis a function is assessed for each criterion separately. The shape of this function is dependent on the specific characteristics of each criterion. Value functions can relate physical scores to an index reflecting the value of these scores. Methods to assess value functions include direct rating techniques and indifference methods such as the difference standard sequence technique and the bisection technique. If the effects of alternatives are uncertain, utility functions can be assessed using, for example, the certainty equivalent or the variable probability method (Keeney and Raiffa, 1976; French, 1988).

Ideal point method

The philosophy underlying the decision methods based on ideal point concepts can be synthesized as follows. It is assumed that there is an ideal level of attributes for objects of choice and that the decision maker's utilities decrease monotonically on both sides of this ideal point. The ideal point procedures are characterized by the following axiom of choice: alternatives that are closer to the ideal are preferred to those that are further away. To be as close as possible to the perceived ideal is the rationale of human choice. Environmental policy is often concerned with removing threats to the environment, trying to reach a certain desired state of the environment rather than maximizing the overall results of alternatives. Assuming that alternatives cover all extremes of the solution space, the ideal point can be found by selecting the single objective maximum for each criterion. If the decision maker can define goals for all criteria, the set of goals can be used to define the ideal point. Various distance measures can be applied to establish the distance between the ideal point and each alternative (Steuer, 1986).

Outranking methods

This approach is based on what Roy calls 'fundamental partial comparability axiom' (Roy, 1985). Outranking methods first translate criterion scores into an outranking relation and, second, analyse this relation. Both steps can be made in a number of ways according to the characteristics of the decision problem and the method used. As an example, in Electre 1, an alternative A outranks an alternative B if A is at least as good as B and B is not as good as A, where 'as good as' is defined by the concordance and discordance indices. In Electre 1 the proposition A outranks B is accepted if the concordant coalition which includes all criteria for which alternative A is equal or better than alternative B is sufficiently important (condition of concordance) and if on the other criteria the difference $g_i(b) - g_i(a)$ is not too large (condition of non-discordance). The importance of a coalition is represented by the sum of the weights of the criteria belonging to that coalition. The concordant coalition can be considered as the summation of the votes of the members in favour of a given option; according to the majority rule of democracies, this option will be approved if it obtains at least more than the 50 per cent of votes. According to the normative tradition in political philosophy, all coalitions, however small, should be given some fraction of the decision power. One measure of this power is the ability to veto certain subsets of outcomes.

The analytic hierarchy process (AHP)

AHP structures the decision problem in levels which correspond to a decision maker's understanding of the situation: goals, criteria, sub-criteria, and alternatives. By breaking the problem into levels, the decision maker can focus on smaller sets of decisions. The AHP is based on four assumptions (Saaty, 1980):

1. Given any pair of alternatives the decision maker is able to provide a pairwise comparison of these alternatives under any criterion on a linguistic scale (better, much better and so on) which can be directly linked to a ratio scale.
2. When comparing any two alternatives, the decision maker never judges one to be infinitely better than another under any criterion.
3. One can formulate the decision problem as a hierarchy.
4. All criteria and alternatives which impact a decision problem are represented in the hierarchy.

Regime method

The Regime method is also based on pairwise comparison of alternatives. For each criterion all pairs of alternatives are compared. The best alternative receives $+1$, the worst -1 and both alternatives receive 0 if they are the same. The sum of criterion weights is used to determine which of the two alternatives is preferred if all criteria are taken into account simultaneously. This is straightforward if quantitative weights are available. If only qualitative weights are available, these weights are interpreted as unknown quantitative weights. A set S is defined containing all sets of quantitative weights that conform to the qualitative priority information. In some cases one alternative will be preferred for the whole set S. In other cases for parts of the set S one alternative is preferred and for other parts the other alternative. The distribution of the weights within S is assumed to be uniform and therefore the relative sizes of the subsets of S can be interpreted as the probability that one alternative in each pair is preferred to the other. Probabilities are aggregated to produce an overall ranking of the alternatives (Nijkamp *et al.*, 1990).

Permutation period

The Permutation method addresses especially the following question: which, of all possible rank orders of alternatives, is most in harmony with the ordinal information contained in the effects table? In the case of I alternatives the total number of possible permutations is equal to $I!$ Each permutation can be numbered as $p(p = 1, ..., I!)$. Each rank order from the permutations is confronted with the ordinal information contained in each of the J rows of the effects table. Kendall's rank correlation coefficient is used to compute the statistical correlation between the $I!$ rank orders and the J columns of the effects table X (Kendall, 1970). This results in $I! \times J$ rank correlation coefficients. The weighted sums of the rank correlation coefficients are used to determine the most attractive of the $I!$ permutations (Ancot, 1988).

The evamix method
The evamix method is designed to deal with an effects table containing both ordinal and quantitative criteria. The set of criteria in the effects table is divided into a set of ordinal criteria O and a set of quantitative criteria Q. A total dominance score is found by combining the indices calculated separately for the qualitative and quantitative scores. To be able to combine the indices they need to be standardized. Voogd (1983) offers various procedures for this standardization. The most straightforward standardization divides qualitative indices by the absolute value of their sum and does the same with quantitative indices. The total dominance score is calculated as the weighted sum of the qualitative and quantitative dominance scores.

Graphic evaluation
Extensive literature exists on the usefulness of graphics for presenting information (Bertin, 1981; Tufte, 1985, 1990). Some of this literature pays specific attention to the use of graphics to support decision making (DeSanctis, 1984; Janssen and van Herwijnen, 1991). Bertin (1981) defines graphic information processing as 'the use of graphics to discover relationships and patterns'. Since evaluation is essentially identical to discovering a pattern in the information on alternatives, graphics can be useful to support or even to perform evaluation. In addition, graphic communication can inform others about what has been discovered. Graphic information processing requires interactive graphic procedures that may be included in a decision support system in the same way as the previously described evaluation methods.

Sensitivity analysis
In problems where the criterion scores and priorities can be estimated with complete certainty and where all evaluation methods yield the same ranking of alternatives, this ranking is certain. In the majority of problems, however, scores and priorities are uncertain and evaluation methods involve different assumptions. Since the aim of evaluation is to provide the decision maker with the best alternative or with a ranking of alternatives, these uncertainties are only relevant in relation to their impact on the ranking. The decision maker is asked to estimate the maximum percentage that actual values may differ from the values included in the elements of the effects table or set of weights. A Monte Carlo approach generates probabilistic rankings of the alternatives which can be used to analyse the sensitivities of ranking of alternatives to overall uncertainty in both effects and priorities (Herwijnen et al., 1995).

4. Multi-criteria evaluation in a fuzzy environment

Zadeh (1965) writes: 'as the complexity of a system increases, our ability to make a precise and yet significant statement about its behaviour diminishes until a threshold is reached beyond which precision and significance (or relevance) become almost mutually exclusive characteristics'. Therefore, in these situations statements such as 'the quality of the environment is good', or 'the unemployment rate is low' are quite common. Fuzzy set theory is a mathematical theory for the modelling of such situations, in which traditional formal modelling languages which are unambiguous in their description cannot be used. Fuzzy information can be represented in decision models by using linguistic variables or by using fuzzy numbers.

In the qualitative information available for an evaluation or decision model, two different types of linguistic variables may be present:

1. The meaning can be translated into a measure on an interval or ratio scale (quantitative base variable), for example, age, distance, and so on.
2. There is no meaning on an interval or ratio scale, and therefore the base variable is also qualitative in nature, for example, appearance, comfort, beauty, and so on.

A fuzzy number is a number to which a membership function in the real line has been associated. For example, instead of the precise number 10, the fuzzy number 'approximately 10' is described by a membership distribution of possible values around the number 10.

The starting point of decision models in a fuzzy environment was the Bellman–Zadeh (1970) model. These authors assume membership functions defined on both goals and constraints, and define a decision in a fuzzy environment as 'the confluence of goals and constraints', that is, as the appropriate aggregation (intersection) of all the fuzzy sets. For an extensive overview of the classical fuzzy multi-criteria methods see Munda et al. (1994), Munda (1995) and Zimmermann (1987).

To support environmental decision making the novel approach to imprecise assessment and decision environments (NAIADE; Munda, 1995) can be considered. The evaluation table used in NAIADE may include either exact, stochastic or fuzzy measurements of the performance of an alternative. This approach is particularly suitable for economic–ecological modelling, incorporating various degrees of precision of the variables taken into consideration. The main steps of NAIADE are:

1. Pairwise comparison of alternatives according to each single criterion.
2. Aggregation of these scores in order to get an overall evaluation of the pair of alternatives according to all the criteria considered.

3.   Final ranking of alternatives in a total or partial pre-order (that is, incomparability relations are allowed).

NAIADE is based on a distance function able to tackle all the different kinds of criterion scores in an equivalent way. All the manipulation rules of the relevant information are quite technical 'approximate reasoning' operations.

In short, the main properties of the NAIADE method can be summarized as follows:

- communication with the decision maker is required to elicit different relevant parameters;
- the method is based on some aspects of the partial comparability axiom; in particular, a pairwise comparison between alternatives is carried out, and incomparability relations are allowed;
- a certain degree of compensation between criteria is allowed; given the characteristics of the method, it may be classified among partial compensatory methods.

5.   An example

A simple example is presented to illustrate the various evaluation methods. A main regional road has insufficient capacity, and as a result frequent traffic jams occur. To improve this situation three alternatives are suggested:

1.   Construction of a four-lane highway parallel to the existing road.
2.   The same as 1 but with two lanes restricted for public transport only.
3.   Construction of a train link along a different route.

The effects of these alternatives are summarized in Table 58.2.

Table 58.2   Evaluation table of a transportation problem

Criteria	Units	Alternatives		
		Highway	Road/bus	Train
Costs	10^6 gld	200	250	400
Travel time	Linguistic	Excellent	Good	Moderate
Capacity	10^6 km/year	20	30	40
NO_x emissions	Ton/year	1000	750	100
Landscape	Linguistic	Bad	Bad	Moderate

Given this decision problem, and given the evaluation methods described in the previous sections, the following approaches can be considered:

1. Quantitative multi-criteria analysis, for example, weighted summation
2. Mixed multi-criteria analysis, for example, the regime method
3. Graphic evaluation, for example, evaluation by histograms
4. Monetary evaluation, for example, cost–benefit analysis
5. Fuzzy multi-criteria evaluation, for example, the NAIADE approach.

Each of these approaches requires additional information and transformation of the available information and each of the approaches generates different types of results.

Quantitative multi-criteria analysis: weighted summation
In order that weighted summation can be applied, the criteria measured on a linguistic scale need to be transformed to a quantitative scale. This can be done by obtaining additional information. It can also be done by transforming the scores to a quantitative scale, for example to an index ranging from 1 (extremely poor) to 10 (excellent). In addition, a quantitative assessment of the criterion weights needs to be provided. If the highest priority (weight = 0.3) is given to capacity and NO_x emissions, an intermediate priority (weight = 0.2) to costs, and a low priority (weight = 0.1) to travel time and landscape, then the final ranking is as follows: Train (0.70) > Road/bus (0.41) > Highway (0.31). The values in parentheses indicate the relative performance of each alternative.

Sensitivity analysis
It is useful to test how sensitive this ranking is to uncertainties in the effect scores. The decision maker estimates that the scores of the criteria costs, capacity and NO_x emissions, may be 25 per cent higher or lower than the scores as included in the evaluation table. Although the information level of ordinal information is low, their certainty is usually high. It is therefore assumed in this example that the preference order of the linguistic variables is certain. Sensitivity analysis shows that under these uncertainties there is a 99 per cent probability that Train is the most preferred alternative.

Mixed multi-criteria analysis: the regime method
Using the regime method, the linguistic scale is interpreted as an ordinal scale. For example; excellent, good and moderate are translated into rank numbers 1, 2 and 3. In this case it is sufficient to determine that capacity and NO_x emissions are considered the most important criteria, followed by costs, and then by travel time and landscape as the least important criteria.

As an intermediate step the regime method generates information that shows for each pair of alternatives the probability that one alternative is better than the other. When all scores are quantitative all probabilities are either 1.00 or 0.00. In the case of qualitative criteria, values are in between these extremes. The degree to which they differ from 1.00 and 0.00 can be interpreted as the uncertainty resulting from the use of a qualitative measurement scale. Table 58.3 shows the pairwise probabilities for the transportation example. The value 1.00 in the comparison between Train and Highway alternatives indicates that, for all quantitative values that comply with the linguistic ordering of travel time and landscape in Table 58.1, the Train alternative ranks above the Highway alternative. For this comparison, therefore, no added value is to be expected from measurement of these criteria on a higher measurement scale. The probability that, given the qualitative information on travel time and landscape, the Road/bus alternative ranks higher than the Highway alternative equals 92 per cent. The overall score of an alternative is calculated as the row average of the relative success indices. The final ranking is Train (1.00) > Road/bus (0.46) > Highway (0.04).

Table 58.3 Pairwise probabilities

	Highway	Road/bus	Train	Total
Highway	–	0.08	0.00	0.04
Road/bus	0.92	–	0.00	0.46
Train	1.00	1.00	–	1.00

Graphic evaluation: evaluation by histograms
One example of graphic presentation of the evaluation table (Table 58.2) is shown in Figure 58.2. To produce this presentation the scores for each criterion in the evaluation table are first standardized between zero (the worst alternative) and one (the best alternative). For each criterion the highest bar represents the most preferred alternative and an empty box the least preferred. In Figure 58.3 the rows of criteria are ordered in such a way that the criteria are shown in descending order of priority. Next the alternatives are ranked visually by exchanging columns until the shaded area in the upper left corner is maximized. All information is shown simultaneously in Figure 58.3: the ranking of the alternatives (the ranking of the columns), the priorities given to the criteria (the ranking of the rows) and the relative performance of the alternatives for all criteria (the size of the bars).

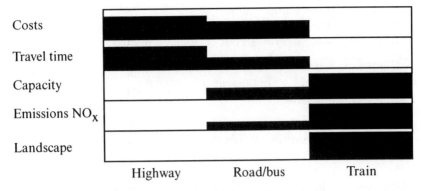

Figure 58.2   A visual representation of the evaluation table

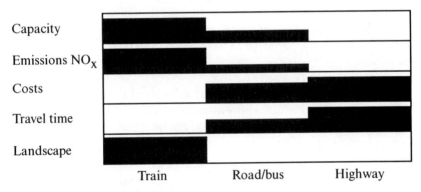

Figure 58.3   A ranked visual representation of the evaluation table

Monetary evaluation: cost–benefit analysis

Cost–benefit analysis requires valuation of all effects (see also Chapter 57 by Hanley in this book). If travel time were scored in minutes it could under certain assumptions be valued according to average production or wage losses. It is, however, not possible to value the linguistic scores. NO_x emissions could be valued according to expected damage. The same holds for capacity which could be valued in relation to possible contribution to economic development. It should be concluded, therefore, that without additional assumptions and research cost–benefit analysis is not feasible.

Fuzzy evaluation: the NAIADE approach

By applying NAIADE, the linguistic scale is represented by means of linguistic variables. For each pair of actions, the following linguistic evaluations are obtained:

Highway is better than Road/bus	$t = 0$
Highway and road/bus are indifferent	$t = 0$
Highway is worse than Road/bus	$t = 0.57$
Highway is better than Train	$t = 0.67$
Highway and Train are indifferent	$t = 0$
Highway is worse than Train	$t = 1$
Road/bus is better than Train	$t = 0.53$
Road/bus and Train are indifferent	$t = 0$
Road/bus is worse than Train	$t = 1$

These numbers indicate the credibility of each assertion of the pairwise comparison. These pairwise comparisons are combined into the following ranking (see Munda, 1995, for technical details):

- the train option is preferred to the road/bus and highway alternatives;
- the road/bus is preferred to the highway option.

6. Conclusions
In this concluding section cost–benefit analysis and multi-criteria analysis are compared on (i) the rationality assumed, (ii) the preference system used and (iii) the way sustainability conditions can be included (see also Janssen, 1992; Munda et al., 1995).

Rationality assumed
Cost–benefit analysis essentially follows the priorities of the market, in which prices are derived directly or indirectly from market prices or are assessed from the willingness of individuals to pay (contingent valuation). To maximize economic efficiency is the central policy objective. Multi-criteria methods revolve around preferences of decision makers. These methods try to consider simultaneously many conflicting criteria. Efficiency is not considered the only aim of the analysis but many different conflictual heterogeneous points of view are considered.

Information
In most environmental decision processes the information to be processed is extensive. This may result in information overload of the decision maker and creates a need for decision support. Using valuation methods to price environmental effects involves large research efforts and often does not succeed in adequately pricing all environmental effects. Many environmental problems involve a mixture of quantitative and qualitative information. This information is often uncertain and in

many cases probability information is not available (Janssen, 1992). This suggests the use of multi-criteria methods and fuzzy evaluation methods.

Preference system and democratic basis
In cost–benefit analysis votes are expressed on the market. The distribution of income is accepted as a means to allocate votes. Multi-criteria evaluation is based on the priorities of decision makers. The way these decision makers have reached their positions is accepted as a way of allocating the right to express these priorities.

Sustainability
Cost–benefit analysis assumes substitution between man-made capital and natural capital. If substitution is not possible, for example, if irreversible effects occur, cost–benefit analysis will lead to unsustainable solutions. In multi-criteria evaluation weak or strong sustainability concepts can be operationalized in the aggregation procedure.

References

Ancot, J.P. (1988), *Micro-Qualiflex; an Interactive Software Package for the Determination and Analysis of the Optimal Solution to Decision Problems*, Dordrecht: Kluwer Academic Publishers.

Bellman, R.E. and L.A. Zadeh (1970), 'Decision-making in a fuzzy environment', *Management Science*, 17, 141–64.

Bertin, J. (1981), *Graphics and Graphic Information Processing*, Berlin: Walter de Gruyter.

Bonte, R.J., J. van den Bergh, R. Janssen, R.H.J. Mooren and J.Th. de Smidt (1997), *Notitie over multi-criteria analyse in milieu-effectrapportage. Commissie voor de milieu-effect rapportage*, Utrecht: Commissie voor de milieueffect rapportage.

DeSanctis, G. (1984), 'Computer graphics as decision aids: directions for research', *Decision Sciences*, 15 (4), 463–87.

Faucheux, S. and M. O'Connor (eds) (1997), *Valuation for Sustainable Development: Methods and Policy Indicators*, Cheltenham, UK and Lyme, US: Edward Elgar.

French, S. (1988), *Decision Theory: an Introduction to the Mathematics of Rationality*, Chichester, UK: Ellis Horwood.

Herwijnen, M. van, P. Rietveld, K. Thevenet and R. Tol (1995), 'Sensitivity analysis with interdependent criteria for multi criteria decision making', *Multi Criteria Decision Making*, 4 (1), 57–70.

Janssen, R. (1992), *Multiobjective Decision Support for Environmental Management*, Dordrecht: Kluwer Academic Publishers.

Janssen, R. and M. van Herwijnen (1991), 'Graphical decision support applied to decisions changing the use of agricultural land', in P. Korhonen, A. Lewandowski and J. Wallenius (eds), *Multiple Criteria Decision Making*, Berlin: Springer, pp. 293–302.

Janssen, R., M. van Herwijnen and E. Beinat (1999), *DEFINITE for Windows. A system to support decisions on a finite set of alternatives (Software package and user manual)*, Amsterdam – Institute for Environmental Studies (IVM), Vrije Universiteit.

Keeney, R.L. and H. Raiffa (1976), *Decisions with Multiple Objectives: Preferences and Value Trade-offs*, New York: Wiley.

Kendall, M.G. (1970), *Rank Correlation Methods*, London: Griffin.

Munda, G. (1995), *Multicriteria Evaluation in a Fuzzy Environment. Theory and Applications in Ecological Economics*. Heidelberg: Physica-Verlag.

Munda, G., P. Nijkamp and P. Rietveld (1994), 'Qualitative multicriteria evaluation for environmental management', *Ecological Economics*, **10**, 97–112.

Munda, G., P. Nijkamp and P. Rietveld (1995), 'Monetary and non-monetary evaluation methods in sustainable development planning', *Economie Appliquée*, **48** (2), 145–62

Nijkamp, P., P. Rietveld and H. Voogd (1990), *Multicriteria Evaluation in Physical Planning*, Amsterdam: North-Holland.

Paruccini, M. (ed.) (1994), *Applying Multiple Criteria Aid for Decision to Environmental Management*, Dordrecht: Kluwer.

Roy, B. (1985),*Methodologie multicritère d'Aide à la Décision*, Paris: Economica.

Saaty, T.L. (1980), *The Analytical Hierarchy Process*, New York: McGraw-Hill.

Steuer, R.E. (1986), *Multiple Criteria Optimization: Theory, Computation and Application*, New York: Wiley.

Tufte, E.R. (1985), *The Visual Display of Quantitative Information*, Cheshire, CT: Graphics Press.

Tufte, E.R. (1990), *Envisioning Information*, Cheshire, CT: Graphics Press.

Voogd, H. (1983), *Multicriteria Evaluation for Urban and Regional Planning*, London: Pion.

Zadeh, L.A. (1965), 'Fuzzy sets', *Information and Control*, **8**,338–53.

Zimmermann, H.J. (1987), *Fuzzy Sets, Decision Making, and Expert Systems*, Dordrecht: Kluwer.

PART VIII

INTERDISCIPLINARY
ISSUES

59 Physical principles and environmental economic analysis
Matthias Ruth

1. Introduction

Advancements in the physical sciences have significantly influenced the history of economic thought (Mirowski, 1989). The fathers of the marginalist revolution have been intrigued by the predictive capacity of physics, and have imitated physics through the development of analogies between economic and physical concepts and processes. Examples include the identification of pleasure, or utility, with energy (Edgeworth, 1881; Fisher, 1892), and comparisons of the equality of the ratios of marginal utility of two goods and their inverted trading ratio to the law of the lever (Jevons, 1970). Following these analogies, certain aspects of production, consumption and exchange were translated into functional forms that had previously been analysed in the physical and engineering sciences (Proops, 1985). With the general acceptance of physical concepts in economic theory came an application of mathematical tools developed in classical mechanics for the analysis of economic processes.

More recently, physical principles have been revisited in an attempt to better understand the nature of economic production and consumption processes and to link these processes to changes in environmental quality (Georgescu-Roegen, 1971; Ayres, 1978; Daly and Umaña, 1981; Faber et al., 1987). These attempts have been spurred both by developments in the physical sciences and the growing dissatisfaction among economists with the treatment of natural resources and the environment in economic models (Boulding, 1981). The physical concepts on which much of recent analyses draw include the laws of conservation of mass and of energy, and the second law of thermodynamics. Each of those laws are discussed briefly in the next section. The remainder of this chapter then outlines in more detail how these laws have made inroads into environmental economic analysis and concludes with comments on recent trends and prospects for future research.

2. Physical principles

The first law of thermodynamics comprises the laws of conservation of mass and energy. Although mass and energy are, according to relativity theory, equivalent, practical applications of the first law deal with mass and energy separately. Mass and energy balances are established in which the outputs of mass and energy from a system are accounted for by inputs and changes in storage. The mass-balance principle helps establish material use and pollution accounts for the economy. In such accounts, the quantity and composition of waste streams, though often unknown, can be deduced by subtracting the mass of desired outputs and storage from the known inputs into a system. The energy-balance principle provides the basis for the calculation of direct and indirect energy requirements for the production of desired products in an economy and ecosystems.

The second law of thermodynamics – the entropy law – deals with the qualitative changes in materials and energy as a process occurs. To calculate system change, a reference environment is defined. The choice of the reference environment can only be made on the basis of first principles in the context of statistical and quantum mechanics (Månsson, 1991). For many practical applications, the reference environment is an idealized system with material composition, pressure and temperature equal to some average of the Earth's crust, atmosphere or oceans (Ahrendts, 1980).

A key concept for second-law analysis of a system is the change in entropy. Entropy is a non-decreasing function that measures the distance of a system from equilibrium with its reference environment. The differences, for example, in pressure, temperature or material composition that exist between a system and its reference environment enable the system to do useful work. Systems with low entropy are highly distinguishable from their reference environment. Increases in entropy are concomitant with a decrease in the physical or chemical gradients between the system and its reference environment. In the absence of an influx of low entropy into a system, the physical and chemical gradients are irreversibly diminished as physical and chemical processes occur, and the potential to do work in the future is reduced.

The continued influx of low entropy into the economy–environment system in the form of solar radiation can help re-establish the gradients that are removed, for example, as metal ores are mined, processed and ultimately discarded, or as fossil fuels are extracted and burned. For example, biogeochemical cycles, driven by the influx of low-entropy solar radiation, continue to contribute to the formation of resource endowments. Biological processes, in particular, help capture that influx through photosynthetic activity. This influx of low entropy establishes an upper bound for all processes on Earth.

For practical applications of the entropy law, the maximum useful work that can be done by a system as it moves from some initial to a final state is calculated. That maximum useful work is called exergy. Given the reference environment, the exergy A of an input into or output from the system of interest is defined as

$$A = \left(E - T_0 S + P_0 V - \sum_{i=1}^{n} N_i \mu_{0i} \right)$$

with E as internal energy, T_0 as the temperature of the reference environment, S as entropy, P_0 as pressure of the reference environment, and N_i as the number of molecules which have in the reference environment chemical potentials μ_{0i} (Gagglioli, 1980; Howell and Buckius, 1992). The exergy is thus the maximum useful work that can be done as the conditions of the reference environment are approached.

Exergy analyses have been developed into powerful means for evaluating engineering systems and identifying potentials for efficiency improvements (Gyftopoulos et al., 1974; Szargut et al., 1988). Together with mass balances, exergy analyses provide a basis to link economic processes with changes in environmental quality irrespective of whether markets are present to establish that link in monetary terms.

3.   The laws of thermodynamics in environmental economic analysis

Analysis of production processes
It is the goal of a production process to change materials from a less desired to a more desired form. Finely distributed pigments are assembled in a highly organized form to establish the text you are reading. Perfumes and paints are mixed and dispersed to create olfactory and optical sensations. In all these cases, energy is required to bring about a change in the thermodynamic state of materials. Since all natural processes occur with an irreversible degradation of exergy, waste is generated and ultimately released into the environment.

Four interrelated aspects of the production process need to be considered if its analysis is to be complete. First, all material and energy flows need to be identified irrespective of whether they are priced or not. Mass and energy balances help identify flows that are typically not accounted for in economic analyses of production processes, and they help trace waste products across the economy–environment boundary. Second, various inputs and outputs can be substituted for each other to generate a constant amount of the desired product. The extent to which this substitution is possible is reflected in the properties of a production function. Third, changes in the quality of material and energy inputs are expressed by changes in their thermodynamic potential. The second law of thermodynamics captures these qualitative changes. The fourth aspect of a production process relevant for its complete description is the effect it has on the environment.

The first of these aspects of a production process has been discussed above. The second and third are the topic of this section. How an assessment of environmental effects can be achieved is discussed below.

Thermodynamic constraints have not yet found widespread application in economic models of production and consumption. Such constraints limit the substitutability of material and energy inputs in economic processes (Berry et al., 1978; Lesourd, 1985; Anderson, 1987; van den Bergh and Nijkamp, 1994). For example, determination of an isoquant based on the observations Q_1, Q_2, Q_3, and statistical criteria may lead to a production function corresponding to the line $Q'Q'$ in Figure 59.1. However, engineering information tells us that there are lower bounds on material and energy use (M^* and E^* respectively) in a given process that produces a given flow of output. These bounds may be derived with equilibrium thermodynamics or, more meaningfully, with finite-time thermodynamics (Andresen, 1983; Andresen et al., 1984). In any event, one can hypothesize the existence of points Q_4 and Q_5 above and to the right of the asymptotes M^* and E^*. These points above and to the right of the asymptotes are characterized by material and energy inputs that exceed those in the

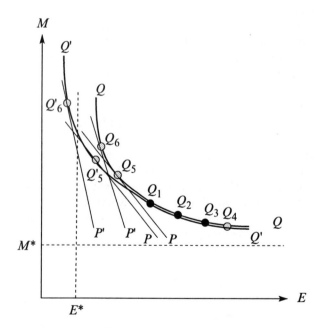

Figure 59.1   Isoquant with thermodynamic limits on material and energy use

thermodynamic ideal. As a result of using more than the thermodynamic minimum, waste materials and waste heat are generated.

In contrast to points above and to the right of the asymptotes M^* and E^*, the point Q'_6 for example, is physically infeasible and can never be observed. It would require that less energy is used in the process than is necessary – according to the laws of thermodynamics – to perform that particular process. Q'_6 violates thermodynamic laws. Consequently, the representation of a production process that obeys the second law of thermodynamics must be constrained by the asymptotes M^* and E^*, and thus must follow isoquants of the type QQ (Berry and Andresen, 1982; Ruth, 1993).

Given a relative price P of materials and energy, different optimal combinations (Q_5 and Q'_5) of material and energy inputs are chosen if thermodynamic limits are disregarded. Even, the physically infeasible input combination Q'_6 may be identified as a goal, if relative prices are expected to change to P' and if thermodynamic information is ignored.

The presence of lower limits on material and energy use has implications for the extent to which technical change can overcome material and energy requirements in production processes. Isoquants can shift downward and to the left up to the point where they approach the thermodynamic limits (M^*, E^*), but cannot pass these asymptotes. Movement towards the asymptotes M^* and E^* may occur by acquiring increasing knowledge about the production process (Ruth and Bullard, 1993) and by reducing the speed at which the process occurs (Spreng, 1993). For example, learning curves must exhibit asymptotes for unit costs, such as material use M^* per unit output flow Y, and energy use E^* per unit output flow Y (Chapman and Roberts, 1983; Ruth, 1995). Given such asymptotes and observations R_1, R_2, R_3, a physically meaningful learning curve (Figure 59.2) must be of the form SS, not SS'.

Inclusion of the thermodynamic limits on material and energy use in the description of production processes is the more relevant the closer the production processes are to those limits (Anderson, 1987). Recognizing these limits is important even in the case where actual production is far from the thermodynamic ideal, because these limits define the technically feasible realm over which efficiency improvements can take place.

Analysis of economy–environment interactions
The laws of thermodynamics provide the physical limits on production, consumption and exchange processes, and link – through mass- and energy-balance equations – economic processes to changes in environmental quality. The linkages between resource extraction, production of goods and services and release of waste into the environment have been

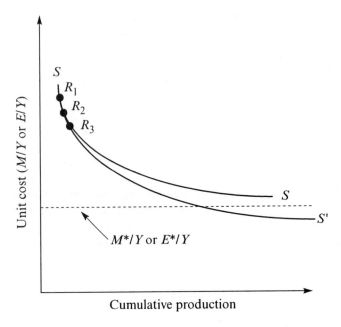

Figure 59.2   Learning curve with thermodynamic limits on unit cost

extensively explored within the framework of input–output analysis (Cumberland, 1966; Leontief, 1970). In input–output approaches the environment is treated similarly to other sectors of the economy, supplying and receiving flows of materials and energy. Early approaches were based on mass balances to establish inter-industry and economy–environment interactions (Ayres and Kneese, 1969; Converse, 1971; Victor, 1972). Subsequently, energy balances were used to calculate the direct and indirect energy embodied in the output of an economic sector (Bullard and Herendeen, 1975). Towards that end, two groups of industries are distinguished. One group consists of m industries extracting energy of type i from their environment. The amount of energy of type i extracted by industry j is E_{ij}. The second group of industries includes those whose output is a non-energy good or service. Thus, if there are no secondary products, $E_{ij} = 0$ unless $i = j$, which implies that industry j is an energy-producing industry. To quantify the energy flows associated with the production of non-energy goods or services, energy intensities ϵ_{ij} are calculated for the energy of type i embodied in the output of sector j. Denoting X_{ij} as the units of good or service i absorbed per unit of output of good or service j and X_j as total output of good j, then the energy-balance equation for the ith energy type in the jth industry is defined as

$$\sum_{k=1}^{n} \epsilon_{ik}X_{ij} + E_{ij} = \epsilon_{ik}X_j, j = 1, ..., n, \text{ and } i = 1, ..., m$$

assuming that there are no secondary products and that the economy consists of a total of n industries out of which m industries extract energy (Casler and Wilbur, 1984).

Solving the system of n energy-balance equations for the economy enables identification of the total energy requirements by fuel type that are necessary for an expansion of the production of a particular good (Bullard et al., 1978; Hannon et al., 1981). Applications of energy input–output analysis and energy intensities range from energy aspects of material recycling (Hannon, 1973) to analyses of the energy efficiency of production processes (Joyce, 1978; Gunn, 1978) and alternative sources for energy supply (Hannon and Perez-Blanco, 1979; Herendeen and Plant, 1981). With notable exceptions (Johnson and Bennet, 1981; Duchin and Lange, 1994), input–output studies of economy–environment interactions have typically been based on assumptions of linearities in the economy and the environment, and have been carried out as comparative static analyses. Besides dealing with non-linearities and dynamics, applications to the combined economy–environment system also make it necessary that input–output models properly capture joint production and measure the multitude of goods and services in units that are appropriate for the respective flows, not just simply either monetary, mass or energy units (Costanza and Hannon, 1989).

Analysis of the long-term potential for economic growth and development
The role of materials and energy for economic growth, development and environmental change is being assessed in the light of the laws of thermodynamics from both a theoretical and an empirical perspective. Implications that thermodynamic constraints have for growth and development have been hotly discussed under the heading of steady-state economics (Georgescu-Roegen, 1982; Young, 1991; Daly, 1992a), and their consequences for the design of human institutions are part of ongoing debate (Daly and Cobb, 1994).

The steady-state view posits that a growing economy increases its material and energy use and thus decreases its potential for future growth to the extent that exergy is degraded faster than it is restored through the influx of low entropy into the economy–environment system (Georgescu-Roegen, 1971, 1977). Economic development, in contrast to growth, does not require that the material and energy flows through the economy increase. Rather, exergy is used to generate information, order and knowledge embodied in humans, capital goods and institutions to offset exergy degradation and to enable the economy to continue to improve the welfare of its members (Daly, 1992b). The extent to which exergy degradation takes place can be used to judge the desirability of alternative production, consumption and exchange processes.

Support for the view that the economy can develop, though not grow, if it is bound by a fixed exergy flow comes from various economic growth models that incorporate physical principles. For example, optimal growth models based on production functions that are consistent with the laws of conservation of mass and energy, and based on the assumption of a finite influx of a renewable resource (exergy), show that an optimal path leads to a stationary state in which resource inputs are not necessarily maximum (Eriksson et al., 1984; Månsson, 1986). Similarly, variants of the von Neumann–Leontief–Sraffa classical general equilibrium model with a jointly determined economy–environment system subject to a conservation of mass constraint demonstrate that the conservation of mass contradicts the free disposal, free gifts, and non-innovation assumptions of such models (Perrings, 1986). Accounting for the conservation of mass destroys the determinacy of the closed, time-variant system in the classical model. An expanding economy causes continuous disequilibrating change in the environment. Since market prices in an interdependent economy–environment system often do not accurately reflect environmental change, such transformations of the environment will often go unnoticed.

4.   Recent trends and prospects for future research
The application of physical principles in environmental economic analysis is currently pursued in at least the following four main directions. First, the laws of thermodynamics highlight the fact that the generation of waste from production and consumption processes can be significantly reduced, though never avoided. To reduce environmental impact of waste requires that firms close material cycles and improve their energy efficiencies. The disciplines of industrial metabolism and industrial ecology attend to these issues with a focus on the product, process and company level (Socolow et al., 1994; Allenby and Richards, 1994; Jelinski et al., 1992; Frosch, 1994; Warnick and Ausubel, 1995).

Second, dynamic, multisector models are developed to trace material cycles and energy flows through the combined economy–environment system to identify upper limits for savings in exergy in the light of endogenous technical change and time lags in the availability of improved technologies (Cleveland and Ruth, 1996; Ruth and Hannon, 1997). These models capture non-linear feedback among system components, rather than restrict analysis to the equilibrium domain or presume linear representations of economic and ecosystem processes. As changes in environmental quality and waste absorption capacities are increasingly taken into account by these models, their ability to reflect complex economy–environment interaction is enhanced. By making economic and environmental processes subject to the same laws and by representing their interactions in physical rather than merely monetary units, the consistency of environmental policies such as pollution taxes and subsidies with the goals of these policies can be assessed (Amir, 1987, 1990).

Third, the exergy concept begins to crystallize as a general measure of the quality of resource flows and reserves, and an indicator of the potential for harm of waste residuals (Ruth and Bullard, 1993; Ayres, 1994; Ayres et al., 1996). The exergy of materials and fuels used by the economy and of the reserves that are at the economy's disposition indicates the maximum useful work that can be done by the economy. The exergy of the waste stream is a measure of its quality and ability to affect physical, chemical and biological processes in the environment. High-exergy waste flows have a high ability to trigger environmental change. Waste flows of zero exergy have a material composition, temperature and pressure that are indistinguishable from the reference environment, and as a result have limited effect on environmental processes if the properties of the ecosystem into which they are released are similar to those of the reference environment. Problems arise in interpreting exergy values of waste streams if the exergy of material flows is dwarfed by the exergy of fuels or solar radiation, and the generalizability of results is impaired by the fact that persistence and eco-toxicity of pollutants are different between different ecosystems. Ongoing research attempts to address these issues (Jørgensen, 1992; Schneider and Kay, 1993, 1994).

Fourth, the relevance of economy–environment interactions for economic growth and development, and the limits to substitution at the level of production processes have prompted inquiries into the substitutability of environmental goods and services by economic goods and services at the local, regional and global scales (Costanza and Daly, 1992). To assess the degree at which human-made capital goods can substitute for environmental resources and waste absorption requires an understanding of the environment's contribution to economic systems and of the resilience of ecosystems and their regenerative capacity. The physical principles that govern all natural processes are but one part in the generation of that understanding.

References

Ahrendts, J. (1980), 'Reference states', *Energy*, 5, 667–77.
Allenby, B.R. and D.J. Richards (eds) (1994), *The Greening of Industrial Systems*, Washington, DC: National Academy Press.

Amir, S. (1987), 'Energy pricing, biomass accumulation, and project appraisal: a thermodynamic approach to the economics of ecosystem management', in G. Pillet (ed.), *Environmental Economics: The Analysis of a Major Interface*, Geneva: R. Leimgruber, pp. 53–108.

Amir, S. (1990), The use of ecological prices and system-wide indicators derived therefrom to quantify man's impact on the ecosystem', *Ecological Economics*, **1**, 203–31.

Anderson, C.L. (1987), 'The production process: inputs and wastes', *Journal of Environmental Economics and Management*, **14**, 1–12.

Andresen, B. (1983), *Finite-Time Thermodynamics*, Ph.D., University of Copenhagen, Sweden.

Andresen, B., P. Salamon and R.S. Berry (1984), 'Thermodynamics in finite time', *Physics Today*, **9**, 62–70.

Ayres, R.U. (1978), *Resources, Environment, and Economics: Applications of the Materials/Energy Balance Principle*, New York: John Wiley and Sons.

Ayres, R.U. (1994), *Information, Entropy, and Progress: A New Evolutionary Paradigm*, New York: American Institute of Physics.

Ayres, R. and A. Kneese (1969), 'Production, consumption, and externalities', *American Economic Review*, **59**, 282–97.

Ayres, R.U., L.W. Ayres and K. Martiñas (1996), *Eco-thermodynamics: Exergy and Life Cycle Analysis*, Working Paper no. 96/04/, INSEAD, Centre for the Management of Environmental Resources.

Bergh, J.C.J.M. van den and P. Nijkamp (1994), 'Dynamic macro modelling and materials balance', *Economic Modelling*, **11**, 283–307.

Berry, R.S. and B. Andresen (1982), 'Thermodynamic constraints in economic analysis, in W.C. Schieve and P.M. Allen (eds), *Self Organization and Dissipative Structures: Applications in the Physical and Social Sciences*, Austin: University of Texas Press.

Berry, S.R., P. Salamon and G. Heal (1978), 'On a relation between economic and thermodynamic optima', *Resources and Energy*, **1**, 125–37.

Boulding, K. (1981), *Evolutionary Economics*, Beverly Hills, CA: Sage Publications.

Bullard, C.W. and R. Herendeen (1975), 'Energy impact of consumption decisions', *Institute of Electrical and Electronic Engineers*, **63**, 484–93.

Bullard, C.W., P.S. Penner and D.A. Pilati (1978), *Net Energy Analysis: a Handbook for Combining Process and Input–Output Analysis*, vol. 1, pp. 267–313.

Casler, S. and S. Wilbur (1984), 'Energy input–output analysis: a simple guide', *Resources and Energy*, **6**, 187–201.

Chapman, P.F. and F. Roberts (1983), *Metal Resources and Energy*, London: Butterworths.

Cleveland, C.J. and M. Ruth (1996), 'Interconnections between the depletion of minerals and fuels: the case of copper production in the U.S.', *Energy Sources*, **18**, 355–73.

Converse, A.O. (1971), 'On the extension of input–output analysis to account for environmental externalities', *American Economic Review*, **61**, 197–8.

Costanza, R. and H.E. Daly (1992), 'Natural capital and sustainable development', *Conservation Biology*, **6**, 37–46.

Costanza, R. and B. Hannon (1989), 'Dealing with the "mixed units" problem in ecosystem network analysis', in F. Wulff, J.G. Field and K.H. Mann (eds), *Network Analysis in Marine Ecology: Methods and Applications*, Berlin: Springer-Verlag, pp. 90–115.

Cumberland, J.H. (1966), 'A regional interindustry model for the analysis of development objectives', *The Regional Science Association Papers*, **17**, 65–94.

Daly, H.E. (1992a), 'Is the entropy law relevant to the economics of natural resource scarcity? – Yes, of course it is', *Journal of Environmental Economics and Management*, **23**, 91–5.

Daly, H.E. (1992b), 'Steady-state economics: concepts, questions, policies', *Gaia*, no. 6, 333–8.

Daly, H.E. and J.B. Cobb (1994), *For the Common Good*, Boston, MA: Beacon Press.

Daly, H.E. and A.F. Umaña (eds), (1981), *Energy, Economics, and the Environment: Conflicting Views of an Essential Interrelationship*, Washington, DC: American Association for the Advancement of Science.

Duchin, F. and G.-M. Lange (1994), *The Future of the Environment: Ecological Economics and Technological Change*, New York: Oxford University Press.

Edgeworth, F.Y. (1881), *Mathematical Physics*, London: Kegan Paul.

Eriksson, K.-E., S. Islam and B. Månsson (1984), 'Development of an economy with a bounded inflow of one essential resource input', *Resources and Energy*, **6**, 235–58.

Faber, M., H. Niemes and G. Stephan (1987), *Entropy, Environment and Resources*, Berlin: Springer-Verlag.

Fisher, I. (1892), 'Mathematical investigations of the theory of values and prices', *Transactions of the Connecticut Academy of Arts and Sciences*, **9**, 11–26.

Frosch, R.A. (1994), 'Industrial ecology: minimizing the impact of industrial waste', *Physics Today*, November, 63–8.

Gagglioli, R.A. (ed.) (1980), *Thermodynamics: Second Law Analysis*, Washington, DC: American Chemical Society.

Georgescu-Roegen, N. (1971), *The Entropy Law and the Economic Process*, Cambridge, MA: Harvard University Press.

Georgescu-Roegen, N. (1977), 'The steady-state and ecological salvation: a thermodynamic analysis', *BioScience*, **27**, 266–70.

Georgescu-Roegen, N. (1982), 'Energetic dogma, energetic economics, and viable technologies', *Advances in Economics of Energy and Resources*, **4**, 1–39.

Gunn, T.L. (1978), *The Energy Optimal Use of Waste Paper* (Document no. 263), Energy Research Group, Office of Vice Chancellor of Research, University of Illinois at Urbana–Champaign, IL.

Gyftopoulos, E.P., L.J. Lazaridis and T.F. Widmer (1974), *Potential Fuel Effectiveness in Industry*, Cambridge, MA: Ballinger Publishing Company.

Hannon, B. (1973), 'An energy standard of value', *The Annals of the American Academy of Political and Social Science*, **410**, 130–53.

Hannon, B. and H. Perez-Blanco (1979), *Ethanol and Methanol as Industrial Feedstocks* (Document no. 268), Energy Research Group, Office of Vice Chancellor of Research, University of Illinois at Urbana–Champaign, IL.

Hannon, B., R. Herendeen and T. Blazek (1981), *Energy and Labor Intensities for 1972* (Document no. 307), Energy Research Group, Office of Vice Chancellor of Research, University of Illinois at Urbana–Champaign, IL.

Herendeen, R. and R. Plant (1981), 'Energy analysis of four geothermal technologies', *Energy*, **6**, 73–82.

Howell, J.R. and R.O. Buckius (1992), *Fundamentals of Engineering Thermodynamics*, New York: McGraw-Hill.

Jelinski, L.W., T.E. Graedel, R.A. Laudise, D.W. McCall, and C.K.N. Patel (1992), 'Industrial ecology: concepts and approaches', *Proceedings of the National Academy of Sciences*, **89**, 793–7.

Jevons, W.S. (1970), *The Theory of Political Economy*, Baltimore, MD: Penguin.

Johnson, M.H. and J.T. Bennett (1981), 'Regional environmental and economic impact evaluation: an input–output approach', *Regional Science and Urban Economics*, **11**, 215–30.

Jørgensen, S.-E. (1992), *Integration of Ecosystem Theories: A Pattern*, Dordrecht: Kluwer Academic Publishers.

Joyce, J. (1978), *Energy Conservation Through Industrial Cogeneration* (Document no. 259), Energy Research Group, Office of Vice Chancellor of Research, University of Illinois at Urbana–Champaign, IL.

Leontief, W.W. (1970), 'Environmental repercussions and the economic structure: an input–output approach', in S. Tsuru (ed.), *A Challenge to Social Scientists*, Tokyo: Asahi, pp. 114–34.

Lesourd, J.B. (1985), 'Energy and resources as production factors in process industries', *Energy Economics*, **7**, 138–44.

Månsson, B.Å.G. (1986), 'Optimal development with flow-based production', *Resources and Energy*, **8**, 109–31.

Månsson, B.Å.G. (1991), 'Fundamental problems with energy theories of value', in L.O. Hansson and B. Jungen (eds), *Human Responsibility and Global Change*, Proceedings of the International Conference in Göteborg, 9–14 June, University of Göteborg, Section of Human Ecology, Göteborg, Sweden, pp. 197–206.

Mirowski, P. (1989), *More Heat than Light: Economics as Social Physics*, Cambridge, UK: Cambridge University Press.

Perrings, C. (1986), 'Conservation of mass and instability in a dynamic economy–environment system', *Journal of Environmental Economics and Management*, **13**, 199–211.

Proops, J.L.R. (1985), 'Thermodynamics and economics: from analogy to physical functioning', in W. v. Gool and J. Bruggink (eds), *Energy and Time in Economics and Physical Sciences*, Amsterdam: North-Holland/Elsevier pp.155–74.

Ruth, M. (1993), *Integrating Economics, Ecology and Thermodynamics*, Dordrecht: Kluwer Academic Publishers.

Ruth, M. (1995), 'Thermodynamic implications for natural resource extraction and technical change in U.S. copper mining', *Environmental and Resource Economics*, **6**, 187–206.

Ruth, M. and C.W. Bullard (1993), 'Information, production and utility', *Energy Policy*, **21**, 1059–67.

Ruth, M. and B. Hannon (1997), *Modeling Dynamic Economic Systems*, New York: Springer-Verlag.

Schneider, E.D. and J.J. Kay (1993), 'Energy degradation, thermodynamics, and the development of ecosystems', *Proceedings of the International Conference on Energy Systems and Ecology*, The American Society of Mechanical Engineers, Advanced Energy Systems, Krakow, Poland.

Schneider, E.D. and J.J. Kay (1994), 'Life as a manifestation of the second law of thermodynamics', *Mathematical and Computer Modelling*, **19**, 25–48.

Socolow, R., C. Andrews, F. Berkhout and V. Thomas (eds) (1994), *Industrial Ecology and Global Change*, Cambridge, UK: Cambridge University Press.

Spreng, D.T. (1993), 'Possibilities for substitution between energy, time and information', *Energy Policy*, **21**, 13–23.

Szargut, J., D.R. Morris and F.R. Steward (1988), *Exergy Analysis of Thermal Chemical and Metallurgical Processes*, New York: Hemisphere Publishing Corporation.

Victor, P.A. (1972), *Pollution: Economy and Environment*, London: Allen and Unwin.

Warnick, I.K. and J.H. Ausubel (1995), 'National material metrics for industrial ecology', *Resources Policy*, **21**, 189–98.

Young, J.T. (1991), 'Is the entropy law relevant to the economics of natural resource scarcity?', *Journal of Environmental Economics and Management*, **21**, 167–79.

60 Materials, economics and the environment
Robert U. Ayres

1. Introduction: the first and second laws of thermodynamics

The laws of physics most constraining to technology (and therefore to economics) are the first and second laws of thermodynamics. The first law of thermodynamics is the law of conservation of mass/energy. Since mass and energy are equivalent (Einstein's equation), this law actually implies that mass and energy are *separately* conserved in every process or transformation except nuclear fission or fusion. Putting it another way, any physical process or transformation that violates this condition is impossible. Something cannot be created from nothing.[1]

This law has surprisingly non-trivial consequences for neoclassical economics. Contrary to the more superficial versions of standard theory, where goods and services are mere abstractions, production of material goods from real raw materials inevitably results in the creation of waste residuals, including waste energy. In other words, 'consumption' is a metaphor insofar as goods other than food or drink are concerned. (Even the consumption of food and drink generates waste effluents, or course.)

The second law of thermodynamics is, in some respects, the more fundamental of the two laws. Its precise statement need not concern us here. (See Chapter 59 in this handbook.) However, roughly speaking, the second law reflects the fact that most physical processes are irreversible in the sense that systems tend towards physical and chemical equilibrium. Differences and gradients tend to be reduced and smoothed out over time. This tendency is reflected in the existence of a function, called entropy. Entropy increases in every real process, and reaches a maximum only when the system reaches final equilibrium with its surroundings. Final equilibrium is a state in which every reaction that can occur has occurred and 'nothing happens, or can happen'.

A further consequences of the second law of thermodynamics – the so-called entropy law – in combination with the first law (mass/energy conservation) is that the useful and economically valuable products from a process tend to have lower entropy than the raw material inputs, while the waste residuals from economic processes have higher entropy than the inputs to the process (Georgescu-Roegen, 1971). But the useful products, too, eventually become wastes. In other words, the economic process converts low-entropy raw materials into high-entropy wastes. Since high-entropy waste residuals have no positive market value to anyone (by definition) but do not disappear by themselves, they tend to be disposed of in non-optimal ways. The usual fate of waste residuals, as well as products that are dissipated in use,[2] is disposal by using common property environmental resources as sinks. This is a built-in and pervasive market failure, or *externality* (Ayres and Kneese, 1969).

In fact, the quantity of wastes associated with raw material extraction often far exceeds the amount of useful product. For instance, over 150 tons of copper ore must now be processed to yield a single ton of virgin copper (global average), not counting large amounts of overburden and process water. For scarcer metals, like silver, gold, platinum and uranium, the quantities of waste material per unit of product are in the tens or hundreds of thousands of tons per ton of metal. Examples of overburden and concentration waste are shown in Table 60.1. The case of zinc is illustrated in Figure 60.1.

Table 60.1   World production of metal ores, 1993 (MMT – million metric tons)

	Gross weight of ore (MMT)	Metal content (%)	Net weight of metal (MMT)	Mine and mill waste (MMT)
Aluminium	106	19.0	19.8	86
Chromium	10	30.0	3.0	7
Copper[a]	>2500	0.4	9.4	>2490
Gold[b]	466	0.0005	0.002	466
Iron	989	52.0	517.0	472
Lead[a]	>45	6.5	2.9	>42
Manganese	22	33.0	7.2	15
Nickel[a]	>130	0.7	0.9	>129
Platinum group[b]	50	0.0005	0.0002	50
Uranium (1978)[c]	1900	0.002	0.04	1900
Zinc[a]	>219	3.2	6.9	>212

Notes:
[a] Extrapolated from US data on ore treated and sold versus marketable product for 1993, using same implied ore grade.
[b] Based on ore grades for mines in South Africa only.
[c] Based on data from Barney (1980). No current data available.

Source: Calculated from data in US Bureau of Mines, *Minerals Yearbook* 1993.

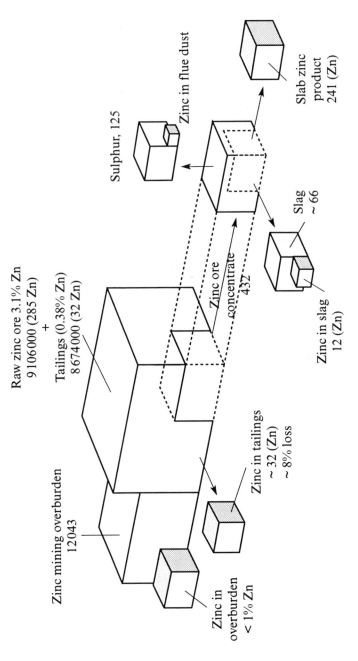

Raw zinc ore 3.1% Zn
9 106000 (285 Zn)
+
Tailings (0.38% Zn)
8 674000 (32 Zn)

Zinc mining overburden
12043

Zinc in
overburden
< 1% Zn

Zinc in tailings
~ 32 (Zn)
~ 8% loss

Zinc ore
concentrate
432

Sulphur, 125

Zinc in flue dust

Slab zinc
product
241 (Zn)

Slag
~ 66

Zinc in slag
12 (Zn)

Source: Adapted from Ayres, (1986).

Figure 60.1   Zinc flow (thousand metric tons) in mining and processing of zinc ores in the US, 1988

The discharge of wastes to the environment creates a variety of possibilities for adverse effects on man and nature, both direct and indirect. Major examples include:

- Disturbance to land (from mining, materials processing construction, or waste disposal).
- Contamination of soil, ground or surface water, used by humans, livestock or for irrigation (by acids, sludges or toxic industrial wastes), with secondary effects on fish, birds, and other species.
- Contamination of air by toxic or irritating combustion products – TSP (total solid particulates) SO_x, NO_x – with direct effects on human health or amenity.
- Disturbance of freshwater ecosystems by eutrophication or acid rain deposition.
- Disturbance of ocean ecosystems due to oil spills, ocean dumping, ocean mining, and so on.
- Climatic disturbance due to build-up of CO_2 and/or other chemical pollutants in the atmosphere.

2. The materials-balance principle
The materials-balance principle, a direct consequence of the first law of thermodynamics, states that, at each physical transformation process, or stage of a process chain, the mass of inputs (including any unpriced materials from the environment) must exactly equal the mass of outputs, including wastes. For continuous process, this balance condition must hold for any arbitrary time period.[3] It also holds for each chemical element independently, since chemical elements do not transmute (except in a nuclear reactor). Moreover, in many processes, non-reactive chemical components, such as process water and atmospheric nitrogen, can also be independently balanced. Thus half a dozen or more independent materials-balance constraints for different chemical elements may have to be satisfied for each batch or steady-state process.[4]

These facts actually provide a powerful tool for estimating waste residuals from industrial processes, since the outputs of one sector become the inputs to another. Even where the process technology is unknown, it may be sufficient to obtain data on purchased inputs and marketed outputs. To cite a practical example of the use of the principle, there are two ways to estimate the emissions of fluorine from the aluminium-smelting process, or the emissions of mercury from the chlorine-production process. The first way is to measure directly the fluoride or mercury contents of all waste streams. This is, however, no easy task since the measurements are inherently difficult and even so-called continuous processes are subject to periods of start-up and shut-down when emissions may be very far from average. The other approach, using the mass-balance principle, is to measure the inputs very carefully. Knowing that all fluorine inputs to the aluminium process, and all mercury inputs to the chlorine-production process, must be to replace losses (none is embodied in either product), it is easy to conclude that average losses (to all media) must equal average inputs, subject only to an inventory correction.

Obviously, if the emissions measurements are done carefully enough, the two methods should agree. But, as a practical matter, they rarely do so. The use of the mass balance is a very helpful means of verification and – in some cases – uncovering measurement of accounting errors. The mass-balance principle is thus applicable to every level of an economic system, from the activity, firm or branch to the industry, region or nation.

3. The sources, uses and emissions of materials

At present, the industrial economy depends largely on extractive resources. There are several generic stages of materials processing. The first stage is, of course, pumping, mining, quarrying or harvesting of some kind. The next stage is a physical concentration process in which unwanted materials such as water (from mines or oil wells), overburden, mine tailings, stems, leaves, husks, pits, branches or bark are discarded. In the next stage the concentrates are both physically and chemically separated from unwanted or less valued elements or contaminants. For instance, unwanted sulphur and ash are removed from fossil fuels. Petroleum is further separated into components, based on volatility, by fractional distillation. Some components are chemically transformed by thermal or catalytic 'cracking', alkylation, reforming, and so on. Petrochemical feedstocks are hydrocarbons mostly produced from natural gas or petroleum refineries. Synthetic chemicals and materials, such as plastics, are essentially recombinations of these elements with a few others (oxygen and nitrogen from the air, chlorine from salt).

In the case of metals, the unwanted sulphur or oxygen to which the metal atoms in the ore are initially bound are removed by a roasting, smelting or electrolytic process, while unwanted contaminants such as silica are floated off the molten metal as slag, with the help of a flux. In the case of calcium and magnesium carbonates, unwanted CO_2 is driven off by heat (calcination). Chlorine and soda ash (caustic soda) are produced by electrolysis of sodium chloride. Ammonia is made from atmospheric nitrogen and natural gas. Most other chemicals are produced from these feedstocks. In the case of other inorganic chemicals, a variety of chemical processes are used, often starting by reaction with a strong acid (sulphuric, hydrochloric or nitric) or a strong alkali like caustic soda or ammonia.

The processing of wood to remove unwanted lignin and produce paper is a process of chemical digestion with the help of strong alkalis and acids. Many agricultural and animal products are further refined, for instance to remove fats and oils, sugars or flavourings (including tea and coffee). Alcoholic beverages are produced by a biological process of fermentation, based on yeasts and natural carbohydrates. Cooking is a combination of chemical processing (for example, to soften and tenderize tough foods) and blending of flavours.

The foregoing process stages yield 'finished' materials. A few such materials – mainly fuels, lubricants, solvents, and so on and foods and beverages – are used as such. Fuels and foods may be said to be truly consumed (that is, chemically transformed into wastes). Others are widely dispersed and dissipated in use. Examples include fuels, pigments, surface coatings, flocculents, water softeners, detergents, anti-freeze, fuel or plastic additives, lubricants, solvents and so on. These materials sometimes cannot *in principle* be recycled (as in the case of fuel additives or detergents), although in many cases recovery opportunities do exist (see note 2).

The recent emphasis on waste reduction and 'clean technologies' depends largely on finding or developing industrial processes that economize on, or eliminate dissipative uses. For instance, major progress has been made recently in reducing emissions of chlorinated solvents used for dry cleaning, by requiring dry cleaners to install closed-cycle machines. Another approach does not eliminate the dissipative use *per se*, but substitutes a biodegradable substance for the non-biodegradable one. This approach is applicable to some industrial cleaning processes and may well be applicable to paints and even packaging materials.

Other materials – notably metals, plastics and some minerals – are physically formed into more or less durable products. These are objects that may perform some function more than once and that lose their value either through wear or obsolescence. These products do offer some potential for recovery and recycling. The materials cycle is illustrated in Figure 60.2. It is logical to suppose that materials recycling will gradually become more widespread as high-quality virgin sources are exhausted or as increasingly strict environmental regulations force processing of combustion products or waterborne waste streams to remove hazardous substances. Nevertheless it is most likely that – for many decades to come – industrial economies will discard significant quantities of materials in forms that are not economically recoverable.

Fuels are, of course, sources of useful energy. Energy is conserved (the first law of thermodynamics), but its useful component – called *exergy* – is not conserved and cannot be recycled.[5] This follows from the second law of thermodynamics. The other examples listed above may be termed *labour-saving*, *capital-saving* or *energy-saving* uses of materials. For

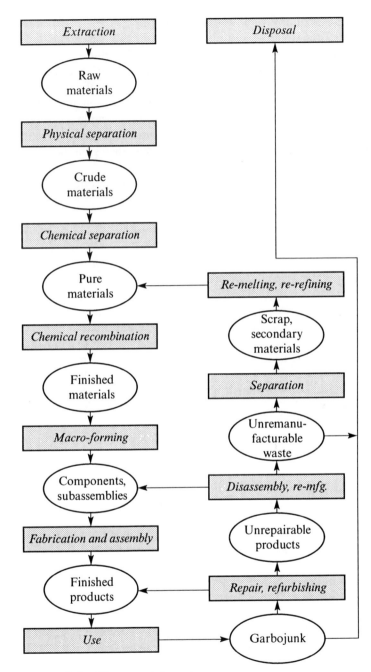

Figure 60.2   The materials cycle

example, lubricants cut down on friction, enabling a machine to function with less energy input and to last longer (saving capital); detergents save scrubbing (labour or energy) and so on (Ayres, 1978). But all these uses are inherently *non-structural*. In non-structural uses the materials are physically or chemically transformed *by use*, usually into low-grade dispersed forms. It is not economically feasible *in principle* to recover a high percentage of the materials now used for these purposes. For example, materials used for paints and surface coatings can never be recovered and recycled, as such. Only a major technological change that eliminates the need for paints or coatings can eliminate the dissipation.

Further discussion can be most usefully conducted by separately considering four major categories of materials:

- Fuels
- Metals
- Non-metallic minerals
- Packaging materials and synthetics

Fuels

In tonnage terms, fossil fuels (petroleum, coal and lignite, natural gas) are consumed in very large amounts. Land disturbance from surface mining of coal must be mentioned as a major environmental impact. For instance, around 6 tons of overburden are removed (albeit usually replaced in the mine) for every ton of coal mined. Cleaning and washing of coal also creates large piles of waste material which can later cause problems, including mud-slides and acid run-off.

However, the major environmental problems associated with fossil fuels are attributable to the combustion process and its waste products. Most air pollution is attributable to combustion of fossil fuels:

- Carbon dioxide (CO_2), the major 'greenhouse gas'
- Carbon monoxide (CO)
- Unburned or partially burned hydrocarbons or volatile organic compounds (Hydrocarbons, Volatile Organic Compounds)
- Total solid particulates (TSP)
- Oxides of nitrogen (NO_x)
- Oxides of sulphur (SO_x)

Some of these effluents, notably SO_x, NO_x and – especially – TSP, cause respiratory/and other health problems in polluted areas. Unburned hydrocarbons, especially in the presence of ultraviolet radiation, can produce a mix of highly reactive, irritating and carcinogenic compounds called 'smog'. Moreover, oxides of sulphur and nitrogen combine with atmospheric moisture and return to earth as acid rain, downwind of major powers plants (or smelters). Acidity slowly, but irreversibly, damages forests – especially conifers – and freshwater lakes. Airborne sulphate particles from anthropogenic sources (SO_x) are estimated to be comparable in mass to natural sources (for example, volcanoes).

It is important to note that atmospheric emissions and other wastes from the combination of natural gas and petroleum products are relatively minor compared to the wastes that are associated with use of coal. Natural gas has little sulphur to begin with, and it is easily removed by the Claus process and sold as elemental sulphur. In the case of petroleum, refining automatically removes the sulphur from most distillate products and, again, most of it is recovered for use. The remainder concentrates in residual fuels, but total sulphur removal is approaching feasibility.

Gas is ash-free and even residual oil has a relatively insignificant ash content, but hard coals average about 10 per cent ash (the range is from a few per cent to 20 per cent or more). In conventional combustion most of this is 'bottom ash', which becomes a solid waste disposal problem because of the large amounts of coal involved. However, some (roughly 10 per cent) of the ash goes up the stack as 'fly ash' and, even with efficient electrostatic precipitators, a small percentage is dissipated to the environment as total solid particulates (TSP). Apart from the undesirable physiological effects of small particles as such, fly ash contains toxic metals, notably zinc, vanadium, copper, nickel, lead, chromium, manganese, arsenic and mercury. Trace elements in typical bituminous (soft) coals are shown in Figure 60.3.

If the world's energy needs are met increasingly from coal in the future, as natural gas and petroleum become relatively scarcer, the environmental health problems associated with coal combustion – especially fly-ash emissions – will become increasingly significant, as they are today in China.

Finally, the build-up of atmospheric carbon dioxide from massive fossil fuel combustion appears to be capable of affecting the heat balance of the Earth itself via the so-called 'greenhouse effect'. While scientific uncertainties remain, evidence seems to be accumulating to support the hypothesis that CO_2 build-up will result in a general climate warming, particularly in the polar regions. This, in turn, is likely to cause increased weather variability, more intense monsoon patterns, northward shifts in the average locations of the jet streams and increased average precipitation in the temperate zones. The desert belt is also likely to move north, for instance. It would also cause some sea-level rise, which would be very threatening to islands and low-lying coastal areas. The resulting climatic impact might be locally favourable for some sparsely populated northern countries (for example, Canada, Siberia) but could be quite

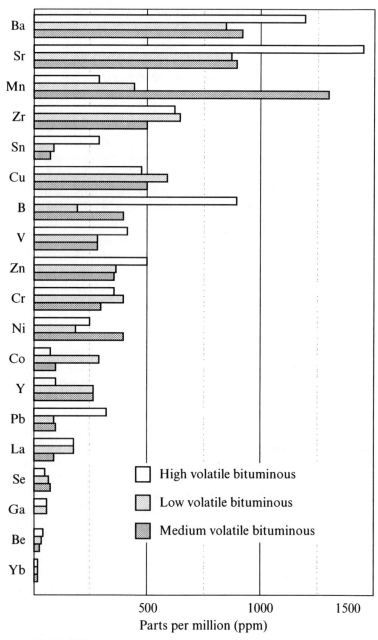

Source:

Source: Bolch (1980).

Figure 60.3   Trace elements in coal

unfavourable for the more heavily populated countries in the temperate zone or tropics.[6]

One semi-optimistic note is worth adding here. A number of technologies have been, and are being, explored to produce pure hydrogen on a large enough scale to replace natural gas and even liquid fuels (via fuel cells). The most promising line of development is to utilize a new generation of photovoltaic cells for the electrolysis of water. The technology is fairly straightforward, but the economics of both production and distribution are as yet unproven. On the production side, it is not yet clear whether major economies of scale can be expected. On the distribution side, liquefaction would be very energy-intensive, but existing natural gas pipelines cannot accommodate hydrogen gas under pressure without costly upgrading. Nevertheless, many experts expect hydrogen to become the second major energy (exergy) carrier – along with electricity – before the end of the next century.

Metals

Metals are worth considering separately because the ferrous metals[7] and aluminium are mainly used in structural applications (that is, embodied in products) and consequently recovery and reuse is often feasible. The major tonnage metals are iron (and steel), aluminium, copper, zinc, lead and nickel. We know, with reasonable accuracy, the annual global output of metal ores, metal content, and mine wastes (Table 60.1). US production of ores, concentrates, concentration waste and smelter waste are shown in Table 60.2. An important point to emphasize at the outset is that the two most important metals in terms of production (iron and aluminium) are obtained from oxide ores. The compounds of these metals are comparatively benign. Environmental problems associated with their extraction and processing are primarily due to the large scale of operations and the need to separate and dispose of significant quantities of economically useless or mildly hazardous materials.

Except for iron and aluminium, the quantities of solid mining and milling wastes produced by mining for metal ores are typically much greater than the quantities of processed metals, as indicated in Table 60.1. In the case of iron/steel facilities, environmental controls are primarily needed to minimize the discharge of toxic gases (mainly CO) from coke ovens and furnaces and waterborne acidic wastes or sludges, from 'pickling' sheet or strip. In the case of aluminium smelting, the most serious environmental problem is to prevent the escape of fluorine from the electrolytic cells (fluorine originates in the breakdown of the molten cryolite bath, not in the aluminium ore). A minor problem is the disposal of so-called 'red mud' from bauxite processing, because of its excess alkalinity.

*Table 60.2   Production and waste allocation for primary US metal
production, 1988 and 1993 (1000 metric tons)*

	US domestic mine production						US domestic	
	Total material handled		Ore treated or sold		Overburden		Production (metal content)	
	A		B		A – B			
	1988	1993	1988	1993	1988	1993	1988	1993
Bauxite/	8246	5610[e,g]	1107	753[e,g]	7140	4857		
aluminium			9139	11917[f]				
Copper	523446	706997	218631	436083	304814	270914	1341	1801
Gold	536146	1027281	117934	254404	418212	772877	0.201	0.331
Lead	9707	4344	6450	4202	3257	142	385	355
Molybdenum	127006	115667[b,g]	72212	65765[g]	54794	49902	43	39
Platinum group	34189	57097	11396	19032[c]	22793	38064	0.005	0.008
Silver	48444	47977[c,g]	15876	15723[g]	32568	32254	1.661	1.645
Zinc	21149	6298[h]	9106	5606[h]	12043	692	244	488
Uranium oxide[a]	22000	22000	15200	15200	6800	6800		
Total non-ferrous	*1330333*	*1993270*	*467912*	*816768*	*862420*	*1176502*		
Iron	300278	284068	197766	102271	102512	181797		
Total	*1630611*	*2277338*	*665678*	*919039*	*964932*	*1358299*		

Notes:
[a] 1980 data.

[b] Assumes 3:1 ratio material handled to ore – as with gold/silver.

[c] Zinc data from page 1159 have been subtracted from 'other' on page 59 of *Minerals Yearbook* 1989 to construct approximate platinum data.

[d] Where direct figures for gross weight of concentrate were unavailable, they were calculated by applying reasonable concentration ratios to the metal content.

[e] Bauxite at US mines. Included in total of 'ore treated'.

Environmental problems associated with end-use consumption and disposal of iron, steel and aluminium are also primarily due to the wide variety of 'small' uses. Scrap from demolished structures, pipelines, worn-out rails and rolling stock, obsolete machinery, junk cars or the like is easily aggregated and recycled via electric furnaces. It is much less easy to recover metal economically from small containers, wire products, foil, fasteners (for example nails), razor blades, mattresses and springs and so forth. These tend to be mixed with other kinds of waste (household refuse) or to be scattered over the landscape as litter. In this context, aluminium cans and bottle caps constitute by far the most serious eyesore since aluminium is highly corrosion-resistant, whereas small iron or carbon steel objects eventually rust away.

concentrate production						US primary metal production (domestic and foreign ores)			
Production (gross weight)d		Concentration wastes		Concentrate consumption (gross weight)d		Primary production total		Smelting/ refining losses	
C		B − C		D		E		D − E	
1988	1993	1988	1993	1988	1993	1988	1993	1988	1993
4575	3695	4564	8222	7730	7242	3944	3695	3786	3547
5364	7206	213267	428877	5794	7023	1406	1704	4388	5319
0.201	0.331	117934	254404	392	305	0.138	0.243	392	305
481	444	5969	3758	490	381	392	305	98	76
172	157	72040	65608	103	91	26	23	77	68
0.005	0.008	11396	19032	0.0003	0.0002	0.0003	0.0002	0	0
1.661	1.645	15874	15721	2	2	1.718	1.712	0	0
432	869	8674	4737	429	428	241	240	188	187
20	20	15180	15180	20	20	5	5	15	15
11046	*12392*	*464898*	*815540*	*14960*	*15491*	*6016*	*5974*	*8944*	*9517*
57515	*55661*	*140251*	*46610*	*83694*	*76793*	*49242*	*52321*	*34452*	*24472*
68561	*68053*	*605149*	*862150*	*98654*	*92284*	*55258*	*58295*	*43396*	*33989*

f Crude bauxite ore, dry equivalent. Includes net imports. Not included in 'ore treated' total.

g 1993 estimate derived from 1988 data by applying 1988 ratio of material handled to ore treated to 1993 data.

h Zinc data from detail 'other' to avoid double counting.

Source: Calculated from data in US Bureau of Mines, *Minerals Yearbooks*, 1988, 1989, 1993.

The other major tonnage metals (copper, zinc, lead, nickel) are geochemically quite different from iron and aluminium (Table 60.3). Technically, they are sulphur-lovers, or 'chalcophiles', meaning that they are typically found in nature as complex sulphides[8] rather than oxides. The sulphides are commonly first converted to oxides by the simple process of 'roasting' the sulphur being oxidized and driven off as SO_2 or recovered for producing sulphuric acid. Copper, zinc, lead and nickel smelters are major sources of air pollution despite recent efforts to improve environmental controls in some countries. For example, the large copper-nickel refineries in the Sudbury district of Ontario have emitted as much as 2.7 million tons of sulphur oxides annually, causing severe damage to forest over 720 square miles and lesser damage over a much larger area.

Table 60.3   By-product and co-product groups

By-product groups			
Copper	Zinc	Lead	Platinum
antimony	antimony	antimony	iridium
arsenic	cadmium	bismuth	osmium
cobalt	gallium	selenium	palladium
gold	germanium	silver	rhodium
rhenium	indium	tellurium	ruthenium
selenium	silver	Nickel	Lithium
silver	thallium	cobalt	rubidium
tellurium	Zirconium	manganese	
Niobium	hafnium		
tantalum			

Co-product groups	
Brine	Rare earths
sodium	yttrium
potassium	europium
boron	erbium
magnesium	terbium
chlorine	dysprosium
bromine	ytterbium

A second significant characteristic of these metals is that they are typically found together with co-products or by-products. Major metal co-product groups are also shown in Table 60.3. Thus a copper, zinc, lead or nickel smelting operation will normally yield tailings slags, ashes flue dust, or sludges that are rich in some of the others, as well as by-product metals such as antimony, arsenic, bismuth, cadmium, selenium, tellurium, silver and gold. These may or may not be highly desirable in themselves (as silver or gold are). Several of these metals are not worth enough to justify highly efficient recovery methods. Thus significant quantities of minor metals are discarded or lost in refinery operations, mainly as smoke, dust and slag.

A third key point is that many compounds of most important metals other than iron and aluminium – including arsenic, cadmium, copper, zinc, lead, nickel, chromium, manganese, cobalt, vanadium, selenium and tin, as well as mercury – are quite toxic to animals and plants. The extreme toxicity of lead, arsenic, cadmium and mercury is well known. But salts of copper, zinc, chromium, tin, bismuth and thallium are also toxic enough to have found medical or agricultural uses as insecticides, fungicides, algicides, rodenticides and so on.

Clearly non-ferrous metal extraction, processing and use all create possibilities of significant environmental damage. The examples of zinc, and its by-product cadmium, are reasonably typical. Figure 60.1 shows, schematically, how and where various fractions of contained zinc (and cadmium) are lost in processing. Much of this may become accessible to biological organisms. Environmental hazards are also associated with end-uses of some metals, especially where the metal is toxic and the use is non-structural. In the case of cadmium, for instance, almost all the existing uses are inherently dissipative. These include electroplating, pigments, and stabilizers for polyvinyl chloride (PVC). Much the same thing can be said of mercury, whose end uses include chlorine production, gold mining, fluorescent lights, small batteries, dentistry, thermometers, electrical switches, pesticides and pharmaceuticals.

Use data are very scarce. But, such data as we have suggest that from half to seven-eighths of the annual consumption of each of the heavy non-ferrous metals is currently dispersed and dissipated beyond economic recoverability. The situation in developing countries might be slightly better due to greater incentives to conserve. In countries like Indonesia, India, China and even Russia, recycling and reuse are far more complete (if informal) than in the West. For example, there is almost no such thing as a junked car. Every part is reused. Bottles, cans, old batteries, wire, electronic parts, rags and so on are collected and sorted by children and professional 'scrap pickers'. But the range of uses in all countries is much the same and for most dissipative uses, from paint to pesticides, recovery is simply not a realistic possibility.

The fact that dissipative uses account for large amounts of these metals (and other non-biodegradables) can be confirmed directly by comparing total production and consumption with uses that are amenable to recovery and recycling. The most obvious example of such a use is tetraethyl and tetramethyl lead (TEL, TML) as gasoline additives to increase octane number and enhance performance. This use has now been banned in the US, but still persists in many countries. Toxic heavy metals have also been extensively used for pigments (for example red and white lead, cadmium red and orange, chrome green and yellow), insecticides (such as lead or zinc arsenate), wood preservers, bactericides, algicides, fungicides, herbicides, catalysts, plastic stabilizers, and so on. Chromium, one of the most toxic of all metals (as chromic acid and its derivatives), is a good example. A comparatively small proportion of annual production is used for metallurgical purposes – mainly stainless steel – where it is biologically harmless and easily recycled. A surprisingly large proportion goes into chemicals, many of which are highly toxic. These chemicals are used for chrome plating, leather tanning, algicides and pigments. All of these uses are essentially dissipative.[9] Mercury, another very toxic metal, has virtually no non-dissipative uses, although small amounts are now being recovered from fluorescent lights and other electronic equipment.

Taking into account extraction, processing and end-use, human activities have sharply increased the natural rates of mobilization of many metals, particularly the more toxic ones. Comparisons of worldwide natural and man-induced rates of mobilization in the environment are given in Table 60.4.

Table 60.4   Indicators of unsustainability (ratios)

Metal	Anthropogenic flow to natural flow		Cumulative extraction to topsoil inventory Azar et al. (1994)
	Galloway et al. (1982)	Azar et al. (1994)	
Antimony (Sb)	38	6.0	—
Arsenic (As)	4	0.33	—
Cadmium	20	3.9	3.0
Chromium (Cr)	2	4.6	2.6
Copper (Cu)	14	24.0	23.0
Lead (Pb)	333	12.0	19.0
Mercury (Hg)	—	6.5	17.0
Nickel (Ni)	4	4.8	2.0
Selenium (Se)	5	2.0	—
Vanadium (V)	3	0.32	—
Zinc (Z)	23	8.3	6.9

Non-metallic minerals

Non-metallic minerals such as stone, gravel, clay and sand are mined in larger quantities than metal ores, although processing losses are smaller and these materials are somewhat more benign. They are used mostly in construction. International trade is minor. Global data are unavailable, but US production, mine waste and use data for 1993 are shown in Table 60.5.

Environmental impacts arise from mining itself, which is mostly on the surface. Significant land disturbances, dust and erosion often accompany such activity. Processing of phosphate rock (to fertilizer) also results in significant further environmental impacts, of several kinds, including toxic fluoride emissions to the atmosphere and accumulation of (mildly) radio-active tailings. It is noteworthy that erosion rates for disturbed land, such as active strip mines, is up to ten times greater than for cropland and perhaps 200 times greater than natural grassland.

Packaging materials and synthetics

It is convenient to consider 'materials' as substances that are used without significant chemical conversion. Packaging materials, synthetic fibres, plastics and rubber fall into this category. Thus we need not consider the complex environmental problems associated with manufacturing chemical intermediates. In the interest of completeness, therefore, it is worthwhile to point out that synthetic polymers – mostly plastics and rubber – are made largely from derivatives of petroleum. Petrochemicals already account for perhaps 5 per cent of world petroleum consumption, and this percentage will increase. The use of synthetics is inseparable from extraction and refining of petroleum. In the future, chemicals may also be manufactured from coal.

The three most important polymers are polyethylene, polystyrene and polyvinyl chloride (PVC). There are, of course, a host of other resins including polyesters, phenolics, acrylics and so on. Neglecting environmental problems associated with the paper and chemical industries, there remains a significant problem of disposal. The physical volumes involved are equal to or greater than the volume of metals produced each year. Plastics are not biodegradable, hence they must be disposed of in landfills or by incineration. Incineration of chlorinated plastics, in particular, is environmentally hazardous because of the emission of toxic or carcinogenic compounds. Tyres are also very difficult to incinerate efficiently. Non-degradable litter, especially polystyrene foams and polyethylene films, is also an increasing problem in many public places, such as beaches.

Paper remains an important material in the economy. It is, of course, made from woodpulp by a process in which unwanted components of the wood (lignin and hemicelluloses) are chemically dissolved and removed. In older pulp and paper mills, this waste material was simply discarded into the nearest river, along with chemicals used for the digestion process. In waterways, this material creates 'biological oxygen demand' (BOD). It removes the dissolved oxygen and kills air-breathing organisms (such as fish) that must have oxygen to survive. In recent years pulp and paper mills in most countries have substantially reduced their waterborne waste output, under pressure of environmental regulations. In Europe, they have also sharply cut their use of chlorine as a bleaching chemical for paper pulp.

4. Closing the materials cycle: the economics of recycling

The notion of a 'materials cycle' is actually based on an analogy with natural biogeochemical cycles involving water, carbon and nitrogen.

Table 60.5 Production and waste allocation for US industrial mineral production from domestic and foreign ores, 1988 and 1993 (1000 metric tons)

	Total material handled A		Ore treated or sold B		Domestic production C		Exports D		Imports E		Apparent consumption C−D+E		Overburden loss A−B		Concentration losses B−C	
	1988	1993	1988	1993	1988	1993	1988	1993	1988	1993	1988	1993	1988	1993	1988	1993
Asbestos	89[b]	70	57[b]	45	17	13	32	28	85	31	71	17	32	25	40	32
Barite	404	1299[i]	404	773	404	315	0	18	1207	834	1611	1131	0	526	0	458
Clays	91900	70653[f]	44617	41074[m]	44515	41074	3535	4154	33	39430	41013	76350	47283	29579	102	0
Diatomite	3429	3267[g]	695	662[a]	629	599	147	165	287	2	769	436	2734	2605	66	63
Feldspar	2782[i]	3328[t,f]	649	3328	649	770	12	18	6	7	643	759	2133	0	0	2558
Gypsum (crude)	20747[k]	22564	14869[m]	15812[m]	14869	15812	246	344	8782	7587	23405	23055	5878	6752	0	0
Magnesium compounds	3770[b]	2169[i]	2221[b]	1627	952	698	37	117	376	495	1292	1076	1549	542	1269	929
Mica (scrap)	130	560[e]	130	388[a]	130	88	6	6	12	22	136	104	0	172	0	300
Perlite	704[i]	872[h]	621	604[b]	585	569	33	26	62	70	614	613	83	269	36	35
Phosphate rock	596733[i]	280586[i]	224075[d]	175225[b]	45389	35494	8092	4831	673	632	37970	31295	372659	105361	178686	139731
Potash and potassium salts	11884[i]	31636[i]	11884	31636[a,c]	2999	3067	579	925	6964	7204	9384	9346	0	0	8885	28569
Pumice	460[k]	537	374	469	353	469	1	18	30	143	382	594	86	68	21	0
Salt	34470[m]	38665[m]	34470[m]	38665[m]	34470	38665	802	688	4966	5868	38634	43845	0	0	0	0
Sand and gravel, total	863640	894920[c]	863640	894920[c]	863531	894920	1837	2882	357	1360	862051	893398	0	0	109	0
Sodium compounds, total	18766[g]	19172[d]	9099[c]	9296[c]	9099	9296	2315	2887	257	252	7041	6661	9667	9876	0	0
Stone, crushed	1222296[g,f,f]	1205037	1134848[a,b]	1118824	1131985	1116000	3304	4824	3268	8400	1131949	1119576	87448	86213	2863	2824
Stone, dimension	1623[g,f]	1853[i,j]	1079[a,b]	1232[c]	1079	1232	510[e]	270[e]	830	310	1399	1272	544	621	0	0
Vermiculite	1769[i]	190	1769[m]	190[m]	275	187	18	7	32	30	289	210	0	0	1494	3
Calculated subtotal	2875597	2577379	2345501	2334770	2151931	2159268	21506	22209	28228	72678			530095	242609	193571	175503
other[l]	141237	309325	103529[c,l]	103725[c,l]	93842	96380							37709	205600	9687	7345

884

Notes:

a,a' 1988 ratio of ore to marketable product used to derive 1993 estimate or vice versa.

b,b' Ratio of 1993 production to 1988 production applied to 1993 data to derive 1993 estimate or vice versa.

c,c' Marketable product for that year assumed equal to production for that year.

d Includes surface mining only.

e Estimated.

f,f' 1988 ratio of crude ore to waste applied to derive 1993 ratio and vice versa.

g,g' Ratio of 1993 to 1988 ore treated applied to 1988 data to derive 1988 estimate or vice versa.

h Surface to underground ratio applied to data in same year to derive estimate.

i,i' Crude ore assumed equal to retreated or sold for that year.

j Ratio for surface data assumed equal to same ratio for underground data in that year.

k,k' 1988 crude ore to waste ratio applied to derive 1993 estimate or vice versa.

l Overall average ratio of crude or to waste for that year applied to derive addition to specific data.

m Maximum calculation. Crude ore = max (crude ore, treated ore, marketable product, production); treated ore = max treated ore, marketable product, production).

Source: Based on data from US Bureau of Mines, *Minerals Yearbooks*, 1988, 1989, 1993.

However, the latter are true cycles, whereas the so-called materials cycle is incomplete except in the very crude sense that materials are extracted from the environment, processed, used, and finally disposed of as waste. It is important to bear in mind that materials are normally returned to the environment in a degraded form very different from (and less useful than) that which was extracted.

The idea of recycling low-grade wastes is intellectually appealing. If the waste stream is easily recovered and processed compared to natural sources, it will generally be exploited, as in the case of steel auto bodies and aluminium cans – and conversely. Not surprisingly, the more economically valuable a material is, the more likely it is to be recycled. Thus it pays to go to considerable lengths to recover platinum from industrial catalysts or silver from film-processing wastes. But, to date, it is cheaper to extract aluminium from bauxite ore than to extract it from fly ash. Similarly, it is cheaper to mine virgin gypsum than to recover it from phosphate rock processing or flue gas desulphurization. And it is cheaper to extract sulphur from natural deposits via the Frasch process[10] than to recover it from combustion products, where it is already oxidized.

To be sure, Malthusian concerns that the world is running out of natural resources have been expressed repeatedly over the last two centuries, and have consistently proved to be premature. Market incentives, via the price system, have sufficed to stimulate effective technological responses to every threat of shortage, up to now. However, high-quality deposits of natural resources are finite. Clearly, extraction of fossil fuels and metal ores will eventually slow down and finally cease, at some future time.

The waste-assimilative capacity of the environment is also finite. Raw materials, once extracted, eventually become process wastes or consumption wastes. The environment cannot tolerate these emissions indefinitely, especially those (such as metals) which are not biodegradable. Unfortunately, waste residuals and environmental assimilative capacity are not a part of the market system. Being 'bads' rather than 'goods', they are unpriced. Thus market incentives have not been applicable in the past to stimulate technological substitutes for environmental services, or technological fixes for environmental damages.

The long-term imperative is to focus on closing the product cycle. This implies creating a system to facilitate the return ('reverse logistics'), reconditioning, reuse, and – where appropriate – remanufacturing of durable manufactured goods so as to maximize the useful life of each component and subsystem. The first requirement to make such a system work effectively is to internalize the cost of environmental damage resulting from extraction and processing, dissipative use or final disposal. There are two basic approaches: regulatory and economic. The regulatory approach limits emissions and thus adds to the costs of waste generators. But this approach is often very inefficient, since a legal requirement to reduce emissions per unit production by 90 per cent (for instance) may be far more costly for some sectors than for others. The economically rational approach would be to tax emissions, thus allowing each emitter to make the optimum trade-off between emission reduction and other objectives.

Unfortunately direct taxation of emissions is often opposed by environmentalists on the fallacious moral grounds that it somehow legitimizes pollution or allows 'the rich' to buy the 'right to pollute'. A more practical objection is that direct taxation of pollution is generally not technically feasible except in a few cases where the polluters are few and where monitoring can be very thorough. Electric power plants, petroleum refineries and steel mills might be examples of this kind. But where the pollution is generated by millions of end-users, taxation of waste production or pollution emissions would be much less practical. Inevitably, the cost of administration, the creation of opportunities for evasion and corruption, and the burden on consumers would compensate for the theoretical advantages. An even more practical objection is that end-users have few options to reduce waste and pollution except by cutting down on consumption. A tax on consumption *per se* would therefore accomplish the same objective as a tax on pollution, but more efficiently and fairly.

However, an even more efficient approach is to regulate the products that create pollution (automobiles, for instance) and to make the manufacturers responsible for the pollution tax, rather than consumers. This makes economic sense because the manufacturers control the design of the products. In terms of recovery and recycling, the role of manufacturers is even more critical, since the economics of materials recovery and recycling is absolutely dependent on product design. The German 'take-back' initiative, to make manufacturers legally liable to take back obsolete durable goods (and packaging materials) at the end of the product's useful life is undoubtedly the most effective scheme that has yet been devised to internalize the costs. Manufacturers are already demonstrating that they can find practical ways to reduce the costs of disassembly, and thus of recycling, by reducing unnecessary design complexity (such as the number of different plastics used), replacing unnecessary welds and bolts by snap fasteners, and so on.

However, more fundamental changes will be needed. The current obsession with labour productivity and 'competitiveness' has increased economic efficiency more than welfare. A balanced approach would put more emphasis on increasing the productivity of material resources – generating more value from less material substance. From a more fundamental perspective, what is needed is a policy of *dematerialization*, from the

Table 60.6   *US recycling statistics and apparent consumption for selected metals, 1987–91*

Year	Recycled metal[1]			Apparent consumption[4]	Recycle % of apparent consumption
	New scrap[2]	Old scrap[3]	Total		
Aluminium[5]					
1987	1134	852	1986	6603	30
1988	1077	1045	2122	6450	33
1989	1043	1011	2054	6000	34
1990	1034	1359	2393	6298	38
1991	979	1522	2501	6214	40
Copper					
1987	716.122	497.937	1214.059	2912.929	42
1988	788.712	518.179	1306.891	3002.257	44
1989	760.894	547.561	1308.455	2945.209	44
1990	773.873	535.656	1309.529	2942.311	45
1991	679.882	533.338	1213.220	2782.942	44
Lead					
1987	52.535	657.532	710.067	1259.029	56
1988	45.274	691.127	736.401	1274.477	58
1989	49.612	841.729	891.341	1382.250	64
1990	48.104	874.093	922.197	1345.344	69
1991	54.172	829.563	883.735	1280.586	69
Nickel[6]					
1987			32.331	155.781	21
1988			41.039	159.019	26
1989			39.784	135.218	29
1990			33.716	145.556	23
1991			32.520	128.048	25
Tin					
1987	4.604	11.462	16.066	59.458	27
1988	3.925	11.350	15.275	60.955	25
1989	2.795	11.545	14.34	47.285	30
1990	4.035	13.200	17.235	53.430	32

Table 60.6 (cont.)

	Quantity (kMT)				Recycle % of apparent consumption
	Recycled metal[1]			Apparent consumption[4]	
Year	New scrap[2]	Old scrap[3]	Total		
			Zinc		
1987	270	82	352	1324	27
1988	240	97	337	1340	25
1989	230	117	347	1311	26
1990	232	109	341	1239	28
1991	233	120	353	1134	31

Notes:
[1] Recycled metal is metal recovered from reported *purchased* new plus old scrap supply.
[2] New scrap is scrap resulting from the manufacturing process, including metal and alloy production.
[3] Old scrap is scrap resulting from consumer products.
[4] Apparent consumption is production plus net imports plus stock change. Apparent consumption is calculated on a contained weight basis.
[5] Recycle quantity is the calculated metallic recovery from aluminium-base scrap, estimated for full industry coverage.
[6] Nickel scrap is nickel contained in ferrous and non-ferrous scrap receipts.

Source: US Bureau of Mines (1991), 'Recycling-nonferrous metals', Tables 1 and 2.

perspective of the whole product life cycle. This means more emphasis on recovery, remanufacturing and recycling. It also means elimination of a non-functional mass – miniaturization – where possible. From the standpoint of environment and employment, too, it is worth pointing out that reconditioning and remanufacturing require roughly half of the energy input, and twice the labour input per physical unit of output, as compared to manufacturing from all-new materials (Stahel, 1982, 1986).

It must be acknowledged that the industrial materials cycle cannot ever (and need not) be completely closed, even at the global level. Some losses are inevitable. Secondary production from new and old scrap in the US and recycling rates as a percentage of apparent consumption are summarized for the US in Table 60.6. The fraction of metal obtained each year from secondary sources has risen fairly sharply between 1987 and 1991 in the case of aluminium (from 30 per cent to 40 per cent) and lead (from 56 per cent to 69 per cent, due to the ban on using lead in gasoline, a dissipative use) but has fluctuated or remained roughly constant in the other cases.

Certainly, there is no realistic possibility of approaching the long-term goal of closing the materials cycle within the next few decades. Indeed, aggregate global use of extractive resources will undoubtedly increase for a number of years to come. Nevertheless, long-term imperatives cast their shadow. Choices will have to be made and distinctions are necessary. For instance, some materials are much more toxic or otherwise environmentally damaging than others.

On a scale of global hazard to economic benefit, the highest (most damaging, least beneficial) materials must be eliminated from commerce first. Similarly, some environmental systems are much more resilient than others. The more fragile ecosystems must be given greater priority for protection, given limited resources. Similarly, some industrial activities and some forms of intermediate consumption are much more dangerous than others. These points are discussed next.

Closing the materials cycle is particularly important for the toxic non-ferrous metals, such as arsenic, bismuth, cadmium, copper, lead, mercury, plutonium, silver, thallium, uranium and zinc, as well as some ferrous metals (such as chromium and nickel). Of these, the artificial element plutonium is by far the most dangerous. It is carcinogenic and toxic to an extreme degree, as well as being fissionable and hence usable for nuclear explosives. Many people now believe that the various risks associated with use of plutonium (or even uranium, from which plutonium is manufactured) are too great to justify its use in nuclear power production. In any case, the closing of the global uranium–plutonium cycle is extremely urgent. However, this subject cannot be realistically discussed without also discussing the entire question of nuclear armaments and their disposition.

Following uranium–plutonium on the list in terms of urgency would be lead, chromium, mercury and those toxic metals (arsenic, bismuth, cadmium, thallium) that are by-products of copper, lead or zinc mining and refining. These metals are widely used in chemical products such as pesticides, pigments and stabilizers, mainly because there is a steady low-cost supply and no constraint on such use. Finally, copper, manganese, nickel, silver, tin and zinc constitute lesser but significant problems worthy of consideration.

One of the problems is that these metals are being dispersed into the environment at very low concentrations that make later recovery for recycling impracticable in most cases, but that nevertheless constitute a threat to the health of humans and other species. With regard to metallic emissions, it should be pointed out that anthropogenic airborne emissions currently exceed natural sources by large factors, even on a global basis (Table 60.4). A similar table for waterborne emissions would show comparable results.

However, if the problem of toxic build-up were not enough, there are other unsustainable features of the present materials system. One is the fact that the industrial world is increasingly import-dependent for critical materials, since economically recoverable deposits in the developed countries are being depleted faster than in the rest of the world. Another problem is that ore grades are gradually declining worldwide, as high-grade deposits are exhausted. In the nineteenth century, copper was being mined from deposits with 10 per cent ore grade. Today the world average is about 0.8 per cent. Much the same situation applies to a number of other non-ferrous metals, including gold, silver, uranium and tin. This means that more and more tons of inert materials must be physically moved, crushed, screened and later dumped, to yield a concentrated fraction. The concentrates must then be smelted or otherwise refined to produce a ton of saleable product. Moving and handling requires energy so that, *ceteris paribus*, energy requirements for primary production must be expected to rise over time.

Technological progress may continue to compensate, to some extent, for declining ore quality – the visible symptom of gradual exhaustion. Costs of most raw materials have actually declined during the past century, in real terms (for example, Barnett and Morse, 1962; Smith 1979). But, in the long run, the cost of further marginal gains in the efficiency of discovery, extraction and refining of raw materials is likely to rise too. Costs for these activities, per unit output, may continue to decline but at a slower and slower rate. At some hypothetical point in the very distant future, the value of the exergy embodied in low-grade ores or mineral fuel deposits in the earth's crust may, in some cases, no longer economically justify the expenditure of solar exergy needed to extract and refine them, for example, from seawater. At that point, if it occurs, the material cycle on earth will necessarily have to be 'closed' for that material. (It can never be closed for all materials, since recycling can never be 100 per cent efficient.)

5. Policy issues

It is not as generally acknowledged as it should be that the environment is also a resource. The fact that it has been available in the past for use as a 'sink' for disposal of industrial and consumption wastes at zero (or very low) cost is a consequence of its indivisibility and the fact that it cannot be contained and privately owned or exchanged in a marketplace. It is, in short, a 'public good', outside the market-pricing mechanism. It is an axiom of economics that (in the absence of cultural restraints) the use of unpriced public goods will be excessive unless regulated by public policy. This is the nub of the problem.

Environmental services to man can be said to include the biosphere –

photosynthesis, the water cycle, the carbon and nitrogen cycles, bio-degradation (decay) of organic materials – the maintenance of oxygen in the atmosphere,[11] the ozone layer in the stratosphere, and a host of local 'public service' functions. There is no question that these environmental functions (and others) are interfered with by large-scale mobilization of toxic materials, erosion, silting, build-up of CO_2 and particulates in the atmosphere, and so on. Unfortunately, much remains to be learned about the specific mechanisms involved and the quantitative impact. Research is therefore the first prerequisite of intelligent environmental policy.

In the absence of the scientific knowledge that would permit us to discriminate between minor and major problems (for example, between reversible and irreversible disturbances), the safest strategy is to limit the mobilization of materials by human activities to levels significantly below the levels found in natural processes. By this criterion, the processing and disposal of heavy toxic metals into surface waters is already excessive. Similarly, combustion and other processes are injecting certain materials into the atmosphere at rates comparable with or greater than natural processes.

Policy instruments for abating these undesirable flows include emissions regulations applicable to particular 'sources' (such as mines or smelters) or on the use of particular substances (for example, phosphates in detergents, chlorofluorocarbons and lead in motor fuel). More broadly, however, policies tending to promote conservation of scarce resources will also tend to reduce environmental problems.

It is important to note that many relevant existing policy instruments have had the opposite effect of encouraging excessive use of materials, especially virgin materials. The mineral depletion allowance (recently reduced, but still in effect) and freight rates favouring transportation of mine products as compared to recycling scrap are two examples. Similarly, regulations tending to increase energy use efficiency without increasing costs (for example, for gasoline) also tend to encourage excessive use of energy – and its associated environmental problems. This is often termed the 'rebound effect'.

Severance taxes on mineral extraction, on the other hand, would tend simultaneously to discourage use of virgin resources and encourage conservation and recycling. Similarly, effluent taxes or disposal fees would tend to discourage the discharges of recoverable wastes into surface waters or atmosphere. This market-based approach is generally preferred by economists over the more common regulatory approaches (permits, standard setting) because it allows greater discretion to the waste generator. As mentioned previously, economic approaches have frequently been opposed by environmentalists, both on the ground that imposition of effluent charges legitimizes pollution and allows the 'rich' to buy the 'right to pollute', and on the ground that taxes or fees would not guarantee meeting desired environmental standards. Both objections are specious. The moral objection is based on a widespread misconception that, in principle, waste and pollution can and should be eliminated entirely.[12] Thanks to the laws of thermodynamics, this would only be possible if the materials cycle were completely closed – which will not happen for a very long time, if ever. The practical objection is easily overcome: if a given fee does not yield the desired result, of course, the answer would be for the public authority to raise the effluent charge until it is effective.

No single approach will suffice. Apart from emissions regulations, taxes, exchangeable quotas, and so on, there is much that can be done to facilitate more efficient use of materials. Take-back legislation on the German model is a very powerful tool for encouraging product redesign to facilitate recovery, reuse, remanufacturing and recycling. Deposit systems can be very effective for encouraging the return and recycling of bottles and cans (as recently demonstrated in Michigan, where a mandatory 10 cent deposit has raised recycling rates for these items to nearly 100 per cent). A similar system would clearly be applicable to troublesome items like used batteries and used motor oil. Waste disposal charges can be extremely potent tools for encouraging recovery and reuse of potentially hazardous industrial wastes, such as chlorinated 'heavy ends' (which can be pyrolized to produce hydrochloric acid) or waste solder flux from the electronics sector (which can be recycled back into the solder itself). Some bottles – such as glass milk and wine bottles – can surely be recovered and reused as such. Some recovered waste packaging materials can, in principle, be used to manufacture products (like highway dividers or park furniture) that are currently made from wood or metal. A combination of policies and approaches will certainly be needed.

Notes
1. Tjalling Koopmans expressed this principle as 'the impossibility of the land of Cockaigne', and made use of the theorem in developing his mathematical treatment of 'activity analysis', an extension of input–output analysis (Koopmans, 1951). However, Koopmans did not discuss the environmental implications.
2. Obviously, products that are used dissipatively cannot be recovered or recycled, even in principle. This topic is discussed later.
3. The case of batch processes or continuous processes with time variability requires more careful consideration. In general, however, the accounting rule holds: stock changes equal inputs minus outputs. When stock changes are zero, or can be neglected, inputs equal outputs.
4. These conditions can be very helpful in filling in missing data. For instance, chemical engineering textbooks (such as Lowenheim and Moran, 1975), tend to provide 'recipes' for standard chemical processes that specify inputs (per unit output) in some detail, but neglect to specify waste products. While a detailed chemical characterization of the wastes requires very complex model calculations (or direct measurements), one can derive some useful information about the elementary composition of the wastes.

5. The formal definition is roughly as follows: exergy is the potential work that can be extracted from a system reversibly as it approaches final equilibrium with its surroundings. For a more complete exposition see Szargut et al. (1988).
6. An extremely *unfavourable* consequence of warming in the far north might be thawing of the (currently) frozen subsoil, or tundra. This would release substantial quantities of methane into the atmosphere, thus further accelerating climate warming.
7. Ferrous metals are chemically (and magnetically) similar to iron, with which they are commonly alloyed. They include chromium, cobalt, manganese, molybdenum, nickel, tungsten and vanadium.
8. Some metals are mined in both forms. The Canadian nickel deposits, for instance, are sulphides. However, the so-called lateritic ores found in tropical countries are oxidized.
9. Plating wastes, in particular, are very toxic and dangerous. Tanning wastes are also toxic. However, chromium-based pigments, and tanning compounds embodied in shoe leather, are probably relatively harmless when dissipated (as dust) by wear and tear.
10. The Frasch process is used to extract sulphur from underground deposits. The technique is to inject high-pressure steam into the well. The steam melts the sulphur, which can them be pumped out as a liquid.
11. The atmosphere of the Earth prior to the evolutionary development of the blue–green algae did not contain free oxygen.
12. Even now, the UN University in Tokyo has adopted a formal research programme under the title 'Zero Emissions Research Initiative' or ZERI. The researchers understand this to be a theoretical target, similar to the target of 'zero defects' that has been widely adopted in the realm of quality management. However, the false implication remains that wastes can be eliminated, in principle.

References

Ayres, Robert U. (1978), *Resources, Environment and Economics: Applications of the Materials/Energy Balance Principle*, New York: John Wiley & Sons.

Ayres, Robert U. and Allan V. Kneese (1969), 'Production, consumption and externalities', *American Economic Review*, June. Reprinted in P. Daltz and H. Perloff (eds), *Benchmark Papers in Electrical Engineering & Computer Science*, Stroudsburg PA: Dowden, Hutchison & Ross Inc., 1974, and New York: Bobbs-Merrill Reprint Series, 1974.

Azar, Christian, John Holmberg and Kristian Lindgren (1994), *Socio-economic Indicators for Sustainability*, Research Report, Institute of Physical Resource Theory, Chalmers University of Technology and University of Göteborg, Göteborg, Sweden.

Barney, Gerald (Study Director) (1980), *The Global 2000 Report to the President*, Technical Report (Vol. 2), Council on Environmental Quality/US Department of State, Washington, DC.

Bolch, William E. Jr (1980), 'Solid waste and trace element impacts', in Alex E.S. Green (ed.), *Coal Burning Issues*, Gainesville FL: University Presses of Florida, pp. 231–48.

Galloway, James N. et al. (1982), 'Trace metals in atmospheric deposition: a review and assessment', *Atmospheric Environment*, **16** (7).

Georgescu-Roegen, Nicholas (1971), *The Entropy Law and the Economic Process*, Cambridge, MA: Harvard University Press.

Koopmans, Tjalling C. (ed.) (1951), *Activity Analysis of Production and Allocation*, Cowles Commission Series, Monograph 13, New York: John Wiley & Sons.

Lowenheim, Frederick A. and Marguerite K. Moran (1975), *Faith, Keyes, and Clark's 'Industrial Chemicals'*, 4th edn, New York: Wiley-Interscience.

Stahel, Walter R. (1982), 'The product life factor', in S. Orr (ed.), *An Inquiry into the Nature of Sustainable Societies: The Role of the Private Sector*, 1982 Mitchell Prize Papers Series, NARC.

Stahel, Walter R. (1986), 'Product life as a variable', *Science and Public Policy*, **13** (4), 185–93.

Szargut, Jan, David R. Morris and Frank R. Steward (1988), *Exergy Analysis of Thermal, Chemical and Metallurgical Processes*, New York: Hemisphere Publishing Corporation.

United States Bureau of Mines (various years), *Minerals Yearbook: Volume I; Metals & Minerals*, United States Government Printing Office, Washington, DC.

61 Ecological principles and environmental economic analysis
Carl Folke

1. Introduction

The rapid expansion of the scale of human actions has radically transformed the Earth (Turner et al., 1990). This transformation has turned the capacity of ecosystems to generate a continuous flow of natural resources and ecosystem services into an increasingly limiting factor for social and economic development (Jansson et al., 1994). But the need for functional ecosystems is scarcely reflected in market prices, seldom perceived by individuals, or fully taken into account by the institutions that provide the framework for human action, whether political or social. Its contribution to economic development and growth is still 'mentally hidden' to many actors of modern society. This is reflected, for example, in most models of economic growth where the necessity of the environmental resource base for human welfare is not accounted for (Dasgupta, 1997).

The escalating globalization of human activities, population growth and large-scale movements of people have placed mankind in an era of unfamiliar dynamics and interdependence of ecological, social and economic systems at regional and even planetary scales (Daily and Ehrlich, 1992; Holling, 1994). They have become so interconnected that rational decisions by individuals locally, or on the project level, may spill over and generate regional and global effects, witnessed in, for example, climate change and the evolution of new diseases (Houghton et al., 1996; McMichael et al., 1996). It is a major challenge in this new situation, and for the prosperous development of human societies, to ensure the capacity of ecosystems to generate natural resources and ecosystem services (de Groot, 1992; Daily, 1997).

In this chapter I shall give a brief introduction to the structure and function of ecosystems, including biological diversity and ecosystem development. The chapter emphasizes the critical role that ecosystems play as essential factors of production for social and economic development, and discusses how the links between this essential resource base and human activity could be improved.

2.   The structure and function of ecosystems

Ecology is the study of living organisms and their environment. Like economics, ecology consists of several sub-branches ranging from the ecology of individuals, to studies of a single population of a species, to communities of populations of several species, to a particular ecosystem, to a mix of ecosystems in the landscape or a drainage basin, all the way up to the biosphere, where, for example, the interactions between the terrestrial and oceanic systems and biogeochemical cycles are studied. The latter includes cycles of carbon, sulphur, nitrogen and important mineral salts. Water is a carrier of many of those compounds, and the water cycle is an essential link between terrestrial environments, the sea and the atmosphere. In Figure 61.1 some of the cycles are illustrated. Obviously, they do not operate in isolation from each other or from biological/ecological systems, and are of utmost importance for life on Earth. But organisms are not only adapted to these cycles. They also actively modify them. The most obvious modification is the pervasive transformation of the cycles caused by *Homo sapiens*.

In this chapter I shall focus on ecosystem and landscape levels since it is those levels of biological organization which most naturally link to human systems. This does not mean that other levels of biological organization are excluded. That would be impossible, since an ecosystem consists of plants, animals and micro-organisms which live in biological communities and which interact with each other and with the physical and chemical environment, with adjacent ecosystems and with the water cycle and the atmosphere (Ehrlich et al., 1977; Odum, 1989).

Solar energy is the driving force of ecosystems, enabling the cyclic use of water, materials and compounds required for system organization and maintenance. The ability of plants in terrestrial ecosystems and plants and algae in aquatic ecosystems to fix solar energy (photosynthesis) is a prerequisite for biological organization. They are called primary producers. All animals (for example, insects, reptiles, mammals) are dependent on the ability of primary producers to fix solar energy. Humans are just as dependent on the primary producers' solar-fixing ability as any other organism. Vitousek et al. (1986) estimated that humans appropriate about 40 per cent of the planet's solar-fixing capacity. Solar energy flow, water and biogeochemical cycling set an upper limit on the quantity and number of organisms, and on the number of trophic levels that can exist in an ecosystem (Pomeroy and Alberts, 1988; Ayres, Chapter 62).

Ecosystems are nested across temporal and spatial scales (O'Neill et al., 1986; Levin, 1992). For example, a wetland ecosystem may consist of several sub-ecosystems such as lakes, areas with reeds, or forested areas. These in turn consist of subsystems. The lakes, for example, have a plankton

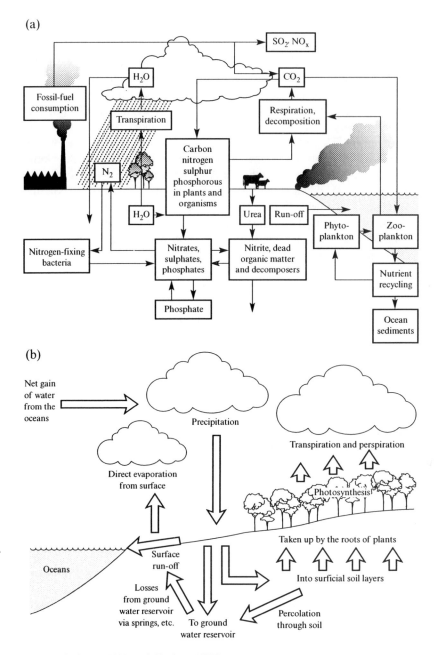

Sources: de Groot (1992) and Clapham (1973).

Figure 61.1   Conceptual representations of (a) the biogeochemical cycle
and (b) the hydrological cycle

community living in the open water. This consists of a food-web (a web of organisms linked to each other for food consumption) (Pimm, 1991). The primary producers in the web are solar-fixing plankton, or phytoplankton, and there are also solar-fixing algae. Primary producers are eaten by a diversity of herbivores such as zooplankton, insect larvae, and snails, which in turn are eaten by carnivores such as fish. The herbivores and carnivores are the consumers. There is also a benthic community of mussels and worms living in the sediments of the lake, to which there is a 'rainfall' of dead plankton, and particles linking it to the plankton community. Dead animals and plants are broken down into basic components like nutrients, carbon and other necessary building blocks for life by a diversity of decomposers such as fungi, and bacteria. The basic components such as nutrients are then recycled back to the primary producers as water mixes, and will become re-incorporated into the primary producers again.

The interactions between producers, consumers and decomposers exist in all ecosystems. The interactions among species in a food-web and their relations to water flow and biogeochemical cycling are complex, non-linear, and contain lags and discontinuities, thresholds and limits. Ecosystems are complex, self-organizing systems. Because these systems are evolutionary (rather than mechanistic), they exhibit a limited degree of predictability (Costanza et al., 1993).

Many scientists use energy flow analysis to describe the interactions between producers, consumers, decomposers and their interactions with water flows and biogeochemical cycling in the ecosystem. These interactions are inherently complex, and energy analysis can provide a first picture of the structure and function of the ecosystem (Odum, 1971). Energy analysis has also been used to analyse human systems and the linkages between humans and nature (Odum, 1971; Hannon, Chapter 63 in this volume; Herendeen, Chapter 64 in this volume). In addition to energy, ecosystem scientists also study the flows of nutrients, organic matter and other basic components in ecosystems and how they are affected by human activities (Schindler, 1990).

Furthermore, ecosystems are linked in time and space. For example, the wetland ecosystem and its lakes discussed above are linked to surrounding ecosystems such as uplands, agricultural land, forests and coastal habitats. As a consequence the system boundary of a landscape or a drainage basin is increasingly used in ecology, since this boundary seems to link most easily to human activities (McDonnell and Pickett, 1993; Groffman and Likens, 1994). Hence ecosystem are open dynamic systems. Ecologists study ecosystems on different scales from microcosms of, for example, one litre to systems of $1m^3$ to large-scale regional ecosystems of many square kilometres (Mooney et al., 1991; Naeem et al., 1994).

3. Ecosystem classification and productivity
It is common to classify ecosystems into biomes, that is the largest ecological unit recognized by the structure of its flora and fauna. The biomes include on the terrestrial side, arctic and alpine tundra, boreal coniferous forests, temperate deciduous forests, temperate grasslands, tropical savanna and grassland, Mediterranean vegetation or chaparal, deserts, semi-evergreen tropical forests and evergreen tropical rainforests. On the aquatic side marine ecosystems consist of open oceans, deep seas, continental shelves including coral reefs, upwelling areas and estuaries, and the freshwater ecosystems of lakes and ponds, rivers and streams, and wetlands (Odum, 1989). There are other ways of classifying ecosystems (Klijn, 1994). The eco-regions approach uses a detailed bioclimatic classification and several features of the landscape, such as soil type and drainage patterns (Bailey and Hogg, 1986). A review of ecosystem classification is given in the Global Biodiversity Assessment (1995). There are also classifications within a certain type of ecosystem. Coastal systems include rocky shores, sandy beaches, kelp forests, subtidal benthos, and the water column over the continental shelf, slope and rise. Lakes are sometimes classified according to their nutritional status. An oligotrophic lake is nutrient-poor and has clear water, whereas a eutrophic lake is often turbid from excess nutrients and plankton. An old-growth mature boreal forest looks very different from a boreal forest managed for timber production. An often-cited ecosystem classification which also provides information on productivity is shown in Table 61.1

4. Ecosystem development

4.1 Succession
The theory of ecological succession describes the development of ecosystems from colonization to mature or so-called climax stages (Odum, 1969). For example, a patch in a coniferous forest that has been clear-cut will go through a regeneration called succession of about 70–100 years from grass species and other opportunistic pioneers of plants and animals to a mature forest with pine trees and a ground-cover habitat dominated by blueberry vegetation. A similar pattern occurs on a much faster time scale for microorganisms. This is described in Figure 61.2.

In agriculture and fisheries human exploitation of living resources often makes use of the rapid growth phase of Figure 61.2. Unfortunately, such exploitation has led to the overexploitation of resources and depletion of ecosystem services, because the complex dynamics of populations and ecosystems that sustain them have been poorly understood and not accounted for (Regier and Baskerville, 1986; Ludwig et al., 1993). In

Table 61.1   Major ecosystems of the world, their area and productivity

Ecosystem type	Area 10^6km^2	Net primary production (dry matter) mean (normal range) gram/m²/year
Tropical rainforest	17.0	2200 (1000–3500)
Tropical seasonal forest	7.5	1600 (1000–2500)
Temperate forest:		
evergreen	5.0	1300 (600–2500)
deciduous	7.0	1200 (600–2500)
Boreal forest	12.0	800 (400–2000)
Woodland and shrubland	8.5	700 (250–1200)
Savanna	15.0	900 (200–2000)
Temperate grassland	9.0	600 (200–1500)
Tundra and alpine	8.0	140 (10–400)
Desert and semi-desert scrub	18.0	90 (10–250)
Extreme desert, rock, sand and ice	24.0	3 (0–10)
Cultivated land	14.0	650 (100–4000)
Swamp and marsh	2.0	3000 (800–6000)
Lake and stream	2.0	400 (100–1500)
Total continental	*149*	*782*
Open oceans	332.0	125 (2–400)
Upwelling zones	0.4	500 (400–1000)
Continental shelf	26.6	360 (200–600)
Algal beds and coral reefs	0.6	2500 (500–4000)
Estuaries	1.4	1500 (200–4000)
Total marine	*361*	*155*
Full total	*510*	*336*

Source: Whittaker and Likens (1975).

addition, as shown by Clark (1973), it makes economic sense (at least according to theory) to treat slowly reproducing living resources, like whales, as a non-renewable resource.

4.2   Dynamics of development
Based on empirical observations, Holling (1986) has described ecosystem behaviour as a dynamic sequential interaction between four system functions: exploitation, conservation, release and reorganization (Figure 61.3).

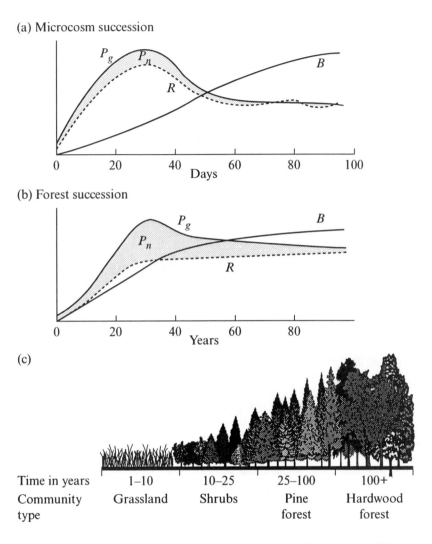

(a) Microcosm succession

(b) Forest succession

(c)

Time in years	1–10	10–25	25–100	100+
Community type	Grassland	Shrubs	Pine forest	Hardwood forest

Note: These two systems show a similar pattern of development, although at very different time-scales. In the microcosm (a) algal cells exploit the temporarily unlimited nutrients and undergo rapid growth. Bacteria, protozoa, nematodes, crustaceans and so on respond likewise so that total biomass increases rapidly. As resources such as space and nutrients reach saturation the rate of production becomes limited by the rate of decomposition and regeneration of nutrients. A similar sequence of forest succession is shown in (b) and illustrated in (c). P = production by photosynthesis, R = respiration or maintenance costs, B = biomass.

Source: Odum (1989).

Figure 61.2 Ecological succession in a forest and a microcosm

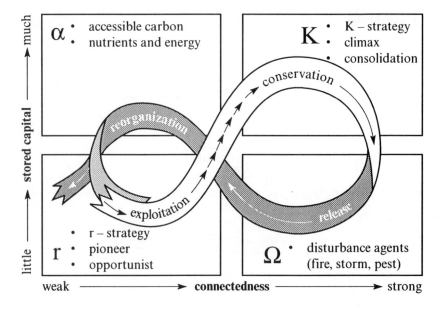

Note: Long arrows represent a rapid change and short arrows slow change. The phase from exploitation to conservation is similar to the ecological succession of Figure 61.2. The exit from the cycle at *x* indicates where loss of resilience (buffer capacity) causes a flip into a different ecosystem configuration.

Source: Holling (1992).

Figure 61.3   The four ecosystem phases and the flow of events among them

The first two are similar to succession. The effectiveness of the release and reorganization phases depend on resilience or the capacity of the system to buffer perturbations, shocks and surprises – its capacity to absorb them. The self-organizing ability of the system, or more particularly the resilience of that self-organization, determines its capacity to respond to stresses and shocks imposed by predation or pollution from external sources. As will be discussed below, biological diversity seems to play an important role in conserving ecosystem resilience, by absorbing disturbances and thereby conserving opportunity for renewal and novelty.

Natural disturbances, such as events triggered by fire, wind and herbivores, are an inherent part of the internal dynamics of ecosystems and in many cases set the timing of successional cycles (Holling, 1986). For example, small fires in a forest ecosystem release nutrients stored in the trees and support a spurt of new growth without destroying all the old growth. Subsystems in the forest are affected but the forest remains. If small fires are blocked out from a forest ecosystem through management, forest biomass will build up to high levels and when the fire does eventually come, it will wipe out the whole forest. Such events may flip the system to a totally new system that will not generate the same level of natural resources and ecosystem services. The dynamics of living resources and ecosystems is complex. Obviously, there are no simple answers, and few linear relationships between harvest of a living resource and regeneration rates. Successful management requires understanding of the ecosystem under exploitation.

5. Biological diversity and ecosystem functioning

Biological diversity plays an important role in ecosystem functions. Wilson (1992) defines biological diversity to include 'the variety of living organisms at all levels – from genetic variants belonging to the same species, through arrays of species, families and genera, and through population, community, habitat and even ecosystems levels. Biological diversity is, therefore, the diversity of life itself.' There is currently much research on the role of biodiversity in ecosystem function, and issues like stability and diversity, critical thresholds of diversity and the spatial and temporal scales over which diversity is particularly important are addressed (Naeem et al., 1994; Schulze and Mooney, 1993; Jones and Lawton, 1995; Holling et al., 1995; Tilman and Downing, 1994).

Ecologists still have insufficient knowledge on the role of particular species, or groups of species, over time, in the generation of ecosystem services. It seems, however, that there are some subgroups of species that are crucial in maintaining the organization and diversity of their ecological communities. These are often referred to as *keystone species* (Paine, 1969) or *keystone process species* (Holling et al., 1995). The effects of keystone species on their communities have been categorized as keystone predator, prey, herbivores, mutualists, competitors, hosts, pathogens, earth movers and modifiers (Bond, 1993; Mills et al., 1993).

The non-keystone process species, that is the remaining species, seem to depend on the niches formed by keystone process species and may not affect the critical structure and functioning of the ecosystem under normal conditions (phases of exploitation and conservation of Figure 61.3). However, although keystone process species are necessary for ecosystem functioning, they may not be sufficient for ecosystem sustainability. The non-keystone species may play an important ecological role by enabling the system to buffer disturbances, including human disturbance. It is in these situations that the buffer capacity, or ecosystem resilience, as defined in the previous section, is essential. In the evolution of the ecosystem over time, non-keystone species may transform into keystone process species through the internal reorganization of the ecosystem. Therefore the role of the non-keystone species in ecosystem resilience and their potential conversion to keystone process species needs to be better understood (Schulze and Mooney, 1993; Holling et al., 1995, Folke et al., 1996). In this way, it can be seen that diversity has two roles. First, it provides the units through which energy and material flow, giving the system its functional properties. Second, it provides the system with the resilience to respond to disturbances.

Biological diversity tends to be reduced in stressed biological communities. The effects of stress on ecosystem structure and function has been discussed by, for example, Odum (1985), and these characteristics have been compared with those of monocultures (Folke and Kautsky, 1992). A diverse mix of species and populations that can change in proportions and distribution has a much better chance of maintaining ecosystem function than a monoculture (Ehrlich and Daily, 1993). Land and water uses that reduce the diversity of the landscape, and with it communities, populations and species, are likely to be less resilient to change in the long run. The reduction and loss of species that are important as a buffer to disturbance may cause detrimental effects to the integrity of the ecosystem, and thereby to its capacity to generate ecosystem services – it implies a loss of opportunity.

6.   Ecosystems: essential factors of production

Ecosystems generate and sustain a flow of natural resources and ecosystem services. The natural resources include fish, trees, crops and wildlife. Ecosystem services include maintenance of the composition of the atmosphere, amelioration of climate, flood controls and water supply, waste assimilation, recycling of nutrients, generation of soils, pollination of crops, predation on pests, provision of food, maintenance of species and a vast genetic library, and also maintenance of the scenery of the landscape, recreational sites, aesthetic and amenity values (Westman, 1977; Folke, 1991; de Groot, 1992; Daily, 1997).

Since they generate a flow of essential natural resources and ecosystem services, ecosystems are essential *factors of production* for social and economic development. Biological diversity is part of these factors of production, and thereby sustains social and economic development, and the resilience – the buffer capacity – that it provides can be viewed as 'natural insurance capital' for securing the generation of essential ecological services under current and future environmental conditions (Barbier et al., 1994; Folke et al., 1996).

Ecosystems are multifunctional in the sense that each system produces several natural resources and ecological services. A forest produces timber but also assimilates nutrients and sequesters carbon dioxide. A fish population in the sea is not just a stock that generates a flow of fish. It is a part of

Table 61.2   Ecosystems generate and sustain essential natural resources and ecosystem services

Natural resources
oxygen
water for drinking, irrigation, industry etc.
crops, fruits, vegetables, meat, fish and shellfish, other food and nutritious
   drinks
fodder and fertilizer
genetic resources
medicinal resources and other biochemicals
fuel and energy
raw materials for clothing and household fabrics
raw materials for building, construction and industrial use etc.

Ecological or ecosystem services
fixation of solar energy
protection against harmful cosmic influences
regulation of the chemical composition of the atmosphere and oceans
modification of the hydrological cycle, including regulation of floods and
   run-off
water catchment and groundwater recharge
regulation of local and global climate and energy balance
formation of topsoil and maintenance of soil fertility
prevention of soil erosion and sediment control
food production by food webs
biomass production
storage and recycling of nutrients and organic matter
assimilation, storage and recycling of waste
maintenance of biological (including genetic) diversity
maintenance of habitats for migration and nursery
maintenance of the scenery of the landscape and recreational sites
provision of historic, spiritual, religious, aesthetic, educational and
   scientific information and of cultural and artistic inspiration, etc.

Source: Modified from de Groot (1992).

the ecosystem in which it lives, in which it is produced. It depends on other parts of the ecosystem, but also contributes to the production of other aquatic resources and services. Without biological diversity, substitution between different renewable resources and different ecosystem services would not be possible.

To reflect the value of the environmental resource base, the issue of joint products of ecosystems has to be addressed, and environmental economists have to collaborate with ecosystem ecologists for this purpose. Ideally this requires knowledge of the internal relationships of ecosystems, analysed for example through so-called network analysis, which consists of many tools and techniques familiar to economists (Wulff et al., 1989). Other modelling approaches are presented in, for example, Braat and van Lierop, 1987; Jörgensen, 1992; Costanza et al., 1990; Groffman and Likens, 1994; Hannon and Ruth, 1994; Bockstael et al., 1995.

The view that ecosystems are essential factors of production differs substantially from the conventional view of natural resources in natural resource economics or the view of the environment in environmental economics. There has been a tendency in environmental economics to focus on amenity values or on the economic consequences of certain pollutants. Natural resource economics has mainly analysed a single resource population in isolation from the ecosystem of which the population is a part, and the field has to a large extent relied on the use of fixed rules for achieving constant yields, as in fixed carrying capacity of animals and fixed maximum sustainable yields of fish and forest products. Methods of resource development and environmental management have treated the environment as discrete boxes of 'resources', the yields from which could be individually maximized.

An increasing number of case studies have shown that in many, if not most, cases of renewable resource and environmental management, the success in managing a resource or services (for example, crops, fish, timber, a nature reserve for recreation) for sustained production has led to an ultimate pathology of (1) more fragile, poorer, and vulnerable ecosystems, (2) more rigid and unresponsive management agencies, and (3) more dependent societies (Holling, 1986; Regier and Baskerville, 1986; Gunderson et al., 1995; Finlayson and McCay, 1998). Examples include the initial decades of chemical control of spruce budworm in Canadian forests – more and more control effort seems to result in larger and larger infestations when they do occur; and forest fire suppression in Yellowstone National Park in the US – almost half of the Park burned down in one major fire in 1988, following a century of fire suppression.

7. Improving the links between humans and ecosystems

The use and misuse of ecosystems affect the flow of resources and ecosystem services. But these changes are not signalled in market prices, generally not perceived by humans, nor in the institutions that provide the framework for human action. Degradation and simplification of ecosystems may not only reduce these flows, but may push the system towards a threshold and flip it into another stability domain, as illustrated in Figure 61.3. Impacts on one ecosystem may spill over into another, and affect the functioning of that system and the services it generates. The human uses of an ecosystem service are dependent on the existence, operation and maintenance of a multifunctional ecosystem, linked to other multifunctional ecosystems, to energy, biogeochemical and hydrological flows, and to other human uses and misuses affecting those flows. Due to the scale of the human dimension, such cross-scale interactions, both temporal and spatial, will increasingly challenge the flow of essential ecosystem services and support on which human welfare depends (Jansson et al., 1994).

Monetary values of the environment are directly or indirectly derived from consumer preferences. Humans are not always aware of the importance of multifunctional ecosystems for human welfare, and do not always perceive their indirect uses of critical resources and ecosystem services, and their dependence on ecosystem support. And even if they do, they may not value it. Preferences are not necessarily linked to biophysical realities.

Most ecologists would argue that ecosystem services and support are essential for society irrespective of whether or not they are perceived as important by humans. There are many ecosystem functions and services which meet the criteria of having economic value (they contribute to well-being and are scarce) but these are not recognized by many people. Therefore economic valuation based on an aggregation of preferences will only capture a part of the ecological preconditions for social and economic development (Costanza and Folke, 1997). Institutions are critical in this context since they provide the framework, the norms and rules for individuals (North, 1990).

The institutions of conventional resource management have been successful in producing yields and economic growth in the short term, but have not been very successful in safeguarding the dynamic capacity of ecosystems or in managing ecological and social systems for long-term well-being (Levin et al., 1998). For example, agricultural output could display a rising trend even when the soils are being mined. Soil erosion, masked by increasing input of fertilizers, irrigation or machinery, may lead to threshold effects, meaning that there can be discontinuities in the flow of services from an agricultural system (Dasgupta et al., 1994).

Clearly, conventional approaches will not suffice to cope with a spectrum of potentially catastrophic and irreversible environmental problems. According to Levin et al. (1998), these problems are characterized by: their unpredictability where surprises are to be expected; the potential importance of threshold effects in ecosystems with multi-equilibria; the difficulty of detecting change early enough to allow effective solutions, or even develop scientific consensus on a time scale rapid enough to allow effective solution; and the likelihood that the signal of change, even when detected, will be displaced in space and time from the source, so that motivation for action is small.

Environmental and renewable resource issues tend to cross temporal and spatial scales, and increasingly so in the light of the intensification of the human dimension. It follows therefore that the problems have to be tackled simultaneously at several levels. Conventional market mechanisms will be inadequate to deal with these problems. They require convexity, continuity and well-defined property rights, conditions that do not necessarily hold for the management of ecosystems. Therefore institutions are needed, and in particular institutions with response systems that are flexible and adaptive (Figure 61.4).

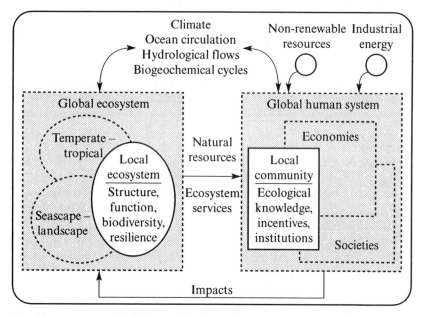

Note: Ecosystems are critical 'factors of production' sustaining society with a flow of essential natural resources and ecosystem services. Only a fraction of this capacity is covered by market prices, perceived by individuals, or taken into account by institutions.

Source: Folke (1998).

Figure 61.4   Combined system of humans and nature

There must be social mechanisms in a society by which information from the environment may be received, processed and interpreted to build resilience of the linked ecological–social–economic system. Combining principles and methods of ecosystem management (Samson and Knopf, 1996) with design principles of robust institutions (Ostrom, 1990; Hanna et al., 1996), with management practices and social mechanisms based on ecological knowledge (Berkes and Folke, 1998), and with insights gained in adaptive management (Gunderson et al., 1995) may provide important lessons for environmental economics, and contribute to improving the economic management and valuation of ecosystems – the essential factors of production for human welfare and existence.

References

Bailey, R.G. and H.C. Hogg (1986), 'A world ecoregion map for resource partitioning', *Environmental Conservation*, **13**, 195–202.

Barbier, E.B., J. Burgess and C. Folke (1994), *Paradise lost? The Ecological Economics of Biodiversity*, London: Earthscan.

Berkes, F. and C. Folke (eds) (1998), *Linking Social and Ecological Systems: Management Practices and Social Mechanisms for Building Resilience*, Cambridge, UK: Cambridge University Press.

Bockstael, N., R. Costanza, I. Strand, W. Boynton, K. Bell and L. Waigner (1995), 'Ecological economic modeling and valuation of ecosystems', *Ecological Economics*, **14**, 143–59.

Bond, W.J. (1993), 'Keystone species', in E.-D. Schulze and H.A. Mooney (eds), *Biodiversity and Ecosystem Function*, New York: Springer.

Braat, L.C. and W.F.J. van Lierop (eds) (1987), *Economic–Ecological Modeling*, Amsterdam: North-Holland.

Clapham, W.B. (1973), *Natural Ecosystems*, New York: Macmillan.

Clark, C.W. (1973), 'The economics of overexploitation', *Science*, **181**, 630–34.

Costanza, R. and C. Folke (1997), 'Valuing ecosystem services with efficiency, fairness and sustainability as goals', in G. Daily (ed.), *Nature's Services: Societal Dependence on Natural Ecosystems*, Washington, DC: Island Press, pp. 49–68.

Costanza, R., F.H. Sklar and M.L. White (1990), 'Modeling coastal landscape dynamics', *BioScience*, **40**, 91–107.

Costanza, R., L. Waigner, C. Folke and K.-G. Mäler (1993), 'Modeling complex ecological economic systems: toward an evolutionary dynamic understanding of people and nature', *BioScience*, **43**, 545–55.

Daily, G. (ed.) (1997), *Nature's Services: Societal Dependence on Natural Ecosystems*, Washington, DC: Island Press.

Daily, G. and P.R. Ehrlich (1992), 'Population, sustainability, and Earth's carrying capacity', *BioScience*, **42**, 761–71.

Dasgupta, P. (1997), 'Economics of the environment', *Environment and Development Economics*, **1**, 387–428.

Dasgupta, P., C. Folke and K.-G. Mäler (1994), 'The environmental resource base and human welfare', in K. Lindahl-Kiessling and H. Landberg (eds), *Population, Economic Development, and the Environment*, Oxford: Oxford University Press, pp. 25–50.

de Groot, R.S. (1992), *Functions of Nature*, Amsterdam: Wolters-Noordhoff.

Ehrlich, P.E. and G.C. Daily (1993), 'Population extinction and saving biodiversity', *Ambio*, **22**, 64–8.

Ehrlich, P.R., A.H. Ehrlich and J.P. Holdren (1977), *EcoScience: Population, Resource, Environment*, San Francisco: Freeman.

Finlayson, A.C. and B.J. McCay (1998), 'Crossing the threshold of ecosystem resilience: the commercial extinction of Northern cod', in F. Berkes and C. Folke (eds), *Linking Social and Ecological Systems: Management Practices and Social Mechanisms for Building Resilience*, Cambridge: Cambridge University Press.

Folke, C. (1991), 'Socioeconomic dependence on the life-supporting environment', in C. Folke and T. Kåberger (eds), *Linking the Natural Environment and the Economy: Essays from the Eco-Eco Group*, Dordrecht: Kluwer Academic Publishers.

Folke, C. (1998), 'Ecosystem approaches to the management and allocation of critical resources', in P.M. Groffman and M.L. Pace (eds), *Successes, Limitations and Frontiers in Ecosystem Science*, Cary Conference 1997, Institute of Ecosystem Studies, New York: Millbrook and Springer-Verlag, pp. 313–45.

Folke, C. and N. Kautsky (1992), 'Aquaculture with its environment: prospects for sustainability', *Ocean and Coastal Management*, **17**, 5–24.

Folke, C., C.S. Holling and C. Perrings (1996), 'Biological diversity, ecosystems, and the human scale', *Ecological Applications*, **6**, 1018–24.

Groffman, P.M. and G.E. Likens (eds) (1994), *Integrated Regional Models: Interactions between Humans and their Environment*, New York: Chapman and Hall.

Gunderson, L., C.S. Holling and S. Light (eds) (1995), *Barriers and Bridges to the Renewal of Ecosystems and Institutions*, New York: Columbia University Press.

Hanna, S., C. Folke and K.-G. Mäler (eds) (1996), *Rights to Nature*, Washington, DC: Island Press.

Hannon, B. and M. Ruth (1994), *Dynamic Modeling*, New York: Springer-Verlag.

Holling, C.S. (1986), 'The resilience of terrestrial ecosystems: local surprise and global change', in W.C. Clark and R.E. Munn (eds), *Sustainable Development of the Biosphere*, London: Cambridge University Press, pp. 292–317.

Holling, C.S. (1992), 'Cross-scale morphology, geometry, and dynamics of ecosystems', *Ecological Monographs*, **62**, 447–502.

Holling, C.S. (1994), 'An ecologists view of the Malthusian conflict', in K. Lindahl-Kiessling and H. Landberg (eds), *Population, Economic Development, and the Environment*, Oxford: Oxford University Press, pp. 79–103.

Holling, C.S., D.W. Schindler, B.H. Walker and J. Roughgarden (1995), 'Biodiversity in the functioning of ecosystems: an ecological synthesis', in C.A. Perrings, K.-G. Mäler, C. Folke, C.S. Holling and B.-O. Jansson (eds), *Biodiversity Loss: Economic and Ecological Issues*, Cambridge, UK: Cambridge University Press.

Houghton, J.T. et al. (eds) (1996), *Climate Change 1995: The Science of Climate Change*, Cambridge, UK: Cambridge University Press.

Jansson, A.M., M. Hammer, C. Folke and R. Costanza (eds) (1994), *Investing in Natural Capital: The Ecological Economics Approach to Sustainability*, Washington, DC: Island Press.

Jones, C.G. and J.H. Lawton (eds) (1995), *Linking Species and Ecosystems*, New York: Chapman and Hall.

Jörgensen, S.-E. (1992), *Integration of Ecosystem Theories: A Pattern*, Dordrecht: Kluwer Academic Publishers.

Klijn, F. (ed.) (1994), *Ecosystem Classification for Environmental Management*, Dordrecht: Kluwer Academic Publishers.

Levin, S.A. (1992), 'The problem of pattern and scale in ecology', *Ecology*, **73**, 1943–67.

Levin, S.A., S. Barrett, S. Aniyar, W. Baumol, C. Bliss, B. Bolin, P. Dasgupta, P. Ehrlich, C. Folke, I.M. Gren, C.S. Holling, A.M. Jansson, B.-O. Jansson, D. Martin, K.-G. Mäler, C. Perrings and E. Sheshinsky (1998), 'Resilience in natural and socioeconomic systems', *Environment and Development Economics*, **3**, 222–35.

Ludwig, D., R. Hilborn and C. Walters (1993), 'Uncertainty, resource exploitation and conservation: lessons from history', *Science*, **260**, 1736.

McDonnell, M.J. and S.T.A. Pickett (eds) (1993), *Humans as Components of Ecosystems: The Ecology of Subtle Human Effects and Populated Areas*, New York: Springer-Verlag.

McMichael, A.J. et al. (1996), *Climate Change and Human Health*, Geneva: WHO.

Mills, L.S., M.E. Soulé and D.F. Doak (1993), 'The keystone-species concept in ecology and conservation', *BioScience*, **43**, 219–24.

Mooney, H.A., E. Medina, D.W. Schindler, E.-D. Schulze and B.H. Walker (eds) (1991), *Ecosystem Experiments. SCOPE 45*, New York: John Wiley & Sons.

Naeem, S., L.J. Thompson, S.P. Lawler, J.H. Lawton and R.M. Woodfin (1994), 'Declining biodiversity can alter the performance of ecosystems', *Nature*, **368**, 734–7.

North, D.C. (1990), *Institutions, Institutional Change and Economic Performance*, Cambridge, UK: Cambridge University Press.

Odum, E.P. (1969), 'The strategy of ecosystem development', *Science*, **164**, 262–70.

Odum, E.P. (1985), 'Trends to be expected in stressed ecosystems', *BioScience*, **35**, 419–22.

Odum, E.P. (1989), *Ecology and Our Endangered Life-Support Systems*, Sunderland, MA: Sinauer Associates.

Odum, H.T. (1971), *Energy, Power and Society*, New York: John Wiley.

O'Neil, R.V., D.L. DeAngelis, J.B. Waide and T.F.H. Allen (1986), *A Hierarchical Concept of Ecosystems*, Princeton, NJ: Princeton University Press.

Ostrom, E. (1990), *Governing the Commons: The Evolution of Institutions for Collective Actions*, Cambridge, UK: Cambridge University Press.

Paine, R.T. (1969), 'A note on trophic complexity and community stability', *American Naturalist*, **103**, 91–93.

Perrings, C., C. Folke and K.-G. Mäler (1992), 'The ecology and economics of biodiversity loss', *Ambio*, **21**, 201–11.

Pimm, S.L. (1991), *The Balance of Nature?*, Chicago: University of Chicago Press.

Pomeroy, L.R. and J.J. Alberts (eds) (1988), *Concepts of Ecosystem Ecology*, Heidelberg: Springer-Verlag.

Regier, H.A. and G.L. Baskerville (1986), 'Sustainable redevelopment of regional ecosystems degraded by exploitative development', in W.C. Clark and R.E. Munn (eds), *Sustainable Development of the Biosphere*, Cambridge, UK: Cambridge University Press.

Samson, F.B. and F.L. Knopf (eds) (1996), *Ecosystem Management: Selected Readings*, New York: Springer-Verlag, pp. 148–63.

Schindler, D.W. (1990), 'Experimental perturbations of whole lakes as tests of hypotheses concerning ecosystem structure and function', *Oikos*, **57**, 25–41.

Schulze, E.-D. and H.A. Mooney (eds) (1993), *Biodiversity and Ecosystem Function*, New York: Springer.

Tilman, D. and J.A. Downing (1994), 'Biodiversity and stability in grasslands', *Nature*, **367**, 363–5.

Turner, B.L., W.C. Clark and W.C. Kates (eds) (1990), *The Earth as Transformed by Human Action: Global and Regional Changes in the Biosphere over the past 300 Years*, Cambridge, UK: Cambridge University Press.

UNEP (1995), *Global Biodiversity Assessment*, Cambridge: Cambridge University Press.

Vitousek, P.M. (1990), 'Biological invasions and ecosystem processes: towards an integration of population ecology and ecosystem studies', *Oikos*, **57**, 7–13.

Westman, W.E. (1977), 'How much are nature's services worth?', *Science*, **197**, 960–64.

Whittaker, R.H. and G.E. Likens (1975), 'The biosphere and man', in H. Lieth and R.H. Whittaker (eds), *Primary Productivity of the Biosphere*, New York: Springer-Verlag, pp. 305–28.

Wilson, E.O. (1992), *The Diversity of Life*, Cambridge, MA: Belknap.

Wulff, F., J.G. Fields and K.H. Mann (eds) (1989), *Network Analysis of Marine Ecosystems: Methods and Applications*, Heidelberg: Springer-Verlag.

62 Industrial metabolism and the grand nutrient cycles

Robert U. Ayres

1. Introduction

The world we live in can be described as a hierarchy of nested non-linear subsystems of a very complex non-linear dynamic system. Each subsystem exhibits variability in several dimensions, including both time and space. Each is a consequence of long-term co-evolution, with links to other subsystems. The earth is part of the solar system, which is a small corner of the galaxy, but life on earth is totally dependent on energy (exergy) from the sun.

Life also depends on the climate, the hydrological cycle and the nutrient cycles. The climate itself is strongly determined by the carbon–oxygen cycle and the hydrological cycle. Thus the biogeochemical system that constitutes the earth as we know it is in many respects self-organized. All these cycles can be characterized, in Prigogine's terms, as 'dissipative systems' that are far from thermodynamic equilibrium (for example, Nicolis and Prigogine, 1977). (If the earth were in thermodynamic equilibrium in the sense that all possible chemical processes among its constituent elements had proceeded as far as possible, it would be uninhabitable and truly dead.) In any case the biosphere and its supporting geochemical cycles exist in a quasi-steady state subject to constant (and largely unpredictable) fluctuations around an 'attractor'. The 'attractor' itself can move unpredictably, as a result of natural forces or human interventions.

The grand nutrient cycles discussed below affect economic activity in several domains, from agriculture and forestry to construction and tourism. Moreover, these cycles are also peculiarly subject to inadvertent human intervention, resulting from agricultural and industrial activity. Thus, it is appropriate – indeed essential – for economic modellers concerned with long-term growth and sustainable development to recognize and take into account these (among other) links between human and natural systems. Indeed, it can be argued that this linkage, taken generally, constitutes the essential core of 'industrial metabolism' or 'industrial ecology'.

2. The nutrient cycles

There are four major elements that are required by the biosphere in significantly greater quantities than they are chemically available in nature. These four are carbon (C), nitrogen (N), sulphur (S) and phosphorus (P). (Hydrogen and oxygen, the other two major ingredients of organic materials, are not scarce in the earth's crust, at least, though oxygen is also recycled along with carbon.) These natural cycles are driven by geological, hydrological, atmospheric and biological processes that have evolved over billions of years. Ultimately, most of these processes are driven by the influx of solar energy (exergy), albeit in different and complexly interrelated ways. Interruption or disturbance of these natural cycles as a consequence of human industrial/economic activity could adversely affect the stability of the biosphere, and might possibly reduce its productivity. (It might also have the opposite effect, but that seems much less likely.) Unfortunately, the interactions between economic activity and nutrient cycles, and between these cycles themselves, have received relatively little attention from scientists up to now.

The nutrient cycles, as they exist today, are consequences of biogeological evolutionary processes that occurred, for the most part, hundreds of millions of years ago. An observer from another galaxy might well regard these cycles as the most significant consequence of that early evolutionary development. In fact, the nutrient elements (C, N, S, P) were *not* recycled during the earth's early history. It should be noted that the atmosphere of the early earth certainly contained no free oxygen, and the Earth's crust certainly contained no free carbon or sulphur. It is currently thought to have consisted of carbon dioxide, nitrogen and water vapour, although the presence of free nitrogen is uncertain. Methane and ammonia may have been present.

The earliest known forms of life, about 3.5 billion years ago, were single-celled prokaryotic[2] organisms – essentially, protobacteria – which obtained the energy needed for their metabolic processes from a supply of simple organic molecules, like glucose. Nobody knows the origin of this primitive food supply. It may have been synthesized on earth by some unknown abiotic process. Or it may have been created originally in cold interplanetary space. The key metabolic process of the first protobacteria was *fermentation*, schematically represented by the sequence:

$$\text{glucose} \rightarrow \text{pyruvate} \rightarrow \text{ethyl alcohol } and/or \text{ lactic acid} + CO_2$$

Since there was no mechanism for replacing the original 'food' supply, this population of fermenting organisms was not stable, or sustainable. Carbon was not recycled. Nothing was.

Fortunately, after the passage of half a billion years or so, the problem was solved by an evolutionary 'great leap forward'. This was the appearance of the first prokaryotic *photobacteria*. These were organisms capable of utilizing the energy of sunlight to create glucose from carbon dioxide. However, there was a waste product from this reaction, namely oxygen. Oxygen was highly toxic to all early forms of life. Luckily, it did not accumulate in the atmosphere at first. For a long time it was removed from circulation almost as fast as it was formed. Oxygen reacted with soluble ferrous iron and/or sulphides to form insoluble ferric iron and calcium sulphates. These materials were deposited on the ocean floor as hematite (iron ore) and gypsum, respectively. We mine these ores today. This is just one of the linkages between human economic activity and biogeochemical activity, although not the closest one.

However, life on planet earth would have self-destructed from oxygen poisoning if a series of other evolutionary developments had not occurred. Perhaps the most important was the appearance of the first oxygen-tolerant photosynthesizers. These were cyanobacteria (2 billion years ago). The next important evolutionary step (1.5 billion years ago) was even more radical: it was an extension of the fermentation process to oxidize the organic waste products (for example lactic acid) to yield carbon dioxide, plus additional metabolic energy. This new process is *aerobic respiration*. As it happens, aerobic respiration is 18 times more efficient (in energy terms) than fermentation. Thus the respirators (eukaryotes) eventually out-competed fermenters in aerobic environments. The fermenters have been relegated to anaerobic environments, such as lake bottoms, sediments and swamps.

The advent of aerobic respiration created a route for the closure of both the oxygen and carbon cycles, for the first time. The evolutionary history of the nitrogen, sulphur and phosphorus cycles is less well known. However, all the grand nutrient cycles did evolve, over billions of years, to a relatively stable state. Thermodynamically they are all oxidation–reduction cycles involving a number of biologically driven steps.

It is convenient for purposes of exposition to describe the grand nutrient cycles in functional terms, as illustrated by Figure 62.1. The cycles differ markedly in terms of the physical and chemical form of the major inorganic reservoir, and the mechanisms for transfer from one reservoir to another. When an element passes from the bio-unavailable inorganic reservoir to the bio-available reservoir it is said to be *mobilized*. In the case of nitrogen, mobilization essentially consists of splitting the dinitrogen N_2 molecule, which is quite stable.[3] When a nutrient moves in the reverse direction it is *sequestrated*. (In the case of carbon, the term is also used in connection with the accumulation of carbon or carbon dioxide in a reser-

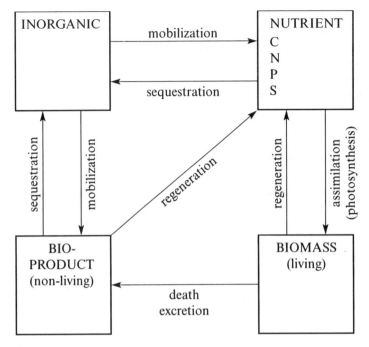

Notes:
INORGANIC:
  Sedimentary rocks, ferric iron, sulphate, carbonate, phosphate
NUTRIENT:
  CO_2 in air or water (O_2), soluble N, P, S
BIO-PRODUCT:
  Organic carbon (humus), Detritus, CH_4, O_2

Figure 62.1   Four-box scheme for biogeochemical cycles

voir from which CO_2 cannot reach the atmosphere.) A nutrient can pass from an organic reservoir (for example dead plant material) to an inorganic reservoir by *decomposition* or (in the case of nitrogen) bacterial *denitrification*.

There are really two generic subcycles. The first is an exchange of the nutrient element between a bio-unavailable reservoir and a bio-available reservoir. For instance, in the case of carbon, there are two bio-unavailable forms. One is the sedimentary calcium and magnesium carbonates (limestone, dolomite), and the other is reduced carbon (kerogen), also in sediments and sedimentary rocks such as shales. The bio-available (nutrient) form of carbon is the dissolved bicarbonate ion (HCO_3^-) in water or atmospheric carbon dioxide. In the case of nitrogen, the bio-unavailable reservoir is atmospheric dinitrogen (N_2) while the bioavailable forms constituting the nutrient pool are dissolved nitrates (NO_3^-) or ammonium (NH_4^+) ions. In the case of sulphur, there are, again, two major reservoirs. The bio-unavailable reservoir consists of insoluble sulphates (for example gypsum) and buried metallic sulphides (for example pyrites). The bio-available reservoir consists of sulphur-containing organic compounds. In the case of phosphorus, the main bio-unavailable reservoir is the mineral apatite $\left(Ca_5(PO_4)_3OH\right)$. Again, the bio-available reservoir consists mainly of organic materials.

Table 62.1 shows the (approximate) quantities of C, N, S, P in the various reservoirs. Table 62.2 shows the ratios of C, N, P in some of the major reservoirs. Apart from reservoirs, it is important to identify carriers. For carbon there are two main gaseous carriers: carbon dioxide (CO_2) and methane CH_4). The water-soluble form of carbon is bicarbonate (HCO_3^-), which is also a carrier. For nitrogen the main gaseous carriers are nitrogen oxides (NO_x) and ammonia (NH_3); most ammonium compounds and nitrates are soluble in water, but the main aqueous form is the nitrate ion (NO_3^-). In the case of sulphur, the inorganic gaseous media are hydrogen sulphide (H_2S), carbonyl sulphide (COS), carbon disulphide (CS_2) and dimethylsulphide $\left(DMS=(CH_3)_2S\right)$ and sulphur dioxide (SO_2); the main aqueous form is the sulphate ion ($SO_4^=$), but DMS is also quite soluble in water. The only phosphorus carriers are phosphate ions ($PO_4^=$). (The aqueous form is phosphoric acid H_3PO_4).

The second generic sub-cycle is an exchange between the bio-available nutrient reservoir and living organisms themselves, which constitute a secondary reservoir of the nutrient. The reverse transfer, by decomposition or mineralization, has already been mentioned. In the case of carbon the conversion of CO_2 to its primary biological form (ribose, a kind of sugar) is accomplished by photosynthetic organisms. Most of the other transfers in this subcycle are carried out by specialized bacteria or by enzymes within cells. For instance, nitrogen in living (or dead) organisms is normally in the amine group ($-NH_2$). A few free living bacteria – notably *Rhizobium* – and some anaerobic cyanobacteria and yeasts have the ability to split the dinitrogen molecule and *fix* nitrogen in a bio-available form.

Aerobic bacteria require oxygen for metabolic purposes. The usual metabolic process is respiration, in which organic material of the general form (CH_2O) is oxidized by molecular oxygen from the atmosphere to CO_2 and H_2O. If atmospheric oxygen is not available, bacteria will obtain it from other molecular sources. In order of decreasing preference – as measured by a quantity called 'redox potential' – these oxygen sources, termed 'electron acceptors', are: NO_3^-, MnO_2, $Fe(OH)_3$, and SO_4^-. Some anaerobic bacteria can also break the CH_2O molecule directly, yielding CO_2 and methane (CH_4). Carbon dioxide and water are the main products in every case, but

Table 62.1 Nutrient reservoirs participating in global cycles (excluding elements in igneous rock)

Nutrient/stable form	Atmosphere	Hydrosphere	Lithosphere	Terrestrial biosphere	Marine biosphere
Carbon (Pg C)					
Carbonate			10^7		
CO_2	750				
CH_4	3		1500	610	3
Organic (DOC, POC)		740+30	10^6		
Fossil organic (kerogen)		150			
Carbonates ($CO_3^=$, HCO_3^-)		38 100			
Nitrogen (Tg N)					
Elemental (N_2)	3.8×10^9	2×10^7			
N_2O	1500				
NO_x	0.6				
Organic (DON, PON)		530+240	95 000	3500	300
Inorganic (DIN, PIN)		530	1.9×10^{11}		
Sulphur (Tg S)					
SO_2	4.8				
Organic		$\left.\begin{array}{c} \\ \end{array}\right\} 1.3 \times 10^9$	3×10^5	760	30
Inorganic, dissolved					
Inorganic sulphate ($SO_4^=$), solid		3×10^8	2×10^{10}		
Phosphorus (Tg P)					
Organic (DOP)		650	96 000	260	50–120
Phosphoric acid (DIP)		89 000			
Inorganic, solid		0.84×10^9	19 000		

DO = Dissolved organic, PO = Particulate organic, DI = Dissolved inorganic, PI = Particulate inorganic

Sources: Den Elzen et al. (1995); IPCC (1995).

Table 62.2   Ratios of C, N and P in various reservoirs

	C	N	P
Terrestrial vegetation[a]	800	5	1
Marine plankton[b]		16	1
Soil[c]	30	2	[d]1
Sediment		15	1
Anthropogenic[e]		15	1

Notes:
[a] C:P from Deevey (1970); the C:N ratio for terrestrial biomass has been calculated to be 160 (Schlesinger, 1991), whence N:P = 5.
[b] Redfield et al. (1963).
[c] The C:N ratio for soil has been estimated to be 15 (Schlesinger, 1991).
[d] Including insoluble P; if only soluble P is included, the C:P and N:P ratios are more than 2 orders of magnitude higher.
[e] Assuming C mobilized by fossil fuel combustion; N mobilized by industrial fixation (fertilizer) and NO_x by combustion; P is mobilized by phosphate rock mining.

Source: Stumm (1977), Table 3, p. 268.

other by-products are generated. For instance, the process of denitrification yields N_2 or N_2O, desulphonation yields H_2S, and so on. These are the gases that transfer nutrients between marine and terrestrial reservoirs.

In principle, anaerobic bacteria could also extract oxygen from the phosphate radical PO_4, yielding a gaseous compound, phosphine (H_3P). However, phosphorus is extraordinarily attracted to oxygen (which is why phosphate groups are oxygen carriers in all living organisms). If phosphine were produced it would be reoxidized very rapidly in today's atmosphere, which limits the possibilities for transport of phosphorus in gaseous form over significant distances.

It is tempting, but potentially misleading, to compare the pre-industrial nutrient 'cycles' (C, N, S) with the current fluxes, on the assumption that these three cycles were in, or very near, a steady state in pre-industrial times. Steady state, in this context, means that each of the major reservoirs remains essentially constant or fluctuates within narrow limits. Inputs and outputs of each species to each reservoir must exactly balance (on average) any chemical transformations from one species to another in a steady-state condition. By this straightforward test, as will be seen, none of the grand nutrient cycles is in steady state now. However, it seems that the grand nutrient cycles are seldom in balance for long, if ever, thanks to geological processes such as continental drift, uplifts, episodic vulcanism and ice ages that occur over geological time scales. Thus it can be quite misleading to compare the current state of imbalance with a hypothetical balance condition.

Brief descriptions of the main cycles follow.

3. The carbon cycle

The 'slow' carbon cycle

The major inorganic reservoir of carbon (Table 62.1) is sedimentary carbonate rocks, such as limestone or calcite ($CaCO_3$) and dolomite $\left(CaMg(CO_3)_2\right)$. This reservoir contains more than 10^5 times more carbon than the atmosphere and the biosphere together. These reservoirs participate in a 'slow' (inorganic) cycle, in which carbon dioxide from the atmosphere is taken up by the weathering of silicate rocks, driven (as mentioned below) by the hydrological cycle. This occurs in a reaction that can be summarized by

$$CaSiO_3 + CO_2 + 2H_2O \rightarrow Ca(OH)_2 + SiO_2 + H_2CO_3 \qquad (62.1)$$

The calcium, magnesium and bicarbonate ions, as well as the dissolved silica, in the surface waters are carried to the oceans. There the dissolved calcium, silica, carbonate and bicarbonate are either precipitated inorganically or picked up by marine organisms and incorporated into their shells as calcium carbonate and opal.[4] The calcium and carbonate part of the marine system can be summarized as:

$$Ca(OH)_2 + H_2CO_3 \rightarrow CaCO_3 + 2H_2O \qquad (62.2)$$

In due course the inorganic precipitates and shells drift down to the ocean floor as sediments, eventually being converted by heat and pressure into limestone, chalk and quartz. The sum of the two reactions is

$$CaSiO_3 + CO_2 \rightarrow CaCO_3 + SiO_2 \qquad (62.3)$$

The observed rate of calcium carbonate deposition would use up all the carbon dioxide in the oceans in about 400 000 years.

However, there is another chemical reaction that occurs at high pressures and temperatures. This reaction reverses the direction of reaction (62.3) and reconverts sedimentary calcium and/or magnesium carbonate rocks (mixed with quartz) into calcium or magnesium silicate, releasing gaseous CO_2. This process occurs when carbonate sedimentary rocks are subducted into the Earth's molten mantle, due to tectonic action in the Earth's crust. The CO_2 is then vented through volcanic eruptions or hot springs. Weathering rates are relatively easier to measure (Holland, 1978; Berner et al., 1983) compared to outgassing rates (Berner, 1990; Gerlach, 1991). But insofar as the data are available, the two rates (CO_2 uptake and emission) appear to agree within a factor of 2 (Kasting and Walker, 1992). The fact that agreement is not closer is an indication that much remains to be learned about the details of these biogeochemical processes.

The silicate weathering rate is directly dependent on climate conditions. In principle, there is a somewhat crude geological mechanism that would tend to keep the silicate weathering rate roughly equal to the volcanic out-gassing rate, over very long time periods. A build-up of CO_2 in the atmos-phere would lead to greenhouse warming. This increases the rate of evaporation (and precipitation) of water, thus accelerating the weathering process, which removes CO_2 from the atmosphere. This would eventually halt the temperature rise. If the atmospheric CO_2 level rises, due to abnor-mal volcanic activity, there will be an increase in the rate of weathering and CO_2 uptake. Conversely, if the CO_2 level drops, so will the temperature and the weathering rate.[5] In fact, it is asserted by some geologists that the inor-ganic carbon cycle is sufficient to explain the major features of paleo-climatic history (Holland, 1978; Berner et al., 1983).

Berner's model failed to explain one major feature, however: the fact that the Earth's climate has actually cooled significantly during the last 50 million years. But thanks to more recent work there is now a strong presumption that the cause of this cooling is also geological (that is, tectonic) in origin. In brief, during that period the Indian subcontinent moved north and collided with Asia (actually, about 35 million years ago), forcing the Tibetan plateau to rise. The rise of this enormous mountain range, in turn, must have sharply increased the rate of CO_2 removal from the atmosphere (Raymo and Ruddiman, 1992). This would account for the observed cooling.[6]

The 'fast' carbon cycle
The geochemical response mechanisms described above are much too slow to account for the strong observed correlation between climate and atmos-pheric CO_2 levels over much shorter periods. These are part of the 'fast' carbon cycle, which is biologically controlled. The observed seasonal cycle of atmospheric CO_2 is an obvious short-term effect of the biosphere. Photosynthetic activity in the spring and summer in the northern hemi-sphere brings about a measurable reduction in the atmospheric CO_2 concentration. Actually, CO_2 is biologically transformed by photosynthesis into sugars and cellulose, with the generic formula CH_2O, that is:

$$CO_2 + H_2O \rightarrow CH_2O + O_2 \qquad (62.4)$$

Aerobic respiration is the reverse of carbon fixation. On a longer time scale, CO_2 fertilization of terrestrial vegetation is a factor (along with temperature) tending to maintain atmospheric CO_2 at a constant level. Rising atmospheric carbon dioxide directly enhances the rate of photosynthesis, other factors being equal.[7] It also causes climate warming, and increased rainfall, both of which further enhance the rate of plant growth, subject to the availability of other nutrients, water, and so on.

However, the organic carbon cycle cannot be understood in terms of the biochemistry of photosynthesis alone. Nor is all sedimentary carbon in the form of carbonates. There is a significant reservoir of reduced organic carbon (kerogen), buried in sediments, some of which has been aggregated by geological processes and transformed by heat or biological activity to form coal, petroleum and (possibly) natural gas.[8] Of course, it is the geologically concentrated sedimentary hydrocarbons that constitute our fossil fuel resources and which are currently being reconverted to CO_2 by combustion.

The methane subcycle

Methane (CH_4) has its own subcycle. In any anaerobic environment – including the guts of cellulose-ingesting animals such as ungulates and termites – organic carbon is broken down by bacteria. The methane is generated according to the reaction:

$$2CH_2O \rightarrow CO_2 + CH_4 \qquad (62.5)$$

In sediments, these anaerobic bacteria produce 'swamp gas' (while the organic nitrogen and sulphur are reduced to ammonia and hydrogen sulphide). In the stomachs and intestines of grazing animals such as cattle and sheep, or termites, the methane is excreted by belching.

As noted previously, the existence of free oxygen in the atmosphere is due to the fact that so much organic carbon has been sequestered over eons by burial in silt. Nevertheless, at least half of all buried organic carbon is recycled to the atmosphere by anaerobic methanation. The methane in the atmosphere is gradually oxidized, via many steps, to CO_2. It is not recycled biologically, as such.

However, at present methane is being emitted to the atmosphere faster than it is being removed. The total atmospheric reservoir is quite disputed, since the residence time is difficult to measure precisely. Global atmospheric concentrations are increasing; they increased 11 per cent between 1978 and 1987 alone (Mackenzie et al., 1993). Annual sources currently exceed sinks by around 10 per cent (ibid.). This is a matter of concern, since methane is a very potent greenhouse gas, much more so than CO_2. Clearly, any mechanism that increases the rate of methane production by anaerobic bacteria will have a pronounced impact on climate, *ceteris paribus*. For instance, the expansion of wet rice cultivation in the orient, together with the spread of cattle and sheep husbandry worldwide, constitute a significant anthropogenic interference in the natural methane cycle.

The carbon cycle as a whole
The carbon cyle as a whole is summarized in Figures 62.2 and 62.3. The carbon cycle is not now in balance. (Whether it was truly balanced in pre-industrial times is debatable; for example Sundquist, 1993). In any case, the carbon dioxide level of the atmosphere has been rising sharply for over a

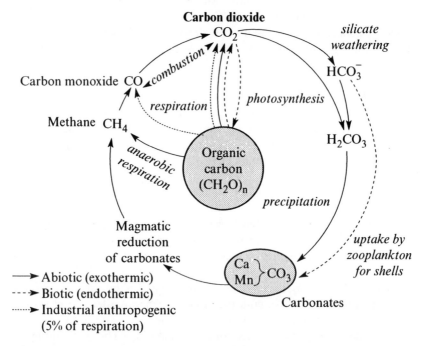

Figure 62.2   Carbon cycle: chemical transformations

century. Anthropogenic extraction and combustion of carbonaceous fuels, together with deforestation to clear land for agriculture, have contributed significantly to altering the atmospheric CO_2 balance. About 5 per cent of total CO_2 emissions from the land to the atmosphere are anthropogenic (Bolin, 1986). The CO_2 concentration is now more than 360 parts per million (ppm), more that 25 per cent above the pre-industrial level (estimated to be 280 ppm). The rate of increase is about 0.4 per cent per year.

As of 1990 approximately 5.4×10^{15}g/yr of carbon was being converted to CO_2 by combustion processes and transferred from underground reser-

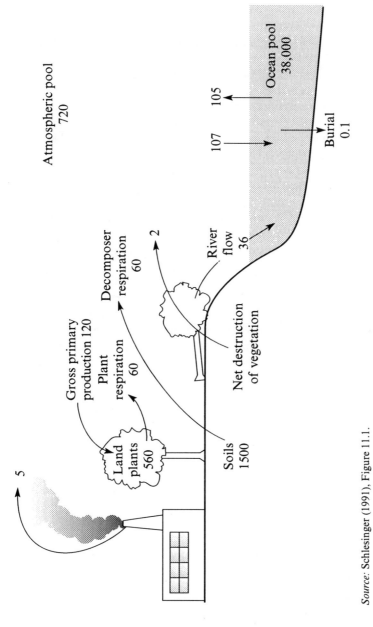

Atmospheric pool
720

Gross primary
production 120

Plant
respiration
60

Decomposer
respiration
60

Land
plants
560

Soils
1500

5

2

River
flow
36

Net destruction
of vegetation

Ocean pool
38,000

105

107

Burial
0.1

Source: Schlesinger (1991), Figure 11.1.

Figure 62.3   Present-day carbon cycle: intermedia fluxes (10^15 g C)

voirs of reduced carbon to the atmosphere. A further 1.6×10^{15}g/yr is attributed to tropical deforestation, for a total of 7×10^{15}g/yr (Stern et al., 1992, Table 3.2).

Roughly half of this excess anthropogenic flux, or 3.5×10^{15}g/yr, is known to be accumulating in the atmosphere. At first glance, it would appear that the remainder must be accumulating either in the oceans or in terrestrial biomass. Although it has been assumed until recently that the ocean must be the ultimate sink (see Peng et al., 1983), there is increasing evidence that the known atmosphere–ocean transfer mechanisms cannot account for all the 'missing' carbon (Tans et al., 1990; Schlesinger, 1991; Sundquist, 1993). Some oceanographers have suggested that the estimates of carbon lost from land may be too high or that the rate of photosynthesis by the remaining vegetation – especially northern forests – may be stimulated by higher atmospheric CO_2 concentrations, climatic warming and/or nitrogen fertilization (from NO_x emissions and deposition of nitrates).

The 1990 IPCC 'business as usual' projections of atmospheric CO_2 concentrations to the year 2100 appear to have neglected or underestimated this fertilization effect, resulting in an overestimate of the order of 66 ppm (that is, the difference between 761 ppm and 827 ppm) (den Elzen, 1994). However, simulation models of the carbon cycle, working both 'forward' and 'backward', have contributed significantly to clarification of the situation. To summarize some recent research, it appears that the most plausible way to balance the carbon budget, within historical emissions and parametric uncertainty ranges, is to introduce a biospheric 'sink' for CO_2 – mostly in the northern hemisphere – probably attributable to a combination of carbon and other fertilization effects (Houghton et al., 1992).

There is also physical evidence to support the hypothesis of enhanced plant growth in the northern hemisphere as a sink for atmospheric CO_2. Notwithstanding increased timber and woodpulp harvesting, the forest biomass of the north temperate zones, North America and northern Europe – and perhaps Russia – is actually *increasing* (Kauppi et al., 1992; Sedjo, 1992). This finding was confirmed by the 1994 IPCC *Scientific Assessment* (Schimel et al., 1994), which no longer considers the terms 'imbalance' or 'missing carbon' to be appropriate. Quantitative estimates now appear to confirm the sufficiency of the N-fertilization hypothesis (Galloway et al., 1995; den Elzen et al., 1995).

4. The nitrogen cycle

In general, vegetation can utilize either soluble nitrates or ammonium compounds, but not elemental nitrogen.[10] Thus all life depends on nitrogen fixation. By the same token, the nitrogen cycle (Figure 62.4) depends intimately on living organisms. Because nitrogen was (and is) a limiting factor in many agricultural regions, it has been relatively easy to increase output by supplementing natural sources of available nitrogen by the addition of synthetic sources. For this reason, however, the imbalances in the nitrogen cycle may prove to be the most difficult to correct (or compensate for) by deliberate human action.

Nitrogen fluxes to the atmosphere (the major reservoir of inorganic nitrogen) are of two kinds. Bacterial denitrification from the decay of

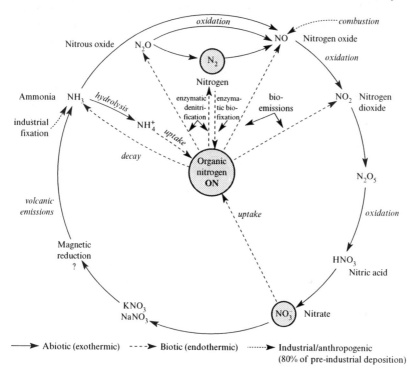

Figure 62.4   Nitrogen cycle: chemical transformations

organic materials and denitrification of nitrate fertilizers return nitrogen to the atmosphere as inert N_2 or N_2O. This loss must be compensated by fixation. On the other hand, ammonia volatilization from the soil, combustion of organic materials (generating NO_x) and bio-emissions from marine organisms are recycled as 'odd' nitrogen. Fluxes from the atmosphere to the land and ocean surface include deposition of nitrate NO_3 (from 'acid rain') and ammonium NH_4. Fluxes to the biosphere include uptake of soluble nitrates and ammonium compounds, recycling of organic detritus (for example manure), and bio-fixation by micro-organisms. None of these fluxes, except the application of synthetic fertilizers, is well quantified.

Synthetic fertilizers from industrial nitrogen fixation (mainly as ammonia, NH_3) became important only in the present century. Current global annual ammonia production is of the order of 110 million metric tons, or 110×10^{12}g/yr (UN Industrial Statistics, 1992). Of this, about 91×10^{12}g is nitrogen content, of which 82×10^{12}g/yr is used for agricultural fertilizer; the remainder is used to manufacture other industrial chemicals, notably explosives, pesticides, plastics (nylon) and so on. These products eventually become wastes and are disposed of, either in landfills or via waterways. This nitrogen eventually finds its way back into the global cycle. As mentioned earlier, the only global reservoir of nitrogen is the atmosphere, which is 78 per cent elemental nitrogen gas, N_2. The total stock of molecular nitrogen (dinitrogen) in the atmosphere (Table 62.1) is estimated to be 3.9 billion teragrams (Tg). Dinitrogen (N_2) and nitrous oxide (N_2O) are not biologically available. There are only four sources of biologically available ('odd') nitrogen compounds. These are (1) biological fixation, (2) atmospheric electrical discharges (lightning), (3) high-temperature combustion and (4) industrial processes for producing synthetic ammonia.

As already mentioned, only a few very specialized bacteria and actinomycetes (yeasts) can utilize (that is, 'fix') elemental dinitrogen. There are some 25 genera of free-living or symbiotic bacteria. The most important is *Rhizobium*, which attaches itself to the roots of legumes, such as alfalfa. In addition, there are 60 genera of anaerobic cyanobacteria, such as *anabaena* (leftovers from the early evolutionary history of earth), and 15 genera of actinomycetes (most prominently, *Frankia*). The range of estimates for bio-fixation in the literature is from 44 Tg/yr to 200 Tg/yr on land and from 1 to 130 Tg/yr in the oceans. Overall, biological N-fixation, from all sources, may be as little as 50 Tg/yr and as much as 365 Tg/yr, although most estimates would be somewhere in the range of 150–200 Tg/yr. The best current estimate (Figure 62.5) is that 140 Tg is fixed by terrestrial vegetation, roughly balanced by 130 Tg dinitrification flux.

The rate of natural atmospheric nitrogen fixation as NO_x by electrical discharges is even less accurately known than the bio-fixation rate. Estimates vary from 0.5 to 30 Tg/yr, although the latter figure is now thought to be much too high. Nitrogen oxides (NO_x) are also produced by high-temperature combustion processes. Anthropogenic activities, mostly automobiles and trucks and electric power generating plants, currently generate around 40 Tg/yr of NO_x. There is a further contribution (estimated to be around 12 Tg/yr from natural forest fires. Finally, of the order 5 Tg/yr of ammonia (NH_3) is also discharged by volcanoes and fumaroles, on average, although this can vary a lot from year to year.

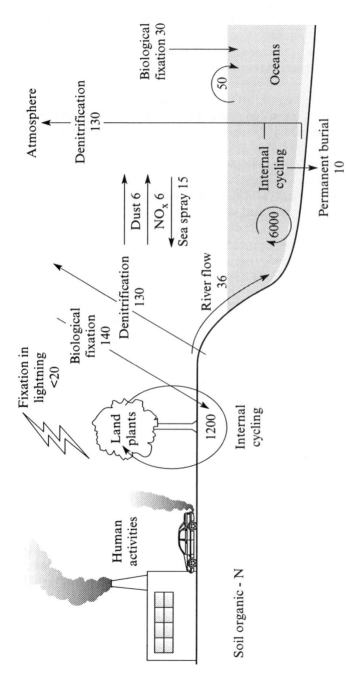

Source: Schlesinger (1991), Figure 12.2.

Figure 62.5   Present-day global nitrogen cycle: intermedia fluxes ($10^{12}g\ N$)

Evidently, known anthropogenic inputs of fixed nitrogen are already comparable in quantity to (and may even be significantly larger than) estimated natural fixation rates. Assuming the nitrogen cycle must have been balanced in pre-industrial times (that is, as recently as 1860), it is safe to say that inputs and outputs to some reservoirs are now out of balance by a large factor. Of course, it would be very difficult to detect any changes in total atmospheric nitrogen content (that is, pressure) over any short period of time. However, it is known that nitrous oxide (N_2O) has increased in recent years, from approximately 300 parts per billion (ppb) in 1978 (Weiss, 1981) to more than 315 ppb today. The annual increase has been measured by several investigators. For example, Khalil and Rasmussen estimated the annual increase at 0.2 per cent; and Schnell put the rate at 0.33 per cent per annum (Khalil and Rasmussen, 1983; Schnell, 1986).

Nitrous oxide is not oxidized in the atmosphere. In the stratosphere it is photolysed yielding N_2 and O, or it is oxidized by ozone to NO_x. In fact, oxidation of nitrous oxide is the major source of stratospheric NO_x. The disappearance rate by these two mechanisms in combination is estimated to be 10 Tg/yr (Weiss, 1981; Liu and Cicerone, 1984; McElroy and Wofsy, 1986). This process has aroused great interest in recent years because of the discovery by Crutzen (Crutzen, 1970, 1974) and others that this set of processes governs the stratospheric ozone level, at least in the absence of chlorine compounds (which also catalytically destroy ozone).

N_2O is a co-product (with N_2) of natural denitrification by anaerobic bacteria and other micro-organisms. Aggregated data on the N_2O/N_2 ratio are scarce. However, such data as do exist (for fertilized land) imply that the ratio of N_2 to N_2O production on land is probably in the range 10–20, with a most likely value of about 16:1 (CAST, 1976). In other words, N_2O is about 1/16 of the total terrestrial denitrification flux. There is no *a priori* reason to assume that this ratio should not hold true for marine conditions or pre-industrial times. It follows that the current N_2O flux of 13 Tg/yr should be accompanied by a corresponding global N_2 flux of about $16 \times 13 = 208$ Tg/yr. (This compares with $130 + 130 = 260$ Tg/yr in Figure 62.5; however, the numbers are subject to considerable uncertainty.)

It now appears that denitrification of nitrate fertilizers accounts for 0.7 Tg/yr of N_2O emissions at present. According to one source, approximately 0.3 per cent of fertilizer nitrogen is converted to N_2O (Galbally, 1985). A calculation by Crutzen sets the figure at 0.4 per cent, which would correspond to N_2O emissions of 0.25 Tg/yr at current fertilizer production levels.[11] An industrial source of N_2O, recently recognized, is the production of adipic acid, an intermediate in nylon manufacture (Thiemens and Trogler, 1991). This source could theoretically account for as much as 0.4 Tg/yr or 10 per cent of the annual increase, in the absence of any emissions controls. However, the actual contribution from this source is probably much less. One other possible source of N_2O is explosives. Virtually all explosives are manufactured from nitrogenated compounds (such as nitrocellulose, ammonium nitrate, trinitroglycerine, and various amines); according to simulation calculations, under conditions of rapid oxidation and decomposition up to 9 per cent of the nitrogen in the explosive may end up as nitrous oxide (Axtell, 1993).

Denitrification is the complementary process to nitrogen fixation (as utilized by plants). Hence the terrestrial contribution to denitrification must have increased in rough proportion to overall terrestrial and atmospheric nitrogen fixation, taking into account both natural and anthropogenic sources. On this basis, pre-industrial natural fixation (approx. 140 Tg/yr) has been increased by anthropogenic contributions, taking into account anthropogenic cultivation of legumes, of the same order of magnitude. In other words, human activity has doubled the amount of biologically available (reactive) nitrogen being produced each year.

It is tempting to assume that global denitrification should increase proportionally, along with the percentage increase in nitrous oxide (N_2O) emissions, since pre-industrial times. This argument is not affected by uncertainties in the $N_2:N_2O$ ratio. On this basis, it would follow that the overall rate of denitrification – including N_2O emissions – could have increased by over 50 per cent in little more than a century.

At first sight this hypothesis seems plausible. Unquestionably, global agricultural activity has increased sharply over the past two centuries, both in scope and intensity. The nitrate content of riverine run-off from land to oceans has increased sharply. At the same time, the organic (humus) content of most agricultural soils has declined. This would seem to be consistent with the notion of accelerated denitrification.

However, there is a problem. The declining organic content of soils is mainly due to ploughing and exposure to oxygen. It is oxidation that is mainly responsible for the loss of organic material in soils. But increased exposure to oxygen would, *ceteris paribus*, probably tend to *decrease* the rate of denitrification (nothwithstanding the fact that some N_2O and NO are apparently produced in aerobic soils). It must be remembered, after all, that denitrification is essentially a process whereby anaerobic bacteria 'steal' oxygen from nitrates in the absence of molecular oxygen (air). Thus the only major agricultural activity that would plausibly result in increased denitrification is wet rice cultivation with nitrate fertilizers. On the other hand, the drainage of wetlands would tend to have the opposite effect, decreasing denitrification. In sum, current evidence suggests that, while denitrification has also increased, it does not keep pace with nitrogen fixation.

The alternative to the hypothesis of compensating global denitrification is that reactive nitrogen is now accumulating. For one thing, global nitrogen fertilization (from acid rain and ammonium sulphate deposition) has increased the reservoir of nitrogen in biomes like grasslands and forests that are not cultivated. This explanation would be qualitatively consistent with the observations of increased forest biomass in the northern hemisphere mentioned previously (for example, Kauppi et al., 1992; Sedjo, 1992). This explanation is now preferred because it also simultaneously provides a satisfactory explanation of the 'missing carbon' problem that worried people a few years ago, as mentioned previously.

Anthropogenic nitrogen fixation from all sources – especially fertilizer use and fossil fuel combustion – is certainly increasing quite rapidly. Not all of this excess is immediately denitrified to N. It is likely to double again within a few decades. For instance, one group has estimated that the anthropogenic fixation rate will increase from 140 Tg in 1990 to 230 Tg by 2020, with no end in sight (Galloway et al., 1995). The consequences are very hard to predict; certainly they vary from one reservoir to another. One predictable consequence of nitrogen fertilization will be a build-up of toxic and carcinogenic nitrates and nitrites in groundwaters. This is already occurring in many agricultural areas. Increased forest and pasture growth rates is another likely consequence already mentioned. But along with the gross fertilization effect, there is a tendency to reduced biodiversity. Regions where nitrogen availability has been the limiting factor for biological productivity are likely to shrink, or even disappear, to be replaced by regions where other plant nutrients are the limiting factor. This shift could lead to major changes in species composition for both plants and animals.

A specific consequence of increased NO_x emissions is predictable: NO_x affects the oxidizing capacity of the atmosphere and, indirectly, increases the tropospheric ozone concentration. This has well-known adverse consequences on cereal crop productivity and on human health, especially for people with respiratory problems.

5. The sulphur cycle

The global sulphur cycle resembles the nitrogen cycle thermodynamically, in so far as reduced forms of sulphur (S, H_2S) are gradually oxidized by atmospheric oxygen, ending in sulphur oxides (So_2, SO_3) and finally sulphuric acid (H_2SO_4). See Figure 62.6. Sulphate (SO_4) is eventually deposited in wet or dry form (for example, as ammonium sulphate). The reverse part of the cycle, which converts sulphur back to states of higher thermodynamic potential, is accomplished either by biological activity or by high-temperature magmatic reactions in the earth's mantle.

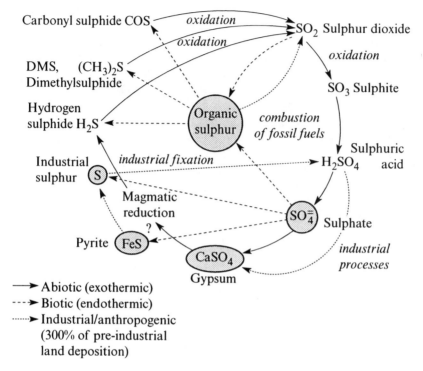

Figure 62.6   Sulphur cycle: chemical transformations

From another perspective, of course, the S cycle consists of transformations of insoluble and biologically unavailable forms of sulphur
(notably sulphides (pyrites) and calcium and magnesium sulphates) to
available forms. These are utilized by organisms and finally returned once
again to unavailable forms. From this perspective, the cycle can also be
seen as a complex set of transfers between air, land and sea, as shown in
Figure 62.7.

Assuming the pre-industrial version of the cycle was really balanced
(which is open to question), the controlling rate, or 'bottleneck' in the
system, must have been the rate at which insoluble sulphides or sulphates
were deposited in oceanic sediments. In the very long run (on the average)
this deposition rate must have been equal to the rate at which sulphur was
remobilized by pre-industrial geochemical processes, with or without biological assistance. It must also equal the pre-industrial net rate of deposition of sulphur compounds on the ocean surface, plus the pre-industrial
run-off from rivers, abrasion of shores, and so on.

The pre-industrial sulphur inputs to the land surface must have been

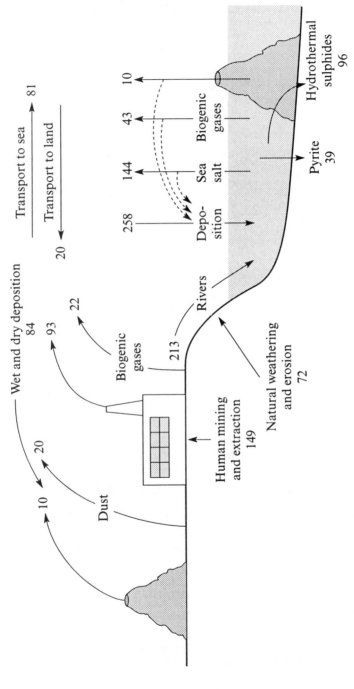

Source: Schlesinger (1991), Figure 13.1.

Figure 62.7 Present-day global sulphur cycle: intermedia fluxes (10^{12} g S/yr)

about 26 Tg/yr, as compared to 84 Tg/yr from atmospheric deposition (in 1980) and a further 28 Tg/yr as fertilizer. In short, the sulphur flux to land has more than quadrupled since the beginning of industrialization. It is likely that river run-off has doubled, for example from 72 Tg/yr pre-industrial to 213 Tg/yr currently. It is clear that the global sulphur cycle is now extremely unbalanced. Inputs to oceans appear to exceed deposition to the ocean bottom by as much as 100 Tg/yr (Schlesinger, 1991).

It must be acknowledged that there is no known or obvious reason to worry unduly about this aspect of the anthropogenic perturbation of the sulphur cycle *per se*, however massive. Clearly, however, the oxidation of large amounts of reduced sulphur will continue to acidify the soils and the ocean. Deposition of heterogeneous sulphite/sulphate (SO_3/SO_4) and nitrate (NO_3) on to the land or water surface as 'acid rain' – with measurable changes in pH – is currently much higher than in the pre-industrial case.

Atmospheric haze, consisting mostly of sulphuric acid/ammonium sulphate aerosols in the micron size range, has probably increased by orders of magnitude over some land areas, due to SO_2 emissions from the combustion of fossil fuels. This was a topic of major concern in the US during the 1980s, due to the association of sulphate particulates with acidification. However, it is not clear whether sulphate haze has increased significantly over the oceans, partly because it is unclear whether oceanic sulphates are attributable to terrestrial industry or marine biology. There is evidence that marine phytoplankton emit dimethylsulphide (DMS), which subsequently oxidizes to sulphate aerosols (Charlson et al., 1987). It has even been suggested that this mechanism contributes to oceanic climate control (for example Schwartz, 1988), although there is no confirming evidence of this (IPCC, 1995, p. 205).

The sulphate haze phenomenon is apparently sufficient measurably to increase the Earth's albedo (that is, its reflectivity to visible radiation) and, possibly, compensate partially for greenhouse warming in recent decades (Wigley, 1989; Taylor and Penner, 1994). It is now incorporated in General Circulation Models (GCMs), where it largely accounts for the fact that climate warming has not occurred as rapidly as the earlier models predicted. On the other hand, sulphate haze is proportional to the current rate of sulphate emissions, whereas the greenhouse phenomenon is a function of the atmospheric concentration, or total build-up, of greenhouse gases. Thus, the greenhouse warming and sulphate cooling will not continue to cancel each other indefinitely.

Sulphate particulates play a different and much subtler role in climate control, however, since microparticulates also act as cloud condensation nuclei (CCNs). These nuclei are known to affect cloud properties, and hence to modify their absorption and reflection of radiation at different wavelengths. But the quantitative aspects and even the aggregate magnitude of these effects are not yet well understood. This remains among the most uncertain aspects of the current generation of GCMs (IPCC, 1995 p. 117).

6. The phosphorus cycle

As was noted earlier, there is no reduced gaseous form of phosphorus that could facilitate transfer from marine to terrestrial reservoirs. Phosphine gas, the only candidate, oxidizes too rapidly in the oxygen atmosphere. Consequently, the phosphorus cycle is only 'closed' by means of geological processes. In the pre-industrial era terrestrial phosphorus was mobilized very slowly from soil by natural processes, mainly driven by carbonic acid. It is taken up by plants and bio-accumulated by animals, especially in bones and teeth. It is recycled, to some extent, by fires.

However, over long periods of time, erosion and run-off gradually moves the biologically available phosphorus from the terrestrial biosphere to the oceans. Again, it is bio-accumulated by marine animals in bones and teeth (especially sharks' teeth). This material gradually falls to the sea floor as detritus. However, ocean currents bring phosphates back to the surface via upwelling. (Upwelling zones, such as the west coast of South America, are famously productive.)

In the very long run, however, organic phosphates tend to accumulate in marine sediments. Only when formerly submerged areas of the sea floor are raised by tectonic processes are these phosphate accumulations – known as 'phosphate rocks' or apatites – mobilizable once again by erosion.

Needless to say, anthropogenic activity has enormously increased the rate of terrestrial phosphate mobilization as well as the rate of phosphate loss, via erosion and run-off, to the oceans. While known reserves of minable phosphate rock are quite large, and appear adequate for the next century or more, phosphate loss will eventually be a limiting factor for agriculture.

7. Thermodynamic equilibrium

One important point needs to be emphasized again with regard to the grand nutrient cycles. It is that the atmosphere and lithosphere are emphatically *not* in thermodynamic equilibrium with the oceans. All three of the cycles discussed above consist of two distinct branches, a geochemical and a biological branch. In the geochemical branch, as schematically represented in Figures 62.2, 62.4 and 62.6, reduced forms of carbon, nitrogen and sulphur are gradually oxidized by a multi-step sequence of processes, approaching the most stable (that is, lowest energy) thermodynamic state. The latter would be one in which buried carbon and sulphur, and atmospheric nitrogen, combined with oxygen (and water) to form acids, that is:

$$C + O_2 + H_2O \rightarrow H_2CO_3 \qquad (62.6)$$

$$H_2O + N_2 + \tfrac{5}{2}O_2 \rightarrow 2HNO_3 \qquad (62.7)$$

$$S + \tfrac{3}{2}O_2 + H_2O \rightarrow H_2SO_4 \qquad (62.8)$$

These acids would react with all alkaline species in the environment and eventually accumulate in the ocean. For instance, if the nitric acid formation reaction, (62.8), alone proceeded to chemical equilibrium, it has been calculated that almost all the oxygen in the atmosphere would be used up and the pH of the ocean would decrease to 1.5 (Lewis and Randall, 1923). More recent equilibrium calculations (below) have confirmed and refined this result.

Fortunately, some of these thermodynamically favoured oxidation reactions do not occur at significant rates on the earth's surface – including the atmosphere and the oceans – under current conditions. In the case of carbon and sulphur, this is because biological reduction processes, combined with sedimentation and burial, regenerate and sequester reduced forms (for example, kerogen and sulphides).

In the case of nitrogen, where physical sequestration is not a factor, there are two barriers. The first is kinetic. The formation of nitric acid is thermodynamically favoured, to be sure. But it can only proceed by a sequence of reversible reactions involving a number of intermediate oxidation stages. The first stage ($N_2 + O_2 \rightarrow 2NO$) is quite endothermic. It only occurs in very hot fires (or in the path of a lightning bolt). Thus the *rate* at which this reaction occurs in nature is very low. Even so, the nitric acid level of the oceans would gradually build up, except for another barrier. There are several enzymatically catalysed biological processes that convert soluble nitrates back to reduced forms, including NH_3 and even N_2, thus restoring the non-equilibrium situation.

In the absence of these biological denitrification processes, most of the atmospheric oxygen would end up as dissolved nitrates in the ocean. Ahrendts has calculated that an atmosphere–ocean–crustal system (equilibrated to a depth of 100 metres) would have an atmosphere of 95 per cent N_2, with only a trace amount of oxygen (0.3 ppm and a pressure of 0.77 atmospheres (Ahrendts, 1980). The atmospheric oxygen would end up mostly as $NaNO_3$ in the ocean, where it would constitute 0.4 per cent of the dissolved solids, and the surface layer would consist largely (54.5 per cent) of silicic acid (H_4SiO_4) (ibid.).

If the equilibrium in the earth's crust were taken to a deeper level (for example, 1000 metres), the silicic acid, ferric iron (hematite) and sulphates would be reduced to silica, magnetite and sulphides respectively. Calcium carbonate and silica would also recombine to produce calcium silicate ($CaSiO_3$) and CO_2 (the reverse of equation 62.3). Essentially all of the sequestered carbon and hydrocarbons in the earth's crust would be oxidized (releasing CO_2 to the atmosphere). Ammonia and methane would also exist in the atmosphere (ibid.). Atmospheric pressure and temperature would then rise. But, in any case, there would be no free oxygen in the atmosphere.

In summary, the Earth system does not (for the present) closely approach thermodynamic equilibrium. This is lucky for us, since the true equilibrium state – or anything close to it – would be antithetical to life. It is possible to estimate roughly what earth would be like if all of the thermodynamically favoured chemical reactions went to completion without biological inter-ference. In addition to Ahrendts's work, noted above, this has been done using two different approaches (Table 62.3). 'World 1' is based on a com-puter simulation of the earth as a chemistry experiment, in which all favourable chemical reactions go to completion (Sillén, quoted by Lovelock, 1979). 'World 2' is based on an interpolation between observed conditions on Mars and Venus, allowing for the earth's intermediate orbit and slightly greater gravitational field (ibid.). It can be seen that the two are very similar to each other, and roughly consistent with Ahrendts's equilib-rium calculations (Ahrendts, op. cit.). The conditions are far different from conditions on the actual earth as we know it.

Table 62.3   The stabilizing influence of the biosphere (Gaia)

Reservoir	Substance	Actual world (%)	Ideal world 1 (%)	Ideal world 2 (%)
Atmosphere	Nitrogen	78	0	1.9
	Oxygen	21	0	trace
	CO_2	0.03	99	98
	Argon	1	1	0.1
Hydrosphere	Water	96	85	Negligible
	NaCl	3.4	13	?
	$NaNO_3$		1.7	?
Temperature	Degrees Celsius	13	290 ± 50	290 ± 50
Pressure	Atmospheres	1	60	60

Note:
Life is impossible if average temperature is too high for liquid water, or if salinity exceeds 6%.

The ability of the biosphere to maintain the earth system far from thermodynamic equilibrium is the essence of the 'Gaia' hypothesis. A thermodynamic measure of the Earth's 'distance from equilibrium' is the exergy (or availability) content of the atmosphere, ocean and crustal layer. Ahrendts has computed the stored exergy values of the major components of the actual state (actually a slightly simplified 'model' version) *vis-à-vis* several possible reference (equilibrium) states (ibid.). Without the biosphere, this stored exergy would be dissipated and lost (as entropy).

Stored environmental exergy has increased, on average, over geological time at least until human industrial activity began in earnest, 200 years ago. Since then, there has been a reversal. Environmental exergy has certainly decreased, although probably not yet by a very significant amount. For example, the amount of free oxygen in the atmosphere is essentially unchanged, and the fraction of sequestered carbon that has been consumed by burning fossil fuels is still infinitesimal compared to the amount stored in shales, not to mention carbonates. Nevertheless, there are potential risks.

8.   Acidification of the environment

Acids are associated with H^+ ions and bases are associated with OH^- ions. A strong acid such as HNO_3 is one that ionizes easily in water, that is $HNO_3 \leftrightarrow H^+ + NO_3^-$. Obviously the total number of positive and negative ions (due to overall charge neutrality) remains constant. However, acidification can increase if the number of H^+ ions increases. For this to happen without a corresponding increase in OH^- ions means that there must be a build-up of other negative ions to balance the positive charges.

Acidification results largely from the oxidation of other atmospheric gases. In particular, reduced gases such as ammonia (NH_3) and hydrogen sulphide (H_2S) were present in the primordial atmosphere.[12] Ammonia dissolved in water is ammonium hydroxide (NH_4OH), a base. These gases can be oxidized (in several steps) to nitric and sulphuric oxides, respectively. In water, these oxides become strong acids. The oxygen build-up, of course, resulted from the evolutionary 'invention' of photosynthesis and the sequestration of carbon (as hydrocarbons) in sediments.

Acid rain is a natural phenomenon, but is closely related to both the sulphur and nitrogen cycles. Hence the anthropogenic acceleration of these cycles has greatly increased the rate of acidification. The basic mechanism for sulphuric acid generation is that sulphur dioxide (SO_2) from combustion products oxidizes in the atmosphere to sulphur trioxide (SO_3) which subsequently dissolves in water droplets to form sulphuric acid (H_2SO_4). In the case of nitrogen, the sequence also starts with combustion, except that the nitrogen is from the air itself. The two nitrogen oxides, NO and NO_2, are also produced by high-temperature combustion with excess air, as in electric generating plants and internal combustion engines operating with lean mixtures. Further reactions with oxygen occur in the atmosphere, by various routes, finally producing N_2O_5 and (with water), nitric acid (HNO_3).

These strong acids ionize to generate nitrate (NO_3^-) and sulphate (SO_4^-) radicals and hydrogen ions (H^+). This process increases soil and water acidity (that is, reduces the pH). The ions react immediately with ammonia or any other base. Many metallic ions – including toxic metals – that are bound quite firmly to soil (especially clay) particles when the soil pH is high (alkaline) are likely to be mobilized as the alkaline 'buffering' capacity (Ca^{++} and Mg^{++} ions) in the soil are used up. Aluminium is one example. Aluminium poisoning, caused indirectly by acid rain, may be one of the causes of the European *Waldsterben* that has decimated some forests in central Europe. Similar problems may arise in the future as toxic heavy metals like Pb, Cd, As and Hg continue to accumulate in soils and sediments.

Although virtually all the literature on acid rain pertains to localized effects, it may be important to consider the global implications. The build-up of NO_3^- and SO_4^- ions in the environment is matched by a corresponding build-up of H^+ ions. This long-term acidification trend has been underway throughout geological time. An hypothetical evolutionary acidification trajectory is indicated schematically in Figure 62.8.

In pre-industrial times, I would speculate that the long-term trend toward environmental acidification was mainly driven by two processes. One was volcanic sulphur (H_2S) emissions. These would have been gradually oxidized and resulted in a build-up of soluble sulphates in the oceans until the rate of removal and sequestration by sedimentation (as insoluble calcium sulphate or in organic materials) matched the rate of input. The fact that large amounts of sulphur have been sequestered in this manner is obvious from the existence of enormous deposits of gypsum and, of course, the sulphur content of all natural hydrocarbon deposits, which ranges from 1 per cent to 3 per cent.

The other important acidification process must have been biological nitrogen fixation followed by ammonia emissions (from anaerobic decay and animal metabolism), which were then partially acidified and converted to nitrate by oxidation. Of course, part of the acid was neutralized by the basic ammonia itself (yielding ammonium sulphate or ammonium nitrate). But the problem is that all nitrates are extremely soluble in water and thus *cannot* be sequestered in insoluble sediments as carbon and sulphur are). Nitrates and nitric acid would have continued to accumulate in the oceans, except for the biological 'denitrification' process, caused by anaerobic soil organisms that derive their metabolic oxygen requirements by decompos-

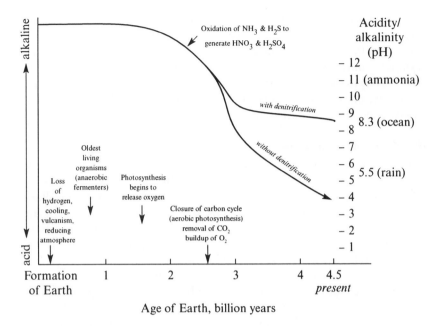

Figure 62.8 Biospheric stabilization by denitrification

ing nitrate molecules. The rate of activity of such organisms would evidently increase with nitrate concentration. This was an evolutionary 'invention' that was necessary to stabilize the system. It was needed to prevent the gradual fixation and conversion of all atmospheric nitrogen to nitric acid.

Natural sources of atmospheric hydrogen ion (H^+) production amount to around 9 Tg/yr[13] (Schlesinger, 1991). Of this amount, only 3 Tg/yr is neutralized by NH_3 from natural sources such as volcanoes and soil volatilization (Warneck, 1988). Thus the natural acidification processes were not in balance with natural sequestration and denitrification processes, even before humans arrived on the scene. Meanwhile, however, anthropogenic sources of H^+ (HNO_3 and H_2SO_4) add another 7.4 Tg/yr to the 9 Tg/yr of natural origin. Since the industrial revolution, of course, the sulphur and nitrogen cycles have been sharply accelerated, by carbonaceous fuel combustion and synthetic fertilizer usage. Moreover, the anthropogenic contribution to acidity is rapidly increasing. It already almost equals the natural contribution.

Indeed, in many locations the very slow carbonic-acid-driven process of rock weathering is now being replaced by a much faster sulphuric- and nitric-acid-driven weathering process. The geological implications of this are difficult to foresee, although there is an obvious implication of increased carbon dioxide removal from the atmosphere. The natural sulphur sequestration process has clearly been reversed, and the biological denitrification process is unlikely to keep up with the rate of injection of synthetic nitrogen into the environment. (However, generalizations are risky: even though most fertilizers are in the form of urea or ammonium and other nitrates, some acid neutralization may occur later when the nitrified organic material decays and releases ammonia.)

9.   Concluding comments

Non-linearity is one of the essential features of a complex system with multiple feedbacks existing in a state far from thermodynamic equilibrium. The earth is such a system. In recent years the dynamics of non-linear systems has been a subject of considerable interest among mathematicians, ecologists and others. There is a well-known tendency for non-linear systems to have multiple 'solutions' or trajectories. They can suddenly 'flip' from one (apparently) stable state – or branch – to another.

Under certain circumstances such systems can also become 'chaotic'. Chaotic trajectories may (or may not) be bounded by 'strange attractors'. It is as though the trajectory were a planetary orbit influenced by large, gravitational masses whose existence can only be inferred from irregularities in the planetary motion. Scientists' ability to predict chaotic behaviour is obviously limited.

The weather is an example of chaotic behaviour within a bounded region. Short-term predictions can be reasonably accurate, and there seems to be some possibility to predict long-term climate changes. The climate of a region is, effectively, the 'strange attractor' for the weather in that region. But the climate itself is probably a chaotic variable on a longer time scale. The Earth system as a whole is so complex, and so non-linear, that accurate predictions of some kinds of behaviour are probably impossible. The best that can be done is to construct models with the requisite degree of non-linearity and to use these models in simulation experiments to explore the bounds of various 'strange attractors' in the system.

Yet models of a system can never capture all the features of the original, and one of the most important features of highly non-linear dynamic systems is that small – even infinitesimal – changes in initial conditions can cause unbounded changes in trajectories after some time has passed. This is called the 'butterfly effect', from the fanciful notion that even the flight of a butterfly in the Amazon forest might have some unpredictable future impact on the weather in Chicago or Tokyo.

Similarly, a seemingly trivial change in the specification of a complex non-linear model can have a surprising – maybe unbounded – impact on the dynamical behaviour of the model. What this means, in effect, is that it is virtually impossible for scientists to determine some of the features of the dynamics of the earth's system. The system may be the only adequate model of itself.

One can envision the present climatic regime as a 'strange attractor' in the above sense. It is a stable state, far from thermodynamic equilibrium. Are there other branches? Other stable states suitable for life support? How far can the system be perturbed before it becomes unstable? How rapidly would the transition ('catastrophe' in Thom's terms) occur? Could it become chaotic? It is impossible to answer such questions definitively now. Because of the complexity and non-linearity of the system, it may never be possible to be certain, no matter how wide the reach of future science.

Meanwhile, humans are perturbing the grand nutrient cycles, and the climate, in major ways. In effect, the whole Earth is undergoing eutrophication. The rate of carbon mobilization has increased by 'only' 5 per cent or so, but the rate of nitrogen mobilization has probably doubled in the past century, while sulphur mobilization has increased still more, and phosphorus mobilization probably most of all. These changes may be harmless. Indeed, to first order, they appear to be increasing biomass production and thus potential food production without any obvious secondary ill effects. But secondary damage may just be slow in appearing. For instance, the build-up of nitrates and nitrites in groundwater may be a significant cause of cancer. The use of synthetic fertilizers is certainly having an adverse impact on natural soil organisms. Many lakes, rivers and estuaries are showing signs of oxygen depletion and disappearance of higher species. Ecological impacts of global eutrophication are virtually unguessable, but unlikely to be negligible.

In this context, it is vital to bear in mind that the time scale of change is probably critical. Biological evolution of higher organisms is a comparatively slow process. This is conspicuously not true of micro-organisms. (The rapidly mutating flu virus is a well-known case in point.) Thus evolutionary adjustment is not possible for our own species as a means of accommodation to environmental changes that occur with extreme rapidity.

Some people seem to have great faith in the ability of a benign 'Mother Nature' to adjust to any perturbation. But there is no rational basis for such confidence. The fact that no great ecological catastrophe has yet occurred is not evidence of inherent stability. The only safe course for Man is to consciously restrain anthropogenic impact on the environment to levels that are within the range of past deviations and excursions of natural origin. This is the so-called 'precautionary principle', which is honoured mainly in the breach.

A few of the implications of all this for economic models of the more traditional kind are worth noting. One is the generic need for adding more feedbacks between economic activity and natural processes, of which the nutrient cycles are only a subset. Another is the possible insight that 'shadow prices' should be estimated not for 'states' of the environment, and still less for hard-to-define 'environmental services', but rather for perturbations in the natural fluxes of nutrient (and other) elements. For instance, it might be feasible to estimate an aggregate economic cost or benefit associated with a given percentage change in the carbon cycle, rather than estimating the cost of a given temperature or sea-level rise.

An important implication of the foregoing is that economic modellers concerned with long-term environmental impacts should drop the assumption that the economic system is always growing in equilibrium. There are several cogent reasons for doing this, but one reason that seems more than sufficient is that the economic system is embedded in a physical environment that is evidently *not* in equilibrium now, and probably never has been.

Notes

1. Much of the technical material in the following sections has been previously published by me and is reprinted here by permission. See Ayres (1997).
2. Prokaryotic cells lack a nucleus.
3. For instance, the oxidation reaction $N_2 + O_2 \rightarrow 2NO$ is highly endothermic. It does not occur spontaneously at normal temperatures and pressures (otherwise the atmosphere could not contain both molecular oxygen and molecular nitrogen). Once NO is formed, however, further oxidation reactions do occur spontaneously, albeit slowly, until the most oxidized form of nitrogen (N_2O_5) is reached. Dissolved in water, this is nitric acid (HNO_3). In thermodynamic equilibrium, oxygen and nitrogen would be combined in this form.
4. Opal is a form of silica used for the shells of diatoms.
5. If the oceans were to freeze, the weathering rate would fall to zero, allowing the atmospheric CO_2 level to rise due to volcanic action. It has been shown that this feedback is sufficient to assure that the oceans would not have been frozen over, even during the Earth's early history when the sun was emitting 30 per cent less energy than it does today (Walker et al., 1981).
6. In fact, some calculations suggest that the weathering of the Tibetan plateau, alone, would remove all the CO_2 from the atmosphere in a few hundred thousand years. Obviously there must be other partially countervailing effects at work which are not yet fully understood.
7. In the more general case, the rate of photosynthesis can be expected to depend on the concentrations of all the essential nutrients – especially C, N, S, P – in biologically available form.
8. The origin of natural gas is currently in doubt. For a long time it was assumed that natural gas was entirely biogenic and associated mainly with petroleum. Now it is known that gas deposits are much more widely distributed than petroleum deposits. It has been suggested by several astronomers that much of the hydrogen in the earth's crust may have originated from the sun (via the 'solar wind' proton bombardment).
9. To be more precise, an environment lacking nitrates, manganese oxide, iron oxides or sulphates. Recall the earlier discussion of 'redox potential' and bacterial sources of oxygen for metabolism.
10. Most bacteria and animals can only utilize organic nitrogen, mainly as amino acids.

11. Denitrification bacteria reduce nitrates (NO_3) to obtain oxygen for metabolic purposes. They do not metabolize ammonia. Thus the denitrification flux from fertilizers depends somewhat on the chemical form in which it is applied. The N_2O/N_2 proportion depends on local factors, such as carbon content of the soil, acidity and dissolved oxygen. It must be acknowledged that the combined uncertainties are quite large. Thus, for instance, a recent US study sets the N_2O emissions from fertilizer at 1.5 Tg/yr, as compared to only 1 Tg/yr from fossil fuel combustion. Other estimates in the literature range from 0.01 to 2.2 Tg/yr (Watson et al., 1992).

12. To be sure, CO_2 was present in the early atmosphere and carbonic acid (H_2CO_3) is CO_2 dissolved in water. But CO_2 is not very soluble, and the oceans are essentially a saturated solution. Moreover, carbonic acid is a very weak acid as compared to sulphuric and nitric acids.

13. A more detailed breakdown of the sources of H^+ in the atmosphere is as follows: carbonic acid 1.25 Tg/yr; volcanic SO_2 1.3 Tg/yr; NO_x formation by atmospheric electrical discharges (lightning) 1.4 Tg/yr; oxidation of biogenic sulphur compounds 4.1 Tg/yr. The total for all the above natural processes is of the order of 9 Tg/yr.

References

Ahrendts, J. (1980), 'Reference states', *Energy,* 5 (5), 667–77.

Axtell, Robert (1993), personal communication to the author, 1993.

Ayres, Robert U. (1997), 'Integrated assessment of the grand nutrient cycles', *Environmental Modeling and Assessment,* (forthcoming).

Berner, R.A., A.C. Lasaga and R.M. Garrels (1983), 'The carbonate–silicate geochemical cycle and its effect on atmospheric carbon dioxide over the past 100 million years', *American Journal of Science,* **283,** 641–83.

Charlson, R.J., J.E. Lovelock, M.O. Andrae and S.G. Warren (1987), 'Oceanic phytoplankton, atmospheric sulfur, cloud albedo and climate', *Nature,* **326,** 655–61.

Council for Agriculture Science and Technology (CAST) (1976), *Effect of Increased Nitrogen Fixation on Stratospheric Ozone,* CAST Report 53, Council for Agriculture Science and Technology, Ames, Ia.

Crutzen, Paul J. (1970), 'The influence of nitrogen oxides on the atmospheric ozone content', *Quarterly Journal of the Royal Meteorological Society,* **96,** 320–25.

Crutzen, Paul, J. (1974), 'Estimates of possible variations in total ozone due to natural causes and human activities', *Ambio,* **3,** 201–210.

Deevey, E.C. (1970), 'Mineral cycles', *Scientific American,* **223,** 148–58.

Den Elzen, Michel G.J. (1994), *Global Environmental Change: An Integrated Modelling Approach,* Utrecht: International Books.

Den Elzen, Michel G.J., J. Rotmans and A. Beusen (1995), *Modelling Global Biogeochemical Cycles: An Integrated Modelling Approach,* Global Dynamics and Sustainable Development Programme GLOBO Report No. 7, National Institute of Public Health and Environment (RIVM), Bilthoven, The Netherlands.

Galbally, I.E. (1985), 'The emission of nitrogen to the remote atmosphere: background paper', in J.N. Galloway et al. (eds), *The Biogeochemical Cycling of Sulfur and Nitrogen in the Remote Atmosphere,* D. Reidel Publishing.

Galloway, James N., William H. Schlesinger, H. Levy, A. Michaels and J.L. Schoor (1995), 'Nitrogen fixation: anthropogenic enhancement–environmental response', *Global Biogeochemical Cycles,* **9** (2), 235–52.

Holland, H.D. (1978), *The Chemical Evolution of the Atmosphere and the Oceans,* New York: John Wiley.

Houghton, J.T., B.A. Callander and S.K. Varney (1992), *Climate Change 1992: The Supplementary Report to the IPCC Scientific Assessment,* Cambridge, UK: Cambridge University Press.

Intergovernmental Panel on Climate Change (IPCC) (1995), 'The science of climate change: contribution of working group I' in *2nd Assessment Report of the Intergovernmental Panel on Climate Change,* Cambridge, UK: Cambridge University Press.

Kasting, James F. and James C.G. Walker (1992), 'The geophysical carbon cycle and the uptake of fossil fuel CO_2', in *Global and Planetary Change*, in press.

Kauppi, P., K. Mielikainen and K. Kuusula (1992), 'Biomass and carbon budget of European forests, 1971 to 1990', *Science*, **256**, 311–14.

Khalil, M.A.K. and R.A. Rasmussen (1983), 'Increase and seasonal cycles of nitrous oxide in the Earth's atmosphere', *Tellus*, **35** (B), 161–9.

Lewis, G.N. and M. Randall (1923), *Thermodynamics*, New York: McGraw-Hill.

Liu, S.C. and R.J. Cicerone (1984), 'Fixed nitrogen cycle', in National Research Council, *Global Tropospheric Chemistry* Washington, DC: National Academy Press, pp. 113–16.

Lovelock, James E. (1979), *Gaia: A New Look at Life on Earth*, London: Oxford University Press.

Mackenzie, F.T., L.M. Ver, C. Sabine, M. Lane and A. Lerman (1993), 'C, N, P, S Global biogeochemical cycles and modeling of global change', in Roland Wollast, Fred T. Mackenzie and Lei Chou (eds), *Interactions of C, N, P and S Biogeochemical Cycles and Global Change* (Series: NATO ASI I: Global Environmental Change), Berlin: Springer-Verlag, pp. 1–62. (Proceedings of the NATO Advanced Research Workshop on Interactions of C, N, P and S Biogeochemical Cycles, Melreux, Belgium, 4–9 March 1991.)

McElroy, M.B. and S.F. Wofsy (1986), 'Tropical forests: interactions with the atmosphere', in G.F. Prance (ed.), *Tropical Forests and World Atmosphere*, Washington, DC: AAAS.

Nicolis, Gregoire and Ilya Prigogine (1977), *Self-Organization in Non-Equilibrium Systems*, New York: Wiley-Interscience.

Peng, T.-H., W.S. Broecker, H.-D. Freyer and S. Trumbore (1983), 'A deconvolution of the tree-ring based BC record', *Journal of Geophysical Research*, **88**, 3609–20.

Raymo, R.E. and W.F. Ruddiman (1992), 'Tectonic forcing of Late Cenozoic climate', *Nature*, **359**, 117–22.

Redfield, A.C., B.H. Ketchum and F.A. Richards (1963), 'The influence of organisms in the composition of seawater', in M.N. Hill (ed.), *Composition of Seawater, Comparative and Descriptive Oceanography* (Series: The Sea) vol. 2, New York: Wiley-Interscience, pp. 26–79.

Schimel, D., I. Enting, M. Heimann, T.M.L. Wigley, D. Raynaud, D. Alves and U. Siegenthaler (1994), 'The carbon cycle', in J.T. Houghton et al. (eds), *Radiative Forcing of Climate*, Cambridge, UK: Cambridge University Press.

Schlesinger, William H. (1991), *Biogeochemistry: An Analysis of Global Change*, New York: Academic Press.

Schnell, R.C. (ed.), *Geophysical Monitoring for Climate Change* (14), Boulder, CO: USOC.

Schwartz, S.E. (1988), 'Are global cloud albedo and climate controlled by marine phytoplankton?', *Nature*, **336**, 441–5.

Sedjo, R.A. (1992), 'Temperate forest ecosystems in the global carbon cycle', *Ambio*, **21**, 274–7.

Sillèn, L.G. (1967), 'The ocean as a chemical system', *Science*, **156**, 1189–97.

Stern, P.C., O.R. Young and D. Druckman (eds), *Global Environmental Change: Understanding the Human Dimension*, Washington, DC: National Academy Press.

Stumm, Werner (ed.), *Global Chemical Cycles and their Alteration by Man*, Berlin: Dahlem Konferenzen.

Sundquist, Eric T. (1993), 'The global carbon dioxide budget', *Science*, **259**, 934–41.

Tans, P.P., I.Y. Fung and T. Takahashi (1990), 'The global atmospheric CO_2 budget', *Science*, **247**, 1431–8.

Taylor, K.E. and J.E. Penner, 'Anthropogenic aerosols and climate change', *Nature*, **369**, 734–7.

Thiemens, Mark H. and William C. Trogler (1991), 'Nylon production: an unknown source of atmospheric nitrous oxide', *Science*, **251**, 932–4.

United Nations Yearbook of Industrial Statistics 1992, New York: UN.

Walker, James C.G., P.B. Hays and James F. Kasting (1981), Title missing, *Journal of Geophysical Research*, **86**, 9776–82.

Warneck, P. (1988), *Chemistry of the Natural Atmosphere*, London: Academic Press.

Watson, R.T., L.G., Filho Meira, E. Sanhueza and A. Janetos (1992), 'Greenhouse gases: sources and sinks', in J.T. Houghton, B.A. Callender and S.K. Varney (eds), *Climate Change*

1992: The Supplementary Report to the IPCC Scientific Assessment, Cambridge, UK: Cambridge University Press.

Weiss, R.F. (1981), 'The temporal and spatial distribution of nitrous oxide', *Journal of Geophysical Resources*, **86**, 7185–95.

Wigley, T.M.L. (1989), 'Possible climate change due to SO_2-derived cloud condensation nuclei', *Nature*, **339**, 365–7.

63 Indicators of economic and ecological health

Bruce Hannon[1]

1. Economic health measures

Ecologists need a consistent focus for their idea of ecosystem health. They must work to achieve consensus on that focus and embed that goal in national and local policy making. I want to propose a candidate for that goal. It is fashioned after the economists' view of the economic system with an attempt to avoid their pitfalls.

Economists refer to the total consumption of the nation by the more general term of national output or, in the terms of this paper, 'net output'. The net output of a modern economy is somewhat arbitrarily but officially defined as the amount of personal and government consumption (cars, food, highways, defence, and so on), plus the amount of net export of goods and services, plus the amount of new capital formed (investment for expansion and replacement), plus any changes in the inventory of goods, in a given period. When taken as an annual sum, this amount is called the gross national product or GNP. The GNP is a flow, not a stock, and it is measured in dollars per year.[2]

All the physical units of things we bought as consumers, the things bought by the government, the exported goods (for example, computers) less the imported goods (for example, oil), the amount of new capital stocks purchased (say, machinery and buildings), the increases in the inventory stocks (such as mined coal), less the decreases of these sorts of stocks (such as unsold cars), are multiplied by their respective prices. This multiplication converts the diverse types of these physical things into a single unit of measure and they can be added together to form the GNP (Peterson, 1962).

If the GNP is high, inflation fears aside, the economy is thought of as more *healthy* than when the GNP is low or negative. The value of, or changes in, the value of the GNP is related to the amount of overall employment and total capital expansion. These sorts of connections are part of the basis on which economic and social welfare policy decisions are made at the national level.

Through various optimization models, used in conjunction with the structure and detail mentioned above, economists are able to make predictions about the effect that certain proposed actions will have on the GNP.

Most economists who follow such approaches agree on the nature of the approach. Usually, controversy is confined to the accuracy of the parameters used in such an analysis. Economic policy can arise through rough consensus among economists over the nature and impact of various proposals. Such consensus allows them to agree on recommendations to those who manage the political forces in the nation. Such recommendations may not be accepted for a variety of reasons, including the reason that the analysis was not sufficiently inclusive of certain social or ecological factors. The economists then try to correct their analytical approach and evaluate the criticisms. This process has been going on for more than a century, and today, economists as professionals have a major influence on policy making around the world. The basic reason for this success is their agreement on a single unifying measure of economic health, underpinned by an explanatory and predictive body of economic theory that is being constantly applied, challenged and refined.

There have been many criticisms of the GNP measure of economic health (for example, American Academy of Political Science, 1967; Nordhaus and Tobin, 1972; Zolotas, 1981; Daly and Cobb, 1989). The criticisms come from many directions. If home-makers join the salaried work force and hire someone to clean the home and care for the children, the GNP increases, though the work in the home has not changed. If people become sicker and use more health care services, the GNP increases. If we deplete the known stock of a valued resource, such as oil or soil, the GNP does not change appropriately.

Is the definition of the GNP a thoroughly good one? No. But the usual conclusion is that the definition could be amended to count a little a more here and a little less there, resulting in a meaningful indicator of economic health. Can we look to the ecologists to find some more appropriate measures of economic health?

2.   Ecosystem health measures: a search for the ecological grail

The control of the economy is a subjective enterprise because the generally agreed-upon measures of economic health are subjectively based. When we subjective creatures look at another system, the ecosystem, one which we tend to observe from outside, can we measure that system's health less subjectively? The above measures of the economic system can be used as a guide. Imperfect as it seems, the economic system measure is the result of a great deal of effort over centuries by some of the best minds in economics. Perhaps a measure of ecosystem health can be found which, by reverse analogy, will reduce the subjectivity of the measure of economic health. As imagined outside observers of the ecosystem, we might assign more objectivity to any conclusions we reach from our observations.

A more difficult problem lies with the ecologists. To gain consensus on a measure of ecological health, they must assume that an ecosystem somehow behaves as though it has a goal or an optimal state. We need to call upon Aristotle's 'final cause'. The ecosystem, at some reasonable level of aggregation, has what seems to be a preferred state, just as the human body seems to have. Disturbances ('disease') are short-term perturbations which the system tries to eliminate and return to its 'optimal' state. This assumption alone would require a very great leap, too subjective a move for many ecologists. But I see no alternative to it. If we do not accept the idea of a goal or accept at least the possibility of one, we are open to the accusation that ecologists are arrogant with regard to nature and can manipulate its processes for the will of man without risk of ultimate failure. Dismissal of the possibility of the existence of such a goal is unscientific. We must assume first that there *is* some internal goal for the development of an ecosystem, some potential description of optimal health. Through a combination of theory and experimentation on specific ecosystems, we should be able to discern if the growth of an ecosystem conforms to predictions based on hypotheses about the goals of growth to that condition. Eventually, this process should allow us to disprove or prove the existence and nature of any internal goals.[3] If we can describe that goal(s),[4] then I believe most ecologists would concede that we have the management basis for their ecosystems.

In an attempt to capture the general system experience of economists and to demonstrate the utility of a single ecosystem goal or health measure, I now sketch out the ecological equivalent of the GNP. Alternative ecological health measures have been proposed by others (Rapport, 1984; Karr, 1991), but these measures are not predictive. For predictive purposes, a model of the ecosystem is needed, preferably dynamic and most likely nonlinear. However, the first predictive modelling steps can be taken with comparative statics (Hannon and Joiris, 1989), using the economist's input–output techniques. The economists have struggled for a long time to provide such a model for economic forecasting. Ecologists are still centred on the idea of an empirical set of ecosystem indicators.

The components of an ecosystem – producers, herbivores, carnivores, decomposers and so on – can be arranged into an economic-like accounting framework (Hannon et al., 1991), with interconnecting flows: herbivores eat producers, carnivores eat herbivores, consumers eat each of them. All components give off heat in the process of using their inputs and the producers absorb sunlight, among other abiotic substances. A net input and a net output can be defined for an ecosystem. Based on these net flows, a set of system-wide indicators or ecosystem 'prices' can be derived (Hannon et al., 1986). The concept of discount rates has also been defined for the ecosystem (Hannon, 1984). The end result of such an approach is a view of the ecological system which is parallel to the economist's view of the economic system. Such congruency is useful if the two systems are ever going to be meaningfully combined into the same framework.

The issue of scale – adequately representing the components of the system that operate at different size and spatial scales – is an important one. The economic accounting system framework has been adapted to regional interactions. The fact that all regions of a landscape are not acting in synchrony is exactly that feature that allows one to talk about the steadiness of the flows and stocks of the collection.

The first step in deriving a measure of ecosystem health is to define precisely what is meant by net ecosystem output. These net outputs should include the net exports of biomass and any abiotic substances and the gross additions to stocks.

But what is the ecological parallel to personal and government consumption? Return to the economic framework for a moment. Imagine an isolated economy at steady state. The imports and exports are zero, and gross capital formation is entirely used to replace worn-out capital. Suppose further that inventory changes were negligible. The only contributions to the GNP would then be the consumption by people and government, and the rate of capital replacement. Some (Costanza, 1980; Costanza and Herendeen, 1984) have argued that consumers and government are simply producing–consuming sectors in the production economy, similar to any other industrial–commercial sector. Consumers supply labour and use housing, food, clothing, transportation, education and so on to do so. Governments consume in order to direct and control. Technically, these two sectors can be considered part of the industrial exchange pattern and removed from direct involvement in the GNP measure. In our closed steady-state economy, the only GNP measure would then be the capital replacement rate.

With the consumption sectors removed from the net output, some of the earlier criticisms of the GNP measure would vanish. Crime, health care and home-maker's labour are considered costs of production of household or government services. By analogy, this reduced GNP definition can be matched in the net output definition for an ecosystem. We have no reason to put any species or trophic level in the net output. To the now-objective human observer, no species or trophic level seems more important than the other. The ecosystem net output for a given period can therefore be defined as the net exports and the gross changes in each of the stocks. For the closed, steady-state ecosystem, the only net output is the replacement rate of the stocks, making up the losses caused by metabolism and decomposition. This replacement rate is exactly analogous to the capital replacement rate used by economists.

Analogous to the net inputs to the economy (wages, taxes, profits and so on) is a list of net inputs to the ecosystem. Think of these net ecosystem inputs as necessary for the production of the ecosystem's net output. Among the various forms of net input to a particular ecosystem, such as nitrogen, phosphorus or sunlight, one of them is generally limiting the size of the system. Assume that the limiting net input is sunlight. With the list of absorbed sunlight quantities, a set of ecosystem sunlight 'prices' can be calculated. This set of prices can be multiplied with the associated terms in the net output. The now-commensurate result can be summed to give an evaluated net output of the ecosystem under study. This evaluated output is analogous to the redefined GNP: it captures all the activities in the ecosystem, in a weighted manner, and gathers them into a single number. That number, the gross ecosystem product (GEP), is a viable candidate for aggregate ecosystem health. But the GEP is not a wholly adequate measure, for the GEP, like the GNP, cannot increase for ever, a problem addressed below.

As an application of this ecosystem health measure, the ecosystem input (GEP) was evaluated for two tidal marshes. One of the marshes existed under natural conditions and the other was elevated on average 6 °C by the waste heat from an electricity generating station (Hannon, 1985). The net output was evaluated for a 17-biotic-sector description of both marshes in terms of absorbed sunlight energy. The evaluated net output of the heated marsh was 33 per cent lower than the same measure for the natural marsh. Unfortunately, this comparison of systems is the only one of its kind. The comparison is based on a detailed exchange between all the components in the companion marsh ecosystems, a rare combination of science and research support. This comparison demonstrates the manner in which the GEP indicates ecosystem health: both marshes are probably close to the steady state but the unheated one has a higher GEP. This comparison also reinforces the fact that my favourite measure of ecosystem and economic health is based directly on system flows, not on stocks. The presence of the system stocks is felt, of course, through the levels of metabolic flows.

3. Conclusion

Rapport's view of size diminution and reversion to juvenile are effects which are also captured in the time-value measures of a dynamic system. Ulanowicz and Hannon (1987) point out that the 'discount' or 'interest' rate of an ecological system captures both the average metabolic rate and the average specific energy content for the living members of the system.

Hannon (1990) argues that this rate is both the average and marginal rate of specific metabolism[5] for the living elements in a steady-state ecosystem, when that system is at steady state. He further argues that the steady-state evaluation would reveal the lowest discount rate ever experienced in the development of that ecosystem. It is well known that larger species have smaller specific metabolic rates compared to those of the physically smaller species. One very general way that the average metabolic rate of an ecosystem becomes smaller is for large individuals to displace the smaller ones.

Climax species seem to have been selected as the least maintenance-requiring as though to store the most order in the climax ecosystem. If this size shift is assumed to be a goal of the system, an additional constraint on the gross ecosystem product measure is required. The GEP should increase continually but less and less rapidly until it becomes steady. At that point, the system has the largest GEP *and* the smallest discount rate possible. The combined requirement ensures that the low entropy retained in the system is maximized. Since the principal low-entropy input to the ecosystem is sunlight, the 'optimal' system would be storing the most converted sunlight possible. This is the opposite side of the same coin as such a system criterion as maximal sunlight degradation (Schneider and Kay, 1994). But this coin is only one of perhaps many goal statements of an ecosystem. My point is that such goal statements should be sharpened for explicit field and laboratory testing (Amir and Hannon, 1991), and that a consistent accounting system for this process is needed before the goals can be clearly stated.

In the system described in this chapter, we have two rate indicators of ecosystem health: increasing net output of the ecosystem (GEP) (albeit at slower and slower rates) and a decreasing aggregate discount rate. For the moment, we have no good ecosystem measure of the discount rate except perhaps at the climax or steady state. But *some* constraint on the GEP is needed, for it clearly cannot increase for ever. The decreasing discount rate concept, however, does tell us that the maturing ecosystem will need increasing amounts of biomass whose unit or specific metabolism is increasingly lower. This is usually the case with the introduction of species with larger members, as Rapport has noted. Therefore, if the larger species are disappearing from an ecosystem, its measured discount rate would probably be rising, all else unchanged.

4.   Grand speculation: combining the measures

We may rest content with the idea of the incompatibility of the economic and the ecological systems and their GNP and GEP 'health' measures as described above. The economic system description with its prices and production measures seem so pertinent to the purposes of man, and we tend to think of the ecological processes as proceeding toward a different and yet unknown goal.

We may want to push the concept further and try to combine these two net output measures in a single system 'health' indicator. It has been suggested (Isard, 1968; Daly, 1968; Hannon et al., 1991) that it is possible to place all economic and ecological transactions in the same matrix or accounting framework. Such a framework would contain the inter-economic and the inter-ecological transactions. It would also have to contain all the important transactions between the economic and ecological systems. The net inputs and outputs of the combined system must be in consistent units of measure. This requirement simply means that the units of measure for each row of the transactions (from the row of steel production to the column of auto production, for example) must be made in the same units of measure (such as dollars). The requirement of identical units of measure for all the exchanges in a given row means that the inputs to the ecosystem of pollution by the steel industry, for example (such as SO_2) must be collected in a special column, the row version of which is the tons of SO_2 absorbed by the various parts of the ecosystem. Likewise, the inputs to the economic system must be measured in consistent units. The wood, for example, harvested from the nation's forests and used in the various manufacturing industries and in the ecological system could be measured in tons of carbon. To make the net output of the combined system sum to a single meaningful number, a set of system-wide prices must be devised. As we learn in the discussion of the ecological system, to calculate this set of prices we must first decide on the limiting net input to the combined system. Is it labour or energy, for example? If such a critical input can be identified, the system-wide prices can be calculated and multiplied by the net outputs, changing each of the net entries into commensurate units. The sum of these converted net outputs is the evaluated net output of the combined system. It is a single measure of the 'health' of the combined system. It is a measure which would show the net effect of pure economic growth, combined with ecological decline: the combined measure may reveal a decline while the economic measure shows an increase.

Notes

1. For a somewhat fuller account of the economic and ecological health measures, see Hannon (1991).
2. We could consider the value of the wealth of a country as a measure of economic health. Wealth is a stock and terribly hard to measure accurately. Since the physical basis for wealth is largely unmarketed on a regular basis, only vague evaluation can be made.
3. I do not see such an existence assumption as a problem. Children learn the complex procedure of 'pumping' their playground swing while the theory to demonstrate such behaviour requires Newtonian mechanics and an understanding of energy principles.

Engineers long ago proved that complex beam deflection can be exactly predicted from a theory that says that the beam deflects in such a way as to minimize its internal strain energy – doing so without a single course in differential equations or optimization techniques!
4. Depending of course on the condition of the environment in which the systems operates (Kay, 1991).
5. The rate of respiration per unit of stock respiring. The units are 1/time.

References

American Academy of Political Science (1967), 'Social goals and indicators for American society', *Annals*, vols 371, 373.

Amir, S. and B. Hannon (1991), 'Biowealth discounting in ecosystems', *Speculations in Science and Technology*, **15** (3), 228–37.

Costanza, R. (1980), 'Embodied energy and economic valuation', *Science*, **210**, 1219–24.

Costanza, R. and R. Herendeen (1984), 'Embodied energy and economic value in the United States economy: 1963, 1967 and 1972', *Resources and Energy*, **6**, 129–64.

Daly, H. (1968), 'Economics as life science', *Journal of Political Economy*, **76**, 392–401.

Daly, H. and J. Cobb (1989), *For the Common Good*, Boston, MA: Beacon Press, pp. 401–55.

Hannon, B. (1984), 'Discounting in ecosystems', in A.-M. Jansson (ed.), *Integration of Economy and Ecology – an Outlook of the Eighties*, University of Stockholm, pp. 73–84.

Hannon, B. (1985), 'Ecosystem flow analysis', *Canadian Bulletin of Fisheries and Aquatic Sciences*, **213**, 97–118.

Hannon, B. (1990), 'Biological time value', *Math. Biosci.*, **100**, 115–40.

Hannon, B. (1991), 'Measures of economic and ecological health', in R. Costanza, B. Norton and B. Haskell (eds), *Ecosystem Health*, Washington, DC: Island Press, pp. 207–222.

Hannon, B. and C. Joiris (1989), 'A seasonal analysis of the Southern North sea ecosystem', *Ecology*, **70** (6), 1916–34.

Hannon, B., R. Costanza and R. Herendeen (1986), 'Measures of cost and value in ecosystems', *Journal of Environmental Economics and Management*, **13**, 391–401.

Hannon, B., R. Costanza and R. Ulanowicz (1991), 'A general accounting framework for ecological systems', *Theoretical Population Biology*, 40–41, 78–104.

Isard, W. (1968), 'Some notes on the linkage of the ecologic and economic system', *The Regional Science Association Papers*, **22**, 85–96.

Karr, J. (1991), 'Biological integrity: a long-neglected aspect of water resource management', *Ecological Applications*, **1** (1), 66–84.

Kay, J. (1991), 'A nonequilibrium thermodynamic framework for discussing ecosystem integrity', *Environmental Management*, **15** (4), 483–95.

Nordhaus, W. and J. Tobin (1972), 'Is growth obsolete?', in *Economic Growth*, National Bureau of Economic Research General Series, no. 96E, New York: Columbia University Press.

Peterson, W. (1962), *Income, Employment and Economic Growth*, New York: Norton & Co., p. 58.

Rapport, D. (1984), 'The interface of economics and ecology', in A.-M. Jansson (ed.), *Integration of Economy and Ecology – an Outlook for the Eighties*, University of Stockholm, pp. 215–23.

Schneider, E. and J. Kay (1994), 'Life as a manifestation of the second law of thermodynamics', *Mathematical Computer Modelling*, **19** (6–8), 25–48.

Ulanowicz, R. and B. Hannon (1987), 'Life and the production of entropy', *Proceedings of the Royal Society of London*, B 232, pp. 181–92.

Zolotas, X. (1981), *Economic Growth and Declining Social Welfare*, New York: New University Press.

64 EMERGY, value, ecology and economics

Robert A. Herendeen

1. Introduction

EMERGY[1] analysis is a bold and broad-reaching attempt to quantify the role of the environment in supporting economic activity. It was developed by Howard T. Odum and his students in a long line of publications, starting with energy in ecosystems in the 1950s and expanding to a societal and global purview in the book *Environment, Power, and Society* (Odum, 1971). The latest output is the edited volume *Maximum Power: The Ideas and Applications of H.T. Odum* (Hall, 1995), and Odum's 1996 book *Environmental Accounting*. Other references include Fontaine (1981); Gilliland (1975); Odum (1983a, 1983b, 1986, 1988, 1995); Odum and Pinkerton (1955); Odum, Lavine et al. (1981); Odum and Odum (1981); Odum and Arding (1991). Various terms have been tried; 'EMERGY' has been used for at least a decade.

The influence of the environment on the economy is the least understood of the connections in the ecological–economic synthesis. To be sure, there are many fruitful attempts, but they tend to be semi-quantitative, linear, and cannot yet answer the fundamental questions: 'How much are environmental services really worth, and how much impact is required to seriously impair them?' Among the useful works are Westman (1985); Archibugi and Nijkamp (1989); de Groot (1992); and Costanza et al. (1997). The latter is an evaluation of the monetary value ($/year) of the world's major ecosystem types.

EMERGY analysis goes far beyond other, partial attempts in a comprehensive method that traces all environmental services back to the sunlight that drives them. (The other attempts include 'green' GDP (Hamilton, 1994), damage costs of residual pollution (Ottinger et al., 1990; Nordhaus, 1994), depletion-corrected GDP (Repetto et al., 1989) or satellite resource accounts (Alfsen et al., 1987), many of which harken back to the mass-balance residual analysis of Kneese et al., 1970 and Ayres, 1978).

H.T. Odum's work for over four decades has been central to what we know about the fascinating, broad and comprehensive analogies between flows in ecosystems and economic systems. Besides its descriptive aspects, EMERGY analysis (hereafter called EMA) is also intended for use in policy decisions. In that connection I became interested in the details, and in the process I have also become a critic (Brown and Herendeen, 1996; Brown is a co-worker of Odum's). EMA is ambitious, but EMA has problems, both internally and as it interacts with other disciplines and viewpoints. Other criticisms are Spreng (1988), Månsson and McGlade (1993), and Patten (1993).

2. Elements of EMERGY analysis

Following is my statement of the elements of EMA, with comments.

Statement: The sun runs the biosphere and thus supports us, not just directly through food crops, the water cycle, and so on, but indirectly through the environment's ability to absorb and process our wastes, even to support evolution and the development of species. The solar energy needed, directly and indirectly, to allow production of a given good or service, is called EMERGY. EMERGY is not the caloric energy of a good. Rather it is the total solar energy that has been needed in all steps of the production process. Most of it is already dissipated. Scienceman (1987) calls it 'energy memory'. EMERGY:

(a)   can be calculated by an algebra specified by EMA (unpublished till recently, but now available (Odum, 1996, pp. 99–102; Brown and Herendeen, 1996));

(b)   is claimed to be an indicator of the true value of that good or service.

Comment: EMA is thus a use-based (or donor-based) valuation scheme, with a single numeraire. For most environmental goods and services, there are no economic markets because they are not perceived as scarce. EMA covers them, and economic goods as well.

Statement: EMA's algebra produces 'transformities', that is, the solar energy needed (directly and indirectly) to provide a unit of the good or service (Odum, 1996). The algebra is explicitly sensitive to indirect effects (as exemplified by the pyramidal energy structure of food chains, for example – Brown and Herendeen, 1996), and tracks many subtle dependences. It is also explicit about pollution solution by dilution; the solar energy to process pollution is often calculated by a free energy/entropy of mixing argument.

Transformities based on the present system are used to determine the solar equivalent EMERGY for new or proposed projects or activities. Some transformities are shown in Table 64.1.

Comment: EMA parallels (but is *not* equivalent to) the calculation of indirect effects in input–output economics (Leontief, 1973), and its extension to energy (Bullard and Herendeen, 1975), pollution (Leontief, 1973), and labour (Bezdek and Hannon, 1974) issues (many of these applications are covered in Miller and Blair, 1985), and to ecological structure (Hannon, 1973; Finn, 1976; Ulanowicz, 1986; Herendeen, 1989; Burns, 1989; Higashi et al., 1992). However, there are unresolved concerns about its bookkeeping, particularly in systems with feedback such as food webs instead of chains (Brown and Herendeen, 1996). Transformities are calculated for a wide range of entities, from economic products to the consequences of evolutionary and geological processes. Thus Table 64.1 lists processes with

Table 64.1   Examples of transformities

Item	Transformity units	Transformity value	Source
In a salt marsh:			Table 7.2
Sunlight	seJ/J	1	
Grass	seJ/J	6962	
Crab	seJ/J	3×10^7	
Wind	seJ/J	1496	Table 3.2
Harvested wood	seJ/J	8009	Table 5.2
Rain	seJ/J	8888	Table 10.2
Tidal energy	seJ/J	23564	Table 10.2
Natural gas	seJ/J	48000	Table 10.2
Electricity			Table 10.2
Hydro	seJ/J	159000	
Fossil fuel	seJ/J	159000	
Nuclear	seJ/J	159000	
Phosphate fertilizer	seJ/J	4.4×10^7	Table 5.2
Metamorphic rock	seJ/g	1.45×10^9	Table 3.6
Goods and services in US economy	seJ/$	3.8×10^{12}	Table 10.2
Species evolution (10000) years	seJ/J	4.8×10^{15}	(Odum, 1995, Table 14.1)

Notes:
seJ = solar equivalent joules. J = Joules. Sunlight is the numeraire; its transformity is 1 by definition. Natural gas and other fossil fuels have EMERGY based on assumed origins in biological production and burial in sediments. Electricity is assumed to be approximately 4 times as EMERGY-intensive as fossil-fuels, mostly because of the thermal efficiency of the steam cycle. The assumed equivalence of hydro and nuclear energy to fossil energy follows engineering convention.

Source: Odum (1996), unless otherwise indicated.

characteristic times ranging from 1 year to ~10^9 years. On one hand using such long time scales satisfies the notion that (say) a species should have a high 'value', but on the other hand the mixing of time scales complicates interpretation of results.

Statement: The goal of nature is to maximize EMERGY flow, and this should be the human objective as well. This is stated in three ways, each with some problems:

1. Maximum power principle: 'Prevailing systems are those whose designs maximize empower by reinforcing intake at the optimum efficiency' (Odum, 1996, p. 26).
2. By use of several normalized indicators which compare EMERGY flows directly from the environment with those via the economy. Figure 64.1 and Table 64.2 show some of these indicators, and a comparison with several from energy analysis. The general impression is that

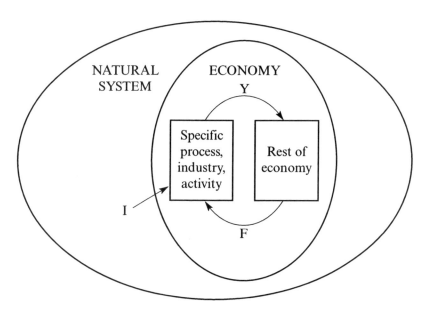

Notes: The symbols I (input from environment), F (input from economy), Y (output economy) follow Odum (1966). A conceptually identical diagram, with different notation, is used for net energy analysis (in which case the specific industry is an energy facility) (Herendeen, 1988).

Figure 64.1   Flows in an economic system embedded in a natural system (environment)

Table 64.2 Comparison of indicators in energy analysis and EMERGY analysis

Description	Energy analysis		EMERGY analysis (EMA)	
	Comment	Formula	Comment	Formula
(Output to economy)/(Input from economy)	Applied to energy industry in net energy analysis. Called IER (incremental energy ratio) in Herendeen (1988), or EROI (energy return on investment) in Hall et al. (1986).	Y/F	Applies to any process. Called EMERGY yield ratio by Odum (1996), pp. 67–71	Y/F
(Output to economy)/(Input from economy plus input directly from environment)	Applied to energy industry in net energy analysis. Called AER (absolute energy ratio) in Herendeen (1988). Typically ≤ 1.0	Y/(I+F)	None	None

958

(Input from economy)/(Input from environment)	None	None	Called EMERGY investment ratio in Odum (1996), pp.67–71	F/I
Ratio of physical flow to monetary flow		(Energy per year)/GDP		(EMERGY per year)/GDP
Monetary flow corresponding to physical flow	None	None	Called Emdollars in Odum (1996)	(Average GDP/EMERGY for nation or region)*(EMERGY flow)
Exports v. imports	Embodied energy of imports v. exports (Herendeen, 1978)	Multiply monetary flows by embodied energy intensities (similar to transformities) of source country or region	Exchange ratio (Odum, 1996, pp.67–71, is defined as the EMERGY of an imported product divided by the EMERGY used by the domestic economy to pay for it	(EMERGY of imported product)/[(EMERGY per year of domestic economy)/(GDP of domestic economy)*(price of product)]

Note: Formulas refer to Figure 64.1.

natural flows are to be preferred over economic ones, but the idea is used casually.

3. By noting that EMERGY flows can be influenced both positively or negatively by an economic activity. For example, constructing a dam produces an EMERGY benefit by increasing agriculture production through irrigation of previously untilled land, but it may reduce agricultural production downriver because the annual flood, which sends fertilizing silt, is now cut off (Brown, Odum, Murphy et al., ch. 22 in Hall, 1995).

Comment: EMA is much more explicit about a maximizing principle than a less-ambitious parallel subdiscipline, energy analysis. Energy analysis, now about 25 years old (Bullard and Herendeen, 1975), has no optimizing principle except the implicit one that because energy has diverse environmental costs, it is desirable to minimize use, everything else being equal. The idea of maximum power reflects the idea that haste makes waste, but that efficient slowness accomplishes vanishingly little in a given time, and that therefore maximum useful output per unit time is accomplished at a speed somewhere between these extremes. There are many examples in physical science, and indeed Odum's first writing on it used a system of weights over a pulley (Odum and Pinkerton, 1955). But there is also an implication that bigger is better; the maximum power principle at first appears to direct one to seek to maximize inputs without constraints, which leads one to ask if it promotes waste. The last part of the principle, 'by reinforcing resource intake at the optimum efficiency' avoids that pitfall by implying that not all power dissipation is desirable. However, it introduces the undefined term 'optimum efficiency' and makes this statement of the priniciple very fuzzy. Other statements of, or references to, the principle[2] do not clarify things adequately for policy application.

Statement: EMA closes the loop back to money by assuming that the ratio of GDP to EMERGY, which is averaged for the entire economy, applies to monetary flows at a much more detailed level. EMA postulates that this ratio can be used to calculate the monetary impact of changing EMERGY flows resulting from human activity. Thus the loss of siltation as a fertilization source downstream from a dam will cause a loss in biological productivity (expressed in EMERGY terms) and this can be converted to the monetary impact on the economy. This is a very explicit connection between environment and economy. I comment on this in the next section.

3. Applications

Using EMERGY analysis to determine the worth of one southern
hemisphere whale (Odum, 1996, Table 7.4)
EMERGY per whale is obtained by first dividing the solar input power to
the ocean frequented by the whales by the number of whales (at a natural
steady state, before the depredations of the past three centuries), giving
3.5×10^{17} seJ whale^{-1} yr^{-1}. Multiplying by the average whale lifetime of 15
years gives an EMERGY of 52.5×10^{17} seJ whale^{-1}. Then multiplying by
the 1990 GDP/EMERGY ratio of the world economy (0.5×10^{12} \$ seJ^{-1})
gives \$2.6 $\times 10^6$ per whale. This assumes that the whale, positioned at the
top of a food chain, can be assigned all of the solar input to the ocean, and
hence implies that this estimate is an upper bound.

Comment: One must admire the attempt to convert EMERGY to money,
but it is extremely problematic in detail. Obvious criticisms are:

(a) The use of a single conversion factor from EMERGY to money for
all products seems unjustified; a typical economy is more inhomo-
geneous.
(b) EMA is silent about when, and to which economic sector(s), the costs
apply if a whale is removed. This makes it difficult to use for policy
discussions because the political battles are usually fought between
constituencies that stand to win or lose, and this calculation does not
identify them.

Benefits of international trade
Different economies have different GDP/EMERGY ratios, so that the
EMERGY being transacted is different from the monetary flows. Applying
this to Ecuadorian shrimp sold to the US, Odum writes (1996, p. 212):

> EMERGY evaluation for the shrimp export trade [pond aquaculture] showed
> 4.1 times more EMERGY going to the United States than received in goods and
> services by Ecuador [when Ecuador assumedly spent the proceeds on American
> goods]. In other words, the coastal zone people were deprived of their
> EMERGY, the regional wealth was reduced to one fourth, and only those oper-
> ating the aquaculture gained.

Comment: First, Odum says EMERGY is wealth. This is revolutionary,
and needs discussion, notwithstanding the physically fundamental aspect
of sunlight. Second, he has injected distributional issues, even though the
results are calculated for averages and therefore should only apply to the
average situation. Third, the reason that Ecuador has a higher ratio of

EMERGY to GDP is that it is poor. In fact, one might draw (standard economic) hope here: if high natural EMERGY means high resources, then Ecuador has a potential to rise too. A poor country with no resources could have a lower EMERGY/GDP and appear to do better in trade, but it would have little chance of development. The 'solution' that EMERGY analysis points towards is for Ecuador to charge more for the shrimp. Conventional economics would support this, but probably object to this definition of wealth.

4. Sustainability and limits

Concern with sustainability is based on the concept of limits, which is predominant in ecology. None the less, EMA does not explicitly confront limits. All human developments combine free and purchased inputs, both expressible in EMERGY terms. EMA seems to say that maximizing total EMERGY is desirable, subject to some as yet unspecified optimality criterion, over an imprecise time scale. In addition, Odum introduces the idea of 'matching'. This says that a new development will do better if it matches the EMERGY investment ratio (see Table 64.2) of its region. Thus a highly developed region, with an average ratio of 10 purchased EMERGY units to 1 unit from nature, say, should continue development with a comparable ratio. There seems to be no room here for less intensive development in developed countries, or for more intensive development in developing countries. Both of these policies would be explicit in a global discussion of sustainability.

5. Conclusion

EMERGY analysis explicitly deals with two areas that have been largely untouched in quantitative terms by economists and ecologists: (1) evaluating environmental services, and (2) relating these to impacts on economic production. EMA goes far beyond attempts from the physical/biological side (such as energy analysis) and from the economic side (such as GDP adjustments). It has helped to spawn a number of fruitful subdisciplines and related activities, such as the nascent field of ecological economics. However, EMA is still a work in progress with problems both internal (statement of the maximum power principle, bookkeeping questions, allocation of economic impacts) and external (interaction with sustainability criteria, definition of real wealth). In my opinion it cannot now be used for policy discussions in detail, but its ideas and thrusts are important and inspirational in the pursuit of better economics. My advice to newcomers is: know its broad-brush outline, but do not yet depend on its details.

Notes

1. The spelling and capitalization follow Odum (1996). EMERGY has the units of energy.
2. Other statements on the maximum power principle, both from H.T. Odum, ch. 28, in Hall (1995):

> During self-organization, system designs develop and prevail that maximize power intake, energy transformation, and those uses that reinforce production and efficiency. (p. 311)

> Maximizing EMERGY production and use at each level of hierarchy at the same time is required to maximize the combined economy of humanity and nature. This means simultaneously maximizing EMERGY production and use at each level's scale of time and space. (p. 319)

References

Alfsen, K., T. Bye and L. Lorentsen (1987), 'Natural resource accounting and analysis, the Norwegian experience 1978–1986' (in English), Central Bureau of Statistics, Oslo, Norway.

Archibugi, F. and P. Nijkamp (eds) (1989), *Economy and Ecology: Towards Sustainable Development*, Dordrecht: Kluwer Academic Publishers.

Ayres, R. (1978), *Resources, Environment, and Economics*, New York: Wiley.

Bezdek, R. and B. Hannon (1974), 'Energy, manpower, and the highway trust fund', *Science*, **85**, 669–75.

Brown, M.T. and R. Herendeen (1996), 'Embodied energy analysis and EMERGY analysis: a comparative view', *Ecological Economics*, **19**, 219–36.

Bullard, C. and R. Herendeen (1975), 'The energy costs of goods and services', *Energy Policy*, **3**, 268–78.

Burns, T. (1989), 'Lindeman's contradiction and the trophic structure of ecosystems', *Ecology*, **70**, 1355–62.

Costanza, R., R. d'Arge, R. de Groot, S. Farber, M. Grasso, B. Hannon, S. Naeem, K. Limburg, J. Paruelo, R.V. O'Neill, R. Raskin, P. Sutton and M. van den Belt (1997), 'The value of the world's ecosystem services and natural capital', *Nature*, **387**, 253–60.

de Groot, R. (1992), *Functions of Nature: Evaluation of Nature in Environmental Planning, Management and Decision Making*, Deventer, Netherlands: Wolters-Noordhoff.

Finn, J.T. (1976), 'Measures of ecosystem structure and function derived from analysis of flows', *Journal of Theoretical Biology*, **56**, 115–24.

Fontaine, T. (1981), 'A self-designing model for testing ecosystem hypotheses', in S. Jorgensen (ed.), *Progress in Ecological Engineering and Management by Mathematical Modelling*, Amsterdam: Elsevier, pp. 281–91.

Gilliland, M. (1975), 'Energy analysis and public policy', *Science*, **189**, 1051–6.

Hall, C. (ed.) (1995), *Maximum Power: The Ideas and Applications of H.T. Odum*, Niwot, Colorado: University Press of Colorado.

Hall, C., C. Cleveland and R. Kaufmann (1986), *Energy and Resource Quality: The Ecology of the Economic Process*, New York: Wiley.

Hamilton, K. (1994), 'Environmental accounting for decision-making', July, Washington, DC: World Bank.

Hannon, B. (1973), 'The structure of ecosystems', *Journal of Theoretical Biology*, **41**, 535–46.

Herendeen, R. (1978), 'Energy balance of trade in Norway', *Energy Systems and Policy*, **2**, 425–32.

Herendeen, R. (1988), 'Net energy considerations', in R. West and F. Kreith (eds), *Economic Analysis of Solar Thermal Energy Systems*, Cambridge, MA: MIT Press, pp. 255–73.

Herendeen, R. (1989), 'Energy intensity, residence time, exergy, and ascendency in dynamic ecosystems', *Ecological Modelling*, **48**, 19–44.

Higashi, M., T. Burns and B. Patten (1992), 'Trophic niches of species and trophic structure of ecosystems: complementary perspectives through food network unfolding', *Journal of Theoretical Biology*, **154**, 57–76.

Kneese, A., R. Ayres and R. d'Arge (1970), *Economics and the Environment: A Materials Balance Approach*, Washington, DC: Resources for the Future.

Leontief, W. (1973), *Input–Output Economics*, New York: Oxford University Press.

Månsson, B. and J. McGlade (1993), 'Ecology, thermodynamics, and H.T. Odum's conjectures', *Oecologia*, **93**, 582–96.

Miller, R. and P. Blair (1985), *Input–Output Analysis: Foundations and Extensions*, Englewood Cliffs, NJ: Prentice-Hall.

Nordhaus, W.D. (1994), *Managing the Global Commons – The Economics of Climate Change*, Cambridge, MA: MIT Press.

Odum, H.T. (1971), *Environment, Power, and Society*, New York: Wiley.

Odum, H.T. (1983a), *Systems Ecology*, New York: Wiley.

Odum, H.T. (1983b), 'Maximum power and efficiency: a rebuttal', *Ecological Modelling*, **20**, 71–82.

Odum, H.T. (1986), 'Enmergy in ecosystems', in N. Polunin (ed.), *Ecosystem Theory and Application*, New York: Wiley, pp. 337–69.

Odum, H.T. (1988), 'Self-organization, transformity, and information', *Science*, **242**, 1132–9.

Odum, H.T. (1995), 'Tropical forest systems and the human economy', in A. Lugo and C. Lowe (eds), *Tropical Forests: Management and Ecology*, New York: Springer, pp. 341–93.

Odum, H.T. (1996), *Environmental Accounting*, New York: Wiley.

Odum, H. and J. Arding (1991), *EMERGY Analysis of Shrimp Mariculture in Ecuador*, Report, Center for Wetlands, University of Florida, Gainesville.

Odum, H.T. and E. Odum (1981), *Energy Basis for Man and Nature*, New York: McGraw-Hill.

Odum, H.T. and R.C. Pinkerton (1955), 'Time's speed regulator: the optimum efficiency for maximum power', *American Scientist*, **43**, 331–43.

Odum, H., M. Lavine, F. Wang, M. Miller, J. Alexander and T. Butler (1981), *A Manual for Using Energy Analysis for Plant Siting*, Report to the Nuclear Regulatory Commission, Contract NRC-04-77-123 Mod. 3. Center for Wetlands, University of Florida, Gainesville.

Ottinger, R., D. Wooley, S. Hodas, N. Robinson and S. Babb (1990), *Environmental Costs of Electricity*, Washington, DC: American Council for an Energy-Efficient Economy.

Patten, B. (1993), 'Toward a more holistic ecology, and science: the contribution of H.T. Odum', *Oecologia*, **93**, 597–602.

Repetto, R., W. Magrath, M. Wells, C. Beer and F. Rossini (1989), *Wasting Assets: Natural Resources in the National Income Accounts*, Report, World Resources Institute, Washington, DC.

Scienceman, D. (1987), 'Energy and emergy', in G. Pillet and T. Murota (eds), *Environmental Economics*, Geneva: Leimgruber, pp. 257–68.

Spreng, D.T. (1988), *Net Energy Analysis and the Energy Requirements of Energy Systems*, New York: Praeger.

Ulanowicz, R. (1986), *Growth and Development: Ecosystems Phenomenology*, New York: Springer.

Westman, W. (1985), *Ecology, Impact Assessment, and Environmental Planning*, New York: Wiley.

65 Evolution, environment and economics
John M. Gowdy

1. Introduction: evolutionary biology and economics

The connections between evolutionary theory and economics go back well over one hundred years. The co-formulators of the theory of evolution by natural selection, Charles Darwin and Alfred Russel Wallace, developed their ideas after reading the economic texts of Thomas Malthus describing competitive markets. Alfred Marshall, the great synthesizer of modern neoclassical economics in the early 1900s, had a keen interest in evolutionary theory. He used Darwin's dictum *natura non facit saltum*, nature does not make leaps, for the frontispiece of his economic textbook. We find in Darwin and Marshall the two ideas which dominated both evolutionary and economic theory for over a century – improvement through competition and gradual change. More important than Darwin to contemporary economics were the ideas of Herbert Spencer who greatly influenced Marshall and Veblen. It was Spencer, not Darwin, who used the term 'evolution' (Darwin preferred the more neutral and accurate phrase 'descent with modification') and who coined the phrase 'survival of the fittest' (Hodgson, 1993). The Spencerian idea of social progress through competition still dominates contemporary thought. To this day neoclassical models of economic change begin with the assumption that the sole driving evolutionary force is competitive selection (see, for example, the explicit statements of this by Geroski, 1989; Telser, 1996).

Until recently, most of the applications of biological metaphors[1] in economics were confined to crude notions of survival of the fittest which were used to validate the main results of neoclassical economic theory, namely, that freely operating markets will 'optimize efficiency' (Friedman, 1953; Hodgson, 1994). Economists have freely used notions from evolutionary biology such as adaptation, selection and variability to describe competitive economies. Certain aspects of selection, such as differences in survival rates through time, work similarly in markets and in ecosystems. Mechanisms of selection work to select the fittest whether or not the individual knows the rules of the game (Alchian, 1950; Friedman 1953). In markets and ecosystems there is also the problem of indeterminacy, that is, what is selected today may not be the fittest tomorrow. The 'Red Queen' (Van Valen, 1973) principle operates in both biology and economics. Firms in a market system and organisms in an ecosystem are under constant pressure from competitors. Like Alice's Red Queen, they must run as fast as they can just to stay in the same place. Critics of biological metaphors have stressed the lack of an equivalent to genetic inheritance in economic change (Penrose, 1952), but as Winter (1988) points out, this does not necessarily rule out the usefulness of biological concepts. Furthermore, if macro-evolution exists in biology, the gene is no longer the exclusive locus of causality for evolutionary change. Thus the search for a gene equivalent in economic evolution may be based in part on an outdated biological metaphor.

Sociobiology, the application of evolutionary biology to human behaviour, has been controversial in biology and in economics (Buchanan, 1996). Because it has so many negative connotations, the term sociobiology is used with decreasing frequency. The application of evolutionary biology to human behaviour is today more often referred to as evolutionary psychology or behavioural ecology (Barkow, 1989). Evolutionary psychologists argue that human psychology evolved as a complex of adaptations to Pleistocene conditions and that this fact constrains the ability of modern cultures to adopt environmentally or socially sustainable behaviour. Behavioural ecologists apply ideas from evolutionary biology, such as optimal foraging theory, to human societies and cultures.

There has been a dramatic shift in recent years regarding the place of evolutionary biology in the philosophy of science. Mayr (1982) notes that most of the major figures in the philosophy of science have been trained in the physical sciences. The influence of the physical science or mechanistic viewpoint has led to a widely held view of what is 'true' science that does not include evolutionary systems. Following the mechanistic viewpoint, the positivist philosophy of neoclassical economics stresses the importance of prediction and falsifiability of economic postulates. In Friedman's (1953, p. 4) view the task of economics is 'to provide a system of generalizations that can be used to make correct predictions about the consequences of any change of circumstance'. Following Karl Popper, Friedman insists that the ability to predict correctly is the only test of validity of a hypothesis. Interestingly, the controversy as to whether a scientific theory must be predictive came to the forefront in the 1970s and 1980s as a result of challenges from so-called 'scientific creationists' who questioned the teaching of evolutionary biology on the grounds that the theory of natural selection does not lead to testable scientific predictions. In court challenges to teaching evolution, creationists quoted Popper's assertion 'I have come to the conclusion that Darwinism is not a testable scientific theory but a metaphysical research programme' (Popper, 1976, p. 168). This turn of events was important because in response to the creationists' attack on evolutionary biology Popper (1978, p. 344) modified his views on the scientific status of the theory of evolution by natural selection and of the historical sciences in general:

> I still believe that natural selection works in this way as a research programme. Nevertheless, I have changed my mind about the testability and the logical status of the theory of natural selection; and I am glad to have an opportunity to make a recantation.

Because of his status as the foremost philosopher of science, Popper's recantation was an important milestone in the elevation of the status of evolutionary theory in the philosophy of science. By the 1980s and 1990s, according to Lewontin (1990), students being trained in the philosophy of science were getting their training in evolutionary biology, not physics.

Another connection between evolutionary theory in biology, economics and the environment centres around the place of *Homo sapiens* in the natural world. Biologists routinely work with the notion of biophysical constraints while most economists accept the notion of 'economic man' isolated from a social and environmental context. Even within the field of economics, however, the theme of environmental contraints to economic activity has a long history. It can be traced at least back to Malthus, who is best known for his theory of population. Among the classical economists it was Malthus who first placed humans within the natural world and who argued that they are subject to the same laws of nature as other species. William Stanley Jevons raised a similar question in his study of the importance of the finite supply of coal to the British economy. The question of whether humans are somehow qualitatively different from other life forms, and are able to circumvent the long-run physical and biological laws which constrain other species, is still the basic point of contention between neoclassical economists and their environmentalist critics. As Page (1991) points out, the fading of the boundary between humans and other species is one of the most significant lessons of contemporary biology. There is growing scientific evidence of highly intelligent behaviour and a range of complex emotions in a number of species (Calvalieri and Singer, 1993; Griffen, 1992; Masson and McCarthy, 1995). Some argue that this means that we have a responsibility to preserve the evolutionary potential not only of humans but also of other life forms. As the length of time considered increases, economic issues blend into ethical ones (Georgescu-Roegen, 1971; Gowdy and Mesner, 1998).

2. Approaches to modelling evolutionary systems
There are several distinct approaches to modelling economic evolution. The first and oldest uses Darwin's theory of natural selection to validate the

neoclassical model of competitive markets. The essays of Alchian (1950), Enke (1951) and Friedman (1953) on the evolution of optimal competitive outcomes are early examples of this approach. The second approach, while seemingly non-neoclassical, merely extends the standard model of optimization at the margin. Even the highly regarded and influential evolutionary models of Nelson and Winter (1982), although allowing for non-optimality and Lamarckian goal-seeking, are fundamentally marginalist in character. Such extensions are interesting but they are based on pre-1970s notions of biological evolution that do not capture the rich and far-reaching implications of contemporary evolutionary theory, particularly the decoupling of macro- from micro-processes.[2] Of the non-neoclassical approaches, there is a clear distinction between those based on evolutionary biology and those grounded in physics and statistical thermodynamics. Those grounded in biology are, in general, sceptical of the ability of formal mathematical models, particularly optimization models, to provide useful economic theories (Gowdy, 1994b; Hodgson, 1993; Victor, 1972). Those grounded in physics are, again in general, much more willing to use optimization models borrowed wholesale from thermodynamics (Faber and Proops, 1990; Ruth, 1993). Ruth (1996) explicitly advocates a move from evolutionary biology to physics in order to understand socioeconomic change.

To a greater or lesser degree, all those interested in modelling economic evolution owe a debt to the Austrian economist Joseph Schumpeter (1974) who argued that economic history was characterized by a process of 'creative destruction'. According to him, there are periods of relative calm when economies are expanding and firms become complacent and are slow to innovate. These periods are broken by economic downturns in which the weakest firms go out of business. After these firms are weeded out by an economic crisis, new niches are available to innovative firms. It is the rush to fill these new niches that is the creative part of creative destruction. So economic history is characterized by waves of expansion and collapse, of creation and destruction. Schumpeter's view of evolutionary change is similar to the new 'punctuated equilibrium' view in evolutionary biology,[3] except that Schumpeter thought that economic change was generated internally.[4] In an oft-quoted passage he states:

> What we are about to consider is that kind of change arising from within the system which so displaces its equilibrium point that the new one cannot be reached from the old one by infinitesimal steps. Add as many mail coaches as you want, you will never get a railroad by doing so. (Schumpeter, 1974, p. 64)

Schumpeter was critical of biological metaphors but it might be that this was because of the inadequate state of evolutionary theory in Schumpeter's time, not because of a dissimilarity in subject matter.

The focus of the neo-Schumpeterian tradition is, for the most part, on the conditions for technical progress and innovation (Day, 1984; Dosi et al., 1988; Iwai, 1984; Nelson and Winter, 1982; Rahmeyer, 1989; Witt, 1992). Unlike Schumpeter, however, and like contemporary neoclassical economics, most of the work of these evolutionary modellers is explicitly based on the metaphor of natural selection. On the other hand, like Schumpeter, most are concerned with change arising endogenously within the economy (Foster, 1993; Saviotti and Metcalfe, 1991; Silverberg et al., 1988). In biological evolution it is now thought that punctuations are caused by external forces, particularly climate change (Vrba, 1984). External forces in economics would include social and environmental influences which envelop the lower hierarchy of the market economy (Gowdy, 1992).

Interestingly both the biological and physical approaches to economic evolution mentioned above are based on the second law of thermodynamics, the entropy law. Thermodynamics entered economic theory in 1971 with the publication of Georgescu-Roegen's *The Entropy Law and the Economic Process*. The entropy law metaphor, challenging the mechanical, reversible, static world of neoclassical analysis, was quickly adopted by a new generation of economists who see the economic process as a one-way flow of low-entropy energy and resources going into the economy and leaving as high-entropy waste. Entropy in one system can decrease only by taking low entropy from another. An obvious example is the dependence of economic activity on fossil fuels. Our industrial economy depends on a steady and apparently increasing flow of raw materials and biological inputs from the lithosphere, atmosphere and biosphere. This entropic relationship also works the other way. Discharges from the economy back into the environment destabilize natural biological and atmospheric systems. If entropy is viewed as information, ecosystem destruction is causing a tremendous loss of genetic information in the biological system surrounding the human economy (Ayres, 1994). Humans are drawing down the natural support systems of the planet in order to subsidize the growth of economic markets (O'Connor, 1993). The net effect of maintaining low entropy in a subsystem is an increase in the total entropy of the system (Ruth, 1996, p. 131).

Georgescu-Roegen, although more familiar with statistics and physics than biology, drew more on biology to build his economic theories. He was quite critical of statistical thermodynamics and the attempt to recast the entropy law in terms of information.[5] The application of thermodynamics to living systems got a boost when Ilya Prigogine won the Nobel prize for chemistry in 1977. Like Georgescu-Roegen, Prigogine argued that far-from-equilibrium systems can achieve a high degree of self-organization by drawing low entropy from an adjacent environment. The implication is that an economic system cannot exist without an open boundary between it and the outside world upon which it depends. The boundary conditions change as low-entropy matter and energy pass into the system and as high-entropy waste passes back across the boundary between the economic system and the biophysical world. Resources become increasingly scarce and the ability of the environment to assimilate wastes from the economic process is reduced.

The physical approach to modelling non-marginal change uses concepts borrowed from thermodynamics but is based on modern physics and chemistry, not biology. The emphasis is on physical processes and the use of energy, materials and information (Ayres, 1989, 1994; Graedel and Allenby, 1995). Ruth (1993) uses a generalized Cobb–Douglas production function with 'thermodynamic constraints' to examine the effects of endogenous technological change. These sorts of models are interesting but are still subject to the criticism made by Victor (1972, p. 41) 25 years ago: 'How can the multifarious outputs of the atmosphere, for example, be aggregated so that it makes sense to talk of 'the' output of the atmosphere which is used as an input by bacteria?'[6]

3. Recent developments in evolutionary theory, economics and the environment

The 1970s and 1980s really ushered in two revolutions in biology, both important to economics. One was the punctuated equilibrium[7] revolution that challenged old notions of adaptation and gradual change (Eldredge and Gould, 1972; Gould and Lewontin, 1979), and the second was the growing recognition among biologists of the environmental crises brought about by economic activity, particularly biodiversity loss (Wilson, 1992). The rapid acceptance of the idea of punctuated equilibria among biologists offers some hope that economists may also be ready to broaden the subject matter of their discipline. Punctuated equilibria does not attack the traditional notion of natural selection as the driving force of evolutionary change. It retains traditional (incremental) explanations of change through time in a broader, more comprehensive theory of evolution. This approach is needed in economics. Neoclassical theory explains the behaviour of individuals and firms acting in well-organized impersonal markets, but it is inadequate as a general theory of economics.

The history of life on Earth has not been one of gradual progression from simpler to more complicated forms of life, but rather a discontinuous path frequently interrupted by cataclysmic events including five or more catastrophic extinction episodes. Biologists have been at the forefront of the attack on the notion of progress itself (Gould, 1988). The idea of progress is central to the standard economic view of evolutionary technological change. Neoclassical economists as well as many of their critics view economic evolution as inherently progressive (Gowdy, 1994a, 1994b). One hundred and thirty years after *The Origin of Species*, the idea that humans are so qualitatively different from other species that they are not subject to the biophysical laws that constrain other life forms is still alive and well. Biologists such as E.O. Wilson and Paul Ehrlich have taken a strong interest in economic theory and are quite critical of the way in which neoclassical economics (and the market system this theory describes) places values on environmental attributes. These two ongoing preoccupations of biology – evolutionary theory and the environmental crisis – have spurred the application of theories of self-organizing systems in economics (Anderson et al., 1988; Foster, 1993; Witt, 1997).

Modelling economic change has a long but heterogeneous history. Only a small portion of this work could be called evolutionary. Most economic forecasting still consists of static projections of past trends to the future using various kinds of multipliers. Some interesting recent work in input–output (IO) analysis goes beyond this approach by bringing in evolutionary concepts from ecology. Perrings (1987) uses a joint production IO framework to examine the workings of an expanding economy constrained by the conservation of mass. O'Connor (1993) has also used a joint production IO model to show the effects of resource depletion and waste production in an economy characterized by uncontrolled technological change. Hewings et al. (1988) describe how the notion of 'fields of influence' may be used to measure the economic impacts of technological change by sector. DeBresson (1989) has used graph theory in IO analysis to examine innovation clusters and their impacts on economic evolution. The concept of total flows, originally developed by ecologists, has been expressed in an input–output system by Szyrmer (1985, 1986). The total flows approach has a fairly long history in models linking the economy and the environment (Cumberland, 1969; Daly, 1968). These approaches have an affinity with evolutionary concepts in biology such as 'keystone' species. Just as certain species seem to have a primary role in the ecosystem, so too do certain sectors seem to drive economic change. Identifying and modelling these fields of influence (Hewings et al., 1988) or fundamental economic structures (Jensen et al., 1988) has the potential to expand our understanding not only of the relationship between the economy and the environment but also of the evolutionary processes involved in this relationship.

Georgescu-Roegen linked concepts of evolutionary theory, economic theory and the environment into a comprehensive world-view, which he called 'bioeconomics' (Georgescu-Roegen, 1977). Following Alfred Lotka (1925), he used the concepts of 'endosomatic' and 'exosomatic' instruments to distinguish humans from other animals. Endosomatic tools such as claws, teeth and fur evolved over eons in an ecological context and through a process of trial and error. Exosomatic tools, 'detachable organs' such as planes, cars and military weapons have evolved with lightning speed and without the usual checks and balances that come with evolving in an ecological context. The work of Kenneth Boulding, particularly his influential paper 'The economics of the coming Spaceship Earth' (1973) also helped lay the foundations of a new entropy-law approach to evolutionary economics.

The two separate but closely related fields of evolutionary economics and ecological economics have grown rapidly since the mid-1980s. In response to a growing awareness of the connections between the environment and the economy, the International Society for Ecological Economics was founded. The intellectual mentors of this school were Georgescu-Roegen and Kenneth Boulding. A leading contemporary spokesman is Herman Daly, whose influential books on steady-state economics have done much to define the new field. The 1980s also saw the formation of the Society for Evolutionary Economics, whose intellectual mentor is Schumpeter. Much of the work done by evolutionary economists in this group may be called neo-Schumpeterian.

Recently, evolutionary economics has turned to the consideration of larger issues such as the evolution of technology and lifestyles (Duchin, 1997), resource constraints on self-organizing systems (Perrings, 1987; Witt, 1997), and the co-evolution of natural and economic systems (Gowdy, 1994b; Norgaard, 1984, 1985, 1994; Söderbaum, 1993). Interestingly, some of the most innovative work linking self-organization, punctuated equilibria and the notion of hierarchies is being done in the field of management. Baum and Singh (1994), Gersick (1991), Hannon and Freeman (1989) and Wollin (1995) have used the idea of nested hierarchies in evolutionary models of organization which account for both incremental and punctuated change.

4.   Future research in evolutionary and environmental economics

The application of evolutionary theory to economic and social systems has provided fruitful insights throughout the history of economic science. Why should economics take into account new ideas from biology? The answer is not simply to borrow metaphors from a more mature field. The physical and social world is one common reality that is split up by the fields of science to make its study more convenient. If the methods of one field of study are based on a deeper understanding of reality, all the other fields should make sure their explanations are consistent with what has been learned. Today evolutionary economics is one of the most exciting and innovative fields of study within economics. Of the many current controversies in evolutionary theory and the environment, the following seem to me to be the most important to economics.

Delineating the mechanism for selection of economic agents through time
Like ultra-Darwinism in evolutionary biology, contemporary neoclassical economics sees evolutionary change as occurring through myriad adaptations at the margin. In the neoclassical view, the movement toward efficiency at the firm level, driven by the profit motive, results in the outward shift of the production possibilities frontier through time. Although there are certainly great differences in approach among economists, for the past quarter century most neoclassical economists have argued that microeconomic principles should provide the foundation of macroeconomics.

Spurred in part by parallel controversies in evolutionary biology, a growing number of economists argue that the Walrasian microfoundation approach to macroeconomics, which insists that the neoclassical theory of the firm should be the basis for a theory of macroeconomics, is inadequate and arbitrary (Foster, 1987; Gowdy, 1992). Colander (1996) and others have called for a 'post-Walrasian' macroeconomics which explicitly recognizes uncertainty and the role of institutions in economic life. Challenging the microfoundations argument, and the argument that striving toward efficiency at the firm level is the sole mechanism driving economic change, is a central theme which links evolutionary theory, economic theory and environmental policy.

Identifying and describing the relevant economic, institutional, and
environmental hierarchies
The study of hierarchical organization is a major concern of contemporary ecology. The natural world seems to be characterized by evolving, overlapping hierarchical systems (Eldredge, 1995). These systems have the following characteristics: (1) entropy in one system can decrease only by taking low entropy from another; (2) different levels in the hierarchy operate on different time scales; and (3) information may be blocked from passing from one hierarchy to another.

Any relevant theory of economic change and the environment must begin by understanding that ecosystems, social systems and markets are discrete elements in a single hierarchical structure and that each element has its own rules that differ across space and time. This is certainly not a new idea, but it is an idea which is yet to be operationalized into a coherent research programme. The work of Herbert Simon (1962, 1973) on hierarchical organization has been very influential in systems theory and in ecology (Allen and Starr, 1982), but has not received the attention it deserves by mainstream economic theory. Some economists are beginning to consider the problem of hierarchical organization in the microfoundations controversy mentioned above. After decades of steady assault by monetarists, members of the rational expectations school, and new classical economists, to mention a few, the tide seems to be turning and new, realistic theories of macroeconomics seem to be emerging. Within ecological economics, influenced by the entropy metaphor of Georgescu-Roegen (1971), innovative work is being done in applying theories of self-organization and chaos (Hinterberger, 1993; Foster, 1993; Perrings, 1987).

Structural economics and industrial ecology
Neoclassical economists have constructed sophisticated models of innovation diffusion, technological change and economy–environment interactions based on neo-Darwinian evolutionary models of marginal change. These models are limited, however, by their limited ability to take into account pure uncertainty and non-marginal change. A new field of economic modelling, structural economics, offers a more realistic and practical method for evaluating the impact on society and ecosystems of real technological choices (Duchin and Lange, 1994). Structural economics uses information contained in input–output tables, natural resource accounts and social accounting matrices to evaluate various scenarios postulated by policy makers. This approach represents a step forward because it begins with a snapshot of the economy and environment as it is, not as it would be if in competitive equilibrium and if populated by rational utility-maximizing consumers. In the structural approach economic well-being may be gauged by a number of variables and environmental attributes may be measured in physical units without forcing inappropriate monetary values on them. Structural analysis can pinpoint the direct and indirect links between various technological choices and changes in environmental features. This is the first step toward determining paths toward environmental sustainability. The next step in structural economics is to delineate the limits of numerical analysis by spelling out the boundaries of uncertainty, the implications of scale and hierarchies, and the characteristics of the different time scales on which markets, human society and ecosystems operate.

Industrial ecology seeks to operate industrial systems in a way that minimizes their negative environmental impacts (Allenby and Richards, 1994). Approaches to industrial ecology include industrial metabolism, which traces the flow of energy and materials through industrial and consumer systems (Ayres, 1989), life cycle assessment (Allenby, 1992), which focuses on quantifying the environmental burdens of particular products and processes, and ecological design of industrial products and processes (van der Ryn et al., 1996).

Human management of natural systems subject to evolution

Perhaps the most important ecological value of diverse ecosystems is the preservation of evolutionary potential. Species diversity, as well as genetic diversity within species, allows species and ecosystems to adapt to environmental changes. Natural systems are not in a state of equilibrium as economists variously use the term. When ecosystems are disturbed, depending on the nature and extent of the disturbance, they do not necessarily revert to their initial state when the disturbance is removed. The flexibility of species to adapt to different environmental conditions has evolved over eons. Geological records show that the Earth is a constantly changing system. Mountains are formed and eroded, ice sheets expand and contract, and volcanoes disrupt climate patterns. Genetic diversity, as well as higher orders of biological diversity, gives ecosystems the ability to adapt to these changes. When we reduce the variability within the biological world through habitat destruction, ecosystem modification, extinction and genetic erosion we limit the possible responses to future environmental change. Evolutionary potential has value to ecosystems, but we cannot quantify its value to the human species (Gowdy, 1997). There are some examples of evolutionary changes which positively affected human prospects for overcoming adverse changes. Palaeolithic human cultures in Europe, whose economies were based on big game hunting, were adversely affected after these animals disappeared with the retreat of the glaciers some 15 thousand years ago. The warmer climate also apparently led to the evolution of certain kinds of plants with larger seeds suitable for agriculture which humans were able to exploit. This kind of evolutionary response depends on nature having a variety of genetic material to work with and illustrates the importance of preserving species *in situ*. Recent controlled experiments by ecologists suggest that species diversity plays an important role in ecosystem resilience not only in natural systems but in agricultural and other human-dominated ecosystems as well (Tilman, 1996).

Many of these considerations are present in the vast literature on sustainable development, a term which by now has numerous interpretations (Tisdell, 1991). As the concept matures, it is being operationalized at the local level in a variety of situations. Not surprisingly, the theory and practice of sustainable development has been most successfully applied to agricultural systems. Agriculture is directly dependent on the environment and the interactions are usually easier to see than in an industrial system. To give a few examples, Serrão et al. (1996) discuss the sustainability conditions for a variety of land-use patterns in the Amazon. van den Bergh and Nijkamp (1994) propose a dynamic simulation model integrating economic development and the natural environment for the Greek Sporades Islands. Hanna (1997) discusses the sustainability of American fisheries in terms of changing governance frontiers. She argues that management regimes must adapt to the evolving condition of the fisheries resource. Berg et al. (1996) present an ecosystem approach to managing aquaculture in Lake Kariba, Zimbabwe. As the number and sophistication of models of local sustainability increases, the better the chances of delineating the common elements of successful projects and formulating general theories.

5. Conclusion

Insights from biology can give us a deeper understanding of economic reality, including its social and environmental context. As Marx put it, however, the point is not to understand reality but to change it. In the context of the above discussion, this means developing public policies which take into account the deeper understanding of reality provided by evolutionary theory. The contribution of economics to environmental policy has been the development of valuation methodologies to be used in public choices. Indeed, cost–benefit analysis, based on real or imputed market values, has come to dominate public policy. The understanding of reality provided by biology leads us to question policies based on an understanding of only one portion of reality, the market economy. The economic concept of value needs to be expanded to include more levels of hierarchy than the behaviour of atomistic agents and their aggregations, and mechanisms of change in addition to efficiency-driven competition (Gowdy, 1997; Bromley, 1990). The greatest policy change economists face is to construct a valuation system which will take into account the various differences and contradictions in natural resource 'values' across hierarchies of space and time. Such a valuation system will necessarily make policy decisions much more complicated. We shall not be able to use a single monetary value to compare various alternatives. Some aspects of natural resource values may be monetized, others may be quantified but not monetized, and others may consist of non-quantifiable descriptions. Whether such a valuation system can lead us to an environmentally sustainable path is an open question.

Notes

1. Following Hodgson (1993), I use the word 'metaphor' rather than 'analogy'. There is an ongoing and frequently sterile debate about various definitions of 'analogy' (Khalil, 1992; Klamer and Leonard, 1994). See the discussion in Hodgson (1993, pp. 32–4).
2. Those who argue for the existence of punctuated equilibrium in biology do not question the fact or even the primacy of natural selection as a driving force in evolutionary change. Rather, they argue that higher-order processes (macro-evolution) are also at work (Vrba and Gould, 1986).
3. Proponents of punctuated equilibria argue that the history of particular species is characterized by long periods of stasis interrupted by abrupt changes to very different forms. According to Gould and Eldredge (1993), the really revolutionary implication of punctuated equilibria is not stasis but the existence of higher-level selection (higher than the individual) as a causal, not only descriptive, phenomenon.

4. For a Schumpeterian model of punctuated equilibrium in biology see Gould et al. (1987).
5. See Georgescu-Roegen's critique of Shannon's theory of information in Appendix B of *The Entropy Law* (1971) and his critique of Boltzman's statistical mechanics in Appendices B, C and D.
6. Quoted in O'Connor (1993, p. 288).
7. For an introduction to the punctuated equilibrium model of biological evolution and its relevance for economic evolution see Eldredge (1997).

References

Alchian, A. (1950), 'Uncertainty, evolution and economic theory', *Journal of Political Economy*, **58**, 211–22.
Allen, T. and T. Starr (1982), *Hierarchy: Perspectives for Ecological Complexity*, Chicago: University of Chicago Press.
Allenby, B. (1992), 'Achieving sustainable development through industrial ecology', *International Environmental Affairs*, **4**, 56–68.
Allenby, B. and D. Richards (1994), *The Greening of Industrial Ecosystems*, Washington, DC: National Academy Press.
Anderson, P., K. Arrow and D. Pines (eds) (1988), *The Economy as an Evolving Complex System*, Reading, MA: Addison Wesley.
Ayres, R. (1989), 'Industrial metabolism', *Technology and the Environment*, 23–49.
Ayres, R. (1994), *Information, Entropy, and Progress: A New Evolutionary Paradigm*, Woodbury, New York: American Institute of Physics, AIP Press.
Barkow, J. (1989), *Darwin, Sex, and Status: Biological Approaches to Mind and Culture*, Toronto: University of Toronto Press.
Baum, J.C. and J.V. Singh (1994), *Evolutionary Dynamics of Organizations*, New York: Oxford University Press.
Berg, H., P. Michélsen, M. Troell, C. Folke and N. Kautsky (1996), 'Managing aquaculture for sustainability in tropical Lake Kariba, Zimbabwe', *Ecological Economics*, **18**, 141–59.
Bergh, J.C.J.M. van den and P. Nijkamp (1994), 'An integrated dynamic model for economic development and natural environment: an application to the Greek Sporades Islands', *Annals of Operations Research*, **54**, 143–74.
Boulding, K. (1973) [1966], 'The economics of the coming Spaceship Earth', in H. Daly (ed.), *Toward a Steady State Economy*, San Francisco: W.H. Freeman.
Bromley, D. (1990), 'The ideology of efficiency', *Journal of Environmental Economics and Management*, **19**, 86–107.
Buchanan, J. (1996), *Ethics of Capitalism and Critique of Sociobiology*, New York: Springer-Verlag.
Calvalieri, P. and P. Singer (eds) (1993), *The Great Ape Project*, New York: Springer-Verlag.
Colander, D. (ed.) (1996), *Beyond Microfoundations: Post Walrasian Macroeconomics*, Cambridge, UK: Cambridge University Press.
Cumberland, J. (1966), 'A regional inter-industry model for analysis of development objectives', *Regional Science Association Papers*, **17**, 65–94.
Daly, H. (1968), 'On economics as a life science', *Journal of Political Economy*, **76**, 392–406.
Day, R.H. (1984), 'Disequilibrium economic dynamics – a post Schumpeterian contribution', *Journal of Economic Behavior and Organization*, March, 57–76.
DeBresson, C. (1989), 'Innovation clusters in Italy, 1981–1985', Working paper, Center for Research on the Development of Industry and Technology (CREDIT), Concordia University, Montreal, Quebec.
Dosi, G., C. Freeman, R. Nelson, G. Silverberg and L. Soete (eds) (1988), *Technical Change and Economic Theory*, London: Pinter Publishers.
Duchin, F. (1997), 'The evolution of technology and lifestyles', mimeo, Rensselaer Polytechnic Institute.
Duchin, F. and G. Lange (1994), *The Future of the Environment*, New York: Oxford University Press.

Eldredge, N. (1995), *Reinventing Darwin*, New York: John Wiley and Sons.

Eldredge, N. (1997), 'Evolution in the marketplace', *Structural Change and Economic Dynamics*, **8** (4), 385–98.

Eldredge, N. and S.J. Gould (1972), 'Punctuated equilibria: an alternative to phyletic gradualism', in T.J.M. Schopf (ed.), *Models in Paleobiology*, San Francisco: W.H. Freeman.

Enke, S. (1951), 'On maximizing profits: a distinction between Chamberlin and Robinson', *American Economic Review*, **41**, 566–78.

Faber, M. and J. Proops (1990), *Evolution, Time, Production and the Environment*, Berlin: Springer-Verlag.

Foster, J. (1987), *Evolutionary Macroeconomics*, London: Unwin Hyman.

Foster, J. (1993), 'Economics and the self organization approach: Alfred Marshall revisited', *The Economic Journal*, **103**, 975–91.

Friedman, M. (1953), 'The methodology of positive economics', in *Essays in Positive Economics*, Chicago: University of Chicago Press.

Georgescu-Roegen, N. (1971), *The Entropy Law and the Economic Process*, Cambridge, MA: Harvard University Press.

Georgescu-Roegen, N. (1977), 'Inequality, limits and growth from a bioeconomic viewpoint', *Review of Social Economy*, **37**, 361–75.

Geroski, P.A. (1989), 'Entry, innovation and productivity growth', *Review of Economics and Statistics*, **71**, 555–64.

Gersick, C.J.G. (1991), 'Revolutionary change theories: a multilevel exploration of the punctuated equilibrium paradigm', *Strategic Management Journal*, **16**, 10–36.

Gould, S.J. (1988), 'On replacing the idea of progress with an operational notion of directionality', in Matthew Nitecki (ed.), *Evolutionary Progress*, Chicago: University of Chicago Press.

Gould, S.J. and N. Eldredge (1993), 'Punctuated equilibrium comes of age', *Nature*, **366**, 223–7.

Gould, S.J. and R. Lewontin (1979), 'The spandrels of San Marco and the Panglossian paradigm', *Proceedings of the Royal Society of London B*, **205**, 581–98.

Gould S.J., N. Gilinsky and R. German (1987), 'Asymmetry of lineages and the direction of evolutionary time', *Science*, **236**, 1437–41.

Gowdy, J. (1992), 'Higher selection processes in evolutionary economic change', *Journal of Evolutionary Economics*, **2**, 1–16.

Gowdy, J. (1994a), 'Progress and environmental sustainability', *Environmental Ethics*, **16**, 41–55.

Gowdy, J. (1994b), *Coevolutionary Economics: Economy, Society, and Environment*, Boston, MA: Kluwer Academic Press.

Gowdy, J. (1997), 'The value of biodiversity: markets, society and ecosystems', *Land Economics*, **73**, 25–41.

Gowdy, J. and S. Mesner (1998), 'The evolution of Georgescu-Roegen's bioeconomics', *Review of Social Economy*, **56** (2), 136–56.

Graedel, T. and B. Allenby (1995), *Industrial Ecology*, Englewood Cliffs, NJ: Prentice-Hall.

Griffen, D. (1992), *Animal Minds*, Chicago: University of Chicago Press.

Hanna, S. (1997), 'The new frontier of American fisheries governance', *Ecological Economics*, **20**, 221–33.

Hannon, M.T. and J. Freeman (1989), *Organisational Ecology*, Cambridge, MA: Harvard University Press.

Hewings, G., M. Sonis and R. Jensen (1988), 'Fields of influence of technological change in input–output models', *Papers of the Regional Science Association*, **64**, 25–36.

Hinterberger, F. (1993), 'On the evolution of open socio-economic systems', in R. Mishra (ed.), *Self-Organization as a Paradigm in Science*, Heidelberg: Springer.

Hodgson, G. (1993), *Economics and Evolution*, Ann Arbor: University of Michigan Press.

Hodgson, G. (1994), 'Optimization and evolution: Winter's critique of Friedman revisited', *Cambridge Journal of Economics*, **18**, 413–30.

Iwai, K. (1984), 'Schumpeterian dynamics: an evolutionary model of innovation and imitation', *Journal of Economic Behavior and Organization*, **5**, 159–90.

Jensen, R., G. West and G. Hewings (1988), 'The study of regional structure using input–output tables', *Regional Studies*, **22**, 209–20.

Khalil, E. (1992), 'Economics and biology: eight areas of research', *Methodus*, **4**, 29–45.

Klamer, A. and T. Leonard (1994). 'So what's an economic metaphor?', in Philip Mirowski (ed.), *Natural Images in Economic Thought*, New York: Cambridge University Press.

Lewontin, R. (1990), 'Fallen Angels: Review of *Wonderful Life*, by S.J. Gould', in *The New York Review of Books*, 14 June.

Lotka, A. (1925), *Elements of Physical Biology*, Baltimore, MD: Williams and Wilkins.

Masson, J. and S. McCarthy (1995), *When Elephants Weep*, New York: Dell.

Mayr, E. (1982), *The Growth of Biological Thought*, Cambridge, MA: Harvard University Press.

Nelson, R. and S. Winter (1982), *An Evolutionary Theory of Economic Change*, Cambridge, MA: Harvard University Press.

Norgaard, R. (1984), 'Coevolutionary development potential', *Land Economics*, **60**, 160–73.

Norgaard, R. (1985), 'Environmental economics: an evolutionary critique and a plea for pluralism', *Journal of Environmental Economics and Management*, **12**, 382–94.

Norgaard, R. (1994), *Development Betrayed*, New York: Routledge.

O'Connor, M. (1993), 'Entropic irreversibility and uncontrolled technological change in economy and environment', *Journal of Evolutionary Economics*, **3**, 285–315.

Page, T. (1991), 'Sustainability and the problem of valuation', in R. Costanza (ed.), *Ecological Economics*, New York: Columbia University Press.

Penrose, E.T. (1952), 'Biological analogies in the theory of the firm', *American Economic Review*, **32**, 809–19.

Perrings, C. (1987), *Economy and Environment*, New York: Cambridge University Press.

Peters, R. and T. Lovejoy (1992), *Global Warming and Biological Diversity*, New Haven, CT: Yale University Press.

Popper, K. (1976), *Unended Quest*, La Salle, IL: Open Court.

Popper, K. (1978), 'Natural selection and the emergence of mind', *Dialectica*, **32**.

Rahmeyer, F. (1989), 'An evolutionary approach to innovation activity', *Journal of Institutional and Theoretical Economics*, **145**, 275–97.

Ruth, M. (1993), *Integrating Economics, Ecology and Thermodynamics*, Boston, MA: Kluwer Academic Press.

Ruth, M. (1996), 'Evolutionary economics at the crossroads of biology and physics', *Journal of Social and Evolutionary Systems*, **19**, 125–44.

Ryn, van der, S. Cowens and S. Cowens (1996), *Ecological Design*, Washington, DC: Island Press.

Saviotti, P. and S. Metcalfe (eds) (1991), *Evolutionary Theories of Economic and Technological Change*, Philadelphia: Harwood Academic Publishers.

Schumpeter, J. (1974) [1934], *The Theory of Economic Development*, Cambridge, MA: Harvard University Press.

Serrão, D. Nepstad and R. Walker (1996), 'Upland agricultural and forestry development in the Amazon: sustainability, criticality and resilience', *Ecological Economics*, **18**, 3–13.

Silverberg, G., G. Dosi and L. Orsenigo (1988), 'Innovation, diversity and diffusion: a self-organization model', *Economic Journal*, **98**, 1032–54.

Simon, H. (1962), 'The architecture of complexity', *Proceedings of the American Philosophical Society*, **106**, 467–82.

Simon, H. (1973), 'The organization of complex systems', in H. Pattee (ed.), *Hierarchy Theory: The Challenge of Complex Systems*, New York: Braziller.

Söderbaum, P. (1993), 'Rethinking economics: from GNP growth to ecological sustainability', in Lars Magnusson (ed.), *Evolutionary and Neo-Schumpeterian Approaches to Economics*, Boston, MA: Kluwer Academic Press.

Stanley, S.M. (1979), *Macroevolution*, San Francisco: W.H. Freeman.

Szyrmer, J. (1985), 'Measuring connectedness of input–output models: 1. Survey of the measures', *Environment and Planning A*, **17**, 1591–612.

Szyrmer, J. (1986), 'Measuring connectedness of input–output models: 2. Total flow concept', *Environment and Planning A*, **18**, 107–21.

Telser, L. (1996), 'Competition and the core', *Journal of Political Economy*, **104**, 85–107.

Tilman, D. (1996), 'Productivity and sustainability influenced by biodiversity in grassland ecosystems', *Nature*, **379**, 718.

Tisdell, C. (1991), *Economics of Environmental Conservation*, New York: Elsevier.

Van Valen, L. (1973), 'A new evolutionary law', *Evolutionary Theory*, **1**, 1–30.

Victor, P. (1972), *Pollution, Economy and Environment*, London: Allen and Unwin.

Vrba, E. (1984), 'What is species selection?', *Systematic Zoology*, **33**, 318–28.

Vrba, E. and S.J. Gould (1986), 'The hierarchical expansion of sorting and selection: sorting and selection cannot be equated', *Paleobiology*, **12**, 217–28.

Wilson, E.O. (1992), *The Diversity of Life*, Cambridge, MA: Harvard University Press.

Winter, S. (1988), 'Economic evolution', *The New Palgrave Dictionary of Economics*, London: Macmillan.

Witt, U. (1992), 'Evolutionary concepts in economics', *Eastern Economic Journal*, **18**, 405–19.

Witt, U. (1997), 'Self-organization and economics – what is new?', *Structural Change and Economic Dynamics*, **8** (4), 489–507.

Wollin, A.S. (1995), 'A hierarchy-based punctuated equilibrium model of emergence and change of new rural industries', unpublished Ph.D. thesis, Griffith University, Brisbane, Australia.

66 Ethical perspectives and environmental policy analysis

Harold Glasser[1]

1. Introduction

Philosophical ethics is concerned with generating and analysing standards for valuing entities and states of affairs. These standards are used by individuals and communities to characterize what is 'good' and 'bad' and to regulate human behaviour. As a discipline that promotes systematic reflection on moral ideas and ideals, ethics can help us define our commitments and reconcile these with our aspirations. As concrete manifestations of social values, ethical principles furnish the normative backbone, the grand social or meta-objectives, upon which our tools for making collective choices are constructed.

In this survey, I review the ethical bases for environmental concern. I also discuss how a special set of moral ideas is embedded in environmental economic theory. More generally, I consider how *any* generic process for making and justifying collective choice decisions about environmental 'goods' must be undergirded by some set of ethical principles and value judgements. Unravelling these principles allows the moral implications of a decision framework to be considered and a search for disparities between people's stated value commitments and the potential of a given tool or method to reflect these value commitments to be initiated.

This chapter is not intended to survey ethics (Frankena, 1973; Hospers, 1996; Beauchamp, 1991), survey environmental ethics (Zimmerman, 1998; Des Jardins, 1997; Pojman, 1994), or even overview the development of ethical attitudes toward the environment (Nash, 1989; Hargrove, 1989). It is simply meant to clarify the role of ethics in forming rational decision strategies for incorporating environmental considerations into public policy analysis. Contrary to recent speculation on the relevance of ethical theory to the determination of policy (Light and Katz, 1996), such an approach may be a prerequisite for sharpening debate on issues increasingly filled with complexity, uncertainty, potential for irreversibility, risk and conflict. While I emphasize the significance of reconnecting ethics and economics (Sen, 1987), the discussion is in the spirit of Norgaard's call for pluralism in methodology (1989).

2. Ethics and collective choice

Public policy analysis is concerned with inspiring, some say simply inducing, individuals to cooperate and coordinate their individual actions to solve social problems (Gilroy and Wade, 1992). In practical terms, its role is to assist society in the evaluation of policies and projects and then recommend what potential course or courses of action are 'socially better'.[2] In logical terms, the process of generating consistent prescriptions for social action requires coupling moral arguments to observations and hypotheses about society and the world. We rely on ethical principles to create coherent bases for resolving conflicts and dilemmas, weighing criteria and prioritizing objectives. Because the ultimate goal of public policy is to prescribe what we, as a collective, *should* or *must* do even if this conflicts with what we, as individuals, may prefer or desire, it is by nature an inherently normative exercise. It is only by combining *defensible* ethical principles with rational analysis – not through dispassionate rational analysis alone – that we create morally credible standards, criteria and aggregation rules for evaluating competing policy options (Schumacher, 1973; Norton, 1987; Bromley, 1991; Anderson, 1993; Funtowicz and Ravetz, 1994; Glasser, 1998).

On the most coarse level, policy frameworks can be viewed as drawing their ethical foundations from two contrasting ethical doctrines, *consequentialism* and *deontology*. A consequentialist policy framework judges the 'goodness' or 'rightness' of policies solely on the basis of the *effects* that are expected to (or do) flow from proposed policies. A consequentialist policy framework allows for the use of questionable means to achieve commendable ends. Examples might be the use of repressive disincentives to reduce burdensome population growth or the use of financial compensation for the taking of environmental goods (which some people view as uncompensatable) to build a new hospital.

A deontological policy framework, on the other hand, drawing on the meaning of the Greek root *deon*, emphasizes *obligations* or *duties*. It judges the rightness of policies in terms of adherence to rules or constraints that are in addition to, or in spite of, any expected consequences. In this case certain commitments may be inviolable. For a deontological policy framework motivations and commitment matter, as do the processes and procedures for coming to decisions. While the reduction of population growth may be viewed as a crucial social goal, the use of repressive or coercive means may be deemed unacceptable. Similarly, the taking of endangered species, even to build a much-needed hospital, may also be viewed as unacceptable. Subsequent discussion will emphasize how these two ethical doctrines suggest contrasting decision strategies.

As environmental policy analyses increasingly invoke non-market values, a series of difficult, dilemma-laden questions is increasingly raised: What things in life are truly important? How do we value nature? Who decides? How do we account for the full spectrum of human motivations? How do we integrate wider equity[3] and ecological sustainability concerns with efficiency considerations? Should future citizens have the same opportunities as we do? How do we make both our decisions and our decision processes fair and equitable? Are there boundaries to the legitimate application of the economic calculus? Answering these questions inevitably involves appeals to normative arguments. For example, everything can be given, or imputed with, a hypothetical commodity value, but this reveals only part of the valuation story.[4] Love, friendship, commitment, respect, community, charity, integrity, stability and beauty are all in some sense unpurchasable and inexplicable in commodity-value terms or language. Yet many authorities believe that such values are critical to rational and defensible policy choice (Anderson, 1993; Funtowicz and Ravetz, 1994; Hodgson, 1997; Kellert, 1996; Leopold, 1949; Sen, 1977; Taylor, 1986; Vatn and Bromley, 1994; Westra, 1994).

When evaluating or designing frameworks and tools for making collective choices about environmental goods, five key questions help structure the analysis. First, can the decision framework adequately reflect contemporary moral and ethical concerns regarding the environment? Second, how broadly or narrowly (in space, time and form) do we define the set of relevant consequences? Third, to what extent can outcomes or consequences be separated from the means or activities used to achieve them? Fourth, to what extent might competing ethical principles inspire different decision methods? Fifth, are the different decision methods likely to generate qualitatively diverse or conflicting policy outcomes?

3.   The significance of coupling ethics and environmental policy analysis

While economic activities are bringing unprecedented material gains, they are, also at unprecedented rates, creating lost cultures and vanished species (Burger, 1987; Wilson, 1992). The complex array of environmental effects resulting from economic activity warrants a more nuanced look at the relationship between ethics and policy analysis (Daly, 1980; Daly and Cobb, 1989; Daly and Townsend, 1993; Bormann and Kellert, 1991; Engel and Engel, 1990; Anderson, 1993; Foster, 1997). This is not simply because the human economy is bound to the physical world and, ultimately, constrained by its laws (Costanza et al, 1997; Daly, 1990; Georgescu-Roegen, 1971), because not all forms of capital are substitutable (Daly, 1990), or because, as some argue, human sustenance – in the broadest of senses – is enmeshed with our relationship to the non-human world (Shepard, 1996; Wilson, 1984; Kellert and Wilson, 1993; Funtowicz and Ravetz, 1994; Mill,

1988). It is also necessary for more immediate reasons, because awareness of environmental problems is heightening, because growth pressures tend to generate irreversible habitat loss, because we act in the face of substantial scientific uncertainty, because resoluble environmental problems often require costly responses, and because conflicts on how to go about 'solving' environmental problems are flourishing.

For example, some respected economists contend that powerful economic arguments that work in the service of the environment are not being exploited effectively (Gillis, 1991; Swanson and Barbier, 1992; Pearce, 1993), while other equally respected economists argue that market-based techniques are insufficient or ultimately inimical to environmental protection (cf. Samuelson, Leontief, Wallerstein and Georgescu-Roegen in Ravaioli, 1995, pp. 36–8). Many authors have, on largely moral grounds, argued that the environmental economic paradigm is ridden with potentially crippling deficiencies. At this point it may be instructive to outline ten of these key 'deficiency claims'.

1. Intertemporal price efficiency is neither a necessary nor a sufficient condition to guarantee the ecological sustainability of economies (Pearce and Turner, 1990).
2. Ecological sustainability can only be guaranteed by dethroning consumer sovereignty and adopting a policy approach that privileges the requirements of the ecological system over those of the individual (Common and Perrings, 1992; Daly and Cobb, 1989).
3. Policy decisions relating to production and consumption increasingly involve the distribution of real physical harm to both humans and non-humans; these impacts can persist for thousands of years and affect many generations (Page, 1977; Kneese et al., 1983; Kneese and Schulze, 1985; Spash, 1993).
4. Environmental risks and hazards are often subtle, difficult to observe, irreversible, potentially catastrophic and highly uncertain – policy responses can generally not rely on clear scientific consensus (Norgaard, 1992).
5. Economics cannot account for the full costs of projects and policies with a single metric because some values are not quantifiable and some quantifiable values have no relevant market surrogates (Kelman, 1981; Kneese and Schulze, 1985; Goodin, 1983; Sagoff, 1988; O'Neil, 1993; Söderbaum, 1992; Funtowicz and Ravetz, 1994).
6. Real humans have, in addition to preference satisfaction, a range of behavioural motivations including: respect for others, charity, altruism, community concern, goodwill, 'right livelihood' (Schumacher, 1973), 'just acquisition' and 'non attachment' (Pryor, 1990, 1991), and

so on (Sen, 1987; Edwards, 1992; Aldred, 1994; Vadnjal and O'Connor, 1994; Anderson, 1993).

7. Human preferences are not fixed and static, but contingent upon our experiences. Realistic models recognize human preferences to be dynamic, adaptive and constructed (Norton, 1987; Brennan, 1992; Gregory and Slovic, 1997).

8. From a moral standpoint, welfare maximization (as maximizing the subjective satisfaction of individual preferences) is an inadequate criterion for social decision making – it requires an ethical reductionism that belies the dilemma-laden, non-compensatory nature of environmental policy decisions (Kapp, 1978; Clark, 1973a, 1973b, Kelman, 1981; Sagoff, 1988; Bromley, 1991; Berry, 1993).

9. Where non-humans are morally considerable or the existence of selfless altruistic motives toward nature is acknowledged, neither cost–benefit analysis, nor any other preference-based, utility-maximizing approach can be applied legitimately (Booth, 1994; Crowards, 1997).

10. Collective choice problems regarding the environment require integrating the preferences, beliefs and commitments of different individuals over multiple generations. Such decision problems are inherently multidimensional and not amenable to solution via standard optimization techniques (Goodin, 1983; Norton, 1994; Vatn and Bromley, 1994; Funtowicz and Ravetz, 1994; Glasser, 1998).

Careful consideration of these claims is important because most of the recent, and otherwise very insightful, discussions devoted to ethics and economics (Farina et al., 1996; Groenewegen, 1996; Hamlin, 1996; Kapur, 1995) neglect to take up the unique *ethical* issues facing the economic analysis of environmental problems. Two notable exceptions are Anderson (1993) and Foster (1997).

4. Ethical bases for environmental concern

What are the moral bases for altering or restricting human activities when we observe or suspect that they have adverse impacts upon nature or one of its constituents? In short, *what kinds of value do things have* and *what, if any, are our obligations and responsibilities to things with these different senses of value?* The ethical foundations for environmental concern can be separated into three principal categories: humanism, ethical extensionism and strong non-anthropocentrism or more-than-human world ethics. Identifying these categories is important because all arguments for defending natural objects, species or ecosystems from exploitation draw their authority from ideas originating in one or more of these categories.

Developing an awareness of these issues also has practical importance for decision making because the premises of certain decision methods may be incompatible with some widely accepted bases for environmental concern. As examples, consider three of the previously identified 'deficiency claims' regarding the economic paradigm. Acceptance of claim 5 requires the introduction of multiple criteria. Acceptance of claim 3 necessitates creating a mechanism for moving beyond potential Pareto compensation so that real trade-offs can be distributed equitably. And acceptance of claim 9 calls for a decision framework that is capable of reflecting human aspirations to consider the needs and interests of non-humans, even when they may be in conflict with human interests.

Humanism

From the perspective of humanism, nature itself has no independent moral status. Nor do any of the myriad entities which compose it, apart from humans. Its claims on us derive solely from the fact that impacts upon nature can affect the health or welfare of human beings, who do have moral status. From this anthropocentric perspective, any responsibilities to non-humans are simply indirect duties to humans (Kant, 1963). We may have special duties *regarding* the environment, but none *to* it. It is nevertheless easy to imagine how the turn-of-the-century resource conservation paradigm of Gifford Pinchot (1967 [1910]) might be expanded within a humanistic framework. A recent example is the effort to characterize nature in very broad instrumental terms, as providing humans with an array of 'services', including food production, raw materials, waste processing, flood control, climate regulation, recreation, scientific research, aesthetic, educational, spiritual, and so on (Costanza et al., 1997; Daily, 1997). The ethical basis for this more expansive, albeit human-centred, valuation of nature has been characterized well by the legal scholar William Baxter (1974, p. 5):

> My criteria are oriented to people, not penguins. Damage to penguins, or sugar pines, or geological marvels, is, without more, simply irrelevant. One must go further, by my criteria, and say: Penguins are important because people enjoy seeing them walk about rocks; and furthermore, the well-being of people would be less impaired by halting use of DDT than by giving up penguins. In short, my observations about environmental problems will be people-oriented, as are my criteria. I have no interest in preserving penguins for their own sake.

What Baxter is asserting is that when making public policy, we need to link *facts* (the potential destruction of species or landscapes) with *values* (the loss of such entities constitutes a 'bad'). For Baxter, the loss of species or landscapes cannot constitute a bad in itself. While Baxter's stated basis for valuing nature is its potential to satisfy the preferences of living humans, anthropocentric bases for valuing nature need not be limited to the present generation or narrow self-interest. If the present generation wants to honour a concern for future generations by restricting the possibility of causing DDT-induced human birth defects or if we believe our grandchildren deserve the opportunity to see penguins, then we must extend traditional ethical theories to reflect our obligations and duties toward future generations. Economists' efforts to characterize and capture option and bequest values, although circumscribed by 'willingness to pay' logic, rest on this assumption of granting future generations moral standing.

A final basis for environmental concern, not directly subsumable under Baxter's 'demand value' or preference-satisfying framework, but still essentially grounded in instrumental anthropocentrism, is Bryan Norton's 'transformative value' (1987). Transformative values are always non-consumptive. Nature's transformative value lies in its potential to promote the examination or alteration of our preferences rather than by simply satisfying them. As Funtowicz and Ravetz (1994, p. 206) explain, part of the worth of a songbird 'lies in its teaching us about ourselves and what we want to do with our lives'. Environmental concern that incorporates both demand and transformative values is frequently referred to as 'weak anthropocentrism' (Norton, 1987).

As malleable as the instrumental anthropocentric view may be, it cannot be expanded to encompass all versions of concern for the environment grounded in humanism. As Hargrove (1989, p. 10) argues,

> [H]umans have for nearly three centuries valued natural beauty for its own sake and without regard to its human uses, and this human or anthropocentric valuing has never depended on any nonanthropocentric factors or arguments.

What Hargrove is claiming is that humans have a basis for environmental concern that is totally non-consumptive and non-instrumental – it need not satisfy or alter any preferences – but is still essentially anthropocentric because it does not view nature as valuable apart from human valuers.

As a defence of Hargrove's assertion regarding the existence of anthropocentric intrinsic value, consider these comments from the political economist John Stuart Mill (1988 [1848], p. 116):

> [There is not] much satisfaction in contemplating the world with nothing left to the spontaneous activity of nature; with every rood of land brought into cultivation, which is capable of growing food for human beings; every flowery waste or natural pasture ploughed up, all quadrupeds or birds which are not domesticated for man's use exterminated as his rivals for food, every hedgerow or superfluous tree rooted out, and scarcely a place left where a wild shrub or flower could grow without being eradicated as a weed in the name of improved agriculture.

Anthropocentric intrinsic value, in contrast to the instrumentalism of Baxter and Norton, offers a clear path for stepping beyond the treatment of nature as a service provider. Efforts to protect or preserve nature can now be grounded in veneration as well as prudence. Anthropocentric intrinsic value, by validating the importance of non-use values, provides economists with a foundation within humanism for developing the notion of existence value – but it does not imply that all things have a commodity value.

The humanistic standpoint values the environment only in so far as it bears on the ideals and interests of humans, but these ideals and interests need not be characterized in terms of 'willingness-to-pay' arguments or even utilitarian evaluation frameworks. Quite the contrary, as with Sagoff's (1988) distinction between consumer preferences and citizen values based on social ideals, Hargrove's concept of anthropocentric intrinsic value, like Sagoff's citizen values, has no justifiable economic surrogate. Both approaches point to a need for alternative metrics and multi-objective evaluation frameworks that integrate *deliberation* with familiar economic and multi-criteria evaluation tools to balance competing interests (Shrader-Frechette, 1985; Glasser, 1998).

Ethical extensionism

From the standpoint of ethical extensionism or 'weak non-anthropocentrism', an expanded form of humanism, nature's or its constituents' moral status, and hence their claim on humans, derives solely from the fact that they manifest characteristics or interests that humans also manifest. Entities that are viewed as sentient, rational, self-conscious, self-reproducing, capable of having their interests represented, or having the ability to experience pleasure, pain, joy or suffering are all potential candidates for independent moral consideration. Possible candidates for independent moral standing, satisfying one or more of these characteristics, include viruses, bacteria, plants, animals, species, rivers, ecosystems, watersheds and the ecosphere.

By 'granting' some non-humans moral standing, we not only have special duties *regarding* them (as with anthropocentric intrinsic value), but we also now have duties and responsibilities *to* entities that possess these characteristics. From this purportedly non-anthropocentric perspective, moral grounds for practising self-restraint toward nature now go beyond prudence and veneration to incorporate general responsibilities to 'not cause harm' or 'respect the needs of others'. These responsibilities would demand revolutionary changes in our treatment of those non-humans that have independent moral status. Most of our contemporary dietary, farming, dress, medical research, entertainment and development practices would need to be radically reconsidered.

Prominent examples of this general view are Christopher Stone's (1974) case for establishing the legal rights of natural objects, Peter Singer's (1975) attempt to incorporate the reduction of animal suffering into the utilitarian calculus, and Tom Regan's (1983) effort to argue that certain animals possess a property, what he refers to as 'inherent value' (value independent from the needs, uses or interests of others), which carries a *prima facie* obligation for humans not to treat them as resources. All three authors differ on where they draw the line of moral considerability. Stone, who is interested in making a case for representing the interests of both mountains and trees, goes the farthest; Regan, who restricts his 'subjects-of-a-life' criterion to healthy mammals more than one year old, is the most restrictive (1983, pp. 77–8).

While some animals possess one or more of the characteristics for moral considerability outlined by these authors, most living things possess none of them. A further difficulty with these animal rights/animal liberation approaches is that they restrict moral considerability to idealized individuals and thus eliminate the possibility of extending moral considerability to environmental collectives – species or ecosystems. Thus, because ethical extensionism is so restrictive, it offers scant moral guidance for the general treatment of non-humans. For instance, it sheds virtually no light on how moral principles could be used to operationalize ecological sustainability. Pointing to these and other limitations, many environmental philosophers have argued that we must search for broader, less individualistic bases for environmental concern (Callicot, 1980; Rodman, 1983).

Strong non-anthropocentrism
From the outlook of 'strong non-anthropocentrism', frequently referred to as 'biocentrism' or 'ecocentrism', nature's and its constituents' claim on humans does not derive from their impact on human well-being, or their possession of particular characteristics chosen by humans. Rather, it originates from the intuition that the continued existence and flourishing of ecosystems, species and individual non-humans, by themselves, constitute a significant good in the world – anything else would simply be speciesism and constitute shear arrogance and chauvinism on the part of humans. The imperiousness of judging the moral considerability of non-human entities on the basis that they possess qualities also possessed by humans has been addressed by many environmental philosophers (Leopold, 1949; Ehrenfeld, 1978; Rodman, 1983; Taylor, 1986).

As Hargrove (1989, p. 10) has pointed out, not all instrumental values in nature are anthropocentric. Coast redwoods provide habitat and climate-stabilizing values that are not only critical to their own survival, but also necessary for the survival of spotted owls, marbled murrelets and coho salmon as well as a host of other endemic species. These biogeophysical systems values would exist even if humans never existed, and they will continue to exist as long as life itself endures. Humans can choose to recognize these values and accord them significance in our decision-making procedures. From the more-than-human world ethics perspective, humans have a moral responsibility to protect these non-anthropocentric instrumental values.

The significant insight of more-than-human-world ethics is not merely that we have special duties *regarding*, and obligations *to*, individual non-humans, but that we have duties and obligations *to* individuals, species, ecosystems and the ecosphere in general. What strong non-anthropocentrism offers, which humanism and ethical extensionism cannot, is a clear moral basis for considering ecological sustainability as a good in itself.

From this perspective, humans do not simply have a duty to use nature efficiently, but they have obligations to use it with respect, restraint and an eye toward nurturing its capacity for self-healing. Furthermore, there may even be times when the above conditions cannot be satisfied and complete non-interference or special intervention is required. From the perspective of strong non-anthropocentrism, humans have responsibilities to protect nature even when these efforts can conflict with their personal wants and even if they create a significant utility loss. This is the moral basis on which the 1973 US Endangered Species Act rests.

Architects of strong non-anthropocentric environmental ethical theories, which are built on premises about nature's intrinsic value, include Aldo Leopold (1949), Paul Taylor (1986), Arne Naess (1973, 1989), Holmes Rolston (1988), and the ecotheologian Thomas Berry (1988). Max Oelschlaeger (1994) derives a similar injunction to 'care for creation' by drawing on religious creation stories from a variety of metaphysically diverse faiths. All these projects, with varying degrees of success, attempt to put forth general principles for guiding (and prohibiting where necessary) the human use of nature. Taylor's (1986, pp. 172–92) four rules of Nonmaleficence, Noninterference, Fidelity and Restitutive Justice come the closest to providing operationalizable suggestions for policy making. Glasser (1996) discusses and develops the environmental policy implications of Naess's 'deep ecology'.

The public's environmental values
An expanding number of public opinion surveys demonstrate that a growing majority of lay people view the non-human world as intrinsically valuable and itself deserving of moral consideration (Kempton et al., 1995; Dunlop et al., 1993; Naess, 1986, 1987).

The most comprehensive survey of environmental values to date, conducted on Americans by Kempton et al. (1995), demonstrates how tightly economics and ethics are interwoven. Three results from the 149-question survey are particularly illustrative. First, 90 per cent of the lay public responded favourably to the statement, 'Preventing species extinction should be our highest environmental priority' (p. 258). Second, 97 per cent of the lay public responded favourably to the statement, 'We have to protect the environment for our children, and for our grandchildren, even if it means reducing our standard of living today' (p. 258). Third, 73 per cent of the lay public responded favourably to the statement, 'We should be more concerned about the environment than the economy because if the environment is all right at least we can survive, even if the economic system is not in good shape' (p. 257).

These environmental concerns can be loosely categorized into three meta-objectives: protection of biodiversity and free nature, reduction of human health and social impacts, and sustainable use of resources. These three meta-objectives are coupled and overlapping but they also raise unique ethical questions that tax existing evaluation methodologies in different ways. The first broaches our responsibilities to and duties toward non-humans. The second broaches both our obligation to diminish the potential for creating physical harm and our responsibility to distribute fairly whatever risk exists – even if it necessitates restricting our own freedom to act. It also underscores our duty to make resource-use decisions that preserve options and opportunities for future generations. The third highlights the need for priority principles by establishing ecological sustainability as a goal superior to economic efficiency. It will be helpful to keep in mind how different evaluation methodologies might treat and prioritize these three meta-objectives, particularly in situations of conflict.

Environmental concern and environmental policy
If we are insufficiently critical of the assumptions underlying our decision methodologies, values can become enshrined *unconsciously* in our tools for policy analysis. Problematic situations are then likely to arise if the values ingrained in such methodologies are highly contested, if they are not widely embraced, or if they support a disregard of ecological constraints (Glasser et al., 1994). Troublesome situations may also arise if social values are evolving rapidly (Gregory and Slovic, 1997). As a case in point, the previously cited ethnographic interviews exploring the fundamental values underlying Americans' concern for the environment demonstrate that both Earth First!ers (a radical environmental group) and unemployed sawmill workers alike unanimously support the statement, 'We have a moral duty to leave the earth in as good or better shape than we found it' (Kempton et al., 1995, p. 257). In such situations, the existing policy methodologies may

be unable to incorporate relevant insights or perspectives. A cognitive dissonance may be created where the resulting policy recommendations clash with contemporary scientific understanding or deeply held beliefs.

Anthropocentric foundations for environmental concern do not necessarily compete with non-anthropocentric ones. There is a strong case to be made that a very significant level of environmental protection can be secured solely on the basis of humanistic environmental concerns. Whether this state of environmental quality could reach that of a world governed by more-than-human-world ethics is debatable. What is clear, however, is that if these concerns are to be adequately reflected in our policy actions, they must first be able to be adequately reflected in our decision-making models.

5.   Consequentialism and deontology

Mainstream environmental economics adopts a very narrow form of consequentialism based on the maximization of individual preferences under the conditions of potential Pareto compensation. This framework, which focuses on instrumental, anthropocentric values, manifests all of the ten 'deficiencies' outlined in Section 2. Consequentialism itself, however, can be conceived in much broader terms. Consequentialist policy frameworks can incorporate a single objective or multiple objectives (Nijkamp et al., 1990; Munda et al., 1994) and a wide range of extra-economic considerations (Ciriacy-Wantrup, 1952; Lichfield, 1996; Shefer and Voogd, 1990; Voogd, 1994). They can be optimizing, as with the many forms of utilitarian decision rules (Kneese and Schulze, 1985), they can be 'satisficing', emphasizing the satisfactory achievement of fixed standards (Simon, 1957), or they can incorporate some combination of the two approaches (Glasser, 1998).

Two key elements of satisficing frameworks bear mention. First, for some dimensions of the decision process, 'good enough' or 'not too much' may be adequate reflections of human aspirations. Second, some dimensions of the decision process may be 'non-tradeoffable' or non-compensatory – they exist as 'go–no-go' constraints. Equity and ecological sustainability are dimensions that admit to such limited 'tradeoffability' – it would be odd, at best, to refer to policy choices as *partly* equitable or *almost* sustainable. An example of a satisficing criterion, albeit embedded in an optimizing framework, is reflected in the strong sustainability constraint, which allows for no net natural capital depletion and prohibits compensation of natural capital losses with human capital gains (Barbier et al., 1990). Another example would be Ciriacy-Wantrup's (1959) 'safe minimum standard' approach for restricting the exploitation of environmental resources, although it includes a caveat stipulating that avoiding the development should not result in excessive social costs (Bishop, 1978; Crowards, 1997).

By creating a framework that stretches the limits of consequentialism, by mixing multiple objectives, satisficing constraints, ethical weights (Kneese et al., 1983; Shrader-Frechette, 1985; Attfield and Dell, 1996), and priority principles for resolving conflicts, it becomes possible, at least theoretically, to address the first seven of the ten deficiencies of environmental economics. The last three deficiencies, having to do with the dilemma-laden, non-compensatory nature of environmental policy problems, are usually associated only with deontological frameworks. Sen (1987), however, makes a compelling case for the possibility of incorporating many such concerns within consequentialism if one adopts a most expansive notion of consequences.[5] Sen is nevertheless aware that no matter how expansively we construct our notion of consequences, some subtle, but possibly significant, distinction always remains (1987, p. 76):

> To say that action *x* should be chosen over action *y* is not the same statement as that the state of affairs resulting from action *x*, including action *x* done, is superior to the state of affairs resulting from action *y*, including *y* done.

Sen's distinction, while somewhat enigmatic, is significant. He is referring to the importance of context and the need to carefully consider how the character of a decision can vary as we draw and redraw the boundaries that define the set of 'net' consequences. After carefully performing an extended cost–benefit analysis, policy *A* is shown to have a much higher cost–benefit ratio than policy *B*. Policy *A* also results in the loss of critical habitat, the loss of a rare cultural site, the displacement of several poor families, and may result in the extinction of several species. From the standpoint of economic efficiency, we *should* choose policy *A*. If we cast our net more broadly, however, if we weigh the negative impacts associated with alternative *A* more heavily or if we do not want to accept the added risk of losing several endangered species, then alternative *B* might be the preferred choice.

With a deontological framework, acts *themselves* can take on moral significance. And some acts are simply not 'right' regardless of whatever consequences are expected to flow. In many societies, actions such as trading in endangered species or the further compromising of their habitat are viewed as unacceptable, regardless of any positive consequences that might result from such actions; trading in tiger penises and rhino horns may be economically efficient, but such actions are now morally unjustifiable in most cultures. Leopold's (1949, pp. 224–5) 'land ethic' functions similarly. An action may be economically efficient, but, according to Leopold, if it does not tend 'to preserve the integrity, stability, and beauty of the biotic community', then it is wrong. From this perspective, certain consequentialist moral principles, particularly those that freely allow trade-offs across all criteria, may not be adequate for governing the choice of competing actions: deontological rules must be considered first and they must take precedence when conflicts arise (Glasser, 1998). While not explicitly deontological, Page (1991) discusses a similar 'two-tiered' approach for achieving wider social goals such as sustainable development and equity. In Page's framework, social imperatives enshrined in the first tier define constraints that circumscribe a valid realm for performing cost–benefit analyses on the second tier.

Deontological reasoning is used much less frequently than consequentialist reasoning and it is almost always coupled with some form of consequentialist analysis, as with discussions of the 'precautionary principle' (O'Riordan and Jordan, 1995). Nevertheless, it has played a key role in decisions involving the environment and it is likely to play a growing role in situations that involve incomparable or non-compensatory criteria (Vatn and Bromley, 1994; Booth, 1994; Owens, 1994), such as when sustainability issues are addressed explicitly (Howarth, 1995). Deontological reasoning underlies some of the most significant, action-forcing environmental legislation in the US, although many of these laws are now under fire on grounds that they unfairly prohibit development. The 1973 Endangered Species Act both instructs the US Fish and Wildlife Service and the National Marine Fisheries Service to carry out rigorous assessments of imperilled species and forbids these agencies from granting permission for any action that would jeopardize the continued existence of a threatened species or result in the loss of critical habitat. Similarly, the 1964 Wilderness Act prohibits human improvements, such as roads and mechanical transportation (except for emergency use) in wilderness areas.

6. Conclusion

Tools for evaluating environmental policies can be viewed as being constructed from six coupled elements – all of which have a normative component. These elements include: (1) a model of human motivations (including a basis for environmental concern); (2) a temporal perspective; (3) a set of decision criteria; (4) a set of decision rules, constraints and aggregation procedures; (5) a strategy for considering the 'fairness' of decisions (including a method for addressing distributional considerations); and (6) a strategy for resolving conflicts and dilemmas through some form of public deliberation.

Neoclassical economists and ethicists have generally been in two separate camps regarding the role that selfless motives do, and should, play in collective choice decision making. If collective choice decision making is to reflect society's legitimate concerns, our decision methods may need to account for non-anthropocentric motives. A rejection of anthropocentrism, however, does not imply a rejection of consequentialism or the importance of human centred concerns. The rationality (and moral responsibility) of evaluating trade-offs under conditions of scarcity is incontestable. Efficiency is an important and necessary consideration for social decision making. The most cogent critiques of environmental economics never contest this claim. What is to be questioned is how welfare maximization fits into the larger framework of consequences that society must consider when making decisions that involve the environment.

The rejection of a particular utilitarian decision rule need not imply a rejection of utilitarianism or a general condemnation of consequentialism. And similarly, the acceptance of a particular deontological standard does not imply a general rejection of the importance of taking consequences into account. We return to a question posed in the introduction – How should society prioritize the meta-goals of efficiency, moral justifiability and ecological sustainability? Do we treat the three goals as separate and non-compensatory, do we allow trade-offs between the categories to be considered freely or do we introduce thresholds that must be satisfied before trade-offs can be considered? Should we develop decision methods that allow for the possibility of accepting reduced economic efficiency for the potential of increased ecological sustainability? Should our decision methods support an explicit consideration of distribution issues or account for the intrinsic value of nature? And finally, what sort of deliberative process should we employ if no pseudo-market valuations can be agreed upon or when other dilemmas and value conflicts arise?[6] All of these questions are inherently normative – there is no escape.

Simply put, different decision methods echo and reinforce different sets of values. Collective decision making is a normative enterprise, but this need not imply a forced relativism, where no firm criteria can be isolated to judge the superiority of one method relative to another (Shrader-Frechette, 1985, p. 74). The crucial question to answer is: Have contemporary environmental problems and our understanding of them outstripped the capacity of the neoclassical paradigm, by itself, to offer efficacious (not morally counter-intuitive or ecologically destructive) policy recommendations? Is the perceived disjunction between our evolving value commitments, policy tools, and the state of physical reality so large that we need a systematic review and overhaul of environmental economics, or is the current system amenable to continued incremental improvements?

Notes

1. The author thanks Jeroen van den Bergh, Mick Common and an anonymous reviewer for helpful criticism and encouragement. This survey could not have been completed without the insight and succour of D. Jones.
2. For a discussion of public economics and environmental policy, see the chapter by Proost in this handbook (Chapter 22).
3. For a discussion of equity in environmental policy, see the chapters in this handbook by Rose and Kverndokk (Chapter 24) and Martínez-Alier and O'Connor (Chapter 25).
4. For a discussion of valuation and ethics in environmental economics, see the chapter by Blamey and Common in this handbook (Chapter 56).
5. In this regard it is wise to keep in mind the distinction between act and rule utilitarianism (Harsanyi, 1982) as the distinction between deontological and consequentialist policy frameworks can become fuzzy in certain instances. Utilitarianism, the branch of consequentialism that dominates contemporary policy analysis, comes in two primary forms. Act utilitarianism is the most common form of utilitarianism and it undergirds economic theory. It judges each individual act by direct appeal to a specific utilitarian criterion. Rule utilitarianism, on the other hand, applies the utilitarian criterion to general rules of conduct governing acts, not individual acts themselves. Thus a morally right act will conform to the correct moral rule for the situation at hand, and this rule, in turn, would maximize social utility if it were followed by everyone in all such situations. Here we see that a policy framework based upon rule utilitarianism could come strikingly close to one based upon deontological rules.
6. The general importance of considering the role of evidence, argument and persuasion in the policy process has been discussed by Majone (1989). A variety of deliberative procedures for resolving conflicts and dilemmas in the policy process have been discussed and proposed. Five of these include: science courts (Schrader-Frechette, 1985), technology tribunals (Shrader-Frechette, 1985), values juries (Brown et al., 1995), deliberative democracy (Jacobs, 1997), and the stakeholder-citizen preference public participation model of Renn et al. (1993). For a discussion of institutions and environmental policy, see the chapter by Dietz and Vollebergh in this handbook (Chapter 23).

References

Aldred, Jonathan (1994), 'Existence value, welfare, and altruism', *Environmental Values*, **3**, 381–402.

Anderson, Elizabeth (1993), *Value in Ethics and Economics*, Cambridge, MA: Harvard University Press.

Attfield, Robin and Katharine Dell (eds), (1996), *Values, Conflict and the Environment*, 2nd edn, Aldershot, UK and Brookfield, US: Avebury.

Barbier, E.B., A. Markandya and D.W. Pearce (1990), 'Environmental sustainability and cost–benefit analysis', *Environment and Planning A*, **22**, 1259–66.

Baxter, William F. (1974), *People or Penguins: The Case for Optimal Pollution*, New York: Columbia University Press.

Beauchamp, Tom L. (ed.) (1991), *Philosophical Ethics: An Introduction to Moral Philosophy*, New York: McGraw-Hill.

Berry, R.J. (ed.) (1993), *Environmental Dilemmas: Ethics and Decisions*, London: Chapman and Hall.

Berry, Thomas (1988), *The Dream of the Earth*, San Francisco: Sierra Club Books.

Bishop, Richard (1978), 'Endangered species uncertainty: the economics of a safe minimum standard', *American Journal of Agricultural Economics*, **60**, 10–18.

Booth, Douglas E. (1994), 'Ethics and the Limits of Environmental Economics', *Ecological Economics*, **9**, 241–52.

Bormann, H. and S. Kellert (eds) (1991), *Ecology, Economics, Ethics: The Broken Circle*, New Haven: Yale University Press.

Brennan, Andrew (1992), 'Moral pluralism and the environment', *Environmental Values*, **1**, 15–33.

Bromley, Daniel W. (1991), *Economy and Environment: Property Rights and Public Policy*, Cambridge, MA: Basil Blackwell.

Brown, Thomas C., George, L. Peterson and Bruce E. Tonn (1995), 'The values jury to aid natural resource decisions', *Land Economics*, **71**, 250–60.

Burger, Julian (1987), *Report from the Frontier: The State of the World's Indigenous Peoples*, London: Zed Books.

Callicott, J. Baird (1980), 'Animal liberation: a triangular affair', *Environmental Ethics*, **2**, 311–38.

Ciriacy-Wantrup, S.V. (1952), *Resource Conservation: Economics and Politics*, Berkeley and Los Angeles: University of California Press.

Clark, Colin W. (1973a), 'The economics of overexploitation', *Science*, **181**, 630–34.

Clark, Colin W. (1973b), 'Profit maximization and the extinction of animal species', *Journal of Political Economy*, **81**, 950–61.

Common, Mick and Charles Perrings (1992), 'Towards an ecological economics of sustainability', *Ecological Economics*, **6**, 7–34.

Costanza, Robert, Ralph d'Arge, Rudolf de Groot, Stephen Farber, Monica Grasso, Bruce Hannon, Karin Limburg, Shahid Naeem, Robert V. O'Neil, Jose Paruelo, Robert G. Raskin, Paul Sutton and Marjan van den Belt (1997), 'The value of the world's ecosystem services and natural capital', *Nature*, **387**, 253–60.

Crowards, Tom (1997), 'Nonuse values and the environment: economic and ethical motivations', *Environmental Values*, **6**, 143–67.

Daily, Gretchen C. (ed.) (1997), *Nature's Services: Societal Dependence on Natural Ecosystems*, Washington, DC: Island Press.

Daly, Herman E. (ed.) (1980), *Ecology, Economics, Ethics: Essays Toward a Steady-State Economy*, New York: W.H. Freeman.

Daly, Herman E. (1990), 'Toward some operational principles of sustainable development', *Ecological Economics*, **2**, 1–6.

Daly, Herman E. and John B. Cobb (1989), *For the Common Good: Redirecting the Economy Toward Community, the Environment, and a Sustainable Future*, Boston, MA: Beacon Press.

Daly, Herman E. and Kenneth N. Townsend (eds) (1993), *Valuing the Earth: Economics, Ecology, Ethics*, Cambridge, MA: MIT Press.

Des Jardins, Joseph (1997), *Environmental Ethics: An Introduction to Environmental Philosophy*, Belmont, CA: Wadsworth.

Dunlop, Riley E., George H. Gallup, Jr and Alec M. Gallup (1993), 'Of global concern: results of the health of the planet survey', *Environment*, **35**, 7–15, 33–39.

Edwards, S.F. (1992), 'Rethinking existence values', *Land Economics*, **68**, 120–22.

Ehrenfeld, David (1978), *The Arrogance of Humanism*, New York: Oxford University Press.

Engel, J. Ronald and Joan Gibb Engel (eds) (1990), *Ethics of Environment and Development: Global Challenges, International Response*, Tucson: University of Arizona Press.

Farina, Francesco, Frank Hahn and Stefano Vannucci (eds) (1996), *Ethics, Rationality, and Economic Behavior*, Oxford: Oxford University Press.

Foster, John (ed.) (1997), *Valuing Nature? Economics, Ethics and Environment*, London and New York: Routledge.

Frankena, William K. (1973). *Ethics*, 2nd edn, Englewood Cliffs, NJ: Prentice-Hall.

Funtowicz, Silvio O. and R. Jerome Ravetz (1994), 'The worth of a songbird: ecological economics as a post-normal science', *Ecological Economics*, **10**, 197–207.

Georgescu-Roegen, Nicholas (1971), *The Entropy Law and the Economic Process*, Cambridge, MA: Harvard University Press.

Gillis, Malcolm (1991), 'Economics, ecology, and ethics: mending the broken circle for tropical forests', in H. Bormann and S. Kellert (eds), *Ecology, Economics, Ethics: The Broken Circle*, New Haven, CT: Yale University Press, pp. 155–79.

Gilroy, John Martin and Maurice Wade (eds) (1992), *The Moral Dimensions of Public Policy Choice: Beyond the Market Paradigm*, Pittsburgh: University of Pittsburgh.

Glasser, Harold (1996), 'Naess's deep ecology approach and environmental policy', *Inquiry*, **39**, 157–87.

Glasser, Harold (1998), 'On the evaluation of "wicked problems": guidelines for integrating qualitative and quantitative factors in environmental policy analysis', in D. Borri, A. Barbanente, A. Khakee, N. Lichfield and A. Prat (eds), *Evaluation and Practice and Urban Interplay in Planning*, Dordrecht: Kluwer, pp. 229–49.

Glasser, Harold, Paul Craig and Willett Kempton (1994), 'Ethics and values in environmental policy: the said and the UNCED', in Jan van der Straaten and Jeroen van den Bergh (eds), *Toward Sustainable Development: Concepts, Methods, and Policy*, Washington, DC: Island Press, pp. 80–103.

Goodin, Robert E. (1983), 'Ethical principles for environmental protection', in R. Elliot and A. Gare (eds), *Environmental Philosophy*, University Park: Penn State University Press, pp. 3–20.

Gregory, Robin and Paul Slovic (1997), 'A constructive approach to environmental valuation'. *Ecological Economics*, **21**, 175–81.

Groenewegen, Peter (ed.) (1996), *Economics and Ethics*, London and New York: Routledge.

Hamlin, Alan P. (ed.) (1996), *Ethics and Economics*, Cheltenham, UK and Lyme, US: Edward Elgar.

Hargrove, Eugene C. (1989), *Foundations of Environmental Ethics*, Englewood Cliffs, NJ: Prentice-Hall.

Harsanyi, John (1982), 'Morality and the theory of rational behavior', in Amartya Sen and Bernard Williams (eds), *Utilitarianism and Beyond*, Cambridge, UK: Cambridge University Press, pp. 39–62.

Hodgson, Geoffrey (1997), 'Economics, environmental policy, and the transcendence of utilitarianism', in John Foster (ed.), *Valuing Nature? Economics, Ethics and Environment*, London and New York: Routledge, pp. 48–63.

Hospers, John (1996), *Human Conduct: Problems of Ethics*, 3rd edn, Fort Worth, Texas: Harcourt Brace.

Howarth, Richard B. (1995), 'Sustainability under uncertainty: a deontological approach', *Land Economics*, **71**, 417–27.

Jacobs, Michael (1997), 'Environmental valuation, deliberative democracy, and decision-making institutions', in John Foster (ed.), *Valuing Nature? Economics, Ethics and Environment*, London and New York: Routledge, pp. 211–31.

Kant, Immanuel (1963), 'Duties to animals and spirits', in *Lectures on Ethics*, translated by Louis Infield, New York: Harper and Row, pp. 239–41.

Kapur, Basant K. (1995), *Communitarian Ethics and Economics*, Aldershot, UK and Brookfield, US: Avebury.

Kapp, K.W. (1978), *The Social Costs of Business Enterprise*, 3rd edn (first published 1950), Nottingham: Spokesman.

Kellert, Stephen R. and E.O. Wilson (eds), *The Biophilia Hypothesis*, Washington, DC: Island Press.

Kelman, Steven (1981), 'Cost–benefit analysis: an ethical critique', *Regulation*, **5**, 33–40.

Kempton, Willett, James S. Boster and Jennifer A. Hartley (1995), *Environmental Values in American Culture*, Cambridge, MA: MIT Press.

Kneese, Allen V. and William D. Schulze (1985), 'Ethics and environmental economics', in Allen V. Kneese and J.L. Sweeney (eds), *Handbook of Natural Resource and Energy Economics*, Amsterdam: North-Holland, pp. 191–220.

Kneese, Allen V., S. Ben-David and William D. Schulze (1983), 'The ethical foundations of benefit–cost analysis', in Douglas MacLean and Peter G. Brown (eds), Totowa, NJ: Rowman and Littlefield, pp. 59–74.

Leopold, Aldo (1949), *A Sand County Alamanac and Sketches Here and There*, New York: Oxford University Press.

Lichfield, Nathaniel (1996), *Community Impact Evaluation*, London: University College of London.

Light, Andrew and Eric Katz (eds) (1996), *Environmental Pragmatism*, London and New York: Routledge.

Majone, Giandomenico (1989), *Evidence, Argument, and Persuasion in the Policy Process*, New Haven, CT: Yale University Press.

Mill, J.S. (1988), *Principles of Political Economy, Books IV and V*. Reprint of 1848 edition, introduced and edited by Donald Winch, New York: Penguin Classics.

Munda, Giuseppe, Peter Nijkamp and Piet Rietveld (1994), 'Qualitative multicriteria evaluation for environmental management', *Ecological Economics*, **10**, 97–112.

Naess, Arne (1973), 'The shallow and the deep, long-range ecology movement. A summary', *Inquiry*, **16**, 95–100.

Naess, Arne (1986), 'Intrinsic nature: will the defenders of nature please rise?', in Michael E. Soulé, (ed), *Conservation Biology: The Science and Scarcity of Diversity*, Sunderand, MA: Sinaeur Associates, pp. 504–15.

Naess, Arne (1987), *Ekspertenes Syn På Naturens Egenverdi* (Expert Views on the Intrinsic Value of Nature), Trondheim: Tapir Forlag. An English translation will appear in *The Selected Works of Arne Naess*, vol. IX, edited by Harold Glasser, Dordrecht: Kluwer, 2000 (forthcoming).

Naess, Arne (1989), *Ecology, Community, and Lifestyle: Outline of an Ecosophy*, edited, translated and revised by David Rothenberg, Cambridge, UK: Cambridge University Press.

Nash, Roderick Frazier (1989), *The Rights of Nature: A History of Environmental Ethics*, Madison: University of Wisconsin Press.

Nijkamp, Peter, Piet Rietveld and Henk Voogd (1990), *Multicriteria Evaluation in Physical Planning*, New York: North-Holland.

Norgaard, Richard B. (1989), 'The case for methodological pluralism', *Ecological Economics*, **1**, 37–58.

Norgaard, Richard B. (1992), 'Environmental science as a social process', *Environmental Monitoring and Assessment*, **20**, 95–110.

Norton, Bryan G. (1987), *Why Preserve Natural Variety?* Princeton: Princeton University Press.

Norton, Bryan G. (1994), 'Economists' preferences and the preferences of economists', *Environmental Values*, **3**, 311–32.

Oelschlaeger, Max (1994), *Caring for Creation: An Ecumenical Approach to the Environmental Crisis*, New Haven, CT: Yale University Press.

O'Neil, John (1993), *Ecology, Policy, and Politics: Human Well-Being and the Natural World*, London and New York: Routledge.

O'Riordan, Timothy and Andrew Jordan (1995), 'The precautionary principle in contemporary environmental politics', *Environmental Values*, **4**, 191–212.

Owens, S. (1994), 'Land, limits, and sustainability: a conceptual framework and some dilemmas for the planning system', *Transactions of the Institute of British Geographers*, **19**, 439–56.

Page, Talbot (1977), *Conservation and Economic Efficiency*, Baltimore, MD: Johns Hopkins University Press.

Page, Talbot (1991), 'Sustainability and the problem of valuation', in Robert Costanza (ed.), *Ecological Economics: The Science and Management of Sustainability*, New York: Columbia University Press, pp. 58–74.

Pearce, David W. (1993), *Economic Values and the Natural World*, London: Earthscan.

Pearce, David W. and R. Kerry Turner (1990), *Economics of Natural Resources and the Environment*, Baltimore, MD: Johns Hopkins University Press.

Pinchot, Gifford (1967), *The Fight for Conservation* (reprint of 1910 edition introduced and edited by Gerald D. Nash), Seattle: University of Washington Press.

Pojman, Louis P. (ed.) (1994), *Environmental Ethics: Readings in Theory and Application*, Boston, MA: Jones and Bartlett.

Pryor, Frederick L. (1990), 'A Buddhist economic system – in principle', *American Journal of Economics and Sociology*, **49**, 339–49.

Pryor, Frederick L. (1991), 'A buddhist economic system – in practice', *American Journal of Economics and Sociology*, **50**, 17–32.

Ravaioli, Carla with a contribution by Paul Ekins (1995), *Economists and the Environment: What Top Economists Say About the Environment*, translated by Richard Bates, London: Zed Books.

Regan, Tom (1983), *The Case for Animal Rights*, Berkeley: University of California Press.

Renn, Ortwin, Thomas Webler, Horst Rakel, Peter Dienel and Branden Johnson (1993),

'Public participation in decision making: a three-step procedure', *Policy Sciences*, **26** (1993), 189–214.

Rodman, John (1983), 'Four forms of ecological consciousness reconsidered', in Donald Scherer and Attig Thomas, (eds), *Ethics and the Environment*, Englewood Cliffs, NJ: Prentice-Hall, pp. 82–92.

Rolston, Holmes, III (1988), *Environmental Ethics: Duties to and Values in the Natural World*, Philadelphia: Temple University Press, 1988.

Sagoff, Mark (1988), *The Economy of the Earth*, Cambridge, UK and New York: Cambridge University Press.

Schumacher, E.F. (1973), *Small is Beautiful: Economics as if People Mattered*, New York: Harper and Row.

Sen, Amartya K. (1977), 'Rational fools: a critique of the behavioral foundations of economic theory', *Philosophy and Public Affairs*, **6**, 317–44.

Sen, Amartya K. (1987), *On Ethics and Economics*, Cambridge, MA: Basil Blackwell.

Shefer, Daniel and Henk Voogd (eds) (1990), *Evaluation Methods for Urban and Regional Plans*, London: Pion.

Shepard, Paul (1996), *The Others: How Animals Made Us Human*, Washington, DC: Island Press.

Shrader-Frechette, Kristin (1985), *Science Policy, Ethics, and Economic Methodology*, Dordrecht: D. Reidel.

Simon, Herbert A. (1957), *Models of Man*, New York: John Wiley.

Singer, Peter (1975), *Animal Liberation: A New Ethics for Our Treatment of Animals*, New York: The New Review.

Söderbaum, Peter (1992), 'Neoclassical and institutional approaches to development and the environment', *Ecological Economics*, **5**, 127–44.

Spash, Clive L. (1993), 'Economics, ethics, and long-term environmental damages', *Environmental Ethics*, **15**, 117–32.

Stone, Christopher D. (1974), *Should Trees Have Standing: Toward Legal Rights for Natural Objects*, Los Altos, CA: William Kaufmann.

Swanson, Timothy M. and Edward B. Barbier (eds) (1992), *Economics of the Wilds*, Washington, DC: Island Press.

Taylor, Paul W. (1986), *Respect for Nature: A Theory of Environmental Ethics*, Princeton, NJ: Princeton University Press.

Vadnjal, Dan and Martin O'Connor (1994), 'What is the value of Rangitoto Island', *Environmental Values*, **3**, 369–80.

Vatn, Arild and Daniel W. Bromley (1994), 'Choices without prices without apologies', *Journal of Environmental Economics and Management*, **26**, 129–48.

Voogd, Henk (ed.) (1994), *Issues in Environmental Planning*, London: Pion.

Westra, Laura (1994), *An Environmental Proposal for Ethics: The Principle of Integrity*, Lanham, MA: Rowman & Littlefield.

Wilson, Edward O. (1984), *Biophilia: The Human Bond with Other Species*, Cambridge, MA: Harvard University Press.

Wilson, Edward O. (1992), *The Diversity of Life*, Cambridge, MA: Harvard University Press.

Zimmerman, Michael E., J. Baird Callicott, George Sessions, Karen J. Warren and John Clark (eds) (1998), *Environmental Philosophy: From Animal Rights to Radical Ecology*, 2nd edn, Englewood Cliffs, NJ: Prentice-Hall.

67 Environmental and ecological economics perspectives

R. Kerry Turner

1. Introduction

While it can be argued that foundational disagreements exist between environmental and ecological economists and that therefore two paradigms are in direct competition with each other (Norton, 1995), this chapter stresses the importance of ensuring a pluralistic and multidisciplinary (potentially leading to interdisciplinary insights) approach to a joint ecological–economic research agenda (Norgaard, 1985). Several writers have sought to show that despite differences in emphasis between resource, environmental and ecological economics (Turner et al., 1997), and in experimental methodologies and philosophies between economics and ecology (Shogren and Nowell, 1992), the joint research and experimental agenda offers significant opportunities for the integration of economics and ecology. Such an integration is a key element in any strategy that seeks to improve the understanding and management of co-evolving interrelated complex ecological and socioeconomic systems (Norgaard, 1981). Indeed ecological economics has recently been defined as an overarching mode of inquiry encompassing both resource economics with its foundations in population ecology and environmental economics with links to systems ecology (Dasgupta, 1996). It is then possible to integrate problems of resource management with problems of environmental pollution and degradation, within the context of the underpinning environment as the provider of an extensive and diverse set of services and capital stock.

Nevertheless, the hypothesis that foundational differences do exist between ecological and mainstream economics finds stronger support in the realms of philosophy, ethics and social policy. The differences between ecological economics and the mainstream school of thought seem to be at their widest in the context of the philosophy, ethics, human psychology and social welfare conditions, as well as policy prescriptions that are supported by the contending camps. Some ecological economists strongly favour the, at least, partial substitution of a collectivist in place of an individualistic perspective. This has important implications for, among others, the neoclassical principle of consumer sovereignty, for the monetary valuation of environmental benefits, for moral codes of conduct and so-called 'social limits' to growth arguments. The 'social limits' position was given prominence in the 1960s and 1970s by orthodox economic writers such as Scitovsky, Hirsch, Mishan and Thurow. They questioned the social desirability of the economic growth society (the 'zero-sum society') centred on market exchanges, and put forward an array of more and less radical policies to restructure the market economy along more communal and egalitarian lines. This line of thought has strongly resonated within ecological economics and has been used to reinforce arguments for the establishment of humanistic 'steady-state' and 'bioeconomic' economic and social systems (Lutz and Lux, 1988).

It is tempting to characterize the wider economic–ecological debate in terms of two polar viewpoints which contrast the economic growth-oriented technological optimism of environmental economics with the steady-state-oriented technological pessimism of ecological economics. The latter position also implies that there is a need for some new environmental ethic to guide action and public policy. Pushing this caricature of mainstream and ecological economics further, it may be argued that growth optimists contend that over the long run, economic growth, trade expansion and environmental protection are not just mutually consistent, but are highly correlated. Some empirical work on long-run economy–environment interactions seems on the surface to support the optimistic worldview. The so-called Kuznets curve models indicate an inverted U-shaped relationship between the emission of some 'flow' pollutants with local to regional scale impacts, for example, sulphur, particulates and fecal coliforms (see Chapter 46 by de Bruyn and Heintz). The inference that has been drawn is that increasing income per capita (economic growth) will, over the long term, reduce an individual's environmental damage impact.

But this cross-sectional evidence is far from sufficient to prove that economic growth will induce generalized environmental improvement, or that an indefinite process of economic growth is feasible. The U-shaped curve finding does not apply to bio-accumulating 'stock' pollutants, or to global-scale emissions such as carbon dioxide, or to resource stocks. The system-wide, global and long-run consequences of localized pollution reductions are also not considered.

Growth pessimists argue that continuous economic growth is neither feasible nor a desirable option. They hold that technological innovation is less important than the capacity of ecological processes to adapt, and that the focus of policy should be technological and institutional measures to reduce the 'throughput' of matter and energy from the environment into the economy and back out into the environment (a thermodynamic imperative). If such switches are not made, then they argue that nature itself will force such changes via an undersupply of food, energy or materials or waste assimilation and an increasingly unstable set of environmental conditions (Daly, 1973, 1991; Ehrlich, 1989). Public policy should already be based on a 'no-growth' objective because the signs are that the planet's carrying capacity has been, or is very close to being, exceeded.

The position taken in this chapter is that neither of these polar views are strongly supported by the bulk of published natural science findings. Nor do they adequately characterize either environmental or ecological economics (Turner et al., 1997). Genuine scientific progress could be made much more rapidly if a pluralistic and multidisciplinary spirit of tolerance was adopted on all sides. There is a new substantive research agenda, straddling resource, environmental and ecological economics, waiting to be tackled and with findings that could be meaningfully and constructively debated. The agenda includes, among others, questions about sustainability and the substitutability of different forms of capital, including natural capital; macro-environmental scale and thermodynamic limits in source and sink terms; future technological and other changes, together with the problems of novelty and 'surprise'; ecosystem resilience, thresholds and chaos. The issues are really important and demand urgent attention, research across a broad multidisciplinary front, with networked researchers. Such efforts could yield significant interdisciplinary insights into the human–nature co-evolutionary process.

A second set of issues to do with value systems, philosophy and ethics and related policy prescriptions are more fundamentally contentious, and represent areas of heated debate between ecological and mainstream economics.

In the rest of this chapter (Sections 3 and 4) the main components of the emergent joint research agenda are addressed in turn, in order to highlight the differences in emphasis that exist between the schools of thought. In Sections 5 and 6 the discussion turns to a review of the other issues that have stimulated substantive differences and much debate between ecological and other economists. In order to set the scene for succeeding sections, the next section briefly surveys the historical development of some of the main elements of ecological–economic thinking as perceived by a variety of analysts.

2.   Ecological–economic thinking: a historical perspective

Historically, economics has been strongly influenced by developments in science as, early on, formal economics followed the mechanistic models of Newtonian physics. More recently developments in population biology and community systems ecology have stimulated new thinking in resource and environmental economics and management (see Chapter 61 by Folke, this volume). Economists have explored the dynamics of the natural systems with which the economy interacts in order to understand optimal rates of resource use and have treated externality effects as a pervasive characteristic of the system. While some environmental economic research focuses on static consumer valuation of externality (in which natural system dynamics are of peripheral interest), other work looks to the dynamics of the natural system to characterize and value externalities.

Economists concerned with environmental problems have accepted the hypothesis that externalities mediated by a common environment are pervasive. The notion that material growth in the economic system necessarily increases both the extraction of environmental resources and the volume of waste deposited in the environment was highlighted in the mass-balance general equilibrium models of Ayres and Kneese (1969) and Mäler (1974). These models, following earlier insights by Leontief (1966), Daly (1968), Georgescu-Roegen (1966) and Marshall (1920), yielded important insights into pollution (waste) externalities, and helped in the development of pollution control instruments. But they did not become a focus for further extensive work in environmental economics. Indeed, such work as was done on both mass-balance and entropy models was out of the mainstream (see Chapter 59 by Ruth, this volume). The so-called 'regional environmental quality models' of the 1970s, for example, never really gained full entry into the core of standard economics (Basta et al., 1978); and Georgescu-Roegen's (1971) work on entropy-based models was very definitely on the fringe. Environmental economists would counter that materials-balance-constraints thinking has influenced work on marketable permit schemes and their practical implementation, as well as underpinning recent integrated modelling research in the context of, for example, climate change. The mass-balance work has generated two ecological–economic axioms. First, since perfect recycling of resources is probably precluded on thermodynamic grounds, the potential growth of physical output is finite. Second, since the waste generated in the process of production is seldom inert, higher rates of physical growth imply higher rates of change in the processes of the environment (Perrings, 1987; and Chapter 60 by Ayres, this volume).

Market failure in the form of externalities has been highlighted by economists as an underlying cause of environmental problems (Baumol and Oates, 1975). For many environmental resources markets fail to operate properly or are simply non-existent. The reasons for this have been identified in terms of a variety of factors such as high transactions costs (caused by temporal and spatial distances), missing, ill-defined or unprotected property rights and inadequate and/or difficult-to-perceive information about environmental change effects. Through some combination of these factors, market prices, when they exist, fail to signal real social scarcities and can mislead policy. Corrections can be made by imposing regulations covering resource use and pollution levels and by the imposition of taxes and other incentive instruments (Cropper and Oates, 1992). But the political economy of public finances and fiscal regimes is complex and mirrors the various stakeholders and political interests present in contemporary societies. In principle, market-based incentive instruments offer efficiency gains over direct regulation measures, although the magnitude of the efficiency advantage is conditioned by the real-world context and application. Moreover, economic efficiency is only one of at least six not necessarily complementary principles (the others being environmental effectiveness, administrative cost-effectiveness, fairness, institutional concordance and revenue raising) that are thought to be relevant in any policy instrument choice situation. So while economic instruments are inherently efficient and effective, the social gains they offer are limited by a policy process typically driven by multiple conflicting objectives (see the chapters in Part III and in particular Chapter 21 by Russell and Powell on this last argument).

It is the case that environmental resource depletion and degradation can also be caused by government (institutional) failures such as inefficient or uncoordinated resource management policies and inappropriate tax exemptions or subsidies of various sorts (Pearce and Warford, 1993). The world's coastal zones, for example, are now under severe pressure from multiple resource demands. In many places this environmental pressure is exacerbated by natural geophysical factors and climate change so that zones have become more vulnerable (less resilient) to further stress and shock. A marked feature of the pollution and resource overexploitation problems in coastal zones is the significance of 'out-of-zone' activities and their effects. Most of the damage occurring in these places is related to activities located in the wider drainage basin areas and beyond. Table 67.1 presents a typology of market and intervention failures relevant to coastal zone resource problems and management (Bower and Turner, 1998; Turner et al., 1996).

In summary, according to Dasgupta (1996), resource allocation mechanisms that cannot or do not assimilate dispersed information, that are insensitive to or inflexible in the face of socioeconomic and ecological interrelationships, that suffer from myopia and that are grossly inequitable, will prove to be environmentally disastrous.

Ecological economists lay great stress on the need for a historical perspective on socioeconomic–natural systems interactions, in order to progress the analysis and debate on the long-run dynamics of human–nature interactions (Faber et al., 1996). They tend to favour an evolutionary perspective and believe that the concept of open systems far from equilibrium is a useful heuristic for describing technological and

Table 67.1   Market and governmental intervention failures in coastal zones

Market failures

1. Pollution externalities:

(a)	air pollution, outside catchment sources	Excess levels of nitrogen, phosphorus and ammonia contributing to eutrophication of water bodies
(b)	Water pollution, land-based within catchment areas	Excess nitrogen and phosphorus from sewage and agricultural sources; industrial wastewater and toxic effluent pollution particularly from the pulp-and-paper and chemical industrial operations, nuclear power plants and research installations, military installations
(c)	Water pollution, coastal and marine sources	Excess nitrogen and phosphorus from coastal sewage outfalls; oil spills and contaminated bilgewater from ships; outside catchment pollutants transported via longshore currents

2. Public goods-type problems:

(a)	Groundwater depletion/surface-water supply diminution	overexploitation on and off site of water supply
(b)	Congestion costs, on-site	Recreation pressure on beaches, wetlands and other sensitive ecosystem areas
(c)	Fisheries yield reduction	Overexploitation due to open access, loss of habitat, water pollution

Intervention failures (including lack of intervention)

3. Intersectoral policy inconsistency:

(a)	Competing sector output prices	Agricultural price fixing and associated land requirements
(b)	Competing sector input prices	Tax breaks or outmoded tax categories on agricultural land; or tax breaks for non-agricultural land development, including forestry; land conversion subsidies; state farming subsidies (historical) and other waste, wastewater and energy subsidies.
(c)	Land-use policy	Zoning; regional development policy; direct conversion or fragmentation of wetlands; waste disposal policy and regulation (uncontrolled waste disposal dumping)

Table 67.1   (cont.)

---

4. *Counterproductive factors:*

(a)	Inefficient policy	For example, strategies that lack a long-term structure; wastewater and industrial effluent combined treatment practices; general lack of enforcement of existing policy rules and regulations
(b)	Institutional failure, due to uncoordinated action by different government ministries, or the lack of an appropriate ministry or agency with a wide enough remit to deal with coastal issues	Non-integrative agencies structure, non-existent agencies; lack of monitoring survey and enforcement because of capacity-inadequate resources such as trained personnel, equipment and operating funds; lack of information dissemination; lack of public awareness and participation

5. *Conflicting perceptions:*

Different perceptions of a problem among stakeholders and management officials, e.g. local inhabitants and local governments do not consider hurricane or coastal storm flooding a major hazard, in contrast to specialists and state/federal/national government officials; or fishermen who do not think overfishing is a problem when state/federal/national agencies do

---

Source: Bower and Turner (1998).

socioeconomic change. Such change is seen to be sensitively dependent on small historical events and characterized by path-dependence ('lock-in' effects) and the unpredictability of outcomes. An attitude of openness is advocated because of the existence of irreducible ignorance and the related concepts of surprise and novelty. In other words, some systems changes may not, in principle, be predictable, but a proper recognition of that unpredictability will still be important and useful for policy responses. Given contexts in which combinations of irreversibility effects, surprise outcomes and irreducible ignorance exist, the appropriate policy response should be a flexible one. Policy should be conditioned by the precautionary principle and notions such as safe minimum standards, with due regard for the cost-effectiveness of option choices and social opportunity costs.

More fundamentally, many ecological economists believe that the key to the mitigation of environmental problems (and in particular pollution and waste assimilative capacity limits problems) lies outside the realm of science and technology. They have focused on the realm of ethics and philosophy. Policy analysis must, in their view, fully incorporate the concept of full and actual compensation for pollution sufferers and should concentrate on the consequences of the distribution of costs and benefits among multiple stakeholders. But justice is not to be seen as exclusively a matter of income distribution; it is also a question of procedures which define the resulting distributional outcome. This then necessarily involves questions about community, social norms and collective preferences. The analytical framework should also be extended to cover the ethical analysis of inter-temporal and interspecies choice (Costanza et al., 1997a).

3. Sustainability, capital substitution and technical change

Sustainable economic development may be characterized as a process of change in an economy that ensures that welfare is non-declining over the long term (Pearce et al., 1990). It is nevertheless the case that the concept is often difficult to pin down in operational terms. The dominant view among both environmental and ecological economists is based on capital theory, and defines sustainable development in terms of the maintenance of the value of a capital stock over time. The definition of capital used encompasses natural capital (the functions, goods and services provided by the environment), manufactured, human and institutional capital (with the latter taken to include ethical or moral capital and cultural capital) (Berkes and Folke, 1992).

While the capital theory approach itself is criticized by some ecological economists, who identify problems in aggregating natural and produced capital, the main difference between analysts concerns the problem of the substitutability of produced and natural capital. The ecological economic concepts of weak and strong sustainability are, for example, defined in terms of the degree to which various capital stocks may be substituted for each other (Daly and Cobb, 1989; Pearce et al., 1990; Turner, 1993). Weak sustainability assumes perfect substitutability between natural and other forms of capital. Under weak sustainability, the maintenance of an aggregate capital stock over time is both a necessary and a sufficient condition for sustainable economic development. Economic growth can continue indefinitely according to this perspective, as long as the 'Hartwick rule' is observed, that is, that the economic rents derived from the exploitation of exhaustible natural resources (fossil fuels and the like) are invested in other forms of capital capable of yielding an equivalent stream of income in the future (Hartwick, 1978).

Strong sustainability assumes well-defined limits to substitution. Under strong sustainability a minimum necessary condition for sustainability is that separate stocks of aggregate natural capital and aggregate 'other' capital must be maintained. Keeping the natural capital base intact over time has been interpreted to mean conserving all 'critical' natural capital (for example, support functions and services and supporting environmental attributes) which by definition is subject to irreversible loss. There are no plausible technological substitutes for climatic stability, stratospheric ozone, topsoil or species diversity. Technological optimism, in this regard, is simply misguided. According to Ayres (1993), these system functions should be regarded as finite resources, vulnerable to human interference. While such functions are potentially renewable, they can be irreversibly destroyed, if not actually consumed. The maintenance of 'critical' natural capital could be achieved via the imposition of environmental standards or regulations mandating lower bounds on appropriate natural capital stocks, including the environment's waste assimilation capacity. It seems better to err on the side of caution and conserve natural capital in order to maintain the options of future generations (Howarth, 1995).

The ecological economics approach to sustainability may be described as a strong sustainability approach with a tendency among some of its advocates to view man-made and natural capital as complements and not just poor substitutes. In part, it is motivated by a perception of high levels of uncertainty about the nature of ecological processes and functions. There is some concern that the capital theory approach to sustainability may serve to delude policy makers into thinking that there are 'simple' rules linked to 'simple' indicators that can guarantee progress along a sustainable path. It is argued that 'true' sustainability conditions and indicators can only be derived from a model that adequately characterizes the limits to long-run substitutability of produced and natural capital, and we currently lack such models. Kaufmann (1995) has recently utilized a neoclassical growth model to examine what he terms an 'environmental life support multiplier'. This multiplier compares the effects of environmental degradation on economic activity. The simulation results suggest that over the long run it is not possible to substitute capital for environmental life support, while simultaneously maintaining material well-being.

Many might argue that putting positive prices on environmental resources on the basis of current market conditions and current preference environmental resources is still better than having zero prices. But, given uncertainty about ecological processes and functions, reliance on preference-based valuation might well mean that aesthetically attractive rather than 'life-supporting' resources get assigned relatively higher prices, thus threatening the sustainability conditions. Critical natural capital would therefore be best protected via standards and regulations rather than by *in situ* valuation. Even if it were possible to assign meaningful monetary valuations to all environmental resources, it may not be prudent to do so if sustainability is the overriding policy goal (Common and Perrings, 1992).

The capital substitution issue therefore is one of the core areas of debate in the modern 'limits to growth' and 'sustainable development' literature going back to the 1960s. The limits position (Meadows et al., 1972, 1992), fairly and coolly interpreted (forgetting the hype on both sides of the argu-ment), is that there are limits to the growth of material throughput for the international economic system. We are offered a conditional warning that without significant reductions in throughput over time (defined in terms of end dates between 2025 and 2050), models suggest that substantial declines in per capita food output, energy use and industrial production can be expected. The basic behaviour mode of the international system as mod-elled is unsustainable; sink and then source limits will become binding. A transition to a more sustainable path is feasible (and desirable) if sub-stantive resources efficiency gains can be realised via a directed technolog-ical R&D effort, buttressed by human value system and lifestyle changes.

For scientific progress to be made, more empirical research undoubtedly needs to be undertaken on substitution elasticities. It is just not helpful, or meaningful, to continue to polarize debate into total substitution versus total complementarity of man-made and natural capital, or to work with time horizons of hundreds/thousands of years. The empirical literature, such as it is, provides a mixed and partial picture. While some studies yield substitution elasticities greater than unity (a necessary condition for eco-nomic growth models to generate sustainable paths) for basic metals such as steel, copper and aluminium (Brown and Field, 1979), others suggest elasticities less than unity and even zero for a variety of 'critical' and strate-gic materials in given applications, for example beryllium, titanium, ger-manium and the like (Deadman and Turner, 1988). Of course technical change and innovation will alter this picture over time, but this begs the empirical question about possible barriers to innovation. The economics of technical change and related science literatures offer some findings in this context (Dosi, 1988; Ausubel and Sladovich, 1989; Skea, 1995).

A growing body of analysis adopts the evolutionary perspective in which the direction of technical progress and economic activity is not seen as an autonomous phenomenon, but as an endogenous process conditioned by the structure of economic incentives, technological opportunities and pre-vailing institutions. Future outcomes are relatively unpredictable because of the complex interaction taking place between different actors who are endogenous to the process of change. Technical innovations are the outcome of learning processes inside firms, but progress is hindered by inertia in the firms' organizational routines and by path-dependence, with the attendant risk of becoming locked into an unsustainable technological trajectory.

The older notions of technology-push and demand-pull driven innovation processes have therefore been supplanted by the concepts of technological paradigms and trajectories. Technical change within a paradigm is biased in certain directions, relies heavily on learning by doing and is a cumulative process. Improvement in techniques is conditioned by input prices, the institutional structure (monopoly and so on) and government regulation (including environmental regulations). But 'localized technical change' ('lock-in' effects) are also common within paradigms and require public investment or grants to release new innovative activities. Sufficiently large changes in the external context in which a firm or industry operates, including environmental pressures, can force a paradigm shift (for example from end-of-pipe to radical 'clean' technologies) in the technology used. Firms which can anticipate changes in environmental regulations can benefit from 'first-mover' advantage (Porter, 1990) and appropriate economic returns from new technology which complies with future standards, gaining both internal cost reductions, new markets and enhanced public image (Arora and Cason, 1996).

Firms that improve their resource-use efficiency (by capital substitution) reduce input costs per unit of output and also minimize waste disposal costs. The trigger can be environmental regulations and changes in wider social values and concerns. The impact of environmental compliance costs on overall competitiveness also appears so far to be insignificant (Jaffe et al., 1995). Even the latest Club of Rome report now claims that resource productivity (reducing waste at all stages in the production–consumption cycle) can, and should, grow fourfold (Von Weizsacker et al., 1997).

According to the 'Factor Four' thesis (Von Weizsacker et al., 1997), existing and new technologies, if properly deployed and encouraged, can achieve significant eco-efficiency savings. Capitalism and technological innovation can in the future be directed to produce such resource productivity gains, just as in the past when economic growth was stimulated by labour productivity improvements. But critics of the eco-efficiency strategy warn that it is not a panacea, even if it did prove feasible to get resource productivity gains of a factor of 4 or more. There may be 'rebound effects' such as reduced pressure on resources, price falls and increased aggregate consumption. A 10 per cent fuel efficiency increase in cars, for example, might stimulate a 1 per cent to 4 per cent increase in driving time and would not necessarily reduce the total number of cars on the road. Congestion costs and possible extra road-building costs would then be incurred.

The role that technology and innovation might play in any future sustainable development strategy is clearly a big question. It underlies the eco-efficiency viewpoint which seeks to challenge the conventional wisdom that improved environmental quality comes at the expense of industrial competitiveness, as firms are forced to carry increasing pollution abatement and related costs. Some analysts argue that stricter environmental regulations have not pushed up industrial costs, or reduced employment levels to any significant extent. Further, according to the 'Porter hypothesis', properly designed environmental regulations can trigger innovation that may partially or more than fully affect the costs of complying with them (Porter and van der Linde, 1995). This hypothesis has spawned a debate in the literature (Oates et al., 1994; Schmalensee, 1993; Jaffe et al., 1995).

It is possible to demonstrate that in the context of a static model of the theory of the firm, more stringent environmental regulations imposed on firms that have already made their cost-minimizing choices will lead to increased cost and reduced industrial competitiveness on world markets (Oates et al., 1994). The simple analysis can, however, be made more complex and realistic by assuming strategic behaviour among polluting firms and the regulatory agency. Such behavioural assumptions, however, need not always lead to results which support the Porter hypothesis. For example, a polling firm might suspect that the regulator has a long-run strategy to ratchet up environmental standards. The firm might then respond by delaying its investment in innovation technology, or it may engage in the development of new techniques which permit existing environmental requirements to be achieved at lower and lower cost, without providing much scope for significant improvements in environmental standards (Heyes and Liston-Heyes, 1997).

Firms might also threaten to relocate abroad if domestic environmental standards are made too stringent. But one recent study has not found any empirical evidence that such movements have occurred since 1970 (Jänicke et al., 1997). The data that exist suggest that there has not been a significant relocation of 'dirty' basic industries (paper and paperboard, petroleum products, primary metals, glass and chemicals and so on) to developing countries. Further, the high-income market economies have remained net exporters of fertilizers, paper and pulp, crude steel and lead and zinc.

Supporters of the Porter hypothesis have deployed two further arguments in support of their case. They argue that tougher environmental regulation is likely to promote an expansion of the pollution control technology industry (external to, but seeking to service the needs of polluting firms). The export potential of this industry is also highlighted, given 'early-mover' advantages in international markets, that is, countries that adopt stricter environmental standards, it is argued, will stimulate firms to provide the necessary technology to reduce pollution; when other countries catch up and want to improve their environmental standards, they provide an export market for firms from the country that first improved its ambient environment.

Second, in the real world firms are not always able or willing to function as the textbooks assume, and as a result unexploited opportunities for cost savings and improvements in product quality are often present (known as the existence of 'slack' or 'X-inefficiency' in the economy; Leibenstein, 1966). If 'slack' is present and properly designed environmental regulations are introduced, then the firms' capacity for innovation and improvement in productivity terms can be harnessed. Many innovations can partially or more than fully offset the costs incurred. According to Porter and van der Linde (1995) such 'innovation offsets' will be common because reducing pollution is often coincident with improving the productivity with which resources are used. Relatively lax environmental regulations have stimulated 'end-of-pipe' or secondary waste treatment investment responses. More stringent regulations could force firms to take a fresh look at their processes and products and adapt accordingly.

The measurement of 'regulatory stringency' across countries is not straightforward. Some studies have looked at the ratios of environmental compliance expenditures to gross domestic product. But there is a danger that compliance costs will be overestimated since the cost data are reported by the polluting firms themselves; and the costs tend not to include innovation benefits which result in lower net compliance costs. Therefore research results relating environmental regulations to the competitiveness of industries or nations are only of limited usefulness. For what it's worth, they do not seem to show that environmental regulations have a significant negative effect on competitiveness, although they do not demonstrate a very positive one either. The available studies tend not to have taken into account initial competitiveness conditions and some of the industries analysed were uncompetitive to start with, quite apart from environmental compliance cost impacts.

To conclude this section, the transition to a more sustainable path will require intervention policy; a mixture of flexible regulations and market-based instruments need to be deployed to steer technological advances. An element of precaution will also be necessary given the problems of ignorance through novelty. New technologies carry with them the potential for 'surprise'. They can lead to a cascade of impacts, with the secondary and tertiary effects being both large and unanticipated.

4. Ecological systems' macro-environmental scale and threshold effects

Another focus of debate among economists concerned with the environment is the issue of scale, and the related issue of the decoupling of economic and environmental systems. Ecological economics accepts the principle of separating scale and allocation decisions in environmental policy (Daly, 1991). Mainstream economics by and large provides no answer to the issue of optimum scale. One of the most frequently cited ecological economic arguments is that current levels of economic activity are such that further growth threatens to overwhelm the carrying capacity of the environment (both as a source of natural resources and in particular as a sink for wastes), and that this could result in environmental collapse (Arrow et al., 1995). The argument is easily misconstrued as a resurrection of the 'limits to growth' arguments of the 1970s. It is more subtle than that.

Economic activities are seen as being embedded within open ecological systems, which themselves are developing and maintaining their own self-organization over time. Therefore the type and overall extent of economic activity is judged acceptable or not according to the severity of their effect on the 'health' (the capacity for self-organizing activity) of the larger ecological system within which the economy operates. Ecological economics predicts that pollution and waste disposal 'sink' limits to growth will prove more recalcitrant than resource availability limits, because of the different types of novelty and ignorance they engender. While resource depletion can be forecasted and adaptive strategies can be encouraged via incentive mechanisms, pollution problems may prove to be more intractable. They may endanger the health of the biospherical system itself and limit adaptive and innovating response strategies.

Ecological economists therefore recognize much more complex 'limits' than those naïvely specified in the earlier 1970s literature. The more recently appreciated limits include total human claims on global primary productivity. The key concept here is net primary product (NPP), which is the energy fixed by photosynthesis minus that required by plants themselves for their life processes. NPP is equivalent to the total supply of food to all living organisms on earth, including humans. The concern lies in the fact that humans currently consume, divert or forego around 40 per cent of global NPP (Vitousek et al., 1986). But it should also be noted that NPP is not exogenously given and fixed; it depends in part on human activity. Other potential 'limits processes' include the erosion of biological diversity, interference in overall temperature control systems and other regulatory systems such as the ozone layer.

Relieving these constraints depends on the extent to which it is possible to decouple growing economic systems from their underpinning ecological foundations. The ecological economics view is that the economy and the environment are jointly determined systems and that the scale of economic activity is now such that this matters (the carrying and assimilative capacity of very many ecological systems are binding constraints). Nevertheless, the biophysical carrying and assimilative capacity of ecological systems are not static but vary with the preferences and technology of the user, as well as with changes in the nature of the ecosystem itself. The real problem appears to lie in the phenomenon of dynamic feedback effects. Ecosystems do not always clearly signal when some carrying or assimilative capacity has been breached, and the feedback effects of so doing are often very indirect and long delayed. They may also be irreversible. In the absence of private indicators of the scarcity of environmental resources – the externality and problems – there is no reason to believe that private resource users will recognize such effects on the global commons. Hence there is no reason to believe that resource users will respect the constraints imposed by carrying and assimilative capacity of the environment. The level of economic activity is currently regulated by reference to a very short-run set of indicators, mainly the stability of market prices. It is argued that it is necessary to take account of the longer-term environmental consequences of current levels of activity precisely because these have important impacts on the future potential of the system to sustain its provision of valuable functions and services.

Ecological processes function in such a way as to provide an array of ecological services on which most economic activity relies. Ecological services include maintenance of the composition of the atmosphere, amelioration of climate, operation of the hydrological cycle including flood controls and drinking water supply, waste assimilation, recycling of nutrients, generation of soils, pollination of crops, provision of food, as well as the maintenance of particular species and landscapes (de Groot, 1992; Daily, 1997). The value of ecological services and the patterns in which they are available, given different institutional contexts, are important components of the economic–ecological research agenda. Figure 67.1 summarizes, using wetlands as an example, the links between ecosystems processes, functions, services and values and provides a basis for an integrated approach to resource management and reduction or damage pollution mitigation (Turner, 1991; Barbier, 1994). Changes in the quality or quantity of ecosystem services have value insofar as they either alter the benefits associated with human activities (such as direct harvesting or indirect flood/storm protection for housing, recreation or industrial activity) or change the cost of those activities. These changes impact human welfare positively or negatively through markets or via non-market activities.

Ecological economists argue that a characteristic feature of the ecological economic system is that its dynamics are discontinuous around critical threshold values for species and their habitats and for ecosystem processes

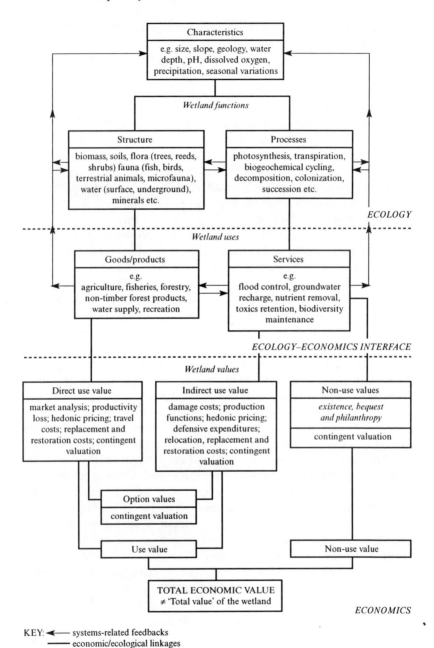

Figure 67.1   General typology and assessment of wetland benefits and ecosystem valuation

and functions (just as they are around economic and institutional thresholds). Such thresholds are the boundaries between locally stable equilibria (Common and Perrings, 1992).

The closer the system is to a threshold, the smaller the perturbation needed to dislodge it. There already exist numerous examples of discontinuous change as a result of a gradual build-up of economic pressure. In many such cases large-scale modifications of ecosystems are the result of many local and disconnected activities (the tyranny of small decisions). The widespread destruction of mangroves in South East Asia and South America for shrimp farming is an example. In this case, the incremental destruction of mangrove systems has had a non-incremental affect on the ability of these systems to provide spawning and nursery grounds for fish and shellfish (Folke et al., 1996). In the Honduras, the incremental transformation of the landscape has induced the outbreak of new diseases by shifting the pattern and abundance of insects (Alemendares et al., 1993). Similarly, in some coastal waters, an incremental build-up of pollutants has changed the structure of plankton communities causing an increase in toxic algal blooms, an incidental effect of which has been the outbreak of infectious diseases including cholera (Epstein et al., 1993).

One consequence of discontinuous change is the novelty of many effects, and this is related to the scale issue. Current rates of human population growth and consequential rates of growth in the demand for environmental resources have increased the interconnectedness of ecological and economic systems in time and space. This is not just a problem for the decoupling of the economy from its environment. It has also moved societies and ecosystems into such novel and unfamiliar territory that the future evolution of both has become more unpredictable. The lack of information about thresholds and the precise consequences of breaching them has led ecological economics to advocate a precautionary approach (in preference to a cost–benefit approach) (O'Riordan and Jordan, 1995). This favours conservation and environmental protection measures, unless the social opportunity costs are 'unacceptably' large. More importantly, it favours protection of the resilience of the joint system.

Some economics is, in part, an outcome of recent developments in community and systems ecology which seek to explain the dynamics of ecological processes. Here, recent research on scale, complexity, stability and resilience is beginning to influence the analysis of ecological economic systems. Work on dryland systems, for example, has shown how stressed systems can flip from one state to another. For example, grazing pressure beyond some critical threshold has been shown, in some cases, to induce an irreversible switch in vegetation type that changes the central characteristics of the system (Perrings and Walker, 1995).

The stability of a system is not the only concern: sustainability has now become a general policy goal (WCED, 1987). It has been argued that the economic growth process typical of high-income economies and characterized by localized stability 'lock-in' features such as an over-reliance on fossil fuels and related technologies may be both unstable and unsustainable over the long run. Equally, some low-income countries can suffer from population pressure and institutional/cultural 'lock-in' constraints which make the system unsustainable in the long term. Economic growth that stresses resource stocks (sources and sinks) beyond their carrying or assimilative capacities risks making the joint system less resilient to external stress and shock (Arrow et al., 1995). Future generations may then be left with a reduced set of opportunities (Page, 1983).

The resilience of a system has been defined in two main ways. According to Pimm (1984), it is the time taken for a disrupted system to return to some initial equilibrium state. Holling (1973), on the other hand, defines resilience in terms of the degree of disturbance (stress and shock) that can be coped with before a system flips from one state to another. The literature has concentrated a great deal of attention on the links between system resilience, biodiversity and the sustainability of different states of a system (Heywood and Watson, 1995). Of particular concern is a situation in which a system close to a threshold suffers extra stress or shock. There is then the potential for a 'catastrophic' change in the system's structure and organization (Arrow et al., 1995; Perrings and Pearce, 1994).

Some scientific work shows that a loss of biodiversity alters the performance of ecosystems (Naeem et al., 1994). Thus Tilman and Downing (1994) have shown that the primary productivity in more diverse grassland communities is more resistant to, and recovers more fully from, a major drought. Agro-ecosystems (containing a species mix tailored to suit cropping regimes) may be at particular risk from sudden stress or shock (Conway, 1993). Other work seems to indicate that many species are functionally redundant. It may be that for many ecosystems, resilience will depend on the retention of keystone species and related keystone processes. The loss of such species may seriously affect the functioning capability of the system under continued environmental change.

The stability and sustainability of joint ecological–economic systems will therefore be determined by a complex set of factors: ecosystem structure; types of stress and shock experienced; the resource usage and management regime that is in place; and the feedback mechanisms that exist (or not) to signal the need for adjustments as environmental conditions change, and in particular as thresholds (carrying or assimilative capacities) are approached.

From the policy viewpoint (with its requirements for the proper identification of resource scarcity and the need for indicators of sustainable development) it is important that progress is made in the measurement of resilience loss, given current market and intervention failures afflicting environmental resources utilization and management. While market price signals are inadequate or absent, there is also a dearth of physical measures of resilience loss. Naeem et al. (1994) have presented some empirical evidence derived from microbial microcosm studies that demonstrates that a simple measure of biodiversity, the number of species (S) per functional or trophic group (F), or S/F, serves as a valuable index of ecosystem reliability. These results support the hypothetical 'insurance' value of biodiversity, that is, insurance against the failure of ecosystems to provide goods and services. The mechanistic basis for such insurance is compensatory growth, a process widely observed in many ecosystems. Greater diversity should therefore enhance the ecosystem's capacity to continue to provide a fixed level of functioning over a given unit of time.

Conservation of an appropriate amount of biodiversity is clearly a necessary condition for the sustainability of a managed resource system. But much scientific research is restricted to the study of biodiversity hotspots and is not concerned with the identification and analysis of the role of keystone species and processes in different ecosystems and different institutional conditions and resource management regimes connected to those ecosystems.

More generally, the search for sustainability indicators can be guided by a theory of sustainable development (defined as non-declining per capita human well-being) and the two interpretations of the conditions necessary to achieve this: strong sustainability (SS) and weak sustainability (WS). Depending on the state of belief about these conditions, a different set of indicators may be deemed important (Pearce et al., 1996). The package currently on offer includes 'green' national income accounts and genuine savings measures (net saving which accounts for the depletion of natural resources and the accumulation of pollution) and some less well-defined ecological indicators linked to resilience, biodiversity, carrying capacity and 'distance to goal' (that is, cost of attaining some pre-emptive sustainability 'targets') concepts (Pearce et al., 1996).

The first two types of indicators fit the WS model and its assumptions about substitutability between natural capital and other capital assets and the lack of threshold effects in ecological processes. The existence of thresholds means that an ecosystem can flip to quite a different state in a short space of time when subjected to stress, with a consequent potentially significant economic loss. An exclusive reliance on accounting price indicators is justified only if production technologies are convex. Threshold effects are examples of non-convexities (Baumol and Bradford, 1972; Starrett, 1972;

Burrows, 1979). From the SS standpoint these accounting price indicators need to be augmented by quantity controls (informed by ecological indicators) on the use of important environmental resources. Given the uncertainty surrounding ecosystem resilience and the rudimentary state of appropriate indicators, a precautionary approach is advocated, perhaps based on the safe minimum standards (SMS) concept or similar ideas (Bishop, 1978).

In principle, the problem posed by threshold effects is the same in ecological and environmental economics. In both cases the problem lies in the fact that market prices do not indicate whether a system is approaching the limits of system resilience. This is partly due to the structure of property rights and other institutions, partly to our lack of understanding of ecosystem dynamics, and partly to the public-good nature of many environmental resources. The difference between ecological and environmental economics in this case lies wholly in the extent and significance accorded to threshold effects. It is still the case that a number of models in environmental economics assume that environmental damage functions are smooth and continuous.

5.   Valuation of environmental resources

The problem of valuation has been the cause of extensive controversy and debate in both academic and policy circles. In environmental economics, a preference-based value system operates in which the benefits of environmental gain (or the damages) are measured by social opportunity cost or total economic value. Within this approach distinctions are made between use values (direct and indirect use values), option value and quasi-option value and non-use values (bequest and existence value); see Figure 67.1. While the meaning of use value (direct and indirect) is straightforward, option and non-use values are somewhat more obscure in both literatures. Option value is essentially the willingness of an individual to pay for an 'insurance premium' to safeguard future resource use and appreciation opportunities. Quasi-option value is a reflection of the conditional expected value of information and is not commensurate with other value components. Bequest value is motivated by a desire to ensure opportunities are kept available for future generations. Existence value covers a number of motivations individuals might hold, not in the context of resource use, but relating to the mere knowledge that certain resources are conserved and will continue to be so.

Debate continues over the precise boundaries between these different components of economic value, but the conventionally accepted approach to the valuation of environmental resources is based on the assumption that households maximize utility deriving from these different sources of value subject to an income constraint; and that their private willingness to pay is a function of prices, income and household tastes (including environmental attitudes), together with conditioning variables such as household size and so on. The social value of environmental resources committed to some use is then defined as the aggregation of private values.

Ecological economies also uses these value categories. But emphasis on the limiting role of ecological processes and the importance of ecological resilience means that it places much greater emphasis on the 'health' of overall systems and life support functions served by ecological processes and biogeochemical cycles. From this perspective it is argued that the aggregation of private values does not adequately capture the 'true' social value of ecosystems and their interrelationships. One formulation of this argument is that total economic value captures only 'secondary' values (associated with useful functions and/or services of an ecosystem) but not 'primary' values (the value of an overall healthy and evolving ecosystem, necessary to support the continuing provision of a range of secondary values) (Turner and Pearce, 1993; Gren et al., 1994). System integrity needs to be conserved by ensuring that sufficiently large 'chunks' of ecosystems are protected so as to retain species diversity and complexity of relationships.

Some positions within ecological economies give greater emphasis to 'intrinsic' values, or values 'in' things compared to purely 'instrumental' values, or values 'of' things. This has led to questions being raised about the nature of the conventional distinction between use and non-use value, and therefore whether there is such a thing as environmental existence value that can be measured. There are variations in the extent to which such wider values are encompassed, partly depending on the practicality of entering intrinsic values into decision making and the problems of choosing a meta-ethical principle that allows trade-offs between intrinsic and instrumental values.

The position adopted in this chapter is that while there are limits to the economic calculus, that is, not everything is amenable to meaningful monetary valuation, economic valuation methods and techniques can and should play a significant role in the project, programme and policy appraisal process which leads to the setting of relative values (including environmental assets values). Constanza et al. (1997b) controversially estimated the current economic value of 17 ecosystem services on a biosphere-wide basis at between US\$16–54 trillion (10^{12}) per year, giving an average annual value some 1.8 times the current global gross national product. The rationale behind this valuation exercise could be based on a number of arguments:

- Due to a lack of adequate market price data (or absence of data), together with inadequate (or absent) property rights regimes which ensure that resource values can be practicably appropriated, ecosystem services are assigned too little or zero value and weight in policy decisions.
- Some important environmental science research and debate, together with related policy making (that is, international agreements and conventions) necessarily takes place at the global scale. There is a need therefore for social science research to 'engage' science and policy at this scale. But such an engagement must, in our view, encompass analysis which will show clearly why globally aggregated social science data/estimates are often not meaningful, if the objective is to move beyond mere dialogue towards a more rational policy process.
- It is important to prove how valuable ecosystem services really are and to formulate mechanisms by which such function-based values can be realistically captured. Such capture must be relevant for everyday socioeconomic and political activity and decision taking, through national income/resource accounting and project cost–benefit appraisal, down to the grass-roots level in developed and developing countries.

Costanza et al.'s study goes some of the way towards meeting the arguments set out above. Their paper has engaged environmental scientists and policy makers, but the global, biome-scale, economic value calculations risk ridicule from both scientists and economists. On the basis of the data and methods cited in the article and supporting inventory, the conclusion that the value of the biosphere services really is, on average, US$33 trillion per year, is not supportable. Apart from raising policy-maker, scientist and citizen awareness about the environment's economic value and the possible significance of the loss of that value over time, the global value calculations do not serve to advance meaningful policy debate in efficiency and equity terms, in practical conservation versus development contexts. Such calculations, with their 'single-number' outcomes, shroud a number of fundamental 'scaling' problems to do with valuation contexts, that is, the temporal, spatial and cultural specificity of economic value estimates. Such values can also only meaningfully be assigned to relatively small ('marginal') changes in ecosystem capabilities (functions/services). The practical problem is that determining precisely what is and what is not a discrete and marginal change in complex ecological systems is not straightforward.

The specificity problem (relative scarcity basis of value) is generic and serves to constrain the transfer of site-based function and/or system services economic values across time and geographical and cultural space. It is not being argued that all such 'benefits transfer' is invalid, but we do believe that such procedures must be handled with extreme caution and have real limits. Many value estimates will not be amenable to legitimate aggregation beyond local to 'regional' (defined biogeographically and including cross-national boundaries where necessary) scales. Further research to more precisely define these limits and to formulate a robust validity and reliability testing protocol is an urgent requirement.

At the core of Costanza et al.'s valuation approach is a conceptual model which links ecosystem processes and functions with outputs of goods and services, which can then be assigned monetary economic values; see Figure 67.1. In principle, both economic use and non-use value estimates can be derived from sustainable or 'healthy' ecosystems. This model does provide a sound basis for future multidisciplinary/interdisciplinary research on ecosystem services valuation expressed as ranges, not point estimates. But the function-based approach must be undertaken on the basis of procedural rules which ensure scientific and economic validity and reliability. Its validity is conditioned by the existence of full knowledge about the relevant ecosystem structure, as well as temporal and spatial scale effects. Thus the raw empirical data inventory on environmental values utilized by Costanza et al. is not amenable to simple translation and aggregation.

The foundation of economic valuation based on a functional approach is a 'proper' appreciation of the links between ecosystem structure, the characteristics of which provide society directly with extractive and/or non-extractive benefits (goods and services) and ecosystem processes providing indirect benefits. This appreciation of the system's underlying dynamics is essential in order to sort out the stocks and flows involved and to ensure against possible double-counting. Both stock and flow value estimates have, for example, been calculated and reported in forest services valuation studies, and researchers seeking to obtain aggregate figures have incorrectly summed both types of numbers. The often-quoted world median value for non-timber forest products (NTFPs) of US$50 ha^{-1} yr^{-1} is an example of such an error (Batagoda and Turner, 1997). There is a need therefore for researchers carefully to unpick the existing value data work, in order to separate out individual function stock and flow estimates. For NTFPs, four types of value exist, but only the last three are economically and policy relevant: (i) the total inventory stock value; (ii) the total extractable stock value (based on some sustainability rule(s)); (iii) the potential extractable flow value (linked to physical accessibility factors and the non-uniformity of species distribution across a forest area); and (iv) the actual extracted flow value (conditioned by market accessibility, market demand and cultural value factors). It may then be legitimate to estimate a mean value for each of the last three value categories, as long as they are further 'regionally' differentiated across the major forest types, that is, tropical rainforests, tropical dry forest and temperate forests (Batagoda and Turner, 1997).

Aggregation across different functions provided by a given ecosystem should be constrained by the danger of double-counting. Exploitation of one function may preclude another, while some keystone processes and related functions may underpin others and the system infrastructure. There may also be possible incompatibilities between different valuation measures (such as opportunity costs, consumer surplus, market prices) as they are applied to different functions. Within a wetland, the exploitation of a particular function service such as wastewater cycling, for example, will preclude, or limit, the provision of other services, such as recreation. The global value of mangroves cited in Costanza et al. (1997b) of $9990 per ha, for example, is in fact made up of substitution cost estimates for the coastal protection function, replacement cost estimates for the nutrient cycling service, market price value of food production and a travel cost estimate of the recreation service.

The issue of double-counting and the extent of control necessary in economic valuation studies of complex ecosystems to account for their characteristics and functional values has been addressed in a recent meta-analysis of wetland valuation studies (Brouwer et al., 1997). In this study, a distinction is made between economic use and non-use values associated with the ecological, biogeochemical and hydrological functions provided by wetlands. The latter were shown to have a significant impact on stated preferences for a large number of wetland conservation projects or programmes in different countries. Average values were derived for different wetland functions after controlling for issues like population sample and procedural valuation characteristics.

Scaling up values of single functions of an ecosystem or, even more ambitiously, aggregate systems value to biogeographical and global scales, on a per hectare basis, increases the difficulties by an order of magnitude. If a single ecosystem service, in economic welfare terms, is relatively independent of location and its sociocultural context, then the scaling-up procedure can be regarded as more or less valid. Thus the economic value of carbon sequestration provided by coastal or terrestrial ecosystems has equal global social value (postponement of possible global climate change and its impacts) wherever it is provided. Or, in the case of coral reefs, the recreation value of reef visits and diving may be conditioned by a reasonably common set of site characteristics, regardless of precise location, and excluding totally inaccessible site cases.

On the other hand, the value of many services is primarily determined by the locational factors. The recreational value of mangroves, for example, is based on a very small number of published studies (Hamilton and Snedaker, 1984). A study in Trinidad and Tobago, for example, used the zonal travel cost method to estimate the recreational use value of Caroni Swamp (Rambial, 1980). This site is of national significance as the only nesting site for the national emblem bird, the scarlet ibis. The large visitation rate at this site can be explained by this symbolic significance value and by its proximity to Port of Spain, the island's largest population centre and magnet for cruise-ship visitors. Clearly, similar site and demand characteristics are not present in all other mangrove forest locations and therefore scaling up site value is very problematic. Although some criteria for 'benefits transfer' have been discussed in the literature, a comprehensive testing protocol is not in prospect (Brouwer and Spaninks, 1997). More research is required on these scaling possibilities and limits. It seems likely that the biogeographical regional scale will be the limit for a large number of service values.

Finally, from a systems perspective, the aggregate and scaling up of individual ecosystem services value estimates does not lead to the quantification of a total ecosystem value. An evolving 'healthy' ecosystem presumably requires some, currently unknown, minimum configuration of structure, processes and functions to retain its resilience property. Economic valuation studies estimate the value of the flow of services assuming the sustainability of ecosystems and their interrelationships between themselves and the abiotic environment. The policy implications are that there is a role for the precautionary principle and the 'safe minimum standards' notion (combined with social opportunity cost assessments). Meanwhile, science works to reduce some aspects of the uncertainty, for example, is it species preservation, or populations, or something else, that should be the basis for conservation policy? (Meyers, 1997; Nee and May, 1997; Hughes et al., 1997). Social scientists are also still required to provide valuation data in order to make more transparent the choices involved in socioeconomic terms. Such choices are made in a number of institutional settings and at and across various levels. Biodiversity conservation policy will be determined just as much by socioeconomic gains and losses and their distribution across humans as by concerns about the loss of evolutionary history *per se*.

Deciding whether or not the social costs of imposing environmental conservation/preservation standards are 'unacceptable' will be a broad social decision, conditioned by the specifications of a given resource conflict situation, including local circumstances. Thus the safe minimum standards (SMS) approach 'is deliberately "fuzzy" because it does not rely on a single criterion for making discrete choices' (Pearce and Turner, 1990,

p. 317). Non-economic criteria, such as an ethical assessment of our obligation to future generations, will also influence the final policy formulation.
By acting as a constraint on economic efficiency objectives, SMS and its
requirement that economic gains be forfeited unless the costs are unacceptable, can provide a framework for addressing the notion that individuals
may foster both consumer and citizen preferences (Sagoff, 1988; Common
et al., 1993; Vatn and Bromley, 1994; Turner, 1998).

Social and not individual preference values will be part of the SMS
setting process and economic analysis can play a constructive role alongside other political and ethical considerations (Turner, 1988, 1993).
Consumer preferences can be measured via economic willingness-to-pay
criteria, from which the social costs of imposing SMS can be assessed. As
Crowards (1995) argues, a social/political procedure will then need to be
instituted to reflect citizen preferences about the acceptability of paying
costs now to avoid exposure to uncertain future losses. The pivotal question is then, how are these citizen preferences to be aired and acknowledged
in a manner that is relevant to each specific location and 'conflict' scenario?
It appears that some degree of community participation will be required in
the decision-making process wherever environmental resources are threatened with irreversible loss.

6.   Ethics, sociology and policy analysis

Ecological economists believe that traditional ethical reasoning is faced
with a number of challenges in the context of the sustainable development
debate. Their adoption of a systems perspective leads to the need for an
ethical re-evaluation of the role and rights of present individual humans,
as against the system's survival and therefore the welfare of future human
generations and present and future non-human species. The welfare of the
current generation will include the existence of poverty and income
inequalities, as well as the institutions that perpetuate such conditions.

So 'concern for others' is an important ethical issue in the debate. Given
that in certain circumstances individuals are, to a greater or lesser extent,
self-interested and greedy, ecological economists have explored the extent
to which such behaviour could be modified and how to achieve the modification. Thus a significant number of ecological economists support a
Rawlsian rather than a utilitarian approach to intergenerational equity.
Sustainable development is seen as a condition imposed on the present
generation in order to satisfy some notion of intergenerational equity. The
present generation can ensure the welfare of future generations by under-
writing the health, diversity, resilience and productivity of natural systems.
The widely held view in ecological economics that the requirements of the
system sometimes outweigh those of its individual components contradicts

the principle of consumer sovereignty by recognizing the bounds within which sovereignty may be exercised. It also lies behind arguments for new environmental ethics or morality. Various candidate ethical codes have been put forward in the 'bioethics' literature, ranging from human-centred stewardship through to 'deep ecology', which in the latter case wishes to ascribe interests and rights to non-human and even inanimate species (Ralston, 1988; Turner, 1988).

The environmental economics valuation literature has addressed the interests of future generations via an investigation of irreversible choices (development versus conservation) and the contradictions between discounting and obligations to the distant future. How societies value the environment is part and parcel of the sustainability question. But incorporating environmental values into decision making will not in itself guarantee sustainability values unless each generation is committed to transferring to the next sufficient reproducible and natural capital to make development sustainable (Howarth and Norgaard, 1992). Howarth (1995) has recently shown that a 'Kantian' approach to intergenerational equity requires the prior imposition of sustainability criteria as a moral constraint on the maximization of social preferences concerning the distribution of welfare between generations. Such an approach precludes actions that yield present benefits but imposes the risk of irreversible future losses when scientific research would permit the effective resolution of uncertainty over generational time.

The search for a modified or new environmental ethical code is buttressed by a range of intervention measures that ecological economists advocate to alter the functioning of the economic system and to push it towards a more sustainable path. A common core feature of the diverse views on intervention seems to be that socioeconomic systems are based exclusively on 'exit' and 'exchange' principles, that is, market systems must be modified/replaced/augmented by 'voice' and 'integrated relationships' systems, say political systems (Boulding, 1963; Hirschman, 1970). The concept of community and collective values needs to be fostered, and greater investment in social capital is required in order to counter the loss of trust in society. The lack of social trust, norms of reciprocity and cooperative networks tend to be mutually reinforcing. A range of resource allocation and institutional failures can be connected to a fundamental lack of trust between the stakeholders involved and the 'authorities'.

Ecological economic methods need to be encompassed within an overarching 'integrated assessment' framework which provides policy-relevant information. The framework must include coupled or integrated models (biogeochemical and socioeconomic) but it is not limited to just this. According to Rotmans and van Asselt (1996), integrated assessment is 'an interdisciplinary and participatory process of combining, interpreting and communicating knowledge from diverse scientific disciplines to achieve a better understanding of complex phenomena'. Valuation in this process is more than the assignment of monetary values and includes multi-criteria assessment methods and techniques to identify practicable trade-offs.

An important long-term goal in ecological economics is the provision of support for environmental sustainability decision making based on the principles of economic efficiency, optimal scale, distributional fairness and justice, participation and legitimacy and precaution. In the face of an increasing degree of environmental risk, uncertainty and ignorance, the distributional incidence of the risks, costs and benefits becomes a key issue. Public consultation and consequent acceptance of the inevitable trade-offs involved will be an important requirement in any legitimization process.

Ecological economists therefore favour a future more active and conciliatory approach to consultation across and between stakeholders in any given resource allocation and environmental decision-making situation. It is argued that there are strong social, political and economic arguments for widening the consultative arrangements and ensuring a more face-to-face participatory role for representative interests. O'Riordan and Ward (1997), for example, have explored the theory of legitimation and legitimacy in negotiative participatory processes in the context of shoreline management planning in the UK. They have sought to justify the development of empowerment through respect, authenticity and trust in the conduct of mediating exercises.

The shoreline management case studies they investigated all posed the policy dilemma of how to provide compensatory equivalents for land and internationally important wildlife resources threatened with inundation because of sea-level rise and/or 'best-practice' shoreline management. It was found that local networks can play an essential role. In many cases incipient networks based on personally cooperative individuals exist and can be mobilized and extended. Such networks are vital for sharing information, formulating positions and for mutual education. This is the basis of empowerment.

7.   Conclusions

The treatment of both technology and consumption preferences as endogenous to the economic growth process is a fundamental change that brings economics much closer to ecology. Economics can no longer be seen as the science of the allocation of an arbitrary set of resources amongst the competing uses given by a fixed institutional structure (the subject matter of politics, anthropology and sociology), technology (the subject matter of engineering, physics and chemistry) and preferences (the subject matter of psychology), within an unchanging environment (the subject matter of ecology, geology, hydrology, climatology and so on). The constraint set within which economists have traditionally analysed the allocation of resources has become part of the system dynamics. What has emerged is a new and potentially very fruitful 'joint' field of inquiry, together with a research agenda, the broad lines of which have derived from ongoing research in a range of scientific disciplines (Turner et al., 1997).

In future, ecological economics will also need to formulate more participatory environmental discussion frameworks, underpinned by integrated ecological–economic modelling. Such frameworks will have to be able to cope with optimal scale, justice and distributional equity and uncertainty and ignorance problems. In order to be legitimate they will need to build trust between stakeholders through real participation and negotiation. Value judgements and ethical differences should be highlighted and debated, rather than being shrouded in overly technical analysis.

References

Alemendares, J., M. Sierra, P.M. Andersson and P.R. Epstein (1993), 'Critical regions, a profile of Honduras', *The Lancet*, **342**, 1400–402.

Arora, S. and T.N. Cason (1996), 'Why do firms volunteer to exceed environmental regulations?', *Land Economics*, **72** (4), 413–32.

Arrow, K., B. Bolin, R. Costanza, P. Dasgupta, C. Folke, C.S. Holling, B.-O. Jansson, S. Leven, K.-G. Mäler, C. Perrings and D. Pimentel (1995), 'Economic growth, carrying capacity and the environment', *Science*, **268**, 520–21.

Ausubel, J.H. and H.E. Sladovich (eds) (1989), *Technology and the Environment*, Washington, DC: National Academy Press.

Ayres, R.U. (1993), 'Cowboys, cornucopians and long-run sustainability', *Ecological Economics*, **8**, 189–207.

Ayres, R.U. and A.V. Kneese (1969), 'Production, consumption and externalities', *American Economic Review*, **59**, 282–97.

Barbier, E.B. (1994), 'Valuing environmental functions: tropical wetlands', *Land Economics*, **70**, 155–75.

Basta, D.J., J.L. Lounsbury and B.T. Bower (1978), 'Analysis for residuals-environmental quality management', Washington, DC: Resources for the Future.

Batagoda, S. and R.K. Turner (1997), 'Towards policy relevant ecosystem services and natural capital values: rainforest', mimeo, CSERGE, University of East Anglia, Norwich, UK.

Baumol, W.M. and D. Bradford (1972), 'Detrimental externalities and non-convexity of the production set', *Economica*, **39**, 160–76.

Baumol, W.M. and W. Oates (1975), *The Theory of Environmental Policy*, Englewood Cliffs, NJ: Prentice-Hall.

Beckerman, W. (1992), 'Economic growth and the environment: whose growth? Whose environment?', *World Development*, **20**, 481–96.

Berkes, F. and C. Folke (1992), 'A systems perspective on the interrelations between natural, human-made and cultural capital', *Ecological Economics*, **5**, 1–8.

Bishop, R.C. (1978), 'Economics of a safe minimum standard', *American Journal of Agricultural Economics*, **57**, 10–18.

Boulding, K.E. (1963), 'Toward a pure theory of threat system', *American Economic Review*,

Papers and Proceedings, **53**, 425–32.

Bower, B.T. and R.K. Turner (1998), 'Characterizing and analysing the benefits of integrated coastal management, *Ocean and Coastal Management*, **38**, 41–66.

Brouwer, R. and F.A. Spaninks (1997), 'The validity of transferring environmental benefits: further empirical testing', Global Environment Change Working Paper GEC 97–07, Centre for Social and Economic Research on the Global Environment (CSERGE), University of East Anglia and University College London.

Brouwer, R., I.H. Langford, I.J. Bateman, T.C. Crowards and R.K. Turner (1997), 'A meta-analysis of wetland contingent valuation studies', Global Environmental Change Working Paper, Centre for Social and Economic Research on the Global Environment (CSERGE), University of East Anglia and University College London.

Brown, G.M. and B. Field (1979), 'The adequacy of measures for signalling the scarcity of natural resources', in U.K. Smith (ed.), *Scarcity and Growth Reconsidered*, Baltimore, MD: Johns Hopkins University Press, pp. 218–48.

Burrows, P. (1979), *The Economic Theory of Pollution Control*, Oxford: Martin Robertson.

Common, M.S. and C. Perrings (1992), 'Towards an ecological economics of sustainability', *Ecological Economics*, **6**, 7–34.

Common, M.S., R.K. Blamey and R.W. Norton (1993), 'Sustainability and environmental valuation', *Environmental Values*, **2**, 299–334.

Conway, G. (1993), 'Sustainable agriculture: the trade-offs with productivity, stability and equitability', in E.B. Barbier (ed.), *Economics and Ecology: New Frontiers and Sustainable Development*, London: Chapman and Hall.

Costanza, R., C. Perrings and C.J. Cleveland (eds) (1997a), *The Development of Ecological Economics*, Cheltenham, UK, and Lyme, US: Edward Elgar.

Costanza, R., R. d'Arge, R. de Groot, S. Forber, M. Grasso, B. Hannon, K. Limburg, S. Naeem, R.V. O'Neil, J. Paruelo, R.G. Raskin, P. Sutton and M. van der Belt (1997b) 'The value of the world's ecosystem services and natural capital', *Nature*, **387**, 253–60.

Cropper, M.L. and W.E. Oates (1992), 'Environmental economics: a survey', *Journal of Economic Literature*, **30**, 675–740.

Crowards, T.M. (1995), 'Safe minimum standards: costs and opportunities', CSERGE Working Paper, University of East Anglia, Norwich.

Daily, G. (ed.) (1997), *Ecosystem Services: Their Nature and Value*, Washington, DC: Island Press.

Daly, H.E. (1968), 'On economics as a life science', *Journal of Political Economy*, **76**, 392–406.

Daly, H.E. (1973), 'The steady state economy: toward a political economy of biophysical equilibrium and moral growth', in H.E. Daly (ed.), *Toward a Steady State Economy*, W.H. Freeman, San Francisco, pp. 149–74.

Daly, H.E. (1991), 'Ecological economics and sustainable development: from concept to policy', Environment Department Divisional Working Paper 1991–24, Washington, DC: World Bank Environment Department.

Daly, H.E. and J.B. Cobb (1989), *For the Common Good*, Boston, MA: Beacon Press.

Dasgupta, P. (1996), 'The economics of the environment', *Environment and Development Economics*, **1**, 387–428.

Deadman, D. and R.K. Turner (1988), 'Resource conservation, sustainability and technical change', in R.K. Turner (ed.), *Sustainable Environmental Management: Principles and Practice*, London: Belhaven Press, pp. 67–101.

de Groot, R.S. (1992), *Functions of Nature*, Amsterdam: Wolters Noordhoff.

Dosi, G. (1988), 'The nature of the innovative process', in G. Dosi et al. (eds), *Technical Change and Economic Theory*, London: Pinter, pp. 221–38.

Ehrlich, P.R. (1989), 'The limits to substitution: meta-response depletion and a new economic–ecological paradigm', *Ecological Economics*, **1**, 9–16.

Epstein, P.R., T.E. Ford and R.R. Colwell (1993), 'Cholera–algae connections', *The Lancet*, **342**, 14–17.

Faber, M., R. Manstetten and J. Proops (1996), *Ecological Economics: Concepts and Methods*, Cheltenham, UK and Brookfield, US: Edward Elgar.

Folke, C., C. Holling and C. Perrings (1996), 'Biological diversity, ecosystems and the human scale', *Ecological Applications*, **6**, 1018–24.

Georgescu-Roegen, N. (1966), *Analytical Economics*, Cambridge, MA: Harvard University Press.

Georgescu-Roegen, N. (1971), *The Entropy Law and the Economic Process*, Cambridge, MA, Harvard University Press.

Gren, I.-M., C. Folke, R.K. Turner and I. Bateman (1994), 'Primary and secondary values of wetland ecosystems', *Environmental and Resource Economics*, **4**, 55–74.

Hamilton, L.S. and S.C. Snedaker (eds) (1984), *Handbook of Mangrove Area Management*. IUCN, Gland and East West Center, Honolulu.

Hartwick, J.M. (1978), 'Substitution among exhaustible resources and intergenerational equity', *Review of Economic Studies*, **45** (2), 347–54.

Heyes, A. and C. Liston-Heyes (1997), 'Regulatory "balancing" and the efficiency of green R and D', *Environmental and Resource Economics*, **9**, 493–507.

Heywood, V. and R. Watson (eds) (1995), *Global Biodiversity Assessment*, Cambridge, UK: Cambridge University Press.

Hirschman, A.O. (1970), 'Exit, voice and loyalty: responses to decline in firms', *Organization and States*, Cambridge, MA: Harvard University Press.

Holling, C.S. (1973), 'Resilience and stability of ecological systems', *Annual Review of Ecology and Systematics*, **4**, 1–23.

Howarth, R.B. (1995), 'Sustainability under uncertainty: a deontological approach', *Land Economics*, **71**, 417–27.

Howarth, R.B. and R.B. Norgaard (1992), 'Environmental valuation under sustainable development', *American Economics Association Papers and Proceedings*, **82**, 473–7.

Hughes, J.B., G.C. Daily and P.R. Ehrlich (1997), 'Population diversity: its extent and extinction', *Science*, **178**, 689–92.

Jaffe, A.B., S.R. Peterson, P.R. Portney and R.N. Stavins (1995), 'Environmental regulation and the competitiveness of U.S. manufacturing: what does the evidence tell us?', *Journal of Economic Literature*, **33**, 132–63.

Jänicke, M., M. Binder and H. Mönch (1997), 'Dirty industries'; patterns of change in industrial countries', *Environmental and Resource Economics*, **9**, 467–91.

Kaufmann, R.K. (1995), 'The economic multiplier of environmental life support: can capital substitute for a degraded environment?', *Ecological Economics*, **12**, 67–79.

Leibenstein, H. (1966), 'Allocative efficiency vs. X-efficiency', *American Economic Review*, **56**, 392–415.

Leontief, W. (1966), *Input–Output Economics*, New York: Oxford University Press.

Lutz, M.A. and K. Lux (1988), *Humanistic Economics: The New Challenge*, New York: The Bootstrap Press.

Marshall, A. (1970), *Principles of Economics*, London: Macmillan.

Mäler, Karl-Goran (1974), *Environmental Economics: A Theoretical Enquiry*, Baltimore, MD: Johns Hopkins University Press.

Meadows, D.H., D.L. Meadows, J. Randers and W. Behrens (1972), *The Limits to Growth*, New York: Universe Books.

Meadows, D.H., D.L. Meadows and J. Randers (1992), *Beyond the Limits: Global Collapse or a Sustainable Future*, New York: Oxford University Press.

Meyers, N. (1997), 'Mass extinction and evolution', *Science*, 278, 597–8.

Naeem, S., L.J. Thompson, S.P. Lawler, J.H. Lawton and R.M. Woodfin (1994), 'Declining biodiversity can alter the performance of ecocystems', *Nature*, **368**, 734–7.

Nee, S. and R.M. May (1997), 'Extinction and the loss of evolutionary history', *Science*, **278**, 692–4.

Norgaard, R.B. (1981), 'Sociosystem and ecosystem coevolution in the Amazon', *Journal of Environmental Economics and Management*, **8**, 238–54.

Norgaard, R.B. (1985), 'Environmental economics: an evolutionary critique and a plea for pluralism', *Journal of Environmental Economics and Management*, **12**, 382–94.

Norton, G. (1995), 'Evaluating ecosystems states: two competing paradigms', *Ecological Economics*, **14**, 113–27.

Oates, W.E., K. Palmer and P.R. Portney (1994), 'Environmental regulation and international competitiveness: thinking about the Porter hypothesis', Resources for the Future Working Paper 94–02, Washington, DC.

O'Riordan, T. and A. Jordan (1995), 'The precautionary principle in contemporary environmental politics', *Environmental Values*, **4**, 191–212.

O'Riordan, T. and R. Ward (1997), 'Building trust in shoreline management', *Land Use Policy*, **14**, 257–76.

Page, T. (1983), 'Intergenerational justice as opportunity', in D. Maclean and P.G. Brown (eds), *Energy and the Future*, Totowa, NJ: Rowman and Littlefield.

Pearce, D.W. and R.K. Turner (1990), *The Economics of Natural Resources and the Environment*, Hemel Hempstead: Harvester Wheatsheaf.

Pearce, D.W. and J. Warford (1993), *World Without End: Economics, Environment and Sustainable Development*, Oxford: Oxford University Press for the World Bank.

Pearce, D.W., A. Markandya and E.B. Barbier (1989), *Blueprint for a Green Economy*, London: Earthscan.

Pearce, D.W., E.B. Barbier and A. Markandya (1990), *Sustainable Development*, London: Earthscan.

Pearce, D.W., K. Hamilton and G. Atkinson (1996), 'Measuring sustainable development: progress on indicators', *Environment and Development Economics*, **1**, 85–101.

Perrings, C. (1987), *Economy and Environment: A Theoretical Essay on the Interdependence of Economic and Environmental Systems*, Cambridge, UK: Cambridge University Press.

Perrings, C. and D. Pearce (1994), 'Threshold effects and incentives for the conservation of biodiversity', *Environmental and Resource Economics*, **4**, 13–28.

Perrings, C. and B. Walker (1995), 'Biodiversity and the economics of discontinuous change in semi-arid rangelands', in C. Perrings, K.-G. Mäler, C. Folke, C.S. Holling and B.-O. Jansson (eds), *Biological Diversity: Economic and Ecological Issues*, Cambridge, UK: Cambridge University Press, pp. 190–210.

Pimm, S.L. (1984), 'The complexity and stability of ecosystems', *Nature*, **307**, 321–6.

Porter, M.E. (1990), *The Competitive Advantage of Nations*, London: Macmillan.

Porter, M. and C. van der Linde (1995), 'Towards a new conception of the environment – competitiveness relationship', *Journal of Economic Perspectives*, **9**, 97–118.

Ralston, H. (1988), *Environmental Ethics*, Philadelphia: Templeton University Press.

Rambial, B.S. (1980), 'The social and economic importance of the Caroni mangrove swamp forest', paper presented at the 11th Commonwealth Forestry Conference, Trinidad and Tobago, September.

Rotmans, J. and M. van Asselt (1996), 'Integrated assessment: a growing child on its way to maturity', *Climate Change*, **34**, 327–36.

Sagoff, M. (1988), *The Economy of the Earth*, Cambridge, UK: Cambridge University Press.

Schmalensee, R. (1993), 'The costs of environmental regulation', Massachusetts Institute of Technology, Centre for Energy and Environmental Policy Research Working Paper 93–015, Cambridge, MA.

Shogren, J.F. and C. Nowell (1992), 'Economics and ecology: a comparison of experimental methodologies and philosophies', *Ecological Economics*, **5**, 101–26.

Skea, J. (1995), 'Environmental technology', in H. Folmer, H. Landis Gabel and H. Opschoor (eds), *Principles of Environmental and Resource Economics*, Aldershot, UK and Brookfield, US: Edward Elgar.

Starrett, D.A. (1972), 'Fundamental non-convexities in the theory of externalities', *Journal of Economic Theory*, **4**, 180–99.

Tilman, D. and J. Downing (1994), 'Biodiversity and stability in grasslands', *Nature*, **367**, 363–5.

Turner, R.K. (1988), 'Wetland conservation: economics and ethics', in D. Collard, D.C.W. Pearce and D. Ulph (eds), *Economics, Growth and Sustainable Development*, London: Macmillan, pp. 121–60.

Turner, R.K. (1991), 'Economics and wetland management', *Ambio*, **20**, 59–63.

Turner, R.K. (1993), 'Sustainability: principles and practice', in R.K. Turner (ed.), *Sustainable Environmental Economics and Management: Principles and Practice*, London: Belhaven Press, pp. 3–36.

Turner, R.K. (1999), 'The place of economic values in environmental valuation', in I. Bateman and K. Willis (eds), *Valuing Environmental Preferences*, Oxford: Oxford University Press.

Turner, R.K. and D.W. Pearce (1993), 'Sustainable economic development: economic and ethical principles', in E.B. Barbier (ed.), *Economics and Ecology*, London: Chapman and Hall, pp. 177–94.

Turner, R.K., S. Subak and N. Adger (1996), 'Pressures trends and impacts in coastal zones', *Environmental Management*, **20**, 159–73.

Turner, R.K., C. Perrings and C. Folke (1997), 'Ecological economics: paradigm or perspective', in J. van den Bergh and J. van der Straaten (eds), *Economy and Ecosystems in Change*, Cheltenham, UK and Lyme, US: Edward Elgar, p. 25–49.

Turner, R.K., N. Adger and R. Brouwer (1998), 'Ecosystem services value, research needs and policy relevance: a commentary', *Ecological Economics*, **25**, 61–5.

Vatn, A. and D.W. Bromley (1994), 'Choices without prices without apologies', *Journal of Environmental Economics and Management*, **26**, 129–48.

Vitousek, P.M., P.R. Ehrlich, A.H. Ehrlich and P.A. Matson (1986), 'Human appropriation of the products of photosynthesis', *Bio Science*, **34**, 368–73.

Von Weizsacker, A.B., A.B. Lovins and L.H. Lovins (1997), *Factor Four: Doubling Wealth, Halving Resource Use*, London: Earthscan.

WCE (1987), *Our Common Future*, Oxford: Oxford University Press.

PART IX

METHODS AND MODELS IN ENVIRONMENTAL AND RESOURCE ECONOMICS

68 Input–output analysis, technology and the environment

Faye Duchin and Albert E. Steenge

1. Introduction

Input–output (I–O) analysis provides a theoretical framework for specific questions about the relationship between economic structure and economic action. Economic structure is defined in terms of industries or sectors (these terms will be used interchangeably) that deliver goods to each other and to final consumers. Each industry's production process is described in terms of the average technology being used in that particular industry. Technologies can be accounted for at different levels of detail, varying between a highly aggregated classification, such as one distinguishing between agriculture, heavy and light industry and services, to a very disaggregated one, at the limit in terms of individual enterprises. Economic action can be described in terms of specified consumption and production activities, involving households, capital formation, government activities, or trade that crosses the borders of the economy in question. The detailed way in which I–O economics is able to examine economic activities opens the way for studies that deal not only with industrial production – the focus established with the earliest I–O studies – but increasingly with other aspects of human activities as well, such as the effects of production and consumption on the physical environment.

The basic theoretical framework of I–O economics was developed by Wassily Leontief in the 1930s. He soon used it for the first empirical implementation of a special sort of empirical general equilibrium model of the US economy (Leontief, 1936). A central place is taken by the I–O table, which quantifies the volume and mix of inputs used in each sector. The table describes inter-industry relations and relations between industries and consumers during a particular period (often a year) for a specific country or region. The standard I–O table is a rectangular matrix with three non-zero quadrants. One quadrant describes the inter-industry deliveries during the period considered, a second one describes the final demand categories, such as production for consumption or investment purposes and a third one registers the use of primary factors, such as labour or capital. The table is discussed in more detail in Section 2.

Much work in I–O economics over the past 60 years has had a strong empirical orientation and directly involves this table. Particularly since the 1960s, many national governments have published I–O tables at periodic intervals. They constitute a database that provides invaluable insights into the structural characteristics of the economies of these countries. I–O analysis makes use of these databases to enable analysts and decison makers to explore the relations between production and consumption activities as parts of larger social and material systems. For example, many instances of environmental degradation can be alleviated, either directly or indirectly, by explicit changes in consumer behaviour. The I–O table also plays a central role in the national accounts which are compiled and maintained in many countries.

Applications of I–O analysis in addressing environmental problems date back to the 1960s and 1970s. A number of I–O model specifications have been proposed, each focusing on particular aspects, such as cost–benefit types of evaluation of the costs of environmental repercussions of economic activities. A well-known model of a general nature dates back to Leontief (1970) or Leontief and Ford (1972), who explicitly introduced pollution (in the form of emissions of noxious substances) and specific pollution abatement activities. In this way price effects of pollution control policy could be estimated.

Much of present-day research related to consumption was stimulated by Richard Stone (1970, 1986), who focused on the actual activities underlying the earning and spending of income. Based on Stone's methodology, statistical offices began compiling social accounting matrices (SAMs) which incorporated many new kinds of information into the existing accounting frameworks. Policies intended to have a direct influence on income distribution will, directly or indirectly, affect consumption behaviour; an I–O analysis can trace these linkages very well.

Contemporary developments include increasing attention to detail, both of inputs and of production diversity on the output side. The increasing attention to detail also applies to consumption patterns and to the tracking of natural substances throughout the economy. The latter is particularly important for environmental analysis, since it enables us to focus on discharges of various types of waste and on actions aimed at changing resource use or reducing pollution.

It may be well to point out here that I–O economics has experienced certain criticisms in its now 60-year-old history. One has to do with the so-called fixed coefficients assumption. In early I–O studies, figures in the coefficient matrix often did not change from one analysis to the next. This meant that an analyst might use the coefficient table for one economy to respresent the structure of a different economy or that of one economy in a given year to represent the same economy in another year. In most modern, empirical analyses, such assumptions are no longer made because tables are available for many economies and there are techniques for projecting changes in coefficients. However, changes in coefficients are not assumed to be automatically responsive to endogenous or exogenous changes in prices, as they would be in other theories about rational economic behaviour. This reflects the fact that I–O economists stress the integrity of a physical structure. Substitution in inputs to consumption or production is not considered a straightforward response to changes in income or prices. 'Structural rigidities' are explicitly recognized as being part of the social and material considerations which call for a framework that is not based solely, or even mainly, on mechanisms reflecting market-clearing assumptions.

Another criticism is that I–O analysis has data requirements that are too extensive to be satisfied realistically, for example, that every economy in every year requires the existence of an official I–O table based on accounting information about purchases and sales that took place in the relevant time period. However, experience has shown that a coefficient matrix can be built directly, in physical or mixed units or in the more common money units, on the basis of technical information about input structures coming from a wide variety of sources. Many research efforts have been devoted to techniques for the estimation and projection of the parameters that correspond to alternative technological options. These projections are indispensable for the construction of scenarios about future technological change and about the choice between technological alternatives. When the choice of parameters is appropriate, even very crude estimates can be useful in empirical analysis.

Below we shall start with an exposition of the basic model, including the duality between prices and quantities. This will be followed by a discussion of extensions of the basic framework which introduce links with the natural environment. Dynamic and institutional aspects will be discussed in the later sections.

2. Input–output table and input–output model

The I–O table describes inter-industry relations during a particular period for a specific country or region. The table's entries are normally given in money flows, but they can be given in physical flows as well. The standard table is a rectangular matrix with three non-zero quadrants, supplemented with a column of totals (see Figure 68.1). In the upper left-hand quadrant (Z), transactions among industries are registered. Outputs are represented along rows, and inputs in columns (so each inter-industry delivery is simultaneously an input and an output). The upper right-hand portion of the figure (F) shows deliveries to final users such as the consumption of

	Industries	Final demand	Total
Industries	**Z**	**F**	**x**
Primary inputs	**V**	–	**V i**

Figure 68.1   The homogeneous input–output table

households and governments, fixed capital formation, changes in stocks and exports. The lower left-hand portion of the table (**V**) shows primary inputs, also called factor inputs. If the table is in money flows, the entries in this portion represent so-called value added, the remuneration for the (in terms of the I–O model) non-produced factors of production such as various types of labour and capital. In the lower right-hand portion primary inputs delivered directly to final users are registered, here supposed to be zero. (The symbol **i** in the column 'Total' denotes the vector that is used for aggregation, all elements being equal to unity.) Often all final demand categories are aggregated in one column, called final destinations. The table can be presented either in physical terms or in money values. In the latter case, if values are at current prices, row totals equal column totals and the total of the row sums equals the total of the column sums.

To investigate the consequences on different parts of the economy of changes in final demand, a model is required. To effect the transition from table to model, a number of assumptions are needed. The main assumption is based on the observation that each sector has a characteristic mix of inputs per unit of output. Another is the assumption of homogeneous production; that is, an industry produces only one characteristic product. This assumption introduces a one-to-one relation between industry and product. Below, for reasons of simplicity, we shall assume that all final demand categories are aggregated into only one category. Similarly, we assume that all factor inputs are aggregated into a single value-added row.

The first step in developing a model based on the I–O table is to derive the input coefficient matrix. This matrix describes the sectoral technologies in terms of the required inputs per unit of output. To this end, all inputs to a sector are divided by the total output of that sector to form a column of technical coefficients. The specific combination of inputs, such as materials, fuels, biomass or water associated with the production of an average unit of output of a particular good or service is said to define a technology. It is a distinguishing characteristic of I–O analysis that industrial production in all sectors is described in terms of these technologies.

The well-known open, static I–O model consists of a matrix of input coefficients, **A**, the (i,j)th element of which is defined as the delivery from sector i to j per unit of sector j's output, and a row **l** of coefficients giving the inputs of the primary factor. (If the table is in money flows, the coefficient matrix is in terms of units each costing one monetary unit, say, dollar or pound; see Dorfman et al., 1958.) Using the symbols of Figure 68.1, dividing each column of **A** by the row totals means post-multiplication by the diagonal matrix $(\hat{\mathbf{x}})^{-1}$. We have:

$$\mathbf{A} = \mathbf{Z}(\hat{\mathbf{x}})^{-1}$$

and

$$\mathbf{l} = \mathbf{V}(\hat{\mathbf{x}})^{-1}$$

The economy can now be represented by the following coefficients matrix:

$$\mathbf{T} = \left[\frac{\mathbf{A}}{\mathbf{l}}\right] \qquad (68.1)$$

Representing the vectors of final demand and total output, respectively, by the symbols **f** and **x**, the physical structure of the economy is modelled as:

$$\mathbf{x} = \mathbf{A}\mathbf{x} + \mathbf{f} \qquad (68.2)$$

The model is made complete by the equation giving the total use (L) of the primary factor:

$$L = \mathbf{l}\mathbf{x} \qquad (68.3)$$

The model is called 'open' because important decisions (for example regarding size and composition of final deliveries and factor prices) are made exogenously, that is, not explained by the model. It is static in the sense that while demand for capacity-increasing investments is taken into account (as part of final demand), it is not explained (in terms of the model). Progressive closure of the model is achieved by endogenizing one exogenous variable after the next, such as investment decisions or consumer demand. Other extensions of the conceptual framework of the I–O model involve its closure for specific phenomena, such as environmental consequences of production or the choice of technology.

A basic property of the model is its duality; that is, price implications of (68.2) are given by the dual

$$p = pA + wl \tag{68.4}$$

where **p** is the vector of unit prices, and w the wage rate, measured, for example, in dollars or pounds. These can be called equilibrium prices in the sense that the price equals the sum of the costs; in other words, if **A** and **l** are measured in current prices, each element of **p** will be equal to 1.0. We directly observe that remuneration for the primary factor inputs is equal to the value of the final demand bundle: $wlx = pf$. (If we identify labour as the primary factor, then the wage sum equals the value of the final demand bundle.) Solving for **x** and **p** gives

$$x = (I - A)^{-1} f \tag{68.5}$$

and

$$p = wl(I - A)^{-1} \tag{68.6}$$

The matrix $(I - A)^{-1}$ is known as the Leontief inverse; its (i, j)th element represents the total amount of commodity i required both directly and indirectly to deliver one unit of final demand of commodity j. This definition highlights a characteristic property of I–O analysis, namely, that it is able to reveal indirect effects, that is, the input needed to produce the inputs (and so forth for an unending number of rounds) required for satisfying final demand. Equation (68.6) tells us that commodity prices are proportional to the amounts of the primary factor 'embodied' in each commodity being produced. If labour is the only primary factor distinguished, prices are thus explained in terms of a 'labour theory of value'. For a further description of this basic model and its properties , see Miller and Blair (1985).

   The above derivation was based on the property that industries were assumed to produce only one, homogeneous product. In many modern applications this assumption is too severe. A solution was found by abandoning the one-to-one relation between industry and commodity. In such developments it is explicitly recognized that an industry can produce more than one commodity, and vice versa, that a particular good can be produced by more than one industry. Outputs and inputs then are registered in so-called make-and-use matrices. As a next step, (commodity-specific) input coefficients tables have – in the context of this make–use framework – to be derived from the use-and-(multiple output)-make matrices. This requires certain additional assumptions, for example regarding market share or input structure. For a recent approach, see Konijn (1994) or Konijn and Steenge (1995).

3. Input–output analysis of the environment

A number of directions in environmental I–O can be distinguished. Cumberland (1966), for example, investigated possibilities for valuing changes in the natural environment as a consequence of human activity. This gave rise to cost–benefit types of approach. Other authors tried to model material flows links between the environment (Daly, 1968; Victor, 1972a, 1972b) or tried to apply I–O methodology to describing interactions in the environment itself (Isard, 1972). (Approaches based on the concept of material balances will be discussed in Section 4.) Many present-day models date back to Leontief (1970) or Leontief and Ford (1972) who explicitly introduced pollution abatement activities to estimate the costs of pollution control policy. Below we shall concentrate on Leontief's approach as it captures the essential features of a number of directions while retaining a close proximity to empirical work. It is characteristic that Leontief does not try to model the influence of economic activities on the natural environment. The focus is on the cost of pollution abatement, not on the way environmental policy is based on our knowledge of nature.

The proposed model is based on the observation that in addition to its characteristic output, an industry often produces a number of substances that may affect the natural environment in the form of discharges into air, water and soil. These substances, such as carbon, nitrogen or sulphur compounds, are associated with both local problems, such as water pollution, and global phenomena, such as the greenhouse effect or the depletion of the ozone layer. To account for such effects, I–O relationships are extended to the production of these substances. That is, the production of the quantities of these substances is recorded per unit of output of 'traditional' goods such as steel or rice. Leontief also investigated the effect of introducing the description of techniques for the abatement of specific pollutants. To accommodate these extensions, the traditional model is incorporated in a larger framework that also accounts for the joint production of pollutants. Let A_{11} now stand for the conventional input coefficients matrix (previously A) and A_{12} for the (rectangular) matrix of input coefficients describing the operations of selected abatement activities. Let the emission of pollutants be registered in A_{21}, a rectangular matrix of emission coefficients. Finally, to complete the system, Leontief allowed for pollution generated by the abatement activities themselves in matrix A_{22}. Let l_1 stand for the vector of direct labour input coefficients for the conventional activities and l_2 for the vector of direct labour input coefficients for the abatement activities. Combining all activities, we obtain, analogous to the standard case (68.1), the following coefficients matrix:

$$
\begin{bmatrix} A_{11} & A_{12} \\ A_{21} & A_{22} \\ l_1 & l_2 \end{bmatrix} \tag{68.7}
$$

Let us denote final consumption of conventional goods by c_1, the tolerated level of pollutants by c_2, total output by x_1 and the total of pollutants being abated by x_2. Corresponding to (68.2), the physical I–O balance for commodities and pollutants now reads

$$
\begin{bmatrix} I - A_{11} & -A_{12} \\ A_{21} & -I + A_{22} \end{bmatrix} \begin{bmatrix} x_1 \\ x_2 \end{bmatrix} = \begin{bmatrix} c_1 \\ c_2 \end{bmatrix} \tag{68.8}
$$

Provided a number of conditions are met, non-negative solutions to this system are guaranteed. We now can determine the consequences of an increase or decrease in certain final demand categories for total pollution; see Proops et al. (1993). Links between c_2, the tolerated level of emmissions, and x_2, the quantity of eliminated pollutants, can be explored in the following way (Steenge, 1978). Assuming that a fraction α ($0 \le \alpha \le 1$) of pollutant outputs are to be eliminated, we may extend the basic model by including as an additional relation:

$$
c_2 = \alpha x_2 \tag{68.9}
$$

The physical balance now can be rewritten in a more compact form in terms of an enlarged input coefficient matrix:

$$
A^* = A_{11} + A_{12} \{(1 + \alpha)I - A_{22}\}^{-1} A_{21} \tag{68.10}
$$

with corresponding enlarged value-added vector:

$$
l^* = l_1 + l_2 \{(1 + \alpha)I - A_{22}\}^{-1} A_{21} \tag{68.11}
$$

Both (68.10) and (68.11) give the additional inputs per unit production of the conventional goods required to oblige with the abatement policy's objectives. We now obtain as the new vector of total outputs

$$
x = A^* x + c_1 \tag{68.12}
$$

and for the required input of the primary factor

$$
L = l^* x. \tag{68.13}
$$

Various extensions are possible. Instead of imposing a uniform rate of abatement, the model can also accommodate sector-specific rates. Prices are readily calculated from

$$\mathbf{p} = \mathbf{p}\mathbf{A}^* + w\mathbf{l}^* \tag{68.14}$$

where w is again the wage rate. This may be called a 'polluter pays' system because the costs of eliminating pollution are charged to the polluting industries. We observe that the above exercises illustrate a fundamental characteristic of environmental I–O studies: the separate but integrated analysis in monetary and physical units. This theme is further elaborated in the next section.

Stone (1972) pointed out that the Leontief model does not enable us to consider the question of how much of each pollutant should be removed in order to reach a balance between the cost of abatement policy and the gains to be expected from reduced pollution. Basically, the community is more interested in the quality of the natural environment after treatment than in the amount of treatment carried out. However, addressing the problem of determining the level of (in our notation) c_2 from this angle would require a large set of valuations in a non-market context. That is, the country or region in question should be able to determine which set of market goods it would be prepared to give up in order to gain something which essentially has no market value. Stone has already indicated that addressing such issues will require a model of a much larger scope and a much larger data set. We shall return to this in Section 7.

Above we have focused on I–O analysis in the direct lineage of Leontief. We should mention that I–O analysis also allows other perspectives on economic production and price formation. We may mention the neo-Austrian approach, which allows us explicitly to model the temporal structure of economic production processes and, in certain cases, of ecological production processes as well. This approach can be particularly valuable in analysing structural change as a consequence of innovations of new capital goods. Such processes can, for example, be observed in the waste treatment and recycling sectors, which are subject to rapid expansion and innovation; see Faber et al. (1987). We may also mention the neo-Ricardian perspective. The literature based on this perspective shares with Leontief-type analysis the view that production is a circular process instead of a linear flow from factors to outputs. Characteristic of neo-Ricardian analysis is the classification of inputs to production as produced and non-produced, the non-produced inputs being in fixed supply. This opens up possibilities for including natural resources within this theoretical framework (England, 1986).

4. Material balances and physical input–output models

In the previous section we discussed I–O models which were extended to quantify the increase in emissions as a consequence of, say, an increase in the demand for steel products. Although these models provide substantial insights for the comparison of alternative economic strategies, they are still rather limited in the range of questions they can address. In particular, while the model is uniquely able to trace intersectoral interactions, the analyst often wants to focus on the path of particular materials, such as chlorine, paper products or heavy metals, one reason being that the processing of these substances is generally energy-intensive and associated with toxic discharges.

By following pathways through an entire production chain, we can analyse the use of exhaustible resources and their effects on the environment. The ability to identify the specific links in the chain makes it possible to represent prospects for reducing material use. This type of analysis requires a description not only of raw materials and basic products, but also of the final products made from these materials. By taking into account the entire chain, including consumer demand, we can investigate in close detail the links between consumption patterns and associated environmental outcomes.

Attention to tracking particular materials or groups of materials through the economy gave rise to the development of the I–O analysis of material flows. In an early contribution Kneese et al. (1970) point out that the inputs of the system can be categorized as fuels, foods and raw materials which are partly converted into final goods and partly become residuals. Except for increases in inventory, final goods also ultimately enter the residuals stream. Thus goods that are 'consumed' really only render certain services; their material substance remains in existence and must be either reused or discharged into the natural environment. The concept of 'material balances' denotes a detailed description of the supply and use of a certain substance or family of substances. For instance, tracing the flow of paper may involve a range of products, including pulp and packaging materials. I–O analysis can accommodate material flows measured in physical units, such as kilograms or joules. For an industry making machines from steel and an electricity plant we may have, respectively:

output of machines (in kg) = input of steel + input of other materials embodied in the machines − scrap of steel − other scrap and waste (all in kg)

and

output of electricity (in PJ) = input of coal or natural gas − energy losses (all in PJ)

The figures measuring specific flows can be compiled into a so-called physical I–O table. This table is based on two distinctions (see Figure 68.2). First, the transformation of materials in the production process is distinguished from their final use, parallel to the distinction between intermediate and final demand in a conventional I–O table. Second, materials which are the outcome of a production process, or secondary materials, are distinguished from primary materials, which – in terms of this model – are directly extracted from nature, usually the soil. The distinction between primary and secondary materials is thus analogous to the distinction between primary and intermediate inputs in a traditional I–O table.

	Use for transformation to secondary materials	Final use by		Total domestic output
		activities	final demand categories	
Secondary materials	Z_s	F_{sa}	F_{sf}	x_s
Primary materials	Z_p	F_{pa}	F_{pf}	x_p

Figure 68.2 The physical input–output table

with

Z_s : use for transformation of secondary materials for the production of secondary materials;
F_{sa} : final use of secondary materials by activities;
F_{sf} : final use of secondary materials by final demand categories;
x_s : domestic production of secondary materials;
Z_p : use for transformation of primary materials for the production of secondary materials;
F_{pa} : final use of primary materials by activities;
F_{pf} : final use of primary materials by final demand categories;
x_p : domestic production of primary materials.

The following identities now hold:

$$Z_s i + F_{sa} i + F_{sf} i = x_s$$
$$Z_p i + F_{pa} i + F_{pf} i = x_p$$

Analogously to the procedure for the standard input–output of Section 2, we now make a number of assumptions regarding the entries in the sectoral matrices $\mathbf{Z}_s$, $\mathbf{Z}_p$, $\mathbf{F}_{sa}$ and $\mathbf{F}_{pa}$. We have, respectively,

$$\mathbf{A}_s = \mathbf{Z}_s(\hat{\mathbf{x}}_s)^{-1}$$
$$\mathbf{A}_p = \mathbf{Z}_p(\hat{\mathbf{x}}_s)^{-1}$$
$$\mathbf{A}_{sa} = \mathbf{F}_{sa}(\hat{\mathbf{x}})^{-1}$$
$$\mathbf{A}_{pa} = \mathbf{F}_{pa}(\hat{\mathbf{x}})^{-1}$$

with:

$\mathbf{A}_s$: use of secondary materials per physical unit of output of secondary materials;

$\mathbf{A}_p$: use of primary materials per physical unit of output of secondary materials;

$\mathbf{A}_{sa}$: final use of secondary materials per money unit of output of activities;

$\mathbf{A}_{pa}$: final use of primary materials per money unit of output of activities.

The symbol $\mathbf{x}$ again represents the total output vector of the standard model of Section 2 and Figure 68.1. We now obtain

$$\mathbf{A}_s\mathbf{x}_s + \mathbf{F}_{sa}\mathbf{i} + \mathbf{F}_{sf}\mathbf{i} = \mathbf{x}_s$$
$$\mathbf{A}_p\mathbf{x}_s + \mathbf{F}_{pa}\mathbf{i} + \mathbf{F}_{pf}\mathbf{i} = \mathbf{x}_p$$

From these equations, we now can straightforwardly calculate $\mathbf{x}_s$ and $\mathbf{x}_p$ as functions of $\mathbf{F}_{sa}$ and $\mathbf{F}_{pa}$, respectively. The link between the above physical input–output model and the standard input–output model of Section 2 is made through the assumptions we made earlier regarding $\mathbf{F}_{sa}$ and $\mathbf{F}_{pa}$ which were defined in terms of the diagonal matrix $(\hat{\mathbf{x}})^{-1}$. Straightforward substitution shows that we have obtained a link between the vectors $\mathbf{x}_p$ and $\mathbf{x}$; that is, between final demand categories in portion $\mathbf{F}$ in Figure 68.1 and $\mathbf{x}_p$. We are now able to calculate the quantities of primary materials needed to satisfy the final demand for the products of activities and the total use of primary materials per final demand category; see further Konijn et al. (1997).

Analysis of energy flows has become a fairly standardized application of I–O analysis (see, for example, Hannon et al., 1984). The use of I–O techniques to describe and analyse material flows is less well known though. An example of the latter, albeit at a still rather aggregate level, is Ayres (1978), which includes physical balances involving the use of iron in kilograms per kilogram of steel, for instance. To calculate the use of iron (in kg) per monetary unit of a specific product requires unit prices – or a comparable table in money values. I–O tables in physical units thus can be used to calculate the total requirements of, say, rolled steel to produce metal products and then the outcomes can be linked to economic data on production, consumption, value added and employment.

Material balances and physical I–O calculations are also useful for representing alternative technologies and examining the consequences of their introduction. In building the relevant databases and balance equations, internal consistency and consistency with the rest of the I–O framework need to be assured. The so-called I–O case study methodology (see the next section) was devised for this purpose.

5.   Dynamic analysis

Different kinds of extensions to the basic framework are needed to provide insight into alternative options available for the growth of an economy and the structural changes associated with development. A dynamic model, which retains many of the features of a static I–O model but at the same time is capable of explaining capacity-expanding investments, requires both considerable modification of the mathematical model and additional kinds of data. A dynamic formulation focuses attention on technological changes, as a response to changes in prices, as a result of new inventions, or as part of an industrialization strategy. Systematic techniques have been developed for describing different technological options in terms of relevant input coefficients and preparing the data to be consistent with the definition of variables and parameters in the dynamic modelling framework.

The models of the previous sections are 'open' with respect to major decision areas such as investment or household consumption. That is, investment and household decisions are specified outside the I–O framework rather than being explained within it. Thus, while investment requirements are fully accounted for as part of final demand even in a static framework, there is no constraint imposing a consistent relationship between those requirements and the future capacity to produce. The dynamic I–O model has been developed to achieve closure with respect to investment decisions. Based on the assumption of commodity-specific capital requirements for the expansion of capacity, investment flows can be calculated using a capital coefficients matrix. The (i,j)th element of the capital matrix represents the quantity of good i required to increase the capacity to produce good j by one unit. A well-known dynamic model specification is (Leontief et al., 1953):

$$\mathbf{x}(t) = \mathbf{A}\mathbf{x}(t) + \mathbf{B}\left[\mathbf{x}(t+1) - \mathbf{x}(t)\right] + \mathbf{f}(t) \qquad (68.15)$$

where $\mathbf{x}(t)$ is output during period t, $\mathbf{f}(t)$ final demand during period t, $\mathbf{A}$ the matrix of intermediate input coefficients, and $\mathbf{B}$ the matrix of capital coefficients. The term $\mathbf{B}[\mathbf{x}(t+1)-\mathbf{x}(t)]$ describes the vector of increments to the capital stock that need to be produced and put in place during period t in order to achieve an increase in production of output of $\Delta\mathbf{x}(t+1)=\mathbf{x}(t+1)-\mathbf{x}(t)$ during period $t+1$. Given a trajectory of projected future values for $\mathbf{f}(t)$, the model solves for output, $\mathbf{x}(t)$. If a rectangular matrix of coefficients describing the discharge of pollutants per unit of output is available, the quantities of associated pollutants can also be determined. The above version of the dynamic model is mainly of didactic value; as it turned out, it is, due to stability problems, not suited to empirical applications. (For a discussion of problem issues, see Steenge, 1990.) A major reason is that capacity is assumed to be fully utilized during each period. This constraining assumption is relaxed in the Duchin and Szyld (1985) specification, which was applied for the first time in Leontief and Duchin (1986). Other applications of this model are found in Costa (1988) and Edler (1990); a discussion of the stability of this non-linear, dynamic formulation is given in Fleissner (1990).

Empirical implementation of a dynamic model often requires the analyst to deal with changing input structures. In situations where technological and organizational changes are experienced in many sectors simultaneously, it is common practice to develop a number of different scenarios. Building sound and well-documented projections of exogenous variables and parameters for each scenario poses a substantial challenge. This challenge is met by the use of new techniques to incorporate information on technical infrastructure, in ways that are consistent with I–O economics. Clearly these alternative technical matrices cannot be calculated from existing I–O tables, since the latter reflect current, actual inter-industry relations. The coefficient matrices have to be built directly on the basis of technical information on input structures coming from a wide variety of sources including engineering studies. Here one advantage of measurement in physical units is apparent in that changes in quantities and in unit prices are readily distinguished.

The I–O case study methodology was developed to provide structure to the task of projecting large numbers of coefficients and to raise the degree of consistency among assumptions underlying the projections of variables and parameters made by different members of a research team. This methodology consists of a series of guidelines and principles to systematically build I–O matrices on the basis of mainly technical data. Each matrix describes future options by way of projections based on specified assumptions about key variables. A typical case study covers a cluster of related sectors. Future technologies relevant to that cluster are identified, and each is described in terms of the major inputs per unit of output. Work of this kind is closely related to the data work underlying material balances. The first application is reported in Duchin and Lange (1994), which includes documented case studies, for all regions of the world economy, on electric power generation, industrial energy conservation, the processing and fabrication of metals, construction, cement, pulp and paper, chemicals, household energy conservation and motor vehicles.

6. Further extensions of the accounting framework

The kinds of extensions to the basic I–O model discussed earlier support scenario-based approaches to analysis. The scope of the scenarios is limited, however, both by the mathematical formulation of the types of model used and by the database. Present-day strategies for resolving environmental challenges focus primarily on changes in consumption behaviour, investments and technology, but they also need to be mindful of other considerations, such as the distribution of incomes (see OECD, 1994). Therefore a broadly conceived database is needed to meet the challenge of such applications.

Richard Stone (1970, 1986) developed the so-called social accounting matrix (SAM) as a data framework to describe the distribution of income in a generalized I–O format. To this end, he divided total value added into several categories, distinguishing factors of production according to different qualifications of labour (such as occupations or skills) and different sources of property-type incomes. Within the categories which constituted consumption demand, several institutions such as households, firms and government agencies were distinguished. The income earned by the primary factors of production is determined by labour requirements, wage rates and levels of production. Any redistribution of income among the institutional sectors is taken into account in determining the value of final consumption expenditure available to each institution. Given the consumption mix and the production input structures, the loop is closed by assuming that consumption of each good is (and this is true to a first approximation) equal to the amount produced and sold. By relating rates of income and labour inputs to income expenditures and consumption patterns, the SAM can provide a complete picture of the circular flow of income at an intermediate or meso-level of detail.

Figure 68.3 gives the general structure of a SAM. The portions A, C and F represent the matrices of intermediate deliveries, consumption categories and factor inputs, respectively. The portion of the matrix designated as W represents ownership of factors by institutions (such as households,

		EXPENDITURES				
		Production activities	Factors of production	Institutions	Other expenditures	Total
RECEIPTS		1	2	3	4	
Production activities	1	A		C	X	X
Factors of production	2	F			X	X
Institutions	3		W	T	X	X
Other	4	X	X	X	X	X
Total		X	X	X	X	X

Note: Submatrices **A**, **F**, **C**, **W** and **T** are discussed in the text. Blank submatrices contain zeros. **X** indicates other non-zero submatrices.

Figure 68.3   Structure of a social accounting matrix

government agencies or corporations), and **T** shows the redistribution of income among the institutional sectors (such as taxes or transfer payments). The residual category in the table (called 'Other') represents net exports, investments and government spending, these are usually given only cursory treatment in a SAM. The blank submatrices contain zeros, the **X**s indicate other non-zero submatrices.

By analogy with the manipulation of an I–O table, a coefficients matrix is normally calculated based on the first three rows and columns of the SAM. Analysis is usually based on interpretation of the figures in the corresponding Leontief inverse. However, calculations can also be made using equations analogous to those of Section 2.

The SAM data framework can be extended to include inputs from and outputs to the environment. A database including such accounts – with substances measured in physical units – makes it possible to investigate interactions between, say, changes in consumption patterns and reductions in pollutant emissions. An example of such an extension is the so-called national accounting matrix, including environmental accounts (NAMEA), a system that integrates physical data on pollution, waste production, and the depletion of natural resources with economic data on production and

		Goods and services	Con-sump-tion	Produc-tion	Income genera-tion	Income distri-bution	Other	Pollu-tants	Environ-mental themes	Total
		1	2	3	4	5	6	7	8	9
Goods and services	1									
Con-sump-tion	2									
Produc-tion	3									
Income genera-tion	4									
Income distri-bution	5									
Other	6									
Pollu-tants	7									
Environ-mental themes	8									
Total	9									

Figure 68.4   Structure of the NAMEA

consumption as described in the National Accounts (de Haan and Keuning, 1996; Keuning and de Haan, 1996).

As the acronym indicates, the NAMEA incorporates a complete system of national flow accounts. Closely related to a SAM, the NAMEA records the distribution of income and also traces particular substances from their origin within the system to their disposal. The general layout is given in Figure 68.4, where the most relevant accounts are shown as shaded areas. As we observe, the NAMEA is based on the make–use framework (see Section 2); the submatrices in the positions (1,3) and (3,1), respectively, are the use-and-make matrices. Accounts 1 to 5 are in monetary units; receipts are shown across the rows and outlays down the columns, with total outlays equalling total receipts for each sector. The real economy is thus described in terms of these five accounts: goods and services, consumption purposes, production activities, income generation, and redistribution of income. The residual (sixth account) contains capital and financial balances and transactions with the rest of the world, while the final account contains environmental pollutants. The seventh column shows the origins of the substances that are monitored; pollution associated directly with consumer activities is presented in submatrix (2,7) while pollution associated with business establishments is registered in (3,7); submatrix (6,7) registers pollution associated with other transactions.

The data in account 7 are weighted and aggregated by column, and the weighted summation is shown as the column totals of this account. In the eighth account the pollutants are reallocated to five environmental 'themes': the greenhouse effect, depletion of the ozone layer, acidification, eutrophication and the accumulation of waste. The NAMEA is also used to calculate indicators measuring environmental pressures and changes in environmental quality. By analogy with the manipulation of the I–O table, a major part of the accounting system can be converted into a coefficients matrix. Models have been developed to investigate possible trade-offs in the relation between production, employment and the level of pollution (Steenge and Voogt, 1995).

7. Structural economics

The SAM and the NAMEA are examples of new frameworks integrating economic, social and environmental data. Both are representative of the wide scope that is needed in modelling increasingly complex issues of the interaction between society and the natural environment. However, for describing and explaining the salient features of today's technological, social and environmental changes even wider frameworks may be needed. Such frameworks then might include links between the economy and the natural environment, or describe relations within the environment itself. Work of the former type started with efforts at modelling at an aggregate level the material flows between an economic system and the natural environment (Daly, 1968; Victor 1972a, 1972b). Work by Isard (1972) on a marine ecosystem suggested the application of I–O methodology to the environment itself. In line with this, Steenge (1977) showed that Isard's data allow an interpretation in terms of a stationary von Neumann model (a generalized I–O model with multiple outputs).

The above approaches are early examples of a new type of I–O model, which integrates economic systems and aspects of ecosystems affected by economic activity. Combining an analysis in terms of material cycles and energy flows with specific aspects of thermodynamics, we obtain a novel type of model integrating core concepts of economics, ecology and physics. Models of this type are capable of integrating in one framework thermo-dynamic concepts regarding materials and energy use and complex feed-back processes among ecosystem components. Ruth (1993) derived conditions for the optimal use of natural resources based on a modelling approach in this tradition. Perrings (1987) proposed a closed economy–

environmental physical I–O system with the conservation of mass condition as the central concept: here the mass of resources potentially available for exploitation in the system, or in any isolated part of it, always remains the same. This model shares certain features with a von Neumann-type I–O model such as the possibility of multiple production. In the model the price system discriminates between environmental resources that are subject to well-defined property rights (and thus have economic value in exchange) and those that are not.

Another example of the new type of analysis that is being developed at the moment is provided by the structural economics approach. In fact, this term may serve as a 'catch-all' for several of the integrated approaches we have discussed. Structural economics provides a conceptual framework for analysing and interpreting interactions of the described type in the context of an economic model that explicitly recognizes the importance of social and behavioural relations (Duchin, 1998). These include activities related to the transformation of natural resources, such as energy feedstocks, materials, and other parts of the natural system like soils and water, to serve human purposes. Structural economics was developed to investigate the socioeconomic and environmental contexts for possible changes in technologies and lifestyles, and the implications of such changes. To this end it makes use of mathematical formulations and techniques for collecting data that grow out of the I–O enterprise while introducing new concepts as required. Data integration is achieved through techniques that ensure the consistent accommodation of primary information from various sources. The relevance to broadly framed questions is ensured by a mathematical framework which is discrete and 'open' (in the sense described earlier).

A main characteristic of structural economics is that it is issue-oriented. This means that it is driven not by methodology or theory as an aim in itself, but by the desire to provide solutions to real-world problems. Scenarios are formulated as possible solution concepts. Then, using appropriate models and data, which may need to be developed for a specific application, the implications of each scenario are analysed and can be compared according to multiple attributes. As increasing attention is focused on scenarios of environmental and social challenges, the inadequacy of various established concepts becomes apparent. In particular, it becomes obvious that the consumer as 'rational man' needs to be replaced by a more complex actor who is concerned not only or mainly with consuming more material goods but also with the quality of life in the form of clean air and water, avoiding traffic congestion, and reasonable ways to dispose of smaller amounts of wastes. This individual lies in a household, generally – although not necessarily – together with other people, and participates in decisions about lifestyle that are taken jointly and reflect household characteristics.

Richard Stone (1986) had envisaged social accounts for 'the systematic quantitative description of social systems, particularly in their economic aspect', emphasizing data collection and integration. Structural economics shares this emphasis and provides a framework for the systematic description of the activities of various categories of households, as well as material use and pollutant generation. One aspect of this involves collecting and estimating data, which it is convenient to arrange in the format shown in Figure 68.5 (Duchin, 1998).

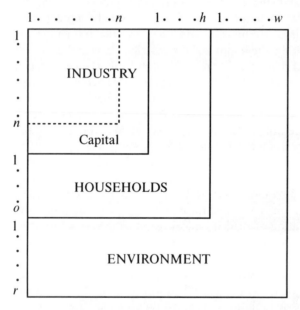

Note: A structural table incorporates elements of an input–output table (*n* sectors), social accounting matrix (*o* occupations and *h* categories of households), and natural resource accounts (*r* resources and *w* categories of wastes). See text.

Figure 68.5   A structural table of an economy

The upper left-hand corner of the figure includes the standard I–O table including capital accounts. The section labelled 'households' represents the inputs and outputs corresponding to various occupations and households categories. The environmental portion of the structural table provides a framework for incorporating the type of information used in the analysis of material balances and in national resource accounting. Here the row and column sums will balance provided that all sources and sinks have been identified. Thus the flow charts usually used to track material balances and the social accounts representing the activities of households (and other social institutions) are conveniently integrated and represented by the figures in the rows and columns of a structural table. In addition, a family of transparently simple linear models and non-linear dynamic models makes use of this table and projected coefficient matrices to analyse alternative scenarios about the future.

8. Conclusion

We have seen a long development in I–O type models, from models focusing on economic structure in a rather narrow sense to models proposing an integration with (models of) natural systems. We may expect to see further developments in this direction, in combination with policy-oriented models, especially in areas such as energy or environmental policy. A relatively new development is the incorporation of input–output elements into computable general equilibrium (CGE) models (Bergman, 1990). These models essentially (only) incorporate the matrix of inter-industry deliveries. In this field we may expect additional developments, because up to now CGE models seem largely to have neglected the additional structure (such as explanation of prices, or, more generally, the role of institutional 'rigidities' in society) that I–O has to offer. Fruitful applications here may be found in the analysis of problems relating to allocation of the costs of environmental policy, including Coasean-type property rights issues (Coase, 1960).

References

Ayres, R.U. (1978), *Resources, Environment and Economics: Applications of the Materials/ Energy Balance Principle*, New York: John Wiley and Sons.

Bergman, L. (1990), 'Energy and environmental constraints on growth: a CGE modeling approach', *Journal of Policy Modeling*, **12**, 671–91.

Coase, R.H. (1960), 'The problem of social cost', *Journal of Law and Economics*, **3**, 1–44.

Costa, P. (1988), 'Using input–output to forecast transport demand', in L. Bianco and A. LaBella (eds), *Freight Transport Planning and Logistics*, Lecture Notes in Economics and Mathematical Systems 217, Berlin: Springer-Verlag.

Cumberland, J.H. (1966), 'A regional inter-industry model for analysis of development objectives', *Papers of the Regional Science Association*, **17**, 65–95.

Daly, H.E. (1968), 'On economics as a life science', *The Journal of Political Economy*, **76**, 392–406.

de Haan, M. and S.J. Keuning (1996), 'Taking the environment into account: the NAMEA approach', *Review of Income and Wealth*, Series 42, pp.131–48.

Dorfman, R., P.A. Samuelson and R.M. Solow (1958), *Linear Programming and Economic Analysis*, New York: McGraw-Hill.

Duchin, F. (1998), *Structural Economics: Measuring Change in Technology, Lifestyles, and the Environment*, Washington, DC: Island Press.

Duchin, F. and G.-M. Lange (1994), *The Future of the Environment: Ecological Economics and Technological Change*, New York: Oxford University Press.

Duchin, F. and D. Szyld (1985), 'A dynamic input–output model with assured positive output', *Metroeconomica*, **37**, 269–82.

Edler, D. (1990), *Ein Dynamisches Input–Output Modell zur Abschätzungen der Auswirkungen Ausgewählter neuer Technologieen auf die Beschäftigung in der Bundesrepublik Deutschland* (A Dynamic Input–Output Model for the Assessment of the Effects of Selected New Technologies on Employment in West Germany), Beiträge zur Strukturforschung, Heft 16, Berlin: Duncker & Humblot.

England, R. (1986), 'Production, distribution, and environmental quality: Mr. Sraffa reinterpreted as an ecologist', *Kyklos*, **39**, 230–44.

Faber, M., H. Niemes and G. Stephan (1987), *Entropy, Environment and Resources: An Essay in Physico-Economics*, Berlin: Springer-Verlag.

Fleissner, P. (1990), 'Dynamic input–output models on the test bed', *Structural Change and Economic Dynamics*, **1**, 321–57.

Hannon, B., T. Blazeck, D. Kennedy and R. Illyes (1984), 'A comparison of energy intensities, 1963, 1967 and 1972', *Resources and Energy*, **5**, 83–102.

Isard, W. (1972), *Ecologic–Economic Analysis for Regional Development*, New York: The Free Press.

Keuning, S.J. and M. de Haan (1996), *What's in a NAMEA?, Recent Results of the NAMEA Approach to Environmental Accounting*, Occasional Paper no. NA-080, National Accounts, Statistics Netherlands, Voorburg.

Kneese, A.V., R.U. Ayres and R. d'Arge (1970), *Economics and the Environment: A Materials Balance Approach*, Washington, DC: Resources for the Future.

Konijn, P.J.A. (1994), *The Make and Use of Commodities by Industries: On the Compilation of Input–Output Data from the National Accounts*, Universiteit Twente, Enschede.

Konijn, P.J.A. and A.E. Steenge (1995), 'Compilation of input–output data from the National Accounts', *Economic Systems Research*, **7**, 31–45.

Konijn, P.J.A., S. de Boer and J. van Dalen (1997), 'Input–output analysis of material flows', *Structural Change and Economic Dynamics*, **8**, 129–53.

Leontief, W. (1936), 'Quantitative input and output relations in the economic system of the United States', *Review of Economics and Statistics*, **18**, 105–25.

Leontief, W. (1970), 'Environmental repercussions and the economic structure: an input–output approach', *Review of Economics and Statistics*, **56**, 262–71.

Leontief, W. and F. Duchin (1986), *The Future Impact of Automation on Workers*, New York: Oxford University Press.

Leontief, W. and D. Ford (1972), 'Air pollution and the economic structure: empirical results of I–O computations', in A. Bródy and A. Carter (eds), *Input–Output Techniques*, Amsterdam: North-Holland.

Leontief, W. et al. (1953), *Studies in the Structure of American Economy*, White Plains, NY: International Arts and Sciences Press.

Miller, R.M. and P.D. Blair (1985), *Input–Output Analysis: Foundations and Extensions*, Englewood Cliffs, NJ: Prentice-Hall.

OECD (1994), *Managing the Environment: The Role of Economic Instruments*, Paris: OECD.

Perrings, Ch. (1987), *Economy and Environment: A Theoretical Essay on the Interdependence of Economic and Environmental Systems*, Cambridge, UK: Cambridge University Press.

Proops, J.L., M. Faber and G. Wagenhals (1993), *Reducing CO_2 Emissions: A Comparative I–O Study for Germany and the UK*, Berlin: Springer-Verlag.

Ruth, M. (1993), *Integrating Economics, Ecology and Thermodynamics*, Dordrecht: Kluwer Academic Publishers.

Steenge, A.E. (1977), 'Economic–ecologic analysis: a note on Isard's approach', *Journal of Regional Science*, **17**, 97–105.

Steenge, A.E. (1978), 'Environmental repercussions and the economic structure: further comments', *Review of Economics and Statistics*, **60**, 482–6.

Steenge, A.E. (1990), 'On the complete instability of empirically implemented dynamic Leontief models', *Economic Systems Research*, **2**, 3–16.

Steenge, A.E. and M.H. Voogt (1995), 'A linear programming model for calculating green national incomes', in U. Derigs, A. Bachem and A. Drexl (eds), *Operations Research Proceedings 1994: Selected Papers of the International Conference on Operations Research*, TU Berlin, 30 August – 2 September 1994, Berlin: Springer-Verlag, pp. 376–81.

Stone, R. (1970), 'Demographic input–output: an extension of social accounting', in A.P. Carter and A. Bródy (eds), *Contributions to Input–Output Analysis*, Amsterdam: North-Holland, vol. 1, pp.293–319.

Stone, R. (1972), 'The evaluation of pollution: balancing gains and losses', *Minerva*, **10**, 412–25.

Stone, R. (1986), 'Social accounting: the state of the art', *Scandinavian Journal of Economics*, **88**, 453–72.

Victor, P.A. (1972a), *Economics of Pollution*, London: Macmillan.

Victor, P.A. (1972b), *Pollution: Economy and Environment*, London: George Allen and Unwin.

69 Computable general equilibrium models for environmental economics and policy analysis

Klaus Conrad

1. Introduction

Given the challenge to realise more restrictive environmental regulation in the near future, it is becoming increasingly important to quantify the costs of such a policy. Policies aimed at significantly reducing environmental problems such as global warming, acid rain, deforestation, waste disposal or any other degradation of the quality of air, water, soil or land most imply drastic emission reductions. Obviously, the implementation of environmental policy instruments to improve the quality of the environment should not hinder other economic goals like GDP growth, international competitiveness or employment. The discussion whether there exists a 'no-regret' policy that improves environmental quality without negative impacts on the economy has been held for a long time but has not yet led to a conclusion. In principle, large emission reductions tend to have a significant impact on costs in one or several sectors of an economy. The implied change in relative prices will induce general equilibrium effects throughout the whole economy. For this reason it is often useful to evaluate the effect of environmental policy measures within the framework of a computable general equilibrium (CGE) model. Models of this type are a computer representation of a national economy or a region of national economies, each of which consists of consumers, producers and a government. Consumers purchase goods from producers, supply factors of production, save, and pay all kinds of taxes to and receive transfer payments from government. Producers supply goods, demand factors of production, invest, and also pay taxes to the government. Although single- and multi-market partial equilibrium models make it possible to estimate the costs of environmental policy measures, taking substitution processes in production and consumption as well as market-clearing conditions into account, CGE models additionally allow for adjustments in all sectors and complete the ties between factor incomes and consumer expenditures. The source of data for these multisectoral economic models is the national accounts and input–output tables which can be comfortably combined in the framework of the social accounting matrix. The practice of model building itself has become increasingly systematized, reflected in the increasing use of standard and rather powerful packages such as MPSGE (Rutherford, 1994) and SOLVER/NTUA (Capros et al., 1992).

CGE models are becoming a widely used tool for quantifying the costs and benefits of environmental policy. Such a study is useful in making obvious that there is no free lunch in pollution control policy. Model builders are concerned with the interactions among fiscal instruments, environmental pollution and the productive economy, as well as with the effects of an ecological tax reform. Since most of the sectors of an economy generate both 'producer–producer' externalities (that is, the damage done to the structure of production as a result of industrial pollution) and 'producer–consumer' externalities (for example, pollution and health), these effects should be part of an environmentally oriented CGE model. Furthermore, the technology of pollution abatement has to be integrated into the theory of cost and production, and the benefits of pollution reduction should be included in welfare calculations (see Ballard and Medema, 1993).

CGE models simulate the impact of a shock (a non-marginal change of a policy variable) on the development of relative prices which leads to a new equilibrium with different levels of production, income and consumption. The main form of an analysis based on CGE models is that of comparative statics. In such a sensitivity analysis one starts from a base solution or scenario as a point of reference (usually the actual values of the economic variables in a given base year). Then one of the exogenous variables or parameters is altered and the model calculates the new values for the endogenous variables. The comparison of the two sets of values of the endogenous variables suggests the estimated economic impact of the exogenous change in environmental policy. Confronting the policy maker with the result will lead to a revised model structure and scenarios until satisfactory results are achieved.

CGE models for assessing cost-effectiveness of environmental policy instruments and loss in economic growth and welfare from reduced international competitiveness in energy-intensive industries, for example, become more and more sophisticated. From a scientific point of view, research to attenuate some of the unrealistic assumptions that general equilibrium models are based on is desirable. From a pragmatic point of view, the variety of approaches to do so makes it more and more difficult to understand why a carbon dioxide reduction target of 10 per cent calls for a CO_2 tax rate of, for example, $20 by one model builder, but $300 by another.

In this chapter I shall present the basic structure of a CGE model and survey some of its methodological alternatives. I shall focus only on some distinct and basic approaches in CGE analysis for environmental policy rather than trying to make a complete account of individual models. Needless to say, this means that several outstanding contributions to CGE modelling will be left out of this survey.

2. Methodological principles

A CGE model is a system of linear and non-linear equations that is solved to simulate market equilibrium. It includes equations describing consumer and producer supply and demand behaviour that are derived explicitly from conditions for profit or utility maximization, and market-clearing conditions in product and input markets. Unlike inter-industry input–output models and other earlier economy-wide planning models, household factor income and expenditures are linked in a theoretically appropriate manner. A common methodological feature in CGE models is an activity analysis approach to model the exchange of commodities by agents. For methodological and data availability reasons, activity analysis is based on the input–output technology typically embedded in CGE models to characterize inter-industry transfers. Next, appropriate mathematical specifications of production or cost function, and of utility functions at the level of the agents, have to be chosen. The optimal demand for production factors (producers) and for commodities (consumers) is then derived through first-order conditions of the optimum. In the case of the producer, the optimizing behaviour may be represented in the form of either the primal problem or the dual problem. Macroeconomic equilibrium models based on the primal approach to production have been used by Shoven and Whalley (1973, 1984), whereas the dual (cost-driven) forms have been prefered by Johansen and Jorgenson.[1] The choice of the primal or the dual representation has an important implication for the mathematical form of the market-clearing mechanism. In the primal problem form, demand as well as supply depends explicitly on prices, which are determined by equating demand and supply. In the dual problem form, the supplier receives the market price of the commodity from the inverse supply function, or, equivalently, from average cost pricing. Demand depends explicitly on prices and determines the quantity to be supplied. Supply enters marginal cost, which influences the price.[2] Although the practical importance of the different schools may seem insigificant, the problems addressed indicate that the Shoven–Whalley type of models have their roots in applied welfare economics, while the Johansen–Jorgenson type of models originate from input–output analysis (see Johansen, 1979; Hudson and Jorgenson, 1974).

Equilibrium models in environmental economics in the Johansen–Jorgenson tradition of the dual problem form have been developed by Jorgenson and Wilcoxen (1990a, 1990b), Burniaux et al. (1992), Bergman (1990a, 1990b, 1991), Conrad and Henseler-Unger (1986), Conrad and

Schröder (1991a, 1991b), and Capros et al. (1996). These models are built around a flexible (price-driven technical coefficient) input–output frame-work and derive equilibrium prices of commodities directly from price (or unit cost) functions. Shephard's lemma is employed for obtaining factor demands (input coefficients). The unit cost pricing of equilibrium is equiv-alent to the zero-profit condition. Primary factor prices are, on the other hand, obtained through supply–demand interaction.[3]

As a point of depature for extensions of this basic framework of a CGE model, it might be useful to state it in mathematical terms. The structure of production of an industry j is characterized by its cost function $C_j (x_j; p_1,..., p_n, p_K, p_L)$ where p_i are the prices for intermediate inputs and p_K and p_L are the prices for the primary inputs capital and labour. From price equal to marginal cost, assuming constant returns to scale, we obtain a system of n equations for the n unknown industry prices p_i:

$$p_j = MC_j (p_1, P_2, ..., P_n; P_K, P_L), \qquad j = 1, ..., n$$

To make things easier for the time being, we assume the prices for the primary inputs to be exogenously given. Next, using Shephard's lemma, that is, by partially differentiating the cost function, input demand or price-dependent input coefficients can be derived:

$$\frac{x_{ij}}{x_j} = a_{ij}\left(\frac{p_j}{p_i}, \sigma, t\right) \qquad i = 1, ..., n+2, j = 1, ..., n$$

where the input coefficients are functions of relative prices, of the elasticity of substitution and of technical change t, represented by the time symbol. The input structure of an industry therefore depends on relative price changes, on the flexibility with respect to substitution, and on the bias of technical change. Finally, supply of an industry must be equal to demand for the product of this industry:

$$x_i = \sum_{j=i}^{n} x_{ij} + FD_i, \qquad i = 1, ..., n$$

where FDi is final demand (consumption (private and public), investment and export). Since intermediate demand can be replaced by $x_{ij} = a_{ij} (\cdot) x_j$, this system of n equations can be solved for the n unknown industry output levels x_j. In order to obtain a basic structure of a CGE model, the above model has to be extended by markets for capital and labour, by a model of consumers' behaviour, by introducing import demand and export supply decisions, and by incorporating a variety of taxes.

If the architecture of the CGE modelling framework is well specified, one can easily add markets and corresponding agents in order to augment

the generality of the equilibrium computed. The framework is fully applicable to any economic, energy or environmental commodity. The degree of
integration between economy, energy and environment is a matter of
formulation of the appropriate markets, commodities and agents. In the
next sections we will discuss certain aspects of such an integration.

3.   Modelling producer behaviour

We begin with a short-run CGE model which is based on the assumption
that not all variables will adjust immediately to their long-run optimal
values. We treat capital as quasi-fixed in the short run so that the economy
is in a short-run equilibrium. Since for environmental policy analysis CGE
models are mostly based on the dual approach, we will characterize the
technology by a cost function whereby environmental policy instruments
will raise marginal costs.

The theory of the firm
The technology of a cost-minimizing firm is characterized by a variable
cost function *VC*

$$VC = VC(x, K, \mathbf{w}, p_L, t)$$

where x is output, $\mathbf{w}$ is the price vector of intermediate inputs, p_L is the price
of labour and t represents technical change. The quasi-fixed factor capital
K is given at the beginning of the period, and the observed variable costs
are $VC = \Sigma w_i v_i + P_L \cdot L$, where v_i are the n intermediate inputs. We assume
constant returns to scale (CRTS) of VC in x and K. Hence $vc = VC(1, (K/x),$
$\mathbf{w}, p_L, t)$ is the average variable cost function with $VC = x \cdot vc(K/x, \mathbf{w}, p_L, t)$.
   From Shephard's lemma we derive short-run demand functions as vari-
able input coefficients:

$$\frac{v_i}{x} = \frac{\partial vc}{\partial \mathbf{w}_i} \qquad i = 1, ..., n, L$$

Assuming profit maximization under perfect competition, $(p = VC_x)$,
profit is zero under the *ex post* price or shadow price of capital $\mathbf{w}_K$
$(\mathbf{w}_K = -VC_K)$:

$$p \cdot x = VC(x, K, \mathbf{w}, p_L) + \mathbf{w}_K \cdot K$$

or

$$p = vc\left(\frac{K}{x}, \mathbf{w}, p_L\right) + \mathbf{w}_K\left(\frac{K}{x}\right) \qquad (69.1)$$

This 'price equal total average cost' condition can be employed to determine the system of n output prices. Since the price vector $\mathbf{w}$ of intermediate inputs is exactly the price vector $(p_1, \ldots, p_n)$ of output prices, equation (69.1) for industry i is:

$$p_i = vc_i\left(\frac{K_i}{x_i}, p_1, \ldots, p_n, p_L\right) + \mathbf{w}_{K,i}\left(\frac{K_i}{x_i}\right) \qquad (69.2)$$

Hence we can solve this system of n prices, given the beginning of year capital stock and the price of labour.

Given the basic approach to modelling producer behaviour in an inter-industry framework, CGE models differ in dealing with the following issues: adjustment of the quasi-fixed capital stock, specification of functional forms, treatment of technical change, the introduction of imperfect competition, and the incorporation of abatement activities.

Adjustment of the quasi-fixed capital stock
The assumptions made about the possibility of adjusting the capital stock in the short run will affect the cost estimates of an environmental policy. Residential and non-residential structures as well as producers' durables cannot be modified without cost. Therefore CGE models with costless adjustment of the capital stock in the same year or in the short run underestimate the cost of an environmental policy.

In a recursive dynamic, that is, not intertemporal model, capital is mobile across industries but total capital is fixed in a certain year. Then, instead of K, the price of capital $\mathbf{w}_K$ enters the cost function. The demand for capital will be derived by Shephard's lemma, and, added up over all industries, will yield total capital demand. Since the supply of capital, the beginning-of-year total capital stock, is fixed, the price $\mathbf{w}_K$ will adjust demand and supply. The price $\mathbf{w}_K$ is a market-clearing price of capital which will be different from the expected price p_K of capital. If a model does not distinguish between $\mathbf{w}_K$ and p_K, then it considers sectoral capital stocks to be at their optimal levels. There are then no investment functions, but the *ex post* identity of savings and investment determines total investment. Hence the closure rule determines the supply of capital in the next period.

Models distinguishing between the *ex post* price $\mathbf{w}_K$ and the *ex ante* price p_K use $\mathbf{w}_K$ to calculate the *ex post* rate of return of capital in the temporary equilibrium for determining capital income. The price of capital $p_K = p_I$ $(r + \delta)$ is a signal for the desired stock of capital resulting in sectoral investment decisions. p_I is the investment goods deflator, r is the nominal rate of return and δ is the rate of replacement. The problem of the firm is to choose the time-path of $K(t)$ which minimizes the present value of total costs including the cost of adjustment. Such an optimal stock is derived from solving $-VK_K(x, K^*, \mathbf{w}, P_L) = p_K$ for the long-run optimal capital stock K^*, neglecting adjustment costs.[4]

For modelling the impact of environmental policy, the choice of a short-run or long-run approach is important. By the envelope theorem we know that the short-run costs are higher than the long-run costs. Adjustment costs can increase the welfare loss for a country during transition to a more energy-efficient structure of production and consumption. To illustrate, consider the estimates of the short-run costs of reducing CO_2 emissions versus the long-run costs. A short-run study is the Manne–Richels (1991) study where the price under the carbon constraint rises to around $600 per ton of carbon in the short run because of difficulties the system has in adapting to stringent constraints before a full adaptation of the capital stock and the technology. Nordhaus (1991) or Jorgenson and Wilcoxen (1992) calculate the long-run costs of reduction, that is, they measure the costs when all factors of production are allowed to adjust fully.

Specification of functional forms

The choice of specification depends on adopting the econometric approach or the calibration approach to CGE modelling. The econometric approach requires time-series or cross-sectional data for estimating the unknown parameters statistically. Calibration may use a mix of econometric results and other data taken from the literature. When choosing the econometric approach, flexible functional forms like the translog specification (Jorgenson and Wilcoxen, 1990a, 1990b; Hazilla and Kopp, 1990) or the generalized Leontief specification of cost functions (Glomsrod et al., 1992) can be used. The estimation procedure of the unknown parameters is based on two-stage budgeting. At the 'top' level there are two inputs, for instance energy and non-energy, or four inputs, say labour, capital, material inputs and energy or agriculture, forestry or land respectively, depending on the focus of the study. At the 'bottom' level, demand for energy, material or for transportation is further divided into its components using flexible sub-functions. Agriculture, for example, can be decomposed into programme crops, livestock and dairy, and all other agricultural production if the user of a CGE model wishes to illustrate some of the difficulties of coordinating agricultural and environmental policies (Hrubovcak et al., 1990). The common approach to CGE modelling is to calibrate the parameters of the model so that one-year observations are sufficient. The preferred specification is a series of nested CES functions but with fixed-input coefficients for some input components (for example, Bergman, 1990 or the GREEN model, Burniaux et al., 1992). In the CES approach, the elasticity of substitution will be guessed, and the distribution parameters depend on the particular year chosen for calibration.[5] The elasticities of price-induced substitution are key parameters and will affect the economic costs and environmental benefits from stricter policies towards sustainable development. In general, input categories and nests in a nested production structure should be selected according to the focus of the model. Those nests one would use for an energy-oriented model may not be the same as for a trade and environmental analysis in a developing country that depends on agriculture, fishery and forestry.

The econometric approach is very demanding in terms of data requirements, but makes it possible to incorporate behavioural responses to changes in energy prices, based on the experience since 1973. However, given the data requirements, and the high degree of aggregation, the knowledge of an estimated elasticity of substitution for chemicals and allied products might be not worth the enormous effort required to explore the production structure from a set of yearly input–output tables. What we know is that a high degree of substitution among inputs implies that the cost of environmental regulation is low, while a low degree of substitutability implies higher costs of environmental regulation. If we simulate the nature of substitutability among inputs by assuming a CES specification first with a low elasticity of substitution and then with a higher one, we get an interval for the economic consequences of regulation. This is perhaps more informative than getting a point forecast under the econometric approach. Furthermore, future research should concentrate on specifications with increasing price and substitution elasticities under stricter environmental policies. The standard argument against a policy of higher energy prices is that empirically estimated price elasticities of energy are rather low. This argument might turn out to be not true if the relative price of energy increases significantly.

Treatment of technological change
Technical change is exogenous in most policy evaluation models. It is traditionally considered to be not the outcome of an endogenous decision process. This obviously hampers thinking about schedules of emission mitigation targets and policies of sustainable development in the presence of uncertainty. The omission of induced technological change might lead to underestimation of the net benefits of tighter environmental policies. Most models either neglect the role of technological change, or introduce exogenous Hicks-neutral technical change. (The increased output of other goods and services per unit of input and the increase in emissions reduction per unit of input are the same.) Most historical data suggest that technical change is biased toward lower emissions per unit of output. One of the few attempts to (partly) endogenize technical change is the approach followed by the Jorgenson and Wilcoxen (1990a, 1990b) model for the US

and later by the G-cubed model of McKibbin and Wilcoxen (1992). Technological development is partly endogenized by the specification of productivity growth as a function of the prices of all inputs of an industry. In this approach substitution away from polluting inputs can affect the rate of productivity growth. A decrease in an industry's productivity level will raise the price of its output relative to its input prices, that is, the industry will become less competitive. If the bias of technical change is input *i*-using and the price of such a pollution intensive input increases (for example by a tax), then cost reduction due to productivity growth will be reduced. Technological development is only partly endogenized in these models because an autonomous trend is included which interacts with the prices of intermediate inputs. The translog unit cost functions are functions of the prices of all inputs and of time *t* as an index of technology. There is price-induced productivity growth in the model which affects input shares. But technological change is not endogenized in terms of leading to new vintages of durable goods, to new products or to different qualities or major breakthroughs.[6]

Autonomous energy-efficiency improvements (AEEI) are more difficult to estimate than those that are induced by price increases. AEEI decouples resource demand and economic output, and so yields resource-saving technical change. Econometric investigations by Jorgenson and Wilcoxen (1990a, 1990b) of the US post-1947 historical record show no evidence for autonomous time trends of this type. Technologically oriented end-use analysts, however, have suggested that non-price efficiency inprovements may be induced by changes in public policy like a mandatory doubling of average fuel efficiency of automobiles during the course of ten years. Manne and Richels (1991) introduce those exogenous efficiency improvements, for example. They also include explicit carbon removal technologies if carbon tax rates are large. Their production function also allows for the possibility of costless AEEI which reduce the share of energy in GNP over time. If environmental policies were to alter technical change, for instance trigger emission- or resource-saving technical change, they would reduce the cost of meeting a given abatement or resource conservation target. Most CGE models, however, assume no difference in the pattern of technical change between the base case and the policy case. This probably leads to an upward bias in the cost estimate of that policy.

An alternative approach to endogenizing technical change is the use of capital vintages involving different technologies. The differentiation of technologies can have effects on the form of the production function, on the input structure, or on flexibility (different elasticities of substitution for the vintages). With new vintages, substitution possibilities among production factors are higher than with old vintages. In Bergman (1990b) the 'old' production units in steel or pulp and paper industries are assumed to have zero elasticities of substitution, whereas the elasticity of substitution of 'new' production units in these industries is positive. In GREEN's dynamic structure, two kinds of capital goods coexist in each period, 'old' capital installed in previous periods, and 'new' capital resulting from current-period investment. This putty-semi-putty technology with substitution before but partially fixed input requirements after installation also implies different substitution possibilities by age of capital.[7]

All these approaches to endogenizing technological change do not provide initiatives to influence the characteristics of future vintages by investing in research and development. The recent literature on endogenous technological change[8] explores the microeconomic foundations of the process of innovation. But even if endogenous technological change in its neoclassical framework could be successfully implemented in CGE models, it would not be very satisfactory. The reason is that decisions based on marginal thinking will never lead to important innovations and breakthroughs.

Imperfect competition
The relevance for policy analysis of models built on the competitive Arrow–Debreu framework has been questioned by Harris (1984). He argued that the disappointingly modest evaluations of trade liberalization effects produced by these models are artefacts of the combined assumptions of price-taking behaviour and constant returns to scale in production. Whereas CGE models with imperfect competition and economies of scale have been extensively used for analysing international trade and development issues (see Mercenier, 1995; Willenbockel, 1994), only a few attempts are known for environmental policy analysis (for example, Conrad and Wang, 1994).

The desirable procedure would be to distinguish between competitive industries with zero profit and marginal cost pricing, and between imperfectly competitive industries. If real economies are characterized by imperfect competition, then the standard Pigouvian tax is second-best because firms cause two types of distortion – prices above marginal cost, and marginal damage above marginal abatement costs. If only an environmental tax is introduced in the face of two distortions, then such a second-best tax should be lower than the Pivouvian tax to reflect the welfare losses associated with restrictions in output under imperfect competition (Lee, 1975). To modify conventional CGE environmental policy analysis by incorporating industrial organization features is necessary in order to underline the robustness of results, for example the impact on growth and on prices under a CO_2 reduction policy or the demonstration of a 'double dividend' from CO_2 taxation, raising employment and environmental quality.

4. Abatement technologies

For an analysis of the impact of environmental regulation on international competitiveness and on growth, the inclusion of the operating costs of pollution control is of importance. Polluting firms can react to standards and/or emission taxes either by factor substitution or by abatement activities or by both. They have abatement cost functions and determine the level of the abatement activity by equating marginal cost of abatement to the uniform tax rate on emissions. Abatement activities also imply demand for intermediate goods, for capital and for labour. Depending on the objective of the study, several approaches to imposing pollution control regulations on the technology can be found in the literature. The easiest way to deal with this problem is to study the economic impact of reducing carbon dioxide emissions. There are no carbon abatement technologies available at reasonable economic costs. This explains the popularity of modelling CO_2 reduction policies.

In determining the impact of environmental restrictions on economic growth, Jorgenson and Wilcoxen (1990a, 1990b) simulated US economic growth with and without pollution control. To eliminate the operating cost of pollution control they estimated the share of pollution abatement in total costs of each industry to compute the share λ_i of costs, pollution abatement excluded, in total costs. To simulate the effect of eliminating the operating costs associated with pollution controls for all industries, they insert the cost shares λ_i into the unit cost functions for these industries, that is,

$$\ln p_i = \ln \lambda_i + \ln c_i (w,t)$$

To simulate the impact of eliminating controls on motor vehicle emissions they reduced the price of motor vehicles in proportion to the cost of pollution control devices. Finally, mandated investment in pollution control equipment has been implemented as an increase in the price of investment goods.

Hazilla and Kopp (1990) also impose pollution control regulations directly on the technologies. They model their impact through modification of the derived input demand equations in each sector. The input structure of each industry is modified to account for increased input usage required by regulation. In Bergman (1990) total emissions of air pollutants (SO_2, NO_x, CO_2) can be reduced by means of separate cleaning activities that are available to all sectors. Technically the reduction of emissions is modelled as a central abatement unit, selling services to the different sectors. The price of these abatement services is equal to marginal cost of abatement. This price will then be determiend on the market for emission permits, implying that marginal cost of abatement will be equal across sources of emissions.

In Conrad and Schröder (1991a, 1993) and in the GEM-E3 model (Capros et al., 1996) abatement activities are modelled so as to increase the user cost of the polluting inputs in terms of additional operating costs. Let d be a degree of abatement which is defined as the ratio of abated emission over potential emissions ($0 \leq d \leq 1$) and $c(d)$ are the cost of abatement measures per unit of emission or waste, measured in base-year prices. They depend on the degree of abatement with $c'(d) > 0$ and $c''(d) > 0$. Then the user cost of fossil fuel, for instance, is $\tilde{w}_F = w_F + w_M \cdot c(d) \cdot d \cdot e$, where w_F is the fuel price, w_M is the price of material or abatement technology and e is an emission or waste coefficient in terms of tons of an air pollutant per unit of energy input. User costs therefore consist of the fuel price w_F and of the additional costs due to environmental regulation when using one unit of the fuel input. This user cost of energy increases over-proportionally with an enforcement in environmental regulation. On the production side this implies an increasing share of complementary material inputs. The change of the user cost of energy will also cause the firm to alter its input choices. A stricter environmental policy will have a substitution effect which will result in a reduced demand for energy and its price complements and in an increased use of its substitutes. This integration of abatement costs in a user cost concept can be used to model the impact of regulation on household and firm behaviour; for the latter each sector should be treated separately.

The user cost approach can be extended to the case of several pollutants. Furthermore, if there is a tax on a pollutant, then there is also a cost component for the emissions released, that is,

$$\tilde{w}_F = w_F + w_M \cdot c(d) \cdot d \cdot e + t \, (1 - d) \cdot e$$

Finally, if there is an energy tax and/or an emission tax on carbon dioxide, t_{co}, where no convenient end-of-pipe measures exist, then d is equal to zero in this user cost of fuel.

This approach permits us to model the effect of alternative environmental policies. If there is a regulated degree of abatement, then users of furnaces have to adhere to governmentally enforced limits of emissions which can be interpreted as a minimum degree of abatement, $\bar{d}$. Then the degree of abatement is given and abatement costs increase the price of energy. If a tax on emission is introduced, the degree d is a decision variable of the firm. Cost minimization with respect to the degree of abatement d yields the optimal degree.

Furthermore, future environmental regulations can be accounted for by modifying the emission coefficients for appropriate sectors. For instance, as new cars are equipped with catalytic converters, the emission of NO_x for a given amount of gasoline will fall gradually (see Glomsrod et al., 1992; Conrad and Schröder, 1991a).

In the user cost approach environmental regulation will have an impact on the composition of the energy aggregate, it will increase the price of the product produced with fuel, and it will reduce the demand for energy.

5.   Modelling consumer behaviour

Usually consumers are assumed to perform a multistage budgeting procedure. At the first level is a model of intertemporal consumer behaviour allocating lifetime wealth endowment across full consumption (consumption and leisure) in different time periods. At a second level is an intratemporal choice between leisure (supply of labour) and consumption. At the final stage of the budgeting process consumption is allocated into several consumption categories, the latter then being transformed into consumption by product according to the industry classification used.[9] In Piggot et al. (1991) even the benefit side of reduced global warming is captured in the specification of preferences by including temperature change (emissions reduced). For the intratemporal allocation of consumption into categories, different specifications can be found; the most frequent ones are the linear expenditure system, nested CES or translog demand functions. In most CGE models the focus of the analysis is on efficiency issues, and all consumers are then aggregated into a single representative consumer. A disaggregation into several types of households is potentially useful in assessing the distributional impacts of policies to restrict air pollution. This requires that the above process is duplicated for several representative consumers to include several social groups. In Jorgenson and Wilcoxen (1990a, 1990b) there are 672 types of households, in Stephan et al. (1992) there are six, and Glomsrod et al. (1992) calculate the effect of the climate convention on the distribution of welfare of 1500 households. They employ a linear expenditure system that includes demographic effects.

On the labour market, aggregate demand is derived from firms' production decisions while aggregate supply is derived from households' preferences for leisure. Almost all CGE models assume a classical labour market with a market-clearing wage rate. One important objective of these models should be, however, to quantify the impact of environmental policy on employment. What do we learn if 'the economy is fully employed in the post-regulation world'? (Hazilla and Kopp, 1990). In puristic CGE models labour supply declines if the relative price of leisure to consumption declines. Voluntary unemployment is then interpreted as good news, for example, in Hazilla and Kopp: 'household leisure consumption increases by 14 billion dollars after environmental regulation'. However, reality shows that downward flexibility of wages is limited and that the labour market adjusts by increasing unemployment.

The debate on environmental tax reforms where the revenue can be used to reduce existing tax distortions on the labour market has influenced some CGE modellers to incorporate labour market imperfections. Instead of assuming a classical labour market where, in spite of millions of unemployed people, the wage rate increases with labour demand, a fixed real wage rate has been assumed.[10] Now, unemployment is a residual variable. An alternative wage rule is a fixed real wage rate multiplied by (one plus the change in labour productivity in the previous year). Other models incorporate some features of wage bargaining in the presence of initial unemployment.[11]

Since environmental regulation affects the use and purchase of consumer durables such as cars, electric appliances and heating, a model of consumer behaviour should integrate demand for durables and for non-durables. Demand for non-durables and for services from durables has to be reconciled with investment demand for durables to modify the stock of durables towards their optimal levels. Such an approach permits us to model the impact of an energy or gasoline tax on growth and on the age of the stock of durables.[12] Since non-durable goods like gasoline or electricity are linked to durable goods such as cars or electric appliances, prices of durables are stated in terms of user costs which include all costs of using durables.[13] The approach is based on the notion of a variable expenditure function $e(u, \mathbf{p}, z)$ which gives minimal expenditure for non-durable goods given the utility level u, the price of vector $\mathbf{p}$ of the non-durable goods and the vector $\mathbf{z}$ of the quasi-fixed stock of durables.

The optimal stock of the durables can be derived from an intertemporal minimization of expenditures. These expenditures consist of expenditures for non-durables, of purchases of new durables as net investment, of purchases for replacement, and of taxes on durables like a motor vehicle tax. The analytical solution is similar to the firm's decision on investment facing a variable cost function with quasi-fixed capital.

Since gasoline, electricity and heating energy are linked to the stock of durables, a composition of these goods into a part linked to the stock, and into a disposable part, is useful (see Conrad and Schröder, 1991c). The idea behind such a composition is that the use of the stock of automobiles ($\mathbf{z}$) involves demand for gasoline. This implies a user cost $\tilde{\mathbf{p}}_z$ for the services of an automobile which consists of the cost of capital $\mathbf{p}_z$ plus the operating costs in terms of the cost of gasoline. The introduction of a tax on CO_2 or NO_x will therefore increase the price of gasoline, hence the user cost of a car, and demand for new cars will decline.

6.   Foreign trade

The cost of a more stringent environmental policy for a country can be significantly affected by the assumptions made about the policies of other countries. Unilateral actions are likely to adversely affect the international competitiveness and to reduce national income, although this conclusion depends on the way the revenue from eco-taxes is recycled. If all countries implement actions, their impact on GDP and relative prices of products will be different in different countries. As a result, trade patterns and domestic production will change. Since the costs of environmental policies will decline as the number of countries implementing them increases, it is of importance to model the impacts on international competitiveness by endogenizing foreign trade. Those CGE models allow the trade pattern to adjust to environmental policy measures.

CGE models for only one country adopt the small open-economy framework. In foreign trade the domestic economy is considered as sufficiently small. Therefore the effects of exports and imports on international prices can be ignored. Foreign export demand and import supply functions are horizontal. For modelling intra-industry foreign trade, the Armington (1969) assumption is widely adopted: domestically produced goods and imported goods are imperfect substitutes (for non-tradable goods there is no Armington assumption and the good is homogeneous). For tradable goods a composite commodity combines domestically produced and imported goods. The unit cost of the composite good determines its selling price. In CGE models based on the cost function approach, a unit cost function is formulated, involving the selling price of the domestic good and the price of imported goods, which is taken as an average over countries of origin. By applying Shephard's lemma, total demand for domestically produced goods and for imported goods is derived. In addition, a domestic supplier has to arbitrate between supplying on the domestic market and exporting. These supply functions are derived from the producer's decision on the profit-maximizing mix of goods subject to a constant elasticity of transformation frontier (CET). CGE models based on the dual approach employ a CET revenue function and derive supply functions from Hotelling's lemma (for example GEM-E3). Thus the Armington equations clear the trade-offs between domestic production and imports, as well as between exports and production for the domestic market.

If imports are further allocated by country of origin (as in the GEM-E3 model), the unit cost formulation is used again. To obtain a trade matrix with import demand functions by good and place of production, a CES import unit cost function can be specified:

$$pim_c = \left[\sum_{j=1}^{C+1} \gamma_j \cdot pim_j^{1-\sigma} \right]^{\frac{1}{1-\sigma}}, \qquad c = 1,2, \ldots, C$$

where pim_j is the price of imports by country j. There are C EU member countries and $C+1$ is the rest of the world. All import prices are expressed in ECU (or euro). As there are import taxes and duties (t_j), it is $pim_j = (1+t_j) \cdot p_j$, where p_j is the price of the good in question in country j. Therefore prices in the EU member states and in the rest of the world (exogenous) determine the import price faced by country c. If a cost-minimizing composition of the import aggregate im_c is the objective of the importing country, then Shephard's lemma can be applied to the cost function in (69.10), which yields the composition:

$$\frac{im_{j,c}}{im_c} = \gamma_j \left(\frac{pim_c}{pim_j} \right)^\sigma, \qquad j = 1, \ldots, C+1$$

where $im_{j,c}$ is import by country c from country j. This approach permits us to fill a trade-flow matrix where, for each commodity considered, the column sums yield the total import of a country and the sum of the row elements yields total export demand. The supplying countries may gain or lose market shares according to their price-setting behaviour.

7. Dynamics and the closure rules

If a model is not based on an explicit intertemporal optimization framework, the system of equations is overdetermined and one of the constraints of the model must be relaxed in order to find a solution (see Dewatripont and Michel, 1987). This requires us to choose a closure rule. Since the closure of a CGE model determines its behaviour, it is a key element and its choice is crucial to the model. The problem is that alternative approaches will almost certainly give different welfare outcomes. The choice of a closure rule follows from the impossibility of guaranteeing the *ex post* identity between investment and savings, although all markets are in equilibrium. One closure could be to allow for unemployment. Most model builders use the identity of private gross domestic production from both the flow-of-cost approach and the flow-of-product approach, and choose a residual variable to close the model. Such a variable could be investment, the public budget or the balance of trade. Equivalently, this closure can be implemented by the addition of a new variable such as the interest rate entering consumption and investment schemes, or by an endogenous exchange rate.

The closure problem arises because of the dynamic nature of the economy, reflected in the possibility for the agents to save or dissave. It can be resolved through the introduction of wealth and expectation effects in a fully dynamic model, where the equilibrium of each period depends both on current stock variables and on expectations of future states of the economy. However, most multi-period CGE models are typically a sequence of static one-period solutions, which implies that intertemporal relative prices do not affect agents' behaviour. The common approach is to limit dynamics to accumulation mechanisms (for capital, population and wealth) (for example, GREEN, GEM-E3). More complete approaches incorporate forward-looking dynamics, divided into models that implement forward-looking expectation (rational or not) and those that assume full perfect foresight. The latter calculate simultaneous solutions for several time periods and take the form of intertemporal optimization pioneered by Jorgenson and Wilcoxen (1990b). In these models current decision making is based on the future path of prices, that is, it is no longer feasable to solve recursively through time.[14] In such models the requirements for actions in a future period (for example global warming) will alter the nature of the environmental policy before the requirements come into effect. In models with perfect foresight the cost estimates of an environmental policy should be lower than for the same model with no foresight because there will be no early, and hence costly, retirement of the capital stock.

8. Global or multiregional models

Most effort to study energy–economy–environment interactions using multiregional models has been made with respect to global warming. Examples in this field are the Nordhaus models DICE (Nordhaus, 1992), the Global 2100 model of Manne and Richels (1990, 1992), the MERGE model of Manne et al. (1995), the OECD model GREEN of Burniaux et al. (1992), the model G-cubed of McKibbin and Wilcoxen (1992a, 1992b), the LEAN model by Welsch and Hoster (1995), and the EU model GEM-E3 (Capros et al., 1996). Since space does not permit describing all the features of these models, I shall sketch only four of them.[15]

The GREEN model is a recursive-dynamic global CGE model and has been developed to assess the economic impacts of imposing limits on carbon dioxide emissions. The global economic activity is divided into 12 regions and the model has been used to analyse the impact of emission constraints in the OECD member countries, of global agreements, and of tradable permits. The Global 2100 model divides the world into five major geopolitical groups: (i) the US, (ii) other OECD countries, (iii) the former Soviet Union, (iv) China, and (v) the rest of the world. Within each region, the analysis is based on the ETA-MACRO approach, a tool to integrate long-term supply and demand projections (Manne and Richels, 1992). ETA is a process model for energy technology assessment and MACRO is based on a macroeconomic production function. The LEAN-TCM4

(LEAN – Low Emission Assessment eNgine) is a multi-country CGE model to simulate macroeconomic impacts of different carbon dioxide reduction strategies in the EU. TCM4 is a two-country model consisting of West Germany and the rest of the EU. It is a recursive-dynamic, 14-sector model with a time horizon up to 2020. The GEM-E3 model (Capros et al., 1996; Conrad and Schmidt 1997a, 1997b) features a disaggregated representation (11 industries) of 14 EU member-state economies linked by trade-flow matrices for each of the 11 goods considered. The model addresses problems of global warming and acidification. Emissions of pollutants CO_2, SO_2 and NO_x are differentiated by country, sector of origin, type of fuel, and by goods (producers' and consumers' durable goods, and non-durable goods). A variety of policy instruments is used to affect transboundary air pollution, deposition, additive (end-of-pipe) and integrated (substitution) abatement. The G-cubed model by McKibbin and Wilcoxen (1992a, 1992b) links the Jorgenson–Wilcoxen model for the US to a global dynamic CGE model. It is a world model with substantial regional disaggregation and sectoral detail and is intended to contribute to the current policy debate on global warming. Countries and regions are linked both temporally and intertemporally through trade and financial markets.

9. Exogenous variables

The response of an economy to changes in environmental regulation depends crucially on assumptions made for exogenous variables. One standard assumption is exogenous (neutral) technical change. Some models (GREEN, Manne and Richels) use exogenous projections of the rate of GDP growth instead of endogenizing it. Its size has a dominant impact on the economic cost of controlling CO_2 emissions, for instance. The costs in terms of economic growth of a carbon policy is low if the CO_2 target is not very restrictive under an assumed small growth in GDP. Countries with stagnant growth are more likely to keep CO_2 emission targets without a CO_2 tax than countries with high growth in GDP.

Of importance for welfare analysis also is the price of crude oil, which is exogenous in most models. In Glomsrod et al. the petroleum sellers' prices are expected to fall. The explanation is that a reduction in CO_2 emissions by a large coalition will result in a reduction in the demand for fuel imports. If the coalition (EU or OECD) is a large net importer of fossil fuels, this will exert downward pressure on world fossil fuel prices. The improvement in the coalition's terms of trade may offset any welfare losses caused by reduced competitiveness in its energy-intensive industries (Pezzey, 1992).

An exogenous transition from carbon-based to carbon-free backstop technologies is also an assumption made in CGE model analyses. In GREEN, each of the four primary sources of energy – coal, oil, natural gas and electricity – can be replaced at some future date by alternative technologies – called 'backstop'. Of course, those assumptions dominate the results from a simulation. Since GREEN runs over the 1985–2050 period, backstop technologies might become available at the end of this period.

Assumptions made for exogenous variables are the main reason why calculated costs and benefits of environmental regulation differ even under the same air pollution target.

10.   Environmental policy instruments and measures of welfare change

Measures to internalize negative externalities are taxes, subsidies or voluntary agreements by the polluters. Other regulation measures are standards or a ban on the polluting product or process. Environmental policy instruments should aim at emissions and not at input or output quantities, and the cost components (the cost of the instrument and abatement costs) should be added to the input prices a firm or a household is facing. The policy instrument will then exert an abatement effect, a substitution effect and an output effect. Most models evaluate the energy-related emissions CO_2, NO_x and SO_2. The emissions are then used to calculate pollutant concentrations or deposition, taking into account the transportation (between countries). Only a few CGE models (for example the GEM-E3 model) compute the damage generated by the concentration/deposition of pollutants.

Although most countries use technical standards to curb SO_2 and NO_x emissions, modelling the effect of market-based instruments like taxes or permits is very popular among CGE modellers because they favour allocation through relative prices. Standards can be imposed on the level of countries, industries and durable goods (that is, cars, heating systems or electrical appliances). They can be based on technical restrictions concerning the concentration of a pollutant in the flue gas of a combustion process or a limit on gasoline consumption for cars (such as 6 litres per 100 km or 10 litres per 100 km for the fleet of a car producer). Standards affect the technology and hence the cost of production. Information on abatement costs per industry and on the cost of regulation using standards is required.[16] A tax rate can be set exogenously and its impact on the environment is endogenous, or a certain emission limit is set by the policy maker and the model determines the tax to achieve it. The latter approach makes it possible to check whether an ambitious goal (for example, a reduction of CO_2 emission by 20 per cent within 10 years) can be reached by a realistic size of a carbon tax rate. When permits for air pollutants are introduced, then the supply of permits is exogenous and the endogenous permit price equilibrates demand and the fixed supply. The permit design varies from undifferentiated emission permits to regionally differentiated ambient discharge permits. GEM-E3, for example, considers the source and the sink of an emission geographically, that is, on a country level. Whereas for taxes the recycling of revenues is an important issue, this is not the case for permits because the initial endowment is based on the grandfathering principle and not on auctioning the permits.

Finally, CGE models are useful in studying the effect of an ecological tax reform. A wide range of fiscal instruments could be designed to support other policy goals such as employment, investment or technological innovation. Such a reform could include a shift of the tax burden from labour and/or capital to energy and/or environment. The objective of this 'double dividend' policy is to raise revenue by environmental taxes (improvement of environment is the first dividend) and use the money to reduce existing tax distortions (reduction in labour taxes with higher employment as the second dividend). If the revenue is used to replace or reduce existing taxes, for example on labour or capital, that impose larger deadweight losses on the economy, national income can be increased. If the revenue is used to reduce taxes, for example on consumption, that impose smaller losses on the economy, national income would be reduced. Since a tax reform requires a large new revenue source, such as a carbon tax, climate change mitigation is one of the limited number of options for realizing the tax reform benefits. All policy instruments can be introduced under different institutional settings. There can be a unilateral action by one country to reduce CO_2 by 10 per cent, or a non-coordinated policy where each country reduces CO_2 by 10 per cent, or a coordinated policy with an EU-wide or OECD-wide reduction of 10 per cent under a uniform CO_2 tax rate or permit market.

In principle, the economic cost of an environmental policy action should be estimated by comparing the welfare of society according to whether the action is implemented or not. However, attempting to measure social welfare raises many difficulties. It involves ethical and policy judgements about the weight given to the welfare of different individuals and generations. Some economists feel that welfare should depend on the distribution of income, and all economists believe that an additional dollar of income spent on the protection of the environment decreases welfare more for a poor person than for a rich person. Finally, for global problems such as climate change, global social welfare should be measured instead of national welfare. Those difficulties associated with the concept of social welfare explain why most CGE models use income or output of the society instead. A few models try to estimate the welfare costs of environmental policies by using the measure of consumer surplus, which considers the costs to consumers of a change in relative prices in a given context. Theoretically more advanced is Hicks's measure of equivalent variation

(EV). The *EV* is based on the (intertemporal) utility-maximization problem and derives money-metric utility using an expenditure function *e*. In period *t*, *EV* is:

$$EV_t = e(p_t^0, u_t^1) - e(p_t^0, u_t^0)$$

EV gives the change in expenditure at base prices p^0 that would be equivalent to the policy implied change in utility. If $EV < 0$, welfare after the policy measure is lower than in the base case. The consumer is willing to pay the maximum amount *EV* at the fixed budget level $e^0 = e(p^0, u^0)$ to avoid the decline of utility from u^0 to u^1. Similarly, if $EV > 0$, the consumer would be willing to pay the maximum amount *EV* to see the change in environmental policy implemented. Finally, despite some attempts to adjust GDP to account for effects such as deterioration of the environment, these adjustments have not yet been incorporated into CGE models.

Since environmental policies are generally aimed at preventing further environmental damage or improving environmental quality, an analysis of the costs of environmental policy emphasizes only the cost but not the benefit side. Of interest is the relation between the costs and the benefits caused by the policy measure in question. Due to the lack of data and of sufficient understanding of the mechanisms by which environmental degradation affects the economy, there are only a few attempts to incorporate the benefits of environmental policies in CGE models. Some models (for example Ballard and Medema, 1993 or GEM-E3) compute environmental damages, but there is no feedback from them to the economy. Experiments on feedback mechanisms of externalities on economic activities and consumer preferences have started. There is a feedback on health with a direct effect of health on the utility of the consumer and an indirect effect through health expenditure. Another impact of externalities is on production efficiency, because a producer–producer externality affects the cost of production of a firm located close by or downstream. Since all non-greenhouse gas components create negative externalities on consumers, producers, structures and vegetation, their reduction under a CO_2 policy will reduce the cost of this policy if lower emissions of other components and their reduced negative externalities are included (see Häkonsen and Mathiesen, 1997).

11. Studies conducted with CGE models

It is impossible to mention all the numerous studies which have tried to identify and to estimate the potential benefits and costs from options designed to improve the quality of the environment. Most studies are intended for quantitative comparative statics analysis of the impact of non-marginal changes in conditions which are exogenous to the modelled economy. The environmental policy issues, pursued in most of the studies, are the following ones:

1. Assessment of the impact of environmental regulations on growth (Jorgenson and Wilcoxen, 1990b). The base case of their model implicitly includes environmental regulation in the 1970s and early 1980s, since it is based on historical data. Thus, to determine the effect of regulation on the performance of the US economy, they conduct counterfactual simulations in which regulation is removed.

2. The increase in world petroleum prices during the 1970s resulted in substantial energy conservation and stabilized carbon dioxide emissions for a period of 15 years between 1972 and 1987. In order to analyse the historical experiment that resulted from higher world petroleum prices since 1973, Jorgenson and Wilcoxen (1993) have simulated the growth of the US economy with and without these price increases. By comparing the results of each of these simulations to their base case (in which world oil prices follow their historical course), they can assess the cost of stabilizing carbon dioxide emissions through high oil prices, for example, by a carbon tax.

3. An important question is the institutional framework of an environmental policy. For instance, the cost-effectiveness of a policy can be analysed under a coordinated policy versus non-coordinated, country-specific policies. Curbing CO_2 emissions by introducing coordinated or non-coordinated pollution permit systems in the European Union is such a topic pursued in studies (see Conrad and Schmidt, 1997a). The main interest of the analysis lay on the national and EU-wide economic impacts of such a policy. In the non-coordinated case each country reduces 10 per cent of its baseline CO_2 emissions: the permits are traded between sectors and households within the country. In the coordinated policy, the permits are traded between all European sectors and households to realize a 10 per cent reduction of the EU's total CO_2 emissions.

4. Curbing SO_2 emissions by introducing coordinated or non-coordinated pollution permit systems is also of interest. An EU-wide permit system for the electricity sector that is operational and in line with the requirements of the Oslo Protocol (convention of Transboundary Air Pollution) was introduced and national and EU-wide economic impacts were studied.

5. The feasibility of a double dividend for environment and employment is an interesting topic for a CGE analysis. The open question is whether the internalization of environmental externalities can be beneficial for

other policy areas as well since the revenues from pollution taxes could be used to cut other distortionary taxes. The non-environmental dividend can be defined in various ways. Given the important unemployment problems, the European Union has given priority to the analysis of distortionary circumstances in the labour market that might explain persisting unemployment. The scenarios that have been conducted were a coordinated or non-coordinated double dividend analysis of a CO_2 tax to reduce 10 per cent of the EU's CO_2 emissions (see Capros et al., 1996; Conrad and Schmidt, 1997a). The prospect for a double dividend of environmental taxation in a small open economy from introducing a unilaterial carbon tax have been investigated by Böhringer et al. (1997b) and by Proost and van Regemorter (1995). Welsch (1996) uses a CGE model of the aggregated European Community member states to test the double dividend hypothesis. In Jorgenson and Wilcoxen (1992) increased CO_2 taxation increases welfare both with labour tax and capital tax redistribution.

6. A different CGE application is to measure the inefficiency of the present regulation by air quality standards by introducing taxes which guarantee the same air quality (Conrad and Schröder, 1993). To measure the cost-effectiveness of such a change in environmental policy, first a base run is produced founded on present emission standards, given by the air quality Acts. These emission standards can be converted into permitted emissions per unit of input. Emissions considered are SO_2, NO_X and particulates. Simulations then show the economic impact of an efficient environmental policy in which all industries are confronted with uniform emission tax rates which have been computed so as to guarantee exactly the air quality under the base run with standards. This minimizes abatement costs given the quality of air from the base run.

7. CGE models have been used to project the effects of trade liberalization on the economy and the environment, concentrating especially on the issues of fertilizers and transportation or on tropical deforestation. Beghin et al. (1995) combine environmental and trade policies for Mexico and show how they interact. Persson and Munasinghe (1995) simulate the effect of government policies on Costa Rican forests to reduce deforestation. As the forest is a carbon sink if it absorbs more carbon than it releases through felling and natural decay, implementing the forests as carbon sinks in a CGE model is another topic. Forests are multiple–use assets because if a forest is used as a carbon sink, it cannot be used as a raw material in the pulp and paper industry. CGE models can evaluate the efficient use of forests as an intertemporal allocation problem (Pohjola, 1996).

8. CGE models for developing economies can be used to analyse the links between growth and environment and between trade policies and the environment. Of special interest are efficient economic policies which can readily be implemented in the context of a developing country. At the OECD Development Centre CGE models for three Latin America economies (Chile, Costa Rica and Mexico), and three Asia Pacific economies (China, Indonesia and Vietnam) have been developed to shed light on the importance of these links, or on the main mechanisms through which changes in trade regimes have impact on the environment (Dessus et al., 1996). In international trade, for example, countries with less stringent environmental regulations may have comparative advantage in dirty industries. This leads to the export of 'pollution services' embodied in goods made with technologies that do not meet the environmental standards of the importing countries. Using a CGE model for Indonesia, Lee and Roland–Holst (1997) show that a combination of trade liberalization and a cost-effective tax policy would not only raise the country's welfare, but could also improve the environmental quality.
9. Issues such as agricultural chemicals, food safety and water quality have brought agriculture and non-point source pollution to the forefront of environmental attention. Significant crop yield increases over the last several decades have been associated with the adoption of pesticides and fertilizers. At the same time, agriculture chemicals may impose economic costs on the environment and human health. Using a CGE model of the US economy, Hrubovcak et al. (1990) weigh such trade-offs for assessing the benefits and costs from integrating agricultural, environmental and food safety policies.

A deficiency of almost all working CGE models is that they focus on industry-based type pollution and ignore other significant environmental issues such as deforestation, soil degradation and erosion, or solid waste and its disposal.

12. Conclusion and future research
Although the general equilibrium framework is the common methodology, there is a variety of economic theories to deal with adjustments of quasi-fixed inputs, with technical change, with imperfect competition, with consumer durables and their user cost, with modelling abatement costs, with dynamics, and with the closure rule. For that reason, empirical results derived from CGE exercises are sometimes difficult to compare or to understand. However, country-specific features and differences in the sectoral structure can often explain different outcomes in spite of the same

methodology used. For instance, the share of hydropower, nuclear power, and coal-fired power plants to produce a country's electricity influences the impact from a carbon tax on the economy. Or, if a country does not produce but only imports cars, then a gasoline tax will not hurt the domestic economy.

The strengths of CGE models are their microeconomic foundation and the disaggregated nature of the analysis. The weaknesses are the deterministic calibration of the parameters, which excludes statistical tests of their quality, the limited usefulness of a comparison between two equilibria in the long run, and the impossibility of using these growth or trend models to stabilize cyclical environmental problems. Furthermore, since there are disequilibria in some markets of an economy, for instance the labour market, standard models of the CGE type have features that make their use questionable. These models do not allow for consideration of change in the level of unemployment or in the utilization of capacities, which are often the short-run consequences of sudden changes in the magnitude of environmental policy instruments. In such cases some CGE model builders modify their approach by allowing explicitly for partial disequilibria in the labour and capital markets (under- or over-utilization of the primary factors of production).

Future research in the area of environmental CGE modelling will be directed towards a more detailed modelling of premature retirement of extant capital and of future technologies. What is required is a better linkage from changes in relative prices to the installation of now profitable, because more energy-efficient, technologies. Instead of smooth transitions, discrete changes might occur. If substitution is the only way to respond to emission taxes because the technology of public utilities is fixed, than tax rates will turn out to be very high. In reality, utilities will then invest in fluid-bed combustion in coal-fired power plants which causes much less emission of SO_2 and NO_x than conventional power plants. Since government proposals to reduce greenhouse gas emissions do not rest on the effect of substitution but on the support from technical change, CGE models have to prove to be superior to simple pocket-calculator forecasts based on future technologies.

Although CGE models cannot be used for economic forecasts, they are indispensable for ranking alternative policy measures. Since these models are based on assumptions concerning the economic development (elasticity of substitution, technical change, the magnitude of exogenous variables), it would be misleading to base policy decisions on a specific numerical result. Rather, CGE models should be used to understand the reasons for particular results, to better frame the policy decisions, and to support the appropriate policy judgements. Using general equilibrium theory, economists can very often get a good idea of the welfare effect and of the qualitative results from a change in a given policy instrument. However, using theory alone, no one is able to evaluate alternative environmental policy approaches and then to rank them according to their welfare effects.

Notes

1. For surveys on the development of CGE modelling see Shoven and Whalley (1984), Robinson (1989) or Bergman (1990a).
2. In prinicple it doesn't matter which approach is used if the equilibrium is unique. A special advantage of the dual is the reduced computational complexity for solving them (a Gauß–Seidel algorithm will do it).
3. I shall also not discuss theoretical issues such as uniqueness of a general equilibrium or externalities as a source of non-convexity. Under concavity–convexity assumptions, Pareto optimality in a basic general equilibrium model with externalities exists and is unique (see Baumol and Oates, 1988, ch. 4). The existence of a competitive solution that is consistent with any particular Pareto optimum has been explored in an extensive literature. The question is, however, whether in GE models calibrated on real-world data, non-existence is a serious problem. A proof of existence of, and computational procedure for finding, a general equilibrium with taxes was derived by Shoven and Whalley (1973). A more serious problem is that any detrimental externalities can produce non-convexity. This breakdown in the concavity–convexity conditions may result in several local optima so that prices may give the wrong signals – directing the economy away from the social optimum.
4. For an inclusion of adjustment costs see Conrad and Schröder (1991a).
5. Nested production functions of the CES type have been employed by Nordhaus (1992), Manne and Richels (1991), Piggot et al. (1991) and Capros et al. (1996).
6. The models by Glomsrod et al. (1992) or by Hazilla and Kopp (1990) endogenize fuel-specific technical change in a similar way, that is, as an incentive for substitution only.
7. A more formal presentation of the idea that the latest vintage, added to the aggregate capital stock, embodies innovation and technical improvement can be found in Conrad and Henseler-Unger (1986). The methodological approach is an integration of price-dependent input coefficients with input coefficients of the latest vintage, both derived from cost functions.
8. For a survey see Barro and Sala-í-Martin (1995).
9. See Jorgenson and Wilcoxen (1990a, 1990b) or Böhringer et al. (1997a).
10. For example, Conrad and Schröder (1991a, 1991b), Conrad and Schmidt (1997b).
11. See Carraro and Galeotti (1994) or Böhringer et al. (1997).
12. Conrad and Schröder (1991b) developed an integrated framework of consumer demand for 20 non-durable goods like food and services, and for three durable goods: cars, heating and electric appliances.
13. The same concept is used in the GEM-E3 model.
14. See Bovenberg and Goulder (1991) on introducing intertemporal features in CGE models.
15. For a more detailed summary of models for studying environmental policy effects, see Jorgenson and Wilcoxen (1993).
16. See, for example, Conrad and Schröder (1993); Jorgenson and Wilcoxen (1990a).

References

Armington, P.S. (1969), 'The geographic pattern of trade and the effect of price changes', IMF Staff Papers, **58**, 179–201.

Ballard, C.L. and S.G. Medema (1993), 'The marginal efficiency effects of taxes and subsidies in the presence of externalities – a CGE approach', *Journal of Public Economics*, **52**, 199–216.

Barro, R.J. and X. Sala-i-Martin (1995), *Economic Growth*, New York: McGraw Hill.

Baumol, W.J. and W.E. Oates (1998), *The Theory of Environmental Policy*, 2nd edn, 1988, Cambridge, UK: Cambridge University Press.

Beghin, J., D. Roland-Holst and D. van der Mensbrugghe (1995), 'Trade liberalization and the environment in the Pacific Basin: coordinated approaches to Mexican trade and environment policy', *American Journal of Agricultural Economics*, **77**, 778–85.

Bergman, L. (1990a), 'The development of computable general equilibrium modeling', in L. Bergman, D.W. Jorgenson and E. Zalai (eds), *General Equilibrium Modeling and Economic Policy Analysis*, Oxford: Basil Blackwell, pp. 3–30.

Bergman, L. (1990), 'Energy and environmental constraints on growth: a CGE modeling approach', *Journal of Policy Modeling*, **12** (4), 671–91.

Bergman, L. (1991), 'General equilibrium effects of environmental policy: a CGE modeling approach', *Environmental and Resource Economics*, **1**, 67–85.

Böhringer, C. and T.F. Rutherford (1997a), 'Carbon taxes with exemptions in an open economy: a general equilibrium analysis of the German tax initiative', *Journal of Environmental and Economic Management*, **32**, 189–203.

Böhringer, C., A. Pahlke and T.F. Rutherford (1997b), 'Enviromental tax reforms and the prospect for a double dividend – an intertemporal general equilibrium analysis for Germany', paper presented at the EAERE Conference, Tilburg.

Bovenberg, A.L. and L.H. Goulder (1991), 'Introducing intertemporal and open economy features in applied general equilibrium models', in F.J.H. Don et al. (eds), *Applied General Equilibrium Modelling*, Dordrecht: Kluwer, pp. 47–64.

Burniaux, J.-M., J.P. Martin, G. Nicoletti and J.O. Martins (1992), 'The cost of reducing CO_2 emissions: evidence from GREEN', OECD Working Paper No. 115.

Capros, P. and G. Atsaves (1992), *Model Solver: User's Manual*, Athens: NTUA.

Capros, P., G. Georgakopoulos, S. Zografakis, S. Proost, D. van Regemorter, K. Conrad, T. Schmidt, Y. Smeers (1996), 'Double dividend analysis: first results of a general equilibrium model (GEM-E3) linking the EU-12 countries', in C. Carraro et al. (eds), *Environmental Fiscal Reform and Unemployment*, Dordrecht: Kluwer, pp. 193–227.

Carraro, C. and M. Galeotti (1994), 'WARM (World Assessment of Resource Management)', Technical Report, GRETA, Venice.

Conrad, K. and I. Henseler-Unger (1986), 'Applied general equilibrium modeling for longterm energy policy in the Fed. Rep. of Germany', *Journal of Policy Modeling*, **8** (4), 531–49.

Conrad, K. and T. Schmidt (1997a), 'National economic impacts of an EU environmental policy – an AGE analysis' in S. Proost and J. Braden (eds), *Climate Change, Transport and Environmental Policy*, Cheltenham, UK and Lyme, US: Edward Elgar.

Conrad, K. and T. Schmidt (1997b), 'The international policy dimension of sustainability – the effect of policy harmonization within the EU using the GEM-E3 model', in J. van den Bergh and M.W. Hofkes (eds), *Economic Modeling of Sustainable Development*, Dordrecht: Kluwer.

Conrad, K. and M. Schröder (1991a), 'An evaluation of taxes on air pollutants emissions: an AGE-approach', *Schweizerische Zeitschrift für Volkswirtschaft und Statistik*, **127**, 199–224.

Conrad, K. and M. Schröder (1991b), 'The control of CO_2-emissions and its economic impact', *Environmental and Resource Economics*, **1**, 289–312.

Conrad, K. and M. Schröder (1991c), 'Demand for durable and non-durable goods, environmental policy and consumer welfare', *Journal of Applied Econometrics*, **6**, 271–86.

Conrad, K. and M. Schröder (1993), 'Environmental policy instruments using general equilibrium models', *Journal of Policy Modeling*, **15**, 521–43.

Conrad, K. and J. Wang (1994), 'Tradable CO_2 emission permits vs. CO_2 taxes: economic impacts and costs by industry – a CGE analysis for West-Germany', in J.-Fr. Hake et al. (eds), *Advances in Systems Analysis: Modeling Energy Related Emissions in a National and Global Level*, Bd. 15, Jülich.

Dessus, S., D. Roland-Host and D. van der Mensbrugge (1996), 'General equilibrium modelling of trade and the environment', Technical Paper no. 116, OECD Development Centre, Paris, September.

Dewatripont, M. and G. Michel (1987), 'On closure rules, homogeneity and dynamics in AGE models', *Journal of Development Economics*, **26**, 65–76.

Glomsrod, S., H. Vennemo and T. Johnsen (1992), 'Stabilization of emissions of CO_2: a computable general equilibrium assessment', *Scandinavian Journal of Economics*, **94** (1), 53–69.

Håkonsen, L. and L. Mathiesen (1997), 'CO_2-stabilization may be a "no-regrets" policy: a general equilibrium analysis of the Norwegian economy', *Environmental and Resource Economics*, **9** (2), 171–98.

Harris, R. (1984), 'AGE analysis of small open economies with scale economies and imperfect competition', *American Economic Review*, **74**, 1016–32.

Hazilla, M. and R.J. Kopp, (1990), 'Social cost of environmental quality regulations: a general equilibrium analysis', *Journal of Political Economy*, **98** (4), 853–73.

Hrubovcak, J., M. Le Blanc and J. Miranowski (1990), 'Limitations in evaluating environmental and agricultural policy coordination benefits', *American Economic Review*, **80**, 208–12.

Hudson, E.A. and D.W. Jorgenson (1974), 'U.S. energy policy and economic growth, 1975–2000', *Bell Journal of Economic and Management Science*, **5**, 461–514.

Johansen, L. (1979), *A Multisectoral Study of Economic Growth*, Amsterdam: North-Holland.

Jorgenson, D.W. and P.J. Wilcoxen (1990a), 'Environmental regulation and U.S. economic growth', *The Rand Journal of Economics*, **21**, 314–40.

Jorgenson, D.W. and P.J. Wilcoxen (1990b), 'Intertemporal general equilibrium modeling of U.S. environmental regulation', *Journal of Policy Modeling*, **12**, 715–44.

Jorgenson, D.W. and P.J. Wilcoxen (1992), 'Reducing U.S. carbon dioxide emissions: the cost of different goals', in J.R. Moroney (ed.), *Energy, Growth, and Environment: Advances in the Economics of Energy and Resources*, **7**, Greenwich, CT: JAI Press, pp. 125–58.

Jorgenson, D.W. and P.J. Wilcoxen (1993), 'Energy, the environment and economic growth', in A.V. Kneese and J.L. Sweeney (eds), *Handbook of Natural Resources and Energy Economics*, vol. 3, ch. 27, Amsterdam: North-Holland.

Lee, H. and D. Roland-Holst (1997), 'The environment and welfare implications of trade and tax policy', *Journal of Development Economics*, **52**, 65–82.

Manne, A.S. and R.G. Richels (1990), 'CO_2 emission limits: an economic analysis for the USA', *The Energy Journal*, **11** (2), 51–74.

Manne, A.S. and R.G. Richels (1991), 'Global CO_2 emission reductions – the impact of rising energy costs', *The Energy Journal*, **12**, 87–108.

Manne, A.S. and R.G. Richels (1992), *Buying Greenhouse Insurance – The Economic Costs of CO_2 Emission Limits*, Cambridge, MA: MIT Press.

Manne, A.S., R. Mendelsohn and R. Richels (1995), 'MERGE: a model for evaluating regional and global effects of GHG reduction policies', *Energy Policy*, **23**, 17–34.

McKibbin, W.J. and P.J. Wilcoxen (1992a), 'The global costs of policies to reduce greenhouse gas emissions', Brookings Discussion Papers, no. 97, The Brookings Institution, October.

McKibbin, W.J. and P.J. Wilcoxen (1992b), 'G-cubed: a dynamic multi-sector general equilibrium model of the global economy (quantifying the costs of curbing CO_2 emissions)', Brookings Discussion Papers, no. 98, Brookings Institution, November.

Mercenier, J., 'Nonuniqueness of solutions in applied general equilibrium models with scale economies and imperfect competition', *Economic Theory*, **6**, 161–77.

Nordhaus, W.D. (1991), 'The cost of slowing climate change: a survey', *The Energy Journal*, **12**, 37–65.

Nordhaus, W.D. (1992), 'The DICE model: background and structure of a dynamic integrated climate – economy model of the economics of global warming', Cowles Foundation Discussion Paper no. 1009, New Haven, Yale University.

Persson, A. and M. Munasinghe (1995), 'Natural resource management and economywide policies in Costa Rica: a computable general equilibrium (CGE) modeling approach', *The World Bank Economic Review*, **9** (2), 259–85.

Pohjola, J. (1996), 'Integrating forests as carbon sinks in a CGE framework: a preliminary analysis for Finland', paper presented at the Meeting of the European Association of Environment and Resource Economists, Lisbon.

Pezzey, J. (1992), 'An analysis of unilateral CO_2 control in the European Community and OECD', *The Energy Journal*, **13** (3), 159–71.

Piggot, J., J. Whalley and R. Wigle (1991), 'How large are the incentives to join sub-global carbon reduction initiatives?', mimeo.

Proost, S. and D. van Regemorter (1995), 'The double dividend and the role of inequality aversion and macroeconomic regimes', *International Tax and Public Finance*, **2**, 207–19.

Robinson, S. (1989), 'Multisectoral models', in H. Chenery and T.N. Srinivasan (eds), *Handbook of Development Economics*, vol. 2, Amsterdam: Elsevier Science Publishers, pp. 885–947.

Rutherford, T. (1994), 'Applied general equilibrium modeling with MPSGE as a GAMS subsystem', mimeo, Department of Economics, University of Colorado.

Shoven, J.B. and J. Whalley (1973), 'General equilibrium with taxes: a computation procedure and an existence proof', *Review of Economics Studies*, **60**, 475–90.

Shoven, J.B. and J. Whalley (1984), 'AGE models of taxation and international trade: an introduction and survey', *Journal of Economic Literature*, **22**, 1007–51.

Stephan, G., R. van Nieuwkoop and T. Wiedmer (1992), 'Social incidence and economic costs of carbon limits. A computable general equilibrium analysis for Switzerland', *Environmental and Resource Economics*, **2**, 569–91.

Welsch, H. (1996), 'Recycling of carbon/energy taxes and the labor market – a general equilibrium analysis for the European Community', *Environmental and Resource Economics*, **8**, 141–55.

Welsch, H. and F. Hoster (1995), 'A general equilibrium analysis of European carbon/energy taxation: model structure and macroeconomic results', *Zeitschrift für Wirtschafts- und Sozialwissenschaften*, **115**, 275–303.

Willenbockel, D. (1994), 'Applied general equilibrium modeling – imperfect competition and European integration', Chichester: Wiley.

70 Game theory in environmental policy analysis

Henk Folmer and Aart de Zeeuw

1. Introduction

Game theory deals with the strategic analysis of multi-agent decision problems. Such problems frequently occur in environmental economics. In the case of transboundary pollution a country's decision whether or not to join an international agreement or to comply with a joint environmental policy depends on the decisions of the other countries involved. The formulation and implementation of domestic environmental policy by the government involves the (expected) decisions of the agents subject to the envisaged policy. Firms, countries and regions compete using environmental issues as strategic instruments.

As can be easily recognized in the above examples, a game is made up of a set of players, a set of strategies available to each player whenever called upon to make a decision, and the payoff that results to each player for each combination of strategies. The payoffs are based on the assumption that the players have a von Neumann–Morgenstern ranking over the set of possible outcomes of the game. The important characteristics of a game are:

- The order of play. If all players make their decisions one after another, we speak of a sequential-move game. Alternatively, if the players have to make their decisions simultaneously, then the game is called a simultaneous-move game.
- The information available to any player at any point during the game. Most common in economics, including environmental economics, are games of perfect recall. This means that it is assumed that no player forgets any information he once knew and all players recall the actions they previously took. Moreover, if every player at every moment he has to conclude a decision knows the actions taken previously by every other player, then the game is one of perfect information.

Two branches can be distinguished: non-cooperative and cooperative game theory. The former focuses on the individual player who maximizes a net benefit function subject to net-benefit-maximizing behaviour of the other players under various technical and economical constraints. Under the assumption of rational behaviour of the players, this branch analyses the plausibility of the possible outcomes of the game. It is typical to resort to Nash equilibrium analysis. A Nash equilibrium is a set of strategies, one for each player, such that for each player his/her strategy is the best response to the strategies specified for the other players. This implies that no player has a unilaterial incentive to deviate from his/her strategy. Most games have a large number of Nash equilibria. Economic analyses that employ game theory usually make assumptions that lead to a unique Nash equilibrium. Moreover, several refinements of the concept have been developed that restrict the possible set of equilibria (van Damme, 1983).

In cooperative game theory, which is less common in economic analysis, including environmental economics, the unit of analysis is the coalition of players and in particular its characteristic function, that is, the total of net benefits that the coalition can achieve for itself. Cooperative games are characterized by the fact that the players can enter into enforceable agreements with each other. In non-cooperative games players cannot do so. Since this latter situation is more common in economics, including environmental economics, non-cooperative game theory has become more popular than cooperative game theory in these areas.

A very important distinction relates to static and dynamic games. In a static setting a game is played only once, whereas dynamic games relate to situations in which strategic interaction over time takes place. In the real world, most problems in environmental economics call for a dynamic approach. In spite of that, static games are used as a first approach. Moreover, static games are the building blocks of dynamic games. For elementary introductions to game theory we refer to Bierman and Fernandes (1995) and Gibbons (1992). Advanced textbooks are Fudenberg and Tirole (1992) and van Damme (1983).

Game theory has turned out to be extremely successful in modelling a variety of typical problems in environmental economics such as property rights and externalities, bargaining, prisoners' dilemma situations, free-rider behaviour and moral hazard. This chapter cannot give a full survey of applications of game theory in environmental economics. We shall only discuss some major areas of application.

In Section 2 some aspects regarding the application of game theory to international environmental economics will be described. Section 3 deals with game-theoretic analysis in the context of the interaction between a regulator and regulated agents, and in Section 4 attention will be paid to competition using environmental issues as a strategic instrument. Conclusions follow in Section 5.

2. International environmental problems

Typical for physical international environmental problems is the existence of externalities in the form of pollutants generated in one country and deposited in another. An essential feature of international environmental problems is the absence of an institution with the international jurisdiction to enforce agreements. This implies that any such agreement must be voluntary and multilateral. Given the environmental interdependencies and institutional setting, non-cooperative game-theoretic models have a strong appeal (see, among others, Mäler, 1989; Barrett, 1990; Hoel, 1992b). Although static models are useful, dynamic models are more appropriate because of the dynamic nature of most environmental problems: the stock of pollutants usually matters more than the flow. These types of models are usually referred to as differential games (for example, van der Ploeg and de Zeeuw, 1992; Kaitala et al., 1992; Hoel, 1992a). An analytical trade-off occurs here. Dynamic games with a stock are technically difficult to solve. Moreover, there exist several unsolved technical problems (see below). On the other hand, important environmental problems such as global warming and acid rain require a stock analysis.

One of the main conclusions of the literature above is that there may be substantial gains associated with efficient international cooperation: the social welfare under the cooperative solution is always equal or higher than under the non-cooperative outcome. However, cooperation may be difficult to achieve and sustain. In spite of their net overall gains, international environmental agreements are not necessarily preferred to the *status quo* by all countries because of free-rider behaviour. Chander and Tulkens (1992) and Barrett (1990), among others, show that the payoff of a cooperating country is usually smaller than the payoff of a free-rider. Game theory has proposed several solutions to this problem. The repeated-game literature provides the folk theorem (Fudenberg and Maskin, 1986), which states that the infinite repetition of an *n*-player static game has equilibria that sustain efficient outcomes (with payoffs that exceed the payoffs in a Nash equilibrium) if the discount rate is small enough. General results similar to the folk theorem for differential games have not yet been obtained. However, Dockner and van Long (1993) show that, for differential games, extension of the strategy spaces to non-linear Markov strategies can yield equilibria that sustain efficient outcomes. Barrett (1994) takes another angle on the problem and specifies stability conditions for international agreements both on the basis of cartel theory and renegotiation proofness in repeated game theory. The former theory relates to the analysis of the stability of a group of countries who have made an explicit agreement on environmental policy. The latter focuses on the question to what extent countries that have concluded an agreement may deviate and then propose abandoning the punishment equilibrium for another equilibrium in which all players are better off (Fudenberg and Tirole, 1992, ch. 5). He shows that agreements of a large number of countries can only be sustained if the benefits of cooperation are small and vice versa. This implies a paradox: when cooperation is possible, it does not matter, and when it matters, cooperation is not possible. This can be seen as follows. For a given number of countries the difference between the abatement levels for the cooperative and the non-cooperative outcomes depends on the ratio of the slopes of the marginal abatement cost and marginal abatement benefit curves. If the ratio is 'large', the cooperative approach will not call for large abatement levels because of the high costs and relatively small benefits involved. In this case the full cooperative approach will not lead to much additional abatement. Hence the discrepancy between the full cooperative and non-cooperative approaches will tend to be small. A similar result holds for a 'small' ratio. This case corresponds to very hazardous pollutants for which abatement yields large benefits at relatively low costs. In this situation countries will usually initiate substantial abatement programmes unilaterally.

It follows that the discrepancy between the full cooperative and non-cooperative abatement levels will tend to be large when the slopes of the marginal abatement cost and marginal abatement benefit curves do not differ very much. This applies to hazardous pollutants that are costly to abate and mildly innocuous pollutants that can be abated at low cost.

In spite of the obstacles to cooperation in the form of incentives to free-riding, small stable coalitions tend to emerge when the game is not a prisoners' dilemma but rather a chicken game (Carraro and Siniscalco, 1993). Moreover, in order to overcome the obstacles, side payments have been suggested (Mäler, 1989). This comes down to transfers from those who incur positive net benefits to those who incur negative net benefits in order to induce the latter to cooperate. Folmer et al. (1993) list several objections to the use of side payments. Therefore Folmer et al. (1993), Carraro and Siniscalco (1994), Folmer and van Mouche (1994), and Cesar and de Zeeuw (1996) suggest issue linkage as a possible alternative for the use of side payments. The possibility of linking issues derives from the fact that countries engaged in a given environmental problem are typically also engaged in several other areas of negotiation which enables them to exchange concessions in fields of relative strength (Krutilla, 1975; Folmer and Howe, 1991).

From the perspective of cooperative game theory side payments should not only yield individual rationality for all countries, but also a form of group rationality. Kaitala et al. (1995) present a transfer scheme with a core property in the sense that no group of countries has an incentive to choose another course of action. Gil and Folmer (1998) show that issue linkage may lead to a non-empty core in situations where the core for each problem separately is empty.

The research on international environmental problems has, with some exceptions, such as Mäler (1989), Kaitala et al. (1992, 1995) and Mäler and de Zeeuw (1998), been theoretical. A major prospect for future research is to analyse the benefits of cooperation and the potential for issue linkage empirically, especially in those situations where it has been difficult to conclude efficient international agreements.

Another important research field relates to modelling international environmental problems as (dynamic) games of incomplete information. Up to now games of complete information have strongly dominated the literature. In these games each player's payoff function is common knowledge to all the players. In most international environmental problems benefit and cost functions are, however, all but common knowledge.

3. The principal–agent approach to environmental policy

A vital aspect of environmental policy is its implementation and enforcement. Its ultimate goal is that firms and consumers comply with regulations and decrees: they should adopt technical standards and pay taxes, invest in environmentally friendly technology and phase out hazardous products.

Implementation and enforcement of environmental policy has been analysed in the context of a structure-of-agency relationship. Accordingly, this branch of game theory is usually referred to as principal–agency theory (see, amongst others, Laffont and Tirole, 1991). It focuses on the public policy obstacles caused by informational asymmetries and imperfect monitoring and designs incentive systems to cope with them.

In the principal–agent structure the principal, that is, the government, maximizes social welfare, including that of industry and consumers. Since they possess information the government needs, firms (that is, the agents) are *de facto* involved in the policy-making process. Since firms know that the information required by the government may negatively impact on them, they have an incentive to overestimate their abatement costs and underestimate their emissions. Therefore the government has to design an incentive system which aims at making firms issue true information.

Within this framework Lévêque and Nadaï (1995) analyse the conditions under which firms

- support environmental policy;
- hinder environmental policy intervention by making use of their obstructive power;
- take voluntary action under the threat of governmental intervention;
- cooperate with the government in defining environmental policies.

Güth and Pethig (1992) analyse a game between a firm and a regulatory agency. The firm considers illegally dumping waste but it does not know about the competence of the agency. It tries to find out by dumping a small amount of illegal waste to test the agency. The main purpose of the paper is to show the potential of advanced game theory with asymmetric information, in particular Harsanyi and Selten's equilibrium selection theory (van Damme, 1983).

Not only has principal–agency theory been applied to model public environmental policy making; it has also been used by, among others, Gabel and Sinclair-Desgagné (1995) to analyse systems of corporate incentives and controls in order to promote a firm's environmental performance. The firm's management is the principal who wants to improve its environmental performance. However, decisions that determine performance are concluded by employees (agents) who are motivated by self-interest. Moreover, a principal can only indirectly and imperfectly monitor the agents' performance. The incentives and control systems to reduce resource depletion and the risks of environmental accidents include the compensation system, monitoring and auditing of environmental objectives, internal pricing, horizontal task restructuring, centralization versus decentralization of decision making, corporate sanctions, corporate culture and human resource management.

Applications of game-theoretic notions can be expected to increase substantially in the area of the firm and the environment. For too long the firm has been viewed as a 'black box' in the environmental economics literature (Gabel and Sinclair-Desgagné, 1995). An active role of firms in the public policy-making process is to be expected. Moreover, the success of environmental policies as far as production is concerned also depends on the allocation decisions within firms. In both areas the principal–agent approach has proved to be a powerful analytical tool.

4. Competition
A major impetus to the development of game theory has been the modelling of strategic interaction among firms. Consequently, game theory has been extensively used to model competition among firms. Applications have focused strongly on traditional forms of competition, such as price and quantity setting. Recently, the game-theoretic approach has been used to model environmental management as a competitive strategy. For instance, Gabel (1995) uses game theory to model competition between Du Pont and ICI in the case of chlorofluorocarbons. Moreover, he includes in his analysis the role of these private firms in influencing public policy formulation. A second strand of research in this area relates to international trade and environmental degradation. The interaction between trade

and environmental policy has been sparked by trade liberalization (WTO, NAFTA) and economic integration (single European Market). The main research and policy problem relates to the question if and to what extent any gains from trade liberalization are outweighed by the damage done to the environment. When modelling strategic behaviour with government involvement, multi-stage games are usually required. At stages 1 and 2 governments choose environmental policy instruments and their levels, respectively. At stage 3 firms choose investments in R&D or plant location and at stage 4 they choose either prices or quantities.

In the literature on environmental issues as a strategic instrument of competition between countries or between regions, the theory of ecological dumping plays a central role. This theory has developed from the literature on the implications for trade policy of imperfectly competitive international markets (see, among others, Helpman and Krugman, 1989). The intuition is as follows. Imperfect competition allows producers to earn rents. This provides incentives for governments to try to shift those rents in favour of their domestic producers. Especially in those cases where conventional trade policies for achieving these objectives have been outlawed by the process of trade liberalization, less stringent environmental policies can give domestic producers a cost advantage on the international markets.

Governments can set their policies prior to the decisions by producers on quantity or prices. Therefore governments can try to manipulate the international markets in a way not available to their domestic producers. Ulph (1997) uses a three-stage game to analyse this kind of strategic behaviour. In stage 1 governments choose the form of their environmental policies and in stage 2 they choose the levels at which they set their instruments. Finally, in stage 3 producers choose output or price. Ulph shows that the intuition outlined above does not hold in general. More specifically, he analyses the conditions under which governments have incentives to set environmental policies that are too lax or too stringent.

Ecchia and Mariotti (1994), Ulph (1994) and Ulph and Ulph (1996) use game theory to address the Porter hypothesis that governments have an incentive to implement stringent environmental policy so as to encourage their producers to invest in environmentally friendly R&D in order to gain a long-term competitive advantage. He shows that the Porter hypothesis does not hold in general. The reason is that there are two opposing factors at work. First, raising environmental taxes may well discourage domestic R&D because the convexity of the cost curve implies that a higher emissions tax reduces the effect of a unit reduction in costs on profits. Second, the higher tax implies that a given amount of environmental R&D may lower the firm's costs and hence stimulate R&D. Hence there is ambiguity about the overall effect. It should be observed, however, that Porter makes historical observations.

Game-theoretic models have also been used to model the location of plants and the impacts on environmental policy in this context (see among others Rauscher, 1993; Markusen et al., 1993). The intuition is that the possibility to relocate plants to other countries increases the pressure on governments to relax their environmental policies. Ulph (1997) shows that there is no general presumption that governments will set emission taxes below marginal damage costs or below the level that would be set if the countries coordinated their environmental policies.

5. Conclusions

Game theory has become one of the major theoretical approaches in environmental economics. Applications of game-theoretic notions and models can be found in virtually any field of environmental economics. In some areas, such as international environmental problems and policy, it is becoming increasingly difficult to gain access to the literature without a profound knowledge of standard game theory.

Application of game theory to environmental problems has led to many important new insights, both from a theoretical and a policy-making point of view. In particular, it has helped expose several intuitively appealing notions, such as the general tenability of ecological dumping.

So far, mainly standard game theory has been applied to environmental problems. However, the nature of many types of environmental problems requires more advanced game-theoretical models. Stock effects which are typical for many environmental problems require differential games whereas uncertainty with respect to benefit and cost functions in transboundary pollution problems calls for the application of games of incomplete information. However, application of stochastic dynamic game theory to environmental problems is still in its infancy. In the context of the analysis of international cooperation, issue linkage is an interesting topic for further research, both theoretically and empirically. Environmental regulation and the analysis of competition between firms, countries and regions also require approaches beyond the standard models. Above all, however, there is an urgent need for applying game-theoretical notions in an empirical setting. An interesting example in this regard is Koskela and Ollikainen (1998), who demonstrate what role game theory can play in the context of the specification of an econometric model. Finally, it is highly desirable that theoretical insights obtained by means of game theory are analysed in an empirical setting.

References

Barrett, S. (1990), 'The problem of global environmental protection', *Oxford Review of Economic Policy*, **6**, 68–79.

Barrett, S. (1994), 'Self-enforcing international environmental agreements', *Oxford Economic Papers*, **46**, 878–94.

Bierman, H.S. and L. Fernandez (1995), *Game Theory with Economic Applications*, Reading, MA: Addison Wesley.

Carraro, C. and D. Siniscalco (1993), 'Strategies for the international protection of the environment', *Journal of Public Economics*, **52**, 309–28.

Carraro, C. and D. Siniscalco (1994), 'R&D cooperation and the stability of international environmental agreements', Nota di Lavoro 65.94, Fondazione Eni Enrico Mattei, Milan.

Cesar, H. and A. de Zeeuw (1996), 'Issue linkage in global environmental problems', in A. Xepapadeas (ed.), *Economic Policy for the Environment and Natural Resources*, Cheltenham, UK and Brookfield, US: Edward Elgar.

Chander, P. and H. Tulkens (1992), 'Theoretical foundations of negotiations and cost sharing in transfrontier pollution problems', *European Economic Review*, **36**, 288–99.

Dockner, E. and N. van Long (1993), 'International pollution control: cooperative versus non-cooperative strategies', *Journal of Environmental Economics and Management*, **24**, 13–29.

Ecchia, G. and M. Mariotti (1994), 'A survey on environmental policy: technological innovation and strategic issues', Nota di Lavoro 44.94, Fondazione Eni Enrico Mattei, Milan.

Folmer, H. and C. Howe (1991), 'Environmental problems and policy in the single European market', *Environmental and Resource Economics*, **1**, 17–42.

Folmer, H. and P. van Mouche (1994), 'Interconnected games and international environmental problems II', *Annals of Operations Research*, **54**, 97–117.

Folmer, H., P. van Mouche and S. Ragland (1993), 'Interconnected games and international environmental problems', *Environmental and Resource Economics*, **3**, 313–35.

Fudenberg, D. and E. Maskin (1986), 'The folk theorem in repeated games with discounting and with incomplete information', *Econometrica*, **54**, 533–54.

Fudenberg, D. and J. Tirole (1992), *Game Theory*, Cambridge, MA: MIT Press.

Gabel, L. (1995), 'Environmental management as a competitive strategy: the case of CFCs', in H. Folmer, L. Gabel and H. Opschoor (eds), *Principles of Environmental and Resource Economics*, Aldershot, UK and Brookfield, US: Edward Elgar.

Gabel, L. and B. Sinclair-Desgagné (1995), 'Corporate responses to environmental concerns', in H. Folmer, H. Gabel and H. Opschoor (eds), *Principles of Environmental and Resource Economics*, Aldershot, UK and Brookfield, US: Edward Elgar.

Gibbons, R. (1992), *Game Theory for Applied Economists*, Princeton, NJ: Princeton University Press.

Gil, J. and H. Folmer (1998), 'Linking environmental and non-environmental problems in an international setting: the interconnected games approach', in H. Folmer and N. Hanley (eds), *Game Theory and the Environment*, Cheltenham, UK and Brookfield, US: Edward Elgar.

Güth, W. and R. Pethig (1992), 'Illegal pollution and monitoring of unknown quality. A signalling game approach', in R. Pethig (ed.), *Conflict and Cooperation in Managing Environmental Resources*, Berlin: Springer-Verlag.

Helpman, E. and P. Krugman (1989), *Trade Policy and Market Structure*, Cambridge, MA: MIT Press.

Hoel, M. (1992a), 'Emission taxes in a dynamic game of CO_2 emissions', in R. Pethig (ed.), *Conflict and Cooperation in Managing Environment Resources*, Berlin: Springer-Verlag.

Hoel, M. (1992b), 'International environment conventions: the case of uniform reductions of emissions', *Environmental and Resource Economics*, **2**, 141–59.

Kaitala, V., M. Pohjola and O. Tahvonen (1992), 'Transboundary air pollution and soil acidification: a dynamic analysis of an acid rain game between Finland and the USSR', *Environmental and Resource Economics*, **2**, 161–8.

Kaitala, V., K.-G. Mäler and H. Tulkens (1995), 'The acid rain game as a resource allocation process with an application to the international cooperation among Finland, Russia and Estonia', *Scandinavian Journal of Economics*, **97**, 325–43.

Koskela, E. and M. Ollikainen (1998), 'A game-theoretic approach to the roundwood market with capital stock determination', in N. Hanley and H. Folmer (eds), *Game Theory and the Environment*, Cheltenham, UK and Lyme, US: Edward Elgar.

Krutilla, J. (1975), 'The international Columbia River treaty: an economic evaluation', in A. Kneese and S. Smith (eds), *Water Research*, Baltimore, MD: Johns Hopkins University Press.

Laffont, J.J. and J. Tirole (1991), 'The politics of government decision-making: a theory of regulatory capture', *Quarterly Journal of Economics*, **56**, 1089–127.

Lévêque, F. and A. Nadaï (1995), 'A firm's involvement in the policy–making process', in H. Folmer, L. Gabel and H. Opschoor (eds), *Principles of Environmental and Resource Economics*, Aldershot, UK and Brookfield, US: Edward Elgar.

Mäler, K.-G. (1989), 'The acid rain game', in H. Folmer and E. van Ierland (eds), *Valuation Methods and Policy Making in Environmental Economics*, Amsterdam: Elsevier.

Mäler, K.-G. and A. de Zeeuw (1998), 'The acid rain differential game', *Environmental and Resource Economics*, **12**, 167–84.

Markusen, J., E. Morey and N. Olewiler (1993), 'Environmental policy when market structure and plant location are endogenous', *Journal of Environmental Economics and Management*, **24**, 69–86.

Rauscher, M. (1993), 'Environmental regulation and international capital allocation', Nota di Lavoro 79.93, Fondazione Eni Enrico Mattei, Milan.

Ulph, A. (1994), 'Strategic environmental policy and international environmental competitiveness', in H. Siebert (ed.), *Elements of a Rational Environmental Policy*, Tübingen: J.C.B. Mohr.

Ulph, A. (1997), 'International trade and the environment', in H. Folmer and T. Tietenberg (eds), *The International Yearbook of Environmental and Resource Economics 1997–1998; A Survey of Current Issues*, Cheltenham, UK and Lyme, US: Edward Elgar.

Ulph, A. and D. Ulph (1996), 'Trade, strategic innovation and strategic environmental policy: a general analysis', in C. Carraro, Y. Katsoulacos and A. Xepapadeas (eds), *Environmental Policy and Market Structure*, Dordrecht: Kluwer.

van Damme, E. (1983), *Refinements of the Nash equilibrium concept*, Lecture Notes in Economics and Mathematical Systems, **219**, Berlin: Springer-Verlag.

Van der Ploeg, F. and A. de Zeeuw (1992), 'International aspects of pollution control', *Environmental and Resource Economics*, **2**, 117–39.

71 Optimal control theory in environmental economics

Talitha Feenstra, Herman Cesar and Peter Kort[1]

1. Introduction

Optimal control theory originated as a mathematical tool to solve problems of dynamic optimization. Applying it to economic problems allows the explicit consideration of time.[2] This makes it suitable for analysing the intertemporal trade-off between current consumption and future pollution or exhaustion of natural resources that is inherent in many environmental problems. Optimal control models consist of an intertemporal objective that must be optimized subject to a set of dynamic equations which specify how some instruments, or control variables, influence the development of the state variables. Examples of control variables in environmental economics are the level of fossil fuel use, the investment in abatement technology and the energy tax rate. State variables are, for instance, the atmospheric concentration of greenhouse gases and the stock of capital. Control theory provides methods of finding optimal levels of the instruments or control variables at each instant of time. Standard references for optimal control theory include Feichtinger and Hartl (1986), Kamien and Schwartz (1991) and Seierstad and Sydsæter (1987). Typically, with the help of Pontryagin's maximum principle,[3] optimality conditions can be formulated in terms of the so-called shadow values of the state variables.

In Section 2 we present a basic model of intertemporal trade-offs and discuss the conclusions that can be drawn from it. Section 3 examines the assumptions that are needed to arrive at these conclusions, such as constant and positive rate of discount and perfect foresight. Section 4 mentions the limitations of optimal control theory in environmental economics. Finally Section 5 reviews some literature in relation to the basic model.

2. A basic model

As regards the application of optimal control theory in environmental economics, it is worthwhile to note that the strands of literature on non-renewable resources (Hotelling, 1931), renewable resources (Gordon, 1954) and environmental resources[4] (Keeler et al., 1972) using optimal control techniques have developed quite separately from each other. Non-renewable and renewable resources are treated elsewhere in this book. The lack of integration in the literature is the more surprising given the analytic similarities between the three, as stressed by Smith (1977) and Dasgupta (1982), among others. These similarities are due to the equivalence of the main problem: to find the optimal trade-off between current and future use of a resource.

Take, for instance, the following optimal control model, where a social planner is supposed to solve the optimization problem:

$$\underset{C}{\text{Max}} \int_0^{\infty} e^{-rt} U(C(t), S(t)) dt \tag{71.1}$$

$$\dot{S}(t) = kG(S(t)) - f(R(t)) \tag{71.2}$$

$$C(t) \leq q(R(t)) \tag{71.3}$$

For notational simplicity, the time dependence of the variables is suppressed hereafter. In this model, the control C is the rate of consumption at t, while the state S is the stock of a natural resource. The variable R denotes the flow of this natural resource and is linked to C by (71.3). The functions $U(\cdot)$, $G(\cdot)$, $q(\cdot)$ and $f(\cdot)$ denote social welfare, the natural regeneration of the resource, production and the transformation of natural resources, respectively. The basic features of any optimal control model are present here: an intertemporal objective function (71.1), to be maximized by the correct choice of a control and a differential equation that describes the development of the state variable (71.2). Additionally the control variable is constrained to be economically meaningful by (71.3). According to whether one wants to discuss a non-renewable, renewable or natural resource, the interpretation and specific characteristics of the functions above change, but the basic model remains the same. Welfare is determined by utility from consumption and costs of extraction, harvest or use. These costs may depend on the resource stock.[5] Moreover, for instance, in the case of environmental resources, the stock itself may influence welfare. In the case of non-renewable resources, the available stock does not grow, so k is zero and $f(R) = R$ is the flow of extraction of the natural resource used for production of $q(R)$ units of output. In the case of renewable resources, k equals unity and $f(R) = R$. The function $q(R)$ denotes the production of goods and services based on resources, for example, fish or timber. In the case of environmental resources, the stock S stands for 'environmental quality'. Accumulated pollution, that is denoted below by P, is another state variable that describes the environmental situation. The basic model is then often further simplified by specifying equation (71.2) as

$$\dot{P} = -\delta P + R \tag{71.2'}$$

This assumes an exponential decay of pollution by natural assimilation. Such a simplification is mathematically convenient. However, it need not be an appropriate description of biological reality.

3. Optimal control theory in economics

We now turn to some remarks on optimal control models in general. Optimal control models applied in economics mostly take the following general form:

$$\underset{u \in U}{\text{Max}} \int_0^\infty e^{-rt} F(x,u)dt \qquad (71.4)$$

subject to

$$\dot{x} = f(x,u) \qquad x(0) = x_0 \qquad (71.5)$$

In the discussion below both x and u are scalars. Thus we restrict the discussion in this section to problems with only one state variable. The discounted stream of some instantaneous objective function $F(x,u)$ is maximized, where the development of the state variable x as steered by the control variable u is described by a differential equation $f(x,u)$. A concept used to derive optimality conditions is the current-value Hamiltonian. For the formulation above, it is given by:

$$H(x,u,\lambda) = F(x,u) + \lambda f(x,u) \qquad (71.6)$$

Here λ is a shadow value or co-state variable and is a function of time. It denotes the increase of the objective function due to a marginal increase of the state variable. At any point in time the decision maker can use the control variable to generate direct contributions to the objective function (represented by the term $F(x,u)$ in the Hamiltonian), or it can use the control variable to change the value of the state variable in order to generate contributions to the objective function in the future. These indirect contributions are measured by the term $\lambda f(x,u)$ in the Hamiltonian. The optimality conditions given by Pontryagin's maximum principle can now loosely be stated as:[6]

If (x^*,u^*) is an optimal solution, then there exists a λ such that

$$u^* = \underset{u \in U}{\text{argmax}} \, H(x^*, u, \lambda) \qquad (71.7)$$

$$\dot{\lambda} = r\lambda - \frac{\partial H(x^*,u^*,\lambda)}{\partial x} \qquad (71.8)$$

Thus the control must maximize the Hamiltonian and one must be able to find a shadow value that satisfies a certain differential equation. The basic model in the previous section has an additional equation that is a constraint on the control variable. Constraints on control or state variables imply that corner solutions should be taken into account. This adds Kuhn–Tucker type of conditions to the optimality conditions.[7] When the optimal value of the control given by (71.7) is inserted in (71.5) and (71.8), we have a system of two differential equations. This is called the modified Hamiltonian system. To be able to solve this system, one needs additional information, namely boundary values for x and λ. For the state variable, its initial value, x_0, is given (in (71.5)). For the shadow value no such initial value exists. In economic applications it frequently holds that the problem has a so-called saddle-point path.[8] This means that there is an optimal path that converges to a steady state. This is a point (x, λ) where the modified Hamiltonian system is stationary, that is, $(\dot{x}, \dot{\lambda}) = (0,0)$. Here the control variable is set such that the value of the state variable does not change, which explains the name steady state. It depends on the characteristics of the specific objective and control functions whether such a point exists, is unique[9] and what are its stability[10] characteristics.[11] If it exists, it gives a boundary value for λ[12] and hence enables us to find one or more candidate optimal solutions.

Some characteristics of the specification of the optimal control problem are worth mentioning. The time horizon is infinite. For trade-off problems, as in the example above, that is probably the most appropriate assumption. In this case, it is unclear where a possibly finite horizon should be located. For other problems, such as those describing a specific project, a finite time horizon may be more suitable.[13] Then the objective function is only evaluated over a finite time period T. It is important to consider the value of the variables at this final time T. The state variables may have some scrap value, since they can either be sold or put to some alternative use. End-point conditions, that describe the properties of an optimal solution at the final time T, should be added to the optimality conditions. Thus some state variables could be required to exactly satisfy a certain value at T, while others should be above some minimum value. To each type of end-point conditions, a different necessary condition on the value of the adjoint shadow value is linked (see, for example, Feichtinger and Hartl, 1986). These are called transversality conditions. They usually provide the additional information that is needed to sort out only a few candidate optimal solutions with the help of the first-order conditions ((71.5), (71.7) and (71.8)).

The instantaneous objective function is discounted at constant and positive rate r. This ensures that the integral converges, provided that $F(x,u)$ is bounded. Especially for environmental economic applications, the assumption of a positive discount rate is disputable. We come back to this in Section 4. When the assumption is dropped, one needs to be careful about the optimality concept used (see Seierstad and Sydsæter, 1987, for alternative optimality concepts).

If the Hamiltonian is concave in (x,u), Pontryagin's maximum principle provides sufficient conditions for an optimum.[14] This holds, for example, for the basic model in Section 2. It avoids one having to check formally whether (x^*, u^*) really is an optimum. When the Hamiltonian is strictly concave, the solution is, moreover, unique. If the Hamiltonian is linear in u, U must be bounded since, otherwise, one cannot solve (71.7). For a one-dimensional problem, U then is a closed interval and u^* can take one of three forms. It equals one of the interval boundaries, or a specific value in between. The latter is called the singular path. Along an optimal path u may jump between these values at certain moments. Such a solution is called a bang–bang solution. It is, for example, relevant for the optimal harvest or renewable resources. For further discussion see, for instance, Feichtinger and Hartl (1986, ch. 3). An application with a linear Hamiltonian in the field of environmental economics is Tahvonen (1997).

4.   Optimal control theory and the environment

Descriptive models used by biologists to model environmental problems (for example, global warming, pollution diffusion, acidification) are often stated as a (large) system of differential equations. Biologists rarely optimize these systems. Economists who include ecological systems in an optimal control model usually make severe simplifying assumptions to keep the model tractable. The question always remains whether essential characteristics of the system are lost in this manner.

 This section mentions a couple of usual simplifications. First, to apply optimal control theory, one assumes rationality and forward-looking behaviour. Second, optimal control assumes a deterministic setting. Decisions are made under perfect foresight. But it is the uncertainty in many environmental resource problems, for example global warming, that causes problems for policy making. Introducing uncertainty drastically complicates the analysis.[15] Third, to apply Pontryagin's maximum principle requires that the objective function and the functions that describe the dynamics are piecewise continuous.[16] But further concavity assumptions are often made, to ensure sufficiency. For a great many environmental problems these convexity requirements are problematic. Often the development over time of environmental stocks is characterized by so-called threshold values,[17] so that the dynamics of a certain environmental stock are better described by non-convex S-shaped curves. Dasgupta (1982) discusses this issue. Another aspect of environmental problems that is hard to put into an optimal control framework is the delay between cause and effect. This introduces time explicitly in the optimal control framework. Most basic theorems still apply, but their practical application becomes quite complex. As a final point, in the objective function, future and current welfare are compared by discounting at a constant[18] annual rate $(1 + r)$. Two questions arise: Is it fair to discount over generations?[19] If so, what is the appropriate discount rate? There is no definite answer to the first question. The second question is relevant, since relatively small changes in the discount rate may lead to considerable variation in the key policy variables.

These remarks are meant to give the reader a sound scepticism with respect to policy implications. The important contribution of optimal control theory models is that they provide insight into the key mechanisms.

5.   Extensions of the basic model

The example in Section 2 is a basic model type to analyse intertemporal trade-offs in resource use which has led to adaptions and extensions. In the basic model, sustainability in the sense of a stable resource base is ensured when the long-term flow of pollution, $f(R^\infty)$, is (less than or) equal to the natural regenerative capacity of the environment, $kG(S^\infty)$. This is a rather simplistic way to model the complex concept of sustainability.[20] A discussion of more sophisticated ways to include the concept of sustainability in optimal control models is given in Pezzey (1989). The modelling of assimilative capacity of the environment is also too simplistic, especially if the linear specification (71.2′) is chosen. How the assimilative capacity of the environment should be modelled has to depend on the described ecosystem and is in principle an empirical matter. Unfortunately, according to biologists, very little is known about the true process of assimilation. Many authors, having stressed that biologists could not supply them with nice quantitative assimilation functions, take the linear specification (71.2′) as a computationally convenient proxy. Exceptions are, among others, Forster (1975), Dasgupta (1982), Barbier and Markandya (1989) and Pethig (1990). For an analysis of the sensitivity of results to various specifications of the assimilation function see Cesar and de Zeeuw (1995).

Another possible extension of the basic model is to include abatement and other forms of emission reduction. Abatement as an additional control variable is included by, among others, Plourde (1972), Barbier and Markandya (1989) and Van de Ploeg and Withagen (1991). Smith (1972) models recycling. Keeler et al. (1972) include process-integrated changes. The standard result of these types of models with one state variable is a unique saddle-point equilibrium with positive levels of pollution and abatement (and/or other forms of emission reduction) brought about by monotonic[21] environmental taxes. The result that positive levels of pollution are optimal hinges on the assumption that marginal damage costs are negligible for very low levels of pollution (formally: $dU/dP(C,0) = 0$ in the utility function $u(C,P)$). This is analysed in a critical note by Forster (1972) regarding the conclusion of Keeler et al. that non-zero levels of pollution are optimal.

Furthermore, the basic model can be extended to include capital accumulation. Capital can be both a complement for and a substitute to environmental resource use. The possibility of endogenous technological progress through investment in human capital can be taken into account too. Human knowledge can be an environmentally friendly substitute for polluting inputs in the production process. This leads to endogenous growth models that take the environment into consideration.[22] Models that are concerned with pollution related to energy use might include the stock of fossil fuels as a state variable. Inclusion of either of these in the analysis implies a two-state variable model. Due to space limitations we refrain from treating such models here. A general characterization of the dynamics in a two-state variable problem is, for example, Feichtinger et al. (1994). Examples of two- (or even three-) state variable models can be found in Tahvonen (1997), Tahvonen and Kuuluvainen (1993) and Van der Ploeg and Withagen (1991). Nordhaus has written a range of contributions concerning global warming. He uses a model where two-state variables summarize the dynamics of the global warming process, including temperature as a state. His book (1994) on this topic includes an extensive discussion of the model.

Finally, the international dimension was ignored as well as other aspects that give rise to strategic behaviour, such as interactions between the private sector and the government. When strategic interaction between various decision makers is introduced the theory of optimal control is no longer appropriate. Instead (dynamic) game theory must be applied (see Chapter 70).

Other applications in the field of environmental economics analyse the issue of biodiversity (Swanson, 1994) and the optimal reaction of a firm to environmental policy (Kort et al., 1991; Xepapadeas, 1992; Hartl and Kort, 1996). Recent applications of more complex models, either with more than one state variable, or with non-linear dynamics in the modified Hamiltonian system, often use numeric simulation of specified cases to exemplify and extend the analytics (one example is Tahvonen's work).

Notes

1. The research of Talitha Feenstra is sponsored by the Netherlands Organization for Scientific Research (NWO). This chapter is an extended and updated version of the introductory chapter of Cesar (1994).
2. Arrow and Kurz (1970) is a seminal work on the application of dynamic optimization methods in economics.
3. To be explained below.
4. Examples of non-renewable or extractable resources are coal and other minerals; of renewable resources forests and fish; and of environmental resources clean air and clean water.
5. For instance, in the case of fish, it is cheaper to obtain the same harvest from richer fishing grounds than from poorer ones.
6. See, for instance, Seierstad and Sydsæter (1987) for a complete specification.
7. The appendices in Van Hilten, Kort and Van Loon (1993) extensively discuss constrained optimal control problems and their solution.
8. See, for instance, Feichtinger and Hartl (1986), p. 105.
9. If more than one steady state exists, the dynamics can be quite complicated (Skiba, 1978).
10. Kamien and Schwartz (1991, ch. 9, part II) give a complete overview of possible types of steady states that can occur for a one-state variable problem.

11. See also Feichtinger and Hartl (1986), ch. 5.
12. Another possibility is that it must satisfy a so-called transversality condition (see also below). However, the validity of such a condition in models with infinite time horizons depends on the structure of the problem. See, for example, Seierstad (1977).
13. For instance, in Caputo and Wilen (1995) an application to clean up waste is presented with fixed final time and a scrap value attached to residual waste at T. In Ready and Ready (1995), T is the moment a landfill is filled. In their model this T is itself a variable to be chosen optimally.
14. See Seierstad and Sydsæter (1987) for a detailed exposition of the sufficiency theorems that are available for optimal control problems.
15. For the theory of stochastic optimal control, see Feichtinger and Hartl (1986, appendix A8) and the references there.
16. See Seierstad and Sydsæter (1987) for a more precise statement of this.
17. Clarke and Reed (1994), for instance, present a model that includes the possibility of an irreversible catastrophe when a threshold is crossed.
18. Weitzman (1994) argues that the appropriate discount rate is decreasing over time.
19. See Toman (1994).
20. A well-known definition of sustainable development is 'development that meets the needs of the present without compromising the ability of future generations to meet their own needs' (World Commission on Environment and Development, 1987).
21. Ulph and Ulph (1994) show that when an exhaustible resource is included in the model the optimal time-path of taxes is no longer monotonic.
22. For example, Bovenberg and Smulders (1995) and Hofkes (1996). Endogenous growth models are discussed in the chapter by Withagen and Smulders on this topic (Chapter 42).

References
Arrow, K.J. and M. Kurz (1970), *Public Investment, the Rate of Return and Optimal Fiscal Policy*, Baltimore, MD: The Johns Hopkins Press.

Barbier, E.B. and A. Markandya (1989), 'The conditions for achieving environmentally sustainable development', LEEC Paper 89–01.

Bovenberg, A.L. and S. Smulders (1995), 'Environmental quality and pollution saving technological change in a two-sector endogenous growth model', *Journal of Public Economics*, **57**, 369–91.

Caputo, M.R. and J.E. Wilen (1995), 'Optimal cleanup of hazardous wastes', *International Economic Review*, **36** (1), 217–43.

Cesar, H.S.J. (1994), *Control and Game Models of the Greenhouse Effect: Economic Essays on the Comedy and Tragedy of the Commons*, Berlin: Springer-Verlag.

Cesar, H. and A. de Zeeuw (1995), 'Sustainability and the greenhouse effect: robustness analysis of the assimilation function', in C. Carraro and J.A. Filar (eds), *Control and Game-theoretic Models of the Environment*, Boston: Birkhäuser.

Clarke, H.R. and W.J. Reed (1994), 'Consumption pollution trade-offs in an environment vulnerable to pollution-related catastrophic collapse', *Journal of Economic Dynamics and Control*, **18** (5), 991–1010.

Dasgupta, P. (1982), *Control of Resources*, Oxford: Basil Blackwell.

Feichtinger, G. and R.F. Hartl (1986), *Optimale Kontrolle Oekonomischer Prozesse*, Berlin: Walter de Gruyter.

Feichtinger, G., A. Novak and F. Wirl (1994), 'Limit cycles in intertemporal adjustment models, theory and applications', *Journal of Economic Dynamics and Control*, **18**, 353–80.

Forster, B.A. (1972), 'A note on the optimal control of pollution', *Journal of Economic Theory*, **5**, 537–9.

Forster, B.A. (1975), 'Optimal pollution control with a nonconstant exponential rate of decay', *Journal of Environmental Economics and Management*, **2**, 1–6.

Gordon, R.L. (1954), 'Economic theory of a common-property resource: the fishery', *Journal of Political Economy*, **62**, 124–42.

Hartl, R.F. and P.M. Kort (1996), 'Capital accumulation of a firm facing an emissions tax', *Journal of Economics*, **63** (1), 1–23.

Hofkes, M.W. (1996), 'Modelling sustainable development: an economy–ecology integrated model', *Economic Modelling*, **13**, 333–53.

Hotelling, H. (1931), 'The economics of exhaustible resources', *Journal of Political Economy*, **39**, 137–75.

Kamien, M.I. and N.L. Schwartz (1991), *Dynamic Optimization, The Calculus of Variations and Optimal Control in Economics and Management*, Amsterdam: North-Holland.

Keeler, E., M. Spence and R. Zeckhauser (1972), 'The optimal control of pollution', *Journal of Economic Theory*, **4**, 19–34.

Kort, P.M., P.J.J. Van Loon and M. Luptaçik (1991), 'Optimal dynamic environmental policies of a profit maximizing firm', *Journal of Economics*, **54**, 195–225.

Nordhaus, W. (1994), *Managing the Global Commons: The Economics of Climate Change*, Cambridge, MA: MIT Press.

Pethig, R. (1990), 'Optimal pollution control, irreversibilities, and the value of future information', Discussion paper no. 6–90. University of Siegen.

Pezzey, J. (1989), 'Economic analysis of sustainable growth and sustainable development', Environmental Department Working Paper no. 5, World Bank.

Plourde, C.G. (1972), 'A model of waste accumulation and disposal', *Canadian Journal of Economics*, **5**, 119–25.

Ready, M.J. and R.C. Ready (1995), 'Optimal pricing of depletable replaceable resources: the case of landfill tipping fees', *Journal of Environmental Economics and Management*, **28**, 307–23.

Seierstad, A. (1977), 'Transversality conditions for optimal control problems with infinite horizons', memorandum, Institute of Economics, University of Oslo.

Seierstad, A. and K. Sydsæter (1987), *Optimal Control Theory with Economic Applications*, Amsterdam: North-Holland.

Skiba, A.K. (1978), 'Optimal growth and a convex–concave production function', *Econometrica*, **46**, 527–39.

Smith, V.L. (1972), 'Dynamics of waste accumulation: disposal versus recycling', *Quarterly Journal of Economics*, **86**, 600–616.

Smith, V.L. (1977), 'Control theory applied to natural and environmental resources: an exposition', *Journal of Environmental Economics and Management*, **4**, 1–24.

Swanson, T.M. (1994), 'The economics of extinction revisited: a generalized framework for the analysis of the problems of endangered species and biodiveristy losses', *Oxford Economic Papers*, **46**, 800–821.

Tahvonen, O. (1997), 'Fossil fuels, stock externalities and backstop technology', *Canadian Journal of Economics*, **30** (4), 855–74.

Tahvonen, O. and J. Kuuluvainen (1993), 'Economic growth, pollution and renewable resources', *Journal of Environmental Economics and Management*, **24**, 101–18.

Toman, M.A. (1994), 'Economics and "sustainability" – balancing trade-offs and imperatives', *Land Economics*, **70** (4), 339–413.

Ulph, A. and D. Ulph (1994), 'The optimal time path of a carbon tax', *Oxford Economic Papers*, **46**, 857–68.

Van der Ploeg, F. and C. Withagen (1991), 'Pollution control and the Ramsey problem', *Environmental and Resource Economics*, **1**, 215–36.

Van Hilten, O., P.M. Kort and P.J.J.M. Van Loon (1993), *Dynamic policies of the firm*, Berlin: Springer-Verlag.

Weitzman, M.L. (1994), 'On the "environmental" discount rate', *Journal of Environmental Economics and Management*, **26**, 200–209.

World Commission on Environment and Development (1987), *Our Common Future*, New York: Oxford University Press.

Xepapadeas, A.P. (1992), 'Environmental policy, adjustment costs and the behaviour of the firm', *Journal of Environmental Economics and Management*, **23**, 258–75.

72 Economic models of sustainable development

*Jeroen C.J.M. van den Bergh and Marjan W. Hofkes**

1. Introduction

This chapter offers an overview of alternative modelling approaches dealing with economic aspects of sustainable development. Sustainable development has become a common term in environmental economics, open to various interpretations, as is discussed in Section 2. When examining suitable models for sustainable development analysis, one can find large differences, due to distinct theoretical starting points and alternative demarcations of the problem associated with the objective of sustainable development. Specific models focus on economic growth *pur sang*, on technology formation, on natural processes and feedback to economic processes, or on evolutionary processes. We do not argue that there is one single best approach, but rather that an array of models is available that provides different, and largely complementary, insights. These different modelling perspectives on sustainable development are discussed in Sections, 3 to 5. They include economic growth models, sectorally disaggregated models, integrated and (co-)evolutionary models, and empirical model-based studies. This distinction is regarded to cover the most important theoretical starting points and disaggregation choices related to the modelling of consumption and welfare, production factors and interactions, and environmental impacts and processes. Comprehensive overviews of specific categories of sustainable development models are presented in Toman et al. (1995), van den Bergh (1996), Faucheux et al. (1996), and van den Bergh and Hofkes (1998).

2. Towards formalizing sustainability

The concept of sustainable development has over a rather short period of time become commonplace in environmental economics. There is, however, some debate about the interpretation of the terms 'sustainability' and 'sustainable development' (see the chapters by Beckerman, Daly, Goodland, and van den Bergh and de Mooij in this book – Chapters 43,

* We acknowledge useful comments by Jason Shogren and Sjak Smulders.

44, 48 and 45, respectively). For many economists sustainable development comes down to issues of equity between generations and as such can be seen as complementary to the concept of efficiency in terms of optimal dynamic allocation. To others the goal of sustainable development is essentially putting a restriction on the physical scale of an economy. In either case, sustainable development asks for an explicit treatment of three elements: (1) materials and energetic processes and transformations (notably mass balance); (2) ecological processes and evolution (notably complexity, uncertainty and irreversibility); and (3) ethical positions and alternative criteria of intra- and intergeneration justice. Most existing models, however, do not deal with all these elements simultaneously.

From a modelling perspective the following distinction of interpretations of sustainable development is useful:

1. *Discounted utilitarianism* The present discounted value of utility is the commonly used criterion in models of optimal economic growth with environment and resources (see, for example, Kamien and Schwarz, 1982). Sustainable development can be integrated in this framework by fully specifying economy–ecology interactions with respect to both production processes and welfare. In this approach a broadly defined welfare function should be used, which also includes environmental quality (see Hofkes, 1996). Furthermore, (normative) restrictions concerning equity between generations and/or (absolute) levels of environmental quality can be added.

2. *Intergenerational equity* In economic growth theory sustainable development is often translated into intergenerational equity. This is operationalized with the restriction of non-decreasing welfare over generations. Intergenerational equity represents a strict criterion, as it regards any temporary decrease of welfare as a sign of unsustainable development.

3. *Weak sustainability* An entirely different starting point is that of maintaining total capital, also referred to as weak sustainability. It typically allows for substitution between man-made and natural capital (see Pearce et al., 1990). The practical expression of this has been to focus attention on equal opportunities for present and future generations. The standard method applied by economists to investigate such equal opportunities has been in terms of substitution of natural resources by man-made capital, and implied utility patterns over time. Common and Perrings (1992) define this case as Solow/Hartwick sustainability (Hartwick, 1977).

4. *Strong sustainability* Under the aspiration of strong sustainability

each type of capital – in any case including economic (man-made) and ecological/natural capital – should be maintained. A motivation for this view is the recognition that natural resources are both unique and essential inputs in economic production, consumption or welfare, implying that they cannot be substituted for by artefacts, labour or knowledge. Alternatively, this view is defended by the acknowledgement of environmental integrity and rights in nature. Although weak and strong sustainability are usually mentioned in one and the same breath, their formalization differs completely, since strong sustainability as opposed to weak sustainability does not allow for any substitution between the different kinds of capital.

5. *Steady state and optimal scale*   Daly has long since forcefully argued in favour of a 'steady state', where population and economic stocks are constant (Daly, 1977/91 and Chapter 44 in this book). In this perspective, the main social aim of development should be to minimize human impacts on the natural environment by minimizing the material and energetic 'throughput' of human production and consumption, subject to some guaranteed (subsistence) income or consumption level. This means an entirely different development objective than that posed by standard economics, although certainly not excluding opportunities for improvement in living conditions and welfare. An alternative viewpoint on this objective is in terms of an optimal physical scale or size of the economy, given carrying capacity constraints. Daly points out this has been neglected in standard economics which focuses instead on optimal allocation issues (for example, Daly, 1992).

6. *Ecological stability and resilience*   Many ecologists would allegedly support the idea that environmental sustainability is mainly a matter of ecological stability, resilience and biotic diversity. Common and Perrings (1992) refer to this as ecological Holling sustainability (Holling 1973, 1986). Resilience can here be considered as a global, structural stability concept, and may cover multiple locally stable equilibria. Standard economic models do not address fluctuations and cycles very much, nor do they incorporate any real ecosystem structure (an exception is Crocker and Tschirhart, 1992). As a result these models are unable to deal with stability and uncertainty in a way consistent with ecological theory. This provides strong support for the view that sustainability should be tackled via a precautionary strategy depending on the assessment of safety margins (see Turner et al., 1997).

It should be noted that the above-mentioned perspectives are not necessarily in disagreement with each other. It is possible that they give rise to similar or identical conclusions on a general level or in specific cases. More important, however, is that they may very well lead to different and possibly conflicting conclusions, so that a choice between them in general or in specific applications, is inevitable.

3. Economic growth theory

The neoclassical Solow/Swan type of growth model has long served as the benchmark in economists' answers to the question whether there are natural resource or environmental limits to growth. Over the last decade attention has shifted to modern growth theory (reviewed by Smulders, Chapter 42 in this book), implying that apart from technology descriptions, the economic and environmental assumptions of the growth model have not essentially altered. The main elements of the growth-with-resources/environment models are as follows (see Kamien and Schwarz, 1982; Toman et al., 1995; Beltratti, 1996): (1) a social objective evaluating welfare over time (possibly of multiple generations), where the standard neoclassical assumption is that of a net present value (discounted utility) function; (2) a production function, combining man-made and environmental stocks and flows to produce final goods and services; (3) a dynamic description of the economy, resulting from investment in, and depreciation of, man-made capital; (4) a dynamic description of the environment, resulting from resource extraction, natural regeneration, waste emission and pollution assimilation; and (5) the distribution of output to consumption, investment and possibly other categories of demand. Item (4) has been dealt with in an intertemporal setting by Siebert (1982), and Barbier and Markandya (1990). Although their models directly link consumption to resource use and exclude capital accumulation – so that they cannot be regarded as growth models in a strict sense – they provide basic insights about sustainability of interactive resource and environmental dynamics. The global model structure may change when additional (disaggregate) activities (production functions) and economic capital are defined, such as those related to recycling, abatement and innovation (the latter leading to endogenous growth theory). Such more complicated models are rare, due to the frequent intractability of analytical solutions.

There are several options to incorporate sustainability in growth theory models and analyses:

(i) Finding the optimal (efficient) dynamic solution and then testing whether it satisfies the chosen definition or interpretation of sustainable development. When the test is negative, one of the problems mentioned under (ii) and (iii) should be solved.

(ii) Explicitly incorporating sustainability as a condition on the stock of environmental resources or assimilative capacity, on consumption patterns or more generally on welfare changes. Then a (complicated) dynamic optimization problem with inequality constraints, reflecting non-decreasing patterns of environmental stocks and/or welfare over time, has to be solved.

(iii) Change the social objective function, for example by explicitly giving a greater weight to the welfare of generations in the distant future. Heal (1996) and Beltratti (1996) refer to the Chichilnisky criterion (Chichilnisky, 1993) as a way to incorporate intergenerational equity in the optimality criterion, that is, without adding any separate condition. This results in a weighted average of a discounted integral of utilities over a finite time (the standard neoclassical criterion) and a term reflecting the stream of utility in the very distant future. The latter term would reflect explicit concern for the long-run future, while the weighted average would ensure that neither the present nor the future were dictatorial.

Each of the above options can be considered in combination with a non-renewable resource, a renewable resource, or a combination of these. The case of non-renewable resources has attained most attention, as it is the most simple representation of the essential features of the growth–environment conflict. With regard to sustainability and non-renewable resources two positions are possible. First, one can argue that strong sustainability implies that these resources are not exploited at all. An alternative position would be to strive for weak sustainability, that is, keeping total capital intact. The most important result for this case is the Hartwick rule, stating that investment of the Hotelling scarcity rents from exploitation of the non-renewable resource in man-made capital results in maximum constant consumption over time, given the initial conditions (Hartwick, 1977; for an overview see Gutés, 1996). This result depends critically on assumptions about the production function. A related concept is the 'Green Golden Rule of Economic Growth' defined as the highest level of consumption that can be indefinitely maintained (independent of initial conditions), given environmental and resource constraints (see Heal, 1996).

The above-mentioned growth models deal with continuous time (optimal control) problems, which means that no clear distinction can be made between generations. A discrete (dynamic programming) approach, in which each generation is supposed to exist during a certain period, allows one to deal with a number of issues, notably, alternative intergenerational welfare functions, overlapping between generations, and altruism (see Howarth and Norgaard, 1995). The neoclassical net present value approach can be replaced by a maximin function, based on an egalitarian or Rawlsian principle (Rawls, 1972), where the objective is to maximize the outcome of the worst-off generation (see Solow, 1974; Asako, 1980; John et al., 1995; Beltratti, 1996). The main lesson from these various contributions is that, based on the maximin criterion, initial conditions may completely dominate the long-run potential development. So if the initial generation is very poor, all future generations will be poor as well, since the maximin criterion does not stimulate the sacrifice of welfare now so as to have more welfare in the future (Solow, 1974). But if such a trade-off is allowed within the time frame of one generation, while maintaining the maximin criterion for strict intergenerational evaluations, things may look less bleak. Multiple arguments in the utility function (including environmental amenities), overlapping generations and altruism may also change the original Solow results, allowing for a wider range than merely egalitarian distributions of consumption between generations (see Dasgupta, 1974; and Beltratti, 1996).

In addition to considering alternative social objectives, we must deal with two other fundamental issues. The first concerns how to formulate aggregate production relationships between all production factors including materials and energy, and aggregate output. Normally shaped isoquants may not apply, because factors cannot be supplied independently of each other as on a micro-level, and because infinite substitution from resource materials to capital or labour is infeasible (see Stern, 1997).

The second issue is mass balance. It is easily shown that physical growth will be bounded when consumption, resource extraction and waste emissions are all interpreted in terms of material units, and satisfy mass-balance conditions. Complementarity of inputs is thus more emphasized so that substitution cannot provide the solution to decreasing resource stocks, and growth has to come to an end at some stage. This was shown mathematically in a Solow-type model with resources by Gross and Veendorp (1990). A mass-balance approach may be required to answer the question to what extent resource scarcity and pollution can be circumvented by producing more value from less materials. Two mechanisms support such trends, namely substitution of materials (and energy) inputs in production by nonmaterial inputs (services obtained from capital and labour) and resource-saving technological progress. Georgescu-Roegen has forcefully argued that capital and labour cannot be set on an equal level with materials as inputs to production functions. The reason is that the services of capital and labour are the real inputs, which are generated by the 'actors', that is, capital and labour. Furthermore, capital and labour are not stocks that can be emptied or filled at any speed, but are 'funds', which can only generate a limited number of services in a given period. Therefore, although substitution among funds or among materials is quite straightforward, substitution between these two categories of production factors is less evident (see van den Bergh, 1996, Section 2.2). Alternative models complying with these insights have been developed by Georgescu-Roegen (1971/76), D'Arge and Kogiku (1973), and van den Bergh and Nijkamp (1994a). The latter two studies use the mass-balance production function in a dynamic growth model. These production specifications are more restrictive than the neoclassical production function which satisfies a necessary condition'. The latter requires that in order to have positive production output, resource input should be strictly positive (Dasgupta and Heal, 1979). As such, neoclassical production functions are very abstract and they may well be consistent with mass balance. However, a more explicit and disaggregate dynamic production model satisfying mass balance and distinguishing between different categories of inputs as outlined above can surely add to our understanding of resources limits to economic growth (see van den Bergh, 1999).

4.   Sectorally disaggregated models

Whereas growth models are generally highly aggregated, it seems useful to employ disaggregated models to deal with other questions in the context of sustainable development. One of the most relevant questions is what a sustainable structure of the economy would look like in terms of sectoral distribution of output and employment. Rather than regarding such an approach as 'blue-printing', one may use the outcome in a qualitative sense, namely to judge in which direction desirable changes would go.

A first approach is the input–output (I–O) model, where sectoral interactions can be included, so that all indirect economic effects, as well as all indirect resource use and emission effects of different economic structures, in terms of final demand composition, can be calculated (see Ayres, 1978). The most important recent study is by Duchin and Lange (1994), where the well-known Leontief world model is extended and adapted to test the Brundtland Commission's statement that growth and sustainability can go together. Their conclusion is negative, and they argue that we should rethink how to integrate development of rich and poor countries with environmental sustainability. The model is used to describe the period 1980 to 2020, and covers 16 regions, 50 sectors and dynamics in the trade of commodities, flows of capital and economic aid. Use of energy and materials (including metals, cement, pulp, paper, chemicals) are calculated as well as emissions of CO_2 (more than doubled worldwide over the studied period), SO_2 (almost constant) and NO_x (almost doubled).

Dutch examples of the I–O type of analysis are WRR (1987) and Dellink et al. (1996). The latter study considers alternative supply-side scenarios for 2010, reflecting different views on sustainability. The model is based on the national accounting matrix including environmental accounts (NAMEA), developed by the Dutch Bureau for Statistics (Keuning, 1993). The I–O matrix is aggregated for the model, resulting in 19 sectors. The model allows us to trace impacts in terms of several important environmental (policy) themes. These include: climate change, acidification, eutrophication, ozone depletion, waste generation, wood use, water use and fishery, and land use. The model optimizes total value added (GNP) by varying the demand for the products of each sector, subject to environmental, economic and other restrictions. Each scenario generates a particular set of environmental constraints. The other restrictions include minimum consumption requirements, maximum productive capacity per sector, limits to trade imbalances, labour market conditions, and so on. Some important results of the scenario optimizations for the period 1991–2030 are that economic growth is compatible with a reduction of the environmental pressure, but requires accelerated technological progress and economic restructuring. Furthermore, sustainable restructuring is found not to be necessarily in conflict with employment objectives. Environmental constraints are most influential on the outcomes in all cases, while the greenhouse gas problem turns out to be the most restrictive constraint. Furthermore, space may become a critical factor for future economic development in the Netherlands.

Related to the I–O approach are multisectoral computable general equilibrium (CGE) models (see also Chapter 69 by Conrad in this book). The advantage of CGE models is that they take account of all interactions, both direct and indirect, in a framework of interacting markets. Furthermore, CGE models are particularly suitable for explicit analysis of the effects of implementation of (regulatory) instruments on economic structure. I–O models have an advantage as compared to CGE models in that they can handle a more disaggregated sector structure, although this advantage is becoming less relevant with current progress in computing power of modern computers. However, both I–O and CGE models are structurally fixed in the sense that sectoral classification and disaggregation, and assumed technologies, cannot change endogenously. Furthermore, both I–O and CGE analyses do not necessarily generate sustainable development solutions. A more explicit linkage of environmental externalities and environmental–ecological systems and processes may be appropriate, for instance, as in the model of Crocker and Tschirhart (1992) and the integrated models discussed below.

5. Disequilibrium, evolutionary and integrated models

An alternative approach to studying sustainable development comes from evolutionary economics (see Gowdy, 1994; Norgaard, 1994). The basic idea is that changes in economic reality arise quickly and via discontinuous jumps. Evolutionary economics regards economic processes as inherently accidental, cumulative and irreversible. Ayres (1997), moreover, regards economic growth and development as fundamentally and unavoidably linked to disequilibrium states of the economy. According to him, only disequilibrium states can explain all economic decisions, ranging from consumers buying goods to investors encouraging technological innovations. The argument used is that if we were really in equilibrium we would have no incentive to make decisions about buying, selling, investing, and so on.

The method of evolutionary economics is based on Darwinian (undirected) and Lamarckian (teleological/goal-oriented) evolutionary theories in biology, as well as on recent developments in evolutionary biology and neo-Schumpeterian economics (Dosi et al., 1988). Recently, sustainable development has also been studied from the perspective of evolutionary economics (Clark et al., 1995; England, 1994). The concept of evolution may be especially important in environmental and ecological economics, with their focus on sustainable development and long-run interactions between evolving economic and ecological systems. All in all, it seems that the Darwinian, gradual and adaptive, approach dominates in evolutionary economics. It should be noted that in biology this approach has long been replaced by a broader perspective on evolution and adaptation (see Gould and Lewontin, 1979). Ayres (1994) and Ruth (1996) argue for an evolutionary approach that is based on physics, in particular thermodynamics, and information theory. Finally, some macro-model analyses specifically focusing on sustainable development issues, notably those including disequilibrium elements, may also be positioned under the present category. A rare example is den Hartog and Maas (1990).

Hodgson (1995) regards evolution as a process consisting of three component principles, namely variation, heredity and selection. This clearly represents a biological metaphor. Variety and diversity, whether fully random or not, are necessary conditions, that is, without them there can be no evolution whatsoever. Variation comes about via mutations and sexual recombination. Heredity means that selected units have some degree of durability and resilience via a mechanism that passes on characteristics to other units. Selection may work on multiple levels, including individual actors, groups, routines and even institutions and policies. In this sense one can also define co-evolution of individuals and systems, such as species and ecosystems, and analogously economic activities and their natural environments (see further Gowdy, Chapter 65 in this book).

Reading about evolutionary models in economics and environmental economics gives one the impression of a large variety of approaches and focal points (see Boulding, 1978; Faber and Proops, 1990; Erdman, 1993;

Gowdy, 1994; Norgaard, 1994). Allen (1998) makes a distinction between three types of models, namely deterministic, such as the standard neo-classical models (characterized by determinism and average behaviour); self-organizing (non-deterministic and average behaviour); and evolutionary (non-deterministic and micro-diversity). Self-organizing systems can show qualitative change only on the level of collective structure (spatio-temporal organization of molecules), whereas the evolutionary type can also qualitatively change at the lowest micro-level. The latter takes places via new genotypes (genetic information or structure) reflected in new phenotypes (realized outer appearance). Evolutionary models are not supposed to be predictive, which is often regarded as a main weakness. But if evolution is the reality, no model will have much predictive power over the long run, irrespective of whether it is based on evolutionary assumptions or not.

In much of the evolutionary economics literature, and also in the modern growth theory literature, technological progress is considered as crucial in the dynamics of both modern and developing economies. Evolutionary approaches regard technological change as an evolutionary process (Nelson and Winter, 1982; Dosi et al., 1988), dating back to ideas of Schumpeter. Such approaches aim at breaking open the black box of technology invention and temporal and spatial diffusion of innovations, using crucial information about patents for inventions and detailed statistics on changes in technologies used in specific sectors. In the context of environmental economics, Faber and Proops (1990) have related long-run interactions between invention, innovation and technical progress to pollution and resource use, using a neo-Austrian approach. This approach is similar to neoclassical economics in its assumption of rational behaviour, but it differs from it in devoting more attention to irreversibility and uncertainty. All in all, evolutionary models pay more attention to substantial and detailed issues of technological invention, innovation and diffusion than modern growth theory models.

Integration and co-evolution of economic and environmental systems may be useful concepts to address environmental sustainability in formal models. Integrated models with a focus on two-way interactions between economic and environmental systems have been applied at spatial scales ranging from local and regional (Zuchetto and Jansson, 1985; Braat and van Lierop, 1987; Giaoutzi and Nijkamp, 1993; van den Bergh and Nijkamp, 1994a and 1994b; Bockstael et al., 1995; van den Bergh, 1996; Reyes et al., 1996; Costanza et al., 1995, 1997) to global scale (Meadows et al., 1982 and 1992). The most recent class of applied models linking to the global scale is in the area of climate change (see Chapter 10 in Bruce et al., 1996; Tol, 1998; and van Ierland, Chapter 41 in this book). Clark et al.

(1995) consider evolution and environmental sustainability in models which combine integrated and evolutionary elements, as well as spatial features. As a result, these models describe co-evolutionary economic–environmental processes.

The integrated and evolutionary models differ from the standard economic growth theory approach to sustainability in that they pay much more attention to a disaggregate treatment of the feedbacks between economic and ecological systems, based on either spatial, ecological, hydrological, evolutionary or technological processes. Stated in a different way, these models endogenize processes which are either excluded, aggregated away, or treated as exogenous in standard growth models. The main problem of the evolutionary approach is that it is still very heterogeneous and lacks a firm theoretical underpinning as well as a sound empirical approach. As a result, the modelling is often quite *ad hoc* and may be seen as merely translating real complexity in model complexity. But the results of this may allow for experiments which can teach us about unexpected outcomes of policies applied to uncertain and complex dynamic environmental–economic systems. Evidently, sustainable development is inherently related to such types of systems.

6.   Empirical issues and further research

For each of the above-discussed approaches it is possible either to test assumptions and implied hypotheses or operationalize the models on the basis of empirical data. Neoclassical growth-with-environment models have seen very few real applications. The work in the area of climate change is a rare exception (Nordhaus, 1994; Tol, 1998). The integrated and evolutionary models have been applied in a variety of ways on local and regional scales. Sectorally disaggregated models have been applied less to real specific sustainability questions than to short-term questions related to concrete instruments of environmental policy. Most of the integrated and evolutionary models discussed represent applied studies. Pure theoretical modelling is less common in this area.

Another line of model-based applied research concerns statistical and systems-descriptive research on the empirical relationship between growth, economic structure, environmental (stress) indicators. A first approach focuses on testing the environmental Kuznets curve hypothesis, that is, the delinking of growth and environmental pressure, for various environmental indicators (see de Bruyn and Heintz, Chapter 46 in this book). Related to this is work on aggregate environmental indicators and economic structure (Jänicke et al., 1993), and on decomposition analysis of 'structural change' (see Ang and Rose, Chapters 74 and 75 in this book). Another stream of literature offers a disaggregate systems analysis, mostly descriptive, of the economic structure and the material and energetic content of economic production and consumption. Terms used in this context are 'dematerialization' and 'industrial metabolism or ecology' (see Ayres, Chapter 62 in this book). This still needs to be linked to economic models and analyses.

Several other issues need attention in future research. First, modelling of sustainable development of open systems has hardly been considered in any systematic way. This requires that more thought be given to what sustainability on a regional or national scale exactly means, and it is evident that this should be considered in the context of international trade and relations (see van den Bergh and Verbruggen, 1999). Next, the consistency of economic growth theory with mass balance remains a debatable topic, for which specific models may have to be developed. More coherence seems necessary with regard to different approaches to evolutionary modelling. Furthermore, a comparison of evolutionary modelling with traditional economic approaches, preferably in applications to similar cases or questions, would be useful, for instance, in the context of the double dividend debate.

References

Allen, P.M. (1998), 'Evolutionary complex systems and sustainable development', in J.C.J.M. van den Bergh and M.W. Hofkes (eds), *Theory and Implementation of Economic Models for Sustainable Development*, Dordrecht: Kluwer Academic Publishers.

Asako, K. (1980), 'Economic growth and environmental pollution under the max-min principle', *Journal of Environmental Economics and Management*, **7**, 157–83.

Ayres, R.U. (1978), *Resources, Environment and Economics: Applications of the Materials/Energy Balance Principle*, New York: Wiley-Interscience.

Ayres, R.U. (1994), *Information, Entropy and Progress: A New Evolutionary Paradigm*, New York: American Institute of Physics, AIP Press.

Ayres, R.U. (1997), 'Theories of economic growth', Working paper 97/13/EPS, Centre for the Management of Environmental Resources, INSEAD, Fontainebleau, France.

Barbier, E.B. and A. Markandya (1990), 'The conditions for achieving environmentally sustainable development', *European Economic Review*, **34**, 659–69.

Beltratti, A. (1996), *Models of Economic Growth with Environmental Assets*, Dordrecht: Kluwer Academic Publishers.

Bergh, J.C.J.M. van den (1996), *Ecological Economics and Sustainable Development: Theory, Methods and Applications*, Cheltenham, UK and Brookfield, US: Edward Elgar.

Bergh, J.C.J.M. van den (1999), 'Materials, capital, direct/indirect substitution and mass balance production functions', *Land Economics*, **74**, November, (forthcoming).

Bergh, J.C.J.M. van den and M.W. Hofkes (eds) (1998), *Theory and Implementation of Economic Models for Sustainable Development*, Dordrecht: Kluwer Academic Publishers.

Bergh, J.C.J.M. van den and P. Nijkamp (1994a), 'Dynamic macro modelling and materials balance: economic–environmental integration for sustainable development', *Economic Modelling*, **11**, 283–307.

Bergh, J.C.J.M. van den and P. Nijkamp (1994b), 'An integrated model for economic development and natural environment: an application to the Greek Sporades Islands', *The Annals of Operations Research*, **54**, 143–74.

Bergh, J.C.J.M. van den and H. Verbruggen (1999), 'Spatial sustainability, trade and indicators: an evaluation of the Ecological Footprint', *Ecological Economics*, **29**, 63–74.

Bockstael, N., R. Costanza, I. Strand, W. Boynton, K. Bell and L. Waigner (1995), 'Ecological economic modeling and valuation of ecosystems', *Ecological Economics*, **14**, 143–59.

Boulding, K.E. (1978), *Ecodynamics: A New Theory of Societal Evolution*, Beverley Hills: Sage Publications.
Braat, L.C. and W.F.J. van Lierop (eds) (1987), *Economic–Ecological Modelling*, Amsterdam: North-Holland.
Bruce, J., H. Lee and E.F. Haites (eds) (1996), *Climate Change 1995: Economic and Social Dimensions of Climate Change*, contribution of Working Group 3 to the Second Assessment Report of the IPCC, Cambridge, UK: Cambridge University Press.
Chichilnisky, G. (1993), 'What is sustainable development?', Working paper, Stanford Institute for Theoretical Economics.
Clark, N., F. Perez-Trejo and P. Allen (1995), *Evolutionary Dynamics and Sustainable Development: A Systems Approach*, Aldershot, UK and Brookfield, US: Edward Elgar.
Common, M. and C. Perrings (1992), 'Towards an ecological economics of sustainability', *Ecological Economics*, **6**, 7–34.
Costanza, R., L. Waigner and N. Bockstael (1995), 'Integrating ecological–economic systems modeling: theoretical issues and practical applications', in J. Shogren and J. Milon (eds), *Integrating Economic and Ecologic Indicators: Practical Methods for Environmental Policy Analysis*, Westport, CT: Praeger Publishing.
Costanza, R., C. Perrings and C.J. Cleveland (eds) (1997), *The Development of Ecological Economics*, Cheltenham, UK and Lyme, US: Edward Elgar.
Crocker, T.D. and J. Tschirhart (1992), 'Ecosystems, externalities and economics', *Environmental and Resource Economics*, **2**, 551–67.
Daly, H.E. (1991), *Steady State Economics*, 2nd edn, Washington, DC: Island Press (1st edn 1977).
Daly, H.E. (1992), 'Allocation, distribution, and scale: towards an economics that is efficient, just and sustainable', *Ecological Economics*, **6**, 185–93.
D'Arge, R.C. and K.C. Kogiku (1973), 'Economic growth and the environment', *Review of Economic Studies*, **40**, 61–77.
Dasgupta, P.S. (1974), 'On some alternative criteria for justice between generations', *Journal of Public Economics*, **3**, 405–23.
Dasgupta, P.S. and G.M. Heal (1979), *Economic Theory and Exhaustible Resources*, Cambridge, UK: Cambridge University Press.
Dellink, R., M. Bennis and H. Verbruggen (1996), 'Sustainable economic structures: scenarios for sustainability in the Netherlands', IVM-report W96/27, Institute for Environmental Studies, Free University, Amsterdam.
Dosi, G., C. Freeman, R. Nelson, G. Silverberg and L. Soete (eds) (1988), *Technical Change and Economic Theory*, London: Pinter Publishers.
Duchin, F. and G.M. Lange, in association with K. Thonstad and A. Idenburg (1994), *The Future of the Environment: Ecological Economics and Technical Change*, Oxford: Oxford University Press.
England, R.W. (1994), 'On economic growth and resource scarcity: lessons from non-equilibrium thermodynamics', in R.W. England (ed.), *Evolutionary Concepts in Contemporary Economics*, Ann Arbor: University of Michigan Press.
Erdman, G. (1993), 'Evolutionary economics as an approach to environmental problems', in H. Giersch (ed.), *Economic Progress and Environmental Concerns*, Berlin: Springer-Verlag.
Faber, M. and J.L.R. Proops (1990), *Evolution, Time, Production and the Environment*, Heidelberg: Springer-Verlag.
Faucheux, S., D.W. Pearce and J.L.R. Proops (1996), *Models of Sustainable Development*, Cheltenham, UK and Brookfield, US: Edward Elgar.
Georgescu-Roegen, N. (1971/76), 'Process analysis and the neoclassical theory of production', in N. Georgescu-Roegen, *Energy and Economic Myths*, New York, Pergamon, pp. 37–52.
Giaoutzi, M. and P. Nijkamp (1993), *Decisions Support Models for Regional Sustainable Development*, Aldershot, UK: Avebury.
Gould, S.J. and R.C. Lewontin (1979), 'The spandrels of San Marco and the Panglossian paradigm: a critique of the adaptationist programme', *Proceedings of the Royal Society of London B*, **205**, 581–98.
Gowdy, J. (1994), *Coevolutionary Economics: The Economy, Society and the Environment*. Dordrecht: Kluwer Academic Publishers.

Gross, L.S. and E.C.H. Veendorp (1990), 'Growth with exhaustible resources and a materials-balance production function', *Natural Resource Modelling*, **4**, 77–94.

Gutés, M.C. (1996), 'The concept of weak sustainability', *Ecological Economics*, **17**, 147–56.

Hartog, H. den and R.J.M. Maas (1990), 'A sustainable economic development: macro-economic aspects of a priority for the environment', in P. Nijkamp and H. Verbruggen (eds), *The Dutch Environment in the European Space*, Leiden: Stenfert Kroese (in Dutch).

Hartwick, J.M. (1977), 'Intergenerational equity and the investing of rents from exhaustible resources', *American Economic Review*, **67**, 972–4.

Heal, G.M. (1996), 'Interpreting sustainability', Plenary presentation, 7th annual conference of the European Association of Environmental Economists (EAERE), 27–29 June, Lisbon, Portugal.

Hodgson, G.M. (1995), 'Introduction', in G.M. Hodgson, *Economics and Biology*, The International Library of Critical Writings in Economics Series, Aldershot, UK and Brookfield, US: Edward Elgar.

Hofkes, M.W. (1996), 'Modelling sustainable development: an economic–ecology integrated model', *Economic Modelling*, **13**, 333–53.

Holling, C.S. (1973), 'Resilience and stability of ecological systems', *Annual Review of Ecological Systems*, **4**, 1–24.

Holling, C.S. (1986), 'The resilience of terrestrial ecosystems: local surprise and global change', in W.C. Clark and R.E. Munn (eds), *Sustainable Development of the Biosphere*, Cambridge UK: Cambridge University Press.

Howarth, R.B. and R.B. Norgaard (1995), 'Intergenerational choices under global environmental change', in D.W. Bromley (ed.), *The Handbook of Environmental Economics*, Oxford: Blackwell.

Jänicke, M., H. Monch and M. Binder (1993), 'Ecological aspects of structural change', *Intereconomics Review of International Trade and Development*, **28**, 159–69.

John, A., R. Pecchenino, D. Schimmelpfennig and S. Schreft (1995), 'Short-lived agents and the long-lived environment', *Journal of Public Economics*, **58**, 127–41.

Kamien, M.I. and N.L. Schwarz (1982), 'The role of common property resources in optimal planning models with exhaustible resources', in V.K. Smith and J.V. Krutilla (eds), *Explorations in Natural Resource Economics*, Baltimore, MD: Johns Hopkins University Press.

Keuning, S.J. (1993), 'An information system for environmental indicators in relation to the national accounts', in W.F.M. de Vries et al. (eds), *The Value Added of National Accounting*, Netherlands Central Bureau of Statistics, Voorburg.

Meadows, D.H., J. Richardson and G. Bruckmann (1982), *Groping in the Dark: The First Decade of Global Modeling*, New York: Wiley.

Meadows, D.H., D.L. Meadows and J. Randers (1992), *Beyond the Limits: Confronting Global Collapse: Envisioning a Sustainable Future*, Post Mills: Chelsea Green Publishing.

Nelson, R. and S. Winter (1982), *An Evolutionary Theory of Economic Change*, Cambridge, MA: Belknap Press of Harvard University Press.

Nordhaus, W.D. (1994), *Managing the Global Commons: The Economics of Climate Change*, Cambridge, MA: MIT Press.

Norgaard, R.B. (1994), *Development Betrayed: The End of Progress and a Coevolutionary Revisioning of the Future*, London and New York: Routledge.

Pearce, D.W., E.B. Barbier and A. Markandya (1990), *Sustainable Development: Economics and Environment in the Third World*, Aldershot, UK and Brookfield, US: Edward Elgar.

Rawls, J. (1972), *A Theory of Justice*, Cambridge, MA: Harvard University Press.

Reyes, E., R. Costanza, L. Waigner, E. Debellevue and N. Bockstael (1996), 'Integrated ecological economics regional modelling for sustainable development', in S. Faucheux, D.W. Pearce and J. Proops (eds), *Models of Sustainable Development*, Cheltenham, UK and Brookfield, US: Edward Elgar.

Ruth, M. (1996), 'Evolutionary economics at the crossroads of biology and physics', *Journal of Social and Evolutionary Systems*, **19**, 125–44.

Siebert, H. (1982), 'Nature as a life support system: renewable resources and environmental disruption', *Journal of Economics*, **42**, 133–42.

Solow, R.M. (1974), 'Intergenerational equity and exhaustible resources', *Review of Economic Studies*, **41**, 29–45.

Stern, D.I. (1997), 'Limits to substitution and irreversibility in production and consumption: a neoclassical interpretation of ecological economics', *Ecological Economics*, **21**, 197–215.

Tol, R.S.J. (1998), 'Economic aspects of global environmental models', in J.C.J.M. van den Bergh and M.W. Hofkes (eds), *Theory and Implementation of Economic Models for Sustainable Development*, Dordrecht: Kluwer Academic Publishers.

Toman, M.A., J. Pezzey and J. Krautkraemer (1995), 'Neoclassical economic growth theory and "sustainability"', in D. Bromley (ed.), *Handbook of Environmental Economics*, Oxford: Blackwell.

Turner, R.K., C. Perrings and C. Folke (1997), 'Ecological economics: paradigm or perspective', in J.C.J.M. van den Bergh and J. van der Straaten (eds), *Economy and Ecosystems in Change: Analytical and Historical Approaches*, Cheltenham, UK and Lyme, US: Edward Elgar.

Wilkinson, R. (1973), *Poverty and Progress: An Ecological Model of Economic Development*, London: Methuen & Co.

WRR (1987), *Capacity for Growth: Opportunities and Threats for the Dutch Economy in the Next Ten Years*, Wetenschappelijke Raad voor het Regeringsbeleid, rapporten aan de regering 1987/29, Staatsuitgeverij, The Hague (in Dutch).

Zuchetto, J. and A.M. Jansson (1985), *Resources and Society: A Systems Ecology Study of the Island of Gotland, Sweden*. New York: Springer-Verlag.

73 Energy–economy–environment models
*Sylvie Faucheux and François Levarlet**

1. Introduction

The fears about depletion of fossil fuel resources, such as oil, at the beginning of the 1970s gave a strong impetus to the development of energy–economy modelling aimed at highlighting decision-making options. Over subsequent years the complexity of modelling has increased, notably with the coverage of global environment issues such as acid rain, ozone depletion and climate change. The accumulation of greenhouse gases in the atmosphere, especially CO_2, whose emissions are largely caused by energy-related activities, could have tremendous implications for both long-run ecological and economic security. The threat of climate change is taking on an increasingly important role in designing economic development strategies and energy policies. In this context, since the 1980s it has become usual to talk about energy–economy–environment models rather than energy–economy models, because analysts now seek to address the complex interactions between the process of energy production and consumption, the economy and the environment.

A typical representation of an energy–economy system is given in Figure 73.1. The economy is presented as an open system with a special focus on energy dimensions. The main features are:

- primary energy inflows into the energy-refining sector and the economy, meaning the inputs of energy resources from the natural environment;
- waste outflows including dissipated energy;
- transformations within the energy–economy system: technical improvements, thermodynamic changes, behaviour changes, and so on;
- interactions between the inflows and outflows through ecological changes taking place in the natural environment.

* We are grateful to Martin O'Connor and Julia Haake for their contributions to the development of this paper.

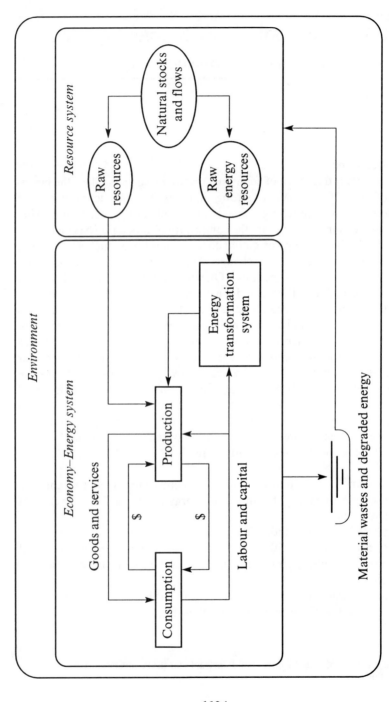

Figure 73.1   A general illustration of an energy–economy–environment system

The main economy system is closely interlinked with the energy transformation system, and both are open to the natural environment which plays the role of a source for raw materials and primary energy, and of a sink where material waste and degraded energy are discharged out of the energy–economy system. When the absorption capacity is overstretched, waste and degraded energy disturb the existing ecological structures and functions, and this can have feedback effects on the quality and the quantity of the natural resources base system upon which the energy–economy system depends.

In this chapter, we present a panorama of energy–economy–environment modelling in the last 20 years. In the 1970s, models could roughly be distinguished into those primarily concerned with inflows to the economy, the resources models (Section 2), and those primarily concerned with outflows from the economy, the pollution models (Section 3). As the complexity of models has increased over time, this distinction cannot be applied so straightforwardly, and there now exist numerous empirically specified as well as conceptual models that combine the two angles. Yet this distinction is still useful, as it allows us to differentiate the stages in recent energy-modelling history. Models belonging to the first category may be further classified according to the type of energy accounting used. Models can also, in general, be classified on the basis of their structure as a partial or comprehensive modelling approach.

Once these basic classifications have been made, we shall focus on the modelling framework. The main features discussed are the aggregation level and geographic scale (Section 4), the distinction between top–down and bottom–up approaches (Section 5), the question of the macroeconomic framing of the various models (Section 6) and the treatment of time (Section 7). As examples, we concentrate mostly on models addressing issues of climate change and related energy–environment policy issues, as these are topical and allow us to bring out the wide range of model forms. Section 8 concludes.

2.   Energy resource modelling

Among the models at the energy–economy interface which focus on the resources side, we can distinguish between, on the one hand, essentially economic approaches which treat energy as an economic variable without specific characteristics, and, on the other hand, those more associated with systems dynamics energy analysis and (more recently) ecological economics, which give a central place to physical accounting and thermodynamic laws.

Models considering energy as an economic input
It is common practice in this subcategory of energy–economy modelling to distinguish between partial equilibrium approaches and integrated or economy-wide energy–economy approaches. The latter attempt to take into account feedback effects between energy sector changes and wider economic dynamics (Destais, 1992).

Among the partial equilibrium models we find a variety of supply-side models, such as the EFOM model (Finon, 1976) and the MARKAL model (Fishbone et al., 1983), which typically use optimization techniques. Demand forecasting models, such as MEDEE (Chateau and Lapillonne, 1982) or SIBILIN (Criqui, 1994), make links between the postulated evolution of the economic system and future energy consumption trends. Many models address only a segment of the energy system, such as TEP (Boucher et al., 1990) for electricity.

Partial equilibrium approaches are useful in investigating specific features or parts of the energy–economy system, but they neglect relationships between supply and demand and, above all, ignore feedback between the energy system and the economy system. An understanding of these whole-economy and dynamic effects is, however, essential for long-run representations of the energy–economy interface.

Towards the end of the 1970s, more attention was focused on the evolution of the energy system and the matching of supply and demand over time. Most of the analyses focus on fossil fuel scarcity and its potential impacts on economic growth, including questions of alternative energy technologies.

By the middle of the 1980s, the emphasis had again changed. National models were increasingly established (this late emergence partly due to the lag between research objectives and their realization in a working model), and much modelling effort concentrated on short- to medium-term disequilibrium of energy markets, and on price and quantity impacts of energy variables on macroeconomic indicators (GNP, investment, employment, trade, and the like). The macro-energy model HERMES, set up in a European context, is a good example of a model which allows us simulate macroeconomic impacts of an oil crisis (Valette and Zagamé, 1994).

Models considering energy as a physical input
Energy analysis of agricultural and industrial economic systems goes back to the nineteenth century, but had a renewed vogue in the 1970s after the first OPEC oil crisis. In fact, modern energy analysis (EA) had already been developing steadily since the 1960s. In EA the central concept is the notion of embodied energy, which is the total energy (direct or indirect) required for the production of economic or environmental goods and services

(Odum, 1971; Costanza, 1980). As a corollary, most approaches of EA focus on thermodynamic efficiency in industrial processes. A major aim is to describe and quantify stocks and energy flows in an economy and, in a policy context, locate prospects for energy-efficiency improvements (Spreng, 1988).

There are several different types of energy accounting (see Faucheux and O'Connor, 1998, ch. 6). The most common of these include enthalpic accounting, as applied in first-law energy balances; and exergetic accounting which takes into account energy quality, in particular the capacity to do useful work (Wall, 1990; Patterson, 1993). Some EA studies deal with physical scarcity evaluations of natural resources (Hall et al., 1986; Cleveland, 1993 and Chapter 7 in this book). They give energy indicators of scarcity and of opportunity cost of resource use, which can be complementary to conventional monetary measures from standard economic analyses.

Energy analysis models can have a single-process perspective, where the analysed unit may be a single production process, an industrial sector, a national economy or the world economy. Or they can be disaggregated, where interactions between different processes are represented. Disaggregated multisector EA models often rely on input–output analysis (Chapman, 1975; Bullard and Herendeen, 1975). Energy input–output tables are numerous and provide precious information on national and sectoral energy consumption (CEREN, 1980; Peet, 1986). More recently they are at the base of the structural economy–environment simulation modelling (SEESM) approach (Crane, 1996; Ryan et al., 1998).

The SEESM approach is a dynamic simulation tool which is concerned with obtaining insight into long-run prospects for economic consumption, capital formation and environmental performance of a national economy, taking into account energy and material resource constraints. In recent years these models have been extended to include the output interface of pollutant emissions and environmental assimilative capacity. These models, which can be calibrated in physical terms using an embodied energy numeraire, allow appraisal of the speed, directions and cumulative effects of changes 'in the longer run' of variables that are mostly taken as 'given' in conventional energy–economy modelling. The purpose here is neither to predict future energy supply or demand, nor to forecast sectoral or national economy output growth rates. Rather, hypotheses about the dynamics of economic change such as improvements in industrial and household energy efficiency, capital requirements for technical change, and pollution abatement targets, are introduced as scenario choices on the basis of independent studies. The models are used to calculate the input–output flows and changes in capital stocks and intersectoral structure that, through time, result from these exogenously specified figures in conjunction with other scenario variables (Ryan et al., 1998; Schembri, 1999).

3.   Modelling focused on the output side of energy–economy systems

The first major efforts to model the interface energy–economy–environment output were spawned by the acid rain questions of the 1970s and 1980s, which particularly concerned countries in the North of Europe and in North America. The RAINS model (Alcamo et al., 1990), for example, gives a good overview of the progress of formalization in this field.

Concerning global climate change, the first modelling formalizations were derived from energy–economy analyses previously presented in Section 2. These are based essentially on carbon accounting from fossil fuel inputs to combustion gas outputs. For example, the IIASA (1981) world energy model presented two scenarios for CO_2 emissions: a high economic growth scenario implying 17 Gt C (billion tonnes CO_2) in 2030 and a pessimistic economic scenario involving 9.5 Gt C. Behind the varied models of the 1980s and 1990s, there are three common goals: (i) modelling the flow of pollutants, notably CO_2 emissions from human activities; (ii) quantifying the macroeconomic and sectoral impacts of pollution reduction policies; (iii) modelling all the feedbacks between the economy and energy systems and their natural environment. The first and second sorts of analysis are typically conducted in a partial systems framework, whereas the third sort requires an integrated analysis of the energy–economy–environment interface.

Among the first group of specific models for climate change were those developed by Nordhaus and Yohe (1983) in a probabilistic macroeconomic framework, and by Edmonds and Reilly (1983) in a very long-run systems dynamics framework (to 2100 AD). The latter work became a basis for a large number of prospective analyses. Since then, a great many models have been proposed. Without claiming to be exhaustive, we cite the following examples:

(i)   technico-economic models such as Goldemberg's model founded on experts' judgements (Goldemberg et al., 1988);

(ii)   computable general equilibrium models such as GLOBAL 2100 (Manne and Richels, 1991) and GREEN, the OECD model (Burniaux et al., 1992);

(iii) the numerous national and regional models such as the European HERMES modelling;

(iv)   structural and energy-based dynamic models such as ECCO applied to the United Kingdom (Slesser et al., 1994) and to the Netherlands (Noorman, 1995), and M3ED applied to France and to the Netherlands (Méral et al., 1994; Faucheux and O'Connor, 1998; Schembri, 1999), and a similar SEESM model for New Zealand (Ryan, 1996).

So-called integrated assessment models (IAMs) developed in the last decade, have the most ambitious goals. These are comprehensive models which attempt to provide an internally consistent, though necessarily selective and aggregated, description of key ecological, social and economic dimensions of the complex biosphere–climate–economic system. IAMs are convenient frameworks for combining knowledge from a wide range of disciplines. As portrayed by Weyant et al. (1996), their intention is to provide a coherent, systematic framework to structure current knowledge, and, on that basis, to address the fundamental policy questions about climate change: how might alternative climate policy measures be compared, and how important is climate change relative to other matters of human concern (Rotmans and van Asselt, 1999)?

There is a wide range of approaches to integrated assessment modelling of climate change. Thus it is possible to distinguish between the *policy evaluation models* and the *optimization models* (Rotmans and van Asselt, 1996). The former emphasize the physical, ecological, economic and social consequences of policies, while the latter optimize over key policy control variables given formulated policy goals (Janssen, 1996). The difficult estimation of monetary environmental damages means that most of the current policy evaluation work adopts a cost-effectiveness framework. There are a few exceptions, where policy options are formulated in terms of intertemporal cost–benefit optimization models, notably DICE (dynamic integrated climate economy) (Nordhaus, 1992), SLICE (Kolstad, 1994) or MERGE (Manne et al., 1995), A representative list of IAMs is given in Table 73.1).

The difficulties associated with modelling the climate process and physical impacts of the possible enhancement of atmosphere and ocean temperatures – such as changes in rainfall, storm and cloud-cover patterns, the rising of sea levels – and their consequences on the spatial occupation, agriculture, biodiversity, and so on, explain, among others, the controversies surrounding the results obtained and the policy messages extracted from the integrated assessment models (O'Connor et al., 1997 and 1998). However, IAMs are at least useful tools for reflection and communication among scientists and between scientists and the rest of society.

As an example, the justifications for and impacts of economic instruments, such as taxes, have often been simulated in energy–economy–environment interface modelling. The results can be highly dispersed, both conceptually and quantitatively, as a function of the hypotheses and the framework chosen by the modeller. For example:

- In the cost–benefit optimization model developed by Nordhaus (1992), the economic optimum would imply a very low control of

Table 73.1   Development status of integrated assessment models

IA model name	Key literature reference
AS/ExM	Lempert et al. (1994)
AIM	Morita et al. (1994); Matsuoka et al. (1995)
CETA	Peek and Teisberg (1992)
Connecticut	Yohe and Wallace (1995)
CRAPS	Hammitt (1995)
CSERGE	Maddison (1995)
DICE	Nordhaus (1994)
FUND	Tol et al. (1995)
DIAM	Grubb et al. (1993); Chapuis et al. (1995)
ICAM-2	Dowlatabadi and Morgan (1993)
IIASA	WEC/IIASA (1995)
IMAGE 2.0	Alcamo (1994)
M3ED	Ryan et al. (1998); Schembri (1999)
MARIA	Mori (1995)
MERGE 2.0	Manne et al. (1995)
MiniCAM	Edmonds et al. (1994); Wigley (1993)
MIT	MIT (1994)
PAGE	Commission of the European Communities (1992)
PEF	Cohen et al. (1994)
ProCAM	Edmonds et al. (1994)
RICE	Nordhaus and Yang (1995)
SLICE	Kolstad (1994)
TARGETS	Rotmans and de Vries (1997)

Source: Weyant et al. (1996).

emissions (between 10 and 20 per cent reduction compared with the business-as-usual output growth path) and a very low tax of around US$6 per ton of carbon as an optimal policy.

- In the model of Manne and Richels (1991) it was estimated that taxes would be needed of between $150 per ton of carbon (for OECD countries excluding the US) and $400 per ton (for the US and Eastern European countries). The model simulated tax levels and their impacts on the GNP that would achieve a much more severe policy target of reducing emissions in 2020 relative to 20 per cent below the 1990 levels in industrialized countries.

- In the GREEN model, the effects of a worldwide tax together with negotiable emission quotas (tradable permits) are simulated. The results are highly sensitive to the initial endowment and to the method to attain carbon emission goals for each country (OECD, 1995).

- Simulations with the HERMES MIDAS (Capros and Karadeloglou, 1991) framework suggest that the linking of spontaneous adaptations (economic agents' responses to price signals) with active policy measures to incite structural change (such as energy-efficiency promoting regulations), together with fiscal measures such as abatements in social costs for firms, can significantly reduce the net macroeconomic impacts of a tax on fossil energy in Europe.

4. Aggregation scale and geographic localization
A classification of energy models can be made on the basis of the criterion 'level of aggregation'. This may be assessed according to the number of model equations, exogenous variables, economic sectors, energy products and pollutants. The aggregation level defines the precision and detail with which interactions between economic activities, consumption, energy production and waste are taken into account (Levarlet, 1996).

For instance, the distinction between different primary energy types (coal, gas, oil, nuclear energy) and different economic sectors (households, transport, industrial production, agriculture, services) is important for estimating the quantity of greenhouse gases released into the atmosphere and also for evaluating economic sector cost abatements.

Among the global greenhouse gas models, the Nordhaus DICE model is a very highly aggregated model. It has one sector and one region, the economic part being essentially a one-good neoclassical growth model for the world economy. The model links a production model for world output, a module of utility maximization by a representative consumer, a climate module and an impact module of climate change and CO_2 emission cost abatements. The very high aggregation disguises some very substantial data, parametric and systemic uncertainties (Funtowicz and Ravetz, 1994). The model of Edmonds and Reilly (1993), by contrast, also a global model, is less aggregated. Its energy module takes into account nine primary energy sources and their corresponding carbon dioxide emission factors, and it also distinguishes nine geographic regions.

On a national level, a good example of a disaggregated model is the Jorgenson–Wilcoxen (1990) general equilibrium model applied to the US. It subdivides the business production sector into 35 industries. This level of industrial disaggregation makes it possible to estimate the impact of alternative policies on relatively narrow segments of the US economy. Similarly, because it is known that energy and environmental policies can have very different impacts on different households, the household sector is subdivided into 672 categories. These households differ by characteristics such as family size, age of head, region of residence, and urban versus rural location.

To show an example of the ranges of disaggregation, Table 73.2 gives the aggregation level for the main French energy–economy models.

A large number of environmental issues originate from energy production and consumption systems, which can express themselves at regional, national and worldwide scales. In integrated assessment modelling (IAM), problems can arise from the juxtaposing of different levels of spatial aggregation and different model components. The energy–economic models may operate on a whole nation or within regional political boundaries, while ecological impact models require data at detailed spatial resolution.

For example, the IMAGE 2.0 model (Alcamo, 1994), a greenhouse gas model, covers the entire globe. But an important goal of the model is also to provide specific regional information, because nearly all potential impacts of climate change, land-use-related greenhouse gas emissions and climate feedbacks vary from location to location. So, economic calculations are performed for 13 world regions.

Abatement costs are also different according to national economies. Global models should, ideally, simulate the different national economic impacts of greenhouse gases abatement policies, for example, taxes or emission rights, according to the level of development. For example, the GREEN model provides a framework to calculate national and worldwide benefits and costs from an international agreement on allocation of emissions entitlements. This means disaggregation into world-region or national units. However, other types of disaggregation and differentiation may also be important. For example general equilibrium models such as GREEN, which are highly sensitive to property rights assumptions (Muir, 1995), have been criticized in so far as they do not take into account the non-market structures of the energy and production–consumption systems in developing countries (Shukla, 1995).

5.   Top–down and bottom-up approaches

Two kinds of approaches predominate in the construction of energy–economy–environment models: top–down models in which macroeconomic features predominate, and bottom–up models which are based substantially on production process information (technical and engineering information). Top–down models attach primary importance to economic variables such as prices and to hypotheses about economic system equilibrium, and usually offer greater endogenization of economic behaviour than bottom–up models. Top–down models include feedbacks

Table 73.2 The degree of disaggregation in French energy–economy models

Model	No. of equations		No. of exogenous variables	No. of non-energy sectors	No. of energy carriers
	Total	Behavioural			
CGP	40	20	no data	1	2
Micro-MELODIE	90	50	110	1	2
MDE	700	175	450	2	5
MELODIE	>600	no data	no data	2	5
HERMES-FRANCE	1500	250	400	7	8

Source: Destais (1992).

1133

between the energy system and the other economic sectors, and with the macroeconomic performance of the economy.

The most significant feature of top–down models is the treatment of capital and technology. Economic capital is considered as a homogeneous input, usually measured in monetary terms. This is a highly abstract treatment, where capital is related to energy only in so far as it possesses a degree of substitutability with energy inputs in production. Technological change (that is, qualitative change in the ratios between inputs and outputs in production) is usually represented as an exogenous trend, sometimes explicitly related to energy consumption, affecting the productivity of the homogeneous capital input. In general, top–down models do not provide much useful information on potential technological improvement in energy systems, focusing instead on prices and incomes as explanatory factors in energy trends.

In bottom–up models capital is given a concrete empirical content and is related to energy in explicit ways, in terms of electricity-generating stocks, other energy-related capital for industrial, household and transportation uses and so on. Technological change is represented as a menu of options presently available or soon to be available which enjoy increasing market penetration. Energy uses and energy supply technologies are thus defined quite precisely, that is, there is a disaggregated analysis of technical options. Bottom–up analyses can thus call on energy analysis to gauge theoretical and practical limits to energy efficiency (Common, 1976; Faucheux, 1993), and to develop estimates of likely costs of efficiency gains or pollution abatement. In general, bottom–up modelling involves the following features:

- detailed representation of end-uses (for example, cooking and lighting for households, thermal energy for industrial processes);
- calculation of the demand for useful and final energy for each previous end-use. This calculation takes into account the efficiency of the consumers' equipment;
- use of models to translate economic and energy policy scenarios into useful energy and final energy demand.

The model of Goldemberg, *Energy for a Sustainable World* (Goldemberg et al., 1988), is a good example of a bottom–up approach. We can also mention MEDEE (Lapillonne, 1978) and EFOM-ENV. This latter model was developed for the DG-XII of the Commission of the European Communities during the last ten years.

Many energy and greenhouse gas abatement studies in developing countries rely on the bottom–up approach. Among the seven UNEP-sponsored

Table 73.3   A comparison of top–down and bottom–up models

Feature	Bottom–up	Top–down
Classifications employed	Engineering-based	Economics-based
Treatment of capital in the model	Precise description of capital equipment	Homogeneous and abstract concept
Treatment of technological change	Menu of technological options introduced	Trend rates (endogenous or exogenous)
Motive force of the model	Discount rate employed by agents	Income and price elasticities
Perception of market in the model	Market imperfections and barriers	Perfect markets
Potential efficiency improvements	Usually high-costless improvements	Usually low constraint on economy

studies, there are five that use bottom–up modelling (see UNEP Collaborating Centre on Energy and Environment, 1992).

Bottom–up models often give more optimistic results concerning the possibilities for implementing negative-cost or 'no-regret' policies, that is, measures whose benefits to those taking the action actually outweigh the costs involved. An important application of this idea is with greenhouse gas mitigation, where 'no-regrets' means that net benefits can be obtained when the benefits of climate change mitigation are excluded from the calculations (thus leading to negative abatement costs; see Grubb et al., 1993). On the other hand, many bottom–up models neglect macroeconomic feedbacks in energy policies, and use numerous exogenous economic variables. Table 73.3 shows a comparison of typical features of top–down and bottom–up models.

In recent years, the limits of both methods have led modellers to develop unified frameworks. The articulation of the HERMES and MIDAS structures, and the MDM 3M model (Barker and Peterson, 1987), are good examples of new integrated approaches that overcome some of the separate bottom–up and top–down limits: more detail is added to top–down models and more behavioural analysis is added to bottom–up models.

6. Macroeconomic dynamics: neo-Keynesianism versus computable general equilibrium modelling

Amongst economy-wide models, a basic distinction may be drawn between neo-Keynesian and computable general equilibrium models. Examples of neo-Keynesian energy models are HERMES, MELODIE (Berthélémy and Devezeaux, 1987) and E3M3 (Barker et al., 1995). The models of the HERMES suite were conceived as a synthesis between rival theories: a neo-classical core and a Keynesian architecture (Valette and Zagamé, 1994). Many features of this neo-Keynesian synthesis have been criticized: the permanence of the 'structural' parameters, the inability to describe non-Keynesian (that is, supply-rationed) situations, the impossibility to include externalities (particularly relevant in the environment field) and the difficulty in taking into account some important long-term factors such as technological progress.

In recent years, notwithstanding the examples just given, the neo-Keynesian approaches have been relatively neglected in energy–economy–environment interface modelling. In contrast, a range of general equilibrium models has been developed, notably in the US. There are several reasons for this. In contrast with the neo-Keynesian models, the general equilibrium models treat supply and demand symmetrically. They can, it is argued, therefore better describe the allocating and redistributing effects of an energy policy measure such as a tax in the case of climate change. Models with a Keynesian structure are focused mostly on the short and medium term and on disequilibrium situations. By contrast, the computable general equilibrium models can have a longer-term orientation, portraying an emergent economic state after the adjustment between supply and demand. By virtue of their long-term vision, these models provide a better frame for variables which have a central place in the energy–economy–environment modelling, such as natural resources, technological change and demography. On the other hand, the CGE models can be criticized from a systems dynamics point of view as overemphasizing market equilibrium dynamics at the expense of technological innovation and structural non-linear feedback effects.

There are a number of computable general equilibrium models portraying the energy–economy–environment interface. The following examples can be given: Jorgenson–Wilcoxen's model (1990) for the US; GLOBAL 2100 models and GREEN, respectively for five and 12 geographic zones; the Stephan et al. (1992) model for Switzerland; Bergman's model (1991) for Sweden; the global SGM model (Edmonds et al., 1994) for 11 regions. More recently, GEM-E3 (Capros et al., 1995), WARM (Carraro and Galeotti, 1995) and MEGAPESTE (Beaumais et al., 1994) are models currently under development in the Joule II programme of DG XII. New national models, such as the model of Böhringer and Rutherford for Germany (1997) or the model of Håkonsen and Mathiesen (1997) for Norway, are appearing sporadically.

Both the macroeconomic energy models and the CGE models depend, for empirical applications, on a large number of econometric calibrations and/or *ex ante* parameter choices. Consider as an example the econometric specification for the energy demand (*E*) which, according to the case, may involve assumptions or estimations for price elasticities, income elasticities and cross-price elasticities. For a Cobb–Douglas demand specification, it is possible to write:

$$E = \gamma A^\alpha P^\beta, \text{ or in linear form: } \text{Log } E = \alpha \text{ Log } A + \beta \text{ Log } P + \text{Log } \gamma$$

where *A* is a macroeconomic performance indicator (income) and *P* an energy price indicator; α is the income elasticity, β the price elasticity and γ a parameter which takes into account time (allowing us to represent technical progress). Generally, taking into account lags makes the structure of the equations more complicated.

The macroeconomic and CGE energy modelling approaches usually assume substitution possibilities between factors of production, particularly between energy inputs and other factors of production. However, the substitution elasticities are dependent on the form of the production function. The most usually used functional form is CES (for example in the GREEN model), or translog. In the case of a translog function, the value of substitution elasticities is not constrained as can be the case with traditional functions such as Cobb–Douglas or CES (Faucheux, 1993; Faucheux et al., 1997). The appropriate value to adopt for substitution elasticities is often a conflictual question between econometric and energy analysts. For the latter, while admitting that there may be possibilities for substitution in the short term, the emphasis is placed on thermodynamic constraints on substitution away from energy as a production and consumption input, and hence on energy and technological constraints on economic system growth paths (Slesser, 1978). However, thermodynamic constraints for most processes will be binding only in the pretty long term (Ryan, 1996).

7. The time dimension in energy–economy–environment modelling

Long time horizons, often important for analyses of energy–economy–environment interfaces, can pose some difficulties for modellers. Ideally, models should take into account all significant feedbacks characterizing the complex phenomena in the long term. This is practically impossible, because of strong uncertainties concerning environmental systems as well as economic evolution. The result is an unresolved tension between, on the one hand, an increase in the complexity of the modelling structure and the number of parameters to estimate (limited only by computational technologies) and, on the other hand, irreducible uncertainty which is, in a sense, revealed through the wide variety of scenarios and the wide range of alternative propositions about appropriate model structures, key dynamic features of the systems in question and possible values for main parameters.

While some process analyses and sectoral models provide a snapshot picture of system functioning, the more recent simulation models give representations of time-paths for key economic and environmental system variables. The passage of time enters into the specification of parameter changes for descriptive or normative aspects. For example, the time dimension is crucial in relation to assumptions about the interest rate for savings, investment and depreciation, notably for specification of a discount rate in optimization models based on the cost–benefit approach. Propositions about technical progress may also be specified as functions of time.

In models applying intertemporal utility optimization criteria, the choice of the social discount rate often dominates the results of the cost–benefit analyses (Muir, 1995). Over the long term, a high discount rate tends to reduce the weight attributed to durable environmental impacts of human activities, giving more importance to economic outputs in the present or near future. In the climate change case, these problems are very relevant. Since precautionary abatement policies can be costly in the short term, such measures may be judged suboptimal. Models do generally agree, at least, about the direction of sensitivity of results to discount rate changes. Higher control costs, lower damage estimates, and higher discount rates generally lead to lower initial control rates, whereas lower control costs, higher damage estimates, and lower discount rates lead to higher initial control rates (Weyant et al., 1996). For example, in the DICE model the initial control rate for 1995 moves from 9 per cent below baseline emissions in the base case to 19 per cent when the pure rate of time preference is changed from its base value of 3 per cent to 1 per cent.

Prospects for technological change have been an enduring preoccupation of energy modelling since the 1970s. Process and sectoral analyses, as well as bottom–up energy–economy modelling, usually incorporate popositions about new technologies, new energy sources and efficiency improvements based on scientific and engineering data. Long-term forecasting and scenario modelling becomes more speculative. In the climate modelling domain, only a few analyses are focused specifically on technical progress – for example POLES and WARM. Most of the integrated models treat technical change in a highly abstract way, due partly to the high aggregation of the economic components of the models. Technical change, measured in terms of change in energy intensity or carbon intensity for a sector, may be set as a fixed rate per year or as a function of the economic growth rate, or as a monotonic decreasing rate of energy intensity. In the GLOBAL 2100 or MERGE modelling (Manne and Richels, 1995), for example, the autonomous energy-efficiency improvements are exogenous modifications for distributional parameters of nested CES–Cobb–Douglas production functions. These parameters represent changes in energy intensity of growth which are not due to changes in prices, such as regulations or tertiarization of the economy. The production on the last capital generation (in t) can be written in the following terms:

$$y = [a(K^\alpha L^{1-\alpha})^\rho + b(E^\beta N^{1-\beta})^\rho]^{1/\rho}$$

where y is the output; K, L, E and N are the inputs respectively in capital, labour, electric energy and non-electric energy; $\rho = (\sigma - 1)/\sigma$, where σ is the elasticity of substitution between the energy aggregate and added value; a is the capital share in the added value and b the electricity share in the energy aggregate. The modification of the energy intensity of growth is achieved by a modification in the parameter b. The latter is hypothesized to decrease according to annual variation in function of the considered region: 0.5 per cent for OECD, 0.25 per cent for ex-USSR countries, 1 per cent for China and 0 per cent for the rest of the world. Such a value for the parameter is an important point of discussion, because the results of the model are very sensitive to the chosen hypotheses.

Uncertainty is a key issue in all prospective studies. It intervenes at a number of levels and stages of modelling. Taking the case of the climate change preoccupations, there are important uncertainties concerning: the forecasts in the volume of greenhouse gas (GHG) emissions; the dynamics of climatic systems and the concentration of gases in the atmosphere; the regional physical impacts of the expected rise in temperature; the economic impacts of climate change; and the agents' behaviour *vis-à-vis* the policies of GHG emissions reduction (IPCC, 1995).

Uncertainty in economics is often treated by means of assigning probabilities to the range of outcomes identified as possible, thus permitting application of concepts of expected value (theory of risk, and so on). However, it is widely argued that environmental problems are characterized by strong uncertainty, where the probabilities of future states of the world are unknown (*ex ante*) or unknowable. In climate change most uncertainty questions belong to this last category (as argued by Edmonds and Reilly, 1985).

Energy–economy–environment modelling can treat uncertainty in a number of ways, including: (i) sensitivity analysis of the exogenous variables and key parameters of the model; (ii) scenario construction with contrasting hypotheses within deterministic models; and (iii) stochastic treatment of exogenous variables and parameters. Stochastic simulation models can be thought of as a statistical form of sensitivity analysis, which can generate a distribution of possible outcomes through 'Monte Carlo' methods – a large number of simulations generated by probability distributions for all major inputs and model parameters.

- A good example of the first case is given by the sensitivity analysis for the CETA model (Peek and Teisberg, 1992) for GHG abatement control rates and carbon taxes. The initial control rate for the years 1990–2000 moves from 0 per cent below baseline emissions in the base case to 7 per cent when the responsiveness of global mean surface temperature to a CO_2 doubling is increased from 1 °C to 5 °C.
- The models PAGE (Hope et al., 1992) and ICAM-2 (Dowlatabadi and Morgan, 1993) are good examples of integrated assessment models that support the stochastic simulation approach. Each input distribution is sampled, the value chosen is used in the subsequent calculations of the model, and the process is continued until probability distributions are derived for each output variable of the model (Weyant et al., 1996).
- The SEESM approach is a good example of a deterministic scenario modelling approach. It links natural resource requirements, economic production, household consumption and environmental pressures, such as pollutant emissions, through a multisectoral dynamic model. Emissions ceilings, primary energy sources, technical change rates, lifestyle or consumption patterns and so on are all set as scenario choices, on the basis of independent studies, and the model then calculates the input–output flows and changes in capital stocks and the intersectoral structure that result. Insights are obtained through identifying the variations in scenario outcomes as a function of the hypotheses introduced (Ryan et al., 1998)

8.   Conclusion

There exists not one but a diversity of energy modelling approaches. While these are often presented as incompatible or exclusive of each other, we suggest that despite the impossibility of making all results compatible or commensurate, there is a certain complementarity (Faucheux et al., 1996). No model can completely represent reality, so a choice has to be made about what key features are to be included in any modelling approach. As Sterman (1991, p. 221) remarks, 'the art of model building is knowing what to cut out, and the purpose of the model acts as the logical knife'. The purpose is the key thing that defines any energy–economic model structure. Models focus on different sorts of phenomena, and investigate processes of change on different levels. For example, single-process models examine prospects for direct energy-efficiency improvements; sectoral models may be used to explore possibilities of new technology penetration and cost; neo-Keynesian models provide an analysis of inertia and resistance to economic change; CGE models can deal with market system responsiveness questions such as those concerning the tradable emission permits; physical–economic SEESM models combine system dynamics with energy input–output analysis in order to portray several features of interlinked economic and ecological structures and processes in an integrated way.

References
Alcamo, J. (ed.) (1994), *IMAGE 2.0: Integrated Modelling of Global Climate Change*, Dordrecht: Kluwer Academic Publishers.
Alcamo, J., R. Shaw and Hordijk (eds) (1990), *The RAINS Model of Acidification: Science and Strategies in Europe*, Dordrecht: Kluwer Academic Publishers.
Barker, T., B. Gardiner and D. Alistair (1995), 'E3ME Version 1.1 (E3ME11) user's manual', final report prepared for CEC DG XII, September.
Barker, T. and W. Peterson (eds) (1987), *The Cambridge Multisectoral Dynamic Model of the British Economy*, Cambridge, UK: Cambridge University Press.
Beaumais, O., L. Ragot and K. Schubert (1994), 'Mégapestes: Manuel de l'utilisateur', working paper, Erasme, Paris, October.
Bergman, L. (1991), 'General equilibrium effects of environmental policy: a CGE-modelling approach', *Environmental and Resource Economics*, **1**, 45–61.
Berthelemy, J.C. and J.G. Devezeaux de Lagrange (1987), 'Le modèle MELODIE: un modèle énergétique de long terme pour l'économie française', *Revue d'Economie Politique*, no. 97, pp. 649–72.
Böhringer, C. and T.F. Rutherford (1997), 'Carbon taxes with exemptions in an open economy: a general equilibrium analysis of the German tax initiative', *Journal of Environmental Economics and Management*, **32**, (2), 189–203.
Boucher, J., D. Gusbin, Y. Smeers and J.-Y. Wei (1990), 'Rapport Final à la Commission des Communautés Européenne', CORE, Université Catholique de Louvain.
Bullard, C.W. and R.A. Herendeen (1975), 'The energy cost of goods and services', *Energy Policy*, **3**, 268–78.
Burniaux, J.M., J.P. Martin, G. Nicoletti and J. Oliviera-Martins (1992), 'GREEN, a multi-sector, multi-regions general equilibrium model for quantifying the costs of curbing CO_2 emissions: a technical manual', Working Paper no. 112, OECD.
Capros, P. and P. Karadeloglou (1991), 'Energy and carbon tax: a quantitative analysis using the HERMES–MIDAS models', National Technical University of Athens, September.
Capros, P., T. Georgakopoulos, S. Zografakis, S. Proost and D. Van Regemorter (1995), 'Co-ordinated versus unco-ordinated European carbon tax solutions analysed with GEM-E3 linking the EU-12 countries', paper presented at the symposium on Economic Aspects of Environmental Policy Making in a Federal System, Leuven, 14–16 June.
Carraro, C. and M. Galeotti (1995), *Un Modello per l'Europa: Occupazione, Ambiente e Progresso Tecnico*, Bologna: Il Mulino.
CEREN (1980), 'Contenu énergétique des biens en 1977', Paris, April.
Chapman, P.F. (1975), 'Energy cost to materials', *Energy Policy*, **6**, 47–57.
Chapuis, T., M. Duong and M. Grubb (1995), 'The greenhouse cost model: an exploration of the implications for climate change policy of inertia and adaptability in energy systems', International Energy Workshop, International Institute for Applied Systems Analysis, Laxenburg, Austria, 20–22 June.

Chateau, B. and B. Lapillone (1982), *Energy Demand Facts and Trends*, Vienna and New York: Springer-Verlag, pp. 181–99.

Cleveland, C.J. (1993), 'An exploration of alternative measures of natural resource scarcity: the case of petroleum resources in the U.S.', *Ecological Economics*, **7** (2), 123–57.

Cohan, D., R.K. Stafford, J.D. Scheraga and S. Herrod (1994), 'The global climate policy evaluation framework', *Proceedings of the 1994 A&WMA Global Climate Change Conference, Phoenix*, Air & Waste Management Association, Pittsburgh, 8 April.

Commission of the European Communities (1992), *PAGE User Masual*, Brussels: CEC.

Common, M. (1976), 'The economics of energy analysis reconsidered', *Energy Policy*, **7**, 158–65.

Costanza, R. (1980), 'Embodied energy and economic valuation', *Science*, **210**, 1219–24.

Crane, D.C. (1996), 'Balancing pollutant emissions and economic growth in a physically conservative world', *Ecological Economics*, **16**, 257–68.

Criqui, P. (1994), 'A detailed simulation approach to world energy modelling: the SIBILIN and POLES experience', in T. Sterner (ed.), *International Energy Economics*, London: Chapman and Hall, pp. 221–37.

Destais, G. (1992), 'A comparison of energy–economy models: the French experience', in T. Sterner (ed.), *International Energy Economics*, London: Chapman and Hall, pp. 185–202.

Dowlatabadi, H. and M.G. Morgan (1993), 'A model framework for integrated assessment of the climate problem', *Energy Policy*, **21**, 209–21.

Edmonds, J.A. and J. Reilly (1983), 'A global energy–economic model of carbon dioxide release', *Energy Economics*, **5** (2), April.

Edmonds, J.A. and J. Reilly (1985), 'Time and uncertainty: analytic paradigms and policy requirements', in W. van Gool and J.J.C. Bruggink (eds), *Energy and Time in the Economic and Physical Sciences*, Amsterdam: North-Holland.

Edmonds, J.A., H.M. Pitcher, Baron R. Barns and M.A. Wise (1994), 'Modelling future greenhouse gas emissions: the second generation model description', Washington Pacific Northwest Laboratory, February.

Faucheux, S. (1993), 'The role of energy in production functions', *International Journal of Global Energy Issues*, Special Issue on Energy Analysis, **5**, (1), 45–55.

Faucheux, S. and M. O'Connor (eds) (1998), *Valuation for Sustainable Development: Methods and Policy Indicators*, Cheltenham, UK and Northampton, US: Edward Elgar.

Faucheux, S., D. Pearce and J. Proops (1996), *Models of Sustainable Development*, Cheltenham, UK: Edward Elgar.

Faucheux, S., E. Muir and M. O'Connor (1997), 'Neoclassical capital theory and *weak* indicators for sustainability', *Land Economics*, **73** (4), 528–52.

Finon, D. (1976), 'Un modèle énergétique pour la France', CNRS, Energie et Société, Paris.

Fishbone, L.G., L. Giesen, G. Goldstein, H.A. Hymmen, K.J. Stocks, H. Vos, D. Wilde, R. Zölcher, C. Balzer and H. Abiloch (1983), 'User's guide for MARKAL (BNL/KFA Version 2.0): a multi-period, linear-programming model for energy system analysis', IEA International Systems Analysis Project, BNL 51701, Brookhaven National Laboratory and Kernforschungsanlage Jülich.

Funtowicz, S.O. and J.R.R. Ravetz (1994), 'The worth of a songbird: ecological economics as a post-normal science', *Ecological Economics*, **10** (3), 197–207.

Goldemberg, J., T.B. Johasson, A.K.N. Reddy and R.H. Williams (1988), *Energy for a Sustainable World*, New Dehli: Wiley Eastern Limited.

Grubb, M., J. Edmonds, P. Ten Brink and M. Morrison (1993), 'The costs of limiting fossil-fuel CO_2 emissions: a survey and analysis', *Annual Review of Energy and Environment*, **18**, 397–478.

Håkonsen, L. and L. Mathiesen (1997), 'CO_2-stabilization may be a "no-regret" policy: a general equilibrium analysis of the Norwegian economy', *Environmental and Resource Economics*, **9** (2), 171–98.

Hall, C.A.S., C.J. Cleveland and R. Kaufman (1986), *Energy and Resource Quality*, New York: J. Wiley & Sons.

Hammitt, J.-K. (1995), 'Outcome and value uncertainties in global change policy', *Climatic Change*, **30** (2), 125–45.

Hope, C., J. Anderson and P. Wenman (1993), 'Policy analysis of the greenhouse effect: an application of the PAGE model', *Energy Policy*, **21**, 327–38.

IIASA (International Institute of Applied Systems Analysis) (1981), *Energy in a Finite World*, Energy Systems Group, Cambridge, MA: Ballinger.

IPCC (Intergovernmental Panel on Climate Change) (1995), *Climate Change 1994: Radiative Forcing of Climate Change and an Evaluation of the IPCC IS92 Emission Scenarios*, edited by J.T. Houghton, L.G. Meira Filho, J. Bruce, H. Lee, B.A. Callander, E. Haites, N. Harris and K. Maskell, Cambridge, UK: Cambridge University Press.

Janssen, M. (1996), 'Meeting targets, tools to support integrated assessment modelling of global change', Ph.D. thesis, University of Maastricht.

Jorgenson, D.W. and P.J. Wilcoxen (1990), 'Environmental regulation and US economic growth', *The Rand Journal of Economics*, **21** (2), 314–40.

Kolstad, C.D. (1994), 'Mitigating climate change impacts: the conflicting effects of irreversibilities in CO_2 accumulation and emission control investment', in N. Nakicenovic, W.D. Nordhaus, R. Richels and R.L. Toth (eds), *Integrative Assessment of Mitigation Impacts and Adaptation to Climate Change*, IIASA, Laxenburg, Austria, pp. 205–18.

Lapillonne, B. (1978), 'MEDEE-2: a model for long term demand evaluation', IIASA, RR 77–78, Laxemburg, Austria.

Lempert, R.J., M.E. Schlesinger and J.K. Hammitt (1994), 'The impacts of potential abrupt climate changes on near-term policy choices', *Climatic Change*, **26**, 351–76.

Levarlet, F. (1996), 'Les modèles éco-énergétiques à l'interface économie environnement', Ph.D. thesis, Université de Paris-I, Panthéon-Sorbonne, Paris.

Maddison, D. (1995), 'A cost benefit analysis of slowing climate change', *Energy Policy*, **23**, 337–46.

Manne, A.S. and R.G. Richels (1991), 'Global CO_2 emission reduction – the impacts of rising costs', *The Energy Journal*, **12** (1), 87–107.

Manne, A.S., R. Mendelson and R.G. Richels (1995), 'MERGE – a model for evaluatinig regional and global effects of GHG reduction policies', *Energy Policy*, **23** (1), 17–34.

Matsuoka, Y., M. Kaimuma and T. Morita (1995), 'Scenario analysis of global warming using the Asian-Pacific integrated model', *Energy Policy*, **23**, 17–34.

Méral, P., P. Schembri and E. Zyla (1994), 'Technological lock-in and complex dynamics: lessons from the French nuclear policy', *Revue Internationale de Systémique*, **8** (4–5), 469–93.

MIT (Massachussetts Institute of Technology) (1994), 'Joint program on the science and technology of global climate change', Center for Global Change Science and Center for Energy and Environmental Policy Research, Cambridge, MA.

Mori, S. (1995), 'Long-term interactions among economy, environment, energy, and land-use changes – an extension of Maria model', Technical Report IA-TR-95-04, Science University of Tokyo, Japan.

Morita, T., Y. Matsuoka, M. Kaihuma, H. Harasawa and K. Kai (1993), 'AIM – Asian Pacific integrated model for evaluating policy options to reduce GHG emissions and global warming impacts', Interim Report, National Institute for Environmental Studies, Tsukuba, Japan.

Muir, E. (1995), 'The question of value: price and output distribution sensitivities in general equilibrium', M.Sc. thesis, Department of Economics/Environmental Science, University of Auckland, New Zealand.

Noorman, K.J. (1995), 'Exploring futures from an energy perspective. A natural capital accounting model study into the long-term economic development potential of the Netherlands', unpublished Ph.D. thesis, University of Groningen.

Nordhaus, W.D. (1992), 'An optimal transition path for controlling greenhouse gases', *Science*, **258**, 1315–19.

Nordhaus, W.D. (1994), *Managing the Global Commons: The Economics of Climate Change*, Cambridge, MA: MIT Press.

Nordhaus, W.D. and Z. Yang (1995), *RICE: A Regional Dynamic General Equilibrium Model of Optimal Climate Change Policy*, New Haven, CT: Yale University Press.

Nordhaus, W.D. and G. Yohe (1983), *Future Paths of Energy and Carbon Dioxide Emissions in Changing Climate*, Washington, DC: National Academy of Sciences.

O'Connor, M., S. Faucheux and S. van den Hove (1997), 'EC pre-Kyoto climate policy process', EU Report, DG-XII.

O'Connor, M., S. Faucheux and S. van den Hove (1998), 'EU climate policy/research interface for Kyoto and beyond', *International Journal of Environment and Pollution*, special issue, **10** (3/4), 12–48.

Odum, H.T. (1971), *Environment, Power and Society*, New York: Wiley Interscience.

OECD (Organization for Economic Cooperation and Development) (1995), *Le Réchauffement Planétaire*, Paris: OECD.

Patterson, M.G. (1993), 'Approaches to energy quality in energy analysis', *International Journal of Global Energy Issues*, **5** (1),19–28.

Peek, S.C. and T.J. Teisberg (1992), 'CETA: a model for carbon emission trajectory assessment', *The Energy Journal*, **13** (1), 55–77.

Peet, J. (1986), 'Energy requirement of output of the New Zealand economy, 1976–1977', *Energy*, **11**, 659–70.

Rotmans, J. and H.J.M. de Vries (1997), *Perspectives on Global Change: the TARGETS Approach*, Cambridge, UK: Cambridge University Press.

Rotmans, J. and M.B.A. van Asselt (1996), 'Integrated assessment: a growing child on its way to maturity', *Climatic Change*, **34** (3–4), 327–36.

Rotmans, J. and M.B.A. van Asselt (1999), 'Perspectives on a sustainable future', *International Journal of Sustainable Development*, (forthcoming).

Ryan, G. (1996), 'Dynamic physical analysis of long term economic environment options', Ph.D. thesis, Department of Chemical and Process Engineering, University of Canterbury, New Zealand.

Ryan, G., P. Méral, P. Schembri and E. Zyla (1998), 'Some exploratory scenarios results', in S. Faucheux and M. O'Connor (eds), *Valuation for Sustainable Development: Methods and Policy Indicators*, chs. 9 and 10, Cheltenham, UK and Northampton, US: Edward Elgar.

Schembri, P. (1997), 'Le processus de destruction créatrice dans les modèles de croissance économique', Ph.D thesis, Université de Paris Panthéon Sorbonne.

Schembri, P. (1999), 'Adaptation costs for sustainable development and ecological transitions: a presentation of the structural model with reference to French energy-economy-carbon dioxide emission prospects', *International Journal of Environment and Pollution*, (forthcoming).

Shukla, P.R. (1995), 'Greenhouse gas models and abatement costs for developing nations', *Energy Policy*, **23** (8), 677–87.

Slesser, M. (1978), *Energy in the Economy*, New York: St Martin's Press.

Slesser, M., J. King, D.C. Crane and C. Revie (1994), *UKECCO Technical User's Manual*, vols 1 and 2, Centre for Human Ecology, University of Edinburgh.

Spreng, D.T. (1988), *Net Energy Analysis and the Energy Requirement of Energy Systems*, New York: Praeger.

Stephan, G., R. Van Nieuwkoop and T. Wiedmer (1992), 'Social incidence and economic costs of carbon limits. A computable general equilibrium analysis for Switzerland', *Environmental and Resource Economics*, **2** (6), 569–91.

Sterman, J.D. (1991), 'A sceptic's guide to computer models', in *Managing a Nation. The Microcomputer Software Catalog*, ch. 14, Oxford: Westview Press.

Tol, R.S.J., T. van der Burg, H.M.A. Jansen and H. Verbruggen (1995), 'The climate fund – some notions on the socio-economic impacts of greenhouse gas emissions and emission reduction in an international context', Institute for Environmental Studies, Report R95/03, Vrije Universiteit, Amsterdam.

UNEP (United Nations Environment Programme) (1992), 'UNEP greenhouse gas abatement costing studies: analysis of abatement costing issues and preparation of a methodology to undertake national greenhouse gas abatement costing studies – Phase Two guidelines',

Collaborating Centre on Energy and Environment, Working Paper, Risø National Laboratory, Denmark.

Valette, P. and P. Zagamé (eds) (1994), *The HERMES Macro-economic Model*, Amsterdam: North-Holland.

Wall, G. (1990), 'Exergy conversion in Japanese society', *Energy*, **15** (5), 435–44.

WEC (World Energy Council) and IIASA (International Institute for Applied Systems Analysis) (1995), *Global Energy Perspectives to 2050 and Beyond*, London; World Energy Council.

Weyant, J., O. Davidson, H. Dowlatabadi, J. Edmonds, M. Grubb, E.A. Parson, R. Richels, J. Rotmans, P.R. Shukla, R.S.J. Tol, W. Cline and S. Fankhauser (1996), 'Integrated assessment, climate change 1995: economic and social dimensions of climate change', Contribution of Working Group III to the *Second Assessment Report of the IPCC*, pp. 367–96, Cambridge University Press.

Wigley, T.M.L. (1993), 'Balancing the carbon budget: implications for projection of future carbon dioxide concentration changes', *Tellus*, **45** (5), 409–25.

Yohe, G. and R. Wallace (1995), 'Near-term mitigation policy for global change under uncertainty: minimizing the expected cost of meeting unknown concentrations', Department of Economics, Wesleyan University, Wesleyan, CT.

74 Decomposition methodology in energy demand and environmental analysis

Beng Wah Ang

1. Introduction

The world oil crisis that took place in 1973/74 has provided a major impetus to energy demand studies. A notable development has been the growing use of quantitative methodologies in economics, statistics, operations research, and industrial and systems engineering to analyse historical and forecast future energy demand. The concern about the effectiveness of energy use has also led to the development and application of various energy performance indicators, such as the energy–output ratio, energy intensity, energy coefficient and energy elasticity.

The energy–output ratio, one of the most commonly used energy performance indicators, is defined as the total energy consumption in the economy divided by the national output. At the level of sectoral energy consumption, such as in the manufacturing industry, it is defined as manufacturing energy consumption divided by manufacturing output and is also referred to as the aggregate energy intensity. A change in the ratio, especially a rapid one, calls for the identification of the contributing factors so that appropriate actions can be taken if needed. Two factors that have often been examined are changes in the composition of activity (that is, structural effect) and changes in sectoral energy intensities (intensity effect). The sectoral energy intensity is the quantity of energy needed to achieve a given level of output for each specific activity/sector. The composition of activity is effectively beyond the control of energy policy makers, while changes in sectoral energy intensities can be influenced through energy policy measures such as taxes, regulatory standards, financial incentives and information programmes.

Various approaches have been proposed to decompose changes in the aggregate energy intensity. The problem is similar to the index number problem in economics and the approaches have been collectively referred to as the decomposition methodology in the energy literature. Since the early 1980s, this methodology has been widely used in industrial energy demand analysis. More recently, with the growing concern about global warming and air pollution, a number of studies using the methodology to study energy-induced emissions of CO_2 and other gases have been reported. As the application of the methodology to industrial energy demand analysis is the best established, this application area will be the main focus of this chapter. Extensions of the methodology to study energy-induced gas emissions will also be discussed. Rose and Casler (1996) considered this methodology as index number analysis, as opposed to a related methodology in input–output economics which they referred to as input–output structural decomposition analysis. For this related methodology, the reader may refer to Rose, Chapter 75 in this handbook.

2. Basic forms of decomposition methods

Define the following variables which are normally measured on an annual basis. Energy consumption is measured in energy units and industrial production in monetary units.

E = Total industrial energy consumption
E_i = Energy consumption in industrial sector i
Y = Total industry production
Y_i = Production of sector i
y_i = Production share of sector i $(= Y_i/Y)$
I = Aggregate energy intensity $(= E/Y)$
I_i = Energy intensity of sector i $(= E_i/Y_i)$

The aggregate energy intensity may be expressed in terms of the disaggregated sectoral data in the form

$$I = \Sigma_i y_i I_i \tag{74.1}$$

Let D_{tot} denote the aggregate energy intensity index, which is defined as the ratio of the intensity of one year to another, say, year T to year 0. Then

$$D_{tot} = I_T/I_0$$
$$= \Sigma_i y_{i,T} I_{i,T} / \Sigma_i y_{i,0} I_{i,0} \tag{74.2}$$

Several decomposition methods have been proposed based on this index and they are described in Ang (1994). The formulation of two of the commonly used methods is described below.

Laspeyres index method
Taking year 0 as the base year and expanding I_T, it can be shown that

$$I_T = \Sigma_i y_{i,T} I_{i,0} + \Sigma_i y_{i,0} I_{i,T} + \Sigma_i (y_{i,T} - y_{i,0})(I_{i,T} - I_{i,0}) - \Sigma_i y_{i,0} I_{i,0} \tag{74.3}$$

Dividing by I_0 equation (74.3) may be expressed in the form

$$D_{tot} = D_{str} + D_{int} + D_{rsd} \tag{74.4}$$

where

$$D_{str} = \Sigma_i y_{i,T} I_{i,0} / I_0 \tag{74.5}$$

$$D_{int} = \Sigma_i y_{i,0} I_{i,T} / I_0 \tag{74.6}$$

$$D_{rsd} = \Sigma_i (y_{i,T} - y_{i,0})(I_{i,T} - I_{i,0}) / I_0 - 1 \tag{74.7}$$

The terms D_{str} and D_{int} respectively denote the decomposed structural effect and intensity effect and they are index numbers expressed in the Laspeyres form. From equation (74.5), with energy intensities held at the respective values in year 0, D_{str} captures the net effect of changes in product mix from year 0 to year T. Likewise, with product mix held unchanged from that in year 0, D_{int} captures the net effect of changes in sectoral energy intensities between the two years. The residual term, D_{rsd}, incorporates the interaction effect of changes in industrial structure and sectoral energy intensity. In the above formulation, the decomposed effects are given in the additive form. Examples of studies using this method or its equivalent are Jenne and Cattell (1983), Bending et al. (1987) and Howarth et al. (1991).

Conventional Divisia index method
This method is based on the Divisia approach (see, for example, Hulten, 1973) and was proposed by Boyd et al. (1987). Applying the theorem of instantaneous growth rate to equation (74.1), as described in Choi et al. (1995), leads to

$$d \ln(I)/dt = \Sigma_i w_i [d \ln(y_i)/dt + d \ln(I_i)/dt] \tag{74.8}$$

where $w_i = E_i/E$. Integrating equation (74.8) over the time interval 0 to T and rearranging the terms yields

$$\ln(I_T/I_0) = \int_0^T \Sigma_i w_i [d \ln(y_i)/dt] \, dt + \int_0^T \Sigma_i w_i [d \ln(I_i)/dt] \, dt \tag{74.9}$$

Taking the exponential, equation (74.9) may be expressed in the multiplicative form

$$D_{tot} = D_{str} D_{int} \tag{74.10}$$

where

$$D_{str} = \exp\left[\int_0^T \Sigma_i w_i \,[d \ln(y_i)/dt]\, dt\right] \qquad (74.11)$$

$$D_{int} = \exp\left[\int_0^T \Sigma_i w_i \,[d \ln(I_i)/dt]\, dt\right] \qquad (74.12)$$

To apply equations (74.11) and (74.12), discrete data are used. A common practice is to adopt the arithmetic mean weight function, which results in

$$D_{str} = \exp\left[\Sigma_i \,(w_{i,T} + w_{i,0})/2 \,\ln(y_{i,T}/y_{i,0})\right] \qquad (74.13)$$

$$D_{int} = \exp\left[\Sigma_i \,(w_{i,T} + w_{i,0})/2 \,\ln(I_{i,T}/I_{i,0})\right] \qquad (74.14)$$

As a result of this approximation, the product of equations (74.13) and (74.14) is no longer exactly equal to D_{tot}. We rewrite equation (74.10) as

$$D_{tot} = D_{str} D_{int} D_{rsd} \qquad (74.15)$$

where D_{rsd} is the residual (no residual if $D_{rsd} = 1$). Examples of studies using this conventional Divisia index method are Boyd et al. (1987), Gardner (1993) and Choi et al. (1995). The term 'conventional' is included to differentiate this method from the refined Divisia index method to be introduced in later sections.

A simple example
Assume that the manufacturing industry is divided into two industrial sectors, one energy-intensive and the other not; the related data are given in Table 74.1. From year 0 to year T, the aggregate energy intensity drops by 20 per cent, the production share of the more energy-intensive sector

Table 74.1   Data for a simple decomposition example (arbitrary units)

	Year 0				Year T			
	E_0	Y_0	y_0	I_0	E_T	Y_T	y_T	I_T
Sector 1	30	10	0.2	3.0	40	20	0.25	2.0
Sector 2	20	40	0.8	0.5	24	60	0.75	0.4
Total	50	50	1.0	1.0	64	80	1.0	0.8

increases from 20 per cent to 25 per cent and the energy intensities of both sectors drop. Thus the structural effect contributes to an increase while the intensity effect causes a drop in the aggregate energy intensity. The effects can be quantified through the application of the Laspeyres and the conventional Divisia index methods. The results, summarized in Table 74.2, confirm the above-mentioned directions and give the contributions of the structural effect and intensity effect. They also show that the intensity effect dominates, and this leads to an overall drop in the aggregate intensity.

Table 74.2   Decomposition results obtained using the energy intensity approach and the data in Table 74.1

Method	D_{tot}	D_{str}	D_{int}	D_{rsd}
Laspeyres index method	0.800	1.125	0.720	-1.045
Conventional Divisia index method	0.800	1.118	0.715	1.000

3.   Review of past studies

Reviews of decomposition studies are given in Boyd et al. (1987), Huntington (1989) and Ang (1995b). Boyd et al. presented a review of eight studies carried out primarily in the early 1980s and discussed the data form and findings. Huntington discussed the causes and effects of structural change, with reference to the US, and compared the levels of sector disaggregation and the estimated contributions of structural change in eight studies. Ang gave detailed discussions on both the methodological and application aspects of the decomposition methodology based on a survey of 51 studies which cover a wide spectrum of countries and decomposition approaches. Comparisons were made among the studies in terms of decomposition approach, indicator decomposed and sector disaggregation. Ang's survey showed that most of the studies dealt with industrial energy analysis, though a few dealt with national energy consumption or energy-induced gas emissions. About a dozen of the studies were devoted to the study of the decomposition methodology, while the rest were primarily application studies.

A review of decomposition approaches is given in the next section; here we shall review the scope, applications and findings of past studies. The survey by Ang showed that an empirical study typically begins with a set of energy and production data defined at a specific level of sector disaggregation. A decomposition method is then chosen which is applied to the data collected. The decomposition results obtained, such as D_{str} and D_{int}, are used to explain the observed changes in the aggregate energy intensity or some other energy-related indicators. The issue of how structural change affects energy demand has attracted the greatest interest. The findings, such as the relative contributions of structural change and changes in sectoral energy intensities, tend to vary between countries. For the same country, these relative contributions also vary with respect to energy type and time period. More studies found a smaller impact of structural change than the impact of changes in sectoral energy intensities. This is not unexpected, as changes in sectoral energy intensities, as compared to structural change, can take place more readily as a result of many possible contributing factors, such as interfuel substitution, changes in actual physical fuel efficiencies, operational changes, as well as changes in product mix within individual industrial sectors. For the industrial countries, past studies showed significant reductions in the aggregate energy intensity over time due to reductions in sectoral energy intensities. Cross-country comparisons of estimated effects are given in Bending et al. (1987), Morovic et al. (1989) and Howarth et al. (1991). Most past studies were concerned with analysing historical developments. Only a few, such as Ang (1987), Huntington (1989) and Ang and Lee (1996), discussed the use of the methodology in energy demand forecasting.

In addition to energy consumption, which is the aggregate consumption of all forms of energy, application studies for specific fuel types, such as electricity, oil and coal, have been reported. It has been common practice to study electricity consumption and total fuel consumption separately since their demand structures are fairly distinct. Industrial production was generally measured in monetary terms, either in terms of constant value added or gross output. Some studies showed large variations between the results given by these two different measures, while others showed insignificant differences. Most studies applied a specific decomposition method to a data set with a specific level of sector disaggregation. As the decomposition results are both method- and database-dependent, it is difficult to make meaningful comparisons between the results given in different studies. A few studies considered more than one method, and some, such as Howarth et al. (1991), Liu et al. (1992a), Ang (1994) and Sinton and Levine (1994) compared the performance of or the results given by different methods. Several multi-level studies, such as Boyd et al. (1987), Ang and Skea (1994), Sinton and Levine (1994) and Ang (1995a), discussed the influence of sector disaggregation.

4. Alternative decomposition approaches

The methods presented in the second section of this chapter are based on what is often called the *energy intensity approach*, as decomposition is performed on the aggregate energy intensity as defined in equation (74.2). Two other approaches which have been reported in the literature are described below. Issues related to the strengths and weaknesses of these approaches are also discussed.

Energy consumption approach
This approach involves the decomposition of the change in energy consumption level over time, that is, $\Delta E_{tot} = E_T - E_0$. Studies using this approach include Hankinson and Rhys (1983), Uchida and Fijii (1986), Reitler et al. (1987), Boyd et al. (1988), Liu et al. (1992a) and Park (1992). The governing formula of the energy consumption approach is

$$\Delta E_{tot} = \Delta E_{pdn} + \Delta E_{str} + \Delta E_{int} + \Delta E_{rsd} \qquad (74.16)$$

where ΔE_{str}, ΔE_{int} and ΔE_{rsd} are equivalent to D_{str}, D_{int} and D_{rsd} in the energy intensity approach, respectively. The term ΔE_{pdn} gives the effect of the change in total production and is called the production effect. The relevant formulae of the effects for the Laspeyres and the conventional Divisia index methods are given below. The derivation can be found in Park (1992) and Boyd et al. (1988), respectively:

Laspeyres index method

$$\Delta E_{pdn} = I_0 (Y_T - Y_0) \qquad (74.17)$$

$$\Delta E_{str} = \Sigma_i (I_{i,0} Y_0) (y_{i,T} - y_{i,0}) \qquad (74.18)$$

$$\Delta E_{int} = \Sigma_i (y_{i,0} Y_0) (I_{i,T} - I_{i,0}) \qquad (74.19)$$

Conventional Divisia index method

$$\Delta E_{pdn} = (E_T + E_0)/2 \ln(Y_T/Y_0) \qquad (74.20)$$

$$\Delta E_{str} = \Sigma_i (E_{i,T} + E_{i,0})/2 \ln (y_{i,T}/y_{i,0}) \qquad (74.21)$$

$$\Delta E_{int} = \Sigma_i (E_{i,T} + E_{i,0})/2 \ln(I_{i,T}/I_{i,0}) \qquad (74.22)$$

Application of equations (74.17)–(74.22) to the data in Table 74.1 gives the results shown in Table 74.3. It can be seen that the estimated effects given by the two methods can be quite different and that the residual term tends to be large in the case of the Laspeyres index method.

Energy elasticity approach
Ang and Lee (1996) proposed another decomposition approach which they called the energy elasticity approach. This is an extension of the energy

Table 74.3 *Decomposition results obtained using the energy consumption approach and the data in Table 74.1*

Method	ΔE_{tot}	ΔE_{pdn}	ΔE_{str}	ΔE_{int}	ΔE_{rsd}
Laspeyres index method	14	30.0	6.3	−14.0	−8.3
Conventional Divisia index method	14	26.8	6.4	−19.1	−0.1

consumption approach and is built upon the concept of energy coefficients and elasticities in energy demand analysis. The idea is to break down the aggregate energy coefficient or elasticity into contributions from production, structural and intensity effects. In the case of the Laspeyres index method, the energy elasticity is defined as

$$C_{tot} = [(E_T - E_0)/E_0] / [(Y_T - Y_0)/Y_0]$$
$$= (\Delta E_{tot}/E_0) / (\Delta Y/Y_0) \tag{74.23}$$

where $\Delta Y = Y_T - Y_0$. Substitute equation (74.16) into equation (74.23) and define

$$C_{tot} = C_{pdn} + C_{str} + C_{int} + C_{rsd} \tag{74.24}$$

We have

$$C_{pdn} = (\Delta E_{pdn}/E_0) / (\Delta Y/Y_0) \tag{74.25}$$

$$C_{str} = (\Delta E_{str}/E_0) / (\Delta Y/Y_0) \tag{74.26}$$

$$C_{int} = (\Delta E_{int}/E_0) / (\Delta Y/Y_0) \tag{74.27}$$

$$C_{rsd} = (\Delta E_{rsd}/E_0) / (\Delta Y/Y_0) \tag{74.28}$$

Equations (74.25)–(74.28) give the factorized energy elasticities which can be interpreted in the same way as the aggregate elasticity except that each is now associated with a specific effect. The data in Table 74.1 show $C_{tot} = 0.47$. Application of equations (74.25)–(74.28) to the data gives the following results: $C_{pdn} = 1.00$, $C_{str} = 0.21$, $C_{int} = -0.47$ and $C_{rsd} = -0.28$.

Approach selection
To study past developments, the energy intensity approach and the energy consumption approach are preferred to the energy elasticity approach. The choice between these two approaches is methodologically inconsequential

and depends more on ease of result presentation and interpretation. In time-series analysis, the energy intensity approach has the advantage of ease of result presentation because the estimated effects are normally expressed in indices. If the decomposition involves only two benchmark years, the results given by the energy consumption approach can be more easily understood by non-specialists since they are given in energy units. When the study period is long or the growth of industrial production is very rapid, the estimated production effect given by the energy consumption appproach tends to be significantly larger than the estimated structural and intensity effects. In such cases and if the objective is to study the impact of structural change, the energy consumption approach may not be as appropriate as the energy intensity approach. The energy elasticity approach gives factorized elasticity estimates which can be readily used to extrapolate future energy demand trends, as described in Ang and Lee (1996).

5.   Alternative methods of formulation

Similar to the index problem pointed out in Fisher (1972), an infinite number of decomposition methods can be formulated. Several methods which are different from those described above have been reported. These include that proposed by Reitler et al. (1987), which is equivalent to the Marshall–Edgeworth index, two general parametric Divisia index methods and the adaptive weighting parametric Divisia index method proposed by Liu et al. (1992a), and a refinement of the conventional Divisia index method as reported in a recent study by Ang and Choi (1997). As the method proposed by Reitler et al. (1987) is straightforward, we shall describe the last three methods. We also briefly discuss the inclusion of additional causal factors in method formulation.

General parametric Divisia index methods

Liu et al. (1992a) transformed the integral path problem in the Divisia index into a parameter estimation problem. Since many traditional indices can be conceived as Divisia line integrals following certain paths, as pointed out by Vogt (1978), defining a set of parameter values in their proposed general methods is equivalent to formulating a specific decomposition method. They showed that many formerly proposed methods, including the Laspeyres, Divisia and Marshall–Edgeworth index methods, were identical or similar to specific cases of their two general methods. Liu et al. formulated the two general methods using the energy consumption approach and Ang (1994) extended the study and formulated the general methods in both the additive and multiplicative forms based on the energy intensity approach. As an illustration and with reference to equation (74.15), their proposed formulae in the multiplicative form for the energy intensity approach are as follows:

General parametric Divisia index method 1

$$D_{str} = \exp\left[\Sigma_i \left[E_{i,0}/E_0 + \beta_i(E_{i,T}/E_T - E_{i,0}/E_0)\right] \ln(y_{i,T}/y_{i,0})\right] \quad (74.29)$$

$$D_{int} = \exp\left[\Sigma_i \left[E_{i,0}/E_0 + \gamma_i(E_{i,T}/E_T - E_{i,0}/E_0)\right] \ln(I_{i,T}/I_{i,0})\right] \quad (74.30)$$

General parametric Divisia index method 2

$$D_{str} = \exp\left[\Sigma_i \left[I_{i,0}/I_0 + \beta_i(I_{i,T}/I_T - I_{i,0}/I_0)\right] (y_{i,T} - y_{i,0})\right] \quad (74.31)$$

$$D_{int} = \exp\left[\Sigma_i \left[y_{i,0}/I_0 + \gamma_i(y_{i,T}/I_T - y_{i,0}/I_0)\right] (I_{i,T} - I_{i,0})\right] \quad (74.32)$$

where $0 \leq \beta_i, \gamma_i \leq 1$. Setting $\beta_i = \gamma_i = 0$ gives the methods in the Laspeyres index form, setting them equal to 1 gives the methods in the Paache index form, and setting them equal to 0.5 gives the Marshall–Edgeworth or Divisia–Törnqvist index form. It can be seen that the conventional Divisia index method is a special case of general parametric Divisia index method 1 with $\beta_i = \gamma_i = 0.5$. Application of the above specific cases of equations (74.29)–(74.32) to the data in Table 74.1 gives the results shown in Table 74.4.

Table 74.4 Decomposition results for specific cases of parametric Divisia index methods obtained using the energy intensity approach and the data in Table 74.1

Parameter values	D_{tot}	D_{str}	D_{int}	D_{rsd}
Parameter method 1				
$\beta_i = \gamma_i = 0$	0.800	1.114	0.717	1.001
$\beta_i = \gamma_i = 0.5$	0.800	1.118	0.715	1.000
$\beta_i = \gamma_i = 1$	0.800	1.122	0.714	0.999
Parametric method 2				
$\beta_i = \gamma_i = 0$	0.800	1.133	0.756	0.934
$\beta_i = \gamma_i = 0.5$	0.800	1.119	0.710	1.008
$\beta_i = \gamma_i = 1$	0.800	1.105	0.666	1.087
Adaptive weighting	0.800	1.118	0.716	1.000

Adaptive weighting parametric Divisia index method
Based on the two general parametric Divisia index methods, both Liu et al. (1992a) and Ang (1994) proposed a new method which they called the adaptive weighting parametric Divisia index method by defining a set of parameter values whereby both the general methods give exactly the same results for a given set of data. In this case, the relevant β_i and γ_i values are obtained by equating equations (74.29) and (74.31), and (74.30) and (74.32). The term 'adaptive' implies that these parametric values are not fixed by the analyst but are dictated by the growth patterns of energy consumption and industrial production. This differs from most, if not all, of the other methods in which the parameter values, or weighting scheme, are predefined. Due to this feature, the adaptive weighting method is appealing on theoretical ground. The results given by the application of this method to the data in Table 74.1 are also included in Table 74.4. A summary of the relevant formulae for the general and adaptive weighting parametric Divisia index methods in both the additive and multiplicative forms and for both the energy consumption and energy intensity approaches is given in Ang (1995b).

Refined Divisia index method
To overcome the problem of the existence of a residual after decomposition, Ang and Choi (1997) recently modified equations (74.13) to (74.14) by replacing the arithmetic mean weight function by a logarithmic one. They called their proposed method the refined Divisia index method since this method gives perfect decomposition with no residual. This logarithmic mean weight scheme is based on the following weight function which gives the logarithmic mean of x and y:

$$L(x,y) = (y - x)/\ln (y/x) \qquad (74.33)$$

Sato (1976) proposed the above weight function and defined that $L(x,x) = x$, which is the limit of $L(x,y)$ as $y \to x$. According to Törnqvist et al. (1985), this logarithmic function, which requires that x and y be positive numbers, was originally proposed in Törnqvist (1935). It can be seen that this weight function is symmetric, that is, $L(x,y) = L(y,x)$.

Replacing x and y in equation (74.33) by $w_{i,0}$ and $w_{i,T}$ respectively yields

$$L(w_{i,0}, w_{i,T}) = (w_{i,T} - w_{i,0})/\ln (w_{i,T}, w_{i,0}) \qquad (74.34)$$

However, the sum of this weight function, when taken over all sectors, is not unity. To fulfil this basic property of weight functions, equation (74.34) is normalized. The normalized weight function can be written as

$$w_i^* = L(w_{i,0}, w_{i,T})/\Sigma_k L(w_{k,0}, w_{k,T}) \tag{74.35}$$

where the summation in the denominator on the right-hand side is taken over all sectors. Hence the formulae for the refined Divisia index method for aggregate energy intensity decomposition are

$$D_{str} = \exp\left[\Sigma_i w_i^* \ln\left(y_{i,T}/y_{i,0}\right)\right] \tag{74.36}$$

$$D_{int} = \exp\left[\Sigma_i w_i^* \ln\left(I_{i,T}/I_{i,0}\right)\right] \tag{74.37}$$

Application of equations (74.36) and (74.37) leaves no residual in equation (74.15), that is, $D_{rsd} = 1$, and the proof of perfect decomposition is given in Ang and Choi (1997). Using the data in Table 74.1, the decomposition results obtained using the conventional and the refined Divisia index methods are compared in Table 74.5. Because of the data set used, the results obtained are very similar. This, however, is not always the case. The refined method also has the advantage that it can handle the value zero in the data set effectively while the conventional method cannot. These two advantages will be discussed in greater detail in later sections.

Table 74.5   Comparisons of the results given by the conventional and refined Divisia index methods using the data in Table 74.1

Method	D_{tot}	D_{str}	D_{int}	D_{rsd}
Conventional Divisia index method	0.80000	1.11814	0.71547	1.00001
Refined Divisia index method	0.80000	1.11816	0.71546	1.00000

Inclusion of other causal factors
Extensions of the basic formulation given by such equations as equations (74.4) and (74.15) to include additional factors have been reported. These include decomposing the structural effect further into the effect of changes in value added and the effect of changes in intra-industrial composition in Uchida and Fijii (1986), and studying the influence of self-generation of electricity or combined heat and power in Bending et al. (1987), the effect of changes in sectoral fuel share in Torvanger (1991), and the effect of changes in fuel efficiency arising from interfuel substitution in Liu et al. (1992b) and Choi et al. (1995).

6.   Decomposition of environment-related indicators
Extensions to the decomposition methodology have recently been made to study energy-induced emissions of CO_2 and other gases. Related studies

include Torvanger (1991), Alcántara and Roca (1995), and Lin and Chang (1996). As an illustration, we describe the use of the conventional and the refined Divisia index methods to decompose the energy-induced aggregate CO_2 intensity for industry. The following variables are defined, in addition to those already defined:

C = Total CO_2 emissions arising from industrial energy consumption
C_i = Total CO_2 emissions arising from energy consumption in industrial sector i
C_{ij} = Total CO_2 emissions arising from consumption of fuel j in sector i
e_{ij} = Consumption share of fuel j in sector i $(= E_{ij}/E_i)$
U_{ij} = Average CO_2 emission coefficient of fuel j in sector i, given by emissions per unit of energy use
Z = Aggregate CO_2 intensity $(= C/Y)$

Total CO_2 emissions from industrial energy consumption are given by

$$C = \Sigma_{ij} U_{ij} E_{ij} \tag{74.38}$$

Divide equation (74.1) by industrial output and expand the equation yields

$$\begin{aligned} Z &= \Sigma_{ij} U_{ij} E_{ij}/Y \\ &= \Sigma_{ij} (U_{ij})(Y_i/Y)(E_{ij}/E_i)(E_i/Y_i) \\ &= \Sigma_{ij} U_{ij} y_i e_{ij} I_i \end{aligned} \tag{74.39}$$

Let $D_{tot} = Z_T/Z_0$, which is the aggregate CO_2 intensity index. Define $w_{ij} = C_{ij}/C$ and

$$D_{tot} = D_{emc} D_{str} D_{fsh} D_{int} D_{rsd} \tag{74.40}$$

Following the steps given in Section 2, the following formulae can be shown.

Conventional Divisia index method

$$D_{emc} = \exp\left[\Sigma_{ij}(w_{ij,T} + w_{ij,0})/2 \ln(U_{ij,T}/U_{ij,0})\right] \tag{74.41}$$

$$D_{str} = \exp\left[\Sigma_{ij}(w_{ij,T} + w_{ij,0})/2 \ln(y_{i,T}/y_{i,0})\right] \tag{74.42}$$

$$D_{fsh} = \exp\left[\Sigma_{ij}(w_{ij,T} + w_{ij,0})/2 \ln(e_{ij,T}/e_{ij,0})\right] \tag{74.43}$$

$$D_{int} = \exp\left[\Sigma_{ij}(w_{ij,T} + w_{ij,0})/2 \ln(I_{i,T}/I_{i,0})\right] \tag{74.44}$$

Refined Divisia index method

$$D_{emc} = \exp\left[\Sigma_{ij}\, w_{ij}^{*}\, \ln(U_{ij,T}/U_{ij,0})\right] \qquad (74.45)$$

$$D_{str} = \exp\left[\Sigma_{ij}\, w_{ij}^{*}\, \ln(y_{i,T}/y_{i,0})\right] \qquad (74.46)$$

$$D_{fsh} = \exp\left[\Sigma_{ij}\, w_{ij}^{*}\, \ln(e_{ij,T}/e_{ij,0})\right] \qquad (74.47)$$

$$D_{int} = \exp\left[\Sigma_{ij}\, w_{ij}^{*}\, \ln(I_{i,T}/I_{i,0})\right] \qquad (74.48)$$

where

$$w_{ij}^{*} = L(w_{ij,0}, w_{ij,T})/\Sigma_{uv}L(w_{uv,0},\, w_{uv,T}) \qquad (74.49)$$

The meanings of the terms D_{str} and D_{int} are similar to those in energy decomposition. The term D_{emc} gives the weighted effect of changes associated with CO_2 emission coefficients and is commonly referred to as the emission coefficient effect. This effect is largely caused by changes in the emission coefficient for electricity, which depends on the fuel mix in electricity generation. The term D_{fsh} gives the weighted effect of changes in sectoral fuel shares and is called the fuel share effect. Using the conventional Divisia index method, Torvanger (1991) showed that D_{int} was the largest of the four effects in nine OECD countries. Ang and Choi (1997) used both the conventional and refined methods to analyse the data for Korea and showed the superiority of the latter to the former.

7. Application issues

Method selection
As shown in Tables 74.2 to 74.5, decomposition results are method-dependent. Result interpretation needs to be made with reference to the method used and the incorporated assumption. Since there can be an infinite number of decomposition methods, the analyst often faces the problem of method selection. Ang (1994) suggested three guidelines in method selection: (a) whether or not the assumptions associated with the chosen method meet the study objective, (b) ease of use, and (c) magnitude of the residual. With reference to the general parametric Divisia methods, parameter values of 0 and 0.5 are obvious choices in studying the evolving patterns of historical energy consumption. A value of 0 for all the parameters (that is, Laspeyres index methods) have the advantage of ease of result interpretation because all estimated effects are measured with reference to the earlier of the two years in a specific decomposition period. A value of 0.5 (that is,

arithmetic mean weight) gives equal weight to both years and decomposition is performed in a symmetrical manner with respect to time. A value of greater than 0.5 for all the parameters gives a greater weight to the relevant variables in year T, which is the more recent year. The concept is analogous to the discounted regression models and the results obtained could better reflect future trends in energy demand and are useful for forecasting purposes. In the case of a value of 1 (Paache index methods), both decomposition and forecasting can be done with reference to the same year.

Issues related to the residual

The purpose of a decomposition study is to decompose a chosen energy or environment-related indicator into several predefined effects. A large part of the change in the indicator appearing as a residual would defeat the study purpose. Ang and Lee (1994) found that the conventional Divisia index method and the adaptive weighting Divisia method normally give a smaller residual term as compared to the Laspeyres or Paache index methods. However, when changes in the data between the decomposition years are drastic, the performance of the conventional and the adaptive weighting Divisia methods can be shown to deteriorate and give a large residual term. This situation can arise when decomposition is carried out using highly disaggregated data or on the aggregate intensity for a specific fuel. An example of the latter case is a study that focuses on coal where the sectoral coal intensities (that is, I_i) are very different between year 0 and year T. The refined Divisia index method always gives perfect decomposition irrespective of the pattern exhibited by the data.

Zero values in the data set

Consider the case where fuel j had not been used in sector i in year 0 and it was introduced in the sector in year T. We then have $e_{ij,0} = 0$ such that D_{fsh} in equations (74.43) and (74.47) are indeterminate. Similarly, the same problem arises when a fuel ceased to be used in year T but it had been used in year 0, that is, $e_{ij,T} = 0$. In both cases, the corresponding $w_{i,j}$, is also equal to zero. These cases can arise even when a limited number of sectors is considered, particularly for fuel types such as coal and natural gas. To overcome these problems, a small value, say δ, may be used to replace the value zero in the data set. As shown in Ang and Choi (1997), application of the refined Divisia index method shows not only perfect decomposition but also converging decomposition results as δ approaches zero. In contrast, the results given by the conventional Divisia index method are highly sensitive to the assumed value of δ and do not converge as δ approaches zero. In studies involving fuel share variables, such as those related to interfuel substitution or energy-induced gas emissions, where the data set is likely to have zero values, the refined Divisia index method is therefore the preferred method.

Period-wise versus time-series decomposition
A decomposition analysis may be carried out simply using the data for the first year and the last year of a time period. This is termed a period-wise analysis and in such an analysis the yearly energy and production growth patterns in the intervening years are not known. In contrast, a time-series analysis involves yearly decomposition using time-series data and, through cumulative analysis, shows how the contributing effects have changed over time. The results given by time-series analysis, as compared to period-wise decomposition, are less dependent on the decomposition method used. However, period-wise analysis remains the more practical procedure in cases when decomposition is done at very fine levels of sector disaggregation when energy and production data are available for selected years and in multi-country studies where data availability may be a problem.

Level of sector disaggregation
Three different approaches to sector classification have been adopted in past studies. They are: (1) following the Standard Industrial Classification, (2) grouping together industrial activities which are related in terms of energy use patterns, and (3) defining a few major energy-intensive sectors and treating the remaining non-energy-intensive industries as a residual group. Studies using highly disaggregated data tend to follow the first approach, the second approach is adopted in studies in which sector classification follows that in national energy statistical yearbooks, and the third approach is often applied in cross-country studies. Arising from the above, Ang (1995a) found large variations in the number of sectors considered, from two to a few hundred, in past studies. Since the choice of disaggregation level dictates the results, result interpretation needs to be made with reference to the level of disaggregation used and generalization should be avoided. Ang (1995a) also proposed some procedures for multi-level analysis which allow estimates of various effects at different disaggregation levels to be made and interpreted in a consistent manner.

8. Conclusion and areas for future research

In the last two decades, decomposition methodology has been widely used in industrial energy demand analysis. Application studies for a large number of countries have been reported and the results obtained are useful in energy policy analysis. More recently, several studies dealing with energy-induced emissions of CO_2 and other gases have been reported. Many different methods have been proposed and two often-used methods are the Laspeyres index method and the conventional Divisia index method. Application of the Laspeyres index method often leads to a large residual, which is undesirable, while the conventional Divisia index methods cannot handle zero values in the data set. These two problems can be effectively overcome using the recently proposed refined Divisia index method which uses a logarithmic weight function.

In industrial energy demand decomposition, the vast majority of studies were concerned with analysing past developments rather than with energy demand forecasting. Application of the methodology to forecasting is an area that clearly deserves further research. In particular, the methodology is conceptually similar to some standard time-series forecasting methods. The concept of decomposition is similar to decomposition of seasonal time-series into trend, seasonal and cyclic components, since it allows the underlying mechanisms of change to be better understood after decomposition. Also, in the case of parametric Divisia index methods, the choice of the parameter values may be compared to that used in determining the smoothing constant, commonly known as α, in exponential smoothing approach in forecasting. The decomposition methodology can also be further extended to other applications areas, such as manpower requirements, and resource and environment-related indicators (for example, water demand and toxic solid wastes), where sectoral data are involved. In industrial engineering and management, these include decomposition of aggregate product defective rate in batch production for quality control purposes and of turnover ratio in inventory control to manage stock effectively, and a recent study was reported in Lai et al. (1998).

References

Alcántara, V. and J. Roca (1995), 'Energy and CO_2 emissions in Spain: methodology of analysis and some results for 1980–90', *Energy Economics*, **17** (3), 221–30.

Ang, B.W. (1987), 'Structural change and energy demand forecasting in industry with applications to two newly industrialized countries', *Energy*, **12** (2), 101–11.

Ang, B.W. (1994), 'Decomposition of industrial energy consumption: the energy intensity approach', *Energy Economics*, **16** (3), 163–74.

Ang, B.W. (1995a), 'Multilevel decomposition of industrial energy consumption', *Energy Economics*, **17** (1), 39–51.

Ang, B.W. (1995b), 'Decomposition methodology in industrial energy demand analysis', *Energy*, **20** (11), 1081–95.

Ang, B.W. and K.H. Choi (1997), 'Decomposition of aggregate energy and gas emission intensities for industry: a refined Divisia index method', *The Energy Journal*, **18** (3), 59–73.

Ang, B.W. and S.Y. Lee (1994), 'Decomposition of industrial energy consumption: some methodological and application issues', *Energy Economics*, **16** (2), 83–92.

Ang, B.W. and P.W. Lee (1996), 'Decomposition of industrial energy consumption: the energy coefficient approach', *Energy Economics*, **18** (1–2), 129–43.

Ang, B.W. and J.F. Skea (1994), 'Structural change, sector disaggregation and electricity consumption in the UK industry', *Energy and Environment*, **5** (1), 1–16.

Bending, R.C., R.K. Cattell and R.J. Eden (1987), 'Energy and structural change in the United Kingdom and Western Europe', *Annual Review of Energy*, **12**, 185–222.

Boyd, G.A., D.A. Hanson and T. Sterner (1988), 'Decomposition of changes in energy intensity – a comparison of the Divisia index and other methods', *Energy Economics*, **10** (4), 309–12.

Boyd, G., J.F. McDonald, M. Ross and D.A. Hanson (1987), 'Separating the changing composition of US manufacturing production from energy efficiency improvements: a Divisia index approach', *The Energy Journal*, **8** (2), 77–96.

Choi, K.H., B.W. Ang and K.K. Ro (1995), 'Decomposition of the energy-intensity index with application for the Korean manufacturing industry', *Energy*, **20** (9), 835–42.

Fisher, I. (1972), *The Making of Index Numbers*, 3rd edn, Boston: Houghton Mifflin.

Gardner, D. (1993), 'Industrial energy use in Ontario from 1962 to 1984', *Energy Economics*, **15** (1), 25–32.

Hankinson, G.A. and J.M.W. Rhys (1983), 'Electricity consumption, electricity intensity and industrial structure', *Energy Economics*, **5** (3), 146–52.

Howarth, R.B., L. Schipper, P.A. Duerr and S. Strom (1991), 'Manufacturing energy use in eight OECD countries', *Energy Economics*, **13** (2), 135–42.

Hulten, C.L. (1973), 'Divisia index numbers', *Econometrica*, **41** (6), 1017–25.

Huntington, H.G. (1989), 'The impact of sectoral shifts in industry on US energy demand', *Energy*, **14** (6), 363–72.

Jenne, J. and R. Cattell (1983), 'Structural change and energy efficiency in industry', *Energy Economics*, **5** (2), 114–23.

Lai, Y.W., B.W. Ang and E.P. Chew (1998), 'Decomposition of aggregate defective rate in batch production', *Production Planning and Control*, **9** (3), 286–92.

Lin, S.J. and T.C. Chang (1996), 'Decomposition of SO_2, NO_x and CO_2 emissions from energy use of major economic sectors in Taiwan', *The Energy Journal*, **17** (1), 1–17.

Liu, X.Q., B.W. Ang and H.L. Ong (1992a), 'The application of the Divisia index to the decomposition of changes in industrial energy consumption', *The Energy Journal*, **13** (4), 161–77.

Liu, X.Q., B.W. Ang and H.L. Ong (1992b), 'Interfuel substitution and decomposition of changes in industrial energy consumption', *Energy*, **17** (7), 689–96.

Morovic, T., G. Gerritse, G. Jaeckel, E. Jochem, W. Mannsbart, H. Poppke and B. Witt (1989), *Energy Conservation Indicators*, vol. 2, Berlin: Springer-Verlag.

Park, S.H. (1992), 'Decomposition of industrial energy consumption – an alternative method', *Energy Economics*, **14** (4), 265–70.

Reitler, W., M. Rudolph and H. Schaefer (1987), 'Analysis of the factors influencing energy consumption in industry – a revised method', *Energy Economics*, **9** (3), 145–8.

Rose, A. and S. Casler (1996), 'Input–output structural decomposition analysis: a critical appraisal', *Economic Systems Research*, **8** (1), 33–62.

Sato, K. (1976), 'The ideal log-change index number', *The Review of Economics and Statistics*, **58**, 223–8.

Sinton, J. and M. Levine (1994), 'Changing energy intensity in Chinese industry: the relative importance of structural shift and intensity change', *Energy Policy*, **22** (3), 239–55.

Törnqvist, L. (1935), 'A memorandum concerning the calculation of Bank of Finland consumption price index' (in Swedish), unpublished memo, Bank of Finland, Helsinki.

Törnqvist, L., P. Vartia and Y. Vartia (1985), 'How should relative changes be measured ?', *The American Statistician*, **39** (1), 43–6.

Torvanger, A. (1991), 'Manufacturing sector carbon dioxide emissions in nine OECD countries, 1973–87', *Energy Economics*, **13** (3), 168–86.

Uchida, M. and Y. Fijii (1986), *Historical Change in Energy Use in Japan*, EY86005, Tokyo: Central Research Institute of Electric Power Industry.

Vogt, A. (1978), 'Divisia indices on different paths', in W. Eichhorn, R. Henn, O. Opitz and R.W. Shephard (eds), *Theory and Applications of Economic Indices*, Wurzburg: Physica-Verlag, pp. 297–305.

75 Input–output structural decomposition analysis of energy and the environment
Adam Rose[1]

1. Introduction

Changes in the patterns of energy use and pollution emissions are influenced by such factors as sociopolitical events, behavioural shifts, technological innovation, resource scarcity and government regulation. Although these stimuli differ from one another, they manifest themselves through a common set of channels within the economic system. These channels correspond to production function responses, and we can examine the effects through a set of stylized 'sources' of change, or the pure form that the changes take in the context of production theory. For example, an OPEC price increase will lead to interfuel substitution, spur the development and subsequent adoption of energy-saving technology, and accelerate the decline of energy-intensive heavy industry. Likewise, a carbon tax will lead to substitution away from fossil fuels and will spur conservation. Once these individual responses are estimated, they can be grouped together to characterize the impact of the original stimulus.

Since the classic work on intermediate energy demand analysis by Hudson and Jorgenson (1974), it has been popular to employ flexible functional forms, inclusive of all inputs, for the production function modelling used in energy and natural resource analysis. The most common example is the translog production function specified in terms of capital, labour, energy and material aggregates, often denoted by the acronym KLEM. Typically, the production function has two decision-making levels, or tiers, with sub-aggregates within some of the KLEM components (for example, coal, oil, gas and nuclear components of the energy aggregate).

Input–output structural decomposition analysis (I–O SDA) is an alternative tool for analysing production responses at the same level of detail as the neoclassical KLEM formulations but with substantially lower data requirements. SDA is capable of quantifying fundamental 'sources' of change in a wide range of variables including economic growth, energy use, material intensity of use and pollution emissions. On the surface, these sources are simple variants of changes in: 1) I–O technical coefficients and 2) mix and 3) level of final demand. Underlying these constructs, however, is a more sophisticated base that goes to the heart of economic theory.

I–O SDA is 'the analysis of economic change by means of a set of comparative static changes in key parameters in an input–output table' (Rose and Chen, 1991a, p. 3). Most early papers on this subject used the simple three-part decomposition and employed *ad hoc* specifications of estimating equations. Such specifications arise naturally because SDA is usually implemented by changing one set of parameters at a time and using the resulting equations as a reference point for the next set of changes.

The advantage of a formal derivation is that it ensures that equations have the desirable properties of being: (a) mutually exclusive and (b) completely exhaustive. The latter is guaranteed by the 'trick' of splitting an identity into various components. The former, however, has not necessarily been verified, given conceptual ambiguities in defining decomposition terms and because of the presence of an interaction term, or joint effect. Still, many empirical studies have lent support to the comprehensiveness of SDA estimating equations by being able to ascribe 100 per cent of the change in key variables to the various 'sources' of change.[2]

The first antecedent of SDA is the analysis of changes in US I–O tables performed by Leontief (1941). More formal dynamic analyses in this vein, focusing on investment and technological change, were undertaken by Carter (1970). The first formal SDA equation derivation is the three-part decomposition of sources of change in air pollution emissions performed by Leontief and Ford (1972). The next major set of contributions was begun by Skolka in the mid-1970s and culminated in an expanded set of estimating equations (Skolka, 1989). Still, these estimating equations were not formally derived, and thus desirable properties were not ensured. The first work to address the properties of the SDA production function and to compare it with neoclassical formulations was undertaken by Rose and Chen (1991a). That paper offers the most extensive formulation and derivation to date in the form of a set of 14 estimating equations in the context of a two-tier KLEM production function.

SDA has become a popular methodology for several reasons. First, it overcomes many of the static features of I–O models and is able to examine changes over time in technical coefficients and sectoral mix. Second, SDA enables the analyst to examine responses to price changes, which are only implicit even in value-based I–O tables. Third, SDA is a pragmatic alternative to econometric estimation, which requires a long time-series of data. In contrast, SDA requires only two I–O tables, one for the initial year and one for the terminal year of the analysis. Moreover, it has been demonstrated heuristically that the SDA estimating equations are only slightly more restrictive than the most advanced of the econometrically estimated production functions – flexible functional forms such as the translog (see Rose and Chen, 1991a).

Still another strength of SDA is its I–O base, which provides a comprehensive accounting of all inputs in production. As environmental and natural resource issues became more prominent, there was a greater need to look at root causes of environmental pollution and resource depletion. These are more readily linked to intermediate sectors of the economy than are more standard approaches that focus on primary factors and GNP. To date, most SDA applications have been to historical analyses, but recent advances indicate potential applications to policy analysis (see, for example, Siegel et al., 1996) and forecasting (see, for example, Rose and Chen, 1991b).

2. Basics of SDA
The change in input requirements in an economy over time can be defined as:

$$\Delta(\mathbf{I} - \mathbf{A})^{-1} = (\mathbf{I} - \mathbf{A}')^{-1} - (\mathbf{I} - \mathbf{A}'^{-1})^{-1} \tag{75.1}$$

In an I–O context, these effects are transmitted from the structural matrix of direct input requirements, $\mathbf{A}$, to the inverse matrix of total input requirements, $(\mathbf{I} - \mathbf{A}^{-1})$. Thus the impact of changes in the input structure of specific sectors can be measured and examined in an economy-wide framework.

Rose and Casler (1996) have characterized two fundamental approaches to decomposing changes in the economy on any of its key components, such as energy use or pollution emissions. The first relies on an additive identity splitting, and is seen in the work of Gowdy and Miller (1987), Rose and Chen (1991a), and Han and Lakshmanan (1994). For simplicity, suppose the structural matrix consists of two sets of mutually exclusive and exhaustive sets of coefficients. The matrix $\mathbf{A}_1^{\prime}$ is formed by using the structural matrix from the original time period $t-1$ and replacing the structural coefficients corresponding to set 1 with their values in the next period. Then, adding and subtracting like terms, the total change in the inverse is estimated as:[3]

$$
\begin{aligned}
\Delta(\mathbf{I} - \mathbf{A})^{-1} = {} & (\mathbf{I} - \mathbf{A}_1^{\prime})^{-1} - (\mathbf{I} - \mathbf{A}'^{-1})^{-1} \quad \text{(Effects of changes in set 1)} \\
& + (\mathbf{I} - \mathbf{A}')^{-1} - (\mathbf{I} - \mathbf{A}_1^{\prime})^{-1} \quad \text{(Effects of changes in set 2)} \quad (75.2)
\end{aligned}
$$

The first term in this sum measures the change in the inverse that would occur given the updated coefficients in $\mathbf{A}_1^{\prime}$. By subtracting out the effects of changes in the first set of coefficients from the inverse in the new period, the second term measures the effects of change in all other coefficients not in set 1, in this case, the effects of changes in the second set of coefficients. If we begin this decomposition using the coefficients in $\mathbf{A}_2^t$ rather than $\mathbf{A}_1^t$, we have:

$$\Delta(\mathbf{I} - \mathbf{A})^{-1} = (\mathbf{I} - \mathbf{A}_2^t)^{-1} - (\mathbf{I} - \mathbf{A}^{t-1})^{-1} \quad \text{(Effects of changes in set 2)}$$
$$+ (\mathbf{I} - \mathbf{A}^t)^{-1} - (\mathbf{I} - \mathbf{A}_2^t)^{-1} \quad \text{(Effects of changes in set 1)} \quad (75.3)$$

Therefore, for this approach to yield unique measures of effects combining equations (75.2) and (75.3), it must be the case that:

$$(\mathbf{I} - \mathbf{A}^t)^{-1} - (\mathbf{I} - \mathbf{A}_2^t)^{-1} = (\mathbf{I} - \mathbf{A}_1^t)^{-1} - (\mathbf{I} - \mathbf{A}^{t-1})^{-1}$$
$$\text{(Effects of changes in set 1)}$$
$$(\mathbf{I} - \mathbf{A}^t)^{-1} - (\mathbf{I} - \mathbf{A}_1^t)^{-1} = (\mathbf{I} - \mathbf{A}_2^t)^{-1} - (\mathbf{I} - \mathbf{A}^{t-1})^{-1}$$
$$\text{(Effects of changes in set 2)} \quad (75.4)$$

or, by substituting equation (75.1), that:

$$\Delta(\mathbf{I} - \mathbf{A})^{-1} = (\mathbf{I} - \mathbf{A}_1^t)^{-1} - (\mathbf{I} - \mathbf{A}^{t-1})^{-1} \quad \text{(Effects of changes in set 1)}$$
$$+ (\mathbf{I} - \mathbf{A}_2^t)^{-1} - (\mathbf{I} - \mathbf{A}^{t-1})^{-1} \quad \text{(Effects of changes in set 2)} \quad (75.5)$$

However, this relationship does not hold for discrete changes, and requires the addition of a joint effect, or interaction term:

$$(\mathbf{I} - \mathbf{A}^t)^{-1} - (\mathbf{I} - \mathbf{A}_1^t)^{-1} = (\mathbf{I} - \mathbf{A}_2^t)^{-1} + (\mathbf{I} - \mathbf{A}^{t-1})^{-1} \quad \text{(Joint Effect)} \quad (75.6)$$

The second inverse decomposition technique, introduced by Casler and Hannon (1989) and found in OTA (1990) and Lin and Polenske (1995), for example, is based on an identity that follows from the product rule, so it can be considered a multiplicative identity splitting as follows:

$$\Delta(\mathbf{I} - \mathbf{A})^{t-1} = (\mathbf{I} - \mathbf{A}^{t-1})^{-1} \Delta\mathbf{A}(\mathbf{I} - \mathbf{A}^{t-1})^{-1} \quad (75.7)$$

where $\Delta\mathbf{A}$ is the change in the $\mathbf{A}$ matrix (the ijth element is $a_{ij}^t - a_{ij}^{t-1}$).
 The change in the structural matrix can be written:

$$\Delta\mathbf{A} = \Sigma\Delta\bar{\mathbf{A}}_i \quad (75.8)$$

where $\Delta\bar{\mathbf{A}}_i$ is composed of the ith set of changes in the structural coefficients to be isolated (for example, technological change in capital) in the comparative static analysis, with zeros everywhere else, that is, no change in other coefficients. Therefore, the total change in the inverse can be written:

$$\Delta(I-A)^{-1} = (I-A'^{-1})^{-1} \Delta\bar{A}_1 (I-A'^{-1})^{-1}$$
$$+ (I-A'^{-1})^{-1} \Delta\bar{A}_2 (I-A'^{-1})^{-1}$$
$$+ \ldots + (I-A'^{-1})^{-1} \Delta\bar{A}_n (I-A'^{-1})^{-1} \qquad (75.9)$$

Each component in this sum represents the change in all inverse coefficients caused by changes in the set of structural coefficients considered, holding constant all other structural changes. For infinitesimal changes, the effects are mutually exclusive and exhaustive. However, an additional effect is present when data are measured over discrete time intervals. This effect is attributable to the interaction between changes in the inverse and changes in the structural matrix, and is written:

$$\Delta(I-A)^{-1} \Delta A (I-A'^{-1})^{-1} \qquad (75.10)$$

The joint effect can be alternatively interpreted as an error term or in relation to the index number problem (see Skolka, 1989; Betts, 1989; Rose and Casler, 1996).

The complete exhaustion of sources of change is guaranteed by the identity-splitting nature of the additive approach and the mathematical rule of the multiplicative approach, both with due care to joint effects. Any empirical analysis in which the sources of change do not add up to 100 per cent of the total change would therefore be suspect. The mutual exclusivity, however, has yet not been demonstrated. In fact, from a theoretical standpoint, there are several serious aspects of the problem. First, the identity-splitting approach is not necessarily unique. That is, there are a number of alternative combinations of additions and subtractions possible, and the specification also depends on the order in which they take place. Related to this is the index number problem facing any analysis of discrete changes (see also Chapter 74 by Ang in this volume). Second, there is the issue of whether the estimating equations actually measure only the production or consumption response intended, for example, pure technical substitution (movement along an isoquant) as opposed to technological change (shift in isoquants), or whether there is some overlap. This is further suspect because of the absence of explicit prices in most I–O formulations.[4] Also, there is a question of the extent to which external factors (such as environmental constraints on input use) affect the outcome, and more generally whether the response to a source of change is an optimal one. Finally, there is the issue of interpreting the joint, or interaction, effects and whether they inter-act further with the 'pure' sources, that is, the individual production func-tion responses. As noted below, however, empirical analyses appear to provide reasonable results on these various aspects.

3. Estimating equations

Extended decomposition
The equations derived by Rose and Chen (1991a) in their analysis of changes in energy use are presented in summary form in Table 75.1. They are based on an additive identity-splitting procedure analogous to equa-tions (75.1)–(75.6) above. Two major categories of distinctions are inherent in the Table 75.1 decompositions. The first is delineation of the separate types of response to endogenous variables and exogenous parameters as typically analysed in production theory. The second is acknowledgement of important differences in major input categories. A vehicle for the analysis of both of these types of distinctions is the KLEM model. Each of these 'aggregates' is further subdivided to several levels in order to capture addi-tional important interactions, as, for example, between individual fuel types. The resulting formulation is known as a 'two-tiered', or 'double-nested', KLEM production function:

$$Q = F[K, L, E(E_1 \ldots E_g), M(M_1 \ldots M_h)] \qquad (75.11)$$

In most neoclassical versions, the production function is assumed to be a positive, twice-differentiable, strictly quasi-concave function. Also, the convention is to assume that the production function is homothetically weakly separable, meaning that the optimal mix of components in each aggregate is independent of the optimal mix of the four aggregate groups. Of course, the linearity feature of the most basic version of the I–O model encompasses homothetic weak separability,[5] thus facilitating the derivation of the theoretical SDA model and its comparison with neoclassical models (see below).

The first two equations of Table 75.1 decompose final demand changes into 'level' and 'mix' components. For example, in Table equation (T1), the effect of a change in the level of economic activity is modelled by utilizing 1972 energy and other technical coefficients, as well as the 1972 mix of final demands, throughout, but with a change in final demand levels in order to isolate the effect of economic growth. In the notation $Y^{82(72)} \equiv Y_i^{82}(\Sigma Y_i^{72}/\Sigma Y_i^{82})$, the first superscript refers to the year that coefficient values (that is, proportions, or the mix) are set, while the superscript in parentheses refers to the year that serves as the control total (level) for final

Table 75.1   Decomposition of change in energy demand

Source	Estimating equation
1. Level of final demand	$\mathbf{B}^{72}\mathbf{G}^{72}\mathbf{Y}^{82} - \mathbf{B}^{72}\mathbf{G}^{72}\mathbf{Y}^{82(72)}$
2. Mix of final demand	$\mathbf{B}^{72}\mathbf{G}^{72}\mathbf{Y}^{82(72)} - \mathbf{B}^{72}\mathbf{G}^{72}\mathbf{Y}^{72}$
3. Interfuel substitution (direct)	$\mathbf{B}^{82(72)}\mathbf{G}^{72}\mathbf{Y}^{72} - \mathbf{B}^{72}\mathbf{G}^{72}\mathbf{Y}^{72}$
4. Interfuel substitution (linkage)	$\mathbf{B}^{82(72)}\mathbf{G}^{72}_{M82(72)}\mathbf{Y}^{72} - \mathbf{B}^{82(72)}\mathbf{G}^{72}\mathbf{Y}^{72}$
5. Material substitution	$\mathbf{B}^{72}\mathbf{G}^{72}_{M82(72)}\mathbf{Y}^{72} - \mathbf{B}^{72}\mathbf{G}^{72}\mathbf{Y}^{72}$
6. Substitution joint effect	$\mathbf{B}^{82(72)}\mathbf{G}^{72}_{M82(72)}\mathbf{Y}^{72} - \mathbf{B}^{82(72)}\mathbf{G}^{72}\mathbf{Y}^{72}$ $- \mathbf{B}^{72}\mathbf{G}^{72}_{M82(72)}\mathbf{Y}^{72} - \mathbf{B}^{72}\mathbf{G}^{72}\mathbf{Y}^{72}$
7. KLEM substitution	$\mathbf{B}^{82(72)}\mathbf{G}^{82(72)}\mathbf{Y}^{72} - \mathbf{B}^{82(72)}\mathbf{G}^{72}\mathbf{Y}^{72}$
8. Tech. change in capital	$\mathbf{B}^{82(72)}\mathbf{G}^{82(72)}_{K82}\mathbf{Y}^{72} - \mathbf{B}^{82(72)}\mathbf{G}^{82(72)}\mathbf{Y}^{72}$
9. Tech. change in labour	$\mathbf{B}^{82(72)}\mathbf{G}^{82(72)}_{L82}\mathbf{Y}^{72} - \mathbf{B}^{82(72)}\mathbf{G}^{82(72)}\mathbf{Y}^{72}$
10. Tech. change in energy (direct)	$\mathbf{B}^{82}\mathbf{G}^{82(72)}\mathbf{Y}^{72} - \mathbf{B}^{82(72)}\mathbf{G}^{82(72)}\mathbf{Y}^{72}$
11. Tech. change in energy (linkage)	$\mathbf{B}^{82}\mathbf{G}^{82(72)}_{E82}\mathbf{Y}^{72} - \mathbf{B}^{82}\mathbf{G}^{82(72)}\mathbf{Y}^{72}$
12. Tech. change in materials	$\mathbf{B}^{82(72)}\mathbf{G}^{82(72)}_{M82}\mathbf{Y}^{72} - \mathbf{B}^{82(72)}\mathbf{G}^{82(72)}\mathbf{Y}^{72}$
13. Tech. change joint effect	$\mathbf{B}^{82}\mathbf{G}^{82}\mathbf{Y}^{72} - \mathbf{B}^{82(72)}\mathbf{G}^{82(72)}_{M82}\mathbf{Y}^{72}$ $- \mathbf{B}^{82(72)}\mathbf{G}^{82(72)}_{K82}\mathbf{Y}^{72}$ $- \mathbf{B}^{82(72)}\mathbf{G}^{82(72)}_{L82}\mathbf{Y}^{72} - \mathbf{B}^{82}$ $\mathbf{G}^{82(72)}_{E82}\mathbf{Y}^{72} + 3(\mathbf{B}^{82(72)}\mathbf{G}^{82(72)}\mathbf{Y}^{72})$
14. Joint effect between final demand and input charge	$(\mathbf{B}^{82}\mathbf{G}^{82} - \mathbf{B}^{72}\mathbf{G}^{72})(\mathbf{Y}^{82} - \mathbf{Y}^{72})$

Notes:
*Variables
  K = capital; L = labour; E = energy; M = materials
  $\mathbf{B}$ = vector of physical energy flows by fuel type
  $\mathbf{G}$ = Leontief inverse $(\mathbf{I}-\mathbf{A})^{-1}$
  $\mathbf{Y}$ = Vector of final demand
The superscripts refer to years of comparison (1972 and 1982), and the subscripts refer to the subset of coefficients that are changed (see the text for additional explanation of subscripts and superscripts).

demand. Equation (T2) also keeps the technical coefficients constant, as well as using constant final demand levels, but with different final demand mixes. This means subtracting actual energy use in 1972 from the calculation of the energy use in the US economy that would have been required given a 1982 mix of final demand, set at its 1972 level, in order to determine the change due to structural shifts across sectors.[6]

Equations (T3) through (T6) refer to substitution within the bottom tier of the energy and material aggregates. In this case, 1982 coefficients of individual components of E and M, respectively, are utilized as weights for the corresponding aggregates, set at 1972 levels, to capture substitution effects, for example, substitution of coal for oil. Again, the energy-related estimation is split into two components. The first refers to the pure inter-fuel substitution effect, which should sum to zero if equivalent fuel-efficiency requirements are assumed. The second refers to the higher-order repercussions of this substitution (that is, impacts on the rest of the economy).

Equation (T7) determines the effects of substitution within the top tier of the production function (for example, capital for energy). Here aggregate coefficients are set at their 1982 proportions, though the components of the energy and material aggregates maintain their 1972 proportions. At the same time, the total of the aggregates is adjusted to its 1972 coefficient level.

Equations (T8) through (T13) isolate technological changes (that is, improvements in productivity) in each of the four KLEM components. Here, the subscript symbols refer to the elements of the extended **A** matrix under scrutiny, all other elements being held constant. In the case of capital and labour there is only a single variable to be set at its 1982 level. Note that there is a pair of equations relating to technological change in energy (energy conservation). Equation (T10) refers to the direct conservation effects operating through the matrix of physical unit energy coefficients, **B**. Equation (T11) covers the indirect and induced (linkage) effects of energy conservation via a change in the energy coefficients of the **A** matrix and hence $\mathbf{G} = (\mathbf{I} - \mathbf{A})^{-1}$. That is, a reduction in energy use per unit of output will lead to a reduction in the demand for energy products and their various direct and indirect suppliers which, in turn, sets off more rounds of energy production (level but not coefficient) reductions. Equation (T14) refers to the joint interaction term between final demand and coefficient change that arises in cases of discrete change analysis.

Further decompositions

Several other decompositions have been developed. For example, final demand has been examined according to its column components – consumption, investment, government and exports (see, for example, Lin and Polenske, 1995). Closely related to this are various approaches to examining trade considerations, especially on the import side (see, for example, Pal, 1991). This has also been the focus of some regional analyses (see, for example, Holland and Cooke, 1992) and interregional analysis (see, for example, Linden and Oosterhaven, 1995). Some of these formulations have been undertaken in the context of the final demand quadrant, as in the Chen and Rose (1990) import substitution measure, while others focus on the matrix of technical coefficients by dividing them into own country and imported goods, as in Rose et al. (1992).

It is possible to extend the nesting of this formulation to deeper levels. One example is recent work by Adams (1997) on a third tier to analyse substitution between virgin and recycled materials.

The counterpart to the basic output balance equation of I–O is a balance equation relating the price of each output to the sum of intermediate input costs and primary factor costs (value added). This is often referred to as the I–O *dual*, but it has much more limited duality features than neoclassical formulations and even linear programming. Still, the price-value-added equation yields substantial insight into price formation and such phenomena as cost-push inflation. SDA can be applied to the dual equation to examine the influence on prices of various sources of change (see, for example, Kanemitsu and Ohnishi, 1989). Although most approaches (for example, Gunluk-Senesen and Kucukcifci, 1994) have involved the simple three-part SDA formulation, the potential exists for a full-blown KLEM two-tiered cost (dual to production) function analysis.

4. Theoretical underpinnings

It is not unusual for production functions to be utilized for empirical work before all their theoretical properties are ascertained. In a recent survey of applied demand analysis, Chambers (1988, p. 15), referring to Leontief and Cobb–Douglas production functions, states 'their widespread use in theoretical analysis only came after their extensive use in empirical analysis. As such, it represents an excellent example of applied production analysts crystallizing a means of research for the entire economics profession after this widespread use.'

Although the SDA estimating equations represent comparative static changes in coefficients of an I–O table, they need not emanate from an underlying production function as restrictive as the Leontief function. Several approaches should be tried to specify the SDA production function and to unambiguously delineate its properties. One is to use modern duality theory to work backward from input demand or cost. The properties of these constructs should be examined, for example, non-negativity, linear homogeneity and concavity, in the case of cost functions, and, say, reciprocity and symmetry to derived input demands. Structural properties should also be explored.

One approach currently in progress is to try to derive the SDA function as a special case of a more general one, such as the generalized Leontief cost function or other flexible functional form (see Rose and Casler, 1997).

This will facilitate theoretical comparisons with related methods, and thus enable us to evaluate the relative restrictiveness of the SDA approach.

Rose and Chen have shown that the I–O SDA model can yield results as extensive as a neoclassical flexible functional form, and with only one additional restriction. The restriction could result in a confusion of some substitution effects for output effects in the I–O approach. The implications for the accuracy of the results depends on the size of output change. For modest changes, the I–O approximation is likely to yield results whose accuracy can rival the neoclassical model. In cases of homogeneous production functions, this issue does not arise, and the two methodologies would yield equivalent results. Again, neoclassical production theory is not the only way to solidify the foundations of SDA. Other promising work extending input–output analysis in a neoclassical direction has been undertaken by ten Raa (1994). For alternative approaches, the reader is referred to the work of Hewings et al. (1988).

5. Applications

Case studies
Of the more than 50 SDA applications over the past decade, more than half have been to energy issues. One example is the study by Rose and Chen (1991a) of changes in US energy demand between 1972 and 1982. The results of this study are presented in Table 75.2, with computations based on the equations presented in Table 75.1. While the overall change in intermediate energy use was only 1 per cent, this belies the major forces at work, which, in this case, offset each other to yield the rather minimal overall change. Rose and Chen found that economic growth in isolation would have led to an 18 per cent increase in energy use, but that this was offset by an 8 per cent decrease due to the final demand mix effect and a 13 per cent decrease attributable to technological change in energy (conservation). Technological change and other factors were minimal, and two of the three joint effects were nearly zero. The direct interfuel substitution effect was by definition zero, but this is the net effect of increases in coal and electricity use and decreases in oil and gas use. The interfuel substitution linkage effect was only 2 per cent. These results were generally consistent with those offered in a more aggregate SDA approach in the 1990 study by the US Congress Office of Technology Assessment (see also Blair and Wyckoff, 1989).

A similar set of estimating equations, with some trade dimensions added, was applied by Chen and Rose (1990) to Taiwan for the period 1971–84. Here also the growth effect (further decomposed to isolate exports) was the strongest positive stimulus, followed closely by technological change in

Table 75.2   Percentage change in intermediate sector energy demand in the US, 1972–82

Source	Coal	Petroleum	Natural gas	Electricity	Weighted avg.
1. Level of final demand	17	19	18	19	18
2. Mix of final demand	−14	−5	−8	−1	−8
3. Interfuel substitution (direct)	20	−5	−16	35	0
4. Interfuel substitution (linkage)	5	*	1	−58	2
5. Material substitution	−7	−4	−7	−4	−5
6. Substitution joint effect	*	*	1	55	*
7. KLEM substitution	10	14	8	17	12
8. Tech. change in capital	−4	−3	−3	−5	−3
9. Tech. change in labour	−5	−4	−4	−6	−4
10. Tech. change in energy (direct)	−3	−17	−10	−26	−13
11. Tech. change in energy (linkage)	*	*	*	*	*
12. Tech. change in materials	1	−14	−7	−21	−10
13. Tech. change in joint effect	3	18	10	27	13
14. Joint effect of FD and input change	7	−1	−3	−6	*
Total	28	−4	−20	27	1

*Less than 0.5 per cent.

Source: Rose and Chen (1991a).

materials. Energy conservation was the strongest negative source of change, and, in this case, final demand mix was minimal. An update of the study by Chen and Wu (1994) indicated a continuation of these trends, though they were substantially muted in the most recent sub-period, due in part to Taiwan's maturation and the relative calm of the international energy situation in the mid-1980s.

Lin and Polenske (1995) performed an SDA analysis for China for the period 1981–87 using an aggregate analysis, though with an energy/non-energy separation as in Gowdy and Miller (1987), as well as a component disaggregation of final demand as discussed earlier. They found the economic growth effect to be strong, especially in the capital investment component. Still, the 84.3 per cent growth effect was offset by more than half by energy conservation. The mix effect was small – 5.8 per cent – probably due in great part to lack of an adequate energy pricing policy in China.

The SDA approach can readily be applied to analysing sources of change and pollution. In fact one of the first SDA studies (Leontief and Ford, 1972) did just that for ordinary air pollutants and the US economy. All that is needed is a set of pollution coefficients (emissions of pollutant k per unit of gross output in sector j) to perform the analysis. Leontief and Ford's SDA was the basic three-part decomposition and indicated that the growth effect was more prominent that structural shifts or an aggregate of technological change.

A major potential application of this methodology is to analyse sources of change in greenhouse gases, since the major GHGs (carbon dioxide and methane) are by-products of energy use. In the global warming context, an energy-based approach is superior to the direct pollution coefficient approach when there is an energy substitution tier capable of examining changes in the otherwise fixed pollution coefficients themselves. Casler and Rose (1998), building on the Casler and Blair (1997) analysis of energy-based pollution coefficients found energy substitution to be the dominant source of change.[7] A similar analysis by Chen and Wu (1995) indicated that growth effects predominated in Taiwan.

Note that some of the SDA energy study results by themselves can be used to perform pollution emission analyses. All that is needed is to append pollution coefficients to the energy use changes, with the further adjustment for interfuel substitution.

Gale (1995) has performed an analysis of the possible effects of trade liberalization of pollution emissions in Mexico, thereby extending SDA from its predominant use in historical analysis to an application to policy analysis. His is an aggregate approach that examines output (level) and composition (mix) effects for three categories: producers, end-users, and other. However, he does tie CO_2 emissions to fuel use. Gale found that CO_2

emissions would expand due to output growth but that there would be a significant shift away from CO_2-intensive goods as a result of the North American Free Trade Agreement (NAFTA).

Practical significance

Rose and Chen (1991b) have suggested that the 'source of change' results of an SDA analysis can serve as the denominators of elasticity measures in relation to the appropriate stimuli in the denominators. Knowledge of the relative ease or difficulty of effecting past changes may then serve as a basis for forecasts or as a useful guide to future policy modeling.

One set of responsiveness measures in SDA analysis of energy use, for example, would be changes in use of individual fuel types in response to price changes. Ordinarily this could be reflected in a simple price elasticity, holding all other factors constant. In most cases the comparative static nature of SDA computations only allows one variable at a time to change, but the interfuel substitution equation calculates the change in the fuel mix for all four fuels simultaneously. This means that relative prices must be used (in this case, a price index denominator). Rose and Chen (1991b) derived a set of elasticity measures for the US and Taiwan. With the exception of the KLEM substitution term for the US all the elasticities were within the range of *a priori* expectations for industrialized and developing countries.

6.   Conclusions

As a means of explaining changes in an economy over time, input–output structural decomposition analysis currently incorporates a wide range of techniques and perspectives. Based on the large number of articles and breadth of topics covered, there is little question that the approaches currently employed provide useful insights. However, it is still imperative to develop a unified theoretical basis for SDA and consistent measures of change effects.

Overall, SDA analyses have shown that policies aimed at reducing energy use have been somewhat effective, and that they have been reinforced by some secular trends (structural economic shifts) but offset even more by others (economic growth). These results then provide direct insights into historical sources of change in pollution as well. More up-to-date analysis needs to be performed, to gauge the effect of more recent measures aimed at reducing major pollutants through interfuel substitution.

Notes

1.   I wish to acknowledge the funding support of the US National Science Foundation under Grant no. SBR-9223856. I also wish to thank Jeroen van den Bergh for his helpful comments on an earlier draft.

2.   This chapter is intended to supplement the chapter by Duchin and Steenge (Chapter 68 in this volume), which introduces the reader to input–output analysis and explains a broad range of applications to the environment. Also, the SDA methodology presented here is closely related to a number of other methodologies. Most prominent is index number decomposition analysis, often applied to energy (see Chapter 74 in this volume by Ang, as well as work by Boyd et al., 1987, and Ang, 1995). The index number approach is less data-intensive than I–O SDA, but is not able to distinguish between direct and indirect impacts and has not been refined to as great a level of detail. Of course, this approach is often applied to issues quite apart from those typically addressed by I–O SDA, as, for example, the impact of changes in electricity generation mix on gaseous emissions. Closely related to the index number approach are well-known approaches to growth accounting, which typically focus on factor productivity rather than considerations of energy and the environment, even though some studies have incorporated natural resources as a primary factor. Another set of approaches to structural change in the context of I–O models has been undertaken by Hewings and his associates, based on entropy, extreme tendency, spatial path analysis, and fields of influence theories (see Hewings et al., 1988).

3.   We remind the reader that $\mathbf{A}^{t-1}$ represents the matrix of both sets of coefficients in its original state and $\mathbf{A}_1^t$, for example, represents the matrix of both sets of coefficients in the next time period but with only the first set changed.

4.   The effects of nominal price changes can be filtered out by simply applying sector deflators to the terminal year I–O table.

5.   The fixed coefficient assumption of the standard I–O model implies strong homotheticity. In contrast, the SDA approach is less restrictive because it only implies weak homothetic separability, but still requires constant returns to scale.

6.   The underlying logic of the identity-splitting technique is illustrated by equations (T1) and (T2). The overall change in energy use is ascertained by $\mathbf{B}^{72}\mathbf{G}^{72}\mathbf{Y}^{72} - \mathbf{B}^{72}\mathbf{G}^{72}\mathbf{Y}^{72}$, where the comparative static analysis focuses on final demand, holding all other terms constant. Adding and substracting $\mathbf{B}^{72}\mathbf{G}^{72}\mathbf{Y}^{82(72)}$ to the equation enables us to split it into two sub-equations to decompose overall final demand change into level and mix effects. Decomposition of other major components proceeds in an analogous, though more complicated, manner. Note also that changes in I–O technical coefficients are applied to the structural matrix, $\mathbf{A}$, rather than the inverse, to allow for the decomposition of direct and indirect effects. The changes in Table 75.1 are presented in relation to the Leontief inverse, $\mathbf{G}$, so that they can be presented in a more compact reduced form manner, that is in equation (8), $\mathbf{G}^{82(72)}_{K^{82}}$ really stands for

$$\left(I - \mathbf{A}^{82(72)}_{K^{82}}\right)^{-1}.$$

7.   Miller and Blair (1985) have shown that the value-based I–O coefficient approach fails to maintain an energy-balance condition, unless energy prices are uniform across sectors. Hence, forming an all-dollar inverse and using direct impact coefficients to transform direct and indirect dollars per dollar of input into direct and indirect energy per dollar of output will not generate accurate energy intensities, as demonstrated by Casler and Blair (1997). Miller and Blair recommend the use of a 'hybrid' matrix consisting of physical units for energy and dollar units for other inputs. The SDA analyses of Casler, Blair, Gowdy and Polenske utilize the hybrid matrix, while Rose, Chen and the other authors whose work is summarized here do not.

References

Adams, G. (1997), 'Structural decomposition analysis of recycling', Department of Energy, Environmental, and Mineral Economics, The Pennsylvania State University, University Park, PA.

Ang, B.W. (1995), 'Multilevel decomposition of industrial energy consumption', *Energy Economics*, **17**, 39–51.

Betts, J.R. (1989), 'Two exact, non-arbitrary and general methods of decomposing temporal change', *Economic Letters*, **30**, 151–6.

Blair, P. and A. Wyckoff (1989), 'The changing structure of the U.S. economy', in R. Miller et al. (eds), *Frontiers of Input–Output Analysis*, New York: Oxford University Press.

Boyd, G., J.F. McDonald, M. Ross and D.A. Hanson (1987), 'Separating the changing composition of U.S. manufacturing production from energy improvements: a divisia index approach', *The Energy Journal*, **8**, 77–96.

Carter, A. (1970), *Structural Change in the American Economy*, Cambridge, MA: Harvard University Press.

Casler, S. and P. Blair (1997), 'Economic structure, fuel combustion, pollution emissions', *Ecological Economics*, **22**, 19–27.

Casler, S. and B. Hannon (1989), 'Readjustment potentials in industrial energy efficiency and structure', *Journal of Environmental Economics and Management*, **17**, 93–108.

Casler, S. and A. Rose (1998), 'Structural decomposition analysis of changes in greenhouse gas emissions in the U.S.', *Environmental and Resource Economics*, **11**, 349–63.

Chambers, B. (1988), *Applied Production Analysis*, New York: Cambridge University Press.

Chen, C.Y. and A. Rose (1990), 'A structural decomposition analysis of energy demand in Taiwan', *The Energy Journal*, **11**, 127–46.

Chen, C.Y. and R.H. Wu (1994), 'Sources of change in industrial electricity use in the Taiwan economy, 1976–86', *Energy Economics*, **16**, 115–20.

Chen, C.Y. and R.H. Wu (1995), 'Effects of restructuring of international trade on changing energy use patterns and CO_2 emissions in Taiwan: 1981–91', *Proceedings of the 18th IAEE International Conference*, pp.351–60.

Gale, L.R. (1995), 'Trade liberalization and pollution: an input–output study of carbon dioxide emissions in Mexico', *Economic Systems Research*, **7**, 309–20.

Gowdy, J.M., and J.L. Miller (1987), 'Technological and demand change in energy use: an input–output analysis', *Environment and Planning A*, **19**, 1387–98.

Gunluk-Senesen, G. and S. Kucukcifci (1994), 'Decomposition of structural change into technology and price components: Turkey, 1973–85', *Economic Systems Research*, **6**, 199–215.

Han, X. and T.K. Lakshmanan (1994), 'Structural changes and energy consumption in the Japanese economy 1975–85: an input–output analysis', *The Energy Journal*, **15**, 165–88.

Hewings, G., M. Sonis and R. Jensen (1988), 'Fields of influence of technological change in input–output models', in P. Nijkamp et al. (eds), *Information Technology: Social and Spatial Perspectives*, Berlin: Springer-Verlag.

Holland, D. and S.C. Cooke (1992), 'Sources of structural change in the Washington economy: an input–output perspective', *Annals of Regional Science*, **26**, 155–70.

Hudson, E.A. and D.W. Jorgenson (1974), 'U.S. energy policy and economic growth, 1975–2000', *Bell Journal of Economics*, **5**, 461–514.

Kanemitsu, H. and H. Ohnishi (1989), 'An input–output analysis of technological change in the Japanese economy: 1970–1980', in R. Miller et al. (eds), *Frontiers of Input–Output Analysis*, New York: Oxford University Press.

Leontief, W. (1941), *Structure of American Economy*, New York: Oxford University Press.

Leontief, W. and D. Ford (1972), 'Air pollution and economic structure', in A. Brody and A. Carter (eds), *Input–Output Techniques*, Amsterdam, North-Holland.

Lin, X. and K.R. Polenske (1995), 'Input–output anatomy of China's energy use changes in the 1980s', *Economic Systems Research*, **7**, 67–83.

Linden, J.A. van der and J. Oosterhaven (1995), 'European community intercountry input–output relations: construction method and main results for 1965–85', **7** (3), 249–69.

Miller, R. and P. Blair (1985), *Input–Output Analysis: Foundations and Extensions*, Englewood Cliffs, NJ: Prentice-Hall.

OTA (Office of Technology Assessment) (1990), *Energy Use and the Economy*, Washington, DC: USGPO.

Pal, D.P. (1991), 'Import substitution and changes in structural independence: a decomposition analysis', in A.W.A. Peterson (ed.), *Advances in Input–Output Analysis*, New York: Oxford University Press.

Rose, A. and S. Casler (1996), 'Input–output structural decomposition analysis: a critical appraisal', *Economic Systems Research*, **8** (1), 33–62.

Rose, A. and S. Casler (1997), 'Theoretical foundations of input–output structural decomposition analysis', report to the US National Science Foundation.

Rose, A. and C.Y. Chen (1991a), 'Sources of change in energy use in the U.S. economy, 1972–1982: a structural decomposition analysis', *Resources and Energy*, **13**, 1–21.

Rose, A. and C.Y. Chen (1991b), 'Modeling the responsiveness of energy use to changing economic conditions', in F. Fesharaki and J. Dorian (eds), *Energy Developments in the 1990s*, Honolulu, HI, pp. 31–51.

Rose, A., C.Y. Chen and S.M. Lin (1992), 'The role of international competition in changing energy use patterns in the U.S.', in O. Guvenan et al. (eds), *Politiques Economiques et Marchés Internationaux de Matières Premières: Analyses Econometriques*, Paris: Economica, pp. 169–86.

Siegel, P., J. Alwang and T. Johnson (1996), 'Decomposing sources of regional growth with an input–output model: a framework for policy analysis', *International Regional Science Review*, **18**, 221–38.

Skolka, J. (1989), 'Input–output structural decomposition analysis for Austria', *Journal of Policy Modeling*, **11**, 45–66.

ten Raa, Thijs (1994), 'Neoclassical input–output analysis', *Regional Science and Urban Economics*, **24**, 135–58.

76 Experiments in environmental economics
Jason F. Shogren and Terrance M. Hurley

1. Introduction
Light a fire, stare at the flames, sift through the ashes, repeat – this is the nature of laboratory experimentation in environmental economics. By choosing what phenomena to explore, institution to evaluate, theory to test, response to measure, a researcher constructs the environment and rules of the game that affect the actual behaviour of economic agents (Smith, 1982, 1991). The researcher's *a priori* expectation of rational economic behaviour is either met or not, triggering a new set of experiments to further understand what assumptions drive rationality and what design features send unintended but influential signals. The lab provides the repetition and control needed to understand the behavioural underpinnings of environmental economic phenomena. See Davis and Holt (1993), Friedman and Sunder (1994), and Kagel and Roth (1995) for extensive surveys covering the major areas in experimental economics.

Environmental and experimental economics evolved during the 1960s and 1970s; both fields on a separate track but both fields led by pragmatic researchers who judged a method by results, not by preconceived methodological principles. As succinctly argued by Plott (1987, p. 194), '[m]ethodological principles should evolve from our experience about what works and what does not work'. The merger of lab experiments into environmental economics began in earnest during the 1980s and continues today. Economists who now turn to the lab to study environmental economic phenomena can look to econometricians from decades past where limited computer capacity, time and money constrained the number of regressions to a handful. Pragmatism ruled because, once the regressions were run, one used the results or tried to fund further exploration. But every curse has its blessing – in this case, an imposed discipline to identify and test the most interesting questions. Experimental economics demands the same discipline today as theoretical presumptions become testable hypotheses that require control not often found outside the lab. One identifies an interesting phenomenon, develops hypotheses, designs an experiment, runs the treatments, pays the subjects, and explores which

* We wish to thank Tom Crocker, Charlie Plott, and two reviewers for comments.

restrictions, if any, best organize the patterns of behaviour. Working along with theory and prior empirical information, experiments become habitual – another productive approach to discipline one's thinking about economics and environmental policy.

Lab experiments help guide environmental economic policy by providing insight into how a proposed change in incentives will affect behaviour. By supplying information on the behavioural links between incentives, preferences, beliefs and choice, experimental markets can inform policy. Since the lab environment differs from the wild by definition, a lab experiment can be used to explore a specific case of a more general phenomenon or theory. Experimental results will be used to complement field data and improve our understanding of the underlying assumptions and incentives that drive behavioural responses to policy. Experiments explore environmental economic phenomena by allowing the researcher to control the rules or general principles that guide the organization of social interaction, given the imperfect and incomplete knowledge of each member of a society.

Sceptics may complain that environmental issues are too complex to be adequately captured in the lab. Two retorts – first, a general theory should explain a specific case. If experimental results cast doubt on the specific validity of a theory, a researcher can begin to question its general application to the more complicated world. The lab often provides the cleanest possible test of these specific cases. Second, complexity is not an argument against experiments, but rather an argument for a certain type of research programme – one where the complexity of the lab experiment gradually increases to isolate and control the factors that reduce the robustness of a model (Plott, 1989). The best guesses guiding environmental policy can be improved with more understanding of the behavioural implications of such economic complexities as institutions and transactions costs, conflicts and strategy, risk and its reduction, and information and value (Shogren, 1993).

2. Experimental method
Economics and environmental sciences such as ecology have quite different views on the proper role of experiments. Historically, economics has been primarily theory-driven, with experimentation coming in a distant second. In contrast, ecology and biology have focused on observation-based lab and field experiments as the primary mechanism of research, almost separate from the development of theoretical ecology. One reason this divergence developed and persists is that economists and ecologists differ in their assumptions regarding the objective function of a model. Economists generally assumed an objective function (for example, profit and utility) is well defined, while environmental sciences usually view the function as unknown (for example, net energy storage, genetic fitness) (Shogren and

Nowell, 1991). The end result is a difference in application – natural scientists usually present experiments as a tool to measure a cause-and-effect relationship; economists often present experiments as a tool to study an interesting phenomenon such as the nature of equilibration in markets, rationality in bargaining and gaming experiments, or the performance of a proposed exchange institution. As such, economists use experiments both to test the specific predictions of alternative stylized models, and as test-beds to measure the performance of new institutions operating in environments too complex to model to the letter (see Plott, 1994).

Figure 76.1 illustrates the basic triad that grounds lab explorations of economic phenomena (Mount and Reiter, 1974). The triad captures the three main components underlying an experiment – the environment,

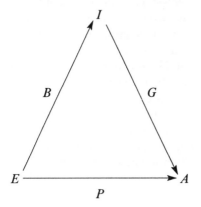

Source: Mount and Reiter (1974).

Figure 76.1   Experimental economic triad

human and natural (E); the institution or mechanism (I); and actual behaviour (A). The environment includes the preferences, endowments, technology, physical constraints, property rights and information structure (such as exchange value and starting quantity of a fictitious commodity). The institution specifies the rules that aggregate and generate information and coordinate actions. It outlines the rules of interaction and consequences: possible actions and messages, allocation rules conditional on messages and actions, and transition rules which may also be conditioned on actions and messages. Repeated experience allows individuals to appraise their own preferences and beliefs in the light of the information generated by the market, a tool that promotes social order by efficiently disseminating knowledge 'which is not given to anyone in totality' (Hayek, 1945). Grether (1994) and Plott (1996) supply several examples of how feedback and repetition in an exchange institution reduce or remove anomalous behaviour as individuals apparently learn that, say in the case of Vickrey's (1961) second-price auction, strategic behaviour does not pay. Given the environment, people send messages (say, bids or prices) that the institution uses to allocate resources and costs, G. Given a performance criterion (P) and a set of behavioural models (B), the experimenter can evaluate the efficiency and rationality of the actual behaviour of the people under these alternative institutional structures.

Often experimentalists chase economic phenomena down dark alleys without a theoretical flashlight because they see the gain in parallelism with reality exceeding the loss in experimental control. Experiments use repeated trials, for example, so that subjects have the opportunity to learn about an institution or environment even though no formal theory of learning is presupposed (although this is changing; see for example Roth and Erev, 1995). This habit of walking the line between realism and control can generate lively exchanges because both can only be achieved within broad limits, given human subjects – realism to one researcher is a lack of control to another; control to one represents an artificial edifice to another. In addition, experimenters must be wary of the subtle and not-so-subtle differences they have created between groups of subjects that can confound results and make interpretations untrustworthy, that is, the classic Hawthorne effect – experimenters examining job performance made changes in the workplace of the Hawthorne plant of the Western Electric Company in Chicago that made people feel important and thus improved their performance (also see Rosenthal and Jacobson, 1968).

And even if the appropriate mix of control and realism can be agreed on, subjects still have preferences, beliefs and skills that differ dramatically from the traditional *homo economicus* inhabiting our analytical frameworks. Some institutions are robust to such variation, that is, the double-oral auction (see Gode and Sunder, 1993). Other institutions are more sensitive, however, as one subject's 'irrational' actions can contaminate the entire environment, that is, gaming experiments with rotating partners that assume 'perfect' information. The challenge is to sort out what makes an institution robust, and how much reality can be added to the lab without losing perceptible control – a task especially relevant to experiments in environmental economics.

3. Institutional experiments

Experiments in environmental economics fall into two general categories – institutional and valuation. Institutional experiments control the environment (E) and then explore how alternative market and non-market mechanisms (I) affect the allocation of scarce resources. Evolving from the classic prisoner's dilemma game (for example, Lave 1962), these experiments address the question of how to design alternative exchange mechanisms to reduce the inefficient allocation of resources in the presence of market failure such as public goods, externalities, asymmetric information and incomplete markets (Plott, 1983); or non-market failure due to the public choice aspects of environmental policy, that is, rent-seeking over subsidies for green technologies.

To illustrate, consider three specific institutional experiments – public goods, emission permit trading, and Coasean bargaining. First, many environmental goods such as clean air or clean water are public goods – goods that are non-rival and non-exclusive in consumption. Received theory predicts that rational, self-interested people will free-ride off the contributions of others, and thus markets will fail to provide the optimal level of the public good, making alternative organizations necessary. While several variants exist on the public-good experiment, the basic design captures the idea that the efficient outcome is to cooperate but the dominant strategy is to free-ride (see Isaac et al., 1984). Suppose four subjects are collected in a room and endowed with $5 each. The subjects are asked to make either a $0 or $5 contribution to a collective programme; this contribution is private information and group discussion is prohibited. The monitor collects the contributions, sums them, doubles them, and redistributes the grand total back to the subjects uniformly. In this design, every $1 contribution returns $2 to the group – $0.50 to the contributor and $1.50 to the other three subjects. The efficient outcome is for everyone to contribute $5, but the dominant strategy is to contribute $0 since the private net return is negative. While the laboratory evidence shows that neither complete self-interest ($0) nor cooperation ($5) dominates behaviour, it reveals that the environment and institutional rules can be manipulated to push behaviour either more toward the games people that theory assumes or the fair people often observed in actual collective programmes (see Ledyard, 1995). Exactly how and why it all works is an open and ongoing research question, but current findings suggest that marginal payoffs, group size and communication matter. Also see the related work on common property regimes (for example, Ostrom et al., 1994), and coordination games (for example, Cooper et al., 1992).

Second, tradable emission permits have long been suggested as an alternative control mechanism for environmental bads (Crocker, 1966). A key question is how to design an emission trading institution that maximizes economic efficiency. Consider Cason's (1995) lab evaluation of the US Environmental Protection Agency's (EPA) sulphur dioxide (SO_2) emission trading programme. Cason designed an experimental market to capture the basic features of the EPA's SO_2 auction: buyers and sellers submit bids and offers for emission permits given their induced preferences; and the intersection of the implied supply and demand curves determines the quantity of permits traded. The EPA sets the market price discriminatively off the demand curve – the EPA first matches the buyer with the highest bid to the seller with the lowest offer. The matching continues – the second-highest bidder to second-lowest offer, and so on, until the equilibrium quantity is reached. Cason showed that this institutional design provides sellers with an incentive to understate their true willingness to accept in order to be matched with a high bidder, thus earning a higher price for their permits. The experimental results confirm his prediction – sellers undercut each other to get into the market. The results suggest that incentive mechanisms depend on the rules defining the institution, and changing the trading rules would make the SO_2 markets more efficient (also see Cason and Plott, 1996).

The third example of an institutional experiment is Coasean bargaining. Recall that the Coase theorem asserts that if a regulator can implement an efficient Pigouvian tax, then economic friction embodied as transaction costs must be sufficiently low such that the disputing parties can bargain to an equally efficient outcome, regardless of who is assigned property rights over the resource (Coase, 1960). The basic lab design has two parties to each bargain, two payoff schedules – the demand and supply for pollution control or pollution emissions depending on which party has property rights, perfect knowledge of payoffs, zero transactions costs, perfect contract enforcement, and no wealth effects. These assumptions create two testable behavioural outcomes: two parties will come to an efficient and mutually advantageous agreement. The first experimental tests observed efficient but equitable bargaining (Hoffman and Spitzer, 1982). Harrison and McKee (1985) revisited the design, and showed that people who are first asked to bargain without property rights quickly grasp the legitimate nature of unilateral property rights so that the next bargains were both efficient and mutually advantageous. But Coase was really interested in how economic friction affects agreements. Experimental evidence suggests that bargaining efficiency is robust to large groups and uncertain payoffs (Hoffman and Spitzer, 1986; Shogren, 1992), but falters under the threat of an imperfectly enforced contract or delay costs (Shogren, 1998).

4.   Valuation experiments

Valuation experiments elicit a person's actual private preference for a market or non-market good by trying to control actual behaviour (A) with the choice of the institution (I). Here researchers focus on how preferences are formed and revealed, given alternative auction institutions with and without market experience. For instance, the second-price auction has been used in lab valuation in the attempt to induce a person truthfully to reveal his or her preferences. Examples of valuation experiments include the expression of preferences and individual choice (Becker et al., 1964); public-good demand (Bohm, 1972, 1984; Brookshire and Coursey, 1987); pre-survey evaluation of elicitation mechanisms (Coursey and Schulze, 1986; Cummings et al., 1995); valuing alternative risk reduction mechanisms (Shogren, 1990); valuing new products (Hoffman et al., 1993; Melton et al., 1996); willingness to pay and willingness to accept measures of value (Kahneman et al., 1990); and hypothetical–actual value comparisons (Bishop and Heberlein, 1979; Dickie et al., 1987).

We consider three examples to illustrate valuation experiments – the expression of preferences, the divergence between measures of value, and the calibration of hypothetical and actual values. First, although the expression of preferences through an exchange institution is the foundation of the economic theory of choice, these institutions do not usually exist for environmental assets. A person can act as if his/her revealed preferences will not be contested by arbitrage, and, therefore, lacks the gravity to hold his/her presumed rationality intact. Economic and psychological evidence is abundant that, absent arbitrage, people commonly engage in anomalous behaviour that is inconsistent with the axiomatic foundation of the economic theory of choice and valuation. Thaler (1992) and Camerer (1995) catalogue the numerous violations of the continuity, completeness, transitivity and independence axioms observed in the lab.

Consider an abridged version of the long history of preference reversals as a motivating example. The transitivity axiom implies that preferences are well defined, and that if an individual's preference ordering exists, it is independent of the method used to recover them. Psychologists Lichtenstein and Slovic (1971) upset this argument by designing a series of experiments showing that it is possible to construct lottery pairs that violate transitivity. Each subject was presented with some variation of the following pair of bets and asked to choose one bet out of the pair, P-bet or $-bet:

P-bet: p chance of $\$X$ $-bet: q chance of $\$Y$
         $1 - p$ chance of $\$x$ $1 - q$ chance of $\$y$

where $X > x$, $Y > y$, $p > q$, and $Y > X$. The subjects were then asked to state their maximum willingness to pay for each bet. Although expected utility requires that the bet selected is also the most valued, many subjects violated this prediction by selecting the P-bet but paid more for the $-bet. This result has been duplicated in numerous settings, including with real gamblers in Las Vegas and by economists sceptical of the initial work (Grether and Plott, 1979), leading some to conclude that traditional willingness-to-pay approaches and choice-based surveys are unreliable (Irwin et al., 1993). And while arbitrage and big-ticket goods can eliminate preference reversals through the discipline of the market (Chu and Chu, 1990; Bohm, 1994), such institutions do not exist for most environmental goods, leaving this debate far from over. The lab provides a useful tool for more research into why different elicitation methods affect the ordering of stated preferences for environmental goods.

The second example is the divergence between the willingness to pay (WTP) for a commodity and the willingness to accept (WTA) compensation to sell the same commodity. While the WTP and WTA should be about equal for goods with close substitutes (Hanemann, 1991), lab evidence is mixed. Using a discrete-choice auction to reveal preferences for a candy bar or mug, Kahneman et al. (1990) reject the WTP–WTA equality hypothesis; attributing the divergence to an 'endowment effect' whereby a person becomes attached to a commodity, demanding more compensation than he or she was originally willing to pay. In contrast, Shogren et al. (1994) observe no significant difference between WTP and WTA for a candy bar or mug, given a second-price auction with market experience, rejecting the endowment effect explanation. The difference in behaviour vividly illustrates that the context of choice matters to valuation. The two lab auctions created two distinct information environments. Bidders receive different signals about the market, given the variation in design parameters such as the auction, monetary incentives and experience. Again the lab is well suited to address how and why alternative auction environments trigger idiosyncratic information flows and data processing that affect revealed values (see Rutström, 1998).

The third example focuses on the calibration of the hypothetical to the actual willingness to pay for market and non-market goods. Understanding whether people overstate their actual preferences for a good when asked a hypothetical question remains an important issue in current policy debates over environmental goods. Earlier work suggested that the average person exaggerates his/her actual willingness to pay (for example, Neill et al., 1994). In response, the National Oceanic and Atmospheric Administration's (NOAA) blue-ribbon panel recommended that hypothetical bids be deflated using a 'divide by 2' rule unless these bids can be calibrated using actual market data. The NOAA rule has served as an *ad hoc* place-holder to motivate more research into the nature of calibrating hypothetical and actual values. To illustrate, consider List and Shogren's (1998) field experiment that compares bidding behaviour in a hypothetical and actual second-price auction for baseball cards – a good with many characteristics favourable for a calibration exercise including familiarity, the ability to deliver and an intangible quality. Three samples were run – 1 card, 1 card among 10, and

1 card bid on by sportscard dealers presumed more experienced with the market than the general population. While the results support the view that people overstate actual bids, the calibration function estimated to correct for this exaggeration is both good- and context-specific, that is, other goods and market experience affect the calibration function. Calibration research will continue to develop in the lab or field, especially for environmental policy debates in which researchers are constrained by the inability to deliver an actual public good.

5. Conclusion

Experiments provide insight into the behavioural underpinnings of environmental policy. The lesson from the lab is unmistakable – the context of choice matters to the wilderness within. And when unexpected results arise or assumptions fail to be supported, the environment and institutions can be scrutinized, shortcomings corrected, the experiment redesigned, and the subject pool resampled. The impact of this lab mindset on environmental economics will continue to grow as more researchers sense that experimental methods can enhance their answers to policy questions.

References

Becker, G., M. DeGroot and J. Marschak (1994), 'Measuring utility by a single response sequential method', *Behavioral Science*, **9**, 226–32.

Bishop, Richard C, and Thomas A. Heberlein (1979), 'Measuring values of extramarket goods: are indirect measures biased?', *American Journal of Agricultural Economics*, **61** (5), 926–30.

Bohm, Peter (1972), 'Estimating demand for public goods: an experiment', *European Economic Review*, **3** (2), 111–30.

Bohm, Peter (1984), 'Revealing demand for an actual public good', *Journal of Public Economics*, **24** (2), 135–51.

Bohm, Peter (1994), 'Behavior under uncertainty without preference reversals: a field experiment', *Empirical Economics*, **19**, 185–200.

Brookshire, David S. and Don L. Coursey (1987), 'Measuring the value of a public good: an empirical comparison of elicitation procedures', *American Economic Review*, **77** (4), 554–66.

Camerer, Colin (1995), 'Individual decision making', in J. Kagel and A. Roth (eds), *The Handbook of Experimental Economics*, Princeton, NJ: Princeton University Press, pp. 587–703.

Cason, Timothy N. (1995), 'An experimental investigation of the seller incentives in the EPA's emission trading auction', *American Economic Review*, **85** (4), 905–22.

Cason, Timothy N. and Charles R. Plott (1996), 'EPA's new emissions trading mechanism: a laboratory evaluation', *Journal of Environmental Economics and Management*, **30** (2), 133–60.

Chu, Yun-Peng and Ruey-Ling Chu (1990), 'The subsidence of preference reversals in simplified and marketlike experimental settings: a note', *American Economic Review*, **80** (4), 902–11.

Coase, R. (1960), 'The problem of social cost', *Journal of Law and Economics*, **3**, 1–44.

Cooper, R., D. DeJong, R. Forsythe and T. Ross (1992), 'Communication in coordination games', *Quarterly Journal of Economics*, **107** (2), 739–71.

Coursey, Don and William Schulze (1986), 'The application of laboratory experimental economics to the contingent valuation of public goods', *Public Choice*, **49**, 47–68.

Crocker, T. (1966), 'The structuring of atmosphere pollution control systems', H. Wolozin (ed.), *The Economics of Air Pollution*, New York: Norton, pp. 61–86.

Cummings, Ronald, W. Glenn Harrison and E. Elisabet Rutström (1995), 'Homegrown values and hypothetical surveys: is the dichotomous choice approach incentive-compatible?', *American Economic Review*, **85** (1), 260–66.

Davis, Douglas D. and Charles A. Holt (1993), *Experimental Economics*, Princeton, NJ: Princeton University Press.

Dickie, Mark, Ann Fisher and Shelby Gerking (1987), 'Market transactions and hypothetical demand data: a comparative study', *Journal of the American Statistical Association*, **82** (397), 69–75.

Friedman, Daniel and Shyam Sunder (1994), *Experimental Methods: A Primer for Economists*. Cambridge, UK and New York: Cambridge University Press.

Gode, Dhananjay K. and Shyam Sunder (1993), 'Allocative efficiency of markets with zero intelligence traders: markets as a partial substitute for individual rationality', *Journal of Political Economy*, **101** (1), 119–37.

Grether, David (1994), 'Individual behavior and market performance', *American Journal of Agricultural Economics*, **76** (5), 1079–83.

Grether, David M. and Charles R. Plott (1979), 'Economic theory of choice and the preference reversal phenomenon', *American Economic Review*, **69** (4), 623–38.

Hanemann, W.M. (1991), 'Willingness to pay and willingness to accept: how much can they differ?', *American Economic Review*, **81**, 635–47.

Harrison, Glenn W. and Michael McKee (1985), 'Experimental evaluation of the Coase theorem', *Journal of Law and Economics*, **28** (3), 653–70.

Hayek, F. (1945), 'The use of knowledge in society', *American Economic Review*, **35**, 519–30.

Hoffman, Elizabeth and Matthew L. Spitzer (1982), 'The Coase theorem: some experimental tests', *Journal of Law and Economics*, **25** (1), 73–98.

Hoffman, Elizabeth and Matthew L. Spitzer (1986), 'Experimental tests of the Coase theorem with large bargaining groups', *Journal of Legal Studies*, **15**, 149–71.

Hoffman, Elizabeth, Dale Menkhaus, D. Chakravarti, R. Field and G. Whipple (1993), 'Using laboratory experimental auctions in marketing research: a case study of new packaging for fresh beef', *Marketing Science*, **12** (3), 318–38.

Irwin, Julie, Paul Slovic, Sarah Lichtenstein and Gary McClelland (1993), 'Preference reversals and the measurement of environmental values', *Journal of Risk and Uncertainty*, **6**, 5–18.

Isaac, R. Mark, James M. Walker and Susan H. Thomas (1984), 'Divergent evidence on free riding: an experimental examination of possible explanations', *Public Choice*, **43** (2), 113–49.

Kagel, John H. and Alvin E. Roth (1995), *The Handbook of Experimental Economics*, Princeton, NJ: Princeton University Press.

Kahneman, Daniel, Jack L. Knetsch and Richard H. Thaler (1990), 'Experimental tests of the endowment effect and the Coase theorem', *Journal of Political Economy*, **98** (6), 1325–48.

Lave, Lester B. (1962), 'An empirical approach to the prisoner's dilemma', *Quarterly Journal of Economics*, **76**, 424–36.

Ledyard, John B. (1995), 'Public goods: a survey of experimental research', in J. Kagel and A. Roth (eds), *The Handbook of Experimental Economics*, Princeton, NJ: Princeton University Press, pp. 111–94.

Lichtenstein, Sarah and Paul Slovic (1971), 'Reversals of preference between bids and choices in gambling decisions', *Journal of Experimental Psychology*, **89**, 46–55.

List, John and Jason F. Shogren (1998), 'Calibration of the difference between actual and hypothetical valuations in a field experiment', *Journal of Economic Organization and Behavior*, **37**, 193–205.

Mount, Kenneth and Stanley Reiter (1974), 'The informational size of message spaces', *Journal of Economic Theory*, **8** (2), June, 161–92.

Melton, Bryan, Wallace Huffman, Jason Shogren and John Fox (1996), 'Consumer preferences for fresh food items with multiple quality attributes: evidence from an experimental auction of pork chops', *American Journal of Agricultural Economics*, **78**, 916–23.

Neill, Helen R, Ronald G. Cummings, Philip T. Ganderton, Glenn W. Harrison and Thomas McGuckin (1994), 'Hypothetical surveys and real economic commitments', *Land Economics*, **70** (2), 145–54.

Ostrom, Elinor, Roy Gardner and James Walker (1994), *Rules, Games, and Common-pool Resources*, Ann Arbor: University of Michigan Press.

Plott, Charles (1983), 'Externalities and corrective policies in experimental markets', *Economic Journal*, **93** (369), 106–27.

Plott, Charles (1987), 'Dimensions of parallelism: some policy applications of experimental methods', in A. Roth (ed.), *Laboratory Experimentation in Economics: Six Points of View*, Cambridge, UK: Cambridge University Press, pp. 193–219.

Plott, Charles (1989), 'An updated review of industrial organization: applications of experimental methods', in R. Schmalensee and R. Willig (eds), *Handbook of Industrial Organization*, vol. 2. Amsterdam: North-Holland, pp. 1109–76.

Plott, Charles R. (1994), 'Market architectures, institutional landscapes and testbed experiments', *Economic Theory*, **4**, 3–10.

Plott, Charles (1996), 'Rational individual behavior in markets and social choice processes', in *The Rational Foundations of Economic Behavior*, London: Macmillan and New York: St Martin's Press.

Rosenthal, Robert and L. Jacobson (1968), *Pygmalion in the Classroom. Teacher Expectations and Pupils' Intellectual Development*, New York: Holt, Rinehart, and Winston.

Roth, Alvin and Ido Erev (1995), 'Learning in extensive form games: experimental data and simple dynamic models in the intermediate term', *Games and Economic Behavior*, **8**, 164–212.

Rutström, E. Elisabet (1998), 'Home-grown values and the design of incentive compatible auctions', *International Journal of Game Theory*, **27**, 427–41.

Shogren, Jason F. (1990), 'The impact of self-protection and self-insurance on individual response to risk.' *Journal of Risk and Uncertainty*, **3** (2), 191–204.

Shogren, Jason F. (1992), 'An experiment on Coasean bargaining over ex ante lotteries and ex post rewards', *Journal of Economic Behavior and Organization*, **17** (1), 153–69.

Shogren, Jason F. (1993), 'Experimental markets and environmental policy', *Agricultural and Resource Economic Review*, **3** (2), 117–29.

Shogren, Jason F. (1998), 'Coasean bargaining with symmetric delay costs', *Resources and Energy Economics*, **20**, 309–26.

Shogren, Jason F. and Clifford Nowell (1991), 'Economics and ecology: a comparison of experimental methodologies and philosophies', *Ecological Economics*, **3**, 1–21.

Shogren, Jason F., Seung Y. Shin, Dermot J. Hayes and James B. Kliebenstein (1994), 'Resolving differences in willingness to pay and willingness to accept', *American Economic Review*, **84** (1), 255–70.

Smith, Vernon L. (1982), 'Microeconomic systems as an experimental science', *American Economic Review*, **72** (5), 523–55.

Smith, Vernon L. (1991), 'Rational choice: the contrast between economics and psychology', *Journal of Political Economy*, **99** (4), 877–97.

Thaler, Richard (1992), *The Winner's Curse. Paradoxes and Anomalies of Economic Life*, New York: Free Press.

Vickrey, William (1961), 'Counterspeculation, auctions, and competitive sealed tenders', *Journal of Finance*, **16** (1), 8–37.

77 Natural resource accounting
Salah El Serafy

1. Issues and coverage

1.1 What are natural resources?

Natural resources are assets which may be defined narrowly as sources of raw materials and energy, or more broadly to include nature's capacity to absorb wastes. More broadly still, natural resources may be taken to include the diversity of biological life and life support systems. Biological diversity and life support systems, however, are not easy to quantify or to attach monetary values to, and will not be covered here. Excluded from coverage too will be the degradation of ecological systems, and such natural resource erosion as the depletion of the ozone layer. These do not lend themselves easily to measurement, and may lie outside *national* accounting systems altogether. Owing to the difficulty of demarcation and the evolving nature of the subject, the discussion here will sometimes conflate natural resource accounting with environmental accounting which is increasingly being called 'green accounting'.

Accounting may be effected in physical units of the measurable stocks of natural resources and their periodic changes, or, more ambitiously, reckoning these in money terms for their integration in the (economic) national accounts. Many institutions and national statistical offices (in Norway, the Netherlands, France, Canada and the US, among others) now collect and publish physical measurements of various aspects of natural resources. Such physical measurements are in themselves a kind of green accounting, and are a *sine qua non* for monetary valuation. However, it is the integration, or intended integration, of money-valued resource accounts into the standard set of national accounts that has attracted much interest of late, and it is this aspect of resource accounting that will be the focus of this chapter.

1.2 Accounting for pollution

The role of nature as an absorber and assimilator of wastes (sometimes referred to as nature's 'sink function') may be viewed as a natural resource of a given capacity which declines progressively as wastes accumulate and become difficult to assimilate. However, the depletion and degradation of

1191

this resource are to a certain extent reversible. For the purpose of accounting, incremental pollution associated with wastes of production and consumption may be assessed directly and given a value based on the cost of raising emission quality to acceptable levels. To the extent that such a cost has not actually been incurred by the polluters and thus not been internalized in their accounts, it may theoretically be 'imputed' as a cost against the gross product.[1] If purity standards are set and effectively policed, most of the costs incurred in this process would automatically be incorporated in the accounts of the polluters, and the gross product, as conventionally reckoned, would require no adjustment. In practice, however, it is unlikely that pollutants will be so totally eradicated from emissions as to obviate the need to adjust the gross product. On the other hand counter-pollution expenditures by consumers would continue to be treated as part of final consumption in parallel, for example, with expenditures by employees on transport to work.

It is worth noting that many of the richer countries, with few natural resources remaining to them, tend to identify environmental stress with pollution, often overlooking the role of the environment *as a source* of natural resources. Their requirements of materials and energy are now largely imported at favourable prices that seldom internalize environmental costs. Thus, with some notable exceptions, developed countries tend to advocate leaving the national accounts unchanged, relying instead on physical indicators of pollution to motivate and shape their *environmental* policies. Developing countries, by contrast, are often in the position where natural resources – normally a major source of their prosperity – are seriously threatened, and the national accounts fail to reflect their unsustainability, with grave implications for measuring output, analysing *macroeconomic* aggregates, and forging appropriate development policies. While pollution is often an additional concern for them, addressing it through the vehicle of the national accounts is not easy and is seldom effective.[2]

2.   The link with the national accounts

2.1   A new system of national accounts

The most tangible advance made recently in resource accounting was marked by the publication in December 1993 of a new *System of National Accounts*, SNA (Commission of the European Communities et al., 1993) and its companion manual, *Integrated Environmental and Economic Accounts* (United Nations Statistical Division, 1993). This advance has been associated with concern for 'sustainability' – a key preoccupation of the Brundtland Report (WCED, 1987). The issue of sustainability was later to receive attention from the United Nations Conference on Environment and Development, 1992, which, in Agenda 21, stressed the need for green accounting. However, the most direct line of development leading to the change of the SNA stemmed from the United Nations Environment Programme (UNEP) which had sponsored a series of workshops jointly with the World Bank during the 1980s to explore the feasibility of adjusting the national accounting framework to reflect natural resource deterioration. A selection of the studies presented at the workshops was published by the World Bank (Ahmad et al., 1989).

2.2 The SEEA

The work of the workshops led to the formation of an inter-agency secretariat representing five leading international institutions for the purpose of amending the SNA.[3] The secretariat, however, came to the conclusion that the old system was largely adequate, with only minor changes needed. Treatment of natural resources was judged to be unsatisfactory under the old SNA, but should be handled, not in the main accounts, but extraneously in 'satellite accounts', an appellation that had originated in France as *comptes satellites*. These would marry the economic and environmental worlds within a 'System of Economic and Environmental Accounts' (SEEA). The unadjusted, so-called *economic*, accounts were viewed as having been estimated rightly all along, while the new *environmental* accounts, implicitly viewed as not quite economic, were to be placed outside the system's core. As the United Nations manual (1993) made clear, the satellite accounts were essentially a depository of information about links between the economic and environmental worlds, useful for a variety of purposes including the adjustment of the income and product accounts.

Methodological controversy persisted on *how* to adjust the accounts for environmental change and, to a certain extent, justified the relegation of the adjustments to the new satellite accounts. Until views converged on the best way to adjust the accounts, it made sense that the adjustments be kept outside the main accounts. However, the implied notion that environmental and resource accounting was not an economic concern was unwarranted. For if the decline of natural resource stocks had no economic import, then this should have no place whatever in the *economic* system of national accounting. The new SNA also did not correct the treatment of commercial natural resource extraction whose products normally exchange hands at market prices. As will be explained below, considering the whole surplus realized in commercial extraction as value added, to be included in the gross product without imputing a cost for depletion, is an economic and accounting fault which had been allowed to persist under the old SNA and was ripe for correction.[4] It should be obvious that proceeds from selling assets (and natural resources are assets) are not totally value-added, and should not be included in GDP before deducting an estimated opportunity cost of liquidating the asset today rather than tomorrow. As a result of counting asset sale proceeds in GDP as if they were value-added, the income of a large number of developing countries which rely heavily on primary production is wrongly estimated – a fact which can impair macro-economic analysis and mislead economic policy prescriptions (El Serafy, 1993, 1997a, 1997b).[5]

2.3   Emphasis on stock accounting

A characteristic of the SEEA is its implicit favouring of accounting for natural resource *stocks* over accounting for periodic *changes* in these stocks. The emphasis on stock accounting seems to follow naturally from concern for 'strong sustainability', which lays stress on resource conservation. Stock accounting, however, does not mix easily with income estimation, which is the main product usually expected from natural accounting. There would be no problem with a stock approach if accounting were done in physical units. But having to put values on stocks, say of fish in the wild or forests, as an initial requirement of resource accounting can be a handicap to prac-tical estimation. Besides, reconciling flows and stocks valued at different prices is problematic, and resort has to be made to artefacts, such as rec-onciliation accounts often of dubious utility.

It should also be noted that it is not the *stocks*, even of commercially exploited resources, but stock *changes* that are normally transacted. Declines due to exploitation are directly observable as they leave one sector of an economy for another, or one country, through exports, for another. They are directly valued by the market so that their value does not have to be inferred from changes in the value of the stock. Moreover, to assume that the entire stock of a resource can be valued at a market price that relates specifically to the amount of the stock exchanging hands is not real-istic. This is because unloading the entire stock (which may be one, two or more orders of magnitude greater than annual extraction) would depress market prices precipitously. Thus the SEEA's emphasis on accounting for the stocks in value terms, though laudable from the point of view of environmental conservation, can do damage to meaningful income esti-mates for resource-dependent countries. These seem to seek not so much a value of their natural resource stocks as a correct reading of their (flow) economic accounts.[6] After all it is the medium of the national accounts, with its traditional focus on macroeconomic aggregate flows, that is being used for the adjustment. Paradoxically, bilateral and other assistance con-tinues to be provided for green accounting exercises in a growing number of developing countries employing disparate and often irreconcilable approaches. And no focal point has emerged for assessing methods and comparing results which are frequently cited uncritically as if they were obtained with reliable methods and based on comparable approaches. Given the past history of debate, the period of methodological experimentation should have ended by now, and a common approach should have emerged. Even the studies conducted by a number of national statistical offices in cooperation with the World Bank and the United Nations Statistical Division, ostensibly as trial runs for the SEEA, had their own weaknesses, and in any case there has been no attempt to subject these and other comparable work to critical and objective scrutiny. It may therefore be significant that the adjusted accounts obtained after such studies have so far almost invariably remained unutilized, with the empirical work ending in new numbers without any serious attempts made to revise previous analyses or derive policy lessons from the new estimates.[7]

3.   Valuation methods

3.1   Accounting in money terms

Accounting for natural resources in physical units is straightforward and yields reliable results if the resources are measurable. Some standardization of quality may be necessary in order to reduce them to a common numeraire. Accounting in money terms, however, can be problematic. This is especially so if we wish to account, not just for resource stocks, but for *income* derived from the exploitation of the stocks. To the extent that a natural resource is marketable, the market price may be used to value the stock at any point in time. As argued earlier, attaching a temporary and unrealizable value to the stock is not particularly illuminating, and may even be harmful if a temporarily booming market encourages unsustainable consumption with disastrous results for the resource owners when prices decline. As to resources that are not marketed, various valuation techniques have been devised for some of them, including 'contingent valuation'. This often relies on asking individuals and groups to set a price they would be prepared to pay for protecting an amenity or cleaning up a specific environment. Such contigent values can suffer from fundamental weaknesses, and while not devoid of merit, they are not always consistent with standard national accounting valuation.[8]

This last point leads up to an important issue, namely the degree to which resource accounting should depart from the conventions of national accounting if the latter's framework is to be used. Assessing pollution damage in monetary terms and imputing it as a cost of output, though possibly relying on uncertain or subjective cost estimates, raises the whole issue of 'imputation' which, though generally frowned upon in national accounting, is nevertheless tolerated for certain activities such as the rental values of owner-occupier homes or production for subsistence. For subject to imputation would also be the estimation of the user cost of natural resource depletion.

Another related problem concerns externalities where the market overlooks the full environmental cost of natural-resource-based production. The value of a felled tree sold as timber, for instance, generally far exceeds the market value of the timber. However, it can be argued that, if the framework of national accounting is to be used for making the adjustments, the rules of national accounting have to be respected, and market values used for resource accounting. Market values are not ideal or optimal for practically any of the goods and services that make up the national output, so why should natural resources be treated differently? However, there is no reason why the whole adjustment exercise should not be conducted outside the constraining conventions of the national accounts, using shadow prices that would internalize environmental costs. Since estimates of environmental costs are bound to vary considerably from analyst to analyst, shadow pricing, which can be invaluable for policy analysis, should remain outside the framework of the national accounts.

3.2   Comparing approaches: the net price method

The net price method is one of two approaches recommended by the SEEA (the other being the user cost method). Apart from the difficulty of having initially to put a money value on the stock (a procedure avoided altogether under the pioneering WRI study of Indonesia), it is a straightforward method that focuses on charging the decline in the natural resource stock as *depreciation* against the gross product. In application the net price method seems to have two variants. First, what may be called the 'pure variant' which was used in the WRI study of Indonesia, where the adjustment to conventional GDP followed exactly the course of the change in stocks: declines due to extraction were fully charged against GDP as a cost, and new discoveries were added to it in the year of discovery. The second variant emerged in the SEEA where extraction was also deducted, but upward re-estimation of the stock did not affect the adjustment, but was recorded instead in 'reconciliation' accounts. That middle course was adopted because 'windfalls' due to stock re-estimation were judged appropriately to be unrelated to output measurement.

In the WRI study of Indonesia (1989) the net price was defined as the market price less 'all factor costs of extracting the resource' and bringing it to the point of sale. In that study it is identified as a 'Ricardian scarcity rent' determined after deducting from the market price 'all factor costs incurred in extraction, including a normal return to capital but excluding taxes, duties, and royalties'. Since net price applies to a unit of extraction, it has to be multiplied by the volume of extraction to get the 'resource rent' being sought. This method has been criticized on account of its use of the average cost of extraction rather than the marginal cost with which Hotelling (1931) had worked his model. This is an unfair criticism, largely because Hotelling's *ex ante* optimization objective has little to do with *ex post* accounting with its focus on actual extraction that is often if not always far removed from optimality. And rather than having to read the so-called aggregate 'Ricardian rent' from average prices net of cost, it can be read directly from aggregate revenue less aggregate cost during the account period, and it is thus only naming the method 'net price' that is unfortunate while the method itself is defensible.[9] Because of its simplicity and conformity with environmentalists' concern for conservation, this method has been frequently applied.

3.3   The user cost approach

As an alternative, the SEEA also recommended the user cost method which relates extraction to the available stock and integrates stock reassessments in income estimates without resort to reconciliation accounts. It recognizes the fact that liquidating, say, 1 per cent of the available stock in one year has *economic* implications for sustainability quite different from liquidating 80 per cent. The user cost method is primarily a device for accounting for income (or product) emanating from natural resource extraction. It also indicates an estimated loss in ('fundist') capital due to extraction.[10] As stated earlier, the user cost is a temporal opportunity cost deriving from the fact that if a unit of a resource is extracted today it will not be available for extraction tomorrow. The user cost approach has been employed by numerous researchers for adjusting the national or sectoral accounts for several countries, including South Africa, Chile, Ecuador, Thailand and the United Kingdom (see Hamilton et al., *c.* 1992). It has been compared with the 'net price method' in doctoral dissertations, including those of Foy (1991); Sadoff (1993); and Kellenberg (1995). It has also been applied, albeit with too high a discount rate, for Papua New Guinea and Mexico for the benefit of developing the SEEA.

The user cost method owes its origins to Hicks (1946) who had stressed the fact that revenues obtained by selling a 'wasting asset' exceed income (El Serafy, 1981). Sale proceeds, or part of them, can be allocated to new investments whose yield would sustain income after the resource has been exhausted. Genuine income may be estimated, Hicks suggested, by converting the revenue obtained during the finite life of a wasting resource into a permanent stream of undiminished receipts by using a discount rate (Hicks, 1946, pp. 185ff.) A formula was proposed (El Serafy, 1981, 1989) indicating income as a proportion of revenue from extraction, and its complement, the user cost, which must be reinvested for generating the same income in future.

Denoting net revenue from extraction as R, true income as X, the life expectancy of the resource at the current year's extraction rate as n, and the discount rate as r, the user cost as a ratio of net revenue for any one year will be: $1 - X/R = 1/(1+r)^{n+1}$; and income, also as a ratio of net revenue, will be: $X/R = 1 - 1/(1+r)^{n+1}$. Both these quantities add up to unity.

The life expectancy of a resource is observable once the stock is known, and it is the product of dividing the stock by annual extraction (both measured in physical units). Life expectancy in practice is apt to change every year, depending on stock reassessments and entrepreneurial decisions regarding extraction. These are normally influenced by the owner's financial requirements and expectations about future costs and prices. Thus an owner may be expected to sell more of the asset than otherwise if pressed for liquid resources, or if future prices are predicted to fall.

Perpetual income defines a constant level of current and future income derived from this particular year's extraction. Controversy about the user cost approach has emanated from writers who thought that it relied on a constant profile of *extraction* (Young and da Motta, 1995). The user cost approach in fact parallels standard accounting methods for treating the *using up* of inventories in the course of production, and this is quite different from depreciation of fixed assets (El Serafy, 1993). Among other things, withdrawals from inventories are accounted for at the stage of estimating *gross* income, whereas depreciation of fixed assets is carried out at the later stage of reckoning *net* income after the gross income has been determined.[11]

Two weaknesses may be said to underlie the user cost method. It is a method of imputation of cost that is not actually transacted; and it rests on an arbitrary choice of a discount rate. Imputation is nevertheless unavoidable in the present context. The discount rate is also unavoidable, but its level can be defended. It should above all be a modest rate expected from the new investments and not a maximal targeted rate, difficult to realize. Keeping faith with the precautionary spirit of accounting, it should be 2 or 3 per cent, representing a real rate that may be reasonably expected as a long-term return on investing the equivalent of the user cost. In a closed economy this rate and the rate of exhausting a relatively *sizeable* natural asset will be interdependent. But such interdependence leading to indeterminacy would not arise if the asset was small relative to the economy concerned, or if the user cost was invested abroad. If invested at home, the long-term real growth rate of an economy would be a useful benchmark indicating a relevant discount rate, provided of course that such a growth rate was correctly reckoned, net of natural asset liquidation.[12]

If the value of natural resource sales (net of extraction costs) is entered in the gross product as if it were value added (which is the current practice) and then, in the absence of any re-estimation of the stock, the same amount (equivalent to the decline of the stock) is deducted for the gross product, the net product will be zero. The user cost approach, by contrast, will always show a positive net income from extraction, relying on the fact that part of the proceeds of asset sales can be treated as income provided that a sufficient portion of the receipts is sunk into new investments for the specific purpose of generating new income. It should be clear that what is being sustained here is not resource stocks, but *income*, which must be sustainable by definition.

3.4   Renewable resources

Significantly, the user cost approach is also applicable to renewable resources. If extraction of a renewable resource is within its capacity to regenerate itself, then no adjustment to the flow accounts will be necessary. Any rise in the stock due to the excess of regeneration over extraction may be safely ignored in the manner accountants assume as guardians of income sustainability. Being conscious of the need to keep capital intact, accountants see no harm in occasionally underestimating income in order to guard against capital consumption. Understandably, economists have little sympathy with such precautionary attitudes, which the accountants observe due to prevailing uncertainties and the knowledge that once a quantity has been certified as income it is indicated as available for consumption. If exploitation of a renewable resource exceeds regeneration and its stock declines, the resource in fact is being 'mined'. The stock *decline* should then be subjected to a user cost estimation. How much this would affect the accounts hinges, as in the standard case, on the life expectancy of the resource as it is being so mined, and of course, on the discount rate.

3.5   Shadow pricing and imputation

Many natural resources are traded at prices that do not internalize their full environmental costs. In fact, generally speaking, the market almost always prices primary products at less than their scarcity value. As large parts of natural resources are not privately owned, including fish stocks in international waters and the ozone layer, or have as yet no market value at all, it would be difficult to capture these in the national accounts. Thus in their monetary form the accounts will not (in fact, cannot) fully reflect environmental and natural resource deterioration. While it is tempting to try to cover as much as possible of natural resources in the national accounts, attaching theoretical values to them is likely to be subjective. If that route is followed, integrating natural resources in the national accounts will always be controversial. A conservative approach would integrate only those parts of the natural world that are amenable to money measurement, beginning with the ones that are actually being transacted, while refraining from any shadow pricing. In this way the national accounting conventions would be observed in the expectation that as methods become refined, larger and larger parts of the natural environment will be brought into the accounts. In this respect, studies such as that by WRI of Indonesia (1989), which focused on a few natural resources of importance to the Indonesian economy, appear to have had the right focus. As stated earlier, using the national accounting framework highlights the *economic* nature of the exercise, and to some extent relegates *environmental* sustainability to the background. Shadow pricing environmental services, relying on accounting values that reflect perceived natural resource scarcities, would still be useful and even necessary, but its place, as argued in subsection 3.1 above, is outside, not within, the national accounts.

3.6   Other related issues

Economists, being often forward-looking and seeking precision in their measurements, tend to want to reflect all natural resource changes in their measurements. When the stock of fish or forests rises in the presence of light or non-existent exploitation, they would add such rises to the unadjusted domestic product. Even improvements in the real burden of external debt due to falling (flexible) interest rates would augment the adjusted product. This kind of adjustment usually depreciates the need for adjusting the conventional accounts since the impression is created that there are positive changes that are not being recorded and somehow these might offset the declines and obviate the need to change the accounts. Related to this argument is the proposal by analysts like Peskin (1989) who would adjust the conventional product upward by environmental services, obtaining a higher figure for the gross product before deducting estimates of stock declines. The accountants, on the other hand, tend to take declines much more seriously than improvements out of their concern for guarding against capital consumption. When in doubt they would rather underestimate than overestimate income, and they may be truly regarded as guardians of (income) sustainability.

4.   Mixed measurements: NAMEA

Resource accounting need not be done exclusively in either physical units or money values. For instance, Statistics Netherlands pioneered a system called NAMEA which is a combination of both. NAMEA is an acronym for a 'national accounting matrix including environmental and economic accounts'. This was endorsed in December 1994 by the Commission of the European Communities, albeit with some reservations.[13] The NAMEA system is claimed to yield all conventional economic aggregates in addition to five summary environmental (in fact pollution) indicators, making it possible to compare the contribution of economic activities with their impact on the environment. It is noteworthy that NAMEA sidesteps adjustments to be made to the macroeconomic aggregates of the SNA as a result of environmental *source* declines. These aggregates, unadjusted, are thought to be useful, only needing broadening with environmental accounts and summary pollution indicators. A planned extension of NAMEA will be the compilation of an integrated social accounts and social indicators in an expanded system called SESAME. It is too early yet to assess the success and potential utility of such a hybrid system, and whether or not it will confirm the judgement earlier stated in this chapter to the effect that the more industralized countries are reluctant to change the core national accounts which for many a developing country is an economic necessity.[14]

While several institutions, including the World Resources Institute and Worldwatch Institute, now regularly publish information about the changing state of natural resources in physical units, others attempt combinations of the physical and the monetary. The earlier involvement of the World Bank in green accounting through collaboration of some of its staff with UNEP had taken place before the establishment of the World Bank's Environment Department and its parent, the Vice-Presidency for Environmentally Sustainable Development. The World Bank's *World Development Report, 1992* was lukewarm on resource accounting, and this seems to have set a trend within the Bank that is still current today. As Sheng (1994) noted, implicitly referring to the World Bank, much is being claimed as green accounting which in reality is not so. Such is the initiative of the World Bank to compile physical indicators of sustainability, and to publish cross-country per capita stocks of wealth, defined to include 'human', 'social' as well as 'environmental capital' (World Bank, 1995, 1996, 1997). Many of these estimates have been imaginative, but more importantly they tend to lack economic or environmental significance. As this chapter has, I hope, shown, the economic accounting for changes in natural capital belongs to an entirely different order of importance, well above that of other so-called categories of capital. There is little danger that the stock of human capital depreciates, and so-called social capital is unwieldy and perhaps also immeasurable.

5.   Concluding remarks

It will be noted that reference to welfare implications of natural resource accounting has been eschewed. This is not because the welfare aspect is unimportant, but because of the emphasis given to national accounts as a medium for the adjustment and the fact that the national accounts are not meant to provide welfare measurements. The particular approach to be selected for the adjustment will depend on the purpose of the analyst. If the aim is to account for resource *stocks*, this can be done entirely in physical units. But if the purpose is to reflect resource declines in the economic measurements, monetary valuation is unavoidable. This can be done by focusing directly on the stock changes taking place during the accounting period, or indirectly by following the course of changes in the value of the stocks. Since not all natural resources lend themselves to monetary valuation, we either have to fall back on hybrid approaches where physical and monetary measurements are juxtaposed without being genuinely integrated, or else be selective, focusing on those few natural resources that are important in individual country situations, and incorporate their changes in the national accounts. Physical indicators, however, are needed for all monetary valuation, but combining them into one physical index is not possible without assigning values to their component parts. Such values would be similar to market prices used for weighting the various economic activities for their aggregation as GDP. Within the national accounting framework, even when such values are underestimates, they would be no different from other components whose market values are far from being optimal. Resort to corrected or shadow prices is feasible, except that this, for arguments already made, should be undertaken outside the national accounts.

Attempts at adjustment, including the SEEA and NAMEA, have so far not been totally successful, and need to be carefully scrutinized against a background of empirical case studies and systematic assessments of results and their policy implications. What we already have, however, reflects progress that is not insubstantial. But since different methodologies are being proposed, the immediate task ahead seems to be to refrain from undertaking fresh empirical work before distilling from the wealth of past experience relevant lessons for illuminating further efforts.

Notes

1.   The idea of estimating the cost of improving the quality of polluting emissions to acceptable standards and charging this cost against output was originally put forward by Hueting (1980), pp. 144ff.) and developed further in Hueting (1989, pp. 35ff.). It should be noted that improving the quality of emissions to acceptable standards during an accounting period is different from raising ambient quality by cleaning up past accumulations of pollutants.

2. This statement has to be qualified somewhat since input–output structures (showing economic flows from sector to sector) which, when available, are appended to the national accounts, have been usefully employed to depict estimated pollution attached to sector activities. See for instance Duchin and Lange (1994), and Resosudarmo and Thorbecke (1996).

3. These were the Commission of the European Communities, the International Monetary Fund, the Organization for Economic Cooperation and Development, the United Nations and the World Bank.

4. Where resources are being depleted in the course of their extraction, proceeds from such extraction cannot all be construed as rent (or income). Marshall (1920) was at pains to stress the fact that Ricardian 'rent' was different from 'royalty', quoting Ricardo himself to the effect that 'mining royalty has no connection with the original and indestructible powers of the land' (Marshall, p. 167n). In Marshall's own words 'the produce of mines is merely a giving up of their stored-up treasures ... The produce of the mine is part of the mine itself' (ibid). Marshall repeats this statement in his *Principles* in various formulations. The royalty argument was extended by Marshall to capital improvements of land (p. 427n): 'That part of the income which is required to cover wear-and-tear bears some resemblance to a royalty, which does no more than cover the injury done to a mine by taking ore out of it.' Keynes (1936), without referring to Marshall, takes up the analogy between wear-and-tear and royalty, and develops it into the 'Appendix on User Cost' which follows Chapter 6 of his *General Theory*.

5. The uncorrected national accounts of natural resource-dependent economies obscure whether an economy is genuinely growing or merely selling its natural assets, thereby undermining its future prosperity. The faster a country sells its natural resources, the higher its income and growth rate appear to be. It should be obvious that countries (and individuals) cannot live for long on the proceeds of liquidating their finite assets. For such countries, the conventional estimates of output, balance of payments on current account and the levels of saving and investment may all be wrongly estimated. Whether a country should or should not liquidate its natural resources, and at what rates, is not an accounting problem, but a managerial one. Environmental considerations apart, such liquidation may be justified if the proceeds are not squandered on consumption, but used judiciously to foster income sustainability and diversify the economy. Needless to say, this kind of *economic* sustainability cannot be generalized, and will certainly not guarantee *environmental* sustainability, especially if a longer view is taken.

6. Similarly, though a little divorced from the national accounts, the World Bank (1997) has published estimates of international per capita natural capital as part of estimates of national wealth including 'human resources' and 'produced assets'. 'Natural capital' valuation is based on contemporary market prices which are normally subject to violent changes, thus undermining the worth of such estimates. Besides, they suffer from the weakness mentioned above, namely that market prices of incremental stock changes that get transacted may be inappropriate for valuing total stocks. The basis for valuing the other categories of capital, notably human capital, are far from robust (cf. Appendix table 1: 'Country-level natural capital estimates'). Whether any economic significance can be attached to such wealth estimates is unclear, and the World Bank itself is careful to label these estimates 'work in progress'.

7. The single conclusion brought out in the pioneering 1989 WRI study of Indonesia (namely, that the environmentally adjusted economic growth rate turned out to be lower than the conventionally estimated one) is not generalizable. Apart from the controversial method of adjustment used in that study (which, *inter alia*, added new petroleum discoveries to output in the year of discovery), the adjusted average growth rate could alternatively have been higher or the same as the old one depending on whether the new estimates of output traced a line against time that is steeper than or parallel to the conventionally estimated growth line – in other words whether environmental deterioration actually declines, increases, or remains the same over the trend. Much more important than the economic growth rate in this respect is the size of the adjustment itself, which would affect the *level* of income, savings, investment and the fiscal and payments balances (El Serafy, 1993, 1995).

8. Contingent valuation usually involves subjective estimates of utility as revealed by respondents' answers to questions. In a market situation such estimates would trace the demand curve and include consumers' surpluses over and above the prices determined by the market. By contrast, national accounting, by convention, is effected at market prices, net of consumers' surpluses. In certain cases, especially where income is not too unevenly distributed and the respondents have fairly homogeneous tastes, contingent valuation can be useful for indicating representative values. For a fuller discussion of the topic see the chapter by Kriström on contingent valuation in this volume – Chapter 54.

9. As mentioned earlier, Ricardian rent is income, arising from the 'indestructible powers of the soil', whereas the surplus realized from extracting a depletable resource relates to the resource itself and cannot qualify as rent. Deducting only 'factor costs' (with an imputation for capital services whose costs are often in reality transparent and already deducted) when in fact there are also many non-factor costs involved, would be an error unless non-factor costs were also netted from revenue.

10. 'Fundist capital', as coined by Hicks (1974), is a value or fund representing all the assets of an entity, including buildings, machines and inventories. It is this value, rather than any specific asset, that must be kept intact from year to year in order to estimate income. Another concept of capital, dubbed by Hicks 'materialist capital', views capital as concrete asset units or categories. These two differing views of capital, which Hicks attributed to different economists over the history of economics, have been brought to bear on recent discussions of strong and weak sustainability (El Serafy, 1991). Weak (or year-to-year income) sustainability relies on a fundist view of capital but, contrary to some interpretations, is unrelated to prescriptive future behaviour or any assumption about substitutability or otherwise among the components of capital (El Serafy, 1996).

11. For summing up a perpetual series of income whose total must equal the sum of the finite series of net revenue from extraction, resort was made to a standard summation formula for a series of income, X, and another of revenue, R, 'accruing in equal amounts' (El Serafy, 1989, p.17). Aside from the formula itself which was only used for summation, actual extraction was left free to vary from year to year. Use of discrete time (a year at a time) parallels the accounting process and, as it turned out, was found not to be a constraint. Later, using continuous time and summation by integration, Hartwick and Hageman (1993; earlier published in 1991) concluded that 'the El Serafy user cost continues to yield the same measure of loss in capital value from extraction as does the economic depreciation concept, $V_{t+1} - V_t$'. In a private communication Hartwick wrote that 'It is pleasing that the attractive intuition underlying the El Serafy measure leads to a concept which has been traditionally derived from a rather different intuition' (letter dated 19 April 1991).

12. It has been suggested (Daly and Cobb, 1989) that the user cost of a depletable resource be reinvested to create renewable substitutes for the resource being depleted. Despite its obvious merit, this 'normative' proposition goes well beyond accounting. Adelman, who totally denies depletability, holds that mineral deposits are so abundant in the Earth's crust that it is only the technology of recovery and cost of development that put a limit on their apparent stocks. He believes that deposits will keep growing with advances in technology (Adelman, 1990; Adelman et al., 1991). An implication of this optimistic view is that the proper user cost is nothing but the present value of expected increases in discovery, development and extraction costs. Adelman remains silent, however, on the depletability of so-called *renewable* resources when these are being mined beyond natural regeneration, and seems to underestimate the practical problem of ascertaining the discounted 'expected increases' in development cost.

13. The EC indicated the existence of a number of methodological difficulties 'which rule it [NAMEA] out as a realistic option for the foreseeable future' (quoted in Keuning, 1995). Instead, the EC proposed a comparable 'European system of integrated economic and environmental indices', using a common European system of environmental pressure indices.

14. It seems that NAMEA will be peripheral to the national accounts which will remain unchanged. Keuning (1995) further states that NAMEA has been used in a linear pro-

gramming model in which sustainable national income was estimated for the Netherlands. However, since work continues on NAMEA which is still developing (Keuning and de Haan, 1996) judgement on NAMEA's worth and potential should be suspended.

References

Adelman, M.A. (1990), 'Mineral depletion with special reference to petroleum', *Review of Economics and Statistics*, **72** (1), 1–10.

Adelman, M.A., H. De Silva and M.F. Koehn (1991), 'User cost in oil production', *Resources and Energy*, **13**, 217–40.

Ahmad, Yusuf J., Salah El Serafy and Ernst Lutz (1989), *Environmental Accounting for Sustainable Development* (A UNEP–World Bank Symposium), Washington, DC: World Bank.

Commission of the European Communities, International Monetary Fund, Organization for Economic Cooperation and Development, United Nations and the World Bank (1993), *System of National Accounts 1993*, Brussels/Luxembourg, New York, Paris, Washington, DC.

Daly, Herman E. and John B. Cobb (1989), *For the Common Good*, Boston, MA: Beacon Press.

Duchin, Faye and G.M. Lange (1994), 'Strategies for environmentally sound economic development', in A.M. Janson et al. (eds), *Investing in Natural Capital*, Washington, DC: Island Press.

El Serafy, Salah (1981), 'Absorptive capacity, the demand for revenue and the supply of petroleum', *Journal of Energy and Development*, **7** (1), 73–88.

El Serafy, Salah (1989), 'The proper calculation of income from depletable natural resources', ch. 3 in Yusuf Ahmad, Salah El Serafy and Ernst Lutz (eds), *Environmental Accounting for Sustainable Development*, Washington, DC: World Bank.

El Serafy, Salah (1991), 'The environment as capital', ch. 12 in Robert Costanza (ed.), *Ecological Economics, the Science and Management of Sustainability*, New York: Columbia University Press.

El Serafy, Salah (1993), 'Depletable resources: fixed capital or inventories?', in Alfred Franz and Carsten Stahmer (eds), *Approaches to Environmental Accounting*, Heidelberg and New York: Physica-Verlag.

El Serafy, Salah (1995), 'Depletion of natural resources', ch. 12 in Wouter van Dieren (ed.), *Taking Nature into Account*, New York: Copernicus Springer-Verlag.

El Serafy, Salah (1996), 'In defence of weak sustainability', *Environmental Values*, **5**, 76–81.

El Serafy, Salah (1997a), 'Natural resources and national accounting: impact on macroeconomic policy – Part II, *Journal of Environmental Taxation and Accounting*, **1** (2), 38–59.

El Serafy, Salah (1997b), 'Green accounting and economic policy', *Ecological economics*, **21** (3), 217–29.

Foy, George E. (1991), 'Accounting for non-renewable natural resources in Louisiana's gross state product', *Ecological Economics*, **3** (1), 25–42.

Hamilton, Kirk, David Pearce, Giles Atkinson, Andres Gomez-Lobo and Carlos Young (undated, *c*.1992), *The Policy Implications of Natural Resource and Environmental Accounting*, Centre for Social and Economic Research on the Global Environment (University College London and Norwich, UK).

Hartwick, John and Anja Hageman (1993), 'Economic depreciation of mineral stocks and the contribution of El Serafy', ch. 12 in *Toward Improved Accounting for the Environment*, Washington, DC: World Bank (published originally in 1991 as World Bank, Environment Department Divisional Working Paper 1991–27).

Hicks, John Richard (1946), *Value and Capital*, 2nd edn, Oxford: The Clarendon Press.

Hicks, John Richard (1974), 'Capital controversies: ancient and modern', *American Economic Review*, May.

Hotelling, Harold (1931), 'The economics of exhaustible resources', *Journal of Political Economy*, April.

Hueting, Roefie (1980), *New Scarcity and Economic Growth*, Amsterdam, New York and Oxford: North-Holland.

Hueting, Roefie (1989), 'Correcting national income for environmental losses: toward a practical solution', ch. 6 in Y.J. Ahmad et al., *Environmental Accounting for Sustainable Development*, Washington, DC: World Bank.

Kellenberg, John V. (1995), 'Accounting for natural resources, Ecuador 1971–90', unpublished doctoral dissertation, Baltimore, MD: Johns Hopkins University.

Keuning, Steven J. (1995), 'Integrated accounts and indicators for the environment and the economy: improved measurement of economic progress in the Netherlands', mimeo, September.

Keuning, Steven J. and Mark de Haan (1996), 'What's in a NAMEA?' Statistics Netherlands, National Accounts Occasional Paper, Voorburg, The Netherlands.

Keynes, John Maynard (1936), *The General Theory of Employment, Interest and Money*, London: Macmillan and Co.

Marshall, Alfred (1920), *Principles of Economics*, 8th edn 1947. London: Macmillan and Co.

Peskin, Henry M. (1989), 'A proposed environmental accounts framework', ch. 10 in Ahmad et al.

Resosudarmo, B.R. and E. Thorbecke (1996), 'The impact of environmental policies on household income for different socio-economic classes: the case of air pollutants in Indonesia', *Ecological Economics*, **17**, (2).

Sadoff, Claudia Winkelman (1993), 'Natural resource accounting: a case study of Thailand forest management', unpublished doctoral dissertation, University of California, Berkeley.

Sheng, Fulai (1994), *Real Value for Nature*. World Wildlife Fund for Nature (WWF), Gland, Switzerland.

United Nations Statistical Division (1993), 'Integrated environmental and economic accounting', (Interim Version), *Studies in Method. Handbook of National Accounting* (Series F, no. 61), New York: UN.

WCED (World Commission on Environment and Development) (1987), *Our Common Future*, Oxford: Oxford University Press.

World Bank (1995), *Monitoring Environmental Progress: A Report on Work on Progress*, Environmentally Sustainable Vice-Presidency, Washington, DC.

World Bank (1996), *Monitoring Environmental Progress: Expanding the Measure of Wealth*. Environment Department. Washington, DC.

World Bank (1997), *Expanding the Measure of Wealth. Indicators of Environmentally Sustainable Development*, Environmentally Sustainable Development Studies and Monography Series no. 17, Washington, DC.

World Resources Institute (various dates), *World Resources*, Washington, DC.

World Watch Institute (various dates), *State of the World*, Washington, DC.

Young, C.E.F. and R.S. da Motta (1995), 'Measuring sustainable income from mineral extraction in Brazil', *Resources Policy*, **21** (2), 113–25.

PART X

PROSPECTS

78 Impacts of economic theories on environmental economics

Domenico Siniscalco

1. Introduction

Environmental economics was the subject of a comprehensive research programme in the 1960s and 1970s. This programme dealt with a wide range of issues and policy problems, such as the economics of natural resources, the methods and problems in the correction of externalities, the management of common property goods, and the economics of nature preservation.

Against this background, suitable analytical tools were provided by economic analysis: the theory of non-renewable and renewable resources; the theory of missing markets; Pigouvian taxation and the theory of property rights; the economics of public goods; and welfare economics. All in all, the research programme was very successful and, in the following decade, it gave rise to several textbooks, from Baumol and Oates (1975, 1988) to Siebert (1987) and Pearce and Turner (1990).

In the early 1990s, however, scientists highlighted a set of 'new' environmental phenomena, such as global warming, ozone layer depletion, acid rain, freshwater and ocean pollution, desertification, deforestation and the loss of biodiversity (for example, IUCN, UNEP, WWF, 1991; EEA, UNECE et al., 1995; IPCC, 1995; UNEP, 1996). Some of these phenomena such as ozone layer depletion, were newly discovered; some others, such as global warming, were known but attracted new attention, due to their unexpected scale and socioeconomic implications.

The new environmental phenomena share a set of common features:

- they are closely related to demography, economic growth and structural change;
- they can have a very long-run dimension, affecting future generations as well as the present one;
- they have an intrinsic transnational or global dimension, due to the nature of the externalities involved;
- they have important international repercussions through trade and factor mobility and involve North–South–East relationships;
- they involve a great deal of uncertainty and information asymmetries.

Given their scale and importance, the new environmental problems entered the agenda of policy makers (World Development Report, 1992) and became the centre of worldwide debate and a massive diplomatic effort, culminating in the UN Conference on Environment and Development held in Rio de Janeiro in 1992, followed by the Cairo UN Conference on Population and Development (1994) and the Istanbul UN Conference on Cities and Sustainable Development (1996).

The economists' community has increasingly recognized that the above common characteristics translate into big challenges for environmental economics: they raise new questions, or pose old questions in a new context. Until then, traditional environmental economics had focused on environmental issues which were 'limited' both in time and space and analysed in a closed, competitive, full-information economy, in isolation from all other economic and social dimensions of human development. The new environmental phenomena 'crowd out' much of the existing knowledge, practice and conventional wisdom, thus requiring new analytical tools and fresh policy analyses (Carraro and Siniscalco, 1992b, 1992c). Most importantly, the general framework for the analysis has changed: environmental issues emerging as a particular dimension of human development.

Against this background, environmental economics has received a new impulse and experienced a kind of breakthrough, both in terms of methods and focus of the analysis. In some cases, the required tools are being taken from other areas of economics: macroeconomics and the theory of growth, applied microeconomics, welfare economics, the theory of property rights, taxation, international, industrial and labour economics, and so on. In other cases, the analytical requirements provide an impulse for original applications and developments. In addition to making connections with many other subdisciplines in economics, environmental economics has gradually broadened its focus by making connections with the social, political, natural and physical sciences, thus attracting a much larger group of contributors (for example, IPCC, 1995).

The 'new' developments of the environmental economics literature, both on analytical and policy grounds, may be grouped into three major research areas: (a) sustainable development; (b) transboundary environmental issues; and (c) uncertainty and information asymmetries.

In the following pages, we shall consider – under the above-mentioned three 'headings' – the theoretical questions posed by the new environmental phenomena, the way in which economic theory and environmental economics have dealt with those questions so far and, finally, the issues that call for further advances in economic theory and, more generally, in environmental economics research.

2. Environment and development

The majority of the new environmental phenomena have a macroeconomic scale; they involve more than one country or more than one continent and their solutions cannot be logically separated from the trends of macroeconomic and demographic variables.

The close links between environment and development call for a new viewpoint, which goes under the name of sustainable development (Brundtland Report, 1987). Sustainability, among other implications, requires analysis of the environment as a dimension of socioeconomic development, and not as a separate issue that can be analysed in partial equilibrium or even in isolation from the rest of the economy.

Substantial work has been undertaken in the environmental economics literature to draw out the theoretical and operational implications of the concept of sustainable development. In particular, three main streams of research efforts may be distinguished: new development in the theory of endogenous growth with natural resources; the study of the role of innovation and technological progress; and new approaches to measuring growth and welfare.

On the theoretical side, recent advancements on the theory of endogenous economic growth provide an interesting natural framework to deal with sustainability issues. The existing literature on economic growth has almost exclusively dealt with environmental issues in traditional neoclassical growth models (van der Ploeg and Withagen, 1991; Tahvonen and Kuuluvainen, 1991). In these models long-run growth is solely determined by exogenous factors, like population growth and technological progress, which compensate for the diminishing returns in the accumulation of capital (for example, Solow, 1956). Thus this class of models offers no scope for policy influence and environmental effects, so that these theories find it hard to come to grips with the issue of sustainable growth. However, the recently developed theories of endogenous growth (Romer, 1986; Barro, 1990; Lucas, 1988; Sala-í-Martin, 1990) give a better explanation of economic growth. This new theory no longer takes the steady-state growth rate as given, but endogenizes this rate to allow for the influence of government policies (such as productive government spending, distortionary taxes) and the impact of economic variables such as knowledge spillovers, R&D, and preference parameters such as the rate of time preference and the elasticity of intertemporal substitution.

The new environmental phenomena and the sustainability issues that they imply have given rise to an increasing number of research works aimed at extending the new growth theory to incorporate environmental considerations. The basic question to be answered could be framed as follows: if one considers environmental assets as a stock of natural capital interconnected with economic activity, can one find new limits to development that are due to an excessive depletion of resources which are necessary to life?

The most recent models of growth with environmental assets differ mainly in their assumptions about the productive structure of the economy and cover the various cases that have been analysed in the literature (that is, constant return to scale to one factor, constant returns to scale to all factors, increasing aggregate returns to scale, production functions with varieties of intermediate goods; for a review of the main contributions see Beltratti, 1996). Part of the literature extends the new growth theory by incorporating renewable resources as a factor of production (see, for example, Bovenberg and Smulders, 1995 which also allows for international environmental and production externalities; Musu, 1995; Musu and Lines, 1995; Vellinga, 1995). Other studies incorporate environmental conservation by focusing on endogenous growth models with varieties of clean and dirty intermediate inputs, that is, they address the issue of the environment as a scarce factor of production in the form of a resource constraint which has major implications for the analysis of growth (cf. Hung et al., 1994). The whole research effort aims at coming to grips with the concept of sustainable economic growth.

The second main stream of studies in the environmental economics literature which has received new impetus from the sustainability dimension of the new environmental phenomena is the analysis of the role of innovation and technological progress. In recent years, several attempts to provide a better theoretical and empirical modelling of technical progress and its repercussions on environmental quality have been carried out (for a review see Chapter 16).

On the theoretical side, further research is needed on issues such as technical progress in endogenous growth models of sustainable development, the link between technical progress, the location of industrial activities and trade, the dissemination and diffusion of technical progress, particularly towards LDCs (research joint ventures, arm's length agreements, technology transfers), the role of market structure and imperfections in the innovation process.

On the empirical side, several attempts have been made to model and endogenize technical progress within models designed to address environmental issues. *Ad hoc* endogenous models link technical progress to past energy prices or to some economic indicators of technological changes (Carraro and Galeotti, 1996; see also Chapter 16). Other models provide a behavioural representation of technical progress, as in the R&D models proposed by Goulder and Shneider (1996) and the learning-by-doing model by Grübler and Gritsevskii (1996). These very recent attempts should be developed further and their implications for the dynamics of environmental phenomena and policies should be better assessed.

Further research effort is also needed in order to understand to what extent the claim that technical progress is the best instrument to preserve the environment and natural resources is valid. This has to be done both through case studies and through the use of models in which technological progress is carefully designed. The policy relevance of the above issues is clear. The dynamics and distribution of emission abatement (for example, CO_2), that is, the 'when' and 'where' of climate change policies, crucially depend on the dynamics and distribution of technical progress. Hence a careful understanding of the latter is necessary to provide recommendations about the former.

Finally, the emergence of sustainability as a development criterion has given rise to the need for new approaches to measuring growth and welfare levels which take all the relevant factors into consideration.

In recent years, a growing part of the economics literature dedicated to environmental and natural resource issues has focused its attention on the design of new methodological frameworks for the internalization of the environmental and social dimension into the traditional accounting systems at the national and local, as well as at the microeconomic (firm) level. Various methodological approaches have been developed. They differ in the object of investigation (for example, stocks or flows of environmental and natural resource goods and services, environmental expenditures), the methods used in the collection and valuation of this object (that is monetary versus physical estimation) and the level of integration of new aggregates in the traditional accounting system (that is, 'satellite accounts' versus 'integrated accounts') (see Repetto et al., 1989; Peskin, 1989; El Serafy, 1989; Mäler, 1991; EUROSTAT, 1992; UNSO, 1996).

The development of monetary techniques for non-marketable natural resources and their application to environmental accounting, 'extended' cost–benefit analysis and environmental regulation are part of this effort (for a thorough review of the state of the art in monetary valuation of changes in environmental goods and services see Markandya, 1992).

Against this background, part of the economics literature has developed a strong case against the integration of the environmental dimension into the traditional accounting system and, more specifically, against the use of 'environmentally corrected' national accounts as a general measure of welfare or progress (for policy to aim to maximize) or as an indicator of sustainability (see, for example, Pezzey, 1994; Asheim, 1994).

Also in response to this criticism, research work has been increasingly dedicated to the development of economic and social indicators at the various jurisdictional and sectoral levels as alternative policy tools to monitor the state of progress towards sustainable development (Kuik and Verbruggen, 1991; Hille, 1996; Spangenberg, 1996).

These contrasting views notwithstanding, further developments are still needed in both directions (that is, environmental accounting and sustainability indicators). In particular, it is important to develop consistent common frameworks and methodologies that can be applied across different realities (countries, regions, local communities, and so on), thus allowing useful comparisons. This is true when the internalization of the environmental and social dimension into the traditional accounting systems or the design of indicators of sustainability is concerned. Much greater efforts are also needed on the empirical side, with a greater and more systematic application of the theoretical and methodological advancements to concrete case studies. The lack of data on the relevant variables may represent a serious problem in this direction, particularly with respect to certain regions and countries of the world. On the other hand, a further development of the theoretical and empirical literature in this field might act as a stimulus to the collection of relevant data.

Before turning to the second major environmental economics research area which has received new impetus as a consequence of the new environmental phenomena, it is worth underlining that the three research streams analysed above and linked to the sustainable development dimension of these phenomena do not of course exhaust the (new) research directions opened by this sustainability dimension. Besides improving the analysis of the interrelationships between economic development and the environment, the literature needs to turn its attention and explore deeply the important links between the environment, the economy, and the other dimensions of human development (that is, the societal and political dimension). We shall come back to this issue and develop it further in the concluding section of this chapter.

3.   Transnational dimension, game theory and coalition formation

The global and international dimension of environmental issues has required further departure from standard analysis: a shift from the standard approach to government intervention to an approach on negotiations between nations (see also Chapter 31 in this volume).

Most of the new environmental phenomena mentioned above have an intrinsic international dimension due to transnational or global spillovers. The depletion of the ozone layer and climate change depend on global aggregate emissions. Acid depositions and marine pollution usually cross the borders of the polluting country. Even deforestation is an international problem as forests are a sink for CO_2 and provide important support for biodiversity.

The international dimension of the environment is a source of substantial interdependence among nations: each country benefits from using the environment as a receptacle for emissions and is damaged by environmental deterioration. While the benefit for any country is primarily related to domestic pollution alone, the environmental damage is related to both domestic and foreign emissions.

Even when emissions have no transnational or global spillovers, the interdependence among countries derives from costly national environmental policies which have important international repercussions through trade and factor mobility (cf. Siebert, 1995; Rauscher, 1990; Carraro and Siniscalco, 1992a).

This problem is not new to economists, and has been analysed in the area of externalities and public goods. What is new is the context in which these problems take place. Currently, the atmosphere and water resources are managed as global common property goods, and no institution possesses the power to regulate their use by means of supranational legislation, economic instruments, or by imposing a system of global property rights.

Because these institutions do not exist, the solution of transnational or global environmental problems calls for coordinated action among sovereign countries. Therefore a further shift in economic analysis is required, from a literature on (optimal) government intervention to a literature on international policy coordination and voluntary agreements among sovereign countries.

The outcome of an international environmental negotiation and, more generally, the interdependence among countries in a common environment, may be analysed in the framework of a game-theory approach, specifying each country's behaviour/strategy and payoff function (for a general discussion see Barrett, 1990a, 1990b; Helm and Pearce, 1990; Siebert, 1995).

In the environmental economics literature, the first attempts to study the protection of the international environment were applied by analogy standard schemes of the prisoner's dilemma, where free-riding behaviour inevitably undermines attempts to cooperate, thus resulting in non-cooperative outcomes and consequent environmental deterioration (for a critical review of this literature see McCay and Acheson, 1987; Ostrom, 1990; Steininger, 1991). Alternatively, the literature has analysed the optimal properties of cooperative agreements supported by (linked to?) binding agreements (Hoel, 1991).

More recently, the literature has turned to the use of models of bargaining to study whether cooperative behaviour among all or some of the players (countries) may emerge and be self-sustaining. In a first phase, the focus has been on the design of worldwide agreements to cut emissions by bargaining solely on emissions (see Barrett, 1992; Heal 1993). These analyses show that it is possible to obtain stable coalitions, but that these are restricted to small groups of (like-minded) countries. The dissatisfaction with such an outcome has been followed by attempts at expanding the agreement by bribing reluctant countries by means of money transfers, again undermined by several problems of free-riding and instability (Carraro and Siniscalco, 1993). Finally, the recent literature has tried to link environmental protection to other international agreements, generally on technological cooperation and trade (Carraro and Siniscalco, 1993; Barrett, 1997), showing that it is possible to enlarge the number of signatory countries in an international agreement. It is interesting to note that the actual practice of environmental negotiations (the Climate Change Convention, the Montreal Protocol, the plan for financial implementation of Agenda 21, the environmental clause in the GATT and so on) seems to confirm these outcomes.

These important and relatively recent developments in the literature notwithstanding, a number of further advancements are required for a better understanding of the mechanisms and policy options which may regulate a coordinated action among sovereign countries. Further research efforts must be made on the development of bargaining schemes allowing the study of the emergence of international cooperation in the absence of binding agreements. Second, economic analyses should be integrated with physical and engineering studies and significant improvements in the field of environmental statistics for empirical studies must be made. Third, uncertainty issues (see the following paragraph) and environment–development links must be integrated into the analysis of the interdependence among nations: the intrinsic uncertainty of the impacts of environmental phenomena, the existence of asymmetric information, the non-separability between environment and development are all aspects which may change the very nature of the interaction among countries. Therefore, considering these aspects as marginal would significantly undermine the effectiveness of international research efforts in this field.

The environmental economics literature which has been analysed so far in this section shows that diverse kinds of global environmental protection may be attained even in the absence of an international institution with the power to regulate the use of environmental resources at the international level. Of course, this does not mean that such an institution would not be useful or desirable to help national policy coordination. Such an institution could take the form, for example, of an international agency or of a new hypothesis on property rights (that is, a scheme of international pollution permits administered at the supranational level). The existing literature is rather poor in this respect and significant advancements are required in the study of new institutions formation, which would be able to achieve efficient management of international environmental and natural resources in the presence of profound structural differences among countries, contrasting interests and incentives to free-riding. To this aim, a better understanding of contractual mechanisms is required, with particular reference to processes leading to cooperative agreements and new institutions.

4. Uncertainty and the role of information

Uncertainty over the new environmental phenomena is of both a scientific and economic nature. It arises due to a poor understanding of the *physical* characteristics and consequences of these phenomena, and an equally poor understanding of the economic consequences of environmental degradation. A third source of uncertainty, which adds to the previous ones, takes the form of *asymmetric information* among countries as far as the costs and benefits of environmental policies are concerned.

The new environmental phenomena are of a complex nature and therefore difficult to model on quantitative grounds. Climate change, ozone depletion, acid depositions and marine pollution represent the combined effects of a number of diverse 'elementary' phenomena which occcur at different points in time and space. Each environmental phenomenon seems to be part of a complex chain which is difficult to model. In addition, scientific knowledge about the different physical components of complex environmental phenomena is still very limited. The problem is further complicated by the fact that many phenomena are time-persistent and have long-run irreversible impacts. This sometimes makes empirical observations useless and may result in a chaotic dynamic of climate models.

From an economic point of view, any attempt to value the economic consequences of environmental problems clashes against various obstacles: inadequacy of standard economic indicators as measurements of human welfare (for example GDP–gross domestic product); lack of attention in existing econometric models to important dimensions of human progress and their economic consequences (such as migration flows, social and political factors, loss of biodiversity and so on); inability of existing econometric models – generally linear and country-specific – to evaluate large departures from equilibrium and complex international impacts. All these factors generate a great variability in the valuations of the economic consequences of environmental phenomena and a general dissatisfaction with this type of studies.

In the presence of uncertainty about the new environmental phenomena, their potential and actual impacts and consequences, two basic questions need to be answered by economists: how much should be invested to insure humanity against the risk of environmental damages, particularly if the consequences of environmental degradation are partially irreversible? And how should policy decisions be taken? The international community is divided over these issues, on technical, political and contractual grounds.

On political grounds, the contrasts among different countries and groups of countries during the Rio Summit and a number of other international negotiations on transnational environmental phenomena (climate change, desertification, and the like) are a clear demonstration of such difficulties, which may represent a serious obstacle to the achievement of an agreement.

On the contractual and technical grounds, insurance companies no more insure this class of risks. The solution, put forward in preliminary work by G. Chichilnisky (1998), consists in cutting risk in 'slices' and identifying appropriate institutions (from the state to private insurance companies) to 'take care' of each 'slice', corresponding to different risk categories.

In addition to these aspects, the new environmental phenomena have highlighted the importance of information from another point of view, that is, the importance that pollution control approaches based on environmental information strategies can play.

The nature of pollution obviously entails many issues related to information. In a first stage, some models have concentrated on the regulator–polluter relationship, by means of principal–agent models. More recently, this role emanates from the increasingly perceived need for more regulatory tools as well as from the falling cost of information collection, aggregation and dissemination. In the industrialized countries pollution control systems based on traditional legal remedies and market-based approaches remain overburdened – in terms of budget and human resources constraints – by the sheer number of substances to be controlled (Tietenberg, 1997). On the other hand, in many developing countries the regulatory infrastructure appears to be insufficiently developed and/or subject to corruption and, in either case, it is unable to handle adequately the burden of designing, implementing, monitoring and enforcing an effective pollution control system. It follows that innovative pollution control policy may involve investment in the provision of information at both the private and the public level. A growing number of agencies are increasingly focusing their resources on providing information about the pollution performance of polluters. There is also a growing international recognition of public disclosure as a regulatory tool (cf. Tietenberg, 1997).

In the past, very few studies have focused attention on the role that information approaches play in creating incentives for pollution control, both on a theoretical and empirical level. Only very recently, part of the literature (mainly applied) on environmental economics has turned attention to the analysis of information strategies (that is, public disclosure), their overall effectiveness and its determinants (Tietenberg, 1997; Dasgupta and Wheeler, 1996; Hamilton, 1995).

A thorough understanding of the role that information approaches play in tackling sustainable development problems requires additional analysis of both the conceptual and empirical issues, and the pros and cons of using information to create incentives for pollution control. Economists, in particular, have to understand the circumstances under which public information is more likely to create those incentives, and the marginal benefits and the marginal costs of different types of information provision strategies.

5. Trends in the environmental economics literature: 1990–97
The above analysis shows that the 'new' environmental phenomena and their common characteristics have given a significant impetus to the environmental economics literature by raising new questions or posing old questions in a new context, thus requiring the development of new analytical tools and policy analyses.

With the purpose of deriving additional insights into the contributions of the more recent environmental economics literature to the study of the theoretical and operational questions posed by the new environmental phenomena, I carried out a survey based on articles presented to international conferences and published in journals on environmental economics.

In particular, the survey considers papers which have been presented at the annual conferences of the European Association of Environmental and Natural Resource Economists (EAERE) from its foundation (1990) to the present (1997), as well as papers published in two main international journals on environmental economics from 1990 to 1996: the *Journal of Environmental Economics and Management* (*JEEM*, the official journal of the American Association of Environmental and Resource Economists), and *Environmental and Resource Economics* (*ERE*, the official journal of the European Association of Environmental and Resource Economists).

Studies have been classified into two major research categories: theoretical and applied studies, where the latter includes works with 'real-world' data and the former includes also theoretical works with numerical examples and scenario analysis having an illustrative purpose. Each of the two categories has been further divided into four research groups. The first three groups correspond to the three major 'new' research areas identified above, that is, environment and development interrelationships; transnational environmental problems, game theory and coalition formation; and uncertainty and information. The fourth category includes contributions not specifically dealing with any of the above topics (that is, theory of environmental policy, policy implementation and instruments, natural resources management, and so on).

In all, 1456 papers have been surveyed. The analysis shows that the contribution of the environmental economics literature to the three major

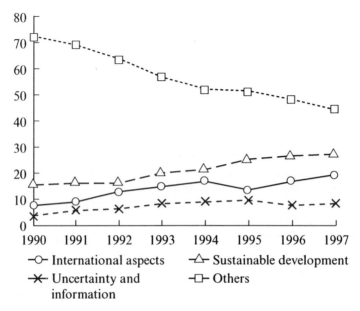

* 'Others' includes papers dealing with natural resource management, theory of environmental policy and policy implementation.

Figure 78.1 Recent trends in the theoretical literature: a survey (% values)

research areas represents a fast-growing share of the total (see Figures 78.1 and 78.2). On the whole time period, the contribution of theoretical work to emerging issues in environmental economics appears to be generally more significant than that of applied studies (68 per cent versus 32 per cent).

Theoretical work in the area of sustainability issues, which represented a relatively minor part of the whole effort at the beginning of the 1990s (about 15 per cent), has constantly increased during the past seven years and now represents about 27 per cent of the total. Similarly, the percentage of theoretical papers dealing with transnational environmental problems and international policy coordination has risen continuously, from 8 per cent in 1990 to 19 per cent in 1997. Also the share of theoretical contributions focusing on uncertainty issues and asymmetric information almost doubled, from 4 per cent in 1990 to 9 per cent in 1997.

Applied research, too, seems to have paid increasing attention to the three research areas considered above, although the majority of the 'real-world' studies appear to focus on 'other' topics (such as valuation issues, natural resource management, policy implementation and policy instruments; cf. Figure 78.2).

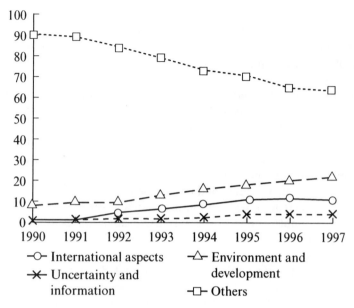

* 'Others' includes papers dealing with natural resource management, theory of environmental policy and policy implementation.

Figure 78.2   Recent trends in the applied literature: a survey (% values)

A comparison of the papers published in the *Journal of Environmental Economics and Management* (*JEEM*) and those published in *Environmental and Resource Economics* (*ERE*) or presented at the annual conferences of the European Association of Environmental and Resource Economists (EAERE) gives additional insights into the geographical distribution of the environmental economics literature. On the whole, a relatively larger part of the studies dealing with transnational and global problems is conducted in (Northern) European countries as opposed to the US (8 per cent versus 5 per cent), while issues of uncertainty and information are studied primarily in the US (5 per cent versus 2 per cent). The sustainability dimension implied by the new environmental phenomena attracts equal attention in Europe and the US, with the former relatively more focused on the development of the theory of endogenous growth with natural resources and the study of the role of innovation and technological progress.

Of course the three sources of information that I have considered in the survey are subject to a major factor of potential bias: they are all 'refereed'. This means that a selection process may have taken place that favours particular types of studies submitted and accepted by these institutions. With this in mind, an additional source of information has been considered: papers submitted at the 1998 World Congress of Environmental and Resource Economists (jointly organized by the European Association of Environmental and Resource Economists and the American Association of Environmental and Resource Economists in cooperation with the Fondazione Eni Enrico Mattei). The call for papers focused on 12 'major subject matter areas': environmental regulation; environment and development; urban environmental problems; empirical modelling of the economy and the environment; environment and technology; natural resource studies; valuation and cost–benefit analysis; international environmental issues; economic theory and the environment; environment politics and law; regional and country studies; and miscellaneous.

In all, 882 abstracts have been submitted from all over the world. The analysis of the sample confirms the increasing attention paid by the environmental economics literature to the relatively new theoretical and policy issues raised by the new environmental phenomena.

Works dealing with issues related to environment–development inter-relationships represent by far the largest share of the papers submitted to the Congress: almost 25 per cent of the total sample as opposed to the 13 per cent of papers focusing on transnational environmental problems and international policy coordination and the 5 per cent dealing with uncertainty and information issues. About 56 per cent of the papers in the sample deal with issues not directly related to the three research areas considered above (that is, theory of environmental policy, policy implementation and instruments, natural resource management studies, valuation and cost–benefit analysis, and so on).

Theoretical contributions still appear to be dominant over applied ones in all the four research areas considered in the analysis, even if the relative share of applied works turns out to be greater than in the previous survey (40 per cent as opposed to 32 per cent).

As far as the geographical distribution of research efforts is concerned, the analysis of the World Congress sample seems to confirm the results of the previous part of the survey. Research efforts from the European (EU) countries are relatively more focused on the study of transnational environmental problems and international policy coordination while contributions dealing with uncertainty issues and information strategies come mainly from the US. The broad area of sustainable development issues is covered equally by the EU and the US.

The new research topics highlighted by the new environmental phenomena and their common characteristics seem to attract relatively little attention from the developing world. Here the greatest share of research contributions focuses on natural resources management (that is, growth, harvesting, pricing, taxation of renewable and non-renewable natural resources) and on the theory and practice of environmental policy (market and non-market environmental policy tools, and so on).

6. Other complementary contributions

Before turning to our conclusions on the contribution of economic analysis to environmental economics, one important remark has to be made. The sample considered in the above survey and, more generally, an overview of the environmental economics literature (volumes, textbooks and journals), gives only a partial picture of the role played and contribution made by economic analysis in the past to the study of environmental and natural resources. To complete the picture one has to consider two additional and relevant complementary research areas that have been attracting growing attention in the last few years: environmental management science and urban socioeconomic studies.

Management science

The first area focuses its attention on the relationships between firms and the environment and, in particular, on the impacts that emerging environmental problems and environmental regulation have on firms' strategies and management tools, and vice versa. This is a relatively new field of study which shifts the attention from the public policymaker to the business policymaker, and which analyses – from a business perspective – the role and the responses of business actors to environmental problems and policies.

In general, economic studies focusing on these themes do not appear in the 'conventional' economics literature dedicated to environmental and natural resources, but rather have 'their own' discussion and dissemination channels, both in terms of specialized journals and in terms of international conferences specifically dedicated to the interrelationships between firms and the environment (the annual 'Greening of Industry' conference and international journals such as *Business Strategy and the Environment, EEMA Review, ENDS Report, Environmental Accounting and Auditing Reporter, Environmental Management, Environmental Quality Management, Greener Management International*).

In the last few years this has been a fast-growing research area focusing in particular on newly designed management strategies and tools in response to environmental concerns: environmental information systems, environmental reporting strategies, eco-management accounting, eco-auditing, environmental performance indicators, full-cost accounting, risk management strategies, and so on (see, for example, Ditz et al., 1995; Fisher and Schot, 1993; Gray, 1993; Malaman and Bartolomeo, 1996; Porter and van der Linde, 1995; Roome, 1994; Schaltegger et al., 1996; Wehrmeyer, 1996; Welford, 1996; Welford and Starkey, 1996; Welford and Gouldson, 1993). Much has still to be done in this field given that firms' activities is one of the major pressure factors on the natural environment and given the proven important and proactive role that firms can play in the pursuit of sustainable development. In particular, economists should analyse in more detail – and from both a theoretical and empirical point of view – the circumstances under which a firm's active involvement within the decision-making process takes place, and the social and private payoffs gained by this involvement. Typically, however, from a management perspective, this literature provides interesting and complementary inputs to the study of the interrelationships between socioeconomic development processes and the natural environment.

Urban socioeconomic studies

Another interesting contribution to the advancement of the understanding of sustainable development issues, their causes, impacts and possible solutions, comes from the recently developed research area of the *urban environment* (see also Chapter 38).

Almost neglected as a specific sustainable development issue and research field until the Rio Conference on Environmental and Development, the study of urban sustainable development has gained increasing momentum in the last few years, with the growing awareness of the key importance of local development patterns on global environmental problems ('think globally, act locally').

Here, even more than in the environmental management field, the analyses of environmental and natural resources issues become truly interdisciplinary, calling for the contribution not just of economists and natural scientists, but also of sociologists, political scientists, geographers, ecologists and the like.

The urban scale is not just a natural studying and 'testing' field for many of the analytical tools and methodological approaches developed in the theoretical literature (environment–development models, environmental policy instruments, environmental accounting and sustainability indicators, and so on). Here the attention is focused on the various social actors (public administration, industries, NGOs, citizens, and others) and the way they interact and affect the local environment. Consensus-building and participatory approaches in the management of urban sustainable development issues are a typical and important area of study to which a growing number of studies are dedicated (see, for example, Abbott, 1996; Gilbert, 1996; Haughton and Hunter, 1994; Nijkamp and Perrels, 1994; UNEP, 1996).

7. Summary and concluding remarks: what can economists do for the environment?

Until the beginning of the 1990s, traditional economic analysis provided environmental economics with suitable tools for the study of environmental issues and related policy problems: the theory of non-renewable and renewable resources; the theory of missing markets; Pigouvian taxation and the theory of property rights; the economics of public goods; welfare economics, and so on.

At the beginning of the present decade, the emergence of 'new' environmental phenomena which have an intrinsic transnational and long-run dimension, which are closely interlinked with human development patterns and which involve a great deal of uncertainty and information asymmetries (climate change, ozone layer depletion, marine pollution, and so on), 'crowd out' much of the existing knowledge, practice and conventional wisdom, thus opening new perspectives for economic analysis and requiring the development of new analytical tools and policy analyses.

The environmental economics discipline has responded to these challenges, experiencing a kind of breakthrough, both in terms of methods and focuses of the analyses.

In the previous pages, the new developments of the literature have been grouped and discussed under three major 'research headings': sustainable development issues; transnational environmental problems and international policy coordination; and uncertainty and information asymmetries. Important contributions to the understanding of environmental phenomena, their causes, effects and possible solutions have been developed from various areas of economic theory and from original applications and developments.

Further theoretical improvements are none the less needed if economists are to provide an increasingly effective contribution to the study and the solution of environmental issues and to the pursuit of sustainable development. These have been discussed in detail in the preceding sections.

Advancements are also needed at the applied level. Indeed, empirical analyses are of fundamental importance both to environmental economics and to the sustainability debate in particular. This point has been made several times in the previous discussion, and it is reiterated here simply to underline its relevance. To implement this, one needs more data sets and more empirical models which can use them. Also, local studies are very important for a better understanding of the interactions between the ecological and the economic systems. This brings us to a further consideration.

Given the interdisciplinary nature of environmental problems and their strong links with the other dimensions of human development, economists will have a significant role in promoting progress in their understanding and solutions only if they further interact and collaborate with natural and social scientists (ecologists, physicians, biologists, jurists and the like). We will fail in our efforts unless better progress is made to integrate the viewpoints of three disciplines:

- The *economists*, whose methods seek to maximize human welfare within the constraints of existing capital stock and technologies. Economists are learning the importance of natural capital.
- The *ecologists*, who stress preserving the integrity of ecological subsystems viewed as critical for the overall stability of the global system. Some argue for the preservation of all ecosystems, although a less extreme view aims at maintaining the resilience and dynamic adaptability of natural life support systems. Here, the units of accounts are physical, not monetary, and the prevailing disciplines are biology, geology, chemistry and the natural sciences generally.
- The *sociologists*, who emphasize that the key actors are human beings, whose patterns of social organization are crucial for devising viable solutions to achieve sustainable development. Indeed, evidence is mounting that failure to pay sufficient attention to social factors in the development process is seriously jeopardizing the effectiveness of various development programmes and projects.

While economists, ecologists and sociologists would all agree that the others' concerns matter, they do not see these concerns through one another's eyes (that is, they interpret the others' concerns through their own lens). For example, social concerns tend to be reduced to questions of inequality and poverty, and environmental concerns to question of natural resource management. Absent from the debate are important concerns such as social cohesion, cultural identity and ecosystem integrity.

As policy makers seek to bring together experts from each of these disciplines, a number of conceptual and methodological questions need to be addressed. The key unresolved questions fall into four broad categories: decision making in the presence of uncertainty and information asymmetries; policy and institutional design – in particular in the presence of international interdependence among countries; proper measurement of human welfare and related valuation issues; and social sustainability (cf. Serageldin and Steer, 1994).

The contribution of economic analysis to the pursuit of sustainable development crucially depends on the capacity of the discipline to respond to the new challenges posed by the new environmental phenomena and to integrate its efforts with those of the other disciplines.

References

Abbott, J. (1996), *Sharing the City: Community Part in Urban Management*, London: Earthscan.

Asheim, G. (1994), 'Net national product as an indicator of sustainability', *Scandinavian Journal of Economics*, **96**, 265–74.

Barrett, S. (1990a), 'The problem of global environmental protection', *Oxford Review of Economic Policy*, **6** (1), 69–79.

Barrett, S. (1990b), 'International environmental agreements as games', paper presented at the symposium on 'Conflicts and Cooperation in Managing Environmental Resources', Siegen, November.

Barrett, S. (1992), 'International environmental agreements as games', in R. Pethig (ed), *Conflicts and Cooperation in Managing Environmental Economics*, Berlin.

Barrett, S. (1997), 'Towards a theory of international environmental cooperation', in C. Carraro and D. Siniscalco (eds), *New Directions in the Economic Theory of the Environment*, Cambridge, UK: Cambridge University Press.

Barro, R.J. (1990), 'Government spending in a simple model of endogenous growth', *Journal of Political Economy*, **98**, S103–25.

Baumol, W.J. and W.E. Oates (1975), *The Theory of Environmental Policy*, Englewood Cliffs, NJ: Prentice-Hall.

Baumol, W.J. and W.E. Oates (1988), *The Theory of Environmental Policy*, Cambridge, UK: Cambridge University Press.

Beltratti, A. (ed.) (1996), *Models of Economic Growth with Environmental Assets*, Dordrecht: Kluwer Academic Publishers.

Bovenberg, A. and S. Smulders (1995), 'Environmental quality and pollution augmenting technological change in a two-sector endogenous growth model', *Journal of Public Economics*, **57**, 369–91.

Brundtland Report, World Commission on Environment and Development (1987), *Our Common Future*, London: Oxford University Press.

Carraro, C. and M. Galeotti (1996), 'WARM: a European model for energy and environmental analysis', *Environmental Modelling and Assessment*, **2**.

Carraro, C. and D. Siniscalco (1992a), 'Environmental innovation policy and international competition', *Environmental and Resource Economics*, **2**, 183–200.

Carraro, C. and D. Siniscalco (1992b), 'Strategies for the international protection of the environment', CEPR Discussion Paper, 586; also *Journal of Public Economics*, **52**, 309–28 (1993).

Carraro, C. and D. Siniscalco (1992c), 'The international dimensions of environmental policy', *European Economic Review*, **36**, 379–87.

Carraro, C. and D. Siniscalco (1993), 'Policy coordination for sustainability: commitments, transfers and linked negotiations', Nota di Lavoro 63.93, Fondazione Eni Enrico Mattei.

Carraro, C. and D. Siniscalco (1993), *The European Carbon Tax: an Economic Assessment*, Dordrecht: Kluwer Academic Publishers.

Chichilnisky, G. (1998), 'Managing unknown risks', *Journal of Portfolio Management*, **24** (4), Summer, 85–91.

Dasgupta, S. and D. Wheeler (1996), *Citizen Complaints as Environmental Indicators*, Washington, DC: World Bank.

Ditz, D., J. Ranganathan and D. Banks (eds) (1995), *Green Ledgers, Case studies in Corporate Environmental Accounting*, Washington, DC: WRI.

EEA, UNECE et al. (eds) (1995), *Europe's Environment: the Dobris Assessment*, European Environmental Agency, Copenhagen.

El Serafy, S. (1989), 'Environment and natural resource accounting', in G. Schramm and J. Warford (eds), *Environmental Management and Economic Development*, Washington, DC: World Bank.

EUROSTAT (1992), *Système européen de rassemblement de l'information économique sur l'environnement – SERIEE*, Luxemburg.

Fischer, K. and J. Schot (eds) (1993), *Environmental Strategies for Industry*, Washington, DC: Island Press.

Gilbert, R. (1996), *Making Cities Work: the Role of Local Authorities in the Urban Environment*, London: Earthscan.

Goulder, L. and S. Shneider (1996), 'Induced technological change, crowding out and the attractiveness of CO_2 emission abatement', working paper, Stanford University, October.

Gray, R. (1993), *Accounting for the Environment*, London: Paul Chapman.

Grübler, A. and A. Gritsevskii (1996), 'A model of endogenous technological change through uncertain returns on learning (R&D and investments), mimeo.

Hamilton, J.T. (1995), 'Pollution as news: media and stock market reactions to the toxics release data', *Journal of Environmental Economics and Management*, **28** (1), 98–113.

Haughton, G. and C. Hunter (1994), *Sustainable Cities*, London: Kingsley.

Heal, G. (1993), 'International negotiations on emission control' in C. Carraro (ed.), *Trade, Innovation and Environment*, Dordrecht: Kluwer Academic Publishers.

Helm, D. and D. Pearce (1990), 'The assessment: economic policy towards the environment', *Oxford Review of Economic Policy*, **6** (1), 1–14.

Hille, J. (1996), 'Environmental space based indicators of sustainable development', a study of the European Environment Agency's expert corner, Copenhagen.

Hoel, M. (1991), 'Global environmental problems: the effects of unilateral actions taken by one country', *Journal of Environmental Economics and Management*, **20** (1), 55–70.

Hung, V., P. Chang and K. Blakburn (1994), 'Endogenous growth, environment and R&D', in C. Carraro (ed.), *Trade, Innovation and Environment*, Dordrecht: Kluwer Academic Publishers.

IPCC (Intergovernmental Panel on Climate Change) (1995), *Report*, Eleventh Session, Rome, 11–15 December.

IUCN, UNEP, WWF (1991), *Caring for the Earth*, Gland, Switzerland: IUCN.

Kuik, O. and H. Verbruggen (eds) (1991), *In Search of Indicators of Sustainable Development*, Dordrecht: Kluwer Academic Publishers.

Lucas, R.E. (1988), 'On the mechanisms of economic growth', *Journal of Monetary Economics*, **22**, 3–42.

Malaman, R. and M. Bartolomeo (eds) (1996), *La strategia ambientale d'impresa*, Milan: Il sole 24 Ore Libri.

Mäler, K. (1991), 'National accounts and environmental resources', *Environmental and Resource Economics*, **1**, 1–15.

Markandya, A. (1992), 'The value of the environment: a state of the art survey', in A. Markandya and J. Richardson (eds), *Environmental Economics*, London: Earthscan.

McCay, B. and J.M. Acheson (1987), *The Question of the Commons*, Tucson: The University of Arizona Press.

Musu, I. (1995), 'Transitional dynamics to optimal sustainable growth', paper presented at the 6th Annual Conference of the European Association for Environmental and Resource Economics, Umeå, Sweden, 24–26 June.

Musu, I. and M. Lines (1995), 'Endogenous growth and environmental preservation', in G. Boero and A. Silberston (eds), *Environmental Economics: Proceedings of European Economic Association at Oxford*, London: St Martin's Press.

Nijkamp, P. and A. Perrels (1994), *Sustainable Cities in EU*, London: Earthscan.

Ostrom, E. (1990), *Governing the Commons*, Cambridge, UK: Cambridge University Press.

Pearce, D. and R.K. Turner (1990), *Economics of Natural Resources and the Environment*, New York: Harvester Wheatsheaf.

Peskin, H.M. (1989), 'Accounting for natural resource depletion and degradation in developing countries', Environmental Department Working Paper, no. 13, Washington, DC, World Resource Institute.

Pezzey, J. (1994), 'Theoretical essays on sustainability and environmental policy', Ph.D. thesis, Department of Economics, University of Bristol.

Ploeg, F. van der and C. Withagen (1991), 'Pollution control and the Ramsey problem', *Environmental and Resource Economics*, **1**, 215–36.

Porter, M. and Claas van der Linde (1995), 'Green and competitive: ending the stalemate', *Harvard Business Review*, September/October.

Rauscher, M. (1990), 'National environmental policies and the effects of economic integration', mimeo, Kiel Institute of World Economics.

Repetto, R. et al. (1989), *Wasting Assets: Natural Resources in the National Income Accounts*, Washington, DC: World Resources Institute.

Romer, P.M. (1986), 'Increasing returns and long-run growth', *Journal of Political Economy*, **94**, 1002–38.

Roome, N. (1994), 'Business strategy, R&D management and environmental imperatives', *R&D Management*, no. 24.

Sala-i-Martin, X. (1990), *Lecture Notes on Economic Growth (I)*, NBER, nos 3563 and 3564.

Schaltegger, S., K. Muller and H. Hindrichsen (1996), *Corporate Environmental Accounting*, New York: John Wiley & Sons.

Serageldin, I. and A. Steer (1994), 'Making development sustainable: from concepts to actions', Environmentally Sustainable Development Occasional Paper Series, no. 2, The World Bank, Washington, DC.

Siebert, H. (1987), *Economics of the Environment: Theory and Policy*, 2nd edn, Berlin: Springer-Verlag.

Siebert, H. (1995), 'Spatial aspects of environmental economics', in A.V. Kneese and J.L. Sweezy, (eds), *Handbook of Natural Resources and Energy Economics*, vol. 1, Amsterdam: North-Holland.

Solow, R.M. (1956), 'A contribution to the theory of growth', *Quarterly Journal of Economics*, **70**, 65–94.

Spangenberg, J.H. et al. (1996), 'Material flows based indicators in environmental reporting', a study of the European Environment Agency's expert corner, Copenhagen.

Steininger, K. (1991), 'Environmental illusion in the depletion of common property resources', mimeo, University of Graz.

Tahvonen, O. and J. Kuuluvainen (1991), 'Optimal growth with renewable resources and pollution', *European Economic Review*, **35**, 650–61.

Tietenberg, T. (1997), *Information strategies for pollution control*, paper presented at the Eighth Annual Conference of the EAERE.

UNEP, Sustainability (1996), *Engaging Stakeholders*, Sustainability UNEP, London.

United Nations Environment Programme (1991), *The State of the Environment*, New York: United Nations.

UNSO (1992), *Integrated Environmental and Economic Accounting*, New York: United Nations.

Vellinga, N. (1995), *Short Run Analysis of Endogenous Environmental Growth*, paper presented at the 6th Annual Conference of the European Association of Environmental and Resource Economics, UMEA, Sweden, 24–26 June.

Wehrmeyer, W. (ed.) (1996), *Greening People, Human Resources and Environmental Management*, Greenleaf Publishing.

Welford, R. (ed.) (1996), *Corporate Environmental Management*, London: Earthscan.

Welford, R. and A. Gouldson (1993), *Environmental Management and Business Strategy*, Pitman.

Welford, R. and R. Starkey (eds) (1996), *Business and the Environment*, London: Earthscan.

World Development Report (1992), *Development and the Environment*, The World Bank, Oxford: Oxford University Press.

Worldwatch (1994), *State of the World 1994: a Worldwatch Institute Report on Progress Toward a Sustainable Society*, London: Earthscan.

79 Integration and communication between environmental economics and other disciplines
John L.R. Proops

1. Introduction

As a social science economics lies at the interface between the natural sciences and the humanities. For example, to analyse the extraction of natural resources, the subsequent production and consumption of goods, and the effects of these activities on the environment, one needs some knowledge of natural science. Similarly, to understand the motivations that inform the decisions of entrepreneurs and consumers, one has to be acquainted with the humanities. I consider it to be significant that classical economics was founded by Adam Smith, who held a chair in moral philosophy; consequently, ethics had a fundamental role in Smith's economics. Further, at its foundation, modern (neoclassical) economics was strongly influenced by Newtonian mechanics, through the natural science backgrounds of Walras, Jevons and Pareto. This, in turn, has led to the emphasis on mathematical formalism we see in modern neoclassical analyses, where economics has been abstracted, even divorced, from its philosophical and natural science roots.

This divorce also holds, to some degree, for environmental economics, which largely derives its concepts and methods from the neoclassical paradigm. (This has led to the emergence of ecological economics, which endeavours to establish communication between environmental economics and other disciplines.) Hence, almost by definition, environmental economics cannot exist as a purely 'economics' discipline. Its subject matter is the relationship between human activity and the natural world, so not only is familiarity with the principles of modern economics a prerequisite for its understanding and advancement; so also is at least some familiarity with the natural sciences which determine how nature constrains, and can be damaged by, economic activity. Also necessary is an insight into the role of philosophy in formulating the area of environmental economics discourse.

In this brief overview I examine four ways in which other disciplines can, and must, influence environmental economics. First, I discuss the need to move from a multidisciplinary to a transdisciplinary approach to the study of human–environment interactions. Second, I note that any economic

1230

activity must be supported by nature, and also have effects on the natural world. Third, concepts from thermodynamics, ecological theory and evolutionary theory are outlined, and their importance for environmental economics noted. Finally, the role of philosophy, as both ethics and epistemology, is noted in forming the mode of discourse, and the limits to application, of environmental economics.

2.   Multidisciplinary, interdisciplinary and transdisciplinary work

Before turning to interrelationships between environmental economics and other disciplines, I make some comments on how work between disciplines can be conducted. Here one often meets the distinction between multidisciplinary, interdisciplinary and transdisciplinary work, which I interpret as follows.

Multidisciplinary work necessarily involves several people, with a variety of disciplinary backgrounds. For example, in environmental impact assessment exercises it is common to form a team containing, say, an ecologist, a hydrologist, a sociologist and a town planner. By each team member bringing to bear their individual and separate skills, with each contributing to the final report, a wider perspective can be taken on the social and environmental effects of some proposed development. In this type of cooperation, the divisions between disciplines are respected, and the team members do not question each other's expertise, nor seek significantly to contribute to each other's input into the analysis.

Interdisciplinary work will often, even usually, also be a team endeavour, though it is feasible by one individual. In my view, the essence of interdisciplinary work is the breaking down of disciplinary boundaries by the individuals concerned. Thus for environmental economics, say the economics of the greenhouse effect, interdisciplinary work will require that all the co-workers are familiar with both the economic tools likely to be useful for such analyses, *and* be familiar with the natural science necessary to understand why the effect, and its consequences, is expected to occur.

It could be argued that for policy discussion of, say, the greenhouse effect, a multidisciplinary approach will suffice. I believe this to be mistaken, as the problems of cooperation between natural scientists and economists are well known. At the simplest level, the different use of terms can lead to great confusion. For example, the word 'equilibrium' has completely different resonances to a chemist and an economist. Even more important, economists and natural scientists perceive the nature of explanation differently. For example, economists focus on the concept of the 'market', while physicists are much more concerned with notions of transformation and time. (For a fuller discussion of these issues, see Faber and Proops, 1996, ch. 10; see Chapter 67 in this volume for an alternative perspective.)

Finally, a transdisciplinary approach takes the integration of disciplines a stage further, where not only does one transcend the boundaries of the disciplines in seeking understanding, but actually generates new concepts and mental structures which subsume and extend the approaches of even an interdisciplinary approach. In particular, if environmental and ecological economics are to integrate the humanities and natural sciences within their mode of analysis, there are sure to arise ethical and epistemological problems that have not previously been attended to. Examples of how a transdisciplinary approach to the study of human–nature interactions can generate new conceptual structures, even new world-views, are apparent in the works of, *inter alia*, Georgescu-Roegen (1971), Clark (1989) and Daly and Cobb (1989).

In summary, interdisciplinary work makes one aware that many concepts and methods are available for studying human–nature interactions. However, for a transdisciplinary approach one must go further, conceiving of new concepts and tools in order coherently to integrate insights from the humanities and the natural sciences. This, in turn, leads to fundamental ethical and epistemological problems, bringing one to the limit of the purely 'scientific' approach. For this reason, for a truly transdisciplinary approach, one needs to bring to one's work such characteristics as attentiveness, openness and flexibility. In particular, it is necessary to be aware of ignorance, both one's own and society's (Faber et al., 1992).

3. The biophysical foundations of economic activity

It is now a triuism that economic activity is not, and cannot be regarded as, independent of the rest of nature. When considering the production process we see that natural resources are necessary in at least two ways. First, any material good has a physical embodiment, so it must be 'made of' something which has its source in nature. Second, any material good, or non-material service, must be made 'with something', that is, production is a 'process', where the desired output is made from material inputs by a transformation that will, itself, require further inputs (usually of low-entropy energy, as discussed below).

These material and energy requirements of production can be met in two distinct ways. First, we can crop living organisms from the earth's surface or oceans; second, we can extract non-living materials from the earth. We can summarize these two contributors to the possibilities of economic production as together constituting the 'biophysical' foundations of economics.

However, as well as this direct dependence of economic production on nature, we can also note extremely important indirect dependence. First, the physical structure of the atmosphere, with its beneficial shielding out of ultraviolent radiation by the ozone layer, and the warming by the 'natural' greenhouse effect, generates a vital and increasingly recognized economic service. Similarly, the global biological system recycles oxygen, nitrogen, and so on, and modifies rainfall patterns. Without these 'services of nature', economic activity would be almost inconceivable, and as economy-derived pollution damages both the physical and biological processes of the earth and its atmosphere, the biophysical foundations of future economic activity are progressively undermined.

In summary, economics is becoming forced to acknowledge the biophysical foundations of economic activity, as that very activity, through resource depletion and pollution, threatens its own future possibility.

4. Natural constraints on the possible: thermodynamics and resilience
Once the effects of economic activity on nature are recognized, and the corresponding threat to future economic activity is identified, the question naturally arises: 'How can we solve these resource and environmental problems, while still maintaining an acceptable level of economic activity into the future?' Another way of putting this is: 'What is the scope for a technical fix of these problems?' To respond to this question, an understanding of the principles of thermodynamics, modern ecosystem analysis and evolutionary theory is indispensable. First we look at thermodynamics.

Thermodynamics
The details of thermodynamics are discussed in detail elsewhere in this volume, by Matthias Ruth (Chapter 59). Here we simply note that all natural systems are constrained by the availability and transformation of energy. In particular, we can refer to the first and second laws of thermodynamics (Georgescu-Roegen, 1971; Balian, 1991; Faber et al., 1996, chs 6 and 7). The first law states that energy can be neither created nor destroyed; it can only be transformed. The second law strictly refers only to systems closed to the in- or outflow of both energy and matter (so-called 'isolated systems'). This law says that in isolated systems, the transformation of energy can be in only one direction; from 'more available' to 'less available' to do work. (Another statement is that the 'entropy' of an isolated system always tends to increase; cf. Ruth.) This law effectively says that, unlike matter, energy cannot be 'recycled'. Once it is 'used', it cannot be used again for the same purpose.

Taken together, the first and second laws of thermodynamics put constraints on economic activity by disallowing the existence of perpetual motion machines (that is, inexhaustible sources of useful, 'available' or 'low-entropy' energy). The first law says that a perpetual motion machine 'of the first sort' is not possible, where new, available, energy is created to replace the old, no-longer-available energy. The second law says that a perpetual motion machine of the second sort is not possible, where old, unavailable, 'high-entropy' energy is recycled to become new, available, low-entropy energy.

Are these important constraints on economic activity? Clearly they are. In their absence we would not need to keep extracting fuels, or collecting biomass, as sources of available energy for running our productive processes. We could simply pull energy 'out of the air', or recycle the energy from a single piece of coal. Further, if we seek to expand productive activity indefinitely, then, even if we allow for increasing efficiency in energy use for production, we shall eventually be constrained by either running out of fossil fuels and/or running out of area to collect solar energy. Indeed, one could go one step further and argue that the 'scarcity' which economics is all about is partly, perhaps even principally, a result of the laws of thermodynamics. (For a debate on the usefulness of thermodynamics to economics, see Young, 1991 and Daly, 1992.)

The further research that these insights suggest is both conceptual and practical. On the conceptual level, can we include the laws of thermodynamics explicitly in our economic models, just as the law of conservation of matter is included by the 'materials-balance' approach? At the practical level, does the close empirical analysis of energy flows and entropy increase aid us in policy making concerning environmental impacts of economic activity? Finally, does the entropy concept undermine simple production models? The issue here is that the second law tells us that it is impossible, even in principle, to produce goods and services without producing high-entropy wastes. As such, all production is joint production, and models of production processes which do not take this into account cannot reflect reality.

The two arrows of time

The thermodynamics described above is that which is most often discussed, if at all, in the environmental economics literature, and derives from the work of nineteenth-century physicists. Such an approach allows one to calculate, with great accuracy, the maximum possible efficiency of electricity generating systems; it also allows one to calculate the minimum (and extremely small) energy input necessary to extract metals from their ores. Clearly, this type of thermodynamics still has great practical and conceptual utility. However, there is a new type of thermodynamics available today, which deals with systems which are 'open' to the through-flow of matter and energy, and which allow for the possibility of the emergence of novel structures (Prigogine and Stengers, 1984). The systems which such thermodynamics describes are altogether more complex than those amenable to analysis by the old 'static' thermodynamics, and include such phe-nomena as the formation of clouds, the structure of flames, the emergence and self-maintenance of organisms, and the functioning of whole economies (Proops, 1985).

As noted above, the second law strictly applies only to systems which are 'isolated', and clearly the earth is not so isolated; it receives a continual inflow of available (low-entropy) energy from the sun. Modern work has shown that such open systems as the earth, while still constrained overall by the second law, need not be constrained locally always to exhibit decreas-ing availability of energy. Instead, such open systems can exhibit local increases of available energy, as reflected in the emergence of structures. We are all familiar with this dichotomy between the natures of isolated systems and open systems. For example, if we plant an acorn, the influx of (low-entropy) sunlight allows the acorn to develop into a large (low-entropy) oak tree, through the accumulation and combination of (high-entropy) carbon dioxide, water and inorganic minerals. On the other hand, we can chop down the grown oak tree and burn it, releasing the stored (available) energy and regenerating carbon dioxide, water and inorganic minerals. It should also be noted that, in both cases, the processes are irreversible; only one direction of change is ever observed.

Now the effect of the second law on isolated systems was dubbed the 'arrow of time' by Eddington, reflecting the unidirectionality of such pro-cesses. If we also consider the nature of open systems, we again have uni-directionality: acorns grow into oak trees, not vice versa. We therefore now speak of the 'two arrows of time': the first arrow is that of dissipation and destructuring; the second arrow is that of the emergence of structure (Layzer, 1976; Faber and Proops, 1998, chs 4–6).

Clearly, environmental economics is closely concerned with both arrows of time. It is concerned with the first arrow, as this corresponds to the using up of natural resources, such as oil and forests. It is also concerned with the second arrow, as this describes processes which, using sunlight, generate again at least some of the resources used in economic activity.

The research opportunities opened up by modern thermodynamics, and the recognition of the two arrows of time, are, in my view, more conceptual than practical. For example, the distinction between systems that are 'running down' (the first arrow) and those that are 'building up' (the second arrow) is clearly related to the use of non-renewable resources (such as oil) and renewables (such as wood). Here, oil, once used, is gone for ever, while wood can regenerate itself through the services of the sun. However, perhaps the key conceptual issue for environmental policy is that of novelty, which is so central to open-system thermodynamics. We all know that novelty can and does arise in real economies, but so far there has been remarkably little work on the implications of the emergence of novelty on how we do environmental economics. It should be stressed that the issue here is not the existence of stochastic disturbances which need modelling; rather it is the possibility that our understanding of the world may cease to hold, because new structures, and new information, arise 'out of nowhere'.

For example, the nature of economic invention and innovation generated chlorofluorocarbons (CFCs), which seemed a great boon because of their volatility, solubility in oils and chemical stability. These properties quickly led to their widespread use as aerosol propellants and refrigerants, degreasers and fire retardants. Only when CFCs had been in production for many years, with significant quantities released into the atmosphere, did we discover that, by a remarkably complex series of chemical and physical interactions, they were leading to the destruction of the ozone layer. This emergence of novelty, of novel problems and perhaps solutions, is an important epistemological issue, to which I return below.

Resilience

Unlike the laws of thermodynamics, which have a nineteenth-century pedigree, ecological resilience (Perrings, 1996; Holling, 1986; see also Chapter 61) is a modern concept, though it has its roots in the discussion of the stability of ecosystems, dating back to Volterra and Lotka early this century. Indeed, perhaps the best way to introduce the concept of resilience is through that of the prior but related concept of stability.

The concept of resilience refers to systems with multiple equilibria, where at least two of these equilibria are locally stable. We might consider a system with exactly two locally stable equilibria, and suppose that we set the system at one of the stable equilibrium states. If we now perturb the system away from the initial equilibrium, what might happen to the system? There are two possible outcomes. First, if the perturbation is not 'too' large, the local stability of the equilibrium prevails, and the system reverts to its original state. Second, if the perturbation is sufficiently large, the system might 'flip' to the other locally stable equilibrium.

A way of envisaging the behaviour of such systems, with multiple stable equilibria, is in terms of 'zones of attraction', where if the system lies in a certain zone it will be 'attracted' towards a particular stable equilibrium, while if it is shifted a little, it might lie in another zone, with a different stable equilibrium. Clearly, if a stable equilibrium has a large zone of attraction, if the system is perturbed by even a quite large amount from that equilibrium, it will still revert to the initial state; that is, the system at that equilibrium is 'resilient' to perturbation. On the other hand, a stable equilibrium with a small zone of attraction will be much less resilient to perturbation.

What does this concept of resilience mean for environmental economics? First, it says that it is important for the economic activity we pursue whether natural systems exhibit more than one stable equilibrium. If there is only one stable equilibrium, then no matter how much we perturb nature by economic activity, nature will 'bounce back'. However, if a natural system has more than one stable equilibrium, then perturbing it may cause it to flip to another, perhaps radically different, state, much to our surprise and, possibly, regret. This is precisely the point, at the global level, addressed by Lovelock's (1979) notion of Gaia.

Second, if we believe that natural systems have more than one equilibrium, we need to know how resilient is the present (known) equilibrium state. If it is very resilient, then again, even major perturbations will not cause the system to flip into another state, or perhaps collapse. Conversely, if the system is not very resilient, we need to resist the temptation to economic activity which generates large perturbations, if we wish to avoid potentially very unpleasant surprises.

The research that the notion of resilience demands of environmental economics is rather obvious. When we set out to model such matters as the optimal exploitation of forests or fish, implicit in most current models is the assumption that such systems have unique and stable equilibria; that is, the systems are extremely resilient. If, as seems likely, most biological systems are not indefinitely resilient to perturbation, then analysis of the optimal use of biological resources will need to take account of the limits to which such systems may be pushed, and the problem of our ignorance, for most biological systems, as to where these limits lie. (For recent empirical work on ecological resilience, see Tilman and Downing, 1994 and Tilman et al., 1994.)

5. Evolutionary modelling

We usually associate the concept of evolution with biology, and the name of Darwin. However, the concept of evolution can have a much broader interpretation, applying to other natural sciences, as well as to economics (Faber and Proops, 1998, chs 2–3; see also Chapter 65 and Chapter 72).

The application of evolutionary concepts has a long pedigree (for example, Marshall, 1890; Nelson and Winter, 1982; Silverberg and Verspagen, 1994). To a greater or lesser extent, much of this literature seeks to replace the 'invisible hand' of economic rationality, as the process of economic interaction, with 'rules of thumb'. In Simon's (1967) terminology, the 'substantive' rationality of conventional economics is replaced with 'bounded' or 'prodedural' rationality. While these reflections on the nature of rationality and decision making are interesting in themselves, I believe they do not reflect the full nature of evolution, which, above all, involves the potential for the emergence of novelty. My discussions below will therefore take a rather different approach from that of the above authors.

In my view, the fundamental distinction for evolutionary analysis is that between a system's genotype, or set of potentialities, and its phenotype, or the realization of those potentialities in the world. For a biological organism, the genotype is normally thought to be determined by the nature of the genetic material of that organism. As the organism develops, the phenotype 'unfolds', deriving from the interaction between the potentialities expressed by the genotype, and the organism's environment. For example, if a person has the genetic potential to be very tall, that person may still grow into a short adult if their diet in youth is very poor.

Over time, the genotype of a species can be altered, by an accumulation of genetic mutations, so that the corresponding species phenotype alters. This is the process Darwin posited, with the progressive alteration of species over time. We note that, as the genotypes of species can alter over time, the observed phenotypes can alter also, although it is generally felt that for most species, the rate of such change is very slow.

This distinction between the genotype and the phenotype can also be applied to physics, where for a physical system the genotype can be thought of as the basic physical laws of nature, and the physical constants. As there is no alteration in the genotype, the phenotype of a physical system will be unchanging.

Finally, for economies we can think of the genotype as being the available production techniques, the preferences of consumers, and the laws and regulations that determine interactions between economic actors. The corresponding phenotype is the outcome of goods produced, at what prices, the distribution of income and wealth, the structure of employment, and so on. Now we know that in economies there is rapid alteration in available techniques, through invention, and also through changing preferences and legal systems. Therefore there is rapid genotypic change, leading to a correspondingly rapid change in the economic phenotype.

From the above evolutionary analysis one can draw some conclusions concerning the problem of prediction, with application to economics, particularly environmental economics. First, we note that to make a prediction one needs understanding of how changes can occur, and for that one needs experience of the process of change, to detect its regularities and structure. Clearly, changes in the phenotype of a system can be understood and predicted if they result from an unchanging genotype (for example, the development of an egg into a bird). On the other hand, the process of alteration of species, deriving from alteration in the genotype, does not give access to prediction in the same way, because experience on the particular nature of genotypic change cannot be accumulated, by the nature of that change. Therefore, predictions of phenotypes when the genotype is unchanging should be possible, while predictions involving systems where the genotype is changing will be impossible, in principle.

For economics, with rapid genotypic change, it is clear that long-run predictions about the (observed) economic phenotype will be very difficult to make. As environmental economics usually deals with issues that are long-run, the problem of prediction will be necessarily a difficult one. It should be noted that this is a difficulty deriving from the way we can understand the world (that is, an epistemological problem), not one that derives from insufficient present knowledge.

The challenge for future research here echoes that noted above, when discussing open systems and resilience. We face certain apparently insurmountable problems of ignorance in environmental policy making. We therefore need to devise ways of conceptualizing and modelling environmental policy which takes explicit account of this problem of ignorance.

6. Environmental philosophy

The impact of economic activity on the rest of nature poses problems not only of a scientific kind, as discussed above, but also of a more philosophical variety, which I divide into two classes. First, there are the very familiar issues of 'right and wrong' concerning economic impacts on nature; these constitute 'environmental ethics' (see Chapters 56 and 66). Second, there are the rather less discussed issues of what we understand about, and to what extent we can predict, economic impacts on nature. As here the issue is one of 'knowledge', we classify such issues as constituting 'environmental epistemology'.

Environmental ethics

One could argue that environmental economics is a very 'ethical' subject. Regarding natural resources, one finds interminable debates in the literature regarding the 'best' discount rate, which takes appropriate account of the well-being of future generations. Similarly, much is written on the socially optimal level of pollution, where the non-marketed effects of pollution are considered somehow to impose an 'unjust' cost. The issue of valuation is also one that vexes economists and philosophers alike, particularly the status of non-economic values for parts of nature, usually summarized as 'intrinsic value'. More recent literature, though not often by economists, also addresses the ethical issues of the relations between humans and the rest of nature. Certainly, the present debate over whaling seems to be driven more by the ethics of killing these apparently highly intelligent mammals than the economics of their historical overexploitation and present scarcity. (The main sources for these debates are the journals *Environmental Ethics* and *Environmental Values.*)

For environmental economists, perhaps the research challenge that is most pressing here is the problem of valuation, though this has both ethical and epistemological aspects. Implicit in much of the economics literature is the assumption that everything has a price, and it is only the problem of imperfect, incomplete or missing markets that stops us being able to observe these prices. As a result, a body of methodology has been established by economists to find the 'real' price of non-marketed goods. Techniques such as contingent valuation and travel cost are those most commonly applied. Philosophers, however, have suggested that it is not necessarily the case that all goods 'really' have prices.

For example, one might, if naïve, assume that all objects have a 'colour', and for those objects that do not have colours seek techniques for finding what the colour 'really is'. However, this is to misunderstand the nature of colour. It simply is not a universal property. For example, a mirror has no 'colour' of its own; it simply reflects the colours around it. Similarly, an electron cannot have a 'colour', as it is too small to interact with visible light.

If one accepts this argument, that economists are in fact trying to discover something (the 'real' price) when non-marketed goods cannot have prices, then clearly the whole use of contingent valuation to aid decision making is not only questionable, but downright wrong and misleading. Thus the challenge to environmental economics is, how do we formulate environmental polices when we *cannot* know the prices of everything? (For further debate on the 'commensurability of wants', see Vatn and Bromley, 1994 and O'Neill, 1993.)

Environmental epistemology
Modern work by mathematicians on 'chaos theory', by evolutionary biologists on the 'emergence of novelty', and by philosophers on the limits to understanding, is leading to a radical reappraisal of the limits to the possibilities of the 'management' of nature and of economies.

Chaos theory (Gleick, 1988) tells us that many systems in nature are likely to be unpredictable *in principle*, and this holds even if the nature of the systems' dynamics is completely understood. This is because such systems exhibit infinite sensitivity to initial conditions, so that if the initial state of the system is not known with infinite precision, the state of the system at some future date becomes completely unknowable. While the existence of such systems in economics or in biology has yet to be conclusively demonstrated, the very possibility of their existence casts a shadow over the modern concern with using environmental economics as a tool for management.

In evolutionary biology (as discussed above), following on from the possibilities of system emergence as discussed under the second arrow of time, it is being strongly argued that the evolution of the global ecosystem in its present form was by no means pre-ordained. Instead, the nature of the biological world is to a large degree the arbitrary outcome of the tendency of complex structures to emerge in open systems, combined with the unpredictable effects on this emergence of large perturbations, such as from the impact of giant asteroids on the earth (Gould, 1989). Some economists (for example, Arthur, 1989) are also coming to believe that the evolution of economic systems is to a large extent 'path-dependent', with small changes having large effects in the long run, through the mechanisms of 'technological lock-in through increasing returns to scale'.

Finally, philosophers have noted further constraints on our ability to understand economies and nature, through problems of the nature of language and mathematics. These difficulties of understanding, and prediction, can be summarized as the 'problem of ignorance'. (These issues are too technical to pursue here; see Smithson, 1988; Faber et al., 1992.)

7.   Concluding comments

At several stages in this discussion, I have noted the problem of knowledge, of epistemology, as being made central through the bringing of other disciplines into environmental economic analysis. This problem of knowledge, its nature, its possibilities and limitations for extension I believe to be the most formidable research challenge facing environmental economists.

Up to the present, most environmental economics has been undertaken within a paradigm that supposes either perfect knowledge, or at least knowledge that is 'perfectible' through further study. We now face the challenge, brought about by the opening up of our world-view to biology, physics and philosophy, that such simple mental models of the world are incomplete, even incorrect. Finding a new way to think about human–nature interactions seems to me the greatest research challenge we face.

References

Arthur, W.B. (1989), 'Competing technologies, increasing returns, and lock-in by historical events', *Economic Journal*, **99**, 116–31.
Balian, R. (1991), *From Microphysics to Macrophysics*, vol. 1, Heidelberg: Springer-Verlag.
Clark, M.E. (1989), *Ariadne's Thread: The Search for New Modes of Thinking*, London: Macmillan.
Daly, H.E. (1992), 'Is the entropy law relevant to the economics of natural resource scarcity? – Yes, of course it is!', *Journal of Environmental Economics and Management*, **23**, 91–5.
Daly, H.E. and J. Cobb (1989), *For the Common Good*, London: Green Print.
Faber, M. and J.L.R. Proops (1998), *Evolution, Time, Production and the Environment*, 3rd edn, Heidelberg: Springer-Verlag.
Faber, M., R. Manstetten and J.L.R. Proops (1992), 'Humankind and the environment: an anatomy of surprise and ignorance', *Environmental Values*, **1**, 217–41.
Faber, M., R. Manstetten and J.L.R. Proops (1996), *Ecological Economics: Concepts and Methods*, Cheltenham, UK and Brookfield, US: Edward Elgar.

Georgescu-Roegen, N. (1971), *The Entropy Law and the Economic Process*, Cambridge, MA: Harvard University Press.

Gleick, J.W. (1988), *Chaos: Making a New Science*, London: Heinemann.

Gould, S.J. (1989), *Wonderful Life: The Burgess Shale and the Nature of History*, Harmondsworth, UK: Penguin.

Holling, C.S. (1986), 'The resilience of terrestrial ecosystems; local surprise and global change', in W.C. Clark and R.E. Munn (eds), *Sustainable Development of the Biosphere*, Cambridge, UK: Cambridge University Press.

Layzer, D. (1976), 'The arrows of time', *Astrophysical Journal*, **206**, 559–64.

Lovelock, J.E.L. (1979), *Gaia: A New Look at Life on Earth*, Oxford: Oxford University Press.

Marshall, A. (1890), *Principles of Economics*, London: Macmillan.

Nelson, R.R. and S.G. Winter (1982), *An Evolutionary Theory of Economic Change*, Cambridge, MA: Harvard University Press.

O'Neill, J. (1993), *Ecology, Policy and Politics*, London: Routledge.

Perrings, C. (1996), 'Ecological resilience in the sustainability of economic development', in S. Faucheux, D.W. Pearce and J.L.R. Proops (eds), *Models of Sustainable Development*, Cheltenham, UK and Brookfield, US: Edward Elgar.

Prigogine, I. and I. Stengers (1984), *Order out of Chaos*, London: Heinemann.

Proops, J.L.R. (1985), 'Thermodynamics and economics: from analogy to physical functioning', in W. van Gool and J.J. Bruggink (eds), *Energy and Time in the Economic and Physical Sciences*, Amsterdam: North-Holland.

Silverberg, G. and B. Verspagen (1994), 'Collective learning, innovation and growth in a boundedly rational, evolutionary world', *Journal of Evolutionary Economics*, **4**, 207–26.

Simon, H.A. (1967), 'Theories of decision-making in economics and behavioural science', in *Surveys of Economic Theory III, Resource Allocation*, London: Macmillan.

Smithson, M. (1988), *Ignorance and Uncertainty: Emerging Paradigms*, Heidelberg: Springer-Verlag.

Tilman, D. and J. Downing (1994), 'Biodiversity and stability in grasslands', *Nature*, **367**, 363–5.

Tilman, D., R. May, C. Lehman and M. Nowak (1994), 'Habitat destruction and extinction debt', *Nature*, **371**, 65–6.

Vatn, A. and D.W. Bromley (1994), 'Choices without prices without apology', *Journal of Environmental Economics and Management*, **26**, 129–48.

Young, J.T. (1991), 'Is the entropy law relevant to the economics of natural resource scarcity?', *Journal of Environmental Economics and Management*, **21**, 169–79.

Name index

Nussbaum, B.D. 277
Nyang'oro, J. 694
Nyborg, K. 364
Nyquist, H. 784
Nzomo, M. 699

Oates, W.E. 3, 6, 20, 36, 191–2, 197,
    199, 206, 223–4, 226, 228, 250,
    295, 312, 330, 339, 342, 412, 444,
    454, 576, 578, 1004–5, 1012,
    1209
O'Connor, J. 383
O'Connor, M. 361, 381, 383–7, 837,
    969, 971, 985, 1127, 1128, 1129
Odum, E.P. 896, 899, 901, 904, 954
Odum, H.T. 17, 185, 898, 954–5,
    956–7, 960–62, 1127
Oelschlaeger, M. 990
Ogus, A. 342
O'Hara, S. 18
Ohnishi, H. 1172
Olewiler, N.D. 5
Ollikainen, M. 1096
Olsen, T. 81
O'Neil, R.V. 670, 831, 896
O'Neil, W. 267
O'Neill, J. 390, 984, 1240
Oosterhaven, J. 1171
Opschoor, J.B. 8, 339, 450, 453, 455,
    597, 658, 671–2, 694, 723
O'Riordan, T. 7, 994, 1017, 1028
Orr, D. 268
O'Ryan, R. 289
Osborne, L. 800, 802–3
Osei, E. 77
Osmundsen, P. 85
Ostrom, E. 150, 412, 909, 1184, 1215
Ott, W.R. 722
Ottinger, R. 954
Owens, S. 994
Ozdemiroglu, E. 96
Ozuna, T. 757, 759

Pack, H. 732
Paelinck, J.H.P. 525
Page, T. 39, 967, 984, 994, 1018
Paine, R.T. 903
Painter, M. 381
Pal, D.P. 1171
Palm, R. 553

Palmer, K. 444
Palmquist, R.B. 553, 766–71, 773
Panagariya, A. 435
Panayotou, T. 658, 659, 662, 664, 666,
    673, 694, 713
Pareto, V. 352, 353, 360, 1230
Parikh, K. 661
Park, S.H. 1152
Park, W.M. 165
Parker, F.L. 257–8
Parks, D.K. 132
Parry, I.W.H. 229, 294
Parry, M. 10, 172, 492
Parsons, G.R. 758, 759
Paruccini, M. 837
Pashigian, B.P. 230
Pasurka, C. 604
Patinkin, D. 748
Patten, B. 955
Patterson, D.A. 778
Patterson, M.G. 1127
Payne, J.W. 815, 818
Pearce, D.W. 10, 14, 25, 197, 205, 211,
    294, 364, 450, 489, 499–502, 511,
    651, 696, 724–5, 832, 834, 984,
    1005, 1008, 1018–19, 1021, 1025,
    1109, 1209, 1215
Pearson, M. 346, 348, 507, 518
Pecchenino, R. 618
Peek, S.C. 475, 497–8, 599–600, 1140
Peet, J. 6, 16, 1127
Peet, R. 381
Pekelney, D.M. 280
Peltzman, S. 229, 341
Peng, T-H. 924
Penner, J.E. 933
Penrose, E.T. 966
Penz, C.P. 810
Perez-Blanco, H. 861
Perman, R. 809
Perman, Y. 25
Perrels, A. 529, 560, 1224
Perrings, C.A. 16, 25, 39, 104, 386, 670,
    696, 811, 831, 862, 971–2, 974,
    984, 1004, 1010, 1017–18, 1054,
    1109–10, 1236
Perroni, C. 428
Perry, A. 553
Persson, A. 429, 696, 700, 1082
Pesaran, M. 38

Subject index

length of trips in UK 563
modes 583
policy 585–9
trade and international transport
399, 402
see also location choice; regional
economics; spatial issues; trade;
urban issues
travel cost models *see* valuation
TRI 324
tropical forests 167, 493, 499, 741
see also biodiversity; forestry; global
environmental issues; renewable
resources

UN
Commission on Sustainable
Development 726
Conference on the Environment and
Development 678, 731, 1193, 1210
Environment Programme 1193, 1201
Framework Convention on Climate
Change 182, 372, 492, 493, 505
Statistical Division 1195
Statistical Office 726
UNCED *see* UN, Conference on the
Environment and Development
uncertainty 212, 1217
and cost–benefit analysis 830–31
and ethics 984
and fisheries 120
and global environmental issues 489,
496, 501–2
and information 1217–19
and non-point source pollution 543
and resource extraction 55
and valuation 25, 759
fuzzy multi-criteria evaluation
845–6, 849–50
risk analysis 501, 557
standards versus taxes 227–9, 343–4
see also asymmetric information;
costs; endogenous environmental
risk; environmental policy; global
environmental issues;
sustainability; sustainable
development; technical change;
valuation
UNEP *see* UN, Environment
Programme

UPF 354
urban issues 560–67, 1224
Almere example 562
brownfield and greenfield sites 71,
563–4
Burgess–Richardson model 554–5,
557
compact city paradox 566
Dutch ABC policy 563
employment 560
energy efficiency 565–6
hedonic models and housing prices
765–74
housing and new settlements 561–2
in-migration to cities 561
Local Agenda *21* 566
meta-analysis 799–801
population density 563
reuse of existing sites 563–4
sustainability 560–67
transport 563, 564–5, 587
zoning 563
see also energy; land use; location
choice; regional economics; spatial
issues; transport
US Fish and Wildlife Service 994
utility 353
CES utility functions 53
commodity versus utility altruism
812
formulations in growth theory 1113
instantaneous 50
intertemporal 612–13
isoelastic utility functions 53
lexicographic preferences 815–16
logarithmic utility functions 53
separable function 473
utility possibility frontier 354
well-behaved functions 810
see also amenities; behavioural
assumptions; consumption;
contingent valuation; endogenous
environmental risk; ethical issues;
valuation; welfare

valuation 14, 24, 35, 36–7, 380,
747–823
and ethics 809–21
and experimental economics 1185–8
and risk reduction 218–19

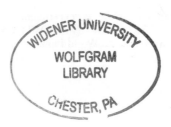